◄ 39TH ANNUAL EDITION ►

NOVEL & SHORT STORY WRITER'S MARKET

2020

Amy Jones, Editor

**WRITER'S DIGEST
BOOKS**

www.penguinrandomhouse.com

ISSN: 0897-9812
ISBN-13: 978-1-4403-5493-9
ISBN-10: 1-4403-5493-6

This book contains information gathered at the time of publication from third parties, including telephone numbers, Internet addresses, and other contact information. Neither the publisher nor the author assume any responsibility for errors, or for changes that occur after publication. Further, the publisher does not have any control over and does not assume any responsibility for author or third-party websites or their content.

Edited by: Amy Jones
Designed by: Wendy Dunning

CONTENTS

MARKETS

RESOURCES

INDEXES

FROM THE EDITOR

Welcome to the 39th Annual Edition of *Novel and Short Story Writer's Market*! The goal for this edition is much the same as in previous years: fit as many fiction listings as possible while also sharing some helpful craft and business articles.

The articles on craft cover topics ranging from antagonistic characters to antagonistic settings, plus addressing political topics and choosing the best title for your work. The business articles will help you work better with your editor, keep track of your submissions, and consider diversity in your writing. Plus you'll find an inspiring collection of interviews with these bestselling authors: Curtis Sittenfeld, Min Jin Lee, N.K. Jemisin, and James Patterson.

The heart of the book, the listings sections, are filled to the brim with literary agents, book publishers, magazines, contests, conferences, and more.

I hope you use the resources in this book to help you make 2020 your most satisfying and productive writing year ever.

Amy Jones
Managing Content Director
Novel & Short Story Writer's Market
http://twitter.com/AmyMJones_5

HOW TO USE *NSSWM*

To make the most of *Novel & Short Story Writer's Market*, you need to know how to use it. And with more than five hundred pages of fiction publishing markets and resources, a writer could easily get lost amid the information. This quick-start guide will help you navigate through the pages of *Novel & Short Story Writer's Market*—as well as the fiction-publishing process—and accomplish your dream of seeing your work in print.

1. READ, READ, READ. Read numerous magazines, fiction collections, and novels to determine if your fiction compares favorably with work currently being published. If your fiction is at least the same caliber as what you're reading, then move on to step two. If not, postpone submitting your work and spend your time polishing your fiction. Reading the work of others is one of the best ways to improve your craft.

You'll find advice and inspiration from best-selling authors and seasoned writers in the articles found in the first few sections of this book (**Craft & Technique**, **Interviews**, and **The Business of Fiction Writing**). *Novel & Short Story Writer's Market* also includes listings for **Literary Agents** who accept fiction submissions, **Book Publishers** and **Magazines** that publish fiction in a variety of genres, **Contests & Awards** to enter, and **Conferences & Workshops** where you can meet fellow writers and attend instructive sessions to hone your skills.

2. ANALYZE YOUR FICTION. Determine the type of fiction you write to target markets most suitable for your work. Do you write literary, genre, mainstream, or one of many other categories of fiction? For definitions and explanations of genres and subgenres, check out the **Glossary** and the **Genre Glossary** in the **Resources** section of the book. Many magazines and presses are currently seeking specialized work in each of these areas as well as numerous others.

For editors and publishers with specialized interests, see the **Category Index** in the back of the book.

3. LEARN ABOUT THE MARKET. Read *Writer's Digest* magazine; *Publishers Weekly*, the trade magazine of the publishing industry; and *Independent Publisher*, which contains information about small- to medium-size independent presses. And don't forget the Internet. The number of sites for writers seems to grow daily, and among them you'll find www.writersdigest.com.

4. FIND MARKETS FOR YOUR WORK. There are a variety of ways to locate markets for fiction. The periodical section in bookstores and libraries is a great place to discover new journals and magazines that might be open to your type of short stories. Read writing-related magazines and newsletters for information about new markets and publications seeking fiction submissions. Also, frequently browse bookstore shelves to see what novels and short story collections are being published and by whom. Check acknowledgment pages for names of editors and agents, too. Online journals often have links to the websites of other journals that may publish fiction. And last, but certainly not least, read the listings found here in *Novel & Short Story Writer's Market*.

5. SEND FOR GUIDELINES. In the listings in this book, we try to include as much submission information as we can get from editors and publishers. Over the course of the year, however, editors' expectations and needs may change. Therefore, it is best to obtain a copy of the submission guidelines. You can check each magazine's and press's website—they usually contain a page with guideline information. Or you can do it the old-fashioned way and send a self-addressed, stamped envelope (SASE) with a request for them.

6. BEGIN YOUR PUBLISHING EFFORTS WITH JOURNALS AND CONTESTS OPEN TO BEGINNERS. If this is your first attempt at publishing your work, your best bet is to begin with local publications or those you know are open to beginning writers. After you have built a pub-

KEY TO ICONS & ABBREVIATIONS

- Ⓐ market accepts agented submissions only
- ⊘ market does not accept unsolicited submissions
- award-winning market
- Canadian market
- market located outside of the U.S. and Canada
- Ⓢ market pays (in magazine sections)
- 💬 comment from the editor of *Novel & Short Story Writer's Market*
- ◯ actively seeking new writers
- ◑ seeks both new and established writers
- ● prefers working with established writers, mostly referrals
- ◎ market has a specialized focus
- ⊙ imprint, subsidiary, or division of larger book publishing house (in book publishers section)
- publisher of graphic novels or comics

lication history, you can try submitting to the more prestigious and nationally distributed magazines. For markets most open to beginners, look for the ⭕ symbol preceding listing titles. Also look for the ◑ symbol, which identifies markets open to exceptional work from beginners as well as work from experienced, previously published writers.

7. SUBMIT YOUR FICTION IN A PROFESSIONAL MANNER. Take the time to show editors that you care about your work and are serious about publishing. By following a publication's or book publisher's submission guidelines and practicing standard submission etiquette, you can increase your chances that an editor will want to take the time to read your work and consider it for publication. Remember: First impressions matter. A carelessly assembled submission packet can jeopardize your chances before your story or novel manuscript has had a chance to speak for itself.

8. KEEP TRACK OF YOUR SUBMISSIONS. Know when and where you have sent fiction and how long you need to wait before expecting a reply. If an editor does not respond in the time indicated in his or her market listing or guidelines, wait a few more weeks before following up with an e-mail or letter (with SASE) asking when the editor anticipates making a decision. If you do not receive a reply from the editor within a month or two, send a letter withdrawing your work from consideration and move on to the next market on your list.

9. LEARN FROM REJECTION. Rejection is the hardest part of the publication process. Unfortunately rejection happens to every writer, and every writer needs to learn to deal with the negativity involved. Believe it or not, rejection can be valuable when used as a teaching tool rather than a reason to doubt yourself and your work. If an editor offers suggestions with his or her rejection slip, take those comments into consideration. You don't have to agree with an editor's opinion of your work. It may be that the editor has a different perspective on the piece than you do. Or you may find that the editor's suggestions give you new insight into your work and help you improve your craft.

10. DON'T GIVE UP. The best advice we can offer you as you try to get published is to be persistent and to always believe in yourself and your work. By continually reading other writers' work, constantly working on the craft of fiction writing, and relentlessly submitting your work, you will eventually find that magazine or book publisher that's the perfect match for your fiction. *Novel & Short Story Writer's Market* will be here to help you every step of the way.

GUIDE TO LISTING FEATURES

Below is an example of the market listings contained in *Novel & Short Story Writer's Market,* with callouts identifying the various format features of the listings. (For an explanation of the icons used, see the sidebar on page 3.)

AT-A-GLANCE REFERENCE ICONS

❶❸❼ THE SOUTHERN REVIEW

Old President's House, Louisiana State University, Baton Rouge, LA 70803-5001. (225)578-5108. Fax: (225)578-5098. E-mail: southernreview@lsu.edu. **Website:** www.lsu.edu/thesouthern review.

E-MAIL AND WEBSITE INFORMATION

Contact Cara Blue Adams, editor. Magazine: 6¼ × 10; 240 pages; 50 lb. Glatfelter paper; 65 lb. #1 grade cover stock. Quarterly. Circ. 3,000.

SPECIFIC CONTACT NAMES

• Several stories published in *The Southern Review* were Pushcart Prize selections.

NEEDS Literary. "We select fiction that conveys a unique and compelling voice and vision." Receives approximately 300 unsolicited mss/month. Accepts 4-6 mss/issue. Reading period: September-June. Publishes ms 6 months after acceptance. Agented fiction 1%. Publishes 10-12 new writers/year. Recently published work by Jack Driscoll, Don Lee, Peter Levine, and Debbie Urbanski. Also publishes literary essays, literary criticism, poetry, and book reviews.

DETAILED SUBMISSION GUIDELINES

HOW TO CONTACT Mail hard copy of ms with cover letter and SASE. No queries. ("Prefer brief letters giving author's professional information, including recent or notable publications. Biographical info not necessary." Responds in 10 weeks to mss. Sample copy for $8. Writer's guidelines online. Reviews fiction, poetry.

TIPS FOR SUBMISSION

PAYMENT/TERMS Pays $30/page. Pays on publication for first North American serial rights. Sends page proof to author via e-mail. Sponsors awards/contests.

TIPS "Careful attention to craftsmanship and technique combined with a developed sense of the creation of story will always make us pay attention."

NO MORE
MR. NICE GUYS

Unlikable characters make for fascinating
protagonists—but their behavior can risk alienating
readers. Follow this blueprint for flawed yet relatable
heroes who can still provoke empathy.

....

by David Corbett

Not so long ago it seemed that every writer agreed: Protagonists must be "likable."

Then something curious happened. Everyone began to realize that "likable" is merely a few degrees from "nice," which in turn nudges perilously close to "boring." People may not like spending 200–500 pages with a wanton wretch, but they don't like wasting time with a Boy Scout's shadow, either.

In truth, protagonists need to be compelling—better yet, fascinating—not necessarily agreeable. And what makes characters compelling or fascinating is their *capacity to surprise*. A character who is predictably *anything* quickly becomes a one-trick pony, incapable of maintaining reader interest for long.

The challenge is especially daunting for characters who may disaffect readers with some particularly repellant trait—a vicious temper, a drinking problem, arrogant self-confidence, outright immorality or even criminality. And yet some such characters are among the most fascinating—and profoundly loved—protagonists of all time. To name just four:

- Holden Caulfield, *Catcher in the Rye* (an aimless, jaded, venomous cynic)
- John Yossarian, *Catch-22* (a World War II bombardier who will do anything to avoid flying combat missions)

- Dexter Morgan, the Dexter novels (the serial killer son of a serial killer)
- Rachel Watson, *The Girl on the Train* (a mysteriously obsessed drunk)

How, then, does one create a potentially reprehensible character who nonetheless fascinates?

THE ALLURE OF TRANSGRESSION

We may tell ourselves that we respect the law and those who uphold it, but there's a little larceny in every heart. The character with a wily knack for seizing a dubious opportunity (or avoiding an odious chore) seldom fails to appeal—as long as no one gets hurt.

This points to two important truths:

1. There's an implicit understanding that we had no part in making the rules, and that many of them are meant not to protect us but to keep us in line. Our intrinsic desire for freedom and autonomy rankles at this sort of benign coercion, and we instinctively recognize that the goal of "the law" is often not just order but conformity, even oppression. The suspicion that there is "rot at the top" and that corruption is the rule, not the exception, never lurks far beneath the surface. And so we admire those who refuse to fall into line.
2. There is a natural limit to the appeal of transgression: the degree of harm to others. We don't mind seeing a greedy plutocrat bilked or a bully brought down a peg, but empathy wanes in direct proportion to the innocence of the victim. Push this too far, you'll need to provide a countering virtue that shows us the character isn't simply a monster.

THE POWER OF CONTRADICTION

That last point can be generalized: We can accept a great deal of unpleasantness in a character as long as we see it balanced against something that inspires empathy or intrigues us.

Charles Portis in *True Grit* employs such contradictions masterfully. Despite Mattie's youth she is indomitable and savvy in business. LaBoeuf is courageous despite a foppish concern for appearance. Cogburn, the one-eyed drunken fat man, is relentless, cunning and, in the end, valiant.

These kinds of incongruities automatically intrigue—and offer the prospect of surprise. We can't help but wonder at what sort of psychological glue holds these supposedly opposite traits together.

This is especially true of transgressive characters. Absent some redemptive quality, they risk alienating readers. To create compelling contradictions, explore the following:

1. **CONTRADICTIONS BASED ON CONTRASTING INFLUENCES.** It's a basic fact of life that we must be "many things to many people." Our behavior at the office risks

serious consequences if it veers too close to our behavior at home—or the local bar. Explore what incompatible environments your character must navigate, and the behavior they exhibit in each. Alternatively, look to the persons who demand or inspire opposing inclinations. Let them be the devil on one shoulder and the angel on the other at every decision point in the story.

2. **CONTRADICTIONS BASED ON COMPETING MORALS OR GOALS.** Don't neglect to explore your character's moral code. In doing so, however, avoid trying to make it too neat and tidy. Explore ways in which he holds opposing views of the same thing—e.g., they may consider innocence in one character nothing but stupidity or naïveté, and yet see it as a kind of gentle nobility in another. Or he may believe in both righteous vengeance and forgiveness, and struggle to know when to apply one or the other.

3. **CONTRADICTIONS THAT RESULT FROM A SECRET OR DECEIT.** Secrets automatically add depth to a character by creating an inside and an outside, what is revealed vs. what is hidden. By making the character act in a way that conceals his secret, you create tension. One great example: Maxim de Winter in Daphne DuMaurier's *Rebecca*. His secret, that he did not love his late wife but hated her to the point of murder, creates the mysterious fits of temper and distance that Rebecca (and the reader) find not just off-putting but repellant. Yet he's the heroine's courtly love interest—how can that be?

Contradiction also alerts the reader that there is more than one side to the character, and thus implicitly suggests that he can change. Readers will extend considerable patience to an otherwise dreadful character if he also possesses the wherewithal to reflect, learn from failure or otherwise turn in a new, more agreeable direction.

THE CONTRADICTORY CHARACTER PAR EXCELLENCE: THE ANTIHERO

The character type referred to as the "antihero" justifies an entire article on its own—I know, I've written one. But for our purposes, the key trait to recognize is what distinguishes them from a protagonist who merely suffers from distinct moral flaws.

The flawed hero is potentially capable, through insight, of recognizing his moral limitation, seeing the damage it does to himself and others, and rectifying his behavior. In fact, this sort of transformational arc lies at the heart of many stories featuring such a character.

In contrast, the antihero stands at the center of an irresolvable moral conflict. Think of him as having a devil on one shoulder, an angel on the other, and neither ever convincingly gains the upper hand.

Homer's Odysseus is just such a character—while capable of heroism and daring, he also exhibits treachery, deceit and cowardice. It's precisely that dual nature that keys our fascination.

In the sixteenth century, the picaresque novel emerged in Hapsburg Spain, epitomized by *The Life of Lazarillo de Tormes and of his Fortunes and Adversities*. Instead of the steadfast knights of the chivalric romance, these novels featured lovable, wandering rogues and thieves, known as *picaros*, and the stories recounted their morally questionable but never explicitly wicked exploits. The appeal of the picaresque novel spread across Europe and took solid root in England, where its popularity survived into the nineteenth century in novels featuring rakish heroes such as Tom Jones, Moll Flanders, Barry Lyndon, and Martin Chuzzlewit.

Lord Byron provided another variation on the type, encapsulated in these lines concerning the pirate hero of his verse tale *The Corsair*:

> He knew himself a villain—but he deem'd
> The rest no better than the thing he seem'd;
> And scorn'd the best as hypocrites

This returns us to the theme of justifiable transgression. When a society's cherished ideals are exposed as serving only the corrupt few, the antihero typically emerges as an antidote to the prevailing hypocrisy. In being neither evil nor virtuous, but revealing instead an uneasy marriage of both tendencies, he seems more genuine and convincing than the more pious and predictable characters the powers-that-be prefer.

Indeed, the recent resurgence in popularity of antiheroes in long-format television—embodied in such characters as Tony Soprano, Jimmy McNulty, Patty Hewes, Don Draper, Nancy Botwin, Ray Donovan, and Walter "Heisenberg" White—reveals not just a need for characters of sufficient moral and psychological complexity to drive a multi-season series, but a newfound awareness that many old American verities (e.g., equal opportunity, fairness, decency) have worn thin, revealing the naked aggression, vanity and greed underneath.

CREATING EMPATHY THROUGH DESIRE, STRUGGLE AND VULNERABILITY

Through some odd magic of the human heart we almost always feel for those struggling in pursuit of a meaningful goal—even if it's a bank heist.

John Yossarian's dogged efforts to escape combat create in the reader a rooting interest, if only because he so doggedly pursues his desire "to live forever or die trying."

Readers initially put off by Rachel Watson's drunken ruminations as she rides the train are soon reeled back in by what is clearly a profound desire to recapture, however fleetingly or futilely, the life and love she lost.

To desire something that requires struggle automatically makes us vulnerable due to the risk that we may fail. That risk may take one or more of several forms:

1. *Existential* (risk of physical harm)
2. *Emotional* (loss of hope, joy, meaning, etc.)
3. *Relational* (risk of loss/disconnection with someone)
4. *Moral* (risk of judgment)

When using struggle and desire to create empathy for an otherwise offensive character, don't neglect to explore just what risks the character faces. The more those risks are emotional, relational, or moral, the better your chances of deepening the empathetic bond.

Finally, another tried-and-true way to create empathy for even a loathsome character is to give him "a kid or a dog"—i.e., give him someone to care about other than himself. We care about those who care about others.

You can also turn this around—we typically empathize with a character if another, more personable character does so as well.

Three Essential Traits

Above and beyond the empathy factor, three key traits can help mitigate the portrayal of an otherwise harsh, off-putting or outright despicable character.

1. Humor: It's amazing how much obnoxious behavior we will put up with from a character who makes us laugh.
2. Lust for Life: A love of food, music, art, travel or any other aspect of an attractive life can reassure us that an otherwise objectionable character is not a rancorous misanthrope stewing in his own bile—or worse.
3. The Intimacy of Insight: We tend to judge less harshly characters who look at themselves and their behavior clearly, honestly and in depth. Even a psychopath like Dexter Morgan becomes a bit less terrifying because we're invited into his thought processes, which are elaborate, detailed, and fascinating.

The importance of insight especially cannot be underestimated. Even if a character possesses a compelling contradiction that suggests he's capable of change, absent insight, it's doubtful he can or will make the effort. A character can't turn in a direction he can't see.

Even if the character doesn't change, the fact that we are invited inside his mind creates an intimacy that is hard to resist. Whether his thoughts are externalized directly to the reader or audience (Richard III, Frank Underwood in *House of Cards*), provided in first person (Freddy Clegg in *The Collector*, Lou Ford in *The Killer Inside Me*), or in close third (Tom in *The Talented Mr. Ripley*), that intimacy creates an implicit, irresistible bond with the reader. It's hard to say no when we're so graciously invited inside.

Bad vs. Worse

We can often accept a certain amount of wickedness in a protagonist if he's pitted against someone genuinely, remorselessly evil.

The entire heist genre is predicated on the fact that the protagonists are clever professionals working to score against a vastly more powerful and largely amoral if not immoral person or entity—another criminal, a bank, an insurance company. This comes with a caveat—the crime involves money, not mayhem.

One of the great innovations of the Dexter series was that it violated this unwritten rule, but did so in an acceptable way. Yes, Dexter's a serial killer, but he only kills other murderers.

This same ethical setup is the premise of a form of moral argument known as *pathos*, in which an everyman employs immoral means to pursue something he considers invaluable in the face of an overwhelmingly powerful person or system. Even though we know the protagonist is doomed to fail, we root for him because we identify with the little guy swinging for the fences, and we all understand that the world isn't fair.

This form of moral argument animates not just the crime genre known as noir, but a great many plays, films, and novels written in the shadow of the Great Depression and World War II, from *The Postman Always Rings Twice* to *Death of a Salesman*. A resurgence followed in the late 1960s and early 1970s with such films as *The King of Marvin Gardens*, *Dog Day Afternoon*, and *Chinatown*, and again in the mid-1990s and early 2000s with novels such as *Mystic River*.

Turning Virtue Into Vice

Often characters who offend readers merely push a virtue to an unacceptable extreme—but the fact that it's a *virtue* that lies at the heart of the problem suggests that it can be corrected if the character has the necessary insight.

Examples of ways virtues can be pushed to an objectionable extreme:

- His loyalty obliges him to overlook the immoral acts of others.
- His courage or ambition leads to recklessness.
- His commitment to honesty makes him hurtful.
- His love of action turns into an addiction to the adrenalin rush.

- His concern for order leads to a rigid, even heartless obsession with rules.
- He is so certain of his moral rectitude he's blind to his own bad acts.

The key to a great protagonist is how *compelling* he is—not how nice. Employing the techniques discussed above, alone or in concert, can help turn even an abhorrent character into one your readers will want to stick with through to the end.

DAVID CORBETT (davidcorbett.com) is the award-winning author of six novels including *The Long-Lost Love Letters of Doc Holliday*, the story collection *Thirteen Confessions* and the writing guide *The Art of Character*. His Writer's Digest guide, *The Compass of Character: Creating Complex Motivation for Compelling Characters in Fiction, Film, and TV* (2019), addresses more topics like the one covered here. This article was previously published in the September 2018 issue of *Writer's Digest*.

CREATING AN ANTAGONISTIC SETTING

by DiAnn Mills

An antagonistic setting is as much a gift to the reader as an unpredictable plot. The explosion of an unforeseen or modified environment forces the protagonist to dig deep for ways to survive. When setting becomes a predator, a character's true inner landscape is revealed, one he cannot deny.

I welcome the task of increasing the stakes to provide an obscure setting. The work is worth every drop of perspiration—and your readers will love you for the professional touch.

Writers search for ways to raise the stakes for the protagonist. We mine weaknesses to make him squirm and pressure him to grow into a true hero—or heroine. Sometimes he fails and sometimes he succeeds. In each instance, the protagonist is caught off guard, and every breath is met with potential disaster.

We writers often turn to obvious means of adding stress, tension, and conflict through characterization, dialogue, plot twists, symbolism, and emotive conflict. These are powerful tools, and our stories must contain stellar treatment of each literary technique to ensure our protagonists are continuously challenged.

Why not add more to defy the protagonist's resolve?

Establishing an antagonistic setting as an additional means of growth and change requires skill. But once mastered, the method offers a new dimension to the story by creating additional stumbling points that add barriers to the character's goal.

Making life easy doesn't keep the reader engaged. I prefer keeping my readers up all night trying to figure out what will happen next.

An antagonistic setting means shaky ground for the protagonist. The problem creeps up to catch the character unaware, stalking him with devious tactics. Survival extends beyond defeating a villain, either mental, physical, or spiritual.

MENTAL ANTAGONISTIC SETTING

- A dream world
- An unconscious state
- A hallucination
- Altered thinking as in mental illness or depression
- A phobia

Phobias provide an ideal backdrop for a hostile setting. The person suffering from one of these fears can experience physical symptoms that can be life-threatening. Dizziness, dread, nausea, chest pains, panic attacks, and a host of other reactions can stop the character and debilitate him from moving forward.

Take a look at a few of these phobias as a possible way to heighten a weakness associated with setting:

- Acrophobia—fear of heights
- Astraphobia—fear of storms
- Claustrophobia—fear of being stuck in a small space
- Ophidiophobia—fear of snakes
- Pteromerhanophobia—fear of flying
- Social Phobia—fear of interacting with people

To ensure a tight, high-stakes scene, use inner and outer fears against him. This intimidates the character to not only struggle but also face an inner and outer antagonist: fear and setting. Watch plot twists emerge that will add levels to the story line. Seek ways to ensure the he faces one difficult situation after another with paralyzing fright.

PHYSICAL ANTAGONISTIC SETTING

- An unexpected storm
- A rough and foreign terrain
- A natural disaster
- An explosive work or home life
- An otherwise harmonious situation that turns hostile
- A limitation of mobility

SPIRITUAL ANTAGONISTIC SETTING

- A belief system that supports superiority of a single race, creed, or culture
- A religious conviction that practices persecution of others
- An ideology presented in childhood has the potential to instill prejudice and strong biases that can be difficult to overcome. An aversion to others who embrace other forms of faith.

An unanticipated change in an environment reveals the true inner self by displaying strengths or weaknesses. Does he run or stand and fight? Sometimes fleeing is a form of courage. The adversity can be obvious or hidden but include the deception in ways that compel him to make tough decisions and then accept responsibility for the consequences.

A wise writer shows enough setting for the reader to envision the story world—and no more. Information overload cheats the reader of vicariously living the adventure of the character and closes the door on imagination. Readers today crave a story of adventure, growth, and unforeseen events.

How does a writer accomplish an antagonistic setting? View the location's description as though it were a characterization sketch. Concentrate on an antagonist's personality traits and use them to disguise what looks like an enticing environment:

- Determination
- Power
- Beauty
- Charm
- Manipulation
- Deception

Setting is vital and full of spirit. Let the character's surroundings whisper, "Be careful for what is ahead." Associate the location with sensory perception, for in the depths of the five senses lie emotions and memories that have the ability to paralyze.

Sight—What does he perceive around him that can alter reality?

A man dreamed of one day living in the mountains. He spent his entire savings building a cabin. During a wildfire, he was forced to evacuate and couldn't find his dog. How does this memory affect his choices today: where will he live or will he ever own another dog?

Smell—What smells trigger pleasant or unpleasant memories? If the smell is unfamiliar, how does the character react?

A twelve-year-old girl was sent to her grandparents' farm at the beginning of summer. She loved helping her grandmother pick strawberries and make preserves. She learned the reason for the visit was so her parents could work out details of a divorce. To this day, the smell of strawberries makes her ill.

Taste—What tastes draw the character to the past? Can a unique taste shake his conscious or unconscious reaction to what is going on around him?

Consider a man who was celebrating his birthday at a restaurant. The meal was served, a steak cooked to perfection, and he received a call that his mother had died. How would he view his birthday, the restaurant, or steak in the future?

Hear—What sounds soothe or disturb the character? Where did the sounds originate to pinpoint the reaction?

A woman's father worked as a professional organist. He played in churches, theaters, and private events, entertaining and inspiring everyone he met. The woman is involved in a high-stress law firm, and the only way she can relax is by listening to organ music.

Feel—How was the character touched in the past that evokes positive or negative memories?

A man was never touched as a child. He was born premature, abandoned in the hospital, and later placed in a foster care home where he didn't receive affection. As he grew, he sought inappropriate means for attention. Now he's considering a serious crime.

When plotting with setting in mind, a writer chooses at least one of the following scenarios to create a story with visceral impact:

- Man vs. man
- Man vs. animal
- Man vs. nature
- Man vs. society
- Man vs. survival
- Man vs. technology
- Man vs. God

Every situation above requires a distinct setting in which the writer can harvest the gems of antagonism. The opposition is often more than one scenario. Write the scene in the point of view of the character who has the most to lose, using staggering conflict. Use dialogue that anchors voice and responses.

A character who is familiar with a particular setting will not make the same observations or mistakes as a novice.

- A veteran police officer understands the demands and evolving nature of his job better than a rookie, who can be either nervous, apprehensive, or overconfident.
- A seasoned teacher welcomes the new school year with experience and wisdom. A new teacher is fearful about her first teaching position. Is she too strong a disciplinarian? Are her students learning? Is she offering them exciting teaching venues?

The following are instances of an antagonistic setting in a few popular genres.

Contemporary: A beautiful afternoon in a park for a family reunion is interrupted when a young girl brings her fiancé, a man who is of a different race and culture. Her father is enraged, and a fight breaks out among family members. The young girl is killed when she attempts to stop the conflict.

Fantasy: In a land faraway, a kindly king is replaced by a tyrant who levies heavy taxes upon his subjects. One man chooses to free the people of the greedy king, but he must find a way to enter the heavily guarded castle.

Historical: A wagon train pulls into a peaceful valley where the weary travelers can rest before heading across a vast prairie. A pack of hungry wolves attack the horses and livestock stopping the travelers from continuing their journey.

Romance: A couple honeymoons on an exotic, deserted island. The white sandy beaches and the call of seagulls appear to be a paradise. An unexpected storm rises, bringing high winds and twenty-foot waves. The couple is trapped with no means of contacting help.

Science-Fiction: An isolated, peaceful planet is invaded by highly intelligent aliens who require the inhabitant's water supply for their own survival. Who can help the weaker people overcome insurmountable odds?

Suspense: A heroine refers to her backyard as a haven. A tall, stone wall frames nature's display of green and flowering plants. But when a killer chases her inside the garden, she is trapped by what she thought was her respite. Can anyone help her?

Thriller: An aid to a popular politician is invited to an isolated mountain retreat center with other staff members. The aid discovers the politician plans to unleash a virus on American citizens that will kill many innocent people. The politician confiscates all devices leaving the aid helpless to tell the world of the devastation to come.

Whatever the setting, the writer strives to keep characters—and the plot—moving in unpredictable directions.

Why place your hero or heroine in an idyllic environment that makes solving the goal easy and pain free? Why not muddy the waters and create an antagonistic setting that keeps readers on the edge of their seats?

DIANN MILLS is a bestselling author who believes her readers should expect an adventure. Her titles have appeared on the CBA and ECPA bestseller lists; won two Christy Awards; and been finalists for the RITA, Daphne Du Maurier, Inspirational Readers' Choice, and Carol award contests. *Firewall*, the first book in her Houston: FBI series, was listed by *Library Journal* as one of the best Christian Fiction books of 2014. DiAnn is a founding board member of the American Christian Fiction Writers, a member of Advanced Writers and Speakers Association, Sisters in Crime, and International Thriller Writers. She is co-director of The Blue Ridge Mountain Christian Writers Conference and The Mountainside Marketing Conference with social media specialist Edie Melson. Learn more at www.diannmills.com.

SHOULD YOU GO THERE?

Politics and religion might not make for polite dinner conversation, but can add depth to your fiction—if handled with care. Here's what to consider and how to proceed.

....

by Elizabeth Sims

Most of us learn fairly early in life that starting a discussion about politics or religion with a stranger will lead to one of three things: cheerful agreement; silence ranging from uncomfortable to icy; disagreement ranging from mild contradiction to fisticuffs. The odds vary.

But what if you're a writer of fiction? If your work gets out into the world, it/you will be "talking" to strangers all the time.

Why do so many authors shy away from dealing with politics and religion? Several good reasons:

- Those subjects are loaded with strong emotion. Many of us picked up religious and political tenets at a young age—or rejected them. In maturity, you figure things out for yourself, and it can be a complex road.
- It's hard to be well informed, and impossible to be perfectly informed. Nobody has witnessed every conflict, read every history book, listened to every analytical podcast, examined every religious text, and prayed to all the different gods.
- Religious and political references—especially political ones—can date a work of fiction. This is fine if you're writing a Civil War romance and somebody swears "by the President's beard!" But if you're writing a contemporary novel and a character prais-

es or condemns "that guy in the White House"—well, in a few years (or less), nobody's going to be sure who that character is talking about. And using the names of real political or religious leaders timestamps your fiction from the start.

- Readers can become alienated if they feel pressured or manipulated. They might also write a nasty review or ask for their money back.
- Doctrine can be tedious. Hammering on the rightness of your beliefs in your fiction—by putting your pet dogma into the mouths of your characters—gets predictable, and therefore boring, fast.

That's the downside. What's to be gained by embracing themes of religion/politics?

- Let's say ten people read your book today. If five of them are either left cold or ticked off by your biases, you've risked losing them. However, if the five that remain are precisely the demographic you want, well, then, that's different. When readers find an author whose work resonates with their ideology, they can become loyal, die-hard fans.
- If you lead an active, engaged life, you feel the impact of political ideas, of government, of the movements within your particular faith (if you are a believer or seeker), and of the movements within other faiths. Therefore, if you want to write about your world, you may feel moved to explore such themes in your art. After all, we artists are supposed to be pursuers of all things true and real. We must find things out for ourselves—and art is our vehicle.
- These themes, if handled with sensitivity and restraint, can bring great depth and immediacy to fiction.

To decide whether to explore political/religious themes in your fiction, consider:

Do you enjoy debating opinions and faiths?

Are you okay with disagreement?

Do you have the knack for looking at your own feelings objectively?

Are you a risk-taker?

Are you more extroverted than introverted?

The more *yes* answers, the more you might be an *embracer* as opposed to an *avoider*. I might note that literary fiction tends to attract embracers, while the commercial mystery and romance genres tend to attract avoiders. Science fiction seems to fall in the middle: Many good sci-fi stories deal with theoretical politics and religion. These are generalizations, of course, but I have noticed them. As a mystery/suspense author myself, I like to let my characters express opinions on religion and politics occasionally—and even carry on minor debates. But given that I abhor dogmatism, I keep it light. That's just me.

Prizewinning and best-selling novelist Ursula K. LeGuin has written, "Art itself is our language for expressing the understandings of the heart, the body and the spirit. Any reduction of that language into intellectual messages is radically, destructively incomplete."

Let's look at some fiction that successfully navigated these dual minefields—what they did, how they did it, and how you might do it too.

REALIZE THAT THE ISSUE IS NOT BY ITSELF THE STORY

Upton Sinclair's progressive-era novel *The Jungle* exposed the dreadful conditions in Chicago's meatpacking industry around the turn of the twentieth century. He hit lots of targets in this one, and became famous. But one could argue the reason the book sold so well was because he wrote a good story. The plot follows one man, a dirt-poor Lithuanian immigrant named Jurgis Rudkus, as he makes his way into the dangerous "jungle" of inhuman working conditions and slum life of his new country. Sinclair took pains to make Rudkus sympathetic—a good man caught in a nightmare of false promises and treachery. However, Rudkus makes mistakes. He permits wishful thinking to overcome his judgment, he takes to drink and self-pity—and thus is not entirely angelic, and not entirely blameless for his pain. Everyone can relate to this!

THE TAKEAWAY: Trace the story of one person against the odds, and don't make your hero unrealistically perfect for fear that readers will reject the story otherwise. Perceptive readers will not throw the baby of your story out with the bathwater of realism; they will appreciate reading about a flawed hero, thrown against an intriguing series of challenges.

ALSO READ: *The Last Hurrah* by Edwin O'Connor, "The Yellow Wallpaper" (short story) by Charlotte Perkins Gilman, *One Flew Over the Cuckoo's Nest* by Ken Kesey.

IN ALLEGORY, TELEGRAPH SOMETHING USEFUL: THIS ISN'T ABOUT WHAT IT'S ABOUT

George Orwell's *Animal Farm* isn't about agriculture and animal husbandry; the farm and its denizens served as a structure for Orwell, a veteran of the Spanish Civil War and democratic socialist, to skewer the totalitarian repressions of post-revolution communism.

Orwell carefully brought literary artistry to *Animal Farm*, knowing that pure propaganda would enjoy a limited reach, and near-zero longevity.

The plot of this novella is remarkably complex, with crises, battles, internecine conflicts, and heroism. The key brilliance of the work is the final twist in which the intelligent pigs, who have led the successful fight for freedom from the human masters, now begin to take on overlord characteristics themselves. The rest of the animals look at one another and go, "Uh-oh."

THE TAKEAWAY: Like Orwell, you can press an ideology beyond its logical conclusion, rather than stopping short at a comfortable place. Alternatively, if your story begins in darkness, you can craft a bright ending as contrast, as Ray Bradbury did in *Fahrenheit 451*. It depends on what you want to communicate to readers: a warning, or a beam of hope? Allegorical stories can go either way.

ALSO READ: *Flatland* by Edwin A. Abbott, *Catch-22* by Joseph Heller, *Lord of the Flies* by William Golding.

YOU CAN CHALLENGE THE STATUS QUO BY SEEMING TO SUPPORT IT

Flannery O'Connor was, personally, as religious as they come, and religion infuses many of her works. But did she ever set out to *tell readers* what to believe? No. In the enduringly disturbing novel *Wise Blood*—which began as separate short stories—she explores mysticism, madness, courage, and cowardice. Although the thirst for redemption is a major theme, O'Connor also rams home the ugly turns faith can take: hypocrisy, violent fanaticism, and self-justification/self-deception. The journeys of the disillusioned preacher Hazel Motes and the terrifyingly clueless and increasingly unhinged Enoch Emery are compelling for their unpredictability and backwoods brutality. Faith is questioned throughout, and answered in varying degrees of certitude. When one turns against one's own tribe, humans know on a very elemental level that trouble is just around the corner.

THE TAKEAWAY: Let your characters plunge down their spiritual paths, even if zealotry is the end game, and let them experience crises of faith.

In real life, believers question themselves; nonbelievers question themselves. A life-changing event can shake a foundation, or create one.

Also, be aware that faith and religion are not one and the same; characters can have lots of spiritual adventures figuring that out.

ALSO READ: *Black Narcissus* by Rumer Godden, *The Screwtape Letters* by C.S. Lewis, *My Name Is Asher Lev* by Chaim Potok.

SYMBOLISM CAN BRING A POLITICAL THEME TO VIVID LIFE

One of my favorite passages in all of Charles Dickens's oeuvre is the Marquis's carriage ride in *A Tale of Two Cities*, a story of the French Revolution. The hypocritical, smug nobleman sits in his heavy coach—pulled by straining horses—and surveys the poverty-stricken countryside. Dickens inserts one moment that serves as both symbolism and foretelling:

> The sunset struck so brilliantly into the travelling carriage when it gained the hill-top, that its occupant was steeped in crimson. "It will die out," said Monsieur the Marquis, glancing at his hands, "directly."

We know the people have had enough humiliation and starvation, and the Marquis and his ilk are doomed. The crimson light suggests, of course, blood. (Note the word *steeped*, which connotes liquid.) Dickens is telling us that the Marquis has blood on his hands; he will be engulfed in blood; however, he persists in believing that the people's unrest will be short-lived. Doomed! Such a little moment can serve a purpose far beyond its literal meaning.

THE TAKEAWAY: Let your subconscious roam. It's much more difficult to invent a symbol than to be open to one appearing more or less on its own. This is a little bit mystical, but once you're open to the multiple meanings of everyday events and things, you'll be able to make use of them. A bullied child's bicycle can be a symbol of freedom. Open-heart surgery can connote repaired love. A constantly-fed woodstove might signify devotion.

ALSO READ: *A Raisin in the Sun* by Lorraine Hansberry (plant on the windowsill), *The Great Gatsby* by F. Scott Fitzgerald (the eyes of Dr. T.J. Eckleburg), *Crime and Punishment* by Fyodor Dostoevsky (Raskolnikov's dreams).

FOR THE LOVE OF LOVE, DON'T FORGET PASSION

When Graham Greene, a former journalist and British intelligence agent, wrote *The Quiet American*, set in Saigon in the early 1950s, he knew exactly what he was doing. The result became the seminal work of fiction on the Vietnam war. The novel renders the complex brew of colonialism, interventionism, and economic realities in a struggling country. But Greene knew that people are more than the sum of their opinions. He injects sexual obsession on the part of the main character, Fowler, with the lead female character, Phuong. The power struggle that erupts upon the arrival of Pyle—the quiet American, who personifies the damage a quixotic outsider can wreak—introduces ambiguity and chance, and *that* makes the novel far more compelling than if it had been a clinical exercise in political ideology and persuasion.

THE TAKEAWAY: Passion makes for unpredictability. You might be surprised by how inventively a love triangle can help you explore sweeping, complex political themes.

ALSO READ: *The Year of Living Dangerously* by Christopher Kock, *The Manchurian Candidate* by Richard Condon, *Gone With the Wind* by Margaret Mitchell.

IF YOU NEED MAGIC, PUT IT IN

Salman Rushdie's *The Satanic Verses*, concerning the immigrant experience, especially that of Indian expatriates in Britain, also deals with the dangers of absolutist religious systems. Rushdie employed satire and magical realism as well as dream sequences to trace the stories of two protagonists, Farishta and Chamcha, whose plane explodes en route from India to Britain. The pair's miraculous survival establishes the first of many layers of meaning, which, for an author aspiring to explore political and religious themes, are instructive. It's as if Rushdie used a giant painter's palette to portray the multiple cultures and reactions experienced by migrants, while also managing to individualize his thematic material: Islam, faith in general, renewal, racism, mental illness, romantic passion. *The Satanic Verses* avoids neatly packaged answers, and makes no disclaimers, which is why it has engendered both attackers and defenders.

THE TAKEAWAY: If you're drawn to unconventional fictional devices, or if you're unsure whether mimetic fiction can carry your story, by all means range into the magical, the hallucinatory, the fantastical. These devices and forms can give you leeway to probe themes that maybe even you don't fully understand. This is the essence of literary exploration.

ALSO READ: *Reservation Blues* by Sherman Alexie, *A Wrinkle in Time* by Madeleine L'Engle, *The Tin Drum* by Günter Grass.

LET HISTORY REPEAT ITSELF

Margaret Atwood digs into both politics and religion in *The Handmaid's Tale*, her speculative novel of totalitarianism, indoctrination, and institutionalized misogyny. Women of a low caste are held captive as breeders for the upper-level rulers, while anyone questioning the regime—male or female—may be disappeared at a moment's notice.

The story could have been written shorter and plainer, almost as an allegory. However, Atwood's details of both political theory and scriptural references—some of them more hinted-at than elaborated—give the novel a solidity, as if to say, "Yes, this could really happen, because—you remember—this and this and this happened at some point in history already. Do you see how close to us this all is?"

THE TAKEAWAY: Do your research. If you're drawn to a particular philosophy or historical period, read, read, read. And make notes! Atwood filled file cabinets with background material for her novels. None of it shows; all of it shows.

ALSO READ: *Atlas Shrugged* by Ayn Rand; *Gulliver's Travels* by Jonathan Swift; *A Clockwork Orange* by Anthony Burgess.

CONSIDER EVERY ANGLE YOU CAN THINK OF

- Do not view, or let your characters view, political and religious issues as dualistic. Get comfortable with the idea that issues have multiple facets, which connect and diverge, complement and contradict. This can be breathtakingly freeing as you explore plotlines, character arcs, beginnings, and endings.
- Bear in mind that hearts/minds/souls are complicated, and sometimes irrational. Celebrate this; make use of it.
- Embrace ambiguity.
- Be prepared to be misinterpreted. Confirmation bias is real.
- Ensure any religious or political theme serves to advance either plot or character development—though it doesn't have to always be in a big way. The use of religion, for instance, can be as simple as a character reliably stopping by the local chapel at precisely 3 p.m. every Wednesday to light a candle for an ancestor. A political theme can appear as easily as a character who collects old campaign buttons.

The ideal work of fiction entertains and enriches its audience. If you've been thinking about venturing into the deep thematic waters of religion and politics, the examples we've discussed here should give you courage and faith for the journey.

ELIZABETH SIMS (elizabethsims.com) is working on her tenth novel, which features a mayoral election in a big city. Her instructional title is *You've Got a Book in You: A Stress-Free Guide to Writing the Book of Your Dreams* (Writer's Digest Books), and she's a contributing editor to *Writer's Digest*. This article previously appeared in the January 2018 issue of *Writer's Digest*.

THE NAME GAME

Book Titles and Their Role

....

by Jennifer D. Foster

///

What's in a name? Nothing? Everything? The essence of success? It's been the theme of countless debates over the centuries, one that even Shakespeare pondered in *Romeo and Juliet* when he wrote: "What's in a name? That which we call a rose by any other name would smell as sweet." And it's one that pertains directly to the titles of novels and short stories. Some titles demand our attention, grabbing us right away with their wit, whimsy, humor, or horror, while others simply provide a connection we can't explain, and still others just fall flat. But how important are titles, and what role do they play in the success (or failure) of a novel or short story? Can a title be a game-changer? And what are some tips for landing a rock-solid title? Myriad authors, as well as a host of others in the publishing industry, including editors, literary agents, writing instructors, publishing consultants, and heads of professional writing organizations, weigh in on this ever-timely topic.

A SHORT HISTORY OF MEMORABLE TITLES

Before getting into the nitty-gritty of the importance and role of titles, a brief history into the naming process of some best-selling stories of all time provides much entertainment and insight. A few of the original titles of Margaret Mitchell's *Gone With the Wind* were *Pansy, Toe the Weary Land*, and *Tomorrow Is Another Day*. (This last one was changed when Mitchell discovered sixteen other books in print that began with "Tomorrow.") F. Scott Fitzgerald's *The Great Gatsby* was almost called *Gold-Hatted Gatsby, The High-Bouncing Lover* and *Trimalchio in West Egg*. George Orwell's original title for *1984* was *The Last Man in Europe*, but he thought that title was too bleak and so he changed it to *1984*, a reversal of the last two digits of the year in which he completed the manuscript, a year far enough into the future to make his fictional world seem possible. Somerset Maugham's first choice for *Of Human Bondage* was *Beauty and Ashes*, but it was already taken. Some of the first titles for Charles Dickens's *Bleak House* were *Tom-All-Alone's: The Ruined House* and *The East Wind*. Jane Austen's *Pride and Prejudice* was once called *First Impressions*, and Peter Benchley, twenty minutes before going to press with *Jaws*, had considered dozens of other titles, including *Leviathan Rising*, *Great White*, and *A Silence in the Water*.

THE IMPORTANCE OF TITLES

Are novel and short story titles really that important? *New York Times* best-selling author Erik Larson thinks so. In a 2015 blog post entitled "The Epic Hunt for an Epic Title for … an Epic," he says: "They should convey not only a sense of the book's subject, but also a feeling—will this be a funny read, or a contemplative one; is it a book I'd like to read at poolside, or in the dentist's chair waiting for the Novocaine to kick in; will it transport me to an imaginary realm, or knock me flat with trauma and despair."

In *The Pleasures of Reading: A Booklover's Alphabet* (Libraries Unlimited, 2014), author Catherine Sheldrick Ross says: "For publishers and booksellers, a title is a lure to attract readers." And she's bang-on. In the few seconds a manuscript/novel/short story has to attract its potential readers, whether it's in the slush pile, on crowded bricks-and-mortar bookshelves, or online, a title needs to be memorable, original, intriguing, easily understood, and appeal to its target market, conveying both the genre and the tone immediately. Taylor Brown, Wilmington, North Carolina–based best-selling author of the novels *Fallen Land*, *The River of Kings*, *Gods of Howl Mountain*, and *Pride of Eden*, stresses that a "well-conceived title … can make a story stand out from the slush pile of an agent or literary magazine. I've heard editors admit that their inboxes become so saturated with submissions that they can't read everything, so they have to choose only the pieces whose titles stand out."

In her book *The Complete Canadian Book Editor* (Brush Education Inc., 2016), Leslie Vermeer says "titles help readers meet books because they signal how the book is positioned in the market." That holds true for Nebraska native K.M. Weiland, an award-winning and internationally-published author who mentors fellow scribes and writes historical and speculative fiction. She says "a title's most important job is signaling genre. A particularly snappy title can act as a hook all its own (e.g., *The Curious Incident of the Dog in the Night-time*)." Anita Purcell, executive director of Canadian Authors Association, shares a similar view. "A good title serves to hook the potential reader—the more intriguing the title is, the better the chance of the book or story being selected by readers." Why is this the case? According to research conducted at Thomas Nelson, consumers first look at the book's title, followed by the cover, the back cover, the flaps, table of contents, the books first few paragraphs, and last, the price.

For Elizabeth Berg, Chicago-based, award-winning, *New York Times* best-selling author of *The Story of Arthur Truluv*, *Night of Miracles*, and *The Confession Club* (to be released in November 2019), titles are "really important. Along with the jacket, the title is the first chance a book has of catching someone's attention. The role of the title is not, as I thought for years, to be poetic. Rather, the role of the title is to give some suggestion of what the book is about." And, she says, "if it's catchy, that helps—or cool, or funny, or interesting in some way. Or beautiful (*Leaves of Grass*)," she notes. "If a reader can remember it so they can ask for it in a bookstore, that helps."

For Brown, "from a craft perspective, I sometimes feel that titles aren't given enough weight. Too many writers think of them as an afterthought. To me, the title is integral to the piece. Much like that idea of the *mot juste*—the exact, appropriate word we're always hunting for in our prose—the title has to be *just right*."

For Linden MacIntyre, award-winning journalist, international best-selling and Scotiabank Prize–winning author, and former host of the award-winning investigative TV documentary, *The Fifth Estate*, the importance of the title is "relative to the importance (familiarity) of the author. The less established the author, the more important the title, which must convey information about content, as well as the promise of originality and reader satisfaction." So, he says, "as an author's reputation grows, one notes the size of the byline grows in relation to the title of the work, which suggests that we eventually presume that an established author will probably deliver satisfaction at some level." He says that "a book title is a form of branding, but so, too, is an author's name." Geoffrey E. Taylor, director of the Toronto International Festival of Authors, agrees. "For a lesser-known writer, the design and title often play an even more important role." And, he adds, "books are still often judged by their covers. Depending on the book, the author's name, the cover design, and the title are all important elements of the packaging. For some readers, the publisher or imprint also has an influence. But, says Taylor, "the work itself is always the most important foundation of any project."

THE ROLE OF BOOK TITLES

Effective titles bring readers immediately and completely into the novel or short story's world, setting readers up for what's between the covers and interacting with the story in a compelling way. Titles may create a sense of inevitability (*A Farewell to Arms*; *Bleak House*), amp up anticipation and pre-set tension (*Gone Girl*; "Graveyard Shift"), or add intensity to the poetic nature of a key phrase (*Gone With the Wind*; *The Catcher in the Rye*). Essentially, a title can be described as the soul of the story, the key to its meaning. Lee Parpart, Toronto, Ontario-based writer, cultural organizer, editor for Iguana Books, and co-president of Canadian Authors Association, Toronto branch, says "titles are a bit like endings. They can't just sum up what the story is about without feeling horribly reductive, but they should hint at something central to the story. A good title should contain multitudes within itself in relation to the story or book." A book or short story's title makes you want to start reading it right away—or not—as the title is a story's best chance at a first impression. Michael Redhill, a Scotiabank Giller Prize–winning novelist (*Bellevue Square*), poet, and playwright who lives in Toronto, Ontario, concurs. "A title is a first impression, so it's very important, and a great title can live forever. It should offer something, or make a kind of promise to the reader. It should, ultimately, be of a piece with the work."

As Michael Hyatt says in *Platform: Get Noticed in a Noisy World* (Thomas Nelson, 2012): "If your title doesn't pull me into the content, what will? Don't be cute; tempt me." In her book *You've Got a Book in You: A Stress-Free Guide to Writing the Book of Your Dreams* (Writer's Digest Books, 2013), American prize-winning novelist and writing authority Elizabeth Sims says "choosing the right title for your book is like choosing the right name for your baby. No single perfect choice exists; several probably do, and as many as a zillion titles might be adequate." Sarah Selecky, author of the novel *Radiant Shimmering Light* and the Scotiabank Giller Prize–nominated short story collection *This Cake Is for the Party*, and the creator of Sarah Selecky Writing School in Prince Edward County, Ontario, also says titles can be akin to people's names, but has this take: "Once you know and love someone, you love the sound of their name because it's so familiar. The name can become an extension of the person. Sometimes a title can remind you of another famous title, which might bring a certain kind of attention to it."

For MacIntyre, "a book, especially a work of fiction, quickly becomes the 'property' of other people—readers who will relate in different ways to the content and form different impressions of what the book is saying." So, he says, "a book title must, if possible, be particular enough to create an idea of what the story is about, but flexible enough to accommodate changes in perception as the story unfolds in other minds."

For Lori Hahnel, Calgary-based author of *After You've Gone*, *Love Minus Zero*, and *Nothing Sacred,* creative writing teacher at Mount Royal University and the Alexandra Writers' Centre Society, and board member of the Writers' Guild of Alberta, "the role of titles is to interest the reader, perhaps get them to ask a question, and possibly to evoke something about the story—the mood, the atmosphere, maybe the era."

Newfoundland-based, award-winning author Charis Cotter feels the same way. She says a good title "needs to sum up the essence of the book in a few words, and it travels with the reader as they read the book, so they will keep referring back to it and connecting it to the story. For years after you read a good book with a really good title, thinking about the title will recall the book, and why you liked it so much." Patti Callahan Henry, a Mountain Brook, Alabama-based, *New York Times* and *USA Today* best-selling author of fourteen books, says "the title should be as clear as possible about what the story is at his heart." And she likes "a bit of surprise" in a title—"a little clue that you find during the story where you smile and say, 'Ah! That's where that title came from.'" Weiland agrees. "The title may make no sense out of context, other than to (hopefully) strike readers as an enticement. But *in* context, the title not only explains itself, but, optimally, adds a nuance of understanding to the story itself. I love it when I'm able to close a book (or finish a series) and suddenly realize: 'Oh, that's what the title meant!'" Purcell concurs: "Sometimes a good title is one that is most appreciated *after* the work has been read."

Parpart agrees, taking it a step further: "I love that a title holds onto its mystery until the end of the story or book, then relates back in a way that magnifies a number of key concerns. A good title actually demands that you go back to it after you're finished reading and think through all the layered ways in which it relates to the book or story." She cites Raymond Carver as a master at this. Parpart says although his titles are "deceptively simple," they "relate to the stories in complex and satisfying ways," referring to "A Small, Good Thing" (in his collection *Cathedral*) as an example of "an entire world of complex human emotion packed into one story." To her, "a good title is one that opens a door onto meanings that are inherent within the story, but that also depend on the title to deepen and become more apparent." Sam Hiyate, president and literary agent at The Rights Factory in Toronto, Ontario, agrees when it comes to short story titles. "Here, the title can have a more intimate relation to the story and can even become part of unraveling the meaning or message in the story at the end." But, adds Parpart, titles of "individual short stories are less important than the title of the collection."

WHOSE "JOB" ARE TITLES, ANYWAY?

While finishing detective novel *The Lady in the Lake*, Raymond Chandler wrote to his publisher, saying, "I'm trying to think up a good title for you to want me to change." When it comes to the responsibility of creating a title, opinions vary. Sims adamantly believes "an author must own that title if at all possible, if only for the sake of pure dignity. And of course, as the author, you've spent the most amount of time with that book, writing drafts, thinking about revisions while waiting for your hamburger at the drive-thru, feverishly contemplating possibilities of success or failure." So, she says, the writer is "the most invested in the project," and they "should never count on *anybody* to come up with a title. It's okay to invite input, though." Berg thinks "it's great when the author comes up with the title. Who better to do that, really? Who knows the intent and the heart of the book better than the author?" And, adds Redhill, "if the author has the 'right' title (i.e., everyone gets why that's the title), hopefully no one interferes."

Vermeer says that "titles are touchy things, frequently a point of fierce debate. Sometimes the author knows best." This was the case for the first novel by Trevor Cole, a Toronto, Ontario-based, award-wining author of *The Whisky King*, *Hope Makes Love*, and *Practical Jean*. "I am very proud of the title of my first novel, *Norman Bray in the Performance of His Life*. It came to me early, and even though it was a little unwieldy, it captured exactly what I wanted the novel to be." But, notes, Cole, "a famous editor, who I won't name, suggested I go with a shorter and more traditional title—*The Narcissist*. It just felt too on-the-nose and too one-note for me, so I refused. I'm glad I did." For Cole, "a literary novel is very much the expression of the author, and the title is part of that." And, he says, "there's also less financial pressure on most literary novels from the publisher's point of view."

But, notes Coles, "non-fiction and commercial fiction books bear a greater burden to deliver financially, so publishers tend to be more involved in crafting titles for these books. That tells you how important titles can be to sales." And, believes Berg, "sometimes an author (like me) needs a little help finding the best title. Sales and marketing departments can help show you what might work best. Editors and agents can help too." As an independent author, Weiland has never been aided in choosing titles. "For the most part, I find this a blessing. But there have been times when I would have appreciated the input of marketing experts." Ultimately, she says, "I think a team approach is best when possible. I dislike the idea of an author having no final say in her own work's title, but objective input is often invaluable."

MacIntyre can relate. "An author must be prepared to entertain and seriously consider other suggestions based on other points of view." His most successful book, *The Bishop's Man*, "had a completely different title up to a point where I thought that it was final. Near the end of the editing process, the publisher confessed she thought the title was too vague—that it said nothing about the theme or content of the book. Eventually, she suggested the one we used." And while MacIntyre feels the original title (which wasn't shared) was more "evocative," he admits he had to agree the title was "unclear to everyone but me precisely what it was evoking."

Callahan Henry also believes "titles should be as collaborative as possible. We are a team. In the end, the author is responsible for her work, but I think we all must feel as though we are a team working together in tandem to bring the novel to life." She says she's had "a couple titles change when the sales and marketing team got a hold of it. Sometimes I've agreed and others I've stuck by my title. Either way, I want to hear what they have to say, and I want their feedback." Her bestselling novel *Becoming Mrs. Lewis* was originally titled *The Consolation of a Happy Ending*, from a J.R.R. Tolkien essay about faerie stories. When she was at dinner with some author friends, one of them said about the original title: "Why isn't it just *Mrs. Lewis*?" And, she says, "I got that chill one gets when someone says something very true. I called my publisher the next morning, and we brainstormed some titles and ended up with 'Becoming,' because that is exactly what the story is about!"

Like Callahan Henry, Hahnel feels "the choice of title should be a collaboration between author and publisher; after all, the publisher likely has experience in marketing books." Parpart, who works for a hybrid publisher, says they "expect writers to take a first serious crack at coming up with a title for their work, but we reserve the right to suggest a new one if we think it will avoid duplication with other books or do a better job of helping the book find its readership." She believes "publishers owe it to writers to work with them to arrive at a consensus, rather than imposing a title on a work that's not their creation." Parpart thinks "it makes the most sense for titles to be negotiated between writers and editors, leaving anyone who hasn't read the book closely (which usually includes the publisher and the marketing team) well out of it. Writers and editors should be given wide latitude to shape titles together. They are the people who know the story best."

Cotter says the publisher's input "is essential only when the author is having trouble coming up with their own title." She says "sometimes a title will elude the author completely and then they need help. I know some writers just can't find their titles. That's when the publisher should step in. But the writer needs to be happy with the final choice." Ideally, she thinks "the author should come up with the right title for their book. Leaving it up to the publisher is like asking your doctor to name your baby! Naming something you create is a vital part of the process of creation." However, she says that since a title is "such an important marketing tool, the publisher should have input if necessary. But the author should do their best first to find the right title."

Purcell believes "the editor as well as the marketing team have the wider experience and knowledge of what works—and what doesn't work—with the target audience, and in most cases, the author should defer to their judgment." Similar to Purcell, Stuart Horwitz, a developmental editor and ghostwriter living in Providence, Rhode Island, who is the author of three books on writing that together comprise The Book Architecture Method, thinks "authors need to have a sense of how their work will be best marketed and become part of the solution of creating a great title that will do the necessary work in the market-place—rather than remaining on the sidelines with a disapproving glare when evolutions to a title have to be made."

Vermeer also notes that "sometimes the editor finds the title or subtitle during the editorial process, as the manuscript comes more fully into focus. Sometimes the sales and marketing staff offer suggestions, too, usually fairly early in the marketing conversations. The publisher may also have an opinion—and the publisher often wins." Taylor shares her sentiments. "Rarely does the title that the author comes up with become the final title. Usually (almost always) the title is selected by the publisher during the editing process. Sometimes titles are changed because there are other works that have a similar title. Or, a similar work is being published around the same publishing season by a different publisher."

Vermeer says that "finding the right title for a book requires both art and science, drawing on both your intellect and your gut." She says that while the title is being refined, "consider both demographics (statistical information about the readers) and psycho-graphics (information about readers' motivations and loyalties): who is 'the tribe' for a given book?" Lloyd D. Kelly, a literary agent and founder of Kelly Consulting Agency in Toronto, Ontario, agrees. "It's very important to think through what best represents the story itself, but will also strike a chord with publishers and ultimately with your readers. Collaboration with others and your agent is very important here, as you will want to ensure that your title is not only meaningful to you, but most of all, to your readers."

Brown sees the responsibility of the title this way. "It's absolutely the author's responsibility—at least at first. Now, the publisher and sales/marketing team may have thoughts or suggestions on the matter, dictated by their own knowledge of the market, and the title may change as a result of those thoughts, but ideally that's a collaborative decision-making process." And, he adds, "I think the goal of the writer should be to come up with a title that's so darn good that the publisher doesn't have to expend any energy trying to change it … easier said than done, I know!"

Hiyate also thinks "the author should have a title, even a preliminary one, as it's very hard to sell a book as *Untitled*—though it's acceptable to sell a second book called that." He once sold a book on proposal with the original title *30 Going on 13*, but it was retitled to *On the Outside Looking Indian*. "Sometimes we go out with the best title we can come up with on proposal, knowing it will likely be improved through the editorial and early sales and marketing processes," says Hiyate. Kelly holds the same philosophy. "It's best that you as the creator of your work put your best thoughts forward for a title and drive the conversation, as you know your manuscript the best. However, be willing to accept help and advice about titles that may work better." Like Hiyate, he typically puts together publishing proposals with a working title, "as often publishers can provide valuable input and collaboration here."

Selecky says she knows "writers who don't care about writing the title as much as the rest of the book; they leave it to the marketing team to decide. In my experience, publishers do like to have a hand in the titling of the books on their list. It's a marketing decision, so I get it. But marketing books is so difficult. Nobody ever really knows what's going to make a book a hit!" And, adds Parpart, "a publisher's determination to change the title of a book is probably directly related to the size of their investment in the project. Publishers are taking a financial risk every time they invest in an author. The title had better do the best possible job of mitigating that risk by drawing in readers, or the whole industry will suffer, and that's bad for everyone."

TITLES AND SELF-PUBLISHED AUTHORS

Purcell says self-published authors don't have the luxury of the expertise and experience of publishing house experts. "When authors are self-publishing, they are best to do as much research as possible to become better informed on the art and science of titles. They should also seriously consider using a freelance editor who has solid experience in the publishing world and can give advice on the workability of the title, as well as other important aspects of the manuscript." And like an author whose work is being traditionally published, self-publishing authors should research whether their proposed title has been already used," she says. "While it is possible to use a title that has been used before, it is rarely something you would want to do unless the other book is a completely different type of book." She points to the title *Prick*, which has also been used for two non-fiction books with the subtitles *Cacti and Succulents: Choosing, Styling, Caring* and *Confessions of a Tattoo Artist*. "Obviously, there is little chance of confusion between the two books and therefore no competition." Taylor suggests self-publishing authors have their "trusted readers read the work without a title. Then, ask them what they think the title should be or evoke."

A FEW WORDS ON COPYRIGHT AND SAME TITLES

Book titles are not protected by U.S. copyright laws, and that's why there are so many books with the same titles. According to Brian A. Klems in his online article "Can You Use a Book Title That's Been Used Before?" a work needs to possess "a significant amount of original expression" in order to qualify for copyright protection. And while that significant amount of originality isn't defined by any strict rules, "the courts have ruled that expressions as short as book titles do not qualify," he says. Some titles, though, do qualify for trademark protection—"specifically, series titles like Chicken Soup for the Soul, Harry Potter, Encyclopedia Brown, etc." And he adds that "the U.S. Patent and Trademark Office states that a trademark protects words, phrases, symbols or designs identifying the source of the goods or services of one party and distinguishing them from those of others. So once a book becomes successful enough to be considered a recognizable brand, it could be eligible for trademark protection."

So, before you consider or even finalize a title for your novel or short story, be sure to do your homework, if for no other reason than to avoid reader confusion when it comes to branding and capturing your target market. A title is a vital component of your book or short story's metadata—it is how your work introduces itself and makes that critical first impression. For Weiland, "searchability is a big consideration in successful titles these days." When she's considering a title, she always searches for it both on Google and on Amazon. "If a dozen books already share the same title, I have to seriously consider if a) I can rank among them and b) I really want a title that obviously isn't unique."

Redhill see it through this lens: "Authors shouldn't be horrified if they discover their title has already been used as a title by someone else. If it was more than ten years ago, wasn't famous, was in another genre, by a now-dead author—or any combination thereof—you shouldn't feel too sheepish about using it." Brown can relate. "For my first novel, *Fallen Land*, I panicked when I learned there was an existing novel with the same title, published just three years earlier. Fortunately, my publisher said this was a common occurrence, and we didn't have to change the title—phew!"

TIPS FOR WRITING EFFECTIVE TITLES

Unfortunately, no perfect formula exists for creating an effective title; the process involves a combination of hard work, research, creativity, and sometimes just plain luck. Sims's advice? "Short and snappy for fiction works best." Purcell concurs, adding that "short and uncomplicated titles seem to work best, including one- to three-word titles." Weiland says titles must "be easy to pronounce, spell, or remember. There are exceptions, of course, but for the most part, if readers can't find you, well, they can't find you." Taylor agrees. He says effectives titles "are not too long and do not use complicated or hard-to-pronounce words." Selecky also loves bold one-word titles. She cites *Rebecca* by Daphne DuMaurier as an example. "Titling a novel with the simple first name of a character makes me immediately intrigued. It's such an audacious choice, and in this novel, it puts you in the same position as the narrator, right away—compelled by the name Rebecca." Redhill agrees on the concept of simplicity. "Often the simplest thing is the best. *Sons and Lovers. The Idiot. The World According to Garp.* Each of these titles captures the essence of the book in the blink of an eye. Titles were memes before there were memes."

Sims says "you want to create a title that's easy to say, has a good rhythm, and isn't too long. One word is not too short, but after, like, four or five words, you're asking a lot of a reader to remember it accurately so they can buy or recommend it." She says one of her favorite titles is *In Cold Blood* by Truman Capote. "It's literally a bit of legalese. It grabs you and informs you that the book is serious; you're going to read things that are shocking, probably. The very word 'blood' triggers you in a primal way. Three short, one-syllable words. Bam, bam, bam." The short story "The Rocking-Horse Winner" by D.H. Lawrence is another example she cites. "I thought from the very first time I heard it, it was kind of beautifully creepy, and indeed the story has this semi-paranormal, dark aspect." Sims also suggests asking your beta readers what they think of your title. If you get consistent feedback saying it's too long or they don't "get it," then she says you need to reconsider. "Sometimes when we live with a title for a long time, we get overly possessive of it. Keep an open mind and play with a few ideas."

Hyatt, in his blog post titled "Four Strategies for Creating Titles that Jump Off the Page," says "great titles are PINC." He believes they must do at least one of the following: "make a promise; create intrigue; identify a need; or state the content." And while he says these strategies are mainly for non-fiction titles, he does state for fiction that "it seems like the strategy is usually to create intrigue, for example, *The Girl Who Kicked the Hornet's Nest* or *What the Night Knows*." The bottom line for Hyatt? "The right title can make you or break you."

In his blog post "7 Tips to Land the Perfect Title for Your Novel," Jacob M. Appel says the "trick is to find a happy balance between the all-too-forgettable and the truly over-the-top." He stresses that "you want to choose something that makes your readers think: *What a fantastic title! Why didn't I come up with it?"* He recommends using active verbs and precise nouns. "Eugene O'Neill's *Desire Under the Elms* is far more compelling than *Love Under the Trees* would have been." He also says to ensure your title crafts two meanings. "Most readers consider your title twice—once before they start reading your work, and again after they have finished." Appel states that many successful titles (he gives Shirley Jackson's "The Lottery" and John Cheever's "The Swimmer" as noteworthy examples) "gain hidden layers of meaning as they're read, so they pack an extra punch when reflected upon for the second time."

Purcell agrees, adding that titles with a double meaning or a play on words "act as teasers. If a title is able to intrigue or engage the mind in some way, making a potential reader curious enough to want to know more, it is more likely to hook the reader into buying and reading it." Sims agrees. "I like double-entendres, which might not be evident until the reader's into the book." Her novel *The Actress* is an example she shares, along with Harlan Coben's *Gone for Good*. "You could read that two ways, and one of them gives the key to the story."

Cole says that "while it can be useful to 'write to' a title in a short work, I think it can be too restrictive, at least when writing book-length fiction, to come up with a title early and then try to write the novel to fit." For Selecky, she prefers to title her work early on. "This is an important part of the creative process for me, and I require it." She also likes a title "to include a concrete word, like a proper name or a noun, so I can remember it. I like to anchor my titles with some kind of detail, so it creates an image in my mind." And she tells her writing students "to title their work as they're writing it, even if they change it later. Working on a story that has a title makes it more significant. You're more likely to show up for it, because it has a name." Redhill has a similar belief: "A good title should make you feel connected to the work." Sims concurs. "I really want a title as I'm going along. A title imbues a sense of reality to the project. You can pick just about any title, so you can at least say, 'Yeah, I'm working on a book. The working title is _____.'" She clarifies that you can "certainly refine a title or change your mind as you go; it's best not to be too rigid. But when you know a title is right, that's nice, and you can relax and enjoy the rest of the trip." Weiland shares their beliefs. "For fiction, it's crucial I find a title as soon as possible. I have a hard time getting a story to 'hang' right if there is no title to hang it on." With some of her earlier novels, she says a working title was enough to get her going, even though she changed them to better-advised alternatives later on. Usually, though, says Weiland, "I know the title from the beginning, and it is instrumental in guiding me to the heart of the story." The opposite holds true for Hahnel: "Very rarely do I have an idea of what a story is going to be called until I'm at least partway through it. Usually, I name the file after the main character until a title emerges."

Callahan Henry says authors "have to relax into the title. The harder we try and come up with something pithy and right, the more we cramp up." Cotter concurs: "Titles need to be inspired. And sometimes you need to wait for that inspiration. Thinking about it too much leads to brain freeze. The right title will slip in when you're not looking." Brown agrees. "Honestly, what's worked best for me is not trying too hard. Instead, it seems like titles will arise quite naturally during the writing process if you let them. This might sound strange, but I sometimes think the book ends up telling you its title, not the other way around."

Hiyate's "favorite title of all time" is *Norwegian Wood* by Haruki Murakami. "Essentially, if you know the lyrics of the song, you know what the book is about—or at least that's the effect the author wants to create," he notes. "I love the idea of using song or movie titles on proposals, and one of my biggest books was called *Girls in White Dresses*, from the song "My Favorite Things" from the movie *The Sound of Music*." Why is it effective for him? "It's because the idea is already resonating with readers and then the book can capitalize on that feeling the song creates."

Kelly cautions, however, not to "just come up with a title that you think will grab the most attention for the sake of being attention seeking. Most importantly, the writer needs to make sure that the title best represents what you have written." And lately, he adds, "there have been a number of best-sellers with "F*ck" or "Sh*t" in them. Just adding an expletive to attract attention can be a turn off." He recommends thinking of titles as a work in progress because "often the content of the book can take a turn in a different direction, and by the time the manuscript is finished, the original title that you had in mind may not best reflect how the story has turned out."

Another no-no, according to Sims, is the use or irony. "I remember seeing Steve Martin's story collection coming out and being titled *Pure Drivel* and thinking, 'Dude, you'll regret that.' Obviously, it's ironic; obviously, it's a joke, but way too few people get that. Even if you're the smartest person in the room, why handicap your book with a difficult title?"

For Redhill, usually a title has occurred to him once he's deep into a new draft, and he works with it until he's "sick of it or something better comes along." He says that "some titles are so obvious, they couldn't be/shouldn't be something else." He cites his award-winning novel *Bellevue Square* as "an example of a title that asserted itself as inevitable, and I called the book by that title before I'd written ten pages."

Horowitz says he congratulates those who happen to get the final title before the end of the drafting process. "You'll know because it continues to check out so often you kind of lose interest in worrying about it, and that worry is replaced by a quietness around it in your mind."

THE LAST WORD

When it comes to book titles and their role, perhaps Parpart summarizes it best: "A great book can survive a forgettable title, but a terrible book is not made less terrible by a great title. Book titles carry a heavy load, but they also work closely with … a host of other factors to draw readers in," she says. "When a strong title works together with compelling cover art and the quality is there in the writing, that's a powerful combination."

JENNIFER D. FOSTER is a Toronto, Canada-based freelance writer and editor, and her company is Planet Word. Her clients are from the book and custom publishing, magazine, and marketing and communications fields and include House of Anansi Press, Art Gallery of Ontario, TC Media Inc., *Quill & Quire*, PwC Management Services, *The Globe and Mail*, and *Canadian Children's Book News*. Some of her favorite titles (which are also some of her favorite novels and short stories) are: *The Bell Jar*; *She's Come Undone*, "The Yellow Wallpaper," *Cat's Eye, What We Keep*, and "The Tell-Tale Heart"). When Jennifer's not busy spilling ink for her first novel, she enjoys mentoring novice editors and writers, theater, traveling, gardening, camping, women's roller derby, urban hiking, baking, and yoga. Jennifer is administrative director of Rowers Reading Series and vice-president of Canadian Authors Association, Toronto branch. Find her online at lifeonplanetword.wordpress.com.

N.K. JEMISIN

The master fantasy world-builder reveals her secrets to success on Patreon and speculates on how the imagination might test-drive our future.

....

by Jera Brown

N.K. Jemisin wants to be a "storyteller of a writer." It's an ambition she claims not to have mastered, but many who have lost themselves in Jemisin's tales of captive gods and stone eaters are sure to disagree.

Through her three epic fantasy series (the Inheritance trilogy, the Dreamblood duology and the Broken Earth trilogy) as well as dozens of short stories and a novella, Jemisin has become known as a master world creator, each world brought to life through their detailed histories and unique mythology. And even though Jemisin's stories are set in universes where magic is commonplace, Jemisin's writing feels pressingly relevant to our own world. Her stories are based on flawed power structures and deeply held prejudices with devastating consequences. There's also hope—a constant theme through Jemisin's latest book, *How Long 'til Black Future Month.* The short story collection, published in November 2018, imagines futures for people of color like herself.

Storytelling is not just about the tales themselves, but also the connection between the storyteller and their audience. Outside of her work, Jemisin cultivates a bond with her readers through means such as her writing groups and outspoken activism in the fantasy and science fiction communities. This bond has paid off. In 2016, Jemisin quit her day job to focus on writing full-time with the generous support of her fans through the Patreon platform.

Among Jemisin's accolades, her debut novel, *The Hundred Thousand Kingdoms,* was short-listed for the James Tiptree Jr. Award, earned the Sense of Gender Award from the Japanese Association for Gender, Fantasy, and Science Fiction, and a Locus Award for Best

First Novel. In 2018, when *The Stone Sky* (the final book in Jemisin's Broken Earth trilogy) won the Best Novel Hugo award, Jemisin became the first author to win three Hugo Best Novel awards in a row. The novel also earned a Nebula Award for Best Novel and a Locus award for Best Fantasy Novel.

Jemisin spoke to Writer's Digest about her relationship to her readers and how she creates other worlds.

You were able to move into writing full time thanks to the support of your fans via Patreon. Can you tell us about making that decision?

It was not my decision 100 percent. I liked my day job [as a career counselor and academic advisor], and I really didn't want to give the job up. But at the time, my mother was ill and deteriorating. And my writing career had become more than full time. *The Fifth Season* came out and sold like gangbusters, which is great. But it meant that I immediately started getting a deluge of interview requests, and when you have a nine-to-five job, you can only do interviews between 5:30 and seven, and you've got to eat somewhere in there, and write on top of that.

Some things had started to give, and the things that had started to give were my health and my sanity. It was to the point where the only reason I hadn't quit already was because I was afraid of the finances of the writer's life, because I had done that before. Back at the beginning of my career, I had taken about a year-and-a-half off after I got the contract for the Inheritance trilogy. I discovered that I did not function well not having structure, not having people to interact with other than family, not having a purpose or sense of fulfillment. Because the thing about my day job was helping real people in real time and working with marginalized kids.

So given the stress that I was under, either I was going to break or I had to do something. That was when I decided to try Patreon.

What was that experience like?

Honestly, I didn't think it was going to work. There were some popular authors and artists who were making a great deal of money through Patreon, but I was just a midlist author. At the time, the Dreamblood series was the only thing that I had the royalty statement for, and I knew the sales of the last book of the series were not fantastic. So I was like, *If I do this, am I going to end up on the street?* That was the fear. I launched it on a Friday afternoon around 5:00 thinking nobody's going to pay any attention and by the end of the weekend, it was fully funded, and I was quitting my job.

Terror was the feeling that I had beforehand going into it and shock afterward. I still am making more than my initial goal of $3,000 a month, which was just enough to cover my rent and health insurance (at least before Trump, that was enough to cover my health insurance).

What advice do you have for other writers considering pursuing fan-based funding?

First and foremost, you do have to be a known person. I've seen friends who were writers that didn't have any books out attempting it, and it doesn't usually go well. The sense that I get from the people who contribute to my Patreon is that they do so out of a sense of personal relationship. They've read my books, and they feel like they know me on some level. And, to a degree, they do, because I put a lot of myself into my books.

They want to contribute to the writer that they've seen already and make sure that that writer produces more work. It's not just an altruistic thing on their part; it's a desire for more of the same.

So if you are a writer who's got some stuff out there and feel like you've built even a small audience, then it can be useful for you. You're not necessarily going to get rent and insurance money, but you are very likely going to get enough to cover a few utility bills. Even just $200 a month can make difference because everybody's living paycheck to paycheck. People should just manage their expectations going into it.

Make sure your story doesn't get too detailed. When you're explaining to people what you need, you don't want them to start, like, trying to work out your budget for you. I've seen mostly women feeling uncomfortable asking about money and so they literally delineate every single line of what they would spend XYZ on, and because they are working in a patriarchal environment, men jump in and start nitpicking how they're spending the money. When you go and look at men's Patreon [profiles], they're not offering you their life story. They're literally saying, "I need X for Y," and that's all you need to say.

What do your supporters expect in return?

You owe your readers whatever you've promised them. Once a month, I post an original vignette or a short story based on the world of the books that I've written so far. But you do have to deliver on that.

Now the readers can be reasonable about it; when I tell my readers I am deep in deadline hell and can't produce the thing that I told them I was going to try and produce for a while, for example.

The people I've seen have trouble with it are the ones that are not able to deliver on anything, and people will vote with their dollars for that.

In the introduction to your newest book, *How Long 'til Black Future Month*, you explained that you write "proof of concept" stories to "test drive potential novel worlds." Once the concept seems viable, where do you go from there?

If you read "Stone Hunger," [from *How Long 'til Black Future Month*] and then read the Broken Earth series, you would see where I did not like the way that "Stone Hunger" depicted the magical form orogeny. In that short story, it was very "sense specific." The character thought of everything in terms of the taste of food, and that wasn't going to work, because I wanted it to be effectively a science that had gone wrong.

Once I finish the proof-of-concept story and have sent it to people and have seen how they react to it, then I decide from there what I need to change or refine in order to make the world building work for a novel. What that usually means is that I simply start writing. I start doing test chapters to see what voices work best. I tried many voices with the Broken Earth until the second person thing just kind of clicked and seemed like the right voice, and that's a purely instinctual thing.

And, as I went forward, I realized that the concept of the magic from the short story wasn't going to work, but the rest of the world was fine.

You took a year off of novel writing to focus on short stories. The process improved your longer fiction by teaching you about the "quick hook and the deep character" and by giving you "space to experiment with unusual plots and story forms." How did you learn to trust whether your experimental forms were working?

Nearly all of the short stories [in *How Long 'til Black Future Month*] were run through one writing group or another. I didn't do a lot of experimental stuff to begin with, because I didn't know what the hell I was doing, and because I didn't even really know how to read experimental stuff at first. That was partly what that year was about. One of the magazines that I read during that year was *Strange Horizons*, for example, which does a lot of wide-ranging styles, everything from the very didactic to slipstream or interstitial, and a lot of new weird stuff. So that helped me learn how to read it, and then I finally felt more willing to try and write it.

In your blog and when you speak publicly, you frequently mention your readers.

Well, we're storytellers. Storytellers work with an audience. That's normal, isn't it?

I'd hope so. I do think that many writers seem to go off into their own world and are less interested in that dialogue and more interested in just presenting something.

Well, that's their personal choice, and not everybody feels comfortable with it. I get it. To me though, I've always wanted to be a storyteller. When I was a teenager, I used to babysit kids, and I would tell them stories to entertain them. I've traveled to lots of different places in the world. I've seen storytellers, and I've always admired the hell out of them. It's a different art form from writing. It is an art form that I have nowhere near mastered, but I try to be a storyteller of a writer and to me that's what it's supposed to be. But everyone's mileage varies, I guess.

In your acceptance speech for your latest Hugo Award, you explain, "As this genre finally, however grudgingly, acknowledges that the dreams of the marginalized matter, and that all of us have a future, so will the world." Do you believe that speculative fiction has the power to change society?

I didn't used to think so, and then I started to realize, first off that I was underestimating it, and then second of all that other people had already done that calculation and were using it for evil. It sounds kind of corny, but I started to realize it when right-wingers tried to take over fandom. When you started trying to take over every bit of media, and you suddenly see Nazis in video games and comic books trying their damnedest to squish out people who are different from young, straight, white boys, and harassing and trying to dox them, there's a reason for that.

I don't necessarily think it's a one-for-one relationship. I don't think that I'll write a book and it'll change the world. But I do tend to think that the things we are capable of imagining and believing are our future are influenced by all of the media that we consume.

Growing up, I had a really hard time imagining a future for myself and for other black people because when you looked at science fiction, you did not see black people in the future. There had been some kind of unspoken apocalypse that wiped us all out, and Asians, and everybody else too. Certainly that's not what the creators of those works intended to convey, but that was what their work did convey by their exclusion.

People often point out—and I don't know how true this is—but one of the reasons that America became comfortable enough with the idea of a black man and the presidency to elect Obama was because, in TV and film, presidents had been black for quite some time. So we pursue in reality the things that we're capable of imagining and those of us who are in industries or fields that play with imagination have a responsibility to depict futures that are for everyone. And I think that if we can manage to start doing that, then it makes it easier for people in the present day who are trying to influence policy to say, "Look, this is just like in *Star Trek*, we can do blah, blah, blah."

Is there anything else you'd like to convey to other writers?

The industry is changing in some good ways. It's still got a lot of the old blind spots, and it's still struggling to fully embrace futures and mythologies other than what it's familiar with, and that's not entirely surprising. Business has always been reactive rather than proactive. Artists may sometimes have to go outside of traditional channels in order to get our vision realized, but I do like the fact that more people now have the ability to get their work out there.

People encouraged you to self-publish after the *Killing Moon*—your first novel that landed you an agent—didn't find a publisher, but you wanted the book to be in libraries ... Is the only channel other than traditional press self-publishing?

There's small press publishing, but small press publishing also doesn't get you in the library. But you decide on the publishing method that satisfies what it is that you want. A lot of people simply want to make the maximum amount of money possible. For them, self-publishing is perfect because they can control how much they spend on production and marketing. And there's no nobody else kind of like taking chunks out of that profit. They're willing to pay in time for that flexibility. I am not willing to pay in time. Time is my most precious resource, not money.

JERA BROWN is a freelance writer and columnist for *Rebellious Magazine*. Selections from her memoir-in-progress have been published in *The Rumpus* and *Big Muddy*. This interview appeared in the May/June 2019 issue of *Writer's Digest*.

MIN JIN LEE

The *Pachinko* author talks finding story ideas that truly provoke your passions, and how to tune out the burden of expectations.

....

by Amy Jones

//

Before becoming the acclaimed author of two bestselling books, Min Jin Lee was used to working obscene hours as a lawyer in a New York firm. So it should be no surprise that as a full-time writer, Lee now throws herself into researching and promoting her books with that same relentless rigor.

When Lee spoke with WD, she was on the last leg of a 12-day tour that included conducting research for her next book at a punk-rock bar in Minneapolis, giving a speech about women in the workplace at the *Wall Street Journal* conference in San Francisco, and accepting the fiction runner-up award at the Dayton Literary Peace Prize.

"I do have an agenda—to make you all Korean," she said during her acceptance speech at the DLPP ceremony. "After all, perhaps it is the job of writers to ask, *Could they be us?*" It's that sentiment that resonates so deeply throughout Lee's work—the ability to provide readers a portal into her character's experience.

In *Free Food for Millionaires*, her 2007 debut, protagonist Casey Han is fresh out of college and trying to make hard choices about career, love, and friendship, but she's also the daughter of Korean immigrants trying to balance their traditional expectations with her very American lifestyle. The characters in *Pachinko*, Lee's 2017 National Book Award finalist, are simultaneously trying to feed their families, pay their bills, and survive life as unwelcome Korean refugees living in war-torn Japan.

These are all topics that hit close to home for Lee. The daughter of a North Korean father and South Korean mother, her family emigrated from Seoul to the U.S. when she was only 7 years old. After growing up in Queens, the author graduated from Yale and attended law school at Georgetown University. Now 50, her writing has been translated into more than 27 languages. *Pachinko* was named a *New York Times* "Top 10 Best Book" of 2017 (and landed on 75 other "best book" lists), received a Medici Book Club Prize, and was also a *New York Times* bestseller.

Yet for Lee, the road to literary success was neither easy nor meteoric. "Having only produced two books in 25 years [of writing], I'm surprised I have readers," Lee laughs. "And I think, in a way, it's kind of a relief. If you don't think about it too much, it allows you this freedom because you don't want to be self-conscious about what you do."

Lee sat down with WD before accepting her Literary Peace Prize, where she opened up about writing for readers instead of reviewers, creating her own writing education, and finding the topics that keep her motivated.

In writing your novels, I read that you threw out many "completed but inefficient" manuscripts.

Yeah. They were terrible!

How do you decide when it's time to throw out a manuscript and what exactly does that mean to you?

I throw out the whole thing, and it's very distressing to people but it's very liberating to me. Because by the time I've done it, I realized something that's kind of cool. You've already internalized a huge pattern in your brain just from the act of doing it. I don't think there's a shortcut to writing novels; I haven't seen that shortcut. I used to think that I was just dumb and I couldn't figure out how to do it. And that if I had a clever teacher or if there was a better lesson then I would be able to figure out how to write faster. But then I realized the kind of books I'm writing are so weird and unusual compared to my peers. I'm really a throwback. Because of that, I realized there was no other way to do it except by learning how to write this omniscient narration. Now that I know how to do it, I don't feel like it was a waste of my time.

That said, when I was throwing the books away, I was really upset and I felt like a failure. It's like, there's only really one way to do it—just by doing it. But it was very awful. [Laughs] I would spare anyone this trial if I could.

How do you know when to throw it away? Well this is the thing—you do know. Because you're a good reader. Everyone who wants to be a writer is usually an amazing reader. That's given me a kind of confidence to say when my work isn't working. When I'm drafting, I'm super nice to myself. I don't judge. I try to put on two different hats: Drafting me, and I'm super nice, and the editing me, and I'm very tough.

Pachinko was a National Book Award Finalist. Your books have been compared to those of George Eliot and Jane Austen. As you work on your third novel, do those sorts of accolades create any unwelcome pressure?

No, no, because you know, people are being nice. And they're being gracious and you can't take yourself that seriously because if you did, you would just stay home! I think that what I can do is, I want to be truthful and I want to honor the subject. I'm writing about education and wisdom, and what it means for Koreans around the world. It is a very painful and a very important topic for Koreans. It's an important topic for every-body, but for Koreans? They kind of hold it almost like some sort of bizarre idol, like they're really attached to what it means. If I could be faithful to the subject and to their intentions and to their feelings, then I feel like I've done my job. As for whether or not people are going to continue to compare me to the greats? That would just become like a funny bonus.

I also want it to be a good read. I care a lot about that, because I hate reading boring books. I mean, you have to read a lot of boring stuff, and I don't want to have to read anything boring. So it's got to be a great topic that I care about, but it has to be a really interesting read because I'm competing against so many things and everybody's busy.

Right, and there's so much competition for people's attention.

Right! It's not even the money. Most people will spend $15 on very fancy coffee drink and a sandwich, right? So I don't think it's the money at all. But for me to ask, "Can you give me 15 hours of your life?" That is *major*! It's almost like asking for marriage! [Laughs] It's such a big deal nowadays to ask someone for their time. So I think, *I need to work for that*. I need to merit *that*.

I've read that you're outlining a new novel, *American Hagwon*. What does the outlining/planning process look like for you?

I always start with a big idea, so [this time] it's education and wisdom. And my meta-physical question, for now is, "How do you live a wise life?" Then it becomes about peo-ple and of course the central thrust of my work is diaspora. How does diaspora figure into these questions because I am asking for these Koreans around the world. They've been ejected from their place of origin and they have consciously either chosen to move, or due to war and colonization, they have decided to go elsewhere. Once they go there, they change and they change others.

Then I interview *constantly* and I do a lot of fieldwork the way journalists and anthro-pologists work. I go somewhere and I spend time, and I think, *Well, what am I feeling? What am I looking at?* That's what fiction can do: I can talk about feelings and weird sit-uations where people don't make any sense because people really don't make any sense. That weird disjuncture is what I think fiction does really well.

AMY JONES is the managing content editor for *Writer's Digest* and former managing content director for Writer's Digest Books. Prior to joining the WD team, Amy was the managing editor for North Light Books and IMPACT Books, where she met lots of talented artists who helped her find her artistic side and encouraged her to buy far more art supplies than she should have. Like most WD staffers, Amy is a voracious reader and has a particular interest in literary fiction, historical fiction, and page-turning mysteries. When she's not reading, Amy can be found daydreaming about Italy or volunteering at the Ohio Alleycat Resource, her local no-kill cat shelter. Find Amy on Twitter at @AmyMJones_5. This interview was previously published in the March/April 2019 issue of *Writer's Digest*.

JAMES PATTERSON

After more than four decades in publishing,
the record-breaking bestseller has this to say:
You can go your own way.

by Bobbi Dempsey

"I never give anyone writing advice." That may seem like a surprising way to open an interview with a magazine for writers, but James Patterson has always avoided casting himself in the role of all-knowing writing guru. He is a firm believer that every author is unique, and each must find a way to use their individual strengths and talents: "I don't tell other people what they should do. I just know what I do. But I can share what works for me."

What works for Patterson also seems to be popular with a massive number of readers. He holds the Guinness World Record for the most No.1 *New York Times* bestsellers, and his books have sold more than 375 million copies worldwide. He is the author of dozens of titles, many of them written with a crew of co-writers that Patterson seems to keep very busy.

He is passionate about promoting literacy and a love of reading, and invests significant resources to support those causes. He has donated more than 1 million books to students and soldiers, and heads up a foundation that has funded some 400 Teacher Education Scholarships at 24 colleges and universities. Plus, he has donated millions of dollars to school libraries and independent bookstores, including giving hundreds of thousands of dollars in surprise bonuses directly to bookstore employees.

Patterson created a children's book imprint, JIMMY Patterson Books for Young Readers—affectionately known as "JIMMY Books"—in 2015. He says the imprint has one simple and important goal: "When a kid finishes a JIMMY book, I want them to say, 'Give me another book.'"

In 2016, Patterson played a central role in launching BookShots, a publishing program offering original, shorter-length (150 pages maximum) stories that each sell for $5 or less.

Some of the stories are written by Patterson and his co-authors and feature his well-known characters like Alex Cross, while other titles are from a stable of authors selected and edited by Patterson himself. He also teamed up with former President Bill Clinton to pen the thriller *The President Is Missing*, which hit stores in June and sold more than 152,000 hardcovers in the first week according to NPD BookScan—the best first-week sale for an adult hardcover fiction title in several years.

The prolific author is enthusiastic about the latest JIMMY Books project, a new line with a super-smart 12-year-old homeless girl as the heroine. *Max Einstein: The Genius Experiment* is the first of a series (co-written with Chris Grabenstein) Patterson will produce in conjunction with the Albert Einstein Archives.

His strongest asset as a writer, Patterson would say, is his love for telling (and hearing) stories. His likeable, relatable personality immediately makes people comfortable. He's the kind of guy you'd gladly spend hours trading tales with over a drink. As we settled in for this interview, he told a fascinating story about his uncle, whose last name was the same as my hometown. Placed for adoption as a child, the uncle—as an adult—tracked down his brother (Patterson's father), then eventually located their long-lost father in a seedy bar near a bridge in Poughkeepsie, only to leave without ever introducing himself.

Wow, that's quite a story, like the real-life start of a novel.

There's a writing lesson from that story. Sometimes people go, "Oh he's not a very good writer." There were no big sentences in that story. But it was a really good story. I write colloquial. I don't tell anyone else they should write colloquial. I write the way we tell stories. If everybody wrote that way, it wouldn't be great. But that's what I do.

I write in a very simple way. I don't *have* to. I was a PhD candidate at Vanderbilt. I know the rules—I could write more complex sentences if I wanted to. But I choose not to, and I think it's a valid approach, in the same way I think James Joyce had a valid approach when he wrote *Ulysses*. It's a *different* tone, a different voice. I think my voice is pretty distinctive.

You don't come from a privileged background, but you credit that for playing a role in your success.

I was poor and middle class, and then I was poor and middle class again. And now I'm rich. And on balance, I prefer being rich. But I don't think I'd be who I am or write what I wrote if I hadn't been brought up the way I was. I think I had a 10-cent allowance when I was a kid. And I had to make that decision: Are you going to have a Pepsi this week? My mom went to the supermarket and she would get one quart of soda a week. For four kids. And she was a teacher at a Catholic school, so there was no money there.

I didn't come to [success] overnight. I was lucky in that the first novel I wrote won an Edgar when I was 26, but I didn't have anything that would have supported my life in terms of making a living until I was in my 40s. I was very practical about it, and humble. I didn't feel that I should expect to make a living, or that I was entitled to anything. That seemed very presumptuous to me. I've always been big on, "Have a dream *and* a backup dream."

I'm very organized. Anybody I work with would tell you, "He's very focused." I'm clear and will say exactly what I want. But there's room for exploring. I think most of [my co-authors] have enjoyed it. It allows me to do what I love, which is telling stories. Most of the time I will lay out the story. And then we'll take that 40 or 60 pages and turn it into 350 pages.

Do you ever worry about running out of ideas?

You see this? [He holds up a stuffed folder, roughly the size of an old-fashioned Manhattan phone book, with the word IDEAS in large capital letter on the front.] I don't think I'll run out anytime soon. I'm not quite as quick as I was, but I still do okay.

You've done a lot for childhood literacy. It seems like a natural fit.

It's a fit, and also I tend to be very efficient and do a lot of things at the same time. With the philanthropy, I try to make it as efficient as I possibly can. To have a really clear-cut mission. So with JIMMY Books, it's a simple mission but I think it's clear and it allows us to function in an appropriate manner. Which is, when a kid fiinshes a JIMMY book, I want them to say, "Give me another," instead of, "I never want to read again." If we can deliver on that, then JIMMY Books is a big deal. Because we've done what we should do, which is putting books in kids' hands so they say, "I like to read."

Your latest kids' project is the Max Einstein book. How did that come about?

The Einstein estate came to three publishers, and they basically said, "We want to do a series of books that would introduce kids around the world to Albert Einstein. And the only thing we're going to give you is the name Max Einstein." So we had to pitch our idea.

And we're little compared to the others. But I figured we have an advantage because I'm going to write them and I'll be in the room, so I can talk about what the books will really be like. When we get in there, I said, "For starters, I'd like to make Max a girl. Because I think that's more useful now. Because there are still a lot of places in the United States, and a lot of places around the world, where girls and women are not encouraged to study math and science. I know in some places it's beginning to even out and that's good, but I think it would be good that Max is a girl." They really liked that a lot. Then I began to tell them the story we had in mind. They were very smart in that they said it's got to be entertaining or kids won't read it. Then you get to the challenge of, how do you write an entertaining book about Einstein's theories?

You've called it the most important work you've ever done.

Because I think it is, if we go around the world and turn on millions of kids to science. For a long time, a lot of the scientists that you would meet, if you asked, "What got you started?" They would say, "Reading science fiction." They read sci-fi and they get turned on. And they say, "I want to do that. I want to build a time machine, or whatever it is." That would be part of the stimulus. I think this series of books will turn a lot of kids on. Boys and girls. And in certain families there are going to be doubts. The way I grew up, my mother encouraged my sisters to become secretaries. We didn't know any better.

To me, that's important. I mean, it's nice to have created Alex Cross and the Women's Murder Club and all that. And Max Ride, my other Max. Now I have two Maxes. And Max Ride, that's another empowered girl who basically becomes the leader of this group of kids who escape from a terrible situation and have to power through life somehow.

Do you find it challenging to write in the voice of female characters?

Not really. I think a piece of it is, I grew up in a house full of women. Mother, grandmother, sisters, female cat. I write about women a lot. I wouldn't feel comfortable writing something like Harlequin [romance]. I don't have the voice. I just spent so much time with women, especially growing up. I think I kind of got it, within reason. I know and empathize with a lot of things that people go through.

BookShots was a new, innovative approach to publishing works that were packaged differently than your normal books. You take a very active role in creating and developing the outlines for all of your full-length books. Was it the same with BookShots?

There they are right there. [He gestures towards shelves filled with books]. That was one year's output. That was insane. To take that on and write a bunch of them, and then to do the outlines. That year, I wrote 2,500 pages of outlines. And all of my outlines are three or four drafts. So that's nuts.

I did all of the outlines. Every outline was 30 or 40 pages. In 90 percent of the cases, I would have [my writers] sending pages every two weeks. And I would call them back that day and either say, "Keep going," or, "Hold up, we're going off the track here." That's the way I work with all of my books, with my co-authors.

But with the BookShots, we're kind of done with them. It was too threatening to publishers, honestly, to have these books for $3.99 and $4.99. They thought people were not going to want to buy a hardback. But I think toward the end, [the books] were really catching on. What we do now is we'll bundle three of them in a paperback. They sell well. We've gone from being in the red to being solidly in the black. But the energy it took was incredible. We're doing an occasional one now. But not a lot.

What do you think of the state of publishing today? There's a trend toward giving content away, especially in the form of ebooks.

People think free books are great, but it's a problem when publishers want to give away writing. Just like what happened with musicians. It's like, *Okay, let's go to your house and take your money*. A lot of free books don't even have editors. That's a problem because if the last six books you read were terrible, you're not going to want to read any more. It turns people off from reading. I think at this point it's important that we still have publishers and editors. That can all be done on the internet, but nobody's *really* doing it yet. Not really doing it, to a big extent.

I wonder who is going to do the Great American Novels in the future. Who's going to develop the next Hemingway or Fitzgerald, or whoever you think is terrific. The reality of it is, if *Infinite Jest* is published today on the internet, it sells five copies, and it disappears. *Ulysses* goes out and sells three copies and disappears.

Originality is a big thing. You get too much of, *Let's do another one of whatever*. Realistic fiction in YA is a hot thing now because of John Green. But people forget that John Green does really, really good dialogue. And if they can't do great dialogue, they might not make it. That's what separates him. Obviously, he promotes really well, too. But his dialogue is great.

How did Bill Clinton compare to your normal co-author situation?

He was very respectful. What sets that book apart, in my opinion, is the authenticity. This book, even though it's a novel, people really get to know what it's like to be president during an unbelievably tense three or four days, where the worst attack ever on the United States is imminent. There's a traitor in the White House. The president disappears. If that kind of attack were about to happen, this is the way it would go.

It's all real stuff. If the motorcade was attacked, this is exactly what the Secret Service would do. [Clinton] has been a joy to work with. It's fun. I think we get a kick out of each other. It's a little different than with my other co-authors. I defer more here than I normally would. And he wants everything to be accurate, which is good. A lot of times, if you're a fiction writer, you just make shit up. But he'll be pushing for accuracy. And he pushed for the characters to be more flesh and blood. There's an assassin in the book, and in the first draft or two, I think she was a little bit more of a thriller device. But she wound up being *very* flesh and blood, and he really helped push for that—to make sure she was a real human being.

Anybody on your wish list you'd like to work with?

Maybe the Pope. I think the two of us could do something good.

....

BOBBI DEMPSEY (bobbidempsey.com) is a freelance writer whose credits include *The New York Times, Harper's, Quartz*, and Parade. She is the author of the Amazon Kindle Single ebook *Degrees of Desperation: The Working-Class Struggle to Pay for College*. This interview was previously published in the November/December 2018 issue of *Writer's Digest*.

....

CURTIS SITTENFELD

The bestselling *Eligible* author explains how her characters keep it "real," and why plumbing the awkward and uncomfortable can lead to the richest social commentary.

....

by Baihley Gentry

Ask Curtis Sittenfeld who she writes for, and the answer is simple: "Other writers, of course!"

If you know Sittenfeld's work—masterful demonstrations of literary prose coupled with insightful, unblinking inquiry into emotion, identity, and the human experience—it's little surprise she aims to please just the crowd most authors would claim among their harshest critics.

"I think writers [in particular] notice and appreciate what other writers are doing," Sittenfeld says. "It's like they can see the machinery, see the scaffolding. So if you can get another writer to suspend disbelief and just read for pleasure or climb into your fictional world, that's a huge achievement."

Sittenfeld has a long history of impressing other scribes: Before her senior year of high school she won *Seventeen* magazine's 1992 fiction contest and, a few years later, was named one of *Glamour*'s Top 10 College Women. After graduating from Stanford in 1997 with a degree in English, she joined the editorial staff at the newly minted *Fast Company*. Two years later she nabbed a coveted spot at the prestigious Iowa Writer's Workshop, where she earned her MFA.

In 2005, at 29, she released her debut novel, *Prep*, a boarding-school set coming-of-age tale that quickly became a *New York Times* bestseller. Five other fiction titles—of which many also became bestsellers; were optioned for film and television; and have been translated into more than 30 languages—were released in regular succession. *Prep* was followed by *The Man of My Dreams*, a story that follows young Hannah Gavener's trials and tribulations in life and love over a decade and a half; *American Wife*, a fictional account of a First Lady loosely based on the life of Laura Bush; *Sisterland*, about psychic twin sisters; and *Eligible*, a modern retelling of Austen's *Pride and Prejudice*, based in the Midwest.

In between writing novels, she's published numerous short stories and essays in such esteemed markets as *The New York Times*, *The Atlantic*, *Slate*, *The Washington Post*, *Time*, *Vanity Fair*, *Esquire*, *The New Yorker*, and more. Several of her short stories that appeared in *The New Yorker* were included in her first short story collection, *You Think It, I'll Say It*, published in April (2018).

Sittenfeld took a break from promoting *You Think It, I'll Say It* to talk with WD about her process, writing cringeworthy moments and crafting unlikeable-yet-empathetic characters.

You've noted that "so much in life that's a little bit awkward … is just ideas for fiction." And that's something we see a lot in your latest book, *You Think It, I'll Say It*, where the characters often find themselves in intensely cringe-worthy situations. How do those sorts of interactions inspire your writing?

I can't imagine writing scenes where the characters are not emotionally invested, even if it's a negative emotion. I think that when people are having awkward feelings, there's potentially a lot of complicated things going on. That that can be interesting. And if you start to unpack why you felt awkward in a certain moment … it's not always multilayered, but it certainly can be.

You do an incredibly skillful job creating characters who are "real" and complex, but are also empathetic (if not necessarily likeable). What's the key to walking that line?

I think that saying who's likable and who isn't is very subjective. And so I actually don't really think I can control that. I guess it's more like I could create pretty inoffensive characters who, to me, would be very boring—but [that] most readers would not find objectionable. That's not really my goal. I'm so lucky I get to write fiction, because the last thing I would want to do is bore myself while writing it. [While] I would never think to myself, "Does this dialogue or gesture make a character likable or unlikable?" I *would* think in terms of, you know, is this character transgressing in a way that I mean for her to transgress? Or you know, is she being fair to other characters? Or is she being mean to other characters? So I wouldn't really think about her likability in terms of the way the reader receives her, but I would within the ecosystem of the story.

That makes sense. Like, are they brimming with malice toward other characters?

Yeah. And if they do have malice, is it serving the story? 'Cause if it is, then that would be left in. [Laughs] But I don't think that I would include malice for the sake of malice. I *would* include it because it made the story interesting. Or revealed something about the characters or advanced the plot. But it's not like my overarching goal is to explore the nastiest side of humanity.

Your latest book is of short fiction, but you're known for your novels. How do you decide whether a piece can sustain a full novel, versus being a better fit for the short form?

For something to be a novel, I have to get an idea that seems like it's this huge thing that I can approach in like 17 different ways. And if someone asks me why I found it interesting, I could spend four hours explaining why, because it feels infinitely interesting. Whereas a short story feels more contained. It still feels intriguing, but [more] like this sort of fleeting or brief thing, instead of feeling infinite. It's more like conceiving of a moment instead of conceiving of a massive topic.

You've talked before about your creative process, saying sometimes an "organizational issue is more to blame for feeling stuck than a content" problem. How can other writers recognize this occurring in their own work, and go about fixing the issue?

It's funny, because I have a friend named Sheena who is also a writer, and she and I talk about this all the time. A phrase that we use a lot with each other is "paper management." I think sometimes a writer, including me, could feel as if maybe they've written 60 percent of a novel. But it's not the first 60 percent—it's sort of out of order. And then maybe 30 percent of it doesn't exist and then 10 percent of it is really messy. And [that makes the] whole document feel kind of intimidating and I don't know where I should enter it or how to tame it. And so something Sheena and I talk about [that helps] is to print out the whole thing, and within that one stack of paper take the sections that are basically finished, and put paper clips around those parts. And then take the sections that are messy and put them in blue folders [or whatever]. And then take the stacks that don't exist and put manila folders as placeholders for them. Then you think to yourself ahead of time, "Okay, I'm gonna go through the blue folders first on these days. And then I'm gonna go to the manila folder."

I find that in general, if I plan ahead what I'm going to do with my own writing or even *when* I'm going to write, it goes more smoothly. If you sit down and you don't know what your plan of attack is, you can feel immobilized and then just decide to check Twitter. And then your day goes down the toilet. I think that there's this element of feeling, from an organizational perspective, as if you're in control of your manuscript and that can actually allow your creativity to proceed.

You have a very different process than most writers I've interviewed. Are you familiar with the "plotting versus pantsing" debate?

Ha! Oh, no, oh, no, is that like flying by the seat of your pants? Oh, God, I don't know if I've heard of that, but I can tell you right now: I do *not* believe in pantsing.

You do seem like more of a plotter, though actually I can maybe see both.

Yeah. I do outlines and then I change the outline as I go along. So it's not as if I'm following a recipe. I mean, think whatever works. I would never tell someone else how to write her novel if asked, nor [give] unsolicited advice, like, "This is how everybody should do it." But I *do* think as a reader—I bet you if you gave me 10 novels and said, "Guess which writer outlined, and which didn't," I don't think I'd have a 100 percent success rate, but I feel like I could probably guess more often than not who did and who didn't.

I think I believe more in pantsing for a short story than for a novel. [In a novel], 300 or 400 pages is a lot of material to manage. [To me] it's almost like, you can get through a day without planning your day. But you can't get through a year without planning your year.

You have an MFA from the Iowa Writer's Workshop, which is well-known for its literary prestige. I'm sure it's so difficult to boil down, but what favorite takeaway(s) did you learn there?

I started at the workshop on my 24th birthday. And I actually naïvely thought to myself [at the time], "I won't learn that much about writing, but I'll have *time* to write." And then I actually learned a tremendous amount about writing. The No. 1 thing that I learned, and it was life-changing for me, it was from Ethan Kanin, who was my professor and my advisor. He leads his workshops by dividing the discussion into talking only about structure, then only about character, then only about language. And that usually covers anything anyone would want to say about a particular manuscript. But the way that he talked about structure made me think about structure, and it gave me control over my own writing. And I think it's usually structure that determines the success or failure of any piece of writing, whether it's fiction or nonfiction.

You once quoted an editor who said, "People think publishing is a business, but it's a casino." How do you take that statement, as an author? In your experience, have you found that to be truly the case?

It's funny because I think a lot of people, including published writers, sometimes think the system is sort of rigged. And to some extent, the system *is* rigged. It's undeniable that if a publisher pays a large amount for a book, it means that they will get behind it, in terms of promoting it. And [even] if there are limited resources, they will use those resources. But that doesn't mean the book will be a bestseller. A publisher can't really manufacture a bestseller out of thin air—because if they could, they would do it every time. Every editor has had their heart broken many times, believing in a book that just doesn't get very much attention or traction. And the inverse is true, where a book doesn't necessarily have much institutional support but then does end up getting attention and finding readers. There are things that a writer can contribute to the overall publication process, but a writer can not control how many books sell. I don't know if that's more disappointing or liberating for writers to hear.

Many of our readers juggle writing on top of another profession, and finding time to write is a challenge. What is your advice for finding and guarding that writing time?

Decide ahead of time when you'll write. Maybe plan out a week or two weeks or a month at a time. Write it into your calendar, whether it's an hour every day or half an hour once a week. Then, treat it like a commitment with another person that you like and are lucky to spend time with. Don't treat it like drinks with your friend that you secretly don't like or are going to bail on. [Laughs] And during your writing time, just sit there— you don't have to write, but just sit there and don't get online. If you think of things that you have to do—whether it's change the laundry, schedule a doctor's appointment, whatever—write it on a little Post-It next to you. You might have to sit there like four times before you really do write, but you just have to train yourself to attack this time. A journalistic trick is putting the letters "TK" as a placeholder. Let's say you want to find a song from 1976. Put "1976 song TK," in your work-in-progress, look it up later, and therefore avoid going down that internet rabbit hole [during your writing time].

Often when I give writing advice, I think "Oh, God, Curtis, this is what *you* should do." [Laughs.]

Your first novel, *Prep*, became a *NYT* bestseller, which tends to put additional pressure on subsequent books. How do you handle that pressure? Looking back, knowing so many of your books have become bestsellers, what would you tell your younger self?

I think the pressure is hard to quantify. You know like what, what does that mean exactly? Does that mean you hope that your other books sell a certain number of copies? Do you hope they get a certain flavor of review? It's hard to say. I think that almost any advice I would've tried to give my younger self, I'm probably much likelier to believe just because of my own experiences. And publishing has changed. My first book came out in 2005. Digital readers didn't exist for my first three books, and it was like 0 percent digital sales. And then when *Sisterland* came out in 2013, it was close to 80 percent digital sales. It was this huge change. You and I were just discussing what the writer can and can't control. Really the only thing I can control is the writing, and so I think I should try to write books that I feel very emotionally invested in, and should work hard to make them the best that I can make them. And beyond that, you know, I should try to be polite and pleasant to work with. [Laughs] I guess if I were to give advice to my younger self, it would be that your own sense of success will wax and wane. The work is the constant. Stay focused on the writing and remember why you became a writer—which is just that you like to write and you like to read.

What's up next for you? I've heard that an adaptation of *You Think It, I'll Say It* is slated to become a 10-episode series for Apple TV, starring Kristen Wiig. Will you play any role in the production of that?

Reese Witherspoon's company Hello Sunshine is [producing it], and Reese Witherspoon and Kristin Wiig and a writer named Colleen McGuinness are all working together and developing it. I'm in contact with Colleen, and sometimes she bounces ideas off me. I would have a title with the show. But I would not work in California and it would not be a full-time job. I'm also writing a novel about Hillary Rodham, who has fallen in love with Bill Clinton. In real life, she declined his marriage proposal a few times and then eventually accepted. In my version it's, *What if she declined his marriage proposals and then went on her own way?* It's occupying my brain, so I guess that's a good sign.

BAIHLEY GENTRY was the associate editor of Writer's Digest. This interview appeared in the October 2018 issue of *Writer's Digest*.

BUSINESS BASICS

Successfully Submit Your
Novels & Short Stories

//

It's true there are no substitutes for talent and hard work. A writer's first concern must always be attention to craft. No matter how well presented, a poorly written story or novel has little chance of being published. On the other hand, a well-written piece may be equally hard to sell in today's competitive publishing market. Talent alone is just not enough.

To be successful, writers need to study the field and pay careful attention to finding the right market. While the hours spent perfecting your writing are usually hours spent alone, you're not alone when it comes to developing your marketing plan. *Novel & Short Story Writer's Market* provides you with detailed listings containing the essential information you'll need to locate and contact the markets most suitable for your work.

Once you've determined where to send your work, you must turn your attention to presentation. We can help here, too. We've included the basics of manuscript preparation, along with information on submission procedures and how to approach markets. We also include tips on promoting your work. No matter where you're from or what level of experience you have, you'll find useful information here on everything from presentation to mailing to selling rights to promoting your work—the "business" of fiction.

APPROACHING MAGAZINE MARKETS

A query letter by itself is usually not required by most magazine fiction editors. If you are approaching a magazine to find out if fiction is accepted, a query is fine, but editors looking for short fiction want to see the actual piece. A cover letter can be useful as a letter of introduction, but the key here is brevity. A successful cover letter is no more than one page (20-lb. bond paper). It should be single-spaced with a double space between paragraphs, proofread carefully, and neatly typed in a standard typeface (not script or italic). The writer's name, address, phone number, and e-mail address must appear at the top, and the letter should be addressed, ideally, to a specific editor. (If the editor's name is unavailable, use "Fiction Editor.")

The body of a successful cover letter contains the name and word count of the story, a brief list of previous publications, if you have any, and the reason you are submitting to this particular publication. Mention that you have enclosed a self-addressed, stamped envelope for reply. Also, let the editor know if you are sending a disposable manuscript (not to be returned; more and more editors prefer disposable manuscripts that save them time and save you postage). Finally, don't forget to thank the editor for considering your story.

Note that more and more publications prefer to receive electronic submissions, both as e-mail attachments and through online submission forms. See individual listings for specific information on electronic submission requirements, and always visit magazines' websites for up-to-date guidelines.

APPROACHING BOOK PUBLISHERS

Some book publishers ask for queries first, but most want a query plus sample chapters or an outline or, occasionally, the complete manuscript. Again, make your letter brief. Include the essentials about yourself: name, address, phone number, e-mail address, and publishing experience. Include a three- or four-sentence "pitch" and only the personal information related to your story. Show that you have researched the market with a few sentences about why you chose this publisher.

BOOK PROPOSALS

A book proposal is a package sent to a publisher that includes a cover letter and one or more of the following: sample chapters, outline, synopsis, author bio, publications list. When asked to send sample chapters, send up to three consecutive chapters. An outline covers the highlights of your book chapter by chapter. Be sure to include details on main characters, the plot, and subplots. Outlines can run up to thirty pages, depending on the length of your novel. The object is to tell what happens in a concise but clear manner. A synopsis is a shorter summary of your novel, written in a way that expresses the emotion of the story in addition to just explaining the essential points. Evan Marshall, literary agent and author of *The Marshall Plan for Getting Your Novel Published* (Writer's Digest Books), suggests you aim for a page of synopsis for every twenty-five pages of manuscript. Marshall also advises you write the synopsis as one unified narrative, without section heads, subheads, or chapters to break up the text. The terms *synopsis* and *outline* are sometimes used interchangeably, so be sure to find out exactly what each publisher wants.

We occasionally receive letters asking why a certain magazine, publisher, or contest is not in the book. Sometimes when we contact listings, the editors do not want to be listed because they:

- do not use very much fiction.
- are overwhelmed with submissions.
- are having financial difficulty or have been recently sold.
- use only solicited material.
- accept work from a select group of writers only.
- do not have the staff or time for the many unsolicited submissions a listing may bring.

Some of the listings do not appear because we have chosen not to list them. We investigate complaints of unprofessional conduct in editors' dealings with writers and misrepresentation of information provided to us by editors and publishers. If we find these reports to be true after a thorough investigation, we will delete the listing from future editions.

There is no charge to the companies that list in this book. Listings appearing in *Novel & Short Story Writer's Market* are compiled from detailed questionnaires, phone interviews, and information provided by editors, publishers, and directors of awards and conferences. The publishing industry is volatile, and changes of address, editor, policies, and needs happen frequently. Many magazine and book publishers offer updated information for writers on their websites. Check individual listings for those website addresses.

Organization newsletters and small magazines devoted to helping writers also list market information. Several offer online bulletin boards, message centers, and chat lines with up-to-the-minute changes and happenings in the writing community.

We rely on our readers, as well, for new markets and information about market conditions. E-mail us if you have any new information or if you have suggestions on how to improve our listings to better suit your writing needs.

A FEW WORDS ABOUT AGENTS

Agents are not usually needed for short fiction and most do not handle it unless they already have a working relationship with you. For novels, you may want to consider working with an agent, especially if you intend to market your book to publishers who do not look at unsolicited submissions. For more on approaching agents and to read listings of agents willing to work with beginning and established writers, see our **Literary Agents** section. You can also refer to this year's edition of *Guide to Literary Agents*, edited by Robert Lee Brewer.

MANUSCRIPT MECHANICS

A professionally presented manuscript will not guarantee publication. But a sloppy, hard-to-read manuscript will not be read—publishers simply do not have the time. Here's a list of suggested submission techniques for polished manuscript presentation:

- For a short story manuscript, your first page should include your name, address, phone number, and e-mail address (single spaced) in the upper left corner. In the upper right, indicate an approximate word count. Center the name of your story about one-third of the way down the page, skip a line, and center your byline (the byline is optional). Skip four lines and begin your story. On subsequent pages, put your last name and page number in the upper right corner.

- For book manuscripts, use a separate title page. Put your name, address, phone number, and e-mail address in the lower right corner and word count in the upper right. If you have representation, list your agent's name and address in the lower right. (This bumps your name and contact information to the upper left corner.) Center your title and byline about halfway down the page. Start your first chapter on the next page. Center the chapter number and title (if there is one) one-third of the way down the page. Include your last name and the novel's title in all caps in the upper left header, and put the page number in the upper right header of this page and each page to follow. Start each chapter with a new page.

- Proofread carefully. Keep a dictionary, thesaurus, and stylebook handy and use the spell-check function on your computer.

- Include a word count. Your word processing program can likely give you a word count.

- Suggest art where applicable. Most publishers do not expect you to provide artwork and some insist on selecting their own illustrators, but if you have suggestions, let them know. Magazine publishers work in a very visual field and are usually open to ideas.

- Keep accurate records. This can be done in a number of ways, but be sure to keep track of where your stories are and when you sent them out. Write down submission dates. If you do not hear about your submission for a long time—about one to two months longer than the reporting time stated in the listing—you may want to contact the publisher. When you do, you will need an accurate record for reference.

Electronic Submissions

- If sending electronic submissions via e-mail or online submission form, check the publisher's website first for specific information and follow the directions carefully.

Hard-Copy Submissions

- Many publications no longer accept hard-copy submissions. Make sure to read the submission guidelines carefully.
- Use white 8½" × 11" bond paper, preferably 16- or 20-lb. weight. The paper must be heavy enough not to show pages underneath and strong enough to take handling by several people.
- Type your manuscript on a computer and print it out using a laser or ink-jet printer (or, if you must, use a typewriter with a new ribbon).
- An occasional spot of white-out is okay, but don't send a marked-up manuscript with many typos.
- Always double-space and leave a 1" margin on all sides of the page.
- Don't forget word count. If you are using a typewriter, there are several ways to count the number of words in your piece. One way is to count the words in five lines and divide that number by five to find an average. Then count the number of lines and multiply to find the total words. For long pieces, you may want to count the words in the first three pages, divide by three, and multiply by the number of pages you have.
- Always keep a copy. Manuscripts do get lost. To avoid expensive mailing costs, send only what is required. If you are including artwork or photos but you are not positive they will be used, send photocopies. Artwork is hard to replace.
- Enclose a self-addressed, stamped envelope (SASE) if you want a reply or if you want your manuscript returned. For most letters, a business-size (#10) envelope will do. Avoid using any envelope too small for an 8½" × 11" sheet of paper. For manuscripts, be sure to include enough postage and an envelope large enough to contain it. If you are requesting a sample copy of a magazine or a book publisher's catalog, send an appropriately sized envelope.
- Consider sending a disposable manuscript that saves editors time (this will also save you money).

RIGHTS

The Copyright Law states that writers are selling one-time rights (in almost all cases) unless they and the publisher have agreed otherwise. A list of various rights follows. Be sure you know exactly what rights you are selling before you agree to the sale.

Copyright is the legal right to exclusive publication, sale, or distribution of a literary work. As the writer or creator of a written work, you need simply to include your name and the date on your piece in order to copyright it. Be aware, however, that most editors today consider placing the copyright symbol on your work the sign of an amateur and many are even offended by it.

To get specific answers to questions about copyright (but not legal advice), you can call the Copyright Public Information Office at (202)707-3000 weekdays between 8:30 A.M. and 5 P.M. EST. Publications listed in *Novel & Short Story Writer's Market* are copyrighted unless otherwise stated. In the case of magazines that are not copyrighted, be sure to keep a copy of your manuscript with your notice printed on it. For more information on copyrighting your work, see *The Copyright Handbook: What Every Writer Needs to Know, 11th edition*, by Stephen Fishman (Nolo Press, 2011).

Some people are under the mistaken impression that copyright is something they have to send away for and that their writing is not properly protected until they have "received" their copyright from the government. The fact is, you don't have to register your work with the Copyright Office in order for your work to be copyrighted; all writing is copyrighted the moment it is put to paper.

Although it is generally unnecessary, registration is a matter of filling out an application form (for writers, that's Form TX). The Copyright Office now recommends filing an online claim at www.copyright.gov/forms. The online service carries a basic claim fee of $35. If you opt for snail mail, send the completed form, a nonreturnable copy of the work in question, and a check for $65 to the Library of Congress, Copyright Office-TX, 101 Independence Ave. SE, Washington, DC 20559-6000. If the thought of paying $35 each to register every piece you write does not appeal to you, you can cut costs by registering a group of your works with one form, under one title, for one $65 fee.

Most magazines are registered with the Copyright Office as single collective entities themselves; that is, the individual works that make up the magazine are not copyrighted individually in the names of the authors. You'll need to register your article yourself if you wish to have the additional protection of copyright registration.

For more information, visit the U.S. Copyright Office online at www.copyright.gov.

First Serial Rights

This means the writer offers a newspaper or magazine the right to publish the article, story, or poem for the first time in a particular periodical. All other rights to the material remain with the writer. The qualifier "North American" is often added to this phrase to specify a geographical limit to the license.

When material is excerpted from a book scheduled to be published and it appears in a magazine or newspaper prior to book publication, this is also called first serial rights.

One-Time Rights

A periodical that licenses one-time rights to a work (also known as simultaneous rights) buys the nonexclusive right to publish the work once. That is, there is nothing to stop the author from selling the work to other publications at the same time. Simultaneous sales would typically be to periodicals with different audiences.

Second Serial (Reprint) Rights

This gives a newspaper or magazine the opportunity to print an article, poem, or story after it has already appeared in another newspaper or magazine. Second serial rights are nonexclusive; that is, they can be licensed to more than one market.

All Rights

This is just what it sounds like. All rights means a publisher may use the manuscript anywhere and in any form, including movie and book club sales, without further payment to the writer (although such a transfer, or assignment, of rights will terminate after thirty-five years). If you think you'll want to use the material more than once, you must avoid submitting to such markets or refuse payment and withdraw your material. Ask the editor whether he is willing to buy first rights instead of all rights before you agree to an assignment or sale. Some editors will reassign rights to a writer after a given period, such as one year. It's worth an inquiry in writing.

Subsidiary Rights

These are the rights, other than book publication rights, that should be covered in a book contract. These may include various serial rights; movie, television, audiotape, and other electronic rights; translation rights, etc. The book contract should specify who controls these rights (author or publisher) and what percentage of sales from the licensing of these subrights goes to the author.

Dramatic, Television, and Motion Picture Rights

This means the writer is selling his material for use on the stage, in television, or in the movies. Often a one-year option to buy such rights is offered (generally for 10 percent of the total price). The interested party then tries to sell the idea to actors, directors, studios, or television networks. Some properties are optioned over and over again, but most fail to become dramatic productions. In such cases, the writer can sell his rights again and again—as long as there is interest in the material.

Electronic Rights

These rights cover usage in a broad range of electronic media, from online magazines and databases to interactive games. The editor should state in writing the specific electronic rights he is requesting. The presumption is that the writer keeps unspecified rights.

Compensation for electronic rights is a major source of conflict between writers and publishers, as many book publishers seek control of them and many magazines routinely include electronic rights in the purchase of print rights, often with no additional payment. Writers can suggest an alternative way of handling this issue by asking for an additional

15 percent to purchase first rights and a royalty system based on the number of times an article is accessed from an electronic database.

MARKETING AND PROMOTION

Everyone agrees writing is hard work whether you are published or not. Yet once you achieve publication, the work changes. Now not only do you continue writing and revising your next project, you must also concern yourself with getting your book into the hands of readers. It's time to switch hats from artist to salesperson.

While even best-selling authors whose publishers have committed big bucks to marketing are asked to help promote their books, new authors may have to take it upon themselves to plan and initiate some of their own promotion, usually dipping into their own pockets. While this does not mean that every author is expected to go on tour, sometimes at their own expense, it does mean authors should be prepared to offer suggestions for promoting their books.

Depending on the time, money, and personal preferences of the author and publisher, a promotional campaign could mean anything from mailing out press releases to setting up book signings to hitting the talk-show circuit. Most writers can contribute to their own promotion by providing contact names—reviewers, hometown newspapers, civic groups, organizations—that might have a special interest in the book or the writer.

Above all, when it comes to promotion, be creative. What is your book about? Try to capitalize on it. Focus on your potential audiences and how you can help them connect with your book.

IMPORTANT LISTING INFORMATION

- Listings are not advertisements. Although the information here is as accurate as possible, the listings are not endorsed or guaranteed by the editors of *Novel & Short Story Writer's Market*.
- *Novel & Short Story Writer's Market* reserves the right to exclude any listing that does not meet its requirements.

SUBMISSION CONTROL

Sending your work to literary magazines puts you at the whim of editors—but there's more in your power than you may realize. Consider these insider tips to blast your entries into another orbit.

....

by Dinty W. Moore

///

The trick is to draw as little attention to your formatting as possible, not the other way around. Unlike kindergarten musicals and best puppy contests, cute does not win any points here.

Here's a vital truth that many writers do not realize about the process of submitting work to literary journals: You are in control.

Yes, submitting to a literary magazine can feel like a game of wait-and-wait-and-wait-some-more, and after many months pass, a rejection may arrive with little or no explanation. But that doesn't mean you're powerless. You wield far more influence than you imagine. For instance:

- You decide when the work is ready to submit.
- You decide where to send it.

- You decide how many magazines to submit the work to simultaneously.
- You decide when a magazine has held your work for too long and when it is time to politely withdraw your submission and send the poem, story, or essay elsewhere.

Let's take these one-by-one.

YOU'VE GOT THE POWER

You decide when the work is ready, and that is not only a crucial step in the publication process, but also something no one else can do on your behalf. Making this choice requires a temporary suspension of ego and a hard-edged editorial eye, which can be difficult at first, but becomes easier with time and practice. Read your work out loud, pretend you aren't the one who wrote it, and ask yourself honestly, *Am I hearing a piece of writing that is as tightly constructed and as elegantly worded as possible? Is the writing clear? Is it saying something fresh?* We all make mistakes and send work around too early, so don't berate yourself if you misjudge here and there, but never forget the power you hold as the first and best critic of what you've written. When it comes to publishing, tough love can be your best friend.

Next, *you* decide where to send your finished work. When I started submitting to literary magazines, this meant navigating the dusty back corners of a university library, flipping through the pages of *The Iowa Review* or *Crazyhorse* to decide if the journal seemed like one that would appreciate my style and point-of-view. Today's digital literary world makes it vastly more convenient to review the aesthetic leanings of a particular magazine (and to find their specific submission guidelines). Even journals that are not primarily online typically have websites that provide excerpts of the work they publish. The trick is to determine as best you can where your work fits, *before* sending it out. Of course, it is the editors who will make the final selection, but it can be helpful and empowering to see the publication process as a shared decision.

Third, it is *you* that decides how many magazines to submit the work to simultaneously. Blasting your stories or poems off to every corner of the literary universe as if you are wielding a t-shirt launcher at a minor league ballgame is a lousy strategy, and given submission fees, also a poor financial choice. But the vast majority of literary journals now accept simultaneous submissions, so how many makes sense for you: three, four, five at a time? There is a trade-off here. Too few and your odds grow thinner. Too many and you risk giving your work up to a magazine on your "B" list because one of your dream markets has yet to respond. Without question, the ideal situation is to have a robust backlog of polished poems or a handful of finished stories or essays, each circulating to a select number of journals you respect and admire. Persistence, and constant attention to improving the quality of what you write, wins out every time. (And always, always, let the editors know when your work has been accepted elsewhere.)

Finally, *you* get to decide when a magazine has had your work for too long without responding, and thus when the time is right to politely withdraw the submission and send the poem, story, or essay elsewhere. It is your work, after all, until an editor asks for the first serial rights and you agree, so it is *your* decision when to withdraw your invitation. After all, you're doing the editor a favor here, not the other way around.

Wait, What Do You Mean I'm Doing the Editor a Favor? Aren't I Begging Editors to Publish Me?

No, you aren't begging them. You are assisting them. Your voice, your words, your ideas, all have value, and at the end of the day, without *your* writing these magazines would not exist.

I have been editing the online nonfiction magazine *Brevity* for more than 20 years, and I can tell you firsthand that it is a happy moment, a thrill actually, each time I find a piece of writing so good that I can't wait to share it with our readers. My job is to showcase the best examples of the flash essay that I can locate, so when you send me work that is polished, powerful and ready-to-go, you are helping me do my job well.

That thrill, by the way, is twofold if the writing comes from a writer *without* a long list of previous publications. Discovering new talent is one reason many editors first become involved with the (eye-straining, low-paying) world of literary publishing, and it remains a motivation for most of us throughout our careers.

So What If I'm Rejected Anyway?

Well, it happens—and unfortunately there is no getting around the inevitability of disappointing news. (Though, come to think of it, would the acceptances be nearly as sweet if there weren't a few sour notes that came first?)

Another aspect of the submission process over which you have the power, however, is how you choose to think about rejection. There are any number of reasons your poem, story, or essay might be returned with a "No Thank You" note. One possible reason is that the editors thought your writing was "amateurish crap," but despite the negative voices in our heads, that's usually not the case.

Maybe the editors liked where your poem was headed but thought it needed a few more rounds of revision. (They'd like to help with that, but most editors are busy people, often doing the work for no pay, with other jobs and responsibilities.) Maybe they liked your story just fine, except it too-closely resembles something the magazine published in its previous issue, or is about to publish in the next. Maybe the editors have decided to publish only experimental essays, or only formal poetry, or only stories highlighting marginalized voices.

Or maybe you've hit the editor on a bad day, when she is dog-tired, overwhelmed, and not making good decisions.

Deciding that each rejection is proof of your complete and undeniable failure as a writer, and your dismal lack of future potential, is unnecessarily punishing yourself when writing and waiting are hard enough as it is. There are thousands of magazines—and tens of thousands of writers—in the world. Not every submission is going to be a good fit for every editor.

SO, ANY OTHER INSIDE TIPS?

Sure, I've got plenty. For instance:

Don't Stress Over Cover Letters

Editors either ignore them, or glance at them quickly before diving into the first line or first sentence of your submission. You will accomplish so much more over time if you take the minutes spent worrying about your cover letter and apply them instead toward improving the submission itself.

In fact, you can simply adapt this boilerplate and be done with any worry about what to say:

> Dear [Name of Literary Journal] Staff:
>
> I have attached my essay/poem/story ["Title Here"] for your consideration.
>
> My work has appeared in *The Mugwump Review, Journal of Fancy Words* and *Sage*. [Or, if your work has not appeared anywhere, just say so: "If accepted, this will be my first literary magazine publication." Editors love discovering new talent.]
>
> This is a simultaneous submission, but I will promptly withdraw my piece if it is accepted elsewhere. Thank you for considering my work for publication in [Name of Literary Journal].
>
> Sincerely,
> [Your Name Here]

If you can sincerely say something meaningful about why you've sent to a particular literary journal—perhaps by mentioning a recent poem or story, or a special issue that you recently read and enjoyed—feel free to add that as well, but only if you really mean it. Otherwise, keep it simple.

Yes, Formatting Matters

The trick is to draw as little attention to your formatting as possible, not the other way around.

Unlike kindergarten musicals and best puppy contests, cute does not win any points here. Editors will read dozens of submissions in a stretch, and eye fatigue is a real thing. You win points by making your work easy to read: All prose should be double-spaced, unless the magazine guidelines request it differently, using a familiar font like Times New Roman or Garamond with standard margins of about one-inch.

In Publishing, There Is No One-Size-Fits-All

I'm an editor, a teacher, and a writer myself, so I'm often asked, "Should I send my work to the tippity-top, most prestigious magazines that pay the most? Or set my sites lower, where the odds may be more in my favor?"

Here's the answer: You need to know your "all of this hard work was worth it" target.

If you are a writer who will not rest or consider your hard work validated until the editors at *The New Yorker* finally accept one of your short stories to sit alongside the work of literary luminaries such as Zadie Smith and George Saunders, then you need to pursue that dream. This means you will likely be rejected for years, and you'll have to repeatedly grit your teeth and go forward—always, always, *always* looking for ways to make your writing more surprising, more current, more gut-punch powerful. And you'll probably need a bit of good luck as well.

If, however, publishing your poems or essays in a mid-size journal—knowing that hundreds of readers will see what you have written, and that you will have a chance to either hold the magazine in your hands, or, if the journal is online, forward a link along to all of your friends and post it on social media—feels like fulfillment to you, then by all means, aim for excellent, well-regarded second-tier journals. (You can always up your game in a few years.)

Or maybe it would be entirely gratifying to publish in a small, regional literary journal, one that is focused on writers from your city, or the northwest corner of your state, or a small digital community of writers who love work centered on paranormal experiences. If this feels right to you, if your reaction will be, *Yes, good for me, and all my hard work was worth it*, then don't let anyone tell you that the journal is too small to matter.

All of them matter.

If we aren't going to get rich writing our essays, stories, and poems, then we have to find other rewards, and feeling proud is the best reward we have.

What Do I Do If an Editor Invites Me to Send More Work?

The first thing you should do is smile. This is good news, and not to be taken lightly.

But then, pause a moment. If an editor says, "No on this one, but we'd love to see more," what you send next should be every bit as polished, every bit as powerful as the work the editor returned to you with the welcome request. Don't squander the opportunity by making the all-too-common mistake of frantically sending the editor every story or poem on your hard drive. If the work you send is less wonderful, the editor is going to lose interest fast.

Take a breath: Ask yourself, *What do you suppose they liked best about this submission, and how does it line up with other work I've seen in that magazine?* If you have something that you think fits the bill, you should wait a week and then send it along. If nothing is ready to go, wait a few months while you revise one of your existing pieces into a near-perfect-as-possible state, then send it with a polite note of your own.

The wheels of publishing grind slowly, so take your time to get it right.

How Can I Decode Submittable's Status Updates?

Don't bother trying. "Received" may mean no one has looked at your submission yet, but that is not always the case. The status "In Progress" may mean editors have read and are considering your submission, but that is not always the case either. Your best bet is to stop compulsively checking Submittable status indicators, and instead focus on what you'll write next.

What Else?

Here's the most important tip: Every few months, ask yourself *why* you're doing this. If writing, waiting, and facing rejection make you truly miserable, maybe you should stop.

But if you don't want to stop, if writing is necessary, like breathing, then change your way of thinking. The long wait, the long odds, the sometimes inscrutable aesthetic tastes of the editorial staff: You have to put all of that aside and write new poems, essays, and stories.

And that's a good thing.

Because the more you write, the better you get.

DINTY W. MOORE is author of the memoir *Between Panic & Desire*, the writing guide *Crafting the Personal Essay*, and other books. He has published essays and stories in *The Georgia Review*, *Harpers*, *The New York Times Sunday Magazine*, *The Iowa Review*, and elsewhere. He edits *Brevity*, a journal of flash nonfiction. This article was previously published in the March/April 2019 issue of *Writer's Digest*.

THE EDITOR BEHIND THE CURTAIN

For first-time authors, the publishing process is often shrouded in mystery. Here's an inside look at what goes on behind the scenes— and how to leverage it for future success.

....

by Alex Field

//

Whether you're currently writing a book, querying agents, or on submission to publishers, allow me to share this small-but-important truth: There's an editor out there right now— sorting stacks of pitch letters, book proposals, and manuscripts, thumbing through literary agent submissions, reading selections of the manuscripts she requested from authors directly—who is seeking to buy a book similar to yours.

So, in a sense, your future editor occasionally thinks about you.

Picture this person for a moment: Perhaps she's an associate editor for a mid-level imprint, working her way up at a growing publishing company. She majored in creative writing or English literature or journalism in college, where she developed a passion for Jane Austen or Jack Kerouac, Joan Didion or Anne Lamott. Whoever her muse, she knows good writing when she sees it. She wrote articles for the school newspaper or poems for the creative journal, nabbed a good internship after college, and she's worked hard ever since to finally land her dream job—acquiring and editing books full time and *getting paid for it*!

Now she fills the role of champion for her authors and books. She pitches the books she discovers to her own internal publishing team, during which time she makes both the editorial case and the business case for acquiring said manuscripts.

Her boss expects her to acquire a handful of books every year, and though she's still learning and growing into the job, in part, her performance is tied to the performance of her selections. If she acquires and takes a huge financial risk on a book and bombs a year later, it reflects on her directly. Of course, like anyone in a new position, she needs time to grow and, sure, she might have more seasoned editors guide her through this journey. But eventually, given a couple of years, her acquisitions become hers to own.

Does all of this create a little pressure on our friendly associate editor? *You bet.*

Every editor's list of acquisitions is viewed (especially by management) as their own personal business within the greater publishing company, complete with its own profit and loss statement. As a result, each individual book might get more or less scrutiny depending on how it fits into the greater scheme. The worse the editor's books perform, the harder time she'll have convincing her team to take risks in the future.

When you're writing a book, preparing a proposal or query (for publishers *or* literary agents, because agents make decisions based on whether they think a publisher will be interested), it's important to think about your future editor. She is a human being, just like you, and every day she is facing the very real difficulties of the changing market, the shifting retail landscape, and her own internal company pressures. She, like many editors in this business, hopes to come across something special—a work of unique power or appeal or finesse or authority—that makes her feel like she did in college when she read Joan Didion.

As someone who once sat in the editor's chair at publishers large and small, I know those simultaneous pressures and hopes firsthand. My first publishing job was as a junior editor acquiring and editing 10–12 books a year for a small, family-owned press. To be honest, for a long time I had no idea what I was doing—but I worked hard and soaked up every lesson I could. Despite my inexperience, over the course of several fairly successful years, I found myself the publisher of this small imprint, hustling to make budgets; publish competitive, influential books; learn the fast-changing worlds of marketing and publicity; and manage a team that shared my goals.

Ten years and a couple of mid-size publishing companies later, I managed two imprints for Penguin Random House as vice president and publisher, working within the largest publisher of trade books in the English-speaking world. While much in this role was new, especially on a corporate level, most everything else remained the same. The art of good publishing is difficult no matter where it's practiced.

My accumulated experience has taught me this: Large and small, all publishers ultimately desire *the same thing.*

Editors are hopeful (if slightly jaded) readers. They're all on the hunt for a carefully crafted manuscript, a clever concept, or an author-influencer with a platform who is ready to write and sell a great book. We're all in this business because of the power of books to change things, inspire people or make the future brighter in some way. We all recognize that fantastic stories help us relate to the world around us, and discover the way others see the world. Most of us in publishing really do *love* books. That's why we do what we do.

But while hopeful, publishing professionals are also pragmatic and deeply skeptical. Why? Well, consider this: Your future editor will go out and buy (and publish) 10 or 12 books a year, and watch as a high percentage of them fail to earn back their initial advances. Industry wide, that number is roughly 70 percent, though it can vary. Editors are full-time talent spotters, but predicting winners is never a sure thing.

Think about the ways in which you can remove hurdles for your future editor in such a way that, first, you actually get her to read your manuscript or book proposal, and second, she finds it good enough to take a personal risk on you—and then is able to convince others at her imprint to join her in publishing your book.

Your future editor faces a few realities every single day: Limited time. Loads of meetings. Corporate politics. An excess of manuscripts to read. And unique financial challenges.

Many publishers face incredibly tight margins, especially small, nonprofit or family-owned press. As they move toward acquiring your book, your future publisher must project your book's future sales long before there's a book cover, an Amazon description or even a final title. If there's a modicum of interest, publishers start to carefully estimate based on similar or competitive titles. Using a combination of the sales history of books similar to yours, editorial, marketing, and sales team feedback, as well as good old-fashioned gut instinct, the publishing team whittles down their submission pile to a few key projects they deem worthy of the risk.

So, with that in mind, here are seven keys to getting (and keeping) your publisher's attention.

1. DO YOUR HOMEWORK

Every category and genre of publishing is governed by unspoken rules. In the world of traditional trade book publishing, fiction and nonfiction aren't the same. For instance, most editors sign nonfiction book deals based on one to two chapters. But for fiction, and especially with first-time novelists, editors typically need to read the full manuscript before a deal is done.

If you're submitting the next high-concept business book to an experienced agent, or an editor at a business book imprint, make sure you've done your research. Do you know what other books the literary agent has represented, or the editor has acquired in the recent past? Has that press recently published a book like yours?

Immerse yourself in books similar to your own. Read in the category, but also study the jacket, the acknowledgments page, the author's blog, and previous books. Conduct industry research on publishing houses, editors, and literary agents through sites like *Publisher's*

Weekly. Attend a conference, watch lectures on YouTube. Read relevant articles, essays and blog posts.

To know a category is to know the world in which your future editor lives every day.

2. USE CONCISE COMMUNICATION

The volume of reading material that accrues on the desks of editors and literary agents is immense. These folks read mountains of content every day, sifting through stacks of submissions for eye-catching queries.

Which is why yours should get right to the point—in such a way that compels them to read more. Don't belabor your initial synopsis or write a three-page email. If in doubt, the fewer words the better. Share a little about yourself, but *only* the most relevant points.

Most important: Any sample writing you include should read fast and clean. Editors aren't *looking* for reasons to reject per se, but when inundated, it's far too easy to dismiss a submission for little things like spelling errors, awkward phrasing, or poor formatting.

3. SIGN WITH AN AGENT

Inking a contract with a good literary agent can help avoid some of the above issues. When on submission to publishers, agents almost always get a faster read than unsolicited queries—especially in certain categories. There are several reasons why this is the case. First, most literary agents take the time to build relationships (and a level of trust) with acquisition editors in the genres they work within. Second, because publishing professionals have such limited time, agents effectively serve as a filter, siphoning in projects with higher caliber content. Plus, most have also taken the time to work with their authors to develop and shape their book concepts, which adds additional value for the publisher.

I've had countless conversations with authors who published their books agentless, and suddenly found themselves in a strange new world with no idea how to navigate it. Their books released to the world and their lofty publishing dreams slowly wilted as they made mistakes, agreed to bad contractual terms, blindly trusted editors, or neglected their marketing and publicity campaigns. The best literary agents act as a trusted guide, thinking through these details long before a deal ever comes to fruition.

4. GROW YOUR PLATFORM

Here's a fact of life in modern publishing: Attracting (and holding) attention is difficult in *any* medium, especially in a world of social media, streaming television, and unlimited self-publishing. As a result, presses look for projects with a built-in audience. It's thus through a *platform* that authors can do just that.

I define platform as any outward-facing method a writer has used to attract a readership prior to publishing—which will, in theory, translate to that readership purchasing the writer's book. It can manifest as anything from a YouTube channel, podcast, blog or Twitter following, to an email newsletter or college classroom.

Think of your writing as a business, and take the initiative to build your influence via a robust platform, which will only increase your chances of publishing.

5. FORGE A RELATIONSHIP

Once you sign a book deal, you'll be assigned a "champion." More often than not, that person is an acquisitions editor or developmental editor, but it may also be the marketing manager or the publisher herself. While every press is different, often that person is your point of contact throughout the publishing process—from beginning to end.

Whoever your point-person, be intentional in building that relationship. If possible, meet your champion face-to-face, or at least set up regular phone calls. Get to know her. This small investment of time and effort on your part can pay off in the long run.

I've seen authors send a nice handwritten note after a meeting or a phone call, thanking the participants for their time. And sometimes I've seen those simple thank yous tacked to the wall of an editor's office *years* later. A small, kind act goes a long way, and when you need a favor down the road, your champion will remember you.

6. REMEMBER TO ENGAGE

Shift your thinking about the publishing process: Turning in your manuscript is not an end, but the beginning. The more engaged you are at every following stage, the better chance your book has of making an impact in the market. Writing a terrific manuscript is step one, but you must also help to market, publicize, and sell.

Seek to be included in the key publishing decisions along the way, including the final title, cover design, marketing and publicity strategy, and so on. Believe it or not, each of these things is regularly decided without the author's input—but becoming a part of these decisions, you can bring your vision to the table.

7. BE YOUR BOOK'S CMO

Remember: You are your book's Chief Marketing Officer—its first and last advocate. Be clear that this book is still your baby, while remaining cordial and professional.

Consider setting aside some of your advance (if you received one) to help market your book when the time comes. Thinking that far ahead is tough, but every bit of marketing is important: strong Book 1 sales pave the way for Book 2.

If you know your publisher's marketing strategy (presuming you've stay engaged in the process), then you can supplement it. For example, if the publisher focuses on store placement, ads in industry magazines, focused banner ads, and a book tour, then perhaps you invest in hiring a freelance publicist to line up TV, radio, or print interviews.

Once you've garnered a book deal, it's easy to sit back and let the professionals handle everything for you. But resist, for your own sake (and the sake of your book). Your book is your baby. When it gets out into the world, you're the best one to teach it how to walk.

ALEX FIELD is principal and founder of The Bindery (thebinderyagency.com) and a former VP and publisher at Penguin Random House. This article was previously published in the March/April 2018 issue of *Writer's Digest*.

DIVERSE BOOKS MATTER

The push to publish a broader range of voices
is no fad—it's an industry course correction
long overdue. Here, a literary agent unpacks the
movement taking books by storm.

....

by Ammi-Joan Paquette

One of the most common questions I'm asked as a literary agent at writers' conferences these days—and one that I'm always happy to hear—is some variation on: "How do you feel about the increased focus on diversity in publishing? What changes are you seeing in this area?"

Why am I happy to hear it? Because it's a question that didn't really come up five years ago, or at least not to this extent. It *should* be coming up, and the fact that it does so with increasing frequency is in itself a sign of the industry's change and forward progress.

But first, a caveat: This won't be an article detailing the history, statistics, or specific trajectory of diversity in publishing. I'm neither a scholar nor an analyst, and while I do love a good spreadsheet, I am not qualified to deliver any type of comprehensive treatise. What I hope to do here is share my broader perspective as an active member of the publishing community—both as a consumer of books and someone who helps funnel them along toward your bookshelves. Thus here's a primer, if you will, for those who may be less familiar with the subject and could use an overview on diversity in publishing today.

WHAT READERS WANT

To begin, someone who may not be up on the movement might be wondering: *What's this all about?* Well, historically, published books have largely focused their lens on white, straight, able-bodied characters. *What's wrong with that*, you ask? It's not what's there that's the problem; it's what's *not* there. Seeing ourselves reflected in the books—and media—we consume can be a way of legitimizing our own journey, struggles and questions. Seeing the reflection of someone else's journey, a journey that may be entirely unlike our own, provides an essential portal into the experiences of others, fostering empathy, understanding and growth. Simply put, readers want, *need*, to see themselves in the books they read. In recent years, that need has begun to be addressed with a growing range of books reflecting a broader, truer lens. A more diverse selection of books means more mirrors to reflect our experiences, and more windows to offer glimpses into lives unlike our own. Win-win, right?

"As someone obsessed with and who writes small-town America, if you don't see diversity in your town, you're not looking hard enough." —Julie Murphy, author of *Dumplin'*

WHAT AGENTS & EDITORS WANT

Certainly I cannot speak for all of the publishing community, but from what I've seen as a literary agent working largely in publishing for young readers, I can safely say: There is a great and a growing hunger for diverse books—in terms of culture, race, sexuality, gender, ability, class, and beyond. When I meet with editors and talk about what they're looking to acquire, almost invariably the conversation will come around to: "I want to see more diverse books, and books by diverse authors."

"We talk about representation every single day. When I started in publishing two decades ago at a different company, we weren't allowed to use the word 'gay' in describing a character unless it was specifically tagged a 'gay book' and was geared toward that community only. Now it feels like there is a real push toward diversity, a focus on and celebration of that." — John Morgan, executive editor at Imprint, a part of Macmillan Children's Publishing Group

This appetite is also seen in the formation of social media campaigns to enhance visibility for underrepresented voices, such as the popular #DVpit event on Twitter (created by literary agent Beth Phelan), where authors can pitch their diverse projects in real-time. Interested agents and editors can—and do—request these manuscripts, and the event already has an impressive rate of authors signing with agents and getting book deals. And initiatives like We Need Diverse Books have provided resources and a rallying point for writers of marginalized communities and beyond.

Bear in mind: This is a process. The skewed balance of worldview in literature didn't happen overnight, and the shift to a more accurate and complete representation will not happen overnight either. But readers are hungry for it. Agents are hungry for it. Editors are hungry for it. What comes next?

WHAT WRITERS CAN DO

Some people have called diversity in publishing a "trend." Let me be clear, it's nothing of the sort. It is, and will continue to be, a gradual shifting—*a correction in the market*, so to speak—an increased awareness for those writing and publishing from a place of privilege that there are important stories out there that were formerly overlooked. It's an initiative that I believe will only grow more as marginalized authors continue to gain confidence and experience and wherewithal to make their stories known, and as publishers continue not only to diversify their acquisitions, but also their staff at every step of the publishing process.

"'Diversity' should just be called 'reality.' Your books, your TV shows, your movies, your articles, your curricula, need to reflect *reality*." —Tananarive Due, author of *The Living Blood*

One contentious issue right now is the debate over whether authors can—or should— write from a perspective that is outside their own race or culture. Those arguing against point to the glut of inauthentic voices crowding the shelves and taking space and attention from those writing from their "own voice" viewpoints. On the other side, some argue that authors writing only their own distinct gender, race, culture and specific background would make for dull books indeed.

On one thing all sides agree, however: Any author writing outside their culture should do so thoughtfully, respectfully, and deliberately. If you're considering doing so, ask: *Why am I the one telling this particular story? What is my touch-point or connection that makes me an authentic narrator for this character?* Next, be willing to put in the work. Research is good, but that alone isn't enough. Talk, interview, experience. Bring in readers of the race or culture in question to critique your work—and then *listen* to what they're saying, and make the necessary changes.

WHAT THE FUTURE HOLDS

One has only to look at *The New York Times* bestsellers list or the National Book Awards list to see how whole-heartedly readers and critics alike are taking to this shift toward greater and more accurate representation. In the last year, books by authors of color have repeatedly sold in high-stakes auctions, with foreign and film deals flocking in their wake. This is especially the case in YA and children's publishing, but adult fiction is catching on as well. It turns out that people like to see themselves in the books—and media—they consume. It makes logical, and financial, sense.

What does this all mean for you? If you're a marginalized writer: There's never been a better time to tell your story. If you're writing from a place of privilege: Be willing to educate yourself, and in the works you do create, strive for honesty, authenticity, inclusivity.

Publishing is experiencing a period of growth. Things are changing, yet more change is still needed. Diversity is not a fad, trend or marketing gimmick. It is a lifestyle; a requirement. The new normal.

AMMI-JOAN PAQUETTE is a senior literary agent with Erin Murphy Literary Agency and the author of many books for young readers. This article previously appeared in the March/April 2018 issue of *Writer's Digest*.

LITERARY AGENTS

Many publishers are willing to look at unsolicited submissions, but most feel having an agent is in the writer's best interest. In this section we include agents who specialize in or represent fiction.

The commercial fiction field is intensely competitive. Many publishers have small staffs and little time. For that reason, many book publishers rely on agents for new talent. Some publishers even rely on agents as "first readers" who must wade through the deluge of submissions from writers to find the very best. For writers a good agent can be a foot in the door—someone willing to do the necessary work to put your manuscript in the right editor's hands.

It would seem today that finding a good agent is as hard as finding a good publisher. Yet writers who have agents say they are invaluable. Not only can an agent help you make your work more marketable, an agent also acts as your business manager and adviser, protecting your interests during and after contract negotiations.

Still, finding an agent can be very difficult for a new writer. If you are already published in magazines, you have a better chance than someone with no publishing credits. (Some agents read periodicals searching for new writers.) Although many agents do read queries and manuscripts from unpublished authors without introduction, referrals from their writer clients can be a big help. If you don't know any published authors with agents, attending a conference is a good way to meet agents. Some agents even set aside time at conferences to meet new writers.

Almost all the agents listed here have said they are open to working with new, previously unpublished writers as well as published writers. They do not charge a fee to cover the time and effort involved in reviewing a manuscript or a synopsis and chapters, but their time is still extremely valuable. Send an agent your work only when you feel it is as complete and polished as possible.

⊘ DOMINICK ABEL LITERARY AGENCY, INC.

146 W. 82nd St., #1A, New York NY 10024. (212)877-0710. **Fax:** (212)595-3133. **E-mail:** agency@dalainc.com. **Website:** www.dalainc.com. **Contact:** Dominick Abel. Estab. 1975. Member of AAR. Represents 50 clients.

REPRESENTS Fiction, novels. **Considers these fiction areas:** action, adventure, crime, detective, mystery, police.

HOW TO CONTACT Query via e-mail. No attachments. "If you wish to submit fiction, describe what you have written and what market you are targeting (you may find it useful to compare your work to that of an established author). Include a synopsis of the novel and the first two or three chapters. If you wish to submit nonfiction, you should, in addition, detail your qualifications for writing this particular book. Identify the audience for your book and explain how your book will be different from and better than already published works aimed at the same market." Accepts simultaneous submissions. Responds in 2-3 weeks.

ADAMS LITERARY

7845 Colony Rd., C4 #215, Charlotte NC 28226. (704)542-1440. **Fax:** (704)542-1450. **E-mail:** info@adamsliterary.com. **Website:** www.adamsliterary.com. **Contact:** Tracey Adams, Josh Adams. Estab. 2004. Member of AAR. Other memberships include SCBWI and WNBA.

MEMBER AGENTS Tracey Adams, Josh Adams, Lorin Oberweger.

REPRESENTS **Considers these fiction areas:** middle grade, picture books, young adult.

☞   Represents "the finest children's book and young adult authors and artists."

HOW TO CONTACT **Submit through online form on website only.** Send e-mail if that is not operating correctly. All submissions and queries should first be made through the online form on website. Will not review—and will promptly recycle—any unsolicited submissions or queries received by mail. Before submitting work for consideration, review complete guidelines online, as the agency sometimes shuts off to new submissions. Accepts simultaneous submissions. Responds in 6 weeks if interested. "While we have an established client list, we do seek new talent—and we accept submissions from both published and aspiring authors and artists."

TERMS Agent receives 15% commission on domestic sales; 20% on foreign sales. Offers written contract.

RECENT SALES *The Cruelty*, by Scott Bergstrom (Feiwel & Friends); *The Little Fire Truck*, by Margery Cuyler (Christy Ottaviano); *Unearthed*, by Amie Kaufman and Meagan Spooner (Disney-Hyperion); *A Handful of Stars*, by Cynthia Lord (Scholastic); *Under Their Skin*, by Margaret Peterson Haddix (Simon & Schuster); *The Secret Horses of Briar Hill*, by Megan Shepherd (Delacorte); *The Secret Subway*, by Shana Corey (Schwartz & Wade); *Impyrium*, by Henry Neff (HarperCollins).

TIPS "Guidelines are posted (and frequently updated) on our website."

AEVITAS CREATIVE MANAGEMENT

19 W. 21st St., Suite 501, New York NY 10010. (212)765-6900. **Website:** aevitascreative.com. Member of AAR. Signatory of WGA.

MEMBER AGENTS Esmond Harmsworth, managing partner; David Kuhn, managing partner; Todd Shuster, managing partner; Jennifer Gates, senior partner; Laura Nolan, senior partner; Janet Silver, senior partner; Lane Zachary, senior partner; Bridget Wagner Matzie, partner; Rick Richter, partner; Jane von Mehren, partner; Rob Arnold, agent; Sarah Bowlin, agent; Michelle Brower, agent; Nick Chiles, agent; Lori Galvin, agent; David Granger, agent; Jim Kelly, agent; Sarah Lazin, agent; Sarah Levitt, agent; Will Lippincott, agent; Jen Marshall, agent; Penny Moore, agent; Lauren Sharp, agent; Becky Sweren, agent; Nan Thornton, agent; Susan Zanger, agent; Erica Bauman, associate agent; Justin Brouckaert, associate agent; Kate Mack, associate agent; Nate Muscato, associate agent.

REPRESENTS Nonfiction, fiction.

HOW TO CONTACT Find specific agents on the Aevitas website to see their specific interests and guidelines. Accepts simultaneous submissions.

THE AHEARN AGENCY, INC.

2021 Pine St., New Orleans LA 70118. (504)861-8395. **Fax:** (504)866-6434. **E-mail:** pahearn@aol.com. **Website:** www.ahearnagency.com. **Contact:** Pamela G. Ahearn. Estab. 1992. Other memberships include MWA, RWA, ITW. Represents 25 clients.

🖸   Prior to opening her agency, Ms. Ahearn was an agent for 8 years and an editor with Bantam Books.

REPRESENTS Novels. **Considers these fiction areas:** crime, detective, romance, suspense, thriller.

☛ Handles general adult fiction, specializing in women's fiction and suspense. Does not deal with any nonfiction, poetry, juvenile material or science fiction.

HOW TO CONTACT Query with SASE or via e-mail. Please send a one-page query letter stating the type of book you're writing, word length, where you feel your book fits into the current market, and any writing credentials you may possess. Please do not send ms pages or synopses if they haven't been previously requested. If you're querying via e-mail, send no attachments unless requested. Accepts simultaneous submissions. Responds in 2-3 months on submissions, 3-4 months on queries. Obtains most new clients through recommendations from others, solicitations, conferences.

TERMS Agent receives 15% commission on domestic sales; 20% commission on foreign and dramatic sales. Offers written contract, binding for 1 year; renewable by mutual consent.

RECENT SALES *Paper Ghosts*, by Julia Heaberlin; *Project Duchess*, by Sabrina Jeffries; *The Dead Girl in 2A*, by Carter Wilson; *Romancing the Laird*, by Gerri Russell; *The Hangman's Secret*, by Laura Joh Rowland; *A Spy's Guide to Seduction*, by Kate Moore; *Just a Breath Away*, by Carlene Thompson.

WRITERS CONFERENCES Romance Writers of America, Thrillerfest, Bouchercon.

TIPS "Be professional! Always send in exactly what an agent/editor asks for—no more, no less. Keep query letters brief and to the point, giving your writing credentials and a very brief summary of your book. If 1 agent rejects you, keep trying—there are a lot of us out there!"

🌀 AITKEN ALEXANDER ASSOCIATES

291 Gray's Inn Rd., Kings Cross, London WC1X 8QJ United Kingdom. (020)7373-8672. **Fax:** (020)7373-6002. **E-mail:** reception@aitkenalexander.co.uk. **E-mail:** submissions@aitkenalexander.co.uk. **Website:** www.aitkenalexander.co.uk. Estab. 1976.

MEMBER AGENTS Gillon Aitken; Clare Alexander (literary, commercial, memoir, narrative nonfiction, history); Matthew Hamilton (literary fiction, suspense, music, politics, and sports); Gillie Russell (middle grade, young adult); Mary Pachnos; Anthony Sheil; Lucy Luck (quality fiction and nonfiction);

Lesley Thorne; Matias Lopez Portillo; Shruti Debi; Leah Middleton.

REPRESENTS Nonfiction, novels. **Considers these fiction areas:** commercial, literary, mainstream, middle grade, suspense, thriller, young adult.

☛ "We specialize in literary fiction and nonfiction." Does not represent illustrated children's books, poetry, or screenplays.

HOW TO CONTACT "If you would like to submit your work to us, please e-mail your covering letter with a short synopsis and the first 30 pages (as a Word document) to submissions@aitkenalexander.co.uk indicating if there is a specific agent who you would like to consider your work. Although every effort is made to respond to submissions, if we have not responded within three months please assume that your work is not right for the agency's list. Please note that the Indian Office does not accept unsolicited submissions." Accepts simultaneous submissions. Obtains most new clients through recommendations from others, solicitations.

RECENT SALES *A Country Row, A Tree*, by Jo Baker (Knopf); *Noonday*, by Pat Barker (Doubleday); *Beatlebone*, by Kevin Barry (Doubleday); *Spill Simmer Falter Wither*, by Sara Baume (Houghton Mifflin).

❷ ALIVE LITERARY AGENCY

7680 Goddard St., Suite 200, Colorado Springs CO 80920. (719)260-7080. **Fax:** (719)260-8223. **E-mail:** info@aliveliterary.com. **E-mail:** submissions@aliveliterary.com. **Website:** www.aliveliterary.com. **Contact:** Rick Christian. Estab. 1989. Member of AAR. Other memberships include Authors Guild.

MEMBER AGENTS Rick Christian president (blockbusters, bestsellers); Andrea Heinecke (thoughtful/inspirational nonfiction, women's fiction/nonfiction, popular/commercial nonfiction & fiction); Bryan Norman (popular nonfiction, biography/memoir/autobiography, spiritual growth, inspirational, literary); Lisa Jackson (popular nonfiction, biography/memoir/autobiography, spiritual growth, inspirational, literary, women's nonfiction).

REPRESENTS Nonfiction, fiction, novels, short story collections, novellas. **Considers these fiction areas:** adventure, contemporary issues, family saga, historical, humor, inspirational, literary, mainstream, mystery, religious, romance, satire, sports, suspense, thriller, young adult.

☞ This agency specializes in inspirational fiction, Christian living, how-to, and commercial nonfiction. Actively seeking inspirational, literary and mainstream fiction, inspirational nonfiction, and work from authors with established track records and platforms. Does not want to receive poetry, scripts, or dark themes.

HOW TO CONTACT "Because all our agents have full client loads, they are only considering queries from authors referred by clients and close contacts. Please refer to our guidelines at http://aliveliterary. com/submissions. Authors referred by an Alive client or close contact are invited to send proposals to submissions@aliveliterary.com." Your submission should include a referral (name of referring Alive client or close contact in the e-mail subject line. In the e-mail, please describe your personal or professional connection to the referring individual), a brief author biography (including recent speaking engagements, media appearances, social media platform statistics, and sales histories of your books), a synopsis of the work for which you are seeking agency representation (including the target audience, sales and marketing hooks, and comparable titles on the market), and the first 3 chapters of your manuscript. Alive will respond to queries meeting the above guidelines within 8-10 weeks.

TERMS Agent receives 15% commission on domestic sales. Offers written contract; two-month notice must be given to terminate contract.

TIPS Rewrite and polish until the words on the page shine. Endorsements, a solid platform, and great connections may help, provided you can write with power and passion. Hone your craft by networking with publishing professionals, joining critique groups, and attending writers' conferences.

AMBASSADOR LITERARY AGENCY

P.O. Box 50358, Nashville TN 37205. (615)370-4700. **E-mail:** info@ambassadoragency.com. **Website:** www.ambassadorspeakers.com/acp/index.aspx. **Contact:** Wes Yoder. Represents 25-30 clients.

◑ Prior to becoming an agent, Mr. Yoder founded a music artist agency in 1973; he established a speakers bureau division of the company in 1984.

REPRESENTS Nonfiction, novels. **Considers these fiction areas:** contemporary issues, religious.

☞ "Ambassador's Literary department represents a select list of best-selling authors and writers who are published by the leading religious and general market publishers in the United States and Europe."

HOW TO CONTACT Authors should e-mail a short description of their ms with a request to submit their work for review. Official submission guidelines will be sent if we agree to review a ms. Direct all inquiries and submissions to info@ambassadoragency.com. Accepts simultaneous submissions.

BETSY AMSTER LITERARY ENTERPRISES

607 Foothill Blvd. #1061, La Cañada Flintridge CA 91012. **E-mail:** b.amster.assistant@gmail.com (for adult titles); b.amster.kidsbooks@gmail.com (for children's and young adult). **Website:** www.amsterlit. com; www.cummingskidlit.com. **Contact:** Betsy Amster (adult); Mary Cummings (children's and young adult). Estab. 1992. Member of AAR. PEN America (Amster); Society of Children's Books Writers and Illustrators (Cummings). Represents more than 75 clients.

◑ Prior to opening her agency, Ms. Amster was an editor at Pantheon and Vintage for 10 years and served as editorial director for the Globe Pequot Press for 2 years. Prior to joining the agency, Mary Cummings served as education director at the Loft Literary Center in Minneapolis for 14 years, overseeing classes, workshops, and conferences. She curated the annual Festival of Children's Literature and selected judges for the McKnight Award in Children's Literature.

REPRESENTS Nonfiction, novels, juvenile books. **Considers these fiction areas:** crime, detective, family saga, juvenile, literary, middle grade, multicultural, mystery, picture books, police, suspense, thriller, women's, young adult.

☞ "Betsy Amster is actively seeking strong narrative nonfiction, particularly by journalists; outstanding literary fiction; witty, intelligent commercial women's fiction; character-driven mysteries and thrillers that open new worlds to us; high-profile self-help, psychology, and health, preferably research-based; and cookbooks and food narratives by West Coast–based chefs and food writers with an original viewpoint and national exposure. Does not want to receive poetry, romances, western, science fiction, action/adventure, screenplays, fantasy, techno-thrillers, spy capers, apocalyptic scenarios, or political or religious arguments. Mary Cummings is actively seeking great read-aloud picture books and middle-grade novels with strong story arcs, a spunky central character, and warmth, humor, or quirky charm as well as picture-book biographies and lyrically written children's nonfiction on science, nature, mindfulness, and social awareness."

HOW TO CONTACT "For adult fiction or memoirs, please embed the first 3 pages in the body of your e-mail. For nonfiction, please embed the overview of your proposal. For children's picture books, please embed the entire text in the body of your e-mail. For longer middle-grade and YA fiction and nonfiction, please embed the first 3 pages." Accepts simultaneous submissions. Responds in 1 month to queries; 2 months to mss. Obtains most new clients through recommendations from others, solicitations, and conferences.

TERMS Agent receives 15% commission on domestic sales; 20% commission on foreign sales. Offers written contract, binding for 1 year; three-month notice must be given to terminate contract. Charges for photocopying, postage, messengers, galleys/books used in submissions to foreign and film agents and to magazines for first serial rights. (Please note that it is rare to incur much in the way of expenses now that most submissions are made by e-mail.)

RECENT SALES Betsy Amster: *Sugarproof: How Sugar Puts Your Kid at Risk—and What You Can Do About It*, by Michael I. Goran, Ph.D. and Emily Ventura, Ph.D., M.P.H. (Avery); *What Makes a Wine Worth Drinking: In Praise of the Sublime*, by Terry Theise (Houghton Mifflin Harcourt); *Good Trouble: Lessons from the Civil Rights Playbook*, by Christopher Noxon (Abrams); *The Lost Gutenberg: The Astounding Story of One Book's Five-Hundred-Year Odyssey*, by Margaret Leslie Davis (TarcherPerigee). **Mary Cummings**: *Counting Elephants*, by Dawn Young (Running Press Kids); *Those Are Not My Underpants!*, by Melissa Martin (Random House Childrens); *We Love Fishing!*, by Ariel Bernstein (Paula Wiseman Books/Simon & Schuster); *Little Things*, by Nick Dyer (Peter Pauper Press);*Small Walt to the Rescue*, by Elizabeth Verdick (Paula Wiseman Books/Simon & Schuster).

WRITERS CONFERENCES SDSU (Amster); Minnesota Writing Workshop and regional SCBWI (Cummings).

⊘ APONTE LITERARY AGENCY

E-mail: agents@aponteliterary.com. **Website:** aponteliterary.com. **Contact:** Natalia Aponte. Member of AAR. Signatory of WGA.

MEMBER AGENTS Natalia Aponte (any genre of mainstream fiction and nonfiction, but she is especially seeking women's novels, historical novels, supernatural and paranormal fiction, fantasy novels, political and science thrillers); Victoria Lea (any category, especially interested in women's fiction, science fiction and speculative fiction).

REPRESENTS Novels. **Considers these fiction areas:** fantasy, historical, paranormal, science fiction, supernatural, thriller, women's.

➥ Actively seeking women's novels, historical novels, supernatural and paranormal fiction, fantasy novels, political and science thrillers, science fiction and speculative fiction. In nonfiction, will look at any genre with commercial potential.

HOW TO CONTACT E-query. Accepts simultaneous submissions. Responds in 6 weeks if interested.

RECENT SALES *The Nightingale Bones*, by Ariel Swan; *An Irish Doctor in Peace and At War*, by Patrick Taylor; *Siren's Treasure*, by Debbie Herbert.

⊘ THE AUGUST AGENCY, LLC

Website: www.augustagency.com. **Contact:** Cricket Freemain, Jeffery McGraw. Estab. 2004. Represents 25-40 clients.

◯ Before opening The August Agency, Ms. Freeman was a freelance writer, magazine editor and independent literary agent. Mr. McGraw worked as an editor for HarperCollins and publicity manager for Abrams.

MEMBER AGENTS Jeffery McGraw, Cricket Freeman.

REPRESENTS Novels. **Considers these fiction areas:** crime, mainstream.

➥ "At this time, we are not accepting the following types of submissions:self-published works, screen plays, children's books, genre fiction, romance, horror, westerns, fantasy, science fiction, poetry, short story collections."

HOW TO CONTACT Currently closed to submissions.

THE AXELROD AGENCY

55 Main St., P.O. Box 357, Chatham NY 12037. (518)392-2100. **E-mail:** steve@axelrodagency.com. **Website:** www.axelrodagency.com. **Contact:** Steven Axelrod. Member of AAR. Represents 15-20 clients.

○ Prior to becoming an agent, Mr. Axelrod was a book club editor.

MEMBER AGENTS Steven Axelrod, representation; Lori Antonson, subsidiary rights.

REPRESENTS Novels. **Considers these fiction areas:** crime, mystery, new adult, romance, women's.

☛ This agency specializes in women's fiction and romance.

HOW TO CONTACT Query via e-mail. Accepts simultaneous submissions. Obtains most new clients through recommendations from others.

TERMS Agent receives 15% commission on domestic sales; 20% commission on foreign sales. No written contract.

WRITERS CONFERENCES RWA National Conference.

AZANTIAN LITERARY AGENCY

Website: www.azantianlitagency.com. **Contact:** Jennifer Azantian. Estab. 2014.

○ Prior to establishing ALA, Ms. Azantian was with the Sandra Dijkstra Literary Agency and Ms. Gunic was an assistant editor at Abrams.

REPRESENTS Novels. **Considers these fiction areas:** fantasy, horror, middle grade, science fiction, urban fantasy, young adult.

☛ Stories that explore meaningful human interactions against fantastic backdrops, underrepresented voices, obscure retold fairy tales, quirky middle grade, modernized mythologies, psychological horror, literary science fiction, historical fantasy, magical realism, internally consistent epic fantasy, and spooky stories for younger readers.

HOW TO CONTACT During open submission windows only: send your query letter, 1-2 page synopsis, and first 10 pages through the form on ALA's website. Accepts simultaneous submissions. Responds within 6 weeks. Please check the submissions page of the agency website before submitting to make sure ALA is currently open to queries.

BARONE LITERARY AGENCY

385 North St., Batavia OH 45103. (513)732-6740. **Fax:** (513)297-7208. **E-mail:** baronelit@outlook.com. **Website:** www.baroneliteraryagency.com. **Contact:** Denise Barone. Estab. 2010. Member of AAR. Signatory of WGA. Member of RWA. Represents 14 clients.

REPRESENTS Fiction, novels. **Considers these fiction areas:** action, adventure, cartoon, comic books, commercial, confession, contemporary issues, crime, detective, erotica, ethnic, experimental, family saga, fantasy, feminist, frontier, gay, glitz, hi-lo, historical, horror, humor, inspirational, juvenile, lesbian, literary, mainstream, metaphysical, military, multicultural, multimedia, mystery, new adult, New Age, occult, paranormal, plays, police, psychic, regional, religious, romance, satire, science fiction, spiritual, sports, supernatural, suspense, thriller, translation, urban fantasy, war, westerns, women's, young adult.

☛ Actively seeking adult contemporary romance. Does not want textbooks.

HOW TO CONTACT "Do not send anything through the mail. I accept only email queries. If I like your query letter, I will ask for the first 3 chapters and a synopsis as attachments." Accepts simultaneous submissions. "I make every effort to respond within 4 months." Obtains new clients by queries/submissions via e-mail only.

TERMS Agency receives 15% commission on domestic sales; 20% on foreign sales. Offers written contract.

RECENT SALES *Haunting You*, by Molly Zenk (Intrigue Publishing); *The Beekeeper*, by Robert E. Hoxie (Six Gun Pictures); *All The Glittering Bones*, by Anna Snow (Entangled Publishing); *Devon's Choice*, by Cathy Bennett (Clean Reads); *Molly's Folly*, by Denise Gwen (Clean Reads); *In Deep*, by Laurie Albano (Solstice Publishing); *The Trouble with Charlie*, by Cathy Bennett (Clean Reads); *The Fairy Godmother Files: Cinderella Complex*, by Rebekah L. Purdy (Clean Reads).

WRITERS CONFERENCES The Sell More Books Show, Chicago, Illinois, 2018; Annual Conference of Romance Writers of America, Orlando, Florida, 2017; Lori Foster's Readers and Authors' Get-Together, West Chester, Ohio; A Weekend with the Authors, Nashville, Tennessee; Willamette Writers' Conference, Portland, Oregon.

TIPS "The best writing advice I ever got came from a fellow writer, who wrote, 'Learn how to edit yourself,' when signing her book to me."

BAROR INTERNATIONAL, INC.

P.O. Box 868, Armonk NY 10504. **E-mail:** heather@barorint.com. **Website:** www.barorint.com. **Contact:** Danny Baror; Heather Baror-Shapiro. Represents 300 clients.

MEMBER AGENTS Danny Baror; Heather Baror-Shapiro.

REPRESENTS Fiction. **Considers these fiction areas:** fantasy, literary, science fiction, young adult, adult fiction, commerical.

☛ This agency represents authors and publishers in the international market. Currently representing commercial fiction, literary titles, science fiction, young adult, and more.

HOW TO CONTACT Submit by e-mail or mail (with SASE); include a cover letter and a few sample chapters Accepts simultaneous submissions.

THE BENT AGENCY

19 W. 21st St., #201, New York NY 10010. **E-mail:** info@thebentagency.com. **E-mail:** Please see website.. **Website:** www.thebentagency.com. **Contact:** Jenny Bent. Estab. 2009. Member of AAR.

○ Prior to forming her own agency, Ms. Bent was an agent and vice president at Trident Media Group.

MEMBER AGENTS Jenny Bent (adult fiction, including women's fiction, romance, and crime/suspense; she particularly likes novels with magical or fantasy elements that fall outside of genre fiction; young adult and middle-grade fiction; memoir; humor); Nicola Barr (literary and commercial fiction for adults and children, and nonfiction in the areas of sports, popular science, popular culture, and social and cultural history); Molly Ker Hawn (young adult and middle-grade books, including contemporary, historical, fantasy, science fiction, thrillers, and mystery); Gemma Cooper (all ages of children's and young adult books, including picture books; likes historical, contemporary, thrillers, mystery, humor, and science fiction); Louise Fury (children's fiction: picture books, literary middle-grade, and all young adult; adult fiction: speculative fiction, suspense/thriller, commercial fiction, and all subgenres of romance including erotic; nonfiction: cookbooks and pop culture); Sarah Manning (commercial and accessible literary adult fiction and nonfiction in the area of memoir, lifestyle, and narrative nonfiction); Beth Phelan (young adult, thrillers, suspense and mystery, romance and women's fiction, literary and general fiction, cookbooks, lifestyle, and pets/animals); Victoria Cappello (commercial and literary adult fiction as well as narrative nonfiction); Heather Flaherty (young adult and middle-grade fiction: all genres; select adult fiction: upmarket fiction, women's fiction, and female-centric thrillers; select nonfiction: pop culture, humorous, and social media–based projects, as well as teen memoir).

REPRESENTS Nonfiction, novels, short story collections, juvenile books. **Considers these fiction areas:** adventure, commercial, crime, erotica, fantasy, feminist, historical, horror, humor, juvenile, literary, mainstream, middle grade, multicultural, mystery, new adult, picture books, romance, short story collections, suspense, thriller, women's, young adult.

HOW TO CONTACT "Tell us briefly who you are, what your book is, and why you're the one to write it. Then include the first 10 pages of your material in the body of your e-mail. We respond to all queries; please resend your query if you haven't had a response within 4 weeks." Accepts simultaneous submissions.

RECENT SALES *Caraval*, by Stephanie Garber (Flatiron); *Rebel of the Sands*, by Alwyn Hamilton (Viking Children's/Penguin BFYR); *The Square Root of Summer*, by Harriet Reuter Hapgood (Roaring Brook/Macmillan); *Dirty Money*, by Lisa Renee Jones (Simon & Schuster); *True North*, by Liora Blake (Pocket Star).

VICKY BIJUR LITERARY AGENCY

27 W. 20th St., Suite 1003, New York NY 10011. **E-mail:** queries@vickybijuragency.com. **Website:** www.vickybijuragency.com. Estab. 1988. Member of AAR.

○ Vicky Bijur worked at Oxford University Press and with the Charlotte Sheedy Literary Agency. Books she represents have appeared on *the New York Times Bestseller List*, in the *New York Times* Notable Books of the Year, *Los Angeles Times* Best Fiction of the Year, *Washington Post* Book World Rave Reviews of the Year.

MEMBER AGENTS Vicky Bijur; Alexandra Franklin.

REPRESENTS Nonfiction, novels. **Considers these fiction areas:** commercial, literary, mystery, new adult, thriller, women's, young adult, Campus novels, coming-of-age.

☛ "We are not the right agency for screenplays, picture books, poetry, self-help, science fiction, fantasy, horror, or romance."

HOW TO CONTACT "Please send a query letter of no more than 3 paragraphs on what makes your book special and unique, a very brief synopsis, its length and genre, and your biographical information, along with the first 10 pages of your manuscript. Please let us know in your query letter if it is a multiple submission, and kindly keep us informed of other agents' interest and offers of representation. If sending electronically, paste the pages in an e-mail as we don't open attachments from unfamiliar senders. If sending by hard copy, please include an SASE for our response. If you want your material returned, include an SASE large enough to contain pages and enough postage to send back to you." Accepts simultaneous submissions. "We generally respond to all queries within 8 weeks of receipt."

RECENT SALES *That Darkness*, by Lisa Black; *Long Upon the Land*, by Margaret Maron; *Daughter of Ashes*, by Marcia Talley.

DAVID BLACK LITERARY AGENCY

335 Adams St., Suite 2707, Brooklyn NY 11201. (718)-852-5500. **Fax:** (718)852-5539. **Website:** www.davidblackagency.com. **Contact:** David Black, owner. Estab. 1989. Member of AAR. Represents 150 clients.

MEMBER AGENTS David Black; Jenny Herrera; Gary Morris; Joy E. Tutela (narrative nonfiction, memoir, history, politics, self-help, investment, business, science, women's issues, GLBT issues, parenting, health and fitness, humor, craft, cooking and wine, lifestyle and entertainment, commercial fiction, literary fiction, MG, YA); Susan Raihofer (commercial fiction and nonfiction, memoir, pop culture, music, inspirational, thrillers, literary fiction); Sarah Smith (memoir, biography, food, music, narrative history, social studies, literary fiction).

REPRESENTS Nonfiction, novels. **Considers these fiction areas:** commercial, literary, middle grade, thriller, young adult.

HOW TO CONTACT "To query an individual agent, please follow the specific query guidelines outlined in the agent's profile on our website. Not all agents are currently accepting unsolicited queries. To query the agency, please send a 1-2 page query letter describing your book, and include information about any previously published works, your audience, and your platform." Do not e-mail your query unless an agent specifically asks for an e-mail. Accepts simultaneous submissions. Responds in 2 months to queries.

RECENT SALES Some of the agency's best-selling authors include: Erik Larson, Stuart Scott, Jeff Hobbs, Mitch Albom, Gregg Olsen, Jim Abbott, and John Bacon.

BOND LITERARY AGENCY

4340 E. Kentucky Ave., Suite 471, Denver CO 80246. (303)781-9305. **E-mail:** queries@bondliteraryagency.com. **Website:** www.bondliteraryagency.com. **Contact:** Sandra Bond.

🗨 Prior to her current position, Ms. Bond worked with agent Jody Rein and was the program administrator at the University of Denver's Publishing Institute.

MEMBER AGENTS Sandra Bond, agent (fiction: adult commercial and literary, mystery/thriller/suspense, women's, historical, young adult; nonfiction: narrative, history, science, business);
Becky LeJeune, associate agent (fiction: horror, mystery/thriller/suspense, science fiction/fantasy, historical, general fiction, young adult).

REPRESENTS Nonfiction, fiction, novels, juvenile books. **Considers these fiction areas:** commercial, crime, detective, family saga, fantasy, historical, horror, juvenile, literary, mainstream, middle grade, multicultural, mystery, police, science fiction, suspense, thriller, urban fantasy, women's, young adult.

☛ Agency does not represent romance, poetry, young reader chapter books, children's picture books, or screenplays.

HOW TO CONTACT Please submit query by e-mail (absolutely no attachments unless requested). No unsolicited mss. "They will let you know if they are interested in seeing more material. No phone calls, please." Accepts simultaneous submissions.

TERMS No Fees

RECENT SALES *The Past is Never*, by Tiffany Quay Tyson; *Cold Case: Billy the Kid*, by W.C. Jameson; *Women in Film: The Truth and the Timeline*, by Jill S. Tietjen and Barbara Bridges; Books 7 & 8 in the Hiro Hattori Mystery Series, by Susan Spann.

BOOK CENTS LITERARY AGENCY, LLC

121 Black Rock Turnpike, Suite #499, Redding Ridge CT 06876. **E-mail:** cw@bookcentsliteraryagency.com. **Website:** www.bookcentsliteraryagency.com. **Contact:** Christine Witthohn. Estab. 2005. Member of AAR. RWA, MWA, SinC, KOD.

REPRESENTS Novels. **Considers these fiction areas:** commercial, mainstream, multicultural, mystery, paranormal, romance, suspense, thriller, women's, young adult.

☛ Actively seeking upmarket fiction, commercial fiction (particularly if it has crossover appeal), women's fiction (emotional and layered), romance (single title or category), mainstream mystery/suspense, thrillers (particularly psychological), and young adult. For a detailed list of what this agency is currently searching for, visit the website. Does not want to receive third party submissions, previously published titles, short stories/novellas, erotica, inspirational, historical, science fiction/fantasy, horror/pulp/slasher thrillers, middle-grade, children's picture books, poetry, or screenplays. Does not want stories with priests/nuns, religion, abuse of children/animals/elderly, rape, or serial killers.

HOW TO CONTACT Submit via agency website. Does not accept mail or e-mail submissions.

TIPS Sponsors the International Women's Fiction Festival in Matera, Italy. See www.womensfictionfestival.com for more information. Ms. Witthohn is also the U.S. rights and licensing agent for leading French publisher Bragelonne, German publisher Egmont, and Spanish publisher Edebe.

BOOKENDS LITERARY AGENCY

Website: www.bookendsliterary.com. **Contact:** Jessica Faust, Kim Lionetti, Jessica Alvarez, Moe Ferrara, Tracy Marchini, Rachel Brooks, Natascha Morris, Naomi Davis, Amanda Jain, James McGowan. Estab. 1999. Member of AAR. RWA, MWA, SCBWI, SFWA. Represents 50+ clients.

MEMBER AGENTS Jessica Faust (women's fiction, mysteries, thrillers, suspense); Kim Lionetti (romance, women's fiction, young adult); Jessica Alvarez (romance, women's fiction, mystery, suspense, thrillers, and nonfiction); Moe Ferrara (middle-grade, young adult, and adult: romance, science fiction, fantasy, horror); Tracy Marchini (picture book, middle-grade, and young adult: fiction and nonfiction); Rachel Brooks (young adult, romance, women's fiction, cozy mysteries); Natascha Morris (young adult, middle grade, picture book); Naomi Davis (science fiction, fantasy, young adult, middle grade, picture books); Amanda Jain (mystery, romance, women's fiction, up-market, historical fiction); James McGowan (literary, upmarket, mystery, suspense, thrillers, young adult).

REPRESENTS Nonfiction, novels, juvenile books. **Considers these fiction areas:** adventure, comic books, commercial, crime, detective, erotica, family saga, fantasy, gay, historical, horror, juvenile, lesbian, mainstream, middle grade, multicultural, mystery, paranormal, picture books, police, romance, science fiction, supernatural, suspense, thriller, urban fantasy, women's, young adult.

☛ "BookEnds is currently accepting queries from published and unpublished writers in the areas of romance, mystery, suspense, science fiction and fantasy, horror, women's fiction, picture books, middle-grade, and young adult. In nonfiction we represent titles in the following areas: current affairs, reference, business and career, parenting, pop culture, coloring books, general nonfiction, and nonfiction for children and teens." BookEnds does not represent short fiction, poetry, screenplays, or techno-thrillers.

HOW TO CONTACT Visit website for the most up-to-date guidelines and current preferences. BookEnds agents accept all submissions through their personal Query Manager forms. These forms are accessible on the agency website under Submissions. Accepts simultaneous submissions. "Our response time goals are 6 weeks for queries and 12 weeks on requested partials and fulls."

THE BOOK GROUP

20 W. 20th St., Suite 601, New York NY 10011. (212)803-3360. **E-mail:** submissions@thebookgroup.com. **Website:** www.thebookgroup.com. Estab. 2015. Member of AAR. Signatory of WGA.

MEMBER AGENTS Julie Barer; Faye Bender; Brettne Bloom (fiction: literary and commercial fiction, select young adult; nonfiction, including cookbooks, lifestyle, investigative journalism, history, biography, memoir, and psychology); Elisabeth Weed (upmarket fiction, especially plot-driven novels with a sense of place); Rebecca Stead (innovative forms, diverse voices, and open-hearted fiction for children, young adults, and adults); Dana Murphy (story-driven fiction with a strong sense of place, narrative nonfiction/essays with a pop-culture lean, and YA with an honest voice).

REPRESENTS **Considers these fiction areas:** commercial, literary, mainstream, women's, young adult.

☛ Please do not send poetry or screenplays.

HOW TO CONTACT Send a query letter and 10 sample pages to submissions@thebookgroup.com, with the first and last name of the agent you are querying in the subject line. All material must be in the body of the e-mail, as the agents do not open attachments. "If we are interested in reading more, we will get in touch with you as soon as possible." Accepts simultaneous submissions.

RECENT SALES *This Is Not Over*, by Holly Brown; *Perfect Little World*, by Kevin Wilson; *City of Saints & Thieves*, by Natalie C. Anderson; *The Runaway Midwife*, by Patricia Harman; *Always*, by Sarah Jio; *The Young Widower's Handbook*, by Tom McAllister.

BOOKS & SUCH LITERARY MANAGEMENT

52 Mission Circle, Suite 122, PMB 170, Santa Rosa CA 95409. **E-mail:** representation@booksandsuch.com. **Website:** www.booksandsuch.com. **Contact:** Janet Kobobel Grant, Wendy Lawton, Rachel Kent, Rachelle Gardner, Cynthia Ruchti. Estab. 1996. CBA, American Christian Fiction Writers Represents 250 clients.

Prior to founding the agency, Ms. Grant was an editor for Zondervan and managing editor for Focus on the Family. Ms. Lawton was an author, sculptor, and designer of porcelain dolls and became an agent in 2005. Ms. Ruchti has written 21 books—both fiction and nonfiction—and was president of ACFW. Now she serves as ACFW's professional relations liaison (since 2011) and became an agent in 2017. Ms. Kent has worked as an agent for ten years and is a graduate of UC Davis majoring in English. Ms. Gardner worked as an editor at NavPress, at General Publishing Group in rights and marketing, and at Fox Broadcasting Company as special programming coordinator before becoming an agent in 2007.

REPRESENTS Nonfiction, fiction, novels, juvenile books. **Considers these fiction areas:** adventure, commercial, crime, family saga, frontier, historical, inspirational, juvenile, literary, mainstream, middle grade, mystery, religious, romance, spiritual, suspense, women's, young adult.

This agency specializes in general and inspirational fiction and nonfiction, and in the Christian booksellers market. Actively seeking well-crafted material that presents Judeo-Christian values, even if only subtly.

HOW TO CONTACT Query via e-mail only; no attachments. Accepts simultaneous submissions. Responds in 1 month to queries. "If you don't hear from us asking to see more of your writing within 30 days after you have sent your e-mail, please know that we have read and considered your submission but determined that it would not be a good fit for us." Obtains most new clients through recommendations from others, conferences.

TERMS Agent receives 15% commission on domestic sales; 20% commission on foreign sales. Offers written contract; two-month notice must be given to terminate contract. No additional charges.

RECENT SALES A full list of this agency's clients (and the awards they have won) is on the agency website.

WRITERS CONFERENCES The Declare Conference, The Why Conference, She Speaks, American Christian Fiction Writers Conference, West Coast Christian Writers Conference.

TIPS "Our agency highlights personal attention to individual clients that includes coaching on how to thrive in a rapidly changing publishing climate, grow a career, and get the best publishing offers possible."

GEORGES BORCHARDT, INC.

136 E. 57th St., New York NY 10022. (212)753-5785. **Website:** www.gbagency.com. Estab. 1967. Member of AAR. Represents 200+ clients.

MEMBER AGENTS Anne Borchardt, Georges Borchardt, Valerie Borchardt, Samantha Shea.

REPRESENTS Nonfiction, fiction, novels, short story collections, novellas.

This agency specializes in literary fiction and outstanding nonfiction.

HOW TO CONTACT No unsolicited submissions. Obtains most new clients through recommendations from others.

TERMS Agent receives 15% commission on domestic sales; 20% commission on foreign sales. Offers written contract.

RECENT SALES *The Relive Box and Other Stories*, by T.C. Boyle; *Nutshell*, by Ian McEwan; *What It Means When a Man Falls From the Sky*, by Lesley Nneka Arimah.

BRADFORD LITERARY AGENCY

5694 Mission Center Rd., #347, San Diego CA 92108. (619)521-1201. **E-mail:** queries@bradfordlit.com.

Website: www.bradfordlit.com. **Contact:** Laura Bradford, Natalie Lakosil, Sarah LaPolla, Kari Sutherland, Jennifer Chen Tran. Estab. 2001. Member of AAR. RWA, SCBWI, ALA Represents 130 clients.

MEMBER AGENTS Laura Bradford (romance [historical, romantic suspense, paranormal, category, contemporary, erotic], mystery, women's fiction, thrillers/suspense, middle grade & YA); Natalie Lakosil (children's literature [from picture book through teen and New Adult], romance [contemporary and historical], cozy mystery/crime, upmarket women's/general fiction and select children's nonfiction); Sarah LaPolla (YA, middle grade, literary fiction, science fiction, magical realism, dark/psychological mystery, literary horror, and upmarket contemporary fiction); Kari Sutherland (children's literature, middle grade, YA, upmarket women's fiction, magical realism, historical dramas, light-hearted contemporary fiction, biography, humor, and parenting); Jennifer Chen Tran (women's fiction, YA, middle grade, graphic novels, narrative nonfiction, parenting, culinary, lifestyle, business, memoir, parenting, psychology).

REPRESENTS Nonfiction, fiction, novels, juvenile books. **Considers these fiction areas:** commercial, crime, ethnic, gay, historical, juvenile, lesbian, literary, mainstream, middle grade, multicultural, mystery, new adult, paranormal, picture books, romance, science fiction, thriller, women's, young adult.

- Laura Bradford does not want to receive poetry, screenplays, short stories, westerns, horror, new age, religion, crafts, cookbooks, gift books. Natalie Lakosil does not want to receive inspirational novels, memoir, romantic suspense, adult thrillers, poetry, screenplays. Sarah LaPolla does not want to receive nonfiction, picture books, inspirational/spiritual novels, romance, or erotica. Kari Sutherland does not want to receive horror, romance, erotica, memoir, adult sci-fi/fantasy, thrillers, cookbooks, business, spiritual/religious, poetry, or screenplays. Jennifer Chen Tran does not want to receive picture books, sci-fi/fantasy, urban fantasy, westerns, erotica, poetry, or screenplays.

HOW TO CONTACT Accepts e-mail queries only; For submissions to Laura Bradford, send to queries@bradfordlit.com. For submissions to Natalie Lakosil, use the form listed on the website under the "How to Submit" page. For submissions to Sarah LaPolla, send to sarah@bradfordlit.com. For submissions to Kari Sutherland, send to kari@bradfordlit.com. For submissions to Jennifer Chen Tran, send to jen@bradfordlit.com. The entire submission must appear in the body of the e-mail and not as an attachment. The subject line should begin as follows: "QUERY: (the title of the ms or any short message that is important should follow)." For fiction: e-mail a query letter along with the first chapter of ms and a synopsis. Include the genre and word count in your query letter. Nonfiction: e-mail full nonfiction proposal including a query letter and a sample chapter. Accepts simultaneous submissions. Responds in 4 weeks to queries; 10 weeks to mss. Obtains most new clients through queries.

TERMS Agent receives 15% commission on domestic sales; 25% commission on foreign sales. Offers written contract. Charges for extra copies of books for foreign submissions.

RECENT SALES Sold 80 titles in the last year, including *Vox* by Christina Dalcher (Berkley); *The Last 8*, by Laura Pohl (Sourcebooks Fire); *You'll Miss Me When I'm Gone*, by Rachel Solomon (Simon Pulse); *Monday's Not Coming*, by Tiffany Jackson (Harper Collins); *Where She Fell*, by Kaitlin Ward (Adaptive); *Into the Nightfell Wood*, by Kristin Bailey (Katherine Tegen Books); *Yasmin the Explorer*, by Saadia Faruqi (Capstone); *Fix Her Up*, by Tessa Bailey (Entangled); *The Protector*, by HelenKay Dimon (Avon); *The Spitfire Girls*, by Soraya Lane (St. Martins); *Highland Wrath*, by Madeline Martin (Diversion); *Everybody's Favorite Book*, by Mike Allegra (Macmillan); *The Hook Up*, by Erin McCarthy (PRH); *Next Girl to Die*, by Dea Poirier (Thomas & Mercer); *The Fearless King*, by Katee Robert (Entangled); *Noble Hops*, by Layla Reyne (Carina Press); *The Rogue on Fifth Avenue*, by Joanna Shupe (Kensington).

WRITERS CONFERENCES RWA National Conference, Romantic Times Booklovers Convention.

BRANDT & HOCHMAN LITERARY AGENTS, INC.

1501 Broadway, Suite 2310, New York NY 10036. (212)840-5760. **Fax:** (212)840-5776. **Website:** brandthochman.com. **Contact:** Gail Hochman or individual agent best suited for the submission. Estab. over a century ago. Member of AAR. Represents 200 clients.

MEMBER AGENTS Gail Hochman (works of literary fiction, idea-driven nonfiction, literary memoir and children's books); Marianne Merola (fiction, non-fiction and children's books with strong and unique narrative voices); Bill Contardi (voice-driven young adult and middle grade fiction, commercial thrillers, psychological suspense, quirky mysteries, high fantasy, commercial fiction and memoir); Emily Forland (voice-driven literary fiction and nonfiction, memoir, narrative nonfiction, history, biography, food writing, cultural criticism, graphic novels, and young adult fiction); Emma Patterson (fiction from dark, literary novels to upmarket women's and historical fiction; narrative nonfiction that includes memoir, investigative journalism, and popular history; young adult fiction); Jody Kahn (literary and upmarket fiction; narrative nonfiction, particularly books related to sports, food, history, science and pop culture—including cookbooks, and literary memoir and journalism); Henry Thayer (nonfiction on a wide variety of subjects and fiction that inclines toward the literary). The e-mail addresses and specific likes of each of these agents is listed on the agency website.

REPRESENTS Nonfiction, novels. **Considers these fiction areas:** fantasy, historical, literary, middle grade, mystery, suspense, thriller, women's, young adult.

☛ No screenplays or textbooks.

HOW TO CONTACT "We accept queries by e-mail and regular mail; however, we cannot guarantee a response to e-mailed queries. For queries via regular mail, be sure to include a SASE for our reply. Query letters should be no more than 2 pages and should include a convincing overview of the book project and information about the author and his or her writing credits. Address queries to the specific Brandt & Hochman agent whom you would like to consider your work. Agent e-mail addresses and query preferences may be found at the end of each agent profile on the 'Agents' page of our website." Accepts simultaneous submissions. Obtains most new clients through recommendations from others.

TERMS Agent receives 15% commission on domestic sales; 20% commission on foreign sales.

RECENT SALES This agency sells 40-60 new titles each year. A full list of their hundreds of clients is on the agency website.

TIPS "Write a letter which will give the agent a sense of you as a professional writer—your long-term interests as well as a short description of the work at hand."

THE BRATTLE AGENCY

P.O. Box 380537, Cambridge MA 02238. (617)721-5375. **E-mail:** christopher.vyce@thebrattleagency.com. **E-mail:** submissions@thebrattleagency.com. **Website:** thebrattleagency.com. **Contact:** Christopher Vyce. Member of AAR. Signatory of WGA.

◐ Prior to being an agent, Mr. Vyce worked for the Beacon Press in Boston as an acquisitions editor.

REPRESENTS Nonfiction, novels. **Considers these fiction areas:** literary.

HOW TO CONTACT Query by e-mail. Include cover letter, brief synopsis, brief CV. Accepts simultaneous submissions. Responds to queries in 72 hours. Responds to approved submissions in 6-8 weeks.

BARBARA BRAUN ASSOCIATES, INC.

7 E. 14th St., #19F, New York NY 10003. **Fax:** (212)604-9023. **E-mail:** bbasubmissions@gmail.com. **Website:** www.barbarabraunagency.com. **Contact:** Barbara Braun. Member of AAR. Authors Guild, PEN Center USA

REPRESENTS Nonfiction, novels. **Considers these fiction areas:** commercial, historical, literary, multicultural, mystery, thriller, women's, young adult, Art-related fiction.

☛ "Our fiction is strong on stories for women, art-related fiction, historical and multicultural stories, and to a lesser extent mysteries and thrillers. We are interested in narrative nonfiction and current affairs books by journalists, as well as YA literature." Does not represent poetry, science fiction, fantasy, horror, or screenplays.

HOW TO CONTACT "We no longer accept submissions by regular mail. Please send all queries via e-mail, marked 'Query' in the subject line. Your query should include: a brief summary of your book, word count, genre, any relevant publishing experience, and the first 5 pages of your manuscript pasted into the body of the e-mail. (No attachments—we will not open these.)" Accepts simultaneous submissions.

TERMS Agent receives 15% commission on domestic sales; 20% commission on foreign sales. No reading fees.

TIPS "Our clients' books are represented throughout Europe, Asia, and Latin America by various sub-agents. We are also active in selling motion picture rights to the books we represent, and work with various Hollywood agencies."

BRESNICK WEIL LITERARY AGENCY

115 W. 29th St., Third Floor, New York NY 10001. (212)239-3166. **Fax:** (212)239-3165. **E-mail:** query@ bresnickagency.com. **Website:** bresnickagency.com. **Contact:** Paul Bresnick.

○ Prior to becoming an agent, Mr. Bresnick spent 25 years as a trade book editor.

MEMBER AGENTS Paul Bresnick; Susan Duff (women's health, food and wine, fitness, humor, memoir); Lisa Kopel (narrative nonfiction, memoir, pop culture, and both commercial and literary fiction); Matthew MiGangi (music, American history, sports, politics, weird science, pop/alternative culture, video games, and fiction).

REPRESENTS Nonfiction, novels. **Considers these fiction areas:** commercial, literary.

☞ Matthew DiGangi does not represent YA, middle grade, or books for children.

HOW TO CONTACT Electronic submissions only. For fiction, submit query and 2 chapters. For nonfiction, submit query with proposal. Accepts simultaneous submissions.

⊘ M. COURTNEY BRIGGS

Derrick & Briggs, LLP, 100 N. Broadway Ave., 28th Floor, Oklahoma City OK 73102. (405)235-1900. **Fax:** (405)235-1995. **Website:** www.derrickandbriggs.com.

CURTIS BROWN, LTD.

10 Astor Place, New York NY 10003. (212)473-5400. **Fax:** (212)598-0917. **Website:** www.curtisbrown.com. Member of AAR. Signatory of WGA.

MEMBER AGENTS Noah Ballard (literary debuts, upmarket thrillers, narrative nonfiction, always looking for honest and provocative new writers); Tess Callero (young adult, upmarket commercial women's fiction, mysteries/ thrillers, romance, nonfiction: pop culture, business, cookbooks, humor, biography, self-help, and food narrative projects); Ginger Clark (science fiction, fantasy, paranormal romance, literary horror, and young adult and middle grade fiction); Kerry D'Agostino (literary and commercial fiction, as well as narrative nonfiction and memoir); Katherine Fausset (literary fiction, upmarket commercial fiction, journalism, memoir, popular science, and narrative nonfiction); Holly Frederick; Peter Ginsberg, president; Elizabeth Harding, vice president (represents authors and illustrators of juvenile, middle-grade and young adult fiction); Ginger Knowlton, executive vice president (authors and illustrators of children's books in all genres—picture book, middle grade, young adult fiction and nonfiction); Timothy Knowlton, CEO; Jonathan Lyons (biographies, history, science, pop culture, sports, general narrative nonfiction, mysteries, thrillers, science fiction and fantasy, and young adult fiction); Sarah Perillo (middle grade fiction and commercial fiction for adults, nonfiction:history, politics, science, pop culture, and humor, and is especially fond of anything involving animals or food); Laura Blake Peterson, vice president (memoir and biography, natural history, literary fiction, mystery, suspense, women's fiction, health and fitness, children's and young adult, faith issues and popular culture); Steven Salpeter (literary fiction, fantasy, graphic novels, historical fiction, mysteries, thrillers, young adult, narrative nonfiction, gift books, history, humor, and popular science); Maureen Walters, senior vice president (working primarily in women's fiction and nonfiction projects on subjects as eclectic as parenting & child care, popular psychology, inspirational/motivational volumes as well as a few medical/nutritional books); Mitchell Waters (literary and commercial fiction and nonfiction, including mystery, history, biography, memoir, young adult, cookbooks, self-help and popular culture); Monika Woods (plot-driven literary novels, non-fiction that is creatively critical, unique perspectives, a great cookbook, and above all, original prose).

REPRESENTS Nonfiction, fiction, novels, short story collections, juvenile books. **Considers these fiction areas:** contemporary issues, ethnic, fantasy, feminist, historical, horror, humor, juvenile, literary, mainstream, middle grade, mystery, paranormal, picture books, religious, romance, spiritual, sports, suspense, thriller, women's, young adult.

HOW TO CONTACT Please refer to the "Agents" page on the website for each agent's submission guidelines. Accepts simultaneous submissions. Responds in 4 weeks to queries; 6 weeks to mss. (but do see Agent page on website for more information) Obtains most new clients through recommendations from others, solicitations, conferences.

TERMS Agent receives 15% commission on domestic sales; 20% on foreign sales. Offers written contract. 75-day notice must be given to terminate contract. Charges for some postage (overseas, etc.).

RECENT SALES This agency prefers not to share information on specific sales.

CURTIS BROWN (AUST) PTY LTD

P.O. Box 19, Paddington NSW 2021 Australia. (+61) (2)9361-6161. **Fax:** (+61)(2)9360-3935. **E-mail:** reception@curtisbrown.com.au. **E-mail:** submission@curtisbrown.com.au. **Website:** www.curtisbrown.com.au.

"Prior to joining Curtis Brown, most of our agents worked in publishing or the film/theatre industries in Australia and the United Kingdom.".

MEMBER AGENTS Fiona Inglis (managing director/agent); Tara Wynne (agent); Pippa Masson (agent); Clare Forster (agent); Grace Heifetz (agent).

"We are Australia's oldest and largest literary agency representing a diverse range of Australian and New Zealand writers and Estates."

HOW TO CONTACT "Please refer to our website for information regarding ms submissions, permissions, theatre rights requests, and the clients and Estates we represent. We are not currently looking to represent poetry, short stories, stage/screenplays, picture books, or translations. We do not accept e-mailed or faxed submissions. No responsibility is taken for the receipt or loss of mss." Accepts simultaneous submissions.

BROWNE & MILLER LITERARY ASSOCIATES

52 Village Place, Hinsdale IL 60521. (312)922-3063. **E-mail:** mail@browneandmiller.com. **Website:** www.browneandmiller.com. **Contact:** Danielle Egan-Miller, president. Estab. 1971. Member of AAR. RWA, MWA, Authors Guild.

Prior to joining the agency as Jane Jordan Browne's partner, Danielle Egan-Miller worked as an editor.

REPRESENTS Nonfiction, fiction.

Browne & Miller is most interested in literary and commercial fiction, women's fiction, women's historical fiction, literary-leaning crime fiction, dark suspense/domestic suspense,romance, and Christian/inspirational fiction by established authors, and a wide range of platform-driven nonfiction by nationally-recognized author-experts. "We do not represent children's books of any kind or Young Adult; no adult Memoirs; we do not represent horror, science fiction or fantasy, short stories, poetry, original screenplays,or articles."

HOW TO CONTACT Query via e-mail only; no attachments. Do not send unsolicited mss. Accepts simultaneous submissions.

ANDREA BROWN LITERARY AGENCY, INC.

E-mail: andrea@andreabrownlit.com; caryn@andreabrownlit.com; lauraqueries@gmail.com; jennifer@andreabrownlit.com; kelly@andreabrownlit.com; jennL@andreabrownlit.com; jamie@andreabrownlit.com; jmatt@andreabrownlit.com; kathleen@andreabrownlit.com; lara@andreabrownlit.com; soloway@andreabrownlit.com. **Website:** www.andreabrownlit.com. Estab. 1981. Member of AAR.

Prior to opening her agency, Ms. Brown served as an editorial assistant at Random House and Dell Publishing and as an editor with Knopf.

MEMBER AGENTS Andrea Brown (president); Laura Rennert (executive agent); Caryn Wiseman (senior agent); Jennifer Laughran (senior agent); Jennifer Rofé (senior agent); Kelly Sonnack (senior agent); Jamie Weiss Chilton (senior agent); Jennifer Mattson (agent); Kathleen Rushall (agent); Lara Perkins (agent, digital manager); Jennifer March Soloway (associate agent).

REPRESENTS Juvenile books. **Considers these fiction areas:** juvenile, middle grade, picture books, young adult, middle-grade, all juvenile genres..

Specializes in all kinds of children's books—illustrators and authors. 98% juvenile books. Considers: nonfiction, fiction, picture books, young adult.

HOW TO CONTACT Writers should review the large agent bios on the agency website to determine which agent to contact. Please choose only one agent to query. The agents share queries, so a no from one agent at Andrea Brown Literary Agency is a no from all. (Note that Jennifer Laughran and Kelly Sonnack only receive queries by querymanager - please visit the agency's website for information.) For picture books, submit a query letter and complete ms in the body of the e-mail. For fiction, submit a query letter and the first 10 pages in the body of the e-mail. For nonfiction, submit proposal, first 10 pages in the body of the e-mail. Illustrators: submit a query letter and 2-3 illustration samples (in jpeg format), link to online portfolio, and text of picture book, if applicable. "We only accept queries via e-mail. No attachments, with the exception of jpeg illustrations from illustrators." Visit the agents' bios on our website and choose only one agent to whom you will submit your e-query. Send a short e-mail query letter to that agent with "QUERY" in the subject field. Accepts simultaneous submissions. If we are interested in your work, we will certainly follow up by e-mail or by phone. However, if you haven't heard from us within 6-8 weeks, please assume that we are passing on your project. Obtains most new clients through queries and referrals from editors, clients and agents. Check website for guidelines and information.

TERMS Agent receives 15% commission on domestic sales; 25% commission on foreign sales. Offers written contract. No fees.

RECENT SALES Supriya Kelkar's middle grade novel *American As Paneer Pie* to Jennifer Ung at Aladdin, at auction, for publication in summer 2020, by Kathleen Rushall. Mitali Perkins's *You Bring the Distant Near* , sold at auction, in a two-book deal, to Grace Kendall at Farrar, Straus Children's, by Laura Rennert. Cynthia Salaysay's YA novel *Private Lessons* to Kate Fletcher at Candlewick, for publication in the spring of 2020, by Jennifer March Soloway. Dev Petty's picture book text, *The Bear Must Go On* to Talia Benamy at Philomel, for publication in spring 2021, by Jennifer Rofe. Carrie Pearson's nonfiction picture book text *A Girl Who Leaped, A Woman Who Soared* to Simon Boughton at Norton Children's by Kelly Sonnack. K. C. Johnson's YA novel, *This is My America* to Chelsea Eberly at Random House Children's in a two-book deal by Jennifer March Soloway. Nancy Castaldo's nonfiction YA, *Water* to Elise Howard at Algonquin Young Readers, by Jennifer Laughran. Kate Messner's picture book text, *The Next President* to Melissa Manlove at Chronicle Children's, in a two book deal, by Jennifer Laughran. Amber Lough's YA novel, *Summer of War* to Amy Fitzgerald at Carolrhoda Lab by Laura Rennert and Jennifer March Soloway. Andrea Zimmerman and David Clemesha's picture book *All Buckled Up!* to Jeffrey Salane at Little Simon, in a two-book deal by Jamie Weiss Chilton. Jennifer Berne's picture book *Dinosaur Doomsday* to Melissa Manlove at Chronicle Children's by Caryn Wiseman. Tami Charles's *Serena Williams—G.O.A.T.: Making the Case for the Greatest of All Time*, a sports biography of Serena Williams to Ada Zhang at Sterling Children's by Lara Perkins. Katy Loutzenhiser's YA *If You're Out There* to Donna Bray at Balzer & Bray in a two-book deal by Jennifer Mattson. Barry Eisler's *The Killer Collective,* as well as a John Rain prequel, and two more in the Livia Lone series, to Gracie Doyle at Thomas & Mercer, in a major deal by Laura Rennert.

Maggie Stiefvater's The Raven Cycle series to Universal Cable Productions by Laura Rennert.

WRITERS CONFERENCES SCBWI, Asilomar; Maui Writers' Conference, Southwest Writers' Conference, San Diego State University Writers' Conference, Big Sur Children's Writing Workshop, William Saroyan Writers' Conference, Columbus Writers' Conference, Willamette Writers' Conference, La Jolla Writers' Conference, San Francisco Writers' Conference, Hilton Head Writers' Conference, Pacific Northwest Conference, Pikes Peak Conference.

SHEREE BYKOFSKY ASSOCIATES, INC.

P.O. Box 706, Brigantine NJ 08203. **E-mail:** shereebee@aol.com. **Website:** www.shereebee.com. **Contact:** Sheree Bykofsky. Estab. 1991. Member of AAR. Author's Guild, Atlantic City Chamber of Commerce, PRC Council. Represents 1,000+ clients.

○ Prior to opening her agency, Sheree Bykofsky served as executive editor of the Stonesong Press and managing editor of Chiron Press. Janet Rosen worked as associate book editor at *Glamour* and as the senior books and fiction editor at *Woman* before turning to agenting at Sheree Bykofsky Associates, where she represents a range of nonfiction and a limited amount of fiction.

MEMBER AGENTS Sheree Bykofsky, Janet Rosen.

REPRESENTS Nonfiction, novels. **Considers these fiction areas:** commercial, contemporary issues, crime, detective, literary, mainstream, mystery, suspense, women's.

○→ This agency is seeking nonfiction, both prescriptive and narrative, and some fiction. Prescriptive nonfiction: primarily health and business. Narrative nonfiction: pop culture, biography, history, popular and social science, language, music, cities, medicine, fashion, military, and espionage. Fiction: women's commercial fiction (with a literary quality) and mysteries. Does not want to receive poetry, children's, screenplays, westerns, science fiction, or horror.

HOW TO CONTACT Query via e-mail to submitbee@aol.com. "We only accept e-queries. We respond only to those queries in which we are interested. No attachments, snail mail, or phone calls, please. We do not open attachments." Fiction: one-page query, one-page synopsis, and first three pages of ms in body of the e-mail. Nonfiction: one-page query in the body of the e-mail. Currently we are focusing much more on our nonfiction portfolio, especially business, prescriptive nonfiction, and popular culture. Accepts simultaneous submissions. Responds in 1 month to requested mss. Obtains most new clients through referrals but still reads all submissions closely.

TERMS Agent receives 15% commission on domestic sales. Agent receives 15% commission on foreign sales, plus international co-agent receives another 10%. Offers written contract, binding for 1 year. Charges for international postage.

RECENT SALES *That Thin, Wild Mercury Sound: Dylan, Nashville, and the Making of Blonde on Blonde* by Daryl Sanders (Chicago Review Press), *A Tangled Web* by Leslie Rule (Kensington), *Sneaky Uses for Everyday Things, 2nd Edition* by Cy Tymony (Andrews McMeel), *Don't Believe Everything you Think* by Rod Evans (Sterling), *Gamer Nation* by Eric Geissinger (Prometheus Books), *Virtual Billions: The Genius, the Drug Lord, and the Ivy League Twins Behind the Rise of Bitcoin* by Eric Geissinger (Prometheus Books), *Thank You, Teacher: Grateful Students Tell the Stories of the Teachers Who Changed Their Lives* by Holly and Bruce Holbert (New World Library), *The Type B Manager: Leading Successfully in a Type A World* by Victor Lipman (Prentice Hall), *Let the Story Do the Work: The Art of Storytelling for Business Success* by Esther Choy (Amacom), *Convicting Avery: The Bizarre Laws and Broken System Behind "Making a Murderer"* by Michael D. Cicchini (Prometheus Books), *The Curious Case of Kiryas Joel: The Rise of a Village Theocracy and the Battle to Defend the Separation of Church and State* by Louis Grumet with John Caher (Chicago Review Press), *Cells are the New Cure* by Robin L. Smith, M.D. and Max Gomez, Ph.D.; dozens of international sales.

WRITERS CONFERENCES Truckee Meadow Community College Keynote, Southwest Florida Writers Conference, Philadelphia Writer's Conference, Push to Publish, Lewes Writers Conference, Pennwriters, League of Vermont Writers, Asilomar, Florida Suncoast Writers' Conference, Whidbey Island Writers' Conference, Florida First Coast Writers' Festival, Agents and Editors Conference, Columbus Writers' Conference, Southwest Writers' Conference, Willamette Writers' Conference, Dorothy Canfield Fisher Conference, Maui Writers' Conference, Pacific Northwest Writers' Conference, IWWG.

KIMBERLEY CAMERON & ASSOCIATES

1550 Tiburon Blvd., #704, Tiburon CA 94920. (415)789-9191. **Website:** www.kimberleycameron. com. **Contact:** Kimberley Cameron. Member of AAR. Signatory of WGA.

Kimberley Cameron & Associates (formerly The Reece Halsey Agency) has had an illustrious client list of established writers, including Aldous Huxley, Upton Sinclair, William Faulkner, and Henry Miller.

MEMBER AGENTS Kimberley Cameron; Elizabeth Kracht (nonfiction: memoir, self-help, spiritual, investigative, creative / fiction: women's, literary, historical, mysteries, thrillers); Amy Cloughley (literary and upmarket fiction, women's, historical, narrative nonfiction, travel or adventure memoir); Mary C. Moore (fantasy, science fiction, upmarket "book club," genre romance, thrillers with female protagonists, and stories from marginalized voices); Lisa Abellera (currently closed to unsolicited submissions); Pooja Menon; Dorian Maffei (only open to submissions requested through Twitter pitch parties, conferences, or #MSWL).

REPRESENTS Nonfiction, fiction, novels. **Considers these fiction areas:** action, adventure, commercial, confession, crime, detective, gay, historical, literary, mainstream, military, mystery, police, romance, science fiction, spiritual, thriller, women's, young adult, LGBTQ.

"We are looking for a unique and heartfelt voice that conveys a universal truth."

HOW TO CONTACT Prefers queries via site. Only query one agent at a time. For fiction, fill out the correct submissions form for the individual agent and attach the first 50 pages and a synopsis (if requested) as a Word doc or PDF. For nonfiction, fill out the correct submission form of the individual agent and attach a full book proposal and sample chapters (includes the first chapter and no more than 50 pages) as a Word doc or PDF. Accepts simultaneous submissions. Obtains new clients through recommendations from others, solicitations.

CYNTHIA CANNELL LITERARY AGENCY

54 W. 40th St., New York NY 10018. (212)396-9595. **E-mail:** info@cannellagency.com. **Website:** www. cannellagency.com. **Contact:** Cynthia Cannell. Estab. 1997. Member of AAR. Women's Media Group and the Authors Guild

Prior to forming the Cynthia Cannell Literary Agency, Ms. Cannell was the vice president of Janklow & Nesbit Associates for 12 years.

REPRESENTS Nonfiction, fiction.

➤ Does not represent screenplays, children's books, illustrated books, cookbooks, romance, category mystery, or science fiction.

HOW TO CONTACT "Please query us with an e-mail or letter. If querying by e-mail, send a brief description of your project with relevant biographical information including publishing credits (if any) to info@cannellagency.com. Do not send attachments. If querying by conventional mail, enclose an SASE." Responds if interested. Accepts simultaneous submissions.

RECENT SALES Check the website for an updated list of authors and sales.

CAPITAL TALENT AGENCY

419 S. Washington St., Alexandria VA 22314. (703)349-1649. **E-mail:** literary.submissions@capitaltalentagency.com. **Website:** capitaltalentagency.com/html/literary.shtml. **Contact:** Cynthia Kane. Estab. 2014. Member of AAR. Signatory of WGA.

Prior to joining CTA, Ms. Kane was involved in the publishing industry for more than 10 years. She has worked as a development editor for different publishing houses and individual authors and has seen more than 100 titles to market.

MEMBER AGENTS Cynthia Kane; Shaheen Qureshi.

REPRESENTS Nonfiction, fiction, movie scripts, stage plays.

HOW TO CONTACT "We accept submissions only by e-mail. We do not accept queries via postal mail or fax. For fiction and nonfiction submissions, send a query letter in the body of your e-mail. Please note that while we consider each query seriously, we are unable to respond to all of them. We endeavor to respond within 6 weeks to projects that interest us." Accepts simultaneous submissions. 6 weeks

CHALBERG & SUSSMAN

115 W. 29th St., Third Floor, New York NY 10001. (917)261-7550. **Website:** www.chalbergsussman.com. Member of AAR. Signatory of WGA.

Prior to her current position, Ms. Chalberg held a variety of editorial positions, and was an agent with The Susan Golomb Literary Agency. Ms. Sussman was an agent with Zachary Shuster Harmsworth. Ms. James was with The Aaron Priest Literary Agency.

MEMBER AGENTS Terra Chalberg; Rachel Sussman (narrative journalism, memoir, psychology, history, humor, pop culture, literary fiction); Nicole James (plot-driven fiction, psychological suspense, uplifting female-driven memoir, upmarket self-help, and lifestyle books); Lana Popovic (young adult, middle grade, contemporary realism, speculative fiction, fantasy, horror, sophisticated erotica, romance, select nonfiction, international stories).

REPRESENTS Nonfiction, fiction, novels. **Considers these fiction areas:** erotica, fantasy, horror, literary, middle grade, romance, science fiction, suspense, young adult, contemporary realism, speculative fiction.

HOW TO CONTACT To query by e-mail, please contact one of the following: terra@chalbergsussman.com, rachel@chalbergsussman.com, nicole@chalbergsussman.com, lana@chalbergsussman.com. To query by regular mail, please address your letter to one agent and include SASE. Accepts simultaneous submissions.

RECENT SALES The agents' sales and clients are listed on their website.

CHASE LITERARY AGENCY

11 Broadway, Suite 1010, New York NY 10004. (212)477-5100. **E-mail:** farley@chaseliterary.com. **Website:** www.chaseliterary.com. **Contact:** Farley Chase.

MEMBER AGENTS Farley Chase.

REPRESENTS Nonfiction, fiction, novels. **Considers these fiction areas:** commercial, historical, literary, mystery.

➤ No romance, science fiction, or young adult.

HOW TO CONTACT E-query farley@chaseliterary.com. If submitting fiction, please include the first few pages of the ms with the query. "I do not response to queries not addressed to me by name. I'm keenly interested in both fiction and nonfiction. In fiction, I'm looking for both literary or commercial projects in either contemporary or historical settings. I'm open to anything with a strong sense of place, voice, and, especially plot. I don't handle science fiction, romance, supernatural or young adult. In nonfiction, I'm especially interested in narratives in history, memoir, journalism, natural science, military history, sports, pop culture, and humor. Whether by first-time writers or long time journalists, I'm excited by original ideas, strong points of view, detailed research, and access to subjects which give readers fresh perspectives on things they think they know. I'm also interested in visually-driven and illustrated books. Whether they involve photography, comics, illustrations, or art I'm taken by creative storytelling with visual elements, four color or black and white." Accepts simultaneous submissions.

RECENT SALES *Devil in the Grove: Thurgood Marshall, the Groveland Boys, and the Dawn of a New America* , by Gilbert King (Harper); *Heads in Beds: A Reckless Memoir of Hotels, Hustles, and So-Called Hospitality*, by Jacob Tomsky (Doubleday); *And Every Day Was Overcast*, by Paul Kwiatowski (Black Balloon); *The Badlands Saloon*, by Jonathan Twingley (Scribner).

CHENEY ASSOCIATES, LLC

78 Fifth Ave., 3rd Floor, New York NY 10011. (212)277-8007. **Fax:** (212)614-0728. **E-mail:** submissions@cheneyliterary.com. **Website:** www.cheneyliterary.com. **Contact:** Elyse Cheney; Adam Eaglin; Alex Jacobs; Alice Whitwham.

○ Prior to her current position, Ms. Cheney was an agent with Sanford J. Greenburger Associates.

MEMBER AGENTS Elyse Cheney; Adam Eaglin (literary fiction and nonfiction, including history, politics, current events, narrative reportage, biography, memoir, and popular science); Alexander Jacobs (narrative nonfiction [particularly in the areas of history, science, politics, and culture], literary fiction, crime, and memoir); Alice Whitwham (literary and commercial fiction, as well as voice-driven narrative nonfiction, cultural criticism, and journalism).

REPRESENTS Nonfiction, novels. **Considers these fiction areas:** commercial, crime, family saga, historical, literary, short story collections, suspense, women's.

HOW TO CONTACT Query by e-mail or snail mail. For a snail mail responses, include a SASE. Include up to 3 chapters of sample material. Do not query more than one agent. Accepts simultaneous submissions.

RECENT SALES *The Love Affairs of Nathaniel P.*, by Adelle Waldman (Henry Holt & Co.); *This Town*, by Mark Leibovich (Blue Rider Press); *Thunder & Lightning*, by Lauren Redniss (Random House).

THE CHUDNEY AGENCY

72 N. State Rd., Suite 501, Briarcliff Manor NY 10510. (914)465-5560. **E-mail:** steven@thechudneyagency.com. **Website:** www.thechudneyagency.com. **Contact:** Steven Chudney. Estab. 2001. SCBWI

○ Prior to becoming an agent, Mr. Chudney held various marketing and sales positions with major publishers.

REPRESENTS Novels, juvenile books. **Considers these fiction areas:** commercial, family saga, gay, historical, juvenile, lesbian, literary, middle grade, picture books, regional, suspense, thriller, young adult.

☞ "At this time, the agency is only looking for author/illustrators (one individual), who can both write and illustrate wonderful picture books. The author/illustrator must really know and understand the prime audience's needs and wants of the child reader! Storylines should be engaging, fun, with a hint of a life lessons and cannot be longer than 800 words. With chapter books, middle grade and teen novels, I'm primarily looking for quality, contemporary literary fiction: novels that are exceedingly well-written, with wonderful settings and developed, unforgettable characters. I'm looking for historical fiction that will excite me, young readers, editors, and reviewers, and will introduce us to unique characters in settings and situations, countries, and eras we haven't encountered too often yet in children's and teen literature." Does not want most fantasy and no science fiction.

HOW TO CONTACT No snail mail submissions for fiction/novels. Queries only. Submission package info from us to follow should we be interested in your project. For children's picture books, we only want author/illustrator projects. Submit a pdf with full text and at least 5-7 full-color illustrations. Accepts simultaneous submissions. Responds if interested in 2-3 weeks to queries.

WM CLARK ASSOCIATES

54 W. 21st St., Suite 809, New York NY 10010. (212)675-2784. **E-mail:** general@wmclark.com. **Website:** www.wmclark.com. **Contact:** William Clark. Estab. 1997. Member of AAR. Member, Board of Directors, Association of Authors Representatives.

○ Prior to opening WCA, Mr. Clark was an agent at the William Morris Agency.

REPRESENTS Nonfiction, novels. **Considers these fiction areas:** historical, literary.

☞ Agency does not represent screenplays or respond to screenplay pitches. "It is advised that before querying you become familiar with the kinds of books we handle by browsing our Book List, which is available on our website."

HOW TO CONTACT Accepts queries via online query form only. "We will endeavor to respond as soon as possible as to whether or not we'd like to see a proposal or sample chapters from your manuscript." Responds in 1-2 months to queries.

TERMS Agent receives 15% commission on domestic sales; 20% commission on foreign sales. Offers written contract.

WRITERS CONFERENCES London Book Fair, Frankfurt Book Fair.

TIPS "Translation rights are sold directly in the German, Italian, Spanish, Portuguese, Latin American, French, Dutch, and Scandinavian territories; and through corresponding agents in China, Bulgaria, Czech Republic, Latvia, Poland, Hungary, Russia, Japan, Greece, Israel, Turkey, Korea, Taiwan, Vietnam, and Thailand."

FRANCES COLLIN, LITERARY AGENT

Sarah Yake, Literary Agent, P.O. Box 33, Wayne PA 19087-0033. **E-mail:** queries@francescollin.com. **Website:** www.francescollin.com. Estab. 1948. Member of AAR. Represents 50 clients.

○ Sarah Yake has been with the agency since 2005 and handles foreign and subsidiary rights as well as her own client list. She holds an M.A. in English Literature and has been a sales rep for a major publisher and a bookstore manager. She currently teaches in the Rosemont College Graduate Publishing Program.

MEMBER AGENTS Frances Collin; Sarah Yake.

REPRESENTS Nonfiction, fiction, novels, short story collections. **Considers these fiction areas:** adventure, commercial, experimental, feminist, gay, historical, juvenile, literary, middle grade, multicultural, science fiction, short story collections, women's, young adult.

○— Actively seeking authors who are invested in their unique visions and who want to set trends not chase them. "I'd like to think that my authors are unplagiarizable by virtue of their distinct voices and styles." Does not want previously self-published work. Query with new mss only, please.

HOW TO CONTACT "We periodically close to queries, so please check our Publishers Marketplace account or other social media accounts before query-ing. When we are open to queries, we ask that writers send a traditional query e-mail describing the project and copy and paste the first 5 pages of the manuscript into the body of the e-mail. We look forward to hearing from you at queries@francescollin.com. Please send queries to that e-mail address. Any queries sent to another e-mail address within the agency will be deleted unread." Accepts simultaneous submissions. Responds in 1-4 weeks for initial queries, longer for full mss.

⊘ COMPASS TALENT

729 7th Ave., New York NY 10019. (646)376-7747. **E-mail:** query@compasstalent.com. **Website:** www. compasstalent.com. **Contact:** Heather Schroder. Member of AAR. Signatory of WGA.

REPRESENTS Considers these fiction areas: commercial, literary, mainstream.

HOW TO CONTACT This agency is currently closed to unsolicited submissions. Accepts simultaneous submissions.

RECENT SALES A full list of agency clients is available on the website.

DON CONGDON ASSOCIATES INC.

110 William St., Suite 2202, New York NY 10038. (212)645-1229. **Fax:** (212)727-2688. **E-mail:** dca@doncongdon.com. **Website:** doncongdon.com. Estab. 1983. Member of AAR.

MEMBER AGENTS Cristina Concepcion (crime fiction, narrative nonfiction, political science, journalism, history, books on cities, classical music, biography, science for a popular audience, philosophy, food and wine, iconoclastic books on health and human relationships, essays, and arts criticism); Michael Congdon (commercial and literary fiction, suspense, mystery, thriller, history, military history, biography, memoir, current affairs, and narrative nonfiction [adventure, medicine, science, and nature]); Katie Grimm (literary fiction, historical, women's fiction, short story collections, graphic novels, mysteries, young adult, middle-grade, memoir, science, academic); Katie Kotchman (business [all areas], narrative nonfiction [particularly popular science and social/cultural issues], self-help, success, motivation, psychology, pop culture, women's fiction, realistic young adult, literary fiction, and psychological thrillers); Maura Kye-Casella (narrative nonfiction, cookbooks, women's fiction, young adult, self-help, and parenting); Susan Ramer (literary fiction, upmarket commercial fiction [contemporary and historical], narrative nonfiction, social history, cultural history, smart pop culture [music, film, food, art], women's issues, psychology and mental health, and memoir).

REPRESENTS Nonfiction, novels, short story collections. **Considers these fiction areas:** crime, hi-lo, historical, literary, middle grade, mystery, short story collections, suspense, thriller, women's, young adult.

☞ Susan Ramer: "Not looking for romance, science fiction, fantasy, espionage, mysteries, politics, health/diet/fitness, self-help, or sports." Katie Kotchman: "Please do not send her screenplays or poetry."

HOW TO CONTACT "For queries via e-mail, you must include the word 'query' and the agent's full name in your subject heading. Please also include your query and sample chapter in the body of the e-mail, as we do not open attachments for security reasons. Please query only one agent within the agency at a time. If you are sending your query via regular mail, please enclose a SASE for our reply. If you would like us to return your materials, please make sure your postage will cover their return." Accepts simultaneous submissions.

RECENT SALES This agency represents many best-selling clients such as David Sedaris and Kathryn Stockett.

CORVISIERO LITERARY AGENCY

275 Madison Ave., at 40th, 14th Floor, New York NY 10016. (646)856-4032. **Fax:** (646)217-3758. **E-mail:** consult@corvisieroagency.com. **Website:** www.corvisieroagency.com. **Contact:** Marisa A. Corvisiero, Founder, Senior Agent, Attorney. Estab. 2012.

MEMBER AGENTS Marisa A. Corvisiero, senior agent and literary attorney (contemporary romance, thrillers, adventure, paranormal, urban fantasy, science fiction, MG, YA, picture books, Christmas themes, time travel, space science fiction, nonfiction, self-help, science, business); Saritza Hernandez, senior agent (all kinds of romance, GLBT, YA, erotica, science fiction, fantasy, thriller, mystery, horror); Doreen Thistle (do not query); Cate Hart (YA, MG, and Adult; romance, fantasy, magical realism, mystery, adventure, historical, upmarket women's fiction, LGBTQ, multicultural; adult and juvenile nonfiction: history, biography, Southern and pop culture); Veronica Park (dark or edgy YA/NA, Commercial adult, adult romance and romantic suspense, and funny

and/or current/controversial nonfiction); Kelly Peterson (MG, fantasy, paranormal, sci-fi, YA, steampunk, historical, dystopian, sword and sorcery, romance, historical romance, adult, fantasy, romance); Justin Wells; Kaitlyn Johnson (upper MG, YA, NA, and Adult; fantasy, urban fantasy, romance, historical fiction, contemporary, LGBTQ+); Kortney Price (MG & YA; fantasy, science fiction, mystery, thriller, suspense, contemporary, romance); Kat Kerr (adult literary and commercial, contemporary, science fiction, fantasy, historical, romance, women's fiction, multicultural, psychological thrillers, mysteries, southern gothic, YA, nonfiction, LGBTQ+, ownvoices, Nonfiction: literary journalism); Maria Heater (Fiction: Adult/YA, literary, contemporary, SFF, mystery/suspense, women's fiction, historical; Nonfiction: Adult/YA, memoir, social/cultural issues, gender/sexuality, psychology, history); Cortney Radocaj (YA and Adult; fantasy, science fiction, steampunk, cyberpunk, urban fantasy, paranormal, contemporary).

REPRESENTS Nonfiction, fiction, novels, juvenile books. **Considers these fiction areas:** action, adventure, commercial, erotica, family saga, fantasy, feminist, gay, historical, humor, juvenile, lesbian, metaphysical, middle grade, multicultural, mystery, new adult, New Age, occult, paranormal, picture books, psychic, religious, romance, science fiction, spiritual, suspense, thriller, urban fantasy, women's, young adult, magical realism, steampunk, dystopian, sword and sorcery.

HOW TO CONTACT Accepts submissions via QueryManager. Include query letter, 5 pages of complete and polished ms, and a 1-2 page synopsis. For nonfiction, include a proposal instead of the synopsis. Each agent profile on website has a button for direct submissions. Accepts simultaneous submissions.

WRITERS CONFERENCES SCWC (San Diego); AuthorPreneur Workshop Charlotte; NJ Fiction Writers; Muse and the Marketplace; RT Convention; LI Romance Writers; BEA; DFW Fort Worth; Thrillerfest NYC; RWA; Writers Digest NYC; AuthorPreneur Workshop Red Bank; SCWC (Los Angeles); NJ Romance Writers; SCBWI.

CREATIVE MEDIA AGENCY, INC.

(212)812-1494. **E-mail:** paige@cmalit.com. **Website:** www.cmalit.com. **Contact:** Paige Wheeler. Estab. 1997. Member of AAR. WMG, RWA, MWA, Authors Guild. Represents about 30 clients.

○ After starting out as an editor for Harlequin Books in NY and Euromoney Publications in London, Paige repped writers, producers, and celebrities as an agent with Artists Agency, until she formed Creative Media Agency in 1997. In 2006 she co-created Folio Literary Management and grew that company for 8 years into a successful mid-sized agency. In 2014 she decided to once again pursue a boutique approach, and she relaunched CMA.

REPRESENTS Nonfiction, fiction, novels. **Considers these fiction areas:** commercial, crime, detective, historical, inspirational, mainstream, middle grade, mystery, new adult, romance, suspense, thriller, women's, young adult, general fiction.

☛ Fiction: All commercial and upscale (think book club) fiction, as well as women's fiction, romance (all types), mystery, thrillers, inspirational/Christian and psychological suspense. I enjoy both historical fiction as well as contemporary fiction, so do keep that in mind. I seem to be especially drawn to a story if it has a high concept and a fresh, unique voice. Nonfiction: I'm looking for both narrative nonfiction and prescriptive nonfiction. I'm looking for books where the author has a huge platform and something new to say in a particular area. Some of the areas that I like are lifestyle, relationship, parenting, business/entrepreneurship, food-subsistence-homesteading topics, popular/trendy reference projects and women's issues. I'd like books that would be a good fit on the *Today* show. Does not want to receive children's books, science fiction, fantasy, or academic nonfiction.

HOW TO CONTACT E-query. Write "query" in your e-mail subject line. For fiction, paste in the first 5 pages of the ms after the query. For nonfiction, paste in an extended author bio as well as the marketing section of your book proposal after the query. Accepts simultaneous submissions. Responds in 4-6 weeks.

⊘ CREATIVE TRUST, INC.

210 Jamestown Park Dr., Suite 200, Brentwood TN 37027. (615)297-5010. **Fax:** (615)297-5020. **E-mail:** info@creativetrust.com. **Website:** www.creative-trust.com.

REPRESENTS Nonfiction, novels, movie scripts. , multimedia, other.

HOW TO CONTACT "Creative Trust Literary Group does not accept unsolicited manuscripts or book proposals from unpublished authors. We do accept unsolicited inquiries from previously published authors under the following requisites; email inquiries only, which must not be accompanied by attachments of any kind, to info@creativetrust.com. Please indicate 'Literary Submission' in your subject line. Due to the volume of queries we receive, we are not able to respond except to request additional materials." Accepts simultaneous submissions.

⊘ RICHARD CURTIS ASSOCIATES, INC.

200 E. 72nd St., Suite 28J, New York NY 10021. (212)772-7363. **Fax:** (212)772-7393. **Website:** www.curtisagency.com. Member of AAR. RWA, MWA, ITW, SFWA. Represents 100 clients.

○ Prior to becoming an agent, Mr. Curtis authored blogs, articles, and books on the publishing business and help for authors.

REPRESENTS Nonfiction, fiction, novels, juvenile books. **Considers these fiction areas:** adventure, commercial, fantasy, romance, science fiction, thriller, young adult.

☛ Actively seeking nonfiction (but no memoir), women's fiction (especially contemporary), thrillers, science fiction, middle-grade, and young adult. Does not want screenplays.

HOW TO CONTACT Use submission procedure on website. "We also read one-page query letters accompanied by SASE." Accepts simultaneous submissions.

TERMS Agent receives 15% commission on domestic sales; 25% commission on foreign sales. Offers written contract. Charges for photocopying, express mail, international freight, book orders.

RECENT SALES Sold 100 titles in the last year, including *The Library*, by D.J. MacHale; *Tylers of Texas*, by Janet Dailey; and *Death of an Heir*, by Philip Jett.

D4EO LITERARY AGENCY

7 Indian Valley Rd., Weston CT 06883. (203)544-7180. **Fax:** (203)544-7160. **Website:** www.d4eoliteraryagency.com. **Contact:** Bob Diforio. Estab. 1990.

○ Prior to opening his agency, Mr. Diforio was a publisher.

MEMBER AGENTS Bob Diforio; Joyce Holland; Pam Victorio; Jessie Devine; Julie Dinneen.

REPRESENTS Nonfiction, novels. **Considers these fiction areas:** adventure, detective, erotica, juvenile, literary, mainstream, middle grade, mystery, new adult, romance, sports, thriller, young adult.

HOW TO CONTACT Each of these agents has a different submission e-mail and different tastes regarding how they review material. See all on their individual agent pages on the agency website. Responds in 1 week to queries if interested. Obtains most new clients through recommendations from others.

TERMS Offers written contract, binding for 2 years; automatic renewal unless 60 days notice given prior to renewal date. Charges for photocopying and submission postage.

LAURA DAIL LITERARY AGENCY, INC.

121 W. 27th St., Suite 1201, New York NY 10001. (212)239-7477. **E-mail:** literary@ldlainc.com. **E-mail:** queries@ldlainc.com. **Website:** www.ldlainc.com. Member of AAR.

MEMBER AGENTS Laura Dail; Tamar Rydzinski; Elana Roth Parker.

REPRESENTS Nonfiction, fiction, novels, juvenile books. **Considers these fiction areas:** commercial, contemporary issues, crime, detective, ethnic, fantasy, feminist, gay, historical, juvenile, lesbian, mainstream, middle grade, multicultural, mystery, picture books, thriller, women's, young adult.

☛ Specializes in women's fiction, literary fiction, young adult fiction, as well as both practical and idea-driven nonfiction. "Due to the volume of queries and mss received, we apologize for not answering every e-mail and letter. None of us handles children's picture books or chapter books. No New Age. We do not handle screenplays or poetry."

HOW TO CONTACT "If you would like, you may include a synopsis and no more than 10 pages. If you are mailing your query, please be sure to include a self-addressed, stamped envelope; without it, you may not hear back from us. To save money, time and trees, we prefer queries by e-mail to queries@ldlainc.com. We get a lot of spam and are wary of computer viruses, so please use the word 'Query' in the subject line and include your detailed materials in the body of your message, not as an attachment." Accepts simultaneous submissions. Responds in 2-4 weeks.

DARHANSOFF & VERRILL LITERARY AGENTS

133 W. 72nd St., Room 304, New York NY 10023. (917)305-1300. **E-mail:** submissions@dvagency.com. **Website:** www.dvagency.com. Member of AAR.

MEMBER AGENTS Liz Darhansoff; Chuck Verrill; Michele Mortimer; Eric Amling.

REPRESENTS Nonfiction, novels. **Considers these fiction areas:** literary, middle grade, suspense, young adult.

HOW TO CONTACT Send queries via e-mail. Accepts simultaneous submissions.

RECENT SALES A full list of clients is available on their website.

🌑 CAROLINE DAVIDSON LITERARY AGENCY

5 Queen Anne's Gardens, London W4 1TU United Kingdom. (44)(0)(20)8995-5768. **Fax:** (44)(0)(20)8994-2770. **E-mail:** enquiries@cdla.co.uk. **Website:** www.cdla.co.uk. **Contact:** Ms. Caroline Davidson. AAA

REPRESENTS Nonfiction, fiction.

☛ Does not want chick lit, romance, erotica, crime and thrillers, science fiction, fantasy, poetry, individual short stories, children's, young adult, misery memoirs and fictionalised autobiography, conspiracy theories, educational textbooks, local history, occult, PhD theses, self-help, 'sob stories,' unfortunate personal experiences, painful lives, true crime, and war stories.

HOW TO CONTACT Send preliminary letter with CV and detailed well thought-out book proposal/synopsis and/or first 50 pages and last 10 pages of novel in hard copy only. No e-mail submissions will be accepted or replied to. No reply without large SASE with correct return postage. No reading fee. Please refer to website for further information. CDLA does not acknowledge or reply to e-mail inquiries. No telephone inquiries.

LIZA DAWSON ASSOCIATES

121 W. 27th St., Suite 1201, New York NY 10001. (212)465-9071. **Website:** www.lizadawsonassociates.com. **Contact:** Caitie Flum. Member of AAR. MWA, Women's Media Group. Represents 50+ clients.

◯ Prior to becoming an agent, Ms. Dawson was an editor for 20 years, spending 11 years at William Morrow as vice president and 2 years at Putnam as executive editor. Ms. Blasdell was a senior editor at HarperCollins and Avon. Ms.

Johnson-Blalock was an assistant at Trident Media Group. Ms. Flum was the coordinator for the Children's Book of the Month club.

MEMBER AGENTS Liza Dawson, queryliza@ lizadawsonassociates.com (plot-driven literary and popular fiction, historical, thrillers, suspense, history, psychology [both popular and clinical], politics, narrative nonfiction, and memoirs); Caitlin Blasdell, querycaitlin@lizadawsonassociates.com (science fiction, fantasy [both adult and young adult], parenting, business, thrillers, and women's fiction); Hannah Bowman, queryhannah@lizadawsonassociates.com (commercial fiction [especially science fiction and fantasy, young adult] and nonfiction in the areas of mathematics, science, and spirituality); Monica Odom, querymonica@lizadawsonassociates.com (nonfiction in the areas of Social Studies, including topics of: identity, race, gender, sexual orientation, socioeconomics, civil rights and social justice, advice/relationships, self-help/self-reflection, how-to, crafting/creativity, food and cooking, humor, pop culture, lifestyle, fashion & beauty, biography, memoir, narrative, business, politics and current affairs, history, science and literary fiction and upmarket fiction, Illustrators with demonstrable platforms, preferably author/illustrators, working on nonfiction, graphic memoirs or graphic novels); Caitie Flum, querycaitie@lizadawsonassociates.com (commercial fiction, especially historical, women's fiction, mysteries, crossover fantasy, young adult, and middle-grade; nonfiction in the areas of theater, current affairs, and pop culture).

REPRESENTS Nonfiction, novels. **Considers these fiction areas:** action, adventure, commercial, contemporary issues, crime, detective, ethnic, family saga, fantasy, feminist, gay, historical, horror, humor, juvenile, lesbian, mainstream, middle grade, multicultural, mystery, new adult, police, romance, science fiction, supernatural, suspense, thriller, urban fantasy, women's, young adult.

☞ This agency specializes in readable literary fiction, thrillers, mainstream historicals, women's fiction, young adult, middle-grade, academics, historians, journalists, and psychology.

HOW TO CONTACT Query by e-mail only. No phone calls. Each of these agents has their own specific submission requirements, which you can find online at the agency's website. Obtains most new clients through recommendations from others, conferences, and queries.

TERMS Agent receives 15% commission on domestic sales; 20% commission on foreign sales. Offers written contract.

THE JENNIFER DE CHIARA LITERARY AGENCY

299 Park Ave., 6th Floor, New York NY 10171. (212)739-0803. **E-mail:** jenndec@aol.com. **Website:** www.jdlit.com. **Contact:** Jennifer De Chiara. Estab. 2001.

MEMBER AGENTS Jennifer De Chiara, jenndec@aol.com (fiction interests include literary, commercial, women's fiction [no bodice-rippers, please], chick-lit, mystery, suspense, thrillers, funny/quirky picture books, middle-grade, and young adult; nonfiction interests include celebrity memoirs and biographies, LGBT, memoirs, books about the arts and performing arts, behind-the-scenes-type books, and books about popular culture); Stephen Fraser, fraserstephena@gmail.com (one-of-a-kind picture books; strong chapter book series; whimsical, dramatic, or humorous middle-grade; dramatic or high-concept young adult; powerful and unusual nonfiction on a broad range of topics; Marie Lamba, marie.jdlit@gmail.com (young adult and middle-grade fiction, along with general and women's fiction and some memoir; interested in established illustrators and picture book authors); Roseanne Wells, queryroseanne@gmail.com (picture book, middle grade, young adult, select literary fiction, narrative nonfiction, select memoir, science (popular or trade, not academic), history, religion (not inspirational or Christian market), travel, humor, food/cooking, and similar subjects); Victoria Selvaggio, vickiaselvaggio@gmail.com (board books, picture books, chapter books, middle-grade, young adult, new adult, and adult; interested in nonfiction and fiction in all genres); Damian McNicholl, damianmcnichollvarney@gmail.com (accessible literary fiction, memoir, narrative nonfiction [especially biography, investigative journalism, cultural, legal, and LGBT]); Alexandra Weiss, alexweiss.jdlit@gmail.com (voice-driven young adult in all genres, silly and smart middle-grade fiction, chapter books, fiction and nonfiction picture books, especially science-based stories, select literary fiction); Cari Lamba, cari.jdlit.@gmail.com (middle-grade fiction, especially contemporary and quirky, fiction and nonfiction picture books, commercial fiction, mysteries, cozies, and foodie novels); David Laurell, dclaurell@gmail.com (celebrity memoir, pop culture, television, broadcasting, all genres of entertainment and sports, inspirational, collecting and strong character-driven fiction).

REPRESENTS Nonfiction, fiction, novels, juvenile books. **Considers these fiction areas:** commercial, contemporary issues, crime, ethnic, family saga, fantasy, feminist, gay, historical, horror, humor, inspirational, juvenile, lesbian, literary, mainstream, middle grade, multicultural, mystery, new adult, New Age, paranormal, picture books, science fiction, suspense, thriller, urban fantasy, women's, young adult.

HOW TO CONTACT Each agent has their own e-mail submission address and submission instructions; check the website for the current updates, as policies do change. Accepts simultaneous submissions. Obtains most new clients through recommendations from others, conferences, query letters.

TERMS Agent receives 15% commission on domestic sales. Offers written contract.

DEFIORE & COMPANY

47 E. 19th St., 3rd Floor, New York NY 10003. (212)925-7744. **Fax:** (212)925-9803. **E-mail:** info@defliterary.com, submissions@defliterary.com. **Website:** www.defliterary.com. Member of AAR. Signatory of WGA.

Prior to becoming an agent, Mr. DeFiore was publisher of Villard Books (1997-1998), editor-in-chief of Hyperion (1992-1997), editorial director of Delacorte Press (1988-1992), and an editor at St. Martin's Press (1984-88).

MEMBER AGENTS Brian DeFiore (popular nonfiction, business, pop culture, parenting, commercial fiction); Laurie Abkemeier (memoir, parenting, business, how-to/self-help, popular science); Matthew Elblonk (young adult, popular culture, narrative nonfiction); Caryn Karmatz-Rudy (popular fiction, self-help, narrative nonfiction); Adam Schear (commercial fiction, humor, young adult, smart thrillers, historical fiction, quirky debut literary novels, popular science, politics, popular culture, current events); Meredith Kaffel Simonoff (smart upmarket women's fiction, literary fiction [especially debut], literary thrillers, narrative nonfiction, nonfiction about science and tech, sophisticated pop culture/humor books); Rebecca Strauss (literary and commercial fiction, women's fiction, urban fantasy, romance, mystery, young adult, memoir, pop culture, select nonfiction); Lisa Gallagher (fiction and nonfiction); Nicole Tourtelot (narrative and prescriptive nonfiction, food, lifestyle, wellness, pop cul-

ture, history, humor, memoir, select young adult and adult fiction); Ashely Collom (women's fiction, children's and young adult, psychological thrillers, memoir, politics, photography, cooking, narrative nonfiction, LGBT issues, feminism, occult); Miriam Altshuler (adult literary and commercial fiction, narrative nonfiction, middle-grade, young adult, memoir, narrative nonfiction, self-help, family sagas, historical novels); Reiko Davis (adult literary and upmarket fiction, narrative nonfiction, young adult, middle-grade, memoir).

REPRESENTS Nonfiction, novels, short story collections, juvenile books, poetry books. **Considers these fiction areas:** comic books, commercial, ethnic, feminist, gay, lesbian, literary, mainstream, middle grade, mystery, paranormal, picture books, poetry, romance, short story collections, suspense, thriller, urban fantasy, women's, young adult.

"Please be advised that we are not considering dramatic projects at this time."

HOW TO CONTACT Query with SASE or e-mail to submissions@defliterary.com. "Please include the word 'query' in the subject line. All attachments will be deleted; please insert all text in the body of the e-mail. For more information about our agents, their individual interests, and their query guidelines, please visit our 'About Us' page on our website." Accepts simultaneous submissions. Obtains most new clients through recommendations from others.

TERMS Agent receives 15% commission on domestic sales; 20% commission on foreign sales. Offers written contract; 10-day notice must be given to terminate contract. Charges clients for photocopying and overnight delivery (deducted only after a sale is made).

JOELLE DELBOURGO ASSOCIATES, INC.

101 Park St., Montclair NJ 07042. (973)773-0836. **E-mail:** joelle@delbourgo.com. **E-mail:** submissions@delbourgo.com. **Website:** www.delbourgo.com. **Contact:** Joelle Delbourgo. Estab. 1999. Member of AAR. Represents more than 500 clients.

Prior to becoming an agent, Ms. Delbourgo was an editor and senior publishing executive at HarperCollins and Random House. She began her editorial career at Bantam Books where she discovered the Choose Your Own Adventure series. Joelle Delbourgo brings more than three decades of experience as an editor and agent. Prior to joining the agency, Jacqueline Flynn was Executive Editor at Amacom for more than 15 years.

MEMBER AGENTS Joelle Delbourgo; Jacqueline Flynn.

REPRESENTS Nonfiction, fiction, novels. **Considers these fiction areas:** adventure, commercial, contemporary issues, crime, detective, fantasy, feminist, juvenile, literary, mainstream, middle grade, military, mystery, new adult, New Age, romance, science fiction, thriller, urban fantasy, women's, young adult.

> "We are former publishers and editors with deep knowledge and an insider perspective. We have a reputation for individualized attention to clients, strategic management of authors' careers, and creating strong partnerships with publishers for our clients." We are looking for strong narrative and prescriptive nonfiction including science, history, health and medicine, business and finance, sociology, parenting, women's issues. We prefer books by credentialed experts and seasoned journalists, especially ones that are research-based. We are taking on very few memoir projects. In fiction, you can send mystery and thriller, commercial women's fiction, book club fiction and literary fiction. Do not send scripts, picture books, poetry.

HOW TO CONTACT E-mail queries only are accepted. Query one agent directly, not multiple agents at our agency. No attachments. Put the word "Query" in the subject line. If you have not received a response in 60 days you may consider that a pass. Do not send us copies of self-published books. Let us know if you are sending your query to us exclusively or if this is a multiple submission. For nonfiction, wait to send your query when you have a completed proposal. For fiction and memoir, embed the first 10 pages of ms into the e-mail after your query letter. Please no attachments. If we like your first pages, we may ask to see your synopsis and more manuscript. Please do not cold call us or make a follow-up call unless we call you. Accepts simultaneous submissions. Our clients come via referral, and occasionally over the transom.

TERMS Agent receives 15% commission on domestic sales and 20% commission on foreign sales as well as television/film adaptation when a co-agent is involved. Offers written contract. Standard industry commissions. Charges clients for postage and photocopying.

RECENT SALES *The Rule of St. Benedict*, translated by Philip Freeman (St. Martins Essentials); *Holly Banks Full of Angst* & Untitled Novel 2, Julie Valerie (Lake Union); *Flat, Fluid & Fast*, Brynne S. Kennedy (McGraw-Hill); *The Dog Went Over the Mountain*, Peter Zheutlin (Pegasus), *The Remarriage Manual*, Terry Gaspard (Sounds True); *The Narcissistic Family*, Julie Hall (Da Capo Lifelong/Hachette); *Queen of the West*, Theresa Kaminski (Rowman & Littlefield); *The Wealth Creator's Playbook*, John C. Christianson (Praeger).

WRITERS CONFERENCES Jewish Writer's Conference (sponsored by the Jewish Book Council).

TIPS "Do your homework. Do not cold call. Read and follow submission guidelines before contacting us. Do not call to find out if we received your material. No e-mail queries. Treat agents with respect, as you would any other professional, such as a doctor, lawyer or financial advisor."

SANDRA DIJKSTRA LITERARY AGENCY
1155 Camino del Mar, PMB 515, Del Mar CA 92014. **E-mail:** queries@dijkstraagency.com. **Website:** www.dijkstraagency.com. Member of AAR. Authors Guild, Organization of American Historians, RWA. Represents 200+ clients.

MEMBER AGENTS President: Sandra Dijkstra (adult only). Acquiring Associate agents: Elise Capron (adult only); Jill Marr (adult only); Thao Le (adult and YA); Roz Foster (adult and YA); Jessica Watterson (subgenres of adult romance, and women's fiction); Suzy Evans (adult and YA); Jennifer Kim (adult and YA).

REPRESENTS Nonfiction, fiction, novels, short story collections, juvenile books, scholarly books. **Considers these fiction areas:** commercial, contemporary issues, detective, family saga, fantasy, feminist, historical, horror, juvenile, literary, mainstream, middle grade, multicultural, mystery, new adult, romance, science fiction, short story collections, sports, suspense, thriller, urban fantasy, women's, young adult.

HOW TO CONTACT "Please see guidelines on our website, www.dijkstraagency.com. Please note that we only accept e-mail submissions. Due to the large number of unsolicited submissions we receive, we are only able to respond those submissions in which we are interested." Accepts simultaneous submissions. Responds to queries of interest within 6 weeks.

TERMS Works in conjunction with foreign and film agents. Agent receives 15% commission on domestic sales and 20% commission on foreign sales. Offers written contract. No reading fee.

TIPS "Remember that publishing is a business. Do your research and present your project in as professional a way as possible. Only submit your work when you are confident that it is polished and ready for prime-time. Make yourself a part of the active writing community by getting stories and articles published, networking with other writers, and getting a good sense of where your work fits in the market."

DONAGHY LITERARY GROUP

(647)527-4353. **E-mail:** stacey@donaghyliterary.com. **Website:** www.donaghyliterary.com. **Contact:** Stacey Donaghy. RWA, PACLA.

Prior to opening her agency, Ms Donaghy served as an agent at the Corvisiero Literary Agency. And before this, she worked in training and education; acquiring and editing academic materials for publication and training. Ms. Noble interned for Jessica Sinsheimer of Sarah Jane Freymann Literary Agency. Ms. Miller previously worked in children's publishing with Scholastic Canada and also interned with Bree Ogden during her time at the D4EO Agency. Ms. Ayers-Barnett is a former Associate Editor for Pocket Books, Acquisitions Editor for Re.ad Publishing, and a freelance book editor for New York Book Editors.

MEMBER AGENTS Stacey Donaghy (women's fiction, romantic suspense, LGBTQ, Diverse and #Ownvoice, thriller, mystery, contemporary romance, and YA); Valerie Noble (historical, science fiction and fantasy [think Kristin Cashore and Suzanne Collins] for young adults and adults); Sue Miller (YA, urban fantasy, contemporary romance); Amanda Ayers Barnett (mystery/thrillers and middle-grade, young adult, new adult and women's fiction).

REPRESENTS Fiction, novels, juvenile books. **Considers these fiction areas:** commercial, contemporary issues, crime, detective, ethnic, family saga, fantasy, feminist, gay, historical, horror, juvenile, lesbian, literary, mainstream, middle grade, multicultural, mystery, new adult, paranormal, police, psychic, romance, science fiction, sports, supernatural, suspense, thriller, urban fantasy, women's, young adult.

HOW TO CONTACT Visit agency website for "new submission guidelines" Do not e-mail agents directly. This agency only accepts submissions through the QueryManager database system. Accepts simultaneous submissions. Time may vary depending on the volume of submissions.

TERMS Agent receives 15% commission on domestic sales; 20% commission on foreign sales. Offers written contract, 30-day notice must be given to terminate contract.

WRITERS CONFERENCES Romantic Times Booklovers Convention, Windsor International Writers Conference, OWC Ontario Writers Conference, SoCal Writers Conference, WD Toronto Writer's Workshop.

TIPS "Only submit to one DLG agent at a time, we work collaboratively and often share projects that may be better suited to another agent at the agency."

JIM DONOVAN LITERARY

5635 SMU Blvd., Suite 201, Dallas TX 75206. **E-mail:** jdliterary@sbcglobal.net. **Contact:** Melissa Shultz, agent. Estab. 1993. Signatory of WGA. Represents 34 clients.

MEMBER AGENTS Jim Donovan (history—particularly American, military and Western; biography; sports; popular reference; popular culture; fiction—literary, thrillers and mystery); Melissa Shultz (all subjects listed above [like Jim], along with parenting and women's issues).

REPRESENTS Nonfiction, fiction, novels. **Considers these fiction areas:** action, adventure, commercial, crime, detective, frontier, historical, mainstream, multicultural, mystery, police, suspense, thriller, war, westerns.

This agency specializes in commercial fiction and nonfiction. "Does not want to receive poetry, children's, sci-fi, fantasy, short stories, memoir, inspirational or anything else not listed above."

HOW TO CONTACT "For nonfiction, I need a well-thought-out query letter telling me about the book: What it does, how it does it, why it's needed now, why it's better or different than what's out there on the subject, and why the author is the perfect writer for it. For fiction, the novel has to be finished, of course; a short (2- to 5-page) synopsis—not a teaser, but a summary of all the action, from first page to last—and the first 30-50 pages is enough. This material should be polished to as close to perfection as possible." Accepts simultaneous submissions. Responds in 2 weeks to queries; 1 month to mss. Obtains most new clients through recommendations from others.

TERMS Agent receives 15% commission on domestic sales. Agent receives 20% commission on foreign sales. Offers written contract, binding for 1 year; 30-day notice must be given to terminate contract. This agency charges for things such as overnight delivery and manuscript copying. Charges are discussed beforehand.

RECENT SALES *The Undiscovered Country*, by Paul Andrew Hutton; *The Road to Jonestown*, by Jeff Guinn (S&S); *The Earth Is All That Lasts*, by Mark Gardner (HarperCollins); *As Good as Dead*, by Stephen Moore (NAL); *James Monroe*, by Tim McGrath (NAL); *The Greatest Fury*, by William C. Davis (NAL); *The Hamilton Affair*, by Elizabeth Cobbs (Arcade); *Resurrection Pass*, by Kurt Anderson (Kensington).

TIPS "Get published in short form—magazine reviews, journals, etc.—first. This will increase your credibility considerably, and make it much easier to sell a full-length book."

DUNHAM LITERARY, INC.

110 William St., Suite 2202, New York NY 10038. (212)929-0994. **E-mail:** query@dunhamlit.com. **Website:** www.dunhamlit.com. **Contact:** Jennie Dunham. Estab. 2000. Member of AAR. SCBWI Represents 50 clients.

○ Prior to opening her agency, Ms. Dunham worked as a literary agent for Russell & Volkening. The Rhoda Weyr Agency is now a division of Dunham Literary, Inc.

MEMBER AGENTS Jennie Dunham, Bridget Smith, Leslie Zampetti.

REPRESENTS Nonfiction, fiction, novels, short story collections, juvenile books. **Considers these fiction areas:** family saga, fantasy, feminist, gay, historical, humor, juvenile, lesbian, literary, mainstream, middle grade, multicultural, mystery, picture books, science fiction, short story collections, sports, urban fantasy, women's, young adult.

☛ "We are not looking for Westerns, genre romance, poetry, or individual short stories."

HOW TO CONTACT E-mail queries preferred, with all materials pasted in the body of the e-mail. Attachments will not be opened. Paper queries are also accepted. Please include a SASE for response and return of materials. Please include the first 5 pages with the query. Accepts simultaneous submissions. Responds in 4 weeks to queries; 2 months to mss. Obtains most new clients through recommendations from others.

TERMS Agent receives 15% commission on domestic sales; 20% commission on foreign sales.

RECENT SALES *The Bad Kitty Series*, by Nick Bruel (Macmillan); *Believe*, by Robert Sabuda (Candlewick); *The Gollywhopper Games* and Sequels, by Jody Feldman (HarperCollins); *Foolish Hearts*, by Emma Mills (Macmillan); *Gangster Nation*, by Tod Goldberg (Counterpoint); *A Shadow All of Light*, by Fred Chappell (Tor).

DUNOW, CARLSON, & LERNER AGENCY

27 W. 20th St., Suite 1107, New York NY 10011. (212)645-7606. **E-mail:** mail@dclagency.com. **Website:** www.dclagency.com. Member of AAR.

MEMBER AGENTS Jennifer Carlson (narrative nonfiction writers and journalists covering current events and ideas and cultural history, as well as literary and upmarket commercial novelists); Henry Dunow (quality fiction–literary, historical, strongly written commercial–and with voice-driven nonfiction across a range of areas–narrative history, biography, memoir, current affairs, cultural trends and criticism, science, sports); Erin Hosier (nonfiction: popular culture, music, sociology and memoir); Betsy Lerner (nonfiction writers in the areas of psychology, history, cultural studies, biography, current events, business; fiction: literary, dark, funny, voice driven); Yishai Seidman (broad range of fiction: literary, postmodern, and thrillers; nonfiction: sports, music, and pop culture); Amy Hughes (nonfiction in the areas of history, cultural studies, memoir, current events, wellness, health, food, pop culture, and biography; also literary fiction); Eleanor Jackson (literary, commercial, memoir, art, food, science and history); Julia Kenny (fiction—adult, middle grade and YA—and is especially interested in dark, literary thrillers and suspense); Edward Necarsulmer IV (strong new voices in teen & middle grade as well as picture books); Stacia Decker; Rachel Vogel (nonfiction, including photography, humor, pop culture, history, memoir, investigative journalism, current events, science, and more); Arielle Datz (fiction—adult, YA, or middle-grade—literary and commercial, nonfiction—essays, unconventional memoir, pop culture, and sociology).

REPRESENTS Nonfiction, fiction, novels, short story collections. **Considers these fiction areas:** commercial, literary, mainstream, middle grade, mystery, picture books, thriller, young adult.

HOW TO CONTACT Query via snail mail with SASE, or by e-mail. E-mail preferred, paste 10 sample pages below query letter. No attachments. Will respond only if interested. Accepts simultaneous submissions. Responds in 4-6 weeks if interested.

RECENT SALES A full list of agency clients is on the website.

DYSTEL, GODERICH & BOURRET LLC

1 Union Square W., Suite 904, New York NY 10003. (212)627-9100. **Fax:** (212)627-9313. **Website:** www.dystel.com. Estab. 1994. Member of AAR. Other membership includes SCBWI. Represents 600+ clients.

MEMBER AGENTS Jane Dystel; Miriam Goderich, miriam@dystel.com (literary and commercial fiction as well as some genre fiction, narrative nonfiction, pop culture, psychology, history, science, art, business books, and biography/memoir); Stacey Glick, sglick@dystel.com (adult narrative nonfiction including memoir, parenting, cooking and food, psychology, science, health and wellness, lifestyle, current events, pop culture, YA, middle grade, children's nonfiction, and select adult contemporary fiction); Michael Bourret, mbourret@dystel.com (middle grade and young adult fiction, commercial adult fiction, and all sorts of nonfiction, from practical to narrative; he's especially interested in food and cocktail related books, memoir, popular history, politics, religion (though not spirituality), popular science, and current events); Jim McCarthy, jmccarthy@dystel.com (literary women's fiction, underrepresented voices, mysteries, romance, paranormal fiction, narrative nonfiction, memoir, and paranormal nonfiction); Jessica Papin, jpapin@dystel.com (plot-driven literary and smart commercial fiction, and narrative non-fiction across a range of subjects, including history, medicine, science, economics and women's issues); Lauren Abramo, labramo@dystel.com (humorous middle grade and contemporary YA on the children's side, and upmarket commercial fiction and well-paced literary fiction on the adult side; adult narrative nonfiction, especially pop culture, psychology, pop science, reportage, media, and contemporary culture; in nonfiction, has a strong preference for interdisciplinary approaches, and in all categories she's especially interested in underrepresented voices); John Rudolph, jrudolph@dystel.com (picture book author/illustrators, middle grade, YA, select commercial fiction, and narrative nonfiction—especially in music, sports, history, popular science, "big think", performing arts, health, business, memoir, military history, and humor); Sharon Pelletier, spelletier@dystel.com (smart commercial fiction, from upmarket women's fiction to domestic suspense to literary thrillers, and strong contemporary romance novels; compelling nonfiction projects, especially feminism and religion); Michael Hoogland, mhoogland@dystel.com (thriller, SFF, YA, upmarket women's fiction, and narrative nonfiction); Amy Bishop, abishop@dystel.com (commercial and literary women's fiction, fiction from diverse authors, historical fiction, YA, personal narratives, and biographies); Kemi Faderin, kfaderin@dystel.com (smart, plot-driven YA, historical fiction/non-fiction, contemporary women's fiction, and literary fiction); Ann Leslie Tuttle, atuttle@dystel.com (romance); Kieryn Ziegler, kziegler@dystel.com (books about exciting new worlds, found families, fantastic female characters, and stories with diverse POVs, especially YA and MG).

REPRESENTS **Considers these fiction areas:** commercial, ethnic, gay, lesbian, literary, mainstream, middle grade, mystery, paranormal, romance, suspense, thriller, women's, young adult.

☛   "We are actively seeking fiction for all ages, in all genres." No plays, screenplays, or poetry.

HOW TO CONTACT Query via e-mail and put "Query" in the subject line. "Synopses, outlines or sample chapters (say, one chapter or the first 25 pages of your manuscript) should either be included below the cover letter or attached as a separate document. We won't open attachments if they come with a blank e-mail." Accepts simultaneous submissions. Responds in 6 to 8 weeks to queries; within 8 weeks to mss. Obtains most new clients through recommendations from others, solicitations, conferences.

TERMS Agent receives 15% commission on domestic sales; 19% commission on foreign sales. Offers written contract.

WRITERS CONFERENCES Backspace Writers' Conference, Pacific Northwest Writers' Association, Pike's Peak Writers' Conference, Writers League of Texas, Love Is Murder, Surrey International Writers Conference, Society of Children's Book Writers and Illustrators, International Thriller Writers, Willamette Writers Conference, The South Carolina Writers Workshop Conference, Las Vegas Writers Conference, Writer's Digest, Seton Hill Popular Fiction, Romance Writers of America, Geneva Writers Conference.

TIPS "DGLM prides itself on being a full-service agency. We're involved in every stage of the publishing process, from offering substantial editing on mss and proposals, to coming up with book ideas for authors looking for their next project, negotiating contracts and collecting monies for our clients. We follow a book from its inception through its sale to a publisher, its publication, and beyond. Our commitment to our writers does not, by any means, end when we have collected our commission. This is one of the many things that makes us unique in a very competitive business."

EDEN STREET LITERARY

P.O. Box 30, Billings NY 12510. **E-mail:** info@edenstreetlit.com. **E-mail:** submissions@edenstreetlit.com. **Website:** www.edenstreetlit.com. **Contact:** Liza Voges. Member of AAR. Signatory of WGA. Represents over 40 clients.

REPRESENTS Nonfiction, fiction, novels, juvenile books. **Considers these fiction areas:** juvenile, middle grade, picture books, young adult.

HOW TO CONTACT E-mail a picture book ms or dummy; a synopsis and 3 chapters of a MG or YA novel; a proposal and 3 sample chapters for nonfiction. Accepts simultaneous submissions. Responds only to submissions of interest.

RECENT SALES *Dream Dog*, by Lou Berger; *Biscuit Loves the Library*, by Alyssa Capucilli; *The Scraps Book*, by Lois Ehlert; *Two Bunny Buddies*, by Kathryn O. Galbraith; *Between Two Worlds*, by Katherine Kirkpatrick.

JUDITH EHRLICH LITERARY MANAGEMENT, LLC

146 Central Park W., 20E, New York NY 10023. (646)505-1570. **Fax:** (646)505-1570. **E-mail:** jehrlich@judithehrlichliterary.com. **Website:** www.judithehrlichliterary.com. Estab. 2002. Member of the Author's Guild and the American Society of Journalists and Authors.

○ Prior to her current position, Ms. Ehrlich was a senior associate at the Linda Chester Agency and is an award-winning journalist; she is the co-author of *The New Crowd: The Changing of the Jewish Guard on Wall Street* (Little, Brown).

MEMBER AGENTS Judith Ehrlich, jehrlich@judithehrlichliterary.com (upmarket, literary and quality commercial fiction, nonfiction: narrative, women's, business, prescriptive, medical and health-related topics, history, and current events).

REPRESENTS Nonfiction, fiction, novels, short story collections, juvenile books. **Considers these fiction areas:** adventure, commercial, contemporary issues, crime, detective, family saga, historical, humor, juvenile, literary, middle grade, mystery, picture books, short story collections, suspense, thriller, women's, young adult.

☛ Does not want to receive novellas, poetry, textbooks, plays, or screenplays.

HOW TO CONTACT E-query, with a synopsis and some sample pages. The agency will respond only if interested. Accepts simultaneous submissions.

RECENT SALES Fiction: *The Bicycle Spy*, by Yona Zeldis McDonough (Scholastic); *The House on Primrose Pond*, by Yona McDonough (NAL/Penguin); *You Were Meant for Me*, by Yona McDonough (NAL/Penguin); *Echoes of Us: The Hybrid Chronicles*, Book 3 by Kat Zhang (HarperCollins); *Once We Were: The Hybrid Chronicles* Book 2, by Kat Zhang (HarperCollins). Nonfiction: *Listen to the Echoes: The Ray Bradbury Interviews (Deluxe Edition)*, by Sam Weller (Hat & Beard Press); *What are The Ten Commandments?*, by Yona McDonough (Grosset & Dunlap); *Little Author in the Big Woods: A Biography of Laura Ingalls Wilder*, by Yona McDonough (Christy Ottaviano Books/Henry Holt); *Ray Bradbury: The Last Interview: And Other Conversations*, by Sam Weller (Melville House); *Who Was Sojourner Truth?*, by Yona McDonough (Grosset & Dunlap); *Power Branding: Leveraging the Success of the World's Best Brands*, by Steve McKee (Palgrave Macmillan); *Confessions of a Sociopath: A Life Spent Hiding in Plain Sight*, by M.E. Thomas (Crown); *Luck and Circumstance: A Coming of Age in New York and Hollywood* and *Points Beyond*, by Michael Lindsay-Hogg (Knopf).

EINSTEIN LITERARY MANAGEMENT

27 W. 20th St., No. 1003, New York NY 10011. (212)221-8797. **E-mail:** info@einsteinliterary.com. **E-mail:** submissions@einsteinliterary.com.. **Website:** http://einsteinliterary.com. **Contact:** Susanna Einstein. Estab. 2015. Member of AAR. Signatory of WGA.

○ Prior to her current position, Ms. Einstein was with LJK Literary Management and the Einstein Thompson Agency.

MEMBER AGENTS Susanna Einstein, Susan Graham, Shana Kelly.

REPRESENTS Nonfiction, fiction, novels, short story collections, juvenile books. **Considers these fiction areas:** comic books, commercial, crime, fantasy, historical, juvenile, literary, middle grade, mystery, picture books, romance, science fiction, suspense, thriller, women's, young adult.

☞ "As an agency we represent a broad range of literary and commercial fiction, including upmarket women's fiction, crime fiction, historical fiction, romance, and books for middle-grade children and young adults, including picture books and graphic novels. We also handle non-fiction including cookbooks, memoir and narrative, and blog-to-book projects. Please see agent bios on the website for specific information about what each of ELM's agents represents." Does not want poetry, textbooks, or screenplays.

HOW TO CONTACT Please submit a query letter and the first 10 double-spaced pages of your manuscript in the body of the e-mail (no attachments). Does not respond to mail queries or telephone queries or queries that are not specifically addressed to this agency. Accepts simultaneous submissions. Responds in 6 weeks if interested.

EMPIRE LITERARY

115 W. 29th St., 3rd Floor, New York NY 10001. (917)213-7082. **E-mail:** abarzvi@empireliterary.com. **E-mail:** queries@empireliterary.com. **Website:** www.empireliterary.com. Estab. 2013. Member of AAR. Signatory of WGA.

MEMBER AGENTS Andrea Barzvi; Carrie Howland; Kathleen Schmidt; Penny Moore.

REPRESENTS Nonfiction, novels. **Considers these fiction areas:** literary, middle grade, women's, young adult.

HOW TO CONTACT Please only query one agent at a time. "If we are interested in reading more we will get in touch with you as soon as possible." Accepts simultaneous submissions.

FELICIA ETH LITERARY REPRESENTATION

555 Bryant St., Suite 350, Palo Alto CA 94301-1700. **E-mail:** feliciaeth.literary@gmail.com. **Website:** ethliterary.com. **Contact:** Felicia Eth. Member of AAR.

○ Worked as agent in NY at Writers House Inc. Prior to that worked in the movie business, Warner Bros NY. and Palomar Pictures for Story Dept.

REPRESENTS Nonfiction, fiction, novels. **Considers these fiction areas:** contemporary issues, historical, literary, mainstream, suspense.

☞ This agency specializes in high-quality fiction (preferably mainstream/contemporary) and provocative, intelligent, and thoughtful nonfiction on a wide array of commercial subjects. "The agency does not represent genre ficiton, including romance novels, sci fi and fantasy, westerns, anime and graphic novels, mysteries."

HOW TO CONTACT For fiction: Please write a query letter introducing yourself, your book, your writing background. Don't forget to include degrees you may have, publishing credits, awards and endorsements. Please wait for a response before including sample pages. "We only consider material where the manuscript for which you are querying is complete, unless you have previously published." For nonfiction: A query letter is best, introducing idea and what you have written already (proposal, manuscript?). "For writerly nonficiton (narratives, bio, memoir) please let us know if you have a finished manuscript. Also it's important you include information about yourself, your background and expertise, your platform and notoriety, if any. We do not ask for exclusivity in most instances but do ask that you inform us if other agents are considering the same material." Accepts simultaneous submissions. Responds in ideally 2 weeks for query, a month if more.

TERMS Agent receives 15% commission on domestic sales; 20% commission on foreign and film sales. Charges clients for photocopying and express mail service

RECENT SALES *Bumper Sticker Philosophy*, by Jack Bowen (Random House); *Boys Adrift*, by Leonard Sax (Basic Books); *The Memory Thief*, by Emily Colin (Ballantine Books); *The World is a Carpet*, by Anna Badkhen (Riverhead).

WRITERS CONFERENCES "Wide array—from Squaw Valley to Mills College."

MARY EVANS INC.

242 E. Fifth St., New York NY 10003. (212)979-0880. **Fax:** (212)979-5344. **E-mail:** info@maryevansinc.com. **Website:** maryevansinc.com. Member of AAR.

MEMBER AGENTS Mary Evans (progressive politics, alternative medicine, science and technology, social commentary, American history and culture); Julia Kardon (literary and upmarket fiction, narrative nonfiction, journalism, and history); Tom Mackay (non-fiction that uses sport as a platform to explore other issues and playful literary fiction).

REPRESENTS Nonfiction, novels. **Considers these fiction areas:** literary, upmarket.

☛ No screenplays or stage plays.

HOW TO CONTACT Query by mail or e-mail. If querying by mail, include a SASE. If querying by e-mail, put "Query" in the subject line. For fiction: Include the first few pages, or opening chapter of your novel as a single Word attachment. For nonfiction: Include your book proposal as a single Word attachment. Accepts simultaneous submissions. Responds within 4-8 weeks.

FAIRBANK LITERARY REPRESENTATION

Post Office Box Six, Hudson NY 12534-0006. (617)576-0030. **E-mail:** queries@fairbankliterary. com. **Website:** www.fairbankliterary.com; www.pub-lishersmarketplace.com/members/SorcheFairbank/. **Contact:** Sorche Elizabeth Fairbank. Estab. 2002. Member of AAR. Author's Guild, the Agents Round Table, and Grub Street's Literary Advisory Council.

MEMBER AGENTS Sorche Fairbank (narrative nonfiction, commercial and literary fiction, memoir, food and wine); Matthew Frederick, matt@fairbankliterary.com (scout for sports nonfiction, architecture, design).

REPRESENTS Nonfiction, fiction, novels, short story collections, juvenile books. **Considers these fiction areas:** commercial, ethnic, feminist, juvenile, literary, mainstream, middle grade, mystery, new adult, picture books, short story collections, suspense, thriller, women's, young adult, International voices. Southern voices.

☛ "I tend to gravitate toward literary fiction and narrative nonfiction, with a strong interest in women's issues and women's voices, international voices, class and race issues, and projects that simply teach me something new about the greater world and society around us. We have a good reputation for working closely and developmentally with our authors, and love what we do." Actively seeking literary fiction, international and culturally diverse voices, narrative nonfiction, topical subjects (politics, current affairs), history, sports, humor, architecture/design and humor/pop culture. Also looking for picture books by artist authors only. Does not want to receive romance, screenplays, po-etry, science fiction or fantasy, or children's works unless by an artist-author.

HOW TO CONTACT Query by e-mail queries@fairbankliterary.com or by mail with SASE. Accepts simultaneous submissions. Obtains most new clients through recommendations from others, solicitations, conferences, ideas generated in-house.

TERMS Agent receives 15% commission on domestic sales; 20% commission on foreign sales. Offers written contract, binding for 12 months; 60-day notice must be given to terminate contract.

RECENT SALES 3-book deal for Terry Border for picture books to Philomel; 2-book deal for Lisa Currie, *Surprise Yourself* and *Notes to Self* to Marian Lizzi at Tarcher Perigee; scratch & sniff spin-off and an early reader adaptation of Terry Border's best-selling *Peanut Butter & Cupcake* to Grosset and Dunlap/Penguin; 10-book deal for Matthew Frederick for his best-selling *101 Things I Learned Series* moving to Crown.

TIPS "Show me that you know your audience—and your competition. Have the writing and/or proposal at the very, very best it can be before starting the querying process. Don't assume that if someone likes it enough they'll 'fix' it. The biggest mistake new writers make is starting the querying process before they—and the work—are ready. Take your time and do it right."

LEIGH FELDMAN LITERARY

E-mail: assistant@lfliterary.com. **E-mail:** query@lfliterary.com. **Website:** http://lfliterary.com. **Contact:** Leigh Feldman. Estab. 2014. Member of AAR. Signatory of WGA.

○ During her 25 years as a literary agent based in New York City, Leigh Feldman has established herself as an invaluable partner to the writers she represents, and is highly respected by her peers in the industry. Her agency, Leigh Feldman Literary, is the culmination of experiences and lessons learned from her 20-plus years at Darhansoff, Verrill, Feldman Literary Agency and Writer's House. In that time, Feldman has represented National Book Award winners and bestsellers of literary fiction, historical fiction, memoir, middle grade, and young adult. No matter the writer or the category, Feldman only represents books she believes in, that captivate her, and that she can best serve with her passion and tenacity.

✚ eigh Feldman Literary is a full service literary agency.

REPRESENTS Nonfiction, fiction, novels, short story collections. **Considers these fiction areas:** commercial, contemporary issues, family saga, feminist, gay, historical, lesbian, literary, mainstream, multicultural, short story collections, women's, young adult.

☛ Does not want mystery, thriller, romance, paranormal, sci-fi.

HOW TO CONTACT E-query. "Please include 'query' in the subject line. Due to large volume of submissions, we regret that we can not respond to all queries individually. Please include the first chapter or the first 10 pages of your manuscript (or proposal) pasted after your query letter. I'd love to know what led you to query me in particular, and please let me know if you are querying other agents as well." Accepts simultaneous submissions.

RECENT SALES List of recent sales and best known sales are available on the agency website.

DIANA FINCH LITERARY AGENCY

116 W. 23rd St., Suite 500, New York NY 10011. (917)544-4470. **E-mail:** diana.finch@verizon.net. **Website:** dianafinchliteraryagency.blogspot.com. **Contact:** Diana Finch. Estab. 2003. Member of AAR. Represents approximately 40 active clients clients.

◯ Seeking to represent books that change lives. Prior to opening her own agency in 2003, Ms. Finch worked at Ellen Levine Literary Agency for 18 years. She started her publishing career in the editorial department at St. Martin's Press.

REPRESENTS Nonfiction, fiction, novels, scholarly books. **Considers these fiction areas:** action, adventure, contemporary issues, crime, detective, ethnic, fantasy, historical, literary, mainstream, middle grade, multicultural, new adult, police, science fiction, sports, thriller, urban fantasy, young adult.

☛ For news about the agency and agency clients, see the agency Facebook page at https://www.facebook.com/DianaFinchLitAg/. "Does not want romance or children's picture books."

HOW TO CONTACT This agency prefers submissions via its online form. Accepts simultaneous submissions. Obtains most new clients through recommendations from others.

TERMS Agent receives 15% commission on domestic sales; 20% commission on foreign sales. Offers written contract. "I charge for overseas postage, galleys, and books purchased, and try to recoup these costs from earnings received for a client, rather than charging outright."

RECENT SALES *The Journeys of the Trees*, by Zach St George (W. W. Norton); *Owls of the Eastern Ice*, by Jonathan SIaght (FSG/Scientific American); *Uncolor: on toxins in personal products*, by Ronnie Citron-Fink (Island Press); *Cutting School*, by Professor Noliwe Rooks (The New Press); *Merchants of Men*, by Loretta Napoleoni (Seven Stories Press); *Beyond $15*, by Jonathan Rosenblum (Beacon Press); *The Age of Inequality*, by the Editors of In These Times (Verso Books); *Seeds of Resistance*, by Mark Schapiro (Hot Books/Skyhorse).

WRITERS CONFERENCES Washington Writers Conference; Writers Digest NYC Conference; CLMP/New School conference, and others on an individual basis.

TIPS "Do as much research as you can on agents before you query. Have someone critique your query letter before you send it. It should be only 1 page and describe your book clearly—and why you are writing it—but also demonstrate creativity and a sense of your writing style."

FINEPRINT LITERARY MANAGEMENT

207 W. 106th St., Suite 1D, New York NY 10025. (212)279-1412. **E-mail:** info@fineprintlit.com. **Website:** www.fineprintlit.com. **Contact:** Peter Rubie. Estab. 2007. Member of AAR.

MEMBER AGENTS Peter Rubie, CEO, peter@fineprintlit.com (nonfiction interests include narrative nonfiction, popular science, spirituality, history, biography, pop culture, business, technology, parenting, health, self help, music, and food; fiction interests include literate thrillers, crime fiction, science fiction and fantasy, military fiction and literary fiction, middle grade and boy-oriented YA fiction); Laura Wood, laura@fineprintlit.com (serious nonfiction, especially in the areas of science and nature, along with substantial titles in business, history, religion, and other areas by academics, experienced professionals, and journalists; select genre fiction only (no poetry, literary fiction or memoir) in the categories of science fiction & fantasy and mystery); June Clark, june@fineprintlit.com (nonfiction projects in the areas of entertainment, self-help, parenting, reference/how-to books, food and wine, style/beauty, and prescriptive business titles); Lauren Bieker, lauren@fineprintlit.com (commercial and upmarket women's fiction and differentiated YA novels).

REPRESENTS Nonfiction, fiction, novels, short story collections. **Considers these fiction areas:** action, adventure, commercial, crime, detective, fantasy, feminist, frontier, historical, literary, mainstream, middle grade, military, multicultural, multimedia, mystery, police, romance, science fiction, suspense, thriller, translation, urban fantasy, war, women's, young adult.

HOW TO CONTACT E-query. For fiction, send a query, synopsis, bio, and 30 pages pasted into the e-mail. No attachments. For nonfiction, send a query only; proposal requested later if the agent is interested. Accepts simultaneous submissions. Obtains most new clients through recommendations from others, solicitations.

TERMS Agent receives 15% commission on domestic sales; 20% commission on foreign sales.

JAMES FITZGERALD AGENCY

118 Waverly Place, #1B, New York NY 10011. **E-mail:** submissions@jfitzagency.com. **Website:** www.jfitzagency.com. **Contact:** Anna Tatelman.

○ Prior to his current position, Mr. Fitzgerald was an editor at St. Martin's Press and Doubleday.

MEMBER AGENTS James Fitzgerald; Dylan Lowy.

REPRESENTS Nonfiction, fiction, novels, juvenile books, scholarly books. , graphic novles, packaged books. **Considers these fiction areas:** action, adventure, cartoon, comic books, commercial, crime, detective, family saga, fantasy, frontier, historical, humor, juvenile, literary, mainstream, middle grade, mystery, picture books, psychic, science fiction, sports, supernatural, suspense, thriller, translation, war, westerns, young adult.

HOW TO CONTACT Query via e-mail or snail mail. This agency's online submission guidelines page explains all the elements they want to see. Accepts simultaneous submissions.

RECENT SALES A full and diverse list of titles are on this agency's website.

FLANNERY LITERARY

1140 Wickfield Ct., Naperville IL 60563. **E-mail:** jennifer@flanneryliterary.com. **Website:** flanneryliterary.com. **Contact:** Jennifer Flannery. Estab. 1992. Represents 40 clients.

REPRESENTS Nonfiction, fiction, novels, juvenile books. **Considers these fiction areas:** juvenile, middle grade, new adult, picture books, young adult.

☛ This agency specializes in children's and young adult fiction and nonfiction. It also accepts picture books. 100% juvenile books. Actively seeking middle grade and young adult novels. No rhyming picture books nor bodily function topics, please. Also I do not open attachments unless instructed.

HOW TO CONTACT Query by e-mail only. "Multiple queries are fine, but please inform us. Please no attachments. If you're sending a query about a novel, please embed in the e-mail the first 5-10 pages; if it's a picture book, please embed the entire text in the e-mail. We do not open attachments unless they have been requested." Accepts simultaneous submissions. Responds in 2-4 weeks to queries; 1 month to mss. Obtains new clients through referrals and queries.

TERMS Agent receives 15% commission on domestic sales; 20% commission on foreign sales. Offers written contract, binding for life of book in print.

TIPS "Write an engrossing, succinct query describing your work. We are always looking for a fresh new voice."

FLETCHER & COMPANY

78 Fifth Ave., 3rd Floor, New York NY 10011. **E-mail:** info@fletcherandco.com. **Website:** www.fletcherandco.com. **Contact:** Christy Fletcher. Estab. 2003. Member of AAR.

MEMBER AGENTS Christy Fletcher (referrals only); Melissa Chinchillo (select list of her own authors); Rebecca Gradinger (literary fiction, up-market commercial fiction, narrative nonfiction, self-help, memoir, Women's studies, humor, and pop culture); Gráinne Fox (literary fiction and quality commercial authors, award-winning journalists and food writers, American voices, international, literary crime, upmarket fiction, narrative nonfiction); Lisa Grubka (fiction—literary, upmarket women's, and young adult; and nonfiction—narrative, food, science, and more); Sylvie Greenberg (literary fiction, business, sports, science, memoir and history); Donald Lamm (history, biography, investigative journalism, politics, current affairs, and business); Todd Sattersten (business books); Eric Lupfer; Sarah Fuentes; Veronica Goldstein; Alyssa Taylor; Erin McFadden.

REPRESENTS Nonfiction, novels. **Considers these fiction areas:** commercial, crime, literary, women's, young adult.

HOW TO CONTACT Send queries to info@fletcherandco.com. Please do not include e-mail attachments with your initial query, as they will be deleted. Address your query to a specific agent. No snail mail queries. Accepts simultaneous submissions.

RECENT SALES *The Profiteers*, by Sally Denton; *The Longest Night*, by Andrea Williams; *Disrupted: My Misadventure in the Start-Up Bubble*, by Dan Lyons; *Free Re-Fills: A Doctor Confronts His Addiction*, by Peter Grinspoon, M.D.; *Black Man in a White Coat: A Doctor's Reflections on Race and Medicine*, by Damon Tweedy, M.D.

FOLIO LITERARY MANAGEMENT, LLC

The Film Center Building, 630 Ninth Ave., Suite 1101, New York NY 10036. (212)400-1494. **Fax:** (212)967-0977. **Website:** www.foliolit.com. Member of AAR. Represents 100+ clients.

○ Prior to creating Folio Literary Management, Mr. Hoffman worked for several years at another agency; Mr. Kleinman was an agent at Graybill & English.

MEMBER AGENTS Claudia Cross (romance novels, commercial women's fiction, cooking and food writing, serious nonfiction on religious and spiritual topics); Scott Hoffman (literary and commercial fiction, journalistic or academic nonfiction, narrative nonfiction, pop culture books, business, history, politics, spiritual or religious-themed fiction and nonfiction, sci-fi/fantasy literary fiction, heartbreaking memoirs, humorous nonfiction); Jeff Kleinman (book-club fiction (not genre commercial, like mysteries or romances), literary fiction, thrillers and suspense novels, narrative nonfiction, memoir); Dado Derviskadic (nonfiction: cultural history, biography, memoir, pop science, motivational self-help, health/nutrition, pop culture, cookbooks; fiction that's gritty, introspective, or serious); Frank Weimann (biography, business/investing/finance, history, religious, mind/body/spirit, health, lifestyle, cookbooks, sports, African-American, science, memoir, special forces/CIA/FBI/mafia, military, prescriptive nonfiction, humor, celebrity; adult and children's fiction); Michael Harriot (com-

mercial nonfiction (both narrative and prescriptive) and fantasy/science fiction); Erin Harris (book club, historical fiction, literary, narrative nonfiction, psychological suspense, young adult); Katherine Latshaw (blogs-to-books, food/cooking, middle grade, narrative and prescriptive nonfiction); Annie Hwang (literary and upmarket fiction with commercial appeal; select nonfiction: popular science, diet/health/fitness, lifestyle, narrative nonfiction, pop culture, and humor); Erin Niumata (fiction: commercial women's fiction, romance, historical fiction, mysteries, psychological thrillers, suspense, humor; nonfiction: self-help, women's issues, pop culture and humor, pet care/pets, memoirs, and anything blogger); Ruth Pomerance (narrative nonfiction and commercial fiction); Marcy Posner (adult: commercial women's fiction, historical fiction, mystery, biography, history, health, and lifestyle, commercial novels, thrillers, narrative nonfiction; children's: contemporary YA and MG, mystery series for boys, select historical fiction and fantasy); Jeff Silberman (narrative nonfiction, biography, history, politics, current affairs, health, lifestyle, humor, food/cookbook, memoir, pop culture, sports, science, technology; commercial, literary, and book club fiction); Steve Troha; Emily van Beek (YA, MG, picture books), Melissa White (general nonfiction, literary and commercial fiction, MG, YA); John Cusick (middle grade, picture books, YA); Jamie Chambliss.

REPRESENTS Nonfiction, novels. **Considers these fiction areas:** commercial, fantasy, horror, literary, middle grade, mystery, picture books, religious, romance, thriller, women's, young adult.

☛ No poetry, stage plays, or screenplays.

HOW TO CONTACT Query via e-mail only (no attachments). Read agent bios online for specific submission guidelines and e-mail addresses, and to check if someone is closed to queries. "All agents respond to queries as soon as possible, whether interested or not. If you haven't heard back from the individual agent within the time period that they specify on their bio page, it's possible that something has gone wrong, and your query has been lost–in that case, please e-mail a follow-up."

TIPS "Please do not submit simultaneously to more than one agent at Folio. If you're not sure which of us is exactly right for your book, don't worry. We work closely as a team, and if one of our agents gets a query that might be more appropriate for someone else, we'll always pass it along. It's important that you check each agent's bio page for clear directions as to how to submit, as well as when to expect feedback."

FOUNDRY LITERARY + MEDIA

33 W. 17th St., PH, New York NY 10011. (212)929-5064. **Fax:** (212)929-5471. **Website:** www.foundry-media.com.

MEMBER AGENTS Peter McGuigan, pmsubmissions@foundrymedia.com (smart, offbeat voices in all genres of fiction and nonfiction); Yfat Reiss Gendell, yrgsubmissions@foundrymedia.com (practical nonfiction: health and wellness, diet, lifestyle, how-to, and parenting; range of narrative nonfiction that includes humor, memoir, history, science, pop culture, psychology, and adventure/travel stories; unique commercial fiction, including young adult fiction, that touch on her nonfiction interests, including speculative fiction, thrillers, and historical fiction); Chris Park, cpsubmissions@foundrymedia.com (memoirs, narrative nonfiction, sports books, Christian nonfiction and character-driven fiction); Hannah Brown Gordon, hbgsubmissions@foundrymedia.com (stories and narratives that blend genres, including thriller, suspense, historical, literary, speculative, memoir, pop-science, psychology, humor, and pop culture); Brandi Bowles, bbsubmissions@foundrymedia.com (nonfiction list ranges from cookbooks to prescriptive books, science, pop culture, and real-life inspirational stories; high-concept novels that feature strong female bonds and psychological or scientific themes); Kirsten Neuhaus, knsubmissions@foundrymedia.com (platform-driven narrative nonfiction, in the areas of memoir, business, lifestyle (beauty/fashion/relationships), current events, history and stories with strong female voices, as well as smart fiction that appeals to a wide market); Jessica Regel, jrsubmissions@foundrymedia.com (young adult and middle grade books, as well as a select list of adult general fiction, women's fiction, and adult nonfiction); Anthony Mattero, amsubmissions@foundrymedia.com (smart, platform-driven nonfiction particularly in the genres of pop culture, humor, music, sports, and pop-business); Peter Steinberg, pssubmissions@foundrymedia.com (narrative nonfiction, commercial and literary fiction, memoir, health, history, lifestyle, humor, sports, and young adult); Roger Freet, rfsubmissions@foundrymedia.com (narrative and idea-driven nonfiction clients in the areas of religion, spirituality, memoir, and cultural issues by leading scholars, pastors, historians, activists and musicians); Adriann Ranta, arsubmissions@foundrymedia.com (accepts all genres and age groups; loves gritty, realistic, true-to-life narratives; women's fiction and nonfiction; accessible, pop nonfiction in science, history, and craft; and smart, fresh, genre-bending works for children).

REPRESENTS Considers these fiction areas: commercial, historical, humor, literary, middle grade, suspense, thriller, women's, young adult.

HOW TO CONTACT Target one agent only. Send queries to the specific submission e-mail of the agent. For fiction: send query, synopsis, author bio, first 3 chapters—all pasted in the e-mail. For nonfiction, send query, sample chapters, TOC, author bio (all pasted). "We regret that we cannot guarantee a response to every submission we receive. If you do not receive a response within 8 weeks, your submission is not right for our lists at this time." Accepts simultaneous submissions.

TIPS "Consult website for each agent's submission instructions."

FOX LITERARY

110 W. 40th St., Suite 2305, New York NY 10018. **E-mail:** submissions@foxliterary.com. **Website:** foxliterary.com.

MEMBER AGENTS Diana Fox.

REPRESENTS Nonfiction, fiction, novels, short story collections, juvenile books, scholarly books. , graphic novels. **Considers these fiction areas:** action, adventure, comic books, commercial, confession, contemporary issues, crime, detective, erotica, fantasy, feminist, gay, historical, juvenile, lesbian, literary, mainstream, middle grade, multicultural, mystery, new adult, paranormal, romance, science fiction, short story collections, spiritual, suspense, thriller, urban fantasy, women's, young adult, general.

HOW TO CONTACT E-mail query and first 5 pages in body of e-mail. E-mail queries preferred. For snail mail queries, must include an e-mail address for response and no response means no. Do not send SASE. No e-mail attachments. Accepts simultaneous submissions.

SARAH JANE FREYMANN LITERARY AGENCY

(212)362-9277. **E-mail:** sarah@sarahjanefreymann.com. **E-mail:** submissions@sarahjanefreymann.com.

Website: www.sarahjanefreymann.com. **Contact:** Sarah Jane Freymann, Steve Schwartz.

MEMBER AGENTS Sarah Jane Freymann (nonfiction: spiritual, psychology, self-help, women/men's issues, books by health experts [conventional and alternative], cookbooks, narrative non-fiction, natural science, nature, memoirs, cutting-edge journalism, travel, multicultural issues, parenting, lifestyle, fiction: literary, mainstream YA); Jessica Sinsheimer, jessica@sarahjanefreymann.com; Steven Schwartz, steve@sarahjanefreymann.com (popular fiction [crime, thrillers, and historical novels], world and national affairs, business books, self-help, psychology, humor, sports and travel).

REPRESENTS Nonfiction, fiction, novels. **Considers these fiction areas:** crime, historical, literary, mainstream, thriller, young adult, Popular fiction.

HOW TO CONTACT Query via e-mail. No attachments. Below the query, please paste the first 10 pages of your work. Accepts simultaneous submissions.

TERMS Charges clients for long distance, overseas postage, photocopying. 100% of business is derived from commissions on ms sales.

FREDRICA S. FRIEDMAN AND CO., INC.

857 Fifth Ave., New York NY 10065. (212)639-9455. **E-mail:** info@fredricafriedman.com. **E-mail:** submissions@fredricafriedman.com. **Website:** www.fredricafriedman.com. **Contact:** Ms. Chandler Smith.

○ Prior to establishing her own literary management firm, Ms. Friedman was the Editorial Director, Associate Publisher and Vice President of Little, Brown & Co., a division of Time Warner, and the first woman to hold those positions.

REPRESENTS Nonfiction, fiction.

☛ Does not want poetry, plays, screenplays, children's picture books, sci-fi/fantasy, or horror.

HOW TO CONTACT Submit e-query, synopsis; be concise, and include any pertinent author information, including relevant writing history. If you are a fiction writer, submit the first 10 pages of your manuscript. Keep all material in the body of the e-mail. Accepts simultaneous submissions. Responds in 6 weeks.

REBECCA FRIEDMAN LITERARY AGENCY

E-mail: queries@rfliterary.com. **Website:** www.rfliterary.com. Estab. 2013. Member of AAR. Signatory of WGA.

○ Prior to opening her own agency in 2013, Ms. Friedman was with Sterling Lord Literistic from 2006 to 2011, then with Hill Nadell Agency.

MEMBER AGENTS Rebecca Friedman (commercial and literary fiction with a focus on literary novels of suspense, women's fiction, contemporary romance, and young adult, as well as journalistic nonfiction and memoir); Susan Finesman, susan@rfliterary.com (fiction, cookbooks, and lifestyle); Abby Schulman, abby@rfliterary.com (YA and nonfiction related to health, wellness, and personal development).

REPRESENTS Nonfiction, fiction, novels. **Considers these fiction areas:** commercial, family saga, fantasy, feminist, gay, historical, juvenile, lesbian, literary, mystery, science fiction, suspense, thriller, women's, young adult.

HOW TO CONTACT Please submit your brief query letter and first chapter (no more than 15 pages, double-spaced). No attachments. Accepts simultaneous submissions. Tries to respond in 6-8 weeks.

RECENT SALES A complete list of agency authors is available online.

THE FRIEDRICH AGENCY

19 W. 21st St., Suite 201, New York NY 10010. (212)317-8810. **E-mail:** mfriedrich@friedrichagency.com; lcarson@friedrichagency.com; kwolf@friedrichagency.com. **Website:** www.friedrichagency.com. **Contact:** Molly Friedrich; Lucy Carson; Kent D. Wolf. Estab. 2006. Member of AAR. Signatory of WGA. Represents 50+ clients.

○ Prior to her current position, Ms. Friedrich was an agent at the Aaron Priest Literary Agency.

MEMBER AGENTS Molly Friedrich, founder and agent (open to queries); Lucy Carson, TV/film rights director and agent (open to queries); Kent D. Wolf, foreign rights director and agent (open to queries).

REPRESENTS Nonfiction, fiction, novels, short story collections. **Considers these fiction areas:** commercial, detective, family saga, feminist, gay, lesbian, literary, multicultural, mystery, science fiction, short story collections, suspense, thriller, women's, young adult.

HOW TO CONTACT Query by e-mail only. Please query only 1 agent at this agency. Accepts simultaneous submissions. Responds in 2-4 weeks.

RECENT SALES *W is For Wasted*, by Sue Grafton; *Olive Kitteridge*, by Elizabeth Strout. Other clients include Frank McCourt, Jane Smiley, Esmeralda Santiago, Terry McMillan, Cathy Schine, Ruth Ozeki, Karen Joy Fowler, and more.

FULL CIRCLE LITERARY, LLC

San Diego CA **Website:** www.fullcircleliterary.com. **Contact:** Stefanie Von Borstel. Estab. 2005. Member of AAR. Society of Children's Books Writers & Illustrators, Authors Guild. Represents 100+ clients.

MEMBER AGENTS Stefanie Sanchez Von Borstel; Adriana Dominguez; Taylor Martindale Kean; Lilly Ghahremani.

REPRESENTS Considers these fiction areas: literary, middle grade, multicultural, young adult.

Actively seeking nonfiction and fiction projects that offer new and diverse viewpoints, and literature with a global or multicultural perspective. "We are particularly interested in books with a Latino or Middle Eastern angle."

HOW TO CONTACT Online submissions only via submissions form online. Please complete the form and submit cover letter, author information and sample writing. For sample writing: fiction please include the first 10 ms pages. For nonfiction, include a proposal with 1 sample chapter. Accepts simultaneous submissions. "Due to the high volume of submissions, please keep in mind we are no longer able to personally respond to every submission. However, we read every submission with care and often share for a second read within the office. If we are interested, we will contact you by email to request additional materials (such as a complete manuscript or additional manuscripts). Please keep us updated if there is a change in the status of your project, such as an offer of representation or book contract."

If you have not heard from us in 6-8 weeks, your project is not right for our agency at the current time and we wish you all the best with your writing.

Thank you for considering Full Circle Literary, we look forward to reading! Obtains most new clients through recommendations from others and conferences.

TERMS Agent receives 15% commission on domestic sales; 25% commission on foreign sales. Offers written contract which outlines responsibilities of the author and the agent.

FUSE LITERARY

Foreword Literary, Inc. dba FUSE LITERARY, P.O. Box 258, La Honda CA 94020. **E-mail:** info@fuseliterary.com. **E-mail:** query[firstnameofagent]@fuseliterary.com. **Website:** www.fuseliterary.com. **Contact:** Contact each agent directly via e-mail. Estab. 2013. RWA, SCBWI. Represents 100+ clients.

Each agent at Fuse had a specific set of interests and jobs prior to becoming a member of Team Fuse. Laurie ran a multi-million dollar publicity agency. Michelle was an editor at a Big Five publisher. Emily worked in the contracts department at Simon & Schuster. Gordon ran a successful independent editing business. Tricia worked in the video game industry. Connor worked in talent management. Carlisle is a youth librarian. Margaret taught English. Check each agent's bio on our website for more specific information.

MEMBER AGENTS Laurie McLean (only accepting referral inquiries and submissions requested at conferences or online events); Gordon Warnock, querygordon@fuseliterary.com (fiction: high-concept commercial fiction, literary fiction (adults through YA), graphic novels (adults through MG); nonfiction: memoir (adult, YA, NA, graphic), cookbooks/food narrative/food studies, illustrated/art/photography (especially graphic nonfiction), political and current events, pop science, pop culture (especially punk culture and geek culture), self-help, how-to, humor, pets, business and career); Connor Goldsmith, queryconnor@fuseliterary.com (fiction: sci-fi/fantasy/horror, thrillers, and upmarket commercial fiction with a unique and memorable hook; books by and about people from marginalized perspectives, such as LGBT people and/or racial minorities; nonfiction (from recognized experts with established platforms): history (particularly of the ancient world), theater, cinema, music, television, mass media, popular culture, feminism and gender studies, LGBT issues, race relations, and the sex industry); Michelle Richter, querymichelle@fuseliterary.com (primarily seeking fiction, specifically book club reads, literary fiction, and mystery/suspense/thrillers; for nonfiction, seeking fashion, pop culture, science/medicine, sociology/social trends, and economics); Emily S. Keyes, queryemily@fuseliterary.com (picture books, middle grade and young adult children's books, plus select commercial fiction, including fantasy & science fiction, women's fiction, new adult fiction, pop culture and humor); Tricia Skinner, querytricia@fuseliterary.com (Romance: science fiction, futuristic, fantasy, military/special ops, medieval historical; brand new relationships; diversity); Margaret Bail, querymargaret@fuseliterary.com (adult fiction in the genres of romance [no Christian or inspirational, please], science fiction [soft sci-fi rather than hard], mystery, thrillers, action adventure, historical fiction [not a fan of WWII era], and fantasy. In nonfiction, memoirs with a unique hook, and cookbooks with a strong platform); Carlisle Webber, querycarlisle@fuseliterary.com (high-concept commercial fiction in middle grade, young adult, and adult; dark thrillers, mystery, horror, dark women's fiction, dark pop/mainstream fiction; especially interested in diverse authors and their stories).

REPRESENTS Nonfiction, fiction, novels, juvenile books, scholarly books, poetry books. **Considers these fiction areas:** action, adventure, cartoon, comic books, commercial, confession, contemporary issues, crime, detective, erotica, ethnic, experimental, family saga, fantasy, feminist, frontier, gay, glitz, hi-lo, historical, horror, humor, inspirational, juvenile, lesbian, literary, mainstream, metaphysical, middle grade, multicultural, multimedia, mystery, new adult, New Age, occult, paranormal, picture books, plays, poetry, poetry in translation, police, psychic, regional, romance, satire, science fiction, spiritual, sports, supernatural, suspense, thriller, urban fantasy, westerns, women's, young adult. "We are committed to expanding storytelling into a wide variety of formats other than books, including video games, movies, television shows, streaming videos, enhanced ebooks, VR, etc."

HOW TO CONTACT E-query an individual agent. Check the website to see if any individual agent has closed themselves to submissions, as well as for a description of each agent's individual submission preferences. (You can find these details by clicking on each agent's photo.) Accepts simultaneous submissions. Usually responds in 4-6 weeks, but sometimes more if an agent is exceptionally busy. Check each agent's bio/submissions page on the website. Only accepts e-mailed queries that follow our online guidelines.

TERMS "We earn 15% on negotiated deals for books and with our co-agents earn between 20-30% on foreign translation deals depending on the territory; 20% on TV/Movies/Plays; other multimedia deals are so new there is no established commission rate. The au-

thor has the last say, approving or not approving all deals." After the initial 90-day period, there is a 30-day termination of the agency agreement clause. No fees.

RECENT SALES Seven-figure and six-figure deals for NYT bestseller Julie Kagawa (YA); six-figure deal for debut Melissa D. Savage (MG); seven-figure and six-figure deals for Kerry Lonsdale (suspense); two six-figure audio deals for fantasy author Brian D. Anderson; *First Watch*, by Dale Lucas (fantasy); *This Is What a Librarian Looks Like*, by Kyle Cassidy (photo essay); *A Big Ship at the Edge of the Universe*, by Alex White (sci-fi); Runebinder Chronicles, by Alex Kahler (YA); *Perceptual Intelligence*, by Dr. Brian Boxler Wachler (science); *The Night Child*, by Anna Quinn (literary); *Hollywood Homicide*, by Kellye Garrett (mystery); Breakup Bash Series, by Nina Crespo (romance); *America's Next Reality Star*, by Laura Heffernan (women's fiction); *Losing the Girl*, by MariNaomi (graphic novel); *Maggie and Abby's Neverending Pillow Fort*, by Will Taylor (MG); *Idea Machine*, by Jorjeana Marie (how-to).

WRITERS CONFERENCES Agents from this agency attend many conferences. A full list of their appearances is available on the agency website.

GALLT AND ZACKER LITERARY AGENCY

273 Charlton Ave., South Orange NJ 07079. **Website:** www.galltzacker.com. **Contact:** Nancy Gallt, Marietta Zacker. Estab. 2000. Represents 100+ clients.

Ms. Gallt was subsidiary rights director of the children's book division at Morrow, Harper and Viking. Ms. Zacker started her career as a teacher, championing children's and YA books, then worked in the children's book world, bookselling, marketing, and editing. Ms. Camacho held positions in foreign rights, editorial, marketing, and operations at Penguin Random House, Dorchester, Simon and Schuster, and Writers House literary agency before venturing into agenting at Prospect Agency. Ms. Phelan got her start at Scott Waxman Agency and Morhaim Literary then spent four years as an agent with The Bent Agency.

MEMBER AGENTS Nancy Gallt; Marietta Zacker; Linda Camacho; Beth Phelan.

REPRESENTS Nonfiction, fiction, novels, juvenile books, scholarly books, poetry books. **Considers these fiction areas:** juvenile, middle grade, picture books, young adult.

☞ Books for children and young adults. Actively seeking author, illustrators, author/illustrators who create books for young adults and younger readers.

HOW TO CONTACT Submission guidelines on our website: http://galltzacker.com/submissions.html. No e-mail queries, please. Accepts simultaneous submissions. We endeavor to respond to all queries within 4 weeks. Obtains new clients through submissions, conferences and recommendations from others.

TERMS Agent receives 15% commission on domestic sales; 20% commission on foreign sales. Offers written contract; 30-day notice must be given to terminate contract.

RECENT SALES Rick Riordan's Books (Hyperion); *Trace*, by Pat Cummings (Harper); *I Got Next*, by Daria Peoples-Riley (Bloomsbury); *Gondra's Treasure*, illustrated by Jennifer Black Reinhardt (Clarion/HMH); *Caterpillar Summer*, by Gillian McDunn (Bloomsbury); *It Wasn't Me*, by Dana Alison Levy (Delacorte/Random House); *Five Midnights*, by Ann Dávila Cardinal (Tor/Macmillan); *Patron Saints of Nothing*, by Randy Ribay (Kokila/Penguin); *Rot*, by Ben Clanton (Simon & Schuster). *The Year They Fell*, by David Kreizman (Imprint/Macmillan); *Manhattan Maps*, by Jennifer Thermes (Abrams); *The Moon Within*, by Aida Salazar (Scholastic); *Artist in Space*, by Dean Robbins (Scholastic); *Where Are You From?*, by Mary Amato (Holiday House); *Where Are You From?*, by Yamile Saied Méndez (Harper); *The Girl King*, by Mimi Yu (Bloomsbury); *Narwhal and Jelly*, by Ben Clanton (Tundra/Penguin Random House Canada).

TIPS "Writing and illustrations stand on their own, so submissions should tell the most compelling stories possible—whether visually, in narrative, or both."

MAX GARTENBERG LITERARY AGENCY

912 N. Pennsylvania Ave., Yardley PA 19067. (215)295-9230. **Website:** www.maxgartenberg.com. **Contact:** Anne Devlin (nonfiction). Estab. 1954. Represents 100 clients.

MEMBER AGENTS Anne G. Devlin (current events, education, politics, true crime, women's issues, sports, parenting, biography, environment, narrative nonfiction, health, lifestyle, and celebrity).

REPRESENTS Nonfiction, juvenile books, scholarly books, textbooks.

HOW TO CONTACT Writers desirous of having their work handled by this agency may query by e-mail to agdevlin@aol.com. Accepts simultaneous submissions. Responds in 2 weeks to queries; 6 weeks to mss.

TERMS Agent receives 15% commission on sales.

RECENT SALES *The Enlightened College Applicant*, by Andrew Belasco (Rowman and Littlefield); *Beethoven for Kids: His Life and Music*, by Helen Bauer (Chicago Review Press); *Portrait of a Past Life Skeptic*, by Robert L. Snow (Llewellyn Books); *Beyond Your Baby's Checkup*, by Luke Voytas, MD (Sasquatch Books); *Unorthodox Warfare: The Chinese Experience*, by Ralph D. Sawyer (Westview Press); *Encyclopedia of Earthquakes and Volcanoes*, by Alexander E. Gates (Facts on File); *Pandas!: Step Into Reading*, by David Salomon (Random House Children's Books).

TIPS "We have recently expanded to allow more access for new writers."

GELFMAN SCHNEIDER/ICM PARTNERS

850 7th Ave., Suite 903, New York NY 10019. **E-mail:** mail@gelfmanschneider.com. **Website:** www.gelfmanschneider.com. **Contact:** Jane Gelfman, Deborah Schneider. Member of AAR. Represents 300+ clients.

MEMBER AGENTS Deborah Schneider (all categories of literary and commercial fiction and nonfiction); Jane Gelfman; Heather Mitchell (particularly interested in narrative nonfiction, historical fiction and young debut authors with strong voices); Penelope Burns, penelope.gsliterary@gmail.com (literary and commercial fiction and nonfiction, as well as a variety of young adult and middle grade).

REPRESENTS Nonfiction, fiction, juvenile books. **Considers these fiction areas:** commercial, fantasy, historical, literary, mainstream, middle grade, mystery, science fiction, suspense, women's, young adult.

☞ "Among our diverse list of clients are novelists, journalists, playwrights, scientists, activists & humorists writing narrative nonfiction, memoir, political & current affairs, popular science and popular culture nonfiction, as well as literary & commercial fiction, women's fiction, and historical fiction." Does not currently accept screenplays or scripts, poetry, or picture book queries.

HOW TO CONTACT Query. Check Submissions page of website to see which agents are open to queries and further instructions. Accepts simultaneous submissions.

TERMS Agent receives 15% commission on domestic sales; 20% commission on foreign sales; 15% commission on film sales. Offers written contract. Charges clients for photocopying and messengers/couriers.

THE GERNERT COMPANY

136 E. 57th St., New York NY 10022. (212)838-7777. **E-mail:** info@thegernertco.com. **Website:** www.thegernertco.com. Estab. 1996.

MEMBER AGENTS Sarah Burnes (literary fiction and nonfiction; children's fiction); Stephanie Cabot (represents a variety of genres, including crime/thrillers, commercial and literary fiction, latte lit, and nonfiction); Chris Parris-Lamb (nonfiction, literary fiction); Seth Fishman (looking for the new voice, the original idea, the entirely breathtaking creative angle in both fiction and nonfiction); Alia Hanna Habib (narrative nonfiction, literary fiction, and culinary titles); Will Roberts (smart, original thrillers with distinctive voices, compelling backgrounds, and fast-paced narratives); Erika Storella (nonfiction projects that make an argument, narrate a history, and/or provide a new perspective); Sarah Bolling (literary fiction, smart genre fiction —particularly sci-fi— memoir, pop culture, and style); Julia Eagleton (literary fiction and nonfiction: science, politics, nature, and memoir); Anna Worrall (smart women's literary and commercial fiction, psychological thrillers, and narrative nonfiction); Ellen Coughtrey (women's literary and commercial fiction, historical fiction, narrative nonfiction and smart, original thrillers, plus. well-written Southern Gothic anything); Jack Gernert (stories about heroes—both real and imagined); Libby McGuire (distinctive storytelling in both fiction and nonfiction, across a wide range of genres). At this time, Courtney Gatewood and Rebecca Gardner are closed to queries. See the website to find out the tastes of each agent.

REPRESENTS Nonfiction, novels. **Considers these fiction areas:** commercial, crime, fantasy, historical, literary, middle grade, science fiction, thriller, women's, young adult.

HOW TO CONTACT Please send us a query letter by e-mail to info@thegernertco.com describing the work you'd like to submit, along with some information about yourself and a sample chapter if appropriate. Please indicate in your letter which agent you are querying. Please do not send e-mails directly to individual agents. It's our policy to respond to your query only if we are interested in seeing more material, usually within 4-6 weeks. See company website for more instructions. Accepts simultaneous submissions. Obtains most new clients through recommendations from others, solicitations.

RECENT SALES *Partners*, by John Grisham; *The River Why*, by David James Duncan; *The Thin Green Line*, by Paul Sullivan; *A Fireproof Home for the Bride*, by Amy Scheibe; *The Only Girl in School*, by Natalie Standiford.

GHOSH LITERARY

E-mail: submissions@ghoshliterary.com. **Website:** www.ghoshliterary.com. **Contact:** Anna Ghosh. Member of AAR. Signatory of WGA.

○ Prior to opening her own agency, Ms. Ghosh was previously a partner at Scovil Galen Ghosh.

REPRESENTS Nonfiction, fiction.

⌲ "Anna's literary interests are wide and eclectic and she is known for discovering and developing writers. She is particularly interested in literary narratives and books that illuminate some aspect of human endeavor or the natural world. Anna does not typically represent genre fiction but is drawn to compelling storytelling in most guises."

HOW TO CONTACT E-query. Please send an e-mail briefly introducing yourself and your work. Although no specific format is required, it is helpful to know the following: your qualifications for writing your book, including any publications and recognition for your work; who you expect to buy and read your book; similar books and authors. Accepts simultaneous submissions.

GLASS LITERARY MANAGEMENT

138 W. 25th St., 10th Floor, New York NY 10001. (646)237-4881. **E-mail:** alex@glassliterary.com; rick@glassliterary.com. **Website:** www.glassliterary.com. **Contact:** Alex Glass or Rick Pascocello. Estab. 2014. Member of AAR. Signatory of WGA.

MEMBER AGENTS Alex Glass; Rick Pascocello.

REPRESENTS Nonfiction, novels.

⌲ Represents general fiction, mystery, suspense/thriller, juvenile fiction, biography, history, mind/body/spirit, health, lifestyle, cookbooks, sports, literary fiction, memoir, narrative nonfiction, pop culture. "We do not represent picture books for children."

HOW TO CONTACT "Please send your query letter in the body of an e-mail and if we are interested, we will respond and ask for the complete manuscript or proposal. No attachments." Accepts simultaneous submissions.

RECENT SALES *100 Days of Cake*, by Shari Goldhagen; *The Red Car*, by Marcy Dermansky; *The Overnight Solution*, by Dr. Michael Breus; *So That Happened: A Memoir*, by Jon Cryer; *Bad Kid*, by David Crabb; *Finding Mr. Brightside*, by Jay Clark; *Strange Animals*, by Chad Kultgen.

BARRY GOLDBLATT LITERARY LLC

320 7th Ave. #266, Brooklyn NY 11215. **E-mail:** query@bgliterary.com. **Website:** www.bgliterary.com. **Contact:** Barry Goldblatt; Jennifer Udden. Estab. 2000. Member of AAR. Signatory of WGA.

MEMBER AGENTS Barry Goldblatt; Jennifer Udden, query.judden@gmail.com (speculative fiction of all stripes, especially innovative science fiction or fantasy; contemporary/erotic/LGBT/paranormal/historical romance; contemporary or speculative YA; select mysteries, thrillers, and urban fantasies).

REPRESENTS Fiction. **Considers these fiction areas:** fantasy, middle grade, mystery, romance, science fiction, thriller, young adult.

☞ "Please see our website for specific submission guidelines and information on our particular tastes."

HOW TO CONTACT "E-mail queries can be sent to query@bgliterary.com and should include the word 'query' in the subject line. To query Jen Udden specifically, e-mail queries can be sent to query.judden@gmail.com. Please know that we will read and respond to every e-query that we receive, provided it is properly addressed and follows the submission guidelines below. We will not respond to e-queries that are addressed to no one, or to multiple recipients. Your e-mail query should include the following within the body of the e-mail: your query letter, a synopsis of the book, and the first 5 pages of your manuscript. We will not open or respond to any e-mails that have attachments. If we like the sound of your work, we will request more from you. Our response time is 4 weeks on queries, 6-8 weeks on full manuscripts. If you haven't heard from us within that time, feel free to check in via e-mail." Accepts simultaneous submissions. Obtains clients through referrals, queries, and conferences.

TERMS Agent receives 15% commission on domestic sales; 20% on foreign and dramatic sales. Offers written contract. 60 days notice must be given to terminate contract.

RECENT SALES *Trolled*, by Bruce Coville; *Grim Tidings*, by Caitlin Kittridge; *Max at Night*, by Ed Vere.

TIPS "We're a hands-on agency, focused on building an author's career, not just making an initial sale. We don't care about trends or what's hot; we just want to sign great writers."

FRANCES GOLDIN LITERARY AGENCY, INC.

214 W. 29th St., Suite 410, New York NY 10001. (212)777-0047. **Fax:** (212)228-1660. **Website:** www.goldinlit.com. Estab. 1977. Member of AAR.

MEMBER AGENTS Frances Goldin, founder/president; Ellen Geiger, vice president/principal (nonfiction: history, biography, progressive politics, photography, science and medicine, women, religion and serious investigative journalism; fiction: literary thriller, and novels in general that provoke and challenge the status quo, as well as historical and multicultural works. Please no New Age, romance, how-to or right-wing politics); Matt McGowan, agent/rights director, mm@goldinlit.com, (literary fiction, essays, history, memoir, journalism, biography, music, popular culture & science, sports [particularly soccer], narrative nonfiction, cultural studies, as well as literary travel, crime, food, suspense and sci-fi); Sam Stoloff, vice president/principal, (literary fiction, memoir, history, accessible sociology and philosophy, cultural studies, serious journalism, narrative and topical nonfiction with a progressive orientation); Ria Julien, agent/counsel; Caroline Eisenmann, associate agent.

REPRESENTS Nonfiction, novels. **Considers these fiction areas:** historical, literary, mainstream, multicultural, suspense, thriller.

☞ "We are hands on and we work intensively with clients on proposal and manuscript development." "Please note that we do not handle screenplays, romances or most other genre fiction, and hardly any poetry. We do not handle work that is racist, sexist, ageist, homophobic, or pornographic."

HOW TO CONTACT There is an online submission process you can find online. Responds in 4-6 weeks to queries.

IRENE GOODMAN LITERARY AGENCY

27 W. 24th St., Suite 700B, New York NY 10010. **E-mail:** miriam.queries@irenegoodman.com, barbara.queries@irenegoodman.com, rachel.queries@irenegoodman.com, kim.queries@irenegoodman.com, victoria.queries@irenegoodman.com, irene.queries@irenegoodman.com, brita.queries@irenegoodman.com. **E-mail:** submissions@irenegoodman.com. **Website:** www.irenegoodman.com. **Contact:** Brita Lundberg. Estab. 1978. Member of AAR. Represents 150 clients.

MEMBER AGENTS Irene Goodman, Miriam Kriss, Barbara Poelle, Rachel Ekstrom, Kim Perel, Brita Lundberg, Victoria Marini.

REPRESENTS Nonfiction, fiction, novels, juvenile books. **Considers these fiction areas:** action, crime, detective, family saga, historical, horror, middle grade, mystery, romance, science fiction, suspense, thriller, urban fantasy, women's, young adult.

- Commercial and literary fiction and nonfiction. No screenplays, poetry, or inspirational fiction.

HOW TO CONTACT Query. Submit synopsis, first 10 pages pasted into the body of the email. E-mail queries only! See the website submission page. No e-mail attachments. Query 1 agent only. Accepts simultaneous submissions. Responds in 2 months to queries. Consult website for each agent's submission guidelines.

TERMS 15% commission.

TIPS "We are receiving an unprecedented amount of e-mail queries. If you find that the mailbox is full, please try again in two weeks. E-mail queries to our personal addresses will not be answered. E-mails to our personal inboxes will be deleted."

DOUG GRAD LITERARY AGENCY, INC.

156 Prospect Park West, #3L, Brooklyn NY 11215. **E-mail:** query@dgliterary.com. **Website:** www.dgliterary.com. **Contact:** Doug Grad. Estab. 2008. Represents 50+ clients.

- Prior to being an agent, Doug Grad spent 22 years as an editor at imprint at 4 major publishing houses—Simon & Schuster, Random House, Penguin, and HarperCollins.

MEMBER AGENTS Doug Grad (narrative nonfiction, military, sports, celebrity memoir, thrillers, mysteries, cozies, historical fiction, music, style, business, home improvement, food, science and theater).

REPRESENTS Nonfiction, fiction, novels. **Considers these fiction areas:** action, adventure, commercial, crime, detective, historical, horror, literary, mainstream, military, mystery, police, romance, science fiction, suspense, thriller, war, young adult.

- Does not want fantasy, young adult, or children's picture books.

HOW TO CONTACT Query by e-mail first. No sample material unless requested; no printed submissions by mail. Accepts simultaneous submissions. Due to the volume of queries, it's impossible to give a response time.

TERMS None

RECENT SALES *Net Force* series created by Tom Clancy and Steve Pieczenik, written by Jerome Preisler (Hanover Square); *A Serial Killer's Daughter* by Kerri Rawson (Thomas Nelson); *The Next Greatest Generation*, by Joseph L. Galloway and Marvin J. Wolf (Thomas Nelson); *All Available Boats* by L. Douglas Keeney (Lyons Press); *Here Comes the Body*, Book 1 in the Catering Hall mystery series, by Agatha Award-winner Ellen Byron writing as Maria DiRico (Kensington); *Please Don't Feed the Mayor* and *Alaskan Catch*, by Sue Pethick (Kensington).

SANFORD J. GREENBURGER ASSOCIATES, INC.

55 Fifth Ave., New York NY 10003. (212)206-5600. **Fax:** (212)463-8718. **Website:** www.greenburger.com. Member of AAR. Represents 500 clients.

MEMBER AGENTS Matt Bialer, querymb@sjga.com (fantasy, science fiction, thrillers, and mysteries as well as a select group of literary writers, and also loves smart narrative nonfiction including books about current events, popular culture, biography, history, music, race, and sports); Brenda Bowen, querybb@sjga.com (literary fiction, writers and illustrators of picture books, chapter books, and middle-grade and teen fiction); Faith Hamlin, fhamlin@sjga.com (receives submissions by referral); Heide Lange, queryhl@sjga.com (receives submissions by referral); Daniel Mandel, querydm@sjga.com (literary and commercial fiction, as well as memoirs and nonfiction about business, art, history, politics, sports, and popular culture); Rachael Dillon Fried, rfried@sjga.com (both fiction and nonfiction authors, with a keen interest in unique literary voices, women's fiction, narrative nonfiction, memoir, and comedy); Stephanie Delman, sdelman@sjga.com (literary/upmarket contemporary fiction, psychological thrillers/

suspense, and atmospheric, near-historical fiction); Ed Maxwell, emaxwell@sjga.com (expert and narrative nonfiction authors, novelists and graphic novelists, as well as children's book authors and illustrators).

REPRESENTS Nonfiction, fiction, novels, juvenile books. **Considers these fiction areas:** commercial, crime, family saga, fantasy, feminist, historical, literary, middle grade, multicultural, mystery, picture books, romance, science fiction, thriller, women's, young adult.

☞ **No screenplays.**

HOW TO CONTACT E-query. "Please look at each agent's profile page for current information about what each agent is looking for and for the correct email address to use for queries to that agent. Please be sure to use the correct query e-mail address for each agent." Agents may not respond to all queries; will respond within 6-8 weeks if interested. Obtains most new clients through recommendations from others.

TERMS Agent receives 15% commission on domestic sales; 20% commission on foreign sales. Charges for photocopying and books for foreign and subsidiary rights submissions.

RECENT SALES *Origin*, by Dan Brown; *Sweet Pea and Friends: A Sheepover*, by **JOHN CHURCHMAN** and Jennifer Churchman; *Code of Conduct*, by Brad Thor.

THE GREENHOUSE LITERARY AGENCY

E-mail: submissions@greenhouseliterary.com. **Website:** www.greenhouseliterary.com. **Contact:** Sarah Davies. Estab. 2008. Member of AAR. Other memberships include SCBWI. Represents 70 clients.

○ Before launching Greenhouse, Sarah Davies had an editorial and management career in children's publishing spanning 25 years; for 5 years prior to launching the Greenhouse she was Publishing Director of Macmillan Children's Books in London, and published leading authors from both sides of the Atlantic.

MEMBER AGENTS Sarah Davies, vice president (fiction and nonfiction by North American authors, chapter books through to middle grade and young adult); Polly Nolan, agent (fiction by North American, UK, Irish, Commonwealth–including Australia, NZ and India–authors, plus European authors writing in English, young fiction series, through middle grade and young adult).

REPRESENTS Juvenile books. **Considers these fiction areas:** juvenile, young adult.

☞ "We represent authors writing fiction and nonfiction for children and teens. The agency has offices in both the US and UK, and the agency's commission structure reflects this—taking 15% for sales to both US and UK, thus treating both as 'domestic' market." All genres of children's and YA fiction. Occasionally, a nonfiction proposal will be considered. Does not want to receive picture books texts (ie, written by writers who aren't also illustrators) or short stories, educational or religious/inspirational work, preschool/novelty material, screenplays. Represents novels and some nonfiction.Considers these fiction areas: juvenile, chapter book series, middle grade, young adult. Does not want to receive poetry, picture book texts (unless by author/illustrators) or work aimed at adults; short stories, educational or religious/inspirational work, preschool/novelty material, or screenplays.

HOW TO CONTACT Query 1 agent only. Put the target agent's name in the subject line. Paste the first 5 pages of your story after the query. Please see our website for up-to-date information as occasionally we close to queries for short periods of time. Accepts simultaneous submissions.

TERMS Agent receives 15% commission on domestic sales; 25% commission on foreign sales. Offers written contract. This agency occasionally charges for submission copies to film agents or foreign publishers.

RECENT SALES *Agents of the Wild*, by Jennifer Bell & Alice Lickens (Walker UK); *Bookshop Girl in Paris*, by Chloe Coles (Hot Key); *Votes for Women*, by Winifred Conkling (Algonquin); *The Monster Catchers*, by George Brewington (Holt); *City of the Plague God*, by Sarwat Chadda (Disney-Hyperion); *Whiteout*, by Gabriel Dylan (Stripes); *The Lying Woods*, by Ashley Elston (Disney-Hyperion); *When You Trap a Tiger*, by Tae Keller (Random House); *We Speak in Storms*, by Natalie Lund (Philomel); *When We Wake*, by Elle Cosimano (HarperCollins); *Carpa Fortuna*, by Lindsay Eagar (Candlewick); *Instructions Not Included*, by Tami Lewis Brown & Debbie Loren Dunn (Disney-Hyperion); *Fake*, by Donna Cooner (Scholastic); *Unicorn Academy*, by Julie Sykes (Nosy Crow); *The Girl Who Sailed the Stars*, by Matilda Woods (Scholastic UK/Philomel US).

WRITERS CONFERENCES Bologna Children's Book Fair, ALA and SCBWI conferences, BookExpo America.

TIPS "Before submitting material, authors should visit the Greenhouse Literary Agency website and carefully read all submission guidelines."

KATHRYN GREEN LITERARY AGENCY, LLC

157 Columbus Ave., Suite 510, New York NY 10023. (212)245-4225. **E-mail:** query@kgreenagency.com. **Website:** www.kathryngreenliteraryagency.com. **Contact:** Kathy Green. Estab. 2004. Other memberships include Women's Media Group.

○ Prior to becoming an agent, Ms. Green was a book and magazine editor.

REPRESENTS Nonfiction, fiction, novels, short story collections, juvenile books. **Considers these fiction areas:** commercial, crime, detective, family saga, historical, humor, juvenile, literary, mainstream, middle grade, multicultural, mystery, police, romance, satire, suspense, thriller, women's, young adult.

☛ "Considers all types of fiction but particularly like historical fiction, cozy mysteries, young adult and middle grade. For nonfiction, I am interested in memoir, parenting, humor with a pop culture bent, and history. Quirky nonfiction is also a particular favorite." Does not want to receive science fiction, fantasy, children's picture books, screenplays, or poetry.

HOW TO CONTACT Query by e-mail. Send no attachments unless requested. Do not send queries via regular mail. Responds in 4 weeks. "Queries do not have to be exclusive; however if further material is requested, please be in touch before accepting other representation." Accepts simultaneous submissions. Obtains most new clients through recommendations from others, solicitations, conferences.

TERMS Agent receives 15% commission on domestic sales; 20% commission on foreign sales.

RECENT SALES *Jigsaw Jungle*, by Kristin Levine; *Jane, Anonymous*, by Laurie Faria, Stolarz; *To Woo a Wicked Widow, Wedding the Widow*, and *What a Widow Wants*, by Jenna Jaxon; *The Pennypackers Take a Vacation*, by Lisa Doan; *Comfort in Hard Times*, by Earl Johnson.

● GREGORY & COMPANY AUTHORS' AGENTS

David Higham Associates, Waverley House, 7–12 Noel St., London W1F 8GQ England. 020 7434 5900.

E-mail: laura@gregoryandcompany.co.uk; sara@gregoryandcompany.co.uk; info@gregoryandcompany.co.uk. **E-mail:** maryjones@gregoryandcompany.co.uk. **Website:** www.gregoryandcompany.co.uk. **Contact:** Laura Darpetti. Estab. 1987. Other memberships include AAA. Represents 60 clients.

MEMBER AGENTS Jane Gregory (English language and Film and TV sales); Claire Morris (Translation rights sales); Stephanie Glencross and Mary Jones (Editorial); Sara Langham (Editorial Assistant); Laura Darpetti (Rights Assistant).

REPRESENTS Fiction, novels. **Considers these fiction areas:** commercial, crime, detective, historical, literary, mystery, police, suspense, thriller, women's.

☛ "As a British agency, we do not generally take on American authors as there are many US based agents who would do this better!" Actively seeking well-written, accessible novels. Does not want to receive horror, science fiction, fantasy, mind/body/spirit, children's books, screenplays, plays, short stories, or poetry.

HOW TO CONTACT Submit outline of the complete plot, the first three chapters or up to 50 pages by e-mail or by post together with publishing history, and a brief author biography. Send submissions to Mary Jones, submissions editor: maryjones@gregoryandcompany.co.uk. If by post, include a SASE. Accepts simultaneous submissions. Allow 3 or 4 weeks for a response. Returns materials only with SASE. Obtains most new clients through recommendations from others.

TERMS Agent receives 15% commission on domestic sales and 20% commission on foreign sales. Offers written contract; 1-month notice must be given to terminate contract. Charges clients for photocopying of whole typescripts and copies of book for submissions.

GREYHAUS LITERARY

3021 20th St., Pl. SW, Puyallup WA 98373. **E-mail:** scott@greyhausagency.com. **E-mail:** submissions@greyhausagency.com. **Website:** www.greyhausagency.com. **Contact:** Scott Eagan, member RWA. Estab. 2003. Member of AAR. Signatory of WGA.

REPRESENTS Novels. **Considers these fiction areas:** new adult, romance, women's.

☛ Greyhaus only focuses on romance and women's fiction. Please review submission information found on the website to know exactly what Greyhaus is looking for. Stories should be 75,000-120,000 words in length or meet the word count requirements for Harlequin found on its website. Greyhaus does not deviate from these genres. Does not want fantasy, single title inspirational, young adult or middle grade, picture books, memoirs, biographies, erotica, urban fantasy, science fiction, screenplays, poetry, authors interested in only e-publishing or self-publishing.

HOW TO CONTACT Submissions to Greyhaus can be done in one of three ways: 1) A standard query letter via e-mail. If using this method, do not attach documents or send anything else other than a query letter. 2) Use the Submission Form found on the website on the Contact page. Or 3) send a query, the first 3 pages and a synopsis of no more than 3-5 pages (and a SASE), using a snail mail submission. Do not submit anything more than asked. Please also understand Greyhaus does not consider queries through social media sites. Accepts simultaneous submissions. Responds in up to 3 months.

TERMS 15%

WRITERS CONFERENCES Scott Eagan is available to assist writing chapters and organizations through conference attendance, teaching workshops, guest blogging, judging contest final rounds, online workshops and certainly listening to pitches. The agency does not make it a practice of just showing up. If you want the Scott to help out, please reach out to the agency.

JILL GRINBERG LITERARY MANAGEMENT, LLC

392 Vanderbilt Ave., Brooklyn NY 11238. (212)620-5883. **E-mail:** info@jillgrinbergliterary.com. **Website:** www.jillgrinbergliterary.com. Estab. 1999. Member of AAR.

○ Prior to her current position, Ms. Grinberg was at Anderson Grinberg Literary Management.

MEMBER AGENTS Jill Grinberg; Cheryl Pientka; Katelyn Detweiler; Sophia Seidner.

REPRESENTS Nonfiction, fiction, novels. **Considers these fiction areas:** fantasy, historical, juvenile, literary, mainstream, middle grade, multicultural, picture books, romance, science fiction, women's, young adult.

☞ "We do not accept unsolicited queries for screenplays."

HOW TO CONTACT "Please send queries via e-mail to info@jillgrinbergliterary.com–include your query letter, addressed to the agent of your choice, along with the first 50 pages of your ms pasted into the body of the e-mail or attached as a doc. or docx. file. We also accept queries via mail, though e-mail is much preferred. Please send your query letter and the first 50 pages of your ms by mail, along with a SASE, to the attention of your agent of choice. Please note that unless a SASE with sufficient postage is provided, your materials will not be returned. As submissions are shared within the office, please only query one agent with your project." Accepts simultaneous submissions.

TIPS "We prefer submissions by electronic mail."

JILL GROSJEAN LITERARY AGENCY

1390 Millstone Rd., Sag Harbor NY 11963. (631)725-7419. **E-mail:** jilllit310@aol.com. **Contact:** Jill Grosjean. Estab. 1999.

○ Prior to becoming an agent, Ms. Grosjean managed an independent bookstore. She also worked in publishing and advertising.

REPRESENTS Novels. **Considers these fiction areas:** historical, literary, mainstream, mystery, women's.

☞ Actively seeking literary novels and mysteries. Does not want serial killer, science fiction or YA novels.

HOW TO CONTACT E-mail queries preferred, no attachments. No cold calls, please. Accepts simultaneous submissions, though when manuscript requested, requires exclusive reading time. Accepts simultaneous submissions. Responds in 1 week to queries; month to mss. Obtains most new clients through recommendations and through recommendations and solicitations.

TERMS Agent receives 15% commission on domestic sales; 20% commission on foreign and film sales.

RECENT SALES *The Gold Pawn*, by L.A. Chandlar (Kensington Books); *Caught in Time*, by Julie McEwain (Pegasus Books); *A Murder in Time*, by Julie McEwain (Pegasus Books); *A Twist in Time*, by Julie McEwain (Pegasus Books); *The Silver Gun*, by LA Chandlar (Kensington Books); *The Edison Effect*, by Bernadette Pajer (Poison Pen Press); *Threading the Needle*, by Marie Bostwick (Kensington Publishing); *Tim Cratchit's Christmas Carol: A Novel of Scrooge's Legacy*, by Jim Piecuch (Simon & Schuster); *The Lighterman's Curse*, by Loretta Marion (Crooked Lane

Books); *Betrayal in Time*, by Julie McEwain (Pegasus Books); *The Strange Case of Eliza Doolittle*, by Timothy Miller (Prometheus Books).

WRITERS CONFERENCES Thrillerfest, Texas Writer's League, Book Passage Mystery's Writer's Conference, Writer's Market Conference.

LAURA GROSS LITERARY AGENCY

E-mail: assistant@lg-la.com. **Website:** www.lg-la.com. Estab. 1988. Represents 30 clients.

○ Prior to becoming an agent, Ms. Gross was an editor and ran a reading series.

MEMBER AGENTS Laura Gross; Lauren Scovel.

REPRESENTS Nonfiction, novels.

⌐ "I represent a broad range of both fiction and nonfiction writers. I am particularly interested in history, politics, and current affairs, and also love beautifully written literary fiction and intelligent thrillers."

HOW TO CONTACT Queries accepted online via online form on LGLA Submittable site. No e-mail queries. "On the submission form, please include a concise but substantive cover letter. You may include the first 6,000 words of your manuscript in the form as well. We will request further sample chapters from you at a later date, if we think your work suits our list." There may be a delay of several weeks in responding to your query. Accepts simultaneous submissions.

TERMS Agent receives 15% commission on domestic sales; 20% commission on foreign sales. Offers written contract.

HARTLINE LITERARY AGENCY

123 Queenston Dr., Pittsburgh PA 15235-5429. (412)829-2483. **E-mail:** jim@hartlineliterary.com. **Website:** www.hartlineliterary.com. **Contact:** James D. Hart. Estab. 1992. ACFW Represents 400 clients.

○ Jim Hart was a production journalist for 20 years; Joyce Hart was the Vice President of Marketing at Whitaker House Publishing.

MEMBER AGENTS Jim Hart, principal agent (jim@hartlineliterary.com); Joyce Hart, founder (joyce@hartlineliterary.com); Linda Glaz (linda@hartlineliterary.com); Cyle Young (cyle@hartlineliterary.com).

REPRESENTS Nonfiction, fiction, novels, novellas, juvenile books, scholarly books. **Considers these fiction areas:** action, adventure, commercial, contemporary issues, crime, detective, family saga, fantasy, frontier, historical, humor, inspirational, literary, mainstream, mystery, new adult, religious, romance, science fiction, suspense, thriller, urban fantasy, westerns, women's, young adult.

⌐ "This agency specializes in the Christian bookseller market." We also represent general market, but no graphic sex or language. Actively seeking adult fiction, all genres, self-help, social issues, Christian living, parenting, marriage, business, biographies, narrative nonfiction, creative nonfiction. Does not want to receive erotica, horror, graphic violence or graphic language.

HOW TO CONTACT E-mail submissions are preferred. Target one agent only. Each agent has specific interests, please refer to our web page for that information. All e-mail submissions sent to Hartline Agents should be sent as a MS Word doc attached to an e-mail with 'submission: title, authors name and word count' in the subject line. A proposal is a single document, not a collection of files. Place the query letter in the email itself. Do not send the entire proposal in the body of the e-mail. Further guidelines online. Accepts simultaneous submissions. Responds in 2 months to queries; 3 months to mss. Obtains most new clients through recommendations from others, and at conferences.

TERMS Agent receives 15% commission on domestic sales. Offers written contract.

RECENT SALES *Coral*, by Sara Ella (Thomas Nelson); *The Dating Charade*, by Melisa Ferguson (Thomas Nelson); *The Beautiful Ashes of Gomez Gomez*, by Buck Storm (Kregel); *The Mr. Rogers Effect*, by Dr. Anita Knight (Baker Books); *People Can Change*, by Dr. Mark W. Baker (Fortress); *Obedience Over Hustle*, by Malinda Fuller (Barbour); *Keller's Heart*, by John Gray, Illustrations Shanna Oblenus (Paraclete); *Create Your Yes*, by Angela Marie Hutchinson (Source Books); *Simply Spirit Filled*, by Dr. Andrew K. Gabriel (Thomas Nelson).

WRITERS CONFERENCES ACFW; Mt. Hermon Christian Writers Conference, Oregon Christian Writers; Realm Makers; Blue Ridge Mountain Christian Writers; Florida Christian Writers; Write to Publish; Mount Hermon Conference; Taylor's Professional Writing Conference; Maranatha Christian Writers Conference; Write His Answer Christian Conferences (Colorado and Philadelphia), St. Davids Christian Writers Conference

TIPS Please follow the guidelines on our web site www.hartlineliterary for the fastest response to your proposal. E-mail proposals only.

ANTONY HARWOOD LIMITED

103 Walton St., Oxford OX2 6EB United Kingdom. (44)(018)6555-9615. **E-mail:** mail@antonyharwood. com. **Website:** www.antonyharwood.com. **Contact:** Antony Harwood; James Macdonald Lockhart; Jo Williamson. Estab. 2000. Represents 52 clients.

○ Prior to starting this agency, Mr. Harwood and Mr. Lockhart worked at publishing houses and other literary agencies.

MEMBER AGENTS Antony Harwood, James Macdonald Lockhart, Jo Williamson (children's).

REPRESENTS Nonfiction, novels. **Considers these fiction areas:** action, adventure, cartoon, comic books, confession, crime, detective, erotica, ethnic, experimental, family saga, fantasy, feminist, frontier, gay, hi-lo, historical, horror, humor, lesbian, literary, mainstream, military, multicultural, multimedia, mystery, occult, picture books, plays, police, regional, religious, romance, satire, science fiction, spiritual, sports, suspense, thriller, translation, war, westerns, young adult, gothic.

HOW TO CONTACT "We are happy to consider submissions of fiction and nonfiction in every genre and category except for screenwriting and poetry. If you wish to submit your work to us for consideration, please send a covering letter, brief outline and the opening 50 pages by e-mail. If you want to post your material to us, please be sure to enclose an SAE or the cost of return postage." Replies if interested. Accepts simultaneous submissions. Responds in 2 months to queries.

TERMS Agent receives 15% commission on domestic sales; 20% commission on foreign sales.

JOHN HAWKINS & ASSOCIATES, INC.

80 Maiden Ln., Suite 1503, New York NY 10038. (212)807-7040. **E-mail:** jha@jhalit.com. **Website:** www. jhalit.com. **Contact:** Moses Cardona (rights and translations); Annie Kronenberg (permissions); Warren Frazier, literary agent; Anne Hawkins, literary agent; William Reiss, literary agent. Estab. 1893. Member of AAR. The Author Guild Represents 100+ clients.

MEMBER AGENTS Moses Cardona, moses@jhalit. com (commercial fiction, suspense, business, science, and multicultural fiction); Warren Frazier, frazier@jhalit.com (fiction; nonfiction, specifically technology, history, world affairs and foreign policy); Anne Hawkins, ahawkins@jhalit.com (thrillers to literary fiction to serious nonfiction; interested in science, history, public policy, medicine and women's issues).

REPRESENTS Nonfiction, fiction, novels, short story collections, novellas, juvenile books. **Considers these fiction areas:** commercial, historical, literary, multicultural, suspense, thriller.

HOW TO CONTACT Query. Include the word "Query" in the subject line. For fiction, include 1-3 chapters of your book as a single Word attachment. For nonfiction, include your proposal as a single attachment. E-mail a particular agent directly if you are targeting one. Accepts simultaneous submissions. Responds in 1 month to queries. Obtains most new clients through recommendations from others.

TERMS Agent receives 15% commission on domestic sales; 20% commission on foreign sales. Charges clients for photocopying.

RECENT SALES *Forty Rooms*, by Olga Grushin; *A Book of American Martyrs*, by Joyce Carol Oates; *City on Edge*, by Stefanie Pintoff; *Cold Earth*, by Ann Cleeves; *The Good Lieutenant*, by Whitney Terrell; *Grief Cottage*, by Gail Godwin.

HELEN HELLER AGENCY INC.

4-216 Heath St. W., Toronto ON M5P 1N7 Canada. (416)489-0396. **E-mail:** info@helenhelleragency.com. **Website:** www.helenhelleragency.com. **Contact:** Helen Heller. Represents 30+ clients.

○ Prior to her current position, Ms. Heller worked for Cassell & Co. (England), was an editor for Harlequin Books, a senior editor for Avon Books, and editor-in-chief for Fitzhenry & Whiteside.

MEMBER AGENTS Helen Heller, helen@helenhelleragency.com (thrillers and front-list general fiction); Sarah Heller, sarah@helenhelleragency.com (front list commercial YA and adult fiction, with a particular interest in high concept historical fiction); Barbara Berson, barbara@helenhelleragency.com (literary fiction, nonfiction, and YA).

REPRESENTS Nonfiction, novels. **Considers these fiction areas:** commercial, crime, historical, literary, mainstream, thriller, young adult.

HOW TO CONTACT E-mail info@helenhelleragency.com. Submit a brief synopsis, publishing history, author bio, and writing sample, pasted in the body of the e-mail. No attachments with e-queries. Accepts simultaneous submissions. Responds within 3 months if interested. Accepts simultaneous submissions. Obtains most new clients through recommendations from others, solicitations.

TIPS "Whether you are an author searching for an agent, or whether an agent has approached you, it is in your best interest to first find out who the agent represents, what publishing houses has that agent sold to recently and what foreign sales have been made. You should be able to go to the bookstore, or search online and find the books the agent refers to. Many authors acknowledge their agents in the front or back or their books."

HILL NADELL LITERARY AGENCY

6442 Santa Monica Blvd., Suite 201, Los Angeles CA 90038. (310)860-9605. **E-mail:** queries@hillnadell.com. **Website:** www.hillnadell.com. Represents 100 clients.

MEMBER AGENTS Bonnie Nadell (nonfiction books include works on current affairs and food as well as memoirs and other narrative nonfiction; in fiction, she represents thrillers along with upmarket women's and literary fiction); Dara Hyde (literary and genre fiction, narrative nonfiction, graphic novels, memoir and the occasional young adult novel).

REPRESENTS Nonfiction, novels. **Considers these fiction areas:** literary, mainstream, thriller, women's, young adult.

HOW TO CONTACT Send a query and SASE. If you would like your materials returned, please include adequate postage. To submit electronically: Send your query letter and the first 5-10 pages to queries@hillnadell.com. No attachments. Due to the high volume of submissions the agency receives, it cannot guarantee a response to all e-mailed queries. Accepts simultaneous submissions.

TERMS Agent receives 15% commission on domestic and film sales; 20% commission on foreign sales. Charges clients for photocopying and foreign mailings.

HOLLOWAY LITERARY

P.O. Box 771, Cary NC 27512. **E-mail:** submissions@ hollowayliteraryagency.com. **Website:** hollowayliteraryagency.com. **Contact:** Nikki Terpilowski. Estab. 2011. Member of AAR. Signatory of WGA. International Thriller Writers and Romance Writers of America Represents 26 clients.

MEMBER AGENTS Nikki Terpilowski (romance, women's fiction, Southern fiction, historical fiction, cozy mysteries, lifestyle no-fiction (minimalism, homesteading, southern, etc.) commercial, upmarket/book club fiction, African-American fiction of all types, literary); Rachel Burkot (young adult contemporary, women's fiction, upmarket/book club fiction, contemporary romance, Southern fiction, nonfiction).

REPRESENTS Nonfiction, fiction, movie scripts, feature film. **Considers these fiction areas:** action, adventure, commercial, contemporary issues, crime, detective, ethnic, family saga, fantasy, glitz, historical, inspirational, literary, mainstream, metaphysical, middle grade, military, multicultural, mystery, new adult, New Age, regional, romance, short story collections, spiritual, suspense, thriller, urban fantasy, war, women's, young adult.

☛ "Note to self-published authors: While we are happy to receive submissions from authors who have previously self-published novels, we do not represent self-published works. Send us your unpublished manuscripts only." Nikki is open to submissions and is selectively reviewing queries for cozy mysteries with culinary, historical or book/publishing industry themes written in the vein of Jaclyn Brady, Laura Childs, Julie Hyzy and Lucy Arlington; women's fiction with strong magical realism similar to Meena van Praag's *The Dress Shop of Dreams*, Sarah Addison Allen's *Garden Spells, Season of the Dragonflies* by Sarah Creech and Mary Robinette Kowal's Glamourist Series. She would love to find a wine-themed mystery series similar to Nadia Gordon's Sunny McCoskey series or Ellen Crosby's Wine County Mysteries that combine culinary themes with lots of great Southern history. Nikki is also interested in seeing contemporary romance set in the southern US or any wine county or featuring a culinary theme, dark, edgy historical romance, gritty military romance or romantic suspense with sexy Alpha heroes and lots of technical detail. She is also interested in acquiring historical fiction written in the vein of Alice Hoffman, Lalita Tademy and Isabel Allende. Nikki is also interested in espionage, military, political and AI thrillers similar to Tom Clancy, Robert Ludlum, Steve Berry, Vince Flynn, Brad Thor and Daniel Silva. Nikki has a special interest in non-fiction subjects related to governance, politics, military strategy and foreign relations; food and beverage, mindfulness, southern living and lifestyle. Does not want horror, true crime or novellas.

HOW TO CONTACT Send query and first 15 pages of ms pasted into the body of e-mail to submissions@ hollowayliteraryagency.com. In the subject header write: (Insert Agent's Name)/Title/Genre. Holloway Literary does accept submissions via mail (query letter and first 50 pages). Expect a response time of at least 3 months. Include e-mail address, phone number, social media accounts, and mailing address on your query letter. Accepts simultaneous submissions. Responds in 6-8 weeks. If the agent is interested, he/she'll respond with a request for more material.

RECENT SALES A list of recent sales are listed on the agency website's "news" page.

HSG AGENCY

37 W. 28th St., 8th Floor, New York NY 10001. **E-mail:** channigan@hsgagency.com; jsalky@hsgagency.com; jgetzler@hsgagency.com; sroberts@hsgagency.com; leigh@hsgagency.com. **Website:** hsgagency.com. **Contact:** Carrie Hannigan; Jesseca Salky; Josh Getzler; Soumeya Roberts; Julia Kardon; Rhea Lyons. Estab. 2011. Member of AAR. Signatory of WGA.

○ Prior to opening HSG Agency, Ms. Hannigan, Ms. Salky. and Mr. Getzler were agents at Russell & Volkening.

MEMBER AGENTS Carrie Hannigan (children's books, illustrators, YA and MG); Jesseca Salky (literary and mainstream fiction); Josh Getzler (foreign and historical fiction; both women's fiction, straight-ahead historical fiction, and thrillers and mysteries); Soumeya Roberts (literary fiction and narrative non-fiction); Julia Kardon (literary fiction, memoir, essays, narrative non-fiction); Rhea Lyons (commercial fiction, pop-culture, health and wellness, science fiction/fantasy).

REPRESENTS Nonfiction, fiction, novels, short story collections, juvenile books. **Considers these fiction areas:** adventure, commercial, contemporary issues, crime, detective, ethnic, experimental, family saga, fantasy, feminist, historical, humor, juvenile, literary, mainstream, middle grade, multicultural, mystery, picture books, science fiction, suspense, thriller, translation, women's, young adult.

☛ Carrie Hannigan: In the kidlit world, right now Carrie is looking for humorous books and

books with warmth, heart and a great voice in both contemporary and fantasy. She is also open to graphic novels and nonfiction. Jesseca Salky: Jesseca is looking for literary fiction submissions that are family stories (she loves a good mother/daughter tale), have a strong sense of place (where the setting feels like its own character), or a daring or unique voice (think Jamie Quatro), as well as upmarket fiction that can appeal to men and women and has that Tropper/Hornby/Matt Norman quality to it. Josh Getzler: Josh is particularly into foreign and historical fiction; both women's fiction (your Downton Abbey/Philippa Gregory Mashups), straight ahead historical fiction (think Wolf Hall or The Road to Wellville); and thrillers and mysteries (The Alienist, say; or Donna Leon or Arianna Franklin). He'd love a strong French Revolution novel. In nonfiction, he's very interested in increasing his list in history (including micro-histories), business, and political thought–but not screeds. Soumeya Roberts: In fiction, Soumeya is seeking literary and upmarket novels and collections, and also represents realistic young-adult and middle-grade. She likes books with vivid voices and compelling, well-developed story-telling, and is particularly interested in fiction that reflects on the post-colonial world and narratives by people of color. In nonfiction, she is primarily looking for idea-driven or voice-forward memoirs, personal essay collections, and approachable narrative nonfiction of all stripes. Leigh Eisenman: Leigh seeks submissions in the areas of literary and upmarket commercial fiction for adults, and is particularly drawn to: flawed protagonists she can't help but fall in love with (Holden Caulfield was her first crush); stories that take place in contemporary New York, but also any well-defined, vivid setting; explorations of relationships (including journeys of self-discovery); and of course, excellent writing. On the nonfiction side, Leigh is interested in cookbooks, food/travel-related works, health and fitness, lifestyle, humor/gift, and select narrative nonfiction. Please note that we do not represent screenplays, romance fiction, or religious fiction.

HOW TO CONTACT Please send a query letter and the first 5 pages of your ms (within the e-mail–no attachments please) to the appropriate agent for your book. If it is a picture book, please include the entire ms. If you were referred to us, please mention it in the first line of your query. Please note that we do not represent screenplays, romance fiction, or religious fiction. If Carrie and Jesseca have not responded to your query within 10 weeks of submission, please consider this a pass. All agents are open to new clients.

RECENT SALES *A Spool of Blue Thread*, by Anne Tyler (Knopf); *Blue Sea Burning*, by Geoff Rodkey (Putnam); *The Partner Track,* by Helen Wan (St. Martin's Press); *The Thrill of the Haunt*, by E.J. Copperman (Berkley); *Aces Wild*, by Erica Perl (Knopf Books for Young Readers); *Steve & Wessley: The Sea Monster*, by Jennifer Morris (Scholastic); *Infinite Worlds*, by Michael Soluri (Simon & Schuster).

⊘ ICM PARTNERS

65 E. 55th St., New York NY 10022. (212)556-5600. **E-mail:** careersny@icmpartners.com. **Website:** www. icmtalent.com. **Contact:** Literary Department. Member of AAR. Signatory of WGA.

REPRESENTS Nonfiction, fiction, novels.

HOW TO CONTACT Accepts simultaneous submissions.

INKLINGS LITERARY AGENCY

3419 Virginia Beach Blvd. #183, Virginia Beach VA 23452. **E-mail:** michelle@inklingsliterary.com. **E-mail:** query@inklingsliterary.com. **Website:** www. inklingsliterary.com. Estab. 2013. RWA, SinC, HRW.

○ "We offer our clients interactive representation for their work, as well as developmental guidance for their author platforms, working with them as they grow. With backgrounds in book selling, business, marketing, publicity, contract negotiation, as well as editing and writing, and script work, we work closely with our clients to build their brands and their careers." The face of publishing is ever-changing, and bending and shifting with the times and staying ahead of the curve are key for Michelle and her agency, Inklings Literary Agency. The agents of Inklings Literary Agency all strictly adhere to the AAR's code of ethics.

MEMBER AGENTS Michelle Johnson, michelle@inklingsliterary.com (in adult and YA fiction, contemporary, suspense, thriller, mystery, horror, fantasy — including paranormal and supernatural elements within those genres), romance of every level, nonfiction in the areas of memoir and true crime); Dr. Jamie Bodnar Drowley, jamie@inklingsliterary.com (new adult fiction in the areas of romance [all subgenres], fantasy [urban fantasy, light sci-fi, steampunk], mystery and thrillers—as well as young adult [all subgenres] and middle grade stories); Naomi Davis, naomi@inklingsliterary.com (romance of any variety—including paranormal, fresh urban fantasy, general fantasy, new adult and light sci-fi; young adult in any of those same genres; memoirs about living with disabilities, facing criticism, and mental illness); Whitley Abell, whitley@inklingsliterary.com (young adult, middle grade, and select upmarket women's fiction); Alex Barba, alex@inklingsliterary.com (YA fiction).

REPRESENTS Nonfiction, fiction, novels, juvenile books. **Considers these fiction areas:** action, adventure, commercial, contemporary issues, crime, detective, erotica, ethnic, fantasy, feminist, gay, historical, horror, juvenile, lesbian, mainstream, metaphysical, middle grade, military, multicultural, multimedia, mystery, new adult, New Age, occult, paranormal, police, psychic, regional, romance, science fiction, spiritual, sports, supernatural, suspense, thriller, urban fantasy, war, women's, young adult.

HOW TO CONTACT E-queries only. To query, type "Query (Agent Name)" plus the title of your novel in the subject line, then please send your query letter, short synopsis, and first 10 pages pasted into the body of the e-mail to query@inklingsliterary.com. Check the agency website to make sure that your targeted agent is currently open to submissions. Accepts simultaneous submissions. For queries, no response in 3 months is considered a rejection.

TERMS Agent takes 15% domestic, 20% subsidiary commission. Charges no fees.

INKWELL MANAGEMENT, LLC

521 Fifth Ave., Suite 2600, New York NY 10175. (212)922-3500. **Fax:** (212)922-0535. **E-mail:** info@inkwellmanagement.com. **E-mail:** submissions@inkwellmanagement.com. **Website:** www.inkwellmanagement.com. Represents 500 clients.

MEMBER AGENTS Stephen Barbara (select adult fiction and nonfiction); William Callahan (nonfiction of all stripes, especially American history and memoir, pop culture and illustrated books, as well as voice-driven fiction that stands out from the crowd);

Michael V. Carlisle; Catherine Drayton (bestselling authors of books for children, young adults and women readers); David Forrer (literary, commercial, historical and crime fiction to suspense/thriller, humorous nonfiction and popular history); Alexis Hurley (literary and commercial fiction, memoir, narrative nonfiction and more); Nathaniel Jacks (memoir, narrative nonfiction, social sciences, health, current affairs, business,religion, and popular history, as well as fiction—literary and commercial, women's, young adult, historical, short story, among others); Jacqueline Murphy; (fiction, children's books, graphic novels and illustrated works, and compelling narrative nonfiction); Richard Pine; Eliza Rothstein (literary and commercial fiction, narrative nonfiction, memoir, popular science, and food writing); David Hale Smith; Kimberly Witherspoon; Jenny Witherell; Charlie Olson; Liz Parker (commercial and upmarket women's fiction and narrative, practical, and platform-driven nonfiction); George Lucas; Lyndsey Blessing; Claire Draper; Kate Falkoff; Claire Friedman; Michael Mungiello; Jessica Mileo; Corinne Sullivan; Maria Whelan.

REPRESENTS Novels. **Considers these fiction areas:** commercial, crime, historical, literary, middle grade, picture books, romance, short story collections, suspense, thriller, women's, young adult.

HOW TO CONTACT "In the body of your e-mail, please include a query letter and a short writing sample (1-2 chapters). We currently accept submissions in all genres except screenplays. Due to the volume of queries we receive, our response time may take up to 2 months. Feel free to put 'Query for [Agent Name]: [Your Book Title]' in the e-mail subject line." Accepts simultaneous submissions. Obtains most new clients through recommendations from others.

TERMS Agent receives 15% commission on domestic sales; 20% commission on foreign sales. Offers written contract.

TIPS "We will not read mss before receiving a letter of inquiry."

INTERNATIONAL TRANSACTIONS, INC.

P.O. Box 97, Gila NM 88038-0097. (845)373-9696. E-mail: Info@internationaltransactions.us. **Website:** www.intltrans.com. **Contact:** Peter Riva. Estab. 1975.

MEMBER AGENTS Peter Riva with Sandra Riva (part-time); JoAnn Collins (women's fiction, medical fiction).

REPRESENTS Nonfiction, fiction, novels, short story collections, juvenile books, scholarly books. , illustrated books, anthologies. **Considers these fiction areas:** action, adventure, commercial, crime, detective, erotica, experimental, family saga, feminist, gay, historical, humor, inspirational, lesbian, literary, mainstream, middle grade, military, multicultural, mystery, new adult, picture books, police, satire, science fiction, spiritual, sports, suspense, thriller, translation, war, westerns, women's, young adult, chick lit.

☛ "We specialize in large and small projects, helping qualified authors perfect material for publication." Actively seeking intelligent, well-written innovative material that breaks new ground. Authors of non-fiction must have an active and wide-reaching platform to help promote their work (since publishers rarely work at that any more). Does not want to receive material influenced by TV (too much dialogue); a rehash of previous successful novels' themes, or poorly prepared material. Does not want to be sent any material being reviewed by others.

HOW TO CONTACT In 2018, we will be extremely selective of new projects. First, e-query with an outline or synopsis. E-queries only. Put "Query: [Title]" in the e-mail subject line. Submissions or emails received without these conditions met are automatically discarded. Responds in 3 weeks to queries if interested; 5 weeks to ms after follow-up request. Obtains most new clients through recommendations from others.

TERMS Agent receives 15% (25%+ on illustrated books) commission on domestic sales; 20% commission on foreign sales and media rights. Offers written contract; 100-day notice must be given to terminate contract. No additional fees, ever.

RECENT SALES Averaging 20+ book placements per year.

TIPS "'Book'—a published work of literature. That last word is the key. Not a string of words, not a book of (TV or film) 'scenes,' and never a stream of consciousness unfathomable by anyone outside of the writer's coterie. A writer should only begin to get 'interested in getting an agent' if the work is polished, literate and ready to be presented to a publishing house. Anything less is either asking for a quick rejection or is a thinly disguised plea for creative assistance—which is often given but never fiscally sound for the agents involved. Writers, even published authors, have difficulty in being objective about their own work. Friends and family are of no assistance in that process either. Writers should attempt to get their work read by the most unlikely and stern critic as part of the editing process, months before any agent is approached. In another matter: the economics of our job have changed as well. As the publishing world goes through the transition to e-books (much as the music industry went through the change to downloadable music)—a transition we expect to see at 95% within 10 years—everyone is nervous and wants 'assured bestsellers' from which to eke out a living until they know what the new e-world will continue to bring. This makes the sales rate and, especially, the advance royalty rates, plummet. Hence, our ability to take risks and take on new clients' work is increasingly perilous financially for us and all agents."

JABBERWOCKY LITERARY AGENCY

49 W. 45th St., 12th Floor, New York NY 10036. **Website:** www.awfulagent.com. **Contact:** Joshua Bilmes. Estab. 1990. Other memberships include SFWA. Represents 80 clients.

MEMBER AGENTS Joshua Bilmes; Eddie Schneider; Lisa Rodgers. Brady McReynolds.

REPRESENTS Nonfiction, fiction, novels, novellas, juvenile books. **Considers these fiction areas:** action, adventure, contemporary issues, crime, detective, ethnic, family saga, fantasy, feminist, gay, glitz, historical, horror, humor, juvenile, lesbian, literary, mainstream, middle grade, mystery, new adult, paranormal, police, psychic, regional, romance, satire, science fiction, sports, supernatural, thriller, women's, young adult.

☛ This agency represents quite a lot of genre fiction (science fiction & fantasy), romance, and mystery; and is actively seeking to increase the amount of nonfiction projects. It does not handle children's or picture books. Book-length material and novellas only—no poetry, articles, or short fiction.

HOW TO CONTACT "We are currently open to unsolicited queries. No e-mail, phone, or fax queries, please. Query with SASE. Please check our website, as there may be times during the year when we are not accepting queries. Query letter only; no manuscript material unless requested." Accepts simultaneous submissions. Responds in 3-6 weeks to queries. Obtains most new clients through solicitations, recommendation by current clients.

TERMS Agent receives 15% commission on domestic sales; 20% commission on foreign sales. Offers written contract, binding for 1 year. Charges clients for book purchases, photocopying, international book/ms mailing.

RECENT SALES *Alcatraz #5* by Brandon Sanderson; *Aurora Teagarden*, by Charlaine Harris; *The Unnoticeables*, by Robert Brockway; *Messenger's Legacy*, by Peter V. Brett; *Slotter Key*, by Elizabeth Moon. Other clients include Tanya Huff, Simon Green, Jack Campbell, Myke Cole, Marie Brennan, Daniel Jose Older, Jim Hines, Mark Hodder, Toni Kelner, Ari Marmell, Ellery Queen, Erin Tettensor, and Walter Jon Williams.

TIPS "In approaching with a query, the most important things to us are your credits and your biographical background to the extent it's relevant to your work. I (and most agents) will ignore the adjectives you may choose to describe your own work."

JANKLOW & NESBIT ASSOCIATES

285 Madison Ave., 21st Floor, New York NY 10017. (212)421-1700. **Fax:** (212)355-1403. **E-mail:** info@janklow.com. **E-mail:** submissions@janklow.com. **Website:** www.janklowandnesbit.com. Estab. 1989.

MEMBER AGENTS Morton L. Janklow; Anne Sibbald; Lynn Nesbit; Luke Janklow; PJ Mark (interests are eclectic, including short stories and literary novels. His nonfiction interests include journalism, popular culture, memoir/narrative, essays and cultural criticism); Paul Lucas (literary and commercial fiction, focusing on literary thrillers, science fiction and fantasy; also seeks narrative histories of ideas and objects, as well as biographies and popular science); Emma Parry (nonfiction by experts, but will consider outstanding literary fiction and upmarket commercial fiction); Kirby Kim (formerly of WME); Marya Spence; Allison Hunter; Melissa Flashman; Stefanie Lieberman.

REPRESENTS Nonfiction, fiction.

HOW TO CONTACT Be sure to address your submission to a particular agent. For fiction submissions, send an informative cover letter, a brief synopsis and the first 10 pages. "If you are sending an e-mail submission, please include the sample pages in the body of the e-mail below your query. For nonfiction submissions, send an informative cover letter, a full outline, and the first 10 pages of the ms. If you are sending an e-mail submission, please include the sample pages in the body of the e-mail below your query. For picture book submissions, send an informative cover letter, full outline, and include a picture book dummy and at least one full-color sample. If you are sending an e-mail submission, please attach a picture book dummy as a PDF and the full-color samples as JPEGs or PDFs." Accepts simultaneous submissions. Due to the volume of submissions received, please note that we cannot respond to every query. We shall contact you if we wish to pursue your submission. Obtains most new clients through recommendations from others.

TIPS "Please send a short query with first 10 pages or artwork."

J DE S ASSOCIATES, INC.

9 Shagbark Rd., Norwalk CT 06854. (203)838-7571. **Fax:** (203)866-2713. **E-mail:** jdespoel@aol.com. **Website:** www.jdesassociates.com. **Contact:** Jacques de Spoelberch. Estab. 1975.

○ Prior to opening his agency, Mr. de Spoelberch was an editor with Houghton Mifflin. And launched International Literary Management for the International Management Group.

REPRESENTS Novels. **Considers these fiction areas:** crime, detective, frontier, historical, juvenile, literary, mainstream, mystery, New Age, police, suspense, westerns, young adult.

HOW TO CONTACT "Brief queries by regular mail and e-mail are welcomed for fiction and nonfiction, but kindly do not include sample proposals or other material unless specifically requested to do so." Accepts simultaneous submissions. Responds in 2 months to queries. Obtains most new clients through recommendations from authors and other clients.

TERMS Agent receives 15% commission on domestic sales; 20% commission on foreign sales. Charges clients for foreign postage and photocopying.

RECENT SALES Joshilyn Jackson's new novel *A Grown-Up Kind of Pretty* (Grand Central); Margaret George's final Tudor historical *Elizabeth I* (Penguin); the fifth in Leighton Gage's series of Brazilian thrillers *A Vine in the Blood* (Soho); Genevieve Graham's romance *Under the Same Sky* (Berkley Sensation); Hilary Holladay's biography of the early Beat Herbert Huncke, *American Hipster* (Magnus); Ron Rozelle's *My Boys and Girls Are In There: The 1937 New London School Explosion* (Texas A&M); the concluding novel in Dom Testa's YA science fiction series, *The Galahad Legacy* (Tor); and Bruce Coston's new collection of animal stories *The Gift of Pets* (St. Martin's Press).

THE CAROLYN JENKS AGENCY

30 Cambridge Park Dr. Unit 3140, Cambridge MA 02140. (617)233-9130. **E-mail:** carolynjenks@comcast. net. **Website:** www.carolynjenksagency.com. **Contact:** Carolyn Jenks. Estab. 1987. Signatory of WGA. Represents 39 clients.

○ Began publishing career working at Scribner's Subsidiary Rights Dept., managing editor Ballantine Books, Literary agent subcontractor William Morris Agency, Partner Kurt Hellmer LIterary Agency. established Jenks Agency in NYC in the 1970's.

REPRESENTS Nonfiction, fiction, novels, short story collections, novellas, feature film, TV movie of the week, documentary, miniseries. **Considers these fiction areas:** contemporary issues, crime, detective, family saga, feminist, gay, historical, literary, mainstream, mystery, short story collections, thriller.

HOW TO CONTACT Please submit a one page query including a brief bio via the form on the agency website. Queries are reviewed on a rolling basis, and we will follow up directly with the author if there is interest. No cold calls.

TERMS Offers written contract, 1-3 years depending on the project. Standard agency commissions. No fees.

RECENT SALES *Snafu, The Land of Forgotten Girls*, by Erin Kelly, Harper Collins; *The Christos Mosaic*, by Vincent Czyz, Blank Slate Press; *A Tale of Two Maidens*, by Anne Echols, Bagwyn Books; *Esther, Magnolia City*, by Duncan Alderson, Kensington Books; *Create My Heart*, Pamela Rivers; *Silo*, by Kate McCamy; *New Circle Theatre, Until The Iris Bloom*, Tina Olton; *American Ghosts*, Edward Santella; *The Ostermann House*, John R. Klein.

WRITERS CONFERENCES Book Club appearance Womens' Writing and The Red Tent, by Anita Diamant. The Villages, Florida.

TIPS E-mail contact only. Do not query for more than one property at a time. Response within two weeks unless otherwise notified.

JET LITERARY ASSOCIATES

941 Calle Mejia, #507, Santa Fe NM 87501. (505)780-0721. **E-mail:** etp@jetliterary.com. **Website:** www. jetliterary.wordpress.com. **Contact:** Liz Trupin-Pulli. Estab. 1975.

MEMBER AGENTS Liz Trupin-Pulli (adult fiction/nonfiction; romance, mysteries, parenting); Jim Trupin (adult fiction/nonfiction, military history, pop culture).

REPRESENTS Nonfiction, fiction, novels, short story collections.

☛ "JET was founded in New York in 1975, so we bring a wealth of knowledge and contacts, as well as quite a bit of expertise to our representation of writers." JET represents the full range of adult fiction and nonfiction. Does not want to receive YA, sci-fi, fantasy, horror, poetry, children's, how-to, illustrated or religious books.

HOW TO CONTACT Only an e-query should be sent at first. Accepts simultaneous submissions. Responds in 1 week to queries; 8-12 weeks to mss. Obtains most new clients through recommendations from others, solicitations, conferences.

TERMS Agent receives 15% commission on domestic sales; 10% commission on foreign sales, while foreign agent receives 10%. Offers written agency contract, binding for 3 years. This agency charges for reimbursement of mailing and any photocopying.

TIPS "Do not write cute queries; stick to a straightforward message that includes the title and what your book is about, why you are suited to write this particular book, and what you have written in the past (if anything), along with a bit of a bio."

⊘ NATASHA KERN LITERARY AGENCY

White Salmon WA 98672. **E-mail:** via website. **Website:** www.natashakern.com. **Contact:** Natasha Kern. Estab. 1986. Other memberships include RWA, MWA, SinC, The Authors Guild, and American Society of Journalists and Authors. Represents 40 clients.

○ Prior to opening her agency, Ms. Kern worked in publishing in New York. This agency has sold more than 1,500 books.

REPRESENTS Fiction, novels. **Considers these fiction areas:** commercial, historical, inspirational, mainstream, multicultural, mystery, romance, suspense, women's, Only Inspirational fiction in these genres.

☛ "This agency specializes in inspirational fiction." Inspirational fiction in a broad range of genres including: suspense and mysteries, historicals, romance, and contemporary novels. By referral only. Does not represent horror, true crime, erotica, children's books, short stories or novellas, poetry, screenplays, technical, photography or art/craft books, cookbooks, travel, or sports books. No nonfiction.

HOW TO CONTACT This agency is currently closed to unsolicited fiction and nonfiction submissions. Submissions only via referral. Obtains new clients by referral only.

TERMS Agent receives 15% commission on domestic sales; 20% commission on foreign sales; 15% commission on film sales.

WRITERS CONFERENCES RWA National Conference; ACFW Conference.

TIPS "Your chances of being accepted for representation will be greatly enhanced by going to our website first. Our idea of a dream client is someone who participates in a mutually respectful business relationship, is clear about needs and goals, and communicates about career planning. If we know what you need and want, we can help you achieve it. A dream client has a storytelling gift, a commitment to a writing career, a desire to learn and grow, and a passion for excellence. We want clients who are expressing their own unique voice and truly have something of their own to communicate. This client understands that many people have to work together for a book to succeed and that everything in publishing takes far longer than one imagines. Trust and communication are truly essential."

HARVEY KLINGER, INC.

300 W. 55th St., Suite 11V, New York NY 10019. (212)581-7068. **E-mail:** queries@harveyklinger.com. **Website:** www.harveyklinger.com. **Contact:** Harvey Klinger. Estab. 1977. Member of AAR. PEN Represents 100 clients.

MEMBER AGENTS Harvey Klinger, harvey@harveyklinger.com; David Dunton, david@harveyklinger.com (popular culture, music-related books, literary fiction, young adult, fiction, and memoirs); Andrea Somberg, andrea@harveyklinger.com (literary fiction, commercial fiction, romance, sci-fi/fantasy, mysteries/thrillers, young adult, middle grade, quality narrative nonfiction, popular culture, how-to, self-help, humor, interior design, cookbooks, health/fitness); Wendy Silbert Levinson, wendy@harveyklinger.com (literary and commercial fiction, occasional children's YA or MG, wide variety of nonfiction); Rachel Ridout, rachel@harveyklinger.com (children's MG and YA).

REPRESENTS Nonfiction, fiction, novels, juvenile books. **Considers these fiction areas:** action, adventure, commercial, contemporary issues, crime, detective, erotica, family saga, fantasy, gay, glitz, historical, horror, juvenile, lesbian, literary, mainstream, middle grade, mystery, new adult, police, romance, suspense, thriller, women's, young adult.

☛ This agency specializes in big, mainstream, contemporary fiction and nonfiction. Great debut or established novelists and in nonfiction, authors with great ideas and a national platform already in place to help promote one's book. No screenplays, poetry, textbooks or anything too technical.

HOW TO CONTACT Use online e-mail submission form on the website, or query with SASE via snail mail. No phone or fax queries. Don't send unsolicited mss or e-mail attachments. Make submission letter to the point and as brief as possible. A bit of biographical information is always welcome, particularly with non-fiction submissions where one's national platform is vitally important. Accepts simultaneous submissions. Responds in 2-4 weeks to queries, if interested. Obtains most new clients through recommendations from others.

TERMS Agent receives 15% commission on domestic sales; 25% commission on foreign sales. Offers written contract. Charges for photocopying mss and overseas postage for mss.

RECENT SALES *The Far River*, by Barbara Wood; *I Am Not a Serial Killer*, by Dan Wells; *Me, Myself and Us*, by Brian Little; *The Secret of Magic*, by Deborah Johnson; *Children of the Mist*, by Paula Quinn. Other clients include George Taber, Terry Kay, Scott Mebus, Jacqueline Kolosov, Jonathan Maberry, Tara Altebrando, Alex McAuley, Eva Nagorski, Greg Kot, Justine Musk, Michael Northrup, Nina LaCour, Ashley Kahn, Barbara De Angelis, Robert Patton, Augusta Trobaugh, Deborah Blum, Jonathan Skariton.

KNEERIM & WILLIAMS

90 Canal St., Boston MA 02114. **Website:** www.kwlit. com. Also located in Santa Fe, NM, with affiliated office in NYC. Estab. 1990.

◯ Prior to becoming an agent, Mr. Williams was a lawyer; Ms. Kneerim was a publisher and editor; Ms. Flynn was pursuing a Ph.D. in history; Ms. Savarese was a publishing executive.

MEMBER AGENTS Katherine Flynn, kflynn@kwlit.com (history, biography, politics, current affairs, adventure, nature, pop culture, science, and psychology for nonfiction and particularly loves exciting narrative nonfiction; literary and commercial fiction with urban or foreign locales, crime novels, insight into women's lives, biting wit, and historical settings); Jill Kneerim, jill@kwlit.com (narrative history; big ideas; sociology; psychology and anthropology; biography; women's issues; and good writing); John Taylor ("Ike") Williams, jtwilliams@kwblit.com (biography, history, politics, natural science, and anthropology); Carol Franco, carolfranco@comcast.net (business; nonfiction; distinguished self-help/how-to); Lucy Cleland, lucy@kwlit.com (literary/commercial fiction, Y/A novels, history, narrative); Carolyn Savarese, carolyn@kwlit.com (riveting narratives in science, technology and medicine; unknown history; big think subjects; memoir; lifestyle and design, literary fiction and short stories); Hope Denekamp (agency manager); Emma Hamilton (literary fiction).

☛ Actively seeking distinguished authors, experts, professionals, intellectuals, and serious writers.

HOW TO CONTACT E-query an individual agent. Send no attachments. Put "Query" in the subject line. Accepts simultaneous submissions. Obtains most new clients through recommendations from others.

THE KNIGHT AGENCY

232 W. Washington St., Madison GA 30650. **E-mail:** deidre.knight@knightagency.net. **E-mail:** submissions@knightagency.net. **Website:** http://knightagency.net/. **Contact:** Deidre Knight. Estab. 1996. Member of AAR. SCWBI, WFA, SFWA, RWA Represents 200+ clients.

MEMBER AGENTS Deidre Knight (romance, women's fiction, erotica, commercial fiction, inspirational, m/m fiction, memoir and nonfiction narrative, personal finance, true crime, business, popular culture, self-help, religion, and health); Pamela Harty (romance, women's fiction, young adult, business, motivational, diet and health, memoir, parenting, pop culture, and true crime); Elaine Spencer (romance (single title and category), women's fiction, commercial "book-club" fiction, cozy mysteries, young adult and middle grade material); Lucienne Diver (fantasy, science fiction, romance, suspense and young adult); Nephele Tempest (literary/commercial fiction, women's fiction, fantasy, science fiction, romantic suspense, paranormal romance, contemporary romance, historical fiction, young adult and middle grade fiction); Melissa Jeglinski (romance [contemporary, category, historical, inspirational], young adult, middle grade, women's fiction and mystery); Kristy Hunter (romance, women's fiction, commercial fiction, young adult and middle grade material), Travis Pennington (young adult, middle grade, mysteries, thrillers, commercial fiction, and romance [nothing paranormal/fantasy in any genre for now]); Janna Bonikowski (romance, women's fiction, young adult, cozy mystery, upmarket fiction).

REPRESENTS Nonfiction, fiction, novels. **Considers these fiction areas:** commercial, crime, erotica, fantasy, gay, historical, juvenile, lesbian, literary, mainstream, middle grade, multicultural, mystery, new adult, paranormal, psychic, romance, science fiction, thriller, urban fantasy, women's, young adult.

☛ Actively seeking Romance in all subgenres, including romantic suspense, paranormal romance, historical romance (a particular love of mine), LGBT, contemporary, and also category romance. Occasionally I represent new adult. I'm also seeking women's fiction with vivid voices, and strong concepts (think me before you). Further seeking YA and MG, and select nonfiction in the categories of personal development, self-help, finance/business, memoir, parenting and health. Does not want to receive screenplays, short stories, poetry, essays, or children's picture books.

HOW TO CONTACT E-queries only. "Your submission should include a one page query letter and the first five pages of your manuscript. All text must be contained in the body of your e-mail. Attachments will not be opened nor included in the consideration of your work. Queries must be addressed to a specific agent. Please do not query multiple agents." Accepts simultaneous submissions. Responds in 1-2 weeks on queries, 6-8 weeks on submissions.

TERMS 15% Simple agency agreement with open-ended commitment. 15% commission on all domestic sales, 20% on foreign and film.

STUART KRICHEVSKY LITERARY AGENCY, INC.

6 E. 39th St., Suite 500, New York NY 10016. (212)725-5288. **Fax:** (212)725-5275. **Website:** www.skagency.com. Member of AAR.

MEMBER AGENTS Stuart Krichevsky, query@skagency.com (emphasis on narrative nonfiction, literary journalism and literary and commercial fiction); Ross Harris, rhquery@skagency.com (voice-driven humor and memoir, books on popular culture and our society,

narrative nonfiction and literary fiction); David Patterson, dpquery@skagency.com (writers of upmarket narrative nonfiction and literary fiction, historians, journalists and thought leaders); Mackenzie Brady Watson, mbwquery@skagency.com (narrative nonfiction, science, history, sociology, investigative journalism, food, business, memoir, and select up-market and literary YA fiction); Hannah Schwartz, hsquery@skagency; Laura Usselman, luquery@skagency.com; Melissa Danaczko; Laura Usselman; Aemilia Phillips.

REPRESENTS Nonfiction, novels. **Considers these fiction areas:** commercial, contemporary issues, literary, young adult.

HOW TO CONTACT Please send a query letter and the first few (up to 10) pages of your ms or proposal in the body of an e-mail (not an attachment) to one of the e-mail addresses. No attachments. Responds if interested. Accepts simultaneous submissions. Obtains most new clients through recommendations from others, solicitations.

KT LITERARY, LLC

9249 S. Broadway, #200-543, Highlands Ranch CO 80129. **E-mail:** contact@ktliterary.com. **E-mail:** katequery@ktliterary.com, saraquery@ktliterary.com, reneequery@ktliterary.com, hannahquery@ktliterary.com, hilaryquery@ktliterary.com. **Website:** www.ktliterary.com. **Contact:** Kate Schafer Testerman, Sara Megibow, Renee Nyen, Hannah Fergesen, Hilary Harwell. Estab. 2008. Member of AAR. Other agency memberships include SCBWI, YALSA, ALA, SFWA and RWA. Represents 75 clients.

MEMBER AGENTS Kate Testerman (middle grade and young adult); Renee Nyen (middle grade and young adult); Sara Megibow (middle grade, young adult, romance, science fiction and fantasy); Hannah Fergesen (middle grade, young adult and speculative fiction); and Hilary Harwell (middle grade and young adult). Always LGBTQ and diversity friendly!.

REPRESENTS Fiction. **Considers these fiction areas:** fantasy, middle grade, romance, science fiction, young adult.

☛ Kate is looking only at young adult and middle grade fiction, especially #OwnVoices, and selective nonfiction for teens and tweens. Sara seeks authors in middle grade, young adult, romance, science fiction, and fantasy. Renee is looking for young adult and middle grade fiction only. Hannah is interested in speculative fiction in young adult, middle grade, and adult. Hilary is looking for young adult and middle grade fiction only. "We're thrilled to be actively seeking new clients with great writing, unique stories, and complex characters, for middle grade, young adult, and adult fiction. We are especially interested in diverse voices." Does not want adult mystery, thrillers, or adult literary fiction.

HOW TO CONTACT "To query us, please select one of the agents at kt literary at a time. If we pass, you can feel free to submit to another. Please e-mail your query letter and the first 3 pages of your manuscript in the body of the e-mail to either Kate at katequery@ktliterary.com, Sara at saraquery@ktliterary.com, Renee at reneequery@ktliterary.com, Hannah at hannahquery@ktliterary.com, or Hilary at hilaryquery@ktliterary.com. The subject line of your e-mail should include the word 'Query' along with the title of your manuscript. Queries should not contain attachments. Attachments will not be read, and queries containing attachments will be deleted unread. We aim to reply to all queries within 4 weeks of receipt. For examples of query letters, please feel free to browse the About My Query archives on the KT Literary website. In addition, if you're an author who is sending a new query, but who previously submitted a novel to us for which we requested chapters but ultimately declined, please do say so in your query letter. If we like your query, we'll ask for the first 5 chapters and a complete synopsis. For our purposes, the synopsis should include the full plot of the book including the conclusion. Don't tease us. Thanks! We are not accepting snail mail queries or queries by phone at this time. We also do not accept pitches on social media." Accepts simultaneous submissions. Responds in 2-4 weeks to queries; 2 months to mss. Obtains most new clients through query slush pile.

TERMS Agent receives 15% commission on domestic sales; 20% commission on foreign sales. Offers written contract; 30-day notice must be given to terminate contract.

RECENT SALES *Most Likely*, by Sarah Watson, *All of Us With Wings*, by Michelle Ruiz Keil, *Postcards for a Songbird*, by Rebekah Crane, *The Tourist Trap*, by Sarah Morgenthaler, *The Last Year of James and Kat*, by Amy Spalding, and many more. A full list of clients and most recent sales are available on the agency website and some recent sales are available on Publishers Marketplace.

WRITERS CONFERENCES Various SCBWI conferences, ALA, BookExpo, Bologna, RWA, WonderCon, ComicCon.

THE LA LITERARY AGENCY

1264 North Hayworth Ave., Los Angeles CA 90046. (323)654-5288. **E-mail:** maureen@laliteraryagency.com. **E-mail:** ann@laliteraryagency.com. **Website:** www.laliteraryagency.com; www.labookeditor.com. **Contact:** Ann Cashman.

Prior to becoming an agent, Eric Lasher worked in broadcasting and publishing in New York and Los Angeles. Prior to opening the agency, Maureen Lasher worked in New York at Prentice-Hall, Liveright, and Random House. Please visit our websites for more information.

MEMBER AGENTS Ann Cashman, Eric Lasher, Maureen Lasher.

REPRESENTS Nonfiction, fiction, novels. **Considers these fiction areas:** action, adventure, commercial, confession, contemporary issues, crime, detective, family saga, feminist, historical, literary, mainstream, mystery, sports, suspense, thriller, war, westerns, women's.

HOW TO CONTACT Nonfiction: query letter and book proposal. Fiction: query letter and full ms as an attachment. Accepts simultaneous submissions.

RECENT SALES *The Fourth Trimester*, by Susan Brink (University of California Press); *Rebels in Paradise*, by Hunter Drohojowska-Philp (Holt); *La Cucina Mexicana*, by Marilyn Tausend (UC Press); *The Orpheus Clock*, by Simon Goodman (Scribner). Please visit the agency website for more information.

PETER LAMPACK AGENCY, INC.

The Empire State Building, 350 Fifth Ave., Suite 5300, New York NY 10118. (212)687-9106. **Fax:** (212)687-9109. **E-mail:** andrew@peterlampackagency.com. **Website:** www.peterlampackagency.com. **Contact:** Andrew Lampack.

REPRESENTS Nonfiction, fiction, novels. **Considers these fiction areas:** action, adventure, commercial, crime, detective, literary, mainstream, mystery, police, suspense, thriller.

"This agency specializes in commercial fiction, and nonfiction by recognized experts." Actively seeking literary and commercial fiction in the following categories: adventure, action, thrillers, mysteries, suspense, and psychological thrillers. Does not want to receive horror, romance, science fiction, westerns, historical literary fiction, or academic material.

HOW TO CONTACT The Peter Lampack Agency no longer accepts material through conventional mail. E-queries only. When submitting, you should include a cover letter, author biography and a 1 or 2 page synopsis. Please do not send more than 1 sample chapter of your ms at a time. "Due to the extremely high volume of submissions, we ask that you allow 4-6 weeks for a response." Obtains most new clients through referrals made by clients.

TERMS Agent receives 15% commission on domestic sales; 20% commission on foreign sales.

RECENT SALES *The Gray Ghost*, by Clive Cussler and Robin Burcell; *Celtic Empire*, by Clive Cussler and Dirk Cussler; *Shadow Tyrants*, by Clive Cussler and Boyd Morrison; *The Rising Sea*, by Clive Cussler and Graham Brown; *Court of Lies*, by Gerry Spence; *Late Essays*, by J.M. Coetzee.

WRITERS CONFERENCES BookExpo America; Mystery Writers of America.

TIPS "Submit only your best work for consideration. Have a very specific agenda of goals you wish your prospective agent to accomplish for you. Provide the agent with a comprehensive statement of your credentials—educational and professional accomplishments."

THE STEVE LAUBE AGENCY

24 W. Camelback Rd., A-635, Phoenix AZ 85013. **E-mail:** krichards@stevelaube.com. **Website:** www.stevelaube.com. Estab. 2004. Represents 330+ clients.

○ Prior to becoming an agent, Mr. Laube worked over a decade as a Christian bookseller (honored as bookstore of the year in the industry) and 11 years as editorial director of nonfiction with Bethany House Publishers (named editor of the year). Also named Agent of the Year in 2009. Mrs. Murray was an accomplished novelist before becoming an agent. She was also named Agent of the Year in 2017. Mr. Hostetler is also an accomplished author with over 50 books in print. Mr. Umstattd has over a decade of internet marketing experience and is an expert in brand management. Combined the agency has over 100 years of experience in the industry.

MEMBER AGENTS Steve Laube (president), Tamela Hancock Murray, Bob Hostetler, Thomas Umstattd, Jr.

REPRESENTS Nonfiction, fiction, novels. **Considers these fiction areas:** inspirational, religious, Christian.

➤ Primarily serves the Christian market (CBA). Actively seeking Christian fiction and Christian nonfiction. Does not want to receive poetry or cookbooks.

HOW TO CONTACT Consult website for guidelines, because queries are sent to assistants, and the assistants' e-mail addresses may change. Submit proposal package, outline, 3 sample chapters, SASE. For e-mail submissions, attach as Word doc or PDF. Accepts simultaneous submissions. Responds in 6-8 weeks to queries. Obtains most new clients through recommendations from others, solicitations, conferences.

TERMS Agent receives 15% commission on domestic sales; 20% commission on foreign sales. Offers written contract; 30-day notice must be given to terminate contract.

RECENT SALES Averages closing a new book deal every two business days, often for multiple titles in a contract. Clients include Susan May Warren, Lisa Bergren, Lynette Eason, Deborah Raney, Vannetta Chapman, Robert Lesslie, Elizabeth Camden, Allison Bottke, Ellie Kay, Karol Ladd, Stephen M. Miller, Nancy Pearcey, William Lane Craig, Elizabeth Goddard, Pamela Tracy, Kim Vogel Sawyer, Nadine Brandes, Mesu Andrews, Mary Hunt, Hugh Ross, Timothy Smith, Roseanna White, Bill & Pam Farrel, Carla Laureano, Stan Jantz, Ronie Kendig.

WRITERS CONFERENCES Mount Hermon Christian Writers' Conference; RealmMakers; American Christian Fiction Writers' Conference (ACFW).

LAUNCHBOOKS LITERARY AGENCY

E-mail: david@launchbooks.com. **Website:** www.launchbooks.com. **Contact:** David Fugate. Estab. 2005. Represents 45 clients.

○ David Fugate has been an agent for over 25 years and has successfully represented more than 1,000 book titles. He left another agency to found LaunchBooks in 2005.

REPRESENTS Nonfiction, fiction, novels. **Considers these fiction areas:** action, adventure, commercial, crime, fantasy, horror, humor, mainstream, military, paranormal, satire, science fiction, sports, suspense, thriller, urban fantasy, war, westerns, young adult.

➤ "We're looking for genre-breaking fiction. Do you have the next *The Martian*? Or maybe the next *Red Rising*, *Ready Player One*, or *Dark Matter*? We're on the lookout for fun, engaging, contemporary novels that appeal to a broad audience. In nonfiction, we're interested in a broad range of topics. Check www.launchbooks.com/submissions for a complete list."

HOW TO CONTACT Query via e-mail. Accepts simultaneous submissions. Responds in 1 week to queries; 4 weeks to mss. Obtains most new clients through recommendations from others, solicitations.

TERMS Agent receives 15% commission on domestic sales; 25% commission on foreign sales. Offers written contract; 30-day notice to terminate contract. Charges occur very seldom. This agency's agreement limits any charges to $50 unless the author gives a written consent.

RECENT SALES *Artemis* and *The Martian*, by Andy Weir (Random House); *Paradox Bound*, by Peter Clines (Crown);*Captivate*, by Vanessa Van Edwards (Portfolio); *Side Hustle*, by Chris Guillebeau (Crown); *The Art of Invisibility*, by Kevin Mitnick (Little, Brown); the 7-book series *Extinction Cycle*, by Nicholas Smith (Orbit); *A History of the United States in Five Crashes*, by Scott Nations (William Morrow); *Gunpowder Moon*, by Dave Pedreira (Voyager); *An Excess Male*, by Maggie Shen King (Voyager); *One of Us*, by Craig DiLouie (Orbit); *Betaball*, by Erik Malinowski (Atria).

SUSANNA LEA ASSOCIATES

331 W. 20th St., New York New York 10011. **E-mail:** inquiries@susannalea.com. **E-mail:** ny@susannalea.com; london@susannalea.com; paris@susannalea.com. **Website:** www.susannalea.com. **Contact:** Submissions Department. South Wing, Somerset House, Strand, London, WC2R 1LA. Estab. Paris: 2000; New York: 2004; London: 2007.. Association of Authors' Agents.

REPRESENTS Nonfiction, fiction, novels.

☛ "Keeps list small; prefers to focus energies on a limited number of projects rather than spreading themselves too thinly. The company is currently developing new international projects—selective, yet broad in their reach, their slogan is: 'Published in Europe, Read by the World.'" Does not want to receive poetry, plays, screenplays, educational text books, short stories or illustrated works.

HOW TO CONTACT To submit your work, please send the following by e-mail: a concise query letter, including your e-mail address, telephone number, any relevant information about yourself (previous publications, etc.), a brief synopsis, and the first 3 chapters and/or proposal. Please check the website for infor-

mation on which office you should submit to. Accepts simultaneous submissions.

TIPS "Your query letter should be concise and include any pertinent information about yourself, relevant writing history, etc."

⊘ THE NED LEAVITT AGENCY

70 Wooster St., Suite 4F, New York NY 10012. (212)334-0999. **Website:** www.nedleavittagency.com. **Contact:** Ned Leavitt; Jillian Sweeney. Member of AAR. Represents 40+ clients.

MEMBER AGENTS Ned Leavitt, founder and agent; Britta Alexander, agent; Jillian Sweeney, agent.

REPRESENTS Novels.

☛ "We are small in size, but intensely dedicated to our authors and to supporting excellent and unique writing."

HOW TO CONTACT This agency now only takes queries/submissions through referred clients. Do not cold query. Accepts simultaneous submissions.

TIPS "Look online for this agency's recently changed submission guidelines."

ROBERT LECKER AGENCY

4055 Melrose Ave., Montreal QC H4A 2S5 Canada. **E-mail:** robert.lecker@gmail.com. **Website:** www.leckeragency.com. **Contact:** Robert Lecker. Estab. 2003. PACLA Represents 50 clients.

○ Prior to becoming an agent, Mr. Lecker was the cofounder and publisher of ECW Press and professor of English literature at McGill University. He has 30 years of experience in book and magazine publishing.

MEMBER AGENTS Robert Lecker (popular culture, music); Mary Williams (travel, food, popular science).

REPRESENTS Nonfiction, novels. , syndicated material. **Considers these fiction areas:** action, adventure, crime, detective, erotica, literary, mainstream, mystery, police, suspense, thriller.

☛ RLA specializes in books about popular culture, popular science, music, entertainment, food, and travel. The agency responds to articulate, innovative proposals within 2 weeks. Nonfiction titles related to politics, history, popular culture, popular science, music-related titles. We do not represent children's literature, screenplays, poetry, self-help books, or spiritual guides.

HOW TO CONTACT E-query. In the subject line, write: "New Submission QUERY." Accepts simultaneous submissions. Responds in 2 weeks to queries; 1 month to mss. Obtains most new clients through recommendations from others, conferences, interest in website.

TERMS Agent receives 15% commission on domestic sales; 15-20% commission on foreign sales. Offers written contract, binding for 1 year; 6-month notice must be given to terminate contract.

THE LESHNE AGENCY

New York NY **E-mail:** info@leshneagency.com. **E-mail:** submissions@leshneagency.com. **Website:** www.leshneagency.com. **Contact:** Lisa Leshne, agent and owner. Estab. 2011. Member of AAR. Women's Media Group

Lisa Leshne has been in the media and entertainment business for over 25 years. Lisa's experience spans the broadest range of the industry. In 1991, she co-founded The Prague Post, the largest English-language newspaper in Central Europe, along with its book division and website, PraguePost.com. Lisa worked in Prague as the newspaper's Publisher for almost a decade. In 1999, she moved to Manhattan to work for Accenture as a Senior Consultant in the Entertainment & Media Group. She later worked in strategy and business development for Dow Jones, and was Executive Director, International, for WSJ.com, the Wall Street Journal Online, responsible for digital business operations in Europe and Asia, where she oversaw advertising, marketing and circulation. Lisa also served as VP, Strategy and Business Development, for Ink2, an industry leader in the print-on-demand industry and the owner of Cardstore.com. Lisa worked for a year after 9/11 at the Partnership for New York City's Financial Recovery Fund, evaluating grant applications and providing strategic advice to small businesses destroyed in the World Trade Center attacks. Prior to founding The Leshne Agency in 2011, she was a literary agent at LJK Literary.

MEMBER AGENTS Lisa Leshne, agent and owner; Sandy Hodgman, director of foreign rights.

REPRESENTS Nonfiction, fiction, novels. **Considers these fiction areas:** commercial, middle grade, young adult.

An avid reader of blogs, newspapers and magazines in addition to books, Lisa is most interested in narrative and prescriptive nonfiction, especially on social justice, sports, health, wellness, business, political and parenting topics. She loves memoirs that transport the reader into another person's head and give a voyeuristic view of someone else's extraordinary experiences. Lisa also enjoys literary and commercial fiction and some young adult and middle-grade books that take the reader on a journey and are just plain fun to read. Wants "authors across all genres. We are interested in narrative, memoir, and prescriptive nonfiction, with a particular interest in sports, wellness, business, political and parenting topics. We will also look at truly terrific commercial fiction and young adult and middle grade books."

HOW TO CONTACT The Leshne Agency is seeking new and existing authors across all genres. "We are especially interested in narrative; memoir; prescriptive nonfiction, with a particular interest in sports, health, wellness, business, political and parenting topics; and truly terrific commercial fiction, young adult and middle-grade books. We are not interested in screenplays; scripts; poetry; and picture books. If your submission is in a genre not specifically listed here, we are still open to considering it, but if your submission is for a genre we've mentioned as not being interested in, please don't bother sending it to us. All submissions should be made through the Authors.me portal by clicking on this link: https://app.authors.me/#submit/the-leshne-agency." Accepts simultaneous submissions.

LEVINE GREENBERG ROSTAN LITERARY AGENCY, INC.

307 Seventh Ave., Suite 2407, New York NY 10001. (212)337-0934. **Fax:** (212)337-0948. **E-mail:** submit@lgrliterary.com. **Website:** www.lgrliterary.com. Member of AAR. Represents 250 clients.

Prior to opening his agency, Mr. Levine served as vice president of the Bank Street College of Education.

MEMBER AGENTS Jim Levine (nonfiction, including business, science, narrative nonfiction, social and political issues, psychology, health, spirituality, parenting); Stephanie Rostan (adult and YA fiction; nonfiction, including parenting, health & wellness, sports, memoir); Melissa Rowland; Daniel Greenberg (nonfiction: popular culture, narrative nonfiction, memoir, and humor; literary fiction); Victoria Skurnick; Danielle Svetcov (nonfiction); Lindsay Edgecombe (narrative nonfiction, memoir, lifestyle and health, illustrated books, as well as literary fiction); Monika Verma (nonfiction: humor, pop culture, memoir, narrative nonfiction and style and fashion titles; some young adult fiction (paranormal, historical, contemporary)); Kerry Sparks (young adult and middle grade; select adult fiction and occasional nonfiction); Tim Wojcik (nonfiction, including food narratives, humor, pop culture, popular history and science; literary fiction); Arielle Eckstut (no queries); Sarah Bedingfield (literary and upmarket commercial fiction, Epic family dramas, literary novels with notes of magical realism, darkly gothic stories, psychological suspense).

REPRESENTS Nonfiction, novels. **Considers these fiction areas:** commercial, literary, mainstream, middle grade, suspense, young adult.

HOW TO CONTACT E-query to submit@lgrliterary.com, or online submission form. "If you would like to direct your query to one of our agents specifically, please feel free to name them in the online form or in the email you send." Cannot respond to submissions by mail. Do not attach more than 50 pages. "Due to the volume of submissions we receive, we are unable to respond to each individually. If we would like more information about your project, we'll contact you within 3 weeks (though we do get backed up on occasion!)." Accepts simultaneous submissions. Obtains most new clients through recommendations from others.

TERMS Agent receives 15% commission on domestic sales; 20% commission on foreign sales. Offers written contract. Charges clients for out-of-pocket expenses—telephone, fax, postage, photocopying—directly connected to the project.

RECENT SALES **Notorious RBG**, by Irin Carmon and Shana Knizhnik; **Pogue's Basics: Life**, by David Pogue; **Invisible City**, by Julia Dahl; **Gumption**, by Nick Offerman; **All the Bright Places**, by Jennifer Niven.

WRITERS CONFERENCES ASJA Writers' Conference.

TIPS "We focus on editorial development, business representation, and publicity and marketing strategy."

PAUL S. LEVINE LITERARY AGENCY

1054 Superba Ave., Venice CA 90291. (310)450-6711. **Fax:** (310)450-0181. **E-mail:** paul@paulslevinelit.com.

Website: www.paulslevinelit.com. **Contact:** Paul S. Levine. Estab. 1992. Other memberships include the State Bar of California. Represents over 100 clients.

MEMBER AGENTS Paul S. Levine (children's and young adult fiction and nonfiction, adult fiction and nonfiction except sci-fi, fantasy, and horror); Loren R. Grossman (archeology, art/photography, architecture, child guidance/parenting, coffee table books, gardening, education/academics, health/medicine/science/technology, law, religion, memoirs, sociology).

REPRESENTS Nonfiction, fiction, novels, TV movie of the week, episodic drama, sitcom, animation, documentary, miniseries, syndicated material, variety show. , comic books; graphic novels. **Considers these fiction areas:** adventure, ethnic, mainstream, mystery, romance, thriller, young adult.

☛ Does not want to receive science fiction, fantasy, or horror.

HOW TO CONTACT E-mail preferred; "snail mail" with SASE is also acceptable. Send a 1-page, single-spaced query letter. In your query letter, note your target market, with a summary of specifics on how your work differs from other authors' previously published work. Accepts simultaneous submissions. Responds in 1 day to queries; 6-8 weeks to mss. Obtains most new clients through conferences, referrals, giving classes and seminars, and listings on various websites and in directories.

TERMS Agent receives 15% commission on domestic sales. Offers written contract. Charges for postage and actual, out-of-pocket costs only.

WRITERS CONFERENCES Willamette Writers Conference; San Francisco Writers Conference; Santa Barbara Writers Conference; Chicago Writers Conference; Atlanta Writers Conference; West Coast Writers Conferences; and many others.

TIPS "Write good, sellable books."

● LIMELIGHT CELEBRITY MANAGEMENT LTD.

10 Filmer Mews, 75 Filmer Rd., London SW6 7JF United Kingdom. (44)(0)207-384-9950. **E-mail:** mail@limelightmanagement.com. **Website:** www.limelightmanagement.com. **Contact:** Fiona Lindsay. Estab. 1991. Other memberships include AAA.

◑ Prior to becoming an agent, Ms. Lindsay was a public relations manager at the Dorchester and was working on her law degree.

MEMBER AGENTS Fiona Lindsay.

REPRESENTS , and selected fiction. **Considers these fiction areas:** crime, historical, literary, mystery, suspense, thriller, women's.

☞ "We are always looking for exciting new authors and read all work submitted. We endeavour to respond within 8 to 10 weeks of receipt, but this time scale is not always possible due to the volume of submissions we receive." This agency will consider women's fiction, as well.

HOW TO CONTACT All work should be typed with double spacing. Ensure that the word "Submission" is clearly marked in the subject line and that any attachments include the title of your work. E-mail a brief synopsis and the first 3 chapters only as a Word or Open Document attachment. Only handles film and TV scripts for existing clients. Accepts simultaneous submissions. Obtains most new clients through recommendations from others.

TERMS Agent receives 15% commission on domestic sales; 25% commission on foreign sales; 10-20% commission on TV and radio deals.

LITERARY MANAGEMENT GROUP, INC.

P.O. Box 41004, Nashville TN 37204. (615)812-4445. **E-mail:** brucebarbour@literarymanagementgroup.com. **Website:** literarymanagementgroup.com. **Contact:** Bruce R. Barbour. Estab. 1996. Represents 100+ clients.

◯ Prior to becoming an agent, Mr. Barbour held executive positions at several publishing houses, including Revell, Barbour Books, Thomas Nelson, and Random House.

REPRESENTS Nonfiction.

☞ Does not want to receive gift books, poetry, children's books, short stories, or juvenile/young adult fiction. No unsolicited mss or proposals from unpublished authors.

HOW TO CONTACT E-mail proposal as an attachment. Consult website for submission guidelines. Accepts simultaneous submissions. "We acknowledge receipt and review proposals within 4 weeks."

TERMS Agent receives 15% commission on domestic sales.

LITERARY SERVICES, INC.

P.O. Box 888, Barnegat NJ 08005. **E-mail:** jwlitagent@msn.com. **E-mail:** john@literaryservicesinc.com. **Website:** www.literaryservicesinc.com. **Contact:** John Willig. Estab. 1991. Other memberships include Author's Guild. Represents 90 clients.

◯ "I started working in publishing in 1977 as a sales representative ('college traveler') in academic publishing and then marketing manager before becoming an editor; shifted to professional/subscription-based publishing as a senior editor and then became an executive editor for business professional and trade books for Prentice Hall/Simon & Schuster. In 1976 I graduated from Brown University and have always been an avid reader with a broad range of interests. With my love of great stories and historical fiction, I have begun to represent a limited number of new projects in this category in addition to nonfiction".

MEMBER AGENTS John Willig (business, personal growth, history, health and lifestyle, science and technology, politics, psychology, true crime, current events and global issues, food and travel, reference and gift books, humor, historical fiction).

REPRESENTS Nonfiction, scholarly books. **Considers these fiction areas:** detective, horror, literary, new adult, translation.

☞ Works primarily with nonfiction and historical fiction authors. "Our publishing experience and 'inside' knowledge of how companies and editors really work sets us apart from many agencies; our specialties are noted above, but we are open to unique research, creative and contrarian approaches, and fresh presentations with expert advice in all nonfiction topic areas. Whether nonfiction topics or historical fiction, I'm especially interested in writers 'shining a light' on new research, perspectives, events or stories. Actively seeking science, history, current events and global issues, health, lifestyle topics, psychology, true crime, business, food and travel, story and research-driven narratives. Does not want to receive fiction (except historical fiction - literary or thriller), children's books, science fiction, religion, or memoirs.

HOW TO CONTACT Query with SASE. For starters, a one-page outline sent via e-mail is acceptable. See our website and our Submissions section to learn more about our questions. Do not send a manuscrpt unless requested. Accepts simultaneous submissions. Thankfully, obtains most new clients through recommendations from others, solicitations, writer's conferences.

TERMS Agent receives 15% commission on domestic sales; 15% commission on foreign sales. Offers written contract. This agency charges an administrative fee for copying, postage, etc.

RECENT SALES Sold 20+ titles in the past year including *Leading in the Global Matrix*, by John Futterknecht; *Saving Washington*, by Chris Formant; *Managing the Message*, by Jim Karrh; *The Art and Power of Acceptance*, by Ashley Davis Bush; *The Energy Clock*, by Molly Fletcher; *Living in a Post-Genomic World*, by Josh Rappoport, PhD; *The Life Ray*, by Todd Neff; *In Fame We Trust*, by Lauren Wright PhD..a full listing of our clients newly published books is available on our website.

WRITERS CONFERENCES ASJA; Writer's Digest Conference (NYC); Thrillerfest.

TIPS "Be focused. In all likelihood, your work is not going to be of interest to 'a very broad audience' or 'every parent,' so I appreciate when writers research and do some homework, i.e., positioning, special features and benefits of your work. Be a marketer. How have you tested your ideas and writing (beyond your inner circle of family and friends)? Have you received any key awards for your work or endorsements from influential persons in your field? What steps, especially social media and speaking, have you taken to increase your presence in the market?"

LKG AGENCY

60 Riverside Blvd., #1101, New York NY 10069. **E-mail:** query@lkgagency.com. **E-mail:** mgya@lkgagency.com (MG/YA); nonfiction@lkgagency.com (nonfiction). **Website:** lkgagency.com. **Contact:** Lauren Galit; Caitlen Rubino-Bradway. Estab. 2005.

MEMBER AGENTS Lauren Galit (nonfiction, middle grade, young adult); Caitlen Rubino-Bradway (middle grade and young adult, some nonfiction).

REPRESENTS Nonfiction, juvenile books. **Considers these fiction areas:** middle grade, young adult.

- ☛ "The LKG Agency specializes in nonfiction, both practical and narrative, as well as middle grade and young adult fiction." Actively seeking parenting, beauty, celebrity, dating & relationships, entertainment, fashion, health, diet & fitness, home & design, lifestyle, memoir, narrative, pets, psychology, women's focused, middle grade & young adult fiction. Does not want history, biography, true crime, religion, picture

books, spirituality, screenplays, poetry any fiction other than middle grade or young adult.

HOW TO CONTACT For nonfiction submissions, please send a query letter to nonfiction@lkgagency.com, along with a TOC and 2 sample chapters. The TOC should be fairly detailed, with a paragraph or 2 overview of the content of each chapter. Please also make sure to mention any publicity you have at your disposal. For middle grade and young adult submissions, please send a query, synopsis, and the three (3) chapters, and address all submissions to mgya@lkgagency.com. On a side note, while both Lauren and Caitlen consider young adult and middle grade, Lauren tends to look more for middle grade, while Caitlen deals more with young adult fiction. Please note: due to the high volume of submissions, we are unable to reply to every one. If you do not receive a reply, please consider that a rejection. Accepts simultaneous submissions.

STERLING LORD LITERISTIC, INC.

115 Broadway, New York NY 10006. (212)780-6050. **Fax:** (212)780-6095. **E-mail:** info@sll.com. **Website:** www.sll.com. Estab. 1987. Member of AAR. Signatory of WGA.

MEMBER AGENTS Philippa Brophy (represents journalists, nonfiction writers and novelists, and is most interested in current events, memoir, science, politics, biography, and women's issues); Laurie Liss (represents authors of commercial and literary fiction and nonfiction whose perspectives are well developed and unique); Sterling Lord; Peter Matson (abiding interest in storytelling, whether in the service of history, fiction, the sciences); Douglas Stewart (primarily fiction for all ages, from the innovatively literary to the unabashedly commercial); Neeti Madan (memoir, journalism, popular culture, lifestyle, women's issues, multicultural books and virtually any intelligent writing on intriguing topics); Robert Guinsler (literary and commercial fiction (including YA), journalism, narrative nonfiction with an emphasis on pop culture, science and current events, memoirs and biographies); Jim Rutman; Celeste Fine (expert, celebrity, and corporate clients with strong national and international platforms, particularly in the health, science, self-help, food, business, and lifestyle fields); Martha Millard (fiction and nonfiction, including well-written science fiction and young adult); Mary Krienke (literary fiction, memoir, and narrative nonfiction, including psychology, popular science, and cultural commentary); Jenny Stephens (nonfiction: cookbooks, practical lifestyle projects, transportive travel and nature writing, and creative nonfiction; fiction: contemporary literary narratives strongly rooted in place); Alison MacKeen (idea-driven research books: social scientific, scientific, historical, relationships/parenting, learning and education, sexuality, technology, the life-cycle, health, the environment, politics, economics, psychology, geography, and culture; literary fiction, literary nonfiction, memoirs, essays, and travel writing); John Maas (serious nonfiction, specifically business, personal development, science, self-help, health, fitness, and lifestyle); Sarah Passick (commercial nonfiction in the celebrity, food, blogger, lifestyle, health, diet, fitness and fashion categories).

REPRESENTS Nonfiction, fiction. **Considers these fiction areas:** commercial, juvenile, literary, middle grade, picture books, science fiction, young adult.

HOW TO CONTACT Query via snail mail. "Please submit a query letter, a synopsis of the work, a brief proposal or the first 3 chapters of the manuscript, a brief bio or resume, and SASE for reply. Original artwork is not accepted. Enclose sufficient postage if you wish to have your materials returned to you. We do not respond to unsolicited e-mail inquiries." Accepts simultaneous submissions.

TERMS Agent receives 15% commission on domestic sales; 20% commission on foreign sales. Offers written contract.

LOWENSTEIN ASSOCIATES INC.

115 E. 23rd St., Floor 4, New York NY 10010. (212)206-1630. **E-mail:** assistant@bookhaven.com. **Website:** www.lowensteinassociates.com. **Contact:** Barbara Lowenstein. Member of AAR.

MEMBER AGENTS Barbara Lowenstein, president (nonfiction interests include narrative nonfiction, health, money, finance, travel, multicultural, popular culture, and memoir; fiction interests include literary fiction and women's fiction); Mary South (literary fiction and nonfiction on subjects such as neuroscience, bioengineering, women's rights, design, and digital humanities, as well as investigative journalism, essays, and memoir).

REPRESENTS Nonfiction, fiction, novels, short story collections. **Considers these fiction areas:** commercial, literary, middle grade, science fiction, women's, young adult.

Barbara Lowenstein is currently looking for writers who have a platform and are leading experts in their field, including business, women's issues, psychology, health, science and social issues, and is particularly interested in strong new voices in fiction and narrative nonfiction. Does not want westerns, textbooks, children's picture books and books in need of translation.

HOW TO CONTACT "For fiction, please send us a 1-page query letter, along with the first 10 pages pasted in the body of the message by e-mail to assistant@bookhaven.com. If nonfiction, please send a 1-page query letter, a table of contents, and, if available, a proposal pasted into the body of the e-mail. Please put the word 'QUERY' and the title of your project in the subject field of your e-mail and address it to the agent of your choice. Please do not send an attachment as the message will be deleted without being read and no reply will be sent." Accepts simultaneous submissions. Will respond if interested. Obtains most new clients through recommendations from others, solicitations, conferences.

TERMS Agent receives 15% commission on domestic sales; 20% commission on foreign sales. Offers written contract. Charges for large photocopy batches, messenger service, international postage.

TIPS "Know the genre you are working in and read!"

ANDREW LOWNIE LITERARY AGENCY, LTD.

36 Great Smith St., London SW1P 3BU United Kingdom. (44)(207)222-7574. **Fax:** (44)(207)222-7576. **E-mail:** lownie@globalnet.co.uk. **Website:** www.andrewlownie.co.uk. **Contact:** Andrew Lownie, nonfiction. Estab. 1988. Society of Authors Represents 200 clients.

Prior to becoming an agent, Mr. Lownie was a journalist, bookseller, publisher and a former director of the Curtis Brown Agency. He is a critically acclaimed writer and President of the Biographers Club, a judge of several nonfiction prizes and regularly speaks at festivals around the world.

REPRESENTS Nonfiction.

This agent has wide publishing experience, extensive journalistic contacts, and a specialty in showbiz/celebrity memoir. Actively seeking showbiz memoirs, narrative histories, and biographies. No fiction, poetry, short stories, children's, academic, or scripts.

HOW TO CONTACT Query by e-mail only. For nonfiction, submit outline and one sample chapter. Accepts simultaneous submissions. Responds in 1 week to queries; 1 month to mss. Obtains most new clients through recommendations from others and unsolicited through website.

TERMS Agent receives 15% commission on domestic sales; 20% commission on foreign sales. Offers written contract; 30-day notice must be given to terminate contract.

RECENT SALES Sells about fifty books a year, with over a dozen top 10 bestsellers including many number ones, as well as the memoirs of Queen Elizabeth II's press officer Dickie Arbiter, Lance Armstrong's masseuse Emma O'Reilly, actor Warwick Davis, Multiple Personality Disorder sufferer Alice Jamieson, round-the-world yachtsman Mike Perham, poker player Dave 'Devilfish' Ulliott, David Hasselhoff, Sam Faiers and Kirk Norcross from TOWIE, Spencer Matthews from Made in Chelsea, singer Kerry Katona. Other clients: Juliet Barker, Guy Bellamy, Joyce Cary estate, Roger Crowley, Patrick Dillon, Duncan Falconer, Cathy Glass, Timothy Good, Robert Hutchinson, Lawrence James, Christopher Lloyd, Sian Rees, Desmond Seward, Daniel Tammet, Casey Watson and Matt Wilven.

DONALD MAASS LITERARY AGENCY

1000 Dean St., Suite 252, Brooklyn NY 11238. (212)727-8383. **E-mail:** query.dmaass@maassagency.com. **Website:** www.maassagency.com. Estab. 1980. Member of AAR. Other memberships include SFWA, MWA, RWA. Represents more than 200 clients.

○ Prior to opening his agency, Mr. Maass worked as an editor at Dell Publishing (New York) and as a reader at Gollancz (London). He is a past president of the Association of Authors' Representatives, Inc. (AAR).

MEMBER AGENTS Donald Maass (mainstream, literary, mystery/suspense, science fiction, romance, women's fiction); Jennifer Jackson (science fiction and fantasy for both adult and YA markets, thrillers that mine popular and controversial issues, YA that challenges traditional thinking); Cameron McClure (literary, mystery/suspense, urban, fantasy, narrative nonfiction and projects with multicultural, international, and environmental themes, gay/lesbian); Katie Shea Boutillier (women's fiction/book club, edgy/dark, realistic/contemporary YA, commercial-scale literary fiction, and celebrity memoir); Paul Stevens (science

fiction, fantasy, horror, mystery, suspense, and humorous fiction, LBGT a plus); Jennie Goloboy (fun, innovative, diverse, and progressive science fiction and fantasy for adults); Caitlin McDonald (SF/F - YA/MG/Adult, genre-bending/cross-genre fiction, diversity); Michael Curry (science fiction and fantasy, near future thrillers).

REPRESENTS Nonfiction, fiction, novels, short story collections, novellas, juvenile books. **Considers these fiction areas:** commercial, contemporary issues, crime, detective, ethnic, family saga, fantasy, feminist, frontier, gay, historical, horror, humor, juvenile, lesbian, literary, mainstream, middle grade, military, multicultural, mystery, new adult, occult, paranormal, police, psychic, regional, religious, romance, satire, science fiction, short story collections, spiritual, supernatural, suspense, thriller, urban fantasy, war, westerns, women's, young adult.

☛ This agency specializes in commercial fiction, especially science fiction, fantasy, thrillers, suspense, women's fiction—for both the adult and YA markets. All types of fiction, including YA and MG. Does not want poetry, screenplays, picture books.

HOW TO CONTACT Query via e-mail only. All the agents have different submission addresses and instructions. See the website and each agent's online profile for exact submission instructions. Accepts simultaneous submissions.

TERMS Agency receives 15% commission on domestic sales; 20% commission on foreign sales.

RECENT SALES *The Aeronaut's Windlass*, by Jim Butcher (Penguin Random House); *City of Blades*, by Robert Jackson Bennett (Crown); *I am Princess X*, by Cherie Priest (Scholastic); *Treachery at Lancaster Gate*, by Anne Perry (Random House); *Marked in Flesh*, by Anne Bishop (Penguin Random House); *We Are the Ants*, by Shaun David Hutchinson (Simon & Schuster); *Binti*, by Nnedi Okorafor (DAW); *Ninefox Gambit*, by Yoon Ha Lee (Solaris); *The Far End of Happy*, by Kathryn Craft (Sourcebooks); *The Traitor Baru Cormorant*, by Seth Dickinson (Tor).

WRITERS CONFERENCES See each agent's profile page at the agency website for conference schedules.

TIPS "We are fiction specialists, also noted for our innovative approach to career planning. We are always open to submissions from new writers." Works with subagents in all principle foreign countries and for film and television.

GINA MACCOBY LITERARY AGENCY

P.O. Box 60, Chappaqua NY 10514. (914)238-5630. E-mail: query@maccobylit.com. **Website:** www.publishersmarketplace.com/members/ginamaccoby/. **Contact:** Gina Maccoby. Estab. 1986. Member of AAR. AAR Board of Directors; Royalties and Ethics and Contracts subcommittees; Authors Guild, SCBWI.

REPRESENTS Nonfiction, fiction, novels, juvenile books. **Considers these fiction areas:** crime, detective, family saga, historical, juvenile, literary, mainstream, middle grade, multicultural, mystery, new adult, suspense, thriller, women's, young adult.

HOW TO CONTACT Query by e-mail only. Accepts simultaneous submissions. Owing to volume of submissions, may not respond to queries unless interested. Obtains most new clients through recommendations.

TERMS Agent receives 15% commission on domestic sales; 20-25% commission on foreign sales, which includes subagents commissions. May recover certain costs, such as purchasing books, shipping books overseas by airmail, legal fees for vetting motion picture contracts, bank fees for electronic funds transfers, overnight delivery services.

WRITERS CONFERENCES ThrillerFest PitchFest, Washington Independent Writers Conference, New England Crime Bake, Ridgefield Writers Conference, CLMP Literary Writers Conference.

CAROL MANN AGENCY

55 Fifth Ave., 18th Floor, New York NY 10003. (212)206-5635. **Fax:** (212)675-4809. **E-mail:** submissions@carolmannagency.com. **Website:** www.carolmannagency.com. **Contact:** Agnes Carlowicz. Member of AAR. Represents Roughly 200 clients.

MEMBER AGENTS Carol Mann (health/medical, religion, spirituality, self-help, parenting, narrative nonfiction, current affairs); Laura Yorke; Gareth Esersky; Myrsini Stephanides (nonfiction areas of interest: pop culture and music, humor, narrative nonfiction and memoir, cookbooks; fiction areas of interest: offbeat literary fiction, graphic works, and edgy YA fiction); Joanne Wyckoff (nonfiction areas of interest: memoir, narrative nonfiction, personal narrative, psychology, women's issues, education, health and wellness, parenting, serious self-help, natural history; also accepts fiction); Lydia Shamah (edgy, modern fiction and timely nonfiction in the areas of business, self-improvement, relationship and gift books, particularly interested in female voices and experiences);

Tom Miller (narrative nonfiction, self-help/psychology, popular culture, body-mind-spirit, wellness, business, and literary fiction).

REPRESENTS Nonfiction, fiction, novels. **Considers these fiction areas:** commercial, literary, young adult, graphic works.

☛ Does not want to receive genre fiction (romance, mystery, etc.).

HOW TO CONTACT Please see website for submission guidelines. Accepts simultaneous submissions. Responds in 4 weeks to queries.

TERMS Agent receives 15% commission on domestic sales; 20% commission on foreign sales. Offers written contract.

MANUS & ASSOCIATES LITERARY AGENCY, INC.

425 Sherman Ave., Suite 200, Palo Alto CA 94306. (650)470-5151. **Fax:** (650)470-5159. **E-mail:** manuslit@manuslit.com. **Website:** www.manuslit.com. **Contact:** Jillian Manus, Jandy Nelson, Penny Nelson. NYC address: 444 Madison Ave., 39th Floor, New York NY 10022. Member of AAR.

○ Prior to becoming an agent, Ms. Manus was associate publisher of two national magazines and director of development at Warner Bros. and Universal Studios; she has been a literary agent for 20 years.

MEMBER AGENTS Jandy Nelson (currently not taking on new clients); Jillian Manus, jillian@manuslit.com (political, memoirs, self-help, history, sports, women's issues, thrillers); Penny Nelson, penny@manuslit.com (memoirs, self-help, sports, nonfiction).

REPRESENTS Nonfiction, novels. **Considers these fiction areas:** thriller.

☛ "Our agency is unique in the way that we not only sell the material, but we edit, develop concepts, and participate in the marketing effort. We specialize in large, conceptual fiction and nonfiction, and always value a project that can be sold in the TV/feature film market." Actively seeking high-concept thrillers, commercial literary fiction, women's fiction, celebrity biographies, memoirs, multicultural fiction, popular health, women's empowerment and mysteries. No horror, romance, science fiction, fantasy, western, young adult, children's, poetry, cookbooks, or magazine articles.

HOW TO CONTACT Snail mail submissions welcome. E-queries also accepted. For nonfiction, send a full proposal via snail mail. For fiction, send a query letter and 30 pages (unbound) if submitting via snail mail. Send only an e-query if submitting fiction via e-mail. If querying by e-mail, submit directly to one of the agents. Accepts simultaneous submissions. Responds in 3 months. Obtains most new clients through recommendations from others, solicitations, conferences.

TERMS Agent receives 15% commission on domestic sales; 20-25% commission on foreign sales. Offers written contract, binding for 2 years; 60-day notice must be given to terminate contract. Charges for photocopying and postage/UPS.

RECENT SALES *Nothing Down for the 2000s* and *Multiple Streams of Income for the 2000s*, by Robert Allen; *Missed Fortune 101*, by Doug Andrew; *Cracking the Millionaire Code*, by Mark Victor Hansen and Robert Allen; *Stress Free for Good*, by Dr. Fred Luskin and Dr. Ken Pelletier; *The Mercy of Thin Air*, by Ronlyn Domangue; *The Fine Art of Small Talk*, by Debra Fine; *Bone Men of Bonares*, by Terry Tamoff.

WRITERS CONFERENCES Maui Writers' Conference; San Diego State University Writers' Conference; Willamette Writers' Conference; BookExpo America; MEGA Book Marketing University.

TIPS "Research agents using a variety of sources."

🌑 MARJACQ SCRIPTS LTD

Box 412, 19/12 Crawford St., London W1H 1PJ United Kingdom. (44)(207)935-9499. **Fax:** (44)(207)935-9115. **E-mail:** enquiries@marjacq.com. **E-mail:** subs@marjacq.com or (preferably) individual agent as shown on website. **Website:** www.marjacq.com. **Contact:** Submissions: individual agent. Business matters: Guy Herbert.. Estab. 1974. AAA Represents 120+ clients.

○ Ms. Beaumont was an editor at Random House and an agent at UTA; Mr. Patterson was a film, TV, and theatre agent at Curtis Brown and sold rights at HarperCollins; Ms. Pelham worked as assistant to the late Gillon Aitken dealing with his very high profile clients; Ms. Pellegrino ran her own agency, and before that was at Rogers Coleridge and White; Ms. Sawicka worked as a rights executive in publishing. Ms Middleton was a senior TV agent at Aitken Alexander.

MEMBER AGENTS Philip Patterson (thrillers, commercial fiction and nonfiction); Sandra Sawicka (commercial, genre, speculative and upmarket fiction); Diana Beaumont (commercial and accessible literary fiction and nonfiction); Imogen Pelham (literary fiction and nonfiction); Catherine Pellegrino (children's, middle grade and young adult); Leah Middleton (Film & TV, commercial fiction, investigative journalism, popular science).

REPRESENTS Nonfiction, fiction, novels, short story collections, novellas, juvenile books, scholarly books, movie scripts, feature film, TV scripts, TV movie of the week, episodic drama, sitcom, documentary, miniseries, syndicated material.

☛ Actively seeking quality fiction, nonfiction, children's books, and young adult books. Does not want to receive stage plays or poetry.

HOW TO CONTACT Email submissions direct to the individual agent who you feel is the best fit. Submit outline, synopsis, 3 sample chapters, bio, covering letter, SASE. "Do not bother with fancy bindings and folders. Keep synopses, bio, and covering letter short." Accepts simultaneous submissions. Responds in 4-6 weeks to mss. Don't send queries without sample. Obtains most new clients through recommendations from others, solicitations, conferences.

TERMS Agent receives 15% commission on direct book sales; 20% on foreign rights, film etc. Offers written contract. Services include in-house business affairs consultant. No service fees other than commission. Recharges bank fees for money transfers.

RECENT SALES 3-book deal for Stuart McBride (HarperCollins UK) (repeated *Sunday Times* #1 bestseller); 3-book deal for Howard Linskey.

TIPS "Keep trying! If one agent rejects you, you can try someone else. Perseverance and self-belief are important, but do listen to constructive criticism, and 'no' does mean no. Be warned, few agents will give you advice as a non-client. We just don't have the time. Be aware of what is being published. If you show awareness of what other writers are doing in your field/genre, you might be able to see how your book fits in and why an editor/agent might be interested in taking it on. Take care with your submissions. Research the agency and pay attention to presentation: Always follow the specific agency submission guidelines. Doing so helps the agent assess your work. Join writers groups. Sharing your work is a good way to get constructive criticism. If you know anyone in the industry, use your contacts. A personal recommendation will get more notice than cold calling."

MARSAL LYON LITERARY AGENCY, LLC

PMB 121, 665 San Rodolfo Dr. 124, Solana Beach CA 92075. **E-mail:** jill@marsallyonliteraryagency.com; kevan@marsallyonliteraryagency.com; patricia@marsallyonliteraryagency.com; deborah@marsallyonliteraryagency.com; shannon@marsallyonliteraryagency.com. **Website:** www.marsallyonliteraryagency.com. Estab. 2009. Represents See agency website for a client listing clients.

MEMBER AGENTS Kevan Lyon (women's fiction, with an emphasis on commercial women's fiction, young adult fiction and all genres of romance); Jill Marsal (all types of women's fiction, book club fiction, stories of family, friendships, relationships, secrets, and stories with strong emotion; mystery, cozy, suspense, psychological suspense, thriller; romance-contemporary, romantic suspense, historical, and category; nonfiction in the areas of current events, business, health, self-help, relationships, psychology, parenting, history, science, and narrative non-fiction); Patricia Nelson (literary fiction and commercial fiction, all types of women's fiction, contemporary and historical romance, young adult and middle grade fiction, LGBTQ fiction for both YA and adult); Deborah Ritchken (lifestyle books, specifically in the areas of food, design and entertaining; pop culture; women's issues; biography; and current events; her niche interest is projects about France, including fiction); Shannon Hassan (literary and commercial fiction, young adult and middle grade fiction, and select nonfiction).

REPRESENTS Nonfiction, fiction, novels, juvenile books. **Considers these fiction areas:** commercial, contemporary issues, crime, detective, family saga, historical, juvenile, literary, mainstream, middle grade, multicultural, mystery, paranormal, romance, suspense, thriller, women's, young adult.

HOW TO CONTACT Query by e-mail. Query only one agent at this agency at a time. "Please visit our website to determine who is best suited for your work. Write 'query' in the subject line of your e-mail. Please allow up to several weeks to hear back on your query." Accepts simultaneous submissions. Query response time is generally up to 2 weeks and submission time varies by agent.

RECENT SALES All sales are posted on Publishers' Marketplace.

TIPS "Our agency's mission is to help writers achieve their publishing dreams. We want to work with authors not just for a book but for a career; we are dedicated to building long-term relationships with our authors and publishing partners. Our goal is to help find homes for books that engage, entertain, and make a difference."

THE EVAN MARSHALL AGENCY

1 Pacio Ct., Roseland NJ 07068-1121. (973)287-6216. **E-mail:** evan@evanmarshallagency.com. **Website:** www.evanmarshallagency.com. **Contact:** Evan Marshall. Estab. 1987. Member of AAR. Novelists, Inc. Represents 50+ clients.

○ Prior to becoming an agent, Evan Marshall held senior editorial positions at Houghton Mifflin, Ariel Books, New American Library, Everest House and Dodd, Mead, where he acquired national and international bestsellers.

REPRESENTS Fiction, novels. **Considers these fiction areas:** action, adventure, crime, detective, erotica, ethnic, family saga, fantasy, feminist, frontier, gay, glitz, historical, horror, humor, inspirational, lesbian, literary, mainstream, military, multicultural, multimedia, mystery, new adult, New Age, occult, paranormal, police, psychic, regional, religious, romance, satire, science fiction, spiritual, sports, supernatural, suspense, thriller, translation, urban fantasy, war, westerns, women's, young adult, romance (contemporary, gothic, historical, regency).

☛ "We represent all genres of adult and young-adult full-length fiction." Represent all genres of adult and young-adult full-length fiction. Does not want articles, children's books, essays, memoirs, nonfiction, novellas, poetry, screenplays, short stories, stage plays.

HOW TO CONTACT "We consider new clients by referral only." Accepts simultaneous submissions. Responds in 1 week to queries if interested; 2 months to mss. Considers new clients by referral only.

TERMS Agent receives 15% commission on domestic sales; 20% commission on foreign and film/TV sales. Offers written contract.

RECENT SALES *The Taster*, by V. S. Alexander (Kensington); *A Man for Honor*, by Emma Miller (Love Inspired); *The Devil's Wind*, by Steve Goble (Seventh Street); *The Maverick's Holiday Surprise*, by Karen Rose Smith (Harlequin); *Nemesis*, by Joe Yogerst (Blank Slate Press); *Echoes of the Haight*, by Max Tomlinson (Oceanview).

THE MARTELL AGENCY

1350 Avenue of the Americas, Suite 1205, New York NY 10019. **Fax:** (212)317-2676. **E-mail:** submissions@themartellagency.com. **Website:** www.themartellagency.com. **Contact:** Alice Martell.

REPRESENTS Nonfiction, fiction, novels.

☛ Seeks the following subjects in fiction: literary and commercial, including mystery, suspense and thrillers. Does not want to receive romance, genre mysteries, genre historical fiction, science fiction or children's books.

HOW TO CONTACT E-query Alice Martell. This should include a summary of the project and a short biography and any information, if appropriate, as to why you are qualified to write on the subject of your book, including any publishing credits. Accepts simultaneous submissions.

MARTIN LITERARY AND MEDIA MANAGEMENT

914 164th St. SE, Suite B12, #307, Mill Creek WA 98012. **E-mail:** sharlene@martinlit.com. **Website:** www.martinlit.com. **Contact:** Sharlene Martin. Estab. 2002.

○ Prior to becoming an agent, Ms. Martin worked in film/TV production and acquisitions.

MEMBER AGENTS Sharlene Martin (nonfiction); Clelia Gore (children's, middle grade, young adult); Adria Goetz (Christian books, lifestyle books, children and YA); Natalie Grazian (adult fiction) Britt Siess (Y/A and Adult Sci-fi/Horror/Mystery).

REPRESENTS Nonfiction, fiction. **Considers these fiction areas:** adventure, contemporary issues, fantasy, feminist, historical, humor, literary, middle grade, science fiction, supernatural, suspense, urban fantasy, women's, young adult.

☛ This agency has strong ties to film/TV. Sharlene Martin has an overall deal with ITV for unscripted television. Actively seeking nonfiction that is highly commercial and that can be adapted to film. "We are being inundated with queries and submissions that are wrongfully being submitted to us, which only results in more frustration for the writers. Please review our Submission Page on our website and direct your query accordingly."

HOW TO CONTACT Query via e-mail with MS Word only. No attachments on queries; place letter in body of e-mail. Accepts simultaneous submissions. Responds in 2 weeks to queries; 3-4 weeks to mss. Obtains most new clients through recommendations from others.

TERMS Agent receives 15% commission on domestic sales. We are exclusive for foreign sales to Taryn Fagerness Agency. Offers written contract, binding for 1 year; 1-month notice must be given to terminate contract. 99% of materials are sent electronically to minimize charges to author for postage and copying.

RECENT SALES *Chasing Cosby*, by Nicole Weisensee Egan; *Taking My Life Back*, by Rebekah Gregory with Anthony Flacco; *Breakthrough*, by Jack Andraka; *In the Matter of Nikola Tesla: A Romance of the Mind*, by Anthony Flacco; *Honor Bound: My Journey to Hell and Back with Amanda Knox*, by Raffaele Sollecito; *Impossible Odds: The Kidnapping of Jessica Buchanan and Dramatic Rescue by SEAL Team Six*, by Jessica Buchanan, Erik Landemalm and Anthony Flacco; *Walking on Eggshells*, by Lisa Chapman; *Newtown: An American Tragedy*, by Matthew Lysiak; *Publish Your Nonfiction Book*, by Sharlene Martin and Anthony Flacco.

TIPS "Have a strong platform for nonfiction. Please don't call. (I can't tell how well you write by the sound of your voice.) I welcome e-mail. I'm very responsive when I'm interested in a query and work hard to get my clients' materials in the best possible shape before submissions. Do your homework prior to submission and only submit your best efforts. Please review our website carefully to make sure we're a good match for your work. If you read my book, *Publish Your Nonfiction Book: Strategies For Learning the Industry, Selling Your Book and Building a Successful Career* (Writer's Digest Books) you'll know exactly how to charm me."

MASSIE & MCQUILKIN

27 W. 20th St., Suite 305, New York NY 10011. **E-mail:** info@lmqlit.com. **Website:** www.lmqlit.com.

MEMBER AGENTS Laney Katz Becker, laney@lmqlit.com (book club fiction, upmarket women's fiction, suspense, thrillers and memoir); Ethan Bassoff, ethan@lmqlit.com (literary fiction, crime fiction, and narrative nonfiction in the areas of history, sports writing, journalism, science writing, pop culture, humor, and food writing); Jason Anthony, jason@lmqlit.com (commercial fiction of all types, including young adult, and nonfiction in the areas of memoir, pop culture, true crime, and general psychology and sociology); Will Lippincott, will@lmqlit.com (narrative nonfiction and nonfiction in the areas of politics, history, biography, foreign affairs, and health); Rob

McQuilkin, rob@lmqlit.com (literary fiction; narrative nonfiction and nonfiction in the areas of memoir, history, biography, art history, cultural criticism, and popular sociology and psychology; Rayhane Sanders, rayhane@lmqlit.com (literary fiction, historical fiction, upmarket commercial fiction [including select YA], narrative nonfiction [including essays], and select memoir); Stephanie Abou (literary and upmarket commercial fiction (including select young adult and middle grade), crime fiction, memoir, and narrative nonfiction); Julie Stevenson (literary and upmarket fiction, narrative nonfiction, YA and children's books). **REPRESENTS** Nonfiction, fiction, novels. **Considers these fiction areas:** commercial, contemporary issues, crime, literary, mainstream, middle grade, suspense, thriller, women's, young adult.

☛ "Massie & McQuilkin is a full-service literary agency that focuses on bringing fiction and nonfiction of quality to the largest possible audience."

HOW TO CONTACT E-query preferred. Include the word "Query" in the subject line of your e-mail. Review the agency's online page of agent bios (lmqlit.com/contact.html), as some agents want sample pages with their submissions and some do not. If you have not heard back from the agency in 4 weeks, assume they are not interested in seeing more. Accepts simultaneous submissions. Obtains most new clients through recommendations from others, solicitations, conferences.

TERMS Agent receives 15% commission on domestic sales; 20% commission on foreign sales. Offers written contract; 30-day notice must be given to terminate contract. Only charges for reasonable business expenses upon successful sale.

RECENT SALES Clients include Roxane Gay, Peter Ho Davies, Kim Addonizio, Natasha Trethewey, David Sirota, Katie Crouch, Uwen Akpan, Lydia Millet, Tom Perrotta, Jonathan Lopez, Chris Hayes, Caroline Weber.

MARGRET MCBRIDE LITERARY AGENCY

P.O. Box 9128, La Jolla CA 92038. (858)454-1550. **E-mail:** staff@mcbridelit.com. **Website:** www.mcbrideliterary.com. Estab. 1981. Member of AAR. Other memberships include Authors Guild.

○ Prior to opening her agency, Ms. McBride worked at Random House and Ballantine Books. Later, she became the Director of Publicity at Warner Books, and Director of Publicity, Promotions and Advertising for Pinnacle Books.

MEMBER AGENTS Margret McBride; Faye Atchison.

REPRESENTS Nonfiction, fiction, novels. **Considers these fiction areas:** action, adventure, comic books, commercial, confession, contemporary issues, crime, detective, family saga, feminist, historical, horror, juvenile, mainstream, multicultural, multimedia, mystery, new adult, paranormal, police, psychic, regional, supernatural, suspense, thriller, young adult.

☛ This agency specializes in mainstream nonfiction and some commercial fiction. Actively seeking commercial nonfiction, business, health, self-help. Does not want screenplays, romance, poetry, or children's.

HOW TO CONTACT Please check our website, as instructions are subject to change. Only e-mail queries are accepted: staff@mcbridelit.com. In your query letter, provide a brief synopsis of your work, as well as any pertinent information about yourself. We recommend that authors look at book jacket copy of professionally published books to get an idea of the style and content that should be included in a query letter. Essentially, you are marketing yourself and your work to us, so that we can determine whether we feel we can market you and your work to publishers. There are detailed nonfiction proposal guidelines on our website, but we recommend author's get a copy of How to Write a Book Proposal by Michael Larsen for further instruction. **Please note: The McBride Agency will not respond to queries sent by mail, and will not be responsible for the return of any material submitted by mail.** Accepts simultaneous submissions. Responds within 8 weeks to queries; 6-8 weeks to requested mss. "You are welcome to follow up by phone or e-mail after 6 weeks if you have not yet received a response."

TERMS Agent receives 15% commission on domestic sales; 25% commission on translation rights sales (15% to agency, 10% to sub-agent). Charges for overnight delivery and photocopying.

RECENT SALES *Millennial Money*, by Grant Sabatier (Atria/Penguin Random House); *Nimble*, by Baba Prasad (Perigee/Penguin Random House—US and World rights excluding India); *Carefrontation*, by Dr. Arlene Drake (Regan Arts/Phaidon); *There Are No Overachievers*, by Brian Biro (Crown Business/Penguin Random House); *Cheech Is Not My Real Name*, by Richard Marin (Grand Central Books/Hachette);

Killing It!, by Sheryl O'Loughlin (Harper Business/HarperCollins); *Scrappy*, by Terri Sjodin (Portfolio/Penguin Random House).

TIPS "E-mail queries only. Please don't call to pitch your work by phone."

SEAN MCCARTHY LITERARY AGENCY

E-mail: submissions@mccarthylit.com. **Website:** www.mccarthylit.com. **Contact:** Sean McCarthy. Estab. 2013.

○ Prior to his current position, Sean McCarthy began his publishing career as an editorial intern at Overlook Press and then moved over to the Sheldon Fogelman Agency.

REPRESENTS Considers these fiction areas: juvenile, middle grade, picture books, young adult.

⊷ Sean is drawn to flawed, multifaceted characters with devastatingly concise writing in YA, and character-driven work or smartly paced mysteries/adventures in MG. In picture books, he looks more for unforgettable characters, offbeat humor, and especially clever endings. He is not currently interested in issue-driven stories or query letters that pose too many questions.

HOW TO CONTACT E-query. "Please include a brief description of your book, your biography, and any literary or relevant professional credits in your query letter. If you are a novelist: Please submit the first 3 chapters of your manuscript (or roughly 25 pages) and a 1-page synopsis in the body of the e-mail or as a Word or PDF attachment. If you are a picture book author: Please submit the complete text of your manuscript. We are not currently accepting picture book manuscripts over 1,000 words. If you are an illustrator: Please attach up to 3 JPEGs or PDFs of your work, along with a link to your website." Accepts simultaneous submissions.

MCCORMICK LITERARY

37 W. 20th St., New York NY 10011. (212)691-9726. **E-mail:** queries@mccormicklit.com. **Website:** mccormicklit.com. Member of AAR. Signatory of WGA. **MEMBER AGENTS** David McCormick; Pilar Queen (narrative nonfiction, practical nonfiction, and commercial women's fiction); Bridget McCarthy (literary and commercial fiction, narrative nonfiction, memoir, and cookbooks); Alia Hanna Habib (literary fiction, narrative nonfiction, memoir and cookbooks); Edward Orloff (literary fiction and narrative nonfiction, especially cultural history, politics, biography,

and the arts); Daniel Menaker; Leslie Falk; Emma Borges-Scott.

REPRESENTS Nonfiction, novels. **Considers these fiction areas:** literary, women's.

HOW TO CONTACT Snail mail queries only. Send an SASE. Accepts simultaneous submissions.

☺⊘ ANNE MCDERMID & ASSOCIATES, LTD

320 Front St. W., Suite 1105, Toronto ON M5V 3B6 Canada. (647)788-4016. **Fax:** (416)324-8870. **E-mail:** admin@mcdermidagency.com. **E-mail:** info@mcdermidagency.com. **Website:** www.mcdermidagency.com. **Contact:** Anne McDermid. Estab. 1996.

MEMBER AGENTS Anne McDermid, Martha Webb, Monica Pacheco, Chris Bucci.

REPRESENTS Novels.

⊷ The agency represents literary novelists and commercial novelists of high quality, and also writers of nonfiction in the areas of memoir, biography, history, literary travel, narrative science, and investigative journalism. "We also represent a certain number of children's and YA writers and writers in the fields of science fiction and fantasy."

HOW TO CONTACT Query via e-mail or mail with a brief bio, description, and first 5 pages of project only. Accepts simultaneous submissions. *No unsolicited manuscripts.* Obtains most new clients through recommendations from others.

MCINTOSH & OTIS, INC.

353 Lexington Ave., New York NY 10016. (212)687-7400. **Fax:** (212)687-6894. **E-mail:** info@mcintoshandotis.com. **Website:** www.mcintoshandotis.com. **Contact:** Elizabeth Winick Rubinstein. Estab. 1928. Member of AAR. Signatory of WGA. SCBWI

MEMBER AGENTS Elizabeth Winick Rubinstein, ewrquery@mcintoshandotis.com (literary fiction, women's fiction, historical fiction, and mystery/suspense, along with narrative nonfiction, spiritual/self-help, history and current affairs); Christa Heschke, chquery@mcintoshandotis.com (picture books, middle grade, young adult and new adult projects); Adam Muhlig, amquery@mcintoshandotis.com (music–from jazz to classical to punk–popular culture, natural history, travel and adventure, and sports).

REPRESENTS Nonfiction, fiction, novels, juvenile books. **Considers these fiction areas:** fantasy, historical, horror, literary, middle grade, mystery, new adult, paranormal, picture books, romance, science fiction, suspense, urban fantasy, women's, young adult.

☛ Actively seeking "books with memorable characters, distinctive voices, and great plots."

HOW TO CONTACT E-mail submissions only. Each agent has their own e-mail address for subs. For fiction: Please send a query letter, synopsis, author bio, and the first 3 consecutive chapters (no more than 30 pages) of your novel. For nonfiction: Please send a query letter, proposal, outline, author bio, and 3 sample chapters (no more than 30 pages) of the ms. For children's & young adult: Please send a query letter, synopsis and the first 3 consecutive chapters (not to exceed 25 pages) of the ms. Accepts simultaneous submissions. Obtains clients through recommendations from others, editors, conferences and queries.

TERMS Agent receives 15% commission on domestic sales; 20% on foreign sales.

WRITERS CONFERENCES Attends Bologna Book Fair, in Bologna Italy in April, SCBWI Conference in New York in February, and regularly attends other conferences and industry conventions.

MENDEL MEDIA GROUP, LLC

115 W. 30th St., Suite 209, New York NY 10001. (646)239-9896. **E-mail:** query@mendelmedia.com. **Website:** www.mendelmedia.com. Estab. 2002. Member of AAR.

○ Prior to becoming an agent, Mr. Mendel was an academic. "I taught American literature, Yiddish, Jewish studies, and literary theory at the University of Chicago and the University of Illinois at Chicago while working on my PhD in English. I also worked as a freelance technical writer and as the managing editor of a healthcare magazine. In 1998, I began working for the late Jane Jordan Browne, a long-time agent in the book publishing world.".

REPRESENTS Nonfiction, fiction, novels. **Considers these fiction areas:** action, adventure, contemporary issues, crime, detective, erotica, ethnic, feminist, gay, glitz, historical, humor, inspirational, juvenile, lesbian, literary, mainstream, mystery, picture books, police, religious, romance, satire, sports, thriller, young adult, commercial and literary fiction..

☛ "I am interested in major works of history, current affairs, biography, business, politics, economics, science, major memoirs, narrative

nonfiction, and other sorts of general nonfiction." Actively seeking new, major or definitive work on a subject of broad interest, or a controversial, but authoritative, new book on a subject that affects many people's lives. "I also represent more light-hearted nonfiction projects, such as gift or novelty books, when they suit the market particularly well." Does not want "queries about projects written years ago that were unsuccessfully shopped to a long list of trade publishers by either the author or another agent. I am specifically not interested in considering serious poetry, original plays, or original film scripts."

HOW TO CONTACT You should e-mail your work to query@mendelmedia.com. We no longer accept or read submissions sent by mail, so please do not send inquiries by any other method. If we want to read more or discuss your work, we will respond to you by e-mail or phone. Fiction queries: If you have a novel you would like to submit, please paste a synopsis and the first twenty pages into the body of your email, below a detailed letter about your publication history and the history of the project, if it has been submitted previously to publishers or other agents. Please do not use attachments, as we will not open them. Nonfiction queries: If you have a completed nonfiction book proposal and sample chapters, you should paste those into the body of an e-mail, below a detailed letter about your publication history and the history of the project, if it has been submitted previously to any publishers or other agents. Please do not use attachments, as we will not open them. If we want to read more or discuss your work, we will call or e-mail you directly. If you do not receive a personal response within a few weeks, we are not going to offer representation. In any case, however, please do not call or email to inquire about your query. Accepts simultaneous submissions. Responds within a few weeks, if interested. Obtains most new clients through referrals.

TERMS Agent receives 15% commission on domestic sales; 20% commission on foreign sales.

WRITERS CONFERENCES BookExpo America; Frankfurt Book Fair; London Book Fair; RWA National Conference; Modern Language Association Convention; Jerusalem Book Fair.

TIPS "While I am not interested in being flattered by a prospective client, it does matter to me that she knows why she is writing to me in the first place. Is one of my clients a colleague of hers? Has she read a book by one of my clients that led her to believe I might be interested in her work? Authors of descriptive nonfiction should have real credentials and expertise in their subject areas, either as academics, journalists, or policy experts, and authors of prescriptive nonfiction should have legitimate expertise and considerable experience communicating their ideas in seminars and workshops, in a successful business, through the media, etc."

HOWARD MORHAIM LITERARY AGENCY

30 Pierrepont St., Brooklyn NY 11201. (718)222-8400. **Fax:** (718)222-5056. **E-mail:** info@morhaimliterary.com. **Website:** www.morhaimliterary.com. Member of AAR.

MEMBER AGENTS Howard Morhaim, howard@morhaimliterary.com; Kate McKean, kmckean@morhaimliterary.com; DongWon Song, dongwon@morhaimliterary.com; Kim-Mei Kirtland, kimmei@morhaimliterary.com.

REPRESENTS Considers these fiction areas: fantasy, historical, literary, middle grade, new adult, romance, science fiction, women's, young adult, LGBTQ young adult, magical realism, fantasy should be high fantasy, historical fiction should be no earlier than the 20th century..

- Kate McKean is open to many subgenres and categories of YA and MG fiction. Check the website for the most details. Actively seeking fiction, nonfiction, and young adult novels.

HOW TO CONTACT Query via e-mail with cover letter and 3 sample chapters. See each agent's listing for specifics. Accepts simultaneous submissions.

MOVEABLE TYPE MANAGEMENT

244 Madison Ave., Suite 334, New York NY 10016. **E-mail:** achromy@movabletm.com. **Website:** www.movabletm.com. **Contact:** Adam Chromy. Estab. 2002.

REPRESENTS Nonfiction, fiction, novels. **Considers these fiction areas:** action, commercial, crime, detective, family saga, hi-lo, historical, humor, literary, mainstream, mystery, police, romance, satire, science fiction, sports, suspense, thriller, women's.

- Mr. Chromy is a generalist, meaning that he accepts fiction submissions of virtually any kind (except juvenile books aimed for middle grade and younger) as well as nonfiction. He has sold books in the following categories: new adult, women's, romance, memoir, pop culture,

young adult, lifestyle, horror, how-to, general fiction, and more.

HOW TO CONTACT E-queries only. Responds if interested. For nonfiction: Send a query letter in the body of an e-mail that precisely introduces your topic and approach, and includes a descriptive bio. For journalists and academics, please also feel free to include a CV. Fiction: Send your query letter and the first 10 pages of your novel in the body of an e-mail. Your subject line needs to contain the word "Query" or your message will not reach the agency. No attachments and no snail mail. Accepts simultaneous submissions.

RECENT SALES *The Wedding Sisters*, by Jamie Brenner (St. Martin's Press); *Rage*, by (AmazonCrossing); *Sons Of Zeus*, by Noble Smith (Thomas Dunne Books); *World Made By Hand And Too Much Magic*, by James Howard Kunstler (Grove/Atlantic Press); *Dirty Rocker Boys*, by Bobbie Brown (Gallery/S&S).

JEAN V. NAGGAR LITERARY AGENCY, INC.

JVNLA, Inc., 216 E. 75th St., Suite 1E, New York NY 10021. (212)794-1082. **Website:** www.jvnla.com. **Contact:** Jennifer Weltz. Estab. 1978. Member of AAR. Other memberships include Women's Media Group, SCBWI, Pace University's Masters in Publishing Board Member. Represents 450 clients.

MEMBER AGENTS Jennifer Weltz (well-researched and original historicals, thrillers with a unique voice, wry dark humor, and magical realism; enthralling narrative nonfiction; voice driven young adult, middle grade); Alice Tasman (literary, commercial, YA, middle grade, and nonfiction in the categories of narrative, biography, music or pop culture); Ariana Philips (nonfiction both prescriptive and narrative); Alicia Brooks (fiction, non-fiction and YA).

REPRESENTS Nonfiction, fiction, novels, short story collections, novellas, juvenile books, scholarly books, poetry books. **Considers these fiction areas:** action, adventure, cartoon, comic books, commercial, contemporary issues, crime, detective, ethnic, family saga, fantasy, feminist, gay, historical, humor, inspirational, juvenile, lesbian, literary, mainstream, middle grade, multicultural, mystery, picture books, romance, satire, science fiction, suspense, thriller, women's, young adult.

- This agency specializes in mainstream fiction and nonfiction and literary fiction with commercial potential as well as young adult, middle grade, and picture books. Does not want to receive screenplays.

HOW TO CONTACT "Visit our website to send submissions and see what our individual agents are looking for. No snail mail submissions please!" Accepts simultaneous submissions. Depends on the agent. No responses for queries unless the agent is interested.

TERMS Agent receives 15% commission on domestic sales; 20% commission on foreign and film sales. Offers written contract. Charges for overseas mailing, messenger services, book purchases, photocopying—all deductible from royalties received.

RECENT SALES *Mort(e)*, by Robert Repino; *The Paying Guests*, by Sarah Waters; *The Third Victim*, by Phillip Margolin; *Every Kind of Wanting*, by Gina Frangello; *The Lies They Tell*, by Gillian French; *Dietland*, by Sarai Walker; *Mr. Rochester*, by Sarah Shoemaker; *Not If I See You First*, by Eric Lindstrom.

TIPS "We recommend courage, fortitude, and patience: the courage to be true to your own vision, the fortitude to finish a novel and polish it again and again before sending it out, and the patience to accept rejection gracefully and wait for the stars to align themselves appropriately for success."

NELSON LITERARY AGENCY

1732 Wazee St., Suite 207, Denver CO 80202. (303)292-2805. **E-mail:** query@nelsonagency.com. **E-mail:** querykristin@nelsonagency.com; querydanielle@nelsonagency.com; queryjoanna@nelsonagency.com; queryquressa@nelsonagency.com. **Website:** www.nelsonagency.com. **Contact:** Kristin Nelson, President. Estab. 2002. Member of AAR. RWA, SCBWI, SFWA. Represents 95 clients.

MEMBER AGENTS Danielle Burby; Joanna MacKenzie; Quressa Robinson.

REPRESENTS Fiction, novels. , young adult, middle grade, literary commercial, upmarket women's fiction, single-title romance, science fiction, fantasy. **Considers these fiction areas:** commercial, family saga, fantasy, gay, historical, horror, literary, mainstream, middle grade, multicultural, mystery, romance, science fiction, suspense, thriller, urban fantasy, women's, young adult.

➥ NLA specializes in representing commercial fiction and high-caliber literary fiction. "We represent many popular genre categories, including historical romance, steampunk, and all subgenres of YA." Regardless of genre, "we are actively seeking good stories well told." Does not want nonfiction, memoir, stage plays, screenplays, short story collections, poetry, children's picture books, early reader chapter books, or material for the Christian/inspirational market.

HOW TO CONTACT "Please visit our website and carefully read our submission guidelines. We do not accept any queries on Facebook or Twitter." Accepts simultaneous submissions. Makes best efforts to respond to all queries within 3 weeks. Response to full mss requested can take up to 3 months.

TERMS Agent charges industry standard commission.

TIPS "If you would like to learn how to write an awesome pitch paragraph for your query letter or would like any info on how publishing contracts work, please visit Kristin's popular industry blog Pub Rants: http://nelsonagency.com/pub-rants/."

NEW LEAF LITERARY & MEDIA, INC.

110 W. 40th St., Suite 2201, New York NY 10018. (646)248-7989. **Fax:** (646)861-4654. **E-mail:** query@newleafliterary.com. **Website:** www.newleafliterary.com. Estab. 2012. Member of AAR.

MEMBER AGENTS Joanna Volpe (women's fiction, thriller, horror, speculative fiction, literary fiction and historical fiction, young adult, middle grade, art-focused picture books); Kathleen Ortiz, Director of Subsidiary Rights and literary agent (new voices in YA and animator/illustrator talent); Suzie Townsend (new adult, young adult, middle grade, romance [all subgenres], fantasy [urban fantasy, science fiction, steampunk, epic fantasy] and crime fiction [mysteries, thrillers]); Pouya Shahbazian, Director of Film and Television (no unsolicited queries); Janet Reid, janet@newleafliterary.com; JL Stermer (nonfiction, smart pop culture, comedy/satire, fashion, health & wellness, self-help, and memoir).

REPRESENTS Nonfiction, fiction, novels, novellas, juvenile books, poetry books. **Considers these fiction areas:** crime, fantasy, historical, horror, literary, mainstream, middle grade, mystery, new adult, paranormal, picture books, romance, thriller, women's, young adult.

HOW TO CONTACT Send query via e-mail. Please do not query via phone. The word "Query" must be in the subject line, plus the agent's name, i.e.–Subject: Query, Suzie Townsend. You may include up to 5 double-spaced sample pages within the body of the e-mail. No attachments, unless specifically requested. Include all necessary contact information. You will receive an auto-response confirming receipt of your query. "We only respond if we are interested in seeing your work." Responds only if interested. All queries read within 1 month.

RECENT SALES *Carve the Mark*, by Veronica Roth (HarperCollins); *Red Queen*, by Victoria Aveyard (HarperCollins); *Lobster is the Best Medicine*, by Liz Climo (Running Press); *Ninth House*, by Leigh Bardugo (Henry Holt); *A Snicker of Magic*, by Natalie Lloyd (Scholastic).

DANA NEWMAN LITERARY

1800 Avenue of the Stars, 12th Floor, Los Angeles CA 90067. **E-mail:** dananewmanliterary@gmail.com. **Website:** dananewman.com. **Contact:** Dana Newman. Estab. 2009. Member of AAR. California State Bar. Represents 30 clients.

○ Prior to becoming an agent, Ms. Newman was an attorney in the entertainment industry for 14 years.

MEMBER AGENTS Dana Newman (narrative nonfiction, business, lifestyle, current affairs, parenting, memoir, pop culture, sports, health, literary and upmarket fiction).

REPRESENTS Nonfiction, fiction, novels. **Considers these fiction areas:** commercial, contemporary issues, family saga, feminist, historical, literary, multicultural, sports, women's.

☞ Ms. Newman has a background as an attorney in contracts, licensing, publishing and intellectual property law. She is experienced in digital content creation and distribution. "We are interested in practical nonfiction (business, health and wellness, psychology, parenting, technology) by authors with smart, unique perspectives and established platforms who are committed to actively marketing and promoting their books. We love compelling, inspiring narrative nonfiction in the areas of memoir, biography, history, pop culture, current affairs/women's interest, sports, and social trends. On the fiction side, we consider a very selective amount of literary fiction and women's upmarket fiction." Does not want religious, children's, poetry, horror, mystery, thriller, romance, or science fiction. Does not represent screenplays.

HOW TO CONTACT E-mail queries only. For both nonfiction and fiction, please submit a query letter including a description of your project and a brief biography. "If we are interested in your project, we will contact you and request a full book proposal (non-fiction) or a synopsis and the first 25 pages (fiction)." Accepts simultaneous submissions. "If we have requested your materials after receiving your query, we will use our best efforts to respond within 4 weeks although response time may vary." Obtains new clients through recommendations from others, queries, and submissions.

TERMS Obtains 15% commission on domestic sales; 20% on foreign sales. Offers 1 year written contract. Notice must be given 1 month prior to terminate a contract.

RECENT SALES *Eat Like a Local: France*, by Lynne Martin and Deborah Scarborough (Countryman Press); *Climbing the Hill*, by Jaime Harrison and Amos Snead (Ten Speed Press); *Nora Murphy's Country House Style*, by Nora Murphy (Vendome Press); *Crawl of Fame*, by Julie Moss and Robert Yehling (Pegasus Books); *Into the Abyss*, by Ginger Lerner-Wren (Beacon Press); *Native Advertising*, by Mike Smith (McGraw-Hill); *Breakthrough: The Making of America's First Woman President*, by Nancy L. Cohen (Counterpoint); *Just Add Water*, by Clay Marzo and Robert Yehling (Houghton Mifflin Harcourt); *A Stray Cat Struts*, by Slim Jim Phantom (St. Martin's Press); *Tuff Juice*, by Caron Butler and Steve Springer (Lyons Press).

HAROLD OBER ASSOCIATES

425 Madison Ave., New York NY 10017. (212)759-8600. **Fax:** (212)759-9428. **Website:** www.haroldober.com. **Contact:** Appropriate agent. Member of AAR. Represents 250 clients.

MEMBER AGENTS Phyllis Westberg; Craig Tenney (few new clients, mostly Ober backlist and foreign rights).

HOW TO CONTACT Submit concise query letter addressed to a specific agent with the first 5 pages of the ms or proposal and SASE. No fax or e-mail. Does not handle filmscripts or plays. Responds as promptly as possible. Obtains most new clients through recommendations from others.

TERMS Agent receives 15% commission on domestic sales; 20% commission on foreign sales. Charges clients for express mail/package services.

PARK LITERARY GROUP, LLC

50 Broadway, Suite 1601, New York NY 10006. (212)691-3500. **Fax:** (212)691-3540. **E-mail:** info@parkliterary.com. **E-mail:** queries@parkliterary.com. **Website:** www.parkliterary.com. Estab. 2005.

MEMBER AGENTS Theresa Park (plot-driven fiction and serious nonfiction); Abigail Koons (popular science, history, politics, current affairs and art, and women's fiction); Peter Knapp (children's and YA).

REPRESENTS Nonfiction, novels. **Considers these fiction areas:** juvenile, middle grade, suspense, thriller, women's, young adult.

☞ The Park Literary Group represents fiction and nonfiction with a boutique approach: an emphasis on servicing a relatively small number of clients, with the highest professional standards and focused personal attention. Does not want to receive poetry or screenplays.

HOW TO CONTACT Please specify the first and last name of the agent to whom you are submitting in the subject line of the e-mail. All materials must be in the body of the e-mail. Responds if interested. For fiction submissions, please include a query letter with short synopsis and the first 3 chapters of your work. Accepts simultaneous submissions.

RECENT SALES This agency's client list is on their website. It includes bestsellers Nicholas Sparks, Soman Chainani, Emily Giffin, and Debbie Macomber.

L. PERKINS AGENCY

5800 Arlington Ave., Riverdale NY 10471. (718)543-5344. **E-mail:** submissions@lperkinsagency.com. **Website:** lperkinsagency.com. Estab. 1987. Member of AAR. Represents 150 clients.

○ Ms. Perkins has been an agent for 25 years. She is also the author of *The Insider's Guide to Getting an Agent* (Writer's Digest Books), as well as 3 other nonfiction books. She has edited 25 erotic anthologies, and is also the founder and publisher of Riverdale Avenue Books, an award-winning hybrid publisher with 9 imprints.

MEMBER AGENTS Tish Beaty, ePub agent (erotic romance–including paranormal, historical, gay/lesbian/bisexual, and light-BDSM fiction; also, she seeks new adult and YA); Sandy Lu, sandy@lperkinsagency.com (fiction: she is looking for dark literary and commercial fiction, mystery, thriller, psychological horror, paranormal/urban fantasy, historical fiction, YA, historical thrillers or mysteries set in Victorian times; nonfiction: narrative nonfiction, history, biography, pop science, pop psychology, pop culture [music/theatre/film], humor, and food writing); Lori Perkins (not currently taking new clients); Leon Husock (science fiction & fantasy, as well as young adult and middle-

grade); Rachel Brooks (picture books, all genres of young adult and new adult fiction, as well as adult romance—especially romantic suspense [NOTE: Rachel is currently closed to unsolicited submissions]); Maximilian Ximinez (fiction: science fiction, fantasy, horror, thrillers; nonfiction: popular science, true crime, arts and trends in developing fields and cultures).

REPRESENTS Nonfiction, fiction, novels, short story collections. **Considers these fiction areas:** commercial, crime, detective, erotica, fantasy, feminist, gay, historical, horror, lesbian, literary, middle grade, mystery, new adult, paranormal, picture books, romance, science fiction, short story collections, supernatural, thriller, urban fantasy, women's, young adult.

☞ "Most of our clients write both fiction and nonfiction. This combination keeps our clients publishing for years. The founder of the agency is also a published author, so we know what it takes to write a good book." Actively seeking erotic romance, romance, young adult, middle grade, science fiction, fantasy, memoir, pop culture, thrillers. Does not want poetry, stand alone short stories or novellas, scripts, plays, westerns, textbooks.

HOW TO CONTACT E-queries only. Include your query, a 1-page synopsis, and the first 5 pages from your novel pasted into the e-mail, or your proposal. No attachments. Submit to only 1 agent at the agency. No snail mail queries. "If you are submitting to one of our agents, please be sure to check the submission status of the agent by visiting their social media accounts listed [on the agency website]." Accepts simultaneous submissions. Obtains most new clients through recommendations from others, solicitations, conferences.

TERMS Agent receives 15% commission on domestic sales; 20% commission on foreign sales. No written contract. Charges clients for photocopying.

RECENT SALES *Arena*, by Holly Jennings; *Taking the Lead*, by Cecilia Tan; *The Girl with Ghost Eyes*, by M. H. Boroson; *Silent Attraction*, by Lauren Brown.

WRITERS CONFERENCES Romantic Times; Romance Writers of America nationals; Rainbow Book Fair; NECON; Killercon; BookExpo America; World Fantasy Convention.

TIPS "Research your field and contact professional writers' organizations to see who is looking for what. Finish your novel before querying agents. Read my book, *An Insider's Guide to Getting an Agent*, to get a sense of how agents operate. Read agent blogs-agentinthemiddle.blogspot.com and ravenousromance.blogspot.com."

RUBIN PFEFFER CONTENT

648 Hammond St., Chestnut Hill MA 02467. **E-mail:** info@rpcontent.com. **Website:** www.rpcontent.com. **Contact:** Rubin Pfeffer. Estab. 2014. Member of AAR. Signatory of WGA.

○ Rubin has previously worked as the vice-president and publisher of Simon & Schuster Children's Books and as an independent agent at East West Literary Agency.

MEMBER AGENTS Melissa Nasson is an associate agent at Rubin Pfeffer Content and an attorney. She previously interned at Zachary Shuster Harmsworth, Perseus Books Group, and East-West Literary Agency before joining Rubin Pfeffer Content. Melissa also works as contracts director at Beacon Press.

REPRESENTS Considers these fiction areas: juvenile, middle grade, picture books, young adult.

☛ High-quality children's fiction and nonfiction, including picture books, middle-grade, and young adult. No manuscripts intended for an adult audience.

HOW TO CONTACT Note: Rubin Pfeffer accepts submissions by referral only. Melissa Nasson is open to queries for picture books, middle-grade, and young adult fiction and nonfiction. To query Melissa, email her at melissa@rpcontent.com, include the query letter in the body of the email, and attach the first 50 pages as a Word doc or PDF. If you wish to query Rubin Pfeffer by referral only, specify the contact information of your reference when submitting. Authors/illustrators should send a query and a 1-3 chapter ms via e-mail (no postal submissions). The query, placed in the body of the e-mail, should include a synopsis of the piece, as well as any relevant information regarding previous publications, referrals, websites, and biographies. The ms may be attached as a .doc or a .pdf file. Specifically for illustrators, attach a PDF of the dummy or artwork to the e-mail. Accepts simultaneous submissions. Strives to respond within 6-8 weeks.

● PONTAS LITERARY & FILM AGENCY

Sèneca, 31, principal 08006, Barcelona Spain. (34)(93)218-2212. **E-mail:** info@pontas-agency.com. **E-mail:** submissions@pontas-agency.com. **Website:** www.pontas-agency.com. Estab. 1992. Represents 70 clients.

REPRESENTS Fiction, novels. **Considers these fiction areas:** action, adventure, commercial, confession, contemporary issues, crime, detective, ethnic, experimental, family saga, feminist, frontier, gay, historical, horror, inspirational, lesbian, literary, mainstream, multicultural, mystery, regional, satire, thriller, translation, women's, young adult.

☛ "At this moment in time, we are only looking for works of adult fiction written in English and French." Please defer to send any materials that do not match this requirement. Does not want original film screenplays, theatre plays, poetry, sci-fi, fantasy, romance, children's, illustrated.

HOW TO CONTACT When submitting work, include a brief cover letter with your name and title of your mss in the e-mail subject, a detailed synopsis of your plot, your biography, and the full work in PDF or Word format. Accepts simultaneous submissions. "Due to the enormous and increasing volume of submissions that we receive, we cannot guarantee a reply. If you do not receive a response 6 weeks from the date of your submission, you can assume we're not interested. It's also important to note that we don't provide specific reasons nor editorial feedback on the submissions received."

PRENTIS LITERARY

PMB 496 6830 NE Bothell Way, Kenmore WA 98028. **Website:** prentisliterary.com. **Contact:** Autumn Frisse, acquisitions; Terry Johnson, business manager. Represents 12-15 clients.

○ Trodayne Northern worked as an English teacher and Academic Advisor prior to being and agent. He also worked as both a fiction and nonfiction freelancer writer and editor. After coming to work for The Literary Group, Mr. Northern started working for Linn Prentis in 2010. Trodayne Northern, Leslie Varney and Terry Johnson took over the agency and rebranded the company after Linn's retirement and eventual passing.

REPRESENTS Nonfiction, fiction, novels. **Considers these fiction areas:** adventure, ethnic, fantasy, gay, historical, horror, humor, lesbian, literary, mainstream, middle grade, mystery, paranormal, romance, science fiction, supernatural, thriller, urban fantasy, young adult.

☛ Special interest in sci-fi and fantasy, but fiction is what truly interests us. Nonfiction projects have to be something we just can't resist. Actively seeking science fiction/fantasy, POC/intersectional, women's fiction, LBGTQ+, literary fiction, children's fiction, YA, MG, mystery, horror, romance, nonfiction/memoir. Please visit website for comprehensive list. Does not want to "receive books for little kids."

HOW TO CONTACT No phone or fax queries. No surface mail. For submission use our submission form posted on our submission page or e-mail acquisitions afrisse@prentisliterary.com. For other business business questions e-mail: tjohnson@prentisliterary.com. Accepts simultaneous submissions. Obtains most new clients through recommendations from others, solicitations.

TERMS Agent receives 15% commission on domestic sales; 20% commission on foreign sales. Offers written contract; 60-day notice must be given to terminate contract.

RECENT SALES Sales include The Relic Hunter: A Gina Miyoko Mystery NYT best selling author, Maya Bohnhoff, Substrate Phantoms for Jessica Reisman, Vienna for William Kirby; Hunting Ground, Frost Burned and Night Broken titles in two series for NY Times bestselling author Patricia Briggs (as well as a graphic novel *Homecoming*) and a story collection; with more coming; a duology of novels for A.M. Dellamonica whose first book, *Indigo Springs*, won Canada's annual award for best fantasy, as well as several books abroad for client Tachyon Publications.

AARON M. PRIEST LITERARY AGENCY

200 W. 41st St., 21st Floor, New York NY 10036. (212)818-0344. **Fax:** (212)573-9417. **E-mail:** info@aaronpriest.com. **Website:** www.aaronpriest.com. Estab. 1974. Member of AAR.

MEMBER AGENTS Aaron Priest, querypriest@aaronpriest.com (thrillers, commercial fiction, biographies); Lisa Erbach Vance, queryvance@aaronpriest.com (contemporary fiction, thrillers/suspense, international fiction, narrative nonfiction); Lucy Childs, querychilds@aaronpriest.com (literary and commercial fiction, memoir, edgy women's fiction); Mitch Hoffman, queryhoffman@aaronpriest.com (thrillers, suspense, crime fiction, and literary fiction, as well as narrative nonfiction, politics, popular science, history, memoir, current events, and pop culture).

REPRESENTS Considers these fiction areas: commercial, contemporary issues, crime, literary, middle grade, suspense, thriller, women's, young adult.

☛ Does not want to receive poetry, screenplays, horror or sci-fi.

HOW TO CONTACT Query one of the agents using the appropriate e-mail listed on the website. "Please do not submit to more than 1 agent at this agency. We urge you to check our website and consider each agent's emphasis before submitting. Your query letter should be about one page long and describe your work as well as your background. You may also paste the first chapter of your work in the body of the e-mail. Do not send attachments." Accepts simultaneous submissions. Responds in 4 weeks, only if interested.

TERMS Agent receives 15% commission on domestic sales.

PROSPECT AGENCY

551 Valley Rd., PMB 377, Upper Montclair NJ 07043. (718)788-3217. **Fax:** (718)360-9582. **E-mail:** https://www.prospectagency.com/submit.html. **Website:** www.prospectagency.com. Estab. 2005. Member of AAR. Signatory of WGA. Represents 130+ clients.

MEMBER AGENTS Emily Sylvan Kim focuses on romance, women's, commercial, young adult, new adult, nonfiction and memoir. She is currently looking for commercial and upmarket women's fiction; self-published authors looking to explore a hybrid career; established and strong debut romance writing mainstream romance; memoir and high interest nonfiction; literary and commercial YA fiction; and select middle grade and early reader fiction with strong commercial appeal. Rachel Orr focuses on picture books, illustrators, middle grade and young adult. She is currently looking for short, punchy picture books (either in prose or rhyme) that are humorous and have a strong marketing hook; non-fiction picture books (especially biographies or stories with a historical angle); illustrators for the trade market; and literary and commercial middle-grade and YA (all time periods and genres.) Ann Rose focuses on middle grade, young adult and commercial adult fiction. She is currently seeking YA of all genres; MG of all genres, especially ones that push the boundaries of middle grade; Swoony romances; Light sci-fi or fantasy; Commercial fiction; Heartwarming (or heart wrenching) contemporaries; any stories with unique voices, diverse perspectives, vivid settings; stories that explore tough topics; and dark and edgy stories with unlikeable characters. Emma Sector focuses on picture books, illustrators, middle grade and young adult. She is currently seeking quirky, character driven chapter books; literary and commercial middle-grade and YA Novels; picture book authors and illustrators; middle-grade graphic novels; and nonfiction middle-grade. Please use the agency form to submit your query: https://www.prospectagency.com/submit.html.

REPRESENTS Nonfiction, fiction, novels, novellas, juvenile books, scholarly books, textbooks. **Considers these fiction areas:** commercial, contemporary issues, crime, ethnic, family saga, fantasy, feminist, gay, hi-lo, historical, horror, humor, juvenile, lesbian, literary, mainstream, middle grade, multicultural, mystery, new adult, picture books, romance, science fiction, suspense, thriller, urban fantasy, women's, young adult.

☞ "We're looking for strong, unique voices and unforgettable stories and characters."

HOW TO CONTACT All submissions are electronic and must be submitted through the portal at prospectagency.com/submit.html. We do not accept any submissions through snail mail. Accepts simultaneous submissions. Obtains new clients through conferences, recommendations, queries, and some scouting.

TERMS Agent receives 15% on domestic sales, 20% on foreign sales sold directly and 25% on sales using a subagent. Offers written contract.

✪ P.S. LITERARY AGENCY

2010 Winston Park Dr., 2nd Floor, Oakville ON L6H 5R7 Canada. **E-mail:** info@psliterary.com. **E-mail:** query@psliterary.com. **Website:** www.psliterary.com. **Contact:** Curtis Russell, principal agent; Carly Watters, senior agent; Maria Vicente, literary agent; Eric Smith; literary agent; Kurestin Armada, associate agent. Estab. 2005.

MEMBER AGENTS Curtis Russell (literary/commercial fiction, mystery, thriller, suspense, romance, young adult, middle grade, picture books, business, history, politics, current affairs, memoirs, health/wellness, sports, humor, pop culture, pop science, pop psychology); Carly Watters (upmarket/commercial fiction, women's fiction, book club fiction, literary thrillers, cookbooks, health/wellness, memoirs, humor, pop science, pop psychology); Maria Vicente (young adult, middle grade, illustrated picture books, graphic novels, pop culture, science, lifestyle, design); Kurestin Armada (magic realism, science fiction, fantasy, illustrated picture books, middle grade, young adult, graphic novels, romance, design, cookbooks, pop psychology, photography, nature, science); Eric Smith (young adult,

new adult, literary/commercial fiction, cookbooks, pop culture, humor, essay collections).

REPRESENTS Nonfiction, fiction, novels, juvenile books. **Considers these fiction areas:** action, adventure, comic books, commercial, crime, detective, erotica, ethnic, experimental, family saga, fantasy, feminist, gay, historical, horror, humor, inspirational, juvenile, lesbian, literary, mainstream, middle grade, multicultural, mystery, new adult, New Age, paranormal, picture books, police, romance, satire, science fiction, sports, supernatural, suspense, thriller, urban fantasy, women's, young adult.

☞ Actively seeking both fiction and nonfiction. Seeking both new and established writers. Does not want to receive poetry or screenplays.

HOW TO CONTACT Query letters should be directed to query@psliterary.com. PSLA does not accept or respond to phone, paper, or social media queries. Responds in 4-6 weeks to queries/proposals. Obtains most new clients through solicitations.

TERMS Agent receives 15% commission on domestic sales; 25% commission on foreign sales. "We offer a written contract, with 30-days notice to terminate."

TIPS "Please review our website for the most up-to-date submission guidelines. We do not charge reading fees. We do not offer a critique service."

⊘ PUBLICATION RIOT GROUP

E-mail: submissions@priotgroup.com. **Website:** www.priotgroup.com. **Contact:** Donna Bagdasarian. Member of AAR. Signatory of WGA.

◗ Prior to being an agent, Ms. Bagdasarian worked as an acquisitions editor. Previously, she worked for the William Morris and Maria Carvainis agencies.

REPRESENTS Nonfiction, novels. **Considers these fiction areas:** ethnic, historical, literary, mainstream, thriller, women's.

☞ "The company is a literary management company, representing their authors in all processes of the entertainment trajectory: from book development, to book sales, to subsidiary sales in the foreign market, television and film." Does not want science fiction and fantasy.

HOW TO CONTACT Currently closed to all submissions. Accepts simultaneous submissions.

RECENT SALES List of sales on agency website.

THE PURCELL AGENCY

E-mail: tpaqueries@gmail.com. **Website:** www.the-purcellagency.com. **Contact:** Tina P. Schwartz. Estab. 2012. SCBWI Represents 42 clients.

MEMBER AGENTS Tina P. Schwartz, Catherine Hedrick.

REPRESENTS Nonfiction, fiction, novels, juvenile books. **Considers these fiction areas:** juvenile, middle grade, women's, young adult.

☛ This agency also takes juvenile nonfiction for MG and YA markets. At this point, the agency is not considering fantasy, science fiction or picture book submissions.

HOW TO CONTACT Check the website to see if agency is open to submissions and for submission guidelines. Accepts simultaneous submissions.

RECENT SALES *Seven Suspects*, by Renee James; *A Kind of Justice*, by Renee James; *Adventures at Hound Hotel*, by Shelley Swanson Sateren; *Adventures at Tabby Towers*, by Shelley Swanson Sateren; *Keys to Freedom*, by Karen Meade.

QUEEN LITERARY AGENCY

30 E. 60th St., Suite 1004, New York NY 10022. (212)974-8333. **Fax:** (212)974-8347. **E-mail:** submissions@queenliterary.com. **Website:** www.queenliterary.com. **Contact:** Lisa Queen.

◯ Prior to her current position, Ms. Queen was a former publishing executive and most recently head of IMG Worldwide's literary division.

REPRESENTS Novels. **Considers these fiction areas:** commercial, historical, literary, mystery, thriller.

☛ Ms. Queen's specialties: "While our agency represents a wide range of nonfiction titles, we have a particular interest in business books, food writing, science and popular psychology, as well as books by well-known chefs, radio and television personalities, and sports figures."

HOW TO CONTACT E-query. Accepts simultaneous submissions.

RECENT SALES A full list of this agency's clients and sales is available on their website.

RED SOFA LITERARY

P.O. Box 40482, St. Paul MN 55104. (651)224-6670. **E-mail:** dawn@redsofaliterary.com laura@redsofaliterary.com; amanda@redsofaliterary.com; stacey@redsofaliterary.com; erik@redsofaliterary.com; liz@redsofaliterary.com. **Website:** www.redsofaliterary.com. **Contact:** Dawn Frederick, owner/literary agent; Laura Zats, literary agent; Amanda Rutter, associate literary agent; Stacey Graham, associate literary agent; Erik Hane, associate literary agent; Liz Rahn, subrights agent. Estab. 2008. Authors Guild and the MN Publishers Round Table Represents 125 clients.

◯ **Dawn:** "Before publishing I was a bookseller in the independent, chain, and specialty stores. I ended up in MN due to my first publishing job, eventually becoming a literary agent at Sebastian Literary Agency. I have B.S. in Human Ecology and a M.S. in Information Sciences from an ALA accredited institution. I'm also the co-founder of the MN Publishing Tweet Up, the News chair for the Twin Cities Advisory Council for MPR, and a teaching artist at Loft Literary. I can be found on Twitter at @redsofaliterary." **Laura:** "I received my B.A. from graduated from Grinnell College with degrees in English and anthropology. She began working in the publishing industry in 2011, joining Red Sofa Literary in 2013. As an agent, she specializes in children's fiction, science fiction and fantasy, and romance. She is also one-half of the weekly publishing podcast, Print Run. In her free time, Laura serves on the board of the Minnesota Book Publishers' Roundtable, teaches classes on writing and publishing, and drinks a lot of tea. Connect with her on Twitter @LZats." **Amanda:** "I have no formal qualifications in literary—in fact, my degree subject was accounting. But my professional history includes acquisition editor for Strange Chemistry, freelance editor for Bubblecow and Wise Ink Publishing, and book blogger." **Bree:** "I have a Bachelors in philosophy, a masters in journalism with an emphasis in editing and I've been working in various areas of journalism for the past 9 years. I started agenting in 2011 (after having interned at a literary agency for a year)." **Stacey:** "I have Bachelors of Science degrees in History and Archaeology/Anthropology from Oregon State University. I am the author of four books and multiple short stories, a screenwriter, ghostwriter, and editor." **Erik:** "Along with working as an agent at Red Sofa, Erik Hane is a freelance editor and writer based in Minneapolis. Since graduating from Knox College and the Denver Publishing Institute in 2012, he has worked as an assistant editor at Oxford University Press and then as an acquiring editor at The Overlook Press, both in New York. This experience at both academic and commercial publishing houses means he's performed editorial work on everything from serious scientific nonfiction to literary novels." **Liz:** "Liz Rahn graduated from Concordia College with degrees in English Literature and History. She was in the 2015 class of the Denver Publishing Institute and does freelance editing in addition to her work with Red Sofa Literary."

MEMBER AGENTS Laura Zats; Amanda Rutter; Stacey Graham; Erik Hane; Liz Rahn.

REPRESENTS Nonfiction, fiction, novels, juvenile books. **Considers these fiction areas:** action, adventure, commercial, contemporary issues, detective, erotica, ethnic, fantasy, feminist, gay, humor, juvenile, lesbian, literary, mainstream, middle grade, multicultural, mystery, picture books, romance, science fiction, suspense, thriller, urban fantasy, young adult.

Dawn Frederick: "I am always in search of a good work of nonfiction that falls within my categories (see my specific list at our website). I especially love pop culture, interesting histories, social sciences/advocacy, humor and books that are great conversation starters. As for fiction, I am always in search of good YA and MG titles. For YA I will go a little darker on the tone, as I enjoy a good gothic, contemporary or historical YA novel. For MG, I will always want something fun and lighthearted, but would love more contemporary themes too." **Laura Zats:** " Diverse YA of all kinds, I'm looking for all genres here, and am especially interested in settings or characters I haven't seen before and queer romantic relationships if there's a romance. Adult science fiction and fantasy. Please note I have an anthropology degree, I'm interested in well-drawn cultures and subverting traditional Chosen One, quest, and colonial narratives. I will fall on the floor and salivate if your writing reminds me of N.K. Jemisin or Nnedi Okorafor. No white dudes on quests, dreams, or Western ideas of Hell, please. Romance/erotica - I am looking for all settings and subgenres here. Must have verbal consent throughout and a twist to traditional romance tropes. If you send me the next The Hating Game, I will be the happiest agent in all the land. Please no rape, querying anything

shorter than 60K, or shifters" **Amanda Rutter:** "Science fiction/fantasy, the non-YA ideas, young adult and middle grade–science fiction/fantasy." **Stacey Graham:** "Middle-grade with a great voice — especially funny and/or spooky, Nonfiction (MG/YA/Adult), Romance, and Mystery with a humorous bent." **Erik Hane:** "Literary fiction, Nonfiction [no memoirs]." These are the things we are not actively seeking: **Dawn:** "Memoirs, it seems everyone ignores this request. I also prefer to represent books that aren't overly sappy, overly romantic, or any type of didactic/moralistic."**Laura:** "Nonfiction, including memoir. Adult mystery/thriller/literary fiction. Fiction without quirky or distinctive hooks. Books that follow or fit in trends." **Amanda:** "I am definitely not a non-fiction person. I rarely read it myself, so wouldn't know where to start where to represent! Also, although I enjoy middle grade fiction and would be happy to represent, I won't take on picture books." **Stacey:** "At this time, I do not want to represent YA, fantasy, sci-fi, or romance." **Erik:** "I definitely don't want to represent fiction that sets out at the start to be 'genre.' I like reading it, but I don't think it's for me as an agent. Bring me genre elements, but I think I'd rather let the classification happen naturally. I also don't want memoir unless you've really, really got something unique and accessible. I also don't want to represent children's lit; that's another thing I really do love and appreciate but don't quite connect with professionally."

HOW TO CONTACT Query by e-mail or mail with SASE. No attachments, please. Submit full proposal (for nonfiction especially, for fiction it would be nice) plus 3 sample chapters (or first 50 pages) and any other pertinent writing samples upon request by the specific agent. Do not sent within or attached to the query letter. Pdf/doc/docx is preferred, no rtf documents please. Accepts simultaneous submissions. Obtains new clients through queries, also through recommendations from others, solicitations.

TERMS Agent receives 15% commission on domestic sales; 20% commission on foreign sales. Offers written contract.

WRITERS CONFERENCES Surrey Writers Conference, Writers Digest, SDSU Writer's Conference, WorldCon, CONvergence, SCWBI (regional conferences), FWA Conference, DFW Writers Conference,

Northern Colorado Writers Conference, Horror World Convention, Loft Literary Conference, Madison Writers Workshop, Emerald City Writers Conference, Missouri Writers Guild, Pike's Peak Conference, Willamette Writers Conference, and more.

TIPS "Always remember the benefits of building an author platform, and the accessibility of accomplishing this task in today's industry. Most importantly, research the agents queried. Avoid contacting every literary agent about a book idea. Due to the large volume of queries received, the process of reading queries for unrepresented categories (by the agency) becomes quite the arduous task. Investigate online directories, printed guides (like *Writer's Market*), individual agent websites, and more, before beginning the query process. It's good to remember that each agent has a vision of what s/he wants to represent and will communicate this information accordingly. We're simply waiting for those specific book ideas to come in our direction."

REES LITERARY AGENCY

14 Beacon St., Suite 710, Boston MA 02108. (617)227-9014. **E-mail:** lorin@reesagency.com. **Website:** reesagency.com. Estab. 1983. Member of AAR. Represents more than 100 clients.

MEMBER AGENTS Ann Collette, agent10702@aol.com (fiction: literary, upscale commercial women's, crime [including mystery, thriller and psychological suspense], upscale western, historical, military and war, and horror; nonfiction: narrative, military and war, books on race and class, works set in Southeast Asia, biography, pop culture, books on film and opera, humor, and memoir); Lorin Rees, lorin@reesagency.com (literary fiction, memoirs, business books, self-help, science, history, psychology, and narrative nonfiction); Rebecca Podos, rebecca@reesagency.com (young adult and middle grade fiction, particularly books about complex female relationships, beautifully written contemporary, genre novels with a strong focus on character, romance with more at stake than "will they/won't they," and LGBTQ books across all genres).

REPRESENTS Novels. **Considers these fiction areas:** commercial, crime, historical, horror, literary, middle grade, mystery, suspense, thriller, westerns, women's, young adult.

HOW TO CONTACT Consult website for each agent's submission guidelines and e-mail addresses, as they differ. Accepts simultaneous submissions.

Obtains most new clients through recommendations from others, conferences, submissions.

TERMS Agent receives 15% commission on domestic sales; 20% commission on foreign sales.

REGAL HOFFMANN & ASSOCIATES LLC

143 West 29th St., Suite 901, New York NY 10001. (212)684-7900. **Website:** www.rhaliterary.com. Estab. 2002. Member of AAR. Represents 70 clients.

MEMBER AGENTS Claire Anderson-Wheeler (nonfiction: memoirs and biographies, narrative histories, popular science, popular psychology; adult fiction: primarily character-driven literary fiction, but open to genre fiction, high-concept fiction; all genres of young adult/middle grade fiction); Markus Hoffmann (international and literary fiction, crime, [pop] cultural studies, current affairs, economics, history, music, popular science, and travel literature); Stephanie Steiker (serious and narrative nonfiction, literary fiction, graphic novels, history, philosophy, current affairs, cultural studies, biography, music, international writing); Grace Ross (literary fiction, historical fiction, international narratives, narrative nonfiction, popular science, biography, cultural theory, memoir); Elianna Kan (Spanish-language fiction and non-fiction writers, literature in translation).

REPRESENTS Nonfiction, fiction, novels, short story collections, juvenile books, scholarly books. **Considers these fiction areas:** literary, mainstream, middle grade, short story collections, thriller, women's, young adult.

☛ We represent works in a wide range of categories, with an emphasis on literary fiction, outstanding thriller and crime fiction, and serious narrative nonfiction. Actively seeking literary fiction and narrative nonfiction. Does not want romance, science fiction, poetry, or screenplays.

HOW TO CONTACT Query with SASE or via Submittable (https://rhaliterary.submittable.com/submit). No phone calls. Submissions should consist of a 1-page query letter detailing the book in question, as well as the qualifications of the author. For fiction, submissions may also include the first 10 pages of the novel or one short story from a collection. Accepts simultaneous submissions. Responds in 4-8 weeks.

TERMS Agent receives 15% commission on domestic sales; 20% commission on foreign sales. We charge no reading fees.

RECENT SALES *Wily Snare*, by Adam Jay Epstein; *Perfectly Undone*, by Jamie Raintree; *A Sister in My House*, by Linda Olsson; *This Is How It Really Sounds*, by Stuart Archer Cohen; *Autofocus*, by Lauren Gibaldi; *We've Already Gone This Far*, by Patrick Dacey; *A Fierce and Subtle Poison*, by Samantha Mabry; *The Life of the World to Come*, by Dan Cluchey; *Willful Disregard*, by Lena Andersson; *The Sweetheart*, by Angelina Mirabella.

TIPS "We are deeply committed to every aspect of our clients' careers, and are engaged in everything from the editorial work of developing a great book proposal or line editing a fiction manuscript to negotiating state-of-the-art book deals and working to promote and publicize the book when it's published. We are at the forefront of the effort to increase authors' rights in publishing contracts in a rapidly changing commercial environment. We deal directly with co-agents and publishers in every foreign territory and also work directly and with co-agents for feature film and television rights, with extraordinary success in both arenas. Many of our clients' works have sold in dozens of translation markets, and a high proportion of our books have been sold in Hollywood. We have strong relationships with speaking agents, who can assist in arranging author tours and other corporate and college speaking opportunities when appropriate."

⊘ THE AMY RENNERT AGENCY

1550 Tiburon Blvd., #302, Tiburon CA 94920. **E-mail:** queries@amyrennert.com. **Website:** www.publishersmarketplace.com/members/amyrennert/. **Contact:** Amy Rennert.

REPRESENTS Nonfiction, novels. **Considers these fiction areas:** literary, mainstream, mystery.

☛ "The Amy Rennert Agency specializes in books that matter. We provide career management for established and first-time authors, and our breadth of experience in many genres enables us to meet the needs of a diverse clientele."

HOW TO CONTACT Amy Rennert is not currently accepting unsolicited submissions. Accepts simultaneous submissions.

TIPS "Due to the high volume of submissions, it is not possible to respond to each and every one. Please understand that we are only able to respond to queries that we feel may be a good fit with our agency."

◐ THE LISA RICHARDS AGENCY

108 Upper Leeson St., Dublin 4 Ireland. (03)(531)637-5000. **Fax:** (03)(531)667-1256. **E-mail:** info@lisarichards.ie. **Website:** www.lisarichards.ie. Estab. 1989.

MEMBER AGENTS Faith O'Grady (literary).

REPRESENTS Nonfiction, fiction, juvenile books. **Considers these fiction areas:** commercial, literary, middle grade, young adult.

☛ "For fiction, I am always looking for exciting new writing–distinctive voices, original, strong storylines, and intriguing characters." Doesn't handle horror, science fiction, screenplays, or children's picture books.

HOW TO CONTACT Contact If sending fiction, please limit your submission to the first three or four chapters, and include a covering letter and an SASE if required. If sending nonfiction, please send a detailed proposal about your book, a sample chapter and a cover letter. Every effort will be made to respond to submissions within 3 months of receipt. Accepts simultaneous submissions.

RECENT SALES Clients include Arlene Hunt, Roisin Ingle, Declan Lynch, Kevin Rafter.

◐ THE RIGHTS FACTORY

P.O. Box 499, Station C, Toronto ON M6J 3P6 Canada. (416)966-5367. **Website:** www.therightsfactory.com. Estab. 2004. Represents ~150 clients.

MEMBER AGENTS Sam Hiyate (President: fiction, nonfiction and graphic novel); Ali McDonald (Kidlit Agent: YA and children's literature of all kinds); Olga Filina (Associate Agent: commercial and historical fiction; great genre fiction in the area of romance and mystery; nonfiction in the field of business, wellness, lifestyle and memoir; and young adult and middle grade novels with memorable characters); Cassandra Rogers (Associate Agent: adult literary and commercial women's fiction; historical fiction; nonfiction on politics, history, science, and finance; humorous, heartbreaking and inspiring memoir); Lydia Moed (Associate Agent: science fiction and fantasy, historical fiction, diverse voices; narrative nonfiction on a wide variety of topics, including history, popular science, biography and travel); Natalie Kimber (Associate Agent: literary and commercial fiction and creative nonfiction in categories such as memoir, cooking, pop-culture, spirituality, and sustainability); Harry Endrulat (Associate Agent: children's literature, especially author/illustrators and Canadian voices); Haskell Nussbaum

(Associate Agent: literature of all kinds); Anna Trader (Associate Agent: literary, general and women's fiction; nonfiction in self-help and memoir); Lindsay Leggett (Associate Agent: SFF, horror, ownvoices, children's).

REPRESENTS Nonfiction, fiction, novels, short story collections, novellas, juvenile books. **Considers these fiction areas:** commercial, crime, family saga, fantasy, gay, hi-lo, historical, horror, juvenile, lesbian, literary, mainstream, middle grade, multicultural, mystery, new adult, paranormal, picture books, romance, science fiction, short story collections, suspense, thriller, urban fantasy, women's, young adult.

☛ Plays, screenplays, textbooks.

HOW TO CONTACT There is a submission form on this agency's website. Accepts simultaneous submissions. Responds in 3-6 weeks.

ANGELA RINALDI LITERARY AGENCY

P.O. Box 7875, Beverly Hills CA 90212-7875. (310)842-7665. **Fax:** (310)837-8143. **E-mail:** info@rinaldiliterary.com. **Website:** www.rinaldiliterary.com. **Contact:** Angela Rinaldi. Member of AAR.

○ Prior to opening her agency, Ms. Rinaldi was an editor at NAL/Signet, Pocket Books and Bantam, and the manager of book development for *The Los Angeles Times*.

REPRESENTS Nonfiction, novels. , TV and motion picture rights (for clients only). **Considers these fiction areas:** commercial, historical, literary, mainstream, mystery, suspense, thriller, women's, contemporary, gothic, women's book club fiction.

☛ Actively seeking commercial and literary fiction, as well as nonfiction. For fiction, we do not want to receive humor, CIA espionage, drug thrillers, techno thrillers, category romances, science fiction, fantasy, horror/occult/paranormal, poetry, film scripts, magazine articles or religion. For nonfiction, please do not send us magazine articles, celebrity bios, or tell alls.

HOW TO CONTACT E-queries only. Include the word "Query" in the subject line. For fiction, please send a brief synopsis and paste the first 10 pages into an e-mail. Nonfiction queries should include a detailed cover letter, your credentials and platform information as well as any publishing history. Tell us if you have a completed proposal. Accepts simultaneous submissions. Responds in 2-4 weeks.

TERMS Agent receives 15% commission on domestic sales; 25% commission on foreign sales. Offers written contract.

ANN RITTENBERG LITERARY AGENCY, INC.

15 Maiden Lane, Suite 206, New York NY 10038. (212)684-6936. **E-mail:** info@rittlit.com. **Website:** www.rittlit.com. **Contact:** Ann Rittenberg, president. Estab. 1992. Member of AAR. Represents 30 clients.

MEMBER AGENTS Ann Rittenberg, Rosie Jonker.

REPRESENTS Nonfiction, fiction, novels, juvenile books. **Considers these fiction areas:** crime, detective, family saga, literary, mainstream, mystery, suspense, thriller, women's.

☛ "We don't represent screenplays, poetry, plays, or self-help."

HOW TO CONTACT Query via e-mail or postal mail (with SASE). Submit query letter with 3 sample chapters pasted into the body of the e-mail. If you query by e-mail, we will only respond if interested. If you are making a simultaneous submission, you must tell us in your query. Accepts simultaneous submissions. Responds in 6-8 weeks. However, as noted above, if you don't receive a response to an emailed query, that means it was a pass. Obtains most new clients through referrals from established writers and editors.

TERMS Agent receives 15% commission on domestic sales, and 20% commission on foreign and film deals. This 20% is shared with co-agents. Offers written contract. No charges except for PDFs or finished books for foreign and film submissions.

RECENT SALES *Since We Fell*, by Dennis Lehane; *Your First Novel - Revised and Expanded Edition*, by Ann Rittenberg and Laura Whitcomb with Camille Goldin; *Paradise Valley*, by C.J. Box; *The Field Guide to Dumb Birds of North America*, by Matt Kracht; *Stay Hidden*, by Paul Doiron.

TIPS "Refrain from sending enormous bouquets of red roses. Elegant bouquets of peonies, tulips, ranunculus, calla lily, and white roses are acceptable."

RIVERSIDE LITERARY AGENCY

41 Simon Keets Rd., Leyden MA 01337. (413)772-0067. **Fax:** (413)772-0969. **E-mail:** rivlit@sover.net. **Website:** www.riversideliteraryagency.com. **Contact:** Susan Lee Cohen. Estab. 1990.

○ Worked at Viking Penguin before becoming an agent at Richard Curtis Associates, and then Sterling Lord Literistic. Founded RLA in 1990.

REPRESENTS Nonfiction, fiction.

☛ This agency sells adult nonfiction and fiction, and has sold books in the categories of science, psychology, spirituality, health, memoir, pop culture, true crime, parenting, history/politics, and narrative.

HOW TO CONTACT E-query. Accepts simultaneous submissions. Obtains most new clients through referrals.

TERMS Agent receives 15% commission on domestic sales. Offers written contract. Charges clients for foreign postage, photocopying large mss, express mail deliveries, etc.

RLR ASSOCIATES, LTD.

420 Lexington Ave., Suite 2532, New York NY 10170. (212)541-8641. **E-mail:** website.info@rlrassociates. net. **Website:** www.rlrassociates.net. **Contact:** Scott Gould. Member of AAR. Represents 50 clients.

REPRESENTS Nonfiction, novels. **Considers these fiction areas:** commercial, literary, mainstream, middle grade, picture books, romance, women's, young adult, genre.

☛ "We provide a lot of editorial assistance to our clients and have connections." Does not want to receive screenplays.

HOW TO CONTACT Query by snail mail. For fiction, send a query and 1-3 chapters (pasted). For nonfiction, send query or proposal. Accepts simultaneous submissions. "If you do not hear from us within 3 months, please assume that your work is out of active consideration." Obtains most new clients through recommendations from others.

TERMS Agent receives 15% commission on domestic sales; 20% commission on foreign sales. Offers written contract.

RECENT SALES Clients include Shelby Foote, The Grief Recovery Institute, Don Wade, David Plowden, Nina Planck, Karyn Bosnak, Gerald Carbone, Jason Lethcoe, Andy Crouch.

TIPS "Please check out our website for more details on our agency."

BJ ROBBINS LITERARY AGENCY

5130 Bellaire Ave., North Hollywood CA 91607-2908. **E-mail:** robbinsliterary@gmail.com. **Website:** www. bjrobbinsliterary.com. **Contact:** (Ms.) BJ Robbins. Estab. 1992. Member of AAR.

○ Prior to becoming an agent, Robbins spent 15 years in publishing, starting in publicity at Simon & Schuster and later as Marketing Director and Senior Editor at Harcourt.

REPRESENTS Nonfiction, fiction, novels. **Considers these fiction areas:** contemporary issues, crime, detective, ethnic, historical, literary, mainstream, multicultural, mystery, sports, suspense, thriller, women's.

☛ "We do not represent screenplays, plays, poetry, science fiction, fantasy, westerns, romance, techno-thrillers, religious tracts, dating books or anything with the word 'unicorn' in the title."

HOW TO CONTACT E-query with no attachments. For fiction, okay to include first 10 pages in body of e-mail. Accepts simultaneous submissions. Only responds to projects if interested. Obtains most new clients through conferences, referrals.

TERMS Agent receives 15% commission on domestic sales; 20% commission on foreign sales. Offers written contract. No fees.

RECENT SALES *Shoot for the Moon: The Perilous Voyage of Apollo 11*, by James Donovan (Little, Brown); *Mongrels*, by Stephen Graham Jones (William Morrow); *Blood Brothers: The Story of the Strange Friendship between Sitting Bull and Buffalo Bill*, by Deanne Stillman (Simon & Schuster); *Reliance, Illinois*, by Mary Volmer (Soho Press), Mapping the Interior by Stephen Graham Jones (Tor).

⊘ THE ROBBINS OFFICE, INC.

509 Madison Ave., New York NY 10022. (212)223-0720. **Fax:** (212)223-2535. **Website:** www.robbinsoffice.com. **Contact:** Kathy P. Robbins, owner.

MEMBER AGENTS Kathy P. Robbins; David Halpern.

REPRESENTS Novels.

☛ This agency specializes in selling serious nonfiction as well as commercial and literary fiction.

HOW TO CONTACT Accepts submissions by referral only. Do not cold query this market. Accepts simultaneous submissions.

TERMS Agent receives 15% commission on domestic, foreign, and film sales. Bills back specific expenses incurred in doing business for a client.

RODEEN LITERARY MANAGEMENT

3501 N. Southport #497, Chicago IL 60657. **E-mail:** info@rodeenliterary.com. **E-mail:** submissions@rodeenliterary.com. **Website:** www.rodeenliterary.com.

Contact: Paul Rodeen. Estab. 2009. Member of AAR. Signatory of WGA.

○ Paul Rodeen established Rodeen Literary Management in 2009 after 7 years of experience with the literary agency Sterling Lord Literistic, Inc.

REPRESENTS Nonfiction, novels, juvenile books. , illustrations, graphic novels. **Considers these fiction areas:** juvenile, middle grade, picture books, young adult, graphic novels, comics.

☛ Actively seeking "writers and illustrators of all genres of children's literature including picture books, early readers, middle-grade fiction and nonfiction, graphic novels and comic books, as well as young adult fiction and nonfiction." This is primarily an agency devoted to children's books.

HOW TO CONTACT Unsolicited submissions are accepted by e-mail only. Cover letters with synopsis and contact information should be included in the body of your e-mail. An initial submission of 50 pages from a novel or a longer work of nonfiction will suffice and should be pasted into the body of your e-mail. Accepts simultaneous submissions.

THE ROSENBERG GROUP

23 Lincoln Ave., Marblehead MA 01945. (781)990-1341. **Fax:** (781)990-1344. **Website:** www.rosenberggroup.com. **Contact:** Barbara Collins Rosenberg. Estab. 1998. Member of AAR. Recognized agent of the RWA. Represents 25 clients.

○ Prior to becoming an agent, Ms. Rosenberg was a senior editor for Harcourt.

REPRESENTS Nonfiction, novels, textbooks. , college textbooks only. **Considers these fiction areas:** romance, women's, chick lit.

☛ Ms. Rosenberg is well-versed in the romance market (both category and single title). She is a frequent speaker at romance conferences. The Rosenberg Group is accepting new clients working in romance fiction (please see my Areas of Interest for specific romance sub-genres); women's fiction and chick lit. Does not want to receive inspirational, time travel, futuristic or paranormal.

HOW TO CONTACT Query via snail mail. Your query letter should not exceed one page in length. It should include the title of your work, the genre and/or sub-genre; the manuscript's word count; and a brief description of the work. If you are writing category romance, please be certain to let her know the line for which your work is intended. Accepts simultaneous submissions. Obtains most new clients through recommendations from others, solicitations, conferences.

TERMS Agent receives 15% commission on domestic and foreign sales. Offers written contract; 1-month notice must be given to terminate contract. Charges maximum of $350/year for postage and photocopying.

RECENT SALES Sold 27 titles in the last year.

WRITERS CONFERENCES RWA National Conference; BookExpo America.

ANDY ROSS LITERARY AGENCY

767 Santa Ray Ave., Oakland CA 94610. (510)238-8965. **E-mail:** andyrossagency@hotmail.com. **Website:** www.andyrossagency.com. **Contact:** Andy Ross. Estab. 2008. Member of AAR. Represents See website for client list. clients.

○ I was the owner of Cody's Books in Berkeley California for 30 years.

REPRESENTS Nonfiction, fiction, novels, juvenile books, scholarly books. **Considers these fiction areas:** commercial, contemporary issues, historical, juvenile, literary, middle grade, picture books, young adult.

☛ "This agency specializes in general nonfiction, politics and current events, history, biography, journalism and contemporary culture as well as literary, commercial, and YA fiction." Does not want to receive poetry.

HOW TO CONTACT Queries should be less than half page. Please put the word "query" in the title header of the e-mail. In the first sentence, state the category of the project. Give a short description of the book and your qualifications for writing. Accepts simultaneous submissions. Responds in 1 week to queries.

TERMS Agent receives 15% commission on domestic sales; 20% commission on foreign sales or other deals made through a sub-agent. Offers written contract.

RECENT SALES See my website.

JANE ROTROSEN AGENCY LLC

318 E. 51st St., New York NY 10022. (212)593-4330. **Fax:** (212)935-6985. **Website:** www.janerotrosen.com. Estab. 1974. Member of AAR. Other memberships include Authors Guild. Represents more than 100 clients.

MEMBER AGENTS Jane Rotrosen Berkey (not taking on clients); Andrea Cirillo, acirillo@janerotrosen.com (general fiction, suspense, and women's fiction);

Annelise Robey, arobey@janerotrosen.com (women's fiction, suspense, mystery, literary fiction, and select nonfiction); Meg Ruley, mruley@janerotrosen.com (commercial fiction, including suspense, mysteries, romance, and general fiction); Christina Hogrebe, chogrebe@janerotrosen.com (young adult, new adult, book club fiction, romantic comedies, mystery, and suspense); Amy Tannenbaum, atannenbaum@janerotrosen.com (contemporary romance, psychological suspense, thrillers, and new adult, as well as women's fiction that falls into that sweet spot between literary and commercial, memoir, narrative and prescriptive non-fiction in the areas of health, business, pop culture, humor, and popular psychology); Rebecca Scherer rscherer@janerotrosen.com (women's fiction, mystery, suspense, thriller, romance, upmarket/literary-leaning fiction); Jessica Errera (assistant to Christina and Rebecca).

REPRESENTS Nonfiction, novels. **Considers these fiction areas:** commercial, literary, mainstream, mystery, new adult, romance, suspense, thriller, women's, young adult.

☛　　Jane Rotrosen Agency is best known for representing writers of commercial fiction: thrillers, mystery, suspense, women's fiction, romance, historical novels, mainstream fiction, young adult, etc. We also work with authors of memoirs, narrative and prescriptive nonfiction.

HOW TO CONTACT Check website for guidelines. Accepts simultaneous submissions. Obtains most new clients through recommendations from others.

TERMS Agent receives 15% commission on domestic sales; 20% commission on foreign sales. Offers written contract, binding for 3 years; 2-month notice must be given to terminate contract. Charges clients for photocopying, express mail, overseas postage, book purchase.

THE RUDY AGENCY

825 Wildlife Ln., Estes Park CO 80517. (970)577-8500. **E-mail:** mak@rudyagency.com; claggett@rudyagency.com; gstone@rudyagency.com. **Website:** www.rudyagency.com. **Contact:** Maryann Karinch. Estab. 2004. Adheres to AAR canon of ethics. Represents 30 clients.

◗　　Prior to becoming an agent, Ms. Karinch was, and continues to be, an author of nonfiction books—primarily covering the subjects of health/medicine and human behavior. Prior to that, she was in public relations and mar-

keting: areas of expertise she also applies in her practice as an agent.

MEMBER AGENTS Maryann Karinch, Hilary Claggett, and Geoffrey Stone.

REPRESENTS Nonfiction, fiction, novels, scholarly books. **Considers these fiction areas:** action, adventure, commercial, contemporary issues, crime, erotica, gay, historical, lesbian, literary, military, multicultural, mystery, sports, thriller, women's.

☛　　"We support authors from the proposal stage through promotion of the published work. We work in partnership with publishers to promote the published work and coach authors in their role in the marketing and public relations campaigns for the book." Actively seeking projects with social value, projects that open minds to new ideas and interesting lives, and projects that entertain through good storytelling. Does not want to receive poetry, screenplays, novellas, religion books, children's lit, and joke books.

HOW TO CONTACT "Query us. If we like the query, we will invite a complete proposal (or complete ms if writing fiction). No phone queries, please. We won't hang up on you, but it makes it easier if you send us a note first." Accepts simultaneous submissions. Responds in under 3 weeks to non-fiction proposals and 12 weeks to invited manuscripts. Obtains most new clients through recommendations from others, solicitations.

TERMS Agent receives 15% commission on domestic sales. Offers written contract, binding for 1 year.

RECENT SALES *The Art of Creating Value*, by Jeffrey Ansell (Rowman & Littlefield); *Palace Coup*, by Max Frumes and Sujeet Indap (Diversion); *Get People to Do What You Want*, by Gregory Hartley (Red Wheel/Weiser).

TIPS "Present yourself professionally. Know what we need to see in a query and what a proposal for a work of non-fiction must contain before you contact us."

VICTORIA SANDERS & ASSOCIATES

440 Buck Rd., Stone Ridge NY 12484. (212)633-8811. **E-mail:** queriesvsa@gmail.com. **Website:** www.victoriasanders.com. **Contact:** Victoria Sanders. Estab. 1992. Member of AAR. Signatory of WGA. Represents 135 clients.

MEMBER AGENTS Victoria Sanders; Bernadette Baker-Baughman; Jessica Spivey.

REPRESENTS Nonfiction, fiction, novels, short story collections, juvenile books. **Considers these fiction areas:** action, adventure, cartoon, comic books, contemporary issues, crime, detective, ethnic, family saga, feminist, gay, historical, humor, inspirational, juvenile, lesbian, literary, mainstream, middle grade, multicultural, multimedia, mystery, new adult, picture books, suspense, thriller, women's, young adult.

HOW TO CONTACT Authors who wish to contact us regarding potential representation should send a query letter with the first 3 chapters (or about 25 pages) pasted into the body of the message to queriesvsa@gmail.com. We will only accept queries via e-mail. Query letters should describe the project and the author in the body of a single, 1-page e-mail that does not contain any attached files. Important note: Please paste the first 3 chapters of your manuscript (or about 25 pages, and feel free to round up to a chapter break) into the body of your e-mail. Accepts simultaneous submissions. Responds in 1-4 weeks, although occasionally it will take longer. "We will not respond to e-mails with attachments or attached files."

TERMS Agent receives 15% commission on domestic sales; 20% commission on foreign/film sales. Offers written contract.

TIPS "Limit query to letter (no calls) and give it your best shot. A good query is going to get a good response."

WENDY SCHMALZ AGENCY

402 Union St., #831, Hudson NY 12534. (518)672-7697. **E-mail:** wendy@schmalzagency.com. **Website:** www.schmalzagency.com. **Contact:** Wendy Schmalz. Estab. 2002. Member of AAR.

REPRESENTS Juvenile books. **Considers these fiction areas:** middle grade, young adult.

☛ Not looking for picture books, science fiction or fantasy.

HOW TO CONTACT Accepts only e-mail queries. Paste synopsis into the e-mail. Do not attach the ms or sample chapters or synopsis. Replies to queries only if they want to read the ms. If you do not hear from this agency within 2 weeks, consider that a no. Accepts simultaneous submissions. I respond to queries within 2 weeks of receipt. If I don't respond within 2 weeks, it means I'm not interested in reading the ms. Obtains clients through recommendations from others.

TERMS Agent receives 15% commission on domestic sales; 20% on foreign sales; 25% for Asia.

SUSAN SCHULMAN LITERARY AGENCY LLC

454 W. 44th St., New York NY 10036. (212)713-1633. **E-mail:** susan@schulmanagency.com. **E-mail:** queries@schulmanagency.com. **Website:** www.publishersmarketplace.com/members/schulman/. **Contact:** Susan Schulman. Estab. 1980. Member of AAR. Signatory of WGA. Other memberships include Dramatists Guild, Writers Guild of America, East, New York Women in Film, Women's Media Group, Agents' Roundtable, League of New York Theater Women.

REPRESENTS Nonfiction, fiction, novels, juvenile books, feature film, TV scripts, theatrical stage play. **Considers these fiction areas:** commercial, contemporary issues, juvenile, literary, mainstream, new adult, religious, women's, young adult.

☛ "We specialize in books for, by and about women and women's issues including nonfiction self-help books, fiction, and theater projects. We also handle the film, television. and allied rights for several agencies as well as foreign rights for several publishing houses." Actively seeking new nonfiction. Considers plays. Does not want to receive poetry, television scripts or concepts for television.

HOW TO CONTACT "For fiction: query letter with outline and three sample chapters, resume and SASE. For nonfiction: query letter with complete description of subject, at least one chapter, resume and SASE. Queries may be sent via regular mail or e-mail. Please do not submit queries via UPS or Federal Express. Please do not send attachments with e-mail queries Please incorporate the chapters into the body of the e-mail." Accepts simultaneous submissions. Responds in less than 1 week generally to a full query and 6 weeks to a full ms. Obtains most new clients through recommendations from others, solicitations, conferences.

TERMS Agent receives 15% commission on domestic sales; 20% commission on foreign sales. Offers written contract; 30-day notice must be given to terminate contract.

RECENT SALES Sold 70 titles in the last year; hundreds of subsidiary rights deals.

WRITERS CONFERENCES Geneva Writers' Conference (Switzerland); Columbus Writers' Conference; Skidmore Conference of the Independent Women's Writers Group. Attends Frankfurt Book Fair, London Book Fair, and BEA annually.

TIPS "Keep writing!" Schulman describes her agency as "professional boutique, long-standing, eclectic."

SCOVIL GALEN GHOSH LITERARY AGENCY, INC.

276 Fifth Ave., Suite 708, New York NY 10001. (212)679-8686. **Fax:** (212)679-6710. **E-mail:** info@sgglit.com. **Website:** www.sgglit.com. **Contact:** Russell Galen. Estab. 1992. Member of AAR. Represents 300 clients.

MEMBER AGENTS Russell Galen, russellgalen@sgglit.com (novels that stretch the bounds of reality; strong, serious nonfiction books on almost any subject that teach something new; no books that are merely entertaining, such as diet or pop psych books; serious interests include science, history, journalism, biography, business, memoir, nature, politics, sports, contemporary culture, literary nonfiction, etc.); Jack Scovil, jackscovil@sgglit.com; Anna Ghosh, annaghosh@sgglit.com (nonfiction proposals on all subjects, including literary nonfiction, history, science, social and cultural issues, memoir, food, art, adventure, and travel; adult commercial and literary fiction); Ann Behar, annbehar@sgglit.com (juvenile books for all ages).

HOW TO CONTACT E-mail queries only. Note how each agent at this agency has their own submission e-mail. Accepts simultaneous submissions.

SCRIBE AGENCY, LLC

5508 Joylynne Dr., Madison WI 53716. **E-mail:** whattheshizzle@scribeagency.com. **E-mail:** submissions@scribeagency.com. **Website:** www.scribeagency.com. **Contact:** Kristopher O'Higgins. Estab. 2004. Represents 8 clients.

○ "With more than 20 years experience in publishing, with time spent on both the agency and editorial sides, with marketing experience to boot, Scribe Agency is a full-service literary agency, working hands-on with its authors on their projects. Check the website (scribeagency.com) to make sure your work matches the Scribe aesthetic.".

MEMBER AGENTS Kristopher O'Higgins.

REPRESENTS Fiction, novels. , anthologies. **Considers these fiction areas:** fantasy, literary, paranormal, science fiction, urban fantasy.

☛ "Scribe is currently closed to nonfiction and short fiction collections, and does not represent humor, cozy mysteries, faith-based fiction, screenplays, poetry, or works based on another's ideas."

HOW TO CONTACT E-queries only: submissions@scribeagency.com. See the website for submission info, as it may change. Accepts simultaneous submissions. Responds approximately 6 weeks to queries.

TERMS Agent receives 15% commission on domestic sales; 20% commission on foreign sales. Offers written contract.

RECENT SALES Juliette Wade's debut novel, and a sequel, sold to Sheila Gilbert at DAW Books. Slated for a 2020 release.

WRITERS CONFERENCES BookExpo America; WisCon; Wisconsin Book Festival; World Fantasy Convention; WorldCon.

SECRET AGENT MAN

P.O. Box 1078, Lake Forest CA 92609-1078. (949)639-9334. **E-mail:** scott@secretagentman.net. **Website:** www.secretagentman.net. **Contact:** Scott Mortenson. Estab. 1999.

REPRESENTS Nonfiction, fiction, novels. **Considers these fiction areas:** action, crime, detective, horror, literary, mainstream, mystery, paranormal, psychic, religious, science fiction, spiritual, supernatural, suspense, thriller, westerns.

☛ Mystery, thriller, suspense, and detective fiction. Select nonfiction projects that interesting and/or thought-provoking. Does not want to receive scripts or screenplays.

HOW TO CONTACT Query via e-mail only; include sample chapters, synopsis and/or outline. Prefers to read the real thing rather than a description, but a synopsis helps with getting an overall feel of the MS. Accepts simultaneous submissions. Responds in 2-6 weeks. Obtains most new clients through recommendations from others.

⊘ SELECTIC ARTISTS

9 Union Square, #123, Southbury CT 06488. **E-mail:** christopher@selectricartists.com. **E-mail:** query@selectricartists.com. **Website:** www.selectricartists.com. **Contact:** Christopher Schelling. Estab. 2011.

REPRESENTS Nonfiction, fiction, novels, short story collections, juvenile books. **Considers these fiction areas:** commercial, fantasy, feminist, gay, historical, horror, humor, juvenile, lesbian, literary, mainstream, multicultural, science fiction, short story collections, suspense, thriller, young adult.

HOW TO CONTACT E-mail only. Consult agency website for status on open submissions. Accepts simultaneous submissions. Responds in 4-6 weeks.

LYNN SELIGMAN, LITERARY AGENT

400 Highland Ave., Upper Montclair NJ 07043. (973)783-3631. **E-mail:** seliglit@aol.com. **Contact:** Lynn Seligman. Estab. 1986. Women's Media Group Represents 35 clients.

○ Prior to opening her agency, Ms. Seligman worked in the subsidiary rights department of Doubleday and Simon & Schuster, and served as an agent with Julian Bach Literary Agency (which became IMG Literary Agency). Foreign rights are represented by Books Crossing Borders, Inc.

REPRESENTS Nonfiction, fiction, novels. **Considers these fiction areas:** commercial, ethnic, fantasy, feminist, historical, horror, humor, literary, mainstream, mystery, new adult, romance, satire, science fiction, women's, young adult.

☞ "This agency specializes in general nonfiction and fiction. I also do illustrated and photography books and have represented several photographers for books."

HOW TO CONTACT Query with SASE or via e-mail with no attachments. Prefers to read materials exclusively but if not, please inform. Answers written and most email queries. Accepts simultaneous submissions. Responds in 2 weeks to queries; 2 months to mss. Obtains new clients through referrals from other writers and editors as well as unsolicited queries.

TERMS Agent receives 15% commission on domestic sales; 25% commission on foreign sales. Charges clients for photocopying, unusual postage, express mail, telephone expenses (checks with author first).

RECENT SALES Sold 10 titles in 2018 including work by Dee Ernst, Dr. Myrna Shure and Roberta Israeloff.

SERENDIPITY LITERARY AGENCY, LLC

305 Gates Ave., Brooklyn NY 11216. **E-mail:** rbrooks@serendipitylit.com; info@serendipitylit.com. **Website:** www.serendipitylit.com; facebook.com/serendipitylit. **Contact:** Regina Brooks. Estab. 2000. Member of AAR. Signatory of WGA. Represents 150 clients.

○ Prior to becoming an agent, Ms. Brooks was an acquisitions editor for John Wiley & Sons, Inc. and McGraw-Hill Companies.

MEMBER AGENTS Regina Brooks; Christina Morgan (literary fiction, crime fiction, and narrative nonfiction in the categories of pop culture, sports, current events and memoir); Jocquelle Caiby (literary fiction, horror, middle grade fiction, and children's books by authors who have been published in the adult market, athletes, actors, journalists, politicians, and musicians).

REPRESENTS Nonfiction, fiction, novels, juvenile books. **Considers these fiction areas:** commercial, gay, historical, lesbian, literary, middle grade, mystery, romance, thriller, women's, young adult, Christian.

HOW TO CONTACT Check the website, as there are online submission forms for fiction, nonfiction and juvenile. Website will also state if we're temporarily closed to submissions to any areas. Accepts simultaneous submissions. Obtains most new clients through conferences, referrals and social media.

TERMS Agent receives 15% commission on domestic sales; 20% commission on foreign sales. Offers written contract; 2-month notice must be given to terminate contract. Charges clients for office fees, which are taken from any advance.

TIPS "See the books *Writing Great Books For Young Adults* and *You Should Really Write A Book: How To Write Sell And Market Your Memoir*. We are looking for high concept ideas with big hooks. If you get writer's block try possibiliteas.co, it's a muse in a cup."

THE SEYMOUR AGENCY

475 Miner St., Canton NY 13617. (239)398-8209. **E-mail:** nicole@theseymouragency.com; julie@theseymouragency.com. **Website:** www.theseymouragency.com. Member of AAR. Signatory of WGA. Other memberships include RWA, Authors Guild, RWA, ACFW, HWA, MWA, SCBWI.

MEMBER AGENTS Nicole Rescinti, nicole@theseymouragency.com; Julie Gwinn, julie@theseymouragency.com; Tina Wainscott, tina@theseymouragency.com; Jennifer Wills, jennifer@theseymouragency.com; Lesley Sabga, lesley@theseymourageency.com.

REPRESENTS Nonfiction, fiction, novels, juvenile books. **Considers these fiction areas:** action, adventure, commercial, contemporary issues, crime, detective, erotica, ethnic, experimental, family saga, fantasy, feminist, frontier, gay, horror, humor, inspirational, lesbian, literary, mainstream, metaphysical, middle grade, military, multicultural, multimedia, mystery, new adult, New Age, occult, paranormal, picture books, police, religious, romance, science fiction, spiritual, sports, supernatural, suspense, thriller, translation, urban fantasy, war, westerns, women's, young adult.

HOW TO CONTACT Accepts e-mail queries. Check online for guidelines. Accepts simultaneous submissions. Responds in 1 month to queries; 3 months to mss.
TERMS Agent receives 12-15% commission on domestic sales.

DENISE SHANNON LITERARY AGENCY, INC.

121 W. 27th St., Suite 303, New York NY 10001. E-mail: info@deniseshannonagency.com. **E-mail:** submissions@deniseshannonagency.com. **Website:** www.deniseshannonagency.com. **Contact:** Denise Shannon. Estab. 2002. Member of AAR.

○ Prior to opening her agency, Ms. Shannon worked for 16 years with Georges Borchardt and International Creative Management.

REPRESENTS Nonfiction, novels. **Considers these fiction areas:** literary.

☞ "We are a boutique agency with a distinguished list of fiction and nonfiction authors."

HOW TO CONTACT "Queries may be submitted by post, accompanied by a SASE, or by e-mail to submissions@deniseshannonagency.com. Please include a description of the available book project and a brief bio including details of any prior publications. We will reply and request more material if we are interested. We request that you inform us if you are submitting material simultaneously to other agencies." Accepts simultaneous submissions.

RECENT SALES *Mister Monkey*, by Francine Prose (Harper); *Hotel Solitaire*, by Gary Shteyngart (Random House); *White Flights*, by Jess Row (Graywolf Press); *The Underworld*, by Kevin Canty (Norton).

TIPS "Please do not send queries regarding fiction projects until a complete manuscript is available for review. We request that you inform us if you are submitting material simultaneously to other agencies."

⊘ KEN SHERMAN & ASSOCIATES

1275 N. Hayworth Ave., Suite 103, Los Angeles CA 90046. (310) 273-8840. **E-mail:** kenshermanassociates@gmail.com. **E-mail:** ksasubmissions@gmail.com. **Website:** www.kenshermanassociates.com. **Contact:** Ken Sherman. Estab. 1989. BAFTA (British Academy of Film and Television Arts). Represents 35 clients.

○ Prior to opening his agency, Mr. Sherman was with The William Morris Agency, The Lantz Office, and Paul Kohner, Inc. He has taught The Business of Writing For Film and Television and The Book Worlds at UCLA and USC.

He also lectures extensively at writer's conferences and film festivals around the U.S. He is currently a Commissioner of Arts and Cultural Affairs in the City of West Hollywood, and is on the International Advisory Board of the Christopher Isherwood Foundation.

REPRESENTS Nonfiction, fiction, novels, novellas, movie scripts, feature film, TV scripts, TV movie of the week, miniseries, theatrical stage play, stage plays. , teleplays, life rights, film/TV rights to books and life rights. **Considers these fiction areas:** action, adventure, commercial, crime, detective, family saga, gay, literary, mainstream, middle grade, mystery, police, romance, satire, science fiction, suspense, thriller, women's, young adult.

☞ Fine writers.

HOW TO CONTACT Contact by referral only, please. Reports in approximately 1 month. Accepts simultaneous submissions. Obtains most new clients through recommendations from others.

TERMS Agent receives 15% commission on domestic and foreign sales; 10-15% commission on film sales. Offers written contract. Charges clients for reasonable office expenses (postage, photocopying, etc.).

WRITERS CONFERENCES Maui Writers' Conference; Squaw Valley Writers' Workshop; Santa Barbara Writers' Conference; Screenwriting Conference in Santa Fe; Aspen Summer Words Literary Festival including The Aspen Institute, the San Francisco Writer's Conference, Eugene International Film Festival, The Chautauqua Institute - Writer's Conference, La Jolla Writer's Conference, Central Coast Writer's Conference (California), etc.

WENDY SHERMAN ASSOCIATES, INC.

138 W. 25th St., Suite 1018, New York NY 10001. (212)279-9027. **E-mail:** submissions@wsherman.com. **Website:** www.wsherman.com. **Contact:** Wendy Sherman. Estab. 1999. Member of AAR.

○ Prior to opening the agency, Ms. Sherman held positions as vice president, executive director, associate publisher, subsidiary rights director, and sales and marketing director for major publishers including Simon & Schuster and Henry Holt.

MEMBER AGENTS Wendy Sherman (women's fiction that hits that sweet spot between literary and mainstream, Southern voices, suspense with a well-developed protagonist, anything related to food, dogs, mothers and daughters).

REPRESENTS Nonfiction, fiction, novels, juvenile books. **Considers these fiction areas:** mainstream, Mainstream fiction that hits the sweet spot between literary and commercial..

☛ "We specialize in developing new writers, as well as working with more established writers. My experience as a publisher has proven to be a great asset to my clients." Does not want genre fiction, picture books.

HOW TO CONTACT Query via e-mail only. "We ask that you include your last name, title, and the name of the agent you are submitting to in the subject line. For fiction, please include a query letter and your first 10 pages copied and pasted in the body of the e-mail. We will not open attachments unless they have been requested. For nonfiction, please include your query letter and author bio. Due to the large number of e-mail submissions that we receive, we only reply to e-mail queries in the affirmative. We respectfully ask that you do not send queries to our individual e-mail addresses." Accepts simultaneous submissions. Obtains most new clients through recommendations from other writers.

TERMS Agent receives standard 15% commission. Offers written contract.

RECENT SALES *All is Not Forgotten*, by Wendy Walker; *Z, A Novel of Zelda Fitzgerald*, by Therese Anne Fowler; *The Charm Bracelet*, by Viola Shipman; *The Silence of Bonaventure Arrow*, by Rita Leganski; *Together Tea*, by Marjan Kamali; *A Long Long Time Ago and Essentially True*, by Brigid Pasulka; *Lunch in Paris*, by Elizabeth Bard; *The Rules of Inheritance*, by Claire Bidwell Smith; *Eight Flavors*, by Sarah Lohman; *How to Live a Good Life*, by Jonathan Fields; *The Essential Oil Hormone Solution*, by Dr. Mariza Snyder.

TIPS "The bottom line is: do your homework. Be as well prepared as possible. Read the books that will help you present yourself and your work with polish. You want your submission to stand out."

BEVERLEY SLOPEN LITERARY AGENCY

131 Bloor St. W., Suite 711, Toronto ON M5S 1S3 Canada. (416)964-9598. **E-mail:** beverly@slopenagency.ca. **Website:** www.slopenagency.com. **Contact:** Beverley Slopen. Represents 100 clients.

Prior to opening her agency, Ms. Slopen worked in publishing and as a journalist.

REPRESENTS Nonfiction, novels. **Considers these fiction areas:** commercial, literary, mystery, suspense.

☛ "This agency has a strong bent toward Canadian writers." Actively seeking serious nonfiction that is accessible and appealing to the general reader. Does not want to receive fantasy, science fiction, or children's books.

HOW TO CONTACT Query by e-mail. Does not return materials. To submit a work for consideration, e-mail a short query letter and a few sample pages. Submit only one work at a time. "If we want to see more, we will contact the writer by phone or e-mail." Accepts simultaneous submissions. Responds in 1 month to queries only if interested.

TERMS Agent receives 15% commission on domestic sales; 10% commission on foreign sales. Offers written contract, binding for 2 years; 3-month notice must be given to terminate contract.

TIPS "Please, no unsolicited manuscripts."

SPECTRUM LITERARY AGENCY

320 Central Park W., Suite 1-D, New York NY 10025. (212)362-4323. **Fax:** (212)362-4562. **Website:** www. spectrumliteraryagency.com. **Contact:** Eleanor Wood, president. Estab. 1976. SFWA Represents 90 clients.

MEMBER AGENTS Eleanor Wood (referrals only; commercial fiction: science fiction, fantasy, suspense, as well as select nonfiction); Justin Bell (science fiction, mysteries, and select nonfiction).

REPRESENTS Novels. **Considers these fiction areas:** commercial, fantasy, mystery, science fiction, suspense.

HOW TO CONTACT Unsolicited mss are not accepted. Send snail mail query with SASE. "The letter should describe your book briefly and include publishing credits and background information or qualifications relating to your work, and the first 10 pages of your work. Our response time is generally 2-3 months." Responds in 1-3 months to queries. Obtains most new clients through recommendations from authors.

TERMS Agent receives 15% commission on domestic sales. Deducts for photocopying and book orders.

TIPS "Spectrum's policy is to read only book-length manuscripts that we have specifically asked to see. Unsolicited manuscripts are not accepted. The letter should describe your book briefly and include publishing credits and background information or qualifications relating to your work, if any."

SPEILBURG LITERARY AGENCY

E-mail: speilburgliterary@gmail.com. **Website:** speilburgliterary.com. **Contact:** Alice Speilburg. Estab. 2012. SCBWI; MWA; RWA; Author's Guild.

MEMBER AGENTS Alice Speilburg worked for John Wiley & Sons and Howard Morhaim Literary Agency, before launching Speilburg Literary. She is a member of Romance Writers of America, Mystery Writers of America, and Society of Children's Book Writers and Illustrators, and she is a board member of Louisville Literary Arts. She represents commercial fiction and narrative nonfiction. Eva Scalzo has a B.A. in the Humanities from the University of Puerto Rico and a M.A. in Publishing and Writing from Emerson College. She has spent her career in scholarly publishing, working for Houghton Mifflin, Blackwell Publishing, John Wiley & Sons, and Cornell University in a variety of roles. Eva is looking to represent all subgenres of Romance, with the exclusion of inspirational romance, as well as Young Adult fiction.

REPRESENTS Nonfiction, fiction, novels. **Considers these fiction areas:** adventure, commercial, detective, fantasy, feminist, historical, horror, mainstream, mystery, police, romance, science fiction, suspense, urban fantasy, westerns, women's, young adult.

☛ Does not want picture books; screenplays; poetry.

HOW TO CONTACT In the subject line of your query e-mail, please include "Query [AGENT'S FIRST NAME]" followed by the title of your project. For fiction, please send the query letter and the first three chapters. For nonfiction, please send the query letter and a proposal, which should include a detailed TOC and a sample chapter. Accepts simultaneous submissions.

SPENCERHILL ASSOCIATES

8131 Lakewood Main St., Building M, Suite 205, Lakewood Ranch FL 34202. (941)907-3700. **E-mail:** submission@spencerhillassociates.com. **Website:** www.spencerhillassociates.com. **Contact:** Karen Solem, Nalini Akolekar, Amanda Leuck, Sandy Harding, and Ali Herring. Estab. 2001. Member of AAR.

◯ Prior to becoming an agent, Ms. Solem was editor-in-chief at HarperCollins and an associate publisher.

MEMBER AGENTS Karen Solem; Nalini Akolekar; Amanda Leuck; Sandy Harding; Ali Herring.

REPRESENTS Fiction, novels, juvenile books. **Considers these fiction areas:** commercial, contemporary issues, crime, detective, erotica, ethnic, family saga, feminist, gay, historical, humor, inspirational, lesbian, literary, mainstream, middle grade, multicultural, mystery, new adult, paranormal, police, religious, romance, supernatural, suspense, thriller, urban fantasy, women's, young adult.

☛ "We handle mostly commercial women's fiction, historical novels, romance (historical, contemporary, paranormal, urban fantasy), thrillers, and mysteries. We also represent Christian fiction only—no nonfiction." No nonfiction, poetry, children's picture books, or scripts.

HOW TO CONTACT "We accept electronic submissions only. Please send us a query letter in the body of an e-mail, pitch us your project and tell us about yourself: Do you have prior publishing credits? Attach the first three chapters and synopsis preferably in .doc, rtf or txt format to your email. Send all queries to submission@spencerhillassociates.com. Or submit through the QueryManager link on our website. We do not have a preference for exclusive submissions, but do appreciate knowing if the submission is simultaneous. We receive thousands of submissions a year and each query receives our attention. Unfortunately, we are unable to respond to each query individually. If we are interested in your work, we will contact you within 12 weeks." Accepts simultaneous submissions. Responds in approximately 12 weeks.

TERMS Agent receives 15% commission on domestic sales; 20% commission on foreign sales. Offers written contract; 3-month notice must be given to terminate contract.

RECENT SALES A full list of sales and clients is available on the agency website.

THE SPIELER AGENCY

27 W. 20 St., Suite 302, New York NY 10011. (212)757-4439, ext. 1. **Fax:** (212)333-2019. **Website:** thespieleragency.com. **Contact:** Joe Spieler. Represents 160 clients.

◗ Prior to opening his agency, Mr. Spieler was a magazine editor.

MEMBER AGENTS Victoria Shoemaker, victoria@thespieleragency.com (environment and natural history, popular culture, memoir, photography and film, literary fiction and poetry, and books on food and cooking); John Thornton, john@thespieleragency.com (nonfiction); Joe Spieler, joe@thespieleragency.com (nonfiction and fiction and books for children and young adults); Helen Sweetland, helen@thespieleragency.com (children's from board books through young adult fiction; adult general-interest nonfiction, including nature, green living, gardening, architecture, interior design, health, and popular science).

REPRESENTS Nonfiction, novels, juvenile books. **Considers these fiction areas:** literary, middle grade, New Age, picture books, thriller, young adult.

HOW TO CONTACT "Before submitting projects to the Spieler Agency, check the listings of our individual agents and see if any particular agent shows a general interest in your subject (e.g. history, memoir, YA, etc.). Please send all queries either by e-mail or regular mail. If you query us by regular mail, we can only reply to you if you include a SASE." Accepts simultaneous submissions. Cannot guarantee a personal response to all queries. Obtains most new clients through recommendations, listing in *Guide to Literary Agents*.

TERMS Agent receives 15% commission on domestic sales. Charges clients for messenger bills, photocopying, postage.

WRITERS CONFERENCES London Book Fair.

PHILIP G. SPITZER LITERARY AGENCY, INC

50 Talmage Farm Ln., East Hampton NY 11937. (631)329-3650. **E-mail:** lukas.ortiz@spitzeragency.com; annelise.spitzer@spitzeragency.com. **E-mail:** kim.lombardini@spitzeragency.com. **Website:** www.spitzeragency.com. **Contact:** Lukas Ortiz. Estab. 1969. Member of AAR.

- Prior to opening his agency, Mr. Spitzer served at New York University Press, McGraw-Hill, and the John Cushman Associates Literary Agency.

MEMBER AGENTS Philip G. Spitzer; Anne-Lise Spitzer; Lukas Ortiz.

REPRESENTS Novels. **Considers these fiction areas:** literary, mainstream, suspense, thriller.

- This agency specializes in mystery/suspense, literary fiction, sports, and general nonfiction (no how-to).

HOW TO CONTACT E-mail query containing synopsis of work, brief biography, and a sample chapter (pasted into the e-mail). Be aware that this agency openly says their client list is quite full. Obtains most new clients through recommendations from others.

TERMS Agent receives 15% commission on domestic sales; 20% commission on foreign sales.

RECENT SALES *New Iberia Blues*, by James Lee Burke (Simon & Schuster); *The Better Sister*, by Alafair Burke (HarperCollins); *Gone So Long*, by Andre Dubus III (Norton); *Two Kinds of Truth*, by Michael Connelly (Little, Brown & Co); *The Emerald Lie*, Ken Bruen (Mysterious Press/Grove-Atlantic); *Terror in the City of Champions*, by Tom Stanton (Lyons Press); *The Brain Defense*, by Kevin Davis (Penguin Press); *The Names of Dead Girls*, by Eric Rickstad (HarperCollins); *Assume Nothing*, Gar Anthony Haywood (Severn House); *The Man on the Stair*, by Gary Inbinder (Norton); *Running in the Dark*, by Sam Reaves (Thomas & Mercer); *Green Sun*, by Kent Anderson (Mulholland Books).

WRITERS CONFERENCES London Bookfair, Frankfurt, BookExpo America, Bouchercon.

NANCY STAUFFER ASSOCIATES

P.O. Box 1203, Darien CT 06820. (203)202-2500. **E-mail:** nancy@staufferliterary.com. **Website:** www.publishersmarketplace.com/members/nstauffer. **Contact:** Nancy Stauffer Cahoon. Other memberships include Authors Guild.

- "Over the course of my more than 20 year career, I've held positions in the editorial, marketing, business, and rights departments of The New York Times, McGraw-Hill, and Doubleday. Before founding Nancy Stauffer Associates, I was Director of Foreign and Performing Rights then Director, Subsidiary Rights, for Doubleday, where I was honored to have worked with a diverse range of internationally known and bestselling authors of all genres.".

REPRESENTS **Considers these fiction areas:** literary.

- We do not represent mysteries, romance, action adventure, historical fiction, or thrillers

HOW TO CONTACT Accepts simultaneous submissions. Obtains most new clients through referrals from existing clients.

TERMS Agent receives 15% commission on domestic sales.

RECENT SALES *You Don't Have To Say You Love Me*, by Sherman Alexie; *Our Souls At Night*, by Kent Haruf

STEPHANIE TADE AGENCY LLC

7A North Bank St., Easton PA 18042. (610)829-0035. **E-mail:** submissions@stephanietadeagency.com. **Website:** stephanietadeagency.com. **Contact:** Stephanie Tade.

○ Prior to becoming an agent, Ms. Tade was an executive editor at Rodale Press. She was also an agent with the Jane Rotrosen Agency.

MEMBER AGENTS Stephanie Tade, president and principal agent; Colleen Martell, editorial director and associate agent (cmartell@stadeagency.com).

REPRESENTS Nonfiction.

☞ Seeks prescriptive and narrative nonfiction, specializing in physical, emotional, psychological and spiritual wellness.

HOW TO CONTACT Query by e-mail. "When you write to the agency, please include information about your proposed book, your publishing history and any media or online platform you have developed." Accepts simultaneous submissions.

STONESONG

270 W. 39th St. #201, New York NY 10018. (212)929-4600. **E-mail:** editors@stonesong.com. **E-mail:** submissions@stonesong.com. **Website:** stonesong.com. Member of AAR. Signatory of WGA.

MEMBER AGENTS Alison Fargis; Ellen Scordato; Judy Linden; Emmanuelle Morgen; Leila Campoli (business, science, technology, and self improvement); Maria Ribas (cookbooks, self-help, health, diet, home, parenting, and humor, all from authors with demonstrable platforms; she's also interested in narrative nonfiction and select memoir); Melissa Edwards (children's fiction and adult commercial fiction, as well as select pop-culture nonfiction); Alyssa Jennette (children's and adult fiction and picture books, and has dabbled in humor and pop culture nonfiction); Madelyn Burt (adult and children's fiction, as well as select historical nonfiction).

REPRESENTS Nonfiction, fiction, novels, juvenile books. **Considers these fiction areas:** action, adventure, commercial, confession, contemporary issues, ethnic, experimental, family saga, fantasy, feminist, gay, historical, horror, humor, juvenile, lesbian, literary, mainstream, middle grade, military, multicultural, mystery, new adult, New Age, occult, paranormal, regional, romance, satire, science fiction, supernatural, suspense, thriller, urban fantasy, women's, young adult.

☞ Does not represent plays, screenplays, picture books, or poetry.

HOW TO CONTACT Accepts electronic queries for fiction and nonfiction. Submit query addressed to a specific agent. Include first chapter or first 10 pages of ms. Accepts simultaneous submissions.

RECENT SALES *Sweet Laurel*, by Laurel Gallucci and Claire Thomas; *Terrain: A Seasonal Guide to Nature at Home*, by Terrain; *The Prince's Bane*, by Alexandra Christo; *Deep Listening*, by Jillian Pransky; *Change Resilience*, by Lior Arussy; *A Thousand Words*, by Brigit Young.

⊘ STRACHAN LITERARY AGENCY

P.O. Box 2091, Annapolis MD 21404. **E-mail:** query@strachanlit.com. **Website:** www.strachanlit.com. **Contact:** Laura Strachan. Estab. 1998.

REPRESENTS Nonfiction, fiction, novels, short story collections, juvenile books. **Considers these fiction areas:** feminist, literary, multicultural, short story collections, translation, young adult.

☞ "This agency specializes in literary fiction and narrative nonfiction."

HOW TO CONTACT Please query with description of project and short biographical statement. Do not paste or attach sample pages. Accepts simultaneous submissions.

ROBIN STRAUS AGENCY, INC.

The Wallace Literary Agency, 229 E. 79th St., Suite 5A, New York NY 10075. (212)472-3282. **Fax:** (212)472-3833. **E-mail:** info@robinstrausagency.com. **Website:** www.robinstrausagency.com. **Contact:** Ms. Robin Straus. Estab. 1983. Member of AAR.

○ Prior to becoming an agent, Robin Straus served as a subsidiary rights manager at Random House and Doubleday. She began her career in the editorial department of Little, Brown.

REPRESENTS **Considers these fiction areas:** commercial, contemporary issues, fantasy, feminist, literary, mainstream, science fiction, translation, women's.

☞ Does not represent juvenile, young adult, horror, romance, Westerns, poetry, or screenplays.

HOW TO CONTACT E-query only. No physical mail accepted. See our website for full submission instructions. Email us a query letter with contact information, an autobiographical summary, a brief synopsis or description of your book project, submission history, and information on competition. If you wish, you may also include the opening chapter of your manuscript (pasted). While we do our best to reply to all queries, you can assume that if you haven't heard from us after six weeks, we are not interested. Accepts simultaneous submissions.

TERMS Agent receives 15% commission on domestic sales; 20% commission on foreign sales. Offers written contract.

THE STRINGER LITERARY AGENCY LLC

P.O. Box 111255, Naples FL 34108. **E-mail:** mstringer@stringerlit.com. **Website:** www.stringerlit.com. **Contact:** Marlene Stringer. Estab. 2008. Member of AAR. RWA, MWA, ITW, SBCWI, The Writers Guild Represents 50 +/- clients.

REPRESENTS Fiction, novels. **Considers these fiction areas:** commercial, crime, detective, fantasy, historical, horror, mainstream, multicultural, mystery, new adult, paranormal, police, romance, science fiction, suspense, thriller, urban fantasy, women's, young adult, No space opera SF..

> This agency specializes in fiction. "We are an editorial agency, and work with clients to make their manuscripts the best they can be in preparation for submission. We focus on career planning, and help our clients reach their publishing goals. We advise clients on marketing and promotional strategies to help them reach their target readership. Because we are so hands-on, we limit the size of our list; however, we are always looking for exceptional voices and stories that demand we read to the end. You never know where the next great story is coming from." This agency is seeking thrillers, crime fiction (not true crime), mystery, women's fiction, single title and category romance, fantasy (all subgenera), grounded science fiction (no space opera, aliens, etc.), and YA/teen. Does not want to receive picture books, MG, plays, short stories, or poetry. This is not the agency for inspirational romance or erotica. No space opera. The agency is not seeking nonfiction as of this time.

HOW TO CONTACT Electronic submissions through website only. Please make sure your ms is as good as it can be before you submit. Agents are not first readers. For specific information on what we like to see in query letters, refer to the information at www.stringerlit.com. Accepts simultaneous submissions. "We strive to respond quickly, but current clients' work always comes first." Obtains new clients through referrals, submissions, conferences.

TERMS Standard commission. "We do not charge fees."

RECENT SALES *Don't Believe It* by Charlie Donlea; *The Waiting Room*, by Emily Bleeker; *The Numina Trilogy*, by Charlie N. Holmberg; *Belle Chasse*, by Suzanne Johnson; *The Evermore Chronicles* by Emily R. King;

Wilds of the Bayou, by Susannah Sandlin; *Death In The Family* by Tessa Wegert; *The Vine Witch* by Luanne Smith; *The Scottish Trilogy*, by Anna Bradley; *Fly By Night*, by Andrea Thalasinos; The Dragonsworn Series, by Caitlyn McFarland; *The Devious Dr. Jekyll*, by Viola Carr; *The Dragon's Price*, by Bethany Wiggins; The Hundredth Queen Series by Emily R. King; Film Rights to *The Paper Magician*, by Charlie N. Holmberg.

WRITERS CONFERENCES Various conferences each year.

TIPS "If your ms falls between categories, or you are not sure of the category, query and we'll let you know if we'd like to take a look. We strive to respond as quickly as possible. If you have not received a response in the time period indicated on website, please re-query."

THE STROTHMAN AGENCY, LLC

63 E. 9th St., 10X, New York NY 10003. **E-mail:** info@strothmanagency.com. **E-mail:** strothmanagency@gmail.com. **Website:** www.strothmanagency.com. **Contact:** Wendy Strothman, Lauren MacLeod. Estab. 2003. Member of AAR. Represents 100+ clients.

> Prior to becoming an agent, Ms. Strothman was head of Beacon Press (1983-1995) and executive vice president of Houghton Mifflin's Trade & Reference Division (1996-2002).

MEMBER AGENTS Wendy Strothman (history, narrative nonfiction, narrative journalism, science and nature, and current affairs); Lauren MacLeod (young adult fiction and nonfiction, middle grade novels, as well as adult narrative nonfiction, particularly food writing, science, pop culture and history).

REPRESENTS Nonfiction, juvenile books. **Considers these fiction areas:** middle grade, young adult.

> Specializes in history, science, biography, politics, narrative journalism, nature and the environment, current affairs, narrative nonfiction, business and economics, young adult fiction and nonfiction, and middle grade fiction and nonfiction. "The Strothman Agency seeks out scholars, journalists, and other acknowledged and emerging experts in their fields. We specialize in history, science, narrative journalism, nature and the environment, current affairs, narrative nonfiction, business and economics, young adult fiction and nonfiction, middle grade fiction and nonfiction. We are not signing up projects in romance, science fiction, picture books, or poetry."

HOW TO CONTACT Accepts queries only via e-mail. See submission guidelines online. Accepts simultaneous submissions. "All e-mails received will be responded to with an auto-reply. If we have not replied to your query within 6 weeks, we do not feel that it is right for us." Accepts simultaneous submissions. Obtains most new clients through recommendations from others.

TERMS Agent receives 15% commission on domestic sales; 20% commission on foreign sales. Offers written contract; 30-day notice must be given to terminate contract.

THE STUART AGENCY

1410 Broadway, 23rd Floor, New York NY 10018. (646)564-2983. **E-mail:** andrew@stuartagency.com. **Website:** stuartagency.com. **Contact:** Andrew Stuart. Estab. 2002.

○ Prior to his current position, Mr. Stuart was an agent with Literary Group International for five years. Prior to becoming an agent, he was an editor at Random House and Simon & Schuster.

MEMBER AGENTS Andrew Stuart (history, science, narrative nonfiction, business, current events, memoir, psychology, sports, literary fiction); Christopher Rhodes, christopher@stuartagency.com (literary and upmarket fiction [including thriller and horror]; connected stories/essays [humorous and serious]; memoir; creative/narrative nonfiction; history; religion; pop culture; and art & design); Rob Kirkpatrick, rob@stuartagency.com (memoir, biography, sports, music, pop culture, current events, history, and pop science).

REPRESENTS Nonfiction, novels. **Considers these fiction areas:** horror, literary, thriller.

HOW TO CONTACT Query via online submission form on the agency website. Accepts simultaneous submissions.

EMMA SWEENEY AGENCY, LLC

245 E 80th St., Suite 7E, New York NY 10075. **E-mail:** info@emmasweeneyagency.com. **E-mail:** queries@emmasweeneyagency.com. **Website:** www.emmasweeneyagency.com. Estab. 2006. Member of AAR. Other memberships include Women's Media Group. Represents 80 clients.

○ Prior to becoming an agent, Ms. Sweeney was director of subsidiary rights at Grove Press. Since 1990, she has been a literary agent. Ms. Sutherland Brown was an Associate Editor at St. Martin's Press/Thomas Dunne Books and a freelance editor. Ms. Watson attended Hunter College where she earned a BA in English (with a focus on Creative Writing) and a BA in Russian Language & Culture.

MEMBER AGENTS Emma Sweeney, president; Margaret Sutherland Brown (commercial and literary fiction, mysteries and thrillers, narrative nonfiction, lifestyle, and cookbook); Hannah Brattesani (poetry, and literary fiction).

REPRESENTS Nonfiction, fiction, novels, poetry books. **Considers these fiction areas:** commercial, contemporary issues, crime, historical, horror, literary, mainstream, mystery, poetry, spiritual, suspense, thriller, women's.

☞ Does not want erotica.

HOW TO CONTACT "We accept only electronic queries, and ask that all queries be sent to queries@emmasweeneyagency.com rather than to any agent directly. Please begin your query with a succinct (and hopefully catchy) description of your plot or proposal. Always include a brief cover letter telling us how you heard about ESA, your previous writing credits, and a few lines about yourself. We cannot open any attachments unless specifically requested, and ask that you paste the first 10 pages of your proposal or novel into the text of your e-mail." Accepts simultaneous submissions.

TALCOTT NOTCH LITERARY SERVICES, LLC

31 Cherry St., Suite 100, Milford CT 06460. (203)876-4959. **Fax:** (203)876-9517. **E-mail:** editorial@talcottnotch.net. **Website:** www.talcottnotch.net. **Contact:** Gina Panettieri, founder. Estab. 2002. SinC, MWA, SCBWI Represents 150 clients.

○ Prior to becoming an agent, Ms. Panettieri was a freelance writer and editor. Ms. Munier was Director of Acquisitions for Adams Media Corporation and had previously worked for Disney. Ms. Sulaiman holds degrees from Wellesley and the University of Chicago and had completed an internship with Sourcebooks prior to joining Talcott Notch. Ms. Mele received her B.A. in English from the University of Connecticut and her Master's in Creative Writing from the University of Southern New Hampshire before completing an internship at Talcott Notch and then joining the agency as an assistant.

MEMBER AGENTS Gina Panettieri, gpanettieri@talcottnotch.net (history, business, self-help, science, gardening, cookbooks, crafts, parenting, memoir, true crime and travel, YA, MG and women's fiction, paranormal, urban fantasy, horror, science fiction, historical, mystery, thrillers and suspense); Paula Munier, pmunier@talcottnotch.net (mystery/thriller, SF/fantasy, romance, YA, memoir, humor, pop culture, health & wellness, cooking, self-help, pop psych, New Age, inspirational, technology, science, and writing); Saba Sulaiman, ssulaiman@talcottnotch.net (upmarket literary and commercial fiction, romance [all subgenres except paranormal], character-driven psychological thrillers, cozy mysteries, memoir, young adult [except paranormal and sci-fi], middle grade, and nonfiction humor); Tia Mele, tmele@talcottnotch.net (YA and MG, fiction and nonfiction, limited adult projects).

REPRESENTS Nonfiction, fiction, novels, short story collections, novellas, juvenile books. **Considers these fiction areas:** action, adventure, comic books, commercial, contemporary issues, crime, detective, erotica, ethnic, family saga, fantasy, feminist, gay, hilo, historical, horror, juvenile, lesbian, literary, mainstream, middle grade, military, multicultural, multimedia, mystery, new adult, New Age, paranormal, police, romance, science fiction, short story collections, sports, supernatural, suspense, thriller, urban fantasy, war, westerns, women's, young adult.

☛ "We are most actively seeking projects featuring diverse characters and stories which expand the reader's understanding of our society and the wider world we live in."

HOW TO CONTACT Query via e-mail (preferred) with first 10 pages of the ms pasted within the body of the e-mail, not as an attachment. Accepts simultaneous submissions. Responds in 2 weeks to queries; 6-10 weeks to mss. We find many of our new clients through conferences and online events that allow us to interact one-on-one with the authors, as well as through referrals by our clients.

TERMS Agent receives 15% commission on domestic sales; 20% commission on foreign sales. Offers written contract, binding for 1 year.

RECENT SALES Agency sold 65 titles in the last year, including *Lies She Told* , by Cate Holahan (Crooked Lane Books); *American Operator*, by Brian Andrews and Jeffrey Wilson (Thomas & Mercer); *Reset*, by Brian Andrews (Thomas & Mercer); *A Lover's Pinch*, by Peter Tupper (Rowman & Littlefield); *Everlasting Nora*, by Marie Cruz (Tor); *A Borrowing of Bones*, by Paula Mu-

nier (St. Martin's); *Muslim Girls Rise*, by Saira Mir (Salaam Reads), *Belabored*, by Lyz Lenz (Nation Books); *Tarnished Are The Stars*, by Rosiee Thor (Scholastic): *The Complicated Math of Two Plus One*, by Cathleen Barnhart (Harper Children's); and many others.

WRITERS CONFERENCES Members of the agency usually appear at BEA, Thrillerfest, Bouchercon, Killer Nashville, New England Mystery Writers Crimebake, New York Pitch, The Monterey Writers Retreat and many other events. Please check each agent's page on our website for updated lists of their appearances.

TIPS "Know your market and how to reach them. A strong platform is essential in your book proposal. Can you effectively use social media/Are you a strong networker: Are you familiar with the book bloggers in your genre? Are you involved with the interest-specific groups that can help you? What can you do to break through the 'noise' and help present your book to your readers? Check our website for more tips and information on this topic."

TESSLER LITERARY AGENCY, LLC

27 W. 20th St., Suite 1003, New York NY 10011. (212)242-0466. **Website:** www.tessleragency.com. **Contact:** Michelle Tessler. Estab. 2004. Member of AAR. Women's Media Group.

○ Prior to forming her own agency, Ms. Tessler worked at the prestigious literary agency Carlisle & Company (now Inkwell Management) and at the William Morris Agency.

REPRESENTS Nonfiction, fiction, novels. **Considers these fiction areas:** commercial, ethnic, family saga, historical, literary, multicultural, women's.

☛ "Tessler Literary Agency represents a select number of best-selling and emerging authors. Based in the Flatiron District in Manhattan, we are dedicated to writers of high quality fiction and nonfiction. Our clients include accomplished journalists, scientists, academics, experts in their field, as well as novelists and debut authors with unique voices and stories to tell. We value fresh, original writing that has a compelling point of view. Our list is diverse and far-reaching. In nonfiction, it includes narrative, popular science, memoir, history, psychology, business, biography, food, and travel. In many cases, we sign authors who are especially adept at writing books that cross many of these categories at once. In fiction, we represent literary, women's, and commercial. If your project is in keeping with the kind of books we take on, we want to hear from you." Does not want genre fiction or children's books or anthologies.

HOW TO CONTACT Submit query through online query form only. Accepts simultaneous submissions. New clients by queries/submissions through the website and recommendations from others.

TERMS Receives 15% commission on domestic sales; 20% on foreign sales. Offers written contract.

THOMPSON LITERARY AGENCY

115 W. 29th St., Third Floor, New York NY 10001. (716)257-8149. **E-mail:** submissions@thompsonliterary.com. **Website:** thompsonliterary.com. **Contact:** Meg Thompson, founder. Estab. 2014. Member of AAR. Signatory of WGA.

○ Before her current position, Ms. Thompson was with LJK Literary and the Einstein Thompson Agency.

MEMBER AGENTS Cindy Uh, senior agent; Kiele Raymond, senior agent; Ashley Collom, Senior Agent; John Thorn, affiliate agent; Sandy Hodgman, director of foreign rights.

REPRESENTS Nonfiction, fiction, novels, juvenile books. **Considers these fiction areas:** commercial, contemporary issues, experimental, fantasy, feminist, historical, juvenile, literary, middle grade, multicultural, picture books, women's, young adult.

~ The agency is always on the lookout for both commercial and literary fiction, as well as young adult and children's books. "Nonfiction, however, is our specialty, and our interests include biography, memoir, music, popular science, politics, blog-to-book projects, cookbooks, sports, health and wellness, fashion, art, and popular culture." "Please note that we do not accept submissions for poetry collections or screenplays, and we only consider picture books by established illustrators."

HOW TO CONTACT "For fiction: Please send a query letter, including any salient biographical information or previous publications, and attach the first 25 pages of your manuscript. For nonfiction: Please send a query letter and a full proposal, including biographical information, previous publications, credentials that qualify you to write your book, marketing information, and sample material. You should address your query to whichever agent you think is best suited for your project." Accepts simultaneous submissions. Responds in 6 weeks if interested.

THREE SEAS LITERARY AGENCY

P.O. Box 444, Sun Prairie WI 53590. (608)834-9317. **E-mail:** threeseaslit@aol.com. **E-mail:** queries@three-seaslit.com. **Website:** threeseasagency.com. **Contact:** Michelle Grajkowski, Cori Deyoe. Estab. 2000. Member of AAR. Other memberships include RWA (Romance Writers of America), SCBWI Represents 55 clients.

○ Since its inception, 3 Seas has sold more than 500 titles worldwide. Ms. Grajkowski's authors have appeared on all the major lists including *The New York Times*, *USA Today* and *Publishers Weekly*. Prior to joining the agency in 2006, Ms. Deyoe was a multi-published author. She represents a wide range of authors and has sold many projects at auction.

MEMBER AGENTS Michelle Grajkowski (romance, women's fiction, young adult and middle grade fiction, select nonfiction projects); Cori Deyoe (all sub-genres of romance, women's fiction, young adult, middle grade, picture books, thrillers, mysteries and select nonfiction); Linda Scalissi (women's fiction, thrillers, young adult, mysteries and romance).

REPRESENTS Nonfiction, novels. **Considers these fiction areas:** middle grade, mystery, picture books, romance, thriller, women's, young adult.

~ "We represent more than 50 authors who write romance, women's fiction, science fiction/fantasy, thrillers, young adult and middle grade fiction, as well as select nonfiction titles. Currently, we are looking for fantastic authors with a voice of their own." 3 Seas does not represent poetry or screenplays.

HOW TO CONTACT E-mail queries only; no attachments, unless requested by agents. For fiction, please e-mail the first chapter and synopsis along with a cover letter. Also, be sure to include the genre and the number of words in your manuscript, as well as pertinent writing experience in your query letter. For nonfiction, e-mail a complete proposal, including a query letter and your first chapter. For picture books, query with complete text. Accepts simultaneous submissions. Obtains most new clients through recommendations from others, conferences.

TERMS Agent receives 15% commission on domestic sales; 20% commission on foreign sales. Offers written contract.

RECENT SALES REPRESENTS Bestselling authors, including Jennifer Brown, Katie MacAlister, Kerrelyn Sparks, and C.L. Wilson.

✪ TRANSATLANTIC LITERARY AGENCY

2 Bloor St. E., Suite 3500, Toronto ON M4W 1A8 Canada. (416)488-9214. **E-mail:** info@transatlanticagency.com. **Website:** transatlanticagency.com.

MEMBER AGENTS Trena White (upmarket, accessible non-fiction: current affairs, business, culture, politics, technology, and the environment); Amy Tompkins (adult: literary fiction, historical fiction, women's fiction including smart romance, narrative non-fiction, and quirky or original how-to books; children's: early readers, middle grade, young adult, and new adult); Stephanie Sinclair (literary fiction, upmarket women's and commercial fiction, literary thriller and suspense, YA crossover; narrative nonfiction, memoir, investigative journalism and true crime); Samantha Haywood (literary fiction and upmarket commercial fiction, specifically literary thrillers and upmarket mystery, historical fiction, smart contemporary fiction, upmarket women's fiction and cross-over novels; narrative nonfiction, including investigative journalism, politics, women's issues, memoirs, environmental issues, historical narratives, sexuality, true crime; graphic novels (fiction/nonfiction): preferably full length graphic novels, story collections considered, memoirs, biographies, travel narratives); Jesse Finkelstein (nonfiction: current affairs, business, culture, politics, technology, religion, and the environment); Marie Campbell (middle grade fiction); Shaun Bradley (referrals only; adult literary fiction and narrative nonfiction, primarily science and investigative journalism); Sandra Bishop (fiction; nonfiction: biography, memoir, and positive or humorous how-to books on advice/relationships, mind/body/spirit, religion, healthy living, finances, life-hacks, traveling, living a better life); Fiona Kenshole (children's and young adult; only accepting submissions from referrals or conferences she attends as faculty); Lynn Bennett (not accepting submissions or new clients); David Bennett (children's, young adult, adult).

REPRESENTS Nonfiction, novels, juvenile books.

☛ "In both children's and adult literature, we market directly into the US, the United Kingdom and Canada." Represents adult and children's authors of all genres, including illustrators. Does not want to receive picture books, musicals, screenplays or stage plays.

HOW TO CONTACT Always refer to the website, as guidelines will change, and only various agents are open to new clients at any given time. Obtains most new clients through recommendations from others.

TERMS Agent receives 15% commission on domestic sales; 20% commission on foreign sales. Offers written contract; 45-day notice must be given to terminate contract. This agency charges for photocopying and postage when it exceeds $100.

RECENT SALES Sold 250 titles in the last year.

TRIADA US

P.O. Box 561, Sewickley PA 15143. (412)401-3376. **E-mail:** uwe@triadaus.com; brent@triadaus.com; laura@triadaus.com; lauren@triadaus.com; amelia@triadaus.com. **Website:** www.triadaus.com. **Contact:** Dr. Uwe Stender, President. Estab. 2004. Member of AAR.

MEMBER AGENTS Uwe Stender; Brent Taylor; Laura Crockett; Lauren Spieller; Amelia Appel.

REPRESENTS Nonfiction, fiction, novels, juvenile books. **Considers these fiction areas:** action, adventure, comic books, commercial, contemporary issues, crime, detective, ethnic, family saga, fantasy, feminist, gay, historical, horror, juvenile, lesbian, literary, mainstream, middle grade, multicultural, mystery, occult, picture books, police, suspense, thriller, urban fantasy, women's, young adult.

☛ Actively seeking fiction and non-fiction across a broad range of categories of all age levels.

HOW TO CONTACT E-mail queries preferred. Please paste your query letter and the first 10 pages of your ms into the body of a message e-mailed to the agent of your choice. Do not simultaneously query multiple Triada agents. Please query one and wait for their response before moving onto another agent within our agency. Triada US agents personally respond to all queries and requested material and pride themselves on having some of the fastest response times in the industry. Obtains most new clients through submission inbox (query letters and requested mss), client referrals, and conferences.

TERMS Triada US retains 15% commission on domestic sales and 20% commission on foreign and translation sales. Offers written contract; 30-day notice must be given prior to termination.

RECENT SALES *Playing Back the 80s* by Jim Beviglia (Rowman & Littlefield), *Game of Stars* by Sayantani DasGupta (Scholastic), *The Voice in My Head* by Dana Davis (Inkyard), *The Sound of Stars* by Alechia Dow (Inkyard), *Fake Blood* by Whitney Gardner (Simon & Schuster), *Maiden & Princess* by Daniel Haack and Isabel Galupo (Little Bee), *Bear No Malice* by Clarissa Harwood (Pegasus), *The Last Chance Dance* by Kate Hattemer (Knopf), *Hunting Annabelle* by Wendy Heard (Mira), *Beside Herself* by Elizabeth LaBan (Lake Union), *Don't Date Rosa Santos* by Nina Moreno (Disney-Hyperion), *Don't Call the Wolf* by Aleksandra Ross (HarperTeen), *Empire of Sand* by Tasha Suri (Orbit), *Ghost Wood Song* by Erica Waters (HarperTeen), *The Light Between Worlds* by Laura Weymouth (HarperTeen), *Going Off-Script* by Jen Wilde (Swoon Reads).

TRIDENT MEDIA GROUP

41 Madison Ave., 36th Floor, New York NY 10010. (212)333-1511. **E-mail:** info@tridentmediagroup.com. **Website:** www.tridentmediagroup.com. **Contact:** Ellen Levine. Member of AAR.

MEMBER AGENTS Kimberly Whalen, ws.assistant@tridentmediagroup (commercial fiction and nonfiction, including women's fiction, romance, suspense, paranormal, and pop culture); Alyssa Eisner Henkin (picture books through young adult fiction, including mysteries, period pieces, contemporary school-settings, issues of social justice, family sagas, eerie magical realism, and retellings of classics; children's/YA nonfiction: history, STEM/STEAM themes, memoir) Scott Miller, smiller@tridentmediagroup.com (commercial fiction, including thrillers, crime fiction, women's, book club fiction, middle grade, young adult; nonfiction, including military, celebrity and pop culture, narrative, sports, prescriptive, and current events); Melissa Flashman, mflashman@tridentmediagroup.com (nonfiction: pop culture, memoir, wellness, popular science, business and economics, technology; fiction: adult and YA, literary and commercial); Don Fehr, dfehr@tridentmediagroup.com (literary and commercial fiction, young adult fiction, narrative nonfiction, memoirs, travel, science, and health); John Silbersack, silbersack.assistant@tridentmediagroup.com (fiction: literary fiction, crime fiction, science fiction and fantasy, children's, thrillers/suspense; nonfiction: narrative nonfiction, science, history, biography, current events, memoirs, finance, pop culture); Erica Spellman-Silverman; Ellen Levine, levine.assistant@tridentmediagroup.com (popular commercial fiction and compelling nonfiction, including memoir, popular culture, narrative nonfiction, history, politics, biography, science, and the odd quirky book); Mark Gottlieb (fiction: science fiction, fantasy, young adult, graphic novels, historical, middle grade, mystery, romance, suspense, thrillers; nonfiction: business, finance, history, religious, health, cookbooks, sports, African-American, biography, memoir, travel, mind/body/spirit, narrative nonfiction, science, technology); Alexander Slater, aslater@tridentmdiagroup.com (children's, middle grade, and young adult fiction); Amanda O'Connor, aoconnor@tridentmediagroup.com; Tara Carberry, tcarberry@tridentmediagroup.com (women's commercial fiction, romance, new adult, young adult, and select nonfiction); Alexa Stark, astark@tridentmediagroup.com (literary fiction, upmarket commercial fiction, young adult, memoir, narrative nonfiction, popular science, cultural criticism and women's issues).

REPRESENTS Considers these fiction areas: commercial, crime, fantasy, historical, juvenile, literary, middle grade, mystery, new adult, paranormal, picture books, romance, science fiction, suspense, thriller, women's, young adult.

☛ Actively seeking new or established authors in a variety of fiction and nonfiction genres.

HOW TO CONTACT Submit through the agency's online submission form on the agency website. Query only one agent at a time. If you e-query, include no attachments. Accepts simultaneous submissions.

TIPS "If you have any questions, please check FAQ page before e-mailing us."

UNITED TALENT AGENCY

888 7th Ave., 7th Floor, New York NY 10106. (212)659-2600. **Website:** www.theagencygroup.com. **Contact:** Marc Gerald.

○ Prior to becoming an agent, Mr. Gerald owned and ran an independent publishing and entertainment agency.

MEMBER AGENTS Marc Gerald (no queries); Juliet Mushens, UK Literary division, juliet.mushens@unitedtalent.com (high-concept novels, thrillers, YA, historical fiction, literary fiction, psychological suspense, reading group fiction, SF and fantasy); Sasha Raskin, sasah.raskin@unitedtalent.com (popular science, business books, historical narrative nonfiction, narrative and/or literary nonfiction, historical fiction, and genre fiction like sci-fi but when it fits the crossover space and isn't strictly confined to its genre); Sarah Manning, sarah.manning@unitedtalent.com (enjoys crime, thrillers, historical fiction, commercial women's fiction, accessible literary fiction, fantasy and YA); Diana Beaumont, UK Literary division, diana.beaumont@unitedtalent.com (accessible literary fiction with a strong hook, historical fiction, crime, thrillers, women's commercial fiction that isn't too marshmallowy, cookery, lifestyle, celebrity books and memoir with a distinctive voice).

REPRESENTS Nonfiction, novels. **Considers these fiction areas:** commercial, crime, fantasy, historical, literary, science fiction, suspense, thriller, women's, young adult.

HOW TO CONTACT To query Juliet: Please send your cover letter, first 3 chapters and synopsis by e-mail. Juliet replies to all submissions, and aims to respond within 8-12 weeks of receipt of e-mail. To query Sasha: e-query. To query Sarah: Please send you cover letter in the body of your e-mail with synopsis and first 3 chapters by e-mail. She responds to all submissions within 8-12 weeks. Accepts simultaneous submissions.

THE UNTER AGENCY

23 W. 73rd St., Suite 100, New York NY 10023. (212)401-4068. **E-mail:** jennifer@theunteragency.com. **Website:** www.theunteragency.com. **Contact:** Jennifer Unter. Estab. 2008. Member of AAR. Women Media Group

○ Ms. Unter began her book publishing career in the editorial department at Henry Holt & Co. She later worked at the Karpfinger Agency while she attended law school. She then became an associate at the entertainment firm of Cowan, DeBaets, Abrahams & Sheppard LLP where she practiced primarily in the areas of publishing and copyright law.

REPRESENTS Nonfiction, fiction, novels, short story collections, juvenile books. **Considers these fiction areas:** action, adventure, cartoon, commercial, family saga, inspirational, juvenile, mainstream, middle grade, mystery, paranormal, picture books, thriller, women's, young adult.

☛ This agency specializes in children's, nonfiction, and quality fiction.

HOW TO CONTACT Send an e-query. There is also an online submission form. If you do not hear back from this agency within 3 months, consider that a

no. Accepts simultaneous submissions. Responds in 3 months.

RECENT SALES A full list of recent sales/titles is available on the agency website.

UPSTART CROW LITERARY

244 Fifth Avenue, 11th Floor, New York NY 10001. **E-mail:** danielle.submission@gmail.com. **Website:** www.upstartcrowliterary.com. **Contact:** Danielle Chiotti, Alexandra Penfold. Estab. 2009. Member of AAR. Signatory of WGA.

MEMBER AGENTS Michael Stearns (not accepting submissions); Danielle Chiotti (all genres of young adult and middle grade fiction; adult upmarket commercial fiction [not considering romance, mystery/suspense/thriller, science fiction, horror, or erotica]; nonfiction in the areas of narrative/memoir, lifestyle, relationships, humor, current events, food, wine, and cooking); Ted Malawer (not accepting submissions); Alexandra Penfold (not accepting submissions); Susan Hawk (books for children and teens only).

REPRESENTS Considers these fiction areas: commercial, mainstream, middle grade, picture books, young adult.

HOW TO CONTACT Submit a query and 20 pages pasted into an e-mail. Accepts simultaneous submissions.

VERITAS LITERARY AGENCY

601 Van Ness Ave., Opera Plaza, Suite E, San Francisco CA 94102. (415)647-6964. **Fax:** (415)647-6965. **E-mail:** submissions@veritasliterary.com. **Website:** www.veritasliterary.com. **Contact:** Katherine Boyle. Member of AAR. Other memberships include Author's Guild and SCBWI.

MEMBER AGENTS Katherine Boyle, kboyle@veritasliterary.com (literary fiction, middle grade, young adult, narrative nonfiction/memoir, historical fiction, crime/suspense, history, pop culture, popular science, business/career); Michael Carr, michael@veritasliterary.com (historical fiction, women's fiction, science fiction and fantasy, nonfiction); Chiara Rosati, literary scout.

REPRESENTS Nonfiction, novels. **Considers these fiction areas:** commercial, crime, fantasy, historical, literary, middle grade, new adult, science fiction, suspense, women's, young adult.

HOW TO CONTACT This agency accepts short queries or proposals via e-mail only. "Fiction: Please include a cover letter listing previously published work, a one-page summary and the first 5 pages in the body of the e-mail (not as an attachment). Nonfiction: If you are sending a proposal, please include an author biography, an overview, a chapter-by-chapter summary, and an analysis of competitive titles. We do our best to review all queries within 4-6 weeks; however, if you have not heard from us in 12 weeks, consider that a no." Accepts simultaneous submissions. If you have not heard from this agency in 12 weeks, consider that a no.

🌑 WADE & CO. LITERARY AGENCY, LTD

33 Cormorant Lodge, Thomas More St., London E1W 1AU United Kingdom. (44)(207)488-4171. **Fax:** (44) (207)488-4172. **E-mail:** rw@rwla.com. **Website:** www. rwla.com. **Contact:** Robin Wade. Estab. 2001.

Ｏ Prior to opening his agency, Mr. Wade was an author.

MEMBER AGENTS Robin Wade.

☛ "We are young and dynamic, and actively seek new writers across the literary spectrum." Does not want to receive poetry, plays, screenplays, children's books, film scripts, or short stories.

HOW TO CONTACT New proposals for full length adult and young adult books (excluding children's books or poetry) are always welcome. We much prefer to receive queries and submissions by e-mail, although we do, of course, accept proposals by post. There is no need to telephone in advance. Please provide a few details about yourself, a synopsis (i.e. a clear narrative summary of the complete story, of between say 1 and 6 pages in length) and the first 10,000 words or so (ideally as word.doc or PDF attachments) over e-mail. Accepts simultaneous submissions. Responds in 1 week to queries; 1 month to mss.

TERMS Agent receives 15% commission on domestic sales; 20% commission on foreign sales. Offers written contract; 1-month notice must be given to terminate contract.

TIPS "We seek manuscripts that are well written, with strong characters and an original narrative voice. Our absolute priority is giving the best possible service to the authors we choose to represent, as well as maintaining routine friendly contact with them as we help develop their careers."

WALES LITERARY AGENCY, INC.

1508 10th Ave. E. #401, Seattle WA 98102. (206)284-7114. **E-mail:** waleslit@waleslit.com. **Website:** www. waleslit.com. **Contact:** Elizabeth Wales; Neal Swain. Estab. 1990. Member of AAR. Other memberships include Authors Guild.

Ｏ Prior to becoming an agent, Ms. Wales worked at Oxford University Press and Viking Penguin.

MEMBER AGENTS Elizabeth Wales; Neal Swain.

REPRESENTS Nonfiction, fiction, novels.

☛ This agency specializes in quality mainstream fiction and narrative nonfiction. "We're looking for more narrative nonfiction writing about nature, science, and animals." Does not handle screenplays, children's picture books, genre fiction, or most category nonfiction (such as self-help or how-to books).

HOW TO CONTACT E-query with no attachments. Submission guidelines can be found at the agency website along with a list of current clients and titles. Accepts simultaneous submissions. Responds in 2 weeks to queries, 2 months to mss.

TERMS Agent receives 15% commission on domestic sales; 20% commission on foreign sales.

RECENT SALES *Half-broke*, by Ginger Gaffney (W.W. Norton); *What Your Food Ate*, by David Montgomery and Anne Bikle (W.W. Norton); *Edgar Martinez: My Life and Baseball* by Edgar Martinez and Larry Stone (Triumph Books); *Every Penguin in the World* by Charles Bergman (Sasquatch/Penguin Random).

TIPS "We are especially interested in work that espouses a progressive cultural or political view, projects a new voice, or simply shares an important, compelling story. We also encourage writers living in the Pacific Northwest, West Coast, Alaska, and Pacific Rim countries, and writers from historically underrepresented groups, such as gay and lesbian writers and writers of color, to submit work (but does not discourage writers outside these areas). Most importantly, whether in fiction or nonfiction, the agency is looking for talented storytellers."

WATERSIDE PRODUCTIONS, INC.

2055 Oxford Ave., Cardiff CA 92007. (760)632-9190. **Fax:** (760)632-9295. **E-mail:** admin@waterside.com. **Website:** www.waterside.com. Estab. 1982.

MEMBER AGENTS Bill Gladstone (big nonfiction books); Margot Maley Hutchinson (computer, health, psychology, parenting, fitness, pop culture, and business); Carole Jelen, carole@jelenpub.com (innovation and thought leaders especially in business, technology, lifestyle and self-help); David Nelson; Jill Kramer, watersideagentjk@aol.com (quality fiction with empowering themes for adults and YA (including crossovers); nonfiction, including mind-body-spirit, self-help, celebrity memoirs, relationships, sociology, finance, psychology, health and fitness, diet/nutrition, inspiration, business, family/parenting issues); Brad Schepp (e-commerce, social media and social commerce, careers, entrepreneurship, general business, health and fitness); Natasha Gladstone, (picture books, books with film tie-ins, books with established animated characters, and educational titles); Johanna Maaghul, johanna@waterside.com (nonfiction and select fiction); Kimberly Brabec, rights@waterside.com (Director of International Rights).

REPRESENTS Considers these fiction areas: mainstream, picture books, young adult.

☞ Specializes in computer and technical titles, and also represent other nonfiction genres, including self-help, cooking, travel, and more. Note that most agents here are nonfiction only, so target your query to the appropriate agent.

HOW TO CONTACT "Please read each agent bio [on the website] to determine who you think would best represent your genre of work. When you have chosen your agent, please write his or her name in the subject line of your e-mail and send it to admin@waterside.com with your query letter in the body of the e-mail, and your proposal or sample material as an attached word document." Nonfiction submission guidelines are available on the website. Accepts simultaneous submissions. Obtains most new clients through referrals from established client and publisher list.

TIPS "For new writers, a quality proposal and a strong knowledge of the market you're writing for goes a long way toward helping us turn you into a published author. We like to see a strong author platform."

⊘ WATKINS LOOMIS AGENCY, INC.

P.O. Box 20925, New York NY 10025. (212)532-0080. **Fax:** (646)383-2449. **E-mail:** assistant@watkinsloomis.com. **Website:** www.watkinsloomis.com. Estab. 1980. Represents 50+ clients.

MEMBER AGENTS Gloria Loomis, president; Julia Masnik, junior agent.

REPRESENTS Nonfiction, novels.

☞ This agency specializes in literary fiction, biography, memoir, and political journalism.

HOW TO CONTACT No unsolicited mss. This agency does not guarantee a response to queries.

TERMS Agent receives 15% commission on domestic sales; 20% commission on foreign sales.

RECENT SALES A list of sales is available on the agency website.

WAXMAN LITERARY AGENCY, INC.

443 Park Ave. S, Suite 1004, New York NY 10016. **Fax:** (212)675-1381. **E-mail:** submit@waxmanagency.com. **Website:** www.waxmanagency.com.

MEMBER AGENTS Scott Waxman (nonfiction: history, biography, health and science, adventure, business, inspirational sports); Byrd Leavell (narrative nonfiction, sports, humor, and select commercial fiction); Ashley Lopez (literary fiction, women's fiction (commercial and upmarket, memoir, narrative nonfiction, pop science/pop culture, cultural criticism).

REPRESENTS Nonfiction, fiction, novels, short story collections. **Considers these fiction areas:** fantasy, historical, literary, mainstream, middle grade, mystery, paranormal, romance, science fiction, suspense, thriller, urban fantasy, women's, young adult.

HOW TO CONTACT To submit a project, please send a query letter only via e-mail to one of the addresses included on the website. Do not send attachments, though for fiction you may include 10 pages of your manuscript in the body of your e-mail. "Due to the high volume of submissions, agents will reach out to you directly if interested. The typical time range for consideration is 6-8 weeks. Please do not query more than 1 agent at our agency simultaneously." (To see the types of projects each agent is looking for, refer to the Agent Biographies page on website.) Accepts simultaneous submissions.

TERMS Agent receives 15% commission on domestic sales; 10% commission on foreign sales. Offers written contract; 2-month notice must be given to terminate contract.

⊘ CHERRY WEINER LITERARY AGENCY

925 Oak Bluff Ct., Dacula GA 30019-6660. (732)446-2096. **Fax:** (732)792-0506. **E-mail:** cherry8486@aol.com. **Contact:** Cherry Weiner. Estab. 1977. Represents 40 clients.

REPRESENTS Fiction, novels. **Considers these fiction areas:** action, adventure, commercial, contemporary issues, crime, detective, family saga, fantasy, frontier, gay, glitz, historical, horror, literary, mainstream, military, mystery, paranormal, police, psychic, romance, science fiction, supernatural, suspense, thriller, urban fantasy, westerns, women's.

☞ *This agency is currently not accepting new clients except by referral or by personal contact at writers' conferences.* Specializes in fantasy, science fiction, westerns, mysteries (both contemporary and historical), historical novels, Native American works, mainstream, and all genre romances.

HOW TO CONTACT Only wishes to receive submissions from referrals and from writers she has met at conferences/events. Responds in 1 week to queries; 2 months to requested mss.

TERMS Agent receives 15% commission on domestic sales; 15% commission on foreign sales. Offers written contract. Charges clients for extra copies of mss, first-class postage for author's copies Mailing of books first class, express mail for important documents/mss.

RECENT SALES This agency prefers not to share information on specific sales.

WRITERS CONFERENCES Western Writers of America; BoucherCon; World Science Fiction Writers Conference; World Fantasy Conference; and many writer group workshops.

TIPS "Meet agents and publishers at conferences. Establish a relationship, then get in touch with them and remind them of the meeting and conference."

THE WEINGEL-FIDEL AGENCY

310 E. 46th St., 21E, New York NY 10017. (212)599-2959. **Contact:** Loretta Weingel-Fidel.

○ Prior to opening her agency, Ms. Weingel-Fidel was a psychoeducational diagnostician.

REPRESENTS Nonfiction, fiction, novels. **Considers these fiction areas:** literary, mainstream.

☞ This agency specializes in commercial and literary fiction and nonfiction. Does not want to receive childrens books, self-help, science fiction, or fantasy.

HOW TO CONTACT Accepts writers by referral only. *No unsolicited mss.* Accepts simultaneous submissions.

TERMS Agent receives 15% commission on domestic sales; 20% commission on foreign sales. Offers written contract, binding for 1 year with automatic renewal.

TIPS "A very small, selective list enables me to work very closely with my clients to develop and nurture talent. I only take on projects and writers about which I am extremely enthusiastic."

WELLS ARMS LITERARY

In association with HSG Agency, New York NY **Website:** www.wellsarms.com. Estab. 2013. Member of AAR. SCBWI, Society of Illustrators. Represents 25 clients.

○ Victoria's career began as an editor at Dial Books for Young Readers, then G. P. Putnam's Sons and then as the founding editorial director and Associate Publisher of Bloomsbury USA's Children's Division. She opened the agency in 2013.

REPRESENTS Nonfiction, fiction, novels, juvenile books. , children's book illustrators. **Considers these fiction areas:** juvenile, middle grade, new adult, picture books, young adult.

☞ "We focus on books for young readers of all ages: board books, picture books, readers, chapter books, middle grade, and young adult fiction." Actively seeking middle grade, young adult, magical realism, contemporary, romance, fantasy. "We do not represent to the textbook, magazine, adult romance or fine art markets."

HOW TO CONTACT Wells Arms Literary is currently closed to queries or submissions "unless you've met me at a conference." Accepts simultaneous submissions. "We try to respond in a month's time." If no response, assume it's a no.

♻ WESTWOOD CREATIVE ARTISTS, LTD.

386 Huron St., Toronto ON M5S 2G6 Canada. (416)964-3302. **E-mail:** wca_office@wcaltd.com. **Website:** www.wcaltd.com. Represents 350+ clients.

MEMBER AGENTS Carolyn Ford (literary fiction, commercial, women's/literary crossover, thrillers, serious narrative nonfiction, pop culture); Jackie Kaiser (President and COO); Michael A. Levine (Chairman); Hilary McMahon (Executive Vice President, fiction, nonfiction, children's); John Pearce (fiction and nonfiction); Bruce Westwood (Founder, Managing Director and CEO).

REPRESENTS Nonfiction, fiction, novels. **Considers these fiction areas:** commercial, juvenile, literary, thriller, women's, young adult.

☞ "We take on children's and young adult writers very selectively. The agents bring their diverse interests to their client lists, but are generally looking for authors with a mastery of language, a passionate, expert or original perspective on their subject, and a gift for storytelling." "Please note that WCA does not represent screenwriters, and our agents are not currently seeking poetry or children's picture book submissions."

HOW TO CONTACT E-query only. Include credentials, synopsis, and no more than 10 pages. No attachments. Accepts simultaneous submissions.

TIPS "We will reject outright complete, unsolicited manuscripts, or projects that are presented poorly in the query letter. We prefer to receive exclusive submissions and request that you do not query more than one agent at the agency simultaneously. It's often best if you approach WCA after you have accumulated some publishing credits."

WHIMSY LITERARY AGENCY, LLC

49 N. 8th St., 6G, Brooklyn NY 11249. (212)674-7162. **E-mail:** whimsynyc@aol.com. **Contact:** Jackie Meyer. Represents 35 clients.

Prior to becoming an agent, Ms. Meyer was a VP at Warner Books (now Grand Central/Hachette) for 20 years.

MEMBER AGENTS Jackie Meyer.

REPRESENTS Nonfiction.

"Whimsy looks for nonfiction projects that are concept- and platform-driven. We seek books that educate, inspire, and entertain." Actively seeking experts in their field with integrated and established platforms.

HOW TO CONTACT Send your proposal via e-mail to whimsynyc@aol.com (include your media platform, table of contents with full description of each chapter). First-time authors: "We appreciate proposals that are professional and complete. Please consult the many fine books available on writing book proposals. We are not considering poetry, or screenplays. Please Note: Due to the volume of queries and submissions, we are unable to respond unless they are of interest to us." Accepts simultaneous submissions. Responds "quickly, but only if interested" to queries. *Does not accept unsolicited mss.* Obtains most new clients through recommendations from others, solicitations.

TERMS Agent receives 15% commission on domestic sales; 20% commission on foreign sales. Offers written contract.

MACKENZIE WOLF

E-mail: queries@mwlit.com. **Website:** mwlit.com. Estab. 2008. Member of AAR. Signatory of WGA.

MEMBER AGENTS Gillian MacKenzie (not accepting new queries); Kirsten Wolf (not accepting queries); Kate Johnson (literary and upmarket fiction, memoir, cultural history, pop science, narrative nonfiction); Allison Devereux (literary and upmarket fiction, narrative nonfiction, cultural history and criticism, memoir, and biography); Rachel Crawford (literary fiction; high concept YA; and narrative nonfiction, particularly environmental and science journalism, and queer and feminist pop culture); Leigh Eisenman (literary and upmarket fiction, prescriptive non-fiction, cooking, lifestyle, illustrated); Elizabeth Rudnick (middle grade fiction focused on the real and relatable; middle grade nonfiction particularly about quirky or less known history; dark, edgy YA fiction; light romantic YA; illustrated picture books).

REPRESENTS Nonfiction, fiction, novels. **Considers these fiction areas:** commercial, contemporary issues, family saga, fantasy, feminist, gay, historical, horror, lesbian, literary, science fiction, suspense, thriller, women's, young adult, LGBTI+.

HOW TO CONTACT To submit a project, please send a query letter along with a 50-page writing sample (for fiction) or a detailed proposal (for nonfiction) to queries@mwlit.com. Samples may be submitted as an attachment or embedded in the body of the e-mail. Accepts simultaneous submissions.

RECENT SALES Dapper Dan of Harlem memoir (Random House); *Hardly Children*, by Laura Adamczyk (Farrar, Straus); *Bloodworth*, by Helen Klein Ross (Little, Brown); *The Only Fact We Have*, by Eric Dean Wilson (Simon & Schuster); *Husbands That Cook*, by Ryan Alvarez and Adam Merrin (St. Martin's Press).

WOLFSON LITERARY AGENCY

P.O. Box 266, New York NY 10276. **E-mail:** query@wolfsonliterary.com. **Website:** www.wolfsonliterary.com. **Contact:** Michelle Wolfson. Estab. 2007. Adheres to AAR canon of ethics.

Prior to forming her own agency in December 2007, Ms. Wolfson spent 2 years with Artists & Artisans, Inc. and 2 years with Ralph Vicinanza, Ltd.

REPRESENTS Nonfiction, fiction. **Considers these fiction areas:** commercial, mainstream, new adult, romance, thriller, women's, young adult.

Actively seeking commercial fiction: young adult, mainstream, women's fiction, romance.

"I am not taking on new nonfiction clients at this time."

HOW TO CONTACT E-queries only. Accepts simultaneous submissions. Responds only if interested. Positive response is generally given within 2-4 weeks. Responds in 3 months to mss. Obtains most new clients through queries or recommendations from others.

TERMS Agent receives 15% commission on domestic sales; 25% commission on foreign sales. Offers written contract; 30-day notice must be given to terminate contract.

TIPS "Be persistent."

WORDSERVE LITERARY GROUP

7500 E. Arapahoe Rd., Suite 285, Centennial CO 80112. **E-mail:** admin@wordserveliterary.com. **Website:** www.wordserveliterary.com. **Contact:** Greg Johnson. Estab. 2003. Represents 180 clients.

⬤ Prior to becoming an agent in 1994, Mr. Johnson was a magazine editor and freelance writer of more than 20 books and 200 articles.

MEMBER AGENTS Greg Johnson, Nick Harrison, Sarah Freese, and Keely Boeving.

REPRESENTS Nonfiction, fiction, novels. **Considers these fiction areas:** historical, inspirational, juvenile, literary, mainstream, military, religious, spiritual, suspense, thriller, war, women's, young adult.

⬤➤ Materials with a faith-based angle, as well as the general market categories of business, health, history, military. No gift books, poetry, short stories, screenplays, graphic novels, children's picture books, science fiction or fantasy. Please do not send mss that are more than 120,000 words.

HOW TO CONTACT E-query admin@wordserveliterary.com. In the subject line, include the word "query." All queries should include the following three elements: a pitch for the book, information about you and your platform (for nonfiction) or writing background (for fiction), and the first 5 (or so) pages of the manuscript pasted into the e-mail. Please view our website for full guidelines: http://www.wordserveliterary.com/submission-guidlines/. Accepts simultaneous submissions. Response within 60 days. Obtains most new clients through recommendations from others.

TERMS Agent receives 15% commission on domestic sales; 10-15% commission on foreign sales. Offers written contract; up to 60-day notice must be given to terminate contract.

TIPS "We are looking for good proposals, great writing and authors willing to market their books. We specialize in projects with a faith element bent. See the website before submitting. Though we are not a member of AAR, we abide by all of the rules for agents."

WRITERS HOUSE

21 W. 26th St., New York NY 10010. (212)685-2400. **Fax:** (212)685-1781. **Website:** www.writershouse.com. Estab. 1973. Member of AAR.

MEMBER AGENTS Amy Berkower; Stephen Barr; Susan Cohen; Dan Conaway; Lisa DiMona; Susan Ginsburg; Susan Golomb; Merrilee Heifetz; Brianne Johnson; Daniel Lazar; Simon Lipskar; Steven Malk; Jodi Reamer, Esq.; Robin Rue; Rebecca Sherman; Geri Thoma; Albert Zuckerman; Alec Shane; Stacy Testa; Victoria Doherty-Munro; Beth Miller; Andrea Morrison; Soumeya Roberts.

REPRESENTS Nonfiction, novels. **Considers these fiction areas:** commercial, fantasy, juvenile, literary, mainstream, middle grade, picture books, science fiction, women's, young adult.

⬤➤ This agency specializes in all types of popular fiction and nonfiction, for both adult and juvenile books as well as illustrators. Does not want to receive scholarly, professional, poetry, plays, or screenplays.

HOW TO CONTACT Individual agent email addresses are available on the website. "Please e-mail us a query letter, which includes your credentials, an explanation of what makes your book unique and special, and a synopsis. Some agents within our agency have different requirements. Please consult their individual Publisher's Marketplace (PM) profile for details. We respond to all queries, generally within six to eight weeks." If you prefer to submit my mail, address it to an individual agent, and please include SASE for our reply. (If submitting to Steven Malk: Writers House, 7660 Fay Ave., #338H, La Jolla, CA 92037.) Accepts simultaneous submissions. "We respond to all queries, generally within 6-8 weeks." Obtains most new clients through recommendations from authors and editors.

TERMS Agent receives 15% commission on domestic sales. Agent receives 20% commission on foreign sales. Offers written contract, binding for 1 year. Agency charges fees for copying mss/proposals and overseas airmail of books.

TIPS "Do not send mss. Write a compelling letter. If you do, we'll ask to see your work. Follow submission guidelines and please do not simultaneously submit your work to more than one Writers House agent."

JASON YARN LITERARY AGENCY

3544 Broadway, No. 68, New York NY 10031. **E-mail:** jason@jasonyarnliteraryagency.com. **Website:** www.jasonyarnliteraryagency.com. Member of AAR. Signatory of WGA.

REPRESENTS Nonfiction, fiction. **Considers these fiction areas:** commercial, fantasy, literary, middle grade, science fiction, suspense, thriller, young adult, graphic novels, comics.

HOW TO CONTACT Please e-mail your query to jason@jasonyarnliteraryagency.com with the word "Query" in the subject line, and please paste the first 10 pages of your manuscript or proposal into the text of your e-mail. Do not send any attachments. "Visit the About page for information on what we are interested in, and please note that JYLA does not accept queries for film, TV, or stage scripts." Accepts simultaneous submissions.

HELEN ZIMMERMANN LITERARY AGENCY

E-mail: submit@zimmagency.com. **Website:** www.zimmermannliterary.com. **Contact:** Helen Zimmermann. Estab. 2003.

○ Prior to opening her agency, Ms. Zimmermann was the director of advertising and promotion at Random House and the events coordinator at an independent bookstore.

REPRESENTS Nonfiction, fiction. **Considers these fiction areas:** family saga, literary, mainstream.

☛ "I am currently concentrating my nonfiction efforts in health and wellness, relationships, popular culture, women's issues, lifestyle, sports, and music. I am also drawn to memoirs that speak to a larger social or historical circumstance, or introduce me to a new phenomenon. And I am always looking for a work of fiction that will keep me up at night!"

HOW TO CONTACT Accepts e-mail queries only. "For nonfiction queries, initial contact should just be a pitch letter. For fiction queries, I prefer a summary, your bio, and the first chapter as text in the email (not as an attachment). If I express interest I will need to see a full proposal for nonfiction and the remainder of the manuscript for fiction." Accepts simultaneous submissions. Responds in 2 weeks to queries, only if interested. Obtains most new clients through recommendations from others, solicitations.

TERMS Agent receives 15% commission on domestic sales. Offers written contract; 30-day notice must be given to terminate contract.

WRITERS CONFERENCES Washington Independent Review of Books Writers Conference; Yale Writers' Conference; American Society of Journalists and Authors Conference; Writer's Digest Conference; LaJolla Writer's Conference; Gulf Coast Writers Conference; Kansas Writers Association Conference; New York Writers Workshop; Self Publishing Book Expo; Burlington Writers' Conference; Southern Expressions Writers' Conference; Literary Writers' Conference, NYC.

MAGAZINES

<hr>

This section contains magazine listings that fall into one of several categories: literary, consumer, small circulation, and online. Our decision to combine magazines under one section was twofold: All of these magazines represent markets specifically for short fiction, and many magazines now publish both print and online versions, making them more difficult to subcategorize.

Selecting the Right Magazine

Once you have browsed through this section and have a list of journals you might like to submit to, read those listings again carefully. Remember, this is information editors provide to help you submit work that fits their needs. Note that you will find some magazines that do not read submissions all year long. Whether limited reading periods are tied to a university schedule or meant to accommodate the capabilities of a very small staff, those periods are noted within listings (when the editors notify us). The staffs of university journals are usually made up of student editors and a managing editor who is also a faculty member. These staffs often change every year. Whenever possible, we indicate this in listings and give the name of the current editor and the length of that editor's term. Also be aware that the schedule of a university journal usually coincides with that university's academic year, meaning that the editors of most university publications are difficult or impossible to reach during the summer.

FURTHERING YOUR SEARCH

Most of the magazines listed here are published in the U.S. You will also find some English-speaking markets from around the world. These foreign publications are denoted with a ◖ symbol at the beginning of listings. To make it easier to find Canadian markets, we include a ◒ symbol at the start of those listings.

30 N

North Central College, Naperville IL 60540. **E-mail:** 30north@noctrl.edu. **Website:** 30northblog.word-press.com. **Contact:** Katie Draves, Crystal Ice. *30 N*, published semiannually, considers work in all literary genres, including occasional interviews, from undergraduate writers globally. The journal's goal is for college-level, emerging creative writers to share their work publicly and create a conversation with each other.

○ Contributors must be currently enrolled as undergraduates at a two- or four-year institution at the time of submission. Reads submissions September-March, with deadlines in February and October.

NEEDS Length: up to 5,000 words.

HOW TO CONTACT Submit complete ms via online submissions manager. "You must be a currently enrolled undergraduate at a two- or four-year institution at the time of submission. Please submit using your .edu e-mail address, your institution, and your year." Include brief bio written in third person.

PAYMENT/TERMS Pays 2 contributor's copies.

TIPS "Don't send anything you just finished moments ago—rethink, revise, and polish. Avoid sentimentality and abstraction. That said, *30 N* publishes beginners, so don't hesitate to submit and, if rejected, submit again."

● 34THPARALLEL MAGAZINE

Indie LitMag Digital & Print, Paris , France. **E-mail:** 34thparallel@gmail.com. **Website:** www.34thparallel. net. **Contact:** Martin Chipperfield. Estab. 2007. *34th-Parallel Magazine*, monthly in digital and print editions, publishes new and emerging writers.

NEEDS Submit via online submissions manager (Submittable).

TIPS "It's all about getting your story out there looking good: your reality (creative nonfiction), fiction, journalism, essays, screenplays, poetry (writing that isn't prose), hip-hop, art, photography, photo stories or essays, graphic stories, comics, or cartoons."

A&U

America's AIDS Magazine, Art & Understanding, Inc., 25 Monroe St., Suite 205, Albany NY 12210-2729. (518)426-9010. **Fax:** (518)436-5354. **E-mail:** chaelneedle@mac.com. **Website:** www.aumag.org. **Contact:** Chael Needle, managing editor. Estab. 1991. Each summer, *A&U* publishes a summer reading issue. Writers are encouraged to submit work to the Chris-topher Hewitt Literary Award contest, held annually. Submissions for the contest open in the spring.

NEEDS Literary electronic submissions, as Word attachments, may be mailed to Brent Calderwood, literary editor, at aumaglit@gmail.com. Pay rate schedule available upon request. Length: up to 1,500 words.

HOW TO CONTACT Send complete ms.

PAYMENT/TERMS Pays $50.

TIPS "We're looking for more articles on youth and HIV/AIDS; more international coverage; celebrity interviews; more coverage of how the pandemic is affecting historically underrepresented communities. We are also looking for literary submissions that address the past and present AIDS epidemic in fresh ways. Each year, we sponsor the Christopher Hewitt Award, given to the best poem, short story, creative nonfiction piece, and drama submitted."

ABLE MUSE

Able Muse Press, 467 Saratoga Ave., #602, San Jose CA 95129-1326. **E-mail:** submission@ablemuse.com. **Website:** www.ablemuse.com. **Contact:** Alex Pepple, editor. Estab. 1999. *Able Muse: A Review of Poetry, Prose & Art*, published twice/year, predominantly publishes metrical poetry complemented by art and photography, fiction, and nonfiction, including essays, book reviews, and interviews with a focus on metrical and formal poetry.

○ Sponsors 2 annual contests: The Able Muse Write Prize for Poetry & Fiction and The Able Muse Book Award for Poetry (in collaboration with Able Muse Press at www.ablemusepress. com). See website for details.

NEEDS "Our emphasis is on literary fiction; *Able Muse* is not a venue for fantasy, romance, horror, action-adventure, gratuitous violence, or inspirational/sentimental genres." Length: up to 4,000 words/ms.

HOW TO CONTACT Send up to 2 ms via online submission form or e-mail. "We will consider longer pieces of exceptional merit."

THE ADIRONDACK REVIEW

Stanhope St., Brooklyn NY 11237. **E-mail:** editors@ theadirondackreview.com. **Website:** www.theadiron-dackreview.com; www.theadirondackreview.submit-table.com. **Contact:** Angela Leroux-Lindsey, editor in chief; Nicholas Samaras, senior poetry editor; Terez Peipins, fiction editor; Sarah Escue, poetry editor; Charles Rammelkamp, reviews editor; Ann Malaspina, copy chief. Estab. 2000. *The Adirondack Review* is an online quarterly literary magazine featuring contemporary art and photography paired with perspective-shifting poetry, fiction, translations, and essays.

NEEDS Length: up to 6,000 words.

HOW TO CONTACT Submit via online submissions manager, include brief bio.

TIPS "See more details about our submission cycle and contests online."

AFRICAN VOICES

African Voices Communications, Inc., 270 W. 96th St., New York NY 10025. (212)865-2982. **E-mail:** africanvoicesart@gmail.com. **Website:** www.africanvoices.com. **Contact:** Angela Kinemore, poetry editor. Estab. 1992. *African Voices*, published quarterly, is an "art and literary magazine that highlights the work of people of color. We publish literature and poetry on any subject. We also consider all themes and styles: avant-garde, free verse, haiku, light verse, and traditional. We do not wish to limit the reader or author." *African Voices* is about 48 pages, magazine-sized, professionally printed, saddle-stapled, with paper cover. Receives about 150 submissions/year, accepts about 30%.

NEEDS Length: 500-2,500 words.

HOW TO CONTACT Send complete ms. Include short bio. Accepts submissions by postal mail. Send SASE for return of ms.

PAYMENT/TERMS Pays contributor's copies.

TIPS "A manuscript stands out if it is neatly typed with a well-written and interesting storyline or plot. Originality is encouraged. We are interested in more horror, erotic, and drama pieces. *AV* wants to highlight the diversity in our culture. Stories must touch the humanity in us all. We strongly encourage new writers/poets to send in their work. Accepted contributors are encouraged to subscribe."

AFTER HAPPY HOUR REVIEW

136 Conneaut Dr., Pittsburgh PA 15239. **E-mail:** hourafterhappyhour@gmail.com. **Website:** afterhappyhourreview.com. **Contact:** Mike Good. Estab. 2014. The *After Happy Hour Review* is an independent, online literary journal that publishes poetry, fiction, creative nonfiction, and visual art. Our headquarters are based in Pittsburgh, and we have published writers from around the United States alongside international writers. Curated by the Hour After Happy Hour Writing Workshop, our editors come from varying backgrounds with their own inclinations, tastes, and preferences. Take your time, read an issue, and send us your best work. We aim to respond as quickly as possible to all submissions and nominate work for all major awards, including the Pushcart Prize and Best of Net."

NEEDS "*AHHR* sets the limit at 6,000, but excessive length is the top reason why we tend to reject short fiction pieces. Oftentimes we run into stories that start strong, but simply go on for too many pages to maintain their effectiveness. Make sure your piece has no fat to cut and send it in. Give us original ideas and uncompromising language. Make an impact and make it early." Length: 6,000 words max.

PAYMENT/TERMS No payment.

$ AGNI

Boston University, 236 Bay State Rd., Boston MA 02215. **E-mail:** agni@bu.edu. **Website:** www.agnimagazine.org. **Contact:** Sven Birkerts, editor. Estab. 1972. Eclectic literary magazine publishing first-rate poems, essays, translations, and stories.

Reading period is September 1-May 31 only. Online magazine carries original content not found in print edition. All submissions are considered for both. Founding editor Askold Melnyczuk won the PEN/Nora Magid Lifetime Achievement Award for Magazine Editing. Work from *AGNI* has been included and cited regularly in the *Pushcart Prize*, *O. Henry*, and *Best American* anthologies.

NEEDS No genre scifi, horror, mystery, or romance.

HOW TO CONTACT Submit online or by regular mail, no more than 1 story at a time. E-mailed submissions will not be considered. Include a SASE or your e-mail address if sending by mail.

PAYMENT/TERMS Pays $20/page up to $300, plus a one-year subscription, and, for print publication, 2 contributor's copies and 4 gift copies.

TIPS "We're also looking for extraordinary translations from little-translated languages. It is important to read work published in *AGNI* before submitting, to see if your own might be compatible."

$ ALASKA QUARTERLY REVIEW

University of Alaska Anchorage, 3211 Providence Dr., Anchorage AK 99508. **E-mail:** uaa_aqr@uaa.alaska.edu. **Website:** www.uaa.alaska.edu/aqr. **Contact:** Ronald Spatz, editor in chief. Estab. 1982. "*Alaska Quarterly Review* is a literary journal devoted to contemporary literary art, publishing fiction, short plays, poetry, photo essays, and literary nonfiction in traditional and experimental styles. The editors encourage new and emerging writers, while continuing to publish award-winning and established writers."

○ Magazine: 6x9; 232-300 pages; 60 lb. Glatfelter paper; 12 pt. C15 black ink or 4-color; varnish cover stock; photos on cover and photo essays. Reads mss August 15-May 15.

NEEDS "Works in *AQR* have certain characteristics: freshness, honesty, and a compelling subject. The voice of the piece must be strong—idiosyncratic enough to create a unique persona. We look for craft, putting it in a form where it becomes emotionally and intellectually complex. Many pieces in *AQR* concern everyday life. We're not asking our writers to go outside themselves and their experiences to the absolute exotic to catch our interest. We look for the experiential and revelatory qualities of the work. We will champion a piece that may be less polished or stylistically sophisticated if it engages me, surprises me, and resonates for me. The joy in reading such a work is in discovering something true. Moreover, in keeping with our mission to publish new writers, we are looking for voices our readers do not know, voices that may not always be reflected in the dominant culture and that, in all instances, have something important to convey." No romance, children's, or inspirational/religious. Length: up to 50 pages.

HOW TO CONTACT Submit complete ms by mail. Include cover letter with contact information and SASE for return of ms.

PAYMENT/TERMS Pays contributor's copies and honoraria when funding is available.

TIPS "Although we respond to e-mail queries, we cannot review electronic submissions."

●⑤ ALBEDO ONE

8 Bachelor's Walk, Dublin 1 , Ireland. **E-mail:** bobn@yellowbrickroad.ie. **Website:** www.albedo1.com. **Contact:** Bob Nielson. Estab. 1993. "We are always looking for thoughtful, well-written fiction. Our definition of what constitutes science fiction, horror, and fantasy is extremely broad, and we love to see material which pushes at the boundaries or crosses between genres."

NEEDS Length: 2,000-8,000 words.

HOW TO CONTACT Submit complete ms by mail or e-mail.

PAYMENT/TERMS Pays €6/1,000 words, to a maximum of 8,000 words, and 1 contributor's copy.

TIPS "We look for good writing, good plot, good characters. Read the magazine, and don't give up."

○ ALBERTA VIEWS

Alberta Views, Ltd., Suite 208, 320 23rd Ave. SW, Calgary AB T2S 0J2, Canada. (403)243-5334; (877)212-5334. **Fax:** (403)243-8599. **E-mail:** queries@albertaviews.ab.ca. **Website:** www.albertaviews.ab.ca. **Contact:** Evan Osenton, editor. Estab. 1997. "We are a regional magazine providing thoughtful commentary and background information on issues of concern to Albertans. Most of our writers are Albertans."

○ No phone queries.

NEEDS Only fiction by Alberta writers via the annual *Alberta Views* fiction contest. Length: 2,500-4,000 words.

HOW TO CONTACT Send complete ms.

PAYMENT/TERMS Pays up to $1,000.

THE ALEMBIC

Providence College, English Department, ATTN: The Alembic Editors, 1 Cunningham Square, Providence RI 02918-0001. **Website:** www.providence.edu/english/pages/alembic.aspx. **Contact:** Magazine has revolving editor. Editorial term: 1 year. Estab. 1940. "*The Alembic* is an international literary journal featuring the work of both established and student writers and photographers. It is published each April by Providence College in Providence, Rhode Island."

○ Magazine: 6x9, 80 pages. Contains illustrations, photographs.

NEEDS "We are open to all styles of fiction." Does not read December 1-July 31. Published Bruce Smith, Robin Behn, Rane Arroyo, Sharon Dolin, Jeff Friedman, and Khalid Mattawa. Length: up to 6,000 words.

HOW TO CONTACT Send complete ms with cover letter. Include brief bio. Send SASE (or IRC) for return of ms. Does not accept online submissions.

PAYMENT/TERMS Pays 2 contributor's copies.

TIPS "We're looking for stories that are wise, memorable, grammatical, economical, poetic in the right places, and end strongly. Take Heraclitus' claim that 'character is fate' to heart and study the strategies, styles, and craft of such masters as Anton Chekov, J. Cheever, Flannery O'Connor, John Updike, Rick Bass, Phillip Roth, Joyce Carol Oates, William Treavor, Lorrie Moore, and Ethan Canin."

ALIMENTUM

The Literature of Food, P.O. Box 210028, Nashville TN 37221. **E-mail:** editor@alimentumjournal.com. **Website:** www.alimentumjournal.com. **Contact:** Peter Selgin, fiction and nonfiction editor; Esther Cohen, poetry editor. Estab. 2005. "*Alimentum* celebrates the literature and art of food. We welcome work from like-minded writers, musicians, and artists."

Ⓞ Essays appearing in *Alimentum* have appeared in *Best American Essays* and *Best Food Writing*.

NEEDS Has published Mark Kurlansky, Oliver Sacks, Dick Allen, Ann Hood, and Carly Sachs. Publishes short shorts. Also publishes literary essays, poetry, spot illustrations. Rarely comments on/critiques rejected mss. Length: up to 2,000 words.

HOW TO CONTACT Send complete ms by mail. Please include SASE.

PAYMENT/TERMS Pays 1 contributor's copy.

TIPS "No e-mail submissions, only snail mail. Mark outside envelope to the attention of Poetry, Fiction, or Nonfiction Editor."

Ⓢ ALIVE NOW

1908 Grand Ave., P.O. Box 340004, Nashville TN 37203. (615)340-7254. **E-mail:** alivenow@upperroom. org. **Website:** www.alivenow.org; alivenow.upperroom.org. **Contact:** Beth A. Richardson, editor. Estab. 1971. *Alive Now*, published bimonthly, is a devotional magazine that invites readers to enter an ever-deepening relationship with God. "*Alive Now* seeks to nourish people who are hungry for a sacred way of living. Submissions should invite readers to see God in the midst of daily life by exploring how contemporary issues impact their faith lives. Each word must be vivid and dynamic and contribute to the whole. We make selections based on a list of upcoming themes. Mss which do not fit a theme will be returned."

NEEDS Length: 400-500 words.

HOW TO CONTACT Prefers electronic submissions attached as Word document. Postal submissions should include SASE. Include name, address, theme on each sheet.

PAYMENT/TERMS Pays $35 minimum.

THE ALLEGHENY REVIEW

Allegheny College Box 32, 520 N. Main St., Meadville PA 16335. **E-mail:** review@allegheny.edu. **Website:** alleghenyreview.wordpress.com. **Contact:** Senior editor. Estab. 1983. "*The Allegheny Review* is one of America's only nationwide literary magazines exclusively for undergraduate works of poetry, fiction, and nonfiction. Our intended audience is persons interested in quality literature."

Ⓞ Annual. Magazine: 6x9; 100 pages; illustrations; photos. Has published work by Dianne Page, Monica Stahl, and DJ Kinney.

NEEDS Receives 50 unsolicited mss/month. Accepts 3 mss/issue. Publishes ms 2 months after deadline. Publishes roughly 90% new writers/year. Also publishes short shorts (up to 20 pages), nonfiction, and poetry. Does not want "fiction not written by undergraduates—we accept nothing but fiction by currently enrolled undergraduate students. We consider anything catering to an intellectual audience." Length: up to 20 pages, double-spaced.

HOW TO CONTACT Submit complete ms via online submissions manager.

PAYMENT/TERMS Pays 1 contributor's copy; additional copies $3. Sponsors awards/contests; reading fee $5.

TIPS "We look for quality work that has been thoroughly revised. Unique voice, interesting topic, and playfulness with the English language. Revise, revise, revise! And be careful how you send it—the cover letter says a lot. We definitely look for diversity in the pieces we publish."

Ⓢ ALLEGORY

P.O. Box 2714, Cherry Hill NJ 08034. **E-mail:** submissions@allegoryezine.com. **Website:** www.allegoryezine.com. **Contact:** Ty Drago, publisher and managing editor. Estab. 1998. "We are an e-zine by writers for writers. Our articles focus on the art, craft, and business of writing. Our links and editorial policy all focus on the needs of fiction authors." *Allegory* (as Peridot Books) won the Page One Award for Literary Contribution.

NEEDS Receives 150 unsolicited mss/month. Accepts 12 mss/issue; 24 mss/year. Agented fiction 5%. Publishes 10 new writers/year. Also publishes literary essays, literary criticism. Often comments on rejected mss. "No media tie-ins (*Star Trek*, *Star Wars*, etc., or space opera, vampires)." Length: 1,500-7,500 words; average length: 2,500 words.

HOW TO CONTACT "All submissions should be sent by e-mail (no letters or telephone calls) in either text or RTF format. Please place 'Submission [Title]-[first and last name]' in the subject line. Include the following in both the body of the e-mail and the attachment: your name, name to use on the story (byline) if different, your preferred e-mail address, your mailing address, the story's title, and the story's word count."

PAYMENT/TERMS Pays $15/story.

TIPS "Give us something original, preferably with a twist. Avoid gratuitous sex or violence. Funny always scores points. Be clever and imaginative, but be able to tell a story with proper mood and characterization. Put your name and e-mail address in the body of the story. Read the site and get a feel for it before submitting."

ALLIGATOR JUNIPER

Prescott College, 220 Grove Ave., Prescott AZ 86301. (928)350-2012. **Website:** alligatorjuniper.org. "*Alligator Juniper* features contemporary poetry, fiction, creative nonfiction, and b&w photography. We encourage submissions from writers and photographers at all levels: emerging, early career, and established." Annual magazine comprised of the winners and finalists of national contests. "All entrants pay an $18 submission fee and receive a complementary copy of that year's issue in the spring. First-place winning writers in each genre receive a $1,000 prize. The first-place winner in photography receives a $500 award. Finalists in writing and images are published and paid in contributor copies. There is currently no avenue for submissions other than the annual contest."

NEEDS "No children's literature or genre work." Length: up to 30 pages, double-spaced.

HOW TO CONTACT Accepts submissions only through annual contest. Submit via online submission form or regular mail. If submitting by regular mail, include $18 entry fee payable to *Alligator Juniper* for each story. Include cover letter with name, address, phone number, and e-mail. Mss should be typed with numbered pages, double-spaced, 12-point font, and 1" margins. Include author's name on first page. "Double-sided submissions are encouraged." No e-mail submissions.

AMBIT MAGAZINE

Staithe House, Main Rd., Brancaster Staithe, Norfolk PE31 8PB, United Kingdom. **E-mail:** contact@ambitmagazine.co.uk. **Website:** www.ambitmagazine.co.uk. **Contact:** Briony Bax, editor; André Naffis-Sahely poetry editor; Kate Pemberton, fiction editor; Olivia Bax and Jean Philippe Dordolo, art editors. Estab. 1959. *Ambit Magazine* is a literary and artwork quarterly published in the UK and read internation-

ally. *Ambit* is put together entirely from previously unpublished poetry and short fiction submissions. "Please read the guidelines on our website carefully concerning submission windows and policies."

NEEDS Length: up to 5,000 words. "We're very enthusiastic about flash and very short fiction, which is under 1,000 words. Stories should not be published elsewhere, including blogs and online."

HOW TO CONTACT Submit complete ms via Submittable. No e-mail submissions.

PAYMENT/TERMS Payment details on website.

TIPS "Read a copy of the magazine before submitting!"

AMERICAN LITERARY REVIEW

University of North Texas, 1155 Union Circle #311307, Denton TX 76203. **E-mail:** americanliteraryreview@gmail.com. **Website:** www.americanliteraryreview.com. **Contact:** Bonnie Friedman, editor in chief. Estab. 1990. "*The American Literary Review* publishes "excellent poetry, fiction, and nonfiction by writers at all stages of their careers." Beginning in fall 2013, *ALR* became an online publication."

○ Reading period is from October 1-May 1.

NEEDS "We would like to see more short shorts and stylistically innovative and risk-taking fiction. We like to see stories that illuminate the various layers of characters and their situations with great artistry. Give us distinctive character-driven stories that explore the complexities of human existence." Looks for "the small moments that contain more than at first possible, that surprise us with more truth than we thought we had a right to expect." Has published work by Marylee MacDonald, Michael Isaac Shokrian, Arthur Brown, Roy Bentley, Julie Marie Wade, and Karin Forfota Poklen. No genre works. Length: up to 8,000 words.

HOW TO CONTACT Submit 1 complete ms through online submissions manager for a fee of $3. Does not accept submissions via e-mail or mail.

TIPS "We encourage writers and artists to examine our journal."

THE AMERICAN READER

E-mail: fiction@theamericanreader.com; poetry@theamericanreader.com; criticism@theamericanreader.com. **Website:** theamericanreader.com. **Contact:** Uzoamaka Maduka, editor in chief. *The American Reader* is a bimonthly print literary journal. The magazine is committed to inspiring literary and critical conversation among a new generation of readers, and restoring literature to its proper place in American cultural discourse.

NEEDS Does not accept unsolicited novel excerpts.

HOW TO CONTACT Submit by e-mail: fiction@ theamericanreader.com.

🟢 AMERICAN SHORT FICTION

Badgerdog Literary Publishing, P.O. Box 301209, Austin TX 78703. **E-mail:** editors@americanshortfiction. org. **Website:** www.americanshortfiction.org. **Contact:** Rebecca Markovits and Adeena Reitberger, editors. Estab. 1991. "Issued triannually, *American Short Fiction* publishes work by emerging and established voices: stories that dive into the wreck, that stretch the reader between recognition and surprise, that conjure a particular world with delicate expertise—stories that take a different way home."

○ Stories published by *American Short Fiction* are anthologized in *Best American Short Stories*, *Best American Non-Required Reading*, *The O. Henry Prize Stories*, *The Pushcart Prize: Best of the Small Presses*, and elsewhere.

NEEDS "Open to publishing mystery or speculative fiction if we feel it has literary value." Does not want young adult or genre fiction. Length: open.

HOW TO CONTACT *American Short Fiction* seeks "short fiction by some of the finest writers working in contemporary literature, whether they are established, new, or lesser-known authors." Also publishes stories under 2,000 words online. Submit 1 story at a time via online submissions manager ($3 fee). No paper submissions.

PAYMENT/TERMS Writers receive $250-500, 2 contributor's copies, free subscription to the magazine. Additional copies $5.

TIPS "We publish fiction that speaks to us emotionally, uses evocative and precise language, and takes risks in subject matter and/or form. Try to read a few issues of *American Short Fiction* to get a sense of what we like. Also, to be concise is a great virtue."

🎧🟢 ANALOG SCIENCE FICTION & FACT

Dell Magazines, 44 Wall St., Suite 904, New York NY 10005-2401. **E-mail:** analogsf@dellmagazines.com. **Website:** www.analogsf.com. **Contact:** Trevor Quachri, editor. Estab. 1930. *Analog* seeks "solidly entertaining stories exploring solidly thought-out speculative ideas. But the ideas, and consequently the stories, are always new. Real science and technology have always been important in *ASF,* not only as the foundation of its fiction but as the subject of articles about real research with big implications for the future."

○ Fiction published in *Analog* has won numerous Nebula and Hugo Awards.

NEEDS "Basically, we publish science fiction stories. That is, stories in which some aspect of future science or technology is so integral to the plot that, if that aspect were removed, the story would collapse. The science can be physical, sociological, psychological. The technology can be anything from electronic engineering to biogenetic engineering. But the stories must be strong and realistic, with believable people (who needn't be human) doing believable things—no matter how fantastic the background might be." No fantasy or stories in which the scientific background is implausible or plays no essential role. Length: 2,000-7,000 words for short stories, 10,000-20,000 words for novelettes and novellas, and 40,000-80,000 for serials.

HOW TO CONTACT Send complete ms via online submissions manager (preferred) or postal mail. Does not accept e-mail submissions.

PAYMENT/TERMS Analog pays 8-10¢/word for short stories up to 7,500 words, 8-8.5¢ for longer material, 6¢/word for serials.

TIPS "I'm looking for irresistibly entertaining stories that make me think about things in ways I've never done before. Read several issues to get a broad feel for our tastes, but don't try to imitate what you read."

🟢 ANCIENT PATHS

E-mail: skylarburris@yahoo.com. **Website:** www.editorskylar.com/magazine/table.html. **Contact:** Skylar H. Burris, editor. Estab. 1998. *Ancient Paths* provides "a forum for quality spiritual poetry and short fiction. We consider works from writers of all religions, but poets and authors should be comfortable appearing in a predominantly Christian publication. Works published in *Ancient Paths* explore themes such as redemption, sin, forgiveness, doubt, faith, gratitude for the ordinary blessings of life, spiritual struggle, and spiritual growth. Please, no overly didactic works. Subtlety is preferred." Please send seasonally themed works for Lent and Advent at least 1 month prior to the start of each season. Works on other themes may be sent at any time.

NEEDS E-mail submissions only. Paste short fiction directly in the e-mail message. Use the subject heading "AP Online Submission (title of your work)." Include name and e-mail address at top of e-mail. Previously published works accepted, provided they are not currently available online. Please indicate if your work has been published elsewhere. Length: under 800 words preferred; up to 2,000 words.

PAYMENT/TERMS Pays $1.25/work published. Published authors also receive discount code for $3 off 2 printed back issues.

TIPS "Read the great religious poets: John Donne, George Herbert, T.S. Eliot, Lord Tennyson. Remember not to preach. This is a literary magazine, not a pulpit. This does not mean you do not communicate morals or celebrate God. It means you are not overbearing or simplistic when you do so."

THE ANNALS OF SAINT ANNE DE BEAUPRE

9795 St. Anne Blvd., St. Anne de Beaupre QC G0A 3C0, Canada. (418)827-4538. **Fax:** (418)827-4530. **E-mail:** mag@revuesainteanne.ca. **Website:** www.annalsofsaintanne.ca. Estab. 1885. "The purpose of The Annals of Saint Anne is to effectively communicate the word of God in the Catholic Tradition by growing and expanding our outreach to Catholics of all ages through print and electronic media. Since the very first publication of The Annals of Saint Anne, our aim was to lead Catholic families toward a deeper union with God through prayer, communion with one another, and a joyful practice of their faith."

HOW TO CONTACT "Be sure to include your complete name, address, phone and/or fax number, and e-mail address. The editing committee will acknowledge your proposal as soon as possible. Please do not send additional material unless it is requested. In the event your manuscript is not accepted, if you want us to return it you, include SASE."

ANOTHER CHICAGO MAGAZINE

P.O. Box 408439, Chicago IL 60640. **E-mail:** editors@anotherchicagomagazine.net. **Website:** www.anotherchicagomagazine.net. **Contact:** Caroline Eick Kasner, managing editor; Matt Rowan, fiction editor; David Welch, poetry editor; Colleen O'Connor, nonfiction editor. Estab. 1977. "*Another Chicago Magazine* is a biannual literary magazine that publishes work by both new and established writers. We look for work that goes beyond the artistic and academic to include and address the larger world. The editors read submissions in fiction, poetry, and creative nonfiction year

round. The best way to know what we publish is to read what we publish. If you haven't read *ACM* before, order a sample copy to know if your work is appropriate." Sends prepublication galleys.

Work published in *ACM* has been included frequently in *The Best American Poetry* and *The Pushcart Prize* anthologies. **Charges $3 submissions fee.**

NEEDS Length: up to 7,500 words.

HOW TO CONTACT Submit complete ms via online submissions manager.

TIPS "Support literary publishing by subscribing to at least 1 literary journal—if not ours, another. Get used to rejection slips, and don't get discouraged. Keep introductory letters short. Make sure ms has name and address on every page, and that it is clean, neat, and proofread. We are looking for stories with freshness and originality in subject angle and style, and work that encounters the world."

THE ANTIGONISH REVIEW

St. Francis Xavier University, P.O. Box 5000, Immaculata Hall, Room 413, Antigonish NS B2G 2W5, Canada. (902)867-3962. **Fax:** (902)867-5563. **E-mail:** tar@stfx.ca. **Website:** www.antigonishreview.com. **Contact:** Gerald Trites, editor. Estab. 1970. *The Antigonish Review*, published quarterly, features the writing of new and emerging writers as well as the ideas of established and innovative thinkers through poetry, stories, essays, book reviews and interviews."

NEEDS Send complete ms only through Submittable on our website. No erotica. Length: 500-5,000 words.

HOW TO CONTACT Send complete ms.

PAYMENT/TERMS Pays $50, 1 print edition and 1 digital edition for stories.

TIPS Contact by e-mail (tar@stfx.ca) and submit through the website using Submittable. There is a submission fee.

ANTIOCH REVIEW

Antioch College, P.O. Box 148, Yellow Springs OH 45387-0148. (937)769-1365. **E-mail:** review@antioch-college.edu. **Website:** www.antiochreview.org. **Contact:** Robert S. Fogarty, editor; Judith Hall, poetry editor. Estab. 1941. Literary and cultural review of contemporary issues and literature for general readership. *The Antioch Review* is an independent quarterly of critical and creative thought. We have a proud 75+ year history of publishing independent writers, exceptional poets, and brilliant thinkers—some only emerging upstarts when originally featured. *The Antioch Review*, founded in 1941, is one of the oldest, continuously publishing literary magazines in America. We publish fiction, essays, and poetry from prominent and promising poets, authors, and critics. Authors published in the *Review* are consistently included in Best American Anthologies and *Pushcart Prizes*. Our writers and poets are routinely recipients of prominent literary awards; and the *Review* has been the recipient of several prominent National Magazine Awards in essays and criticism and fiction. We have an international readership and reputation of publishing the "best words in the best order" for over 75 years. As a result, the competition is keen. We receive thousands of submissions each year from around the world. Form and content are so inseparable and reaction is so personal, it is difficult to state requirements or limitations. Studying prior issues of *The Antioch Review* and reviewing our "Writer's Guidelines" should be helpful.

NEEDS Quality fiction only, distinctive in style with fresh insights into the human condition. No science fiction, fantasy, or confessions.

HOW TO CONTACT Send complete ms with SASE, preferably mailed flat. Fiction submissions are not accepted between June 1-August 31.

PAYMENT/TERMS Pays $20/printed page, plus 2 contributor's copies.

APALACHEE REVIEW

Apalachee Press, P.O. Box 10469, Tallahassee FL 32302. (850)644-9114. **E-mail:** chayes@fsu.edu; mtrammell@fsu.edu. **E-mail:** arsubmissions@gmail.com (for queries outside the U.S.). **Website:** apalacheereview.org. **Contact:** Chris Hayes, chief editor; Mary Jane Ryals, fiction editor; Jenn Bronson, poetry editor; Michael Trammell, advisory & managing editor. Estab. 1976. "At *Apalachee Review*, we are interested in outstanding literary fiction, but we especially like poetry, fiction, and nonfiction that address intercultural issues in a domestic or international setting or context."

○ *Apalachee Review*, published annually, is 90 pages, digest-sized, professionally printed, perfect-bound, with card cover. Press run is 300-400. Includes photographs. Member CLMP.

NEEDS Receives 60-100 mss/month. Accepts 5-10 mss/issue. Agented fiction: 0.5%. Publishes 1-2 new writers/year. "We prefer fiction that is no longer than

15 pages in length." Has published Michael Martone, Lu Vickers, Joe Clark, Joe Taylor, Jane Arrowsmith Edwards, Vivian Lawry, Linda Frysh, Charles Harper Webb, Reno Raymond Gwaltney. Also publishes flash fictions and flash memoirs. Does not want cliché-filled, genre-oriented fiction. Length: 600-3,300 words; average length: 2,200 words. Average length of short shorts: 250 words.

HOW TO CONTACT Send complete ms with cover letter. Include brief bio, list of publications. Send either SASE (international authors should see website for "international" guidelines: no IRCs, please) for return of ms, or disposable copy of ms and #10 SASE for reply only; however, we may be switching to the Submittable online platform soon. Please check the website.

PAYMENT/TERMS Pays 2 contributor's copies.

APEX MAGAZINE

Apex Publications, LLC, P.O. Box 24323, Lexington KY 40524. **E-mail:** lesley@apex-magazine.com. **Website:** www.apex-magazine.com. **Contact:** Lesley Conner, managing editor. Estab. 2004. "An elite repository for new and seasoned authors with an other-worldly interest in the unquestioned and slightly bizarre parts of the universe. We want science fiction, fantasy, horror, and mash-ups of all three of the dark, weird stuff down at the bottom of your little literary heart."

NEEDS Length: 100-7,500 words.

HOW TO CONTACT Send complete ms.

PAYMENT/TERMS Pays 6¢/word.

APPALACHIAN HERITAGE

CPO 2166, Berea KY 40404. **E-mail:** appalachianheritage@berea.edu. **Website:** appalachianheritage.net. **Contact:** Jason Howard, editor. Estab. 1973. "We are seeking poetry, short fiction, literary criticism and biography, book reviews, and creative nonfiction, including memoirs, opinion pieces, and historical sketches. Unless you request not to be considered, all poems, stories, and articles published in *Appalachian Heritage* are eligible for our annual Plattner Award. All honorees are rewarded with a sliding bookrack with an attached commemorative plaque from Berea College Crafts, and first-place winners receive an additional stipend of $200."

○ Submission period: August 15-December 15.

NEEDS "We do not want to see fiction that has no ties to Southern Appalachia." No genre fiction. Length: up to 7,500 words.

HOW TO CONTACT Submit through online submissions manager only.

PAYMENT/TERMS Pays 3 contributor's copies.

TIPS "Sure, we are *Appalachian Heritage* and we do appreciate the past, but we are a forward-looking contemporary literary quarterly, and, frankly, we receive too many nostalgic submissions. Please spare us the 'Papaw Was Perfect' poetry and the 'Mamaw Moved Mountains' manuscripts and give us some hard-hitting prose, some innovative poetry, some inventive photography, and some original art. Help us be the ground-breaking, stimulating kind of quarterly we aspire to be."

APPLE VALLEY REVIEW

A Journal of Contemporary Literature, 88 South Third St., Suite 336, San Jose CA 95113. **E-mail:** editor@leah-browning.net. **Website:** www.applevalleyreview.com. **Contact:** Leah Browning, editor. Estab. 2005. *Apple Valley Review: A Journal of Contemporary Literature*, published semiannually online, features "beautifully crafted poetry, short fiction, and essays."

NEEDS Receives 100+ mss/month. Accepts 1-4 mss/issue; 2-8 mss/year. Published Siamak Vossoughi, Arndt Britschgi, Robert Radin, Sue Hyon Bae, Jessica Rafalko, Thomas Andrew Green, and Inderjeet Mani. Also publishes short shorts/flash, translations, and writing with genre elements (e.g., fabulism/magical realism). Does not want strict genre fiction, erotica, work containing explicit language, or anything "particularly violent or disturbing." Length: 100-4,000 words. Average length: 2,000 words. Average length of short shorts: 800 words.

HOW TO CONTACT Send complete ms with cover letter.

ARKANSAS REVIEW

A Journal of Delta Studies, Department of English and Philosophy, P.O. Box 1890, Office: Humanities and Social Sciences, State University AR 72467-1890. (870)972-3043; (870)972-2210. **Fax:** (870)972-3045. **E-mail:** mtribbet@astate.edu. **Website:** arkreview.org. **Contact:** Dr. Marcus Tribbett, general editor. Estab. 1998. "All material, creative and scholarly, published in the *Arkansas Review* must evoke or respond to the natural and/or cultural experience of the Mississippi River Delta region." *Arkansas Review* is 92 pages, magazine-sized, photo offset-printed, saddle-stapled, with 4-color cover. Press run is 400; 50 distributed free to contributors.

NEEDS Receives 30-50 unsolicited mss/month. Accepts 2-3 mss/issue; 5-7 mss/year. Agented fiction 1%. Publishes 3-4 new writers/year. Has published work by Susan Henderson, George Singleton, Scott Ely, and Pia Erhart. "No genre fiction. Must have a Delta focus." Length: up to 10,000 words.

HOW TO CONTACT Send complete ms.

PAYMENT/TERMS Pays 2 contributor's copies.

TIPS "Immerse yourself in the literature of the Delta, but provide us with a fresh and original take on its land, its people, its culture. Surprise us. Amuse us. Recognize what makes this region particular as well as universal, and take risks. Help us shape a new Delta literature."

💲 ARTS & LETTERS JOURNAL OF CONTEMPORARY CULTURE

Georgia College & State University, Milledgeville GA 31061. (478)445-1289. **Website:** al.gcsu.edu. **Contact:** Laura Newbern, editor; Faith Thompson, managing editor. Estab. 1999. *Arts & Letters Journal of Contemporary Culture*, published semiannually, is devoted to publishing contemporary work from established and emerging writers. Our editors seek work that doesn't try too hard to grab our attention, but rather guides it toward the human voice and its perpetual struggle into language. We're open to both formal and experimental fiction, nonfiction, and poetry; we're also open to work that defies classification. Above all, we look for work in which we can feel writers surprising themselves. Work published in *Arts & Letters Journal* has received the Pushcart Prize.

NEEDS No genre fiction. Length: up to 25 pages typed and double-spaced.

HOW TO CONTACT Submit complete ms via online submissions manager.

PAYMENT/TERMS Pays $10/printed page (minimum payment: $50) and 1 contributor's copy.

💲 ART TIMES

arttimesjournal, P.O. Box 730, Mount Marion NY 12456. (845)246-6944. **Fax:** (845)246-6944. **E-mail:** info@arttimesjournal.com. **Website:** www.arttimesjournal.com. **Contact:** Raymond J. Steiner, editor. Estab. 1984. "*Art Times*, now an online-only publication, covers the arts fields with essays about music, dance, theater, film, and art, and includes short fiction and poetry as well as editorials. Our readers are creatives looking for resources and people who appreciate good writing."

NEEDS Looking for quality short fiction that aspires to be literary. Publishes up to 4 stories a month. Nothing violent, sexist, erotic, juvenile, racist, romantic, political, off-beat, or related to sports or juvenile fiction. Length: up to 1,000 words.

HOW TO CONTACT Send complete ms.

PAYMENT/TERMS Pays $25.

ASIMOV'S SCIENCE FICTION

Dell Magazines, 44 Wall St., Suite 904, New York NY 10005. **E-mail:** asimovs@dellmagazines.com. **Website:** www.asimovs.com. **Contact:** Sheila Williams, editor; Victoria Green, senior art director. Estab. 1977. "Magazine consists of science fiction and fantasy stories for adults and young adults. Publishes the best short science fiction available."

NEEDS Wants "science fiction primarily. Some fantasy and humor. It is best to read a great deal of material in the genre to avoid the use of some very old ideas." Submit ms via online submissions manager or postal mail; no e-mail submissions. No horror or psychic/supernatural, sword and sorcery, explicit sex or violence that isn't integral to the story. Would like to see more hard science fiction. Length: 750-15,000 words.

PAYMENT/TERMS Pays 8-10¢/word for short stories up to 7,500 words; 8-8.5¢/word for longer material. Works between 7,500-10,000 words by authors who make more than 8¢/word for short stories will receive a flat rate that will be no less than the payment would be for a shorter story.

TIPS "In general, we're looking for 'character-oriented' stories, those in which the characters, rather than the science, provide the main focus for the reader's interest. Serious, thoughtful, yet accessible fiction will constitute the majority of our purchases, but there's always room for the humorous as well."

ASSIGNMENT

The Literary Magazine of Southern New Hampshire University, 2500 N. River Rd., Manchester NH 03106. **E-mail:** assignmentlitmag@gmail.com. **Website:** www.assignmentmag.com. **Contact:** Benjamin Nugent, editor. Estab. 2015. "*Assignment* is a literary magazine published annually by Southern New Hampshire University. It's so named because, in addition to short stories and essays by established and up-and-coming authors, and interviews, it will include creative writing assignments (i.e., exercises) generated by the contributors. Said assignments might be as conventional as 'Write a story entirely in dialogue,' or as unconventional as 'Walk across Europe.' Each issue will also feature the winner of the annual contest for students of SNHU's Master in Fine Arts program." *Assignment* is not accepting unsolicited submissions at this time.

THE ATA MAGAZINE

11010 142nd St. NW, Edmonton Alberta T5N 2R1, Canada. (780)447-9400. **Fax:** (780)455-6481. **E-mail:** government@teachers.ab.ca. **Website:** www.teachers.ab.ca. Estab. 1920.

THE ATLANTIC MONTHLY

The Watergate, 600 New Hampshire Ave., NW, Washington DC 20037. (202)266-6000. **Fax:** (202)266-6001. **E-mail:** submissions@theatlantic.com; pitches@theatlantic.com. **Website:** www.theatlantic.com. **Contact:** Scott Stossel, magazine editor; Ann Hulbert, literary editor. Estab. 1857. General magazine for an educated readership with broad cultural and public-affairs interests. "*The Atlantic* considers unsolicited mss, either fiction or nonfiction. A general familiarity with what we have published in the past is the best guide to our needs and preferences."

NEEDS "Seeks fiction that is clear, tightly written with strong sense of 'story' and well-defined characters." No longer publishes fiction in the regular magazine. Instead, it will appear in a special newsstand-only fiction issue. Receives 1,000 unsolicited mss/month. Accepts 7-8 mss/year. **Publishes 3-4 new writers/year.** Preferred length: 2,000-6,000 words.

HOW TO CONTACT Submit via e-mail with Word document attachment to submissions@theatlantic.com. Mss submitted via postal mail must be typewritten and double-spaced.

PAYMENT/TERMS Payment varies.

TIPS "Writers should be aware that this is not a market for beginner's work (nonfiction and fiction), nor is it truly for intermediate work. Study this magazine before sending only your best, most professional work. When making first contact, cover letters are sometimes helpful, particularly if they cite prior publications or involvement in writing programs. Common mistakes: melodrama, inconclusiveness, lack of development, unpersuasive characters and/or dialogue."

AUTHORSHIP

National Writers Association, 10940 S. Parker Rd., #508, Parker CO 80134. **E-mail:** natlwritersassn@hotmail.com. **Website:** www.nationalwriters.com. Estab. 1950s. "Association magazine targeted to beginning and professional writers. Covers how-to, humor, marketing issues. Disk and e-mail submissions preferred."

TIPS "Members of National Writers Association are given preference."

THE AVALON LITERARY REVIEW

CCI Publishing, P.O. Box 780696, Orlando FL 32878. **E-mail:** submissions@avalonliteraryreview.com. **Website:** www.avalonliteraryreview.com. **Contact:** Valerie Rubino, managing editor. Estab. 2011. "*The Avalon Literary Review* welcomes work from both published and unpublished writers and poets. We accept submissions of poetry, short fiction, and personal essays. While we appreciate the genres of fantasy, historical romance, science fiction, and horror, our magazine is not the forum for such work." Quarterly magazine.

NEEDS No erotica, science fiction, or horror. Length: 250-2,500 words.

HOW TO CONTACT Submit complete ms. Only accepts electronic submissions.

PAYMENT/TERMS Pays 3 contributor's copies to residents of the United States. PDF for any contributor outside the US

TIPS "The author's voice and point of view should be unique and clear. We seek pieces that spring from the author's life and experiences. Fiction submissions that explore both the sweet and bitter of life with a touch of humor, and poetry with vivid imagery, are a good fit for our review."

THE AWAKENINGS REVIEW

Awakenings Project, The, P.O. Box 177, Wheaton IL 60187. (630)606-8732. **E-mail:** ar@awakeningsproject. org. **Website:** www.awakeningsproject.org. **Contact:** Robert Lundin, editor. Estab. 1999. *The Awakenings Review* is published by the Awakenings Project. Begun in cooperation with the University of Chicago Center for Psychiatric Rehabilitation in 2000, *The Awakenings Review* has been acclaimed internationally and draws writers from all over the United States and from several other countries including Israel, South Africa, Australia, Finland, Switzerland, the United Kingdom, and Canada.

NEEDS Length: 5,000 words max.

HOW TO CONTACT No e-mail submissions. Cover letter is preferred. Include SASE and short bio.

PAYMENT/TERMS Pays 1 contributor's copy, plus discount on additional copies.

⊙ ⑤ BABYBUG

Cricket Media, Inc., 7926 Jones Branch Dr., Suite 870, McLean VA 22102. (703)885-3400. **Website:** www. cricketmedia.com. Estab. 1994. "*Babybug*, a look-and-listen magazine, presents simple poems, stories, nonfiction, and activities that reflect the natural playfulness and curiosity of babies and toddlers."

NEEDS Wants very short, clear fiction. Length: up to 6 sentences.

HOW TO CONTACT Submit complete ms via online submissions manager.

PAYMENT/TERMS Pays up to 25¢/word.

TIPS "We are particularly interested in mss that explore simple concepts, encourage very young children's imaginative play, and provide opportunities for adult readers and babies to interact. We welcome work that reflects diverse family cultures and traditions."

⑤ THE BALTIMORE REVIEW

6514 Maplewood Rd., Baltimore MD 21212. **E-mail:** editor@baltimorereview.org. **Website:** www.baltimorereview.org. **Contact:** Barbara Westwood Diehl, senior editor. Estab. 1996. *The Baltimore Review* publishes poetry, fiction, and creative nonfiction from Baltimore and beyond. Submission periods are August 1-November 30 and February 1-May 31.

NEEDS Length: 100-5,000 words.

HOW TO CONTACT Send complete ms using online submission form. Publishes 16-20 mss (combination of poetry, fiction, and creative nonfiction) per online issue. Work published online is also published in annual anthology.

PAYMENT/TERMS Pays $40.

TIPS "See editor preferences on staff page of website."

● THE BANGALORE REVIEW

Spanning Minds Media Private Limited, No. 149, 2nd Floor, 4th Cross, Kasturi Nagar, Bangalore Karnataka , India. **Website:** www.bangalorereview.com. **Contact:** Suhail Rasheed, managing editor; Maitreyee Choudhury and Fehmida Zakeer, co-editors; Mithun Jayaram, arts editor.. Estab. 2013. *The Bangalore Review* is a monthly online magazine aimed at promoting literature, arts, culture, criticism, and philosophy at a deeper level.

NEEDS Does not want erotica. Length: 250-5,000.

HOW TO CONTACT Query with complete ms.
PAYMENT/TERMS Does not offer payment.

BARBARIC YAWP

BoneWorld Publishing, 3700 County Rt. 24, Russell NY 13684. **Website:** www.boneworldpublishing.com. Estab. 1997. "We publish what we like. Fiction should include some bounce and surprise. Our publication is intended for the intelligent, open-minded reader."

○ *Barbaric Yawp*, published quarterly, is digest-sized; 44 pages; matte cover stock.

NEEDS "We don't want any pornography, gratuitous violence, or whining."

HOW TO CONTACT Submit complete ms by mail. Send SASE for reply and return of ms, or send a disposable copy of ms. Accepts simultaneous, multiple submissions, and reprints.

PAYMENT/TERMS Pays 1 contributor's copy; additional copies $3.

TIPS "Don't give up. Read much, write much, submit much. Observe closely the world around you. Don't borrow ideas from TV or films. Revision is often necessary—grit your teeth and do it. Never fear rejection."

BARKING SYCAMORES

Autonomous Press, 3488 Gateway Lakes Dr., Grove City OH 43123. **E-mail:** barkingsycamores@gmail.com. **Website:** barkingsycamores.wordpress.com. **Contact:** N.I. Nicholson and V. E. Maday, editors. Estab. 2014. *Barking Sycamores* is a literary journal whose mission is to publish poetry, short fiction (1,000 words or less), creative nonfiction, hybrid genre, and artwork by neurodivergent contributors. "We also seek to add positively to the public discussion about neurodivergence as a whole in the form of essays on literature and the interrelationship between it and the creative process. Additionally, we also publish book reviews (1,000 words or less) of titles either written by or focused on neurodivergent individuals. We pay contributors once their work is included in the yearly print anthology. Payment comes from the Autonomous Press anthology fund."

PAYMENT/TERMS We pay contributors once their work is included in the yearly print anthology. Payment comes from the Autonomous Press anthology fund.

BARRELHOUSE

E-mail: yobarrelhouse@gmail.com. **Website:** www.barrelhousemag.com. **Contact:** Dave Housley, Joe Killiany, and Matt Perez, fiction editors; Tom McAl-lister, nonfiction editor; Dan Brady, poetry editor. Estab. 2004. *Barrelhouse* is a biannual print journal featuring fiction, poetry, interviews, and essays about music, art, and the detritus of popular culture.

○ Stories originally published in *Barrelhouse* have been featured in *The Best American Nonrequired Reading*, *The Best American Science Fiction and Fantasy*, and the Million Writer's Award.

NEEDS Length: open, but prefers pieces under 8,000.

HOW TO CONTACT Submit complete ms via online submissions manager. DOC or RTF files only.

PAYMENT/TERMS Pays $50 and 2 contributor copies.

BATEAU

105 Eden St., Bar Harbor ME 04609. **E-mail:** dan@bateaupress.org. **Website:** bateaupress.org. **Contact:** Daniel Mahoney, editor in chief. Estab. 2007. "*Bateau*, published annually, subscribes to no trend but serves to represent as wide a cross-section of contemporary writing as possible. For this reason, readers will most likely love and hate at least something in each issue. We consider this a good thing. To us, it means *Bateau* is eclectic, open-ended, and not mired in a particular strain."

○ *Bateau* is around 80 pages, digest-sized, offset print, perfect-bound, with a 100% recycled letterpress cover. Press run is 250.

HOW TO CONTACT Submit via online submissions manager. Brief bio is encouraged but not required.

PAYMENT/TERMS Pays contributor's copies.

TIPS "Send us your best work. Send us funny work, quirky work, outstanding work, work that is well punctuated or lacks punctuation. Fearless work. Work that wants to crash on our sofa."

○○ THE BEAR DELUXE MAGAZINE

Orlo, 240 N. Broadway, #112, Portland OR 97227. **E-mail:** beardeluxe@orlo.org. **Website:** www.orlo.org. **Contact:** Tom Webb, editor-in-chief; Kristin Rogers Brown, art director. Estab. 1993. "*The Bear Deluxe Magazine* is a national independent environmental arts magazine publishing significant works of reporting, creative nonfiction, literature, visual art, and design. Based in the Pacific Northwest, it reaches across cultural and political divides to engage readers on vital issues effecting the environment. Published twice per year, *The Bear Deluxe* includes a wider array and a higher percentage of visual artwork and design than many other publications. Artwork is included both as editorial support and as standalone or independent art. It has included nationally recognized artists as well as emerging artists. As with any publication, artists are encouraged to review a sample copy for a clearer understanding of the magazine's approach. Unsolicited submissions and samples are accepted and encouraged."

NEEDS "We are most excited by high-quality writing that furthers the magazine's goal of engaging new and divergent readers. We appreciate strong aspects of storytelling and are open to new formats, though we wouldn't call ourselves publishers of 'experimental fiction.'" No traditional sci-fi, horror, romance, or crime/action. Length: up to 4,000 words.

HOW TO CONTACT Query or send complete ms. Prefers postal mail submissions.

PAYMENT/TERMS Pays free subscription to the magazine, contributor's copies, and $25-400, depending on piece; additional copies for postage.

TIPS "Offer to be a stringer for future ideas. Get a copy of the magazine and guidelines, and query us with specific nonfiction ideas and clips. We're looking for original, magazine-style stories, not fluff or PR. Fiction, essay, and poetry writers should know we have an open and blind review policy and they should keep sending their best work even if rejected once. Be as specific as possible in queries."

BEATDOM

Beatdom Books, 426 Blowrie St., Dundee Scotland DD3 1AH, United Kingdom. **E-mail:** editor@beatdom.com. **Website:** www.beatdom.com. **Contact:** David Wills, editor. Estab. 2007. Beatdom is a Beat Generation-themed literary journal that publishes essays, short stories, and poems related to the Beats. "We publish studies of Beat texts, figures, and legends; we look at writers and movements related to the Beats; we support writers of the present who take their influence from the Beats."

NEEDS Length: up to 5,000 words.

HOW TO CONTACT Submit complete ms via e-mail.

PAYMENT/TERMS Pays $50.

BELLINGHAM REVIEW

Mail Stop 9053, Western Washington University, Bellingham WA 98225. (360)650-4863. **E-mail:** bellingham.review@wwu.edu. **Website:** wwww.bhreview.org. **Contact:** Susanne Paola Antonetta, editor-in-

chief; Bailey Cunningham, managing editor. Estab. 1977. Nonprofit magazine published once/year in the Spring. Seeks "literature of palpable quality: poems, stories, and essays so beguiling they invite us to touch their essence. *Bellingham Review* hungers for a kind of writing that nudges the limits of form or executes traditional forms exquisitely." The editors are actively seeking submissions of creative nonfiction, as well as stories that push the boundaries of the form. Open submission period is from September 15-December 1.

NEEDS Length: up to 6,000 words. For prose that is 1,500 words or fewer, submit up to three in one entry. Does not want anything nonliterary. Length: up to 6,000 words.

HOW TO CONTACT Submit complete ms via online submissions manager.

PAYMENT/TERMS Pays as funds allow, plus contributor's copies.

TIPS "The *Bellingham Review* holds 3 annual contests: the 49th Parallel Award for poetry, the Annie Dillard Award for Nonfiction, and the Tobias Wolff Award for Fiction. See the individual listings for these contests under Contests & Awards for full details."

BELOIT FICTION JOURNAL

Box 11, Beloit College, 700 College St., Beloit WI 53511. (608)363-2079. **E-mail:** bfj@beloit.edu. **Website:** www.beloit.edu/bfj. **Contact:** Chris Fink, editor-in-chief. Estab. 1985. "*The Beloit Fiction Journal* publishes the best in contemporary short fiction. Traditional and experimental narratives find a home in our pages. We publish new writers alongside established writers. Our fiction-only format allows us to consider very long as well as very short stories. We occasionally publish excerpts."

Reading period: August 1-December 1. Work first appearing in *Beloit Fiction Journal* has been reprinted in award-winning collections, including the Flannery O'Connor and the Milkweed Fiction Prize collections, and has won the Iowa Short Fiction award. Has published work by Dennis Lehane, Silas House, and David Harris Ebenbach.

NEEDS Receives 200 unsolicited mss/month. Accepts 14 mss/year. Publishes ms 9 months after acceptance. **Publishes new writers every year.** Sometimes comments on rejected mss. Wants more experimental and short shorts. Would like to see more "stories with a focus on both language and plot, unusual metaphors and vivid characters." No pornography, religious dogma, science fiction, horror, political propaganda, or genre fiction. Length: 1-60 pages.

HOW TO CONTACT Submit complete ms via online submissions manager ($3 fee) or postal mail.

PAYMENT/TERMS Pays contributor copies.

TIPS "Many of our contributors are writers whose work we had previously rejected. Don't let 1 rejection slip turn you away from our—or any—magazine."

BERKELEY FICTION REVIEW

Berkeley Fiction Review
c/o ASUC Student Union FMO
432 Eshleman, MC 4500, University of California, Berkeley, Berkeley CA 94720, United States. **E-mail:** berkeleyfictionreview@gmail.com. **Website:** berkeleyfictionreview.com. Estab. 1981. "The *Berkeley Fiction Review* is a UC Berkeley undergraduate, student-run publication. We look for innovative short fiction that plays with form and content, as well as traditionally constructed stories with fresh voices and original ideas."

○ *BFR* nominates to O.Henry, *Best American Short Stories* and *Pushcart* prizes. Sponsored by the ASUC.

NEEDS Length: no more than 25 pages.

HOW TO CONTACT Submit via e-mail with "Submission: Name, Title" in subject line. Include cover letter in body of e-mail, with story as an attachment.

PAYMENT/TERMS Pays 1 contributor's copy.

TIPS "Our criteria is fiction that resonates. Voices that are strong and move a reader. Clear, powerful prose (either voice or rendering of subject) with a point. Unique ways of telling stories—these capture the editors. Work hard, don't give up. Ask an honest person to point out your writing weaknesses, and then work on them. We look forward to reading fresh new voices."

○$ BEYOND CENTAURI

White Cat Publications, LLC, 33080 Industrial Rd., Suite 101, Livonia MI 48150. (734)237-8522. **Fax:** (313)557-5162. **E-mail:** beyondcentauri@whitecatpublications.com. **Website:** www.whitecatpublications.com/guidelines/beyond-centauri. Estab. 2003. *Beyond Centauri*, published quarterly, contains fantasy, science fiction, sword and sorcery, very mild horror short stories, poetry, and illustrations for readers ages 10 and up.

○ *Beyond Centauri* is 44 pages, magazine-sized, offset printed, perfect-bound, with paper cover

for color art, includes ads. Press run is 100; 5 distributed free to reviewers.

NEEDS Looks for themes of science fiction or fantasy. "Science fiction and especially stories that take place in outer space will find great favor with us." Length: up to 2,500 words.

HOW TO CONTACT Submit in the body of an e-mail, or as an RTF attachment.

PAYMENT/TERMS Pays $6/story, $3/reprints, and $2/flash fiction (under 1,000 words), plus 1 contributor's copy.

BIG BRIDGE

Big Bridge Press, P.O. 2724, Tallahassee FL 32304. **E-mail:** walterblue@bigbridge.org. **Website:** www.bigbridge.org. **Contact:** Michael Rothenberg and Terri Carrion, editors. "*Big Bridge* is one of the oldest and most respected online literary arts magazines. For over 20 years, Big Bridge has published the best in poetry, fiction, nonfiction essays, journalism, and art (photos, line drawings, performance, installations, site-works, comics, graphics)."

HOW TO CONTACT Only accepts electronic submissions. Submit via e-mail.

TIPS "Big Bridge publishes one very big issue each year. Each issue features an online chapbook. We are interested in anthology concepts and thematic installations as well as individual submissions. Send query to propose installations and anthology ideas for consideration. All individual submissions should include a bio and bio photo."

BIG MUDDY

A Journal of the Mississippi River Valley, Southeast Missouri State University Press, One University Plaza, MS 2650, Cape Girardeau MO 63701. (573)651-2044. **E-mail:** upress@semo.edu. **Website:** bigmuddyjournal.com. Estab. 2000. "*Big Muddy* explores multidisciplinary, multicultural issues, people, and events mainly concerning, but not limited to, the 10-state area that borders the Mississippi River. We publish fiction, poetry, historical essays, creative nonfiction, environmental essays, biography, regional events, photography, art, etc."

NEEDS No romance, fantasy, or children's.

PAYMENT/TERMS Pays 2 contributor's copies; additional copies $5. Annual short story ($1,000) and flash fiction ($500) contests.

TIPS "We look for clear language, avoidance of clichés, a fresh vision of the theme or issue. Find some excellent and honest readers to comment on your work-in-progress and final draft. Consider their viewpoints carefully. Revise if needed."

⑤ BIG PULP

Exter Press, P.O. Box 92, Cumberland MD 21501. E-mail: editors@bigpulp.com. **Website:** www.bigpulp. com. **Contact:** Bill Olver, editor. Estab. 2008. *Big Pulp* defines "pulp fiction" very broadly: It's lively, challenging, thought provoking, thrilling, and fun, regardless of how many or how few genre elements are packed in. It doesn't subscribe to the theory that genre fiction is disposable; a great deal of literary fiction could easily fall under one of their general categories. Places a higher value on character and story than genre elements.

○ "Submissions are only accepted during certain reading periods. Our website is updated to reflect when we are and are not reading, and what we are looking for."

NEEDS Does not want generic slice-of-life, memoirs, inspirational, political, pastoral odes. Length: up to 2,500 words.

HOW TO CONTACT Submit complete ms.

PAYMENT/TERMS Pays $5-25.

TIPS "We like to be surprised, and we have few boundaries. Fantasy writers may focus on the mundane aspects of a fantastical creature's life or the magic that can happen in everyday life. Romances do not have to be requited or have happy endings, and the object of one's obsession may not be a person. Mysteries need not focus on 'whodunit?' We're always interested in science or speculative fiction focusing on societal issues, but writers should avoid being partisan or shrill. We also like fiction that crosses genre; for example, a science fiction romance or a fantasy crime story. We have an online archive for fiction and poetry and encourage writers to check it out. That said, *Big Pulp* has a strong editorial bias in favor of stories with monkeys. Especially talking monkeys."

BILINGUAL REVIEW

Arizona State University, Hispanic Research Center, P.O. Box 875303, Tempe AZ 85287-5303. (480)965-3867. **Fax:** (480)965-0315. **E-mail:** brp@asu.edu. **Website:** www.asu.edu/brp/submit. **Contact:** Gary Francisco Keller, publisher. Estab. 1974. *Bilingual Review* is "committed to publishing high-quality writing by both established and emerging writers."

○ Magazine: 7x10; 96 pages; 55 lb. acid-free paper; coated cover stock.

NEEDS Receives 50 unsolicited mss/month. Accepts 3 mss/issue; 9 mss/year. "We do not publish literature about tourists in Latin America and their perceptions of the 'native culture.' We do not publish fiction about Latin America unless there is a clear tie to the U.S."

HOW TO CONTACT Submit via mail. Send 2 copies of complete ms with SAE and loose stamps. Does not usually accept e-mail submissions except through special circumstance/prior arrangement.

PAYMENT/TERMS Pays 2 contributor's copies; 30% discount for additional copies.

THE BITTER OLEANDER

4983 Tall Oaks Dr., Fayetteville NY 13066. **E-mail:** info@bitteroleander.com. **Website:** www.bitteroleander.com. **Contact:** Paul B. Roth, editor and publisher. "We're reading to find a language uncommitted to the commonplace and more integrated with the natural world. A language that helps define the same particulars in nature that exist in us and have not been socialized out of us." Biannual magazine covering poetry and short fiction and translations of contemporary poetry and short fiction.

NEEDS Wants short, imaginative fiction of no more than 2,500 words. Does not want family or college stories with moralistic plots or fantasy that involve hyper-reality of any sort. Length: up to 2,500 words.

HOW TO CONTACT Submit through online Submittable portal.

PAYMENT/TERMS Pays 1 contributor's copy.

TIPS "If you are writing poems or short fiction in the tradition of 98% of all journals publishing in this country, then your work will usually not fit for us. If within the first 400 words our minds start to drift, the rest rarely makes it. Be yourself, and listen to no one but yourself."

BLACKBIRD

Virginia Commonwealth University Department of English, P.O. Box 843082, Richmond VA 23284. (804)827-4729. **E-mail:** blackbird@vcu.edu. **Website:** www.blackbird.vcu.edu. Estab. 2001. *Blackbird* is published twice a year. Reading period: August 1 to March 15.

NEEDS "We primarily look for short stories, but novel excerpts are acceptable if self-contained."

HOW TO CONTACT Submit using online submissions manager or by mail. Online submission is preferred.

TIPS "We like a story that invites us into its world, that engages our senses, soul, and mind. We are able to publish long works in all genres, but query *Blackbird* before you send a prose piece over 8,000 words or a poem exceeding 10 pages."

⑤ BLACK WARRIOR REVIEW

P.O. Box 862936, Tuscaloosa AL 35486. (205)348-4518. **E-mail:** interns.bwr@gmail.com. **Website:** www.bwr.ua.edu. **Contact:** Cat Ingrid Leeches, editor. Estab. 1974. "We publish contemporary fiction, poetry, reviews, essays, and art for a literary audience. We publish the freshest work we can find." Work that appeared in the *Black Warrior Review* has been included in the *Pushcart Prize* anthology, *Harper's Magazine, Best American Short Stories, Best American Poetry,* and *New Stories from the South.*

NEEDS "We are open to good experimental writing and short-short fiction. No genre fiction please." Publishes novel excerpts if under contract to be published. Length: up to 7,000 words.

HOW TO CONTACT One story/chapter per envelope. Wants work that is conscious of form and well-crafted.

PAYMENT/TERMS Pays one-year subscription and nominal lump-sum fee.

TIPS "We look for attention to language, freshness, honesty, a convincing and sharp voice. Send us a clean, well-printed, proofread ms. Become familiar with the magazine prior to submission."

BLUE COLLAR REVIEW

Partisan Press, P.O. Box 11417, Norfolk VA 23517. **E-mail:** red-ink@earthlink.net. **Website:** www.partisanpress.org. **Contact:** A. Markowitz, editor; Mary Franke, co-editor. Estab. 1997. *Blue Collar Review (Journal of Progressive Working Class Literature)*, published quarterly, contains poetry, short stories, and illustrations "reflecting the working-class experience— a broad range from the personal to the societal. Our purpose is to promote and expand working-class literature and an awareness of the connections between workers of all occupations and the social context in which we live. Also to inspire the creativity and latent talent in 'common' working people."

NEEDS Submit ms via mail. Name and address should appear on every page. Cover letter is help-ful but not required. Size 10 SASE is required for response. Length: up to 1,000 words.

PAYMENT/TERMS Pays contributor's copies.

BLUELINE

120 Morey Hall, SUNY Potsdam, Postdam NY 13676. **E-mail:** blueline@potsdam.edu. **Website:** bluelinemagadk.com. **Contact:** Donald J. McNutt, editor and nonfiction editor; Caroline Downing, art editor; Stephanie Coyne-DeGhett, fiction editor; Rebecca Lehmann, poetry editor. Estab. 1979. "*Blueline* seeks poems, stories, and essays relating to the Adirondacks and regions similar in geography and spirit, or focusing on the shaping influence of nature. Submission period is July-November. *Blueline* welcomes electronic submissions as Word document (DOC or DOCX) attachments. Please identify genre in subject line. Please avoid using compression software." Annual literary magazine publishing fiction, poetry, personal essays, book reviews, and quality visual art for those interested in the Adirondacks or well-crafted nature writing in general.

○ "Proofread all submissions. It is difficult for our editors to get excited about work containing typographical and syntactic errors."

NEEDS Receives 8-10 unsolicited mss/month. Accepts 2-3 mss/issue. Does not read January-June. Publishes 2 new writers/year. Recently published work by Jim Meirose, Amber Timmerman, Gail Gilliland, Matthew J. Spireng, Roger Sheffer, and Mason Smith. No urban stories or erotica. Length: 500-3,000 words. Average length: 2,500 words.

PAYMENT/TERMS Pays 1 contributor's copy; charges $9 each for 3 or more copies.

TIPS "We look for concise, clear, concrete prose that tells a story and touches upon a universal theme or situation. We prefer realism to romanticism but will consider nostalgia if well done. Pay attention to grammar and syntax. Avoid murky language, sentimentality, cuteness, or folksiness. We would like to see more good, creative nonfiction centered on the literature and/or culture of the Adirondacks, Northern New York, New England, or Eastern Canada. If ms has potential, we work with author to improve and reconsider for publication. Our readers prefer fiction to poetry (in general) or reviews. Write from your own experience, be specific and factual (within the bounds of your story), and if you write about universal features such as love, death, change, etc., write about them in a fresh way. You'll catch our attention if your writing is interesting, vigorous, and polished."

BLUE MESA REVIEW

Department of Language and Literature, Humanities Building, Second Floor, MSC03 2170, 1 University of New Mexico, Albuquerque NM 87131. **Website:** bluemesareview.org. **Contact:** Has rotating editorial board; see website for current masthead. Estab. 1989. "Originally founded by Rudolfo Anaya, Gene Frumkin, David Johnson, Patricia Clark Smith, and Lee Bartlette in 1989, the *Blue Mesa Review* emerged as a source of innovative writing produced in the Southwest. Over the years the magazine's nuance has changed, sometimes shifting towards more craft-oriented work, other times realigning with its original roots."

○ Open for submissions from September 30-March 31. Contest: June 1-August 31. Only accepts submissions through online submissions manager.

NEEDS Length: up to 6,000 words.

HOW TO CONTACT Submit via online submissions manager.

TIPS "In general, we are seeking strong voices and lively, compelling narrative with a fine eye for craft. We look forward to reading your best work!"

BLUESTEM

English Deptartment, Eastern Illinois University, **Website:** www.bluestemmagazine.com. **Contact:** Olga Abella, editor. Estab. 1966. *Bluestem*, formerly known as *Karamu*, produces a quarterly online issue (December, March, June, September) and an annual spring print issue.

○ Only accepts submissions through online submissions manager.

NEEDS Length: up to 5,000 words.

HOW TO CONTACT Submit only 1 short story at a time. Include bio (less than 100 words) with submission. Query if longer than 5,000 words.

PAYMENT/TERMS Pays 1 contributor's copy and discount for additional copies.

BODY LITERATURE

Website: bodyliterature.com. Estab. 2012. *BODY* is an international online literary journal. "We publish the highest-quality poetry and prose from emerging and established writers."

NEEDS Length: up to 10 pages typed and double-spaced.

HOW TO CONTACT Submit through online submissions manager. Include short cover letter and short third-person bio.

BOMBAY GIN

Naropa University, Creative Writing and Poetics Department, 2130 Arapahoe Ave., Boulder CO 80302. **E-mail:** bgin@naropa.edu. **Website:** www.bombayginjournal.com. **Contact:** Jade Lascelles, editor in chief. Estab. 1974. *Bombay Gin*, published annually, is the literary journal of the Jack Kerouac School of Disembodied Poetics at Naropa University. Produced and edited by MFA students, *Bombay Gin* publishes established writers alongside unpublished and emerging writers. We have a special interest in works that push conventional literary boundaries. Submissions of poetry, prose, visual art, translation, and works involving hybrid forms and cross-genre exploration are encouraged. Translations are also considered. Guidelines are the same as for original work. Translators are responsible for obtaining any necessary permissions."

○ *Bombay Gin* is 150-200 pages, digest-sized, professionally printed, perfect-bound, with color card cover. Has published work by Amiri Baraka, Lisa Robertson, CA Conrad, Sapphire, Fred Moten, Anne Waldman, Diane di Prima and bell hooks, among others.

NEEDS Length: up to 15 pages.

HOW TO CONTACT Submit through online submissions manager. Include 100-word bio, e-mail, and mailing address.

BOMB MAGAZINE

80 Hanson Place, Ste. 703, Brooklyn NY 11217. (718)636-9100. **Fax:** (718)636-9200. **E-mail:** saul@bombsite.com. **Website:** www.bombmagazine.com. **Contact:** Saul Anton, senior editor. Estab. 1981. "Written, edited, and produced by industry professionals and funded by those interested in the arts, *BOMB Magazine* publishes work which is unconventional and contains an edge, whether it be in style or subject matter."

NEEDS No genre fiction: romance, science fiction, horror, western. Length: up to 25 pages.

HOW TO CONTACT *BOMB Magazine* accepts unsolicited poetry and prose submissions for our literary supplement *First Proof* by online submission manager in January and August. Submissions sent outside these months will not be read. Submit complete ms via online submission manager. E-mailed submissions will not be considered.

PAYMENT/TERMS Pays $100 and contributor's copies.

TIPS "Mss should be typed, double-spaced, and proofread, and should be final drafts. Purchase a sample issue before submitting work."

⑤ BOULEVARD

Opojaz, Inc., 6614 Clayton Rd., Box 325, Richmond Heights MO 63117. **E-mail:** editors@boulevardmagazine.org. **Website:** www.boulevardmagazine.org; boulevard.submittable.com/submit. **Contact:** Jessica Rogen, editor. Estab. 1985. Hosts the Short Fiction Contest for Emerging Writers. **Prize:** $1,500 and publication in *Boulevard.* **Postmarked deadline:** December 31. **Entry fee:** $15 for each individual story, with no limit per author. Entry fee includes a one-year subscription to *Boulevard* (1 per author). Make check payable to *Boulevard.* For contests, make check payable to *Boulevard* or submit online at boulevard.submittable.com/submit. "*Boulevard* is a diverse literary magazine presenting original creative work by well-known authors as well as by writers of exciting promise." Triannual magazine featuring fiction, poetry, and essays. Sometimes comments on rejected mss. *Boulevard* has been called "one of the half-dozen best literary journals" by Poet Laureate Daniel Hoffman in *The Philadelphia Inquirer.* "We strive to publish the finest in poetry, fiction, and nonfiction. We frequently publish writers with previous credits, and we are very interested in publishing less experienced or unpublished writers with exceptional promise. We've published everything from John Ashbery to Donald Hall to a wide variety of styles from new or lesser known poets. We're eclectic. We are interested in original, moving poetry written from the head as well as the heart. It can be about any topic." *Boulevard* is 175-250 pages, digest-sized, flat-spined, with glossy card cover. Receives over 600 unsolicited mss/month. Accepts about 10 mss/issue. Publishes 10 new writers/year. Recently published work by Joyce Carol Oates, Floyd Skloot, John Barth, Stephen Dixon, David Guterson, Albert Goldbarth, Molly Peacock, Bob Hicok, Alice Friman, Dick Allen, and Tom Disch.

NEEDS Submit by mail or Submittable. Accepts multiple submissions. Does not accept mss May 1-October 1. SASE for reply. "We do not want erotica, science fiction, romance, western, horror, or children's stories." Length: up to 8,000 words.

PAYMENT/TERMS Pays $50-500 (sometimes higher) for accepted work.

TIPS "Read the magazine first. The work *Boulevard* publishes is generally recognized as among the finest in the country. We continue to seek more good literary or cultural essays. Send only your best work."

THE BRIAR CLIFF REVIEW

3303 Rebecca St., Sioux City IA 51104. (712)279-1651. **E-mail:** tricia.currans-sheehan@briarcliff.edu. **Website:** bcreview.org. **Contact:** Tricia Currans-Sheehan, editor; Jeanne Emmons, poetry editor; Phil Hey, fiction editor; Paul Weber, Siouxland and nonfiction editor. Estab. 1989. *The Briar Cliff Review,* published annually in April, is "an attractive, eclectic literary/art magazine." It focuses on, but is not limited to, "Siouxland writers and subjects. We are happy to proclaim ourselves a regional publication. It doesn't diminish us; it enhances us."

◉ Member: CLMP, Humanities International Complete.

NEEDS Accepts 5 mss/year. **Publishes 10-14 new writers/year.** Publishes ms 3-4 months after acceptance. Recently published work by Leslie Barnard, Daryl Murphy, Patrick Hicks, Siobhan Fallon, Shelley Scaletta, Jenna Blum, Brian Bedard, Rebecca Tuch, Scott H. Andrews, and Josip Novakovich. "No romance, horror, or alien stories." Length: up to 5,000 words.

HOW TO CONTACT Submit by (send SASE for return of ms) or online submissions manager. Does not accept e-mail submissions (unless from overseas). Seldom comments on rejected mss.

PAYMENT/TERMS Pays 2 contributor's copies; additional copies available for $12.

TIPS "So many stories are just telling. We want some action. It has to move. We prefer stories in which there is no gimmick, no mechanical turn of events, no moral except the one we would draw privately."

BRILLIANT CORNERS: A JOURNAL OF JAZZ & LITERATURE

Lycoming College, 700 College Place, Williamsport PA 17701. **Website:** www.lycoming.edu/brilliantcorners. **Contact:** Sascha Feinstein, editor. Estab. 1996. "We publish jazz-related literature—fiction, poetry, and nonfiction. We are open as to length and form." Semiannual.

◉ Reading period: September 1-May 15.

NEEDS Receives 10-15 unsolicited mss/month. Accepts 1-2 mss/issue; 2-3 mss/year.

HOW TO CONTACT Submit with SASE for return of ms, or send disposable copy of ms. Accepts unpublished work only. No e-mail or fax submissions. Cover letter is preferred.

TIPS "We look for clear, moving prose that demostrates a love of both writing and jazz. We primarily publish established writers, but we read all submissions carefully and welcome work by outstanding young writers."

THE BROADKILL REVIEW

c/o John Milton & Company, 104 Federal St., Milton DE 19968. **E-mail:** broadkillreview@gmail.com. **Website:** broadkillreview.com, www.thebroadkillreview.blogspot.com; sites.google.com/site/thebroadkillreview. **Contact:** James C.L. Brown, founding editor; Stephen Scott Whitaker, managing editor; Linda Blaskey, poetry and interview editor, HA Maxson, fiction editor. Estab. 2005.

    "The Broadkill Review accepts the best fiction, poetry, and nonfiction by new and established writers. We have published Pushcart-nominated fiction and poetry." TBR publishes many writers from the Mid-Atlantic region, but does not limit itself to work from this region, as they are an internationally read publication that publishes a wide variety of work from around the globe, including Canada, U.S., Western and Eastern Europe, China, Vietnam, Australia, and Pakistan.

NEEDS No erotica, fantasy, science fiction "unless these serve some functional literary purpose; most do not." Length: up to 6,000 words.

HOW TO CONTACT Send complete ms with cover letter through online submissions manager. Include estimated word count, brief bio, list of publications.

PAYMENT/TERMS Pays contributor's copy.

TIPS "Query the editor first. Visit our website to familiarize yourself with the type of material we publish. Request and read a copy of the magazine first!"

BUENOS AIRES REVIEW

E-mail: editors@buenosairesreview.org. **Website:** buenosairesreview.org. *The Buenos Aires Review* presents the best and latest work by emerging and established writers from the Americas, in both Spanish and English. "We value translation and conversation. We're bilingual. And we're passionate about the art and craft that allows us to be, so we provide a dedicated space for translators to discuss their recent projects."

BUGLE

Rocky Mountain Elk Foundation, 5705 Grant Creek, Missoula MT 59808. (406)523-4500. **Fax:** (800)225-5355. **E-mail:** bugle@rmef.org. **E-mail:** conservationeditor@rmef.org; huntingeditor@rmef.org; assistanteditor@rmef.org; photos@rmef.org. **Website:** www.rmef.org. Estab. 1984. *Bugle* is the membership publication of the Rocky Mountain Elk Foundation, a nonprofit wildlife conservation group. "Our readers are predominantly hunters, many of them conservationists who care deeply about protecting wildlife habitat." Bimonthly. Magazine: 114-212 pages; 55 lb. Escanaba paper; 80 lb. Sterling cover, b&w, 4-color illustrations; photos.

NEEDS "We accept fiction and nonfiction stories pertaining in some way to elk, other wildlife, hunting, habitat conservation, and related issues. We would like to see more humor." Length: 1,500-5,000 words; average length: 2,500 words.

HOW TO CONTACT Query or submit complete ms to appropriate e-mail address; see website for guidelines.

PAYMENT/TERMS Pays 30¢/word and 3 contributor's copies.

TIPS "Hunting stories and essays should celebrate the hunting experience, demonstrating respect for wildlife, the land, and the hunt. Articles on elk behavior or elk habitat should include personal observations and should entertain as well as educate. No freelance product reviews or formulaic how-to articles accepted. Straight action-adventure hunting stories are in short supply, as are 'Situation Ethics' mss."

BURNSIDE REVIEW

P.O. Box 1782, Portland OR 97207. **Website:** www.burnsidereview.org. **Contact:** Sid Miller, founder and editor; Dan Kaplan, managing editor. Estab. 2004. *Burnside Review*, published every 9 months, prints "the best poetry and short fiction we can get our hands on. We tend to publish writing that finds beauty in truly unexpected places; that combines urban and natural imagery; that breaks the heart."

    Burnside Review is 80 pages, 6x6, professionally printed, perfect-bound. Charges a $3 submission fee to cover printing costs.

NEEDS "We like bright, engaging fiction that works to surprise and captivate us." Length: up to 5,000 words.

HOW TO CONTACT Submit complete ms via online submissions manager.

PAYMENT/TERMS Pays $25 and 1 contributor's copy.

🖲 THE CAFE IRREAL

E-mail: editors@cafeirreal.com. **Website:** www.cafeirreal.com. **Contact:** G.S. Evans and Alice Whittenburg, co-editors. Estab. 1998. "Our audience is composed of people who read or write literary fiction with fantastic themes, similar to the work of Franz Kafka, Kobo Abe, or Ana María Shua. This is a type of fiction (irreal) that has difficulty finding its way into print in the English-speaking world and defies many of the conventions of American literature especially. As a result, ours is a fairly specialized literary publication, and we would strongly recommend that prospective writers look at our current issue and guidelines carefully." Recently published work by Tamara K. Walker, Jeff Friedman, Vanessa Gebbie, Viki Shock, JB Mulligan, Tess Gunty, Jiří Kratochvil, Ian Seed.

NEEDS Accepts submissions by e-mail. No attachments; include submission in body of e-mail. Include estimated word count. Accepts 6-8 mss/issue; 24-32 mss/year. No horror or "slice-of-life" stories; no genre or mainstream science fiction or fantasy. Length: up to 2,000 words.

PAYMENT/TERMS Pays 1¢/word, $2 minimum.

TIPS "Forget formulas. Write about what you don't know, take me places I couldn't possibly go, don't try to make me care about the characters. Read short fiction by writers such as Franz Kafka, Jorge Luis Borges, Donald Barthelme, Leonora Carrington, Magnus Mills, and Stanislaw Lem. Also read our website and guidelines."

CALLALOO

A Journal of African Diaspora Arts & Letters, Texas A&M University, 249 Blocker Hall, College Station TX 77843-4212, United States. (979)458-3108. **Fax:** (979)458-3275. **E-mail:** callaloo@tamu.edu. **Website:** callaloo.tamu.edu. Estab. 1976. *Callaloo: A Journal of African Diaspora Arts & Letters*, published quarterly, is devoted to poetry dealing with the African Diaspora, including North America, Europe, Africa, Latin and Central America, South America, and the Caribbean. Features about 15-20 poems (all forms and styles) in each issue along with short fiction, interviews, literary criticism, and concise critical book reviews.

NEEDS Would like to see more experimental fiction, science fiction, and well-crafted literary fiction particularly dealing with the black middle class, immigrant communities, and/or the black South. Accepts 3-5 mss/issue; 10-20 mss/year. **Publishes 5-10 new writers/year.** Recently published work by Charles Johnson, Edwidge Danticat, Thomas Glave, Nallo Hopkinson, John Edgar Wideman, Jamaica Kincaid, Percival Everett, and Patricia Powell. Also publishes poetry. Length: up to 10,000 words excluding title page, abstract, bio, and references.

HOW TO CONTACT Submit ms via online submissions manager: callaloo.expressacademic.org/login.php. All fiction submissions are now limited to 1 manuscript per submission with a maximum of 3 submissions by a single author per calendar year.

TIPS "We look for freshness of both writing and plot, strength of characterization, plausibility of plot. Read what's being written and published, especially in journals such as *Callaloo*."

CALYX

P.O. Box B, Corvallis OR 97339. (541)753-9384. **E-mail:** info@calyxpress.org; editor@calyxpress.org. **Website:** www.calyxpress.org. **Contact:** Brenna Crotty, senior editor. Estab. 1976. *"CALYX exists to publish fine literature and art by women and is dedicated to publishing the work of all women, including women of color, older women, working-class women and other voices that need to be heard. We are committed to discovering and nurturing developing writers."*

🗨 Annual open submission (poetry and prose) period is October 1 - December 31.

➕ois Cranston Memorial Poetry Prize ($300 cash prize) is open March 1 - June 30.

🗨argarita Donnelly Prize for Prose Writing ($500 cash prize) is open July 1 - September 30.

NEEDS Length: no more than 5,000 words.

HOW TO CONTACT All submissions should include author's name on each page and be accompanied by a brief (50-word or less) biographical statement, phone number, and e-mail address. Submit using online submissions manager.

PAYMENT/TERMS Pays in contributor's copies and one-volume subscription.

TIPS "A forum for women's creative work—including work by women of color, lesbian and queer women, young women, old women—*CALYX* breaks new ground. Each issue is packed with new poetry, short stories, full-color artwork, photography, essays, and reviews."

🔄🖲 THE CAPILANO REVIEW

102-281 Industrial Ave., Vancouver BC V6A 2P2, Canada. **E-mail:** contact@thecapilanoreview.ca. **E-mail:** online through submittable. **Website:** www.thecapilanoreview.com. **Contact:** Matea Kulic, managing editor. Estab. 1972. Triannual visual and literary arts magazine that "publishes only what the editors consider to be the very best fiction, poetry, drama, or visual art being produced. *TCR* editors are interested in fresh, original work that stimulates and challenges readers. Over the years, the magazine has developed a reputation for pushing beyond the boundaries of traditional art and writing. We are interested in work that is new in concept and in execution. We no longer accept submissions by mail. Please review our submission guidelines on our website and submit online through submittable."

NEEDS No traditional, conventional fiction. Wants to see more innovative, genre-blurring work. Length: up to 5,000 words.

PAYMENT/TERMS Pays $50-150.

O THE CARIBBEAN WRITER

University of the Virgin Islands, RR 1, P.O. Box 10,000, Kingshill, St. Croix USVI 00850. (340)692-4152. **E-mail:** info@thecaribbeanwriter.org. **Website:** www.thecaribbeanwriter.org. **Contact:** Alscess Lewis-Brown, editor in chief. Estab. 1986. *The Caribbean Writer* features new and exciting voices from the region and beyond that explore the diverse and multiethnic culture in poetry, short fiction, personal essays, creative nonfiction, and plays. Social, cultural, economic, and sometimes controversial issues are also explored, employing a wide array of literary devices.

O Poetry published in *The Caribbean Writer* has appeared in *The Pushcart Prize*. *The Caribbean Writer* is 300+ pages, digest-sized, handsomely printed on heavy stock, perfect-bound, with glossy card cover. Press run is 1,200.

NEEDS Submit complete ms through online submissions manager. Name, address, phone number, e-mail address, and title of ms should appear in cover letter along with brief bio. Title only on ms. All submissions are eligible for the Virgin Islands Daily News Prize ($500) for a fiction or nonfiction essay to an author residing in the U.S. or British Virgin Islands, the David Hough Literary Prize to a Caribbean author ($500), the Canute A. Brodhurst Prize for Fiction ($400), the Cecile Dejongh Literary Prize to an author whose work best expresses the spirit of the Caribbean ($500), and the Marvin Williams Literary Prize for first-time publication in the Caribbean ($500). Length: up to 3,500 words or 10 pages.

PAYMENT/TERMS Pays 1 contributor's copy.

THE CAROLINA QUARTERLY

CB #3520 Greenlaw Hall, University of North Carolina, Chapel Hill NC 27599-3520. (919)408-7786. **E-mail:** carolina.quarterly@gmail.com. **Website:** www.thecarolinaquarterly.com; thecarolinaquarterly.submittable.com/submit. **Contact:** Sarah George-Waterfield, editor-in-chief; Travis Alexander, nonfiction editor; Laura Broom, fiction editor; Calvin Olsen, poetry editor. Estab. 1948. *The Carolina Quarterly*, published 2 times/year, prints fiction, poetry, reviews, nonfiction, and visual art. No specifications regarding form, length, subject matter, or style. Considers translations of work originally written in languages other than English. *The Carolina Quarterly* is about 100 pages, digest-sized, professionally printed, perfect-bound, with glossy cover; includes ads. Press run is 1,000. Accepts submissions September through May.

NEEDS Length: up to 7,500 words.

HOW TO CONTACT Submit 1 complete ms via online submissions manager or postal mail (address submissions to Fiction Editor).

CAVEAT LECTOR

400 Hyde St., #606, San Francisco CA 94109. **E-mail:** caveatlectormagazine@gmail.com. **Website:** www.caveat-lector.org. **Contact:** Christopher Bernard, co-editor. Estab. 1989. *Caveat Lector*, published 2 times/year, is devoted to the arts and cultural and philosophical commentary. As well as literary work, it publishes art, photography, music, streaming audio of selected literary pieces, and short films. "Don't let those examples limit your submissions. Send what you feel is your strongest work, in any style and on any subject." All submissions should be sent with a brief bio and SASE, or submitted electronically at caveatlectormagazine@gmail.com. (Poetry submissions are only accepted through postal mail.) Reads poetry submissions February 1-June 30; reads all other submissions year round.

NEEDS Accepts prose submissions (short stories, excerpts from longer works) throughout the year. Submit complete ms, preferably by e-mail. Interested in authors who have a distinct, engaging voice, regardless of subject or genre.

PAYMENT/TERMS Pays contributor's copies.

CC&D: CHILDREN, CHURCHES & DADDIES

The Unreligious, Non-Family-Oriented Literary and Art Magazine, Scars Publications and Design, 1316 Porterfield Dr., Austin TX 78753. **E-mail:** ccandd96@

scars.tv. **Website:** scars.tv/ccd. **Contact:** Janet Kuypers. Estab. 1993. 99% of our submissions are vias email and we prefer email submissions to snail mail submissions. Our biases are works that relate to issues such as politics, sexism, society, and the like, but are definitely not limited to such. We publish good work that makes you think, that makes you feel like you've lived through a scene instead of merely reading it. If it relates to how the world fits into a person's life (political story, a day in the life, coping with issues people face), it will probably win us over faster. We have received comments from readers and other editors saying that they thought some of our stories really happened. They didn't, but it was nice to know they were so concrete, so believable that people thought they were nonfiction. Do that to our readers. Publishes every other month online and in print (though sometimes it may vary and we will publish monthly); issues sold via Amazon.com throughout the U.S., U.K., and continental Europe (online web page issues are available for free to view any time). Publishes short shorts, essays, and stories, as well as artwork. Also publishes poetry. Always comments on/critiques rejected mss if asked. Has published Patrick Fealey, Linda M. Crate, Kenneth DiMaggio, Linda Webb Aceto, Brian Looney, Joseph Hart, Fritz Hamilton, G.A. Scheinoha, Ken Dean and many more (see the writings section of http://scars.tv directly at http://scars.tv/cgi-bin/framesmain.pl?writers for a listing of writers published through Scars Publications' "cc&d" magazine and "Down in the Dirt" magazine over the years.

NEEDS Does not want religious, rhyming, or family-oriented material. Average length: 1,000 words. "Contact us if you are interested in submitting very long stories or parts of a novel. (If you are accepted, it would appear in parts in multiple issues.)"

HOW TO CONTACT Send complete ms with cover letter, or query with clips of published work. Prefers submissions by e-mail. "If you have e-mail and send us a snail-mail submission, we will accept writing only if you e-mail it to us. 99.5% of all submissions are via e-mail only, so if you do not have electronic access, there is a strong chance you will not be considered. We recommend you e-mail submissions to us, either as an attachment (TXT, RTF, DOC, or DOCX, but not PDF) or by placing it directly in the e-mail letter). Send either SASE (or IRC) for return of ms or disposable copy of ms and #10 SASE for reply only." Reviews fiction, essays, journals, editorials, short fiction.

THE CHAFFIN JOURNAL

E-mail: nancy.jensen@eku.edu. **Website:** www.english.eku.edu/chaffin_journal. **Contact:** Nancy Jensen, editor. Estab. 1998; revised and re-established in 2017. *The Chaffin Journal* is a print journal for literary fiction, poetry, and creative nonfiction, published annually through the English Department at Eastern Kentucky University. "We seek diverse and original poetry, fiction, and creative nonfiction rooted in literary tradition. We value strong voices, freshness of vision, precision in language, and a sense of urgency in the literary fiction, poetry, and creative nonfiction we publish." Online submission period: April 1-July 15. Use the Submittable link on website. No postal mail or e-mailed submissions will be considered.

NEEDS Wants literary fiction, primarily short stories. Novel excerpts that can stand alone may be considered. No children's fiction, young adult fiction, formula fiction, fanfiction, or erotica. Length: up to 6,000 words

HOW TO CONTACT Submit 1 work of fiction up to 6,000 words per reading period.

PAYMENT/TERMS Pays 1 contributor's copy.

THE CHARITON REVIEW

Truman State University Press, 100 E. Normal Ave., Kirksville MO 63501. (660)785-7336. **Fax:** (660)785-4480. **E-mail:** chariton@truman.edu. **Website:** tsup.truman.edu/product/chariton-review/. Estab. 1975. *The Chariton Review* is an international literary journal publishing the best in short fiction, essays, poetry, and translations in 2 issues each year.

NEEDS No flash fiction. Length: up to 7,000 words.

HOW TO CONTACT Submit 1 complete ms through online submissions manager. English only.

CHAUTAUQUA

Chautauqua Institution and University of North Carolina at Wilmington, Department of Creative Writing, 601 S. College Rd., Wilmington NC 28403. **E-mail:** chautauquajournal@gmail.com. **Website:** ciweb.org. **Contact:** Jill Gerard and Philip Gerard, editors. Estab. 2003. *Chautauqua*, published annually in June, prints poetry, short fiction, and creative nonfiction. The editors actively solicit writing that expresses the values of Chautauqua Institution broadly construed: a sense of inquiry into questions of personal, social, political, spiritual, and aesthetic importance, regardless of genre. Considers the work of any writer, whether or not affiliated with Chautauqua Institution. Looking for a mastery of craft, attention to vivid and accurate language, a true lyric "ear," an original and compelling vision, and strong narrative instinct. Above all, it values work that is intensely personal, yet somehow implicitly comments on larger public concerns, like work that answers every reader's most urgent question: Why are you telling me this? Reads submissions February 15-April 15 and August 15-November 15. Work published in *Chautauqua* has been included in *The Pushcart Prize* anthology; notable work in Best American Series; notable issues Best American Series.

NEEDS "*Chautauqua* short stories, self-contained novel excerpts, or flash fiction demonstrate a sound storytelling instinct, using suspense in the best sense, creating a compulsion in the reader to continue reading. Wants to engage readers' deep interest in the characters and their actions, unsettled issues of action or theme, or in some cases simple delight at the language itself. A superior story will exhibit the writer's attention to language—both in style and content—and should reveal a masterful control of diction and syntax." Length: up to 25 double-spaced pages or 7,000 words.

HOW TO CONTACT Submit through online submissions manager.

PAYMENT/TERMS Pays 2 contributor's copies.

TIPS "*Chautauqua* has added a new section, which celebrates young writers, ages 12-18. Work should be submitted by a teacher, mentor, or parent. Please confirm on the entry that the piece can be classified as a Young Voices entry. We ask that young writers consider the theme. Essays and stories should remain under 1,500 words. For poetry, please submit no more than 3 poems and/or no more than 6 pages."

CHICAGO QUARTERLY REVIEW

517 Sherman Ave., Evanston IL 60202. **E-mail:** cqr@icogitate.com. **Website:** www.chicagoquarterlyreview.com. **Contact:** S. Afzal Haider and Elizabeth McKenzie, senior editors. Estab. 1994. "The *Chicago Quarterly Review* is a nonprofit, independent literary journal publishing the finest short stories, poems, translations, and essays by both emerging and established writers. We hope to stimulate, entertain, and inspire."

○   The *Chicago Quarterly Review* is 6x9; 225 pages; illustrations; photos. Receives 250 unsolicited mss/month. Accepts 10-15 mss/issue; 20-30

mss/year. Agented fiction 5%. **Publishes 8-10 new writers/year.**

NEEDS Length: up to 5,000 words; average length: 2,500 words.

HOW TO CONTACT Submit through online submissions manager only.

PAYMENT/TERMS Pays 2 contributor's copies.

TIPS "The writer's voice ought to be clear and unique and should explain something of what it means to be human. We want well-written stories that reflect an appreciation for the rhythm and music of language, work that shows passion and commitment to the art of writing."

CHICAGO REVIEW

Taft House, 935 E. 60th St., Chicago IL 60637. **E-mail:** editors@chicagoreview.org. **Website:** chicagoreview.org. **Contact:** Gerónimo Sarmiento Cruz, managing editor. Estab. 1946. "Since 1946, *Chicago Review* has published a range of contemporary poetry, fiction, and criticism. Each year typically includes two single issues and a double issue with a special feature section."

NEEDS "We will consider work in any literary style but are typically less interested in traditional narrative approaches." Length: up to 5,000 words.

HOW TO CONTACT Submit 1 short story or up to 5 short short stories submitted in 1 file. Submit via online submissions manager. Prefers electronic submissions.

PAYMENT/TERMS Pays contributor's copies.

TIPS "We strongly recommend that authors familiarize themselves with recent issues of *Chicago Review* before submitting. Submissions that demonstrate familiarity with the journal tend to receive more attention than those that appear to be part of a carpet-bombing campaign."

CHIRON REVIEW

Chiron, Inc., 522 E. South Ave., St. John KS 67576-2212. **E-mail:** editor@chironreview.com. **Website:** www.chironreview.com. **Contact:** Michael Hathaway, publisher. Estab. 1982 as *The Kindred Spirit*. *Chiron Review*, published quarterly, presents the widest possible range of contemporary creative writing—fiction and nonfiction, traditional and off-beat—in an attractive, perfect-bound digest, including artwork and photographs. No taboos.

NEEDS Submit complete ms by mail with SASE, or by e-mail as DOC attachment. Length: up to 2,500 words.

PAYMENT/TERMS Pays 1 contributor's copy.

CIMARRON REVIEW

205 Morrill Hall, English Department, Oklahoma State University, Stillwater OK 74078. **E-mail:** cimarronreview@okstate.edu. **Website:** cimarronreview.okstate.edu. **Contact:** Toni Graham, editor and fiction editor; Lisa Lewis, poetry editor; Sarah Beth Childers, nonfiction editor. Estab. 1967. "One of the oldest quarterlies in the nation, *Cimarron Review* publishes work by writers at all stages of their careers, including Pulitzer Prize winners, writers appearing in the Best American Series and the Pushcart anthologies, and winners of national book contests. Since 1967, *Cimarron* has showcased poetry, fiction, and nonfiction with a wide-ranging aesthetic. Our editors seek the bold and the ruminative, the sensitive and the shocking, but above all they seek imagination and truth-telling, the finest stories, poems, and essays from working writers across the country and around the world."

○ *Cimarron Review* is 6.5x8.5; 110 pages. Accepts 3-5 mss/issue; 12-15 mss/year. Publishes 2-4 new writers/year. Eager to receive mss from both established and less experienced writers "who intrigue us with their unusual perspective, language, imagery, and character." Has published work by Molly Giles, Gary Fincke, David Galef, Nona Caspers, Robin Beeman, Edward J. Delaney, William Stafford, John Ashbery, Grace Schulman, Barbara Hamby, Patricia Fargnoli, Phillip Dacey, Holly Prado, and Kim Addonizio.

NEEDS "We are interested in any strong writing of a literary variety but are especially partial to fiction in the modern realist tradition and poetry that engages the reader through a distinctive voice—be it lyric, narrative, etc. When submitting fiction, please do not include a summary of your story in the cover letter. Allow the work to stand on its own." No juvenile or genre fiction. "We have no set page lengths for any genre, but we seldom publish short shorts or pieces longer than 25 pages. There are, however, exceptions to every rule. Our guiding aesthetic is the quality of the work itself."

HOW TO CONTACT Send complete ms with SASE, or submit online through submission manager; include cover letter.

PAYMENT/TERMS Pays 2 contributor's copies.

TIPS "All electronic and postal submissions should include a cover letter. Postal submissions must include a SASE. We do not accept submissions by e-mail. Please follow our guidelines as they appear on our website. In order to get a feel for the kind of work we publish, please read several issues before submitting."

⑤ THE CINCINNATI REVIEW

P.O. Box 210069, Cincinnati OH 45221-0069. **E-mail:** editors@cincinnatireview.com. **Website:** www.cincinnatireview.com. **Contact:** Michael Griffith, fiction editor; Rebecca Lindenberg, poetry editor; Kristen Iversen, literary nonfiction editor; Brant Russell, drama editor. Estab. 2003. A journal devoted to publishing the best new literary fiction, creative nonfiction, and poetry, as well as a short play, book reviews, essays, and occasional interviews.

○ *The Cincinnati Review* is 200-360 pages, digest-sized, perfect-bound, with matte paperback cover with full-color art. Press run is 1,500. Reads submissions September 1-March 1.

NEEDS Does not want genre fiction. Length: up to 40 double-spaced pages.

HOW TO CONTACT Submit complete ms via online submissions manager only.

PAYMENT/TERMS Pays $25/page.

◑ THE CLAREMONT REVIEW

1581-H Hillside Ave., Suite 101, Victoria BC V8T 2C1, Canada. **E-mail:** claremontreview@gmail.com. **Website:** www.theclaremontreview.ca. **Contact:** Ali Blythe, Editor-in-chief. Estab. 1992. The editors of *The Claremont Review* publish the best poetry, short stories, visual art and photography by youth ages 13-19, from anywhere in the English-speaking world. "We publish work in many styles that range from traditional to modern. We prefer edgy pieces that take chances, show your commitment to craft, explore real characters, and reveal authentic emotion. Read the samples in our resources or in past issues for a clearer understanding of what we accept. We strongly encourage readers to subscribe to our magazine, to read, connect with and support youth writing from all over the world."

NEEDS Only accepts submissions from writers ages 13-19. Length: up to 2,000 words.

PAYMENT/TERMS Pays $10.

TIPS "We love: Wild minds like yours..don't be afraid to try something new with form or thinking. Images, metaphor, leaps, research, specificity, images, sensory details, images. Writing that reveals YOUR artistic spirit..are you formal? Tricky? Elusive? Allusive? Quiet? Bold? Clean writing: read your piece word by word, then line by line, and fix spelling or grammatical errors. Entries that meet all our guidelines, read them."

CLOUD RODEO

E-mail: jakesyersak@gmail.com. **E-mail:** submit@cloudrodeo.org. **Website:** cloudrodeo.org. **Contact:** Jake Syersak, editor. "*Cloud Rodeo* is an irregularly published journal of the irregular. So let's get weird."

HOW TO CONTACT Submit 1 prose piece via e-mail as a DOC or PDF attachment.

○ COAL CITY REVIEW

Coal City Press, English Department, University of Kansas, Lawrence KS 66045. **Website:** coalcitypress.wordpress.com. **Contact:** Brian Daldorph, editor. *Coal City Review*, published annually, usually late in the year, publishes poetry, short stories, reviews: "the best material I can find."

NEEDS Accepts mainly mainstream fiction: "Please don't send 'experimental' work our way." Length: up to 4,000 words.

PAYMENT/TERMS Pays contributor's copies.

COLD MOUNTAIN REVIEW

Department of English, Appalachian State University, ASU Box 32052, Boone NC 28608. (828)262-7687. **E-mail:** coldmountain@appstate.edu. **Website:** www.coldmountainreview.org. **Contact:** Mark Powell, editor; Katherine Abrams, managing editor; Rachel Sasser, assistant editor. Estab. 1972. *Cold Mountain Review*, published twice/year (in spring and fall), features fiction, nonfiction, poetry, and b&w art. "Themed fall issues rotate with general spring issues, but all work is considered beneath our broad social- and eco-justice umbrella." *Cold Mountain Review* is about 130 pages, digest-sized, perfect-bound, with light cardstock cover. Reading period is August and January.

NEEDS Considers novel excerpts if the submissions is "an exemplary stand-alone piece." Length: up to 6,000 words.

HOW TO CONTACT Submit 1 piece at a time through online submissions manager or by mail.

PAYMENT/TERMS Pays contributor's copies.

THE COLLAGIST

Dzanc Books, **E-mail:** editor@thecollagist.com; poetry@thecollagist.com; bookreviews@thecollagist.com. **Website:** thecollagist.com. **Contact:** Gabriel Blackwell, editor in chief; Marielle Prince, poetry editor; Michael Jauchen, book review editor. Estab. 2009. *The Collagist* is a monthly journal published on the 15th of each month, containing short fiction, poetry, essays, book reviews, and one of more excerpts from novels forthcoming from (mostly) independent presses.

HOW TO CONTACT Submit short stories through online submissions manager.

⑤ COLORADO REVIEW

Center for Literary Publishing, Colorado State University, 9105 Campus Delivery, Fort Collins CO 80523. (970)491-5449. **E-mail:** creview@colostate.edu. **Website:** coloradoreview.colostate.edu. **Contact:** Stephanie G'Schwind, editor-in-chief and nonfiction editor; Steven Schwartz, fiction editor; Don Revell, Sasha Steensen, and Matthew Cooperman, poetry editors; Harrison Candelaria Fletcher, nonfiction editor; Dan Beachy-Quick, poetry book review editor; Jennifer Wisner Kelly, fiction and nonfiction book review editor. Estab. 1956. Literary magazine published 3 times/year. Work published in *Colorado Review* has been included in *Best American Essays*, *Best American Short Stories*, *Best American Poetry*, *Best New American Voices*, *Best Travel Writing*, *Best Food Writing*, and the *Pushcart Prize Anthology*.

NEEDS No genre fiction. Length: up to 10,000 words.

HOW TO CONTACT Send complete ms. Fiction mss are read August 1-April 30. Mss received May 1-July 31 will be returned unread. Send no more than 1 story at a time.

PAYMENT/TERMS Pays $200.

COLUMBIA

A Journal of Literature and Art, Columbia University, New York NY 10027. **E-mail:** info@columbiajournal.org. **Website:** columbiajournal.org. **Contact:** Staff rotates each year. Estab. 1977. "*Columbia: A Journal of Literature and Art* is an annual publication that features the very best in poetry, fiction, nonfiction, and art. We were founded in 1977 and continue to be one of the few national literary journals entirely edited, designed, and produced by students. You'll find that our minds are open, our interests diverse. We solicit mss from writers we love and select the most exciting finds from our virtual submission box. Above all, our commitment is to our readers—to producing a collection that informs, surprises, challenges, and inspires." ⚪ Reads submissions March 1-September 15.

NEEDS Accepts all forms of short fiction: short stories, flash fiction, prose poetry. Length: up to 5,000 words.

HOW TO CONTACT Submit complete ms via online submissions manager. Include short bio.

COMMON GROUND REVIEW

Western New England University, H-5132, Western New England University, 1215 Wilbraham Rd., Springfield MA 01119. **E-mail:** editors@cgreview.org. **Website:** cgreview.org. **Contact:** Janet Bowdan, editor. Estab. 1999. *Common Ground Review*, published twice yearly (Spring/Summer, Fall/Winter), prints poetry and 1 short nonfiction piece in the Fall issue and 1 short fiction piece in the Spring issue. Holds annual poetry contest.

NEEDS Length: up to 12 pages double-spaced.

HOW TO CONTACT Submit via online submissions manager or mail.

PAYMENT/TERMS Pays 1 contributor's copy.

TIPS "For poems, use a few good images to ground and convey ideas; take ideas further than the initial thought. Poems should be condensed and concise, free from words that do not contribute. The subject matter should be worthy of the reader's time and should appeal to a wide range of readers. Form should be an extension of content. Sometimes the editors may suggest possible revisions."

CONCEIT MAGAZINE

Perry Terrell Publishing, P.O. Box 884223, San Francisco CA 94188-4223. **E-mail:** conceitmagazine2007@yahoo.com and conceitmagazine@yahoo.com. **Website:** https://sites.google.com/site/conceitmagazine/; http://conceitmagazine.weebly.com. **Contact:** Perry Terrell, editor. Estab. 2006. "We are a literary sharing organization. Magazine publishes poetry, short stories, articles, cartoons and essays. Very few guidelines—let me see your creative work. We will decide after reading."

NEEDS List of upcoming themes available for SASE and on website. Receives 60-70 mss/month. Accepts 20-30 mss/issue; up to 640+ mss/year. Ms published 3-10 months after acceptance. Publishes 250 new

writers/year. Published Terry Lee, D. Neil Simmers, Tamara Fey Turner, William Howard, Eve J. Blohm, Barbara Hantman, David Body, Milton Kerr, Marlon Jackson, Michael Shane Love and Juanita Torrence-Thompson. Does not want profanity, porn, gruesomeness. Length: 100-4,000 words. Average length: 1,500-2,000 words. Publishes short shorts. Average length of short shorts: 50-500 words.

HOW TO CONTACT Will read and review your books. "Send review copies to Perry Terrell." Query first or send complete ms with cover letter. Accepts submissions by e-mail and snail mail. Include estimated word count, brief bio, list of publications.

PAYMENT/TERMS Pays 1 contributor's copy. Additional copies $3.00. Pay via PayPal to conceitmagazine@yahoo.com or checks and money orders payable to: PERRY TERRELL. Also accepts payment through VENMO payable to: perryterrell@perryterrell and CASH APP payable to: $epterrell. Pays writers through contests. Send SASE or check blog on websites for details.

TIPS "We are a 'literary sharing' organization. Uniqueness and creativity makes a manuscript stand out. Be brave and confident. Let me see what you created. Also, patience is ultimately required."

CONCHO RIVER REVIEW

Angelo State University, ASU Station #10894, San Angelo TX 76909. **E-mail:** ageyer@usca.edu; haleya@acu.edu; jerry.bradley@lamar.edu; roger.jackson@angelo.edu. **Website:** conchoriverreview.org. **Contact:** R. Mark Jackson, general editor and book review editor; Andrew Geyer, fiction editor; Albert Haley, nonfiction editor; Jerry Bradley, poetry editor. Estab. 1987. "*CRR* aims to provide its readers with escape, insight, laughter, and inspiration for many years to come. We urge authors to submit to the journal and readers to subscribe to our publication."

NEEDS "Editors tend to publish traditional stories with a strong sense of conflict, finely drawn characters, and crisp dialogue." Length: 1,500-5,000 words.

HOW TO CONTACT Submit only 1 ms at a time. Electronic submissions preferred. See website for appropriate section editor.

PAYMENT/TERMS Pays 1 contributor's copy.

💲 CONFRONTATION

English Department, LIU Post, Brookville NY 11548. **E-mail:** confrontationmag@gmail.com. **Website:**

www.confrontationmagazine.org. **Contact:** Jonna G. Semeiks, editor in chief; Belinda Kremer, poetry editor; Terry Kattleman, publicity director/production editor. Estab. 1968. *"Confrontation* has been in continuous publication since 1968. Our taste and our magazine is eclectic, but we always look for excellence in style, an important theme, a memorable voice. We enjoy discovering and fostering new talent. Each issue contains work by both well-established and new writers. We read August 16-April 15. Do not send mss or e-mail submissions between April 16 and August 15."

Confrontation has garnered a long list of awards and honors, including the Editor's Award for Distinguished Achievement from CLMP (given to Martin Tucker, the founding editor of the magazine) and NEA grants. Work from the magazine has appeared in numerous anthologies, including the *Pushcart Prize, Best Short Stories,* and *The O. Henry Prize Stories.* "We also publish the work of 1 visual artist per issue, selected by the editors."

NEEDS "We judge on quality of writing and thought or imagination, so we will accept genre fiction. However, it must have literary merit or must transcend or challenge genre." No "proselytizing" literature or conventional genre fiction. Length: up to 7,200 words.

HOW TO CONTACT Send complete ms.

PAYMENT/TERMS Pays $175-250; more for commissioned work.

TIPS "We look for literary merit. Keep honing your skills, and keep trying."

CONJUNCTIONS

Bard College, 21 E. 10th St., #3E, New York NY 10003. (845)758-7054. **E-mail:** conjunctions@bard.edu. **Website:** www.conjunctions.com. Estab. 1981. "We provide a forum for writers and artists whose work challenges accepted forms and modes of expression, experiments with language and thought, and is fully realized art." Unsolicited mss cannot be returned unless accompanied by SASE. Electronic and simultaneous submissions will not be considered.

TIPS "Final selection of the material is made based on the literary excellence, originality, and vision of the writing. We have maintained a consistently high editorial and production quality with the intention of attracting a large and varied audience."

CONNOTATION PRESS

Website: www.connotationpress.com. **Contact:** Ken Robidoux, publisher. *Connotation Press* accepts submissions in poetry, fiction, creative nonfiction, playwriting, screenplay, interview, book review, music review, etc. "Basically, we're looking at virtually every genre or crossover genre you can create."

NEEDS Submit 1 story of any length, a chapter or excerpt from a novel, or 1-5 flash fiction pieces through online submission manager. Include headshot and short bio.

CONTRARY

The Journal of Unpopular Discontent, Chicago IL **E-mail:** chicago@contrarymagazine.com. **Website:** www.contrarymagazine.com. **Contact:** Jeff McMahon, editor; Frances Badgett, fiction editor; Shaindel Beers, poetry editor. Estab. 2003. *Contrary* publishes fiction, poetry, and literary commentary, and prefers work that combines the virtues of all those categories. Founded at the University of Chicago, it now operates independently and not-for-profit on the South Side of Chicago. Quarterly. Member CLMP. "We like work that is not only contrary in content but contrary in its evasion of the expectations established by its genre. Our fiction defies traditional story form. For example, a story may bring us to closure without ever delivering an ending. We don't insist on the ending, but we do insist on the closure. And we value fiction as poetic as any poem."

NEEDS Receives 650 mss/month. Accepts 6 mss/issue; 24 mss/year. Publishes 14 new writers/year. Has published Sherman Alexie, Andrew Coburn, Amy Reed, Clare Kirwan, Stephanie Johnson, Laurence Davies, and Edward McWhinney. Length: up to 2,000 words. Average length: 750 words. Publishes short shorts. Average length of short shorts: 750 words.

HOW TO CONTACT Accepts submissions through website only. Include estimated word count, brief bio, list of publications.

PAYMENT/TERMS Pays $20-60.

TIPS "Beautiful writing catches our eye first. If we realize we're in the presence of unanticipated meaning, that's what clinches the deal. Also, we're not fond of expository fiction. We prefer to be seduced by beauty, profundity, and mystery than to be presented with the obvious. We look for fiction that entrances, that stays the reader's finger above the mouse button. That is, in part, why we favor microfiction, flash fiction, and short shorts. Also, we hope writers will remember that most editors are looking for very particular species of work. We try to describe our particular species in our mission statement and our submission guidelines, but those descriptions don't always convey nuance. That's why many editors urge writers to read the publication itself, in the hope that they will intuit an understanding of its particularities. If you happen to write that particular species of work we favor, your submission may find a happy home with us. If you don't, it does not necessarily reflect on your quality or your ability. It usually just means that your work has a happier home somewhere else."

THE COPPERFIELD REVIEW

A Journal for Readers and Writers of Historical Fiction, **E-mail:** copperfieldreview@gmail.com. **Website:** www.copperfieldreview.com. **Contact:** Meredith Allard, executive editor. Estab. 2000. "We are an online literary journal that publishes historical fiction, reviews, and interviews related to historical fiction. We believe that by understanding the lessons of the past through historical fiction, we can gain better insight into the nature of our society today, as well as a better understanding of ourselves."

"Remember that we are a journal for readers and writers of historical fiction. We only consider submissions that are historical in nature."

NEEDS "We will consider submissions in most fiction categories, but the setting must be historical in nature. We don't want to see anything not related to historical fiction." Receives 40 unsolicited mss/month. Publishes 80% new writers/year. Publishes short shorts. Length: 500-3,000 words.

HOW TO CONTACT Send complete ms. Name and e-mail address should appear on the first page of the submission. Accepts submissions pasted into an e-mail only. "Do not query first. Send the complete ms according to our guidelines."

PAYMENT/TERMS Pays $20.

TIPS "We wish to showcase the very best in historical fiction. Stories that use historical periods to illuminate universal truths will immediately stand out. We are thrilled to receive thoughtful work that is polished, poised, and written from the heart. Be professional, and only submit your very best work. Be certain to adhere to a publication's submission guidelines, and always treat your e-mail submissions with the same care you would use with a traditional publisher."

COPPER NICKEL

English Department, Campus Box 175, CU Denver, P.O. Box 173364, Denver CO 80217. (303)315-7358. **E-mail:** wayne.miller@ucdenver.edu. **Website:** copper-nickel.org. **Contact:** Wayne Miller, editor/managing editor; Brian Barker and Nicky Beer, poetry editors; Joanna Luloff, fiction and nonfiction editor; Teague Bohlen, fiction editor. Estab. 2002. *Copper Nickel*—the national literary journal housed at the University of Colorado Denver—was founded by poet Jake Adam York in 2002. Work published in *Copper Nickel* has appeared in *Best American Poetry*, *Best American Short Stories*, and *Pushcart Prize* anthologies. Contributors to *Copper Nickel* have received numerous honors for their work, including the National Book Critics Circle Award; the Kingsley Tufts Poetry Award; the American, California, Colorado, Minnesota, and Washington State Book Awards; the Georg Büchner Prize; the T.S. Eliot and Forward Poetry Prizes; the Anisfield-Wolf Book Award; the Whiting Writers Award; the Alice Fay Di Castagnola Award; the Lambda Literary Award; and fellowships from the National Endowment for the Arts; the MacArthur, Guggenheim, Ingram Merrill, Witter Bynner, Soros, Rona Jaffe, Bush, and Jerome Foundations; the Bunting Institute; Cave Canem; and the American Academy in Rome. Submission period: September 1 to December 15; January 15 to March 1.

HOW TO CONTACT Submit 1 story or 3 pieces of flash fiction at a time through submittable.

PAYMENT/TERMS Pays $30/printed page, 2 contributor's copies, and a one-year subscription.

CRAB CREEK REVIEW

7315 34th Ave. NW, Seattle WA 98117. **E-mail:** crabcreekreview@gmail.com. **Website:** www.crabcreekreview.org. **Contact:** Jenifer Lawrence, editor-in-chief; Laura Read, poetry editor. Estab. 1983. *Crab Creek Review* is a 100-page, perfect-bound paperback. "We are a literary journal based in the Pacific Northwest that is looking for poems, stories, and essays that pay attention to craft. We appreciate risk-taking, wild originality, and consummate craftsmanship. We publish established and emerging writers." Nominates for the Pushcart Prize. Annual *Crab Creek Review* poetry prize: $500.

NEEDS Accepts only the strongest fiction. 2,500 word maximum; prefers shorter work and flash fiction (750 word max). Has published fiction by Shann Ray, Sharma Shields, Daniel Homan, Leyna Krow. Length: 2,500 words.

HOW TO CONTACT Send complete ms.

PAYMENT/TERMS Pays 1 contributor's copy.

⊛ CRAB ORCHARD REVIEW

Southern Illinois University Carbondale, Department of English, Faner Hall 2380, Mail Code 4503, 1000 Faner Dr., Carbondale IL 62901. (618)453-6833. **Fax:** (618)453-8224. **E-mail:** jtribble@siu.edu. **Website:** www.craborchardreview.siu.edu. **Contact:** Allison Joseph, editor-in-chief and poetry editor; Carolyn Alessio, prose editor; Jon Tribble, managing editor. Estab. 1995. "We are a general-interest literary journal published twice/year. We strive to be a journal that writers admire and readers enjoy. We publish fiction, poetry, creative nonfiction, fiction translations, interviews, and reviews."

NEEDS No science fiction, romance, western, horror, gothic, or children's. Wants more novel excerpts that also stand alone. Length: up to 25 pages double-spaced.

HOW TO CONTACT Submit through online submissions manager.

PAYMENT/TERMS Pays $25/published magazine page ($100 minimum), 2 contributor's copies, and one-year subscription.

CRAZYHORSE

College of Charleston, Department of English, 66 George St., Charleston SC 29424. (843)953-4470. **E-mail:** crazyhorse@cofc.edu. **Website:** crazyhorse.cofc.edu. **Contact:** Jonathan Bohr Heinen, managing editor; Emily Rosko, poetry editor; Anthony Varallo, fiction editor; Bret Lott, nonfiction editor. Estab. 1960. "We like to print a mix of writing regardless of its form, genre, school, or politics. We're especially on the lookout for original writing that doesn't fit the categories and that engages in the work of honest communication."

◐ Reads submissions September 1-May 31.

NEEDS "We are open to all narrative styles and forms, and are always on the lookout for something we haven't seen before. Send a story we won't be able to forget." Submit 1 story through online submissions manager. Length: 2,500-8,500 words.

PAYMENT/TERMS Pays $20/page ($200 maximum) and 2 contributor's copies.

TIPS "Write to explore subjects you care about. The subject should be one in which something is at stake. Before sending, ask, 'What's reckoned with that's important for other people to read?'"

CREAM CITY REVIEW

University of Wisconsin-Milwaukee, Department of English, P.O. Box 413, Milwaukee WI 53201. E-mail: info@creamcityreview.org. **Website:** uwm.edu/creamcityreview. **Contact:** Caleb Nelson, editor-in-chief; Su Cho, managing editor. Estab. 1975. *Cream City Review* publishes "memorable and energetic fiction, poetry, and creative nonfiction. Features reviews of contemporary literature and criticism as well as author interviews and artwork. We are particularly interested in camera-ready art depicting themes appropriate to each issue."

◐ Reading periods: August 1-November 1 for fall/winter issue; January 1-April 1 for spring/summer issue.

NEEDS "No horror, formulaic, racist, sexist, pornographic, homophobic, and romance." Length: up to 20 pages.

HOW TO CONTACT Submit ms via online submissions manager.

PAYMENT/TERMS Pays one-year subscription beginning with the issue in which the author's work appears.

CREATIVE WITH WORDS PUBLICATIONS

P.O. Box 223226, Carmel CA 93922. **E-mail:** geltrich@mbay.net. **Website:** creativewithwords.tripod.com. **Contact:** Brigitta Gisella Geltrich-Ludgate, publisher and editor. Estab. 1975. *Creative with Words* publishes "poetry, prose, illustrations, photos by all ages."

NEEDS No violence or erotica, overly religious fiction, or sensationalism. Length: up to 800 words.

HOW TO CONTACT Submit complete ms by mail or e-mail. Always include SASE and legitimate address with postal submissions. Cover letter preferred.

TIPS "We offer a great variety of themes. We look for clean family-type fiction and poetry. Also, we ask the writer to look at the world from a different perspective, research the topic thoroughly, be creative, apply brevity, tell the story from a character's viewpoint, tighten dialogue, be less descriptive, proofread before submitting, and be patient. We will not publish every ms we receive. It has to be in standard English, well written, and proofread. We do not appreciate receiving mss where we have to do the proofreading and correct the grammar."

CRUCIBLE

Barton College, P.O. Box 5000, Wilson NC 27893. E-mail: crucible@barton.edu. **Website:** www.barton.edu/crucible. Estab. 1964. *Crucible*, published annually in the fall, publishes poetry and fiction as part of its Poetry and Fiction Contest run each year. Deadline for submissions is May 1.

○ *Crucible* is under 100 pages, digest-sized, professionally printed on high-quality paper, with matte card cover. Press run is 500.

NEEDS Length: up to 8,000 words.

HOW TO CONTACT Submit ms by e-mail. Do not include name on ms. Include separate bio.

PAYMENT/TERMS Pays $150 for first prize, $100 for second prize, contributor's copies.

CUMBERLAND RIVER REVIEW

Trevecca Nazarene University, Department of English, 333 Murfreesboro Rd., Nashville TN 37210. **E-mail:** crr@trevecca.edu. **Website:** crr.trevecca.edu. **Contact:** Graham Hillard, editor; Torri Frye, managing editor. *The Cumberland River Review* is a quarterly online publication of new poetry, fiction, essays, and art. The journal is produced by the department of English at Trevecca Nazarene University and welcomes submissions from both national and international writers and artists. Reading period: September through April.

NEEDS Length: up to 5,000 words.

HOW TO CONTACT Submit 1 story through online submissions manager or mail (include SASE).

CURA

A Literary Magazine of Art and Action, 441 E. Fordham Rd., English Department, Dealy 541W, Bronx NY 10548. **E-mail:** curamag@fordham.edu. **Website:** www.curamag.com. **Contact:** Sarah Gambito, editor. Estab. 2011. *CURA: A Literary Magazine of Art and Action* is a multimedia initiative based at Fordham University committed to integrating the arts and social justice. Featuring creative writing, visual art, new media, and video in response to current news, we seek to enable an artistic process that is rigorously engaged with the world at the present moment. *CURA* is taken from the Ignatian educational principle of "cura personalis," care for the whole person. On its own, the word *cura* is defined as guardianship, solicitude, and significantly, written work.

○ Reading period: October 15-March 15.

NEEDS Length: up to 6,000 words.

HOW TO CONTACT Submit complete ms through online submissions manager.

PAYMENT/TERMS Pays 1 contributor's copy.

❂ CURRENT ACCOUNTS

Current Accounts, Apt. 2D, Bradshaw Hall, Hardcastle Gardens, Bolton BL2 4NZ, United Kingdom.

E-mail: fjameshartnell@aol.com. **Website:** www.bankstreetwriters.uk. **Contact:** James Hartnell, editor. Estab. 1994. *Current Accounts*, an online publication, prints poetry, drama, fiction, and nonfiction by members of Bank Street Writers, and other contributors. E-mail submissions please. Receives about 200 poems and stories/plays per year; accepts about 5%.

NEEDS Length: up to 1,500 words, and preferably under 1,000 words for short stories. Plays should be 1 act and no longer than 4 minutes read aloud.

HOW TO CONTACT E-mail submissions only. "Stories need to be well-constructed with good believable characters, an awareness of 'show, don't tell' dialogue that is real, a plot that moves along, and an ending that is neither obvious nor ridiculously far-fetched. Too many stories are overwritten and leave nothing unexplained for the reader to work out and enjoy. All genres (within the word length) are acceptable. We don't get enough plays."

PAYMENT/TERMS Pays 1 contributor's copy.

TIPS Bank Street Writers meets once/month and offers workshops, guest speakers, and other activities. E-mail for details. "We like originality of ideas, images, and use of language. No inspirational or religious verse unless it's also good in poetic terms."

CUTTHROAT

A Journal of the Arts, P.O. Box 2414, Durango CO 81302. (970)903-7914. **E-mail:** cutthroatmag@gmail.com. **Website:** www.cutthroatmag.com. **Contact:** Pamela Uschuk, editor in chief; Beth Alvarado, fiction editor; William Luvaas, online fiction editor; William Pitt Root, poetry editor. Estab. 2005. Sponsors the Rick DeMarinis Short Fiction Prize ($1,250 first prize). See separate listing and website for more information. "We publish only high-quality fiction, creative nonfiction, and poetry. We are looking for the cutting edge, the endangered word, fiction with wit, heart, soul, and meaning." *CUTTHROAT* is a literary magazine/journal and "one separate online edition of poetry, translations, short fiction, essays, and book reviews yearly."

○ Member CLMP.

NEEDS Send review copies to Pamela Uschuk. List of upcoming themes available on website. Receives 100+ mss/month. Accepts 6 mss/issue; 10-12 mss/year. Does not read October 1-March 1 and June 1-July 15. **Publishes 5-8 new writers/year.** Published Michael Schiavone, Rusty Harris, Timothy Rien, Summer

Wood, Peter Christopher, Jamey Genna, Doug Frelke, Sally Bellerose, and Marc Levy. Publishes short shorts and book reviews. Does not want romance, horror, historical, fantasy, religious, teen, or juvenile. Length: 500-5,000 words.

HOW TO CONTACT Submit complete ms through online submissions manager (preferred) or mail (include SASE).

PAYMENT/TERMS Pays contributor copies. Additional copies: $10.

TIPS "Read our magazine, and see what types of work we've published. The piece must have heart and soul, excellence in craft. "

◷ THE DALHOUSIE REVIEW

Dalhousie University, 6420 Coburg Road, Halifax NS B3H 4R2, Canada. **E-mail:** dalhousie.review@dal.ca. **Website:** dalhousiereview.dal.ca. **Contact:** Lynne Evans, production manager. Estab. 1921. *Dalhousie Review*, published 3 times/year, is a journal of criticism publishing poetry and fiction. Considers works from both new and established writers.

◔ *Dalhousie Review* is 144 pages, digest-sized. Press run is 500.

NEEDS Length: up to 8,000 words.

HOW TO CONTACT Submit by e-mail. Writers are encouraged "to follow whatever canons of usage might govern the particular work in question and to be inventive with language, ideas, and form."

PAYMENT/TERMS Pays 2 contributor's copies.

DARGONZINE

E-mail: dargon@dargonzine.org. **Website:** dargonzine.org. **Contact:** Jon Evans, editor. "*DargonZine* is an e-zine that prints original fantasy fiction by aspiring fantasy writers. The Dargon Project is a shared world anthology whose goal is to provide a way for aspiring fantasy writers to meet and improve their writing skills through mutual contact and collaboration as well as through contact with a live readership via the Internet. Our goal is to write fantasy fiction that is mature, emotionally compelling, and professional. Membership in the Dargon Project is a requirement for publication."

◔ Publishes 1-3 new writers/year.

NEEDS Must be a member of the Dargon Project to submit fiction for publication. See website for details and guidelines.

PAYMENT/TERMS "As a strictly noncommercial magazine, our writers' only compensation is their growth and membership in a lively writing community."

TIPS "The Readers and Writers FAQs on our website provide much more detailed information about our mission, writing philosophy, and the value of writing for *DargonZine*."

⑤ THE DARK

Prime Books, P.O. Box 1152, Germantown MD 20875. **E-mail:** thedarkmagazine@gmail.com. **Website:** www.thedarkmagazine.com. **Contact:** Silvia Moreno-Garcia and Sean Wallace, editors. Estab. 2013.

NEEDS "Don't be afraid to experiment or to deviate from the ordinary; be different—try us with fiction that may fall out of 'regular' categories. However, it is also important to understand that despite the name, *The Dark* is not a market for graphic, violent horror." Length: 2,000-6,000 words.

HOW TO CONTACT Send complete ms by e-mail attached in Microsoft Word DOC only. No multiple submissions.

PAYMENT/TERMS Pays 6¢/word.

TIPS "All fiction must have a dark, surreal, fantastical bend to it. It should be out of the ordinary and/or experimental. Can also be contemporary."

THE DEAD MULE SCHOOL OF SOUTHERN LITERATURE

The Dead Mule Literary Journal, NC 27889. **E-mail:** deadmule@gmail.com. **Website:** www.deadmule.com. **Contact:** Valerie MacEwan, publisher and editor. Estab. 1996. The *Mule* sponsors flash fiction contests with no entry fees. See the site for specifics. Chapbooks published by invitation, also short fiction compilations. "No good southern fiction is complete without a dead mule." *The Dead Mule* is one of the oldest, if not *the* oldest, continuously published online literary journals alive today. Publisher and editor Valerie MacEwan welcomes submissions. *The Dead Mule School of Southern Literature* wants flash fiction, visual poetry, essays, and creative nonfiction. Twenty-three Years Online, 1996-2019. Celebrate With a Dead Mule. 2019 means 23 years online—that's a century in cyber-time. "*The Dead Mule School of Southern Literature* Institutional Alumni Association recruits year round. We love reading what you wrote."

NEEDS "We welcome the ingenue and the established writer. It's mostly about you entertaining us and capturing our interest. Everyone is South of Somewhere; go ahead, check us out." No soft porn, no erotica, no ethnic slurs and all that the term implies. The Dead Mule is read in high schools, writers are encouraged to consider the audience when they submit. 2,500 word limit, but we're flexible. We love short fiction, 750 words or less.

HOW TO CONTACT All submissions must be accompanied by a "southern legitimacy statement," details of which can be seen within each page on *The Dead Mule* and within the submishmash entrypage.

PAYMENT/TERMS Pays sporadically "whenever CafePress/*Dead Mule* sales reach an agreeable amount."

TIPS "Read the site to get a feel for what we're looking to publish. Read the guidelines. We look forward to hearing from you. We are nothing if not for our writers. *The Dead Mule* strives to deliver quality writing in every issue. It is in this way that we pay tribute to our authors. Send us something original."

⑤ DECEMBER

A Literary Legacy Since 1958, December Publishing, P.O. Box 16130, St. Louis MO 63105-0830. (314)301-9980. **E-mail:** editor@decembermag.org. **Website:** decembermag.org. **Contact:** Gianna Jacobson, editor; Jennifer Goldring, managing editor. Estab. 1958. Committed to distributing the work of emerging writers and artists, and celebrating more seasoned voices through a semiannual nonprofit literary magazine featuring fiction, poetry, creative nonfiction, and visual art.

NEEDS Does not want genre fiction. Length: up to 10,000 words.

HOW TO CONTACT Send complete ms.

PAYMENT/TERMS Pays $10/page (minimum $40; maximum $200).

⑤ DELAWARE BEACH LIFE

Endeavours LLC, P.O. Box 417, Rehoboth Beach DE 19971. (302)227-9499. **E-mail:** info@delaware-beachlife.com. **Website:** www.delawarebeachlife.com. **Contact:** Terry Plowman, publisher/editor. Estab. 2002. "*Delaware Beach Life* focuses on coastal Delaware: Fenwick to Lewes. You can go slightly inland as long as there's water and a natural connection to the coast, e.g., Angola or Long Neck."

○ "*Delaware Beach Life* is the only full-color glossy magazine focused on coastal Delaware's culture and lifestyle. Created by a team of the best freelance writers, the magazine takes a deeper look at the wealth of topics that interest coastal residents. *Delaware Beach Life* features such top-notch writing and photography that it inspires 95% of its readers to save it as a 'coffee-table' magazine."

NEEDS Does not want anything not coastal. Length: 1,000-2,000 words.

HOW TO CONTACT Query with published clips.

①⊙ DESCANT

Fort Worth's Journal of Poetry and Fiction, TCU Department of English, Box 297270, Ft. Worth TX 76129. **E-mail:** descant@tcu.edu. **Website:** www.descant.tcu.edu. **Contact:** Matthew Pitt, editor in chief and fiction editor; Alex Lemon, poetry editor. Estab. 1956. "*descant* seeks high-quality poems and stories in both traditional and innovative form."

○ Member CLMP. Magazine: 6x9; 120-150 pages; acid-free paper; paper cover. Reading period: September 1-April 1. Offers 4 annual cash awards for work already accepted for publication in the journal: The $500 Frank O'Connor Award for the best story in an issue, the $250 Gary Wilson Award for an outstanding story in an issue, the $500 Betsy Colquitt Award for the best poem in an issue, and the $250 Baskerville Publishers Award for outstanding poem in an issue. Several stories first published by *descant* have appeared in *Best American Short Stories*.

NEEDS Receives 20-30 unsolicited mss/month. Accepts 3-5 mss/year. Publishes ms 1 year after acceptance. Publishes 50% new writers/year. Recently published work by William Harrison, Annette Sanford, Miller Williams, Patricia Chao, Vonesca Stroud, and Walt McDonald. No horror, romance, fantasy, erotica. Length: up to 5,000 words.

HOW TO CONTACT Send complete ms through online submissions manager or mail.

PAYMENT/TERMS Pays 2 contributor's copies; additional copies $6.

TIPS "We look for character and quality of prose. Send your best short work."

DEVIL'S LAKE

600 N. Park St., Suite 6195, Madison WI 53706. **E-mail:** devilslake.editor@gmail.com. **Website:** english.wisc.edu/devilslake.

NEEDS Length: up to 4,500 words.

HOW TO CONTACT Submit complete ms through online submissions manager.

DIAGRAM

Department of English, University of Arizona, P.O. Box 210067, ML 445, Tucson AZ 85721-0067. **E-mail:** editor@thediagram.com. **Website:** www.thediagram.

com. **Contact:** Ander Monson, editor; T. Fleischmann and Nicole Walker, nonfiction editors; Sarah Blackman and Thomas Mira y Lopez, fiction editors; Heidi Gotz, Rafael Gonzalez, and Katie Jean Shinkle, poetry editors. Estab. 2000. "*DIAGRAM* is an electronic journal of text and art, found and created. We're interested in representations, naming, indicating, schematics, labeling and taxonomy of things; in poems that masquerade as stories; in stories that disguise themselves as indices or obituaries. We specialize in work that pushes the boundaries of traditional genre or work that is in some way schematic. We do publish traditional fiction and poetry, too, but hybrid forms (short stories, prose poems, indexes, tables of contents, etc.) are particularly welcome! We also publish diagrams and schematics (original and found)." Publishes 15 new writers/year. Bimonthly. Member CLMP. "We cosponsor a yearly chapbook contest for prose, poetry, or hybrid work with New Michigan Press with a Spring deadline. Guidelines on website."

NEEDS Receives 200 unsolicited mss/month. Accepts 3-4 mss/issue; 20 mss/year. "We don't publish genre fiction unless it's exceptional and transcends the genre boundaries." Length: open.

HOW TO CONTACT Send complete ms. Accepts submissions by online submissions manager; no e-mail. If sending by snail mail, send SASE for return of the ms or send disposable copy of the ms and #10 SASE for reply only.

TIPS "Submit interesting text, images, sound, and new media. We value the insides of things, vivisection, urgency, risk, elegance, flamboyance, work that moves us, language that does something new, or does something old—well. We like iteration and reiteration. Ruins and ghosts. Mechanical, moving parts, balloons, and frenzy. We want art and writing that demonstrates interaction; the processes of things; how functions are accomplished; how things become or expire, move or stand. We'll consider anything."

THE DOS PASSOS REVIEW

Briery Creek Press, Longwood University, Department of English and Modern Languages, 201 High St., Farmville VA 23909. **E-mail:** brierycreek@gmail.com. **E-mail:** dospassosreview@gmail.com. **Website:** brierycreekpress.wordpress.com/the-dos-passos-review. **Contact:** Managing Editor. "We are looking for writing that demonstrates characteristics found in the work of John Dos Passos, such as an intense and original

exploration of specifically American themes, an innovative quality, and a range of literary forms, especially in the genres of fiction and creative nonfiction. We are not interested in genre fiction or prose that is experiment for the sake of experiment. We are also not interested in nonfiction that is scholarly or critical in nature. Send us your best unpublished literary prose or poetry."

○ Reading periods: April 1-July 31 for Fall issue; February 1-May 31 for Spring issue.

NEEDS No genre fiction. Length: up to 3,000 words for short stories; up to 1,000 for flash fiction.

HOW TO CONTACT Submit 1 short story or 3 flash fiction pieces by e-mail as attachment. Include cover letter and brief bio.

PAYMENT/TERMS Pays 2 contributor's copies.

DOWN IN THE DIRT

E-mail: dirt@scars.tv. **Website:** www.scars.tv/dirt. **Contact:** Janet Kuypers, editor. Estab. 2000. 99% of our submissions are vias email and we prefer email submissions to snail mail submissions. *Down in the Dirt*, published every other month online and in print issues sold via Amazon.com throughout the U.S., U.K., and continental Europe, prints "good work that makes you think, that makes you feel like you've lived through a scene instead of merely read it." Also considers poems. *Down in the Dirt* is published "electronically as well as in print, either as printed magazines sold through our printer over the Internet, on the Web, or sold through our printer. And for prose, because we get so much of it, all we can suggest is, the shorter the better." Has published work by Mel Waldman, Ken Dean, Jon Brunette, John Ragusa, and Liam Spencer.

NEEDS No religious, rhyming, or family-oriented material. Average length: 1,000 words. "Contact us if you are interested in submitting very long stories or parts of a novel (if accepted, it would appear in parts in multiple issues)."

HOW TO CONTACT Query editor with e-mail submission. "99.5% of all submissions are via e-mail only, so if you do not have electronic access, there is a strong chance you will not be considered. We recommend you e-mail submissions to us, either as an attachment (TXT, RTF, DOC, or DOCX files, but not PDF) or by placing it directly in the e-mail letter. For samples of what we've printed in the past, visit our website."

DOWNSTATE STORY

1825 Maple Ridge, Peoria IL 61614. (309)688-1409. **E-mail:** ehopkins7@prodigy.net. **Website:** www.downstatestory.com; www.wiu.edu/users/mfgeh/dss. Estab. 1992.

NEEDS Does not want porn. Length: 300-2,000 words.

HOW TO CONTACT Submit complete ms with cover letter and SASE via postal mail.

TIPS "We want more political fiction. We also publish short shorts and literary essays."

DRAMATICS MAGAZINE

Educational Theatre Association, 2343 Auburn Ave., Cincinnati OH 45219. (513)421-3900. **E-mail:** gbossler@schooltheatre.org. **Website:** schooltheatre. org. **Contact:** Gregory Bossler, editor-in-chief. Estab. 1929. *Dramatics* is for students (mainly high school age) and teachers of theater. The magazine wants student readers to grow as theater artists and become a more discerning and appreciative audience. Material is directed to both theater students and their teachers, with strong student slant. Tries to portray the theater community in all its diversity.

NEEDS Young adults: drama (one-act and full-length plays). "We prefer unpublished scripts that have been produced at least once." Does not want to see plays that show no understanding of the conventions of the theater. No plays for children, no Christmas or didactic "message" plays. Length: 10 minutes to full length.

HOW TO CONTACT Submit complete ms. Buys 5-9 plays/year. Emerging playwrights have better chances with résumé of credits.

PAYMENT/TERMS Pays $100-500 for plays.

TIPS "Obtain our writer's guidelines and look at recent back issues. The best way to break in is to know our audience—drama students, teachers, and others interested in theater—and write for them. Writers who have some practical experience in theater, especially in technical areas, have an advantage, but we'll work with anybody who has a good idea. Some freelancers have become regular contributors."

DUCTS

P.O. Box 3203, Grand Central Station, New York NY 10163. **E-mail:** vents@ducts.org. **Website:** www.ducts. org. **Contact:** Mary Cool, editor in chief; Tim Tomlinson, fiction editor; Lisa Kirchner, memoir editor; Amy Lemmon, poetry editor; Jacqueline Bishop, art editor. Estab. 1999. *Ducts* is a semiannual webzine of personal stories, fiction, essays, memoirs, poetry, humor, profiles, reviews, and art. "*Ducts* was founded in 1999 with the intent of giving emerging writers a venue to regularly publish their compelling, personal stories. The site has been expanded to include art and creative works of all genres. We believe that these genres must and do overlap. *Ducts* publishes the best, most compelling stories, and we hope to attract readers who are drawn to work that rises above."

NEEDS No novel excerpts.

HOW TO CONTACT Submit by e-mail to julie@ ducts.org.

PAYMENT/TERMS Pays $20.

TIPS "We prefer writing that tells a compelling story with a strong narrative drive."

ECLECTICA MAGAZINE

E-mail: editors@eclectica.org. **Website:** www.eclectica.org. **Contact:** Tom Dooley, managing editor. Estab. 1996. "*Eclectica* is a sterling-quality quarterly electronic literary magazine on the World Wide Web, not bound by formula or genre, harnessing technology to further the reading experience without distracting from its dynamic, global content. Founded in 1996, *Eclectica* has been devoted to showcasing the best writing on the Web regardless of genre for over two decades, and it remains one of a handful of still active publications from the earliest days of the Internet. 'Literary' and 'genre' work appear side-by-side in each issue, along with pieces blurring the distinctions between such categories. Pushcart Prize, National Poetry Series, and Pulitzer Prize winners, as well as Nebula Award nominees, have shared issues with previously unpublished authors. On the fiction front, *Eclectica* has been recognized for more Million Writers Award notable and top ten stories than any other site." Submission deadlines: December 1 for January/February issue, March 1 for April/May issue, June 1 for July/August issue, September 1 for October/November issue.

NEEDS Needs "high-quality work in any genre." Accepts short stories and novellas. Length: up to 20,000 words for short fiction; longer novella-length pieces accepted.

HOW TO CONTACT Submit via online submissions manager.

TIPS "We pride ourselves on giving everyone (high schoolers, convicts, movie executives, etc.) an equal shot at publication, based solely on the quality of their work. Because we like eclecticism, we tend to favor the varied perspectives that often characterize the work of international authors, people of color, women, alternative lifestylists—but others who don't fit into these categories often surprise us."

ECOTONE, REIMAGINING PLACE

University of North Carolina Wilmington, Department of Creative Writing, 601 S. College Rd., Wilmington NC 28403. **E-mail:** info@ecotonejournal.com. **Website:** www.ecotonemagazine.org. **Contact:** Anna Lena Phillips Bell, editor. Estab. 2005. "*Ecotone*'s mission is to publish and promote the best place-based work being written today. Founded at the University of North Carolina Wilmington in 2005, the award-winning magazine features writing and art that reimagine place, and our authors interpret this charge expansively. An ecotone is a transition zone between two adjacent ecological communities, containing the characteristic species of each. It is therefore a place of danger or opportunity, a testing ground. The magazine explores the ecotones between landscapes, literary genres, scientific and artistic disciplines, modes of thought. Semiannual.

○ Literary magazine/journal: 6x9. For 2019–20, our windows are August 26–September 1, 2019, and January 26–February 1, 2020. *Ecotone* charges a small fee for electronic submissions. If you are unable to pay this fee, please submit by postal mail.

NEEDS Has published Kevin Brockmeier, Michael Branch, Brock Clarke, Daniel Orozco, Steve Almond, and Pattiann Rogers. Does not want genre (fantasy, horror, science fiction, etc.) or young adult fiction. Length: up to 30 pages. "We are now considering shorter prose works (under 2,500 words) as well."

HOW TO CONTACT Submit via online submissions manager or postal mail with SASE. Include brief cover letter, listing both the title of the piece and the word count. Do not include identifying information on or within the ms itself. Also publishes literary essays, poetry.

⑤ ELLIPSIS

Westminster College, 1840 S. 1300 E., Salt Lake City UT 84105. (801)832-2321. **E-mail:** ellipsis@westminstercollege.edu. **Website:** ellipsis.westminstercollege.edu. Estab. 1965. *Ellipsis*, published annually in April, needs good literary poetry, fiction, essays, plays, and visual art.

○ Reads submissions August 1-November 1. Staff changes each year; check website for an updated list of editors. *Ellipsis* is 120 pages, digest-sized, perfect-bound, with color cover. Accepts about 5% of submissions received. Press run is 2,000; most distributed free through college.

NEEDS Length: up to 6,000 words.

HOW TO CONTACT Submit complete ms via online submissions manager. Include cover letter.

PAYMENT/TERMS Pays $50 and 2 contributor's copies.

EPOCH

251 Goldwin Smith Hall, Cornell University, Ithaca NY 14853-3201. (607)255-3385. **Website:** www.epoch.cornell.edu. **Contact:** Michael Koch, editor; Heidi E. Marschner, managing editor. Estab. 1947. Looking for well-written literary fiction, poetry, personal essays. Newcomers welcome. Open to mainstream and avant-garde writing.

○ Magazine: 6×9; 128 pages; good quality paper; good cover stock. Receives 500 unsolicited mss/month. Accepts 15-20 mss/issue. Reads unsolicited submissions September 15-April 15. Publishes 3-4 new writers/year. Has published work by Antonya Nelson, Doris Betts, Heidi Jon Schmidt.

NEEDS No genre fiction. Would like to see more Southern fiction (Southern U.S.).

HOW TO CONTACT Send complete ms. Considers fiction in all forms, short short to novella length.

PAYMENT/TERMS Pay varies; pays up to $150/unsolicited piece.

TIPS "Tell your story, speak your poem, straight from the heart. We are attracted to language and to good writing, but we are most interested in what the good writing leads us to, or where."

EVANSVILLE REVIEW

University of Evansville Creative Writing Department, 1800 Lincoln Ave., Evansville IN 47722. (812)488-1042. **E-mail:** evansvillereview@evansville.edu. **Website:** https://theevansvillereview.submittable.com/submit. **Contact:** Amanda Alexander, editor in chief; Sari Baum, editor in chief; Brittney Kaleri, nonfiction editor; William Capella, fiction editor; Beth Brunmeier, poetry editor. Estab. 1990. "*The Evansville Review* is an annual literary journal published at the University of Evansville. Our award-winning journal includes poetry, fiction, nonfiction, plays, and interviews by a wide range of authors, from emerging writers to Nobel Prize recipients. Past issues have included work by Joyce Carol Oates, Arthur Miller, John Updike, Joseph Brodsky, Elia Kazan, Edward Albee, Willis Barnstone, Shirley Ann Grau, and X.J. Kennedy."

O   Reading period: September 1-October 31.

NEEDS "We are open to a wide range of styles, though our aim is always the highest literary quality. Hit us with your best language, your most compelling characters. Make us remember your story." Does not want erotica, fantasy, experimental, or children's fiction. Submit up to 3 pieces of flash fiction (1,000 words each) or 1 story (up to 9,000 words).

HOW TO CONTACT Submit online at theevansvillereview.submittable.com/submit.

PAYMENT/TERMS Pays contributor's copies.

EVENING STREET REVIEW

Evening Street Press, Inc., 2881 Wright St, Sacramento CA 95821. (614)937-2124. **E-mail:** editor@eveningstreetpress.com. **Website:** www.eveningstreetpress.com. **Contact:** Barbara Bergmann, managing editor. Estab. 2007. "Intended for a general audience, *Evening Street Press* is centered on Elizabeth Cady Stanton's 1848 revision of the Declaration of Independence: 'that all men and women are created equal,' with equal rights to 'life, liberty, and the pursuit of happiness.' It focuses on the realities of experience, personal and historical, from the most gritty to the most dreamlike, including awareness of the personal and social forces that block or develop the possibilities of this new culture."

HOW TO CONTACT Send complete ms. E-mail submissions preferred.

PAYMENT/TERMS Pays 1 contributor's copy.

TIPS "Does not want to see male chauvinism. Mss are read year round. See website for chapbook and book competitions."

FEMINIST STUDIES

4137 Susquehanna Hall, University of Maryland, College Park MD 20742. (301)405-7415. **Fax:** (301)405-8395. **E-mail:** info@feministstudies.org; brittany@feministstudies.org. **E-mail:** kmantilla@feministstudies.org. **Website:** www.feministstudies.org. **Contact:** Ashwini Tambe, editorial director; Karla Mantilla, managing editor. Estab. 1974. Over the years, *Feminist Studies* has been a reliable source of significant writings on issues that are important to all classes and races of women. Those familiar with the literature on women's studies are well aware of the importance and vitality of the journal and the frequency with which articles first published in *Feminist Studies* are cited and/or reprinted elsewhere. Indeed, no less than 4 anthologies have been created from articles originally published in *Feminist Studies: Clio's Consciousness Raised: New Perspectives on the History of Women*; *Sex and Class in Women's History*; *U.S. Women in Struggle: A Feminist Studies Anthology*; and *Lesbian Subjects: A Feminist Studies Reader. Feminist Studies* is committed to publishing an interdisciplinary body of feminist knowledge that sees intersections of gender with racial identity, sexual orientation, economic means, geographical location, and physical ability as the touchstone for our politics and our intellectual analysis. Whether work is drawn from the complex past or the shifting present, the articles and essays that appear in *Feminist Studies* address social and political issues that intimately and significantly affect women and men in the United States and around the world."

NEEDS "We are interested in work that addresses questions of interest to the Feminist Studies audience, particularly work that pushes past the boundaries of what has been done before." Length: up to 15 pages or 5,500 words.

HOW TO CONTACT Submit complete ms by mail and e-mail (creative@feministstudies.org). FS has published Meena Alexander, Nicole Brossard, Jayne Cortez, Toi Derricotte, Diane Glancy, Marilyn Hacker, Lyn Hejinian, June Jordan, Audre Lorde, Cherrie Moraga, Sharon Olds, Grace Paley, Ruth Stone, and Mitsuye Yamada, among others.

FICTION

Department of English, City College of New York, Convent Ave. & 138th St., New York NY 10031. **E-mail:** fictionmageditors@gmail.com. **Website:** www.fictioninc.com. **Contact:** Mark J. Mirsky, editor. Estab. 1972. "As the name implies, we publish only fiction; we are looking for the best new writing available, leaning toward the unconventional. *Fiction* has traditionally attempted to make accessible the inaccessible, to bring the experimental to a broader audience." Reading period for unsolicited mss is September 15-June 15.

O   Stories first published in *Fiction* have been selected for the *Pushcart Prize: Best of the Small Presses*, *O. Henry Prize Stories*, and *Best American Short Stories*.

NEEDS No romance, science fiction, etc. Length: reads any length, but encourages lengths under 5,000 words.

HOW TO CONTACT Submit complete ms via mail or online submissions manager.

TIPS "The guiding principle of *Fiction* has always been to go to terra incognita in the writing of the imagination and to ask that modern fiction set itself serious questions, if often in absurd and comedic voices, interrogating the nature of the real and the fantastic. It represents no particular school of fiction, except the innovative. Its pages have often been a harbor for writers at odds with each other. As a result of its willingness to publish the difficult, experimental, and unusual, while not excluding the well known, *Fiction* has a unique reputation in the U.S. and abroad as a journal of future directions."

FICTION INTERNATIONAL

San Diego State University, San Diego State University, Department of English and Comp. Lit, 5500 Campanile Dr., San Diego CA 92182-6020. **E-mail:** fictioninternational@gmail.com. **E-mail:** https://fictioninternational.submittable.com/submit. **Website:** fictioninternational.sdsu.edu. **Contact:** Harold Jaffe, editor. Estab. 1973. "*Fiction International* is the only literary journal in the United States emphasizing formal innovation and social activism. Each issue revolves around a theme and features a wide variety of fiction, nonfiction, indeterminate prose, and visuals by leading writers and artists from around the world." Has published works by William Burroughs, Clarice Lispector (Brazil), Robert Coover, Edmund White, Joyce Carol Oates, Walter Abish, and Kathy Acker.

NEEDS Each issue is themed; see website for details. No genre fiction. Length: up to 5,500 words.

HOW TO CONTACT Submit complete ms via online submissions manager.

➕ FICTION TERRIFICA

7956 Cross Creek Dr., Glen Burnie MD 21061. (443)875-4524. **E-mail:** dschaff@fictionterrifica.com. **E-mail:** subs@fictionterrifica.com. **Website:** www.fictionterrifica.com. **Contact:** Dana Schaff, managing editor. Estab. 2014. "*Fiction Terrifica* is a website/bimonthly e-zine dedicated to helping small press writers and previously unpublished writers publish their mss. We are a royalty-based publishing site. We promote writers on Facebook and Twitter, along with any works they may have currently for sale. Our only requirement for acceptance is that the work be horror, dark fiction, science fiction, or fantasy related. We

host links to our authors works available at other sites. We also offer Kindle publishing on a royalty basis."

NEEDS Length: 1,500-15,000 words.

HOW TO CONTACT Query before submitting.

TIPS "The best advice I can give is to write a good story, article, or personal experience publishing piece and submit it. We are always looking to promote new and upcoming writers. Have your piece polished and ready for publication."

➊➍ THE FIDDLEHEAD

Campus House, 11 Garland Crt, PO Box 4400, University of New Brunswick, Fredericton NB E3B 5A3, Canada. (506)453-3501. **E-mail:** fiddlehd@unb.ca. **Website:** www.thefiddlehead.ca. **Contact:** Kathryn Taglia, managing editor or Ian LeTourneau, design & layout. Estab. 1945. *The Fiddlehead* is open to good writing in English or translations into English from all over the world and in a variety of styles, including experimental genres. Our editors are always happy to see new unsolicited works in fiction (including novel excerpts), creative nonfiction, and poetry. We also publish reviews, and occasionally other selected creative work such as excerpts from plays. Work is read on an ongoing basis; the acceptance rate is around 1-2% (we are, however, famous for our rejection notes!). We particularly welcome submissions from Indigenous writers, writers of colour, writers with disabilities, LGBTQQIA+ writers, and writers from other intersectional and under-represented communities. If you are comfortable identifying yourself as one or more of the above, please feel free to mention this in your cover letter. *The Fiddlehead*'s mandate is to publish accomplished poetry, short fiction, and Canadian literature reviews; to discover and promote new writing talent; to represent the Atlantic Canada's lively cultural and literary diversity; and to place the best of new and established Canadian writing in an international context. *The Fiddlehead* has published works from a long list of Canadian authors including Margaret Atwood, George Elliott Clarke, Kayla Czaga, Eden Robinson, Gregory Scofield, and Clea Young alongside international authors such as Jorie Graham, Jaki McCarrick, Thylias Moss, Les Murray, and Daniel Woodrell. *The Fiddlehead* also sponsors annual writing contests for creative nonfiction, poetry, and short fiction.

NEEDS A short fiction submission should be one story, double spaced. Unless a story is very, very short (under 1,000 words), please send only one story per submission. Please specify at the top of the first page the number of words in the story submitted. No fiction aimed at children or teens. Length: up to 6,000 words. Rarely publishes flash fiction.

HOW TO CONTACT Send SASE with Canadian postage for response or self-addressed envelope with cheque/money to cover postage (US or CA dollars). May request e-mail response if you do not want ms. returned. No e-mail or faxed submissions. Simultaneous submissions only if stated on cover letter; must contact immediately if accepted elsewhere. *The Fiddlehead* is now accepts online submissions via Submittable.com, please check website for details.

PAYMENT/TERMS Pays up to $60 (Canadian)/published page and 2 contributor's copies.

TIPS "If you are serious about submitting to *The Fiddlehead*, you should subscribe or read several issues to get a sense of the journal. Contact us if you would like to order sample back issues."

✪⑤ FILLING STATION

P.O. Box 22135, Bankers Hall RPO, Calgary AB T2P 4J5, Canada. **E-mail:** mgmt@fillingstation.ca. **Website:** www.fillingstation.ca. **Contact:** Kyle Flemmer, managing editor. Estab. 1993. *filling Station*, published 3 times/year, prints contemporary poetry, fiction, visual art, interviews, reviews, and articles. "We are looking for all forms of contemporary writing, but especially that which is innovative and/or experimental."

〇 *filling Station* is 60 - 80 pages, 8.5x11, perfectbound, with card cover, includes photos and artwork. Receives about 100 submissions for each issue, accepts approximately 10%. Press run is 500.

NEEDS Length: up to 10 pages (submissions at the upper end of this length spectrum will need to be of exceptional quality to be considered).

HOW TO CONTACT Submit fiction via Submittable.

PAYMENT/TERMS Pays $25 honorarium and three-issue subscription.

TIPS "*filling Station* accepts singular or simultaneous submissions of previously unpublished poetry, fiction, creative nonfiction, nonfiction, or art. We are always on the hunt for great writing!"

⑤ THE FIRST LINE

Blue Cubicle Press, LLC, P.O. Box 250382, Plano TX 75025. (214)455-4324. **E-mail:** info@thefirstline.com. **E-mail:** submission@thefirstline.com. **Website:** www.

thefirstline.com. **Contact:** Robin LaBounty, manuscript coordinator. Estab. 1999. *"The First Line* is an exercise in creativity for writers and a chance for readers to see how many different directions we can take when we start from the same place. The purpose of *The First Line* is to jump start the imagination—to help writers break through the block that is the blank page. Each issue contains short stories that stem from a common first line; it also provides a forum for discussing favorite first lines in literature."

NEEDS "We only publish stories that start with the first line provided. We are a collection of tales—of different directions writers can take when they start from the same place." "Stories that do not start with our first line." Length: 300-5,000 words.

HOW TO CONTACT Submit complete ms.

PAYMENT/TERMS Pays $25-50.

TIPS "Don't just write the first story that comes to mind after you read the sentence. If it is obvious, chances are other people are writing about the same thing. Don't try so hard. Be willing to accept criticism."

FIVE POINTS

Georgia State University, P.O. Box 3999, Atlanta GA 30302-3999. **Website:** www.fivepoints.gsu.edu. **Contact:** David Bottoms, co-editor. Estab. 1996. *Five Points*, published 3 times/year, is committed to publishing work that compels the imagination through the use of fresh and convincing language.

〇 Magazine: 6x9; 200 pages; cotton paper; glossy cover; photos. Has published Alice Hoffman, Natasha Tretheway, Pamela Painter, Billy Collins, Philip Levine, George Singleton, Hugh Sheehy, and others. All submissions received outside of our reading periods are returned unread.

NEEDS Receives 250 unsolicited mss/month. Accepts 4 mss/issue; 15-20 mss/year. Reads fiction August 15-December 1 and January 3-March 31. Publishes 1 new writer/year. Sometimes comments on rejected mss. Sponsors awards/contests. Length: up to 7,500 words.

HOW TO CONTACT Submit through online submissions manager. Include cover letter.

PAYMENT/TERMS Pays $15/page ($250 maximum), plus free subscription to magazine and 2 contributor's copies; additional copies $4.

TIPS "We place no limitations on style or content. Our only criteria is excellence. If your writing has an original voice, substance, and significance, send it to us. We will publish distinctive, intelligent writing that has something to say and says it in a way that captures and maintains our attention."

FLINT HILLS REVIEW

Department of English, Modern Languages, and Journalist, Emporia State University, 1 Kellogg Circle, Emporia KS 66801. **E-mail:** awebb@emporia.edu. **E-mail:** bluestem@emporia.edu. **Website:** www.emporia.edu/fhr. **Contact:** Amy Sage Webb and Kevin Rabas, editors. Estab. 1996. *Flint Hills Review*, published annually, is "a regionally focused journal presenting writers of national distinction alongside new authors. *FHR* seeks work informed by a strong sense of place or region, especially Kansas and the Great Plains region. We seek to provide a publishing venue for writers of the Great Plains and Kansas while also publishing authors whose work evidences a strong sense of place, writing of literary quality, and accomplished use of language and depth of character development." Magazine: 6x9; 75-200 pages; perfect-bound; 60 lb. paper; glossy cover; illustrations; photos. Has published work by Julene Bair, Elizabeth Dodd, Dennis Etzel Jr., Patricia Lawson, and Amanda Frost. Reads mss November to mid-March.

NEEDS Wants writing of literary quality with a strong sense of place. Publishes short stories and flash fiction. Include short bio (150 words or less). No religious, inspirational, children's. Length: 1-3 pages for short shorts; 7-25 pages for short stories.

HOW TO CONTACT Submit complete ms by mail or as e-mail attachment.

PAYMENT/TERMS Pays 1 contributor's copy; additional copies at discounted price.

TIPS "Submit writing that has strong imagery and voice, writing that is informed by place or region, writing of literary quality with depth of character development. Hone the language to the most literary depiction possible in the shortest space that still provides depth of development without excess length."

THE FLORIDA REVIEW

Department of English, University of Central Florida, P.O. Box 161346, Orlando FL 32816-1346. **E-mail:** flreview@ucf.edu. **Website:** floridareview.cah.ucf.edu. **Contact:** Lisa Roney, editor. Estab. 1972. "*The Florida Review* publishes exciting new work from around the world from writers both emerging and well known. We are not Florida-exclusive, though we acknowledge having a jungle mentality and a preference for grit,

and we have provided and continue to offer a home for many Florida writers."

Has published work by Gerald Vizenor, Billy Collins, Sherwin Bitsui, Kelly Clancy, Denise Duhamel, Tony Hoagland, Baron Wormser, Marcia Aldrich, and Patricia Foster. Accepts mailed submissions only if author does not have regular access to the Internet.

NEEDS No genre fiction. Length: 3-20 pages.

HOW TO CONTACT Submit complete ms via online submissions manager.

TIPS "We're looking for writers with fresh voices and original stories. We like risk. Please visit our website and/or read a back issue of our magazine to understand what we seek."

FLOYD COUNTY MOONSHINE

720 Christiansburg Pike, Floyd VA 24091. (540)745-5150. **E-mail:** floydshine@gmail.com. **Website:** www.floydcountymoonshine.com. **Contact:** Aaron Lee Moore, editor-in-chief. Estab. 2008. *Floyd County Moonshine*, published biannually, is a "literary and arts magazine in Floyd, Virginia, and the New River Valley. We accept poetry, short stories, and essays addressing all manner of themes; however, preference is given to those works of a rural or Appalachian nature. *Floyd County Moonshine* publishes a variety of homegrown Appalachian writers in addition to writers from across the country. The mission of *Floyd County Moonshine* is to publish thought-provoking, well-crafted, free-thinking, uncensored prose and poetry. Our literature explores the dark and Gothic as well as the bright and pleasant in order to give an honest portrayal of the human condition. We aspire to publish quality literature in the local color genre, specifically writing that relates to Floyd, Virginia, and the New River Valley. Floyd and local Appalachian authors are given priority consideration; however, to stay versatile we also aspire to publish some writers from all around the country in every issue. We publish both well-established and beginning writers." Wants literature addressing rural or Appalachian themes. Has published poetry by Steve Kistulentz, Louis Gallo, Ernie Wormwood, R.T. Smith, Chelsea Adams, and Justin Askins.

NEEDS "Any and all subject matter is welcome, although we gravitate toward Local Color (especially stories set in Floyd, the New River Valley, or a specific rural setting) and the Southern Gothic." Length: up to 8,000 words.

HOW TO CONTACT Accepts e-mail (preferred). Submit a Word document as attachment. Accepts previously published works and simultaneous submissions on occasion. Cover letter is unnecessary. Include brief bio. Reads submissions year round.

PAYMENT/TERMS Pays 1 contributor's copy.

FLYWAY

Journal of Writing and Environment, Department of English, 206 Ross Hall, Iowa State University, Ames IA 50011-1201. (515)294-8273. **Fax:** (515)294-6814. **E-mail:** flywayjournal@gmail.com. **Website:** www.flywayjournal.org. **Contact:** Zachary Lisabeth, managing editor. Estab. 1995. Based out of Iowa State University, *Flyway: Journal of Writing and Environment* publishes poetry, fiction, nonfiction, and visual art exploring the many complicated facets of the word environment—at once rural, urban, and suburban—and its social and political implications. Also open to all different interpretations of environment.Reading period is August 15-May 15. Has published work by Rick Bass, Jacob M. Appel, Madison Smartt Bell, Jane Smiley. Also sponsors the annual fall Notes from the Field contest in creative nonfiction, the spring Sweet Corn Prize in Fiction and Poetry contest and a themed winter contest. Details on website. "We look for stories that bring in environment as a character or central element. Does this mean we only take stories about ecology/nature/treehuggers? Nope. We want stories that wouldn't be remarkable or couldn't happen in another place than where they happen. We want writing that shows tension between character and surroundings, that shows how changes in living space affect actions and interactions in that living space. This environment could be an abandoned school, a strip mall comic bookstore, a thinning forest or a hiking trail—if it shapes the characters, affects events, and if it's of interest to us. We are open to work of all genres and subjects if it fits our aesthetic, and we are always happy to be surprised."

NEEDS Length: up to 5,000 words. Average length: 3,000 words. Also publishes short shorts of up to 1,000 words. Average length: 500 words.

HOW TO CONTACT Submit mss only via online submission manager. Receives 50-100 mss monthly. Accepts 3-5 stories per issue; up to 10 per year. Also reviews novels and short-story collections. Submit 1 short story or up to 3 short shorts.

PAYMENT/TERMS Pays one-year subscription to *Flyway.*

TIPS "For *Flyway*, there should be tension between the environment or setting of the story and the characters in it. A well-known place should appear new, even alien and strange through the eyes and actions of the characters. We want to see an active environment, too—a setting that influences actions, triggers its own events."

FOGGED CLARITY

Fogged Clarity and Nicotine Heart Press, P.O. Box 1016, Muskegon MI 49443-1016. (231)670-7033. **E-mail:** editor@foggedclarity.com; submissions@foggedclarity.com. **Website:** www.foggedclarity.com. **Contact:** Editors. Estab. 2008. "*Fogged Clarity* is an arts review that accepts submissions of poetry, fiction, nonfiction, music, visual art, and reviews of work in all mediums. We seek art that is stabbingly eloquent. Our print edition is released once every year, while new issues of our online journal come out at the beginning of every month. Artists maintain the copyrights to their work until they are monetarily compensated for said work. If your work is selected for our print edition and you consent to its publication, you will be compensated."

"By incorporating music and the visual arts and releasing a new issue monthly, *Fogged Clarity* aims to transcend the conventions of a typical literary journal. Our network is extensive, and our scope is as broad as thought itself; we are, you are, unconstrained. With that spirit in mind, *Fogged Clarity* examines the work of authors, artists, scholars, and musicians, providing a home for exceptional art and thought that warrants exposure."

NEEDS Length: up to 8,000 words.

HOW TO CONTACT Submit 1-2 complete ms by e-mail (submissions@foggedclarity.com) as attached .DOC or .DOCX file. Subject line should be formatted as: "Last Name: Medium of Submission." For example, "Evans: Fiction." Include brief cover letter, complete contact information, and a third-person bio.

TIPS "The editors appreciate artists communicating the intention of their submitted work and the influences behind it in a brief cover letter. Any artists with proposals for features or special projects should feel free to contact Ben Evans directly at editor@foggedclarity.com."

FOLIATE OAK LITERARY MAGAZINE

University of Arkansas-Monticello, Arts & Humanities, 562 University Dr., Monticello AR 71656. (870)460-1247. **E-mail:** foliateoak@gmail.com. **Website:** www.foliateoak.com. **Contact:** Diane Payne, faculty advisor. Estab. 1973. The *Foliate Oak Literary Magazine* is an online student-run magazine accepting hybrid prose, poetry, fiction, flash, creative nonfiction, and artwork. "After you receive a rejection/acceptance notice, please wait 1 month before submitting new work. **Submission Period: August 1-April 24.** We do not read submissions during summer break. If you need to contact us for anything other than submitting your work, please write to foliateoak@gmail.com." No e-mail submissions.

NEEDS Does not want pornographic, racist, or homophobic content. We avoid genre fiction. Length: 200-2,500 words.

HOW TO CONTACT Send complete ms through online submission manager. "Remember to include your brief third-person bio."

TIPS "Please submit all material via our online submission manager. Read our guidelines before submitting. We are eager to include multimedia submissions of videos, music, and collages. Submit your best work."

FOURTEEN HILLS

Department of Creative Writing, San Francisco State University, 1600 Holloway Ave., San Francisco CA 94137. **E-mail:** hills@sfsu.edu. **Website:** www.14hills.net. Estab. 1994. "*Fourteen Hills* publishes the highest-quality innovative fiction and poetry for a literary audience."

○ Annual magazine: 6x9; 200 pages; 60 lb. paper; 10-point C15 cover. Reading periods: March 1-June 1 for following year spring magazine release.

NEEDS Has published work by Susan Straight, Yiyun Li, Alice LaPlante, Terese Svoboda, Peter Rock, Stephen Dixon, and Adam Johnson. Length: up to 6,000 words or 20 pages for short stories; up to 1,000 words or 10 pages each for flash fiction.

HOW TO CONTACT Submit 1 short story or 3 flash fiction pieces via online submissions manager.

PAYMENT/TERMS Pays 2 contributor's copies and offers discount on additional copies.

TIPS "Please read an issue of *Fourteen Hills* before submitting."

THE FOURTH RIVER

Chatham University, Woodland Rd., Pittsburgh PA 15232. **E-mail:** 4thriver@gmail.com. **Website:** thefourthriver.com. Estab. 2005. *The Fourth River*, an annual publication of Chatham University's MFA in Creative Writing Programs, features literature that engages and explores the relationship between humans and their environments. Wants writings that are richly situated at the confluence of place, space, and identity, or that reflect upon or make use of landscape and place in new ways.

○ *The Fourth River* is digest-sized, perfect-bound, with full-color cover by various artists. *The Fourth River*'s contributors have been published in *Glimmer Train*, *Alaska Quarterly Review*, *The Missouri Review*, *The Best American Short Stories*, *The O. Henry Prize Stories*, and *The Best American Travel Writing*. Reading periods: November 1-January 1 (fall online issue) and July 1-September 1 (spring print issue).

NEEDS Length: up to 7,000 words.

HOW TO CONTACT Submit complete ms via online submissions manager.

○$ FREEFALL MAGAZINE

FreeFall Literary Society of Calgary, 460, 1720 29th Ave. SW, Calgary AB T2T 6T7, Canada. **E-mail:** editors@freefallmagazine.ca. **Website:** www.freefallmagazine.ca. **Contact:** Ryan Stromquist, managing editor. Estab. 1990. Magazine published triannually containing fiction, poetry, creative nonfiction, essays on writing, interviews, and reviews. "We are looking for exquisite writing with a strong narrative."

NEEDS Length: up to 4,000 words.

HOW TO CONTACT Submit via online submissions manager.

PAYMENT/TERMS Pays $10/printed page in the magazine ($100 maximum) and 1 contributor's copy.

TIPS "Our mission is to encourage the voices of new, emerging, and experienced Canadian writers and provide a platform for their quality work."

● FREEXPRESSION

Peter F Pike T/As FreeXpresSion, 44 Hambledon Circuit, Harrington Park NSW 2567, Australia. 0425-273-703. **E-mail:** editor@freexpression.com.au. **Website:** www.freexpression.com.au. **Contact:** Peter F. Pike, managing editor. Estab. 1993. *FreeXpresSion*, published monthly, contains creative writing, how-to articles, short stories, and poetry, including cinquain, haiku, etc., and bush verse. Open to all forms. "Christian themes OK. Humorous material welcome. No gratuitous sex; bad language OK. We don't want to see anything degrading." *FreeXpres-Sion* also publishes books up to 200 pages **through subsidy arrangements with authors**. Some poems published throughout the year are used in *Yearbooks* (annual anthologies). *FreeXpresSion* is 32 pages, magazine-sized, offset-printed, saddle-stapled, full color. Receives about 3,500 poems/year, accepts about 30%.

HOW TO CONTACT Submit prose via e-mail.

THE FRIEND MAGAZINE

The Church of Jesus Christ of Latter-day Saints, 50 E. North Temple St., Salt Lake City UT 84150. (801)240-2210. **Fax:** (801)240-2270. **E-mail:** friend@ldschurch. org. **Website:** www.lds.org/friend. **Contact:** Paul B. Pieper, editor; Mark W. Robison, art director. Estab. 1971. "The *Friend* is published by The Church of Jesus Christ of Latter-day Saints for boys and girls up to 3-12 years of age."

NEEDS Wants illustrated stories and "For Little Friends" stories. See guidelines online.

THE FROGMORE PAPERS

The Frogmore Press, 21 Mildmay Rd., Lewes, East Sussex BN7 1PJ, England. **E-mail:** frogmorepress@gmail. com (accepted from outside UK only). **Website:** www. frogmorepress.co.uk. **Contact:** Jeremy Page, editor. Estab. 1983. *The Frogmore Papers*, published semiannually, is a literary magazine with emphasis on new poetry, short stories and flash fiction. *The Frogmore Papers* is 42 pages, photocopied in photo-reduced typescript, saddle-stapled, with matte card cover. Accepts 2% of poetry received. Press run is 500. Reading periods: October 1-31 for March issue and April 1-30 for September issue.

NEEDS Length: up to 2,000 words.

HOW TO CONTACT Submit by e-mail or mail (email submissions only accepted from outside the UK).

PAYMENT/TERMS Pays 1 contributor's copy.

FUGUE LITERARY JOURNAL

200 Brink Hall, University of Idaho, P.O. Box 44110, Moscow ID 83844. **E-mail:** fugue@uidaho.edu. **Website:** www.fuguejournal.com. **Contact:** Alexandra Teague, faculty advisor. Estab. 1990. "Begun in 1990 by the faculty in the Department of English at University of Idaho, *Fugue* has continuously published

poetry, plays, fiction, essays, and interviews from established and emerging writers biannually. We take pride in the work we print, the writers we publish, and the presentation of each and every issue. Working in collaboration with local and national artists, our covers display some of the finest art from photography and digital art to ink drawings and oil paintings. We believe that each issue is a print and digital artifact of the deepest engagement with our culture, and we make it our personal goal that the writing we select and presentation of each issue reflect the reverence we have for art and letters." Work published in *Fugue* has won the Pushcart Prize and has been cited in *Best American Essays*. Submissions are accepted online only. Poetry, fiction, and nonfiction submissions are accepted September 1-May 1. All material received outside of this period will not be read. $3 submission fee per entry. See website for submission instructions.

HOW TO CONTACT Submit complete ms via online submissions manager. "Please send no more than 2 short shorts or 1 story at a time. Submissions in more than 1 genre should be submitted separately. All multiple submissions will be returned unread. Once you have submitted a piece to us, wait for a response on this piece before submitting again."

PAYMENT/TERMS Pays 1 contributor's copy and $15 per published piece.

TIPS "The best way, of course, to determine what we're looking for is to read the journal. As the name *Fugue* indicates, our goal is to present a wide range of literary perspectives. We like stories that satisfy us both intellectually and emotionally, with fresh language and characters so captivating that they stick with us and invite a second reading. We are also seeking creative literary criticism which illuminates a piece of literature or a specific writer by examining that writer's personal experience."

FUNNY TIMES

Funny Times, Inc., P.O. Box 18530, Cleveland Heights OH 44118. (216)371-8600. **E-mail:** info@funnytimes. com. **Website:** www.funnytimes.com. **Contact:** Ray Lesser and Susan Wolpert, publishers. Estab. 1985. "*Funny Times* is a monthly review of America's funniest cartoonists and writers. We are a unique voice in modern American humor with a progressive/peace-oriented/environmental/politically activist slant."

NEEDS Wants anything funny. Length: 600-800 words.

HOW TO CONTACT Query with published clips.

PAYMENT/TERMS Pays $50-150.

TIPS "Send us a small packet (1-3 items) of only your very funniest stuff. If this makes us laugh, we'll be glad to ask for more. We particularly welcome previously published material that has been well received elsewhere."

GARBLED TRANSMISSIONS MAGAZINE

5813 NW 20th St., Margate FL 33063. **E-mail:** jamesrobertpayne@yahoo.com. **E-mail:** editor@garbledtransmission.com. **Website:** www.garbledtransmission.com. **Contact:** James Payne, editor in chief. Estab. 2011. Daily online literary magazine featuring fiction and book, movie, and comic book reviews.

"Stories should have a dark/strange/twisted slant to them and should be original ideas, or have such a twist to them that they redefine the genre. We like authors with an original voice. That being said, we like Stephen King, Richard Matheson, Neil Gaiman, A. Lee Martinez, Chuck Palahniuk, and Clive Barker. Movies and TV shows that inspire us include "Lost," *The Matrix*, *Fight Club*, *3:10 to Yuma*, *Dark City*, *The Sixth Sense*, "X-Files," and *Super 8*."

NEEDS "No romance or corny sci-fi or fantasy. Nothing contrived or a blatant rip-off." Length: 500-15,000 words.

HOW TO CONTACT Send complete ms by e-mail with subject line "Garbled Transmissions Submission."

TIPS "The best way to see what we like is to visit our website and read some of the stories we've published to get a taste of what style we seek."

GARGOYLE

Paycock Press, 3819 13th St. N, Arlington VA 22201. (703) 380-4893. **E-mail:** rchrdpeabody9@gmail.com. **Website:** www.gargoylemagazine.com. **Contact:** Richard Peabody, editor/publisher. Estab. 1976. "*Gargoyle* has always been a scallywag magazine, a maverick magazine, a bit too academic for the underground and way too underground for the academics. We are a writer's magazine in that we are read by other writers and have never worried about reaching the masses." Annual. The submission window opens each year in August and remains open until full. Recently published works by: Jill Adams, Roberta Allen, Cathy Alter, Jacob Appel, Donna Baier Stein, Stacy Barton, C.L. Bledsoe, Caroline Bock, Jamie Brown, Grace Cavalieri, Laura Cesarco Eglin, Patrick Chapman, Juliet

Cook, Rachel Dacus, Michael Dailey, Kristina Marie Darling, William Virgil Davis, Glenn Deutsch, Andrew Gifford, Sid Gold, Suzanne Feldman, Heather Fowler, Susan Gubernat, Myronn Hardy, Abhay K. George Kalamaras, Jesse Lee Kercheval, Leonard Kress, W. F. Lantry, Lyn Lifshin, Susan Neville, Kevin O'Cuinn, Donaji Olmedo, Frances Park, Pedro Ponce, Glen Pouricau, Melissa Reddish, Aria Riding, Bruce Sager, John Saul, Marija Stajic, Liza Nash Taylor, Susan Tepper, Sally Toner, Gretchen A. Van Lente, Idea Vilarino, Jesse Waters, Kathleen Wheaton, Andrea Wyatt, Katherine E. Young, and Bonnie ZoBell.

NEEDS Wants "edgy realism or experimental works. We run both." Wants to see more Canadian, British, Australian, and Third World fiction. Receives 300 unsolicited mss/week during submission period. Accepts 20-50 mss/issue. Agented fiction 5%. **Publishes 2-3 new writers/year.** Publishes 1-2 titles/year. Format: trade paperback originals. No romance, horror, science fiction. Length: up to 5,000 words. "We have run 2 novellas in the past 40 years."

PAYMENT/TERMS Pays 1 contributor's copy and offers 50% discount on additional copies.

TIPS "We have to fall in love with a particular fiction."

A GATHERING OF THE TRIBES

P.O. Box 20693, Tompkins Square Station, New York NY 10009. (212)777-2038. **E-mail:** gatheringofthetribes@gmail.com. **Website:** www.tribes.org. **Contact:** Steve Cannon. Estab. 1992. *A Gathering of the Tribes* is a multicultural and multigenerational publication featuring poetry, fiction, interviews, essays, visual art, and musical scores. The audience is anyone interested in the arts from a diverse perspective.

Magazine: 8.5x10; 130 pages; glossy paper and cover; illustrations; photos. Receives 20 unsolicited mss/month. Publishes 40% new writers/year. Has published work by Carl Watson, Ishle Park, Wang Pang, and Hanif Kureishi.

NEEDS "Would like to see more satire/humor. We are open to all work; just no poor writing/grammar/syntax." Length: 2,500-5,000 words.

HOW TO CONTACT Send complete ms by postal mail or e-mail.

PAYMENT/TERMS Pays 1 contributor's copy.

TIPS "Make sure your work has substance."

THE GEORGIA REVIEW

The University of Georgia, Main Library, Room 706A, 320 S. Jackson St., Athens GA 30602. (706)542-3481. **Fax:** (706)542-0047. **E-mail:** garev@uga.edu. **Website:** thegeorgiareview.com. **Contact:** Stephen Corey, editor. Estab. 1947. "*The Georgia Review* is a literary quarterly committed to the art of editorial practice. We collaborate equally with established and emerging authors of essays, stories, poems, and reviews in the pursuit of extraordinary works that engage with the evolving concerns and interests of intellectually curious readers from around the world. Our aim in curating content is not only to elevate literature, publishing, and the arts, but also to help facilitate socially conscious partnerships in our surrounding communities." $3 online submission fee waived for subscribers. No fees for manuscripts submitted by post. Reading period: August 15-May 15.

NEEDS "We seek original, excellent short fiction not bound by type. Ordinarily we do not publish novel excerpts or works translated into English, and we discourage authors from submitting these."

HOW TO CONTACT Send complete ms via online submissions manager or postal mail.

PAYMENT/TERMS Pays $50/published page.

GERTRUDE

Queer Literary Journal and Book Club, 4857 NE 13th Ave., Portland OR 97211. **E-mail:** editorgertrudepress@gmail.com. **Website:** www.gertrudepress.org. **Contact:** Tammy Lynne Stoner. Estab. 1999. *Gertrude* is a "literary journal featuring the voices and visions of LGBTQA writers and artists" whose editors also make selections from the best of new and notable queer, literary novels for GERTIE - their 'quarterly, queer book club.'"

NEEDS Had published over 300 writers from 10 countries, launching many careers. romance. christian. erotica. abuse stories. Length: up to 3,000 words.

HOW TO CONTACT Submit 1-2 pieces via online submissions manager, double-spaced. Include word count for each piece in cover letter.

TIPS "We look for strong characterization and imagery, and new, unique ways of writing about universal experiences. Or anything bizarre."

THE GETTYSBURG REVIEW

Gettysburg College, Gettysburg College, 300 N. Washington St., Gettysburg PA 17325. (717)337-6770. E-mail: mdrew@gettysburg.edu. **Website:** www.gettysburgreview.com. **Contact:** Mark Drew, editor; Jess L. Bryant, managing editor. Estab. 1988. Published quarterly, *The Gettysburg Review* considers unsolicited submissions of poetry, fiction, and essays. "Our concern is quality. Mss submitted here should be extremely well written." Reading period September 1-May 31.

NEEDS Wants high-quality literary fiction. "We require that fiction be intelligent and aesthetically written." No genre fiction. Length: 2,000-7,000 words.

HOW TO CONTACT Send complete ms with SASE.

PAYMENT/TERMS Pays $25/printed page, a one-year subscription, and 1 contributor's copy.

GINOSKO LITERARY JOURNAL

Ginosko, P.O. Box 246, Fairfax CA 94978. (415)785-3160. **E-mail:** editorginosko@aol.com. **Website:** www.ginoskoliteraryjournal.com. **Contact:** Robert Paul Cesaretti, editor. Estab. 2002. *Ginosko* Flash Fiction Contest: Deadline is March 1; $5 entry fee; $250 prize. "*Ginosko* (ghin-océ-koe): To perceive, understand, realize, come to know; knowledge that has an inception, a progress, an attainment. The recognition of truth by experience." Accepting short fiction and poetry, creative nonfiction, interviews, social justice concerns, and literary insights for www.ginoskoliteraryjournal.com. Reads year round. Length of articles flexible; accepts excerpts. Publishing as semiannual e-zine. Print anthology every 2 years. Check downloadable issues on website for tone and style. Downloads free; accepts donations. Member CLMP.

NEEDS Download issue for tone and style. Length: 25-5,000 words.

HOW TO CONTACT Online submissions manager Submittable (ginosko.submittable.com/submit, see website http://GinoskoLiteraryJournal.

PAYMENT/TERMS No payment.

TIPS "Read several issues for tone and style."

GIRLS' LIFE

3 S. Frederick St., Suite 806, Baltimore MD 21202. (410)426-9600. **Fax:** (866)793-1531. **E-mail:** writeforgl@girlslife.com. **Website:** www.girlslife.com. **Contact:** Karen Bokram, founding editor and publisher; Kelsey Haywood, senior editor; Chun Kim, art director. Estab. 1994.

NEEDS "We accept short fiction. They should be stand-alone stories and are generally 2,500-3,500 words."

TIPS "Send thought-out queries with published writing samples and detailed résumé. Have fresh ideas and a voice that speaks to our audience—not down to them. And check out a copy of the magazine or visit girlslife.com before submitting."

GRASSLIMB

P.O. Box 420816, San Diego CA 92142-0816. **E-mail:** editor@grasslimb.com. **Website:** www.grasslimb.com. **Contact:** Valerie Polichar, editor. Estab. 2002. *Grasslimb* publishes literary prose, poetry, and art. Fiction is best when it is short and avant-garde or otherwise experimental.

Submit full mss—no queries. Although general topics are welcome, we're less likely to select work regarding romance, sex, aging, and children. Fiction in an experimental, avant-garde or surreal mode is often more interesting to us than a traditional story. When submitting poetry, 4-6 pieces are preferred; line count is not necessary. For artwork, please submit photocopies or electronic versions (if electronic, 600 dpi preferred) only. Prose must include a word count and should not exceed 2,500 words; 1,000-2,000 is best for us. Submissions over 3,000 words will be returned unread. Reviews of 500-1,000 words are preferred. Please do not submit work to us more often than once every six months unless you have had work accepted previously to our publication, in which case you are not subject to a limit.

NEEDS "Fiction in an experimental, avant-garde, or surreal mode is often more interesting to us than a traditional story." "Although general topics are welcome, we're less likely to select work regarding romance, sex, aging, and children." Length: up to 2,500 words; average length: 1,500 words.

HOW TO CONTACT Send complete ms via e-mail or postal mail with SASE.

PAYMENT/TERMS Pays $10-70 and 2 contributor's copies.

TIPS "We publish brief fiction work that can be read in a single sitting over a cup of coffee. Work is generally 'literary' in nature rather than mainstream. Experimental work welcome. Remember to have your work proofread and to send short work. We cannot read over 3,000 words and prefer under 2,000 words. Include word count."

GREEN HILLS LITERARY LANTERN

Truman State University, Department of English, Truman State University, Kirksville MO 63501. **E-mail:** adavis@truman.edu. **Website:** ghll.truman.edu. **Contact:** Adam Brooke Davis, prose editor/managing editor; Joe Benevento, poetry editor. Estab. 1990. *Green Hills Literary Lantern* is published annually, in June, by Truman State University. Historically, the print publication ran between 200-300 pages, consisting of poetry, fiction, reviews, and interviews. The digital magazine is of similar proportions and artistic standards. Open to the work of new writers, as well as more established writers.

NEEDS "We are interested in stories that demonstrate a strong working knowledge of the craft. Not especially interested in genre fiction, inspirational, or religious fiction—but if you've got something in those categories that goes beyond the conventions in interesting ways, send it. Otherwise, we are open to short stories of various settings, character conflict, and styles, including experimental." No word limit.

HOW TO CONTACT Submit complete ms.

GREEN MOUNTAINS REVIEW

Northern Vermont University- Johnson, 337 College Hill, Johnson VT 05656. (802)635-1350. **E-mail:** gmr@northernvermont.edu. **Website:** greenmountainsreview.com. **Contact:** Elizabeth Powell, editor; Darcie Abbene, nonfiction and managing editor; Jensen Beach, fiction editor; Didi Jackson, assistant poetry editor. Semiannual magazine covering poems, stories, and creative nonfiction by both well-known authors and promising newcomers.

The editors are open to a wide range of styles and subject matter. Open reading period: September 1-March 1.

NEEDS Recently published work by Tracy Daugherty, Terese Svoboda, Walter Wetherell, T.M. McNally, J. Robert Lennon, Louis B. Jones, and Tom Whalen. Publishes short shorts. Also publishes literary criticism, poetry. Sometimes comments on rejected mss. Length: up to 25 pages, double-spaced.

HOW TO CONTACT Submit ms via online submissions manager.

PAYMENT/TERMS Pays contributor's copies, one-year subscription, and small honorarium, depending on grants.

TIPS "We encourage you to order some of our back issues to acquaint yourself with what has been accepted in the past."

GREENPRINTS

P.O. Box 1355, Fairview NC 28730. (828)628-1902. E-mail: pat@greenprints.com. **Website:** www.greenprints.com. **Contact:** Pat Stone, managing editor. Estab. 1990. "*GreenPrints* is the 'Weeder's Digest.' We share the human—*not* how-to—side of gardening. We publish true personal gardening stories and essays: humorous, heartfelt, insightful, inspiring. We love good, true, well-told personal *stories*—all must be about gardening!"

NEEDS "We run very little fiction."

HOW TO CONTACT Submit complete ms.

PAYMENT/TERMS Pays $75-200.

TIPS Wants "a great, true, *unique* personal *story* with dialogue, a narrative, and something special that happens to make it truly stand out."

◑◔ THE GREENSBORO REVIEW

MFA Writing Program, 3302 MHRA Building, UNC-Greensboro, Greensboro NC 27402. **E-mail:** jlclark@uncg.edu. **Website:** tgronline.net. **Contact:** Jim Clark, editor. Estab. 1965. "A local lit mag with an international reputation. We've been 'old school' since 1965."

◔ Stories for *The Greensboro Review* have been included in *Best American Short Stories, The O. Henry Awards Prize Stories, New Stories from the South*and *Pushcart Prize*. Does not accept e-mail submissions.

NEEDS Length: up to 7,500 words.

HOW TO CONTACT Submit complete ms via online submission form or postal mail. Include cover letter and estimated word count.

PAYMENT/TERMS Pays contributor's copies.

TIPS "We want to see the best being written regardless of theme, subject, or style."

❺ GRIST: A JOURNAL OF THE LITERARY ARTS

English Dept., 301 McClung Tower, Univ. of Tennessee, Knoxville TN 37996-0430. **E-mail:** gristeditors@gmail.com. **Website:** www.gristjournal.com. Estab. 2007. *Grist* is a nationally distributed journal of fiction, nonfiction, poetry, interviews, and craft essays. We seek work of high literary quality from both emerging and established writers, and we welcome all styles and aesthetic approaches. Each issue is accompanied by Grist Online, which features some of the best work we receive during our reading period. In addition to general submissions, *Grist* holds the Pro-Forma Contest every spring, recognizing unpublished creative work that explores the relationship between content and form, whether in fiction, nonfiction, poetry, or a hybrid genre. Throughout the year, we publish interviews, craft essays, and reviews on our blog, The Writing Life.

NEEDS Length: 7,000 words.

HOW TO CONTACT Send complete ms.

PAYMENT/TERMS Pays 1 cent per word up to $50.

TIPS "*Grist* seeks work from both emerging and established writers, whose work is of high literary quality."

GULF STREAM MAGAZINE

English Department, FIU, Biscayne Bay Campus, 3000 NE 151 St., AC1-335, North Miami FL 33181. **E-mail:** gulfstreamlitmag@gmail.com. **Website:** www.gulfstreamlitmag.com. **Contact:** T.C. Jones, editor in chief. Estab. 1989. "*Gulf Stream Magazine* has been publishing emerging and established writers of exceptional fiction, nonfiction, and poetry since 1989. We also publish interviews and book reviews. Past contributors include Sherman Alexie, Steve Almond, Jan Beatty, Lee Martin, Robert Wrigley, Dennis Lehane, Liz Robbins, Stuart Dybek, David Kirby, Ann Hood, Ha Jin, B.H. Fairchild, Naomi Shihab Nye, F. Daniel Rzicznek, and Connie May Fowler. *Gulf Stream Magazine* is supported by the Creative Writing Program at Florida International University in Miami, Florida."

NEEDS Does not want romance, historical, juvenile, or religious work.

HOW TO CONTACT "Submit online only. Please read guidelines on website in full. Submissions that do not conform to our guidelines will be discarded. We do not accept e-mailed or mailed submissions. We read from September 1-November 1 and January 1-March 1."

PAYMENT/TERMS Pays contributor's copies.

TIPS "We look for fresh, original writing: well-plotted stories with unforgettable characters, fresh poetry, and experimental writing."

HADASSAH MAGAZINE

Hadassah, WZOA, 40 Wall St., Eighth Floor, New York NY 10005. **Fax:** (212)451-6257. **E-mail:** magazine@hadassah.org. **Website:** www.hadassahmagazine.org. **Contact:** Elizabeth Barnea. Bimonthly publication of the Hadassah Women's Zionist Organization of America. Emphasizes Jewish life, Israel. Readers are 85% females who travel and are interested in Jewish affairs, average age 59.

NEEDS Wants short stories with strong plots and positive Jewish values. Receives 20-25 unsolicited mss/month. Publishes some new writers/year. No personal memoirs, "schmaltzy" or shelter magazine fiction. Length: 1,500-2,000 words.

PAYMENT/TERMS Pays $500 minimum.

TIPS "Stories on a Jewish theme should be neither self-hating nor schmaltzy."

HAIGHT ASHBURY LITERARY JOURNAL

558 Joost Ave., San Francisco CA 94127. (415)584-8264. **E-mail:** haljeditor@gmail.com. **Website:** haightashburyliteraryjournal.wordpress.com. **Contact:** Alice Rogoff and Cesar Love, editors. Estab. 1979. *Haight Ashbury Literary Journal*, publishes well-written poetry and fiction. *HALJ*'s voices are often of people who have been marginalized, oppressed, or abused. *HALJ* strives to bring literary arts to the general public, to the San Francisco community of writers, to the Haight Ashbury neighborhood, and to people of varying ages, genders, ethnic groups, and sexual preferences. The Journal is produced as a tabloid to maintain an accessible price for low-income people.

NEEDS Submit 1-3 short stories or 1 long story. Submit only once every 6 months. No e-mail submissions (unless overseas); postal submissions only. "Put name and address on first page, and include SASE. No bio." Sometimes publishes theme issues (each issue changes its theme and emphasis).

HOW TO CONTACT Submit under 20 pages.

⑤ HANGING LOOSE

Hanging Loose Press, 231 Wyckoff St., Brooklyn NY 11217. (347)529-4738. **Fax:** (347)227-8215. **E-mail:** print225@aol.com. **Website:** www.hangingloosepress.com. **Contact:** Robert Hershon and Mark Pawlak, editors. Estab. 1966. *Hanging Loose*, published in April and October, concentrates on the work of new writers. Wants excellent, energetic poems and short stories.

💬 *Hanging Loose* is 120 pages, offset-printed on heavy stock, flat-spined, with 4-color glossy card cover.

HOW TO CONTACT Submit 1 complete ms by postal mail with SASE.

PAYMENT/TERMS Pays small fee and 2 contributor's copies.

HARVARD REVIEW

Harvard University, Lamont Library, Harvard University, Cambridge MA 02138. **E-mail:** info@harvardreview.org. **Website:** harvardreview.fas.harvard.edu. **Contact:** Christina Thompson, editor; Suzanne Berne, fiction editor; Major Jackson, poetry editor; Chloe Garcia Roberts, managing editor. Estab. 1992. Semiannual magazine covering poetry, fiction, essays, drama, graphics, and reviews in the spring and fall by an eclectic range of international writers. "Previous contributors include John Updike, Alice Hoffman, Joyce Carol Oates, Miranda July, and Jim Crace. We also publish the work of emerging and previously unpublished writers." Does not accept e-mail submissions.

NEEDS No genre fiction (romance, horror, detective, etc.). Length: up to 7,000 words.

HOW TO CONTACT Submit by online submissions manager or mail (with SASE).

TIPS "Writers at all stages of their careers are invited to apply; however, we can only publish a very small fraction of the material we receive. We recommend that you familiarize yourself with *Harvard Review* before you submit your work."

HAWAI'I PACIFIC REVIEW

1060 Bishop St., Honolulu HI 96813. **Website:** hawaiipacificreview.org. **Contact:** Tyler McMahon, editor; Christa Cushon, managing editor. Estab. 1987. "*Hawai'i Pacific Review* is the online literary magazine of Hawai'i Pacific University. It features poetry and prose by authors from Hawai'i, the mainland, and around the world. *HPR* was started as a print annual in 1987. In 2013, it began to publish exclusively online. *HPR* publishes work on a rolling basis. Poems, stories, and essays are posted 1 piece at a time, several times a month. All contents are archived on the site."

NEEDS Prefers literary work to genre work. Length: up to 4,000 words.

HOW TO CONTACT Submit 1 ms via online submissions manager.

TIPS "We look for the unusual or original plot, and prose with the texture and nuance of poetry. Character development or portrayal must be unusual/original; humanity shown in an original, insightful way (or characters); sense of humor where applicable. Be sure it's a draft that has gone through substantial changes, with supervision from a more experienced writer, if you're a beginner. Write about intense emotion and feeling, not just about someone's divorce or shaky relationship. No soap-opera-like fiction."

HAWAI'I REVIEW

University of Hawaii Board of Publications, 2445 Campus Rd., Hemenway Hall 107, Honolulu HI 96822. (808)956-3030. **Fax:** (808)956-3083. **E-mail:** hawaiireview@gmail.com. **Website:** http://hawaiireview.org/. Estab. 1973. *Hawai'i Review* is a student-run biannual literary and visual arts print journal featuring national and international writing and visual art, as well as regional literature and visual art of Hawai'i and the Pacific.

Accepts submissions online through Submittable only. Offers yearly award with $500 prizes in poetry and fiction.

NEEDS Length: up to 7,000 words for short stories, up to 2,500 words for flash fiction.

HOW TO CONTACT Send 1 short story or 2 pieces of flash fiction via online submission manager.

TIPS "Make it new."

HAYDEN'S FERRY REVIEW

Arizona State University, c/o Dept. of English,, Arizona State University, P.O. Box 871401, Tempe AZ 85287. **E-mail:** hfr@asu.edu. **Website:** haydensferryreview. com. **Contact:** Katie Berta. Estab. 1986. *"Hayden's Ferry Review* publishes the best-quality fiction, poetry, and creative nonfiction from new, emerging, and established writers." Work from *Hayden's Ferry Review* has been selected for inclusion in *Pushcart Prize* anthologies and the *Best American* series. No longer accepts postal mail or e-mail submissions (except in the case of the incarcerated and the visually impaired).

NEEDS Does not want genre fiction. Word length open, but typically does not accept submissions over 25 pages.

HOW TO CONTACT Send complete ms via online submissions manager.

PAYMENT/TERMS Pays 1 contributor's copy.

HELIOTROPE

E-mail: heliotropeditor@gmail.com. **Website:** www. heliotropemag.com. Estab. 2006. *Heliotrope* is a quarterly e-zine that publishes fiction, articles, and poetry.

NEEDS "If your story is something we can't label, we're interested in that, too." Length: up to 5,000 words.

HOW TO CONTACT Submit complete ms via e-mail.

PAYMENT/TERMS Pays 10¢/word.

THE HELIX

Central Connecticut State University, 1615 Stanley St., New Britain CT 06053. **E-mail:** helixmagazine@gmail.com. **Website:** helixmagazine.org. **Contact:** See website for current editorial staff.. "The *Helix* is a Central Connecticut State University undergraduate publication that puts out an issue every semester. The magazine features writing from CCSU students, writing from the Hartford County community, and an array of submissions from all over the world. The magazine publishes multiple genres of literature and art, including poetry, fiction, drama, nonfiction, paintings, photography, watercolor, collage, stencil, and computer-generated artwork. It is a student-run publication and is funded by the university."

NEEDS Length: up to 3,000 words.

HOW TO CONTACT Submit by online submissions manager.

TIPS "Please see our website for specific deadlines, as it changes every semester based on a variety of factors, but we typically leave the submission manager open sometime starting in the summer to around the end of October for the Fall issue, and during the winter to late February or mid-March for the Spring issue. Contributions are invited from all members of the campus community, as well as the literary community at large."

HELLOHORROR

Houston TX (512)537-0504. **E-mail:** info@hellohorror.com. **E-mail:** submissions@hellohorror.com. **Website:** www.hellohorror.com. **Contact:** Brent Armour, editor-in-chief. Estab. 2012. *"HelloHorror* is an online literary magazine. We are currently in search of literary pieces, photography, and visual art, including film from writers and artists that have a special knack for inducing goose bumps and raised hairs. This genre has become, especially in film, noticeably saturated in gore and high shock-value aspects as a crutch to avoid the true challenge of bringing about real psychological fear to an audience that's persistently more and more numb to its tactics. While we are not opposed to the extreme, blood and guts need bones and cartilage. Otherwise it's just a sloppy mess. Specifically, we are looking for pieces grounded in psychological fear induced by surreal situations unusual to horror rather than gore. We will not automatically pass on a gore-drenched story, but it needs to have its foundations in psychological horror."

NEEDS "We don't want fiction that can in no way be classified as horror. Some types of dark science fiction are acceptable, depending on the story." Length: 6-20 pages for short stories; up to 1,000 words for flash fiction.

HOW TO CONTACT Submit complete ms via e-mail.

TIPS "We like authors that show consideration for their readers. A great horror story leaves an impression on the reader long after it is finished. Consider your reader and consider yourself. What really scares you as opposed to what's stereotypically supposed to scare you? Bring us and our readers into that place of fear with you."

⑤ HIGHLIGHTS FOR CHILDREN

803 Church St., Honesdale PA 18431. (570)253-1080. **Fax:** (570)251-7847. **E-mail:** eds@highlights.com (Do not send submissions to this address.). **E-mail:** Highlights.submittable.com. **Website:** www.highlights.com. **Contact:** Christine French Cully, editor-in-chief. Estab. 1946. "This book of wholesome fun is dedicated to helping children grow in basic skills and knowledge, in creativeness, in ability to think and reason, in sensitivity to others, in high ideals, and worthy ways of living—for children are the world's most important people." We publish stories and articles for beginning and advanced readers. Up to 400 words for beginning readers, up to 750 words for advanced readers. Guidelines updated regularly at Highlights.submittable.com.

NEEDS Stories appealing to girls and boys ages 6-12. Vivid, full of action. Engaging plot, strong characterization, lively language. Prefers stories in which a child protagonist solves a dilemma through his or her own resources. No stories glorifying war, crime or violence. Up to 475 words for beginning readers. Up to 750 words for advanced readers.

HOW TO CONTACT See Highlights.submittable.com.

PAYMENT/TERMS Pays $175 and up.

TIPS "We update our guidelines and current needs regularly at Highlights.submittable.com. Read several recent issues of the magazine before submitting. In addition to fiction, nonfiction, and poetry, we purchase crafts, puzzles, and activities that will stimulate children mentally and creatively. We judge each submission on its own merits. Expert reviews and complete bibliography are required for nonfiction. Include special qualifications, if any, of author. Speak to today's kids. Avoid didactic, overt messages. Even though our general principles haven't changed over the years, we are contemporary in our approach to issues."

ALFRED HITCHCOCK'S MYSTERY MAGAZINE

Dell Magazines, 44 Wall St., Suite 904, New York NY 10005. **E-mail:** alfredhitchcockmm@dellmagazines.com. **Website:** www.themysteryplace.com/ahmm. Estab. 1956.

NEEDS Wants "original and well-written mystery and crime fiction. Because this is a mystery magazine, the stories we buy must fall into that genre in some sense or another. We are interested in nearly every kind of mystery: stories of detection of the classic kind, police procedurals, private eye tales, suspense, courtroom dramas, stories of espionage, and so on. We ask only that the story be about crime (or the threat or fear of one). We sometimes accept ghost stories or supernatural tales, but those also should involve a crime." No sensationalism. Length: up to 12,000 words.

HOW TO CONTACT Send complete ms.

PAYMENT/TERMS Payment varies.

TIPS "No simultaneous submissions, please. Submissions sent to *Alfred Hitchcock's Mystery Magazine* are not considered for or read by *Ellery Queen's Mystery Magazine*, and vice versa."

HOME PLANET NEWS ONLINE

E-mail: homeplanetnewsol@gmail.com. **Website:** homeplanetnews.org/AOnLine.html. **Contact:** Frank Murphy, chief editor. Estab. 1979. *Home Planet News* publishes mainly poetry along with some fiction, as well as reviews (books, theater, and art) and articles of literary interest. Home Planet News Online was created when the print edition could no longer be published. Donald Lev ask Frank Murphy (who had been doing an online version of some of the magazine) to continue the magazine online. We have just finished our 5th Issue.

NEEDS Length: 500-2,500 words; average length: 2,000 words.

TIPS "Read an Issue before sending in to us. It will give you an idea of what we are looking for."

⑤ HOOT

A Postcard Review of (Mini) Poetry and Prose, 4234 Chestnut St., Apt. 1 R, Philadelphia PA 19104. **E-mail:** info@hootreview.com. **Website:** www.hootreview.

com. **Contact:** Jane-Rebecca Cannarella, editor in chief; Amanda Vacharat and Dorian Geisler, editors/co-founders. Estab. 2011. *HOOT* publishes 1 piece of writing, designed with original art and/or photographs, on the front of a postcard every month, as well as 2-3 pieces online. The postcards are intended for sharing, to be hung on the wall, etc. Therefore, *HOOT* looks for very brief, surprising-yet-gimmick-free writing that can stand on its own, that also follows "The Refrigerator Rule"—something that you would hang on your refrigerator and would want to read and look at for a whole month. This rule applies to online content as well.

○ Costs $2 to submit up to 2 pieces of work. Submit through online submissions manager or postal mail.

NEEDS Length: up to 150 words.

HOW TO CONTACT Submit complete ms.

PAYMENT/TERMS Pays $10-100 for print publication.

TIPS "We look for writing with audacity and zest from authors who are not afraid to take risks. We appreciate work that is able to go beyond mere description in its 150 words. We offer free online workshops every other Wednesday for authors who would like feedback on their work from the *HOOT* editors. We also often give feedback with our rejections. We publish roughly 6-10 new writers each year."

HOTEL AMERIKA

Columbia College Chicago, The Department of Creative Writing, 600 S. Michigan Ave., Chicago IL 60605. (312)369-8175. **Website:** www.hotelamerika.net. **Contact:** David Lazar, editor; Jenn Tatum, managing editor. Estab. 2002. *Hotel Amerika* is a venue for both well-known and emerging writers. Publishes exceptional writing in all forms. Strives to house the most unique and provocative poetry, fiction, and nonfiction available.

○ Mss will be considered between September 1 and May 1. Materials received after May 1 and before September 1 will be returned unread. Work published in *Hotel Amerika* has been included in *The Pushcart Prize* and *The Best American Poetry*, and featured on *Poetry Daily*.

NEEDS Welcomes submissions in all genres of creative writing, generously defined. Does not publish book reviews as such, although considers review-like essays that transcend the specific objects of consideration.

HOW TO CONTACT Submit complete ms through online submissions manager.

💲 THE HUDSON REVIEW

33 W. 67th St., New York NY 10023. (212)650-0020. **E-mail:** info@hudsonreview.com. **Website:** hudsonreview.com. **Contact:** Paula Deitz, editor. Estab. 1948. Since its beginning, the magazine has dealt with the area where literature bears on the intellectual life of the time and on diverse aspects of American culture. It has no university affiliation and is not committed to any narrow academic aim or to any particular political perspective. The magazine serves as a major forum for the work of new writers and for the exploration of new developments in literature and the arts. It has a distinguished record of publishing little-known or undiscovered writers, many of whom have become major literary figures. Each issue contains a wide range of material including poetry, fiction, essays on literary and cultural topics, book reviews, reports from abroad, and chronicles covering film, theater, dance, music, and art. *The Hudson Review* is distributed in 25 countries. Unsolicited mss are read according to the following schedule: April 1 through June 30 for poetry, September 1 through November 30 for fiction, and January 1 through March 31 for nonfiction.

NEEDS If you go through our archives, most of the short stories fall into the nebulous category of "literary fiction." Many stories have elements of mystery, romance, historical fiction, science fiction/speculative fiction, etc. For novel excerpts, we ask that the work be able to stand on its own. For genre stories, we ask that the work go beyond its genre—a religious story would have to be more than a conversion narrative or cautionary tale; a comic story would ideally have a little pathos; a romance or mystery or sci-fi story would have some ambiguities or aesthetic concerns or experimentation. In general, we want stories that a writer has put a lot of thought into, and that readers will think about long after they've finished. Length: up to 10,000 words.

HOW TO CONTACT Send complete ms by mail or online submissions manager from **September 1 through November 30** only.

TIPS "We do not specialize in publishing any particular 'type' of writing; our sole criterion for accepting unsolicited work is literary quality. The best way for you to get an idea of the range of work we publish is to read a current issue. Unsolicited mss submitted outside of specified reading times will be returned unread. Do not send submissions via e-mail."

HUNGER MOUNTAIN

Vermont College of Fine Arts, 36 College St., Montpelier VT 05602. (802)828-8517. **E-mail:** hungermtn@vcfa.edu. **Website:** www.hungermtn.org. **Contact:** Cameron Finch, managing editor. Estab. 2002. Accepts high-quality work from unknown, emerging, or successful writers. Publishing fiction, creative nonfiction, poetry, and young adult & children's writing. Four writing contests annually. *Hunger Mountain* is a print and online journal of the arts. The print journal is about 200 pages, 7x9, professionally printed, perfect-bound, with full-bleed color artwork on cover. Press run is 1,000. Over 10,000 visits online monthly. Uses online submissions manager (Submittable). Member: CLMP.

NEEDS "We look for work that is beautifully crafted and tells a good story, with characters that are alive and kicking, storylines that stay with us long after we've finished reading, and sentences that slay us with their precision." No genre fiction, meaning science fiction, fantasy, horror, detective, erotic, etc. Length: up to 10,000 words.

HOW TO CONTACT Submit ms using online submissions manager: https://hungermtn.submittable.com/submit.

PAYMENT/TERMS Pays $50 for general fiction.

TIPS "Mss must be typed, prose double-spaced. Poets submit poems as one document. No multiple genre submissions. Fresh viewpoints and human interest are very important, as is originality and diversity. We are committed to publishing an outstanding journal of the arts. Do not send entire novels, mss, or short story collections. Do not send previously published work."

I-70 REVIEW

Writing from the Middle and Beyond, 913 Joseph Dr., Lawrence KS 66049. **E-mail:** i70review@gmail.com. **Website:** www.fieldinfoserv.com. **Contact:** Gary Lechliter, Maryfrances Wagner, Greg Field, Gay Dust, editors; Jan Duncan-O'Neal editor emeritus. Estab. 1998. *I-70 Review* is an annual literary magazine. "Our interests lie in writing grounded in fresh language, imagery, and metaphor. We prefer free verse in which the writer pays attention to the sound and rhythm of the language. We appreciate poetry with individual voice and a good lyric or a strong narrative. In fiction, we like short pieces that are surprising and uncommon. We want writing that captures the human spirit with unusual topics or familiar topics with a different perspective or approach. We reject stereotypical and clichéd writing, as well as sentimental work or writing that summarizes and tells instead of shows. We look for writing that pays attention to words, sentences, and style. We publish literary writing. We do not publish anything erotic, religious, or political." Open submission period is July 1-December 31.

NEEDS Rejects anything over 1,500 words, unless solicited. Not interested in anything political, religious, spiritual, didactic, or erotic. Accepts mainly flash fiction and very short literary fiction. Pays in contributor copies. Length: up to 1,500 words.

HOW TO CONTACT Submit complete ms by e-mail.

PAYMENT/TERMS Pays contributor copies.

TIPS "Read a copy of the issue or check our website to see writers we've featured to get a good idea of what we publish."

ICONOCLAST

1675 Amazon Rd., Mohegan Lake NY 10547-1804. **Website:** www.iconoclastliterarymagazine.com. **Contact:** Phil Wagner, editor and publisher. Estab. 1992. *Iconoclast* seeks and chooses the best new writing and poetry available—of all genres and styles and entertainment levels. Its mission is to provide a serious publishing opportunity for unheralded, unknown, but deserving creators, whose work is often overlooked or trampled in the commercial, university, or Internet marketplace.

NEEDS "Subjects and styles are completely open (within the standards of generally accepted taste—though exceptions, as always, can be made for unique and visionary works)." No slice-of-life stories, stories containing alcoholism, incest, and domestic or public violence. Accepts most genres, "with the exception of mysteries."

HOW TO CONTACT Submit by mail; include SASE. Cover letter not necessary.

PAYMENT/TERMS Pays 1¢/word and 2 contributor's copies. Contributors get 40% discount on extra copies.

TIPS "Please don't send preliminary drafts—rewriting is half the job. If you're not sure about the story, don't truly believe in it, or are unenthusiastic about the subject (we will not recycle your term papers or thesis), then don't send it. This is not a lottery (luck has nothing to do with it)."

THE IDAHO REVIEW

Boise State University, 1910 University Dr., Boise ID 83725. **E-mail:** mwieland@boisestate.edu. **Website:** idahoreview.org. **Contact:** Mitch Wieland, editor. Estab. 1998. *The Idaho Review* is the literary journal of Boise State University. Recent stories appearing in *The Idaho Review* have been reprinted in *The Best American Short Stories, The O. Henry Prize Stories, The Pushcart Prize,* and *New Stories from the South.* Recent contributors include Joyce Carol Oates, Rick Moody, Ann Beattie, T.C. Boyle, and Joy Williams. Reading period: September 15-March 15.

NEEDS No genre fiction of any type. Length: up to 25 double-spaced pages.

HOW TO CONTACT Submit through online submissions manager.

PAYMENT/TERMS Pays $300-$500/story and contributor's copies.

TIPS "We look for strongly crafted work that tells a story that needs to be told. We demand vision and intelligence and mystery in the fiction we publish."

IDIOM 23

Central Queensland University, P.O. Box 172, 554-700 Yaamba Rd., Rockhampton QLD 4702, Australia. **E-mail:** idiom@cqu.edu.au; n.anae@cqu.edu.au. **Website:** www.cqu.edu.au/idiom23. **Contact:** Dr. Nicole Anae, editor. Estab. 1988. *Idiom 23*, published annually, is "named for the Tropic of Capricorn and is dedicated to developing the literary arts throughout the Central Queensland region. Submissions of original short stories, poems, articles, and b&w drawings and photographs are welcomed by the editorial collective. *Idiom 23* is not limited to a particular viewpoint but, on the contrary, hopes to encourage and publish a broad spectrum of writing. The collective seeks out creative work from community groups with as varied backgrounds as possible."

NEEDS Length: up to 3,000 words.

HOW TO CONTACT Submit complete ms via online submissions manager.

ILLUMINATIONS

Department of English, College of Charleston, 66 George St., Charleston SC 29424-0001. (843)953-1920. **E-mail:** illuminations@cofc.edu. **Website:** illuminations.cofc.edu. **Contact:** Simon Lewis, editor. Estab. 1982. "Over these many years, *Illuminations* has remained consistently true to its mission statement to publish new writers alongside some of the world's finest, including Nadine Gordimer, James Merrill, Carol Ann Duffy, Dennis Brutus, Allen Tate, interviews with Tim O'Brien, and letters from Flannery O'Connor and Ezra Pound. A number of new poets whose early work appeared in *Illuminations* have gone on to win prizes and accolades, and we at *Illuminations* sincerely value the chance to promote the work of emerging writers."

"As a magazine devoted primarily to poetry, we publish only 1-2 pieces of short fiction and/or nonfiction in any given year, and sometimes publish none at all. "

HOW TO CONTACT Submit complete ms by mail, or online submissions manager.

PAYMENT/TERMS Pays 2 contributor's copies of current issue and 1 copy of subsequent issue.

IMAGE

3307 Third Ave. W., Seattle WA 98119. (206)281-2988. **Fax:** (206)281-2979. **E-mail:** image@imagejournal. org. **Website:** www.imagejournal.org. **Contact:** Gregory Wolfe, publisher and editor. Estab. 1989. "*Image* is a unique forum for the best writing and artwork that is informed by—or grapples with—religious faith. We have never been interested in art that merely regurgitates dogma or falls back on easy answers or didacticism. Instead, our focus has been on writing and visual artwork that embody a spiritual struggle, that seek to strike a balance between tradition and a profound openness to the world. Each issue explores this relationship through outstanding fiction, poetry, painting, sculpture, architecture, film, music, interviews, and dance. *Image* also features 4-color reproductions of visual art." Magazine: 7×10; 136 pages; glossy cover stock; illustrations; photos.

NEEDS No sentimental, preachy, moralistic, obvious stories, or genre stories (unless they manage to transcend their genre). Length: 3,000-6,000 words.

HOW TO CONTACT Send complete ms by postal mail (with SASE for reply or return of ms) or online submissions manager at www.imagejournal.org/journal/submit. Does not accept e-mail submissions.

PAYMENT/TERMS Pays $20/page and 4 contributor's copies.

TIPS "Fiction must grapple with religious faith, though subjects need not be overtly religious."

⑨ INDIANA REVIEW

Ballantine Hall 529, 1020 E. Kirkwood Ave., Indiana University, Bloomington IN 47405. **E-mail:** inreview@indiana.edu. **Website:** indianareview.org. **Contact:** See masthead for current editorial staff.. Estab. 1976. *"Indiana Review*, a nonprofit organization run by IU graduate students, is a journal of innovative fiction, nonfiction, and poetry. We're interested in energy, originality, and careful attention to craft. While we publish many well-known authors, we also welcome new and emerging poets and fiction writers." See website for open reading periods.

NEEDS "We look for daring stories which integrate theme, language, character, and form. We like polished writing, humor, and fiction which has consequence beyond the world of its narrator." No genre fiction. Length: up to 8,000 words.

HOW TO CONTACT Submit via online submissions manager.

PAYMENT/TERMS Pays $5/page ($10 minimum), plus 2 contributor's copies.

TIPS "We're always looking for more nonfiction. We enjoy essays that go beyond merely autobiographical revelation and utilize sophisticated organization and slightly radical narrative strategies. We want essays that are both lyrical and analytical, where confession does not mean nostalgia. Read us before you submit. Back issues are available for $10. Our most recent issues have online previews available for free and accessible through the "Shop" page on our website. Often reading is slower in summer and holiday months. Submit work that 'stacks up' with the work we've published."

INTERNATIONAL EXAMINER

409 Maynard Ave. S., #203, Seattle WA 98104. (206)624-3925. **Fax:** (206)624-3046. **E-mail:** editor@iexaminer.org. **Website:** www.iexaminer.org. **Contact:** Travis Quezon, editor in chief. Estab. 1974. *"International Examiner* is about Asian American issues and things of interest to Asian Americans. We do not want stuff about Asian things (stories on your trip to China, Japanese Tea Ceremony, etc. will be rejected). Yes, we are in English."

NEEDS Asian American authored fiction by or about Asian Americans only.

HOW TO CONTACT Query.

TIPS "Write decent, suitable material on a subject of interest to the Asian American community. All sub-missions are reviewed; all good ones are contacted. It helps to call and run an idea by the editor before or after sending submissions."

⑨ INTERPRETER'S HOUSE

'Scrimshaw', 63 Strait Path, Gardenstown Aberdeenshire AB45 3ZQ, Scotland. **E-mail:** theinterpretershouse@aol.com. **Website:** www.theinterpretershouse.com. **Contact:** Martin Malone, editor. Estab. 1996. *The Interpreter's House*, published 3 times/year spring, summer, and autumn, prints short stories and poetry. Submission windows: October for the Spring issue, February for the Summer issue, June for the Autumn issue.

NEEDS Length: up to 2,000 words.

HOW TO CONTACT Submit up to 2 short stories by mail (with SASE) or e-mail.

PAYMENT/TERMS Pays contributor's copies.

⑨ THE IOWA REVIEW

308 EPB, The University of Iowa, Iowa City IA 52242. (319)335-0462. **E-mail:** iowa-review@uiowa.edu. **Website:** www.iowareview.org. **Contact:** Harilaos Stecopoulos. Estab. 1970. *The Iowa Review*, published 3 times/year, prints fiction, poetry, essays, reviews, and, occasionally, interviews. Receives about 5,000 submissions/year, accepts up to 100. Press run is 2,900; 1,500 distributed to stores.

○ This magazine uses the help of colleagues and graduate assistants. Its reading period for unsolicited work is September 1-December 1. From January through April, the editors read entries to the annual Iowa Review Awards competition. Check the website for further information.

NEEDS "We are open to a range of styles and voices and always hope to be surprised by work we then feel we need." Receives 600 unsolicited mss/month. Accepts 4-6 mss/issue; 12-18 mss/year. Does not read mss January-August. Publishes ms an average of 12-18 months after acceptance. Agented fiction less than 2%. **Publishes some new writers/year.** Recently published work by Johanna Hunting, Bennett Sims, and Pedro Mairal.

HOW TO CONTACT Send complete ms with cover letter. Don't bother with queries. SASE for return of ms. Accepts mss by snail mail (SASE required for response) and online submission form at iowareview.submittable.com/submit; no e-mail submissions.

PAYMENT/TERMS Pays 8¢/word ($100 minimum), plus 2 contributor's copies.

TIPS "We publish essays, reviews, novel excerpts, stories, poems, and photography. We have no set guidelines regarding content but strongly recommend that writers read a sample issue before submitting."

IRIS

E-mail: submissions@creatingiris.org. **E-mail:** editorial@creatingiris.org. **Website:** www.creatingiris.org. Estab. 2014. "*Iris* seeks works of fiction and poetry that speak to LGBT young adults and their allies. We are interested in creative, thoughtful, original work that engages our young readers. We seek writing that challenges them and makes them think. We're looking for stories that capture their imaginations and characters that are relatable. We think there's a need in the young adult literary market for writing that speaks to the everyday experiences of LGBT adolescents: Themes of identity, friendship, coming out, families, etc., are especially welcome. The protagonist need not identify as LGBT, but we do ask that there be some kind of LGBT angle to your story. We welcome all genres of fiction and poetry!"

○ "Because we publish for a young demographic, work submitted to *Iris* may not include depictions of sex, drug use, and violence. They can certainly be discussed and referenced, but not directly portrayed."

NEEDS Length: up to 3,000 words.

HOW TO CONTACT Submit complete ms via e-mail as attachment. Include cover letter in text of e-mail.

☁ ISLAND

Island Magazine, P.O. Box 4703, Hobart Tasmania 7000, Australia. (+61)(03)6234-1462. **E-mail:** admin@islandmag.com. **Website:** www.islandmag.com. **Contact:** Kate Harrison, general manager. Estab. 1979. *Island* seeks quality fiction, poetry, and essays. It is "one of Australia's leading literary magazines, tracing the contours of our national, and international, culture while still retaining a uniquely Tasmanian perspective." Only publishes the work of subscribers; you can submit if you are not currently a subscriber, but if your piece is chosen, the subscription will be taken from the fee paid for the piece.

NEEDS "Although we are not strict about word limits, we tend not to publish flash fiction or microfiction at time. In terms of upper limits, we are less likely to publish works longer than 5,000 words. This is a general guideline: We do not have a formal cut-off

for submissions. However, please be aware that if you submit a work longer than 4,000 words, we may not read beyond this length if we feel certain the work is not suited for publication with us."

HOW TO CONTACT Submit 1 piece via online submissions manager.

PAYMENT/TERMS Pay varies.

JABBERWOCK REVIEW

Department of English, PO Box E, Mississippi State MS 39762. **E-mail:** jabberwockreview@english.msstate.edu. **Website:** www.jabberwock.org.msstate.edu. **Contact:** Michael Kardos, editor. Estab. 1979. *Jabberwock Review* is a literary journal published semi-annually by students and faculty of Mississippi State University. Each issue features an eclectic mix of poetry, fiction, and creative nonfiction. Submissions accepted August 15-October 20 and January 15-March 15.

○ Send us your best work! We're open to everything from traditional to experimental. We look forward to reading.

NEEDS Does not publish romance or erotica. There is no word limit, but we rarely publish works of more than 30 pages. The entire journal is about 100 pages.

HOW TO CONTACT Submit no more than 1 story at a time.

PAYMENT/TERMS Pays contributor's copies.

TIPS "It might take a few months to get a response from us, but your work will be read with care. Our editors enjoy reading submissions (really!) and will remember writers who are persistent and committed to getting a story 'right' through revision."

⑤ JACK AND JILL

U.S. Kids, P.O. Box 88928, Indianapolis IN 46208. (317)634-1100. **E-mail:** jackandjill@uskidsmags.com. **Website:** www.uskidsmags.com. Estab. 1938. *Jack and Jill* is an award-winning magazine for children ages 6-12. It promotes the healthy educational and creative growth of children through interactive activities and articles. The pages are designed to spark a child's curiosity in a wide range of topics through articles, games, and activities. Inside you will find: current real-world topics in articles in stories; challenging puzzles and games; and interactive entertainment through experimental crafts and recipes. Please do not send artwork. "We prefer to work with professional illustrators of our own choosing. Write entertaining and imaginative stories for kids, not just about them. Writers should understand what is funny to kids, what's important to them, what excites them. Don't write from an adult 'kids are so cute' perspective. We're also looking for health and healthful lifestyle stories and articles, but don't be preachy."

NEEDS Submit complete ms via postal mail; no e-mail submissions. The tone of the stories should be fun and engaging. Stories should hook readers right from the get-go and pull them through the story. Humor is very important! Dialogue should be witty instead of just furthering the plot. The story should convey some kind of positive message. Possible themes could include self-reliance, being kind to others, appreciating other cultures, and so on. There are a million positive messages, so get creative! Kids can see preachy coming from a mile away, though, so please focus on telling a good story over teaching a lesson. The message—if there is one—should come organically from the story and not feel tacked on. Length: 600-800 words.

PAYMENT/TERMS Pays $25 minimum.

TIPS "We are constantly looking for new writers who can tell good stories with interesting slants—stories that are not full of outdated and time-worn expressions. We like to see stories about kids who are smart and capable but not sarcastic or smug. Problem-solving skills, personal responsibility, and integrity are good topics for us. Obtain current issues of the magazine and study them to determine our present needs and editorial style."

JEWISH CURRENTS

P.O. Box 111, Accord NY 12404. (845)626-2427. **E-mail:** editor@jewishcurrents.org. **Website:** jewishcurrents.org. **Contact:** Lawrence Bush, editor; Jacob Plitman, associate editor. Estab. 1946. *Jewish Currents*, published 4 times/year, is a progressive Jewish quarterly magazine that carries on the insurgent tradition of the Jewish left through independent journalism, political commentary, and a 'countercultural' approach to Jewish arts and literature. Our website is an active magazine in its own right, with new material published daily. *Jewish Currents* is 88 pages, magazine-sized, offset-printed, saddle-stapled with a full-color arts section, "JCultcha & Funny Pages." The Winter issue is a 12-month arts calendar.

HOW TO CONTACT Send complete ms with cover letter. "Writers should include brief biographical information."

PAYMENT/TERMS Pays contributor's copies or small honoraria.

J JOURNAL: NEW WRITING ON JUSTICE

524 W. 59th St., Seventh Floor, New York NY 10019. (212)237-8697. **E-mail:** jjournal@jjay.cuny.edu. **E-mail:** submissionsjjournal@gmail.com. **Website:** www.jjournal.org. **Contact:** Adam Berlin and Jeffrey Heiman, editors. Estab. 2008. "*J Journal* publishes literary fiction, creative nonfiction, and poetry on the justice theme—social, political, criminal, gender, racial, religious, economic. While the justice theme is specific, it need not dominate the work. We're interested in innovative writing that examines justice from all creative perspectives. Tangential connections to justice are often better than direct." Several works from *J Journal* have been recognized in *Pushcart Prize* anthologies.

NEEDS Receives 100 mss/month. Accepts 5-8 mss/issue; 10-16 mss/year. Length: 750-6,000 words. Average length: 4,000 words.

HOW TO CONTACT Send complete ms with cover letter. Include estimated word count, brief bio, list of publications.

PAYMENT/TERMS Pays 2 contributor's copies. Additional copies $10.

TIPS "We're looking for literary fiction, memoir, personal narrative, or poetry with a connection, direct or tangential, to the theme of justice."

⑤ THE JOURNAL

The Ohio State University, 164 Annie and John Glenn Ave., Columbus OH 43210. **E-mail:** managingeditor@thejournalmag.org. **Website:** thejournalmag.org. Estab. 1973. "We are interested in quality fiction, poetry, nonfiction, art, and reviews of new books of poetry, fiction, and nonfiction. We impose no restrictions on category, type, or length of submission for fiction, poetry, and nonfiction. We are happy to consider long stories and self-contained excerpts of novels. Please double-space all prose submissions. Please send 3-5 poems in 1 submission. We only accept online submissions and will not respond to mailed submissions."

○ "We're open to all forms; we tend to favor work that gives evidence of a mature and sophisticated sense of the language."

NEEDS No romance, science fiction, or religious/devotional. Length: up to 10,000 words.

HOW TO CONTACT Send full ms via online submissions manager. "Mss are rejected because of lack of understanding of the short story form, shallow plots, undeveloped characters. Cure: Read as much well-written fiction as possible. Our readers prefer 'psychological' fiction rather than stories with intricate plots. Take care to present a clean, well-typed submission."

PAYMENT/TERMS Pays 2 contributor's copies and one-year subscription.

KAIMANA

Literary Arts Hawai'i, Hawai'i Literary Arts Council, P.O. Box 11213, Honolulu HI 96828. **E-mail:** reimersa001@hawaii.rr.com. **Website:** www.hawaii.edu/hlac. Estab. 1974. *Kaimana: Literary Arts Hawai'i*, published annually, is the magazine of the Hawai'i Literary Arts Council. Wants submissions with "some Pacific reference—Asia, Polynesia, Hawai'i—but not exclusively."

○ *Kaimana* is 64-76 pages, 7.5x10, saddle-stapled, with high-quality printing. Press run is 1,000. "Poets published in *Kaimana* have received the Pushcart Prize, the Hawaii Award for Literature, the Stefan Baciu Award, the Cades Award, and the John Unterecker Award."

HOW TO CONTACT Submit ms with SASE. No e-mail submissions. Cover letter is preferred.

PAYMENT/TERMS Pays 2 contributor's copies.

TIPS "Hawai'i gets a lot of 'travelling regionalists,' visiting writers with inevitably superficial observations. We also get superb visiting observers who are careful craftsmen anywhere. *Kaimana* is interested in the latter, to complement our own best Hawai'i writers."

⑤ KALEIDOSCOPE

United Disability Services, 701 S. Main St., Akron OH 44311-1019. (330)762-9755. **Fax:** (330)762-0912. **E-mail:** kaleidoscope@udsakron.org. **Website:** www. kaleidoscopeonline.org. **Contact:** Editor. Estab. 1979. Kaleidoscope magazine creatively focuses on the experiences of disability through literature and the fine arts. As a pioneering literary resource for the field of disability studies, this award-winning publication expresses the diversity of the disability experience from a variety of perspectives including: individuals, families, friends, caregivers, educators, and healthcare professionals, among others."

○ Kaleidoscope has received awards from the Great Lakes Awards Competition and Ohio Public Images; received the Ohioana Award of Editorial Excellence.

NEEDS Wants short stories with a well-crafted plot and engaging characters. No fiction that is stereotypi-

cal, patronizing, sentimental, erotic, or maudlin. No romance, religious or dogmatic fiction; no children's literature. Length: up to 5,000 words.

HOW TO CONTACT Submit complete ms by website or e-mail. Include cover letter.

PAYMENT/TERMS Pays $25.

TIPS "The material chosen for Kaleidoscope challenges and overcomes stereotypical, patronizing, and sentimental attitudes about disability. We accept the work of writers with and without disabilities; however the work of a writer without a disability must focus on some aspect of disability. The criteria for good writing apply: effective technique, thought-provoking subject matter, and, in general, a mature grasp of the art of storytelling. Writers should avoid using offensive language and always put the person before the disability."

KANSAS CITY VOICES

Whispering Prairie Press, P.O. Box 410661, Kansas City MO 64141. **E-mail:** info@wppress.org. **Website:** www.wppress.org. **Contact:** Tom Sullivan, managing editor. Estab. 2003. *Kansas City Voices*, published annually, features an eclectic mix of fiction, poetry, and art. "We seek exceptional written and visual creations from established and emerging voices." Submission period: December 15 through March 15. Note: We will not be publishing KCV in 2018. Our next submission period begins December 15, 2018, for publication in 2019.

NEEDS Length: up to 2,500 words.

HOW TO CONTACT Submit up to 2 complete mss via online submissions manager.

PAYMENT/TERMS Pays small honorarium and 1 contributor's copy.

TIPS "There is no 'type' of work we are looking for, and while we would love for you to read through our previous issues, it is not an indicator of what kind of work we actively seek. Our editors rotate, our tastes evolve, and good work is just *good work*. We want to feel something when we encounter a piece. We want to be excited, surprised, thoughtful, and interested. We want to have a reaction. We want to share the best voices we find. Send us that one."

♻ KASMA MAGAZINE

E-mail: editors@kasmamagazine.com. **Website:** www.kasmamagazine.com. **Contact:** Alex Korovessis, editor. Estab. 2009. Online magazine. "We publish the best science fiction from promising new and established writers. Our aim is to provide stories that are well written, original, and thought provoking."

NEEDS No erotica or excessive violence/language. Length: 1,000-5,000 words.

HOW TO CONTACT Submit complete ms via e-mail.

PAYMENT/TERMS Pays $25 CAD.

TIPS "The type of stories I enjoy the most usually come as a surprise: I think I know what is happening, but the underlying reality is revealed to me as I read on. That said, I've accepted many stories that don't fit this model. Sometimes I'm introduced to a new story structure. Sometimes the story I like reminds me of another story, but it introduces a slightly different spin on it. Other times, the story introduces such interesting and original ideas that structure and style don't seem to matter as much."

THE KELSEY REVIEW

Liberal Arts Division, Mercer County Community College, P.O. Box 17202, Trenton NJ 08690. **E-mail:** kelsey.review@mccc.edu. **Website:** www.mccc.edu/community_kelsey-review.shtml; kelseyreview.com. **Contact:** Jacqueline Vogtman, editor. Estab. 1988. *The Kelsey Review*, published annually in print and online formats by Mercer County Community College, serves as an outlet for literary talent of people living and working in the larger Mercer County, New Jersey, area. Submissions are open between January 15-May 15 via our Submittable site.

NEEDS Has no specifications as to form, subject matter, or style. Length: up to 4,000 words.

HOW TO CONTACT Submit via online submissions manager. Submissions are limited to people who live, work, or give literary readings in Mercer County, New Jersey.

TIPS "See *The Kelsey Review* website for current guidelines. Note: We only accept submissions from the Mercer County, New Jersey, area."

🟢 KENTUCKY MONTHLY

Vested Interest Publications, P.O. Box 559, 100 Consumer Lane, Frankfort KY 40602-0559. (502)227-0053; (888)329-0053. **Fax:** (502)227-5009. **E-mail:** kymonthly@kentuckymonthly.com; steve@kentuckymonthly.com. **E-mail:** patty@kentuckymonthly.com. **Website:** www.kentuckymonthly.com. **Contact:** Stephen Vest, editor; Patricia Ranft, associate editor. Estab. 1998. "We publish stories about Kentucky and

by Kentuckians, including stories written by those who live elsewhere."

NEEDS We publish stories about Kentucky and by Kentuckians, including stories written by those who live elsewhere." Length: 1,000-5,000 words.

HOW TO CONTACT Query with published clips. Accepts submissions by e-mail.

TIPS "Please read the magazine to get the flavor of what we're publishing each month. We accept articles via e-mail. Approximately 70% of articles are assigned."

🟢 THE KENYON REVIEW

Finn House, 102 W. Wiggin, Gambier OH 43022. (740)427-5208. **Fax:** (740)427-5417. **E-mail:** kenyonreview@kenyon.edu. **Website:** www.kenyonreview.org. **Contact:** Alicia Misarti. Estab. 1939. "An international journal of literature, culture, and the arts, dedicated to an inclusive representation of the best in new writing (fiction, poetry, essays, interviews, criticism) from established and emerging writers." The *Kenyon Review* receives about 8,000 submissions/year. Also publishes KROnline, a separate and complementary online literary magazine.

NEEDS Receives 800 unsolicited mss/month. Unsolicited mss accepted September 15-November 1 only. Recently published work by Leslie Blanco, Karl Taro Greenfeld, Charles Johnson, Amit Majmudar, Joyce Carol Oates, and Rion Amilcar Scott. Length: 3-15 typeset pages preferred.

HOW TO CONTACT Only accepts mss via online submissions manager; visit website for instructions. Do not submit via e-mail or mail.

PAYMENT/TERMS Pays 8¢/published word of prose (minimum payment $80; maximum payment $450); word count does not include title, notes, or citations.

TIPS "We no longer accept mailed or e-mailed submissions. Work will only be read if it is submitted through our online program on our website. Reading period is September 15 through November 1. We look for strong voice, unusual perspective, and power in the writing."

KEYS FOR KIDS DEVOTIONAL

Keys for Kids Ministries, PO Box 1001, Grand Rapids MI 49501. **E-mail:** editorial@keysforkids.org. **Website:** www.keysforkids.org. **Contact:** Courtney Lasater, editor. Estab. 1982. Quarterly devotional featuring stories and Scripture verses for children ages 6-12 that help kids dig into God's Word and apply it to their lives.

Please put your name and contact information on the first page of your submission. "We prefer to receive submissions via our website." Story length is typically 340-375 words. To see full guidelines or submit a story, please go to www.keysforkids.org/writersguidelines.

NEEDS Need short contemporary stories with spiritual applications for kids. Please suggest a key verse and an appropriate Scripture passage, generally 3-10 verses, to reinforce the theme of your story. (See guidelines for more details on our devotional format.) Length: Up to 375 words.

PAYMENT/TERMS Pays $30.

TIPS "We love devotional stories that use an everyday object/situation to illustrate a spiritual truth (especially in a fresh, unique way) with characters that pull the reader into the story."

LADY CHURCHILL'S ROSEBUD WRISTLET

Small Beer Press, 150 Pleasant St., #306, Easthampton MA 01027. **E-mail:** info@smallbeerpress.com. **Website:** www.smallbeerpress.com/lcrw. **Contact:** Gavin Grant, editor. Estab. 1996. *Lady Churchill's Rosebud Wristlet* accepts fiction, nonfiction, poetry, and b&w art. "The fiction we publish tends toward, but is not limited to, the speculative. This does not mean only quietly desperate stories. We will consider items that fall out with regular categories. We do not accept multiple submissions." Semiannual.

NEEDS Receives 100 unsolicited mss/month. Accepts 4-6 mss/issue; 8-12 mss/year. Publishes 2-4 new writers/year. Also publishes literary essays, poetry. Has published work by Ted Chiang, Gwenda Bond, Alissa Nutting, and Charlie Anders. "We do not publish gore, sword and sorcery, or pornography. We can discuss these terms if you like. There are places for them all; this is not one of them." Length: 200-7,000 words.

HOW TO CONTACT Send complete ms with a cover letter. Include estimated word count. Send SASE (or IRC) for return of ms, or send a disposable copy of ms and #10 SASE for reply only.

PAYMENT/TERMS Pays $0.03 per word, $25 minimum.

TIPS "We recommend you read *Lady Churchill's Rosebud Wristlet* before submitting. You can pick up a copy from our website or from assorted book shops."

LAKE EFFECT

An International Literary Journal, School of Humanities & Social Sciences, Penn State Erie, The Behrend College, Erie PA 16563-1501. **E-mail:** gol1@psu.edu; alp248@psu.edu. **Website:** psbehrend.psu.edu/school-of-humanities-social-sciences/academic-programs-1/creative-writing/cw-student-organizations/lake-effect. **Contact:** George Looney, editor in chief. Estab. 1978. *Lake Effect* is a publication of the School of Humanities and Social Sciences at Penn State Erie, The Behrend College.

NEEDS "*Lake Effect* is looking for stories that emerge from character and language as much as from plot. *Lake Effect* does not, in general, publish genre fiction, but literary fiction. *Lake Effect* seeks work from both established and new and emerging writers." Query first for stories longer than 15 pages.

HOW TO CONTACT Submit via online submissions manager.

LAKE SUPERIOR MAGAZINE

Lake Superior Port Cities, Inc., P.O. Box 16417, Duluth MN 55816-0417. (218)722-5002. **Fax:** (218)722-4096. **E-mail:** edit@lakesuperior.com. **Website:** www.lakesuperior.com. **Contact:** Konnie LeMay, editor. Estab. 1979. We are a family-owned business sustained with book and magazine publications as well as a Lake Superior Collection of retail items.

NEEDS Must be targeted regionally. Wants stories that are Lake Superior related. Rarely uses fiction stories. Length: 300-2,500 words.

HOW TO CONTACT Query with published clips.

PAYMENT/TERMS Pays $50-125.

TIPS "Well-researched queries are attended to. We actively seek queries from writers in Lake Superior communities. We prefer queries. Provide enough information on why the subject is important to the region and our readers, or why and how something is unique. We want details. The writer must have a thorough knowledge of the subject and how it relates to our region. We prefer a fresh, unused approach to the subject that provides the reader with an emotional involvement. Almost all of our articles feature quality photography in color or b&w. It is a prerequisite of all nonfiction. All submissions should include a *short* biography of author/photographer; mug shot sometimes used. Blanket submissions need not apply."

THE LAND

Free Press Co., P.O. Box 3169, Mankato MN 56002-3169. (507)345-4523. **Fax:** (507)345-1027. **E-mail:** editor@thelandonline.com. **Website:** www.thelandonline.com. Estab. 1976. "Although we're not tightly focused on any one type of farming, our articles must be of interest to farmers. In other words, will your article topic have an impact on people who live and work in rural areas?" Prefers to work with Minnesota or Iowa writers.

TIPS "Be enthused about rural Minnesota and Iowa life and agriculture, and be willing to work with our editors. We try to stress relevance. When sending me a query, convince me the story belongs in a Minnesota farm publication."

● LANDFALL: NEW ZEALAND ARTS AND LETTERS

Otago University Press, P.O. Box 56, Dunedin 9054, New Zealand. (64)(3)479-4155. **E-mail:** landfall.press@otago.ac.nz. **Website:** www.otago.ac.nz/press/landfall. **Contact:** Editor. Estab. 1947. *Landfall: New Zealand Arts and Letters* contains literary fiction and essays, poetry, extracts from works-in-progress, commentary on New Zealand arts and culture, work by visual artists including photographers and reviews of local books. (*Landfall* does not accept unsolicited reviews.)

◯ Deadlines for submissions: January 10 for the May issue, July 10 for the November issue. "*Landfall* is open to work by New Zealand and Pacific writers or by writers whose work has a connection to the region in subject matter or location. Work from Australian writers is occasionally included as a special feature."

NEEDS Length: up to 3,000 words.

HOW TO CONTACT Submit up to 3 pieces at a time. Prefers e-mail submissions. Include cover letter with contact info and bio of about 30 words.

● LEADING EDGE MAGAZINE

Brigham Young University, 4087 JKB, Provo UT 84602. **E-mail:** editor@leadingedgemagazine.com; fiction@leadingedgemagazine.com; art@leadingedgemagazine.com; poetry@leadingedgemagazine.com; nonfiction@leadingedgemagazine.com. **Website:** www.leadingedgemagazine.com. **Contact:** Abigail Miner, editor-in-chief. Estab. 1981. "*Leading Edge* is a magazine dedicated to new and upcoming talent in the fields of science fiction, fantasy, and horror. We strive to encourage developing and established talent and provide high-quality speculative fiction to our readers." Does not accept mss with sex, excessive violence, or profanity. Accepts unsolicited submissions.

NEEDS Length: up to 15,000 words.

HOW TO CONTACT Send complete ms with cover letter and SASE. Include estimated word count.

PAYMENT/TERMS Pays 1¢/word; $50 maximum.

TIPS "Buy a sample issue to know what is currently selling in our magazine. Also, make sure to follow the writer's guidelines when submitting."

LE FORUM

University of Maine, Franco-American Center, Orono ME 04469-5719. (207)581-3789. **Fax:** (207)581-3791. **E-mail:** lisa_michaud@umit.maine.edu. **Website:** umaine.edu/francoamerican/le-forum. **Contact:** Lisa Desjardins Michaud, editor. Estab. 1972. "We will consider any type of short fiction, poetry, and critical essay having to do with the Franco-American experience. They must be of good quality in French or English. We are also looking for Canadian writers with French-North American experiences."

HOW TO CONTACT Include SASE.

PAYMENT/TERMS Pays 3 contributor's copies.

TIPS "Write honestly. Start with a strongly felt personal Franco-American experience. If you make us feel what you have felt, we will publish it. We stress that this publication deals specifically with the Franco-American experience."

LIGHTHOUSE DIGEST

Lighthouse Digest, P.O. Box 250, East Machias ME 04630. (207)259-2121. **E-mail:** Editor@LighthouseDigest.com. **Website:** www.lighthousedigest.com. **Contact:** Tim Harrison, editor. Estab. 1989. Full color lighthouse news and history magazine.

NEEDS 2,500 words maximum.

HOW TO CONTACT Send complete ms.

TIPS "Read our publication and visit the website."

LILITH MAGAZINE: INDEPENDENT, JEWISH & FRANKLY FEMINIST

119 West 57th St., Suite 1210, New York NY 10019. (212)757-0818. **Fax:** (212)757-5705. **E-mail:** info@lilith.org. **Website:** www.lilith.org. **Contact:** Susan Weidman Schneider, editor in chief; Naomi Danis, managing editor. Estab. 1976. *Lilith Magazine: Independent, Jewish & Frankly Feminist*, published quarterly, welcomes submissions of high-quality, lively writing: reportage, opinion pieces, memoirs, fiction, and poetry on subjects of interest to Jewish women.

◯ *Lilith Magazine* is 48 pages, magazine-sized, with glossy color cover. Press run is about 10,000 (about 6,000 subscribers). Subscription: $26/year.

For all submissions: Make sure name and contact information appear on each page of mss. Include a short bio (1-2 sentences), written in third person. Accepts submissions year round.

NEEDS Length: up to 3,000 words.

HOW TO CONTACT Send complete ms via online submissions form or mail.

TIPS "Read a copy of the publication before you submit your work. Please be patient."

THE LISTENING EYE

Kent State University Geauga Campus, 14111 Claridon-Troy Rd., Burton OH 44021. (440)286-3840. **E-mail:** grace_butcher@msn.com. **E-mail:** Only from other countries. **Contact:** Grace Butcher, editor. Estab. 1970. "We look for powerful, unusual imagery, content, and plot in our short stories. In poetry, we look for tight lines that don't sound like prose, unexpected images or juxtapositions, the unusual use of language, noticeable relationships of sounds, a twist in viewpoint, an ordinary idea in extraordinary language, an amazing and complex idea simply stated, play on words and with words, an obvious love of language. Poets need to read the 'Big Three'—Cummings, Thomas, Hopkins—to see the limits to which language can be taken. Then read the 'Big Two'—Dickinson to see how simultaneously tight, terse, and universal a poem can be, and Whitman to see how sprawling, cosmic, and personal. Then read everything you can find that's being published in literary magazines today, and see how your work compares to all of the above."

○ Magazine: 5.5×8.5; 60 pages; photographs. "We publish the occasional very short stories (750 words/3 pages double-spaced) in any subject and any style, but the language must be strong, unusual, free from cliché and vagueness. We are a shoestring operation from a small campus, but we publish high-quality work." Reads submissions January 1-April 15 only.

NEEDS "Pretty much anything will be considered except porn." Recently published work by Simon Perchik, Lyn Lifshin, and John Hart. Publishes short shorts. Also publishes poetry. Sometimes comments on rejected mss.

HOW TO CONTACT Send SASE for return of ms or disposable copy of ms with SASE for reply only.

LITERAL LATTÉ

200 E. 10th St., Ste. 240, New York NY 10003. (212)260-5532. **E-mail:** litlatte@aol.com. **Website:** www.literal-latte.com. **Contact:** Jenine Gordon Bockman and Jeffrey Michael Bockman, editors and publishers. Estab. 1994. Bimonthly online publication. Print anthologies featuring the best of the website. "We want great writing in all styles and subjects. A feast is made of a variety of flavors."

NEEDS Accepts all styles and genres. Length: up to 10,000 words.

HOW TO CONTACT Submit via online submissions manager or postal mail.

PAYMENT/TERMS Pays anthology copies. Cash prizes for contests.

TIPS "Keeping free thought free and challenging entertainment are not mutually exclusive. Words make a ms stand out, words beautifully woven together in striking and memorable patterns."

◉ LITERARY MAMA

E-mail: lminfo@literarymama.com. **E-mail:** Specific to departments; see website. **Website:** www.literarymama. com. **Contact:** Karna Converse, editor-in-chief. Estab. 2003. Online monthly magazine that features writing about the complexities and many faces of motherhood. Departments include columns, creative nonfiction, fiction, literary reflections, poetry, profiles, and book reviews. "We prefer previously unpublished work and are interested in work that offers a fresh perspective."

○ "*Literary Mama* is not currently a paying market. We are all volunteers here: editors, writers, and editorial assistants. With the publication of each issue, we make a concerted effort to promote the work of our contributors via Facebook, Twitter, and our newsletter."

NEEDS "We love stories with strong narrative structure, great characters, interesting settings, beautiful language, and complicated themes." Length: up to 5,000 words.

THE LITERARY REVIEW

285 Madison Ave., Madison NJ 07940. (973)443-8564. **E-mail:** info@theliteraryreview.org. **Website:** www. theliteraryreview.org. **Contact:** Minna Proctor, editor. Estab. 1957. *The Literary Review* is published by Fairleigh Dickinson University. Work published in *The Literary Review* has been included in *Editor's Choice*, *Best American Short Stories*, and *Pushcart Prize* anthologies. Uses online submissions manager.

NEEDS Wants works of high literary quality only. Does not want to see "overused subject matter or pat resolutions to conflicts." Length: up to 7,000 words.

HOW TO CONTACT Submit electronically only. Does not accept paper submissions.

PAYMENT/TERMS Pays 2 contributor's copies and a one-year subscription.

TIPS "We want original dramatic situations with complex moral and intellectual resonance and vivid prose. We don't want versions of familiar plots and relationships. Too much of what we are seeing today is openly derivative in subject, plot, and prose style. We pride ourselves on spotting new writers with fresh insight and approach."

THE LITERARY REVIEW

An International Journal of Contemporary Writing, Fairleigh Dickinson University, 285 Madison Ave., Madison NJ 07940. (973)443-8564. **E-mail:** info@ theliteraryreview.org. **Website:** www.theliteraryreview.org. **Contact:** Minna Proctor, editor. Estab. 1957. *The Literary Review*, published quarterly, is "interested in innovative writing, engaging stories, and work that feels as if it had to be written. In other words, we like writing that has the courage of its convictions." *TLR Online*, available on the website, features original work not published in the print edition. *The Literary Review* is about 200 pages, digest-sized, professionally printed, flat-spined, with glossy color cover. Receives about 1,200 submissions/year, accepts 100-150. Press run is 2,000 (800 subscribers, one-third are overseas).

NEEDS Length: up to 7,000 words.

HOW TO CONTACT Submit via online submissions manager.

PAYMENT/TERMS Pays 2 contributor's copies and one-year subscription.

LITTLE PATUXENT REVIEW

P.O. Box 6084, Columbia MD 21045. **E-mail:** editor@ littlepatuxentreview.org. **Website:** www.littlepatuxentreview.org. **Contact:** Steven Leyva, editor. Estab. 2006. "*Little Patuxent Review* (*LPR*) is a community-based, biannual print journal devoted to literature and the arts, primarily in the Mid-Atlantic region. We profile the work of a major poet or fiction writer and a visual artist in each issue. We celebrate the launch of each issue with a series of readings and broadcast highlights on *LPR*'s YouTube channel. All forms and styles considered. Please see our website for the current theme." *LPR* is about 120 pages; digest-sized; 100# finch cover; artwork (varies depending on featured artist). Has published poetry by Lucille Clifton,

Martín Espada, Donald Hall, Joy Harjo, Marie Howe, Myra Sklarew, Clarinda Harriss, and Alan King.

NEEDS Length: up to 5,000 words.

HOW TO CONTACT Submit complete ms by online submissions manager; no mail or e-mail submissions. Include word count and 75-word bio.

PAYMENT/TERMS Pays 1 contributor's copy.

TIPS "Please see our website for the current theme. Poetry and prose must exhibit the highest quality to be considered. Please read a sample issue before submitting."

⑤ LIVE

Gospel Publishing House, 1445 N. Boonville Ave., Springfield MO 65802-1894. (417)862-1447. **E-mail:** rl-live@gph.org. **Website:** www.gospelpublishing.com. Estab. 1928. "*LIVE* is a take-home paper distributed weekly in young adult and adult Sunday school classes. We seek to encourage Christians in living for God through fiction and true stories which apply Biblical principles to everyday problems."

NEEDS No preachy fiction, fiction about Bible characters, or stories that refer to religious myths (e.g., Santa Claus, Easter Bunny, etc.). No science or Bible fiction. No controversial stories about such subjects as feminism, war, or capital punishment. Length: 800-1,200 words.

HOW TO CONTACT Send complete ms.

PAYMENT/TERMS Pays 7-10¢/word.

TIPS "Don't moralize or be preachy. Provide human interest articles with Biblical life application. Stories should consist of action, not just thought-life, interaction, or insight. Heroes and heroines should rise above failures, take risks for God, prove that scriptural principles meet their needs. Conflict and suspense should increase to a climax! Avoid pious conclusions. Characters should be interesting, believable, and realistic. Avoid stereotypes. Characters should be active, not just pawns to move the plot along. They should confront conflict and change in believable ways. Describe the character's looks and reveal his personality through his actions to such an extent that the reader feels he has met that person. Readers should care about the character enough to finish the story. Feature racial, ethnic, and regional characters in rural and urban settings."

● ⑤ THE LONDON MAGAZINE

11 Queen's Gate, London SW7 5EL, United Kingdom. (44)(0)20 7584 5977. **E-mail:** info@thelondonmaga-

zine.org. **Website:** www.thelondonmagazine.org. **Contact:** Steven O'Brien, editor. Estab. 1732. "The Oldest Literary Magazine, established 1732. We publish literary writing of the highest quality. We look for poetry and short fiction that startles and entertains us. Reviews, essays, memoir pieces, and features should be erudite, lucid, and incisive. We are obviously interested in writing that has a London focus, but not exclusively so, since London is a world city with international concerns."

NEEDS "Short fiction should address mature and sophisticated themes. Moreover, it should have an elegance of style, structure and characterization. We do not normally publish science fiction or fantasy writing, or erotica." Length: up to 4,000 words.

HOW TO CONTACT Send complete ms. Submit via online submissions manager, e-mail (as an attachment), or postal mail (enclose SASE).

TIPS "Please look at *The London Magazine* before you submit work so that you can see the type of material we publish."

LONG LIFE

Longevity through Technology, The Immortalist Society, 24355 Sorrentino Ct., Clinton Township MI 48035. **E-mail:** info@cryonics.org. **Website:** www.cryonics.org/resources/long-life-magazine. Estab. 1968. "*Long Life* magazine is a publication for people who are particularly interested in cryonic suspension: the theory, practice, legal problems, etc. associated with being frozen when you die in the hope of eventual restoration to life and health. Many people who receive the publication have relatives who have undergone cryonic preparation or have made such arrangements for themselves or are seriously considering this option. Readers are also interested in other aspects of life extension such as anti-aging research and food supplements that may slow aging. Articles we publish include speculation on what the future will be like; problems of living in a future world, and science in general, particularly as it may apply to cryonics and life extension."

NEEDS "We occasionally publish short fiction, but cryonics and life extension should be essential to the story. We are not interested in horror, in stories where the future is portrayed as gloom and doom, end-of-the-world stories, or those with an inspirational theme." Length: up to 2,500 words.

PAYMENT/TERMS Pays 1 contributor's copy.

TIPS "We are a small magazine but with a highly intelligent and educated readership which is socially and economically diverse. We currently don't pay for material but are seeking new authors and provide contributors with copies of the magazine with the contributor's published works. Look over a copy of *Long Life*, or talk with the editor to get the tone of the publication. There is an excellent chance that your ms will be accepted if it is well written and 'on theme.' Pictures to accompany the article are always welcome, and we like to publish photos of the authors with their first ms."

LONG STORY SHORT, AN E-ZINE FOR WRITERS

P.O. Box 475, Lewistown MT 59457. **E-mail:** alongstory_short@aol.com. **Website:** www.alongstoryshort.net. **Contact:** Anisa Claire, Kim Bussey, editors. Estab. 2003. *Long Story Short, An E-zine for Writers* publishes "the best fiction and poetry from both emerging and established writers.

Free newsletter with poetry of the month chosen by poetry editor; includes author's bio and web page listed in the e-zine. Offers light critique of submissions upon request and a free writing forum.

NEEDS Accepts all genres of flash fiction or prose. Length: up to 2,000 words.

HOW TO CONTACT Submit by e-mail; no attachments.

PAYMENT/TERMS Pays $10-15 and 1 contributor's copy for short stories 1,000-2,000 words. Pays 1 contributor's copy for flash fiction.

THE LOS ANGELES REVIEW

P.O. Box 2458, Redmond WA 98073. (626)356-4760. **Fax:** (626)356-9974. **E-mail:** lareview.trager.editor@gmail.com. **Website:** losangelesreview.org. **Contact:** Alisa Trager, managing editor. Estab. 2003.

NEEDS "We're looking for hard-to-put-down shorties under 500 words and lengthier shorts up to 4,000 words—lively, vivid, excellent literary fiction." Does not accept multiple submissions. Does not want pornography. Length: 500-4,000 words.

HOW TO CONTACT "Submishmash, our online submission form, is now our preferred method of submission, though you may still submit through postal mail. Please see our guidelines online."

TIPS "Read a few recent issues to see what we're about. Pay close attention to the submission guidelines. We like cover letters, but please keep them brief."

LOST LAKE FOLK OPERA

Shipwreckt Books Publishing Company, 309 W. Stevens Ave., Rushford MN 55971. **E-mail:** contact@shipwrecktbooks.com. **Website:** www.shipwrecktbooks.press. **Contact:** Tom Driscoll, managing editor. Estab. 2013. *Lost Lake Folk Opera* magazine, published twice annually, accepts submissions of critical journalism, short fiction and plays, poetry, B&W photography and graphic art. Seeks high-quality submissions. For journalistic pieces, please query first.

NEEDS Length: 500-5,000 words.

HOW TO CONTACT Use submissions portal at www.shipwrecktbooks.press; follow guidelines. Paper submissions are no longer accepted.

PAYMENT/TERMS Pays contributor copy.

TIPS "When in doubt, edit and cut. Please remember to read your submission. Don't expect *LLFO* to wash your car and detail it. Send clean copies of your work."

LOUISIANA LITERATURE

SLU Box 10792, Hammond LA 70402. **E-mail:** lalit@selu.edu. **Website:** www.louisianaliterature.org. **Contact:** Jack B. Bedell, editor. Estab. 1984. "Since 1984, *Louisiana Literature* has featured some of the finest writing published in America. The journal has always striven to spotlight local talent alongside nationally recognized authors. Whether it's work from established writers or from first-time publishers, *Louisiana Literature* is always looking to print the finest poetry and fiction available."

○ Biannual magazine: 6x9; 150 pages; 70 lb. paper; card cover; illustrations. Receives 100 unsolicited mss/month. May not read mss June-July. Publishes 4 new writers/year. Publishes theme issues. Has published work by Anthony Bukowski, Aaron Gwyn, Robert Phillips, and R.T. Smith. Work first published in *Louisiana Literature* is regularly reprinted in collections and is nominated for prizes from the National Book Awards for both genres and the Pulitzer. Recently, stories by Aaron Gwyn and Robert Olen Butler were selected for inclusion in *New Stories from the South.*

NEEDS Reviews fiction. "No sloppy, ungrammatical mss." Length: 1,000-6,000 words; average length: 3,500 words.

HOW TO CONTACT Submit ms via online submissions manager. Ms should be double-spaced.

PAYMENT/TERMS Pays 2 contributor's copies.

TIPS "Cut out everything that is not a functioning part of the story. Make sure your ms is professionally presented. Use relevant, specific detail in every scene. We love detail, local color, voice, and craft. Any professional ms stands out."

THE LOUISIANA REVIEW

Louisiana State University Eunice, Division of Liberal Arts, P.O. Box 1129, Eunice LA 70535. (337)550-1315. **E-mail:** bfonteno@lsue.edu. **Website:** web.lsue.edu/la-review. **Contact:** Dr. Billy Fontenot, editor and fiction editor; Dr. Jude Meche, poetry editor; Dr. Diane Langlois, art editor. Estab. 1999. *The Louisiana Review*, published annually during the fall or spring semesters, offers "Louisiana poets, writers, and artists a place to showcase their most beautiful pieces. Others may submit Louisiana- or Southern-related poetry, stories, and art. Publishes photographs. Sometimes publishes nonfiction." Wants "strong imagery, metaphor, and evidence of craft."

○ *The Louisiana Review* is 100 pages, digest-sized, professionally printed, perfect-bound. Press run is 300-600.

NEEDS Receives 25 unsolicited mss/month. Accepts 5-7 mss/issue. Reads year round. Has published work by Ronald Frame, Tom Bonner, Laura Cario, and Sheryl St. Germaine. Also publishes short shorts. No length restrictions.

HOW TO CONTACT Send SASE for return of ms. Accepts multiple submissions.

PAYMENT/TERMS Pays 1 contributor's copy.

TIPS "We do like to have fiction play out visually as a film would rather than be static and undramatized. Louisiana or Gulf Coast settings and themes preferred."

LULLWATER REVIEW

Emory University, P.O. Box 122036, Atlanta GA 30322. **E-mail:** emorylullwaterreview@gmail.com. **Website:** emorylullwaterreview.com. **Contact:** Aneyn M. O'Grady, editor in chief. Estab. 1990. "We're a small, student-run literary magazine published out of Emory University in Atlanta, Georgia, with 2 issues yearly—once in the fall and once in the spring. You can find us in the *Index of American Periodical Verse*, the *American Humanities Index* and as a member of the Council of Literary Magazines and Presses. We welcome work that brings a fresh perspective, whether through language or the visual arts."

NEEDS Recently published work by Greg Jenkins, Thomas Juvik, Jimmy Gleacher, Carla Vissers, and Judith Sudnolt. No romance or science fiction, please. Length: up to 5,000 words.

HOW TO CONTACT Send complete ms via e-mail. *Does not accept postal mail submissions.*

PAYMENT/TERMS Pays 3 contributor's copies.

TIPS "We at the *Lullwater Review* look for clear, cogent writing, strong character development, and an engaging approach to the story in our fiction submissions. Stories with particularly strong voices and well-developed central themes are especially encouraged. Be sure that your ms is ready before mailing it to us. Revise, revise, revise! Be original, honest, and, of course, keep trying."

LUMINA JOURNAL

Sarah Lawrence College, 1 Mead Way, Bronxville NY 10708. **E-mail:** lumina@gm.slc.edu. **Website:** luminajournal.com. **Contact:** Victoria Johnson, editor-in-chief. Estab. 2000. "*LUMINA*'s mission is to provide a journal where emerging and established writers and visual artists come together in exploration of the new and appreciation of the traditional. We want to see sonnets sharing space with experimental prose; we want art that pushes boundaries and bends rules with eloquence."

NEEDS Length: up to 5,000 words.

HOW TO CONTACT Submit via online submissions manager. All submissions are read blind; do not include personal information on submission documents.

LUNGFULL!MAGAZINE

316 23rd St., Brooklyn NY 11215. **E-mail:** customerservice@lungfull.org. **Website:** lungfull.org. **Contact:** Brendan Lorber, editor/publisher. Estab. 1994. "*LUNGFULL!* Magazine World Headquarters in Brooklyn is home to a team of daredevils who make it their job to bring you only the finest in typos, misspellings, and awkward phrases. That's because *LUNGFULL!magazine* is the only literary and art journal in America that prints the rough drafts of people's work so you can see the creative process as it happens."

○ *LUNGFULL!* was the recipient of a grant from the New York State Council for the Arts.

NEEDS Publishes rough drafts.

HOW TO CONTACT Submit up to 15 pages of prose. Include cover letter.

⑨ LYRICAL PASSION POETRY E-ZINE

Arlington VA **E-mail:** lpezinesubmissions@gmail.com. **Website:** lyricalpassionpoetry.yolasite.com. **Contact:** Raquel D. Bailey, founder & editor-in-chief.

Estab. 2007. Founded by award-winning poet Raquel D. Bailey, *Lyrical Passion Poetry E-Zine* is an attractive monthly online literary magazine specializing in Japanese short-form poetry. Publishes quality artwork, well-crafted short fiction, and poetry in English by emerging and established writers. Literature of lasting literary value will be considered. Welcomes the traditional to the experimental. Poetry works written in German will be considered if accompanied by translations. Offers annual short fiction and poetry contests.

HOW TO CONTACT Send complete ms, typed in the body of your email or as pdf attachment. Cover letter preferred.

⑨ MĀNOA

A Pacific Journal of International Writing, University of Hawaii at Mānoa, English Department, Honolulu HI 96822. **E-mail:** mjournal-l@lists.hawaii.edu. **Website:** manoajournal.hawaii.edu. **Contact:** Frank Stewart, editor. Estab. 1989. *Mānoa* is seeking high-quality literary fiction, poetry, essays, and translations for an international audience. In general, each issue is devoted to new work from an area of the Asia-Pacific region. Because we feature different places and have guest editors, please contact us to see if your submission is appropriate for what we're working on. *Mānoa* has received numerous awards, and work published in the magazine has been selected for prize anthologies. Please see our website for recently published issues.

NEEDS Query first. No Pacific exotica. Length: 1,000-7,500 words.

HOW TO CONTACT Send complete ms.

PAYMENT/TERMS Pays $100-500 ($25/printed page).

TIPS "Not accepting unsolicited mss at this time because of commitments to special projects. Please query before sending mss as e-mail attachments. If you would like to view a copy of the journal, you may do so at Project Muse or JSTOR, online archives available through universities, community libraries, and other institutions."

THE MACGUFFIN

Schoolcraft College, 18600 Haggerty Rd., Livonia MI 48152. (734)462-4400, ext. 5327. **E-mail:** macguffin@schoolcraft.edu. **Website:** www.schoolcraft.edu/macguffin. **Contact:** Steven A. Dolgin, editor; Gordon Krupsky, managing editor;. Estab. 1984. "Our purpose is to encourage, support, and enhance the literary arts in the Schoolcraft College community, the region, the state, and the nation. We also sponsor annual literary events and give voice to deserving new writers as well as established writers."

NEEDS Preferences range from flash and experimental to mainstream. Length: up to 5,000 words.

HOW TO CONTACT Submit ms via e-mail or postal mail. Ms should be double-spaced.

PAYMENT/TERMS Pays 2 contributor's copies.

◑ MAD HATTERS' REVIEW

Edgy and Enlightened Art, Literature and Music in the Age of Dementia, **E-mail:** askalice@madhatarts. com; marc@madhatarts.com. **Website:** www.madhattersreview.com. **Contact:** Marc Vincenz, publisher and editor in chief. *Mad Hatters' Review* "seeks to foster the work of writers and poets: explosive, lyrical, passionate, deeply wrought voices and aesthetic experiments that stretch the boundaries of language, narrative, and image, vital and enduring literary voices that sing on the page as well as in the mind. The name of our annual reflects our view of the world as essentially demented and nonsensical, too frequently a nightmare or 'non-dream' that needs to be exposed to the light for what it is, as well as what it is not. We're particularly interested in risky, thematically broad (i.e., saying something about the world and its creatures), psychologically and philosophically sophisticated works. Humor, satire, irony, magical realism, and surrealism are welcome. We look for originality, surprise, intellectual and emotional strength, lyricism, and rhythm. We love writers who stretch their imaginations to the limits and challenge conventional notions of reality and style; we care little for categories. We also adore collaborative ventures, between/among writers, visual artists, and composers."

NEEDS Submissions are open briefly for each issue: check guidelines periodically for dates. **Publishes 1 new writer/year.** Has published Alastair Gray, Kass Fleisher, Vanessa Place, Harold Jaffe, Andrei Codrescu, Sheila Murphy, Simon Perchik, Terese Svoboda, Niels Hav, Martin, Nakell, and Juan Jose Millas (translated from the Spanish). Does not want mainstream prose/story that doesn't exhibit a love of language and a sophisticated mentality. No religious or inspirational writings, confessionals, boys sowing oats, sentimental and coming-of-age stories. Length: up to 3,000 words. Average length: 1,500-2,500 words. Publishes short shorts. Average length of short shorts: 500-800 words.

HOW TO CONTACT Submit via online submissions manager.

TIPS "Imagination, skill with and appreciation of language, inventiveness, rhythm, sense of humor/irony/satire, and compelling style make a manuscript stand out. Read the magazine. Don't necessarily follow the rules you've been taught in the usual MFA program or workshop."

THE MADISON REVIEW

University of Wisconsin, 600 N. Park St., 6193 Helen C. White Hall, Madison WI 53706. **E-mail:** madisonrevw@gmail.com. **Website:** www.english.wisc.edu/madisonreview. **Contact:** Abigail Zemach and John McCracken, fiction editors; Fiona Sands and Kiyoko Reidy, poetry editors. Estab. 1972. *The Madison Review* is a student-run literary magazine that looks to publish the best available fiction and poetry.

◑ Does not publish unsolicited interviews or genre fiction. Send all submissions through online submissions manager.

NEEDS Wants well-crafted, compelling fiction featuring a wide range of styles and subjects. Does not read May-September. No genre: horror, fantasy, erotica, etc. Length: 500-30,000 words, up to 30 pages.

HOW TO CONTACT Send complete ms.

PAYMENT/TERMS Pays 2 contributor's copies, $5 for additional copies.

TIPS "Our editors have very eclectic tastes, so don't specifically try to cater to us. Above all, we look for original, high-quality work."

THE MAGNOLIA QUARTERLY

Gulfport MS 39505.

NEEDS Length: about 700 words.

HOW TO CONTACT E-mail submissions in DOC format as attachments.

PAYMENT/TERMS No payment.

THE MAIN STREET RAG

Douglass-Rausch, Ent. LLC, P.O. Box 690100, Charlotte NC 28227-7001. (704)573-2516. **E-mail:** editor@mainstreetrag.com. **Website:** www.mainstreetrag.com. **Contact:** M. Scott Douglass, publisher/managing editor. Estab. 1996. *The Main Street Rag*, published quarterly, prints "poetry, short fiction, essays, interviews, reviews, photos, and art. We like publishing good material from people who are interested in more than notching another publishing credit, people who support small independent publishers like ourselves." Will consider "almost anything," but prefers "writing with an edge—either gritty or bitingly humorous. Contributors are advised to visit our website prior to submission to confirm current needs." *The Main Street Rag* receives about 5,000 submissions/year; publishes 50+ poems and 3-5 stories per issue, a featured interview, photos, and an occasional nonfiction piece. Press run is about 500 (250 subscribers, 15 libraries).

NEEDS Length: up to 6,000 words.

HOW TO CONTACT No hard copy submissions—all electronic. See website for details.

PAYMENT/TERMS Pays 1 contributor's copy.

◑❸ THE MALAHAT REVIEW

The University of Victoria, P.O. Box 1700, STN CSC, Victoria BC V8W 2Y2, Canada. (250)721-8524. **E-mail:** malahat@uvic.ca (for queries only). **Website:** www.malahatreview.ca. **Contact:** Iain Higgins, editor. Estab. 1967. Quarterly magazine covering poetry, fiction, creative nonfiction, and reviews. "We try to achieve a balance of views and styles in each issue. We strive for a mix of the best writing by both established and new writers."

NEEDS Length: up to 8,000 words.

HOW TO CONTACT Submit via Submittable link on Submissions page.

PAYMENT/TERMS Pays $60/magazine page.

TIPS "Please do not send more than 1 submission at a time: 3-6 poems, 1 piece of creative nonfiction, or 1 short story (do not mix poetry and prose in the same submission). See *The Malahat Review*'s Contests section of our website for more info on our annual contests involving poetry, short fiction, creative nonfiction, long poems, and novellas."

❶◐❸ THE MASSACHUSETTS REVIEW

University of Massachusetts, Photo Lab 309, 211 Hicks Way, Amherst MA 01003. (413)545-2689. **E-mail:** massrev@external.umass.edu. **Website:** www.massreview.org. **Contact:** Emily Wojcik, managing editor. Estab. 1959. Seeks a balance between established writers and promising new ones. Interested in material of variety and vitality relevant to the intellectual and aesthetic questions of our time. Aspire to have a broad appeal.

◑ Does not respond to mss without SASE.

NEEDS Wants short stories. Accepts 1 short story per submission. Include name and contact information on the first page. Encourages page numbers. Has

published work by Ahdaf Soueif, Elizabeth Denton, and Nicholas Montemarano. Length: up to 30 pages or 8,000 words.

HOW TO CONTACT Send complete ms.

PAYMENT/TERMS Pays $50 and 2 contributor's copies.

TIPS "No manuscripts are considered May-September. Electronic submission process can be found on website. No fax or e-mail submissions. Shorter rather than longer stories preferred (up to 28-30 pages)." Looks for works that "stop us in our tracks." Manuscripts that stand out use "unexpected language, idiosyncrasy of outlook, and are the opposite of ordinary."

MCSWEENEY'S

849 Valencia St., San Francisco CA 94110. **E-mail:** custservice@mcsweeneys.net. **E-mail:** websubmissions@mcsweeneys.net (for humor website only). https://mcsweeneysquarterly.submittable.com/submit (for Print Quarterly). **Website:** www.mcsweeneys.net. **Contact:** Christopher Monks, humor website editor; Claire Boyle, print editor. Estab. 1998. Online literary journal. "Timothy McSweeney's *Internet Tendency* is an offshoot of Timothy McSweeney's *Quarterly Concern*, a journal created by nervous people in relative obscurity, and published four times a year." McSweeney's Internet Tendency is our humor/satire site.

NEEDS literate humor. Sometimes comments on rejected mss. Sometimes comments on rejected mss. Length: 1,500 words maximum; preference for pieces significantly shorter (700-1,000 words).

HOW TO CONTACT For submissions to the website, paste the entire piece into the body of an e-mail.

TIPS "Please read the writer's guidelines before submitting, and send your submissions to the appropriate address. Do not submit your work to both the print submissions address and the Web submissions address, as seemingly hundreds of writers have been doing lately. If you submit a piece of writing intended for the magazine to the web submissions address, you will confuse us, and if you confuse us, we will accidentally delete your work without reading it."

MERIDIAN

University of Virginia, P.O. Box 400145, Charlottesville VA 22904-4145. **E-mail:** meridianuva@gmail.com; meridianpoetry@gmail.com; meridianfiction@gmail.com. **Website:** www.readmeridian.org. Estab. 1998. *Meridian* Editors' Prize Contest offers annual $1,000 award. Submit online only; see website for formatting details. **Entry fee:** $8.50, includes one-year electronic subscription to *Meridian* for all U.S. entries or 1 copy of the prize issue for all international entries. **Deadline:** December or January; see website for current deadline. *Meridian*, published semiannually, prints poetry, fiction, nonfiction, interviews, and reviews. "*Meridian* is interested in writing that is vibrant, moving, and alive, and welcomes contributions from a variety of aesthetic approaches. Has published such poets as Alexandra Teague, Gregory Pardlo, Sandra Meek, and Bob Hicok, and such fiction writers as Matt Bell, Kate Milliken, and Ron Carlson. Has recently interviewed C. Michael Curtis, Ann Beatty, and Claire Messud, among other luminaries. Also publishes a recurring feature called 'Lost Classic,' which resurrects previously unpublished work by celebrated writers and which has included illustrations from the mss of Jorge Luis Borges, letters written by Elizabeth Bishop, Stephen Crane's deleted chapter from *The Red Badge of Courage*, and a letter written by Flannery O'Connor about her novel *Wise Blood*."

Meridian is 130 pages, digest-sized, offset-printed, perfect-bound, with color cover. Receives about 2,500 poems/year, accepts about 40 (less than 1%). Press run is 1,000 (750 subscribers, 15 libraries, 200 shelf sales); 150 distributed free to writing programs. Work published in *Meridian* has appeared in *The Best American Poetry* and *The Pushcart Prize Anthology*.

NEEDS Submit complete ms via online submissions manager. Length: up to 6,500 words.

PAYMENT/TERMS Pays 2 contributor's copies (additional copies available at discount).

⑨ MICHIGAN QUARTERLY REVIEW

0576 Rackham Bldg., 915 E. Washington, Ann Arbor MI 48109-1070. (734)764-9265. **E-mail:** mqr@umich. edu. **Website:** www.michiganquarterlyreview.com. **Contact:** Jonathan Freedman, editor; Vicki Lawrence, managing editor. Estab. 1962. *Michigan Quarterly Review* is an eclectic interdisciplinary journal of arts and culture that seeks to combine the best of poetry, fiction, and creative nonfiction with outstanding critical essays on literary, cultural, social, and political matters. The flagship journal of the University of Michigan, *MQR* draws on lively minds here and elsewhere, seeking to present accessible work of all varieties for sophisticated readers from within and without the academy.

The Laurence Goldstein Award is a $500 annual award to the best poem published in *MQR* during the previous year. The Lawrence Foundation Award is a $1,000 annual award to the best short story published in *MQR* during the previous year. The Page Davidson Clayton Award for Emerging Poets is a $500 annual award given to the best poet appearing in *MQR* during the previous year who has not yet published a book.

NEEDS "No restrictions on subject matter or language. We are very selective. We like stories that are unusual in tone and structure, and innovative in language. No genre fiction written for a market. Would like to see more fiction about social, political, and cultural matters, not just centered on a love relationship or dysfunctional family." Receives 300 unsolicited mss/month. Accepts 3-4 mss/issue; 12-16 mss/year. Publishes 1-2 new writers/year. Has published work by Rebecca Makkai, Peter Ho Davies, Laura Kasischke, Gerald Shapiro, and Alan Cheuse. Length: 1,500-7,000 words; average length: 5,000 words.

HOW TO CONTACT Send complete ms.

PAYMENT/TERMS Payment varies but is usually in the range of $50-$150.

TIPS "Read the journal and assess the range of contents and the level of writing. We have no guidelines to offer or set expectations; every ms is judged on its unique qualities. On essays, query with a very thorough description of the argument and a copy of the first page. Watch for announcements of special issues, which are usually expanded issues and draw upon a lot of freelance writing. Be aware that this is a university quarterly that publishes a limited amount of fiction and poetry and that it is directed at an educated audience, one that has done a great deal of reading in all types of literature."

MID-AMERICAN REVIEW

Bowling Green State University, Department of English, Bowling Green OH 43403. (419)372-2725. **E-mail:** mar@bgsu.edu. **E-mail:** marsubmissions.bgsu. edu. **Website:** www.bgsu.edu/midamericanreview. **Contact:** Abigail Cloud, editor-in-chief; Bridget Adams, fiction editor. Estab. 1981. "We aim to put the best possible work in front of the biggest possible audience. We publish contemporary fiction, poetry, creative nonfiction, translations, and book reviews." Contests: The Fineline Competition for Prose Poems, Short Shorts, and Everything In Between (June 1 deadline, $10 per 3 pieces, limit 500 words each); The Sherwood Anderson Fiction Award (November 1 deadline, $10 per piece); and the James Wright Poetry Award (November 1 deadline, $10 per 3 pieces).

NEEDS Publishes traditional, character-oriented, literary, experimental, prose poem, and short-short stories. No genre fiction. Length: up to 6,000 words.

HOW TO CONTACT Submit ms by mail with SASE, or through online submission manager. Agented fiction 5%. Recently published work by Mollie Ficek and J. David Stevens.

TIPS "We are seeking translations of contemporary authors from all languages into English; submissions must include the original and proof of permission to translate. We would also like to see more creative nonfiction."

MIDWAY JOURNAL

216 Banks St. #2, Cambridge MA 02138. (763)516-7463. **E-mail:** editors@midwayjournal.com. **Website:** www.midwayjournal.com. **Contact:** Christopher Lowe, nonfiction editor; Ralph Pennel, fiction editor; Paige Riehl, poetry editor. Estab. 2006. "Just off of I-94 and on the border between St. Paul and Minneapolis, the Midway, like any other state fairgrounds, is alive with a mix of energies and people. Its position as mid-way, as a place of boundary crossing, also reflects our vision for this journal. The work here complicates and questions the boundaries of genre, binary, and aesthetic. It offers surprises and ways of re-seeing, re-thinking, and re-feeling: a veritable banquet of literary fare. Which is why, in each new issue, we are honored to present work by both new and established writers alike." Member CLMP.

NEEDS No length limit.

HOW TO CONTACT Submit 1 piece of fiction or 2 pieces of flash/sudden fiction via online submissions manager.

TIPS "An interesting story with engaging writing, both in terms of style and voice, make a ms stand out. Round characters are a must. Writers who take chances either with content or with form grab an editor's immediate attention. Spend time with the words on the page. Spend time with the language. The language and voice are not vehicles; they, too, are tools."

MINAS TIRITH EVENING-STAR

Journal of the American Tolkien Society, American Tolkien Society, P.O. Box 97, Highland MI 48357-0097. **E-mail:** americantolkiensociety@yahoo.com.

E-mail: editor@americantolkiensociety.org. **Website:** www.americantolkiensociety.org. **Contact:** Amalie A. Helms, editor. Estab. 1967. *Minas Tirith Evening-Star: Journal of the American Tolkien Society*, published occasionally, publishes poetry, book reviews, essays, and fan fiction. *Minas Tirith Evening-Star* is now online at www.americantolkiensociety.org. There is no charge to website users, Society membership is $5 US per year.

HOW TO CONTACT Submit complete ms by mail or e-mail.

PAYMENT/TERMS Pays 1 contributor's copy.

THE MINNESOTA REVIEW

Virginia Tech, **E-mail:** editors@theminnesotareview.org. **E-mail:** submissions@theminnesotareview.org. **Website:** minnesotareview.wordpress.com. **Contact:** Janell Watson, editor. Estab. 1960. *The Minnesota Review*, published biannually, is a journal featuring creative and critical work from writers on the rise or who are already established. Each issue is about 200 pages, digest-sized, flat-spined, with glossy card cover. Press run is 1,000 (400 subscribers). Also available online. Subscription: $30 for 2 years for individuals, $60/year for institutions. Sample: $15.

Open to submissions August 1-November 1 and January 1-April 1.

NEEDS Length: up to 5,000 words for short stories, up to 1,000 words for short shorts or flash fiction.

HOW TO CONTACT Submit up to 1 short story or 4 short shorts or flash fiction pieces per reading period via online submissions manager.

PAYMENT/TERMS Pays 2 contributor's copies.

❸ THE MISSOURI REVIEW

357 McReynolds Hall, University of Missouri, Columbia MO 65211. (573)882-4474. **E-mail:** question@moreview.com. **Website:** www.missourireview.com. **Contact:** Kate McIntyre. Estab. 1978. The William Peden Prize of $1,000 is awarded annually to the best piece of fiction to have appeared in the previous volume year. The winner is chosen by an outside judge. There is no separate application process. Publishes contemporary fiction, poetry, interviews, personal essays, and special features—such as History as Literature series, Found Text series, and Curio Cabinet art features—for the literary and the general reader interested in a wide range of subjects.

NEEDS Length: No restrictions, but longer mss (9,000-12,000 words) or flash fiction ms (up to 2,000 words) must be truly exceptional to be published.

HOW TO CONTACT Send complete ms.

PAYMENT/TERMS Pays $40/printed page.

TIPS "Send your best work."

MOBIUS

The Journal of Social Change, 149 Talmadge St., Madison WI 53704. **E-mail:** fmschep@charter.net (fiction); demiurge@fibitz.com (poetry). **Website:** www.mobiusmagazine.com. **Contact:** Fred Schepartz, publisher and executive editor. Estab. 1989. *Mobius: The Journal of Social Change* is an online-only journal, published quarterly in March, June, September, and December. "At *Mobius* we believe that writing is power and good writing empowers both the reader and the writer. We feel strongly that alternatives are needed to an increasingly corporate literary scene. *Mobius* strives to provide an outlet for writers disenfranchised by a bottom-line marketplace and challenging writing for those who feel that today's literary standards are killing us in a slow, mind-numbing fashion."

NEEDS Wants fiction dealing with themes of social change. "We like social commentary, but mainly we like good writing. No porn or work that is racist, sexist or any other kind of *-ist*. No Christian or spirituality proselytizing fiction." Length: up to 5,000 words.

HOW TO CONTACT Submit up to 1 story at a time via e-mail (preferred) or mail.

TIPS "We like high impact. We like plot- and character-driven stories that function like theater of the mind. We look first and foremost for good writing. Prose must be crisp and polished; the story must pique my interest and make me care due to a certain intellectual, emotional aspect. *Mobius* is about social change. We want stories that make some statement about the society we live in, either on a macro or micro level. Not that your story needs to preach from a soapbox (actually, we prefer that it doesn't), but it needs to have something to say."

THE MOCHILA REVIEW

Missouri Western State University, Department of English & Modern Languages, 4525 Downs Dr., St. Joseph MO 64507. **E-mail:** mochila@missouriwestern. edu. **Website:** www.missouriwestern.edu/orgs/mochila/homepage.htm. **Contact:** Dr. Marianne Kunkel, editor in chief. Estab. 2000. "*The Mochila Review* is an annual international undergraduate journal published with support from the English and Modern Languages department at Missouri Western State University. Our goal is to publish the best short stories, poems, and essays from the next generation of important authors: student writers. Our staff, comprised primarily of undergraduate students, understands the publishing challenges that emerging writers face and is committed to helping talented students gain wider audiences in the pages of *The Mochila Review* and on our website."

NEEDS Length: up to 5,000 words.

HOW TO CONTACT Submit complete ms via online submissions manager.

PAYMENT/TERMS Pays contributor's copies.

TIPS "Mss with fresh language, energy, passion, and intelligence stand out. Study the craft, and be entertaining and engaging."

MSLEXIA

Mslexia Publications Ltd, P.O. Box 656, Newcastle upon Tyne NE99 1PZ, United Kingdom. (+44) (191)204-8860. **E-mail:** postbag@mslexia.co.uk. **E-mail:** submissions@mslexia.co.uk. **Website:** www. mslexia.co.uk. **Contact:** Debbie Taylor, editorial director. Estab. 1997. "*Mslexia* tells you all you need to know about exploring your creativity and getting into print. No other magazine provides *Mslexia*'s unique mix of advice and inspiration; news, reviews, interviews; competitions, events, grants; all served up with a challenging selection of new poetry and prose. *Mslexia* is read by authors and absolute beginners. A quarterly master class in the business and psychology of writing, it's the essential magazine for women who write. We accept submissions from any woman from any country writing in English. There are 14 ways of submitting to the magazine, for every kind of writing, and we pay for everything we publish. Submissions guidelines are on our website. We also run a series of women's fiction competitions with top cash prizes and career development opportunities for finalists."

NEEDS See guidelines on website. "Submissions not on 1 of our current themes will be returned (if submitted with a SASE) or destroyed." Length: 50-2,200 words.

HOW TO CONTACT Send complete ms.

PAYMENT/TERMS Pays £15 per 1,000 words prose plus contributor's copies.

TIPS "Read the magazine; subscribe if you can afford it. *Mslexia* has a particular style and relationship with its readers which is hard to assess at a quick glance. The majority of our readers live in the UK, so feature pitches should be aware of this. We never commission work without seeing a written sample first. We rarely accept unsolicited manuscripts, but prefer a short letter suggesting a feature, plus a brief bio and writing sample."

$ MUZZLE BLASTS

P.O. Box 67, Friendship IN 47021. (812)667-5131. **Fax:** (812)667-5136. **E-mail:** llarkin@nmlra.org. **Website:** www.nmlra.org. **Contact:** Lee A. Larkin, editor. Estab. 1939. "Articles must relate to muzzleloading or the muzzleloading era of American history."

NEEDS Must pertain to muzzleloading. Length: 2,500 words.

HOW TO CONTACT Query.

PAYMENT/TERMS Pays $50-300.

N+1

The Editors, 68 Jay St., Suite 405, Brooklyn NY 11201. **E-mail:** editors@nplusonemag.com. **E-mail:** submissions@nplusonemag.com. **Website:** www.nplusonemag.com. **Contact:** Nikil Saval and Dayna Tortorici, editors.

NEEDS Submit queries or finished pieces by e-mail.

TIPS "Most of the slots available for a given issue will have been filled many months before publication. If you would like to brave the odds, the best submission guidelines are those implied by the magazine itself. Read an issue or two through to get a sense of whether your piece might fit into *n+1*."

❶$ NA'AMAT WOMAN

21515 Vanowen Street, Suite 102, Canoga Park CA 91303. (818)431-2200. **E-mail:** naamat@naamat.org; judith@naamat.org. **Website:** www.naamat.org. **Contact:** Judith Sokoloff, editor. Estab. 1926. "Magazine covering a wide variety of subjects of interest to the Jewish community—including political and social issues, arts, profiles; many articles about Israel and women's issues. Fiction must have a Jewish theme. Readers are the American Jewish community." Circ. 15,000. "Magazine covering a wide variety of subjects of interest to the Jewish community— including political and social issues, arts, profiles; many articles about Israel and women's issues. Fiction must have a Jewish theme. Readers are the American Jewish community."

NEEDS Ethnic/multicultural, historical, humor/satire, literary, novel excerpts, women-oriented. Receives 10 unsolicited mss/month. Accepts 1-3 mss/year. "We want serious fiction, with insight, reflection and consciousness." "We do not want fiction that is mostly dialogue. No corny Jewish humor. No Holocaust fiction." Length: 2,000-3,000 words.

HOW TO CONTACT Query with published clips or send complete mss. Responds in 6 months to queries; 6 months to mss. Sample copy for 9×11½ SAE and $2 postage or look online. Sample copy for $2. Writer's guidelines for #10 SASE, or by e-mail. Query with published clips or send complete ms.

PAYMENT/TERMS Pays 10¢/word and 2 contributor's copies. Pays on publication for first North American serial, first, one time, second serial (reprint) rights, makes work-for-hire assignments. Pays 10-20¢/word for assigned articles and for unsolicited articles.

TIPS "No maudlin nostalgia or romance; no hackneyed Jewish humor."

NARRATIVE MAGAZINE

2443 Fillmore St., #214, San Francisco CA 94115. **E-mail:** contact@narrativemagazine.com. **Website:** www.narrativemagazine.com. **Contact:** Michael Croft, senior editor; Mimi Kusch, managing editor; Michael Wiegers, poetry editor. Estab. 2003. *"Narrative publishes high-quality contemporary literature in a full range of styles, forms, and lengths. Submit poetry, fiction, and nonfiction, including stories, short shorts, novels, novel excerpts, novellas, personal essays, humor, sketches, memoirs, literary biographies, commentary, reportage, interviews, and short audio recordings of short-short stories and poems. We welcome submissions of previously unpublished mss of all lengths, ranging from short-short stories to complete book-length works for serialization. In addition to submissions for issues of Narrative itself, we also encourage submissions for our Story of the Week, Poem of the Week, literary contests, and Readers' Narratives. Please read our Submission Guidelines for all information on mss formatting, word lengths, author payment, and other policies. We accept submissions only through our electronic submission system. We do not accept submissions through postal services or e-mail. You may send us mss for the following submission categories: General Submissions, Narrative Prize, Story of the Week, Poem of the Week, Readers' Narrative, iPoem, iStory, Six-Word Story, or a specific Contest. Your mss must be in one of the following file forms: DOC, RTF, PDF, DOCX, TXT, WPD, ODF, MP3, MP4, MOV, or FLV."*

◯   *Narrative has received recognitions in New Stories from the South, Best American Mystery Stories, O. Henry Prize Stories, Best American Short Stories, Best American Essays, and the Pushcart Prize Collection. In an article on the* business of books, the National Endowment for the Arts featured *Narrative* as the model for the evolution of both print and digital publishing.

NEEDS Has published work by Alice Munro, Tobias Wolff, Marvin Bell, Jane Smiley, Joyce Carol Oates, E.L. Doctorow, and Min Jin Lee. Publishes new and emerging writers.

HOW TO CONTACT Send complete ms.

PAYMENT/TERMS Pays on publication between $150-1,000, $1,000-5,000 for book length, plus annual prizes of more than $28,000.

TIPS "Log on and study our magazine online. Narrative fiction, graphic art, and multimedia are selected, first and foremost, for quality."

NATURAL BRIDGE

Department of English, University of Missouri-St. Louis, 1 University Blvd., St. Louis MO 63121. **E-mail:** natural@umsl.edu. **Website:** www.umsl.edu/~natural. Estab. 1999. *Natural Bridge*, published biannually in April and December, invites submissions of poetry, fiction, personal essays, and translations.

○ No longer accepts submissions via e-mail. Accepts submissions through online submission manager and postal mail only.

NEEDS Submit year round; however, "we do not read May 1-August 1." Recently published work by Tayari Jones, Steve Stern, Jamie Wriston Colbert, Lex Williford, and Mark Jay Mirsky. Also publishes literary essays, poetry. Sometimes comments on rejected mss.

HOW TO CONTACT Submit 1 ms through online submissions manager ($3 fee for nonsubscribers) or postal mail (free).

PAYMENT/TERMS Pays 2 contributor's copies and one-year subscription.

NEBO

Arkansas Tech University, Department of English, Russellville AR 72801. **E-mail:** nebo@atu.edu. **E-mail:** nebo@atu.edu. **Website:** www.atu.edu/world-languages/Nebo.php. **Contact:** Editor. Estab. 1983. *Nebo*, published in the spring and fall, publishes fiction, poetry, creative nonfiction, drama, comics, and art from Arkansas Tech students and unpublished writers as well as nationally known writers.

○ Reads submissions August 15-May 1.

NEEDS Accepts all genres. Length: up to 5,000 words.

HOW TO CONTACT Submit complete ms by e-mail or postal mail.

TIPS "Avoid pretentiousness. Write something you genuinely care about. Please edit your work for spelling, grammar, cohesiveness, and overall purpose. Many of the mss we receive should be publishable with a little polishing. Mss should never be submitted handwritten or on 'onion skin' or colored paper."

●⑤ NEON MAGAZINE

Neon Books, , UK. **E-mail:** info@neonmagazine. co.uk. **E-mail:** subs@neonmagazine.co.uk. **Website:** www.neonmagazine.co.uk. **Contact:** Krishan Coupland. Twice-yearly online and print magazine featuring alternative work of any form of poetry and prose, short stories, flash fiction, artwork, and reviews. "*Neon* sits on the edge of horror and science-fiction, but with strong literary leanings. If you have a taste for the magical realist or uncanny, *Neon* is the magazine for you."

NEEDS "No nonsensical prose; we are not appreciative of sentimentality." No word limit.

HOW TO CONTACT Full guidelines online.

PAYMENT/TERMS Pays royalties.

TIPS "Send several poems, 1-2 pieces of prose, or several images via e-mail. Include the word 'submission' in your subject line. Include a short biographical note (up to 100 words). Read submission guidelines before submitting your work."

⑤ THE NEW CRITERION

900 Broadway, Ste. 602, New York NY 10003. **Website:** www.newcriterion.com. **Contact:** Roger Kimball, editor and publisher; David Yezzi, poetry editor. Estab. 1982. "A monthly review of the arts and intellectual life, *The New Criterion* began as an experiment in critical audacity—a publication devoted to engaging, in Matthew Arnold's famous phrase, with 'the best that has been thought and said.' This also meant engaging with those forces dedicated to traducing genuine cultural and intellectual achievement, whether through obfuscation, politicization, or a commitment to nihilistic absurdity. We are proud that *The New Criterion* has been in the forefront both of championing what is best and most humanely vital in our cultural inheritance and in exposing what is mendacious, corrosive, and spurious. Published monthly from September through June, *The New Criterion* brings together a wide range of young and established critics whose common aim is to bring you the most incisive criticism being written today."

The New Criterion is 90 pages, 7x10, flat-spined. Single copy: $12.

NEW ENGLAND REVIEW

Middlebury College, Middlebury VT 05753. (802)443-5075. **E-mail:** nereview@middlebury.edu. **Website:** www.nereview.com. **Contact:** Marcia Pomerance, managing editor. Estab. 1978. *New England Review* is a prestigious, nationally distributed literary journal. Reads September 1-May 31 (postmarked dates). *New England Review* is 200+ pages, 7x10, printed on heavy stock, flat-spined, with glossy cover with art. Receives 3,000-4,000 poetry submissions/year, accepts about 70-80 poems/year. Receives 550 unsolicited mss/month, accepts 6 mss/issue, 24 fiction mss/year. Does not accept mss June-August, December-January. Agented fiction less than 5%.

NEEDS Send 1 story at a time, unless it is very short. Wants only serious literary fiction and novel excerpts. Publishes approximately 10 new writers/year. Has published work by Steve Almond, Christine Sneed, Roy Kesey, Thomas Gough, Norman Lock, Brock Clarke, Carl Phillips, Lucia Perillo, Linda Gregerson, and Natasha Trethewey. Length: not strict on word count.

HOW TO CONTACT Send complete ms via online submission manager. No e-mail submissions. "Will consider simultaneous submissions, but it must be stated as such and you must notify us immediately if the ms is accepted for publication elsewhere."

PAYMENT/TERMS Pays $20/page ($20 minimum), and 2 contributor's copies.

TIPS "We consider short fiction, including short shorts, novellas, and self-contained extracts from novels in both traditional and experimental forms. In nonfiction, we consider a variety of general and literary but not narrowly scholarly essays; we also publish long and short poems, screenplays, graphics, translations, critical reassessments, statements by artists working in various media, testimonies, and letters from abroad. We are committed to exploration of all forms of contemporary cultural expression in the U.S. and abroad. With few exceptions, we print only work not published previously elsewhere."

NEW LETTERS

University of Missouri-Kansas City, 5101 Rockhill Rd., Kansas City MO 64110. (816)235-1168. **Fax:** (816)235-2611. **E-mail:** newletters@umkc.edu. **Website:** www.newletters.org. **Contact:** Robert Stewart, editor-in-chief. Estab. 1934. "*New Letters*, published quarterly, continues to seek the best new writing, whether from established writers or those ready and waiting to be discovered. In addition, it supports those writers, readers, and listeners who want to experience the joy of writing that can both surprise and inspire us all." Submissions are not read June 1st through July 30th.

NEEDS No genre fiction. Length: up to 5,000 words.

HOW TO CONTACT Send complete ms.

PAYMENT/TERMS Pays $30-75.

TIPS "We aren't interested in essays that are footnoted or essays usually described as scholarly or critical. Our preference is for creative nonfiction or personal essays. We prefer shorter stories and essays to longer ones (an average length is 3,500-4,000 words). We have no rigid preferences as to subject, style, or genre, although commercial efforts tend to put us off. Even so, our only fixed requirement is good writing."

NEW MADRID

Journal of Contemporary Literature, Murray State University, Department of English and Philosophy, 7C Faculty Hall, Murray KY 42071-3341. (270)809-4730. **E-mail:** msu.newmadrid@murraystate.edu. **Website:** newmadridjournal.org. **Contact:** Ann Neelon, editor; Jacque E. Day, managing editor. "*New Madrid* is the national journal of the low-residency MFA program at Murray State University. It takes its name from the New Madrid seismic zone, which falls within the central Mississippi Valley and extends through western Kentucky."

See website for guidelines and upcoming themes. "We have 2 reading periods, August 15-October 15 and January 15-March 15." Also publishes poetry and creative nonfiction. Rarely comments on/critiques rejected mss.

NEEDS Length: up to 20 pages double-spaced.

HOW TO CONTACT Accepts submissions by online submissions manager only. Include brief bio, list of publications. Considers multiple submissions.

PAYMENT/TERMS Pays 2 contributor's copies.

TIPS "Quality is the determining factor for breaking into *New Madrid*. We are looking for well-crafted, compelling writing in a range of genres, forms, and styles."

NEW OHIO REVIEW

English Department, 201 Ellis Hall; 45 University Terrace, Ohio University, Athens OH 45701. **E-mail:**

noreditors@ohio.edu. **Website:** www.ohiou.edu/nor. **Contact:** David Wanczyk, editor. Estab. 2007. *New Ohio Review*, published biannually in spring and fall, publishes fiction, nonfiction, and poetry. Member CLMP. Reading period is September 15-December 15 and January 15-April 15. Annual contests, Jan 15th-Apr 15th ($1,000 prizes).

NEEDS Considers literary short fiction; no novel excerpts.

HOW TO CONTACT Send complete ms.

PAYMENT/TERMS Pays $30 minimum in addition to 2 contributor's copies and one-year subscription.

❸ NEW ORLEANS REVIEW

Box 195, Loyola University, New Orleans LA 70118. (504)865-2295. **E-mail:** noreview@loyno.edu. **Website:** neworleansreview.org. **Contact:** Heidi Braden, managing editor; Mark Yakich, Editor. Estab. 1968. *New Orleans Review* is an annual journal of contemporary literature and culture, publishing new poetry, fiction, nonfiction, art, photography, film, and book reviews.

The journal has published an eclectic variety of work by established and emerging writers, including Walker Percy, Pablo Neruda, Ellen Gilchrist, Nelson Algren, Hunter S. Thompson, John Kennedy Toole, Richard Brautigan, Barry Spacks, James Sallis, Jack Gilbert, Paul Hoover, Rodney Jones, Annie Dillard, Everette Maddox, Julio Cortazar, Gordon Lish, Robert Walser, Mark Halliday, Jack Butler, Robert Olen Butler, Michael Harper, Angela Ball, Joyce Carol Oates, Diane Wakoski, Dermot Bolger, Roddy Doyle, William Kotzwinkle, Alain Robbe-Grillet, Arnost Lustig, Raymond Queneau, Yusef Komunyakaa, Michael Martone, Tess Gallagher, Matthea Harvey, D. A. Powell, Rikki Ducornet, and Ed Skoog.

NEEDS Length: up to 6,500 words.

HOW TO CONTACT Submit complete ms using online submissions manager ($3 fee).

PAYMENT/TERMS Pays 2 contributor's copies.

TIPS "We're looking for dynamic writing that demonstrates attention to the language and a sense of the medium, writing that engages, surprises, moves us. We're not looking for genre fiction or academic articles. We subscribe to the belief that in order to truly write well, one must first master the rudiments: grammar and syntax, punctuation, the sentence, the paragraph, the line, the stanza. We receive about 3,000 mss a year and publish about 3% of them. Check out a recent issue, send us your best, proofread your work, be patient, be persistent."

◐❸ THE NEW QUARTERLY

St. Jerome's University, 290 Westmount Rd. N., Waterloo ON N2L 3G3, Canada. (519)884-8111, ext. 28290. **E-mail:** editor@tnq.ca; info@tnq.ca. **Website:** www.tnq.ca. Estab. 1981. "Emphasis on emerging writers and genres, but we publish more traditional work as well if the language and narrative structure are fresh." Open to Canadian writers only. Reading periods: March 1-August 31; September 1-February 28.

NEEDS "*Canadian work only*. We are not interested in genre fiction. We are looking for innovative, beautifully crafted, deeply felt literary fiction."

HOW TO CONTACT Send complete ms with submission cover sheet and bio. Does not accept submissions by e-mail. Accepts simultaneoues submissions if indicated in cover letter.

PAYMENT/TERMS Pays $250/story.

TIPS "Reading us is the best way to get our measure. We don't have preconceived ideas about what we're looking for other than that it must be Canadian work (Canadian writers, not necessarily Canadian content). We want something that's fresh, something that will repay a second reading, something in which the language soars and the feeling is complexly rendered."

NEW SOUTH

Georgia State University, Campus Box 1894, MSC 8R0322 Unit 8, Atlanta GA 30303-3083. **E-mail:** newsoutheditors@gmail.com. **Website:** www.newsouthjournal.com. Estab. 1980. Semiannual magazine dedicated to finding and publishing the best work from artists around the world. Wants original voices searching to rise above the ordinary. Seeks to publish high-quality work, regardless of genre, form, or regional ties. *New South* is 160+ pages. Press run is 1,500, and free to GSU students. The *New South* Annual Writing Contest offers $1,000 for the best poem and $1,000 for the best story or essay; one-year subscription to all who submit. Submissions must be unpublished. Submit up to 3 poems, 1 story, or 1 essay on any subject or in any form. Guidelines available online. Competition receives 300 entries. Past judges include Sharon Olds, Jane Hirschfield, Anthony Hecht, Phillip Levine, Mark Doty, and Jake Adam York. Winners will be published in the Fall issue.

NEEDS Receives 200 unsolicited mss/month. Publishes and welcomes short shorts. Length: up to 9,000 words (short stories); up to 1,000 words (short shorts).

HOW TO CONTACT Submit 1 short story or up to 5 short shorts through Submittable.

PAYMENT/TERMS Pays 2 contributor's copies.

TIPS "We want what's new, what's fresh, and what's different—whether it comes from the Southern United States, the South of India, or the North, East or West of Anywhere."

◗ NEW WELSH REVIEW

P.O. Box 170, Aberystwyth, Ceredigion SY23 1 WZ, United Kingdom. 01970-628410. **E-mail:** editor@newwelshreview.com. **E-mail:** submissions@newwelshreview.com. **Website:** www.newwelshreview.com. **Contact:** Gwen Davies, editor. "*New Welsh Review*, a literary magazine published 3 times/year and ranked in the top 5 British literary magazines, publishes stories, poems, and critical essays. The best of Welsh writing in English, past and present, is celebrated, discussed, and debated. We seek poems, short stories, reviews, special features/articles, and commentary."

HOW TO CONTACT Submit complete ms by e-mail.

PAYMENT/TERMS Pays direct to account or sends check on publication and 1 copy at discounted contributor's rate of £5 inc p&p."

NIMROD INTERNATIONAL JOURNAL

International Journal of Prose and Poetry, University of Tulsa, 800 S. Tucker Dr., Tulsa OK 74104-3189. (918)631-3080. **E-mail:** nimrod@utulsa.edu. **Website:** https://nimrod.utulsa.edu. **Contact:** Eilis O'Neal, editor-in-chief; Cassidy McCants, associate editor. Estab. 1956. Since its founding in 1956 at The University of Tulsa, *Nimrod International Journal of Prose and Poetry*'s mission has been the discovery, development, and promotion of new writing. On a national and international scale, *Nimrod* helps new writers find their audiences through publication in our semiannual journal. We offer new and promising work that may be unfamiliar to readers, such as writing from countries not well represented in the American mainstream, writing in translation, and writing from people of under-represented ages, races, and sexual identities. *Nimrod* supports and defends the literary tradition of small magazines, spotlighting lesser-known poets and writers and providing foundations for their literary careers. We promote a living literature, believing

that it is possible to search for, recognize, and reward contemporary writing of imagination, substance, and skill. Semiannual magazine: 200 pages; perfect-bound; 4-color cover. Receives 300 unsolicited mss/month. **Publishes 50-120 new writers/year.** Reading period: January 1 through November 30. Online submissions accepted at nimrodjournal.submittable.com/submit. Does not accept submissions by email unless the writer is living outside the U.S. and cannot submit using the submissions manager.

NEEDS Wants "vigorous writing, characters that are well developed, dialogue that is realistic without being banal." Length: up to 7,500 words.

HOW TO CONTACT Submit complete ms by mail or through the online submissions manager. Include SASE for work submitted by mail.

PAYMENT/TERMS Pays $10/page and 2 contributor's copies.

⑤ NINTH LETTER

Department of English, University of Illinois, 608 S. Wright St., Urbana IL 61801. **E-mail:** info@ninthletter.com; editor@ninthletter.com; fiction@ninthletter.com; poetry@ninthletter.com; nonfiction@ninthletter.com. **Website:** www.ninthletter.com. **Contact:** Editorial staff rotates; contact genre-specific e-mail address with inquiries. "*Ninth Letter* accepts submissions of fiction, poetry, and essays from September 1-February 28 (postmark dates). *Ninth Letter* is published semiannually at the University of Illinois, Urbana-Champaign. We are interested in prose and poetry that experiment with form, narrative, and nontraditional subject matter, as well as more traditional literary work."

> *Ninth Letter* won Best New Literary Journal 2005 from the Council of Editors of Learned Journals (CELJ) and has had poetry selected for *Best American Poetry*, *The Pushcart Prize*, *Best New Poets*, and *The Year's Best Fantasy and Horror*.

NEEDS Length: up to 8,000 words.

HOW TO CONTACT "Please send only 1 story at a time. All mailed submissions must include an SASE for reply."

PAYMENT/TERMS Pays $25/printed page and 2 contributor's copies.

NITE-WRITER'S INTERNATIONAL LITERARY ARTS JOURNAL

158 Spencer Ave., Suite 100, Pittsburgh PA 15227. **E-mail:** nitewritersliteraryarts@gmail.com. **Website:**

https://sites.google.com/site/nitewriterinternational/home. **Contact:** John Thompson. Estab. 1994. *Nite-Writer's International Literary Arts Journal* is "dedicated to the emotional intellectual with a creative perception of life."

○ Journal is open to beginners as well as professionals.

NEEDS Length: up to 1,200 words.

HOW TO CONTACT All literary works should be in DOC format in 12-point font.

TIPS "Read a lot of what you write—study the market. Don't fear rejection, but use it as a learning tool to strengthen your work before resubmitting."

THE NORMAL SCHOOL

The Press at the California State University - Fresno, 5245 North Backer Ave., M/S PB 98, Fresno CA 93740-8001. **E-mail:** editors@thenormalschool.com. **Website:** thenormalschool.com. **Contact:** Sophie Beck, managing editor. Estab. 2008. Semiannual magazine that accepts outstanding work by beginning and established writers.

○ Mss are read September 1-December 1 and January 15-April 15. Address submissions to the appropriate editor. Charges $3 fee for each online submission, due to operational costs.

NEEDS "We consider literary short fiction with contemporary themes and styles. We tend to prefer character-driven work and pieces that explore marginalized voices." Does not want any genre writing. Length: up to 7,000 words.

HOW TO CONTACT Submit complete ms via online submissions manager.

PAYMENT/TERMS Pays 2 contributor's copies and one-year subscription.

⑤ NORTH AMERICAN REVIEW

University of Northern Iowa, 1200 W. 23th St., Cedar Falls IA 50614. (319)273-6455. **E-mail:** nar@uni.edu. **Website:** northamericanreview.org. Estab. 1815. "The *North American Review* is the oldest literary magazine in America and one of the most respected; though we have no prejudices about the subject matter of material sent to us, our first concern is quality."

○ This is the oldest literary magazine in the country and one of the most prestigious. Also one of the most entertaining—and a tough market for the young writer.

NEEDS Wants to see more "well-crafted literary stories that emphasize family concerns. We'd also like

to see more stories engaged with environmental concerns." Reads fiction mss during academic year. **Publishes 2 new writers/year.** Recently published work by Lee Ann Roripaugh, Dick Allen, and Rita Welty Bourke. "No flat narrative stories where the inferiority of the character is the paramount concern." Length: up to 30 pages.

HOW TO CONTACT Submit ms via online submissions manager.

TIPS "We like stories that start quickly and have a strong narrative arc. Poems that are passionate about subject, language, and image are welcome, whether they are traditional or experimental, whether in formal or free verse (closed or open form). Nonfiction should combine art and fact with the finest writing."

⑤ NORTH CAROLINA LITERARY REVIEW

East Carolina University, Mailstop 555 English, Greenville NC 27858-4353. (252)328-1537. **Fax:** (252)328-4889. **E-mail:** bauerm@ecu.edu; nclruser@ecu.edu. **E-mail:** nclrsubmissions@ecu.edu. **Website:** www.nclr.ecu.edu. **Contact:** Margaret Bauer. Estab. 1992. "Articles should have a North Carolina slant. Fiction, creative nonfiction, and poetry accepted through yearly contests. First consideration is always for quality of work. Although we treat academic and scholarly subjects, we do not wish to see jargon-laden prose; our readers, we hope, are found as often in bookstores and libraries as in academia. We seek to combine the best elements of a magazine for serious readers with the best of a scholarly journal." Accepts submissions through Submittable.

NEEDS Length: up to 6,000 words.

HOW TO CONTACT Submit fiction for the Doris Betts Fiction Prize competition via Submittable.

PAYMENT/TERMS First-place winners of contests receive a prize of $250. Other writers whose stories are selected for publication receive contributor's copies.

TIPS "By far the easiest way to break in is with special issue sections. We are especially interested in reports on conferences, readings, meetings that involve North Carolina writers, and personal essays or short narratives with a strong sense of place. See back issues for other departments. Interviews are probably the other easiest place to break in; no discussions of poetics/theory, etc., except in reader-friendly (accessible) language. Interviews should be personal, more like conversations, and extensive, exploring connections between a writer's life and his or her work."

NORTH DAKOTA QUARTERLY

University of North Dakota, 276 Centennial Dr. Stop 7209, Merrifield Hall Room 15, Grand Forks ND 58202. (701)777-3322. **E-mail:** ndq@und.edu. **Website:** www.ndquarterly.org. **Contact:** William Caraher, editor; Gilad Elbom, fiction editor; Heidi Czerwiec, poetry editor; Sharon Carson, book reviews editor. Estab. 1911. *North Dakota Quarterly* strives to publish the best fiction, poetry, and essays that in our estimation we can. Our tastes and interests are best reflected in what we have been recently publishing, and we suggest that you look at some current issues for guidance.

○ Work published in *North Dakota Quarterly* was selected for inclusion in *The O. Henry Prize Stories*, *The Pushcart Prize Series*, and *Best American Essays*.

NEEDS Literary preferences are very subjective. There are no fixed, universal, or objective criteria that we use when we read fiction submissions. In recent issues of NDQ we have published stories in which the setting is clearly identified, characters are properly named and introduced, the action progresses on a linear axis, and things, generally speaking, are far from confusing. We're not against that. But we've also published a partially hallucinatory story about an incompetent broomball player, a theologically equivocal story about a Jesuit novice on an Indian reservation, a story from the perspective of a twice-kidnapped boy, a 4,000-word one-sentence story, a story about an imaginary novel, and a story about sheep in Scotland—from the perspective of a sheep. Ultimately, we're looking for multiple perspectives, different voices, and a variety of approaches to fiction. These approaches can revolve around uncertainty, ambiguity, fragmentation, polyphony, contradictory information, structural experimentation, and all the other things that teachers of freshman composition tell us we must eliminate or avoid. In other words, we value the willingness to treat fiction as textual art and take literary risks. Naturally, there is no guarantee that innovation will yield good results. But when it comes to art, it might be better to fail with something original than to play it safe with a predictable formula. No length restrictions.

HOW TO CONTACT Submit completed manuscript via https://ndquarterly.submittable.com/submit/112686/north-dakota-quarterly-fiction-submissions

⑨ NOTRE DAME REVIEW

University of Notre Dame, B009C McKenna Hall, Notre Dame IN 46556. **Website:** ndreview.nd.edu. Estab. 1995. "The *Notre Dame Review* is an independent, noncommercial magazine of contemporary American and international fiction, poetry, criticism, and art. Especially interested in work that takes on big issues by making the invisible seen, that gives voice to the voiceless. In addition to showcasing celebrated authors like Seamus Heaney and Czeław Milosz, the *Notre Dame Review* introduces readers to authors they may have never encountered before but who are doing innovative and important work. In conjunction with the *Notre Dame Review*, the online companion to the printed magazine, the *nd[re]view*, engages readers as a community centered in literary rather than commercial concerns, a community we reach out to through critique and commentary as well as aesthetic experience."

○ Does not accept e-mail submissions. Only reads hardcopy submissions September through November and January through March.

NEEDS "We're eclectic. Upcoming theme issues planned. List of upcoming themes or editorial calendar available for SASE." No genre fiction. Length: up to 3,000 words.

HOW TO CONTACT Submit complete ms via online submissions manager.

PAYMENT/TERMS Pays $5-25.

TIPS "Excellence is our sole criteria for selection, although we are especially interested in fiction and poetry that take on big issues."

NOW & THEN

The Appalachian Magazine, East Tennessee State University, Box 70556, Johnson City TN 37614-1707. (423)439-5348. **Fax:** (423)439-7074. **E-mail:** nowandthen@etsu.edu; sandersr@etsu.edu. **Website:** www.etsu.edu/cas/cass/nowandthen. **Contact:** Randy Sanders, managing editor. Estab. 1984. *Now & Then* accepts a variety of writing genres: fiction, poetry, nonfiction, essays, interviews, memoirs, and book reviews. All submissions must relate to Appalachia and to the issue's specific theme. Readership is educated and interested in the region.

○ "At this time, the magazine is in the process of transitioning to an online-only publication. Therefore, we are currently not accepting submissions. Follow our progress by visiting the

Now & Then website at www.etsu.edu/cas/cass/nowandthen."

NTH DEGREE

2770 Buckstone Dr., Powhatan VA 23139. **E-mail:** submissions@nthzine.com. **Website:** www.nthzine.com. **Contact:** Michael D. Pederson. Estab. 2002. Free online fanzine to promote up-and-coming new science fiction and fantasy authors and artists. Also supports the world of fandom and conventions. No longer accepts hard copy submissions.

NEEDS Length: up to 7,500 words.

HOW TO CONTACT Submit complete ms via e-mail.

PAYMENT/TERMS Pays in contributor's copies.

TIPS "Don't submit anything that you may be ashamed of 10 years later."

NUTHOUSE

P.O. Box 119, Ellenton FL 34222. **Website:** www.nuthousemagazine.com. *Nuthouse*, published every 3 months, uses humor of all kinds, including homespun and political.

Nuthouse is 12 pages, digest-sized, photocopied from desktop-published originals. Receives about 500 poems/year, accepts about 100. Press run is 100. Subscription: $5 for 4 issues.

NEEDS "We publish all genres, from the homespun to the horrific. We don't automatically dismiss crudity or profanity. We're not prudes. Yet we consider such elements cheap and insulting unless essential to the gag. *NuTHOuSe* seeks submissions that are original, tightly written, and laugh-out-loud funny." Length: up to 1,000 words. "The shorter, the better."

HOW TO CONTACT Send complete ms with SASE and cover letter. Include estimated word count, bio (paragraph), and list of publications. No e-mail submissions.

PAYMENT/TERMS Pays 1 contributor's copy.

OBSIDIAN

Brown University, **E-mail:** obsidianatbrown@gmail.com. **Website:** obsidian-magazine.tumblr.com. **Contact:** Staff rotates each year; see website for current masthead. Estab. 1975. *Obsidian* is a "literary and visual space to showcase the creativity and experiences of black people, specifically at Brown University, formed out of the need for a platform made for us, by us." It is "actively intersectional, safe, and open: a space especially for the stories and voices of black women, black queer and trans people, and black people with disabilities."

NEEDS Length: up to 4,000 words.

HOW TO CONTACT Submit by e-mail as attachment. Include brief bio up to 3 sentences long.

TIPS "Following proper format is essential. Your title must be intriguing and text clean. Never give up. Some of the writers we publish were rejected many times before we published them."

OHIO TEACHERS WRITE

Department of English, University of Dayton, 300 College Park, Dayton OH 45469. (937)229-3463. **E-mail:** pthomas1@udayton.edu. **Website:** octela.org/publications/ohio-teachers-write. **Contact:** Patrick Thomas. Estab. 1995. "*Ohio Teachers Write* is a literary magazine published annually by the Ohio Council of Teachers of English Language Arts. This publication seeks to promote both poetry and prose of Ohio teachers and to provide an engaging collection of writing for our readership of educators and other like-minded adults. Invites electronic submissions from both active and retired Ohio educators for our annual literary print magazine."

NEEDS Submissions are limited to Ohio Educators. Length: up to 1,500 words.

HOW TO CONTACT Submit by e-mail.

PAYMENT/TERMS Pays 2 contributor's copies.

TIPS Check website for yearly theme.

OLD RED KIMONO

Georgia Highlands College, 3175 Cedartown Hwy. SE, Rome GA 30161. **E-mail:** napplega@highlands.edu. **Website:** www.highlands.edu/site/ork. **Contact:** Dr. Nancy Applegate. Estab. 1972. *Old Red Kimono*, published annually, prints original, high-quality poetry and fiction. *Old Red Kimono* is 72 pages, magazine-sized, professionally printed, color cover and 16 color pages. Receives about 250 submissions/year, accepts about 60-70. Sample: $3. Contributors receive two copies.

NEEDS Length: up 1,500 words.

HOW TO CONTACT Submit via mail or e-mail.

PAYMENT/TERMS Pays 2 contributor's copies.

⑤ ONE STORY

232 3rd St., #A108, Brooklyn NY 11215. **Website:** www.one-story.com. **Contact:** Maribeth Batcha, publisher. Estab. 2002. "*One Story* is a literary magazine that contains, simply, 1 story. Approximately every 3-4 weeks, subscribers are sent *One Story* in the mail. *One Story* is artfully designed, lightweight, easy to

carry, and ready to entertain on buses, in bed, in subways, in cars, in the park, in the bath, in the waiting rooms of doctor's offices, on the couch, or in line at the supermarket. Subscribers also have access to a website where they can learn more about *One Story* authors and hear about *One Story* readings and events. There is always time to read *One Story*."

Reading period: September 1-May 31.

NEEDS *One Story* only accepts short stories. Do not send excerpts. Do not send more than 1 story at a time. Length: 3,000-8,000 words.

HOW TO CONTACT Send complete ms using online submission form.

PAYMENT/TERMS Pays $500 and 25 contributor's copies.

TIPS "*One Story* is looking for stories that are strong enough to stand alone. Therefore they must be very good. We want the best you can give."

ON SPEC

P.O. Box 4727, Station South, Edmonton AB T6E 5G6, Canada. (780)628-7121. **E-mail:** onspec@onspec.ca. **Website:** www.onspec.ca. Estab. 1989. . "We publish speculative fiction and poetry by new and established writers, with a strong preference for Canadian-authored works."

See website guidelines for submission announcements. "Please refer to website for information regarding submissions, as we are not open year round."

NEEDS No media tie-in or shaggy-alien stories. No condensed or excerpted novels, religious/inspirational stories, fairy tales. Length: 1,000-6,000 words.

HOW TO CONTACT Send complete ms. Electronic submissions preferred.

TIPS "We want to see stories with plausible characters, a well-constructed, consistent, and vividly described setting, a strong plot, and believable emotions; characters must show us (not tell us) their emotional responses to each other and to the situation and/or challenge they face. Also: Don't send us stories written for television. We don't like media tie-ins, so don't watch TV for inspiration! Read instead! Strong preference given to submissions by Canadians."

OPEN MINDS QUARTERLY

36 Elgin St., 2nd Floor, Sudbury ON P3C 5B4, Canada. (705)222-6472, ext. 303. **E-mail:** openminds@nisa. on.ca. **Website:** www.openmindsquarterly.com. **Con-**tact: Sarah Mann, editor. Estab. 1997. *Open Minds Quarterly* provides a venue for individuals who have experienced mental illness to express themselves via poetry, short fiction, essays, first-person accounts of living with mental illness, and book/movie reviews. Wants unique, well-written, provocative work. Does not want overly graphic or sexual violence.

Open Minds Quarterly is 24 pages, magazine-sized, saddle-stapled, with 100 lb. stock cover with original artwork, includes ads. Press run is 550; 150 distributed free to potential subscribers, published writers, NISA member, advertisers, and conferences and events.

NEEDS Length: 1,000-3,000 words.

HOW TO CONTACT Submit through website. Cover letter is required. Information in cover letter: indicate your lived experience with mental illness. Reads submissions year round.

PAYMENT/TERMS Pays contributor's copies.

ORBIS

17 Greenhow Ave., West Kirby Wirral CH48 5EL, United Kingdom. **E-mail:** carolebaldock@hotmail.com. **Website:** www.orbisjournal.com. **Contact:** Carole Baldock, editor; Noel Williams, reviews editor. Estab. 1969. "*Orbis* has long been considered one of the top 20 small-press magazines in the U.K. We are interested in social inclusion projects and encouraging access to the arts, young people, under 20s, and 20-somethings. Subjects for discussion: 'day in the life,' technical, topical."

Please see guidelines on website before submitting.

NEEDS Submit by postal mail or e-mail (overseas submissions only). Include cover letter. Length: up to 1,000 words.

TIPS "Any publication should be read cover to cover because it's the best way to improve your chances of getting published. Enclose SAE with all correspondence. Overseas: 2 IRCs, 3 if work is to be returned."

OVERTIME

Blue Cubicle Press, LLC, P.O. Box 250382, Plano TX 75025. **E-mail:** overtime@workerswritejournal.com. **Website:** www.workerswritejournal.com/overtime. htm. **Contact:** David LaBounty, editor. Estab. 2006.

NEEDS Length: 5,000-12,000 words.

HOW TO CONTACT Query; send complete ms.

PAYMENT/TERMS Pays $35-50 and one-year print subscription.

OXFORD MAGAZINE

Miami University, Oxford OH 45056. **E-mail:** ox-mag@miamioh.edu. **Website:** www.oxfordmagazine. org. Estab. 1984. *Oxford Magazine*, published annu-ally online in May, is open in terms of form, content, and subject matter. "Since our premiere in 1984, our magazine has received Pushcart Prizes for both fic-tion and poetry and has published authors such as Charles Baxter, William Stafford, Robert Pinsky, Ste-phen Dixon, Helena Maria Viramontes, Andre Dubus, and Stuart Dybek."

◑ Work published in *Oxford Magazine* has been included in the *Pushcart Prize* anthology. Does not read submissions July through August.

NEEDS Length: up to 3,000 words.

HOW TO CONTACT Submit complete ms via on-line submissions manager.

OYEZ REVIEW

Roosevelt University, Dept. of Literature & Languag-es, 430 S. Michigan Ave., Chicago IL 60605. **E-mail:** oyezreview@roosevelt.edu. **Website:** oyezreview. wordpress.com. Estab. 1965. Annual magazine of the Creative Writing Program at Roosevelt Univer-sity, publishing fiction, creative nonfiction, poetry, and art. There are no restrictions on style, theme, or subject matter.

◑ Reading period is August 1-October 1. Each is-sue has 104 pages: 92 pages of text and an 8-page spread of 1 artist's work (in color or b&w). Work by the issue's featured artist also appears on the front and back cover, totaling 10 pieces. The journal has featured work from such writers as Charles Bukowski, James McManus, Carla Pan-ciera, Michael Onofrey, Tim Foley, John N. Miller, Gary Fincke, and Barry Silesky, and visual artists Vivian Nunley, C. Taylor, Jennifer Troyer, and Frank Spidale. Accepts queries by e-mail.

NEEDS "We publish short stories and flash fiction on their merit as contemporary literature rather than the category within the genre." Length: up to 5,000 words.

HOW TO CONTACT Send complete ms via online submissions manager or postal mail.

PAYMENT/TERMS Pays 2 contributor's copies.

OYSTER BOY REVIEW

P.O. Box 550060, South Lake Tahoe CA 96155. **E-mail:** email@oysterboyreview.com. **Website:** www. oysterboyreview.com. **Contact:** Damon Sauve, editor/publisher. Estab. 1993. Electronic and print magazine.

Oyster Boy Review, published annually, is interested in "the underrated, the ignored, the misunderstood, and the varietal. We'll make some mistakes."

NEEDS Wants fiction that revolves around charac-ters in conflict with themselves or each other; a plot that has a beginning, a middle, and an end; a narrative with a strong moral center (not necessarily 'moralis-tic'); a story with a satisfying resolution to the con-flict; and an ethereal something that contributes to the mystery of a question but does not necessarily seek or contrive to answer it. Submit complete ms by postal mail or e-mail. No genre fiction.

PAYMENT/TERMS Pays two contributor's copies.

TIPS "Keep writing, keep submitting, keep revising."

PACIFICA LITERARY REVIEW

E-mail: pacificalitreview@gmail.com. **Website:** www. pacificareview.com. **Contact:** Matt Muth, editor-in-chief; Sarina Sheth and Paul Vega, managing editors. Estab. 2012. "*Pacifica Literary Review* is a small liter-ary arts magazine based in Seattle. *Pacifica* publishes three web issues annually in September, January, and May, and one print editon. *PLR* is now accepting sub-missions of poetry, fiction, creative nonfiction, and art/photography. Submission period: year-round."

NEEDS Wants literary fiction and flash fiction. Length: up to 5,000 words for literary fiction; 300-1,000 words for flash fiction.

HOW TO CONTACT Submit complete ms.

PAYMENT/TERMS Pays copy of issue in which au-thor was published and copy of next issue.

PACKINGTOWN REVIEW

111 S. Lincoln St., Batavia IL 60510. **E-mail:** packing-townreview@gmail.com. **Website:** www.packing-townreview.com. Estab. 2008. *Packingtown Review* publishes imaginative and critical prose and poetry by emerging and established writers. Welcomes sub-missions of poetry, scholarly articles, drama, creative nonfiction, fiction, and literary translation, as well as genre-bending pieces.

◑ Literary magazine/journal: 8.5 x 11, 250 pages. Press run: 500.

NEEDS Does not want to see uninspired or unre-vised work. Wants to avoid fantasy, science fiction, overtly religious, or romantic pieces. Length: up to 4,000 words.

HOW TO CONTACT Send complete ms as attach-ment. Include cover letter in body of e-mail.

PAYMENT/TERMS Pays 2 contributor's copies.

TIPS "We are looking for well-crafted prose. We are open to most styles and forms. We are also looking for prose that takes risks and does so successfully. We will consider articles about prose."

❸ PAINTED BRIDE QUARTERLY

Drexel University, Department of English and Philosophy, 3141 Chestnut St., Philadelphia PA 19104. **E-mail:** info@pbqmag.org. **Website:** pbqmag.org. **Contact:** Kathleen Volk Miller and Marion Wrenn, editors. Estab. 1973. *Painted Bride Quarterly* seeks literary fiction (experimental and traditional), poetry, and artwork and photographs.

NEEDS Publishes theme-related work; check website. Holds annual fiction contests. Length: up to 5,000 words.

HOW TO CONTACT Send complete ms through online submissions manager.

PAYMENT/TERMS Pays $20.

TIPS "We look for freshness of idea incorporated with high-quality writing. We receive an awful lot of nicely written work with worn-out plots. We want quality in whatever—we hold experimental work to as strict standards as anything else. Many of our readers write fiction; most of them enjoy a good reading. We hope to be an outlet for quality. A good story gives, first, enjoyment to the reader. We've seen a good many of them lately, and we've published the best of them."

PANK

PANK, Department of Humanities, 1400 Townsend Dr., Houghton MI 49931-1200. **Website:** www.pankmagazine.com. Estab. 2006. "*PANK* Magazine fosters access to emerging and experimental poetry and prose, publishing the brightest and most promising writers for the most adventurous readers. To the end of the road, up country, a far shore, the edge of things, to a place of amalgamation and unplumbed depths, where the known is made and unmade, and where unimagined futures are born, a place inhabited by contradictions, a place of quirk and startling anomaly. *PANK*, no soft pink hands allowed."

NEEDS "Bright, new, energetic, passionate writing, writing that pushes our tender little buttons and gets us excited. Push our tender buttons, excite us, and we'll publish you."

HOW TO CONTACT Send complete ms through online submissions manager.

PAYMENT/TERMS Pays $20, a one-year subscription, and a *PANK* t-shirt.

TIPS "To read *PANK* is to know *PANK*. Or, read a lot within the literary magazine and small-press universe—there's plenty to choose from. Unfortunately, we see a lot of submissions from writers who have clearly read neither *PANK* nor much else. Serious writers are serious readers. Read. Seriously."

❂ PAPERPLATES

19 Kenwood Ave., Toronto ON M6C 2R8, Canada. **E-mail:** magazine@paperplates.org. **Website:** www.paperplates.org. **Contact:** Bernard Kelly, publisher. Estab. 1990. *paperplates* is a literary journal published once a year. "We make no distinction between veterans and beginners. Some of our contributors have published several books; some have never before published a single line." No longer accepts IRCs.

NEEDS Length: no more than 7,500 words.

HOW TO CONTACT Submit by mail or e-mail. "Do not send fiction as an e-mail attachment. Copy the first 300 words or so into the body of your message. If you prefer not to send a fragment, you have the option of using surface mail." Include short bio with submission.

THE PARIS REVIEW

544 West 27th St., New York NY 10001. (212)343-1333. **E-mail:** queries@theparisreview.org. **Website:** www.theparisreview.org. **Contact:** Lorin Stein, editor; Robyn Creswell, poetry editor. *The Paris Review* publishes "fiction and poetry of superlative quality, whatever the genre, style, or mode. Our contributors include prominent, as well as less well-known and previously unpublished writers. The Writers at Work interview series includes important contemporary writers discussing their own work and the craft of writing."

○ Address submissions to proper department. Do not make submissions via e-mail.

NEEDS Study the publication. Annual Plimpton Prize award of $10,000 given to a new voice published in the magazine. Recently published work by Ottessa Moshfegh, John Jeremiah Sullivan, and Lydia Davis. Length: no limit.

HOW TO CONTACT Send complete ms.

PAYMENT/TERMS Pays $1,000-3,000.

PASSAGER

Passager, 1420 N. Charles St., Baltimore MD 21201. **E-mail:** editors@passagerbooks.com. **Website:** www.

passagerbooks.com. **Contact:** Kendra Kopelke, Mary Azrael, Christine Drawl. Estab. 1990. "*Passager* has a special focus on older writers. Its mission is to encourage, engage, and strengthen the imagination well into old age and to give mature readers opportunities that are sometimes closed off to them in our youth-oriented culture. We are dedicated to honoring the creativity that takes hold in later years and to making public the talents of those over the age of 50." *Passager* publishes 2 issues/year, an Open issue (winter) and a Poetry Contest issue (summer). Open to writers over 50.

NEEDS Accepts literary fiction submissions from writers over 50. Length: up to 4,000 words.

HOW TO CONTACT Send complete ms with cover letter, or use Submittable. Check website for guidelines. Include estimated word count, brief bio, list of publications. Send either SASE or email for reply only.

PAYMENT/TERMS Pays 1 contributor's copy.

TIPS "Stereotyped images of old age will be rejected. Read the publication, or at least visit the website."

PASSAGES NORTH

English Department, Northern Michigan University, 1401 Presque Isle Ave., Marquette MI 49855. (906)227-1203. **E-mail:** passages@nmu.edu. **Website:** www.passagesnorth.com. **Contact:** Jennifer A. Howard, editor-in-chief; Ethan Brightbill & Willow Grosz, managing editors; Matthew Gavin Frank & Rachel May, nonfiction and hybrids editors; Patricia Killelea, poetry editor; Monica McFawn, fiction editor. Estab. 1979. *Passages North*, published annually in spring, prints poetry, short fiction, creative nonfiction, essays, hybrids, and interviews.

○ Magazine: 7×10; 200-350 pgs; 60 lb. paper. Publishes work by established and emerging writers.

NEEDS "Don't be afraid to surprise us." Length: up to 7,000 words.

HOW TO CONTACT Send 1 short story or as many as 3 short-short stories (paste them all into 1 document).

TIPS "We look for voice, energetic prose, writers who take risks. We look for an engaging story in which the author evokes an emotional response from the reader through carefully rendered scenes, complex characters, and a smart, narrative design. Revise, revise. Read what we publish."

THE PATERSON LITERARY REVIEW

Passaic County Community College, 1 College Blvd., Paterson NJ 07505. (973)684-6555. **Website:** www.patersonliteraryreview.com. **Contact:** Maria Mazziotti Gillan, editor/executive director. *Paterson Literary Review*, published annually, is produced by the The Poetry Center at Passaic County Community College.

○ Work for *PLR* has been included in the *Pushcart Prize* anthology and *Best American Poetry*.

NEEDS "We are interested in quality short stories, with no taboos on subject matter." Receives 60 unsolicited mss/month. Publishes 5% new writers/year. Length: up to 1,500 words.

HOW TO CONTACT Send SASE for reply or return of ms. "Indicate whether you want story returned."

PAYMENT/TERMS Pays contributor's copies.

⑤ THE PEDESTAL MAGAZINE

6815 Honors Court, Charlotte NC 28210. **E-mail:** pedmagazine@carolina.rr.com. **Website:** www.thepedestalmagazine.com. **Contact:** John Amen, editor in chief. Estab. 2000. Committed to promoting diversity and celebrating the voice of the individual.

○ See website for reading periods for different forms. Member: CLMP.

NEEDS "We are receptive to all sorts of high-quality literary fiction. Genre fiction is encouraged as long as it crosses or comments upon its genre and is both character-driven and psychologically acute. We encourage submissions of short fiction, no more than 3 flash fiction pieces at a time. There is no need to query prior to submitting; please submit via online submissions manager—no e-mail to the editor." Length: up to 4,000 words for short stories; up to 1,000 words for flash fiction.

PAYMENT/TERMS Pays 3¢/word.

TIPS "If you send us your work, please wait for a response to your first submission before you submit again."

⑤ PENNINE INK MAGAZINE

1 Neptune St., Burnley BB11 1SF, England. **E-mail:** piwwmag40@gmail.com. **Website:** www.pennine-ink.weebly.com. **Contact:** Alex Marsh, compiling editor. Estab. 1983. *Pennine Ink*, published annually in November, prints poems and short prose pieces. *Pennine Ink* is 48 pages, A5, with b&w illustrated cover. Receives about 400 poems/year, accepts about 40. Press run is 200. "Contributors wishing to purchase a copy of *Pennine Ink* should go to the Amazon website and search for Pennine Ink. More information on our website."

PAYMENT/TERMS Pays 1 contributor's copy.

PENNSYLVANIA ENGLISH

Indiana University of Pennsylvania, Department of English, Indiana University of Pennsylvania, HSS 506A, 981 Grant St., Indiana PA 15705. (724)357-5913. **E-mail:** mtwill@iup.edu. **Website:** paenglish.submittable.com/submit. **Contact:** Dr. Michael T. Williamson, editor (mtwill@iup.edu); Dr. Michael Cox, creative prose editor (mwcox@pitt.edu); Tony Vallone, MFA, poetry editor (avallone@psu.edu); Dr. Ann Rea (anr@pitt.edu) and Dr. Michael T. Williamson, literary criticism editors. Estab. 1985. *Pennsylvania English*, published annually, is "sponsored by the Pennsylvania College English Association. Our philosophy is quality. We publish literary fiction (and poetry and nonfiction) and essays about literature. Our intended audience includes people who love literature and writing, university professors, college professors, Community College professors, temporary faculty, K-12 teachers, and literate readers from around the world." *Pennsylvania English* is 6x9 up to 175 pages, perfect-bound, full-color cover featuring the artwork of a Pennsylvania artist. Reads mss during the summer. Publishes 4-6 new writers/year. Has published work by Marcia Loughran, Benjamin Goluboff, Evalyn Lee, Gary Grieve Carlson, Glen Adelson, Simon Perchik, Len Lawson, Dave Kress, Dan Leone, Paul West, Liz Rosenberg, Walt MacDonald, Amy Pence, Jennifer Richter, and Jeff Schiff.

NEEDS No genre fiction or romance.

HOW TO CONTACT Submit via online submissions manager. "For all submissions, please include a brief bio for the contributors' page. Be sure to include your name, address, phone number, e-mail address, institutional affiliation (if you have one), the title of your short story, and any other relevant information. We will edit if necessary for space."

PAYMENT/TERMS Pays 1 contributor's copy.

TIPS "Quality of the writing is our only measure. We're not impressed by long-winded cover letters detailing awards and publications we've never heard of. Beginners and professionals have the same chance with us. We receive stacks of competently written but boring fiction. For a story to rise from the rejection pile, it takes more than the basic competence."

PENNSYLVANIA LITERARY JOURNAL

Anaphora Literary Press, 1108 W 3rd St., Quanah TX 79252. (470)289-6395. **E-mail:** director@anaphoraliterary.com. **Website:** anaphoraliterary.com. **Contact:** Anna Faktorovich, editor/director. Estab. 2009. *Pennsylvania Literary Journal* is a printed, peer-reviewed journal that publishes critical essays, book reviews, short stories, interviews, photographs, art, and poetry. Published tri-annually, it features special issues on a wide variety of different fields from film studies to literary criticism to interviews with bestsellers. Submissions in all genres from emerging and established writers are warmly welcomed.

NEEDS Detailed, descriptive, and original short stories are preferred. No word limit.

HOW TO CONTACT Send complete ms via e-mail.

PAYMENT/TERMS Does not provide payment.

TIPS "We are just looking for great writing. Send your materials; if they are good and you don't mind working for free, we'll take it."

PENNY DREADFUL

Tales & Poems of Fantastic Terror, P.O. Box 719, Radio City Station, Hell's Kitchen NY 10101-0719. **E-mail:** mmpendragon@aol.com. **Website:** www.mpendragon.com/pennydreadful.html. Estab. 1996. *Penny Dreadful: Tales & Poems of Fanastic Terror*, published irregularly (about once a year), features goth-romantic poetry and prose. Publishes poetry, short stories, essays, letters, listings, reviews, and b&w artwork "which celebrate the darker aspects of Man, the World, and their Creator." Wants "literary horror in the tradition of Poe, M.R. James, Shelley, M.P. Shiel, and LeFanu—dark, disquieting tales and verses designed to challenge the reader's perception of human nature, morality, and man's place within the Darkness. Stories and poems should be set prior to 1910 and/or possess a timeless quality." Does not want "references to 20th- and 21st-century personages/events, graphic sex, strong language, excessive gore and shock elements."

"Works appearing in *Penny Dreadful* have been reprinted in *The Year's Best Fantasy and Horror*." *Penny Dreadful* nominates best tales and poems for Pushcart Prizes. *Penny Dreadful* is over 100 pages, digest-sized, desktop-published, perfect-bound. Press run is 200.

NEEDS Length: up to 5,000 words.

HOW TO CONTACT Submit complete ms by mail or e-mail. "Mss should be submitted in the standard, professional format: typed, double-spaced, name and address on the first page, name and title of work on all subsequent pages, etc. Include SASE for reply. Also include brief cover letter with a brief bio and publication history."

PAYMENT/TERMS Pays 1 contributor's copy.

PEREGRINE

Amherst Writers & Artists Press, P.O. Box 1076, Amherst MA 01004. (413)253-3307. **E-mail:** peregrine-journal@gmail.com. **E-mail:** peregrine@amherstwriters.com. **Website:** amherstwriters.info/peregrine. **Contact:** Kate Eliza Frank, managing editor; Milo Muise, fiction editor, Rachelle Parker, poetry editor. Estab. 1983. *Peregrine*, published annually, features poetry and fiction. "*Peregrine* has provided a forum for national and international writers since 1983 and is committed to finding excellent work by emerging as well as established writers. We welcome work reflecting diversity of voice. We like to be surprised. We look for writing that is honest, unpretentious, and memorable. All decisions are made by the editors."

◯ Magazine: 6x9; 100+ pages; 60 lb. white offset paper; glossy cover. Member: CLMP. Reading period: March 15-May 15.

NEEDS Length: up to 750 words.

HOW TO CONTACT Submit via e-mail. Include word count on first page of submissions. "Shorter stories have a better chance."

PAYMENT/TERMS Pays 2 contributor's copies.

TIPS "Check guidelines before submitting your work. Familiarize yourself with *Peregrine*. We look for heart and soul as well as technical expertise. Trust your own voice."

PERMAFROST: A LITERARY JOURNAL

America's Farthest North Literary Magazine, University of Alaska Fairbanks, c/o English Dept., Univ. of Alaska Fairbanks, P.O. Box 755720, Fairbanks AK 99775. **E-mail:** editor@permafrostmag.com. **Website:** permafrostmag.uaf.edu. Estab. 1977. *Permafrost Magazine*, a literary journal, contains poems, short stories, hybrid pieces, creative nonfiction, b&w drawings, photographs, and prints. We print both new and established writers, hoping and expecting to see the best work out there. We have published work by E. Ethelbert Miller, W. Loran Smith, Peter Orlovsky, Jim Wayne Miller, Allen Ginsberg, and Andy Warhol. *Permafrost* is about 200 pages, digest-sized, professionally printed, flat-spined. Also publishes summer online edition.

NEEDS Length: up to 8,000 words.

HOW TO CONTACT Submit complete ms via online submissions manager at permafrostmag.submittable.com; "e-mail submissions will not be read."

PAYMENT/TERMS Pays 1 contributor's copy. Reduced contributor rate of $5 on additional copies.

PERSIMMON TREE

Magazine of the Arts by Women Over Sixty, 255 E. 78th St, New York NY 10075. (212)472-0692. **E-mail:** editor@persimmontree.org. **E-mail:** submissions@persimmontree.org. **Website:** www.persimmontree.org. **Contact:** Sue Leonard, editor. *Persimmon Tree*, an online magazine, is a showcase for the creativity and talent of women over sixty. Too often older women's artistic work is ignored or disregarded, and only those few who are already established receive the attention they deserve. Yet many women are at the height of their creative abilities in their later decades and have a great deal to contribute. *Persimmon Tree* is committed to bringing this wealth of fiction, nonfiction, poetry, and art to a broader audience, for the benefit of all.

NEEDS Length: under 3,500 words.

HOW TO CONTACT Submit complete ms via e-mail. Note: You must be signed onto the e-mail newsletter to be considered for publication.

TIPS "High quality of writing and an interesting or unique point of view make a manuscript stand out. Make it clear that you're familiar with the magazine. Tell us why the piece would work for our audience."

PERSPECTIVES

P.O. BOX 441130 #94102, DETROIT MI 48244-1130. **E-mail:** editors@perspectivesjournal.org. **E-mail:** submissions@perspectivesjournal.org. **Website:** perspectivesjournal.org. **Contact:** Jason Lief, Sara Tolsma. "*Perspectives* is a journal of theology in the broad Reformed tradition. We seek to express the Reformed faith theologically; to engage issues that Reformed Christians meet in personal, ecclesiastical, and societal life; and thus to contribute to the mission of the church of Jesus Christ. The editors are interested in submissions that contribute to a contemporary Reformed theological discussion. Our readers tend to be affiliated with the Presbyterian Church (USA), the Reformed Church in America, and the Christian Reformed Church. Some of our subscribers are academics or pastors, but we also gear our articles to thoughtful, literate laypeople who want to engage in Reformed theological reflection on faith and culture."

◯ *Perspectives* is 24 pages, magazine-sized, Web offset-printed, saddle-stapled, with paper cover containing b&w illustration. Receives about 300 poems/year, accepts 6-20. Press run is 1,575.

NEEDS Length: up to 3,000 words.

HOW TO CONTACT Submit complete ms by e-mail.

PHILADELPHIA STORIES

Fiction/Nonfiction/Art/Poetry of the Delaware Valley, 93 Old York Rd., Suite 1/#1-753, Jenkintown PA 19046. **E-mail:** info@philadelphiastories.org. **Website:** www.philadelphiastories.org. **Contact:** Christine Weiser, executive director/co-publisher. Estab. 2004. *Philadelphia Stories*, published quarterly, publishes "fiction, poetry, creative nonfiction, and art written by authors living in, or originally from, Pennsylvania, Delaware, or New Jersey. *Philadelphia Stories* also hosts 2 national writing contests: The Marguerite McGlinn Short Story Contest ($2,500 first-place prize; $750 second-place prize; $500 third-place prize) and the Sandy Crimmins National Poetry Contest ($1,000 first-place prize, 3 $100 runner-up prizes). Visit our website for details." Literary magazine/journal: 8.5x11; 32 pages; 70# matte text, all 4-color paper; 70# matte text cover. Contains illustrations, photographs. Subscription: "We offer $20 memberships that include home delivery." Make checks payable to *Philadelphia Stories*. Member: CLMP.

NEEDS Receives 45-80 mss/month. Accepts 3-4 mss/issue for print, additional 1-2 online; 12-16 mss/year for print, 4-8 online. Publishes 50% new writers/year. "We will consider anything that is well written but are most inclined to publish literary or mainstream fiction. We are *not* particularly interested in most genres (science fiction, fantasy, romance, etc.)." Length: up to 5,000 words; 4,000 words average. Also publishes short shorts; average length: 800 words.

PAYMENT/TERMS Pays $25 honorarium from the Conrad Weiser Author Fund and 2 contributor's copies.

TIPS "We look for exceptional, polished prose, a controlled voice, strong characters and place, and interesting subjects. Follow guidelines. We cannot stress this enough. Read every guideline carefully and thoroughly before sending anything out. Send out only polished material. We reject many quality pieces for various reasons; try not to take rejection personally. Just because your piece isn't right for one publication doesn't mean it's bad. Selection is an extremely subjective process."

PHOEBE

A Journal of Literature and Art, MSN 2C5, George Mason University, 400 University Dr., Fairfax VA 22030. **Website:** www.phoebejournal.com. **Contact:** Kate Branca, editor-in-chief; Rachel Purdy, assistant editor. Estab. 1971. Publishes poetry, fiction, nonfiction, and visual art. "*Phoebe* prides itself on supporting up-and-coming writers, whose style, form, voice, and subject matter demonstrate a vigorous appeal to the senses, intellect, and emotions of our readers."

NEEDS No romance or erotica. Length: up to 4,000 words.

HOW TO CONTACT Submit 1 fiction submission via online submission manager.

PAYMENT/TERMS Pays 2 contributor's copies and $400 for contest winner.

PILGRIMAGE MAGAZINE

Colorado State University-Pueblo, Dept. of English, 2200 Bonforte Blvd., Pueblo CO 81001. **E-mail:** info@pilgrimagepress.org. **Website:** www.pilgrimagepress.org. **Contact:** Juan Morales, editor. Estab. 1976. Serves an eclectic fellowship of readers, writers, artists, naturalists, contemplatives, activists, seekers, adventurers, and other kindred spirits.

NEEDS Length: up to 6,000 words. "Shorter works are easier to include, due to space constraints."

TIPS "Our interests include wildness in all its forms; inward and outward explorations; home ground, the open road, service, witness, peace, and justice; symbols, story, and myth in contemporary culture; struggle and resilience; insight and transformation; wisdom wherever it is found; and the great mystery of it all. We like good storytellers and a good sense of humor. No e-mail submissions, please."

THE PINCH

English Department, University of Memphis, Memphis TN 38152. **E-mail:** editor@pinchjournal.com. **Website:** www.pinchjournal.com. Estab. 1980. Semi-annual literary magazine. "We publish fiction, creative nonfiction, poetry, and art of literary quality by both established and emerging artists."

◯ "The Pinch Literary Awards in Fiction, Poetry, and Nonfiction offer a $1,000 prize and publication. Check our website for details."

NEEDS Wants "character-based" fiction with a "fresh use of language." No genre fiction. Length: up to 5,000 words.

HOW TO CONTACT Submit complete ms (or up to 3 flash fiction pieces) via online submissions manager.

PAYMENT/TERMS Pays 2 contributor's copies. "One work from each genre will be awarded a $200 Featured Writer award, as determined by the editors."

TIPS "We have a new look and a new edge. We're soliciting work from writers with a national or international reputation as well as strong, interesting work from emerging writers."

THE PINK CHAMELEON

The Pink Chameleon On Line, **E-mail:** dpfreda@juno.com. **Website:** www.thepinkchameleon.com. **Contact:** Dorothy Paula Freda, editor/publisher. Estab. 2000. *The Pink Chameleon*, published annually online, contains family-oriented, upbeat poetry, stories, essays, and articles, any genre in good taste that gives hope for the future. Reading period is February 1-March 31 and September 1-October 31.

NEEDS Accepts fiction that follows *The Pink Chameleon* online guidelines. No violence for the sake of violence. No novels or novel excerpts. Length: 500-2,500 words; average length: 2,000 words.

HOW TO CONTACT Send complete ms in the body of the e-mail. No attachments. Accepts reprints as long as author retains rights to reprints. Has published work by Deanne F. Purcell, Martin Green, Albert J. Manachino, James W. Collins, Ron Arnold, Sally Kosmalski, Susan Marie Davniero, and Glenn D. Hayes, among many others.

PAYMENT/TERMS No payment.

TIPS Wants "simple, honest, evocative emotion; upbeat fiction and nonfiction submissions that give hope for the future; well-paced plots; stories, poetry, articles, essays that speak from the heart. Read guidelines carefully. Use a good, but not ostentatious, opening hook. Stories should have a beginning, middle, and end that make the reader feel the story was worth his or her time. This also applies to articles and essays. In the latter 2, wrap your comments and conclusions in a neatly packaged final paragraph. Turnoffs include violence and bad language. Simple, genuine, and sensitive work does not need to shock with vulgarity to be interesting and enjoyable."

PISGAH REVIEW

Division of Humanities, Brevard College, 1 Brevard College Dr., Brevard NC 28712. (828)577-8324. **E-mail:** tinerjj@brevard.edu. **Website:** www.pisgahreview.com. **Contact:** Jubal Tiner, editor. Estab. 2005. "*Pisgah Review* publishes primarily literary short fiction, creative nonfiction, and poetry. Our only criteria is quality of work; we look for the best." Has published Ron Rash, Thomas Rain Crowe, Joan Conner, Gary Fincke, Steve Almond, and Fred Bahnson. Also published Rick Bass, Marjorie Hudson, Ron Rash, Jane Smiley, Robert Morgan, Sy Montgomey and others in our Looking Glass Rock Writer's Conference special issues.

NEEDS Receives 85 mss/month. Accepts 6-8 mss/issue; 12-15 mss/year. Publishes 5 new writers/year. Does not want genre fiction or inspirational stories. Length: 2,000-7,500 words. Accepts Flash Fiction as well.

HOW TO CONTACT "Send complete ms to our submission manager on our website."

PAYMENT/TERMS Writers receive 2 contributor's copies. Additional copies $7.

TIPS "We select work of only the highest quality. Grab us from the beginning and follow through. Engage us with your language and characters. A clean ms goes a long way toward acceptance. Stay true to the vision of your work, revise tirelessly, and submit persistently."

☯☯ PLANET: THE WELSH INTERNATIONALIST

Berw Ltd., P.O. Box 44, Aberystwyth Ceredigion SY23 3ZZ, United Kingdom. 01970 622408. **E-mail:** admin@planetmagazine.org.uk. **E-mail:** submissions@planetmagazine.org.uk. **Website:** www.planetmagazine.org.uk. **Contact:** Emily Trahair, editor. Estab. 1970. A literary/cultural/political journal centered on Welsh affairs but with a strong interest in minority cultures in Europe and elsewhere. *Planet: The Welsh Internationalist*, published quarterly, is a cultural magazine centered on Wales, but with broader interests in arts, sociology, politics, history, and science. *Planet* is 96 pages, A5, professionally printed, perfect-bound, with glossy colour card cover. Receives about 500 submissions/year, accepts about 5%. Press run is 1,000 (800 subscribers, about 10% libraries, 200 shelf sales).

NEEDS Would like to see more inventive, imaginative fiction that pays attention to language and experiments with form. No magical realism, horror, science fiction. Length: 1,500-2,750 words.

HOW TO CONTACT Submit complete ms via mail or e-mail (with attachment). For postal submissions, no submissions returned unless accompanied by an SASE. Writers submitting from abroad should send at least 3 IRCs for return of typescript; 1 IRC for reply only.

PAYMENT/TERMS Pays £50/1,000 words.

TIPS "We do not look for fiction that necessarily has a 'Welsh' connection, which some writers assume from our title. We try to publish a broad range of fiction, and our main criterion is quality. Try to read copies of any magazine you submit to. Don't write out of the blue to a magazine which might be completely inappropriate for your work. Recognize that you are likely to have a high rejection rate, as magazines tend to favor writers from their own countries."

⑨ PLEIADES

Literature in Context, University of Central Missouri, Department of English, Martin 336, 415 E. Clark St., Warrensburg MO 64093. (660)543-4268. **E-mail:** clintoncrockettp@gmail.com (nonfiction inquiries); pnguyen@ucmo.edu (fiction inquiries); pleiadespoetryeditor@gmail.com (poetry inquiries). **Website:** www.pleiadesmag.com. **Contact:** Clinton Crockett Peters, nonfiction editor; Phong Nguyen, fiction editor; and Jenny Molberg, poetry editor. Estab. 1991. "We publish contemporary fiction, poetry, interviews, literary essays, special-interest personal essays, and reviews for a general and literary audience from authors from around the world." Reads in the months of July for the summer issue and December for the winter issue.

NEEDS Reads fiction year-round. No science fiction, fantasy, confession, erotica. Length: 2,000-6,000 words.

HOW TO CONTACT Send complete ms via online submission manager.

PAYMENT/TERMS Pays $10 and contributor's copies.

TIPS "Submit only 1 genre at a time to appropriate editors. Show care for your material and your readers—submit quality work in a professional format. Cover art is solicited directly from artists. We accept queries for book reviews."

⑨ PLOUGHSHARES

Emerson College, 120 Boylston St., Boston MA 02116. (617)824-3757. **E-mail:** pshares@pshares.org. **Website:** www.pshares.org. **Contact:** Ladette Randolph, editor-in-chief/executive director; Ellen Duffer, managing editor. Estab. 1971. *Ploughshares* publishes issues four times a year. 2 of these issues are guest-edited by different, prominent authors. A third issue, a mix of both prose and poetry, is edited by our staff editors. The fourth issue is a collection of longform work edited by our Editor-in-chief, Ladette Randolph; these stories and essays are first published as e-books known as Ploughshares Solos. Translations are welcome if permission has been granted. We accept electronic submissions—there is a $3 fee per submission, which is waived if you are a subscriber. Ploughshares is 200 pages, digest-sized. Receives about 11,000 poetry, fiction, and essay submissions/year. Reads submissions June 1-January 15 (postmark); hosts the Emerging Writer's Contest, for writers who have yet to publish a book-length work, March 1-May 15; mss submitted at all other times will be returned unread. A competitive and highly prestigious market. Rotating and guest editors make cracking the line-up even tougher, since it's difficult to know what is appropriate to send.

NEEDS Has published work by ZZ Packer, Antonya Nelson, and Stuart Dybek. Length: up to 6,000 words

HOW TO CONTACT Submit via online submissions form or by mail.

PAYMENT/TERMS Pays $45/printed page ($90 minimum, $450 maximum); 2 contributor's copies; and one-year subscription.

PMS

University of Alabama at Birmingham, HB 217, 1530 Third Ave. S., Birmingham AL 35294. (205)934-2641. **Fax:** (205)975-8125. **E-mail:** poemmemoirstory@gmail.com. **Website:** www.uab.edu/cas/englishpublications/pms-poemmemoirstory. **Contact:** Kerry Madden, editor in chief. "*PMS poemmemoirstory* appears once a year. We accept unpublished, original submissions of poetry, memoir, and short fiction during our January 1-March 31 reading period. We accept simultaneous submissions; however, we ask that you please contact us immediately if your piece is published elsewhere so we may free up space for other authors. While *PMS* is a journal of exclusively women's writing, the subject field is wide open."

○ "*PMS* has gone all-digital on Submittable. There is now a $3 fee, which covers costs associated with our online submissions system. Please send all submissions to poemmemoirstory.submittable.com/submit."

NEEDS Length: up to 15 pages or 4,300 words.

HOW TO CONTACT Submit through online submissions manager.

PAYMENT/TERMS Pays 2 contributor's copies.

TIPS "We strongly encourage you to familiarize yourself with *PMS* before submitting. You can find links to some examples of what we publish in the pages of *PMS 8* and *PMS 9*. We look forward to reading your work."

○⑨ POCKETS

The Upper Room, P.O. Box 340004, Nashville TN 37203. (615)340-7333. **E-mail:** pockets@upperroom.org. **Website:** pockets.upperroom.org. **Contact:** Lynn

W. Gilliam, editor. Estab. 1981. In addition to receiving regular submissions, *Pockets* sponsors a fiction contest each year. Magazine published 11 times/year. "*Pockets* is a Christian devotional magazine for children ages 6-12. All submissions should address the broad theme of the magazine. Each issue is built around a theme with material which can be used by children in a variety of ways. Scripture stories, fiction, poetry, prayers, art, graphics, puzzles and activities are included. Submissions do not need to be overtly religious. They should help children experience a Christian lifestyle that is not always a neatly wrapped moral package but is open to the continuing revelation of God's will. Seasonal material, both secular and liturgical, is desired."

◯   Does not accept e-mail or fax submissions.

NEEDS "Stories should contain lots of action, use believable dialogue, be simply written, and be relevant to the problems faced by this age group in everyday life." Length: 600-1,000 words.

HOW TO CONTACT Submit complete ms by mail. No e-mail submissions.

TIPS "Theme stories, role models, and retold scripture stories are most open to freelancers. Poetry is also open. It is very helpful if writers read our writers' guidelines and themes on our website."

POETICA MAGAZINE

Contemporary Jewish Writing, Mizmor L'David Anthology, 5215 Colley Ave. #138, Norfolk VA 23508. (757)617-0821. **E-mail:** poeticapublishing@aol.com. **Website:** www.poeticamagazine.com. **Contact:** Michal Mahgerefteh, publisher. Estab. 2002. *Poetica Magazine, Contemporary Jewish Writing,* is the publisher of the annual Mizmor L'David Anthology, offers "an outlet for the many writers who draw from their Jewish background and experiences to create poetry/prose/short stories, giving both emerging and recognized writers the opportunity to share their work with the larger community." *Poetica* is 80 pages, perfect-bound, full-color cover. Receives about 300 poems/year, accepts about 80%. Press run is 350.

HOW TO CONTACT Submit ms through online submissions manager. Include e-mail, bio, and mailing address.

TIPS "We publish original, unpublished works by Jewish and non-Jewish writers alike. We are interested in works that have the courage to acknowledge, challenge, and celebrate modern Jewish life beyond distinctions of secular and sacred. We like accessible works that find fresh meaning in old traditions that recognize the challenges of our generation. We evaluate works on several levels, including its skillful use of craft, its ability to hold interest, and layers of meaning."

POETS & WRITERS MAGAZINE

90 Broad St., Suite 2100, New York NY 10004. (212)226-3586. **E-mail:** editor@pw.org. **Website:** www.pw.org/magazine. **Contact:** Kevin Larimer, editor. Estab. 1987.

◯   No poetry or fiction submissions.

TIPS "We typically assign profiles to coincide with an author's forthcoming book publication. We are not looking for the Get Rich Quick or 10 Easy Steps variety of writing and publishing advice."

POINTED CIRCLE

Portland Community College, Cascade Campus, SC 206, 705 N. Killingsworth St., Portland OR 97217. **Website:** www.pcc.edu/about/literary-magazines/pointed-circle. **Contact:** Wendy Bourgeois, faculty advisor. Estab. 1980. Publishes "anything of interest to educationally/culturally mixed audience. We will read whatever is sent, but we encourage writers to remember we are a quality literary/arts magazine intended to promote the arts in the community. No pornography, nothing trite. Be mindful of deadlines and length limits." Accepts submissions by e-mail, mail; artwork in high-resolution digital form.

◯   Reading period: October 1-February 7. Magazine: 80 pages; b&w illustrations; photos.

NEEDS Length: up to 3,000 words.

HOW TO CONTACT Submitted materials will not be returned; include SASE for notification only. Accepts multiple submissions.

PAYMENT/TERMS Pays 2 contributor's copies.

THE PORTLAND REVIEW

Portland State University, P.O. Box 751, Portland OR 97207. **E-mail:** editor@portlandreview.org. **Website:** portlandreview.org. **Contact:** Alex Dannemiller, eidor-in-chief. Estab. 1956. Portland Review has been publishing exceptional writing and artwork by local and international artists since 1956.

NEEDS Publishes 40 manuscripts per year.

PAYMENT/TERMS Pays contributor's copies.

TIPS "Please visit portlandreview.org for access to our submission manager and for more information."

◯◉   THE PRAIRIE JOURNAL

A Magazine of Canadian Literature, P.O. Box 68073, 28 Crowfoot Terrace NW, Calgary AB T3G 3N8, Canada.

E-mail: editor@prairiejournal.org (queries only); prairiejournal@yahoo.com. **Website:** www.prairiejournal.org. **Contact:** Anne Burke, literary editor. Estab. 1983. "The audience is literary, university, library, scholarly, and creative readers/writers. We welcome newcomers and unsolicited submission of writing and artwork. In addition to the print issues, we publish online long poems, fiction, interviews, drama, and reviews."

NEEDS No genre: romance, horror, western—sagebrush or cowboys—erotic, science fiction, or mystery. Length: 100-3,000 words.

HOW TO CONTACT Send complete ms. No e-mail submissions.

PAYMENT/TERMS Pays $10-75.

TIPS "We publish many, many new writers and are always open to unsolicited submissions because we are 100% freelance. Do not send U.S. stamps; always use IRCs. We have poems, interviews, stories, and reviews online (query first)."

PRAIRIE SCHOONER

University of Nebraska–Lincoln, 123 Andrews Hall, Lincoln NE 68588. (402)472-0911. **Fax:** (402)472-1817. **E-mail:** prairieschooner@unl.edu. **Website:** prairieschooner.unl.edu. **Contact:** Ashley Strosnider, managing editor. Estab. 1926. "We look for the best fiction, poetry, and nonfiction available to publish, and our readers expect to read stories, poems, and essays of extremely high quality. We try to publish a variety of styles, topics, themes, points of view, and writers with a variety of backgrounds in all stages of their careers. We like work that is compelling—intellectually or emotionally—either in form, language, or content."

Submissions must be received between September 1 and May 1. Poetry published in *Prairie Schooner* has been selected for inclusion in *The Best American Poetry* and the *Pushcart Prize* anthologies. "All mss published in *Prairie Schooner* will automatically be considered for our annual prizes." These include The Strousse Award for Poetry ($500), the Bernice Slote Prize for Beginning Writers ($500), the Hugh J. Luke Award ($250), the Edward Stanley Award for Poetry ($1,000), the Virginia Faulkner Award for Excellence in Writing ($1,000), the Glenna Luschei Prize for Excellence ($1,500), and the Jane Geske Award ($250). Also, each year 10 Glenna Luschei Awards ($250 each) are given for poetry, fiction, and nonfiction. All contests are open only to those writers whose work was published in the magazine the previous year. Editors serve as judges. Also sponsors The *Prairie Schooner* Book Prize.

NEEDS "We try to remain open to a variety of styles, themes, and subject matter. We look for high-quality writing, 3-D characters, well-wrought plots, setting, etc. We are open to realistic and/or experimental fiction."

HOW TO CONTACT Send complete ms through mail, e-mail, or online submissions manager.

PAYMENT/TERMS Pays 3 copies of the issue in which the writer's work is published.

TIPS "Send us your best, most carefully crafted work, and be persistent. Submit again and again. Constantly work on improving your writing. Read widely in literary fiction, nonfiction, and poetry. Read *Prairie Schooner* to know what we publish."

PRISM INTERNATIONAL

Dept. of Creative Writing, Buch E462, 1866 Main Mall, University of British Columbia, Vancouver BC V6T 1Z1, Canada. (604)822-2514. **Fax:** (604)822-3616. **E-mail:** prismcirculation@gmail.com. **Website:** www.prismmagazine.ca. Estab. 1959. A quarterly international journal of contemporary writing—fiction, poetry, drama, creative nonfiction and translation. *PRISM international* is digest-sized, elegantly printed, flat-spined, with original colour artwork on a nylon card cover. Readership: public and university libraries, individual subscriptions, bookstores—a world-wide audience concerned with the contemporary in literature. "We have no thematic or stylistic allegiances: Excellence is our main criterion for acceptance of manuscripts." Receives 1,000 submissions/year, accepts about 80. Circulation is for 1,200 subscribers. Subscription: $35/year for Canadian subscriptions, $40/year for US subscriptions, $45/year for international. Sample: $13.

NEEDS Experimental, traditional. New writing that is contemporary and literary. Short stories and self-contained novel excerpts (up to 25 double-spaced pages). Works of translation are eagerly sought and should be accompanied by a copy of the original. Would like to see more translations. "No gothic, confession, religious, romance, pornography, or sci-fi." Also looking for creative nonfiction that is literary, not journalistic, in scope and tone. Receives over 100 unsolicited mss/month. Accepts 70 mss/year. "PRISM publishes both new and established writers; our contributors have included Franz Kafka, Gabriel Garciía Maárquez, Michael Ondaatje, Margaret Laurence, Mark Anthony Jarman, Gail Anderson-Dargatz and Eden Robinson." Publishes ms 4 months after acceptance. **Publishes 7 new writers/year.** Recently published work by Ibi Kaslik, Melanie Little, Mark Anthony Jarman. Publishes short shorts. Also publishes poetry. For Drama: one-acts/excerpts of no more than 1,500 words preferred. Also interested in seeing dramatic monologues. "New writing that is contemporary and literary. Short stories and self-contained novel excerpts. Works of translation are eagerly sought and should be accompanied by a copy of the original. Would like to see more translations. No gothic, confession, religious, romance, pornography, or science fiction." Length: 25 pages maximum.

HOW TO CONTACT "Keep it simple. U.S. contributors take note: Do not send SASEs with U.S. stamps, they are not valid in Canada. Send International Reply Coupons instead." Responds in 4 months to queries; 3-6 months to mss. Sample copy for $13 or on website. Writer's guidelines online. Send complete ms.

PAYMENT/TERMS Pays $20/printed page of prose, $40/printed page of poetry, and 2 copies of issue. Pays on publication for first North American serial rights. Selected authors are paid an additional $10/page for digital rights. Cover art pays $300 and 2 copies of issue. Sponsors awards/contests, including annual short fiction, poetry, and nonfiction contests. Pays $30/printed page, and 2 copies of issue.

TIPS "We are looking for new and exciting fiction. Excellence is still our No. 1 criterion. As well as poetry, imaginative nonfiction and fiction, we are especially open to translations of all kinds, very short fiction pieces and drama which work well on the page. Translations must come with a copy of the original language work."

A PUBLIC SPACE

323 Dean St., Brooklyn NY 11217. (718)858-8067. **E-mail:** general@apublicspace.org. **Website:** www.apublicspace.org. **Contact:** Brigid Hughes, founding editor; Anne McPeak, managing editor. *A Public Space*, published quarterly, is an independent magazine of literature and culture. "In an era that has relegated literature to the margins, we plan to make fiction and poetry the stars of a new conversation. We believe that stories are how we make sense of our lives and how we learn about other lives. We believe that stories matter."

Accepts unsolicited submissions from September 15-April 15. Submissions accepted through Submittable or by mail (with SASE).

NEEDS No word limit.

HOW TO CONTACT Submit 1 complete ms via online submissions manager.

PUERTO DEL SOL

New Mexico State University, English Dept., P.O. Box 30001, MSC 3E, Las Cruces NM 88003. **E-mail:** puertodelsoljournal@gmail.com. **Website:** www.puertodelsol.org. **Contact:** Richard Greenfield, editor-in-chief; Marissa Bond, prose editor; Caroline Chavatel, poetry editor; Jill Mceldowney, managing editor. Estab. 1964. Publishes innovative work from emerging and established writers and artists. Wants poetry, fiction, nonfiction, drama, theory, artwork, interviews, reviews, and interesting combinations thereof. *Puerto del Sol* is 150 pages, digest-sized, professionally printed, flat-spined, with matte card cover with art. Press run is 1,250 (300 subscribers, 25-30 libraries). Reading period for the print issue is June-October 15. General submissions reading period is variable.

NEEDS Accepts 8-12 mss/issue; 16-24 mss/year. Publishes several new writers/year. Has published work by David Trinidad, Molly Gaudry, Ray Gonzalez, Cynthia Cruz, Steve Tomasula, Denise Leto, Rae Bryant, Joshua Cohen, Blake Butler, Trinie Dalton, and Rick Moody.

HOW TO CONTACT Send 1 short story or 2-4 short short stories at a time through online submission manager.

PAYMENT/TERMS Pays 1 contributor copy.

TIPS "We are especially pleased to publish emerging writers who work to push their art form or field of study in new directions."

QUARTER AFTER EIGHT

Ohio University, 306 Ellis Hall, Athens OH 45701. **E-mail:** editor@quarteraftereight.org. **Website:** www.quarteraftereight.org. **Contact:** Derek Robbins, editor; Justin Mundhenk, editor; Kristin Distel, assistant editor. "*Quarter After Eight* is an annual literary journal devoted to the exploration of innovative writing. We celebrate work that directly challenges the conventions of language, style, voice, or idea in literary forms. In its aesthetic commitment to diverse forms, *QAE* remains a unique publication among contemporary literary magazines." Reading period: October 15-April

15. Holds annual short prose (any genre) contest with grand prize of $1,008.15. Deadline is November 30.

HOW TO CONTACT Submit through online submissions manager.

TIPS "We look for prose and poetry that is innovative, exploratory, and—most importantly—well written. Please subscribe to our journal and read what is published to get acquainted with the *QAE* aesthetic."

⑤ QUARTERLY WEST

University of Utah, 255 S. Central Campus Dr., Room 3500, Salt Lake City UT 84112. **E-mail:** quarterlywest@gmail.com. **Website:** www.quarterlywest.com. **Contact:** Sara Eliza Johnson and J.P. Grasser, editors. Estab. 1976. "We publish fiction, poetry, nonfiction, and new media in long and short formats, and will consider experimental as well as traditional works."

◗ *Quarterly West* was awarded first place for Editorial Content from the American Literary Magazine Awards. Work published in the magazine has been selected for inclusion in the *Pushcart Prize* anthology, the *Best of the Net* anthology, and *The Best American Short Stories* anthology.

NEEDS No preferred lengths; interested in longer, fuller short stories and short shorts. Accepts 6-10 mss/year. No detective, science fiction, or romance.

HOW TO CONTACT Send complete ms using online submissions manager only.

TIPS "We publish a special section of short shorts every issue, and we also sponsor an annual novella contest. We are open to experimental work—potential contributors should read the magazine! Don't send more than 1 story per submission. Novella competition guidelines available online. We prefer work with interesting language and detail—plot or narrative are less important. We don't do religious work."

⭘ ⑥ ⑤ ELLERY QUEEN'S MYSTERY MAGAZINE

44 Wall St., Suite 904, New York NY 10005-2401. **E-mail:** elleryqueenmm@dellmagazines.com. **Website:** www.themysteryplace.com/eqmm. Estab. 1941. "*Ellery Queen's Mystery Magazine* welcomes submissions from both new and established writers. We publish every kind of mystery short story: the psychological suspense tale, the deductive puzzle, the private eye case—the gamut of crime and detection from the realistic (including the policeman's lot and stories of police procedure) to the more imaginative (including 'locked rooms' and 'impossible crimes'). We look for strong writing, an original and exciting plot, and professional craftsmanship. We encourage writers whose work meets these general criteria to read an issue of *EQMM* before making a submission."

NEEDS "We always need detective stories. Special consideration given to anything timely and original." Publishes ms 6-12 months after acceptance. Agented fiction 50%. **Publishes 10 new writers/year.** Recently published work by Jeffery Deaver, Joyce Carol Oates, and Margaret Maron. Sometimes comments on rejected mss. No explicit sex or violence, no gore or horror. Seldom publishes parodies or pastiches. "We do not want true detective or crime stories." Length: 2,500-8,000 words, but occasionally accepts longer and shorter submissions—including minute mysteries of 250 words, stories up to 12,000 words, and novellas of up to 20,000 words from established authors.

HOW TO CONTACT "*EQMM* uses an online submission system (eqmm.magazinesubmissions.com) that has been designed to streamline our process and improve communication with authors. We ask that all submissions be made electronically, using this system, rather than on paper. All stories should be in standard ms format and submitted in .DOC format. We cannot accept .DOCX, .RTF, or .TXT files at this time."

PAYMENT/TERMS Pays 5-8¢/word; occasionally higher for established authors.

TIPS "*EQMM*'s range in the mystery genre is extensive: Almost any story that involves crime or the threat of crime comes within our purview. However, like all magazines, *EQMM* has a distinctive tone and style, and you can only get a sense of whether your work will suit us by reading an issue."

⭘ ⑤ QUEEN'S QUARTERLY

402D - Douglas Library, 93 University Ave., Queen's University, Kingston ON K7L 5v4, Canada. (613)533-2667. **E-mail:** queens.quarterly@queensu.ca. **Website:** www.queensu.ca/quarterly. **Contact:** Dr. Boris Castel, editor; Joan Harcourt, literary editor. Estab. 1893. *Queen's Quarterly* is "a general-interest intellectual review featuring articles on science, politics, humanities, arts and letters, extensive book reviews, and some poetry and fiction." Has published work by Gail Anderson-Dargatz, Tim Bowling, Emma Donohue, Viktor Carr, Mark Jarman, Rick Bowers, and Dennis Bock.

NEEDS Length: up to 2,500 words.

HOW TO CONTACT Send complete ms with SASE and/or IRC. No reply with insufficient postage. Accepts 2 mss/issue; 8 mss/year. Publishes 5 new writers/year. **PAYMENT/TERMS** "Payment to new writers will be determined at time of acceptance."

THE RAG

P.O. Box 17463, Portland OR 97217. **E-mail:** submissions@raglitmag.com; seth@raglitmag.com. **Website:** raglitmag.com. **Contact:** Seth Porter, managing editor; Dan Reilly, editor. Estab. 2011. *The Rag* focuses on the grittier genres that tend to fall by the wayside at more traditional literary magazines. *The Rag*'s ultimate goal is to put the literary magazine back into the entertainment market while rekindling the social and cultural value short fiction once held in North American literature.

◯ Fee to submit online ($3) is waived if you subscribe or purchase a single issue.

NEEDS Accepts all styles and themes. Length: up to 10,000 words.

HOW TO CONTACT Send complete ms.

PAYMENT/TERMS Pays 5¢/word, $250 average/story.

TIPS "We like gritty material: material that is psychologically believable and that has some humor in it, dark or otherwise. We like subtle themes, original characters, and sharp wit."

⑤ RALEIGH REVIEW LITERARY & ARTS MAGAZINE

Box 6725, Raleigh NC 27628-6725. **E-mail:** info@raleighreview.org. **Website:** www.raleighreview.org. **Contact:** Rob Greene, editor; Landon Houle, fiction editor; Bryce Emley, poetry editor. Estab. 2010. "*Raleigh Review* is a national nonprofit magazine of poetry, short fiction (including flash), and art. We believe that great literature inspires empathy by allowing us to see the world through the eyes of our neighbors, whether across the street or across the globe. Our mission is to foster the creation and availability of accessible yet provocative contemporary literature. We look for work that is emotionally and intellectually complex."

NEEDS "We prefer work that is physically grounded and accessible, though complex and rich in emotional or intellectual power. We delight in stories from unique voices and perspectives. Any fiction that is born from a relatively unknown place grabs our attention. We are not opposed to genre fiction, so long as

it has real, human characters and is executed artfully." Length: 250-7,500 words. "While we accept fiction up to 7,500 words, we are more likely to publish work in the 4,500- to 5,000-word range."

HOW TO CONTACT Submit complete ms.

PAYMENT/TERMS Pays $15 per accepted title.

TIPS "Please be sure to read the guidelines and look at sample work on our website. Every piece is read for its intrinsic value, so new/emerging voices are often published alongside nationally recognized, award-winning authors."

⑤ RATTAPALLAX

Rattapallax Press, 217 Thompson St., Suite 353, New York NY 10012. **E-mail:** devineni@rattapallax.com. **Website:** www.rattapallax.com. **Contact:** Ram Devineni, founder & president; Flávia Rocha, editor in chief. Estab. 1999. Receives 15 unsolicited mss/month. Accepts 3 mss/issue; 6 mss/year. Agented fiction 15%. Receives about 5,000 poems/year; accepts 2%. Publishes 3 new writers/year. Has published work by Stuart Dybek, Howard Norman, Molly Giles, Rick Moody, Anthony Hecht, Sharon Olds, Lou Reed, Marilyn Hacker, Billy Collins, and Glyn Maxwell. *Rattapallax*, published semiannually, is named for "Wallace Stevens's word for the sound of thunder. The magazine includes a DVD featuring poetry films and audio files. *Rattapallax* is looking for the extraordinary in modern poetry and prose that reflect the diversity of world cultures. Our goals are to create international dialogue using literature and focus on what is relevant to our society."

◯ *Rattapallax* is 112 pages, magazine-sized, offset-printed, perfect-bound, with 12-pt. CS1 cover; some illustrations; photos. Press run is 2,000 (100 subscribers, 50 libraries, 1,200 shelf sales); 200 distributed free to contributors, reviews, and promos.

NEEDS Length: up to 2,000 words.

HOW TO CONTACT Submit via online submissions manager at rattapallax.submittable.com/submit.

PAYMENT/TERMS Pays 2 contributor's copies.

RATTLING WALL

c/o PEN USA, 269 S. Beverly Dr. #1163, Beverly Hills CA 90212. **E-mail:** therattlingwall@penusa.org. **Website:** therattlingwall.com. **Contact:** Michelle Meyering, editor. Estab. 2010.

◯ Magazine: 6x9, square bound.

NEEDS Length: up to 15 pages.

HOW TO CONTACT Submit 1 complete story; no excerpts. Submissions should be double-spaced. Include cover letter with contact information, brief bio, writing sample.

PAYMENT/TERMS Pays 2 contributor's copies.

✪ THE RAVEN CHRONICLES

A Journal of Art, Literature, & the Spoken Word, 15528 12th Ave. NE, Shoreline WA 98155. (206)941-2955. **E-mail:** editors@ravenchronicles.org. **E-mail:** https://ravenchronicles.submittable.com/submit. **Website:** www.ravenchronicles.org. **Contact:** Phoebe Bosché, managing editor; Priscilla Long, nonfiction editor; Kathleen Alcalá, fiction editor; Gary Lilley, poetry editor. Estab. 1991. *"The Raven Chronicles* publishes work which reflects the cultural diversity of the Pacific Northwest, Canada, and other areas of North America. We promote art, literature, and the spoken word for an audience that is hip, literate, funny, informed, and lives in a society that has a multicultural sensibility. We publish fiction, talk art/spoken word, poetry, essays, reflective articles, reviews, interviews, and contemporary art. We look for work that reflects the author's experiences, perceptions, and insights."

NEEDS "Experimental work is always of interest." Length: up to 4,000 words, or 3 flash fiction/lyric prose fiction. "Check with us for maximum length. We sometimes print longer pieces."

HOW TO CONTACT Submit complete ms via online submissions manager.

◗ THE READER

The Reader Organisation, Calderstones Mansion, Calderstones Park, Liverpool L18 3JB, United Kingdom. **E-mail:** magazine@thereader.org.uk; info@thereader.org.uk. **Website:** www.thereader.org.uk. **Contact:** Grace Frame. Estab. 1997. *"The Reader* is a quarterly literary magazine aimed at the intelligent 'common reader'—from those just beginning to explore serious literary reading to professional teachers, academics, and writers. As well as publishing short fiction and poetry by new writers and established names, the magazine features articles on all aspects of literature, language, and reading; regular features, including a literary quiz and a section on the Reading Revolution, reporting on The Reader Organisation's outreach work; reviews; and readers' recommendations of books that have made a difference to them. *The Reader* is unique among literary magazines in its focus on reading as a creative, important, and pleasur-

able activity, and in its combination of high-quality material and presentation with a genuine commitment to ordinary but dedicated readers." Also publishes literary essays, literary criticism, poetry.

NEEDS Wants short fiction and (more rarely) novel excerpts. Has published work by Karen King Arbisala, Ray Tallis, Sasha Dugdale, Vicki Seal, David Constantine, Jonathan Meades, and Ramesh Avadhani. Length: 1,000-2,500 words. Average length: 2,300 words. Publishes short shorts. Average length of short shorts: 1,500 words.

HOW TO CONTACT No e-mail submissions. Send complete ms with cover letter. Include estimated word count, brief bio, list of publications.

TIPS "The style or polish of the writing is less important than the deep structure of the story (though, of course, it matters that it's well written). The main persuasive element is whether the story moves us—and that's quite hard to quantify. It's something to do with the force of the idea and the genuine nature of enquiry within the story. When fiction is the writer's natural means of thinking things through, that'll get us. "

REAL

Regarding Arts & Letters, Stephen F. Austin State University, Nacogdoches TX 75962-3007. **Website:** regardingartsandletters.wordpress.com. **Contact:** Mark Sanders, editor. Estab. 1968. *"REAL: Regarding Arts & Letters* was founded in 1968 as an academic journal which occasionally published poetry. Now, it is an international creative magazine dedicated to publishing the best contemporary fiction, poetry, and nonfiction." Features both established and emerging writers. Magazine: semiannual, 120 pages, perfect-bound.

NEEDS "We're not interested in genre fiction—science fiction or romance or the like—unless you're doing some cheeky genre-bending. Otherwise, send us your best literary work." Publishes short shorts. Length: up to 6,000 words.

HOW TO CONTACT Submit via online submissions manager.

PAYMENT/TERMS Pays contributor's copies

TIPS "We are looking for the best work, whether you are established or not."

REDIVIDER

Department of Writing, Literature, and Publishing, Emerson College, 120 Boylston St., Boston MA 02116. **E-mail:** editor@redividerjournal.org. **Website:**

www.redividerjournal.org. Estab. 1986. *Redivider*, a journal of literature and art, is published twice a year by graduate students in the Writing, Literature, and Publishing Department of Emerson College. Prints new art, fiction, nonfiction, and poetry from new, emerging, and established artists and writers. Every spring, *Redivider* hosts the Beacon Street Prize Writing Contest, awarding a cash prize and publication to the winning submission in fiction, poetry, and nonfiction categories. Hosts the Blurred Genre Contest each fall, awarding cash prizes and publication for flash fiction, flash nonfiction, and prose poetry. See website for details.

NEEDS Length: up to 8,000 words.

HOW TO CONTACT Submit via online submissions manager.

PAYMENT/TERMS Pays 2 contributor's copies.

TIPS "To get a sense of what we publish, pick up an issue!"

RED ROCK REVIEW

College of Southern Nevada, CSN Department of English, J2A, 3200 E. Cheyenne Ave., North Las Vegas NV 89030. (702)651-4094. **Fax:** (702)651-4455. **E-mail:** redrockreview@csn.edu. **Website:** sites.csn.edu/english/redrockreview. **Contact:** Todd Moffett, senior editor; Erica Vital-Lazare, associate editor. Estab. 1994. Dedicated to the publication of fine contemporary literature. Accepts fine poetry and short fiction year round.

○ *Red Rock Review* is about 130 pages, magazine-sized, professionally printed, perfect-bound, with 10-pt. CS1 cover.

NEEDS "We're looking for the very best literature. Stories need to be tightly crafted, strong in character development, built around conflict." Length: up to 5,000 words.

HOW TO CONTACT Send ms via e-mail as Word, RTF, or PDF file attachment.

PAYMENT/TERMS Pays 2 contributor's copies.

RED WHEELBARROW

De Anza College, 21250 Stevens Creek Blvd., Cupertino CA 95014. **Website:** www.deanza.edu/redwheelbarrow. Estab. 1976 as *Bottomfish*; 2000 as *Red Wheelbarrow*.

○ "We seek to publish a diverse range of styles and voices from around the country and the world." Publishes a student edition and a national edition.

NEEDS Length: up to 4,000 words.

HOW TO CONTACT Send complete ms by mail (include SASE) or e-mail with brief bio.

TIPS "Write freely, rewrite carefully. Resist clichés and stereotypes. We are not affiliated with Red Wheelbarrow Press or any similarly named publication."

REED MAGAZINE

San Jose State University, Dept. of English, One Washington Square, San Jose CA 95192. **E-mail:** mail@reedmag.org; cathleen.miller@sjsu.edu. **Website:** www.reedmag.org. **Contact:** Cathleen Miller, editor-in-chief. Estab. 1867. *Reed Magazine* is California's oldest literary journal. "We publish works of short fiction, nonfiction, poetry, and art, and offer cash prizes in each category." Accepts electronic submissions only.

NEEDS Does not want children's, young adult, fantasy, or erotica. Length: up to 5,000 words.

HOW TO CONTACT Submit complete ms via online submissions manager.

PAYMENT/TERMS Contest contributors receive 1 free copy; additional copies: $15.

TIPS "Well-writen, original, clean grammatical prose is essential. We are interested in established authors as well as fresh new voices. Keep submitting!"

RHINO

The Poetry Forum, Inc., P.O. Box 591, Evanston IL 60204. **E-mail:** editors@rhinopoetry.org. **Website:** rhinopoetry.org. **Contact:** Ralph Hamilton, editor-in-chief. "This independent, eclectic annual journal of 40 plus years accepts poetry, flash fiction (up to 500 words), and poetry-in-translation that experiments, provokes, compels. Emerging and established poets are showcased." Accepts general submissions April 1-July 31 and Founders' Prize submissions September 1-October 31.

NEEDS Length: up to 500 words.

PAYMENT/TERMS Pays 1 contributor's copy and offers contributor discounts for additional copies.

TIPS "Our diverse group of editors looks for the very best in contemporary writing, and we have created a dynamic process of soliciting and reading new work by local, national, and international writers. We are open to all styles and look for idiosyncratic, rigorous, well-crafted, lively, and passionate work."

⊙ ROANOKE REVIEW

221 College Lane, Miller Hall, Salem VA 24153. **E-mail:** review@roanoke.edu. **Website:** roanokereview.

org. Estab. 1967. "The *Roanoke Review* is an online literary journal that is dedicated to publishing new and established voices in fiction, nonfiction, visual poetry, and poetry." Recent work by Henry Taylor, Adrian Blevins, Sharbari Ahmed, John Sibley Williams, and Karl Harshbarger.

NEEDS Length: 1,000-5,000 words. Average length: 3,000 words.

HOW TO CONTACT Submit via Submittable, e-mail, or send SASE for reply only.

TIPS "Send us something you love."

THE ROCKFORD REVIEW

Rockford Writers' Guild, P.O. Box 858, Rockford IL 61105. **E-mail:** sally@rockfordwritersguild.org. **Website:** www.rockfordwritersguild.org. **Contact:** Sally Hewitt. Estab. 1947. Since 1947, the Rockford Writers' Guild has published The Rockford Review twice a year. Anyone may submit to the winter-spring edition of The Rockford Review from July 15-October 15. If published, payment is one contributor copy of journal and $5 per published piece. We also publish a "Members Only" edition in the summer which is open to members of Rockford Writers' Guild. Anyone may be a member of RWG and we have over 100 members from the United States, England, Canada, and Mexico. Members are guaranteed publication at least once a year. Check website for frequent updates at www.rockfordwritersguild.org. Follow us Facebook under Rockford Writers' Guild or Twitter and Instagram @ guildypleasures. Poetry 50 lines or less, prose 1,300 words or less. No racist, supremacist, pornographic or sexist content. If published in the winter-spring edition of *The Rockford Review*, writer receives one copy of journal and $5 per published piece. Pays on publication. Credit line given. Buys first North American serial rights.

NEEDS Prose should express fresh insights into the human condition. No sexist, pornographic, or supremacist content. Length: no more than 1,300 words.

TIPS "We're wide open to new and established writers alike."

○ ○ ROOM

West Coast Feminist Literary Magazine Society, P.O. Box 46160, Station D, Vancouver BC V6J 5G5, Canada. **E-mail:** contactus@roommagazine.com. **Website:** www.roommagazine.com. Estab. 1975. "*Room* is Canada's oldest feminist literary journal. Published quarterly by a collective based in Vancouver, *Room* showcases fiction, poetry, reviews, artwork, interviews, and profiles by writers and artists who identify as women or genderqueer. Many of our contributors are at the beginning of their writing careers, looking for an opportunity to get published for the first time. Some later go on to great acclaim. *Room* is a space where women can speak, connect, and showcase their creativity. Each quarter we publish original, thought-provoking works that reflect women's strength, sensuality, vulnerability, and wit."

○ *Room* is digest-sized; contains illustrations, photos. Press run is 1,600 (900 subscribers, 50-100 libraries, 100-350 shelf sales).

NEEDS Accepts literature that illustrates the female experience—short stories, creative nonfiction, poetry—by, for, and about women.

HOW TO CONTACT Submit complete ms via online submissions manager.

PAYMENT/TERMS Pays $50-120 CAD, 2 contributor's copies, and a one-year subscription.

ROSEBUD

N3310 Asje Rd., Cambridge WI 53523. (608)423-9780. **Website:** www.rsbd.net. **Contact:** Rod Clark, managing editor & publisher. Estab. 1993. *Rosebud*, published 2-3 times/year has presented many of the most prominent voices in the nation and has been listed as among the very best markets for writers. Publishes fiction, poetry, and art. Since 2018, Rosebud includes a full-color section featuring art, including graphic art. Rosebud administers a number of literary prizes each year.

○ *Rosebud* is elegantly printed with full-color cover. Press run is 5,000.

NEEDS Has published work by Ray Bradbury, X.J. Kennedy, and Nikki Giovanni. Publishes short shorts. Also publishes literary essays. Often comments on rejected mss. "No formula pieces."

HOW TO CONTACT Send up to 3 stories to Roderick Clark by postal mail. Include SASE for return of ms and $1 handling fee.

TIPS "Each issue has 6 or 7 flexible departments (selected from a total of 16 departments that rotate). We are seeking stories; articles; profiles; and poems of love, alienation, travel, humor, nostalgia, and unexpected revelation. Something has to 'happen' in the pieces we choose, but what happens inside characters is much more interesting to us than plot manipulation. We like good storytelling, real emotion, and authentic voice."

⑤ THE SAINT ANN'S REVIEW

Saint Ann's School, 129 Pierrepont St., Brooklyn NY 11201. Best to email. **Fax:** (718)522-2599. **E-mail:** sareview@saintannsny.org. **Website:** www.saintannsreview.com. Estab. 2000. *"The Saint Ann's Review* publishes short fiction, poetry, essays, drama, novel excerpts, reviews, translations, interviews, and experimental works."

◯ We seek honed work that conveys a sense of its necessity.

NEEDS Length: up to 6,000 words for short stories; up to 25 pages for excerpts.

HOW TO CONTACT Guidelines online.

PAYMENT/TERMS Pays $50/contributor and 2 contributor copies.

ST. ANTHONY MESSENGER

Franciscan Media, 28 W. Liberty St., Cincinnati OH 45202-6498. (513)241-5615. **Fax:** (513)241-0399. **E-mail:** magazineeditors@franciscanmedia.org. **Website:** www.stanthonymessenger.org. **Contact:** Pat McCloskey, OFM, Franciscan Editor. Estab. 1893. *St. Anthony Messenger* is a Catholic family magazine which aims to help its readers lead more fully human and Christian lives. "We publish articles that report on a changing church and world, opinion pieces written from the perspective of Christian faith and values, personality profiles, and fiction which entertains and informs. Take our writer's guidelines very seriously. We do!"

NEEDS "We do not want mawkishly sentimental or preachy fiction. Stories are most often rejected for poor plotting and characterization, bad dialogue (listen to how people talk), and inadequate motivation. Many stories say nothing, are 'happenings' rather than stories. No fetal journals, no rewritten Bible stories." Length: 2,000 words maximum.

HOW TO CONTACT Send complete ms.

PAYMENT/TERMS Pays 20¢/word.

TIPS "The freelancer should consider why his or her proposed article would be appropriate for us, rather than for *Redbook* or *Saturday Review.* We treat human problems of all kinds, but from a religious perspective. Articles should reflect Catholic theology, spirituality, and employ a Catholic terminology and vocabulary. We need more articles on prayer, scripture, Catholic worship. Get authoritative information (not merely library research); we want interviews with experts. Write in popular style; use lots of examples, stories, and personal quotes. Word length is an important consideration."

SALMAGUNDI

Skidmore College, 815 N. Broadway, Saratoga Springs NY 12866. **Fax:** (518)580-5188. **E-mail:** salmagun@skidmore.edu. **Website:** https://salmagundi.skidmore.edu. **Contact:** Marc Woodworth, associate editor. Estab. 1965. *"Salmagundi* publishes an eclectic variety of materials, ranging from short-short fiction to novellas from the surreal to the realistic, as well as poems, essays, symposia and interviews. Authors include Allan Gurganus, Phillip Lopate, Lincoln Perry, Max Nelson, David Bromwich, J.M. Coetzee, Russell Banks, Rick Moody, Binnie Kirschenbaum, Akeel Bilgrami, Carolyn Forché, Chase Twichell, Linda Pastan, Debora Greger, William Logan, Bina Gogenini, Thomas Chatterton Williams, Marilynne Robinson, Orlando Patterson, Gordon Lish, Anthony Appiah, Clark Blaise, Henri Cole, Mary Gordon, Frank Bidart, Louise Glück, George Steiner, Robert Pinsky, Joyce Carol Oates, Mary Gaitskill, Amy Hempel, Nadine Gordimer, George Scialabba, Rochelle Gurstein, Catherine Pond, Richard Howard, Jennifer Delton and Cynthia Ozick. Our audience is a generally literate population of people who read for pleasure and enjoy the occasional bracing argument." Magazine: 8x5; illustrations; photos. *Salmagundi* authors are regularly represented in *Pushcart* collections and *Best American Short Story* collections. Reading period: November 1-December 1.

NEEDS Length: up to 12,000 words.

HOW TO CONTACT Submit hard copy only by snail mail with SASE.

PAYMENT/TERMS Pays 6-10 contributor's copies and one-year subscription.

TIPS "I look for excellence and a very unpredictable ability to appeal to the interests and tastes of the editors. Be brave. Don't be discouraged by rejection. Keep stories in circulation. Of course, it goes without saying: Work hard on the writing. Revise tirelessly. Study other magazines as well as this one, and send only to those whose sensibility matches yours."

SALT HILL JOURNAL

Creative Writing Program, Syracuse University, English Department, 401 Hall of Languages, Syracuse University, Syracuse NY 13244. **E-mail:** salthilljournal@gmail.com. **E-mail:** salthill.submittable.com. **Website:** salthilljournal.net. **Contact:** Ariel Chu, Myriam Lacroix, Rainie Oet, Ally Young, editors-in-chief. *Salt Hill* is a biannual literary journal publishing outstanding new fiction, poetry, creative nonfiction, and art by people at various stages in their literary and artistic careers. We publish new and emerging writers alongside those with long, illustrious careers in the literary arts. Previous contributors include Terrance Hayes, Patricia Smith, Eduardo C. Corral, Laura Kasischke, W. S. Merwin, Aimee Nezhukumatathil, Mary Ruefle, Sam Sax, Charles Simic, James Tate, Jean Valentine, Dean Young, and even Stephen King, among so many brilliant others. *Salt Hill* is produced by writers in and affiliated with the Graduate Creative Writing Program at Syracuse University and is funded in part by the College of Arts & Sciences and the Graduate Student Organization of Syracuse University.

○ We are interested in work that shines, work that represents a broad spectrum of experience, and work that makes us feel in new and exciting ways. In order to put out the best magazine we can, full of all that is glimmering, we believe it is critical to lift up the voices of writers and artists who have been traditionally underrepresented in the literary arts. As such, we feel a strong urgency to read and consider work by people of color, women, queer/trans people, non-binary folks, and anyone else who has been marginalized by the institutions which have, for so long, dominated the publishing scene.

NEEDS Length: up to 30 double-spaced pages.

HOW TO CONTACT Submit via online submissions manager; contact fiction editor via e-mail for retractions and queries only.

THE SAME

P.O. Box 494, Mount Union PA 17066. **E-mail:** editors@thesamepress.com. **E-mail:** submissions@thesamepress.com. **Website:** www.thesamepress.com. **Contact:** Nancy Eldredge, managing editor. Estab. 2000. *The Same*, published biannually, prints nonfiction (essays, reviews, literary criticism), poetry, and short fiction.

○ *The Same* is 50-100 pages, desktop-published, perfect-bound.

HOW TO CONTACT Query before submitting.

SANDY RIVER REVIEW, THE

University of Maine at Farmington, 114 Prescott St., Farmington ME 04938. **E-mail:** thesandyriverreview@gmail.com. **E-mail:** sandyriversubmissions@gmail.com. **Website:** sandyriverreview.com. **Contact:** Alexandra Dupuis and Elayna Chamberlin, print editors; Richard Southard and Meagan Jones, the River editors. "*The Sandy River Review* seeks prose, poetry, and art submissions once a year for our annual print issue. *The River*, our regularly flowing stream of high-quality digital content, accepts these as well, along with podcasts and music. Deadline for the print issue is in December, while *The River* has rolling submissions. Prose submissions may be either fiction or creative nonfiction and should be a maximum of 3,500 words in length, 12-point, Times New Roman font, and double-spaced. Most of our art is published in b&w and must be submitted as 300-dpi quality, CMYK color mode, and saved as a TIFF file. We publish a wide variety of work from students as well as professional, established writers. Your submission should be polished and imaginative with strongly drawn characters and an interesting, original narrative. The review is the face of the University of Maine at Farmington's venerable BFA Creative Writing program, and we strive for the highest quality prose and poetry standard."

NEEDS Submit via e-mail. "The review is a literary journal—please, no horror, science fiction, romance." Length: up to 3,5000 words.

HOW TO CONTACT Send complete ms.

PAYMENT/TERMS Pays 3 contributor's copies.

TIPS "We recommend that you take time with your piece. As with all submissions to a literary journal, submissions should be fully completed, polished final drafts that require minimal to no revision once accepted. Double-check your prose pieces for basic grammatical errors before submitting."

SANTA MONICA REVIEW

Santa Monica College, 1900 Pico Blvd., Santa Monica CA 90405. **Website:** www.smc.edu/sm_review. **Contact:** Andrew Tonkovich, editor. Estab. 1988. The *Santa Monica Review*, published twice yearly in fall and spring, is a nationally distributed literary arts journal sponsored by Santa Monica College. It currently features fiction and nonfiction.

NEEDS "No crime and detective, mysogyny, footnotes, TV, dog stories. We want more self-conscious, smart, political, humorous, digressive, meta-fiction."

HOW TO CONTACT Submit complete ms with SASE. No e-mail submissions.

PAYMENT/TERMS Pays contributor's copies and subscription.

THE SARANAC REVIEW

Dept. of English, SUNY Plattsburgh, 101 Broad St., Plattsburgh NY 12901. (518)564-2241. **Fax:** (518)564-2140. **E-mail:** saranacreview@plattsburgh.edu. **Website:** www.saranacreview.com. **Contact:** Aimee Baker, executive editor. Estab. 2004. "*The Saranac Review* is committed to dissolving boundaries of all kinds, seeking to publish a diverse array of emerging and established writers from Canada and the U.S. *The Saranac Review* aims to be a textual clearing in which a space is opened for cross-pollination between American and Canadian writers. In this way the magazine reflects the expansive, bright spirit of the etymology of its name, Saranac, meaning 'cluster of stars.' *The Saranac Review* is digest-sized, with color photo or painting on cover. Publishes both digital and print-on-demand versions. Has published Lawrence Raab, Jacob M. Appel, Marilyn Nelson, Tom Wayman, Colette Inez, Louise Warren, Brian Campbell, Gregory Pardlo, Myfanwy Collins, William Giraldi, Xu Xi, Julia Alvarez, and other fine emerging and established writers." Published annually.

NEEDS "We're looking for well-crafted fiction that demonstrates respect for and love of language. Fiction that makes us feel and think, that edifies without being didactic or self-indulgent and ultimately connects us to our sense of humanity." No genre material (fantasy, sci-fi, etc.) or light verse. Length: up to 7,000 words.

HOW TO CONTACT Submit complete ms via online submissions manager (Submittable).

PAYMENT/TERMS Pays $5/printed page.

SCREAMINMAMAS

Harmoni Productions, LLC, 1911 Cleveland St., Hollywood FL 33020. **E-mail:** screaminmamas@gmail.com. **Website:** www.screaminmamas.com. **Contact:** Darlene Pistocchi, editor; Lena, submissions coordinator. Estab. 2012. "We are the voice of everyday moms. We share their stories, revelations, humorous rants, photos, talent, children, ventures, etc."

NEEDS Does not want vulgar, obscene, derogatory, or negative fiction. Length: 800-1,200 words.

HOW TO CONTACT Send complete ms.

TIPS "Visit our submissions page and themes page on our website."

THE SEATTLE REVIEW

Box 354330, University of Washington, Seattle WA 98195. (206)543-2302. **E-mail:** seattlereview@gmail.com. **Website:** www.seattlereview.org. **Contact:** Andrew Feld, editor in chief. Estab. 1978. *The Seattle Review* includes poetry, fiction, and creative nonfiction.

The Seattle Review will only publish long works. Poetry must be 10 pages or longer, and prose must be 40 pages or longer. *The Seattle Review* is 8x10; 175-250 pages. Receives 200 unsolicited mss/month. Accepts 10-15 mss/issue; 20-30 mss/year. Publishes ms 6 months-1 year after acceptance.

NEEDS Only publishes novellas. "Currently, we do not consider, use, or have a place for genre fiction (sci-fi, detective, etc.) or visual art." Length: at least 40 double-spaced pages.

HOW TO CONTACT Send complete ms. Accepts electronic submissions only.

PAYMENT/TERMS Pays 2 contributor's copies and 1-year subscription.

TIPS "Know what we publish; no genre fiction. Look at our magazine and decide if your work might be appreciated. Beginners do well in our magazine if they send clean, well-written manuscripts. We've published a lot of 'first stories' from all over the country and take pleasure in discovery."

SEEMS

Lakeland University, W 3718 South Dr., Plymouth WI 53073-4878. (920)565-1000 x2295 or (920)565-3871. **Fax:** (920)565-1206. **E-mail:** seems@lakeland.edu. **Website:** seemsmagazine.wixsite.com/seems. Estab. 1971. *SEEMS*, published irregularly, prints poetry, fiction, and essays. Focuses on work that integrates economy of language, "the musical phrase," forms of resemblance, and the sentient. Will consider unpublished poetry, fiction, and creative nonfiction. See the editor's website at www.karlelder.com. "Links to my work and an interview may provide insight for the potential contributor."

NEEDS Length: up to 5,000 words.

HOW TO CONTACT Submit by mail or e-mail.

PAYMENT/TERMS Pays 1 contributor's copy.

SEQUESTRUM

Sequestrum Publishing, 1023 Garfield Ave., Ames IA 50014. **E-mail:** sequr.info@gmail.com. **Website:** www.sequestrum.org. **Contact:** R.M. Cooper, managing editor. Estab. 2014. All publications are paired with a unique visual component. Regularly holds contests and features well-known authors, as well as promising new and emerging voices.

NEEDS Length: 12,000 words max.

HOW TO CONTACT Submit complete ms via online submissions manager.

PAYMENT/TERMS Pays $10-15/story.

TIPS "Reading a past issue goes a long way; there's little excuse not to. Our entire archive is available online to preview, and subscription rates are variable. Send your best, most interesting work. General submissions are always open, and we regularly hold contests and offer awards which are themed."

THE SEWANEE REVIEW

735 University Ave, Sewanee TN 37383. (931)598-1185. **E-mail:** sewaneereview@sewanee.edu. **Website:** thesewaneereview.com. **Contact:** Adam Ross, editor. Estab. 1892. *The Sewanee Review* is America's oldest continuously published literary quarterly. Publishes original fiction, poetry, essays, and interviews. Does not accept submissions June 1-Aug 31.

NEEDS Length: up to 10,000 words.

HOW TO CONTACT Submit complete ms via online submissions manager.

PAYMENT/TERMS Pays $25/page, $300 minimum.

SHENANDOAH

Washington and Lee University, Lexington VA 24450. (540)458-8908. **E-mail:** shenandoah@wlu.edu. **Website:** shenandoahliterary.org. **Contact:** Beth Staples, editor. Estab. 1950. Sponsors the Shenandoah Prize for Fiction, awarded annually to the best story published in a volume year of *Shenandoah*, and the Bevel Summers Prize for the Short Short Story, awarded annually to the best short short story of up to 1,000 words. Prizes for both contests are $1,000. For nearly 70 years,*Shenandoah* has been publishing poems, stories, essays, and reviews which display passionate understanding, formal accomplishment, and serious mischief. As of 2018, under new editor Beth Staples, *Shenandoah* aims to to showcase a wide variety of voices and perspectives in terms of gender identity, race, ethnicity, class, age, ability, nationality, regionality, sexuality, and educational background. We're excited to consider short stories, essays, excerpts of novels in progress, poems, comics, and translations of all the above.

NEEDS Length: Up to 8,000 words.

HOW TO CONTACT Send complete ms via online submissions manager.

PAYMENT/TERMS Pays $100 for every 1,000 words up to $500.

SHINE BRIGHTLY

GEMS Girls' Clubs, 1333 Alger St., SE, Grand Rapids MI 49507. (616)241-5616. **Fax:** (616)241-5558. **E-mail:** shinebrightly@gemsgc.org. **Website:** www.gemsgc.org. **Contact:** Kelli Gilmore, managing editor. Estab. 1970. "Our purpose is to lead girls into a living relationship with Jesus Christ and to help them see how God is at work in their lives and the world around them. Puzzles, crafts, stories, and articles for girls ages 9-14."

NEEDS Does not want "unrealistic stories and those with trite, easy endings. We are interested in manuscripts that show how real girls can change the world." Believable only. Nothing too preachy. Length: 700-900 words.

HOW TO CONTACT Submit complete ms in body of e-mail. No attachments.

PAYMENT/TERMS Pays up to $35, plus 2 copies.

TIPS Writers: "Please check our website before submitting. We have a specific style and theme that deals with how girls can impact the world. The stories should be current, deal with pre-adolescent problems and joys, and help girls see God at work in their lives through humor as well as problem-solving." Prefers not to see anything on the adult level, secular material, or violence. Writers frequently oversimplify the articles and often write with a Pollyanna attitude. An author should be able to see his/her writing style as exciting and appealing to girls ages 9-14. The style can be fun, but also teach a truth. Subjects should be current and important to *SHINE brightly* readers. Use our theme update as a guide. We would like to receive material with a multicultural slant."

SIERRA NEVADA REVIEW

999 Tahoe Blvd., Incline Village NV 89451. **E-mail:** sncreview@sierranevada.edu. **Website:** blog.sierranevada.edu/sierranevadareview. Estab. 1990. "*Sierra Nevada Review*, published annually in May, features poetry, short fiction, and literary nonfiction by new and established writers. Wants "writing that leans toward the unconventional, surprising, and risky." Reads submissions September 1-February 15 only.

NEEDS Length: up to 4,000 words.

HOW TO CONTACT Submit ms via online submissions manager.

PAYMENT/TERMS Pays 2 contributor's copies.

SINISTER WISDOM

2333 McIntosh Rd., Dover FL 33527. (813)502-5549. **E-mail:** julie@sinisterwisdom.org. **Website:** www.

sinisterwisdom.org. Estab. 1976. *Sinister Wisdom* is a quarterly lesbian-feminist journal providing fiction, poetry, drama, essays, journals, and artwork. Past issues include "Lesbians of Color," "Old Lesbians/Dykes," and "The Lesbian Body." *Sinister Wisdom* is 5.5x8.5; 128-144 pages; 55 lb. stock; 10 pt. C1S cover; with illustrations, photos.

NEEDS List of upcoming themes available on website. Receives 30 unsolicited mss/month. Accepts 6 mss/issue; 24 mss/year. Recently published work by Jacqueline Miranda, Amanda Esteva, and Sharon Bridgforth. No heterosexual or male-oriented fiction; no 1970s Amazon adventures; nothing that stereotypes or degrades women. Length: 500-5,000 words; average length: 2,000 words.

HOW TO CONTACT Send complete ms. Strongly prefers submissions through online submissions manager. Publishes short shorts. Also publishes literary essays, literary criticism, poetry. Sometimes comments on rejected mss. Reviews fiction.

PAYMENT/TERMS Pays 1 contributor's copy and one-year subscription.

TIPS *Sinister Wisdom* is "a multicultural lesbian journal reflecting the art, writing, and politics of our communities."

SKIPPING STONES

A Multicultural Literary Magazine, Skipping Stones. Inc., P.O. Box 3939, Eugene OR 97403-0939. (541)342-4956. **E-mail:** editor@skippingstones.org. **Website:** www.skippingstones.org. **Contact:** Arun Toké, editor. Estab. 1988. "*Skipping Stones* is an award-winning multicultural, nonprofit magazine designed to promote cooperation, creativity and celebration of cultural and ecological richness. We encourage submissions by children of color, minorities and under-represented populations. We want material meant for children and young adults/teenagers with multicultural or ecological awareness themes. Think, live and write as if you were a child, tween or teen. We want material that gives insight to cultural celebrations, lifestyle, customs and traditions, glimpse of daily life in other countries and cultures. Photos, songs, artwork are most welcome if they illustrate/highlight the points. Translations are invited if your submission is in a language other than English." Themes may include cultural celebrations, living abroad, challenging disability, hospitality customs of various cultures, cross-cultural understanding, African, Asian and Latin American cultures, humor,

international understanding, turning points and magical moments in life, caring for the earth, spirituality, and multicultural awareness. *Skipping Stones* is magazine-sized, saddle-stapled, printed on recycled paper. Published quarterly during the school year (4 issues).

NEEDS Middle readers, young adult/teens: contemporary, meaningful, humorous. All levels: folktales, multicultural, nature/environment. Multicultural needs include: bilingual or multilingual pieces; use of words from other languages; settings in other countries, cultures or multi-ethnic communities. No suspense or romance stories. Length: 1,000 words maximum.

HOW TO CONTACT Send complete ms.

PAYMENT/TERMS Pays 6 contributor's copies.

TIPS "Be original and innovative. Use multicultural, nature, or cross-cultural themes. Multilingual submissions are welcome."

SNREVIEW

197 Fairchild Ave., Fairfield CT 06825-4856. **E-mail:** editor@snreview.org. **Website:** www.snreview.org. **Contact:** Joseph Conlin, editor. Estab. 1999. *SNReview* is a quarterly literary e-zine created for writers of non-genre fiction, nonfiction, and poetry. Quarterly.

NEEDS Receives 300 unsolicited mss/month. Accepts 40+ mss/issue; 150 mss/year. Publishes 75 new writers/year. Has published work by Frank X. Walker, Adrian Louis, Barbara Burkhardt, E. Lindsey Balkan, Marie Griffin, and Jonathan Lerner. "No romance, mystery, science fiction, fantasy, or horror genre fiction." Length: up to 7,000 words.

HOW TO CONTACT Submit via e-mail; label the e-mail "SUB: Name of Story." Copy and paste work into the body of the e-mail. Don't send attachments. Include 100-word bio and list of publications.

SONORA REVIEW

University of Arizona, Dept. of English, Tucson AZ 85721. **Website:** sonorareview.com/. Estab. 1980. "We look for the highest-quality poetry, fiction, and nonfiction, with an emphasis on emerging writers. Our magazine has a long-standing tradition of publishing the best new literature and writers. Check out our website for a sample of what we publish and our submission guidelines."

NEEDS Length: up to 4,000 words.

HOW TO CONTACT Send complete ms via online submissions manager.

PAYMENT/TERMS Pays 2 contributor's copies.

SO TO SPEAK

George Mason University, 4400 University Dr., MSN 2C5, Fairfax VA 22030. **E-mail:** sotospeak@sotospeakjournal.org. **Website:** sotospeakjournal.org. **Contact:** Kristen Brida, editor in chief. Estab. 1993. *So to Speak*, published semiannually, prints "high-quality work relating to feminism, including poetry, fiction, nonfiction (including book reviews and interviews), photography, artwork, collaborations, lyrical essays, and other genre-questioning texts." Wants "work that addresses issues of significance to women's lives and movements for women's equality. Especially interested in pieces that explore issues of race, class, and sexuality in relation to gender."

O *So to Speak* is 100-128 pages, digest-sized, photo-offset-printed, perfect-bound, with glossy cover; includes ads. Press run is 1,000 (75 subscribers, 100 shelf sales); 500 distributed free to students/contributors. Reads submissions September 15-November 15 for spring issue and January 1-April 15 for fall issue.

NEEDS Receives 100 unsolicited mss/month. Accepts 3-5 mss/issue; 6-10 mss/year. **Publishes 7 new writers/year.** Sponsors awards/contests. No science fiction, mystery, genre romance. Length: up to 4,000 words.

HOW TO CONTACT Submit ms via online submissions manager. Include cover letter.

PAYMENT/TERMS Pays 2 contributor's copies.

TIPS "Every writer has something they do exceptionally well; do that and it will shine through in the work. We look for quality prose with a definite appeal to a feminist audience. We are trying to move away from strict genre lines. We want high-quality fiction, nonfiction, poetry, art, innovative and risk-taking work."

SOUL FOUNTAIN

E-mail: soulfountain@antarcticajournal.com. **Website:** www.antarcticajournal.com/soul-fountain/. **Contact:** Tone Bellizzi, editor. Estab. 1997. *Soul Fountain* is produced by The Antarctica Journal, a not-for-profit arts project of the Hope for the Children Foundation, committed to empowering young and emerging artists of all disciplines at all levels to develop and share their talents through performance, collaboration, and networking. Digitally publishes poetry, art, photography, short fiction, and essays on the antarcticajournal.com website. Open to all. Publishes quality submitted work, and specializes in emerging voices. Favors visionary, challenging, and consciousness-expanding material.

HOW TO CONTACT Submit by e-mail only. No cover letters, please.

SOUNDINGS EAST

Salem State University, English Department, MH249, 352 Lafayette St., Salem MA 01970. **E-mail:** soundingseast@salemstate.edu. **Website:** www.salemstate.edu/soundingseast. **Contact:** Kevin Carey (kcarey@salemstate.edu). Estab. 1973. *Soundings East* is the literary journal of Salem State University, published annually with support from the Center for Creative and Performing Arts.

O Reading period: September 1-Feburary 15.

NEEDS Length: up to 10,000 words.

HOW TO CONTACT Submit ms via online submissions manager or by postal mail.

THE SOUTH CAROLINA REVIEW

Center for Electronic and Digital Publishing, 801 Strode Tower, Clemson SC 29634-0522. **Fax:** (864)656-1345. **E-mail:** screv@clemson.edu. **Website:** http://www.clemson.edu/caah/sites/south-carolina-review/index.html. **Contact:** Elizabeth Stansell, managing editor (eander3@clemson.edu). Estab. 1967. Since 1968, *The South Carolina Review* has published fiction, poetry, interviews, unpublished letters and mss, essays, and reviews from well-known and aspiring scholars and writers. *The South Carolina Review* is 7.5 x 9.25; 150-200 pages. Semiannual. Does not read mss June-August or December.

NEEDS Submit complete ms as PDF or Word file. Cover letter is preferred. Do not submit during June, July, August, or December. Recently published work by Thomas E. Kennedy, Ronald Frame, Dennis McFadden, Dulane Upshaw Ponder, and Stephen Jones. Rarely comments on rejected mss.

THE SOUTHEAST REVIEW

Department of English, Florida State University, Tallahassee FL 32306. **E-mail:** southeastreview@gmail.com. **Website:** southeastreview.org. **Contact:** Alex Quinlan, editor in chief. Estab. 1979. "The mission of *The Southeast Review* is to present emerging writers on the same stage as well-established ones. In each semiannual issue, we publish literary fiction, creative nonfiction, poetry, interviews, book reviews, and art. With nearly 60 members on our editorial staff who come from throughout the country and the world, we strive to publish work that is representative of our diverse interests and aesthetics, and we celebrate the eclectic mix this produces. We receive approximately 400 submissions per month, and we accept less than 1-2% of them."

○ Publishes 4-6 new (not previously published) writers/year. Accepts submissions year round, "though please be advised that the response time is slower during the summer months." Has published work by A.A. Balaskovits, Hannah Gamble, Michael Homolka, Brandon Lingle, and Colleen Morrissey.

NEEDS Submit Length: up to 7,500 words.

HOW TO CONTACT Submit complete ms through online submissions manager. "All submissions must be typed (prose should be double-spaced) and properly formatted, then uploaded to our online submissions manager as a DOC or RTF file only. Submission manager restricts you from sending us your work more than twice per year. Please wait until you receive a reply regarding a submission before you upload the next." Does not accept e-mail, paper, or previously published submissions.

PAYMENT/TERMS Pays 2 contributor's copies.

TIPS "Avoid trendy experimentation for its own sake (present-tense narration, observation that isn't also revelation). Fresh stories, moving and interesting characters, and a sensitivity to language are still fiction mainstays. We also publish the winner and runners-up of the World's Best Short Story Contest, Poetry Contest, and Creative Nonfiction Contest."

SOUTHERN HUMANITIES REVIEW

Auburn University, 9088 Haley Center, Auburn University AL 36849. (334)844-9088. **Fax:** (334)844-9027. **E-mail:** shr@auburn.edu. **Website:** www.southernhumanitiesreview.com. **Contact:** Aaron Alford, managing editor. Estab. 1967. *Southern Humanities Review* publishes fiction, essays, and poetry.

⑤ THE SOUTHERN REVIEW

338 Johnston Hall, Louisiana State University, Baton Rouge LA 70803. (225)578-6453. **Fax:** (225)578-6461. **E-mail:** southernreview@lsu.edu. **Website:** thesouthernreview.org. **Contact:** Jessica Faust, coeditor and poetry editor; Sacha Idell, coeditor and prose editor. Estab. 1935. "*The Southern Review* is one of the nation's premiere literary journals. Hailed by *Time* as 'superior to any other journal in the English language,' we have made literary history since our founding in 1935. We publish a diverse array of fiction, nonfiction, poetry, and translation by the country's—and the world's—most respected contemporary writers." Unsolicited submissions period: September 1 through December 1 (prose); September 1 through January 1 (poetry and translation). All mss submitted outside the reading period will be recycled.

NEEDS Wants short stories of lasting literary merit, with emphasis on style and technique; novel excerpts. "We emphasize style and substantial content. No fantasy or religious mss." Length: up to 8,000 words.

HOW TO CONTACT Submit 1 ms at a time through online submission form. "We rarely publish work that is longer than 8,000 words. We consider novel excerpts if they stand alone."

PAYMENT/TERMS Pays $50 for first pages and $25 for each subsequent printed page (max $200), 2 contributor's copies, and 1-year subscription.

TIPS "Careful attention to craftsmanship and technique combined with a developed sense of the creation of story will always make us pay attention."

SOUTHWESTERN AMERICAN LITERATURE

Center for the Study of the Southwest, Texas State University, Brazos Hall, 601 University Dr., San Marcos TX 78666-4616. (512)245-2224. **Fax:** (512)245-7462. **E-mail:** wj13@txstate.edu. **Website:** www.txstate.edu/cssw/publications/sal.html. **Contact:** William Jensen, editor. Estab. 1971. *Southwestern American Literature* is a biannual scholarly journal that includes literary criticism, fiction, poetry, and book & film reviews concerning the Greater Southwest. "We are interested only in material dealing with the **Southwest**."

NEEDS Fiction must deal with the Southwest. Stories set outside our region will be rejected. We are always looking for stories that examine the relationship between the tradition of Southwestern American literature and the writer's own imagination. We like stories that move beyond stereotype. Length: no more than 6,000 words/25 pages.

HOW TO CONTACT Submit using online submissions manager.

PAYMENT/TERMS Pays 2 contributor's copies.

TIPS "Fiction and poetry must deal with the greater Southwest. We look for crisp language, an interesting approach to material. Read widely, write often, revise carefully. We seek stories that, as William Faulkner noted in his Nobel Prize acceptance speech, treat subjects central to good literature—the old verities of the human heart, such as honor and courage and pity and suffering, fear and humor, love and sorrow."

SOU'WESTER

Department of English, Box 1438, Southern Illinois University Edwardsville, Edwardsville IL 62026. **Website:** souwester.org. **Contact:** Joshua Kryah, poetry editor; Valerie Vogrin, prose editor. Estab. 1960. *Sou'wester* appears biannually in spring and fall.

○ *Sou'wester* is professionally printed, flat-spined, with textured matte card cover, press run is 300 for 500 subscribers of which 50 are libraries. Open to submissions in mid-August for fall and spring issues.

HOW TO CONTACT Submit 1 piece of prose at a time. Will consider a suite of 2-3 flash fiction pieces.

PAYMENT/TERMS Pays 2 contributor's copies and a one-year subscription.

Ⓢ SPACE AND TIME

458 Elizabeth Ave., Somerset NJ 08873. **Website:** www.spaceandtimemagazine.com. **Contact:** Hildy Silverman, publisher. Estab. 1966. *Space and Time* is the longest continually published small-press genre fiction magazine still in print. "We pride ourselves in having published the first stories of some of the great writers in science fiction, fantasy, and horror."

○ "We love stories that blend elements—horror and science fiction, fantasy with science fiction elements, etc. We challenge writers to try something new and send us their hard to classify works-—what other publications reject because the work doesn't fit in their 'pigeonholes.'"

NEEDS "We are looking for creative blends of science fiction, fantasy, and/or horror." "Do not send children's stories." Length: 1,000-10,000 words. Average length: 6,500 words. Average length of short shorts: 1,000 words.

HOW TO CONTACT Submit electronically as a Word doc or .rtf attachment only during open reading periods. Anything sent outside those period will be rejected out of hand.

PAYMENT/TERMS Pays 1¢/word.

SPITBALL

The Literary Baseball Magazine, 536 Lassing Way, Walton KY 41094. **E-mail:** spitball5@hotmail.com. **Website:** www.spitballmag.com. **Contact:** Mike Shannon, editor-in-chief. Estab. 1981. *Spitball: The Literary Baseball Magazine*, published semiannually, is a unique magazine devoted to poetry, fiction, and book reviews exclusively about baseball. Newcomers are very welcome, but they must know the subject. "Perhaps a good place to start for beginners is one's personal reactions to the game, a game, a player, etc., and take it from there." Writers submitting to *Spitball* for the first time must buy a sample copy (waived for subscribers). "This is a one-time-only fee, which we regret, but economic reality dictates that we insist those who wish to be published in *Spitball* help support it, at least at this minimum level." *Spitball* is 48 pages, digest-sized, computer-typeset, perfect-bound. Receives about 1,000 submissions/year, accepts about 40. Press run is 1,000.

NEEDS Length: 5-15 pages, double-spaced. Short stories longer than 20 pages must be exceptionally good.

HOW TO CONTACT Submit ms with bio and SASE.

PAYMENT/TERMS Pays 2 contributor's copies.

TIPS "Take the subject seriously. We do. In other words, get a clue (if you don't already have one) about the subject and about the poetry that has already been done and published about baseball. Learn from it— think about what you can add to the canon that is original and fresh—and don't assume that just anybody with the feeblest of efforts can write a baseball poem worthy of publication. And most importantly, stick with it. Genius seldom happens on the first try."

SPORTS AFIELD

Field Sports Publishing, P.O. Box 271305, Fort Collins CO 80527. **Website:** www.sportsafield.com. Estab. 1887. "We cater to the upscale hunting market, especially hunters who travel to exotic destinations like Alaska and Africa. We are not a deer hunting magazine, and we do not cover fishing."

SPOTLIGHT ON RECOVERY MAGAZINE

R. Graham Publishing Company, 9602 Glenwood Rd., #140, Brooklyn NY 11236. (347)831-9373. **E-mail:** rgraham_100@msn.com. **Website:** www.spotlight-onrecovery.com. **Contact:** Robin Graham, publisher and editor-in-chief. Estab. 2001. "This is the premiere outreach and resource magazine in New York. Its goal is to be the catalyst for which the human spirit could heal. Everybody knows somebody who has mental illness, substance abuse issues, parenting problems, educational issues, or someone who is homeless, unemployed, physically ill, or the victim of a crime. Many people suffer in silence. *Spotlight on Recovery* will provide a voice to those who suffer in silence and begin the dialogue of recovery."

TIPS "Send a query and give a reason why you would choose the subject posted to write about."

⚓ STAND MAGAZINE

School of English, University of Leeds, Leeds LS2 9JT, United Kingdom. (44)(113)343-4794. **E-mail:** editors@standmagazine.org. **Website:** www.stand-magazine.org. **Contact:** Jon Glover, managing editor. Estab. 1952. *Stand Magazine* is concerned with what happens when cultures and literatures meet, with translation in its many guises, with the mechanics of language, with the processes by which the policy receives or disables its cultural makers. *Stand* promotes debate of issues that are of radical concern to the intellectual community worldwide. U.S. submissions can be made through the Virginia office (see separate listing). Does not accept e-mail submissions except from subscribers.

NEEDS Does not want genre fiction. Length: up to 3,000 words.

HOW TO CONTACT Submit ms by mail. Include SASE if from U.K; email address otherwise

⭕ STEPPING STONES MAGAZINE

P.O. Box 902, Norristown PA 19404-0902. **E-mail:** info@ssmalmia.com. **Website:** ssmalmia.com. **Contact:** Trinae Ross, publisher. Estab. 1996. "*Stepping Stones Magazine* is a not-for-profit organization dedicated to presenting awesome writing and art created by people from all lifestyles." Publishes fiction, nonfiction, and poetry."

⭕ Has published poetry by Richard Fenwick, Karlanna Lewis, and Stephanie Kaylor. Receives about 600 poems/year, accepts about 10-15%.

NEEDS Fiction should be able to hold the reader's interest in the first paragraph and sustain that interest throughout the rest of the story. Length: up to 4,000 words.

HOW TO CONTACT Send up to 3 mss via postal mail, e-mail (fiction@ssmalmia.com), or online submissions manager. Include brief bio.

STILL CRAZY

(614)746-0850. **E-mail:** editor@crazylitmag.com. **Website:** www.crazylitmag.com. **Contact:** Barbara Kussow, editor. Estab. 2008. *Still Crazy*, published biannually in January and July, features poetry, short stories, and essays written by or about people over age 50. The editor is particularly interested in material that challenges the stereotypes of older people and that portrays older people's inner lives as rich and rewarding. Wants writing by people over age 50

and writing by people of any age if the topic is about people over 50.

⭕ Accepts 3-4 short stories per issue; 5-7 essays; 12-14 poems. Reads submissions year round.

NEEDS Publishes short shorts. Ms published 6-12 months after acceptance. Sometimes features a "First Story," a story by an author who has not been published before. Does not want material that is "too sentimental or inspirational, 'Geezer' humor, or anything too grim." Length: up to 3,500 words, but stories fewer than 3,000 words are more likely to be published.

HOW TO CONTACT Upload submissions via submissions manager on website. Include estimated word count, brief bio, age of writer or "Over 50."

PAYMENT/TERMS Pays 1 contributor's copy.

TIPS Looking for interesting characters and interesting situations that might interest readers of all ages. Humor and lightness welcomed.

STIRRING

Sundress Publications, **E-mail:** stirring@sundress-publications.com. **E-mail:** stirring.nonfiction@gmail.com; reviews@sundresspublications.com; stirring.fiction@gmail.com; stirring.poetry@gmail.com; stirring.artphoto@gmail.com. **Website:** www.stirringlit.com. **Contact:** Luci Brown and Andrew Koch, managing editors and poetry editors; Shaun Turner, fiction editor; Donna Vorreyer, reviews writer; Katie Culligan, reviews editor; Gabe Montesanti, nonfiction editor. Estab. 1999. "*Stirring* is one of the oldest continually published literary journals on the Web. *Stirring* is a quarterly literary magazine that publishes poetry, short fiction, creative nonfiction, reviews and visual art by established and emerging writers and artists."

NEEDS Length: up to 5,000 words.

HOW TO CONTACT Submit complete ms by e-mail to stirring.fiction@gmail.com

STONE SOUP

The magazine inspiring creative kids around the world, Children's Art Foundation, P.O. Box 83, Santa Cruz CA 95063-0083. **E-mail:** editor@stonesoup.com. **Website:** https://stonesoup.com. **Contact:** Emma Wood, editor. Estab. 1973. *Stone Soup*, a digital magazine with a print annual, is the national magazine of writing and art by kids, founded in 1973. Receives 5,000 poetry submissions/year, accepts about 20. Subscription: $24.99/year (U.S.). "We have a preference for writing and art based on real-life experiences; no formula stories or poems. We only publish writing by children up to (and including) age 13. We do not publish writing by adults." Subscription includes downloadable PDFs of each issue as well as more than 15 years of back issues online.

NEEDS "We do not like assignments or formula stories of any kind." Length: 150-5,000 words.

HOW TO CONTACT We only accept submissions through Submittable.

PAYMENT/TERMS Pays in a contributor copy of the print annual (a collection of the years' issues along with bonus content from the blogs), discounted subscription rates.

TIPS "All writing we publish is by young people ages 13 and under. We do not publish any writing by adults. We can't emphasize enough how important it is to read a couple of issues of the magazine. You can read stories and poems from past issues online. We have a strong preference for writing on subjects that mean a lot to the author. If you feel strongly about something that happened to you or something you observed, use that feeling as the basis for your story or poem. Stories should have good descriptions, realistic dialogue, and a point to make. In a poem, each word must be chosen carefully. Your poem should present a view of your subject, and a way of using words that are special and all your own."

STORY BYTES

E-mail: editor@storybytes.com. **Website:** www.storybytes.com. **Contact:** Mark Stanley Bubein. "A monthly e-zine and weekly electronic mailing list presenting the Internet's (and the world's) shortest stories—fiction ranging from 2 to 2,048 words. Just as eyes, art often provides a window to the soul. *Story Bytes*' very short stories offer a glimpse through this window into brief vignettes of life, often reflecting or revealing those things which make us human."

NEEDS "Story length must fall on a power of 2.That's 2, 4, 8, 16, 32, 64, 128, 256, 512, 1,024, and 2,048 words long. Stories must match one of these lengths exactly." See website for examples. No sexually explicit material. Length: 2-2,048 words.

HOW TO CONTACT Submit story as plain text via e-mail. "The easiest way to do so is to simply copy it from your word processor and paste it into an e-mail message. Specify the word count below the title."

TIPS "In *Story Bytes* the very short stories themselves range in topic. Many explore a brief event—a vignette of something unusual, unique, and at times even commonplace. Some stories can be bizarre, while others quite lucid. Some are based on actual events, while others are entirely fictional. Try to develop conflict early on (in the first sentence if possible!), and illustrate or resolve this conflict through action rather than description."

STORYSOUTH

3302 MHRA Building, UNCG, Greensboro NC 27412, USA. **E-mail:** terry@storysouth.com; fiction@storysouth.com; poetry@storysouth.com;. **Website:** www.storysouth.com. **Contact:** Terry Kennedy, editor; Cynthia Nearman, creative nonfiction editor; Drew Perry, fiction editor; Luke Johnson, poetry editor. Estab. 2001. "*storySouth* accepts unsolicited submissions of fiction, poetry, and creative nonfiction during 2 submission periods annually: May 15-July 1 and November 15-January 1. Long pieces are encouraged. Please make only 1 submission in a single genre per reading period."

NEEDS No word-count limit.

HOW TO CONTACT Submit 1 story via online submissions manager.

TIPS "What really makes a story stand out is a strong voice and a sense of urgency—a need for the reader to keep reading the story and not put it down until it is finished."

THE STORYTELLER

65 Highway 328 W., Maynard AR 72444. (870)647-2137. **E-mail:** storytelleranthology@gmail.com. **Website:** www.thestorytellermagazine.com. **Contact:** Regina Riney, editor. Estab. 1996. "We are here to help writers however we can and to help start them on their publishing career. Proofread! Make sure you know what we take and what we don't and also make sure you know the word count."

NEEDS Does not want pornography, erotica, horror, graphic language or violence, children's stories, or anything deemed racial or biased toward any religion, race, or moral preference. 3,000

HOW TO CONTACT Send complete ms with cover letter and SASE.

TIPS "*The Storyteller* is one of the best places you will find to submit your work, especially new writers. Our best advice, be professional. You have one chance to make a good impression. Don't blow it by being unprofessional."

THE STRAND MAGAZINE

P.O. Box 1418, Birmingham MI 48012-1418. (800)300-6652. **E-mail:** strandmag@strandmag.com. **Website:** www.strandmag.com. Estab. 1998. "After an absence of nearly half a century, the magazine known to millions for bringing Sir Arthur Conan Doyle's ingenious detective, Sherlock Holmes, to the world has once again appeared on the literary scene. First launched in 1891, *The Strand* included in its pages the works of some of the greatest writers of the 20th century: Agatha Christie, Dorothy Sayers, Margery Allingham, W. Somerset Maugham, Graham Greene, P.G. Wodehouse, H.G. Wells, Aldous Huxley, and many others. In 1950, economic difficulties in England caused a drop in circulation, which forced the magazine to cease publication."

NEEDS "We are interested in mysteries, detective stories, tales of terror and the supernatural as well as short stories. Stories can be set in any time or place, provided they are well written, the plots interesting and well thought." Occasionally accepts short shorts and short novellas. "We are not interested in submissions with any sexual content." Length: 2,000-6,000 words.

HOW TO CONTACT Submit complete ms by postal mail. Include SASE. No e-mail submissions.

PAYMENT/TERMS Pays $25-150.

TIPS "No gratuitous violence, sexual content, or explicit language, please."

🌑 STRANGE HORIZONS

Strange Horizons, Inc., P.O. Box 1693, Dubuque IA 52004-1693. **E-mail:** management@strangehorizons.com; fiction@strangehorizons.com. **Website:** strangehorizons.com. **Contact:** Jane Crowley and Kate Dollarhyde, editors-in-chief. Estab. 2000. **E-mail:** fiction@strangehorizons.com. "*Strange Horizons* is a magazine of and about speculative fiction and related nonfiction. Speculative fiction includes science fiction, fantasy, horror, slipstream, and other flavors of fantastica." Work published in *Strange Horizons* has been shortlisted for or won Hugo, Nebula, Rhysling, Theodore Sturgeon, James Tiptree Jr., and World Fantasy Awards.

NEEDS "We love, or are interested in, fiction from or about diverse perspectives and traditionally underrepresented groups, settings, and cultures, written from a nonexoticizing and well-researched position; unusual yet readable styles and inventive structures and narratives; stories that address political issues in complex and nuanced ways, resisting oversimplification; and hypertext fiction." No excessive gore. Length: up to 10,000 words (under 5,000 words preferred).

HOW TO CONTACT Submit via online submissions manager; no e-mail or postal submission accepted.

PAYMENT/TERMS Pays 8¢/word, $50 minimum.

STRAYLIGHT

UW-Parkside, English Department, University of Wisconsin-Parkside, 900 Wood Rd., Kenosha WI 53141. **E-mail:** submissions@straylightmag.com. **Website:** www.straylightmag.com. **Contact:** Dean Karpowicz. Estab. 2005. *Straylight*, published biannually, seeks fiction and poetry of almost any style "as long as it's inventive."

○ Literary magazine/journal: 6x9, 115 pages, quality paper, uncoated index stock cover. Contains illustrations, photographs.

NEEDS "*Straylight* is interested in publishing high-quality, character-based fiction of any style. We tend not to publish strict genre pieces, though we may query them for future special issues. We do not publish erotica." Publishes short shorts and novellas. Does not read May through August. Agented fiction 10%. Length: 1,000-5,000 words for short stories; under 1,000 words for flash fiction; 17,500-45,000 words for novellas. Average length: 1,500-3,000 words.

HOW TO CONTACT Send complete ms with cover letter. Accepts submissions by online submission manager or mail (send either SASE or IRC for return of ms, or disposable copy of ms and #10 SASE for reply only). Include brief bio, list of publications.

PAYMENT/TERMS Pays 2 contributor's copies.

TIPS "We tend to publish character-based and inventive fiction with cutting-edge prose. We are unimpressed with works based on strict plot twists or novelties. Read a sample copy to get a feel for what we publish."

STRUGGLE

A Magazine of Proletarian Revolutionary Literature, P.O. Box 28536, Detroit MI 48228. (313)273-9039. **E-mail:** timhall11@yahoo.com. **Website:** www.strugglemagazine.net. **Contact:** Tim Hall, editor. Estab. 1985. "Irregularly published now after 30 years of existence funded solely by writers and activists, but planning to resume as a twice-yearly magazine featuring African American, Latino, and other writers of color; prisoners; disgruntled workers; activists in the anti-war, anti-racist, and other mass movements; and many writers discontented with the Democrats and with the Republicans, their joint austerity campaign against the workers and the poor, the racist police murders against people of color, the unending destruction of the environment, and their continuing aggressive wars and drone murders abroad. While we urge literature in the direction of revolutionary working-class politics and a vision of socialism as embodying a genuine workers' power, in distinction to the state-capitalist regimes of the former Soviet Union, present-day China, North Korea, Cuba, etc., we accept a broader range of rebellious viewpoints in order to encourage creativity and dialogue."

NEEDS "Readers would like fiction about anti-globalization, the fight against racism, global militarism including the war dangers under Trump, the struggle of immigrants, and the disillusionment with the Democratic and Republican administrations as they reveal their craven service to the rich billionaires. Would also like to see more fiction that depicts life, work, and struggle of the working class of every background, especially young workers in the struggle for a $15/hour wage and unionization in fast food and Walmart; also the struggles of the 1930s and 1960s illustrated and brought to life." No romance, psychic, mystery, western, erotica, or religious. Length: 4,000 words; average length: 1,000-3,000 words.

HOW TO CONTACT Submit ms via e-mail or postal mail.

PAYMENT/TERMS Pays 1 contributor's copy.

◗ STUDIO

A Journal of Christians Writing, 727 Peel St., Albury NSW 2640, Australia. (61)(2)6021-1135. **E-mail:** studio00@bigpond.net.au. **Contact:** Paul Grover, publisher. Estab. 1980. *Studio, A Journal of Christians Writing*, published three times a year, prints poetry and prose of literary merit, offering a venue for previously published, new, and aspiring writers and seeking to create a sense of community among Christians writing. Also publishes occasional articles as well as news and reviews of writing, writers, and events of interest to members. People who send material should be comfortable being published under this banner: *Studio, A Journal of Christians Writing*. *Studio* is 60-80 pages, digest-sized, professionally printed on high-quality paper, saddle-stapled, with matte card cover. Press run is 300 (all subscriptions).

NEEDS Cover letter is required. Include brief details of previous publishing history, if any. SAE with IRC required. "Submissions must be typed and double-spaced on 1 side of A4 white paper. Name and address must appear on the reverse side of each page submitted."

PAYMENT/TERMS Pays 1 contributor's copy.

◖◗ SUBTERRAIN

Strong Words for a Polite Nation, P.O. Box 3008, MPO, Vancouver BC V6B 3X5, Canada. (604)876-8710. **Fax:** (604)879-2667. **E-mail:** subter@portal.ca. **Website:** www.subterrain.ca. **Contact:** Brian Kaufman, editor-in-chief; Jessica Key, editorial and marketing assistant. Estab. 1988. "*subTerrain* magazine is published 3 times/year from modest offices just off of Main Street in Vancouver, BC. We strive to produce a stimulating fusion of fiction, poetry, photography, and graphic illustration from uprising Canadian, U.S., and international writers and artists."

○ Magazine: 8.5×11; 80 pages; colour matte stock paper; colour matte cover stock; illustrations; photos. "Strong words for a polite nation."

NEEDS Receives 100 unsolicited mss/month. Accepts 4 mss/issue; 10-15 mss/year. Recently published work by J.O. Bruday, Lisa Pike, and Peter Babiak. Does not want genre fiction or children's fiction. 3,000 words max.

HOW TO CONTACT Send complete ms. Include disposable copy of the ms and SASE for reply only. Accepts multiple submissions.

PAYMENT/TERMS Pays $50/page for prose.

TIPS "Read the magazine first. Get to know what kind of work we publish."

◖ SUBTROPICS

University of Florida, P.O. Box 112075, 4008 Turlington Hall, Gainesville FL 32611-2075. **E-mail:** subtropics@english.ufl.edu. **Website:** www.english.ufl.edu/subtropics. **Contact:** David Leavitt, editor. Estab. 2005. *Subtropics* seeks to publish the best literary fiction, essays, and poetry being written today, both by established and emerging authors. Will consider works of fiction of any length, from short shorts to novellas and self-contained novel excerpts. Gives the same latitude to essays. Appreciates work in translation and, from time to time, republishes important and compelling stories, essays, and poems that have lapsed out of print by writers no longer living. Member: CLMP.

○ Literary magazine/journal: 9x6, 160 pages. Includes photographs. Submissions accepted from September 1-April 15.

NEEDS Does not read May 1-August 31. Agented fiction 33%. **Publishes 1-2 new writers/year.** Has published John Barth, Ariel Dorfman, Tony D'Souza, Allan Gurganus, Frances Hwang, Kuzhali Manickavel, Eileen Pollack, Padgett Powell, Nancy Reisman, Jarret Rosenblatt, Joanna Scott, and Olga Slavnikova. No genre fiction. Length: up to 15,000 words. Average length: 5,000 words. Average length of short shorts: 400 words.

HOW TO CONTACT Submit complete ms via on-line submissions manager.

PAYMENT/TERMS Pays $500 for short shorts; $1,000 for full stories; 2 contributor's copies.

TIPS "We publish longer works of fiction, including novellas and excerpts from forthcoming novels. Each issue includes a short-short story of about 250 words on the back cover. We are also interested in publishing works in translation for the magazine's English-speaking audience."

THE SUN

107 N. Roberson St., Chapel Hill NC 27516. (919)942-5282. **Fax:** (919)932-3101. **Website:** www.thesunmagazine.org. **Contact:** Sy Safransky, editor. Estab. 1974. *The Sun* publishes essays, interviews, fiction, and poetry. "We are open to all kinds of writing, though we favor work of a personal nature."

NEEDS Open to all fiction. Receives 800 unsolicited mss/month. Accepts 20 short stories/year. Recently published work by Sigrid Nunez, Susan Straight, Lydia Peelle, Stephen Elliott, David James Duncan, Linda McCullough Moore, and Brenda Miller. No science fiction, horror, fantasy, or other genre fiction. "Read an issue before submitting." Length: up to 7,000 words.

HOW TO CONTACT Send complete ms. Accepts reprint submissions.

PAYMENT/TERMS Pays $300-1,500 and 1-year subscription.

TIPS "Do not send queries except for interviews. We're open to unusual work. Read the magazine to get a sense of what we're about. Our submission rate is extremely high. Please be patient after sending us your work and include return postage."

SUSPENSE MAGAZINE

Suspense Publishing, 26500 W. Agoura Rd., Suite 102-474, Calabasas CA 91302. **E-mail:** editor@suspensemagazine.com; john@suspensemagazine.com. **E-mail:** stories@suspensemagazine.com. **Website:** www.suspensemagazine.com. **Contact:** John Raab, publisher/CEO/editor-in-chief. Estab. 2007. *Suspense Magazine* was designed to bring fans closer to the authors they love. We cover the entire suspense, thriller, mystery, horror genre not only with our magazine but with Suspense Radio. We have something for everyone that loves to dive into the unknown. We also have a publishing company that has published several bestsellers and won several awards. When you submit either a short story or a manuscript to Suspense Pub-lishing, the one thing the author needs to make sure of? Editing! I can't say this strong enough. Almost 80% of our entries have not been edited and it shows. If you misspell a word in your query letter, we are not to excited to read your manuscript or short story. And most times we never get that far, we just simply reject it. Just write the absolute best book you can. Don't worry about trends in the market, etc. If you write a great book, people will find it. Just be patient.

NEEDS No explicit scenes. Length: 1,500-5,000 words.

HOW TO CONTACT Submit story in body of e-mail. "Attachments will not be opened."

TIPS "Unpublished writers are welcome and encouraged to query. Our emphasis is on horror, suspense, thriller, and mystery."

SYCAMORE REVIEW

Purdue University Department of English, 500 Oval Dr., West Lafayette IN 47907. (765) 494-3783. **Fax:** (765) 494-3780. **E-mail:** sycamore@purdue.edu. **Website:** www.sycamorereview.com. **Contact:** Anthony Sutton, editor in chief; Bess Cooley, managing editor. *Sycamore Review* is Purdue University's internationally acclaimed literary journal, affiliated with Purdue's College of Liberal Arts and the Dept. of English. Strives to publish the best writing by new and established writers. Looks for well-crafted and engaging work, works that illuminate our lives in the collective human search for meaning. Would like to publish more work that takes a reflective look at national identity and how we are perceived by the world. Looks for diversity of voice, pluralistic worldviews, and political and social context.

Reading period: September 1-March 31.

NEEDS No genre fiction.

HOW TO CONTACT Submit complete ms via on-line submissions manager.

PAYMENT/TERMS Pays in contributor's copies and $50/short story.

TIPS "We look for originality, brevity, significance, strong dialogue, and vivid detail. We sponsor the Wabash Prize for Poetry (deadline: December 1) and Fiction (deadline: April 17), $1,000 award for each. All contest submissions will be considered for regular inclusion in the *Sycamore Review*."

⑨⑤ TAKAHĒ

P.O. Box 13-335, Christchurch 8141, New Zealand. **E-mail:** admin@takahe.org.nz. **E-mail:** essays@takahe.org.nz; fiction@takahe.org.nz; poetry@takahe.org.nz. **Website:** www.takahe.org.nz. **Contact:** Jane Seaford and Rachel Smith, fiction editors. *Takahē* magazine is a New Zealand-based literary and arts magazine that appears 3 times/year with a mix of print and online issues. It publishes short stories, poetry, and art by established and emerging writers and artists as well as essays, interviews, and book reviews (by invitation) in these related areas. The Takahē Collective Trust is a nonprofit organization that aims to support emerging and published writers, poets, artists, and cultural commentators.

NEEDS "We look for stories that have something special about them: an original idea, a new perspective, an interesting narrative style or use of language, an ability to evoke character and/or atmosphere. Above all, we like some depth, an extra layer of meaning, an insight—something more than just an anecdote or a straightforward narration of events." Length: 1,500-3,000 words, "Stories up to 5,000 words may be considered for publication in the online magazine only."

HOW TO CONTACT E-mail submissions are preferred (fiction@takahe.org.nz). Overseas submissions are only accepted by e-mail.

PAYMENT/TERMS Pays small honorarium.

TIPS "Editorials, book reviews, artwork, and literary commentaries are by invitation only."

◐ TALKING RIVER

Lewis-Clark State College, 500 Eighth Ave., Lewiston ID 83501. (208)792-2716. **E-mail:** talkingriver@lcmail.lcsc.edu. **Website:** www.lcsc.edu/talking-river. **Contact:** Kevin Goodan, editorial advisor. Estab. 1994. *"Talking River*, Lewis-Clark State College's literary journal, seeks examples of literary excellence and originality. Theme may and must be of your choosing. Send us your mss of poetry, fiction, and creative nonfiction. The journal is a national publication, featuring creative work by some of this country's best contemporary writers."

◑ Reads mss August 1-April 1 only.

NEEDS Wants more well-written, character-driven stories that surprise and delight the reader with fresh, arresting yet un-self-conscious language, imagery, metaphor, revelation. Recently published work by Chris Dombrowski, Sherwin Bitsui, and Lia Purpura, Jim Harrison, David James Duncan, Dan Ger-

ber, Alison Hawthorne Deming. No stories that are sexist, racist, homophobic, erotic for shock value; no genre fiction. Length: up to 4,000 words.

HOW TO CONTACT Send complete ms with cover letter by postal mail. Include estimated word count, two-sentence bio, and list of publications. Send SASE for reply and return of ms, or send disposable copy of ms.

PAYMENT/TERMS Pays contributor's copies; additional copies $6.

TIPS "We look for the strong, the unique; we reject clichéd images and predictable climaxes."

TAMPA REVIEW

University of Tampa Press, 401 W. Kennedy Blvd., Tampa FL 33606. (813)253-6266. **Fax:** (813)258-7593. **E-mail:** utpress@ut.edu. **Website:** www.ut.edu/tampareview. **Contact:** Richard Mathews, editor; Daniel Dooghan, nonfiction editor; Shane Hinton and Yuly Restrepo, fiction editors; Geoff Bouvier and Elizabeth Winston, poetry editors.. Estab. 1988. An international literary journal publishing art and literature from Florida and Tampa Bay as well as new work and translations from throughout the world. "We no longer accept paper submissions. Please submit all work via the online submission manager. You will find it on our website under the link titled 'How to Submit.'"

NEEDS "We are far more interested in quality than in genre. Nothing sentimental as opposed to genuinely moving, nor self-conscious style at the expense of human truth." Length: up to 5,000 words.

HOW TO CONTACT Send complete ms via online submissions manager. We no longer accept submissions by mail.

PAYMENT/TERMS Pays $10/printed page, 1 contributor's copy, and offers 40% discount on additional copies.

TIPS "Send a clear cover letter stating previous experience or background. Our editorial staff considers submissions between September and December for publication in the following year."

◑ TEARS IN THE FENCE

Portman Lodge, Durweston, Blandford Forum, Dorset DT11 0QA, United Kingdom. **E-mail:** tearsinthefence@gmail.com. **Website:** tearsinthefence.com. Estab. 1984. *Tears in the Fence*, published 3 times/year, is a "small-press magazine of poetry, prose poetry, creative non-fiction, fiction, interviews, essays, and reviews. We are open to a wide variety of poetic styles and work that shows social and poetic awareness whilst prompting close and divergent readings." *Tears in the Fence* is 184 pages, A5, digitally printed on 110-gms. paper, perfect-bound, with matte card cover. Press run is 600.

NEEDS Length: up to 3,000 words.

HOW TO CONTACT Submit complete ms via e-mail as attachment.

PAYMENT/TERMS Pays 1 contributor's copy.

TERRAIN.ORG: A JOURNAL OF THE BUILT + NATURAL ENVIROMENTS

Terrain.org, P.O. Box 19161, Tucson AZ 85731-9161. **E-mail:** contact2@terrain.org. **Website:** www.terrain.org. **Contact:** Simmons B. Buntin, editor in chief. Receives 25 mss/month. Accepts 12-15 mss/year. Agented fiction 5%. **Publishes 1-3 new writers/year.** Published Al Sim, Jacob MacAurthur Mooney, T.R. Healy, Deborah Fries, Andrew Wingfield, Braden Hepner, Chavawn Kelly, Tamara Kaye Sellman. *Terrain.org* is based on, and thus welcomes quality submissions from, new and experienced authors and artists alike. Our online journal accepts only the finest poetry, essays, fiction, articles, artwork, and other contributions' material that reaches deep into the earth's fiery core, or humanity's incalculable core, and brings forth new insights and wisdom. *Terrain.org* is searching for that interface—the integration among the built and natural environments, that might be called the soul of place. The works contained within *Terrain.org* ultimately examine the physical realm around us and how those environments influence us and each other physically, mentally, emotionally, and spiritually."

Beginning March 2014, publication schedule is rolling; we will no longer be issue-based. Sends galleys to author. Publication is copyrighted. Sponsors *Terrain.org* Annual Contest in Poetry, Fiction, and Nonfiction. **Deadline:** August 1. Submit via online submissions manager.

NEEDS Does not want erotica. Length: up to 6,000 words. Average length: 5,000 words. Publishes short shorts. Average length of short shorts: 750 words.

HOW TO CONTACT Accepts submissions online at sub.terrain.org. Include brief bio. Send complete ms with cover letter. Reads September 1-May 30 for regular submissions; contest submissions open year round.

TIPS "We have 3 primary criteria in reviewing fiction: (1) The story is compelling and well crafted. (2) The story provides some element of surprise; whether in content, form, or delivery we are unexpectedly delighted in what we've read. (3) The story meets an upcoming theme, even if only peripherally. Read fiction in the current issue and perhaps some archived work, and if you like what you read—and our overall enviromental slant—then send us your best work. Make sure you follow our submission guidelines (including cover note with bio), and that your mss is as error-free as possible."

THEMA

Thema Literary Society, P.O. Box 8747, Metairie LA 70011-8747. **E-mail:** thema@cox.net. **E-mail:** For writers living outside the U.S.. **Website:** themaliterarysociety.com. **Contact:** Virginia Howard, editor; Gail Howard, poetry editor. Estab. 1988. *"THEMA* is designed to stimulate creative thinking by challenging writers with unusual 'themes, such as "The Critter in the Attic' and 'Six before Eighty.' Appeals to writers, teachers of creative writing, artists, photographers, and general reading audience." *THEMA* is 100 pages, digest-sized professionally printed, with glossy card cover. Receives about 400 poems/year, accepts about 8%. Press run is 300 (180 subscribers, 30 libraries). Subscription: $30 U.S./$40 foreign. Has published poetry by Rosalie Calabrese, Deborah H. Doolittle, David Subacchi, and Wally Swist. Has published fiction/nonfiction by Virginia Butler, Madonna Dries Christensen, Tony Concannon, Diane Jackman, and Margaret Nelson. Has published photographs by Kathleen Gunton, Stanley Horowitz, and John McCluskey.

NEEDS All stories must relate to one of *THEMA*'s upcoming themes (**indicate the target theme on submission of manuscript**). See website for themes. No erotica. Length: 300-6,000 words (1-20 double-spaced pages).

HOW TO CONTACT Send complete ms with SASE, cover letter; include "name and address, brief introduction, **specifying the intended target issue for the mss**." SASE. Accepts simultaneous, multiple submissions, and reprints. Does not accept e-mailed submissions except from non-USA addresses.

PAYMENT/TERMS Payment: $10 for under 1,000 words; $25 for stories over 1,000 words, plus one contributor copy.

THIRD COAST

Western Michigan University, English Department, Kalamazoo MI 49008-5331. **E-mail:** editors@thirdcoastmagazine.com. **Website:** www.thirdcoastmagazine.com. **Contact:** S.Marie LaFata-Clay, editor in chief. Estab. 1995. Sponsors an annual fiction contest. First prize: $1,000 and publication. Guidelines available on website. **Entry fee:** $16, which includes one-year subscription to *Third Coast*. "*Third Coast* publishes poetry, fiction (including traditional and experimental fiction, shorts, and novel excerpts, but not genre fiction), creative nonfiction (including reportage, essay, memoir, and fragments), drama, and translations."

○ *Third Coast* is 176 pages, digest-sized, professionally printed, perfect-bound, with 4-color cover with art. Reads mss from September through December of each year.

NEEDS Has published work by Bonnie Jo Campbell, Peter Ho Davies, Robin Romm, Lee Martin, Caitlin Horrocks, and Peter Orner. No genre fiction. Length: up to 7,500 words or 25 pages. Query for longer works.

HOW TO CONTACT Send complete ms via online submissions manager.

PAYMENT/TERMS Pays 2 contributor's copies and one-year subscription.

TIPS "We will consider many different types of fiction and favor those exhibiting a freshness of vision and approach."

THE THREEPENNY REVIEW

P.O. Box 9131, Berkeley CA 94709. (510)849-4545. **E-mail:** wlesser@threepennyreview.com. **Website:** www.threepennyreview.com. **Contact:** Wendy Lesser, editor. Estab. 1980. "We are a general-interest, national literary magazine with coverage of politics, the visual arts, and the performing arts." Reading period: January 1-June 30.

NEEDS No fragmentary, sentimental fiction. Length: 800-4,000 words.

HOW TO CONTACT Send complete ms.

PAYMENT/TERMS Pays $400.

TIPS "Nonfiction (political articles, memoirs, reviews) is most open to freelancers."

TIMBER JOURNAL

University of Colorado Boulder, **E-mail:** timberjournal@gmail.com. **Website:** www.colorado.edu/timberjournal. **Contact:** Staff changes regularly; see website for current staff members. *Timber* is a literary journal run by students in the MFA program at the University of Colorado Boulder and dedicated to the promotion of innovative literature. Publishes work that explores the boundaries of poetry, fiction, creative nonfiction, and digital literatures. Produces both an online journal that explores the potentials of the digital medium and an annual print anthology.

○ Reading period: August-March (submit once during this time).

NEEDS Length: up to 4,000 words.

HOW TO CONTACT Submit via online submissions manager. Include 30- to 50-word bio.

PAYMENT/TERMS Pays 1 contributor's copy.

TIPS "We are looking for innovative poetry, fiction, creative nonfiction, and digital lit (screenwriting, digital poetry, multimedia lit, etc.)."

TIN HOUSE

McCormack Communications, P.O. Box 10500, Portland OR 97296. (503)219-0622. **E-mail:** info@tinhouse.com. **Website:** www.tinhouse.com. **Contact:** Cheston Knapp, managing editor; Holly MacArthur, founding editor. Estab. 1999. "We are a general-interest literary quarterly. Our watchword is quality. Our audience includes people interested in literature in all its aspects, from the mundane to the exalted."

○ Reading period: September 1-May 31.

NEEDS Length up to 10,000 words.

HOW TO CONTACT Submit via online submissions manager or postal mail. Include cover letter with word count.

PAYMENT/TERMS Pays $200-800.

TOASTED CHEESE

E-mail: editors@toasted-cheese.com. **E-mail:** submit@toasted-cheese.com. **Website:** www.toasted-cheese.com. Estab. 2001. *Toasted Cheese* accepts submissions of previously unpublished fiction, flash fiction, creative nonfiction, poetry, and book reviews. See site for book review requirements and guidelines. "Our focus is on quality of work, not quantity. Some issues will therefore contain fewer or more pieces than previous issues. We don't restrict publication based on subject matter. We encourage submissions from innovative writers in all genres and actively seek diverse voices." No simultaneous submissions. Be mindful that final notification of acceptance or rejection may take four months. No chapters or excerpts unless they read as a stand-alone story. No first drafts.

NEEDS Toasted Cheese actively seeks submissions from those with diverse voices. See site for submission guidelines and samples of what Toasted Cheese publishes. No fan fiction. No chapters or excerpts unless they read as a stand-alone story. No first drafts.

HOW TO CONTACT See site for submission guidelines and samples of what Toasted Cheese publishes.

PAYMENT/TERMS Toasted Cheese is a non-paying market.

TIPS "We are looking for clean, professional work from writers and poets of any experience level. Accepted stories and poems will be concise and compelling with a strong voice. We're looking for writers who are serious about the craft: tomorrow's literary stars before they're famous.See site for submission guidelines and samples of what Toasted Cheese publishes."

TRIQUARTERLY

School of Professional Studies, Northwestern University, 339 E. Chicago Ave., Chicago IL 60611. **E-mail:** triquarterly@northwestern.edu. **Website:** www.triquarterly.org. **Contact:** Carrie Muehle, managing editor. Estab. 1964. "*TriQuarterly*, the literary magazine of Northwestern University, welcomes submissions of fiction, creative nonfiction, poetry, short drama, and hybrid work. We also welcome short-short prose pieces." Reading period: November 15-May 1.

NEEDS Length: up to 5,000 words.

HOW TO CONTACT Submit complete ms via online submissions manager.

PAYMENT/TERMS Pays honoraria.

TIPS "We are especially interested in work that embraces the world and continues, however subtly, the ongoing global conversation about culture and society that *TriQuarterly* pursued from its beginning in 1964."

TULANE REVIEW

Tulane University, Suite G08A Lavin-Bernick Center, Tulane University, New Orleans LA 70118. **E-mail:** litsoc@tulane.edu. **Website:** www.tulane.edu/~litsoc/index.html. Estab. 1988. *Tulane Review*, published biannually, is a national literary journal seeking quality submissions of prose, poetry, and art.

○ *Tulane Review* is the recipient of an AWP Literary Magazine Design Award. *Tulane Review* is 70 pages, 7x9, perfect-bound, with 100# cover with full-color artwork.

NEEDS Length: up to 4,000 words.

HOW TO CONTACT Submit via online submissions manager only. Include a brief biography, an e-mail address, and a return address in cover letter.

PAYMENT/TERMS Pays 2 contributor's copies.

UPSTREET

Ledgetop Publishing, P.O. Box 105, Richmond MA 01254-0105. (413)441-9702. **E-mail:** editor@upstreet-mag.org. **Website:** www.upstreet-mag.org. **Contact:** Vivian Dorsel, Founding Editor/Publisher. Estab. 2005.

NEEDS Does not want run-of-the-mill genre, children's, anything but literary. Length: 5,000 words.

HOW TO CONTACT Send complete ms.

PAYMENT/TERMS Pays $50-250.

TIPS "Get sample copy, submit electronically, and follow guidelines."

⊙ U.S. CATHOLIC

Claretian Publications, 205 W. Monroe St., Chicago IL 60606. (312)236-7782. **Fax:** (312)236-8207. **E-mail:** literaryeditor@uscatholic.org. **E-mail:** submissions@claretians.org. **Website:** www.uscatholic.org. Estab. 1935. "*U.S. Catholic* puts faith in the context of everyday life. With a strong focus on social justice, we offer a fresh and balanced take on the issues that matter most in our world, adding a faith perspective to such challenges as poverty, education, family life, the environment, and even pop culture."

○ Please include SASE with written ms.

NEEDS Accepts short stories. "Topics vary, but unpublished fiction should be no longer than 1,500 words and should include strong characters and cause readers to stop for a moment and consider their relationships with others, the world, and/or God. Specifically religious themes are not required; subject matter is not restricted. E-mail submissions@uscatholic.org." Length: 700-1,500 words.

HOW TO CONTACT Send complete ms.

PAYMENT/TERMS Pays minimum $200.

◑ VAN GOGH'S EAR

Best World Poetry & Prose, French Connection Press, 12 Rue Lamartine, Paris 75009, France. (33)(1)4016-1147. **E-mail:** tinafayeayres@gmail.com. **Website:** www.frenchcx.com/press; theoriginalvangoghsearanthology.com. Estab. 2002. *Van Gogh's Ear*, published annually in April, is an anthology series "devoted to publishing powerful poetry and prose in English and English translations by major voices and innovative new talents from around the globe."

○ *Van Gogh's Ear* is 280 pages, digest-sized, offset-printed, perfect-bound, with 4-color matte cover with commissioned artwork. Poetry published in *Van Gogh's Ear* has appeared in *The Best American Poetry*.

NEEDS Length: up to 1,500 words.

HOW TO CONTACT Submit up to 2 prose pieces by e-mail. Cover letter is preferred, along with a brief bio of up to 120 words.

PAYMENT/TERMS Pays 1 contributor's copy.

TIPS "As a 501(c)(3) nonprofit enterprise, *Van Gogh's Ear* needs the support of individual poets, writers, and readers to survive. Any donation, large or small, will help *Van Gogh's Ear* continue to publish the best cross-section of contemporary poetry and prose. Because of being an anglophone publication based in France, *Van Gogh's Ear* is unable to get any grants or funding. Your contribution will be tax-deductible. Make donation checks payable to Committee on Poetry-*VGE*, and mail them (donations **only**) to the Allen Ginsberg Trust, P.O. Box 582, Stuyvesant Station, New York NY 10009."

🌓 VANILLEROTICA LITERARY EZINE

Cleveland OH 44111. (216)203-4166. **E-mail:** talentdripseroticpublishing@yahoo.com. **Website:** eroticatalentdrips.wordpress.com. **Contact:** Kimberly Steele, founder. Estab. 2007. *Vanillerotica*, published bi-monthly online, focuses solely on showcasing new romantic erotic fiction.

NEEDS Length: 5,000-10,000 words.

HOW TO CONTACT Submit short stories by e-mail to talentdripseroticpublishing@yahoo.com. Stories should be pasted into body of message. Reads submissions during publication months only.

PAYMENT/TERMS Pays $15 for each accepted short story.

TIPS "Please read our take on the difference between *erotica* and *pornography* on the website. *Vanillerotica* does not accept pornography. And please keep poetry 30 lines or less."

⚫ VERANDAH LITERARY & ART JOURNAL

Faculty of Arts, Deakin University, 221 Burwood Hwy., Burwood VIC 3125, Australia. (614)2381-1048. **E-mail:** verandah@deakin.edu.au. **Website:** verandahjournal.wordpress.com. **Contact:** Verandah 34. Estab. 1985. *Verandah*, published annually, is a high-quality literary and art journal edited by professional writing students. It aims to give voice to new and innovative writers and artists.

O Submission period: April 1 through June 30. Has published work by Margaret Atwood, Christos Tsiolka, Dorothy Porter, Seamus Heaney, Les Murray, Ed Burger, and John Muk Muk Burke. *Verandah* is a print journal roughly pages, professionally printed often on glossy stock, flat-spined, with full-color glossy card cover.

NEEDS Maximum 2,500 words.

HOW TO CONTACT Submit via Submittable, see our wordpress website for information www.verandahjournal.wordpress.com. Reads submissions by June 30 deadline.

PAYMENT/TERMS Pays 1 contributor's copy, "with prizes awarded accordingly." Aims to pay ~$30 per piece this year.

TIPS "Check our website!"

VESTAL REVIEW

P.O. Box 35369, Brighton MA 02135. **E-mail:** submissions@vestalreview.net. **Website:** www.vestalreview.org. **Contact:** Mark Budman, editor. Estab. 2000. Semi-annual print magazine specializing in flash fiction. The oldest magazine of flash fiction. A paying market. Our reading periods are February-May and August-November.

O Please read our guidelines and send all submissions through the Submittable. Do not use our email address for submissions.

NEEDS Only flash fiction under 500 words. No porn, racial slurs, excessive gore, or obscenity. No children's or preachy stories. Nothing over 500 words. Length: 50-500 words.

HOW TO CONTACT Publishes flash fiction. "We accept submissions only through our submission manager."

PAYMENT/TERMS Pays $25 and 1 contributor's copy.

TIPS "We like literary fiction with a plot that doesn't waste words. Don't send jokes masked as stories."

🌓 THE VIRGINIA QUARTERLY REVIEW

VQR, P.O. Box 400223, Charlottesville VA 22904. **E-mail:** editors@vqronline.org. **Website:** www.vqronline.org. **Contact:** Allison Wright, executive editor. Estab. 1925. "*VQR*'s primary mission has been to sustain and strengthen Jefferson's bulwark, long describing itself as 'A National Journal of Literature and Discussion.' And for good reason. From its inception in prohibition, through depression and war, in prosperity and peace, *The Virginia Quarterly Review* has been a haven—and home—for the best essayists, fiction writers, and poets, seeking contributors from every section of the United States and abroad. It has not limited itself to any special field. No topic has been alien: literary, public affairs, the arts, history, the economy. If it could be approached through essay or discussion, poetry or prose, *VQR* has covered it." Press run is 4,000.

NEEDS "We are generally not interested in genre fiction (such as romance, science fiction, or fantasy)." Length: 2,000-10,000 words.

HOW TO CONTACT Accepts online submissions only at virginiaquarterlyreview.submittable.com/submit.

PAYMENT/TERMS Pays $1,000-2,500 for short stories; $1,000-4,000 for novellas and novel excerpts.

WEST BRANCH

Stadler Center for Poetry, Bucknell University, Lewisburg PA 17837-2029. (570)577-1853. **Fax:** (570)577-1885. **E-mail:** westbranch@bucknell.edu. **Website:** www.bucknell.edu/westbranch. **Contact:** G.C. Waldrep, editor. *West Branch* publishes poetry, fiction, and nonfiction in both traditional and innovative styles.

○ Reading period: August 15 through April 1. No more than 3 submissions from a single contributor in a given reading period.

NEEDS No genre fiction. Length: no more than 30 pages.

HOW TO CONTACT Send complete ms.

PAYMENT/TERMS Pays 5¢/word, with a maximum of $100.

TIPS "All submissions must be sent via our online submission manager. Please see website for guidelines. We recommend that you acquaint yourself with the magazine before submitting."

WESTERN HUMANITIES REVIEW

University of Utah, 3528 LNCO / English Department, 255 S. Central Campus Dr., Salt Lake City UT 84112-0494. (801)581-6168. **Fax:** (801)585-5167. **E-mail:** managingeditor.whr@gmail.com. **Website:** www.westernhumanitiesreview.com. **Contact:** Michael Mejia, editor; Emily Dyer Barker, managing editor. Estab. 1947. *Western Humanities Review* is a journal of contemporary literature and culture housed in the University of Utah English Department. Publishes poetry, fiction, nonfiction essays, artwork, and work that resists categorization. Submissions are open year-round. All submissions must be sent through online submissions manager.

NEEDS Does not want genre (romance, science fiction, etc.). Length: 5,000 words.

HOW TO CONTACT Send complete ms.

TIPS "Because of changes in our editorial staff, we urge familiarity with recent issues of the magazine. We do not publish writer's guidelines because we think that the magazine itself conveys an accurate picture of our requirements. Please, no e-mail submissions."

WHISKEY ISLAND MAGAZINE

English Dept., Cleveland State University, 2121 Euclid Ave., Cleveland OH 44115. (216)687-3951. **E-mail:** whiskeyisland@csuohio.edu. **Website:** whiskeyislandmagazine.com. **Contact:** Dan Dorman. *Whiskey Island* is a nonprofit literary magazine that has been published in one form or another by students of Cleveland State University for over 30 years.

○ Reading periods: August 15 through November 15 and January 15 through April 15. Paper and e-mail submissions are not accepted. No multiple submissions.

NEEDS No translations, please. Length: 1,500-8,000 words for short stories; up to 1,500 words for flash fiction.

HOW TO CONTACT Submit via online submissions manager.

PAYMENT/TERMS Pays 2 contributor's copies.

WICKED ALICE

Dancing Girl Press & Studio, 410 S. Michigan #921, Chicago IL 60605. **E-mail:** wickedalicepoetry@yahoo.com. **Website:** www.sundresspublications.com/wickedalice. **Contact:** Kristy Bowen, editor. Estab. 2001. "*Wicked Alice* is a women-centered online journal dedicated to publishing quality work by both sexes, depicting and exploring the female experience." Wants "work that has a strong sense of image and music. Work that is interesting and surprising, with innovative, sometimes unusual, use of language. We love humor when done well, strangeness, wackiness. Hybridity, collage, intertexuality."

HOW TO CONTACT Submit complete ms by e-mail.

WILD VIOLET

P.O. Box 39706, Philadelphia PA 19106. **E-mail:** wildvioletmagazine@yahoo.com. **Website:** www.wildviolet.net. **Contact:** Alyce Wilson, editor. Estab. 2001. *Wild Violet*, published monthly online, aims "to make the arts more accessible, to make a place for the arts in modern life, and to serve as a creative forum for writers and artists. Our audience includes English-speaking readers from all over the world who are interested in both 'high art' and pop culture."

NEEDS Receives 30 unsolicited mss/month. Accepts 3-5 mss/issue; 135 mss/year. **Publishes 70 new writers/year.** Recently published work by Aaron Sokoloff, Josh Karaczewski, Jason Howell and Megan Sierra Smith. Also publishes literary essays, literary criticism, poetry. Sometimes comments on rejected mss. "No stories where sexual or violent content is just used to shock the reader. No racist writings." Length: 500-6,000 words; average length: 3,000 words.

HOW TO CONTACT Send complete ms. Accepts submissions by e-mail and postal mail. Include estimated word count and brief bio. Send SASE for return of ms or send a disposable copy of ms and #10 SASE for reply only. Accepts simultaneous, multiple submissions.

PAYMENT/TERMS Writers receive bio and links on contributor's page. Sponsors awards/contests.

TIPS "We look for stories that are well-paced and show character and plot development. Even short shorts should do more than simply paint a picture. Manuscripts stand out when the author's voice is fresh and engaging. Avoid muddying your story with too many characters, and don't attempt to shock the reader with an ending you have not earned. Experiment with styles and structures, but don't resort to experimentation for its own sake."

WILLOW REVIEW

College of Lake County Publications, College of Lake County, 19351 W. Washington St., Grayslake IL 60030-1198. (847)543-2956. **E-mail:** com426@clcillinois.edu. **Website:** www.clcillinois.edu/community/willowreview.asp. **Contact:** Michael Latza, editor. Estab. 1969. Prizes totaling $400 are awarded to the best poetry and short fiction/creative nonfiction in each issue. *Willow Review*, published annually, is interested in poetry, creative nonfiction, and fiction of high quality. "We have no preferences as to form, style, or subject, as long as each piece stands on its own as art and communicates ideas." The editors award prizes for best poetry and prose in the issue. Prize awards vary contingent on the current year's budget but normally range from $100-400. There is no reading fee or separate application for these prizes. All accepted mss are eligible."*Willow Review* can be found on EBSCOhost databases, assuring a broader targeted audience for our authors' work. *Willow Review* is a nonprofit journal partially supported by a grant from the Illinois Arts Council (a state agency), College of Lake County Publications, private contributions, and sales."

NEEDS Accepts short fiction. Considers simultaneous submissions "if indicated in the cover letter" and multiple submissions.

HOW TO CONTACT Send complete ms with cover letter. Include estimated word count, brief bio, list of publications. Send either SASE (or IRC) for return of ms or disposable copy of ms and #10 SASE for reply only.

PAYMENT/TERMS Pays 2 contributor's copies.

⑤ WILLOW SPRINGS

668 N. Riverpoint Blvd. #259, Spokane WA 99202. (509)828-1486. **E-mail:** willowspringsewu@gmail.com. **Website:** willowsprings.ewu.edu. **Contact:** Samuel Ligon, editor. Estab. 1977. *Willow Springs* is

a semiannual magazine covering poetry, fiction, literary nonfiction and interviews of notable writers. Published twice a year, in spring and fall. Reading period: September 1 through May 31 for fiction and poetry; year-round for nonfiction. Reading fee: $3/submission.

NEEDS "We accept any good piece of literary fiction. Buy a sample copy." Does not want to see genre fiction that does not transcend its subject matter. Length: open for short stories; up to 750 words for short shorts.

HOW TO CONTACT Submit via online submissions manager.

PAYMENT/TERMS Pays $100 and 2 contributor's copies for short stories; $40 and 2 contributor's copies for short shorts.

TIPS "While we have no specific length restrictions, we generally publish fiction and nonfiction no longer than 10,000 words and poetry no longer than 120 lines, though those are not strict rules. *Willow Springs* values poems and essays that transcend the merely autobiographical and fiction that conveys a concern for language as well as story."

WITCHES AND PAGANS

BBI Media, Inc., P.O. Box 687, Forest Grove OR 97116. (503)430-8817. **E-mail:** editor2@bbimedia.com. **Website:** www.witchesandpagans.com. **Contact:** Anne Newkirk Niven. Estab. 2002. "Devoted exclusively to promoting and covering contemporary Pagan culture, *W&P* features exclusive interviews with the teachers, writers, and activists who create and lead our traditions, visits to the sacred places and people who inspire us, and in-depth discussions of our ever-evolving practices. You'll also find practical daily magic, ideas for solitary ritual and devotion, God/dess-friendly craft-projects, Pagan poetry and short fiction, reviews, and much more in every 88-page issue. *W&P* is available in either traditional paper copy sent by postal mail or as a digital PDF e-zine download that is compatible with most computers and readers."

NEEDS Does not want faction (fictionalized retellings of real events). Avoid gratuitous sex, violence, sentimentality, and pagan moralizing. Don't beat our readers with the Rede or the Threefold Law. Length: 1,000-5,000 words.

HOW TO CONTACT Send complete ms.

TIPS "Read the magazine, do your research, write the piece, send it in. That's really the only way to get started as a writer; everything else is window dressing."

WOODS READER

P.O. Box 46, Warren MN 56762. **E-mail:** editor@wood-sreader.com. **Website:** www.woodsreader.com. **Contact:** S Sedgwick. Estab. 2017. A quarterly publication for those who love woodland areas: whether a public preserve, forest, tree farm, backyard woodlot or other patch of trees and wildlife. Will only consider articles based on woodlands. "We are looking for positive, whimsical, interesting articles. Our readers like to hear about others' experiences and insights. Please visit submissions page on website. We encourage stories of personal experience. We also buy forest ecology mss of general interest, DIY (photos must accompany), personal essays, book reviews (query first)."

NEEDS Short fiction based on woodland setting. Will buy longer fiction for serialization over four issues. Length: 500-2,000 words.

PAYMENT/TERMS Payment varies.

THE WORCESTER REVIEW

P.O. Box 804, Worcester MA 01613. **E-mail:** editor.worcreview@gmail.com. **Website:** www.theworcesterreview.org. **Contact:** Diane Vanaskie Mulligan, managing editor. Estab. 1972. *The Worcester Review*, published annually by the Worcester County Poetry Association, encourages "critical work with a New England connection; no geographic limitation on poetry and fiction." Wants "work that is crafted, intuitively honest and empathetic. We like high-quality, creative poetry, artwork, and fiction. Critical articles should be connected to New England." *The Worcester Review* is 160 pages, digest-sized, professionally printed in dark type on quality stock, perfect-bound, with matte card cover. Press run is 600.

NEEDS Accepts about 5% unsolicited mss. Length: 1,000-4,000 words. Average length: 2,000 words.

HOW TO CONTACT Send complete ms via online submissions manager. "Send only 1 short story—reading editors do not like to read 2 by the same author at the same time. We will use only 1."

PAYMENT/TERMS Pays 2 contributor's copies and honorarium if possible.

TIPS "We generally look for creative work with a blend of craftsmanship, insight, and empathy. This does not exclude humor. We won't print work that is shoddy in any of these areas."

⑤ WORKERS WRITE!

Blue Cubicle Press, LLC, P.O. Box 250382, Plano TX 75025. **E-mail:** info@workerswritejournal.com. **Web-**site: www.workerswritejournal.com. **Contact:** David LaBounty, managing editor. Estab. 2005. "*Workers Write!* is an annual print journal published by Blue Cubicle Press, an independent publisher dedicated to giving voice to writers trapped in the daily grind. Each issue focuses on a particular workplace; check website for details. Submit your stories via e-mail or send a hard copy."

NEEDS "We need your stories (5,000-12,000 words) about the workplace from our Overtime series. Every 3 months, we'll release a chapbook containing 1-2 related stories that center on work." Length: 500-5,000 words.

HOW TO CONTACT Send complete ms.

PAYMENT/TERMS Payment: $5-50 (depending on length and rights requested).

THE WRITE PLACE AT THE WRITE TIME

E-mail: questions@thewriteplaceatthewritetime.org. **E-mail:** submissions@thewriteplaceatthewritetime.org. **Website:** www.thewriteplaceatthewritetime.org. **Contact:** Nicole M. Bouchard, editor-in-chief. Estab. 2008. Online literary magazine, published 3 times/year. Publishes fiction, personal nonfiction, craft essays by professionals, and poetry that "speaks to the heart and mind. Our writers come from around the world and range from previously unpublished to having written for *The New York Times*, *Time* magazine, *The New Yorker*, *The Wall Street Journal*, *Glimmer Train*, *Newsweek*, *Business Week*, Random House, and Simon and Schuster. Interview subjects include *NYT* best-selling authors such as Tracy Chevalier, Dennis Lehane, Mona Simpson, Janet Fitch, Alice Hoffman, Joanne Harris, Arthur Golden, Jodi Picoult, and Frances Mayes."

NEEDS Considers literary and most genre fiction if thought-provoking and emotionally evocative. No erotica, explicit horror/gore/violence, political. Length: up to 3,500 words. Average length of stories: 3,000 words. Average length of short-shorts: 1,000 words. "If we feel the strength of the submission merits added length, we are happy to consider exceptions."

HOW TO CONTACT Send complete ms with cover letter by e-mail—no attachments. Include estimated word count and brief bio. Accepts multiple submissions, up to 3 stories at a time. Accepts simultaneous submissions if indicated; other publications must be notified immediately upon acceptance. "If accepted elsewhere, we must be notified." Accepts 90-100 mss/year; receives 500-700 mss/year.

TIPS "Through our highly personalized approach to content, feedback, and community, we aim to give a very human visage to the publishing process. We wish to speak deeply of the human condition through pieces that validate the entire spectrum of emotions and the real circumstances of life. Every piece has a unique power and presence that stands on its own; we've had writers write about surviving an illness, losing a child, embracing a foreign land, learning of their parent's suicide, discovering love, finding humor in dark hours, and healing from abuse. Our collective voice, from our aesthetic to our artwork to the words, looks at and highlights aspects of life through a storytelling lens that allows for or promotes a universal understanding."

WRITER'S BLOC

MSC 162, Fore Hall Rm. 110, 700 University Blvd., Texas A&M University-Kingsville, Kingsville TX 78363. (361)593-2516. **E-mail:** kfmrj00@tamuk.edu; connie.salgado@tamuk.edu. **E-mail:** WritersBloc-LitMag@hotmail.com. **Website:** www.tamuk.edu/artsci/langlit/writers_bloc.html. **Contact:** Dr. Michelle Johnson Vela. *Writer's Bloc*, published annually, prints poetry, short fiction, flash fiction, one-act plays, interviews, and essays. "About half of our pages are devoted to the works of Texas A&M University-Kingsville students and half to the works of writers and artists from all over the world." Wants quality poetry; no restrictions on content or form.

○ *Writer's Bloc* is 96 pages, digest-sized. Press run is 300. Reading period: February through May.

NEEDS Submit via e-mail or postal mail. Include cover letter with contact info, short bio. Accepts about 6 mss/year. Publishes short shorts. Also publishes literary essays, poetry. No pornography, genre fiction, or work by children. Length: up to 3,500 words. Average length is 2,500 words.

PAYMENT/TERMS Pays 1 contributor's copy.

WRITER'S DIGEST

F+W Media, Inc., 10151 Carver Rd., Suite #200, Blue Ash OH 45242. (513)531-2690. **E-mail:** wdsubmissions@fwmedia.com. **Website:** www.writersdigest.com. Estab. 1920. *Writer's Digest*, the No. 1 magazine for writers, celebrates the writing life and what it means to be a writer in today's publishing environment.

○ The magazine does not accept or read e-queries with attachments.

TIPS "*InkWell* is the best place for new writers to break in. We recommend you consult our editorial calendar before pitching feature-length articles. Check our writer's guidelines for more details."

THE WRITING DISORDER

A Literary Journal, P.O. Box 93613, Los Angeles CA 90093. **E-mail:** submit@thewritingdisorder.com. **Website:** www.writingdisorder.com. **Contact:** C.E. Lukather, editor; Paul Garson, managing editor; Julianna Woodhead, poetry editor. Estab. 2009. "*The Writing Disorder* is an online literary journal devoted to literature, art, and culture. Our mission is to showcase new and emerging writers—particularly those in writing programs—as well as established ones. We feature new fiction, poetry, nonfiction and art. Although we strive to publish original and experimental work, *The Writing Disorder* remains rooted in the classic art of storytelling. Send us your best work. Have someone proof your work before submitting. No limit on word count."

NEEDS Does not want to see romance or fluff. No limit.

HOW TO CONTACT Query.

PAYMENT/TERMS Pays contributor's copies.

TIPS "We are looking for work from new writers, writers in writing programs, and students and faculty of all ages."

THE YALE REVIEW

The Yale Review, P.O. Box 208243, New Haven CT 06520-8243. (203)432-0499. **Fax:** (203)432-0510. **Website:** www.yale.edu/yalereview. **Contact:** J.D. McClatchy, editor. Estab. 1911. "Like Yale's schools of music, drama, and architecture, like its libraries and art galleries, *The Yale Review* has helped give the University its leading place in American education. In a land of quick fixes and short view and in a time of increasingly commercial publishing, the journal has an authority that derives from its commitment to bold established writers and promising newcomers, to both challenging literary work and a range of essays and reviews that can explore the connections between academic disciplines and the broader movements in American society, thought, and culture. With independence and boldness, with a concern for issues and ideas, with a respect for the mind's capacity to be surprised by speculation and delighted by elegance, *The Yale Review* proudly continues into its third century."

HOW TO CONTACT Submit complete ms with SASE. All submissions should be sent to the editorial office.

PAYMENT/TERMS Pays $400-500.

THE YALOBUSHA REVIEW

University of Mississippi, **E-mail:** yreditors@gmail.com. **Website:** yr.olemiss.edu. Estab. 1995.

NEEDS Length: up to 5,000 words for short stories; up to 1,000 words for flash fiction.

HOW TO CONTACT Submit 1 short story or up to 3 pieces of flash fiction via online submissions manager.

YEMASSEE

University of South Carolina, Department of English, Columbia SC 29208. **E-mail:** editor@yemassee-journal.com. **Website:** yemasseejournal.com. Estab. 1993. "*Yemassee* is the University of South Carolina's literary journal. Our readers are interested in exceptional fiction, poetry, creative nonfiction, and visual art. We publish in the fall and spring. We tend to solicit reviews and interviews but welcome unsolicited queries. We do not favor any particular aesthetic or school of writing."

NEEDS "We are open to a variety of subjects and writing styles. Our essential consideration for acceptance is the quality of the work." No romance, religious/inspirational, young adult/teen, children's/juvenile, erotica. We want more experimental work. Length: up to 5,000 words.

HOW TO CONTACT Send complete ms. Submissions for all genres should include a cover letter that lists the titles of the pieces included, along with your contact information (including author's name, address, e-mail address, and phone number). Yemassee Short Fiction Contest: $750 award. Check website for deadline.

PAYMENT/TERMS Pays 2 contributor's copies.

ZEEK

A Jewish Journal of Thought and Culture, 125 Maiden Ln., 8th Floor, New York NY 10038. (212)453-9435. **E-mail:** zeek@zeek.net. **Website:** www.zeek.net. **Contact:** Erica Brody, editor in chief. Estab. 2001. *ZEEK* "relaunched in late February 2013 as a hub for the domestic Jewish social justice movement, one that showcases the people, ideas, and conversations driving an inclusive and diverse progressive Jewish community. At the same time, we've reaffirmed our commitment to building on *ZEEK*'s reputation for original, ahead-of-the-curve Jewish writing and arts, culture and spirituality content, incubating emerging voices and artists, as well as established ones." *ZEEK* seeks "great writing in a variety of styles and voices, original thinking, and accessible content. That means we're interested in hearing your ideas for first-person essays, reflections and commentary, reporting, profiles, Q&As, analysis, infographics, and more. For the near future, *ZEEK* will focus on domestic issues. Our discourse will be civil."

NEEDS "Calls for fiction submissions are issued periodically. Follow *ZEEK* on Twitter @ZEEKMag for announcements and details."

ZOETROPE: ALL-STORY

Zoetrope: All-Story, The Sentinel Bldg., 916 Kearny St., San Francisco CA 94133. **Website:** www.all-story.com. **Contact:** fiction editor. Estab. 1997. Quarterly magazine specializing in the best of contemporary short fiction. Winner of the National Magazine Award for Fiction as the finest literary publication in the United States.

NEEDS Length: up to 7,000 words. Excerpts from larger works, screenplays, treatments, and poetry will be returned unread.

HOW TO CONTACT Writers should submit only one story at a time. We do not accept artwork or design submissions. We do not accept unsolicited revisions nor respond to writers who don't include an SASE. Send complete ms by postal mail.

PAYMENT/TERMS Pays $1,000.

ZYZZYVA

57 Post St., Suite 604, San Francisco CA 94104. (415)757-0465. **E-mail:** editor@zyzzyva.org. **Website:** www.zyzzyva.org. **Contact:** Laura Cogan, editor; Oscar Villalon, managing editor. Estab. 1985. "Every issue is a vibrant mix of established talents and new voices, providing an elegantly curated overview of contemporary arts and letters with a distinctly San Francisco perspective."

Accepts submissions January 1-May 31 and August 1-November 30. Does not accept online submissions.

NEEDS Length: no limit.

HOW TO CONTACT Send complete ms by mail. Include SASE and contact information.

PAYMENT/TERMS Pays $50.

TIPS "We are not currently seeking work about any particular theme or topic; that said, reading recent issues is perhaps the best way to develop a sense for the length and quality we are looking for in submissions."

BOOK PUBLISHERS

In this section, you will find many of the "big name" book publishers. Many of these publishers remain tough markets for new writers or for those whose work might be considered literary or experimental. Indeed, some only accept work from established authors, and then often only through an author's agent. Although having your novel published by one of the big commercial publishers listed in this section is difficult, it is not impossible. The trade magazine *Publishers Weekly* regularly features interviews with writers whose first novels are being released by top publishers. Many editors at large publishing houses find great satisfaction in publishing a writer's first novel.

Also listed here are "small presses," which publish four or more titles annually. Included among them are independent presses, university presses, and other nonprofit publishers. Introducing new writers to the reading public has become an increasingly important role of these smaller presses at a time when the large conglomerates are taking fewer chances on unknown writers. Many of the successful small presses listed in this section have built their reputations and their businesses in this way and have become known for publishing prize-winning fiction.

These smaller presses also tend to keep books in print longer than larger houses. And, since small presses publish a smaller number of books, each title is equally important to the publisher and each is promoted in much the same way and with the same commitment. Editors also stay at small presses longer because they have more of a stake in the business—often they own the business. Many smaller book publishers are writers themselves and know firsthand the importance of a close editor-author or publisher-author relationship.

⊘ ABBEVILLE FAMILY

Abbeville Press, 116 W. 23rd St., New York NY 10011. (646)375-2136. **Fax:** (646)375-2359. **E-mail:** abbeville@abbeville.com. **Website:** www.abbeville.com. Estab. 1977. Our list is full for the next several seasons. *Not accepting unsolicited book proposals at this time.*

NEEDS Picture books: animal, anthology, concept, contemporary, fantasy, folktales, health, hi-lo, history, humor, multicultural, nature/environment, poetry, science fiction, special needs, sports, suspense. Average word length 300-1,000 words.

HOW TO CONTACT Please refer to website for submission policy.

ABDO PUBLISHING CO.

8000 W. 78th St., Suite 310, Edina MN 55439. (800)800-1312. **Fax:** (952)831-1632. **E-mail:** nonfiction@abdopublishing.com. **E-mail:** fiction@abdopublishing.com; illustrations@abdopublishing.com. **Website:** www.abdopublishing.com. Estab. 1985. ABDO publishes nonfiction children's books (prekindergarten to 8th grade) for school and public libraries—mainly history, sports, biography, geography, science, and social studies. "Please specify each submission as either nonfiction, fiction, or illustration. Publishes hardcover originals. Guidelines online.

ABINGDON PRESS

Imprint of The United Methodist Publishing House, 201 Eighth Ave. S., P.O. Box 801, Nashville TN 37202. (615)749-6000. **Fax:** (615)749-6512. **E-mail:** submissions@umpublishing.org. **Website:** www.abingdonpress.com. Estab. 1789. Abingdon Press, America's oldest theological publisher, provides an ecumenical publishing program dedicated to serving the Christian community—clergy, scholars, church leaders, musicians, and general readers—with quality resources in the areas of Bible study, the practice of ministry, theology, devotion, spirituality, inspiration, prayer, music and worship, reference, Christian education, and church supplies. Publishes hardcover and paperback originals. Book catalog available free. Guidelines online.

NEEDS Publishes stories of faith, hope, and love that encourage readers to explore life.

HOW TO CONTACT Agented submissions only for fiction.

TERMS Pays 7½% royalty on retail price. Responds in 2 months to queries.

⊘ ABRAMS

115 W. 18th St., 6th Floor, New York NY 10011. (212)206-7715. **Fax:** (212)519-1210. **E-mail:** abrams@abramsbooks.com. **Website:** www.abramsbooks.com. **Contact:** Managing Editor. Estab. 1951. Publishes hardcover and a few paperback originals.

○ Does not accept unsolicited materials.

IMPRINTS Stewart, Tabori & Chang: Abrams Appleseed; Abrams Books for Young Readers; Abrams Image; STC Craft; Amulet Books.

NEEDS Publishes hardcover and "a few" paperback originals. Averages 150 total titles/year.

TIPS "We are one of the few publishers who publish almost exclusively illustrated books. We consider ourselves the leading publishers of art books and high-quality artwork in the U.S. Once the author has signed a contract to write a book for our firm the author must finish the manuscript to agreed-upon high standards within the schedule agreed upon in the contract."

⊘ ABRAMS BOOKS FOR YOUNG READERS

195 Broadway, 9th floor, New York NY 10007. **Website:** www.abramsyoungreaders.com.

○ Abrams no longer accepts unsolicited mss or queries.

ACADEMY CHICAGO PUBLISHERS

814 N. Franklin St., Chicago IL 60610. (312)337-0747. **Fax:** (312)337-5985. **Website:** www.chicagoreviewpress.com. **Contact:** Yuval Taylor, senior editor. Estab. 1975. "We publish quality fiction and nonfiction. Our audience is literate and discriminating. No novelized biography, history, or science fiction. No electronic submissions." Publishes hardcover and some paperback originals and trade paperback reprints. Book catalog online. Guidelines online.

NEEDS "We look for quality work, but we do not publish experimental, avant garde, horror, science fiction, thrillers novels."

HOW TO CONTACT Submit proposal package, synopsis, 3 sample chapters, and short bio.

TERMS Pays 7-10% royalty on wholesale price. Responds in 3 months.

TIPS "At the moment, we are looking for good nonfiction; we certainly want excellent original fiction, but we are swamped. No fax queries, no disks. No electronic submissions. We are always interested in reprinting good out-of-print books."

✪⊘ ACE SCIENCE FICTION AND FANTASY

Imprint of Penguin Random House LLC, 1745 Broadway, New York NY 10019. (212)782-9000. **Website:** www.penguinrandomhouse.com. Estab. 1953. Ace publishes science fiction and fantasy exclusively. Publishes hardcover, paperback, and trade paperback originals and reprints.

⬤ As imprint of Penguin, Ace is not open to unsolicited submissions.

NEEDS No other genre accepted. No short stories.

HOW TO CONTACT Due to the high volume of manuscripts received, most Penguin Group (USA) Inc. imprints do not normally accept unsolicited mss.

TERMS Pays royalty. Pays advance.

⊘ ALADDIN

Simon & Schuster, 1230 Avenue of the Americas, 4th Floor, New York NY 10020. (212)698-7000. **Website:** www.simonandschuster.com. **Contact:** Acquisitions Editor. Aladdin publishes picture books, beginning readers, chapter books, middle grade and tween fiction and nonfiction, and graphic novels and nonfiction in hardcover and paperback, with an emphasis on commercial, kid-friendly titles. Publishes hardcover/paperback originals and imprints of Simon & Schuster Children's Publishing Children's Division.

HOW TO CONTACT Simon & Schuster does not review, retain or return unsolicited materials or artwork. "We suggest prospective authors and illustrators submit their mss through a professional literary agent."

⊘ ALGONQUIN BOOKS OF CHAPEL HILL

Workman Publishing, P.O. Box 2225, Chapel Hill NC 27515-2225. (919)967-0108. **Website:** www.algonquin.com. **Contact:** Editorial Department. Algonquin Books publishes quality literary fiction and literary nonfiction. Publishes hardcover originals. Guidelines online.

IMPRINTS Algonquin Young Readers.

HOW TO CONTACT Does not accept unsolicited submissions at this time.

ALGONQUIN YOUNG READERS

P.O. Box 2225, Chapel Hill NC 27515. **Website:** algonquinyoungreaders.com. Algonquin Young Readers is a new imprint that features books for readers 7-17. "From short illustrated novels for the youngest independent readers to timely and topical crossover young adult fiction, what ties our books together are unforgettable characters, absorbing stories, and superior writing. Guidelines online.

NEEDS Algonquin Young Readers publishes ficiton and a limited number of narrative nonfiction titles for middle grade and young adult readers. "We don't publish poetry, picture books, or genre fiction."

HOW TO CONTACT Query with 15-20 sample pages and SASE.

◗ ALLEN & UNWIN

406 Albert St., East Melbourne VIC 3002, Australia. (61)(3)9665-5000. **E-mail:** fridaypitch@allenandunwin.com. **Website:** www.allenandunwin.com. Allen & Unwin publish over 80 new books for children and young adults each year, many of these from established authors and illustrators. "However, we know how difficult it can be for new writers to get their work in front of publishers, which is why we've decided to extend our innovative and pioneering Friday Pitch service to emerging writers for children and young adults. Guidelines online.

AMBERJACK PUBLISHING

P.O. Box 4668 #89611, New York NY 10163. (888)959-3352. **Website:** www.amberjackpublishing.com. Amberjack Publishing offers authors the freedom to write without burdening them with having to promote the work themselves. They retain all rights. "You will have no rights left to exploit, so you cannot resell, republish or use your story again."

NEEDS Amberjack Publishing is always on the lookout for the next great story. "We are interested in fiction, children's books, graphic novels, science fiction, fantasy, humor, and everything in between."

HOW TO CONTACT Submit via online query form with book proposal and first 10 pages of ms.

AMERICAN QUILTER'S SOCIETY

5801 Kentucky Dam Rd., Paducah KY 42003. (270)898-7903. **Fax:** (270)898-1173. **Website:** www.americanquilter.com. Estab. 1984. American Quilter's Society publishes how-to and pattern books for quilters (beginners through intermediate skill level). We are not the publisher for non-quilters writing about quilts. We now publish quilt-related craft cozy romance and mystery titles, series only. Humor is good. Graphic depictions and curse words are bad. Publishes trade paperbacks. Guidelines online.

⬤ Accepts simultaneous nonfiction submissions. Does not accept simultaneous fiction submissions.

HOW TO CONTACT Submit a synopsis and 2 sample chapters, plus an outline of the next 2 books in the series.

TERMS Pays 5% royalty on retail price for both nonfiction and fiction. Responds in 2 months to proposals.

⚠️⊘ AMULET BOOKS

Imprint of Abrams, 115 W. 18th St., 6th Floor, New York NY 10001. **Website:** www.amuletbooks.com. Estab. 2004. *Does not accept unsolicited mss or queries.*

NEEDS Middle readers: adventure, contemporary, fantasy, history, science fiction, sports. Young adults/teens: adventure, contemporary, fantasy, history, science fiction, sports, suspense.

🌍 ANDERSEN PRESS

20 Vauxhall Bridge Rd., London SW1V 2SA, United Kingdom. **E-mail:** andersoneditorial@penguinrandomhouse.co.uk. **Website:** www.andersenpress.co.uk. Andersen Press is a specialist children's publisher. "We publish picture books, for which the required text would be approximately 500 words (maximum 1,000), juvenile fiction for which the text would be approximately 3,000-5,000 words and older fiction up to 75,000 words. We do not publish adult fiction, nonfiction, poetry, or short story anthologies." Guidelines online.

HOW TO CONTACT Send all submissions by post: Query and full ms for picture books; synopsis and 3 chapters for longer fiction.

ANKERWYCKE

American Bar Association, 321 N. Clark St., Chicago IL 60654. **Website:** www.ababooks.org. Estab. 1878. In 1215, the Magna Carta was signed underneath the ancient Ankerwycke Yew tree, starting the process which led to rule by constitutional law—in effect, giving rights and the law to the people. And today, the ABA's Ankerwycke line of books continues to bring the law to the people. With legal fiction, true crime books, popular legal histories, public policy handbooks, and prescriptive guides to current legal and business issues, Ankerwycke is a contemporary and innovative line of books for everyone from a trusted and vested authority. Publishes hardcover and trade paperback originals. Book catalog and ms guidelines online.

NEEDS "We're actively acquiring legal fiction with extreme verisimilitude."

HOW TO CONTACT Query with cover letter; outline or TOC; and CV/bio including other credits. Include e-mail address for response.

TERMS Responds in 1 month to queries and proposals; 3 months to mss.

🔵⊘ ANNICK PRESS, LTD.

15 Patricia Ave., Toronto ON M2M 1H9, Canada. (416)221-4802. **Fax:** (416)221-8400. **Website:** www.annickpress.com. **Contact:** The Editors. Annick Press maintains a commitment to high quality books that entertain and challenge. Our publications share fantasy and stimulate imagination, while encouraging children to trust their judgment and abilities. *Does not accept unsolicited mss.* Publishes picture books, juvenile and YA fiction and nonfiction; specializes in trade books. Book catalog and guidelines online.

NEEDS Publisher of children's books. Not accepting picture books at this time.

TERMS Pays authors royalty of 5-12% based on retail price. Offers advances (average amount: $3,000). Pays illustrators royalty of 5% minimum.

🔵 ANVIL PRESS

P.O. Box 3008 MPO, Vancouver BC V6B 3X5, Canada. (604)876-8710. **Fax:** (604)879-2667. **E-mail:** info@anvilpress.com. **Website:** www.anvilpress.com. Estab. 1988. Anvil Press publishes contemporary adult fiction, poetry, and drama, giving voice to up-and-coming Canadian writers, exploring all literary genres, discovering, nurturing, and promoting new Canadian literary talent. Currently emphasizing urban/suburban themed fiction and poetry; de-emphasizing historical novels. Canadian authors only. No e-mail submissions. Publishes trade paperback originals. Book catalog for 9×12 SAE with 2 first-class stamps. Guidelines online.

NEEDS Contemporary, modern literature; no formulaic or genre.

HOW TO CONTACT Query with 20-30 pages and SASE.

TERMS Pays advance. Average advance is $500-2,000, depending on the genre. Responds in 2 months to queries; 6 months to mss.

TIPS "Audience is informed, educated, aware, with an opinion, culturally active (films, books, the performing arts). No U.S. authors. Research the appropriate publisher for your work."

ARBORDALE PUBLISHING

612 Johnnie Dodds, Suite A2, Mt. Pleasant SC 29464. (843)971-6722. **Fax:** (843)216-3804. **E-mail:** submissions@arbordalepublishing.com. **Website:** www.arbordalepublishing.com. **Contact:** Acquisitions Editor.

Estab. 2004. "The picture books we publish are usually, but not always, fictional stories with nonfiction woven into the story that relate to science or math. All books should subtly convey an educational theme through a warm story that is fun to read and that will grab a child's attention. Each book has a 4-page 'For Creative Minds' section to reinforce the educational component. This section will have a craft and/or game as well as 'fun facts' to be shared by the parent, teacher, or other adult. Authors do not need to supply this information with their submission, but if their ms is accepted, they may be asked to provide additional information for this section. Mss should be less than 1,000 words and meet all of the following 4 criteria: fun to read—mostly fiction with nonfiction facts woven into the story; national or regional in scope; must tie into early elementary school curriculum; must be marketable through a niche market such as a zoo, aquarium, or museum gift shop." Publishes hardcover, trade paperback, and electronic originals. Book catalog and guidelines online.

NEEDS Picture books: animal, folktales, nature/environment, science- or math-related. No more than 1,000 words. Holiday-specific, cats or dogs

HOW TO CONTACT All mss should be submitted via e-mail to Acquisitions Editor. Mss should be less than 1,000 words.

TERMS Pays 6-8% royalty on wholesale price. Pays small advance. Accepts electronic submissions only. Snail mail submissions are discarded without being opened. Acknowledges receipt of ms submission within 1 month.

TIPS "Please make sure that you have looked at our website to read our complete submission guidelines and to see if we are looking for a particular subject. Manuscripts must meet all four of our stated criteria. We look for fairly realistic, bright and colorful art-no cartoons. We want the children excited about the books. We envision the books being used at home and in the classroom."

ARCADE PUBLISHING

Skyhorse Publishing, 307 W. 36th St., 11th Floor, New York NY 10018. (212)643-6816. **Fax:** (212)643-6819. **E-mail:** arcadesubmissions@skyhorsepublishing.com. **Website:** www.arcadepub.com. **Contact:** Acquisitions Editor. Estab. 1988. Arcade prides itself on publishing top-notch literary nonfiction and fiction, with a significant proportion of foreign writers. Publishes hardcover originals, trade paperback reprints. Book catalog and ms guidelines for #10 SASE.

NEEDS No romance, historical, science fiction.

HOW TO CONTACT Submit proposal with brief query, 1-2 page synopsis, chapter outline, market analysis, sample chapter, bio.

TERMS Pays royalty on retail price and 10 author's copies. Pays advance. Responds in 2 months if interested.

✪ ARCHAIA

Imprint of Boom! Studios, 5670 Wilshire Blvd., Suite 450, Los Angeles CA 90036. **Website:** www.archaia.com. Use online submission form.

NEEDS Looking for graphic novel submissions that include finished art. "Archaia is a multi-award-winning graphic novel publisher with more than 75 renowned publishing brands, including such domestic and international hits as *Artesia, Mouse Guard*, and a line of Jim Henson graphic novels including *Fraggle Rock* and *The Dark Crystal*. Publishes creator-shared comic books and graphic novels in the adventure, fantasy, horror, pulp noir, and science fiction genres that contain idiosyncratic and atypical writing and art. *Archaia does not generally hire freelancers or arrange for freelance work, so submissions should only be for completed book and series proposals."*

ARROW PUBLICATIONS, LLC

7716 Bells Mill Rd., Bethesda MD 20817. (301)299-9422. **E-mail:** arrow_info@arrowpub.com. **Website:** www.arrowpub.com. **Contact:** Tom King, managing editor. Estab. 1987. No graphic novels until further notice. Guidelines online.

NEEDS "We are looking for outlines of stories heavy on romance with elements of adventure/intrigue/mystery. We will consider other romance genres such as fantasy, western, inspirational, and historical as long as the romance element is strong."

HOW TO CONTACT Query with outline first with SASE. Consult submission guidelines online before submitting.

TERMS Makes outright purchase of accepted completed scripts. Responds in 2 month to queries; 1 month to mss sent upon request.

TIPS "Our audience is primarily women 18 and older. Send query with outline only."

✪ ARSENAL PULP PRESS

#202-211 East Georgia St., Vancouver BC V6A 1Z6, Canada. (604)687-4233. **Fax:** (604)687-4283. **E-mail:** info@arsenalpulp.com. **Website:** www.arsenalpulp.com. **Contact:** Editorial Board. Estab. 1980. "We are interested in literature that traverses uncharted territories, publishing books that challenge and stimulate and ask probing questions about the world around us." Publishes trade paperback originals, and trade paperback reprints. Book catalog for 9×12 SAE with IRCs or online. Guidelines online.

NEEDS No children's books or genre fiction, i.e., westerns, romance, horror, mystery, etc.

HOW TO CONTACT Submit proposal package, outline, clips, 2-3 sample chapters.

TERMS Responds in 2-4 months.

ARTE PUBLICO PRESS

University of Houston, 4902 Gulf Fwy, Bldg 19, Rm 100, Houston TX 77204-2004. **Fax:** (713)743-2847. **E-mail:** submapp@uh.edu. **Website:** artepublicopress. com. Estab. 1979. Arte Publico Press is the oldest and largest publisher of Hispanic literature for children and adults in the United States. "We are a showcase for Hispanic literary creativity, arts and culture. Our endeavor is to provide a national forum for U.S.-Hispanic literature." Publishes hardcover originals, trade paperback originals and reprints. Book catalog available free. Guidelines online.

NEEDS "Written by U.S.-Hispanics."

HOW TO CONTACT Submissions made through online submission form.

TERMS Pays 10% royalty on wholesale price. Provides 20 author's copies; 40% discount on subsequent copies. Pays $1,000-3,000 advance. Responds in 1 month to queries and proposals; 4 months to mss.

TIPS "Include cover letter in which you 'sell' your book—why should we publish the book, who will want to read it, why does it matter, etc. Use our ms submission online form. Format files accepted are: Word, plain/text, rich/text files. Other formats will not be accepted. Manuscript files cannot be larger than 5MB. Once editors review your ms, you will receive an e-mail with the decision. Revision process could take up to 4 months."

ASABI PUBLISHING

Asabi Publishing, **E-mail:** submissions@asabipublishing.com. **Website:** https://asabipublishing.com. **Contact:** Tressa Sanders, publisher. Estab. 2004. Publishes hardcover, mass market and trade paperback originals. Book catalog online. Guidelines online.

IMPRINTS Solomon Publishing Group-Sweden.

NEEDS "We will only consider publishing a fiction title if it is a part of a series." The series should not already exist (except for the first unpublished title). There should be a plan/outline for at least two more

titles in the series beyond the initial title. Does not want anything religious or spiritual, astrology, ghosts, aliens, vampires or werewolves.

HOW TO CONTACT Submit professional query letter.

TERMS Pays 40% royalty on wholesale or list price. Pays up to $500 advance. Responds in 1 month to queries and proposals, 2-6 months to mss.

Ⓐ⊘ ATHENEUM BOOKS FOR YOUNG READERS

Simon & Schuster, 1230 Avenue of the Americas, New York NY 10020. **Website:** kids.simonandschuster.com. Estab. 1961. Publishes hardcover originals. Guidelines for #10 SASE.

NEEDS All in juvenile versions. "We have few specific needs except for books that are fresh, interesting and well written. Fad topics are dangerous, as are works you haven't polished to the best of your ability. We also don't need safety pamphlets, ABC books, coloring books and board books. In writing picture book texts, avoid the coy and 'cutesy,' such as stories about characters with alliterative names." Agented submissions only. No paperback romance-type fiction.

TIPS "Study our titles."

AUTUMN HOUSE PRESS

5530 Penn Ave., Pittsburgh PA 15206. (412)362-2665. **E-mail:** info@autumnhouse.org. **Website:** www.autumnhouse.org. **Contact:** Christine Stroud, editor-in-chief. Estab. 1998. A nonprofit literary publisher, Autumn House Press was launched in 1998 when prominent American publishers, driven by economic concerns, dramatically reduced their poetry lists. Since our launch, Autumn House has expanded to publish fiction (2008) and nonfiction titles (2010). These books receive the same attention to design and manufacturing as our award-winning poetry titles. Autumn House publications have received a great deal of recognition and acclaim. In 2011, we earned a Certificate of Appreciation from the Pennsylvania legislature recognizing our contribution to the arts. Our books are regularly reviewed in *Ploughshares, Brevity, London Grip Review, The Women's Review of Books, The Jewish Review of Books,* and *Poets Quarterly.* Many of our poems have been featured in *The New York Times Magazine,* on *The Writer's Almanac,* and Ted Kooser's *American Life in Poetry.* Our titles also circulate within the local Pittsburgh community, with reviews in *The Pittsburgh City Paper* and *The Pittsburgh Post-Gazette.* Our books have won numerous awards over the years, such as *Love for Sale and Other Essays* by Clifford Thompson, which won the 2013 Whiting Award. Publishes trade paperback and electronic originals. Format: acid-free paper; offset printing. Catalog online. Guidelines online.

IMPRINTS Coal Hill Review.

HOW TO CONTACT Submit through our annual contest or open-call period. See guidelines online.

TERMS Pays 8% royalty on wholesale price. Pays $0-2,500 advance. Responds in 1-3 days on queries and proposals; 3 months on mss.

TIPS "Though we are open to all styles of poetry, fiction, and nonfiction, we suggest you familiarize yourself with previous Autumn House publications before submitting. We are committed not just to publishing the prominent voices of our age, but also to publishing first books and lesser-known authors who will become the important writers of their generation. Many of our past winners have been first-book authors. We encourage writers from all backgrounds to submit; it is our goal at Autumn House to develop a rich and varied literary tradition."

AVON ROMANCE

Harper Collins Publishers, 10 E. 53 St., New York NY 10022. **E-mail:** info@avonromance.com. **Website:** www.avonromance.com. Estab. 1941. Avon has been publishing award-winning books since 1941. It is recognized for having pioneered the historical romance category and continues to bring the best of commercial literature to the broadest possible audience. Publishes paperback and digital originals and reprints.

HOW TO CONTACT Submit a query and ms via the online submission form.

BAEN BOOKS

P.O. Box 1188, Wake Forest NC 27588. (919)570-1640. **E-mail:** info@baen.com. **Website:** www.baen.com. Estab. 1983. "We publish only science fiction and fantasy. Writers familiar with what we have published in the past will know what sort of material we are most likely to publish in the future: powerful plots with solid scientific and philosophical underpinnings are the sine qua non for consideration for science fiction submissions. As for fantasy, any magical system must be both rigorously coherent and integral to the plot, and overall the work must at least strive for originality."

NEEDS "Style: Simple is generally better; in our opinion good style, like good breeding, never calls attention to itself. Length: 100,000-130,000 words

Generally we are uncomfortable with manuscripts under 100,000 words, but if your novel is really wonderful send it along regardless of length."

HOW TO CONTACT "Query letters are not necessary. We prefer to see complete manuscripts accompanied by a synopsis. We prefer not to see simultaneous submissions. Electronic submissions are strongly preferred. *We no longer accept submissions by e-mail.* Send ms by using the submission form at: http://ftp.baen.com/Slush/submit.aspx. No disks unless requested. Attach ms as a Rich Text Format (.rtf) file. Any other format will not be considered."

TERMS Responds to mss within 12-18 months.

BAEN PUBLISHING ENTERPRISES

P.O. Box 1188, Wake Forest NC 27588. (919)570-1640. **E-mail:** info@baen.com; toni@baen.com. **Website:** www.baen.com. Estab. 1983. Publishes hardcover, trade paperback and mass market paperback originals and reprints. Book catalog available free. Guidelines online.

HOW TO CONTACT Submit synopsis and complete ms. "Electronic submissions are strongly preferred. Attach manuscript as a Rich Text Format (.rtf) file. Any other format will not be considered." Additional submission guidelines online. Include estimated word count, brief bio. Send SASE or IRC. Responds in 9-12 months. No simultaneous submissions. Sometimes comments on rejected mss.

TERMS Yes. Responds in 9-12 months to mss.

TIPS "Keep an eye and a firm hand on the overall story you are telling. Style is important but less important than plot. Good style, like good breeding, never calls attention to itself. Read *Writing to the Point*, by Algis Budrys. We like to maintain long-term relationships with authors."

BAILIWICK PRESS

309 East Mulberry St., Fort Collins CO 80524. (970)672-4878. **Fax:** (970)672-4731. **E-mail:** info@bailiwickpress.com. **E-mail:** aldozelnick@gmail.com. **Website:** www.bailiwickpress.com. "We're a micro-press that produces books and other products that inspire and tell great stories. Our motto is 'books with something to say.' We are now considering submissions, agented and unagented, for children's and young adult fiction. We're looking for smart, funny, and layered writing that kids will clamor for. Authors who already have a following have a leg up. We are only looking for humorous children's fiction. Please

do not submit work for adults. Illustrated fiction is desired but not required. (Illustrators are also invited to send samples.) Make us laugh out loud, ooh and aah, and cry, 'Eureka!'"

HOW TO CONTACT "Please read the Aldo Zelnick series to determine if we might be on the same page, then fill out our submission form. Please do not send submissions via snail mail or phone calls. You must complete the online submission form to be considered. If, after completing and submitting the form, you also need to send us an e-mail attachment (such as sample illustrations or excerpts of graphics), you may e-mail them to aldozelnick@gmail.com."

TERMS Responds in 6 months.

Ⓐ BALLANTINE BOOKS

Imprint of Penguin Random House, Inc., 1745 Broadway, 18th Floor, New York NY 10019. (212)782-9000. **Website:** www.penguinrandomhouse.com. Estab. 1952. Ballantine Bantam Dell publishes a wide variety of nonfiction and fiction. Publishes hardcover, trade paperback, mass market paperback originals. Guidelines online.

HOW TO CONTACT Agented submissions only.

Ⓐ BALZER & BRAY

HarperCollins Children's Books, 10 E. 53rd St., New York NY 10022. **Website:** www.harpercollinschildrens.com. Estab. 2008. "We publish bold, creative, groundbreaking picture books and novels that appeal directly to kids in a fresh way."

NEEDS Picture Books, Young Readers: adventure, animal, anthology, concept, contemporary, fantasy, history, humor, multicultural, nature/environment, poetry, science fiction, special needs, sports, suspense. Middle readers, young adults/teens: adventure, animal, anthology, contemporary, fantasy, history, humor, multicultural, nature/environment, poetry, science fiction, special needs, sports, suspense.

HOW TO CONTACT Agented submissions only.

TERMS Offers advances. Pays illustrators by the project.

Ⓐ BANCROFT PRESS

P.O. Box 65360, Baltimore MD 21209-9945. (410)358-0658. **Fax:** (410)764-1967. **E-mail:** bruceb@bancroftpress.com. **Website:** www.bancroftpress.com. **Contact:** Bruce Bortz, editor/publisher (memoirs, health, investment, politics, history, humor, literary novels, mystery/thrillers, chick lit, young adult). Estab. 1992.

"Bancroft Press is a general trade publisher. Our only mandate is 'books that enlighten.' Our most recent emphasis, with 'The Missing Kennedy' and 'Both Sides of the Line,' has been on memoirs." Publishes hardcover and trade paperback originals as well as e-books and audiobooks. Guidelines online.

HOW TO CONTACT Submit complete ms.

TERMS Pays 8-15% royalty on retail price. Pays $750-2,500 advances. Responds in 6-12 months.

TIPS "We advise writers to visit our website and to be familiar with our previous work. Patience is the number one attribute contributors must have. It takes us a very long time to get through submitted material, because we are such a small company. Also, we only publish 4-6 books per year, so it may take a long time for your optioned book to be published. We like to be able to market our books to be used in schools and in libraries. We prefer fiction that bucks trends and moves in a new direction. We are especially interested in mysteries and humor (especially humorous mysteries)."

ⒶⓄ BANTAM BOOKS

Imprint of Penguin Random House, Inc., 1745 Broadway, New York NY 10019. (212)782-9000. **Website:** www.randomhousebooks.com. *Not seeking mss at this time.*

Ⓞ BARBOUR PUBLISHING, INC.

P.O. Box 719, Urichsville OH 44683. **E-mail:** submissions@barbourbooks.com. **Website:** www.barbourbooks.com. Estab. 1981. "Barbour Books publishes inspirational/devotional material that is nondenominational and evangelical in nature. We're a Christian evangelical publisher." Specializes in short, easy-to-read Christian bargain books. "Faithfulness to the Bible and Jesus Christ are the bedrock values behind every book Barbour's staff produces."

◗ "We no longer accept unsolicited submissions unless they are submitted through professional literary agencies. For more information, we encourage new fiction authors to join a professional writers organization like American Christian Fiction Writers."

FREDERIC C. BEIL, PUBLISHER, INC.

609 Whitaker St., Savannah GA 31401. (912)233-2446. **E-mail:** fcb@beil.com. **Website:** www.beil.com. **Contact:** Frederic Beil. Estab. 1982. Beil publishes books in the fields of biography, history, and fiction. While under way, Beil has published authors of meaningful

works and adhered to high standards in bookmaking craftsmanship. Publishes original titles in hardcover, softcover, and e-book. Catalog online. Upon agreement with author, Beil will provide guidelines to author.

IMPRINTS The Sandstone Press.

HOW TO CONTACT Query with SASE.

TERMS Pays 7.5% royalty on retail price. Does not pay advance. Responds in 1 week to queries received via postal mail.

TIPS "Our objectives are to offer carefully selected texts; to adhere to high standards in the choice of materials and in bookmaking craftsmanship; to produce books that exemplify good taste in format and design; and to maintain the lowest cost consistent with quality."

BELLEBOOKS

P.O. Box 300921, Memphis TN 38130. (901)344-9024. **Fax:** (901)344-9068. **E-mail:** bellebooks@bellebooks. com. **Website:** www.bellebooks.com. Estab. 1999. BelleBooks began by publishing Southern fiction. It has become a "second home" for many established authors, who also continue to publish with major publishing houses. Guidelines online.

NEEDS "Yes, we'd love to find the next Harry Potter, but our primary focus for the moment is publishing for the teen market."

HOW TO CONTACT Query e-mail with brief synopsis and credentials/credits with full ms attached (RTF format preferred).

TIPS "Our list aims for the teen reader and the crossover market. If you're a 'Southern Louise Rennison,' that would catch our attention. Humor is always a plus. We'd love to see books featuring teen boys as protagonists. We're happy to see dark edgy books on serious subjects."

BELLEVUE LITERARY PRESS

Website: https://blpress.org/. Estab. 2005. Bellevue Literary Press is devoted to publishing literary fiction and nonfiction at the intersection of the arts and sciences because we believe that science and the humanities are natural companions for understanding the human experience. With each book we publish, our goal is to foster a rich, interdisciplinary dialogue that will forge new tools for thinking and engaging with the world. Guidelines online.

NEEDS We publish literary fiction at the intersection of the arts and sciences, or in other words, excellently written books of ideas. We do not publish books for children or young adults, poetry, single short stories, or commercial fiction (such as thrillers or romances). Please see our fiction catalog for examples of the books we're looking for on our website.

HOW TO CONTACT Please submit the complete manuscript during one of our open reading periods.

BERKLEY

An imprint of Penguin Rnadom House LLC. 1745 Broadway, New York NY 10019. **Website:** penguinrandomhouse.com. Estab. 1955. The Berkley Publishing Group publishes a variety of general nonfiction and fiction including the traditional categories of romance, mystery and science fiction. Publishes paperback and mass market originals and reprints.

"Due to the high volume of manuscripts received, most Penguin Group (USA) Inc. imprints do not normally accept unsolicited mss. The preferred and standard method for having mss considered for publication by a major publisher is to submit them through an established literary agent."

IMPRINTS Ace; Jove; Heat; Sensation; Berkley Prime Crime; Berkley Caliber.

NEEDS No occult fiction.

HOW TO CONTACT Prefers agented submissions.

BETHANY HOUSE PUBLISHERS

Division of Baker Publishing Group, 6030 E. Fulton Rd., Ada MI 49301. (616)676-9185. **Fax:** (616)676-9573. **Website:** bakerpublishinggroup.com/bethanyhouse. Estab. 1956. Bethany House Publishers specializes in books that communicate Biblical truth and assist people in both spiritual and practical areas of life. Considers unsolicited work only through a professional literary agent or through manuscript submission services, Authonomy or Christian Manuscript Submissions. Guidelines online. *All unsolicited mss returned unopened.* Publishes hardcover and trade paperback originals, mass market paperback reprints. Book catalog for 9 x 12 envelope and 5 first-class stamps.

TERMS Pays royalty on net price. Pays advance. Responds in 3 months to queries.

TIPS "Bethany House Publishers' publishing program relates Biblical truth to all areas of life—whether in the framework of a well-told story, of a challenging book for spiritual growth, or of a Bible reference work. We are seeking high-quality fiction and nonfiction that will inspire and challenge our audience."

Ⓐⵁ BEYOND WORDS PUBLISHING, INC.

20827 NW Cornell Rd., Suite 500, Hillsboro OR 97124. (503)531-8700. **Fax:** (503)531-8773. **E-mail:** info@beyondword.com. **Website:** www.beyondword. com. **Contact:** Submissions Department (for agents only). Estab. 1984. "At this time, we are not accepting any unsolicited queries or proposals, and recommend that all authors work with a literary agent in submitting their work." Publishes hardcover and trade paperback originals and paperback reprints.

HOW TO CONTACT Agent should submit query letter with proposal, including author bio, 5 sample chapters, complete synopsis of book, market analysis, SASE.

BILINGUAL REVIEW PRESS

Hispanic Research Center, Arizona State University, P.O. Box 875303, Tempe AZ 85287-5303. (480)965-3867. **Fax:** (480)965-0315. **E-mail:** brp@asu.edu. **Website:** www.asu.edu/brp. **Contact:** Gary Francisco Keller, publisher. Estab. 1973. "We are always on the lookout for Chicano, Puerto Rican, Cuban American, or other U.S. Hispanic themes with strong and serious literary qualities and distinctive and intellectually important topics."

HOW TO CONTACT Query with SASE. Query should describe book, plot summary, sample chapter, and any other information relevant to the rationale, content, audience, etc., for the book.

TERMS Responds in 3-4 weeks for queries; 3-4 months on requested mss.

TIPS "Writers should take the utmost care in assuring that their manuscripts are clean, grammatically impeccable, and have perfect spelling. This is true not only of the English but the Spanish as well. All accent marks need to be in place as well as other diacritical marks. When these are missing it's an immediate first indication that the author does not really know Hispanic culture and is not equipped to write about it. We are interested in publishing creative literature that treats the U.S Hispanic experience in a distinctive, creative, revealing way. The kind of books that we publish we keep in print for a very long time irrespective of sales. We are busy establishing and preserving a U.S. Hispanic canon of creative literature."

ⵁ BIRCH BOOK PRESS

Birch Brook Impressions, P.O. Box 81, Delhi NY 13753. **Fax:** (607)746-7453. **E-mail:** birchbrook@copper.net. **Website:** www.birchbrookpress.info. **Contact:** Tom Tolnay, editor/publisher; Leigh Eckmair, art & research editor; Joyce Tolnay, account services. Estab. 1982. Birch Brook Press "is a book printer/typesetter/designer that uses monies from these activities to publish several titles of its own each year with cultural and literary interest." Specializes in literary work, fly-fishing, baseball, outdoors, themed short fiction anthologies, and books about books. *Not considering any new mss in the foreseeable future.* Occasionally publishes trade paperback originals. Book catalog online.

NEEDS "Mostly we do anthologies around a particular theme generated inhouse. We make specific calls for fiction when we are doing an anthology." Currently, BBP is not seeking manuscripts on any subject. Overstocked.

HOW TO CONTACT *Not currently accepting any submissions.*

TERMS Pays modest royalty on acceptance. Responds in 3-6 months.

BKMK PRESS

University of Missouri - Kansas City, 5101 Rockhill Rd., Kansas City MO 64110-2499. (816)235-2558. **Fax:** (816)235-2611. **E-mail:** bkmk@umkc.edu. **Website:** newletters.org/bkmk. Estab. 1971. "BkMk Press publishes fine literature. Reading period February-June." Publishes trade paperback originals. Guidelines online.

HOW TO CONTACT Query with SASE.

TERMS Responds in 4-6 months to queries.

TIPS "We skew toward readers of literature, particularly contemporary writing. Because of our limited number of titles published per year, we discourage apprentice writers or 'scattershot' submissions."

Ⓢ BLACK LAWRENCE PRESS

E-mail: editors@blacklawrencepress.com. **Website:** www.blacklawrencepress.com. **Contact:** Diane Goettel, executive editor. Estab. 2003. Black Lawrence press seeks to publish intriguing books of literature—novels, short story collections, poetry collections, chapbooks, anthologies, and creative nonfiction. Will also publish the occasional translation from German. Publishes 22-24 books/year, mostly poetry and fiction. Mss are selected through open submission and competition. Books are 20-400 pages, offset-printed or high-quality POD, perfect-bound, with 4-color cover. Catalog online.

HOW TO CONTACT Submit complete ms.

TERMS Pays royalties. Responds in 6 months to mss.

BLACK LYON PUBLISHING, LLC

P.O. Box 567, Baker City OR 97814. **E-mail:** info@ blacklyonpublishing.com. **E-mail:** queries@black-lyonpublishing.com. **Website:** www.blacklyonpublishing.com. **Contact:** The Editors. Estab. 2007. "Black Lyon Publishing is a small, independent publisher. We are currently closed to all except existing Black Lyon authors through 2017." Publishes paperback and e-book originals. Guidelines online.

BLACK ROSE WRITING

P.O. Box 1540, Castroville TX 78009. **E-mail:** creator@ blackrosewriting.com. **Website:** www.blackrosewriting.com/home. **Contact:** Reagan Rothe. Estab. 2006. Black Rose Writing is an independent publishing house that strongly believes in developing a personal relationship with their authors. The Texas-based publishing company doesn't see authors as clients or just another number on a page, but rather as individual people.. people who deserve an honest review of their material and to be paid traditional royalties without ever paying any fees to be published. Black Rose Writing, established in 2006, features books from an array of fiction, nonfiction, and children's book genres, all having one thing in common, an individual's originality and hardship. It can take endless hours to finish a deserving manuscript, and Black Rose Writing applauds each and every author, giving them a chance at their dream. Because Black Rose Writing takes full advantage of modern printing technology, the company has an infinite print run via print-on-demand services. Black Rose Writing's success with their authors is due mainly to their many lines of promotion, (examples: showcasing book titles at festivals, scheduling book events, flexible marketing programs, and sending out press releases and review copies, etc.) and they provide a broad distribution (Ingram, Baker & Taylor, Amazon, Barnes & Noble, and more..) that larger book publishers also reach. We are proud members of IBPA (Independent Book Publishers Association), a recognized ITW (International Thriller Writers) publisher, members of Publishers Marketplace, and currently serving on the Ingram Publisher Advisory Board. Publishes fiction, nonfiction, and illustrated children's books. Catalog online. Guidelines online.

IMPRINTS DigiTerra Publishing, Bookend Design.

HOW TO CONTACT "Our preferred submission method is via Authors.me, please click 'Submit Here' on our website."

TERMS Royalties start at 20%, e-book royalties 25% Responds in 3-6 weeks on queries; 3-6 months on mss.

BLACK VELVET SEDUCTIONS PUBLISHING

E-mail: ric@blackvelvetseductions.com. **E-mail:** submissions@blackvelvetseductions.com. **Website:** www. blackvelvetseductions.com. **Contact:** Richard Savage, CEO. Estab. 2005. "We publish across a wide range of romance sub-genres, from soft sweet romance to supernatural romance, domestic discipline to highly erotic romance stories containing D/s and BDSM relationships. We are looking for authors who take something ordinary and make it extraordinary. We want stories with well-developed multi-dimensional characters with back-stories, a high degree of emotional impact, with strong sexual tension between the heroine and hero, and stories that contain strong internal conflict. We prefer stories told in the third person viewpoint, but will consider first person narratives. We put the emphasis on romance, rather than just the erotic. Although we will consider a high level of erotic content, it needs to be in the context of a romance story line. The plots may twist and turn and be full of passion, but please remember that our audience likes a happy ending. Do not be afraid to approach us with a non-traditional character or plot." Publishes trade paperback and electronic originals and reprints. Catalog free or online. Guidelines online.

NEEDS All stories must have a strong romance element. "There are very few sexual taboos in our erotic line. We tend to give our authors the widest latitude. If it is safe, sane, and consensual we will allow our authors latitude to show us the eroticism. However, we will not consider manuscripts with any of the following: bestiality (sex with animals), necrophilia (sex with dead people), pedophillia (sex with children)."

HOW TO CONTACT Only accepts electronic submissions.

TERMS Pays 10% royalty for paperbacks; 50% royalty for electronic books. Responds as swiftly as possible

TIPS "We publish romance and erotic romance. We look for books written in very deep point of view. Shallow point of view remains the number one reason we reject manuscripts in which the storyline generally works."

JOHN F. BLAIR, PUBLISHER

1406 Plaza Dr., Winston-Salem NC 27103. (336)768-1374. **Fax:** (336)768-9194. **E-mail:** editorial@blairpub.com. **Website:** www.blairpub.com. **Contact:** Carolyn

Sakowski, president. Estab. 1954. No poetry, young adult, children's, science fiction. Fiction must be set in southern U.S. or author must have strong Southern connection. Catalog online. Guidelines online.

NEEDS "We specialize in regional books, with an emphasis on nonfiction categories such as history, travel, folklore, and biography. We publish only one or two works of fiction each year. Fiction submitted to us should have some connection with the Southeast. We do not publish children's books, poetry, or category fiction such as romances, science fiction, or spy thrillers. We do not publish collections of short stories, essays, or newspaper columns." Does not want fiction set outside southern U.S.

HOW TO CONTACT Accepts unsolicited mss. Any fiction submitted should have some connection with the Southeast, either through setting or author's background. Send a cover letter, giving a synopsis of the book. Include the first 2 chapters (at least 50 pages) of the ms. "You may send the entire ms if you wish. If you choose to send only samples, please include the projected word length of your book and estimated completion date in your cover letter. Send a biography of the author, including publishing credits and credentials."

TERMS Pays royalties. Pays negotiable advance. Responds in 3-6 months.

TIPS "We are primarily interested in nonfiction titles. Most of our titles have a tie-in with North Carolina or the southeastern United States, we do not accept short story collections. Please enclose a cover letter and outline with the ms. We prefer to review queries before we are sent complete mss. Queries should include an approximate word count."

BLAZEVOX [BOOKS]

131 Euclid Ave., Kenmore NY 14217. **E-mail:** editor@ blazevox.org. **Website:** www.blazevox.org. **Contact:** Geoffrey Gatza, editor/publisher. Estab. 2005. "We are a major publishing presence specializing in innovative fictions and wide-ranging fields of innovative forms of poetry and prose. Our goal is to publish works that are challenging, creative, attractive, and yet affordable to individual readers. Articles of submission depend on many criteria, but overall items submitted must conform to one ethereal trait, your work must not suck. This put plainly, bad art should be punished; we will not promote it. However, all submissions will be reviewed and the author will receive feedback. We are human too." Guidelines online.

NEEDS Submit complete ms via e-mail.

TERMS Pays 10% royalties on fiction and poetry books, based on net receipts. This amount may be split across multiple contributors. "We do not pay advances."

TIPS "We actively contract and support authors who tour, read and perform their work, play an active part of the contemporary literary scene, and seek a readership."

BLIND EYE BOOKS

1141 Grant St., Bellingham WA 98225. **E-mail:** editor@ blindeyebooks.com. **Website:** www.blindeyebooks. com. **Contact:** Nicole Kimberling, editor. Estab. 2007. "Blind Eye Books publishes science fiction, fantasy and paranormal romance novels featuring gay or lesbian protagonists. We do not publish short story collections, poetry, erotica, horror or nonfiction. We would hesitate to publish any manuscript that is less than 70,000 or over 150,000 words." Guidelines online.

HOW TO CONTACT Submit complete ms with cover letter. Accepts queries by snail mail. Send disposable copy of ms and SASE for reply only. Does not return rejected mss. Authors living outside the U.S. can e-mail the editor for submission guidelines.

❷❷ BLOOMSBURY CHILDREN'S BOOKS

Imprint of Bloomsbury USA, 1385 Broadway, 5th Floor, New York NY 10018. **Website:** www.bloomsbury.com/us/childrens. No phone calls or e-mails. *Agented submissions only.* Book catalog online. Guidelines online.

HOW TO CONTACT *Agented submissions only.*

TERMS Pays royalty. Pays advance. Responds in 6 months.

BLUE LIGHT PRESS

P.O. Box 150300, San Rafael CA 94915. **E-mail:** bluelightpress@aol.com. **Website:** www.bluelightpress. com. **Contact:** Diane Frank, chief editor. Estab. 1988. "We like poems that are imagistic, emotionally honest, and push the edge—where the writer pushes through the imagery to a deeper level of insight and understanding. No rhymed poetry." Has published poetry by Stephen Dunn, Kim Addonizio, Jane Hirshfield, Rustin Larson, Mary Kay Rummel, Thomas Centolella,, Loretta Walker, Prartho Sereno, and K.B. Ballentine. "Books are elegantly designed and artistic. Our books are professionally printed, with original cover art, and we publish full-length books of poetry and chapbooks." Catalog online. Guidelines by e-mail.

NEEDS We have published flash fiction and micro fiction.

TERMS Poetry books retail at 15.95. Authors receive a 30% royalty of profits (not of cover price). Author copies are available at close to a 50% discount, for sale at readings and book events. Does not pay advance.

TIPS "To see more than 100 poets we love, get a copy of *River of Earth and Sky: Poems for the Twenty-First Century*. It is full of examples of poems we like to publish. It's like a box of chocolates for poets."

BOA EDITIONS, LTD.

250 N. Goodman St., Suite 306, Rochester NY 14607. (585)546-3410. **Fax:** (585)546-3913. **E-mail:** contact@boaeditions.org. **Website:** www.boaeditions.org. **Contact:** Ron Martin-Dent, director of publicity and production; Peter Conners, publisher. Estab. 1976. BOA Editions, Ltd., a not-for-profit publisher of poetry, short fiction, and poetry-in-translation, fosters readership and appreciation of contemporary literature. By identifying, cultivating, and publishing both new and established poets and selecting authors of unique literary talent, BOA brings high quality literature to the public. Publishes hardcover, trade paperback, and digital e-book originals. Book catalog online. Guidelines online.

NEEDS BOA publishes literary fiction through its American Reader Series. While aesthetic quality is subjective, our fiction will be by authors more concerned with the artfulness of their writing than the twists and turns of plot. Our strongest current interest is in short story collections (and short-short story collections). We strongly advise you to read our published fiction collections. *BOA does not accept novel submissions.*

HOW TO CONTACT Check BOA's website for reading periods for the American Reader Series and the BOA Short Fiction Prize. Please adhere to the general submission guidelines for each series. Guidelines online.

TERMS Negotiates royalties. Pays variable advance. Responds in 1 week to queries; 5 months to mss.

TIPS "Please adhere to the general submission guidelines on BOA's website for each series. BOA cannot accept unsolicited manuscript submissions outside of contests or open-reading periods."

BOLD STROKES BOOKS, INC.

P.O. Box 249, Valley Falls NY 12094. (518)677-5127. **Fax:** (518)677-5291. **E-mail:** sandy@boldstrokesbooks.com. **E-mail:** submissions@boldstrokesbooks.com.

Website: www.boldstrokesbooks.com. **Contact:** Sandy Lowe, senior editor. Estab. 2004. Publishes trade paperback originals and reprints; electronic originals and reprints. Guidelines online.

IMPRINTS BSB Fiction; Victory Editions Lesbian Fiction; Liberty Editions Gay Fiction; Soliloquy Young Adult; Heat Stroke Erotica.

NEEDS "Submissions should have a gay, lesbian, transgendered, or bisexual focus and should be positive and life-affirming." We do not publish any non-lgbtqi focused works.

HOW TO CONTACT Submit completed ms with bio, cover letter, and synopsis—electronically only.

TERMS Sliding scale based on sales volume and format. Pays advance. Responds in 1 month to queries; 2 months to proposals; 4 months to mss.

TIPS "We are particularly interested in authors who are interested in craft enhancement, technical development, and exploring and expanding traditional genre definitions and boundaries and are looking for a long-term publishing relationship. LGBTQ-focused works only."

BOOKFISH BOOKS

E-mail: bookfishbooks@gmail.com. **Website:** bookfishbooks.com. **Contact:** Tammy Mckee, acquisitions editor. BookFish Books is looking for novel lengthed young adult, new adult, and middle grade works in all subgenres. Both published and unpublished, agented or unagented authors are welcome to submit. "Sorry, but we do not publish novellas, picture books, early reader/chapter books or adult novels." Responds to every query. Guidelines online.

HOW TO CONTACT Query via e-mail with a brief synopsis and first 3 chapters of ms.

TIPS "We only accept complete manuscripts. Please do not query us with partial manuscripts or proposals."

BOOKOUTURE

StoryFire Ltd., 23 Sussex Rd., Ickenham UB10 8P, United Kingdom. **Website:** www.bookouture.com. **Contact:** Oliver Rhodes, founder and publisher. Estab. 2012. Publishes mass market paperback and electronic originals and reprints. Book catalog online.

IMPRINTS Imprint of StoryFire Ltd.

NEEDS "We are looking for entertaining fiction targeted at modern women. That can be anything from Steampunk to Erotica, Historicals to thrillers. A distinctive author voice is more important than a particular genre or ms length."

HOW TO CONTACT Submit complete ms.

TERMS Pays 45% royalty on wholesale price. Responds in 1 month.

TIPS "The most important question that we ask of submissions is why would a reader buy the next book? What's distinctive or different about your storytelling that will mean readers will want to come back for more. We look to acquire global English language rights for e-book and Print on Demand."

BOOKS FOR ALL TIMES, INC.

Box 202, Warrenton VA 20188. (540)428-3175. E-mail: staff@bfat.com. **Website:** www.bfat.com. **Contact:** Joe David, publisher & editor. Estab. 1981. One-man operation. Publishes paperback originals.

NEEDS literary, mainstream/contemporary, short story collections. "No novels at the moment; hopeful, though, of publishing a collection of quality short stories. No popular fiction or material easily published by the major or minor houses specializing in mindless entertainment. Only interested in stories of the Victor Hugo or Sinclair Lewis quality."

HOW TO CONTACT Query with SASE. Responds in 1 month to queries. Sometimes comments on rejected mss. Joe David, publisher.

TERMS Pays negotiable advance. "Publishing/payment arrangement will depend on plans for the book."

TIPS Interested in "controversial, honest stories which satisfy the reader's curiosity to know. Read Victor Hugo, Fyodor Dostoyevsky and Sinclair Lewis for example."

BOTTOM DOG PRESS, INC.

P.O. Box 425, Huron OH 44839. (419)602-1556. E-mail: lsmithdog@smithdocs.net. **Website:** smithdocs. net. **Contact:** Larry Smith, director; Susanna Sharp-Schwacke, associate editor. Estab. 1985. Bottom Dog Press, Inc., "is a nonprofit literary and educational organization dedicated to publishing the best writing and art from the Midwest and Appalachia. Query via e-mail first with 2 paragraphs on book and author." Publishes fiction, poetry, and memoirs.

TERMS Pays 10 copies and 15% royalty. Does not pay advance.

GEORGE BRAZILLER, INC.

277 Broadway, Suite 708, New York NY 10007. **Website:** www.georgebraziller.com. Publishes hardcover and trade paperback originals and reprints.

NEEDS "We rarely do fiction but when we have published novels, they have mostly been literary novels."

HOW TO CONTACT Submit 4-6 sample chapter(s), SASE. Agented fiction 20%. Responds in 3 months to proposals.

✪⊘ BROADWAY BOOKS

Penguin Random House, 1745 Broadway, New York NY 10019. (212)782-9000. **Fax:** (212)782-9411. **Website:** crownpublishing.com/imprint/broadway-books. Estab. 1995. "Broadway publishes high quality general interest nonfiction and fiction for adults." Publishes hardcover and trade paperback books.

IMPRINTS Broadway Books; Broadway Business; Doubleday; Doubleday Image; Doubleday Religious Publishing; Main Street Books; Nan A. Talese.

HOW TO CONTACT *Agented submissions only.*

TERMS Pays royalty on retail price. Pays advance.

BRONZE MAN BOOKS

Millikin University, 1184 W. Main, Decatur IL 62522. (217)424-6264. **E-mail:** sfrech@millikin.edu. **Website:** www.bronzemanbooks.com. **Contact:** Dr. Randy Brooks, publisher; Stephen Frech, editorial board, Edwin Walker, editorial board. Estab. 2006. A student-owned and operated press located on Millikin University's campus in Decatur, Ill., Bronze Man Books is dedicated to integrating quality design and meaningful content. The company exposes undergraduate students to the process of publishing by combining the theory of writing, publishing, editing and designing with the practice of running a book publishing company. This emphasis on performance learning is a hallmark of Millikin's brand of education. Publishes hardcover, trade paperback, literary chapbooks and mass market paperback originals.

NEEDS Subjects include art, graphic design, exhibits, general.

HOW TO CONTACT Submit completed ms.

TERMS Outright purchase based on wholesale value of 10% of a press run. Responds in 1-3 months.

TIPS "The art books are intended for serious collectors and scholars of contemporary art, especially of artists from the Midwestern US. These books are published in conjunction with art exhibitions at Millikin University or the Decatur Area Arts Council. The children's books have our broadest audience, and the literary chapbooks are intended for readers of contemporary fiction, drama, and poetry."

THE BRUCEDALE PRESS

P.O. Box 2259, Port Elgin ON N0H 2C0, Canada. (519)832-6025. **E-mail:** info@brucedalepress.ca. **Website:** brucedalepress.ca. Estab. 1994. The Brucedale Press publishes books and other materials of regional interest and merit, as well as literary, historical, and/or pictorial works. Accepts works by Canadian authors only. Book submissions reviewed November to January. Submissions to *The Leaf Journal* accepted in September and March only. Manuscripts must be in English and thoroughly proofread before being sent. Use Canadian spellings and style. Publishes hardcover and trade paperback originals. Book catalog online. "Unless responding to an invitation to submit, query first by Canada Post with outline and sample chapter to book-length manuscripts. Send full manuscripts for work intended for children." Guidelines online.

TERMS Pays royalty.

TIPS "Our focus is very regional. In reading submissions, I look for quality writing with a strong connection to the Queen's Bush area of Ontario. All authors should visit our website, get a catalog, and read our books before submitting. Except for contest entries, we do not review manuscripts sent from outside Canada."

BULLITT PUBLISHING

P.O. Box, Austin TX 78729. **E-mail:** bullittpublishing@yahoo.com. **E-mail:** submissions@bullittpublishing.com. **Website:** bullittpublishing.com. **Contact:** Pat Williams, editor. Estab. 2012. "Bullitt Publishing is a royalty-offering publishing house specializing in smart, contemporary romance. We are proud to provide print on demand distribution through the world's most comprehensive distribution channels. Whether this is your first novel or your 101st novel, Bullitt Publishing will treat you with the same amount of professionalism and respect. While we expect well-written entertaining manuscripts from all of our authors, we promise to provide high quality, professional product in return." Publishes trade paperback and electronic originals.

IMPRINTS Tempo Romance.

BUSTER BOOKS

16 Lion Yard, Tremadoc Rd., London WA SW4 7NQ, United Kingdom. (020)7720-8643. **Fax:** (022)7720-8953. **E-mail:** enquiries@mombooks.com. **Website:** www.busterbooks.co.uk. **Contact:** Buster Submissions. "We are dedicated to providing irresistible and fun books for children of all ages. We typically publish black & white nonfiction for children aged 8-12 novelty titles-including doodle books."

TIPS "We do not accept picturebook or poetry submissions. Please do not send original artwork as we cannot guarantee its safety." Visit website before submitting.

BY LIGHT UNSEEN MEDIA

325 Lakeview Dr., Winchendon MA 01475. (978)433-8866. **Fax:** (978)433-8866. **E-mail:** vyrdolak@bylightunseenmedia.com. **Website:** bylightunseenmedia.com. **Contact:** Inanna Arthen, owner/editor-in-chief. Estab. 2006. The only small press owned and operated by a recognized expert in vampire folklore, media and culture, By Light Unseen Media was founded in 2006. "Our mission is to explore and celebrate the variety, imagination and ambiguities of the vampire theme in fiction, history and the human psyche." No other mythic trope remotely approaches the vampire as an ever-changing and evolving mirror of the zeitgeist, deepest fears and most fervent fantasies of each successive generation—and none ever will. Particular trends and treatments rise and fall in popularity, but the vampire will never go out of style. By Light Unseen Media offers fiction and non-fiction that transcends the popular cliches of the day and demonstrates the creative variety and infinite potential of the vampire motif. Publishes hardcover, paperback and electronic originals. Catalog online. Ms guidelines online.

NEEDS "We are a niche small press that *only* publishes fiction relating in some way to vampires. Within that guideline, we're interested in almost any genre that includes a vampire trope, the more creative and innovative, the better. Restrictions are noted in the submission guidelines (no derivative fiction based on other works, such as Dracula, no gore-for-gore's-sake 'splatter' horror, etc.) We do not publish anthologies." Does not want anything that does not focus on vampires as the major theme.

HOW TO CONTACT Submit proposal package including synopsis, 3 sample chapters, brief author bio. "We encourage electronic submissions." *Unsolicited mss will not be considered.*

TERMS Pays royalty of 50-70% on net as explicitly defined in contract. Payment quarterly. No advance. Responds in 3 months.

TIPS "We strongly urge authors to familiarize themselves with the vampire genre and not imagine that they're doing something new and amazingly different just because they're not imitating the current fad."

⊘ CALAMARI PRESS

Via Titta Scarpetta #28, Rome 153, Italy. **E-mail:** derek@calamaripress.com. **Website:** www.calamaripress.com. **Contact:** Derek White. Calamari Press publishes books of literary text and art. Mss are selected by invitation. Occasionally has open submission period—check website. Helps to be published in *SleepingFish* first. Publishes paperback originals. Guidelines online.

HOW TO CONTACT Query with outline/synopsis and 3 sample chapters. Accepts queries by e-mail only. Include brief bio. Send SASE or IRC for return of ms.

TERMS Pays in author's copies. Responds to mss in 2 weeks.

CALKINS CREEK

Boyds Mills Press, 815 Church St., Honesdale PA 18431. **Website:** www.boydsmillspress.com. Estab. 2004. "We aim to publish books that are a well-written blend of creative writing and extensive research, which emphasize important events, people, and places in U.S. history." Guidelines online.

HOW TO CONTACT Submit outline/synopsis and 3 sample chapters.

TERMS Pays authors royalty or work purchased outright.

TIPS "Read through our recently published titles and review our catalog. When selecting titles to publish, our emphasis will be on important events, people, and places in U.S. history. Writers are encouraged to submit a detailed bibliography, including secondary and primary sources, and expert reviews with their submissions."

⊘ CALYX BOOKS

P.O. Box B, Corvallis OR 97339-0539. (541)753-9384. **Fax:** (541)753-0515. **E-mail:** info@calyxpress.org. **E-mail:** editor@calyxpress.org. **Website:** www.calyxpress.org. **Contact:** The Editor. Estab. 1986.

⊘ "Due to the high volume of book manuscripts received, CALYX Books is currently closed for manuscript submissions until further notice except for the Sarah Lantz Poetry Book Prize."

HOW TO CONTACT Closed to submissions until further notice.

⊘⊘ CANDLEWICK PRESS

99 Dover St., Somerville MA 02144. (617) 661-3330. **Fax:** (617) 661-0565. **E-mail:** bigbear@candlewick.com. **Website:** www.candlewick.com. Estab. 1991. "Candlewick Press publishes high-quality, illustrated children's books for ages infant through young adult.

We are a truly child-centered publisher." Publishes hardcover and trade paperback originals, and reprints.

⊘ *Candlewick Press is not accepting queries or unsolicited mss at this time.*

IMPRINTS Big Picture Press, Candlewick Entertainment, Candlewick Studio, Nosy Crow, Templar Books.

NEEDS Picture books: animal, concept, contemporary, fantasy, history, humor, multicultural, nature/environment, poetry. Middle readers, young adults: contemporary, fantasy, history, humor, multicultural, poetry, science fiction, sports, suspense/mystery.

HOW TO CONTACT "We currently do not accept unsolicited editorial queries or submissions. If you are an author or illustrator and would like us to consider your work, please read our submissions policy (online) to learn more."

TERMS Pays authors royalty of 2½-10% based on retail price. Offers advance.

TIPS *"We no longer accept unsolicited mss. See our website for further information about us."*

CANTERBURY HOUSE PUBLISHING, LTD.

4535 Ottawa Trail, Sarasota FL 34233. (941)312-6912. **Website:** www.canterburyhousepublishing.com. **Contact:** Sandra Horton, editor. Estab. 2009. "Our audience is made up of readers looking for wholesome fiction with good southern stories, with elements of mystery, romance, and inspiration and/or are looking for true stories of achievement and triumph over challenging circumstances. We are very strict on our submission guidelines due to our small staff, and our target market of Southern regional settings." Publishes hardcover, trade paperback, and electronic originals. Book catalog online. Guidelines online.

HOW TO CONTACT Query with SASE and through website.

TERMS Pays 10-15% royalty on wholesale price. Responds in 1 month to queries; 3 months to mss.

TIPS "Because of our limited staff, we prefer authors who have good writing credentials and submit edited manuscripts. We also look at authors who are business and marketing savvy and willing to help promote their books."

CARNEGIE MELLON UNIVERSITY PRESS

5032 Forbes Ave., Pittsburgh PA 15289. (412)268-2861. **Fax:** (412)268-8706. **E-mail:** carnegiemellonuniversitypress@gmail.com. **Website:** www.cmu.edu/universitypress/. **Contact:** Poetry Editor or Nonfiction Editor. Estab. 1972. Publishes hardcover and trade paperback originals. Book catalog and guidelines online.

CAROLINA WREN PRESS

120 Morris St., Durham NC 27701. (919)560-2738. E-mail: carolinawrenpress@earthlink.net. Website: www.carolinawrenpress.org. Contact: Robin Miura, Editor & Director. Estab. 1976. "We publish poetry, fiction, and memoirs by or about people of color, women, gay/lesbian issues, and work by writers from, living in, or writing about the U.S. South." Accepts simultaneous submissions, but "let us know if work has been accepted elsewhere." Guidelines online.

NEEDS "We are no longer publishing children's literature of any topic." Books: 6×9 paper; typeset; various bindings; illustrations. Distributes titles through John F. Blair, Amazon.com, Barnes & Noble, Baker & Taylor, and on their website. "We very rarely accept any unsolicited manuscripts, but we accept submissions for the Doris Bakwin Award for Writing by a Woman in Jan-June of even-numbered years and submissions for the Lee Smith Novel Prize in Jan-June of odd-numbered years."

HOW TO CONTACT "We will accept e-mailed queries—a letter in the body of the e-mail describing your project—but please do not send large attachments." All other submissions are accepted via Submittable as part of our annual contests.

TERMS We pay our authors an honorarium. Responds in 3 months to queries; 6 months to mss.

TIPS "Best way to get read is to submit to a contest."

ⓐⓄ CARTWHEEL BOOKS

Imprint of Scholastic Trade Division, 557 Broadway, New York NY 10012. (212)343-6100. Website: www.scholastic.com. Estab. 1991. Cartwheel Books publishes innovative books for children, up to age 8. "We are looking for 'novelties' that are books first, play objects second. Even without its gimmick, a Cartwheel Book should stand alone as a valid piece of children's literature." Publishes novelty books, easy readers, board books, hardcover and trade paperback originals. Guidelines available free.

NEEDS Again, the subject should have mass market appeal for very young children. Humor can be helpful, but not necessary. Mistakes writers make are a reading level that is too difficult, a topic of no interest or too narrow, or mss that are too long.

HOW TO CONTACT *Accepts mss from agents only.*

CAVE HOLLOW PRESS

P.O. Drawer J, Warrensburg MO 64093. E-mail: gbcrump@cavehollowpress.com. Website: www.cavehollowpress.com. Contact: G.B. Crump, editor. Estab. 2001. Publishes trade paperback originals. Catalog online. Guidelines available free.

NEEDS "We publish fiction by Midwestern authors and/or with Midwestern themes and/or settings. Our website is updated frequently to reflect the current type of fiction Cave Hollow Press is seeking."

HOW TO CONTACT Query with SASE.

TERMS Pays 7-12% royalty on wholesale price. Pays negotiable amount in advance. Responds in 1-2 months to queries and proposals; 3-6 months to mss.

TIPS "Our audience varies based on the type of book we are publishing. We specialize in Missouri and Midwest regional fiction. We are interested in talented writers from Missouri and the surrounding Midwest. Check our submission guidelines on the website for what type of fiction we are interested in currently."

CEDAR FORT, INC.

2373 W. 700 S, Springville UT 84663. (801)489-4084. Website: www.cedarfort.com. Estab. 1986. "Each year we publish well over 100 books, and many of those are by first-time authors. At the same time, we love to see books from established authors. As one of the largest book publishers in Utah, we have the capability and enthusiasm to make your book a success, whether you are a new author or a returning one. We want to publish uplifting and edifying books that help people think about what is important in life, books people enjoy reading to relax and feel better about themselves, and books to help improve lives. Although we do put out several children's books each year, we are extremely selective. Our children's books must have strong religious or moral values, and must contain outstanding writing and an excellent storyline." Publishes hardcover, trade paperback originals and reprints, mass market paperback and electronic reprints. Catalog and guidelines online.

IMPRINTS Council Press, Sweetwater Books, Bonneville Books, Front Table Books, Hobble Creek Press, CFI, Plain Sight Publishing, Horizon Publishers, Pioneer Plus.

HOW TO CONTACT Submit completed ms.

TERMS Pays 10-12% royalty on wholesale price. Pays $2,000-50,000 advance. Responds in 1 month on queries; 2 months on proposals; 4 months on mss.

TIPS "Our audience is rural, conservative, mainstream. The first page of your ms is very important because we start reading every submission, but good-writing and plot keep us reading."

CHANGELING PRESS LLC

Website: changelingpress.com/submissions.php. **Contact:** Margaret Riley, publisher. Estab. 2004. "We publish sci-fi/futuristic, dark and urban fantasy, paranormal, action/adventure, BDSM, and guilty pleasures (contemporary) women's erotic romance. All submissions must be targeted for at least one of these genres and must be women's erotic romance. We accept submissions from 12 to 30 thousand words for single titles. Serials from unsigned authors must be submitted as a completed set." Publishes e-books. Catalog online. Guidelines online.

NEEDS Electronic submissions only. No lesbian fiction submissions without prior approval, please. Absolutely no lesbian fiction written by men. Child pornography will be reported to local authorities and the FBI.

HOW TO CONTACT Please read and follow our submissions guidelines online. All submissions which do not follow the submissions guidelines will be rejected unread.

TERMS Pays 35% gross royalties on site, 50% gross off site monthly. Does not pay advance. Responds in 1 week to queries.

CHARLESBRIDGE PUBLISHING

85 Main St., Watertown MA 02472. (617)926-0329. **Fax:** (617)926-5720. **E-mail:** tradeeditorial@charlesbridge.com. **E-mail:** yasubs@charlesbridge.com. **Website:** www.charlesbridge.com. Estab. 1980. "Charlesbridge publishes high-quality books for children, with a goal of creating lifelong readers and lifelong learners. Our books encourage reading and discovery in the classroom, library, and home. We believe that books for children should offer accurate information, promote a positive worldview, and embrace a child's innate sense of wonder and fun. To this end, we continually strive to seek new voices, new visions, and new directions in children's literature. We are now accepting young adult novels for consideration." Publishes hardcover and trade paperback nonfiction and fiction, children's books for the trade and library markets. Guidelines online. https://charlesbridge.com/pages/submissions

IMPRINTS Charlesbridge Teen: Charlesbridge Teen features storytelling that presents new ideas and an evolving world. Our carefully curated stories give voice to unforgettable characters with unique perspectives. We publish books that inspire teens to cheer or sigh, laugh or reflect, reread or share with a friend, and ultimately, pick up another book. Our mission—to make reading irresistible!

NEEDS Strong stories with enduring themes. Charlesbridge publishes both picture books and transitional bridge books (books ranging from early readers to middle-grade chapter books). Our fiction titles include lively, plot-driven stories with strong, engaging characters. No alphabet books, board books, coloring books, activity books, or books with audiotapes or CD-ROMs.

HOW TO CONTACT Please submit only 1 ms at a time. For picture books and shorter bridge books, please send a complete ms. For fiction books longer than 30 ms pages, please send a detailed plot synopsis, a chapter outline, and 3 chapters of text. If sending a young adult novel, mark the front of the envelope with "YA novel enclosed." Please note, for YA, e-mail submissions are preferred to the following address; yasubs@charlesbridge.com. Only responds if interested. Full guidelines on site. https://charlesbridge.com/pages/submissions

TERMS Pays royalty. Pays advance. Responds in 3 months.

TIPS "To become acquainted with our publishing program, we encourage you to review our books and visit our website where you will find our catalog."

⊘ CHILDREN'S BRAINS ARE YUMMY (CBAY) BOOKS

Children's Brains are Yummy Productions, LLC, P.O. Box 670296, Dallas TX 75367. **E-mail:** submissions@cbaybooks.com. **Website:** www.cbaybooks.blog. **Contact:** Madeline Smoot, publisher. Estab. 2008. "CBAY Books currently focuses on quality fantasy and science fiction books for the middle grade and teen markets. We are not currently accepting unsolicited submissions. We do not publish picture books." "We are distributed by IPG. Our books can be found in their catalog at www.ipgbooks.com." Brochure and guidelines online.

TERMS Pays authors royalty 10-15% based on wholesale price. Offers advances against royalties. Average amount $500. Pays advance. Responds in 2 months.

◐⊘ CHILD'S PLAY (INTERNATIONAL) LTD.

Child's Play, Ashworth Rd. Bridgemead, Swindon, Wiltshire SN5 7YD, United Kingdom. 01793 616286. **E-mail:** neil@childs-play.com; office@childs-play.com.

Website: www.childs-play.com. **Contact:** Sue Baker, Neil Burden, manuscript acquisitions. Estab. 1972. Specializes in nonfiction, fiction, educational material, multicultural material. Produces 30 picture books/year; 10 young readers/year. "A child's early years are more important than any other. This is when children learn most about the world around them and the language they need to survive and grow. Child's Play aims to create exactly the right material for this all-important time."

❍ "Due to a backlog of submissions, Child's Play is currently no longer able to accept anymore manuscripts."

NEEDS Picture books: adventure, animal, concept, contemporary, folktales, multicultural, nature/environment. Young readers: adventure, animal, anthology, concept, contemporary, folktales, humor, multicultural, nature/environment, poetry. Average word length: picture books—1,500; young readers—2,000.

TIPS "Look at our website to see the kind of work we do before sending. Do not send cartoons. We do not publish novels. We do publish lots of books with pictures of babies/toddlers."

◔ CHRISTIAN FOCUS PUBLICATIONS

Geanies House, Fearn, Tain Ross-shire Scotland IV20 1TW, United Kingdom. (44)1862-871-011. **Fax:** (44)1862-871-699. **E-mail:** submissions@christianfocus.com. **Website:** www.christianfocus.com. **Contact:** Director of Publishing. Estab. 1975. Specializes in Christian material, nonfiction, fiction, educational material.

NEEDS Picture books, young readers, adventure, history, religion. Middle readers: adventure, problem novels, religion. Young adult/teens: adventure, history, problem novels, religion. Average word length: young readers—5,000; middle readers—max 10,000; young adult/teen—max 20,000.

TERMS Responds to queries in 2 weeks; mss in 3-6 months.

TIPS "Be aware of the international market as regards writing style/topics as well as illustration styles. Our company sells rights to European as well as Asian countries. Fiction sales are not as good as they were. Christian fiction for youngsters is not a product that is performing well in comparison to nonfiction such as Christian biography/Bible stories/church history, etc."

CHRONICLE BOOKS

680 Second St., San Francisco CA 94107. **E-mail:** submissions@chroniclebooks.com. **Website:** www.chroniclebooks.com. "We publish an exciting range of books, stationery, kits, calendars, and novelty formats. Our list includes children's books and interactive formats; young adult books; cookbooks; fine art, design, and photography; pop culture; craft, fashion, beauty, and home decor; relationships, mind-body-spirit; innovative formats such as interactive journals, kits, decks, and stationery; and much, much more." Book catalog for 9x12 SAE and 8 first-class stamps. Ms guidelines for #10 SASE.

NEEDS Only interested in fiction for children and young adults. No adult fiction.

HOW TO CONTACT Submit complete ms (picture books); submit outline/synopsis and 3 sample chapters (for older readers). Will not respond to submissions unless interested. Will not consider submissions by fax, e-mail or disk. Do not include SASE; do not send original materials. No submissions will be returned.

TERMS Generally pays authors in royalties based on retail price, "though we do occasionally work on a flat fee basis." Advance varies. Illustrators paid royalty based on retail price or flat fee. Responds to queries in 1 month.

CHRONICLE BOOKS FOR CHILDREN

680 Second St., San Francisco CA 94107. (415)537-4200. **Fax:** (415)537-4460. **Website:** www.chronicle-kids.com. "Chronicle Books for Children publishes an eclectic mixture of traditional and innovative children's books. Our aim is to publish books that inspire young readers to learn and grow creatively while helping them discover the joy of reading. We're looking for quirky, bold artwork and subject matter." Publishes hardcover and trade paperback originals. Book catalog for 9x12 envelope and 3 first-class stamps. Guidelines online.

NEEDS Does not accept proposals by fax, via e-mail, or on disk. When submitting artwork, either as a part of a project or as samples for review, do not send original art.

TERMS Pays variable advance. Responds in 2-4 weeks to queries; 6 months to mss.

TIPS "We are interested in projects that have a unique bent to them—be it in subject matter, writing style, or illustrative technique. As a small list, we are looking for books that will lend our list a distinctive flavor. Primarily we are interested in fiction and nonfiction picture books for children ages up to 8 years, and nonfiction books for children ages up to 12 years. We publish board, pop-up, and other novelty formats as well as picture books. We are also interested in early chapter books, middle grade fiction, and young adult projects."

CITY LIGHTS BOOKS

261 Columbus Ave., San Francisco CA 94133. (415)362-8193. **Fax:** (415)362-4921. **Website:** www. citylights.com. Estab. 1953. Publishes paperback originals. Plans 1-2 first novels this year. Averages 12 total titles, 4-5 fiction titles/year.

NEEDS Fiction, essays, memoirs, translations, poetry and books on social and political issues.

HOW TO CONTACT Submit one-page description of the book and a sample chapter or two with SASE. Does not accept unsolicited mss. Does not accept queries by e-mail. See website for guidelines.

CLARION BOOKS

Houghton Mifflin Co., 215 Park Ave. S., New York NY 10003. **Website:** www.hmhco.com. Estab. 1965. "Clarion Books publishes picture books, nonfiction, and fiction for infants through grade 12. Avoid telling your stories in verse unless you are a professional poet. *We are no longer responding to your unsolicited submission unless we are interested in publishing it. Please do not include a SASE. Submissions will be recycled, and you will not hear from us regarding the status of your submission unless we are interested. We regret that we cannot respond personally to each submission, but we do consider each and every submission we receive.*" Publishes hardcover originals for children. Guidelines online.

NEEDS "Clarion is highly selective in the areas of historical fiction, fantasy, and science fiction. A novel must be superlatively written in order to find a place on the list. Mss that arrive without an SASE of adequate size will *not* be responded to or returned. Accepts fiction translations."

HOW TO CONTACT Submit complete ms. No queries, please. Send to only *one* Clarion editor.

TERMS Pays 5-10% royalty on retail price. Pays minimum of $4,000 advance. Responds in 2 months to queries.

TIPS "Looks for freshness, enthusiasm—in short, life."

CLEIS PRESS

101 Hudson St., 37th Floor, Suite 3705, Jersey City NJ 07302. **Fax:** (510)845-8001. **Website:** www.cleispress. com. Estab. 1980. Cleis Press publishes provocative, intelligent books in the areas of sexuality, gay and lesbian studies, erotica, fiction, gender studies, and human rights. Publishes books that inform, enlighten, and entertain. Areas of interest include gift, inspira-

tion, health, family and childcare, self-help, women's issues, reference, cooking. "We do our best to bring readers quality books that celebrate life, inspire the mind, revive the spirit, and enhance lives all around. Our authors are practical visionaries; people who offer deep wisdom in a hopeful and helpful manner."

NEEDS "We are looking for high quality fiction and nonfiction."

HOW TO CONTACT Submit complete ms. Include brief bio, list of publishing credits. Send SASE for return of ms or send a disposable ms and SASE for reply only.

TERMS Responds in 2 month to queries.

TIPS "Be familiar with publishers' catalogs; be absolutely aware of your audience; research potential markets; present fresh new ways of looking at your topic; avoid 'PR' language and include publishing history in query letter."

◑ COACH HOUSE BOOKS

80 bpNichol Ln., Toronto ON M5S 3J4, Canada. (416)979-2217. **Fax:** (416)977-1158. **E-mail:** mail@ch-books.com. **E-mail:** editor@chbooks.com. **Website:** www.chbooks.com. **Contact:** Alana Wilcox, editorial director. Independent Canadian publisher of innovative poetry, literary fiction, nonfiction, and drama. Publishes trade paperback originals by Canadian authors. Guidelines online.

HOW TO CONTACT We much prefer to receive electronic submissions. Please put your cover letter and CV into one Word or PDF file along with the manuscript and e-mail it to editor@chbooks.com. We'd appreciate it if you would name your file following this convention: Last Name, First Name - MS Title. For fiction and poetry submissions, please send your complete manuscript, along with an introductory letter that describes your work and compares it to at least two current Coach House titles, explaining how your book would fit our list, and a literary CV listing your previous publications and relevant experience.

TERMS Pays 10% royalty on retail price. Responds in 6-8 months to queries.

TIPS "We are not a general publisher, and publish only Canadian poetry, fiction, select nonfiction and drama. We are interested primarily in innovative or experimental writing."

COFFEE HOUSE PRESS

79 13th Ave. NE, Suite 110, Minneapolis MN 55413. (612)338-0125. **Fax:** (612)338-4004. **Website:** www.

coffeehousepress.org. Estab. 1984. This successful nonprofit small press has received numerous grants from various organizations including the NEA, the McKnight Foundation and Target. Books published by Coffee House Press have won numerous honors and awards. Example: *The Book of Medicines*, by Linda Hogan won the Colorado Book Award for Poetry and the Lannan Foundation Literary Fellowship. Publishes hardcover and trade paperback originals. Book catalog and ms guidelines online.

NEEDS Seeks literary novels, short story collections and poetry.

HOW TO CONTACT Query first with outline and samples (20-30 pages) during annual reading periods (March 1-31 and September 1-30).

TERMS Responds in 4-6 weeks to queries; up to 6 months to mss.

TIPS "Look for our books at stores and libraries to get a feel for what we like to publish. No phone calls, e-mails, or faxes."

CONSTABLE & ROBINSON, LTD.

50 Victoria Embankment, London EC4Y 0DZ, United Kingdom. **E-mail:** info@littlebrown.co.uk. **Website:** https://www.littlebrown.co.uk/ConstableRobinson/about-constable-publisher.page. Publishes hardcover and trade paperback originals. Book catalog available free.

NEEDS Publishes "crime fiction (mysteries) and historical crime fiction." Length 80,000 words minimum; 130,000 words maximum.

HOW TO CONTACT *Agented submissions only.*

TERMS Pays royalty. Pays advance. Responds in 1-3 months.

COTEAU BOOKS

Thunder Creek Publishing Co-operative Ltd., 2517 Victoria Ave., Regina SK S4P 0T2, Canada. (306)777-0170. **Fax:** (306)522-5152. **E-mail:** coteau@coteaubooks.com. **Website:** www.coteaubooks.com. **Contact:** Geoffrey Ursell, publisher. Estab. 1975. "Our mission is to publish the finest in Canadian fiction, nonfiction, poetry, drama, and children's literature, with an emphasis on Saskatchewan and prairie writers. De-emphasizing science fiction, picture books." Publishes chapter books for young readers aged 9-12 and novels for older kids ages 13-15 and for ages 15 and up. Publishes trade paperback originals and reprints. Book catalog available free. Guidelines online.

NEEDS No science fiction. No children's picture books.

HOW TO CONTACT Query.

TERMS Pays 10% royalty on retail price. Responds in 3 months.

TIPS "Look at past publications to get an idea of our editorial program. We do not publish romance, horror, or picture books but are interested in juvenile and teen fiction from Canadian authors. Submissions, even queries, must be made in hard copy only. We do not accept simultaneous/multiple submissions. Check our website for new submission timing guidelines."

COVENANT COMMUNICATIONS, INC.

Deseret Book Company, 1226 South 630 East Suite #4, P.O. Box 416, American Fork UT 84003. (801)756-1041. **Fax:** (801)756-1049. **E-mail:** samantham@covenant-lds.com. **E-mail:** submissionsdesk@covenant-lds.com. **Website:** www.covenant-lds.com. **Contact:** Samantha Millburn, managing editor. Estab. 1958. "Currently emphasizing inspirational, doctrinal, historical, biography, and fiction." Guidelines online.

NEEDS "Manuscripts do not necessarily have to include LDS/Mormon characters or themes, but cannot contain profanity, sexual content, gratuitous violence, witchcraft, vampires, and other such material." We do not accept nor publish young adult, middle grade, science fiction, fantasy, occult, steampunk, or gay/lesbian/bisexual/transgender themes.

HOW TO CONTACT Submit complete ms.

TERMS Pays 6-15% royalty on retail price. Responds in 1 month on queries; 2-6 months on mss.

TIPS "We are actively looking for new, fresh Regency romance authors."

CRAIGMORE CREATIONS

PMB 114, 4110 SE Hawthorne Blvd., Portland OR 97124. (503)477-9562. **E-mail:** info@craigmorecreations.com. **Website:** www.craigmorecreations.com. Estab. 2009.

HOW TO CONTACT Submit proposal package. See website for detailed submission guidelines.

CRESCENT MOON PUBLISHING

P.O. Box 1312, Maidstone Kent ME14 5XU, United Kingdom. (44)(162)272-9593. **E-mail:** cresmopub@yahoo.co.uk. **Website:** www.crmoon.com. **Contact:** Jeremy Robinson, director (arts, media, cinema, literature); Cassidy Hughes (visual arts). Estab. 1988. "Our mission is to publish the best in contemporary work, in poetry, fiction, and critical studies, and selections from the great writers. Currently emphasizing nonfiction (media, film, music, painting). De-emphasizing children's books." Publishes hardcover and trade paperback originals. Book catalog and ms guidelines free.

IMPRINTS Joe's Press; Pagan America Magazine; Passion Magazine.

NEEDS "We do not publish much fiction at present but will consider high quality new work."

HOW TO CONTACT Query with SASE. Submit outline, clips, 2 sample chapters, bio.

TERMS Pays royalty. Pays negotiable advance. Responds in 2 months to queries; 4 months to proposals and mss.

TIPS "Our audience is interested in new contemporary writing."

CRESTON BOOKS

P.O. Box 9369, Berkeley CA 94709. **E-mail:** submissions@crestonbooks.co. **Website:** crestonbooks. co. Estab. 2013. Creston Books is author-illustrator driven, with talented, award-winning creators given more editorial freedom and control than in a typical New York house. Catalog online. Guidelines online.

HOW TO CONTACT Please paste text of picture books or first chapters of novels in the body of e-mail. Words of Advice for submitting authors listed on the site.

TERMS Pays advance.

CRIMSON ROMANCE

Simon & Schuster, Inc., 57 Littlefield St., Avon MA 02322. **E-mail:** crimsonsubmissions@simonandschuster.com. **Website:** crimsonromance.com. **Contact:** Tara Gelsomino, Executive Editor. Estab. 2012. Direct to e-book romance imprint of Simon & Schuster, Inc. Publishes electronic originals and print-on-demand copies. Guidelines online.

NEEDS Crimson seeks submissions featuring strong characters, smart stories, and satisfying romance in five popular subgenres: contemporary, historical, paranormal, romantic suspense, and spicy. We're looking for previously unpublished novellas (between 20,000 – 50,000 words) and full-length novels (between 50,000 – 90,000 words). All authors—agented or unagented, beginner or veteran writers—are welcome to submit any works that have not been previously published in whole or in part in any media, including self-publishing (Kindle, CreateSpace, etc.). While your work can include other genre elements, Crimson Romances must focus first and foremost on

a couple's emotional journey together towards love. Romances, by nature, must be between consenting adults of any gender, race, creed, etc., and have a happily-ever-after or at least happy-for-now ending. We are strictly a romance publisher and will not look at manuscripts for memoirs or other non-fiction, women's fiction or chick lit, young adult, mysteries and thrillers, horror, or general fiction. We're specifically seeking diverse romances (own voices preferred).

HOW TO CONTACT Please see current submission guidelines online.

TERMS Does not pay advance.

CROSS-CULTURAL COMMUNICATIONS

Cross-Cultural Literary Editions, 239 Wynsum Ave., Merrick NY 11566-4725. (516)869-5635. **Fax:** (516)379-1901. **E-mail:** info@cross-culturalcommunications.com; cccpoetry@aol.com. **Website:** www.cross-culturalcommunications.com. **Contact:** Stanley H. Barkan; Bebe Barkan. Estab. 1971. Publishes hardcover and trade paperback originals. Book catalog (sample flyers) for #10 SASE. Inquire for specifics. Prefer submissions with a query letter including full contact data and brief bio. Focus on bilingual poetry: include original and translations, 3-6 samples.

◯ Focua on bilingual poetry.

IMPRINTS Ostrich editions. Cooperative editions with The Seventh Quarry and the Feral and the New Feral Press.

HOW TO CONTACT Query with SASE.

TERMS Responds in 1 month to proposals; 2 months to mss.

TIPS "Best chance: poetry from a translation."

⊗⊘ CROWN PUBLISHING GROUP

Penguin Random House, 1745 Broadway, New York NY 10019. (212)782-9000. **Website:** crownpublishing. com. Estab. 1933. Publishes popular fiction and nonfiction hardcover originals. *Agented submissions only.* See website for more details.

IMPRINTS Amphoto Books; Back Stage Books; Billboard Books; Broadway Books; Clarkson Potter; Crown; Crown Archetype; Crown Business; Crown Forum; Harmony Books; Image Books; Potter Craft; Potter Style; Ten Speed Press; Three Rivers Press; Waterbrook Multnomah; Watson-Guptill.

CRYSTAL SPIRIT PUBLISHING, INC.

P.O. Box 12506, Durham NC 27709. **E-mail:** crystalspiritinc@gmail.com. **Website:** www.crystalspiritinc.

com. **Contact:** V. S. O'Neal, Senior Managing Editor. Estab. 2004. "Our readers are lovers of high-quality books that are sold as direct sales, in bookstores, gift shops and placed in libraries and schools. They support independent authors and they expect works that will provide them with entertainment, inspiration, romance, and education. Our audience loves to read and will embrace niche authors that love to write." Publishes hardcover, trade paperback, mass market paperback, and electronic originals. Book catalog and ms guidelines online. Submissions are only accepted via the website. Please see guidelines as stated on the website. Postal mail submissions are not allowed and will not be reviewed. We do not acknowledge or respond to queries.

HOW TO CONTACT Submissions are only accepted via the website. Please see guidelines as stated on the website. Postal mail submissions are not allowed and will not be reviewed. We do not acknowledge or respond to queries.

TERMS Pays 20-45% royalty on retail price. Responds in 15-30 days

TIPS "Submissions are accepted for publication throughout the year. Works should be positive and non-threatening. All submissions are accepted via the website only! Ensure that all contact information is correct, abide by the submission guidelines and do not send follow-up e-mails or calls." Do not send queries as they will not be acknowledged or receive a response.

CURIOSITY QUILLS

Whampa, LLC, P.O. Box 2160, Reston VA 20195. (800)998-2509. **Fax:** (800)998-2509. **E-mail:** editor@curiosityquills.com. **E-mail:** acquisitions@curiosityquills.com. **Website:** curiosityquills.com. **Contact:** Alisa Gus. Estab. 2011. Curiosity Quills is a publisher of hard-hitting dark sci-fi, speculative fiction, and paranormal works aimed at adults, young adults, and new adults. Firm publishes sci-fi, speculative fiction, steampunk, paranormal and urban fantasy, and corresponding romance titles under its new Rebel Romance imprint. Catalog available. Guidelines online.

IMPRINTS Curiosity Quills Press, Rebel Romance.

NEEDS Looking for "thought-provoking, mind-twisting rollercoasters—challenge our mind, turn our world upside down, and make us question. Those are the makings of a true literary marauder."

HOW TO CONTACT Submit ms using online submission form or e-mail to acquisitions@curiosityquills.com.

TERMS Pays variable royalty. Does not pay advance. Responds in 1-6 weeks.

CURIOUS FOX

Brunel Rd., Houndmills, Basingstoke Hants RG21 6XS, United Kingdom. **E-mail:** submissions@curious-fox.com. **Website:** www.curious-fox.com. "Do you love telling good stories? If so, we'd like to hear from you. Curious Fox is on the lookout for UK-based authors, whether new talent or established authors with exciting ideas. We take submissions for books aimed at ages 3-young adult. If you have story ideas that are bold, fun, and imaginative, then please do get in touch!" Guidelines online.

HOW TO CONTACT "Send your submission via e-mail to submissions@curious-fox.com. Include the following in the body of the email, not as attachments: Sample chapters, Résumé, List of previous publishing credits, if applicable. We will respond only if your writing samples fit our needs."

DARK HORSE COMICS, INC.

10956 SE Main St., Milwaukie OR 97222. (503)652-8815. **Fax:** (503)654-9440. **E-mail:** dhcomics@darkhorse.com. **E-mail:** dhsubsproposals@darkhouse.com. **Website:** www.darkhorse.com. "In addition to publishing comics from top talent like Frank Miller, Mike Mignola, Stan Sakai and internationally-renowned humorist Sergio Aragonés, Dark Horse is recognized as the world's leading publisher of licensed comics."

NEEDS Comic books, graphic novels. Published *Astro Boy Volume 10 TPB*, by Osamu Tezuka and Reid Fleming; *Flaming Carrot Crossover #1* by Bob Burden and David Boswell.

HOW TO CONTACT Submit synopsis to dhcomics@darkhorse.com. See website (www.darkhorse.com) for detailed submission guidelines and submission agreement, which must be signed. Include a full script for any short story or single-issue submission, or the first eight pages of the first issue of any series. Submissions can no longer be mailed back to the sender.

TIPS "If you're looking for constructive criticism, show your work to industry professionals at conventions."

DAW BOOKS, INC.

Penguin Random House, 1745 Broadway., New York NY 10019. (212)782-9000. **Fax:** (212)366-2090. **E-mail:** daw@penguinrandomhouse.com. **Website:** www.dawbooks.com. **Contact:** Peter Stampfel, submissions editor. Estab. 1971. DAW Books publishes science fiction and fantasy. Publishes hardcover and paperback originals and reprints. Guidelines online.

NEEDS "Currently seeking modern urban fantasy and paranormals. We like character-driven books with appealing protagonists, engaging plots, and well-constructed worlds. We accept both agented and un-agented manuscripts."

HOW TO CONTACT Submit entire ms, cover letter, SASE. "Do not submit your only copy of anything. The average length of the novels we publish varies but is almost never less than 80,000 words."

TERMS Pays in royalties with an advance negotiable on a book-by-book basis. Responds in 3 months.

KATHY DAWSON BOOKS

Penguin Random House, 1745 Broadway, New York NY 10019. (212)782-9000. **Website:** penguinrandomhouse.com. **Contact:** Kathy Dawson, vice-president and publisher. Estab. 2014. Mission statement: Publish stellar novels with unforgettable characters for children and teens that expand their vision of the world, sneakily explore the meaning of life, celebrate the written word, and last for generations. The imprint strives to publish tomorrow's award contenders: quality books with strong hooks in a variety of genres with universal themes and compelling voices—books that break the mold and the heart. Guidelines online.

HOW TO CONTACT Accepts fiction queries via snail mail only. Include cover sheet with one-sentence elevator pitch, main themes, author version of catalog copy for book, first 10 pages of ms (double-spaced, Times Roman, 12 point type), and publishing history. No SASE needed. Responds only if interested.

TERMS Responds only if interested.

⊘ DC UNIVERSE

1700 Broadway, New York NY 10019. **Website:** www. dccomics.com. Imprints: Vertigo, Wildstorm, CMX Manga, DC Direct, Mad, DC Kids, Zuda.

HOW TO CONTACT *No unsolicited submissions.* Recycles unsolicited manuscripts. Artists should contact through Comic Con conventions. See submission guidelines on website for more information. International Comic-Cons.

TERMS Artist's guidelines on website.

ⒶⓄ DELACORTE PRESS

an imprint of Random House Children's Books, a division of Penguin Random House LLC, New York, 1745

Broadway, New York NY 10019. (212)782-9000. **Website:** randomhousekids.com; randomhouseteens.com. Publishes middle grade and young adult fiction in hard cover, trade paperback, mass market and digest formats.

⌑ All query letters and manuscript submissions must be submitted through an agent or at the request of an editor.

ⒶⓄ DEL REY BOOKS

Penguin Random House, 1745 Broadway, 18th Floor, New York NY 10019. (212)782-9000. **Website:** www. penguinrandomhouse.com. Estab. 1977. Del Rey publishes top level fantasy, alternate history, and science fiction. Publishes hardcover, trade paperback, and mass market originals and mass market paperback reprints.

IMPRINTS Del Rey/Manga, Del Rey/Lucas Books.

HOW TO CONTACT *Agented submissions only.*

TERMS Pays royalty on retail price. Pays competitive advance.

TIPS "Del Rey is a reader's house. Pay particular attention to plotting, strong characters, and dramatic, satisfactory conclusions. It must be/feel believable. That's what the readers like. In terms of mass market, we basically created the field of fantasy bestsellers. Not that it didn't exist before, but we put the mass into mass market."

DIAL BOOKS FOR YOUNG READERS

Imprint of Penguin Random House, 1745 Broadway., New York NY 10019. (212)782-9000. **Website:** www. penguinrandomhouse.com. Estab. 1961. "Dial Books for Young Readers publishes quality picture books for ages 18 months-6 years; lively, believable novels for middle readers and young adults; and occasional nonfiction for middle readers and young adults." Publishes hardcover originals. Book catalog and guidelines online.

NEEDS Especially looking for lively and well-written novels for middle grade and young adult children involving a convincing plot and believable characters. The subject matter or theme should not already be overworked in previously published books. The approach must not be demeaning to any minority group, nor should the roles of female characters (or others) be stereotyped, though we don't think books should be didactic, or in any way message-y. No topics inappropriate for the juvenile, young adult, and middle grade audiences. No plays.

HOW TO CONTACT Accepts unsolicited queries and up to 10 pages for longer works and unsolicited mss for picture books. Will only respond if interested.

TERMS Pays royalty. Pays varies advance. Responds in 4-6 months to queries.

TIPS "Our readers are anywhere from preschool age to teenage. Picture books must have strong plots, lots of action, unusual premises, or universal themes treated with freshness and originality. Humor works well in these books. A very well-thought-out and intelligently presented book has the best chance of being taken on. Genre isn't as much of a factor as presentation."

⊕⊘ DIAL PRESS

1745 Broadway, New York NY 10019. **Website:** www. randomhouse.com/bantamdell/. Estab. 1924.

HOW TO CONTACT *Agented submissions only.*

DIGITAL MANGA PUBLISHING

1487 West 178th St., Suite 300, Gardenia CA 90248. **Website:** www.dmpbooks.com. "Submissions must be original and not infringe on copyrighted works by other creators. Please note that we are a manga publisher; we do not distribute Western style comics or literary novels. Completed works must contain a minimum of 90 pages of content. Submissions may be in black and white or full color. We accept submissions for all genres of manga which comply to US law and we only accept submissions from persons aged 18 and over. Please do not send your original copies as we cannot return them to you. If your work is published online elsewhere, please feel free to include a link for us to further view your portfolio."

DIVERTIR

P.O. Box 232, North Salem NH 03073. **E-mail:** info@divertirpublishing.com. **E-mail:** query@divertirpublishing.com. **Website:** www.divertirpublishing.com. **Contact:** Kenneth Tupper, publisher. Estab. 2009. Divertir Publishing is an independent publisher located in Salem, NH. "Our goal is to provide interesting and entertaining books to our readers, as well as to offer new and exciting voices in the writing community the opportunity to publish their work. We seek to combine an understanding of traditional publishing with a unique understanding of the modern market to best serve both our authors and readers." Publishes trade paperback and electronic originals. Catalog online. Guidelines online.

NEEDS "We are particularly interested in the following: science fiction, fantasy, historical, alternate history, contemporary mythology, mystery and suspense, paranormal, and urban fantasy." Does not consider erotica or mss with excessive violence.

HOW TO CONTACT Electronically submit proposal package, including synopsis and query letter with author's bio.

TERMS Pays 10-15% royalty on wholesale price (for novels and nonfiction). Does not pay advance. Responds in 1-3 months on queries; 3-4 months on proposals and mss.

TIPS "Please see our Author Info page (online) for more information."

⊕⊙ DOUBLEDAY CANADA

1 Toronto St., Suite 300, Toronto ON M5C 2V6, Canada. **Website:** www.randomhouse.ca. Random House of Canada, 1 Toronto Street, Suite 300, Toronto ON M5C 2V6 Canada. (416)364-4449. **Website:** www.randomhouse.ca. Publishes hardcover and paperback originals. Averages 50 total titles/year.

HOW TO CONTACT Does not accept unsolicited mss. *Agented submissions only.*

DOWN THE SHORE PUBLISHING

P.O. Box 100, West Creek NJ 08092. **Fax:** (609)812-5098. **E-mail:** info@down-the-shore.com. **Website:** www.down-the-shore.com. **Contact:** Acquisitions Editor. "Bear in mind that our market is regional-New Jersey, the Jersey Shore, the mid-Atlantic, and seashore and coastal subjects." Publishes hardcover and trade paperback originals and reprints. Book catalog online. Guidelines online.

HOW TO CONTACT Query with SASE. Submit proposal package, clips, 1-2 sample chapters.

TERMS Pays royalty on wholesale or retail price, or makes outright purchase. Responds in 3 months to queries.

TIPS "Carefully consider whether your proposal is a good fit for our established market."

⊙ DRAGON MOON PRESS

3521 43A Ave., Red Deer AB T4N 3E9, Canada. **Website:** www.dragonmoonpress.com. Estab. 1994. "Dragon Moon Press is dedicated to new and exciting voices in science fiction and fantasy." Publishes trade paperback and electronic originals. Books: 60 lb. offset paper; short run printing and offset printing. Average print order: 250-3,000. **Published several debut authors within the last year.** Plans 5 first novels this year. Averages 4-6 total titles, 4-5 fiction titles/year. Distributed through Baker & Taylor. Promoted locally through authors and online at leading retail bookstores like Amazon, Barnes & Noble, Chapters, etc.

NEEDS "At present, we are only accepting solicited manuscripts via referral from our authors and partners. All manuscripts already under review will still be considered by our readers, and we will notify you of our decision." For solicited submissions: Market: "We prefer manuscripts targeted to the adult market or the upper border of YA. No middle grade or children's literature, please. Fantasy, science fiction (soft/sociological). No horror or children's fiction, short stories or poetry."

TIPS "First, be patient. Read our guidelines. Not following our submission guidelines can be grounds for automatic rejection. Second, be patient, we are small and sometimes very slow as a result, especially during book launch season. Third, we view publishing as a family affair. Be ready to participate in the process and show some enthusiasm and understanding in what we do. Remember also, this is a business and not about egos, so keep yours on a leash! Show us a great story with well-developed characters and plot lines, show us that you are interested in participating in marketing and developing as an author, and show us your desire to create a great book and you may just find yourself published by Dragon Moon Press."

DUFOUR EDITIONS

P.O. Box 7, 124 Byers Rd., Chester Springs PA 19425. (610)458-5005. **Website:** www.dufoureditions.com. Estab. 1948. Publishes hardcover originals, trade paperback originals and reprints. Book catalog available free.

NEEDS "We like books that are slightly off-beat, different and well-written."

HOW TO CONTACT Query with SASE.

TERMS Pays $100-500 advance. Responds in 3-6 months.

☺ THE DUNDURN GROUP

3 Church St., Suite 500, Toronto ON M5E 1M2, Canada. **Website:** www.dundurn.com. Estab. 1972. Dundurn prefers work by Canadian authors. First-time authors are welcome. Publishes hardcover and trade paperback originals and reprints.

HOW TO CONTACT Query with SASE or submit 3 sample chapter(s), synopsis. Accepts queries by mail. Include estimated word count. Responds in 3-4 months to queries. Accepts simultaneous submissions. No electronic submissions.

❶❷ THOMAS DUNNE BOOKS

Imprint of St. Martin's Press, 175 Fifth Ave., New York NY 10010. (212)674-5151. **E-mail:** thomasdunnebooks@stmartins.com. **Website:** www.thomasdun-

nebooks.com. Estab. 1986. "Thomas Dunne Books publishes popular trade fiction and nonfiction. His group covers a range of genres including commercial and literary fiction, thrillers, biography, politics, sports, popular science, and more. The list is intentionally eclectic and includes a wide range of fiction and nonfiction, from first books to international bestsellers." Publishes hardcover and trade paperback originals, and reprints. Book catalog and ms guidelines free.

HOW TO CONTACT *Accepts agented submissions only.*

❶❷ DUTTON ADULT TRADE

Penguin Random House, 1745 Broadway, New York NY 10019. (212)782-9000. **Website:** penguinrandomhouse.com. Estab. 1852. "Dutton currently publishes 45 hardcovers a year, roughly half fiction and half nonfiction." Publishes hardcover originals. Book catalog online.

HOW TO CONTACT Agented submissions only. *No unsolicited mss.*

TERMS Pays royalty. Pays negotiable advance.

TIPS "Write the complete ms and submit it to an agent or agents. They will know exactly which editor will be interested in a project."

DUTTON CHILDREN'S BOOKS

Penguin Random House, 375 Hudson St., New York NY 10014. **Website:** www.penguin.com. Estab. 1852. Dutton Children's Books publishes high-quality fiction and nonfiction for readers ranging from preschoolers to young adults on a variety of subjects. Currently emphasizing middle grade and young adult novels that offer a fresh perspective. De-emphasizing photographic nonfiction and picture books that teach a lesson. Publishes hardcover originals as well as novelty formats.

☺   "Cultivating the creative talents of authors and illustrators and publishing books with purpose and heart continue to be the mission and joy at Dutton."

NEEDS Dutton Children's Books has a diverse, general interest list that includes picture books; easy-to-read books; and fiction for all ages, from first chapter books to young adult readers.

HOW TO CONTACT Query. Responds only if interested.

TERMS Pays royalty on retail price. Pays advance.

DYNAMITE ENTERTAINMENT

113 Gaither Dr., Suite 205, Mt. Laurel NJ 8054. **E-mail:** submissions@dynamite.com. **Website:** www.dynamiteentertainment.com.

HOW TO CONTACT Query first. Does not accept unsolicited submissions. Include brief bio, list of publishing credits.

DZANC BOOKS

Dzanc Books, Inc., 2702 Lillian, Ann Arbor MI 48104. **Website:** www.dzancbooks.org.

NEEDS "We're an independent non-profit publishing literary fiction. We also set up writer-in-residence programs and help literary journals develop their subscription bases." Publishes paperback originals.

HOW TO CONTACT Query with outline/synopsis and 35 sample pages. Accepts queries by e-mail. Include brief bio. Agented fiction: 3%. Accepts unsolicited mss. Considers simultaneous submissions, submissions on CD or disk. Rarely critiques/comments on rejected mss. Responds to mss in 5 months.

TIPS "Every word counts—it's amazing how many submissions have poor first sentences or paragraphs and that first impression is hard to shake when it's a bad one."

ⓐⓞ THE ECCO PRESS

195 Broadway, New York NY 10007. (212)207-7000. **Fax:** (212)702-2460. **Website:** www.harpercollins.com. Estab. 1970. Publishes hardcover and trade paperback originals and reprints.

NEEDS Literary, short story collections. "We can publish possibly 1 or 2 original novels a year."

HOW TO CONTACT *Does not accept unsolicited mss.*

TERMS Pays royalty. Pays negotiable advance.

TIPS "We are always interested in first novels and feel it's important that they be brought to the attention of the reading public."

ⓒ EDGE SCIENCE FICTION AND FANTASY PUBLISHING

Hades Publications, Box 1414, Calgary AB T2P 2L7, Canada. (403)254-0160. **E-mail:** publisher@hadespublications.com. **Website:** www.edgewebsite.com. **Contact:** Editorial Manager. Estab. 1996. EDGE publishes thought-provoking full length novels and anthologies of Science Fiction, Fantasy and Horror. Featuring works by established authors and emerging new voices, EDGE is pleased to provide quality literary entertainment in both print and pixels. Publishes trade paperback and e-book originals. Catalog online. Guidelines online.

IMPRINTS EDGE, EDGE-Lite, Tesseracts Books, Absolute XPress.

NEEDS "We are looking for all types of fantasy, science fiction, and horror - except juvenile, erotica, and religious fiction. Short stories and poetry are only required for announced anthologies." Length: 75,000-100,000/words. Does not want juvenile, erotica, and religious fiction.

HOW TO CONTACT Submit first 3 chapters and synopsis. Check website for guidelines. Include estimated word count.

TERMS Pays royalty on net price for distributed printed and eBook editions. Negotiable advance. Responds in 4-5 months to mss.

WILLIAM B. EERDMANS PUBLISHING CO.

2140 Oak Industrial Dr. NE, Grand Rapids MI 49505. (616)459-4591. **Fax:** (616)459-6540. **E-mail:** info@eerdmans.com. **E-mail:** submissions@eerdmans.com. **Website:** www.eerdmans.com. Estab. 1911. "The majority of our adult publications are religious and most of these are academic or semi-academic in character (as opposed to inspirational or celebrity books), though we also publish general trade books on the Christian life. Our nonreligious titles, most of them in regional history or on social issues, aim, similarly, at an educated audience." Publishes hardcover and paperback originals and reprints. Book catalog and ms guidelines free.

HOW TO CONTACT Query with SASE.

TERMS Responds in 4 weeks.

ELLYSIAN PRESS

E-mail: publisher@ellysianpress.com. **E-mail:** submissions@ellysianpress.com. **Website:** www.ellysianpress.com. **Contact:** Maer Wilson. Estab. 2014. "Ellysian Press is a speculative fiction house. We seek to create a sense of home for our authors, a place where they can find fulfillment as artists. Just as exceptional mortals once sought a place in the Elysian Fields, now exceptional authors can find a place here at Ellysian Press. We are accepting submissions in the following genres only: Fantasy, Science Fiction, Paranormal, Paranormal Romance, Horror, along with Young/New Adult in these genres. Please submit polished manuscripts. It's best to have work read by critique groups or beta readers prior to submission. PLEASE NOTE: We do not publish children's books, picture books, or Middle Grade books. We do not publish books outside the genres listed above." Publishes fantasy, science fiction, paranormal, paranormal romance, horror, and young/new adult in these genres. Catalog online. Guidelines online.

HOW TO CONTACT "We accept online submissions only. Please submit a query letter, a synopsis and the first ten pages of your manuscript in the body of your e-mail. The subject line should be as follows: QUERY – Your Last Name, TITLE, Genre." If we choose to request more, we will request the full manuscript in standard format. This means your manuscript should be formatted as per the guidelines on our website. Please do not submit queries for any genres not listed above. Please do not submit children's books, picture books or Middle Grade books. You may email queries to submissions(at)ellysianpress(dot)com.

TERMS Pays quarterly. Does not pay advance. Responds in 1 week for queries; 4-6 weeks for partials and fulls.

ELM BOOKS

1175 Hwy. 130, Laramie WY 82070. (610)529-0460. **E-mail:** leila.elmbooks@gmail.com. **Website:** www.elm-books.com. **Contact:** Leila Monaghan, publisher. "Follow us on Facebook to learn about our latest calls for science fiction, mystery and romance stories. We also welcome submissions of middle grade fiction featuring diverse children. No picture book submissions."

NEEDS "Follow us on Facebook to learn about our latest calls for science fiction, mystery and romance stories. We also welcome submissions of middle grade fiction featuring diverse children. No picture book submissions."

HOW TO CONTACT Send inquiries for middle grade fiction featuring diverse children via e-mail to Leila.elmbooks@gmail.com. No mail inquiries.

TERMS Pays royalties.

ENTANGLED TEEN

Website: www.entangledteen.com. "Entangled Teen and Entangled digiTeen, our young adult imprints publish the swoonworthy young adult romances readers crave. Whether they're dark and angsty or fun and sassy, contemporary, fantastical, or futuristic. We are seeking fresh voices with interesting twists on popular genres."

IMPRINTS Teen Crush; Teen Crave.

NEEDS "We are seeking novels in the subgenres of romantic fiction for contemporary, upper young adult with crossover appeal."

HOW TO CONTACT E-mail using site. "All submissions must have strong romantic elements. YA novels should be 50K to 100K in length. Revised backlist titles will be considered on a case by case basis." Agented and unagented considered.

TERMS Pays royalty.

EYEWEAR PUBLISHING

E-mail: info@eyewearpublishing.com. **Website:** store.eyewearpublishing.com. **Contact:** Dr. Todd Swift, managing director and editor. Estab. 2012. Eyewear Publishing Ltd. is a small press founded in 2012 by Todd Swift, based in London, UK, with distribution in the USA. Our books have been recommended by such literary figures as Kaveh Akbar, Stephen Fry, Louis Theroux, Salman Rushdie, Clare Pollard, Vicki Feaver, Thomas Lux, Suhayl Saadi and The Rev. Jesse Jackson. We search for emerging talent, and neglected out-of-work authors, as well as well-established figures. We are welcoming, with a commitment to diversity. In 2019 we have acquired the famous Black Spring Press. Since 1985, Black Spring Press has produced work by Nick Cave, Anaïs Nin, Charles Baudelaire, Kyril Bonfiglioli, Carolyn Cassady and Leonard Cohen, among many impressive others. Firm publishes fiction, non-fiction, and poetry. Guidelines online.

IMPRINTS Maida Vale Publishing.

TERMS Royalties vary from 10-20%. Pays variable advance. Response time varies.

FAMILIUS

1254 Commerce Way, Sanger CA 93657. (559)876-2170. **Fax:** (559)876-2180. **E-mail:** bookideas@familius.com. **Website:** familius.com. **Contact:** Acquisitions. Estab. 2012. Familius is a value's driven trade publishing house, publishing in children's, parenting, relationships, cooking, health and wellness, and education. The company's mission is to help families be happy. Publishes hardcover, trade paperback, and electronic originals and reprints. Catalog online and print. Guidelines online.

NEEDS All picture books must align with Familius values statement listed on the website footer.

HOW TO CONTACT Submit a proposal package, including a synopsis, 3 sample chapters, and your author platform.

TERMS Authors are paid 10-30% royalty on wholesale price. Advances periodically paid to participating illustrators. Responds in 1 month to queries and proposals; 2 months to mss.

FANTAGRAPHICS BOOKS, INC.

7563 Lake City Way NE, Seattle WA 98115. (206)524-1967. **Fax:** (206)524-2104. **Website:** www.fantagraphics.com. **Contact:** Submissions Editor. Estab. 1976. Publishes comics for thinking readers. Does not want mainstream genres of superhero, vigilante, horror, fantasy, or science fiction. Publishes original trade paperbacks. Book catalog online. Guidelines online.

NEEDS "Fantagraphics is an independent company with a modus operandi different from larger, factory-like corporate comics publishers. If your talents are limited to a specific area of expertise (i.e. inking, writing, etc.), then you will need to develop your own team before submitting a project to us. We want to see an idea that is fully fleshed-out in your mind, at least, if not on paper. Submit a minimum of 5 fully-inked pages of art, a synopsis, SASE, and a brief note stating approximately how many issues you have in mind."

TERMS Responds in 2-3 months to queries.

TIPS "Take note of the originality and diversity of the themes and approaches to drawing in such Fantagraphics titles as *Love & Rockets* (stories of life in Latin America and Chicano L.A.), *Palestine* (journalistic autobiography in the Middle East), *Eightball* (surrealism mixed with kitsch culture in stories alternately humorous and painfully personal), and *Naughty Bits* (feminist humor and short stories which both attack and commiserate). Try to develop your own, equally individual voice; originality, aesthetic maturity, and graphic storytelling skill are the signs by which Fantagraphics judges whether or not your submission is ripe for publication."

FARRAR, STRAUS & GIROUX

18 W. 18th St., New York NY 10011. (646)307-5151. **Website:** us.macmillan.com/fsg. **Contact:** Editorial Department. Estab. 1946. "We publish original and well-written material for all ages." Publishes hardcover originals and trade paperback reprints. Catalog available by request. Guidelines online.

NEEDS Do not query picture books; just send ms. Do not fax or e-mail queries or mss.

HOW TO CONTACT Send cover letter describing submission with first 50 pages.

TERMS Pays 2-6% royalty on retail price for paperbacks, 3-10% for hardcovers. Pays $3,000-25,000 advance. Responds in 2-3 months.

FARRAR, STRAUS & GIROUX FOR YOUNG READERS

Macmillan Children's Publishing Group, 175 Fifth Ave., New York NY 10010. (212)741-6900. **Fax:** (212)633-2427. **E-mail:** childrens.editorial@fsgbooks.com. **Website:** www.fsgkidsbooks.com. Estab. 1946. Book catalog available by request. Ms guidelines online.

NEEDS All levels: all categories. "Original and well-written material for all ages."

HOW TO CONTACT Submit cover letter, first 50 pages by mail only.

TIPS "Study our catalog before submitting. We will see illustrators' portfolios by appointment. Don't ask for criticism and/or advice—due to the volume of submissions we receive, it's just not possible. Never send originals. Always enclose SASE."

↩ FAT FOX BOOKS

The Den, P.O. Box 579, Tonbridge TN9 9NG, United Kingdom. (44)(0)1580-857249. **E-mail:** hello@fatfoxbooks.com. **Website:** fatfoxbooks.com. "Can you write engaging, funny, original and brilliant stories? We are looking for fresh new talent as well as exciting new ideas from established writers and illustrators. We publish books for children from 3-14, and if we think the story is brilliant and fits our list, then as one of the few publishers who accepts unsolicited material, we will take it seriously. We will consider books of all genres." Guidelines online. Currently closed to submissions.

HOW TO CONTACT For picture books, send complete ms; for longer works, send first 3 chapters and estimate of final word count.

FATHER'S PRESS

590 N.W. 1921 St. Rd., Kingsville MO 64063. (816)550-1138. **E-mail:** mike@fatherspress.com. **Website:** www.fatherspress.com. **Contact:** Mike Smitley, owner (fiction, nonfiction, Christian). Estab. 2006. Publishes hardcover, trade paperback, and mass market paperback originals and reprints. Guidelines online.

HOW TO CONTACT Query with SASE. Unsolicited mss returned unopened. Call or e-mail first.

TERMS Pays 10-15% royalty on wholesale price. Responds in 1-3 months.

ⒶØ FEIWEL AND FRIENDS

Macmillan Children's Publishing Group, 175 Fifth Ave., New York NY 10010. (646)307-5151. **Website:** us.macmillan.com. Feiwel and Friends is a publisher of innovative children's fiction and nonfiction literature, including hardcover, paperback series, and individual titles. The list is eclectic and combines quality and commercial appeal for readers ages 0-16. The imprint is dedicated to "book by book" publishing, bringing the work of distinctive and oustanding authors, illustrators, and ideas to the marketplace. This market does not accept unsolicited mss due to the volume of submissions; they also do not accept unsolicited queries for interior art. The best way to submit a ms is through an agent. Catalog online.

FENCE BOOKS

Science Library 320, Univ. of Albany, 1400 Washington Ave., Albany NY 12222. (518)591-8162. **E-mail:** jessp.fence@gmail.com. **Website:** www.fenceportal.org. **Contact:** Submissions Manager. "Fence Books publishes poetry, fiction, and critical texts and anthologies, and prioritizes sustained support for its authors, many of whom come to us through our book contests and then go on to publish second, third, fourth books." Publishes hardcover originals. Guidelines online.

HOW TO CONTACT Submit via contests and occasional open reading periods.

DAVID FICKLING BOOKS

31 Beamont St., Oxford OX1 2NP, United Kingdom. (018)65-339000. **Fax:** (018)65-339009. **Website:** www.davidficklingbooks.co.uk. **Contact:** Simon Mason, managing director. David Fickling Books is a story house."For nearly twelve years DFB has been run as an imprint—first as part of Scholastic, then of Random House. Now we've set up as an independent business." Guidelines online. Closed to submissions. Check website for when they open to submissions and for details on the Inkpot competition.

NEEDS Considers all categories.

HOW TO CONTACT Submit cover letter and 3 sample chapters as PDF attachment saved in format "Author Name_Full Title."

TERMS Responds to mss in 3 months, if interested.

TIPS "We adore stories for all ages, in both text and pictures. Quality is our watch word."

FILBERT PUBLISHING

Box 326, Kandiyohi MN 56251-0326. **E-mail:** filbertpublishing@filbertpublishing.com. **Website:** filbertpublishing.com. **Contact:** Maurice Erickson, acquisitions. Estab. 2001. "We really like to publish books that creative entrepreneurs can use to help them make a living following their dream. This includes books on marketing, anything that encourages living a full life, freelancing, self-help, we'll consider a fairly wide range of subjects under this umbrella. The people who purchase our titles (and visit our website) tend to be in their fifties, female, well-educated; many are freelancers who want to make a living writing. Any well-written manuscript that would appeal to that audience is nearly a slam dunk to get reviewed." Publishes trade paperback and electronic originals and reprints. Catalog online. Guidelines online.

NEEDS "We're thrilled when we find a story that sweeps us off our feet. Good fiction queries have been sparse the last couple of years, and we're keen on expanding our current mystery/suspense line in the coming year."

HOW TO CONTACT Query, include SASE with a proposal package, including a synopsis, 5 sample chapters, information regarding your web platform, and a brief mention of your current marketing plan. "If you'd like to submit a query via e-mail, that's fine. However, we get a lot of e-mail and if you don't receive a reply within a couple weeks, don't hesitate to resend."

TERMS Paperback authors receive 10% royalty on retail price. E-books receive 50% net. Does not pay advance. Responds in 1-2 months. Sometimes we get really behind on this. If after a couple months you haven't heard from us, feel free to resend.

TIPS "Get to know us. Subscribe to Writing Etc./The Creative Entrepreneur to capture our preferred tone. Dig through our website, you'll get many ideas of what we're looking for. We enjoy nurturing new talent and most of our authors have stuck with us since our humble beginning. All new authors begin their journey with us with e-book publication. If that goes well, we move on to print. We love words. We enjoy marketing. We really love the publishing business. If you share those passions, feel free to query."

FIRST SECOND

Macmillan Children's Publishing Group, 175 5th Ave., New York NY 10010. **E-mail:** mail@firstsecondbooks.com. **Website:** www.firstsecondbooks.com. First Second is a publisher of graphic novels and an imprint of Macmillan Children's Publishing Group. First Second does not accept unsolicited submissions. Catalog online.

TERMS Responds in about 6 weeks.

FLASHLIGHT PRESS

527 Empire Blvd., Brooklyn NY 11225. (718)288-8300. **Fax:** (718)972-6307. **E-mail:** submissions@flashlightpress.com. **Website:** www.flashlightpress.com. **Contact:** Shari Dash Greenspan, editor. Estab. 2004. Publishes hardcover original children's picture books for 4-8 year olds. Book catalog online. Guidelines online.

NEEDS Average word length: 1,000 words. Picture books: contemporary, humor, multicultural.

HOW TO CONTACT "Query by e-mail only, after carefully reading our submission guidelines online. Do not send anything by snail mail."

TERMS Pays 8-10% royalty on net. Pays advance. "Only accepts e-mail queries according to submission guidelines."

✪ FLYING EYE BOOKS

62 Great Eastern St., London EC2A 3QR, United Kingdom. (44)(0)207-033-4430. **E-mail:** picturbksubs@nobrow.net. **Website:** www.flyingeyebooks.com. Estab. 2013. Flying Eye Books is the children's imprint of award-winning visual publishing house Nobrow. FEB seeks to retain the same attention to detail and excellence in illustrated content as its parent publisher, but with a focus on the craft of children's storytelling and nonfiction. Guidelines online.

FORWARD MOVEMENT

412 Sycamore St., Cincinnati OH 45202. (513)721-6659; (800)543-1813. **Fax:** (513)721-0729. **E-mail:** editorialstaff@forwardmovement.org. **Website:** www.forwardmovement.org. Estab. 1934. "Forward Movement was established to help reinvigorate the life of the church. Many titles focus on the life of prayer, where our relationship with God is centered, death, marriage, baptism, recovery, joy, the Episcopal Church and more. Currently emphasizing prayer/spirituality." Book catalog free. Guidelines online.

TERMS Responds in 1 month.

TIPS "Audience is primarily Episcopalians and other Christians."

FOUR WAY BOOKS

Box 535, Village Station, New York NY 10014. (212)334-5430. **E-mail:** editors@fourwaybooks.com. **Website:** www.fourwaybooks.com. Estab. 1993. "Four Way Books is a not-for-profit literary press dedicated to publishing poetry and short fiction by emerging and established writers. Each year, Four Way Books publishes the winners of its national poetry competitions, as well as collections accepted through general submission, panel selection, and solicitation by the editors."

NEEDS Open reading period: June 1-30. Book-length story collections and novellas. Submission guidelines will be posted online at end of May. Does not want novels or translations.

✪ FRANCES LINCOLN CHILDREN'S BOOKS

Frances Lincoln, 74-77 White Lion St., London N1 9PF, United Kingdom. (44)(20)7284-4009. **Website:** www. franceslincoln.com. Estab. 1977. "Our company was founded by Frances Lincoln in 1977. We published our

first books two years later, and we have been creating illustrated books of the highest quality ever since, with special emphasis on gardening, walking and the outdoors, art, architecture, design and landscape. In 1983, we started to publish illustrated books for children. Since then we have won many awards and prizes with both fiction and nonfiction children's books."

NEEDS Average word length: picture books—1,000; young readers— 9,788; middle readers— 20,653; young adults— 35,407.

HOW TO CONTACT Query by e-mail.

TERMS Responds in 6 weeks to mss.

FREE SPIRIT PUBLISHING, INC.

6325 Sandburg Rd., Suite 100, Minneapolis MN 55427-3674. (612)338-2068. **Fax:** (612)337-5050. **E-mail:** acquisitions@freespirit.com. **Website:** www.freespirit. com. Estab. 1983. "Free Spirit is the leading publisher of learning tools that support young people's social-emotional health and educational needs. We help children and teens think for themselves, overcome challenges, and make a difference in the world." Free Spirit does not accept general fiction, poetry or storybook submissions. Publishes trade paperback originals and reprints. Book catalog and guidelines online.

NEEDS "Please review catalog and author guidelines (both available online) for details before submitting proposal. If you'd like material returned, enclose a SASE with sufficient postage."

TERMS Responds to proposals within 6 months.

TIPS "Our books are issue-oriented, jargon-free, and solution-focused. Our audience is children, teens, teachers, parents and youth counselors. We are especially concerned with kids' social and emotional well-being and look for books with ready-to-use strategies for coping with today's issues at home or in school—written in everyday language. We are not looking for academic or religious materials, or books that analyze problems with the nation's school systems. Instead, we want books that offer practical, positive advice so kids can help themselves, and parents and teachers can help kids succeed."

GERTRUDE PRESS

P.O. Box 28281, Portland OR 97228. (503)515-8252. **E-mail:** editorgertrudepress@gmail.com. **Website:** www.gertrudepress.org. Estab. 2005. "Gertrude Press is a nonprofit organization developing and showcasing the creative talents of lesbian, gay, bisexual, trans, queer-identified and allied individuals. We publish limited-edition fiction and poetry chapbooks plus the biannual literary journal, *Gertrude*." Reads chapbook mss only through contests.

TIPS Sponsors poetry and fiction chapbook contest. Prize is $175 and 50 contributor's copies. Submission guidelines and fee information on website. "Read the journal and sample published work. We are not impressed by pages of publications; your work should speak for itself."

GIVAL PRESS

Gival Press, LLC, P.O. Box 3812, Arlington VA 22203. (703)351-0079. **E-mail:** givalpress@yahoo.com. **Website:** www.givalpress.com. **Contact:** Robert L. Giron, editor-in-chief (area of interest: literary). Estab. 1998. "We publish literary works: fiction, nonfiction (essays, academic), and poetry in English, Spanish, and French." Publishes trade paperback, electronic originals, and reprints. Book catalog online. Guidelines online.

HOW TO CONTACT Always query first via e-mail; provide description, author's bio, and supportive material.

TERMS Pays royalty. Per the contest prize, amount per the content. Outside of contests, yes. Responds in 3-5 months. If we get behind, it's okay to remind us. Prefer submissions via Submittable or e-mail (after query).

TIPS "Our audience is those who read literary works with depth to the work. Visit our website—there is much to be read/learned from the numerous pages."

THE GLENCANNON PRESS

P.O. Box 1428, El Cerrito CA 94530. (510)455-9027. **E-mail:** merships@yahoo.com. **Website:** www.glencannon.com. **Contact:** Bill Harris (maritime, maritime children's). Estab. 1993. "We publish quality books about ships and the sea." Average print order: 300. Member PMA, BAIPA. Promotes titles through direct mail, magazine advertising and word of mouth. Accepts unsolicited mss. Often comments on rejected mss. Publishes hardcover and paperback originals and hardcover reprints. Available on request. Submit complete paper ms with SASE. "We do not look at electronic submissions due to the danger of computer viruses."

IMPRINTS Smyth: perfect binding; illustrations.

HOW TO CONTACT Submit complete ms. Include brief bio, list of publishing credits. Send SASE for return of ms or send a disposable ms and SASE for reply only.

TERMS Pays 10-20% royalty. Does not pay advance. Responds in 1 month to queries; 2 months to mss.

TIPS "Write a good story in a compelling style."

DAVID R. GODINE, PUBLISHER

15 Court Square, Suite 320, Boston MA 02108. (617)451-9600. **Fax:** (617)350-0250. **E-mail:** info@godine.com. **Website:** www.godine.com. Estab. 1970. "We publish books that matter for people who care." This publisher is no longer considering unsolicited mss of any type. Only interested in agented material.

IMPRINTS Black Sparrow Books, Verba Mundi, Nonpareil.

GOLDEN BOOKS FOR YOUNG READERS GROUP

1745 Broadway, New York NY 10019. **Website:** www.penguinrandomhouse.com. Estab. 1935. "Random House Books aims to create books that nurture the hearts and minds of children, providing and promoting quality books and a rich variety of media that entertain and educate readers from 6 months to 12 years." *Random House-Golden Books does not accept unsolicited mss, only agented material.* They reserve the right not to return unsolicited material. Book catalog free on request.

TERMS Pays authors in royalties; sometimes buys mss outright.

GOOSE LANE EDITIONS

500 Beaverbrook Ct., Suite 330, Fredericton NB E3B 5X4, Canada. (506)450-4251. **Fax:** (506)459-4991. **E-mail:** info@gooselane.com. **Website:** www.gooselane.com. Estab. 1954. "Goose Lane publishes literary fiction and nonfiction from well-read and highly skilled Canadian authors." Publishes hardcover and paperback originals and occasional reprints.

NEEDS Our needs in fiction never change: Substantial, character-centered literary fiction. No children's, YA, mainstream, mass market, genre, mystery, thriller, confessional or science fiction.

HOW TO CONTACT Query with SAE with Canadian stamps or IRCs. No U.S. stamps.

TERMS Pays 8-10% royalty on retail price. Pays $500-3,000, negotiable advance. Responds in 6 months to queries.

TIPS "Writers should send us outlines and samples of books that show a very well-read author with highly developed literary skills. Our books are almost all by Canadians living in Canada; we seldom consider submissions from outside Canada. We consider submissions from outside Canada only when the author is Canadian and the book is of extraordinary interest to Canadian readers. We do not publish books for children or for the young adult market."

GRAYWOLF PRESS

250 Third Ave. N., Suite 600, Minneapolis MN 55401. (651)641-0077. **Fax:** (651)641-0036. **Website:** www.graywolfpress.org. Estab. 1974. "Graywolf Press is an independent, nonprofit publisher dedicated to the creation and promotion of thoughtful and imaginative contemporary literature essential to a vital and diverse culture." Publishes trade cloth and paperback originals. Book catalog free. Guidelines online.

NEEDS "Familiarize yourself with our list first." No genre books (romance, western, science fiction, suspense)

HOW TO CONTACT Agented submissions only.

TERMS Pays royalty on retail price. Pays $1,000-25,000 advance. Responds in 3 months to queries.

GREENWILLOW BOOKS

HarperCollins Publishers, 10 E. 53rd St., New York NY 10022. (212)207-7000. **Website:** www.greenwillowblog.com. Estab. 1974. *Does not accept unsolicited mss.* "Unsolicited mail will not be opened and will not be returned." Publishes hardcover originals, paperbacks, e-books, and reprints.

HOW TO CONTACT *Agented submissions only.*

TERMS Pays 10% royalty on wholesale price for first-time authors. Offers variable advance.

GREY GECKO PRESS

38 S. Blue Angel Parkway, Suite 312, Pensacola FL 32506. **E-mail:** info@greygeckopress.com. **E-mail:** submissions@greygeckopress.com. **Website:** www.greygeckopress.com. **Contact:** Submissions Coordinator. Estab. 2011. Not open for submissions; check website for updates. Grey Gecko focuses on new and emerging authors and great books that might not otherwise get a chance to see the light of day. "We publish all our titles in hardcover, trade paperback, and e-book formats, as well as audiobook and foreign-language editions. Our books are available worldwide, for readers of all types, kinds, and interests." Publishes hardcover, trade paperback, audiobook, and electronic originals. Catalog online. Guidelines online.

NEEDS Not accepting submissions. "We do not publish extreme horror, erotica, or religious fiction. New and interesting stories by unpublished authors will always get our attention. Innovation is a core value of our company." Does not want extreme horror (e.g. *Saw* or *Hostel*), religious, or erotica.

HOW TO CONTACT Not currently accepting submissions. When open, use online submission page.

TERMS Pays 50-75% royalties on net revenue. Does not pay advance. Responds in 6-12 months.

TIPS "Be willing to be a part of the Grey Gecko family. Publishing with us is a partnership, not indentured servitude. Authors are expected and encouraged to be proactive and contribute to their book's success."

GROSSET & DUNLAP PUBLISHERS

Penguin Random House, 1745 Broadway, New York NY 10019. **Website:** www.penguinrandomhouse.com. Estab. 1898. Grosset & Dunlap publishes children's books that show children that reading is fun, with books that speak to their interests, and that are affordable so that children can build a home library of their own. Focus on licensed properties, series and readers. "Grosset & Dunlap publishes high-interest, affordable books for children ages 0-10 years. We focus on original series, licensed properties, readers and novelty books." Publishes hardcover (few) and mass market paperback originals.

HOW TO CONTACT *Agented submissions only.*

TERMS Pays royalty. Pays advance.

GROUNDWOOD BOOKS

128 Sterling Rd., Lower Level, Attention: Submissions, Toronto ON M6R 2B7, Canada. (416)363-4343. **Fax:** (416)363-1017. **E-mail:** submissions@groundwoodbooks.com. **Website:** groundwoodbooks.com. "We are always looking for new authors of novel-length fiction for children of all ages. Our mandate is to publish high-quality, character-driven literary fiction. We do not generally publish stories with an obvious moral or message, or genre fiction such as thrillers or fantasy." Publishes 19 picture books/year; 2 young readers/year; 3 middle readers/year; 3 young adult titles/year, approximately 2 nonfiction titles/year. Visit website for guidelines.

HOW TO CONTACT Submit a cover letter, synopsis and sample chapters via e-mail. "Due to the large number of submissions we receive, Groundwood regrets that we cannot accept unsolicited manuscripts for picture books."

TERMS Offers advances. Responds to mss in 6-8 months.

GROVE/ATLANTIC, INC.

154 W. 14th St., 12th Floor, New York NY 10011. **E-mail:** info@groveatlantic.com. **Website:** www.groveatlantic.com. Estab. 1917. "Due to limited resources of time and staffing, Grove/Atlantic cannot accept manuscripts that do not come through a literary agent. In today's publishing world, agents are more important than ever, helping writers shape their work and

navigate the main publishing houses to find the most appropriate outlet for a project." Publishes hardcover and trade paperback originals, and reprints. Book catalog available online.

IMPRINTS Black Cat, Atlantic Monthly Press, Grove Press.

HOW TO CONTACT Agented submissions only.

TERMS Pays 7 ½-12 ½% royalty. Makes outright purchase of $5-500,000. Responds in 1 month to queries; 2 months to proposals; 4 months to mss.

GUERNICA EDITIONS

1569 Heritage Way, Oakville ON L6M 2Z7, Canada. (905)599-5304. **E-mail:** michaelmirolla@guernicaeditions.com. **Website:** www.guernicaeditions.com. **Contact:** Michael Mirolla, editor/publisher (poetry, nonfiction, short stories, novels). Estab. 1978. Guernica Editions is a literary press that produces works of poetry, fiction and nonfiction often by writers who are ignored by the mainstream. "We feature an imprint (MiroLand) which accepts memoirs, how-to books, graphic novels, genre fiction with the possibility of children's and cook books." A new imprint, Guernica World Editions, features writers who are non-Canadian. Publishes trade paperback originals and reprints. Book catalog online. Queries and submissions accepted via e-mail January 1-April 30.

IMPRINTS MiroLand, Guernica World Editions.

NEEDS "We wish to open up into the literary fiction world and focus less on poetry." Does not want fantasy, YA.

HOW TO CONTACT E-mail queries only.

TERMS Pays 10% royalty on either cover or retail price. Pays $450-750 advance. Responds in 1 month to queries; 6 months to proposals; 1 year to mss.

HACHAI PUBLISHING

527 Empire Blvd., Brooklyn NY 11225. (718)633-0100. **Fax:** (718)633-0103. **E-mail:** info@hachai.com; dlr@hachai.com. **Website:** www.hachai.com. **Contact:** Devorah Leah Rosenfeld, editor. Estab. 1988. Hachai is dedicated to producing high quality Jewish children's literature, ages 2-10. Story should promote universal values such as sharing, kindness, etc. Publishes hardcover originals. Guidelines online.

"All books have spiritual/religious themes, specifically traditional Jewish content. We're seeking books about morals and values; the Jewish experience in current and Biblical times; and Jewish observance, Sabbath and holidays."

NEEDS Picture books and young readers: contemporary, historical fiction, religion. Middle readers: adventure, contemporary, problem novels, religion. Does not want to see fantasy, animal stories, romance, problem novels depicting drug use or violence.

HOW TO CONTACT Submit complete ms.

TERMS Work purchased outright from authors for $800-1,000. Responds in 2 months to mss.

TIPS "We are looking for books that convey the traditional Jewish experience in modern times or long ago; traditional Jewish observance such as Sabbath and holidays and mitzvos such as mezuzah, blessings etc.; positive character traits (middos) such as honesty, charity, respect, sharing, etc. We are also interested in historical fiction for young readers (7-10) written with a traditional Jewish perspective and highlighting the relevance of Torah in making important choices. Please, no animal stories, romance, violence, preachy sermonizing. Write a story that incorporates a moral, not a preachy morality tale. Originality is the key. We feel Hachai publications will appeal to a wider readership as parents become more interested in positive values for their children."

HADLEY RILLE BOOKS

P.O. Box 25466, Overland Park KS 66225. **E-mail:** contact@hadleyrillebooks.com. **E-mail:** subs@hadleyrillebooks.com. **Website:** https://hadleyrillebks.wordpress.com. **Contact:** Eric T. Reynolds, editor/publisher. Estab. 2005. Currently closed to submissions. Check website for future reading periods.

TIPS "We aim to produce books that are aligned with current interest in the genres. Anthology markets are somewhat rare in SF these days, we feel there aren't enough good anthologies being published each year and part of our goal is to present the best that we can. We like stories that fit well within the guidelines of the particular anthology for which we are soliciting manuscripts. Aside from that, we want stories with strong characters (not necessarily characters with strong personalities, flawed characters are welcome). We want a sense of wonder and awe. We want to feel the world around the character and so scene description is important (however, this doesn't always require a lot of text, just set the scene well so we don't wonder where the character is). We strongly recommend workshopping the story or having it critiqued in some way by readers familiar with the genre. We prefer clichés be kept to a bare minimum in the prose and avoid re-working old story lines."

HAMPTON ROADS PUBLISHING CO., INC.

65 Parker St, Suite 7, Newburyport MA 01950. **E-mail:** submissions@rwwbooks.com. **Website:** www.redwheelweiser.com. Estab. 1989. "Our reason for being is to impact, uplift, and contribute to positive change in the world. We publish books that will enrich and empower the evolving consciousness of mankind. Though we are not necessarily limited in scope, we are most interested in manuscripts on the following subjects: Body/Mind/Spirit, Health and Healing, Self-Help. Please be advised that at the moment we are not accepting fiction or novelized material that does not pertain to body/mind/spirit, channeled writing." Publishes and distributes hardcover and trade paperback originals on subjects including metaphysics, health, complementary medicine, and other related topics. Guidelines online.

TERMS Pays royalty. Pays $1,000-50,000 advance. Responds in 2-4 months to queries; 1 month to proposals; 6-12 months to mss.

✪ HARLEQUIN BLAZE

225 Duncan Mill Rd., Don Mills ON M3B 3K9, Canada. (416)445-5860. **Website:** www.harlequin.com. **Contact:** Kathleen Scheibling, senior editor. "Harlequin Blaze is a red-hot series. It is a vehicle to build and promote new authors who have a strong sexual edge to their stories. It is also the place to be for seasoned authors who want to create a sexy, sizzling, longer contemporary story." Publishes paperback originals. Guidelines online.

NEEDS "Sensuous, highly romantic, innovative plots that are sexy in premise and execution. The tone of the books can run from fun and flirtatious to dark and sensual. Submissions should have a very contemporary feel—what it's like to be young and single today. We are looking for heroes and heroines in their early 20s and up. There should be a a strong emphasis on the physical relationship between the couples. Fully described love scenes along with a high level of fantasy and playfulness." Length: 55,000-60,000 words.

TIPS "Are you a *Cosmo* girl at heart? A fan of *Sex and the City*? Or maybe you have a sexually adventurous spirit. If so, then Blaze is the series for you!"

HARLEQUIN DESIRE

233 Broadway, Suite 1001, New York NY 10279. (212)553-4200. **Website:** www.harlequin.com. **Contact:** Stacy Boyd, senior editor. Always powerful, passionate, and provocative. "Desire novels are sensual reads and a love scene or scenes are still needed. But there is no set number of pages that needs to be fulfilled. Rather, the level of sensuality must be appropriate to the storyline. Above all, every Silhouette Desire novel must fulfill the promise of a powerful, passionate and provocative read." Publishes paperback originals and reprints. Guidelines online.

NEEDS Looking for novels in which "the conflict is an emotional one, springing naturally from the unique characters you've chosen. The focus is on the developing relationship, set in a believable plot. Sensuality is key, but lovemaking is never taken lightly. Secondary characters and subplots need to blend with the core story. Innovative new directions in storytelling and fresh approaches to classic romantic plots are welcome." Manuscripts must be 50,000-55,000 words.

TERMS Pays royalty. Offers advance.

✪ HARLEQUIN INTRIGUE

225 Duncan Mill Rd., Don Mills ON M3B 3K9, Canada. **Website:** www.harlequin.com. **Contact:** Denise Zaza, senior editor. Wants crime stories tailored to the series romance market packed with a variety of thrilling suspense and whodunit mystery. Word count: 55,000-60,000. Guidelines online.

HOW TO CONTACT Submit online.

✪ HARLEQUIN SUPERROMANCE

225 Duncan Mill Rd., Don Mills ON M3B 3K9, Canada. **Website:** www.harlequin.com. **Contact:** Victoria Curran, senior editor. "The Harlequin Superromance line focuses on believable characters triumphing over true-to-life drama and conflict. At the heart of these contemporary stories should be a compelling romance that brings the reader along with the hero and heroine on their journey of overcoming the obstacles in their way and falling in love. Because of the longer length relevant subplots and secondary characters are welcome but not required. This series publishes a variety of story types—family sagas, romantic suspense, Westerns, to name a few—and tones from light to dramatic, emotional to suspenseful. Settings also vary from vibrant urban neighborhoods to charming small towns. The unifying element of Harlequin Superromance stories is the realistic treatment of character and plot. The characters should seem familiar to readers—similar to people they know in their own lives—and the circumstances within the realm of possibility. The stories should be layered and complex in that the conflicts should not be easily resolved. The best way to get an idea of we're look-

ing for is to read what we're currently publishing. The aim of Superromance novels is to produce a contemporary, involving read with a mainstream tone in its situations and characters, using romance as the major theme. To achieve this, emphasis should be placed on individual writing styles and unique and topical ideas." Publishes paperback originals. Guidelines online.

NEEDS "The criteria for Superromance books are flexible. Aside from length (80,000 words), the determining factor for publication will always be quality. Authors should strive to break free of stereotypes, clichés and worn-out plot devices to create strong, believable stories with depth and emotional intensity. Superromance novels are intended to appeal to a wide range of romance readers."

HOW TO CONTACT Submit online.

TERMS Pays royalties. Pays advance.

TIPS "A general familiarity with current Superromance books is advisable to keep abreast of ever-changing trends and overall scope, but we don't want imitations. We look for sincere, heartfelt writing based on true-to-life experiences the reader can identify with. We are interested in innovation."

HARMONY INK PRESS

Dreamspinner Press, 5032 Capital Circle SW, Suite 2 PMB 279, Tallahassee FL 32305. (850)632-4648. **Fax:** (888)308-3739. **E-mail:** submissions@harmonyinkpress. com. **Website:** harmonyinkpress.com. **Contact:** Anne Regan. Estab. 2010. Teen and new adult fiction featuring at least 1 strong LGBTQ+ main character who shows significant personal growth through the course of the story.

NEEDS "We are looking for stories in all subgenres, featuring primary characters across the whole LGBTQ+ spectrum between the ages of 14 and 21 that explore all the facets of young adult, teen, and new adult life. Sexual content should be appropriate for the characters and the story."

HOW TO CONTACT Submit complete ms.

TERMS Pays royalty. Pays $500-1,000 advance.

Ⓐ⦸ HARPERCOLLINS

195 Broadway, New York NY 10007. (212)207-7000. **Website:** www.harpercollins.com. HarperCollins, one of the largest English language publishers in the world, is a broad-based publisher with strengths in academic, business and professional, children's, educational, general interest, and religious and spiritual

books, as well as multimedia titles. Publishes hardcover and paperback originals and paperback reprints.

NEEDS "We look for a strong story line and exceptional literary talent."

HOW TO CONTACT Agented submissions only. *All unsolicited mss returned.*

TERMS Pays royalty. Pays negotiable advance.

TIPS "We do not accept any unsolicited material."

⦾⦸ HARPERCOLLINS CANADA, LTD.

2 Bloor St. E., 20th Floor, Toronto ON M4W 1A8, Canada. (416)975-9334. **Fax:** (416)975-5223. **Website:** www. harpercollins.ca. Estab. 1989. *HarperCollins Canada is not accepting unsolicited material at this time.*

Ⓐ HARPERCOLLINS CHILDREN'S BOOKS/ HARPERCOLLINS PUBLISHERS

195 Broadway, New York NY 10007. (212)207-7000. **Website:** www.harpercollins.com. HarperCollins, one of the largest English language publishers in the world, is a broad-based publisher with strengths in academic, business and professional, children's, educational, general interest, and religious and spiritual books, as well as multimedia titles. Publishes hardcover and paperback originals and paperback reprints. Catalog online.

IMPRINTS **HarperCollins Australia/New Zealand:** Angus & Robertson, Fourth Estate, HarperBusiness, HarperCollins, HarperPerenniel, HarperReligious, HarperSports, Voyager; **HarperCollins Canada:** HarperFlamingoCanada, PerennialCanada; **HarperCollins Children's Books Group:** Amistad, Julie Andrews Collection, Avon, Joanna Cotler Books, Eos, Laura Geringer Books, Greenwillow Books, HarperAudio, HarperCollins Children's Books, HarperFestival, HarperTempest, HarperTrophy, Rayo, Katherine Tegen Books; **HarperCollins General Books Group:** Access, Amistad, Avon, Caedmon, Ecco, Eos, Fourth Estate, HarperAudio, HarperBusiness, HarperCollins, HarperEntertainment, HarperLargePrint, HarperResource, HarperSanFrancisco, HarperTorch, Harper Design International, Perennial, PerfectBound, Quill, Rayo, ReganBooks, William Morrow, William Morrow Cookbooks; **HarperCollins UK:** Collins Bartholomew, Collins, HarperCollins Crime & Thrillers, Collins Freedom to Teach, HarperCollins Children's Books, Thorsons/Element, Voyager Books; **Zondervan:** Inspirio, Vida, Zonderkidz, Zondervan.

NEEDS "We look for a strong story line and exceptional literary talent."

HOW TO CONTACT Agented submissions only. *All unsolicited mss returned.*

TERMS Negotiates payment upon acceptance. Responds in 1 month, will contact only if interested. Does not accept any unsolicted texts.

TIPS "We do not accept any unsolicited material."

⚠️⃝ HARPER VOYAGER

Imprint of HarperCollins General Books Group, 195 Broadway, New York NY 10007. (212)207-7000. **Website:** www.harpercollins.com. Estab. 1998. Eos publishes quality science fiction/fantasy with broad appeal. Publishes hardcover originals, trade and mass market paperback originals, and reprints. Guidelines online.

NEEDS No horror or juvenile.

HOW TO CONTACT Agented submissions only. *All unsolicited mss returned.*

TERMS Pays royalty on retail price. Pays variable advance.

⚠️⃝ HARVEST HOUSE PUBLISHERS

990 Owen Loop, Eugene OR 97402. (541)343-0123. **Fax:** (541)302-0731. **Website:** www.harvesthousepublishers. com. Estab. 1974. Publishes hardcover, trade paperback, and mass market paperback originals and reprints.

NEEDS *No unsolicited mss, proposals, or artwork.*

HOW TO CONTACT Agented submissions only.

TERMS Pays royalty.

TIPS "For first time/nonpublished authors we suggest building their literary résumé by submitting to magazines, or perhaps accruing book contributions."

HENDRICK-LONG PUBLISHING CO., INC.

10635 Tower Oaks, Suite D, Houston TX 77070. (832)912-READ. **Fax:** (832)912-7353. **E-mail:** hendrick-long@att.net. **Website:** hendricklongpublishing. com. Estab. 1969. "Hendrick-Long publishes historical fiction and nonfiction about Texas and the Southwest for children and young adults." Publishes hardcover and trade paperback originals and hardcover reprints. Book catalog available. Guidelines online.

HOW TO CONTACT Query with SASE. Submit outline, clips, 2 sample chapters.

TERMS Pays royalty on selling price. Pays advance. Responds in 3 months to queries.

HOLIDAY HOUSE, INC.

425 Madison Ave., New York NY 10017. (212)688-0085. **Fax:** (212)421-6134. **E-mail:** info@holidayhouse.com. **Website:** holidayhouse.com. Estab. 1935. "Holiday House publishes children's and young adult books for the school and library markets. We have a commitment to publishing first-time authors and illustrators. We specialize in quality hardcovers from picture books to young adult, both fiction and nonfiction, primarily for the school and library market." Publishes hardcover originals and paperback reprints. Guidelines for #10 SASE.

NEEDS Children's books only.

HOW TO CONTACT Query with SASE. No phone calls, please.

TERMS Pays royalty on list price, range varies. Responds in 4 months.

TIPS "We need manuscripts with strong stories and writing."

⚠️⃝ HENRY HOLT

175 Fifth Ave., New York NY 10011. (646)307-5095. **Fax:** (212)633-0748. **Website:** www.henryholt.com. *Agented submissions only.*

HOPEWELL PUBLICATIONS

P.O. Box 11, Titusville NJ 08560. **Website:** www.hopepubs.com. **Contact:** E. Martin, publisher. Estab. 2002. "Hopewell Publications specializes in classic reprints—books with proven sales records that have gone out of print—and new titles of interest. Our catalog spans from 1 to 60 years of publication history. We print fiction and nonfiction, and we accept agented and unagented materials. Submissions are accepted online only." Format publishes in hardcover, trade paperback, and electronic originals; trade paperback and electronic reprints. Catalog online. Guidelines online.

IMPRINTS Hopewell Publications, Egress Books, Legacy Classics.

HOW TO CONTACT Query online using our online guidelines.

TERMS Pays royalty on retail price. Responds in 3 months to queries; 6 months to proposals; 9 months to mss.

HOUGHTON MIFFLIN HARCOURT BOOKS FOR CHILDREN

Imprint of Houghton Mifflin Trade & Reference Division, 222 Berkeley St., Boston MA 02116. (617)351-5000. **Fax:** (617)351-1111. **Website:** www.houghtonmifflinbooks.com. Houghton Mifflin Harcourt gives shape to ideas that educate, inform, and above all, delight. *Does not respond to or return mss unless interest-*

ed. Publishes hardcover originals and trade paperback originals and reprints. Guidelines online.

HOW TO CONTACT Submit complete ms.

TERMS Pays 5-10% royalty on retail price. Pays variable advance. Responds in 4-6 months to queries.

⊙⊘ HOUSE OF ANANSI PRESS

128 Sterling Rd., Lower Level, Toronto ON M6R 2B7, Canada. (416)363-4343. **Fax:** (416)363-1017. **Website:** www.anansi.ca. Estab. 1967. House of Anansi publishes literary fiction and poetry by Canadian and international writers.

NEEDS Publishes literary fiction that has a unique flair, memorable characters, and a strong narrative voice.

HOW TO CONTACT Query with SASE.

TERMS Pays 8-10% royalties. Pays $750 advance and 10 author's copies.

☺ IDW PUBLISHING

2765 Truxtun Rd., San Diego CA 92106. **E-mail:** letters@idwpublishing.com. **Website:** www.idwpublishing.com. Estab. 1999. IDW Publishing currently publishes a wide range of comic books and graphic novels including titles based on GI Joe, Star Trek, Terminator: Salvation, and Transformers. Creator-driven titles include Fallen Angel by Peter David and JK Woodward, Locke & Key by Joe Hill and Gabriel Rodriguez, and a variety of titles by writer Steve Niles including Wake the Dead, Epilogue, and Dead, She Said. Publishes hardcover, mass market and trade paperback originals.

ILIUM PRESS

2407 S. Sonora Dr., Spokane WA 99037. (509)701-8866. **E-mail:** iliumpress@outlook.com. **Contact:** John Lemon, owner/editor. Estab. 2010. "Ilium Press is a small, 1-person press that I created to cultivate and promote the relevance of epic poetry in today's world. My focus is book-length narrative poems in blank (non-rhyming) metered verse, such as iambic parameter or sprung verse. I am very selective about my projects, but I provide extensive editorial care to those projects I take on." Publishes trade paperback originals and reprints, electronic originals and reprints.

TERMS Pays 20-50% royalties on receipts. Does not pay advance. Responds in 6 months.

☻ IMAGE COMICS

2701 NW Vaughn St., Suite 780, Portland OR 97210. **E-mail:** submissions@imagecomics.com. **Website:** www.imagecomics.com. Estab. 1992. Publishes creator-owned comic books, graphic novels. See this company's website for detailed guidelines. Does not accept writing samples without art.

HOW TO CONTACT Query with 1-page synopsis and 5 pages or more of samples. "We do not accept writing (that is plots, scripts, whatever) samples! If you're an established pro, we might be able to find somebody willing to work with you but it would be nearly impossible for us to read through every script that might find its way our direction. Do not send your script or your plot unaccompanied by art—it will be discarded, unread."

TIPS "We are not looking for any specific genre or type of comic book. We are looking for comics that are well written and well drawn, by people who are dedicated and can meet deadlines."

IMBRIFEX BOOKS

Flattop Productions, Inc., 8275 S. Eastern Ave., Suite 200, Las Vegas NV 89123. (702)309-0130. **E-mail:** acquisitions@imbrifex.com. **Website:** https://imbrifex.com. **Contact:** Mark Sedenquist. Estab. 2016. Based in Las Vegas, Nevada, Imbrifex Books publishes both fiction and nonfiction, with a particular interest in books for road trip aficionados and books that have a connection with Las Vegas and the desert Southwest. Titles are distributed world-wide through Pacific Group West, (PGW), and Audible.com. Guidelines online.

TERMS Pays advance. Responds in 2 months.

IMMEDIUM

P.O. Box 31846, San Francisco CA 94131. (415)452-8546. **Fax:** (360)937-6272. **Website:** www.immedium.com. **Contact:** Submissions Editor. Estab. 2005. "Immedium focuses on publishing eye-catching children's picture books, Asian-American topics, and contemporary arts, popular culture, and multicultural issues." Publishes hardcover and trade paperback originals. Catalog online. Guidelines online.

HOW TO CONTACT Submit complete ms.

TERMS Pays 5% royalty on wholesale price. Pays on publication. Responds in 1-3 months.

TIPS "Our audience is children and parents. Please visit our site."

⊙ INSOMNIAC PRESS

520 Princess Ave., London ON N6B 2B8, Canada. (416)504-6270. **Website:** www.insomniacpress.com. Estab. 1992. Publishes trade paperback originals and reprints, mass market paperback originals, and electronic originals and reprints. Guidelines online.

NEEDS "We publish a mix of commercial (mysteries) and literary fiction."

HOW TO CONTACT Query via e-mail, submit proposal.

TERMS Pays 10-15% royalty on retail price. Pays $500-1,000 advance.

TIPS "We envision a mixed readership that appreciates up-and-coming literary fiction and poetry as well as solidly researched and provocative nonfiction. Peruse our website and familiarize yourself with what we've published in the past."

INTERLINK PUBLISHING GROUP, INC.

46 Crosby St., Northampton MA 01060. (413)582-7054. **E-mail:** info@interlinkbooks.com. **E-mail:** submissions@interlinkbooks.com. **Website:** www.interlinkbooks.com. Estab. 1987. Interlink is an independent publisher of general trade adult fiction and nonfiction with an emphasis on books that have a wide appeal while also meeting high intellectual and literary standards. "Our list is devoted to works of literature, history, contemporary politics, travel, art, and cuisine from around the world, often from areas underrepresented in Western media." Publishes hardcover and trade paperback originals. Book catalog and guidelines online.

IMPRINTS Olive Branch Press; Crocodile Books; Interlink Books.

NEEDS "We are looking for translated works relating to the Middle East, Africa or Latin America. The only fiction we publish falls into our 'Interlink World Fiction' series. Most of these books, as you can see in our catalog, are translated fiction from around the world. The series aims to bring fiction from other countries to a North American audience. In short, unless you were born outside the United States, your novel will not fit into the series." No science fiction, romance, plays, erotica, fantasy, horror.

HOW TO CONTACT Query by e-mail. Submit outline, sample chapters.

TERMS Pays 6-8% royalty on retail price. Pays small advance. Responds in 3-6 months to queries.

TIPS "Any submissions that fit well in our publishing program will receive careful attention. A visit to our website, your local bookstore, or library to look at some of our books before you send in your submission is recommended."

INVERTED-A

P.O. Box 267, Licking MO 65542. **E-mail:** katzaya@gmail.com. **Website:** inverteda.com. **Contact:** Aya Katz, chief editor (poetry, novels, political); Nets Katz, science editor (scientific, academic). Estab. 1985. Books: POD. Distributes through Amazon, Bowker, Barnes Noble. Publishes paperback originals. Guidelines for SASE.

HOW TO CONTACT Does not accept unsolicited mss. Query with SASE. Reading period open from January 2 to March 15. Accepts queries by e-mail. Include estimated word count.

TERMS Pays 10 author's copies. Responds in 1 month to queries; 3 months to mss.

TIPS "Read our books. Read the *Inverted-A Horn*. We are different. We do not follow industry trends."

ITALICA PRESS

99 Wall St., Suite 650, New York NY 10005. (917)371-0563. **E-mail:** inquiries@italicapress.com. **Website:** www.italicapress.com. Estab. 1985. "Italica Press publishes English translations of modern Italian fiction and medieval and Renaissance nonfiction." Publishes hardcover and trade paperback originals. Book catalog and guidelines online.

NEEDS "First-time translators published. We would like to see translations of Italian writers who are well-known in Italy who are not yet translated for an American audience."

HOW TO CONTACT Query via e-mail.

TERMS Pays 7-15% royalty on wholesale price; author's copies. Responds in 1 month to queries; 4 months to mss.

TIPS "We are interested in considering a wide variety of medieval and Renaissance topics (not historical fiction), and for modern works we are only interested in translations from Italian fiction by well-known Italian authors. Only fiction that has been previously published in Italian. A brief e-mail saves a lot of time. 90% of proposals we receive are completely off base—but we are very interested in things that are right on target."

JEWISH LIGHTS PUBLISHING

LongHill Partners, Inc., Sunset Farm Offices, Rt. 4, P.O. Box 237, Woodstock VT 05091. (802)457-4000. **Fax:** (802)457-4004. **E-mail:** submissions@turner-publishing.com. **Website:** www.jewishlights.com. Estab. 1990. "Jewish Lights publishes books for people of all faiths and all backgrounds who yearn for books that attract, engage, educate and spiritually inspire. Our authors are at the forefront of spiritual thought and deal with the quest for the self and for meaning in life by drawing on the Jewish wisdom tradition.

Our books cover topics including history, spirituality, life cycle, children, self-help, recovery, theology and philosophy. We do not publish autobiography, biography, fiction, haggadot, poetry or cookbooks. At this point we plan to do only two books for children annually, and one will be for younger children (ages 4-10)." Publishes hardcover and trade paperback originals, trade paperback reprints. Book catalog and guidelines online.

NEEDS Picture books, young readers, middle readers: spirituality. "We are not interested in anything other than spirituality."

HOW TO CONTACT Query with outline/synopsis and 2 sample chapters; submit complete ms for picture books.

TERMS Pays authors royalty of 10% of revenue received; 15% royalty for subsequent printings. Responds in 6 months to queries.

TIPS "We publish books for all faiths and backgrounds that also reflect the Jewish wisdom tradition. Explain in your cover letter why you're submitting your project to us in particular. Make sure you know what we publish."

JOURNEYFORTH

Imprint of BJU Press, 1430 Wade Hampton Blvd., Greenville SC 29609. **E-mail:** journeyforth@bjupress. com. **Website:** www.journeyforth.com. **Contact:** Nancy Lohr. Estab. 1974. JourneyForth Books publishes fiction and nonfiction that reflects a worldview based solidly on the Bible and that encourages Christians to live out their faith. JourneyForth is an imprint of BJU Press. Publishes paperback originals. Book catalog available free in SASE or online. Guidelines online—https://www.bjupress.com/books/freelance.php

NEEDS "Our fiction is for the youth market only and is based on a Christian worldview. Our catalog ranges from first chapter books to YA titles." Does not want picture books, short stories, romance, speculative fiction, poetry, or fiction for the adult market.

HOW TO CONTACT Submit proposal with synopsis, market analysis of competing works, and first 5 chapters. Will look at simultaneous submissions, but not multiple submissions.

TERMS Pays royalty. Pays advance. Responds in 1 month to queries; 3 months to mss.

TIPS "Study the publisher's guidelines. We are looking for engaging text and a biblical worldview. Will

read hard copy submissions, but prefer e-mail queries/proposals/submissions."

JUST US BOOKS, INC.

P.O. Box 5306, East Orange NJ 07019. (973)672-7701. **Fax:** (973)677-7570. **Website:** justusbooks.com. Estab. 1988. "Just Us Books is the nation's premier independent publisher of Black-interest books for young people. Our books focus primarily on the culture, history, and contemporary experiences of African Americans." Guidelines online.

IMPRINTS Marimba Books.

NEEDS Just Us Books is currently accepting queries for chapter books and middle reader titles only. "We are not considering any other works at this time."

TIPS "We are looking for realistic, contemporary characters; stories and interesting plots that introduce both conflict and resolution. We will consider various themes and story-lines, but before an author submits a query we urge them to become familiar with our books."

KAEDEN BOOKS

P.O. Box 16190, Rocky River OH 44116. **Website:** www.kaeden.com. Estab. 1986. "Children's book publisher for education K-3 market: reading stories, fiction/nonfiction, chapter books, science, and social studies materials." Publishes paperback originals. Book catalog and guidelines online.

NEEDS "We are looking for stories with humor, surprise endings, and interesting characters that will appeal to children in kindergarten through third grade." No sentence fragments. Please do not submit: queries, ms summaries, or résumés, mss that stereotype or demean individuals or groups, mss that present violence as acceptable behavior.

HOW TO CONTACT Submit complete ms. "Can be as minimal as 25 words for the earliest reader or as much as 2,000 words for the fluent reader. Beginning chapter books are welcome. Our readers are in kindergarten to third grade, so vocabulary and sentence structure must be appropriate for young readers. Make sure that all language used in the story is of an appropriate level for the students to read independently. Sentences should be complete and grammatically correct."

TERMS Work purchased outright from authors. Pays royalties to previous authors. Responds only if interested.

TIPS "Our audience ranges from kindergarten-third grade school children. We are an educational publisher. We are particularly interested in humorous stories with surprise endings and beginning chapter books."

④ KANE/MILLER BOOK PUBLISHERS

4901 Morena Blvd., Suite 213, San Diego CA 92117. (858)456-0540. **Fax:** (858)456-9641. **E-mail:** submissions@kanemiller.com. **Website:** www.kanemiller.com. **Contact:** Editorial Department. Estab. 1985. "Kane/Miller Book Publishers is a division of EDC Publishing, specializing in award-winning children's books from around the world. Our books bring the children of the world closer to each other, sharing stories and ideas, while exploring cultural differences and similarities. Although we continue to look for books from other countries, we are now actively seeking works that convey cultures and communities within the US. We are committed to expanding our picture book list and are interested in great stories with engaging characters, especially those with particularly American subjects. When writing about the experiences of a particular community, we will express a preference for stories written from a first-hand experience." Submission guidelines on site.

NEEDS Picture Books: concept, contemporary, health, humor, multicultural. Young Readers: contemporary, multicultural, suspense. Middle Readers: contemporary, humor, multicultural, suspense. "At this time, we are not considering holiday stories (in any age range) or self-published works."

TERMS If interested, responds in 90 days to queries.

TIPS "We like to think that a child reading a Kane/Miller book will see parallels between his own life and what might be the unfamiliar setting and characters of the story. And that by seeing how a character who is somehow or in some way dissimilar—an outsider—finds a way to fit comfortably into a culture or community or situation while maintaining a healthy sense of self and self-dignity, she might be empowered to do the same."

⑤ KAR-BEN PUBLISHING

Lerner Publishing Group, 241 North First St., Minneapolis MN 55401. **E-mail:** editorial@karben.com. **Website:** www.karben.com. **Contact:** Joni Sussman. Estab. 1974. Kar-Ben publishes exclusively Jewish-themed children's books. Publishes hardcover, trade paperback, board books and e-books. Book catalog online; free upon request. Guidelines online.

NEEDS "We seek picture book mss 800-1,000 words on Jewish-themed topics for children." Picture books:

Adventure, concept, folktales, history, humor, multicultural, religion, special needs; must be on a Jewish theme. Average word length: picture books–1,000. Recently published titles: *The Count's Hanukkah Countdown*, *Sammy Spider's First Book of Jewish Holidays*, *The Cats of Ben Yehuda Street*.

HOW TO CONTACT Submit full ms. Picture books only.

TERMS Pays 5% royalty on NET sale. Pays $500-2,500 advance. Only responds if interested.

TIPS "Authors: Do a literature search to make sure similar title doesn't already exist. Illustrators: Look at our online catalog for a sense of what we like—bright colors and lively composition."

KAYA PRESS

c/o USC ASE, 3620 S. Vermont Ave. KAP 462, Los Angeles CA 90089. (213) 740-2285. **E-mail:** info@kaya.com. **E-mail:** acquisitions@kaya.com. **Website:** www.kaya.com. Estab. 1994. Kaya is an independent literary press dedicated to the publication of innovative literature from the Asian Pacific diaspora. Publishes hardcover originals and trade paperback originals and reprints. Book catalog available free. Guidelines online.

HOW TO CONTACT Submit 2-4 sample chapters, clips, SASE.

TERMS Responds in 6 months to mss.

TIPS "Audience is people interested in a high standard of literature and who are interested in breaking down easy approaches to multicultural literature."

KELSEY STREET PRESS

Poetry by Women, 2824 Kelsey St., Berkeley CA 94705. **Website:** www.kelseyst.com. Estab. 1974. "A Berkeley, California press publishing collaborations between women poets and artists. Many of the press's collaborations focus on a central theme or conceit, like the sprawl and spectacle of New York in *Arcade* by Erica Hunt and Alison Saar." Hardcover and trade paperback originals and electronic originals.

KENSINGTON PUBLISHING CORP.

119 W. 40th St., New York NY 10018. (212)407-1500. **Fax:** (212)935-0699. **E-mail:** jscognamiglio@kensingtonbooks.com. **Website:** www.kensingtonbooks.com. **Contact:** John Scognamiglio, editorial director, fiction (historical romance, Regency romance, women's contemporary fiction, gay and lesbian fiction and nonfiction, mysteries, suspense, mainstream fiction); Michaela Hamilton, editor-in-chief, Citadel Press (thrillers, mysteries, mainstream fiction, true crime,

current events); Selena James, executive editor, Dafina Books (African American fiction and nonfiction, inspirational, young adult, romance); Peter Senftleben, assistant editor (mainstream fiction, women's contemporary fiction, gay and lesbian fiction, mysteries, suspense, thrillers, romantic suspense, paranormal romance). Estab. 1975. "Kensington focuses on profitable niches and uses aggressive marketing techniques to support its books." Publishes hardcover and trade paperback originals, mass market paperback originals and reprints. Book catalog and guidelines online.

NEEDS No science fiction/fantasy, experimental fiction, business texts or children's titles.

HOW TO CONTACT Query.

TERMS Pays 6-15% royalty on retail price. Makes outright purchase. Pays $2,000 and up advance. Responds in 1 month to queries and proposals; 4 months to mss.

TIPS "Agented submissions only, except for submissions to romance lines. For those lines, query with SASE or submit proposal package including 3 sample chapters, synopsis."

KIDS CAN PRESS

25 Dockside Dr., Toronto ON M5A 0B5, Canada. (416)479-7000. **Fax:** (416)960-5437. **Website:** www.kidscanpress.com. **Contact:** Corus Quay, acquisitions. Estab. 1973.

Kids Can Press is currently accepting unsolicited mss from Canadian adult authors only.

NEEDS Picture books, young readers: concepts. "We do not accept young adult fiction or fantasy novels for any age." Adventure, animal, contemporary, folktales, history, humor, multicultural, nature/environment, special needs, sports, suspense/mystery. Average word length: picture books 1,000-2,000; young readers 750-1,500; middle readers 10,000-15,000; young adults over 15,000.

HOW TO CONTACT Submit outline/synopsis and 2-3 sample chapters. For picture books submit complete ms.

TERMS Responds in 6 months only if interested.

DENIS KITCHEN PUBLISHING CO., LLC

P.O. Box 2250, Amherst MA 01004. (413)259-1627. **Fax:** (413)259-1812. **E-mail:** help@deniskitchen.com. **Website:** www.deniskitchen.com. **Contact:** Denis Kitchen, publisher. Publishes hardcover and trade paperback originals and reprints.

This publisher strongly discourages e-mail submissions.

NEEDS "We do not want pure fiction. We seek cartoonists or writer/illustrator teams who can tell compelling stories with a combination of words and pictures." No pure fiction (meaning text only).

HOW TO CONTACT Query with SASE. Submit sample illustrations/comic pages. Submit complete ms.

TERMS Pays 6-10% royalty on retail price. Occasionally makes deals based on percentage of wholesale if idea and/or bulk of work is done in-house. Pays $1-5,000 advance. Responds in 4-6 weeks.

TIPS "Our audience is readers who embrace the graphic novel revolution, who appreciate historical comic strips and books, and those who follow popular and alternative culture. We like to discover new talent. The artist who has a day job but a great idea is encouraged to contact us. The pop culture historian who has a new take on an important figure is likewise encouraged. We have few preconceived notions about manuscripts or ideas, though we are decidedly selective. Historically, we have published many first-time authors and artists, some of whom developed into award-winning creators with substantial followings. Artists or illustrators who do not have confidence in their writing should send us self-promotional postcards (our favorite way of spotting new talent)."

KNOPF

Imprint of Penguin Random House LLC. 1745 Broadway, New York NY 10019. **Fax:** (212)940-7390. **Website:** knopfdoubleday.com/imprint/knopf. Estab. 1915. Publishes hardcover and paperback originals.

NEEDS Publishes book-length fiction of literary merit by known or unknown writers. Length: 40,000-150,000 words.

HOW TO CONTACT Usually only accepts mss submitted by agents. However, writers may submit sample 25-50 pages with SASE.

TERMS Royalties vary. Offers advance. Responds in 2-6 months to queries.

KREGEL PUBLICATIONS

2450 Oak Industrial Dr. NE, Grand Rapids MI 49505. (616)451-4775. **Fax:** (616)451-9330. **E-mail:** kregelbooks@kregel.com. **Website:** www.kregelpublications.com. Estab. 1949. "Our mission as an evangelical Christian publisher is to provide—with integrity and excellence—trusted, Biblically based resources that challenge and encourage individuals in their Christian lives. Works in theology and Biblical studies should reflect the historic, orthodox Protestant tradition." Publishes hardcover and trade paperback originals and reprints. Guidelines online.

IMPRINTS Kregel Publications, Kregel Academic, Kregel Childrens, Kregel Classics.

NEEDS Fiction should be geared toward the evangelical Christian market. Wants books with fast-paced, contemporary storylines presenting a strong Christian message in an engaging, entertaining style.

HOW TO CONTACT Finds works through The Writer's Edge and Christian Manuscript Submissions ms screening services.

TERMS Pays royalty on wholesale price. Pays negotiable advance. Responds in 2-3 months.

TIPS "Our audience consists of conservative, evangelical Christians, including pastors and ministry students."

🖊 LANTANA PUBLISHING

London , United Kingdom. **E-mail:** info@lantanapublishing.com. **E-mail:** submissions@lantanapublishing.com. **Website:** www.lantanapublishing.com. Estab. 2014. Lantana Publishing is a young, independent publishing house producing inclusive picture books for children. "Our mission is to publish outstanding writing for young readers by giving new and aspiring BAME authors and illustrators a platform to publish in the UK and by working with much-loved authors and illustrators from around the world. Lantana's award-winning titles have so far received high praise, described as 'dazzling', 'delectable', 'enchanting' and 'exquisite' by bloggers and reviewers. They have been nominated for a Kate Greenaway Medal (three times), received starred Kirkus reviews (three times), been shortlisted for the Teach Early Years Awards, the North Somerset Teachers' Book Awards, and the Sheffield Children's Books Awards, and won the Children's Africana Best Book Award. Lantana's founder, Alice Curry, is the recipient of the 2017 Kim Scott Walwyn Prize for women in publishing." Guidelines online.

NEEDS "We primarily publish picture books for 4-8 year-olds with text no longer than 500 words (and we prefer 200-400 words). We love writing that is contemporary and fun. We particularly like stories with modern-day settings in the UK or around the world, especially if they feature BAME families, and stories that lend themselves to great illustration."

TERMS Pays royalty. Pays advance. Responds in 6 weeks.

LEAPFROG PRESS

Box 505, Fredonia NY 14063. **E-mail:** leapfrog@leapfrogpress.com. **Website:** www.leapfrogpress.com.

Contact: Nathan Carter, acquisitions editor; Lisa Graziano, publicity. Estab. 1996. Guidelines online. Submissions through Submittable only.

NEEDS "We search for beautifully written literary titles and market them aggressively to national trade and library accounts. We also sell film, translation, foreign, and book club rights." Publishes paperback originals. Books: acid-free paper; sewn binding. Print runs range from about 1,000 to 4,000. Distributes titles through Consortium Book Sales and Distribution, St. Paul, MN. Promotes titles through all national review media, bookstore readings, author tours, website, radio shows, chain store promotions, advertisements, book fairs. "Genres often blur; look for good writing. We are most interested in works that are quirky, that fall outside of any known genre, and of course well written and finely crafted. We are most interested in literary fiction." Genre romance, fantasy, and Western. Religious. Occult. Picture books.

HOW TO CONTACT Query with several chapters or stories through Submittable.

TERMS Pays 10% royalty on net receipts. Average advance: negotiable. Response time varies. One week to several months.

TIPS "We like anything that is superbly written and genuinely original. We like the idiosyncratic and the peculiar. We rarely publish nonfiction. Send only your best work, and send only completed work that is ready. That means the completed ms has already been through extensive editing and is ready to be judged. We consider submissions from both previously published and unpublished writers, and both agented and unagented submissions. We do not accept submissions through postal mail and cannot return physical letters or manuscripts."

LEE & LOW BOOKS

95 Madison Ave., #1205, New York NY 10016. (212)779-4400. **E-mail:** general@leeandlow.com. **Website:** www.leeandlow.com. Estab. 1991. "Our goals are to meet a growing need for books that address children of color, and to present literature that all children can identify with. We only consider multicultural children's books. Sponsors a yearly New Voices Award for first-time picture book authors of color. Contest rules online at website or for SASE." Publishes hardcover originals and trade paperback reprints. Book catalog available online. Guidelines available online or by written request with SASE.

NEEDS Picture books, young readers: anthology, contemporary, history, multicultural, poetry. Picture book, middle reader: contemporary, history, multicultural, nature/environment, poetry, sports. Average word length: picture books—1,000-1,500 words. "We do not publish folklore or animal stories."

HOW TO CONTACT Submit complete ms.

TERMS Pays net royalty. Pays authors advances against royalty. Pays illustrators advance against royalty. Photographers paid advance against royalty. Responds in 6 months to mss if interested.

TIPS "Check our website to see the kinds of books we publish. Do not send mss that don't fit our mission."

⊘ LES FIGUES PRESS

P.O. Box 7736, Los Angeles CA 90007. **E-mail:** info@lesfigues.com. **Website:** www.lesfigues.com. **Contact:** Teresa Carmody, director. Estab. 2005. Les Figues Press is an independent, nonprofit publisher of poetry, prose, visual art, conceptual writing, and translation. With amission is to create aesthetic conversations between readers, writers, and artists, Les Figues Press favors projects which push the boundaries of genre, form, and general acceptability. "We are currently closed to all submissions."

LETHE PRESS

118 Heritage Ave., Maple Shade NJ 8052. (609)410-7391. **Website:** www.lethepressbooks.com. Estab. 2001. "Welcomes submissions from authors of any sexual or gender identity." Guidelines online.

NEEDS "Named after the Greek river of memory and forgetfulness (and pronounced Lee-Thee), Lethe Press is a small press devoted to ideas that are often neglected or forgotten by mainstream, profit-oriented publishers." Distributes/promotes titles. Lethe Books are distributed by Ingram Publications and Bookazine, and are available at all major bookstores, as well as the major online retailers.

HOW TO CONTACT Query via e-mail.

ARTHUR A. LEVINE BOOKS

Scholastic, Inc., 557 Broadway, New York NY 10012. (212)343-4436. **Fax:** (212)343-6143. **Website:** www.arthuralevinebooks.com. Estab. 1996. Publishes hardcover, paperback, and e-book editions. Picture Books: Query letter and full text of pb. Novels: Send Query letter, first 2 chapters and synopsis. Other: Query letter, 10-page sample and synopsis/proposal.

NEEDS "Arthur A. Levine is looking for distinctive literature, for children and young adults, for whatever's extraordinary." Averages 18-20 total titles/year.

HOW TO CONTACT Query.

TERMS Responds in 1 month to queries; 5 months to mss.

LILLENAS PUBLISHING CO.

Imprint of Lillenas Drama Resources, P.O. Box 419527, Kansas City MO 64141. (800)877-0700. **Fax:** (816)412-8390. **E-mail:** drama@lillenas.com. **Website:** www.lillenasdrama.com. "We purchase only original, previously unpublished materials. Also, we require that all scripts be performed at least once before it is submitted for consideration. We do not accept scripts that are sent via fax or e-mail. Direct all manuscripts to the Drama Resources Editor." Publishes mass market paperback and electronic originals. Guidelines online.

NEEDS "Looking for sketch and monologue collections for all ages – adults, children and youth. For these collections, we request 12 - 15 scripts to be submitted at one time. Unique treatments of spiritual themes, relevant issues and biblical messages are of interest. Contemporary full-length and one-act plays that have conflict, characterization, and a spiritual context that is neither a sermon nor an apologetic for youth and adults. We also need wholesome so-called secular full-length scripts for dinner theatres and schools." No musicals.

TERMS Pays royalty on net price. Makes outright purchase. Responds in 4-6 months to material.

TIPS "We never receive too many manuscripts."

ⒶⓄ LITTLE, BROWN AND CO. ADULT TRADE BOOKS

1290 Avenue of the Americas, New York NY 10104. **Website:** www.littlebrown.com. Estab. 1837. "The general editorial philosophy for all divisions continues to be broad and flexible, with high quality and the promise of commercial success as always the first considerations." Publishes hardcover originals and paperback originals and reprints. Guidelines online.

HOW TO CONTACT *Agented submissions only.*

TERMS Pays royalty. Offer advance.

ⒶⓄ LITTLE, BROWN BOOKS FOR YOUNG READERS

Hachette Book Group USA, 1290 Avenue of the Americas, New York NY 10104. (212)364-1100. **Fax:** (212)364-0925. **Website:** littlebrown.com. Estab. 1837.

"Little, Brown and Co. Children's Publishing publishes all formats including board books, picture books, middle grade fiction, and nonfiction YA titles. We are looking for strong writing and presentation, but no predetermined topics." *Only interested in solicited agented material.*

NEEDS Average word length: picture books—1,000; young readers—6,000; middle readers—15,000-50,000; young adults—50,000 and up.

HOW TO CONTACT *Agented submissions only.*

TERMS Pays authors royalties based on retail price. Pays illustrators and photographers by the project or royalty based on retail price. Sends galleys to authors; dummies to illustrators. Pays negotiable advance. Responds in 1-2 months.

TIPS "In order to break into the field, authors and illustrators should research their competition and try to come up with something outstandingly different."

LITTLE PICKLE PRESS

3701 Sacramento St., #494, San Francisco CA 94118. (415)340-3344. **Fax:** (415)366-1520. **E-mail:** info@march4thinc.com. **Website:** www.littlepicklepress.com. Little Pickle Press is a 21st Century publisher dedicated to helping parents and educators cultivate conscious, responsible little people by stimulating explorations of the meaningful topics of their generation through a variety of media, technologies, and techniques. Submit through submission link on site. Includes YA imprint Relish Media. Uses Author.me for submissions for Little Pickle and YA imprint Relish Media. Guidelines available on site.

TIPS "We have lots of manuscripts to consider, so it will take up to 8 weeks before we get back to you."

Ⓐⓞ LITTLE SIMON

Imprint of Simon & Schuster, 1230 Avenue of the Americas, New York NY 10020. (212)698-1295. **Fax:** (212)698-2794. **Website:** www.simonandschuster.com/kids. "Our goal is to provide fresh material in an innovative format for preschool to age 8. Our books are often, if not exclusively, format driven." Publishes novelty and branded books only.

NEEDS Novelty books include many things that do not fit in the traditional hardcover or paperback format, such as pop-up, board book, scratch and sniff, glow in the dark, lift the flap, etc. Children's/juvenile. No picture books. Large part of the list is holiday-themed.

HOW TO CONTACT *Currently not accepting unsolicited mss.*

TERMS Offers advance and royalties.

Ⓖⓞ LITTLE TIGER PRESS

1 The Coda Centre, 189 Munster Rd., London SW6 6AW, United Kingdom. (44)(20)7385-6333. **Website:** www.littletigerpress.com. Little Tiger Press is a dynamic and busy independent publisher. Also includes imprints: Caterpillar Books and Stripes Publishing.

NEEDS Picture books: animal, concept, contemporary, humor. Average word length: picture books—750 words or less.

HOW TO CONTACT "We are no longer accepting unsolicited manuscripts. We will however, continue to accept illustration submissions and samples."

LIVINGSTON PRESS

University of West Alabama, 100 N. Washington St., Station 22, University of West Alabama, Livingston AL 35470. **Fax:** (205)652-3717. **E-mail:** jwt@uwa.edu. **Website:** https://livingstonpress.uwa.edu. **Contact:** Joe Taylor, director. Estab. 1974. "Livingston Press, as do all literary presses, looks for authorial excellence in style. Currently emphasizing novels." Reading year around. We do recommend simultaneous submissions, since we can publish only eight or so titles per year. Publishes hardcover and trade paperback originals, plus Kindle. Book catalog online. Guidelines online.

IMPRINTS Swallow's Tale Press.

NEEDS "We are interested in form and, of course, style." No genre or children's fiction, please.

TERMS Pays 80 contributor's copies, after sales of 1,000, standard royalty. Responds in 4 months to queries; 6-12 months to mss.

TIPS "Our readers are interested in literature, often quirky literature that emphasizes form and style. Please visit our website for current needs."

LOOSE ID

P.O. Box 806, San Francisco CA 94104. **E-mail:** submissions@loose-id.com. **Website:** www.loose-id.com. **Contact:** Treva Harte, editor-in-chief. Estab. 2004. "*Loose Id* is love unleashed. We're taking romance to the edge." Publishes e-books and some print books. Distributes/promotes titles. "The company promotes itself through web and print advertising wherever readers of erotic romance may be found, creating a recognizable brand identity as the place to let your id run free and the people who unleash your fantasies. It is currently pursuing licensing agreements for foreign translations, and has a print program of 2 to 5 titles per month." Guidelines online.

○ "Loose Id is actively acquiring stories from both aspiring and established authors."

NEEDS Wants nontraditional erotic romance stories, including gay, lesbian, heroes and heroines, multiculturalism, cross-genre, fantasy, and science fiction, straight contemporary or historical romances.

HOW TO CONTACT Query with outline/synopsis and 3 sample chapters. Accepts queries by e-mail. Include estimated word count, list of publishing credits, and why your submission is love unleashed. "Before submitting a query or proposal, please read the guidelines on our website. Please don't hesitate to contact us by e-mail for any information you don't see there."

TERMS Pays e-book royalties of 40%. Responds to queries in 1 month.

MAGE PUBLISHERS, INC.

1780 Crossroads Dr., Odenton MD 21113. (202)342-1642. **Fax:** (202)342-9269. **E-mail:** as@mage.com. **Website:** www.mage.com. Estab. 1985. Mage publishes books relating to Persian/Iranian culture. Publishes hardcover originals and reprints, trade paperback originals. Book catalog available free. Guidelines online.

NEEDS Must relate to Persian/Iranian culture.

HOW TO CONTACT Submit outline, SASE. Query via mail or e-mail.

TERMS Pays royalty. Responds in 1 month to queries.

TIPS "Audience is the Iranian-American community in America and Americans interested in Persian culture."

MAGINATION PRESS

750 First St. NE, Washington DC 20002. (202)336-5618. **Fax:** (202)336-5624. **E-mail:** magination@apa.org. **Website:** www.apa.org. Estab. 1988. Magination Press is an imprint of the American Psychological Association. "We publish books dealing with the psycho/therapeutic resolution of children's problems and psychological issues with a strong self-help component." Submit complete ms. Full guidelines available on site. Materials returned only with SASE.

NEEDS All levels: psychological and social issues, self-help, health, parenting concerns and, special needs. Picture books, middle school readers.

TERMS Responds to queries in 1-2 months; mss in 2-6 months.

MANDALA PUBLISHING

Mandala Publishing and Earth Aware Editions, 800 A St., San Rafael CA 94901. **E-mail:** info@mandalapublishing.com. **Website:** www.mandalaeartheditions.com. Estab. 1989. "In the traditions of the East, wisdom, truth, and beauty go hand in- hand. This is reflected in the great arts, music, yoga, and philosophy of India. Mandala Publishing strives to bring to its readers authentic and accessible renderings of thousands of years of wisdom and philosophy from this unique culture-timeless treasures that are our inspirations and guides. At Mandala, we believe that the arts, health, ecology, and spirituality of the great Vedic traditions are as relevant today as they were in sacred India thousands of years ago. As a distinguished publisher in the world of Vedic literature, lifestyle, and interests today, Mandala strives to provide accessible and meaningful works for the modern reader." Publishes hardcover, trade paperback, and electronic originals. Book catalog online.

HOW TO CONTACT Query with SASE.

TERMS Pays 3-15% royalty on retail price. Responds in 6 months.

◯ MANOR HOUSE PUBLISHING, INC.

452 Cottingham Crescent, Ancaster ON L9G 3V6, Canada. (905)648-2193. **E-mail:** mbdavie@manorhouse.biz. **Website:** www.manor-house-publishing.com. **Contact:** Mike Davie, president (novels and nonfiction). Estab. 1998. Manor House is currently looking for new fully edited, ready-to-run titles to complete our spring-fall release lineup. This is a rare opportunity for authors, including self-published, to have existing or ready titles picked up by Manor House and made available to retailers throughout the world, while our network of rights agents provide more potential revenue streams via foreign language rights sales. We are currently looking for titles that are ready or nearly ready for publishing to be released this season. Such titles should be written by Canadian citizens residing in Canada and should be profitable or with strong market sales potential to allow full cost recovery and profit for publisher and author. Of primary interest are business and self-help titles along with other nonfiction, including new age. We will also consider non-Canadian writers provided the manuscript meets literary standards and profitability is a certainty. Publishes hardcover, trade paperback, and mass market paperback originals (and reprints if they meet specific criteria - best to inquire with publisher). Book catalog online. Guidelines available.

NEEDS Stories should mainly be by Canadian authors residing in Canada, have Canadian settings and characters should be Canadian, but content should have universal appeal to wide audience. In some cases, we will consider publishing non-Canadian fiction authors - provided they demonstrate publishing their book will be profitable for author and publisher. We will also consider non-Canadian writers provided the manuscript meets literary standards and profitability is a certainty.

HOW TO CONTACT Query via e-mail. Submit proposal package, clips, bio, 3 sample chapters. Submit complete ms.

TERMS Pays 10% royalty on retail price. Queries and mss to be sent by e-mail only. "We will respond in 30 days if interested-if not, there is no response. Please do not follow up unless asked to do so."

TIPS "Our audience includes everyone-the general public/mass audience. Self-edit your work first, make sure it is well written and well edited with strong Canadian content and/or content of universal appeal (preferably with a Canadian connection of some kind)." We will also consider non-Canadian writers provided the manuscript meets literary standards and profitability is a certainty.

MARINER BOOKS

222 Berkeley St., Boston MA 2116. (617)351-5000. **Website:** www.hmco.com. Estab. 1997.

Mariner Books' *Interpreter of Maladies*, by debut author Jhumpa Lahiri, won the 2000 Pulitzer Prize for fiction and *The Caprices*, by Sabina Murray, received the 2003 PEN/Faulkner Award. Mariner Books' *Interpreter of Maladies*, by debut author Jhumpa Lahiri, won the 2000 Pulitzer Prize for fiction and *The Caprices*, by Sabina Murray, received the 2003 PEN/Faulkner Award.

NEEDS Literary, mainstream/contemporary. Recently published Timothy Egan, Donald Hall, Amitav Ghosh, and Edna O'Brien.

HOW TO CONTACT *Agented submissions only.* Responds in 4 months to mss.

TERMS Pays royalty on retail price or makes outright purchase. Average advance: variable.

MARVEL COMICS

135 W. 50th St., 7th Floor, New York NY 10020. **Website:** www.marvel.com. Publishes hardcover originals and reprints, trade paperback reprints, mass market comic book originals, electronic reprints. Guidelines online.

NEEDS Our shared universe needs new heroes and villains; books for younger readers and teens needed.

HOW TO CONTACT Submit inquiry letter, idea submission form (download from website), SASE.

TERMS Pays on a per page work for hire basis or creator-owned which is then contracted. Pays negotiable advance. Responds in 3-5 weeks to queries.

MAVERICK MUSICALS AND PLAYS

18 Almaden Lane, Maroochydore QLD 4558, Australia. Phone/Fax: (61)(7)54791874. **E-mail:** tahlia@maverickmusicals.com. **Website:** www.maverickmusicals.com. **Contact:** Tahlia Wilkins. Estab. 1978. Guidelines online.

NEEDS "Looking for two-act musicals and one- and two-act plays. See website for more details."

MCBOOKS PRESS

ID Booth Building, 520 N. Meadow St., Ithaca NY 14850. (607)272-2114. **E-mail:** mcbooks@mcbooks.com. **E-mail:** alex@mcbooks.com. **Website:** www.mcbooks.com. **Contact:** Alexander G. Skutt, publisher. Estab. 1979. McBooks Press has been publishing books independently for over 30 years in Ithaca, New York. McBooks' extensive list of publications features works of historical fiction—including naval and military fiction in series. We continue to seek excellent historical naval adventures that are suitable for publication in series. In the past, we have also published nonfiction, including books on boxing, food and health, and the Finger Lakes Region of New York State. Publishes trade paperback and hardcover originals and reprints. Guidelines online.

"Currently not accepting submissions or queries for fiction or nonfiction." The only exceptions that we would look at are: 1) well-written nautical historical fiction that could grow into a series 2) great books about the Finger Lakes or adjacent regions of Upstate New York.

NEEDS Publishes Julian Stockwin, John Biggins, Colin Sargent, and Douglas W. Jacobson. Distributes titles through Independent Publishers Group.

TERMS Pays a percentage of cover price for physical books plus a percentage of net income for e-books. Pays advance. Responds in 2 months.

TIPS "We are currently only publishing authors with whom we have a pre-existing relationship. If this policy changes, we will announce the change on our website."

MCCLELLAND & STEWART, LTD.

The Canadian Publishers, 320 Front St. W., Suite 1400, Toronto ON M5V 3B6, Canada. (416)364-4449. **Fax:**

(416)598-7764. **Website:** www.mcclelland.com. Publishes hardcover, trade paperback, and mass market paperback originals and reprints.

NEEDS "We publish work by established authors, as well as the work of new and developing authors."

HOW TO CONTACT Query. *All unsolicited mss* returned unopened.

TERMS Pays 10-15% royalty on retail price (hardcover rates). Pays advance. Responds in 3 months to proposals.

THE MCDONALD & WOODWARD PUBLISHING CO.

695 Tall Oaks Dr., Newark OH 43055. (740)641-2691. **Fax:** (740)641-2692. **E-mail:** mwpubco@mwpubco.com. **Website:** www.mwpubco.com. **Contact:** Jerry N. McDonald, publisher. Estab. 1986. McDonald & Woodward publishes books in natural history, cultural history, and natural resources. Currently emphasizing travel, natural and cultural history, and natural resource conservation. Publishes hardcover and trade paperback originals. Book catalog online. Guidelines free on request; by e-mail.

HOW TO CONTACT Query with SASE.

TERMS Pays 10% royalty. Responds in less than 1 month.

TIPS "Our books are meant for the curious and educated elements of the general population."

⊘ MARGARET K. MCELDERRY BOOKS

Imprint of Simon & Schuster Children's Publishing Division, 1230 Sixth Ave., New York NY 10020. (212)698-7200. **Website:** imprints.simonandschuster.biz/margaret-k-mcelderry-books. Estab. 1971. "Margaret K. McElderry Books publishes hardcover and paperback trade books for children from pre-school age through young adult. This list includes picture books, middle grade and teen fiction, poetry, and fantasy. The style and subject matter of the books we publish is almost unlimited. We do not publish textbooks, coloring and activity books, greeting cards, magazines, pamphlets, or religious publications." Guidelines for #10 SASE.

NEEDS *No unsolicited mss.*

HOW TO CONTACT *Agented submissions only.*

TERMS Pays authors royalty based on retail price. Pays illustrator royalty of by the project. Pays photographers by the project. Original artwork returned

at job's completion. Offers $5,000-8,000 advance for new authors.

TIPS "Read! The children's book field is competitive. See what's been done and what's out there before submitting. We look for high quality: an originality of ideas, clarity and felicity of expression, a well organized plot, and strong character-driven stories. We're looking for strong, original fiction, especially mysteries and middle grade humor. We are always interested in picture books for the youngest age reader. Study our titles."

MELANGE BOOKS, LLC

White Bear Lake MN 55110-5538. **E-mail:** melangebooks@melange-books.com. **E-mail:** submissions@melange-books.com. **Website:** www.melange-books.com. **Contact:** Nancy Schumacher, publisher and acquiring editor for Melange and Satin Romance; Caroline Andrus, acquiring editor for Fire and Ice for Young Adult.. Estab. 2011. Melange is a royalty-paying company publishing e-books and print books. Publishes trade paperback originals and electronic originals. Send SASE for book catalog. Guidelines online.

IMPRINTS Fire and Ice (young and new adult) www.fireandiceya.com; Satin Romance www.satinromance.com.

NEEDS Submit a clean mss by following guidelines on website.

HOW TO CONTACT Query electronically by clicking on "submissions" on website. Include a synopsis and 4 chapters.

TERMS Authors receive a minimum of 20% royalty on print sales, 40% on electronic book sales. Does not offer an advance. Responds in 1 month on queries; 2 months on proposals; 4-6 months on mss.

MERRIAM PRESS

489 South St., Hoosick Falls NY 12090. **E-mail:** ray@merriam-press.com. **Website:** www.merriam-press.com. **Contact:** Ray Merriam, owner. Estab. 1988. Merriam Press specializes in military history, particularly World War II history. We are also branching out into other genres, including fiction, historical fiction, poetry, children. Provide brief synopsis of ms. Never send any files in body of e-mail. Send manuscript as attachment to email. Publisher will ask for full ms for review. Publisher requires unformatted mss. Mss must be thoroughly edited and error-free. Publishes hardcover and softcover trade paperback original works and reprints. Titles are also made available in e-book editions. Book catalog available in print and

PDF editions. Author guidelines and additional information are available on publisher's website.

NEEDS Especially but not limited to military history.

HOW TO CONTACT Query with SASE or by e-mail first. Do not send ms (in whole or in part) unless requested to do so.

TERMS Pays 10% royalty for printed editions and 50% royalty for e-book editions. Royalty payment is based on the amount paid to the publisher, not the retail or list prices. Does not pay advance. Responds quickly (e-mail preferred) to queries.

TIPS "Our military history books are geared for military historians, collectors, model kit builders, wargamers, veterans, general enthusiasts. We now publish some historical fiction and poetry and will consider well-written books on a variety of non-military topics."

MESSIANIC JEWISH PUBLISHERS

6120 Day Long Ln., Clarksville MD 21029. (410)531-6644. **E-mail:** editor@messianicjewish.net. **Website:** www.messianicjewish.net. Publishes hardcover and trade paperback originals and reprints. Guidelines via e-mail.

NEEDS "We publish very little fiction. Jewish or Biblical themes are a must. Text must demonstrate keen awareness of Jewish culture and thought."

HOW TO CONTACT Query with SASE. Unsolicited mss are not return.

TERMS Pays 7-15% royalty on wholesale price.

⊜ METHUEN PUBLISHING LTD

Editorial Department, 35 Hospital Fields Rd., York YO10 4DZ, United Kingdom. **E-mail:** editorial@metheun.co.uk. **Website:** www.methuen.co.uk. Estab. 1889. Guidelines online.

◐   No unsolicited mss; synopses and ideas welcome. Prefers to be approached via agents or a letter of inquiry. No first novels, cookery books or personal memoirs.

NEEDS No first novels.

HOW TO CONTACT Query with SASE. Submit proposal package, outline, outline/proposal, resume, publishing history, clips, bio, SASE.

TERMS Pays royalty.

TIPS "We recommend that all prospective authors attempt to find an agent before submitting to publishers and we do not encourage unagented submissions."

MICHIGAN STATE UNIVERSITY PRESS

1405 S. Harrison Rd., Suite 25, East Lansing MI 48823. (517)355-9543. **Fax:** (517)432-2611. **E-mail:** msupress@msu.edu. **Website:** msupress.org. **Contact:** Alex Schwartz and Julie Loehr, acquisitions. Estab. 1947. Michigan State University Press has notably represented both scholarly publishing and the mission of Michigan State University with the publication of numerous award-winning books and scholarly journals. In addition, they publish nonfiction that addresses, in a more contemporary way, social concerns, such as diversity and civil rights. They also publish literary fiction and poetry. Publishes hardcover and softcover originals. Book catalog and ms guidelines online.

NEEDS Publishes literary fiction.

HOW TO CONTACT Submit proposal.

TERMS Pays variable royalty.

MILKWEED EDITIONS

1011 Washington Ave. S., Suite 300, Minneapolis MN 55415. (612)332-3192. **Fax:** (612)215-2550. **Website:** www.milkweed.org. Estab. 1979. "Milkweed Editions publishes with the intention of making a humane impact on society, in the belief that literature is a transformative art uniquely able to convey the essential experiences of the human heart and spirit. To that end, Milkweed Editions publishes distinctive voices of literary merit in handsomely designed, visually dynamic books, exploring the ethical, cultural, and esthetic issues that free societies need continually to address." Publishes hardcover, trade paperback, and electronic originals; trade paperback and electronic reprints. Book catalog online. Only accepts submissions during open submission periods. See website for guidelines.

NEEDS Novels for adults and for readers 8-13. High literary quality. For adult readers: literary fiction, nonfiction, poetry, essays. Middle readers: adventure, contemporary, fantasy, multicultural, nature/environment, suspense/mystery. Average length: middle readers—90-200 pages. No romance, mysteries, science fiction.

HOW TO CONTACT "Please submit a query letter with three opening chapters (of a novel) or three representative stories (of a collection). Publishes YR."

TERMS Pays authors variable royalty based on retail price. Offers advance against royalties. Pays varied advance from $500-10,000. Responds in 6 months.

TIPS "We are looking for excellent writing with the intent of making a humane impact on society. Please read submission guidelines before submitting and acquaint yourself with our books in terms of style and quality before submitting. Many factors influence our selection process, so don't get discouraged. Nonfiction is focused on literary writing about the natural world, including living well in urban environments."

MILKWEED FOR YOUNG READERS

Milkweed Editions, Open Book Building, 1011 Washington Ave. S., Suite 300, Minneapolis MN 55415. (612)332-3192. **Fax:** (612)215-2550. **Website:** www.milkweed.org. Estab. 1984. "We are looking first of all for high quality literary writing. We publish books with the intention of making a humane impact on society." Publishes hardcover and trade paperback originals. Book catalog for $1.50. Guidelines online.

HOW TO CONTACT "Milkweed Editions now accepts manuscripts online through our Submission Manager. If you're a first-time submitter, you'll need to fill in a simple form and then follow the instructions for selecting and uploading your manuscript. Please make sure that your manuscript follows the submission guidelines."

TERMS Pays 7% royalty on retail price. Pays variable advance. Responds in 6 months to queries.

⑤ MONDIAL

203 W. 107th St., Suite 6C, New York NY 10025. 212-864-7095. **Fax:** (208)361-2863. **E-mail:** contact@mondialbooks.com. **Website:** www.mondialbooks.com; www.librejo.com. **Contact:** Andrew Moore, editor. Estab. 1996. Mondial publishes fiction and non-fiction in English, Esperanto, and Hebrew: novels, short stories, poetry, textbooks, dictionaries, books about history, linguistics, and psychology, among others. Since 2007, it has been publishing a literary magazine in Esperanto. Publishes hard cover, trade paperback originals and reprints. Guidelines online.

HOW TO CONTACT Query through online submission form.

TERMS Pays 10% royalty on wholesale price. Does not pay advance. Responds to queries in 3 months, only if interested.

◗ MONSOON BOOKS

No.1 Duke of Windsor Suite, Burrough Court, Burrough on the Hill Leicestershire LE14 2QS, United Kingdom. **E-mail:** sales@monsoonbooks.co.uk. **Website:** www.monsoonbooks.co.uk. **Contact:** Philip Tatham, Publisher. Estab. 2002. Monsoon Books is a UK-based trade publisher of English-language fiction and narrative nonfiction relating to Asia. All titles have an Asian, usually a SE Asian, angle. Guidelines online.

HOW TO CONTACT Query with outline/synopsis and submit complete ms with cover letter. Accepts queries by snail mail, fax, and e-mail (submissions@monsoonbooks.com.sg. Please include estimated word count, brief bio, list of publishing credits, and list of three comparative titles. Send hard copy submissions to: Monsoon Books Pte Ltd, 71 Ayer Rajah Crescent #01-01, Mediapolis Phase, Singapore 139951. We are not able to return hard copy manuscripts. We do not encourage hand deliveries. Agented fiction 20%. Responds in 8 weeks to your submissions. If you do not hear from us by then, e-mail us. Accepts simultaneous submissions, submissions on CD or disk. Rarely comments on rejected manuscripts. Monsoon Books regularly works with literary agents from the UK and Australia (such as David Higham Associates in London and Cameron's Management in Sydney) and we are particularly keen to hear from agents with manuscripts set in Southeast or North Asia as well as mss written by authors from this region.

TIPS "Monsoon welcomes unsolicited manuscripts from agented and unagented authors writing books set in Asia, particularly Southeast Asia."

Ⓐ⊘ MOODY PUBLISHERS

Moody Bible Institute, 820 N. LaSalle Blvd., Chicago IL 60610. (800)678-8812. **Fax:** (312)329-4157. **Website:** www.moodypublishers.org. **Contact:** Acquisitions Coordinator. Estab. 1894. "The mission of Moody Publishers is to educate and edify the Christian and to evangelize the non-Christian by ethically publishing conservative, evangelical Christian literature and other media for all ages around the world, and to help provide resources for Moody Bible Institute in its training of future Christian leaders." Publishes hardcover, trade, and mass market paperback originals. Book catalog for 9×12 envelope and 4 first-class stamps. Guidelines online.

HOW TO CONTACT *Agented submissions only.*

TERMS Royalty varies. Responds in 2-3 months to queries.

TIPS "In our fiction list, we're looking for Christian storytellers rather than teachers trying to present a message. Your motivation should be to delight the reader. Using your skills to create beautiful works is glorifying to God."

NBM PUBLISHING

160 Broadway, Suite 700, East Bldg., New York NY 10038. **E-mail:** nbmgn@nbmpub.com. **Website:** nbmpub.com. **Contact:** Terry Nantier, editor. Estab. 1976. Publishes graphic novels for an audience of YA/adults. Types of books include fiction, mystery, biographies and social parodies. Catalog online.

TERMS Advance negotiable. Responds to e-mail 1-2 days; mail 1 week.

⚫⚫ ⊘ THOMAS NELSON, INC.

HarperCollins Christian Publishing, Box 141000, Nashville TN 37214. (615)889-9000. **Website:** www.thomasnelson.com. Thomas Nelson publishes Christian lifestyle nonfiction and fiction, and general nonfiction. Publishes hardcover and paperback orginals.

NEEDS Publishes authors of commercial fiction who write for adults from a Christian perspective.

HOW TO CONTACT *Does not accept unsolicited mss.* No phone queries.

TERMS Rates negotiated for each project. Pays advance.

⊘ TOMMY NELSON

Imprint of Thomas Nelson, Inc., P.O. Box 141000, Nashville TN 37214-1000. (615)889-9000. **Fax:** (615)902-2219. **Website:** www.tommynelson.com. "Tommy Nelson publishes children's Christian nonfiction and fiction for boys and girls up to age 14. We honor God and serve people through books, videos, software and Bibles for children that improve the lives of our customers." Publishes hardcover and trade paperback originals. Guidelines online.

NEEDS No stereotypical characters.

HOW TO CONTACT *Does not accept unsolicited mss.*

TIPS "Know the Christian Booksellers Association market. Check out the Christian bookstores to see what sells and what is needed."

NEW DIRECTIONS

80 Eighth Ave., New York NY 10011. **Fax:** (212)255-0231. **E-mail:** editorial@ndbooks.com. **Website:** www.ndbooks.com. **Contact:** Editorial Assistant. Estab. 1936. "Currently, New Directions focuses primarily on fiction in translation, avant garde American fiction, and experimental poetry by American and foreign authors. If your work does not fall into one of those categories, you would probably do best to submit your work elsewhere." Hardcover and trade paperback originals. Book catalog and guidelines online.

NEEDS No juvenile or young adult, occult or paranormal, genre fiction (formula romances, sci-fi or westerns), arts & crafts, and inspirational poetry.

HOW TO CONTACT Brief query only.

TERMS Responds in 3-4 months to queries.

TIPS "Our books serve the academic community."

◌ NEWEST PUBLISHERS LTD.

201, 8540-109 St., Edmonton AB T6G 1E6, Canada. (780)432-9427. **Fax:** (780)433-3179. **E-mail:** info@newestpress.com. **E-mail:** submissions@newestpress.com. **Website:** www.newestpress.com. Estab. 1977. NeWest publishes Western Canadian fiction, nonfiction, poetry, and drama. Publishes trade paperback originals. Book catalog for 9×12 SASE. Guidelines online.

HOW TO CONTACT Submit complete ms.

TERMS Pays 10% royalty. Responds in 6-8 months to queries.

⊘ NEW HOPE PUBLISHERS

Iron Stream Media, 100 Missionary Ridge Dr., Birmingham AL 35242. (888)811-9934. **E-mail:** info@newhopepublishers.com. **E-mail:** proposals@newhopepublishers.com. **Website:** www.newhopepublishers.com. **Contact:** Ramona Richards, associate publisher. Iron Stream Media/New Hope Publishers is a Christian media company providing resources to advance the Gospel of Jesus Christ, making disciples as we go. Catalog online. Guidelines online.

IMPRINTS Ascender Books, New Hope Kids.

HOW TO CONTACT Please follow our online submission guidelines.

TERMS Royalty-based payment. Pays occasional advance; established authors only. Responds in 3-6 months.

NEW ISSUES POETRY & PROSE

Western Michigan University, 1903 W. Michigan Ave., Kalamazoo MI 49008-5463. (269)387-8185. **E-mail:** new-issues@wmich.edu. **Website:** newissuespress.com. **Contact:** Managing Editor. Estab. 1996. Guidelines online.

HOW TO CONTACT Only considers submissions to book contests.

◗ NEW LIBRI PRESS

4907 Meridian Ave. N., Seattle WA 98103. **E-mail:** query@newlibri.com. **Website:** www.newlibri.com. **Contact:** Michael Muller, editor; Stanislav Fritz, editor. Estab. 2011. "We only accept e-mail submissions, not USPS. We have recently changed our publishing model to a HYBRID model. This means a shared risk model on expenses. Do not submit if you are uncomfortable with this model. We still curate submissions in this model, which means we still reject more than we accept. We are very small and eclectic. We tend to like slightly 'quirky' stuff. While we have only published a bit of non-fiction, we are open to more, but (as a reminder) we are a HYBRID publisher and thus there are no advances of any kind and the author shares the financial risks." Publishes trade paperback, electronic original, electronic reprints. Catalog online. Guidelines online. Electronic submissions only. "We are a hybrid publisher. Don't submit if you are not comfortable with that model."

NEEDS "Open to most ideas right now; this will change as we mature as a press. As a new press, we are more open than most and time will probably shape the direction. That said, trite as it is, we want good writing that is fun to read. While we currently are not looking for some sub-genres, if it is well written and a bit off the beaten path, submit to us. We are now a hybrid publisher, which means shared financial risk. Don't submit if you are uncomfortable with that model."

HOW TO CONTACT Submit query, synopsis, and full manuscript (so we don't have to ask for it later if we like it. We will read about 50 pages to start).

TERMS Pays 20-35% royalty on wholesale price. No advance. Responds in 3 months to mss.

TIPS "Our audience is someone who is comfortable reading an e-book, or someone who is tired of the recycled authors of mainstream publishing, but still wants a good, relatively fast, reading experience. The industry is changing, while we accept for the traditional model, we are searching for writers who are interested in sharing the risk and controlling their own destiny. We embrace writers with no agent."

NEW RIVERS PRESS
1104 Seventh Ave. S., Moorhead MN 56563. **Website:** www.newriverspress.com. **Contact:** Nayt Rundquist, managing editor. Estab. 1968. New Rivers Press publishes collections of poetry, novels, nonfiction, translations of contemporary literature, and collections of short fiction and nonfiction. "We continue to publish books regularly by new and emerging writers, but we also welcome the opportunity to read work of every

character and to publish the best literature available nationwide. Each fall through the Many Voices Project competition, we choose 2 books: 1 poetry and 1 prose."

NEEDS Sponsors American Fiction Prize to find best unpublished short stories by American writers.

NIGHTSCAPE PRESS
P.O. Box 1948, Smyrna TN 37167. **E-mail:** info@ nightscapepress.com. **E-mail:** submissions@night-scapepress.com. **Website:** www.nightscapepress. com. Estab. 2012. Nightscape Press is seeking quality book-length words of at least 50,000 words (40,000 for young adult). Guidelines online. Currently closed to submissions. Will announce on site when they reopen to submissions.

NEEDS "We are not interested in erotica or graphic novels."

HOW TO CONTACT Query.

TERMS Pays monthly royalties. Offers advance.

😊 NORTIA PRESS
Santa Ana CA **E-mail:** acquisitions@nortiapress.com. **Website:** www.nortiapress.com. Estab. 2009. Publishes trade paperback and electronic originals.

NEEDS "We focus mainly on nonfiction as well as literary and historical fiction, but are open to other genres. No vampire stories, science fiction, or erotica, please."

HOW TO CONTACT Submit a brief e-mail query. Please include a short bio, approximate word count of book, and expected date of completion (fiction titles should be completed before sending a query, and should contain a sample chapter in the body of the e-mail). All unsolicited snail mail or attachments will be discarded without review.

TERMS Pays negotiable royalties on wholesale price. Responds in 1 month.

TIPS "We specialize in working with experienced authors who seek a more collaborative and fulfilling relationship with their publisher. As such, we are less likely to accept pitches form first-time authors, no matter how good the idea. As with any pitch, please make your e-mail very brief and to the point, so the reader is not forced to skim it. Always include some biographic information. Your life is interesting."

⚠️⊘ W.W. NORTON & COMPANY, INC.
500 Fifth Ave., New York NY 10110. (212)354-5500. **Fax:** (212)869-0856. **Website:** www.wwnorton.com. Estab. 1923. "W. W. Norton & Company, the oldest and largest publishing house owned wholly by its

employees, strives to carry out the imperative of its founder to 'publish books not for a single season, but for the years' in fiction, nonfiction, poetry, college textbooks, cookbooks, art books and professional books. Due to the workload of our editorial staff and the large volume of materials we receive, *Norton is no longer able to accept unsolicited submissions*. If you are seeking publication, we suggest working with a literary agent who will represent you to the house."

❾ NOSY CROW PUBLISHING

The Crow's Nest, 10a Lant St., London SE1 1QR, United Kingdom. (44)(0)207-089-7575. **Fax:** (44)(0)207-089-7576. **E-mail:** hello@nosycrow.com. **E-mail:** submissions@nosycrow.com. **Website:** nosycrow.com. "We publish books for children 0-14. We're looking for 'parent-friendly' books, and we don't publish books with explicit sex, drug use or serious violence, so no edgy YA or edgy cross-over. And whatever New Adult is, we don't do it. We also publish apps for children from 2-7, and may publish apps for older children if the idea feels right." Guidelines online.

NEEDS "As a rule, we don't like books with 'issues' that are in any way overly didactic."

HOW TO CONTACT Prefers submissions by e-mail, but post works if absolutely necessary.

TIPS "Please don't be too disappointed if we reject your work! We're a small company and can only publish a few new books and apps each year, so do try other publishers and agents: publishing is necessarily a hugely subjective business. We wish you luck!"

OCEANVIEW PUBLISHING

595 Bay Isles Rd., Suite 120-G, Longboat Key FL 34228. **E-mail:** mail@oceanviewpub.com. **E-mail:** submissions@oceanviewpub.com. **Website:** www.oceanviewpub.com. Estab. 2006. "Independent publisher of nonfiction and fiction, with primary interest in original mystery, thriller and suspense titles. Accepts new and established writers." Publishes hardcover and electronic originals. Catalog and guidelines online.

NEEDS Accepting adult mss with a primary interest in the mystery, thriller and suspense genres—from new and established writers. No children's or YA literature, poetry, cookbooks, technical manuals or short stories.

HOW TO CONTACT Within body of e-mail only, include author's name and brief bio (Indicate if this is an agent submission), ms title and word count, author's mailing address, phone number and e-mail address. Attached to the e-mail should be the following:

A synopsis of 750 words or fewer. The first 30 pages of the ms. Please note that we accept only Word documents as attachments to the submission e-mail. Do not send query letters or proposals.

TERMS Responds in 3 months on mss.

OHIO UNIVERSITY PRESS

30 Park Place, Suite 101, Athens OH 45701. **Fax:** (740)593-4536. **E-mail:** huard@ohio.edu. **Website:** www.ohioswallow.com. **Contact:** Gillian Berchowitz, director. Estab. 1947. "In addition to scholarly works in African studies, Appalachian studies, US history, and other areas, Ohio University Press publishes a wide range of creative works as part of its Hollis Summers Poetry Prize (yearly deadline in December), its Modern African Writing series, and under its trade imprint, Swallow Press." Publishes hardcover and trade paperback originals and reprints. Catalog online. Guidelines online.

IMPRINTS Swallow Press.

TERMS Sometimes pays advance. Responds in 1-3 months.

TIPS "Rather than trying to hook the editor on your work, let the material be compelling enough and well-presented enough to do it for you."

OMNIDAWN PUBLISHING

2200 Adeline St., Suite 150, Oakland CA 94607. **Website:** www.omnidawn.com. Estab. 1999. Guidelines online.

TIPS "Check our website for latest information."

ONSTAGE PUBLISHING

927 Highland Dr., Madison AL 35758. (256)542-3213. **E-mail:** submissions@onstagepublishing.com. **Website:** www.onstagepublishing.com. **Contact:** Dianne Hamilton, senior editor. Estab. 1999. "At this time, we only produce fiction books for ages 8-18. We have added an e-book only side of the house for mysteries for grades 6-12. See our website for more information. We will not do anthologies of any kind. Query first for nonfiction projects as nonfiction projects must spark our interest. We no longer are accepting written submissions. We want e-mail queries and submissions. For submissions: Put the first 3 chapters in the body of the e-mail. Do not use attachments! We will delete any submission with an attachment without acknowledgment." Suggested ms lengths: Chapter books: 3,000-9,000 words, Middle Grade novels: 10,000-40,000 words, Young adult novels: 40,000-60,000 words. Guidelines online.

NEEDS Middle readers: adventure, contemporary, fantasy, history, nature/environment, science fiction, suspense/mystery. Young adults: adventure, contemporary, fantasy, history, humor, science fiction, suspense/mystery. Average word length: chapter books—4,000-6,000 words; middle readers—5,000 words and up; young adults—25,000 and up. Recently published *Mission: Shanghai* by Jamie Dodson (an adventure for boys ages 12+); *Birmingham, 1933: Alice* (a chapter book for grades 3-5). "We do not produce picture books."

TERMS Pays authors/illustrators/photographers advance plus royalties. Pays advance. Responds in 1-6 months.

TIPS "Study our titles and get a sense of the kind of books we publish, so that you know whether your project is likely to be right for us."

✪ OOLICHAN BOOKS

P.O. Box 2278, Lantzville BC V0B 1M0, Canada. (250)423-6113. **E-mail:** info@oolichan.com. **Website:** www.oolichan.com. Estab. 1974. Publishes hardcover and trade paperback originals and reprints. Book catalog online. Guidelines online.

◔ Only publishes Canadian authors.

NEEDS "We try to publish at least 2 literary fiction titles each year. We receive many more deserving submissions than we are able to publish, so we publish only outstanding work. We try to balance our list between emerging and established writers, and have published many first-time writers who have gone on to win or be shortlisted for major literary awards, both nationally and internationally."

HOW TO CONTACT Submit proposal package, publishing history, clips, bio, cover letter, 3 sample chapters, SASE.

TERMS Pays royalty on retail price. Responds in 1-3 months.

TIPS "Our audience is adult readers who love good books and good literature. Our audience is regional and national, as well as international. Follow our submission guidelines. Check out some of our titles at your local library or bookstore to get an idea of what we publish. Don't send us the only copy of your manuscript. Let us know if your submission is simultaneous, and inform us if it is accepted elsewhere. Above all, keep writing!"

OOLIGAN PRESS

369 Neuberger Hall, 724 SW Harrison St., Portland OR 97201. (503)725-9410. **E-mail:** acquisitions@ooliganpress.pdx.edu. **Website:** ooligan.pdx.edu. **Contact:** Acquisitions Co-Managers. Estab. 2001. "We seek to publish regionally significant works of literary, historical, and social value. We define the Pacific Northwest as Northern California, Oregon, Idaho, Washington, British Columbia, and Alaska. We recognize the importance of diversity, particularly within the publishing industry, and are committed to building a literary community that includes traditionally underrepresented voices; therefore, we are interested in works originating from, or focusing on, marginalized communities of the Pacific Northwest." Publishes trade paperbacks, electronic originals, and reprints. Catalog online. Guidelines online.

NEEDS "We seek to publish regionally significant works of literary, historical, and social value. We define the Pacific Northwest as Northern California, Oregon, Idaho, Washington, British Columbia, and Alaska." We recognize the importance of diversity, particularly within the publishing industry, and are committed to building a literary community that includes traditionally underrepresented voices; therefore, we are interested in works originating from, or focusing on, marginalized communities of the Pacific Northwest. Does not want romance, horror, westerns, incomplete mss.

HOW TO CONTACT Query with SASE. *"At this time we cannot accept science fiction or fantasy submissions."*

TERMS Pays negotiable royalty on retail price. Responds in 3 weeks for queries; 3 months for proposals.

TIPS "Search the blog for tips."

✪◑ ORCA BOOK PUBLISHERS

1016 Balmoral Rd., Victoria BC V8T 1A8, Canada. (800)210-5277. **Fax:** (877)408-1551. **E-mail:** orca@orcabook.com. **Website:** www.orcabook.com. **Contact:** Amy Collins, editor (picture books); Sarah Harvey, editor (young readers); Andrew Wooldridge, editor (juvenile and teen fiction); Bob Tyrrell, publisher (YA, teen); Ruth Linka, associate editor (rapid reads).. Estab. 1984. Only publishes Canadian authors. Publishes hardcover and trade paperback originals, and mass market paperback originals and reprints. Book catalog for 8½x11 SASE. Guidelines online.

NEEDS Picture books: animals, contemporary, history, nature/environment. Middle readers: contemporary, history, fantasy, nature/environment, problem novels, graphic novels. Young adults: adventure, contemporary, hi-lo (Orca Soundings), history, multicultural, nature/environment, problem novels, suspense/mystery, graphic novels. Average word length: picture books—500-1,500; middle readers—20,000-35,000; young adult—25,000-45,000; Orca Soundings—13,000-15,000; Orca Currents—13,000-15,000. No romance, science fiction.

HOW TO CONTACT Query with SASE. Submit proposal package, outline, clips, 2-5 sample chapters, SASE.

TERMS Pays 10% royalty. Responds in 1 month to queries; 2 months to proposals and mss.

TIPS "Our audience is students in grades K-12. Know our books, and know the market."

⊘⊘ ORCHARD BOOKS (US)

557 Broadway, New York NY 10012. **Website:** www.scholastic.com. *Orchard is not accepting unsolicited mss.*

NEEDS Picture books, early readers, and novelty: animal, contemporary, history, humor, multicultural, poetry.

TERMS Most commonly offers an advance against list royalties.

◐◑◕◔ RICHARD C. OWEN PUBLISHERS, INC.

P.O. Box 585, Katonah NY 10536. (914)232-3903; (800)262-0787. **E-mail:** richardowen@rcowen.com. **Website:** www.rcowen.com. **Contact:** Richard Owen, publisher. Estab. 1982. "We publish child-focused books, with inherent instructional value, about characters and situations with which 5, 6, and 7-year-old children can identify—books that can be read for meaning, entertainment, enjoyment and information. We include multicultural stories that present minorities in a positive and natural way. Our stories show the diversity in America." Not interested in lesson plans, or books of activities for literature studies or other content areas. Submit complete ms and cover letter. Book catalog available with SASE. Ms guidelines with SASE or online.

◔ "Due to high volume and long production time, we are currently limiting to nonfiction submissions only."

TERMS Pays authors royalty of 5% based on net price or outright purchase (range: $25-500). Offers no advances. Pays illustrators by the project (range: $100-2,000) or per photo (range: $50-150). Responds to mss in 1 year.

◑ PETER OWEN PUBLISHERS

81 Bridge Rd., London N8 9NP, United Kingdom. (44)(208)350-1775. **Fax:** (44)(208)340-9488. **E-mail:** info@peterowen.com. **Website:** www.peterowen.com. "We are far more interested in proposals for nonfiction than fiction at the moment. No poetry or short stories." Publishes hardcover originals and trade paperback originals and reprints. Book catalog for SASE, SAE with IRC or on website.

NEEDS "No first novels. Authors should be aware that we publish very little new fiction these days."

HOW TO CONTACT Query with synopsis, sample chapters.

TERMS Pays 7½-10% royalty. Pays negotiable advance. Responds in 2 months to queries; 3 months to proposals and mss.

PACIFIC PRESS PUBLISHING ASSOCIATION

Trade Book Division, 1350 N. Kings Rd., Nampa ID 83687. (208)465-2500. **Fax:** (208)465-2531. **Website:** www.pacificpress.com. Estab. 1874. "We publish books that fit Seventh-day Adventist beliefs only. All titles are Christian and religious. For guidance, see www.adventist.org/beliefs/index.html. Our books fit into the categories of this retail site: www.adventistbookcenter.com." Publishes hardcover and trade paperback originals and reprints. Guidelines online.

NEEDS "Pacific Press rarely publishes fiction, but we're interested in developing a line of Seventh-day Adventist fiction in the future. Only proposals accepted; no full manuscripts."

TERMS Pays 8-16% royalty on wholesale price. Responds in 3 months to queries.

TIPS "Our primary audience is members of the Seventh-day Adventist denomination. Almost all are written by Seventh-day Adventists. Books that do well for us relate the Biblical message to practical human concerns and focus more on the experiential rather than theoretical aspects of Christianity. We are assigning more titles, using less unsolicited material—although we still publish manuscripts from freelance submissions and proposals."

PAGESPRING PUBLISHING

P.O. Box 2113, Columbus OH 43221. **E-mail:** sales@pagespringpublishing.com. **E-mail:** submissions@pagespringpublishing.com. **Website:** www.pagespringpublishing.com. **Contact:** Lucky Marble Books Editor or Cup of Tea Books Editor. Estab. 2012. PageSpring Publishing publishes women's fiction under the Cup of Tea Books imprint and YA/middle grade titles under the Lucky Marble Books imprint. Visit the PageSpring Publishing website for submission details. Publishes trade paperback and electronic originals. Catalog online. Guidelines online.

IMPRINTS Cup of Tea Books, Lucky Marble Books.

NEEDS Cup of Tea Books publishes women's fiction. Lucky Marble Books specializes in middle grade and young adult fiction.

HOW TO CONTACT Send submissions for both Cup of Tea Books and Lucky Marble Books to submissions@pagespringpublishing.com. Send a query, synopsis, and the first 30 pages of the manuscript in the body of the email. please. NO attachments.

TERMS Pays royalty on wholesale price. Endeavors to respond to queries within 3 months.

TIPS Cup of Tea Books would love to see more cozy mysteries and humor. Lucky Marble Books is looking for humor and engaging contemporary stories for middle grade and young adult readers.

PAGESPRING PUBLISHING

PageSpring Publishing, P.O. Box 21133, Columbus OH 43221. **E-mail:** submissions@pagespringpublishing.com. **Website:** www.pagespringpublishing.com. Estab. 2012. PageSpring Publishing is a small independent publisher with two imprints: Cup of Tea Books and Lucky Marble Books. Cup of Tea Books publishes women's fiction, with particular emphasis on mystery and humor. Lucky Marble Books publishes young adult and middle grade fiction. "We are looking for engaging characters and well-crafted plots that keep our readers turning the page. We accept e-mail queries only; see our website for details." Publishes trade paperback and electronic originals. Guidelines online.

IMPRINTS Cup of Tea Books and Lucky Marble Books.

NEEDS Cup of Tea Books publishes women's fiction. Lucky Marble Books publishes middle grade and young adult novels. No children's picture books.

HOW TO CONTACT Submit proposal package via e-mail only. Include synopsis and 30 sample pages.

TERMS Pays royalty. Responds in 3 months.

TIPS "Cup of Tea Books is particularly interested in cozy mystery novels. Lucky Marble Books is looking for funny, age-appropriate tales for middle grade and young adult readers."

✪ PAJAMA PRESS

181 Carlaw Ave., Suite 207, Toronto ON M4M 2S1, Canada. 4164662222. **E-mail:** annfeatherstone@pajamapress.ca. **Website:** pajamapress.ca. **Contact:** Ann Featherstone,

senior editor. Estab. 2011. "We publish picture books—both for the very young and for school-aged readers, as well as novels for middle grade readers and contemporary or historical fiction for young adults aged 12+. Our nonfiction titles typically contain a strong narrative element. Pajama Press is also looking for mss from authors of diverse backgrounds. Stories about immigrants are of special interest." Guidelines online.

NEEDS vampire novels; romance (except as part of a literary novel); fiction with overt political or religious messages

TERMS Pays advance. Responds in 6 weeks.

ⓐ ⊘ PANTHEON BOOKS

Penguin Random House, 1745 Broadway, New York NY 10019. **Website:** www.pantheonbooks.com. Estab. 1942. Publishes hardcover and trade paperback originals and trade paperback reprints.

○ Pantheon Books publishes both Western and non-Western authors of literary fiction and important nonfiction. "We only accept mss submitted by an agent."

HOW TO CONTACT *Does not accept unsolicited mss. Agented submissions only.*

PANTS ON FIRE PRESS

2062 Harbor Cove Way, Winter Garden FL 34787. (863)546-0760. **E-mail:** submission@pantsonfirepress.com. **Website:** www.pantsonfirepress.com. **Contact:** Becca Goldman, senior editor; Emily Gerety, editor. Estab. 2012. Pants On Fire Press is an award-winning book publisher of picture, middle-grade, young adult, and adult books. Publishes hardcover originals and reprints, trade paperback originals and reprints, and electronic originals and reprints. Catalog online. Guidelines online.

○ Pants On Fire Press is an award-winning boutique book publisher of middle-grade, young adult and fictional books for adults. We publish in both print and e-book format. We love big story ideas and meaty characters. We are always on the lookout for the following subjects: Action, Adventure, Christian, Detective, Drama, Dystopian, Fantasy, Historical Fiction, Horror, Humor, Jewish, Love, Mystery, Paranormal, Romance, Science Fiction, Supernatural, Suspense and Thriller stories.

NEEDS Publishes big story ideas with high concepts, new worlds, and meaty characters for children, teens, and discerning adults.

HOW TO CONTACT Submit a proposal package including a synopsis, 3 sample chapters, and a query letter via e-mail.

TERMS Pays 10-50% royalties on wholesale price. Responds in 3 months.

PAPERCUTZ

160 Broadway, Suite 700E, New York NY 10038. (646)559-4681. **Fax:** (212)643-1545. **E-mail:** papercutz@papercutz.com. **Website:** www.papercutz.com. Estab. 2004. Publisher of graphic novels for kids and teens. Publishes major licenses and author created comics.

IMPRINTS SuperGenius, Charmz.

NEEDS "Independent publisher of graphic novels including popular existing properties aimed at the teen and tween market."

TERMS Pays advance. Responds in 2-4 weeks.

TIPS "Be familiar with our titles—that's the best way to know what we're interested in publishing. If you are somehow attached to a successful tween or teen property and would like to adapt it into a graphic novel, we may be interested. We also take submissions for new series preferably that have already a following online."

PARADISE CAY PUBLICATIONS

P.O. Box 29, Arcata CA 95518-0029. (800)736-4509. **Fax:** (707)822-9163. **Website:** www.paracay.com. "Paradise Cay Publications, Inc. is a small independent publisher specializing in nautical books, videos, and art prints. Our primary interest is in manuscripts that deal with the instructional and technical aspects of ocean sailing. We also publish and will consider fiction if it has a strong nautical theme." Publishes hardcover and trade paperback originals and reprints. Book catalog and ms guidelines free on request or online.

IMPRINTS Pardey Books.

NEEDS All fiction must have a nautical theme.

HOW TO CONTACT Query with SASE. Submit proposal package, clips, 2-3 sample chapters.

TERMS Pays 10-15% royalty on wholesale price. Makes outright purchase of $1,000-10,000. Does not normally pay advances to first-time or little-known authors. Responds in 1 month to queries/proposals; 2 months to mss.

TIPS "Audience is recreational sailors. Call Matt Morehouse (publisher)."

⊘ PAUL DRY BOOKS

1700 Sansom St., Suite 700, Philadelphia PA 19103. (215)231-9939. **Fax:** (215)231-9942. **E-mail:** editor@pauldrybooks.com. **E-mail:** pdry@pauldrybooks.com. **Website:** pauldrybooks.com. "We publish fiction, both novels and short stories, and nonfiction, biography, memoirs, history, and essays, covering subjects from Homer to Chekhov, bird watching to jazz music, New York City to shogunate Japan." Hardcover and trade paperback originals, trade paperback reprints. Book catalog online.

HOW TO CONTACT "We do not accept unsolicited manuscripts."

TIPS "Our aim is to publish lively books 'to awaken, delight, and educate'—to spark conversation. We publish fiction and nonfiction, and essays covering subjects from Homer to Chekhov, bird watching to jazz music, New York City to shogunate Japan."

PAULINE BOOKS & MEDIA

50 St. Paul's Ave., Boston MA 02130. (617)522-8911. **Fax:** (617)541-9805. **E-mail:** design@paulinemedia.com; editorial@paulinemedia.com. **Website:** www.pauline.org. Estab. 1932. "Submissions are evaluated on adherence to Gospel values, harmony with the Catholic faith tradition, relevance of topic, and quality of writing." For board books and picture books, the entire manuscript should be submitted. For easy-to-read, young readers, and middle reader books and teen books, please send a cover letter accompanied by a synopsis and two sample chapters. "Electronic submissions are encouraged. We make every effort to respond to unsolicited submissions within 2 months." Publishes trade paperback originals and reprints. Book catalog online. Guidelines online.

NEEDS Children's and teen fiction only. "We are now accepting submissions for easy-to-read and middle reader chapter, and teen well documented historical fiction. We would also consider well-written fantasy, fairy tales, myths, science fiction, mysteries, or romance if approached from a Catholic perspective and consistent with church teaching. Please see our writer's guidelines."

HOW TO CONTACT "Submit proposal package, including synopsis, 2 sample chapters, and cover letter; complete ms."

TERMS Varies by project, but generally are royalties with advance. Flat fees sometimes considered for smaller works. Responds in 2 months.

TIPS "Manuscripts may or may not be explicitly catechetical, but we seek those that reflect a positive worldview, good moral values, awareness and appreciation of diversity, and respect for all people. All material must be relevant to the lives of readers and must conform to Catholic teaching and practice."

PAYCOCK PRESS

3819 N. 13th St., Arlington VA 22201. (703)525-9296. **E-mail:** rchrdpeabody9@gmail.com. **E-mail:** gargoyle@gargoylemagazine.com. **Website:** www.gargoylemagazine.com. **Contact:** Richard Peabody. Estab. 1976. "Too academic for the underground, too outlaw for the academic world. We tend to be edgy and look for ultra-literary work." Publishes paperback originals. Books: POD printing. Average print order: 500. Averages 1 total title/year. Member CLMP. Distributes through Amazon and website.

HOW TO CONTACT Accepts unsolicited mss. Accepts queries by e-mail. Include brief bio. Send SASE for return of ms or send a disposable ms and SASE for reply only.

TERMS Responds to queries in 1 month; mss in 4 months.

TIPS "Check out our website. Two of our favorite writers are Paul Bowles and Jeanette Winterson."

PEACHTREE PUBLISHING COMPANY INC.

Peachtree Publishing Company Inc., 1700 Chattahoochee Ave., Atlanta GA 30318. (404)876-8761. **Fax:** (404)875-2578. **E-mail:** hello@peachtree-online.com. **Website:** www.peachtree-online.com. **Contact:** Helen Harriss, submissions editor. "We publish a broad range of subjects and perspectives, with emphasis on innovative plots and strong writing." Publishes hardcover and trade paperback originals. Book catalog for 6 first-class stamps. Guidelines online.

NEEDS Looking for very well-written middle grade and young adult novels. No adult fiction. No collections of poetry or short stories; no romance or science fiction.

HOW TO CONTACT Submit complete ms with SASE.

TERMS Pays royalty on retail price. Responds in 6 months and mss.

PEACHTREE PUBLISHING COMPANY INC.

1700 Chattahoochee Ave., Atlanta GA 30318. (404)876-8761. **Fax:** (404)875-2578. **E-mail:** hello@peachtree-online.com. **Website:** www.peachtree-online.com. Estab. 1977.

NEEDS Picture books, young readers: adventure, animal, concept, history, nature/environment. Middle readers: adventure, animal, history, nature/environment, sports. Young adults: fiction, mystery, adventure. Does not want to see science fiction, romance.

HOW TO CONTACT Submit complete manuscript by postal mail only.

TERMS Responds in 6-9 months.

⊙∅ PEDLAR PRESS

113 Bond St., St. John's NL A16 1T6, Canada. (709)738-6702. **E-mail:** feralgrl@interlog.com. **Website:** www.pedlarpress.com. **Contact:** Beth Follett, owner/editor. Estab. 1996. A consistently award-winning independent Canadian literary publishing house, based in St John's NL, Pedlar Press was begun, and continues, with the following house vision: to acquire works of exceptional literary quality that also break silences regarding widespread failures of social and political systems: to make books with serious intellectual and emotional content, in other words, that are also works of art. So much injustice cries out for attention, so much suffering, so many affronts to human dignity need to be met with strong literary force. Pedlar combines high aesthetic standards with a praxis of action; the press means to foster humane social and political ends. It has been possible, over the twenty-two years of Pedlar's existence, to combine an editorial vision that seeks out both works that are strong in literary quality and also distinctive, often avant-garde, and socially engaged. With everyone working together— author, publisher, editor, copyeditor and designer—the aim is to produce literary works of integrity that will make a pronounced difference in the lives of Pedlar's readers. Catalog online.

NEEDS Experimental, feminist, gay/lesbian, literary, short story collections. Canadian writers only.

HOW TO CONTACT Query with SASE, sample chapter(s), synopsis.

TERMS Pays 10% royalty on retail price. Average advance: $200-400.

TIPS "I select manuscripts according to my taste, which fluctuates. Be familiar with some if not most of Pedlar's recent titles."

PELICAN PUBLISHING COMPANY

1000 Burmaster St., Gretna LA 70053. (504)368-1175. **Fax:** (504)368-1195. **E-mail:** editorial@pelicanpub.com. **Website:** www.pelicanpub.com. Estab. 1926. "We believe ideas have consequences. One of the consequences is that they lead to a best-selling book. We publish books to improve and uplift the reader. Currently emphasizing business and history titles." Publishes 20 young readers/year; 1 middle reader/year. "Our children's books (illustrated and otherwise) include history, biography, holiday, and regional. Pelican's mission is to publish books of quality and permanence that enrich the lives of those who read them." Publishes hardcover, trade paperback and mass market paperback originals and reprints. Book catalog and ms guidelines online.

NEEDS We publish no adult fiction. Young readers: history, holiday, science, multicultural and regional. Middle readers: Louisiana History. Multicultural needs include stories about African-Americans, Irish-Americans, Jews, Asian-Americans, and Hispanics. Does not want animal stories, general Christmas stories, "day at school" or "accept yourself" stories. Maximum word length: young readers—1,100; middle readers—40,000. No young adult, romance, science fiction, fantasy, gothic, mystery, erotica, confession, horror, sex, or violence. Also no psychological novels.

HOW TO CONTACT Submit outline, clips, 2 sample chapters, SASE. Full guidelines on website.

TERMS Pays authors in royalties; buys ms outright "rarely." Illustrators paid by "various arrangements." Advance considered. Responds in 1 month to queries; 3 months to mss. Requires exclusive submission.

TIPS "We do extremely well with cookbooks, popular histories, and business. We will continue to build in these areas. The writer must have a clear sense of the market and knowledge of the competition. A query letter should describe the project briefly, give the author's writing and professional credentials, and promotional ideas."

PENGUIN GROUP: SOUTH AFRICA

P.O. Box 9, Parklands 2121, South Africa. (27)(11)327-3550. **Fax:** (27)(11)327-3660. **E-mail:** fiction@penguinrandomhouse.co.za. **E-mail:** nonfiction@penguinrandomhouse.co.za. **Website:** www.penguinbooks.co.za. Seeks adult fiction (literary and mass market titles) and adult nonfiction (travel, sports, politics, current affairs, business). No children's, young adult, poetry, or short stories.

HOW TO CONTACT Submit intro letter, 3 sample chapters.

TERMS Pays royalty.

PENGUIN RANDOM HOUSE, LLC

Division of Bertelsmann Book Group, 1745 Broadway, New York NY 10019. (212)782-9000. **Website:** www.penguinrandomhouse.com. Estab. 1925. Penguin Random House LLC is the world's largest English-language general trade book publisher. *Agented submissions only. No unsolicited mss.*

IMPRINTS Crown Publishing Group; Knopf Doubleday Publishing Group; Random House Publishing Group; Random House Children's Books; RH Digital Publishing Group; RH International.

THE PERMANENT PRESS

Second Chance Press, Attn: Judith Shepard, 4170 Noyac Rd., Sag Harbor NY 11963. (631)725-1101. **E-mail:** judith@thepermanentpress.com; shepard@thepermanentpress.com. **Website:** www.thepermanentpress.com. **Contact:** Judith and Martin Shepard, acquisitions/co-publishers. Estab. 1978. Mid-size, independent publisher of literary fiction. "We keep titles in print and are active in selling subsidiary rights." Average print order: 1,000-2,500. Averages 16 total titles. Accepts unsolicited mss. Pays 10-15% royalty on wholesale price. Offers $1,000 advance. *Will not accept simultaneous submissions.* Publishes hardcover originals. Catalog available.

NEEDS Promotes titles through reviews. Literary, mainstream/contemporary, mystery. Especially looking for high-line literary fiction, "artful, original and arresting." Accepts any fiction category as long as it is a "well-written, original full-length novel."

TERMS Pays 10-15% royalty on wholesale price. Offers $1,000 advance. Responds in weeks or months.

TIPS "We are looking for good books—be they 10th novels or first ones, it makes little difference. The fiction is more important than the track record. Send us the first 25 pages; it's impossible to judge something that begins on page 302. Also, no outlines—let the writing present itself."

PERSEA BOOKS

277 Broadway, Suite 708, New York NY 10007. (212)260-9256. **Fax:** (212)267-3165. **E-mail:** info@perseabooks.com. **Website:** www.perseabooks.com. Estab. 1975. The aim of Persea is to publish works that endure by meeting high standards of literary merit and relevance. "We have often taken on important books other publishers have overlooked, or have made significant discoveries and rediscoveries, whether of a single work or writer's entire oeuvre. Our books cover a wide range of themes, styles, and genres. We have published poetry, fiction, essays, memoir, biography, titles of Jewish and Middle Eastern interest, women's studies, American Indian folklore, and revived classics, as well as a notable selection of works in translation." Guidelines online.

HOW TO CONTACT Queries should include a cover letter, author background and publication history, a detailed synopsis of the proposed work, and a sample chapter. Please indicate if the work is simultaneously submitted.

TERMS Responds in 8 weeks to proposals; 10 weeks to mss.

PHILOMEL BOOKS

Imprint of Penguin Group (USA), Inc., 375 Hudson St., New York NY 10014. (212)414-3610. **Website:** www.penguin.com. **Contact:** Michael Green, president/publisher. Estab. 1980. "We look for beautifully written, engaging manuscripts for children and young adults." Publishes hardcover originals.

HOW TO CONTACT *No unsolicited mss.*

TERMS Pays authors in royalties. Average advance payment "varies." Illustrators paid by advance and in royalties. Pays negotiable advance.

PIANO PRESS

P.O. Box 85, Del Mar CA 92014. (619)884-1401. **Fax:** (858)755-1104. **E-mail:** pianopress@pianopress.com. **Website:** www.pianopress.com. **Contact:** Elizabeth C. Axford, editor. Estab. 1984. "We publish music-related books, either fiction or nonfiction, music-related coloring books, songbooks, sheet music, CDs, and music-related poetry." Book catalog online.

NEEDS Picture books, young readers, middle readers, young adults: folktales, multicultural, poetry, music. Average word length: picture books—1,500-2,000.

TERMS Pays authors, illustrators, and photographers royalties based on the retail price. Responds if interested.

TIPS "We are looking for music-related material only for the juvenile market. Please do not send non-music-related materials. Query by e-mail first before submitting anything."

PIATKUS BOOKS

Little, Brown Book Group, Carmelite House, 50 Victoria Embankment, London EC4Y 0DZ, United Kingdom. (020)3122-7000. **Fax:** (020)3122-7000. **E-mail:** info@littlebrown.co.uk. **Website:** piatkus.co.uk. Estab. 1979. Publishes hardcover originals, paperback originals, and paperback reprints. Guidelines online.

NEEDS Romance fiction, women's fiction, bookclub fiction.

HOW TO CONTACT *Agented submissions only.*

PICADOR USA

MacMillan, 175 Fifth Ave., New York NY 10010. (212)674-5151. **Website:** us.macmillan.com/picador. Estab. 1994. Picador publishes high-quality literary fiction and nonfiction. "We are open to a broad range of subjects, well written by authoritative authors." Publishes hardcover and trade paperback originals and reprints. Does not accept unsolicited mss. *Agented submissions only.*

TERMS Pays 7-15% on royalty. Advance varies.

PIÑATA BOOKS

Imprint of Arte Publico Press, University of Houston, 4902 Gulf Fwy., Bldg. 19, Room 100, Houston TX 77204-2004. (713)743-2845. **Fax:** (713)743-3080. **E-mail:** submapp@uh.edu. **Website:** www.artepublicopress.com. Estab. 1994. "Piñata Books is dedicated to the publication of children's and young adult literature focusing on U.S. Hispanic culture by U.S. Hispanic authors. Arte Publico's mission is the publication, promotion and dissemination of Latino literature for a variety of national and regional audiences, from early childhood to adult, through the complete gamut of delivery systems, including personal performance as well as print and electronic media." Publishes hardcover and trade paperback originals. Book catalog and guidelines online.

HOW TO CONTACT Submissions made through online submission form.

TERMS Pays 10% royalty on wholesale price. Pays $1,000-3,000 advance. Responds in 2-3 months to queries; 4-6 months to mss.

TIPS "Include cover letter with submission explaining why your manuscript is unique and important, why we should publish it, who will buy it, etc."

PINEAPPLE PRESS, INC.

P.O. Box 3889, Sarasota FL 34230. (941)706-2507. **Fax:** (800)746-3275. **Website:** www.pineapplepress.com. **Contact:** June Cussen, executive editor. Estab. 1982. "We are seeking quality nonfiction on diverse topics for the library and book trade markets. Our mission is to publish good books about Florida." Publishes hardcover and trade paperback originals. Book catalog for 9×12 SAE with $1.32 postage. Guidelines online.

NEEDS Picture books, young readers, middle readers, young adults: animal, folktales, history, nature/environment.

HOW TO CONTACT Query or submit outline/synopsis and 3 sample chapters.

TERMS Pays authors royalty of 10-15%. Responds in 2 months.

TIPS "Quality first novels will be published, though we usually only do one or two novels per year and they must be set in Florida. We regard the author/editor relationship as a trusting relationship with communication open both ways. Learn all you can about the publishing process and about how to promote your book once it is published. A query on a novel without a brief sample seems useless."

🌒 PLAYLAB PRESS

P.O. Box 3701, South Brisbane BC 4101, Australia. **E-mail:** info@playlab.org.au. **Website:** www.playlab.org.au. Estab. 1978. Guidelines online.

HOW TO CONTACT Submit 2 copies of ms, cover letter.

TERMS Responds in 3 months to mss.

TIPS "Playlab Press is committed to the publication of quality writing for and about theatre and performance, which is of significance to Australia's cultural life. It values socially just and diverse publication outcomes and aims to promote these outcomes in local, national, and international contexts."

PLEXUS PUBLISHING, INC.

143 Old Marlton Pike, Medford NJ 08055. (609)654-6500. **Fax:** (609)654-4309. **E-mail:** rcolding@plexuspublishing.com. **Website:** www.plexuspublishing.com. **Contact:** Rob Colding, Book Marketing Manager. Estab. 1977. Plexus publishes regional-interest (southern New Jersey and the greater Philadelphia area) fiction and nonfiction including mysteries, field guides, nature, travel and history. Publishes hardcover and paperback originals. Book catalog and book proposal guidelines for 10x13 SASE.

NEEDS Mysteries and literary novels with a strong regional (southern New Jersey) angle.

HOW TO CONTACT Query with SASE.

TERMS Pays $500-1,000 advance. Responds in 3 months to proposals.

⊕⊘ POCKET BOOKS

Simon & Schuster, 1230 Avenue of the Americas, New York NY 10020. (212)698-7000. **Website:** www.simonandschuster.com. Estab. 1939. Pocket Books publishes commercial fiction and genre fiction (WWE, Downtown Press, Star Trek). Publishes paperback originals and reprints, mass market and trade paperbacks. Book catalog available free. Guidelines online.

HOW TO CONTACT *Agented submissions only.*

POCOL PRESS

3911 Prosperity Ave., Fairfax VA 22031. (703)870-9611. **E-mail:** info@pocolpress.com. **Website:** www.pocolpress.com. **Contact:** J. Thomas Hetrick, editor. Estab. 1999. "Pocol Press is dedicated to producing high-quality print books and e-books from first-time, non-agented authors. However, all submissions are welcome. We're dedicated to good storytellers and to the written word, specializing in short fiction and baseball. Several of our books have been used as literary texts at universities and in book group discussions around the nation. Pocol Press does not publish children's books, romance novels, or graphic novels. Our authors are comprised of veteran writers and emerging talents." Publishes trade paperback originals. Book catalog and guidelines online.

NEEDS "We specialize in thematic short fiction collections by a single author, westerns, war stories, and baseball fiction. Expert storytellers welcome."

HOW TO CONTACT Does not accept or return unsolicited mss. Query with SASE through US Mail or submit 1 sample chapter. No email queries accepted.

TERMS Pays 10-12% royalty on wholesale price. Does not pay advance. Responds in 1 month to queries; 2 months to mss.

TIPS "Our audience is aged 18 and over. Pocol Press is unique; we publish good writing and great storytelling. Write the best stories you can. Read them to you friends/peers. Note their reaction. Publishes some of the finest fiction by a small press."

POISONED PEN PRESS

4014 N. Goldwater Blvd., Suite 201, Scottsdale AZ 85251. **E-mail:** submissions@poisonedpenpress.com. **Website:** www.poisonedpenpress.com. **Contact:** Diane DiBiase, Assistant Publisher. Estab. 1997. "Our publishing goal is to offer well-written mystery novels of crime and/or detection where the puzzle and its resolution are the main forces that move the story forward." *Not currently accepting submissions. Check website.* Publishes hardcover and trade paperback originals, and hardcover and trade paperback reprints. Book catalog and guidelines online.

NEEDS Mss should generally be longer than 65,000 words and shorter than 100,000 words. Member Publishers Marketing Associations, Arizona Book Publishers Associations, Publishers Association of West. Distributes through Ingram, Baker & Taylor, Brodart. Does not want novels centered on serial killers, spousal or child abuse, drugs, or extremist groups, although we do not entirely rule such works out.

HOW TO CONTACT Accepts unsolicited mss. Electronic queries only. "Submit clips, first 3 pages. We must receive both the synopsis and ms pages electronically as separate attachments to an e-mail message."

TERMS Pays 9-15% royalty on retail price. Responds in 2-3 months to queries and proposals; 6 months to mss.

TIPS "Audience is adult readers of mystery fiction."

POLIS BOOKS

E-mail: info@polisbooks.com. **E-mail:** submissions@polisbooks.com. **Website:** www.polisbooks.com. Estab. 2013. "Polis Books is an independent publishing company actively seeking new and established authors for our growing list. We are actively acquiring titles in mystery, thriller, suspense, procedural, traditional crime, science fiction, fantasy, horror, supernatural, urban fantasy, romance, erotica, commercial women's fiction, commercial literary fiction, young adult and middle grade books." Guidelines online.

HOW TO CONTACT Query with 3 sample chapters and bio via e-mail.

TERMS Offers advance against royalties. Only responds to submissions if interested

PRESS 53

560 N. Trade St., Suite 103, Winston-Salem NC 27101. (336)770-5353. **E-mail:** editor@press53.com. **Website:** www.press53.com. **Contact:** Kevin Morgan Watson, Publisher and Editor in Chief. Estab. 2005. "Press 53 was founded in October 2005 and quickly earned a reputation for publishing quality short fiction and poetry collections." Poetry and short fiction collections only. Catalog online. Guidelines online.

NEEDS "We publish roughly 4-5 short fiction collections each year by writers who are active and earning recognition through publication and awards, plus the winner of our Press 53 Award for Short Fiction." Collections should be between 100 and 250 pages (give or take). Including a novella is fine, but only one. Does not want novels or novellas.

HOW TO CONTACT Finds mss through contests, referrals, and scouting magazines, journals, and other contests.

TERMS Pays 10% royalty on gross sales. Pays advance only for contest winners.

TIPS "We are looking for writers who are actively involved in the writing community, writers who are submitting their work to journals, magazines and contests, and who are getting published, building readership, and earning a reputation for their work."

Ⓐⵔ PRICE STERN SLOAN, INC.

Penguin Random House LLC, 1745 Broadway, New York NY 10019. (212)782-9000. **Website:** www.penguinrandomhouse.com. Estab. 1963. "Price Stern Sloan publishes quirky mass market novelty series for childrens as well as licensed movie tie-in books." Price Stern Sloan only responds to submissions it's interested in publishing. Book catalog online.

NEEDS Publishes picture books and novelty/board books.

HOW TO CONTACT *Agented submissions only.*

TIPS "Price Stern Sloan publishes unique, fun titles."

PRUFROCK PRESS, INC.

P.O. Box 8813, Waco TX 76714. (800)988-2208. **Fax:** (800)240-0333. **Website:** www.prufrock.com. "Prufrock Press offers award-winning products focused on gifted education, gifted children, advanced learning, and special needs learners, including trade nonfiction (not narrative nonfiction, however) for adults and children/teens. For more than 20 years, Prufrock has supported gifted children and their education and development. The company publishes more than 300 products that enhance the lives of gifted children and the teachers and parents who support them." Accepts simultaneous submissions, but must be notified about it. Book catalog available. Guidelines online.

NEEDS Prufrock Press "offers award-winning products focused on gifted education, gifted children, advanced learning, and special needs learners. For more than 20 years, Prufrock has supported gifted children and their education and development. The company publishes more than 300 products that enhance the lives of gifted children and the teachers and parents who support them." No picture books.

HOW TO CONTACT "Prufrock Press does not consider unsolicited manuscripts."

Ⓐⵔ PUFFIN BOOKS

Imprint of Penguin Random House LLC. 1745 Broadway, New York NY 10019. (212)782-9000. **Website:** www.penguinrandomhouse.com. "Puffin Books publishes high-end trade paperbacks and paperback reprints for preschool children, beginning and middle readers, and young adults." Publishes trade paperback originals and reprints.

HOW TO CONTACT *No unsolicited mss. Agented submissions only.*

TIPS "Our audience ranges from little children 'first books' to young adult (ages 14-16). An original idea has the best luck."

⊘⊘ G.P. PUTNAM'S SONS HARDCOVER

Imprint of Penguin Random House LLC. 1745 Broadway, New York NY 10019. (212)782-9000. **Fax:** (212)366-2664. **Website:** www.penguinrandomhouse. com. Publishes hardcover originals. Request book catalog through mail order department.

HOW TO CONTACT *Agented submissions only.*

TERMS Pays variable royalties on retail price. Pays varies advance.

⊘⊘ RANDOM HOUSE CHILDREN'S BOOKS

1745 Broadway, New York NY 10019. (212)782-9000. **Website:** www.penguinrandomhouse.com. Estab. 1925. "Producing books for preschool children through young adult readers, in all formats from board to activity books to picture books and novels, Random House Children's Books brings together world-famous franchise characters, multimillion-copy series and top-flight, award-winning authors, and illustrators." Submit mss through a literary agent.

IMPRINTS Kids@Random; Golden Books; Princeton Review; Sylvan Learning.

NEEDS "Random House publishes a select list of first chapter books and novels, with an emphasis on fantasy and historical fiction." Chapter books, middle-grade readers, young adult.

HOW TO CONTACT *Does not accept unsolicited mss.*

TIPS "We look for original, unique stories. Do something that hasn't been done before."

⊘⊘⊘ RANDOM HOUSE CHILDREN'S PUBLISHERS UK

20 Vauxhall Bridge Rd., London SW1V 2SA, United Kingdom. **Website:** www.randomhousechildrens. co.uk. *Only interested in agented material.*

IMPRINTS Bantam, Doubleday, Corgi, Johnathan Cape, Hutchinson, Bodley Head, Red Fox, Tamarind Books.

NEEDS Picture books: adventure, animal, anthology, contemporary, fantasy, folktales, humor, multicultural, nature/environment, poetry, suspense/mystery. Young readers: adventure, animal, anthol-ogy, contemporary, fantasy, folktales, humor, multicultural, nature/environment, poetry, sports, suspense/mystery. Middle readers: adventure, animal, anthology, contemporary, fantasy, folktales, humor, multicultural, nature/environment, problem novels, romance, sports, suspense/mystery. Young adults: adventure, contemporary, fantasy, humor, multicultural, nature/environment, problem novels, romance, science fiction, suspense/mystery. Average word length: picture books—800; young readers—1,500-6,000; middle readers—10,000-15,000; young adults—20,000-45,000.

TERMS Pays authors royalty. Offers advances.

TIPS "Although Random House is a big publisher, each imprint only publishes a small number of books each year. Our lists for the next few years are already full. Any book we take on from a previously unpublished author has to be truly exceptional. Manuscripts should be sent to us via literary agents."

⊘⊘ RANDOM HOUSE PUBLISHING GROUP

Division of Penguin Random House, Inc., 1745 Broadway, New York NY 10019. (212)782-9000. **Website:** www.penguinrandomhouse.com. Estab. 1925. Random House is the world's largest English-language general trade book publisher. It includes an array of prestigious imprints that publish some of the foremost writers of our time. Publishes hardcover and paperback trade books.

IMPRINTS Ballantine Books; Bantam; Delacorte; Dell; Del Rey; Modern Library; One World; Presidio Press; Random House Trade Group; Random House Trade Paperbacks; Spectra; Spiegel & Grau; Triumph Books; Villard.

HOW TO CONTACT *Agented submissions only.*

RAZORBILL

Penguin Young Readers Group, 1745 Broadway, New York NY 10019. (212)782-9000. **E-mail:** asanchez@penguinrandomhouse.com; bschrank@penguinrandomhouse.com; jharriton@penguinrandomhouse.com. **Website:** www.razorbillbooks.com. **Contact:** Jessica Almon, executive editor; Casey McIntyre, associate publisher; Deborah Kaplan, vice president and executive art director, Marissa Grossman; assistant editor, Tiffany Liao; associate editor. Estab. 2003. "This division of Penguin Young Readers is looking for the best and the most original of commercial contemporary fiction titles for middle grade and YA readers. A select quantity of nonfiction titles will also be considered."

NEEDS Middle Readers: adventure, contemporary, graphic novels, fantasy, humor, problem novels. Young adults/teens: adventure, contemporary, fantasy, graphic novels, humor, multicultural, suspense, paranormal, science fiction, dystopian, literary, romance. Average word length: middle readers—40,000; young adult—60,000.

HOW TO CONTACT Submit cover letter with up to 30 sample pages.

TERMS Offers advance against royalties. Responds in 1-3 months.

TIPS "New writers will have the best chance of acceptance and publication with original, contemporary material that boasts a distinctive voice and well-articulated world. Check out website to get a better idea of what we're looking for."

⊙ REBELIGHT PUBLISHING, INC.

23-845 Dakota St., Suite 314, Winnipeg Manitoba R2M 5M3, Canada. **Website:** www.rebelight.com. **Contact:** Editor. Estab. 2014. Rebelight Publishing is interested in "crack the spine, blow your mind" manuscripts for middle grade, young adult and new adult novels. *Only considers submissions from Canadian writers.* Publishes paperback and electronic originals. Catalog online or PDF available via e-mail request. Guidelines online.

NEEDS All genres are considered, provided they are for a middle grade, young adult, or new adult audience. "Become familiar with our books. Study our website. Stick within the guidelines. Our tag line is 'crack the spine, blow your mind'—we are looking for well-written, powerful, fresh, fast-paced fiction. Keep us turning the pages. Give us something we just have to spread the word about."

HOW TO CONTACT Submit proposal package, including a synopsis and 3 sample chapters. Read guidelines carefully.

TERMS Pays 12-22% royalties on retail price. Does not offer an advance. Responds in 3 months to queries and mss. Submissions accepted via email only.

TIPS "Review your manuscript for passive voice prior to submitting! (And that means get rid of it.)"

⊙⊘ RED DEER PRESS

195 Allstate Pkwy., Markham ON L3R 4TB, Canada. (905)477-9700. **Fax:** (905)477-9179. **E-mail:** rdp@reddeerpress.com. **Website:** www.reddeerpress.com.

Contact: Richard Dionne, publisher. Estab. 1975. Book catalog for 9 x 12 SASE.

⊙   Red Deer Press is an award-winning publisher of children's and young adult literary titles.

NEEDS Publishes young adult, adult science fiction, fantasy, and paperback originals "focusing on books by, about, or of interest to Canadians." Books: offset paper; offset printing; hardcover/perfect-bound. Average print order: 5,000. First novel print order: 2,500. Distributes titles in Canada and the US, the UK, Australia and New Zealand. Young adult (juvenile and early reader), contemporary. No romance or horror.

TERMS Pays 8-10% royalty.

TIPS "We're very interested in young adult and children's fiction from Canadian writers with a proven track record (either published books or widely published in established magazines or journals) and for manuscripts with regional themes and/or a distinctive voice. We publish Canadian authors exclusively."

RED HEN PRESS

P.O. Box 40820, Pasadena CA 91114. (626)356-4760. **Fax:** (626)356-9974. **Website:** www.redhen.org. **Contact:** Mark E. Cull, publisher/executive director. Estab. 1993. "At this time, the best opportunity to be published by Red Hen is by entering one of our contests. Please find more information in our award submission guidelines." Publishes trade paperback originals. Book catalog available free. Guidelines online.

HOW TO CONTACT Query with synopsis and either 20-30 sample pages or complete ms using online submission manager.

TERMS Responds in 1-2 months.

TIPS "Audience reads poetry, literary fiction, intelligent nonfiction. If you have an agent, we may be too small since we don't pay advances. Write well. Send queries first. Be willing to help promote your own book."

REDLEAF LANE

Redleaf Press, 10 Yorkton Ct., St. Paul MN 55117. (800)423-8309. **E-mail:** info@redleafpress.org. **E-mail:** acquisitions@redleafpress.org. **Website:** www.redleafpress.org. **Contact:** David Heath, director. Redleaf Lane publishes engaging, high-quality picture books for children. "Our books are unique because they take place in group-care settings and reflect developmentally appropriate practices and research-based standards." Guidelines online.

RED SAGE PUBLISHING, INC.

P.O. Box 4844, Seminole FL 33775. (727)391-3847. **E-mail:** submissions@eredsage.com. **Website:** www.eredsage.com. **Contact:** Alexandria Kendall. Estab. 1995. Publishes books of romance fiction, written for the adventurous woman. Guidelines online and all submissions via e-mail.

HOW TO CONTACT Read guidelines.

TERMS Pays author royalty.

◔◑ REVELL

Division of Baker Publishing Group, 6030 E. Fulton Rd., Ada MI 49301. (616)676-9185. **Fax:** (616)676-9573. **Website:** www.bakerbooks.com. Estab. 1870. "Revell publishes to the heart (rather than to the head). For 125 years, Revell has been publishing evangelical books for the personal enrichment and spiritual growth of general Christian readers." Publishes hardcover, trade paperback and mass market paperback originals. Book catalog and ms guidelines online.

◔ *No longer accepts unsolicited mss.*

RIPPLE GROVE PRESS

P.O. Box 910, Shelburne VT 05482. **E-mail:** submit@ripplegrovepress.com. **Website:** www.ripplegrovepress.com. **Contact:** Robert Broder. Estab. 2013. Ripple Grove Press is an independent, family-run children's book publisher. "We started Ripple Grove Press because we have a passion for well-told and beautifully illustrated stories for children. Our mission is to bring together great writers and talented illustrators to make the most wonderful books possible. We hope our books find their way to the cozy spot in your home." Publishes hardcover originals. Catalog online. Guidelines online.

NEEDS We are looking for something unique, that has not been done before; an interesting story that captures a moment with a timeless feel. We are looking for picture driven stories for children ages 2-6. Please do not send early readers, middle grade, or YA mss. No religious stories. Please do not submit your story with page breaks or illustration notes. Do not submit a story with doodles or personal photographs. Do not send your "idea" for a story, send your story in manuscript form.

HOW TO CONTACT Submit completed mss. Accepts submissions by mail and e-mail. E-mail preferred. Please submit a cover letter including a summary of your story, the age range of the story, a brief biography of yourself, and contact information.

TERMS Authors and illustrators receive royalties on net receipts. Pays negotiable advance. "Given the volume of submissions we receive we are no longer able to individually respond to each. Please allow 5 months for us to review your submission. If we are interested in your story, you can expect to hear from us within that time. If you do not hear from us after that time, we are not interested in publishing your story. It's not you, it's us! We receive thousands of submissions and only publish a few books each year. Don't give up!"

TIPS "Please read children's picture books. Please read our books to see what we look for in a story and in art. We create books that capture a moment, so that a child can create their own."

RIVER CITY PUBLISHING

1719 Mulberry St., Montgomery AL 36106. **E-mail:** fnorris@rivercitypublishing.com. **Website:** www.rivercitypublishing.com. **Contact:** Fran Norris, editor. Estab. 1989. Midsize independent publisher. River City publishes literary fiction, regional, short story collections. No poetry, memoir, or children's books. We also consider narrative histories, sociological accounts, and travel; however, only biographies and memoirs from noted persons will be considered. Publishes hardcover and trade paperback originals.

NEEDS No poetry, memoir, or children's books.

HOW TO CONTACT Send appropriate-sized SASE or IRC, "otherwise, the material will be recycled." Also accepts queries by e-mail. "Please include your electronic query letter as inline text and not an as attachment; we do not open unsolicited attachments of any kind." No multiple submissions. Rarely comments on rejected mss.

TERMS Responds within 9 months.

TIPS "Only send your best work after you have received outside opinions. From approximately 1,000 submissions each year, we publish no more than 8 books and few of those come from unsolicited material. Competition is fierce, so follow the guidelines exactly. First-time novelists are also encouraged to send work."

◔◑ RIVERHEAD BOOKS

Penguin Random House LLC. 1745 Broadway, New York NY 10019. **Website:** www.penguinrandomhouse.com.

HOW TO CONTACT *Submit through agent only. No unsolicited mss.*

○⊘ ROARING BROOK PRESS

Macmillan Children's Publishing Group, 175 Fifth Ave., New York NY 10010. (646)307-5151. **Website:** us.macmillan.com. Estab. 2000. Roaring Brook Press is an imprint of MacMillan, a group of companies that includes Henry Holt and Farrar, Straus & Giroux. *Roaring Brook is not accepting unsolicited mss.*

NEEDS Picture books, young readers, middle readers, young adults: adventure, animal, contemporary, fantasy, history, humor, multicultural, nature/environment, poetry, religion, science fiction, sports, suspense/mystery.

HOW TO CONTACT *Not accepting unsolicited mss or queries.*

TERMS Pays authors royalty based on retail price.

TIPS "You should find a reputable agent and have him/her submit your work."

○ RONSDALE PRESS

3350 W. 21st Ave., Vancouver BC V6S 1G7, Canada. (604)738-4688. **Fax:** (604)731-4548. **E-mail:** ronsdale@shaw.ca. **Website:** ronsdalepress.com. **Contact:** Ronald B. Hatch (fiction, poetry, nonfiction, social commentary); Veronica Hatch (YA novels and short stories). Estab. 1988. "Ronsdale Press is a Canadian literary publishing house that publishes 12 books each year, four of which are young adult titles. Of particular interest are books involving children exploring and discovering new aspects of Canadian history or Canadian social issues." Publishes trade paperback originals. Book catalog for #10 SASE. Guidelines online. Please, no first drafts or uneditited drafts.

NEEDS Young adults: Canadian novels. Average word length: middle readers and young adults—50,000 to 70,000. fantasy, science fiction

HOW TO CONTACT Submit complete MS if you are certain it is right for Ronsdale Press.

TERMS Pays 10% royalty on retail price. Responds to queries in 2 weeks; mss in 2 months.

TIPS "Ronsdale Press is a literary publishing house, based in Vancouver, and dedicated to publishing books from across Canada, books that give Canadians new insights into themselves and their country. We aim to publish the best Canadian writers."

SADDLEBACK EDUCATIONAL PUBLISHING

3120-A Pullman St., Costa Mesa CA 92626. (888)735-2225. **E-mail:** contact@sdlback.com. **Website:** www.sdlback.com. Saddleback is always looking for fresh, new talent. "Please note that we primarily publish books for kids ages 12-18."

NEEDS "We look for diversity for our characters and content."

HOW TO CONTACT Mail typed submission along with a query letter describing the work simply and where it fits in with other titles.

SAGUARO BOOKS, LLC

16845 E. Ave. of the Fountains, Ste. 325, Fountain Hills AZ 85268. **E-mail:** mjnickum@saguarobooks.com. **Website:** www.saguarobooks.com. **Contact:** Mary Nickum, CEO. Estab. 2012. Saguaro Books, LLC is a publishing company specializing in middle grade and young adult ficiton by first-time authors. Publishes trade paperback and electronic originals. Catalog online. Guidelines by e-mail.

○   Only first-time authors (previously unpublished) authors will be considered. No Agents, please.

NEEDS Ms should be well-written; signed letter by a professional editor is required. Does not want agented work.

HOW TO CONTACT Query via e-mail before submitting work. Any material sent before requested will be ignored.

TERMS Pays 20% royalties after taxes and publication costs. Does not offer advance. Responds within 3 months only if we're interested.

TIPS "Visit our website before sending us a query. Pay special attention to the For Authors Only page."

○⊘ ST. MARTIN'S PRESS, LLC

Holtzbrinck Publishers, 175 Fifth Ave., New York NY 10010. (212)674-5151. **Fax:** (212)420-9314. **Website:** www.stmartins.com. Estab. 1952. General interest publisher of both fiction and nonfiction. Publishes hardcover, trade paperback and mass market originals.

HOW TO CONTACT *Agented submissions only. No unsolicited mss.*

TERMS Pays royalty. Pays advance.

SAKURA PUBLISHING & TECHNOLOGIES

805 Lindaraxa Park North, Alhambra CA 91801. (330)360-5131. **E-mail:** skpublishing124@gmail.com. **Website:** www.sakura-publishing.com. **Contact:** Derek Vasconi, submissions coordinator. Estab. 2007. Visit our website for query guidelines. Mss that don't follow guidelines will not be considered. Sakura Publishing is a traditional, independent book publishing company that seeks to publish Asian-themed books, particularly Asian-Horror, or anything dealing with

Japan, Japanese culture, and Japanese horror. Publishes trade paperback, mass market paperback and electronic originals and reprints. Currently accepts only the following genres: Asian fiction, Japanese fiction (in English), and Japanese non-fiction (stories about living in Japan in particular are of interest). Please do not send queries for any other genres. Book catalog available for #10 SASE. Guidelines online.

NEEDS Only looking for Asian horror, with preference given to Japanese horror, as well as Japanese fiction, Japanese erotica, Asian erotica. Will consider other types of Asian-centered fiction, but top preference will be on fiction centered in or dealing with Japan or Japanese people living in America.

HOW TO CONTACT Follow guidelines online.

TERMS Royalty payments on paperback, e-book, wholesale, and merchandise Does not pay advance. Responds in 1 week.

TIPS "When submitting, only include a short query letter, the first three chapters of your manuscript included in the body of the email (no attachments will be opened), and your marketing plan. If you do not include these things, your manuscript will not be considered for publication. Also, please note we are looking only for Asian themed horror, Asian themed fiction, Japanese nonfiction and in particular, anything that has to deal with Japan. If you have a Japanese horror manuscript, or you have a nonfiction book about living in Japan or dating in Japan, your manuscript will be given the highest preference and priority."

SALINA BOOKSHELF

1120 W. University Ave., Suite 102, Flagstaff AZ 86001. (877)527-0070. **Fax:** (928)526-0386. **Website:** www.salinabookshelf.com. Publishes trade paperback originals and reprints.

NEEDS Submissions should be in English or Navajo. "All our books relate to the Navajo language and culture."

HOW TO CONTACT Query with SASE.

TERMS Pays varying royalty. Pays advance. Responds in 3 months to queries.

SALVO PRESS

An imprint of Start Publishing, 101 Hudson St., 37th Floor, Suite 3705, Jersey City NJ 07302. **E-mail:** info@salvopress.com. **Website:** www.salvopress.com. Estab. 1998. Salvo Press proudly publishes mysteries, thrillers, and literary books in e-book and audiobook formats. Book catalog and ms guidelines online.

NEEDS "We are a small press specializing in mystery, suspense, espionage and thriller fiction. Our press publishes in trade paperback and most e-book formats."

HOW TO CONTACT Query by e-mail.

TERMS Pays 10% royalty. Responds in 5 minutes to 1 month to queries; 2 months to mss.

SARABANDE BOOKS, INC.

822 E. Market St., Louisville KY 40206. (502)458-4028. **E-mail:** info@sarabandebooks.org. **Website:** www.sarabandebooks.org. **Contact:** Sarah Gorham, editor-in-chief. Estab. 1994. "Sarabande Books was founded to publish poetry, short fiction, and creative nonfiction. We look for works of lasting literary value. Please see our titles to get an idea of our taste. Accepts submissions through contests and open submissions." Publishes trade paperback originals. Book catalog available free. Contest guidelines for #10 SASE or on website.

NEEDS "We consider novels and nonfiction in a wide variety of genres. We do not consider genre fiction such as science fiction, fantasy, or horror. Our target length is 70,000-90,000 words."

HOW TO CONTACT Queries can be sent via e-mail, fax, or regular post.

TERMS Pays royalty. 10% on actual income received. Also pays in author's copies. Pays $500-3,000 advance. Responds within 8 months.

TIPS "Sarabande publishes for a general literary audience. Know your market. Read-and buy-books of literature. Sponsors contests for poetry and fiction. Make sure you're not writing in a vacuum, that you've read and are conscious of contemporary literature. Have someone read your manuscript, checking it for ordering, coherence. Better a lean, consistently strong manuscript than one that is long and uneven. We like a story to have good narrative, and we like to be engaged by language."

SASQUATCH BOOKS

1904 Third Ave., Suite 710, Seattle WA 98101. (206)467-4300. **Fax:** (206)467-4301. **E-mail:** custserv@sasquatchbooks.com. **Website:** www.sasquatchbooks.com. Estab. 1986. "Sasquatch Books publishes books for and from the Pacific Northwest, Alaska, and California is the nation's premier regional press. Sasquatch Books' publishing program is a veritable celebration of regionally written words. Undeterred by political or geographical borders, Sasquatch defines its region as the magnificent area that stretches from the Brooks Range to the Gulf of California and from the Rocky

Mountains to the Pacific Ocean. Our top-selling Best Places® travel guides serve the most popular destinations and locations of the West. We also publish widely in the areas of food and wine, gardening, nature, photography, children's books, and regional history, all facets of the literature of place. With more than 200 books brimming with insider information on the West, we offer an energetic eye on the lifestyle, landscape, and worldview of our region. Considers queries and proposals from authors and agents for new projects that fit into our West Coast regional publishing program. We can evaluate query letters, proposals, and complete mss." Publishes regional hardcover and trade paperback originals. Guidelines online.

NEEDS Young readers: adventure, animal, concept, contemporary, humor, nature/environment.

TERMS Pays royalty on cover price. Pays wide range advance. Responds to queries in 3 months.

TIPS "We sell books through a range of channels in addition to the book trade. Our primary audience consists of active, literate residents of the West Coast."

SCHOLASTIC, INC.

557 Broadway, New York NY 10012. (212)343-6100. **Website:** www.scholastic.com.

○ Scholastic Trade Books is an award-winning publisher of original children's books. Scholastic publishes approximately 600 new hardcover, paperback and novelty books each year. The list includes the phenomenally successful publishing properties Harry Potter, Goosebumps, Captain Underpants, Dog Man, and The Hunger Games; best-selling and award-winning authors and illustrators, including Suzanne Collins, Christopher Paul Curtis, Ann M. Martin, Dav Pilkey, J.K. Rowling, Pam Muñoz Ryan, Lauren Tarshis, Brian Selznick, David Shannon, Mark Teague, and Walter Wick, among others; as well as licensed properties such as Star Wars and Rainbow Magic.

IMPRINTS Arthur A. Levine Books, Cartwheel Books®, Chicken House®, David Fickling Books, Graphix™, Little Shepherd™, Orchard Books®, Point™, PUSH, Scholastic en Español, Scholastic Licensed Publishing, Scholastic Nonfiction, Scholastic Paperbacks, Scholastic Press, Scholastic Reference™, and The Blue Sky Press® are imprints of the Scholastic Trade Books Division. In addition, Scholastic Trade Books included Klutz®, a highly innovative publisher and creator of "books plus" for children.

Ⓐ SCHOLASTIC PRESS

Imprint of Scholastic, Inc., 557 Broadway, New York NY 10012. (212)343-6100. **Fax:** (212)343-4713. **Website:** www.scholastic.com. Scholastic Press publishes fresh, literary picture book fiction and nonfiction; fresh, literary nonseries or nongenre-oriented middle grade and young adult fiction. Currently emphasizing subtly handled treatments of key relationships in children's lives; unusual approaches to commonly dry subjects, such as biography, math, history, or science. De-emphasizing fairy tales (or retellings), board books, genre, or series fiction (mystery, fantasy, etc.). Publishes hardcover originals.

NEEDS Looking for strong picture books, young chapter books, appealing middle grade novels (ages 8-11) and interesting and well-written young adult novels. Wants fresh, exciting picture books and novels—inspiring, new talent.

HOW TO CONTACT *Agented submissions only.*

TERMS Pays royalty on retail price. Pays variable advance. Responds in 3 months to queries; 6-8 months to mss.

TIPS "Read *currently* published children's books. Revise, rewrite, rework and find your own voice, style and subject. We are looking for authors with a strong and unique voice who can tell a great story and have the ability to evoke genuine emotion. Children's publishers are becoming more selective, looking for irresistible talent and fairly broad appeal, yet still very willing to take risks, just to keep the game interesting."

Ⓢ SCRIBE PUBLICATIONS

18-20 Edward St., Brunswick VIC 3056, Australia. (61)(3)9388-8780. **E-mail:** info@scribepub.com.au. **E-mail:** submissions@scribepub.com.au. **Website:** www.scribepublications.com.au. **Contact:** Anna Thwaites. Estab. 1976. Scribe has been operating as a wholly independent trade-publishing house for almost 40 years. What started off in 1976 as a desire on publisher Henry Rosenbloom's part to publish 'serious non-fiction' as a one-man band has turned into a multi-award-winning company with 20 staff members in two locations — Melbourne, Australia and London, England — and a scout in New York. Scribe publishes over 65 nonfiction and fiction titles annually in Australia and about 40 in the United Kingdom. "We currently have acquiring editors working in both our Melbourne and London offices. We spend each day sifting through submissions and manuscripts from around the world, and commissioning and editing local titles, in an uncompromising pursuit of the best books we can find, help create, and deliver to readers. We love what we do, and we hope you will, too." Guidelines online.

IMPRINTS Scribble.

HOW TO CONTACT Submit synopsis, sample chapters, CV.

TIPS "We are only able to consider unsolicited submissions if you have a demonstrated background of writing and publishing for general readers."

⊘⊘ SCRIBNER

Imprint of Simon & Schuster Adult Publishing Group, 1230 Avenue of the Americas, 12th Floor, New York NY 10020. (212)698-7000. **Website:** www.simonsays.com. Publishes hardcover originals.

HOW TO CONTACT *Agented submissions only.*

TERMS Pays 7-15% royalty. Pays variable advance. Responds in 3 months to queries

♻ SECOND STORY PRESS

20 Maud St., Suite 401, Toronto ON M5V 2M5, Canada. (416)537-7850. **Fax:** (416)537-0588. **E-mail:** info@secondstorypress.ca. **Website:** www.secondstorypress.ca. "Please keep in mind that as a feminist press, we are looking for non-sexist, non-racist and non-violent stories, as well as historical fiction, chapter books, novels and biography."

NEEDS Considers non-sexist, non-racist, and non-violent stories, as well as historical fiction, chapter books, picture books.

SEEDLING CONTINENTAL PRESS

520 E. Bainbridge St., Elizabethtown PA 17022. (800)233-0759. **Website:** www.continentalpress.com. "Continental publishes educational materials for grades K-12, specializing in reading, mathematics, and test preparation materials. We are not currently accepting submissions for Seedling leveled readers or instructional materials."

NEEDS Young readers: adventure, animal, folktales, humor, multicultural, nature/environment. Does not accept texts longer than 12 pages or over 300 words. Average word length: young readers—100.

HOW TO CONTACT Submit complete ms.

TERMS Work purchased outright from authors. Responds to mss in 6 months.

TIPS "See our website. Follow writers' guidelines carefully and test your story with children and educators."

SEVEN STORIES PRESS

140 Watts St., New York NY 10013. (212)226-8760. **Fax:** (212)226-1411. **E-mail:** info@sevenstories.com. **Website:** www.sevenstories.com. **Contact:** Acquisitions. Estab. 1995. Founded in 1995 in New York City, and named for the seven authors who committed to a home with a fiercely independent spirit, Seven Stories Press publishes works of the imagination and political titles by voices of conscience. While most widely known for its books on politics, human rights, and social and economic justice, Seven Stories continues to champion literature, with a list encompassing both innovative debut novels and National Book Award–winning poetry collections, as well as prose and poetry translations from the French, Spanish, German, Swedish, Italian, Greek, Polish, Korean, Vietnamese, Russian, and Arabic. Publishes hardcover and trade paperback originals. Book catalog and ms guidelines free.

HOW TO CONTACT Submit cover letter with 2 sample chapters.

TERMS Pays 7-15% royalty on retail price. Pays advance. Responds in 1 month.

⊘♥⊘ SEVERN HOUSE PUBLISHERS

Salatin House, 19 Cedar Rd., Sutton, Surrey SM2 5DA, United Kingdom. (44)(208)770-3930. **Fax:** (44)(208)770-3850. **Website:** www.severnhouse.com. Severn House is currently emphasizing suspense, romance, mystery. Large print imprint from existing authors. Publishes hardcover and trade paperback originals and reprints. Book catalog available free.

HOW TO CONTACT *Agented submissions only.*

TERMS Pays 7-15% royalty on retail price. Pays $750-5,000 advance. Responds in 3 months to proposals.

SHAMBHALA PUBLICATIONS, INC.

4720 Walnut St., Boulder CO 80304. **E-mail:** submissions@shambhala.com. **Website:** www.shambhala.com. Estab. 1969. Publishes hardcover and trade paperback originals and reprints. Book catalog free. Guidelines online.

IMPRINTS Roost Books; Snow Lion.

TERMS Pays 8% royalty on retail price. Responds in 4 months.

SHIPWRECKT BOOKS PUBLISHING COMPANY LLC

309 W. Stevens Ave., Rushford MN 55971. **E-mail:** contact@shipwrecktbooks.com. **Website:** www.shipwrecktbooks.press. **Contact:** Tom Driscoll, manag-

ing editor. Publishes trade paperback originals, mass market paperback originals, and electronic originals. Catalog and guidelines online.

IMPRINTS Rocket Science Press (literary); Up On Big Rock Poetry Series; Lost Lake Folk Art (memoir, biography, essays, fiction and nonfiction).

HOW TO CONTACT Use submissions portal at www.shipwrecktbooks.press; follow guidelines. Paper submissions are no longer accepted.

TERMS Authors receive 35% royalties unless otherwise negotiated. Responds to queries within 6 months.

TIPS "Quality writing. Please follow our guidelines. Manuscript development and full editorial services available."

Ⓐ⊘ SIMON & SCHUSTER

1230 Avenue of the Americas, New York NY 10020. (212)698-7000. **Website:** www.simonandschuster. com. *Accepts agented submissions only.*

IMPRINTS Aladdin; Atheneum Books for Young Readers; Atria; Beach Lane Books; Folger Shakespeare Library; Free Press; Gallery Books; Howard Books; Little Simon; Margaret K. McElderry Books; Pocket; Scribner; Simon & Schuster; Simon & Schuster Books for Young Readers; Simon Pulse; Simon Spotlight; Threshold; Touchstone; Paula Wiseman Books.

Ⓐ⊘ SIMON & SCHUSTER BOOKS FOR YOUNG READERS

Imprint of Simon & Schuster Children's Publishing, 1230 Avenue of the Americas, New York NY 10020. (212)698-7000. **Fax:** (212)698-2796. **Website:** www.simonsayskids. com. "Simon and Schuster Books For Young Readers is the Flagship imprint of the S&S Children's Division. We are committed to publishing a wide range of contemporary, commercial, award-winning fiction and nonfiction that spans every age of children's publishing. BFYR is constantly looking to the future, supporting our foundation authors and franchises, but always with an eye for breaking new ground with every publication. We publish high-quality fiction and nonfiction for a variety of age groups and a variety of markets. Above all, we strive to publish books that we are passionate about." *No unsolicited mss.* All unsolicited mss returned unopened. Publishes hardcover originals. Guidelines online.

HOW TO CONTACT *Agented submissions only.*

TERMS Pays variable royalty on retail price.

TIPS "We're looking for picture books centered on a strong, fully-developed protagonist who grows or changes during the course of the story; YA novels that are challenging and psychologically complex; also imaginative and humorous middle-grade fiction. And we want nonfiction that is as engaging as fiction. Our imprint's slogan is 'Reading You'll Remember.' We aim to publish books that are fresh, accessible and family-oriented; we want them to have an impact on the reader."

◑ SIMPLY READ BOOKS

501-5525 W. Blvd., Vancouver BC V6M 3W6, Canada. **E-mail:** go@simplyreadbooks.com. **Website:** www. simplyreadbooks.com. Simply Read Books is current seeking mss in picture books, early readers, early chapter books, middle grade fiction, and graphic novels.

HOW TO CONTACT Query or submit complete ms.

SKINNER HOUSE BOOKS

The Unitarian Universalist Association, 24 Farnsworth St., Boston MA 02210. (617)742-2100, ext. 603. **Fax:** (617)948-6466. **E-mail:** bookproposals@uua.org. **Website:** www.uua.org/publications/skinnerhouse. **Contact:** Betsy Martin. Estab. 1975. "We publish titles in Unitarian Universalist faith, liberal religion, history, biography, worship, and issues of social justice. Most of our children's titles are intended for religious education or worship use. They reflect Unitarian Universalist values. We also publish inspirational titles of poetic prose and meditations. Writers should know that Unitarian Universalism is a liberal religious denomination committed to progressive ideals. Currently emphasizing social justice concerns." Publishes trade paperback originals and reprints. Book catalog for 6×9 SAE with 3 first-class stamps. Guidelines online.

NEEDS Only publishes fiction for children's titles for religious instruction.

HOW TO CONTACT Query.

TERMS Responds to queries in 1 month.

TIPS "From outside our denomination, we are interested in manuscripts that will be of help or interest to liberal churches, Sunday School classes, parents, ministers, and volunteers. Inspirational/spiritual and children's titles must reflect liberal Unitarian Universalist values."

SKY PONY PRESS

307 W. 36th St., 11th Floor, New York NY 10018. (212)643-6816. **Fax:** (212)643-6819. **Website:** skyponypress.com. Estab. 2011. Sky Pony Press is the children's book imprint of Skyhorse Publishing. "Following in the footsteps of our parent company, our goal is to provide books for readers with a wide variety of interests." Guidelines online.

NEEDS "We will consider picture books, early readers, midgrade novels, novelties, and informational books for all ages."

HOW TO CONTACT Submit ms or proposal.

SLEEPING BEAR PRESS

2395 South Huron Parkway #200, Ann Arbor MI 48104. (800)487-2323. **Fax:** (734)794-0004. **E-mail:** submissions@sleepingbearpress.com. **Website:** www.sleepingbearpress.com. **Contact:** Manuscript Submissions. Estab. 1998. Book catalog available via e-mail.

NEEDS Picture books: adventure, animal, concept, folktales, history, multicultural, nature/environment, religion, sports. Young readers: adventure, animal, concept, folktales, history, humor, multicultural, nature/environment, religion, sports. Average word length: picture books—1,800.

HOW TO CONTACT Accepts unsolicited queries 3 times per year. See website for details. Query with sample of work (up to 15 pages) and SASE. Please address packages to Manuscript Submissions.

SMALL BEER PRESS

150 Pleasant St., #306, Easthampton MA 01027. (413)203-1636. **Fax:** (413)203-1636. **E-mail:** info@smallbeerpress.com. **Website:** www.smallbeerpress.com. Estab. 2000. Small Beer Press also publishes the zine *Lady Churchill's Rosebud Wristlet*. "SBP's books have recently received the Tiptree and Crawford Awards."

HOW TO CONTACT Does not accept unsolicited novel or short story collection mss. Send queries with first 10-20 pages and SASE.

TERMS Advance and standard royalties.

TIPS "Please be familiar with our books first to avoid wasting your time and ours, thank you. E-mail queries will be deleted. Really."

SMITH AND KRAUS PUBLISHERS, INC.

177 Lyme Rd., Hanover NH 03755. (603)643-6431. **E-mail:** editor@smithandkraus.com. **E-mail:** carolb@smithandkraus.com. **Website:** smithandkraus.com. Estab. 1990. Publishes hardcover and trade paperback originals. Book catalog available free.

NEEDS Does not return submissions.

HOW TO CONTACT Query with SASE.

TERMS Pays 7% royalty on retail price. Pays $500-2,000 advance. Responds in 1 month to queries; 2 months to proposals; 4 months to mss.

SOFT SKULL PRESS INC.

Counterpoint, 2650 Ninth St., Suite 318, Berkeley CA 94710. (510)704-0230. **Fax:** (510)704-0268. **E-mail:** info@counterpointpress.com. **Website:** www.softskull.com. "Here at Soft Skull we love books that are new, fun, smart, revelatory, quirky, groundbreaking, cage-rattling and/or/otherwise unusual." Publishes hardcover and trade paperback originals. Book catalog and guidelines online.

NEEDS Does not consider poetry.

HOW TO CONTACT Soft Skull Press no longer accepts digital submissions. Send a cover letter describing your project in detail and a completed ms. For graphic novels, send a minimum of five fully inked pages of art, along with a synopsis of your storyline. "Please do not send original material, as it will not be returned."

TERMS Pays 7-10% royalty. Average advance: $100-15,000. Responds in 2 months to proposals; 3 months to mss.

TIPS "See our website for updated submission guidelines."

SOHO PRESS, INC.

853 Broadway, New York NY 10003. (212)260-1900. **E-mail:** soho@sohopress.com. **Website:** www.sohopress.com. **Contact:** Bronwen Hruska, publisher; Mark Doten, senior editor. Estab. 1986. Soho Press publishes primarily fiction, as well as some narrative literary nonfiction and mysteries set abroad. No electronic submissions, only queries by e-mail. Publishes hardcover and trade paperback originals; trade paperback reprints. Guidelines online.

NEEDS Adventure, ethnic, feminist, historical, literary, mainstream/contemporary, mystery (police procedural), suspense, multicultural.

HOW TO CONTACT Submit 3 sample chapters and cover letter with synopsis, author bio, SASE. *No e-mailed submissions.*

TERMS Pays 10-15% royalty on retail price (varies under certain circumstances). Responds in 3 months.

TIPS "Soho Press publishes discerning authors for discriminating readers, finding the strongest possible writers and publishing them. Before submitting, look at our website for an idea of the types of books we publish, and read our submission guidelines."

SOURCEBOOKS CASABLANCA

Sourcebooks, Inc., 232 Madison Ave., Suite 1100, New York NY 10016. **E-mail:** romance@sourcebooks.

com. **Website:** www.sourcebooks.com. **Contact:** Deb Werksman (deb.werksman@sourcebooks.com). "Our romance imprint, Sourcebooks Casablanca, publishes single title romance in all subgenres." Guidelines online.

NEEDS "Our editorial criteria call for: a heroine the reader can relate to, a hero she can fall in love with, a world gets created that the reader can escape into, there's a hook that we can sell within 2-3 sentences, and the author is out to build a career with us."

TERMS Responds in 2-3 months.

TIPS "We are actively acquiring single-title and single-title series romance fiction (90,000-100,000 words) for our Casablanca imprint. We are looking for strong writers who are excited about marketing their books and building their community of readers, and whose books have something fresh to offer in the genre of romance."

SOURCEBOOKS FIRE

1935 Brookdale Rd., Suite 139, Naperville IL 60563. (630)961-3900. **Fax:** (630)961-2168. **E-mail:** submissions@sourcebooks.com. **Website:** www.sourcebooks. com. "We're actively acquiring knockout books for our YA imprint. We are particularly looking for strong writers who are excited about promoting and building their community of readers, and whose books have something fresh to offer the ever-growing young adult audience. We are not accepting any unsolicited or unagented manuscripts at this time. Unfortunately, our staff can no longer handle the large volume of manuscripts that we receive on a daily basis. We will continue to consider agented manuscripts." See website for details.

HOW TO CONTACT Query with the full ms attached in Word doc.

SOURCEBOOKS LANDMARK

Sourcebooks, Inc., Sourcebooks, Inc., 232 Madison Ave., Suite 1100, New York NY 10016. **E-mail:** editorialsubmissions@sourcebooks.com. **Website:** www. sourcebooks.com. "Our fiction imprint, Sourcebooks Landmark, publishes a variety of commercial fiction, including specialties in historical fiction and Austenalia. We are interested first and foremost in books that have a story to tell."

NEEDS "We are actively acquiring contemporary, book club, and historical fiction for our Landmark imprint. We are looking for strong writers who are excited about marketing their books and building their community of readers."

HOW TO CONTACT Submit synopsis and full ms preferred. Receipt of e-mail submissions acknowledged within 3 weeks of e-mail.

TERMS Responds in 2-3 months.

SPENCER HILL PRESS

27 W. 20th St., Suite 1102, New York NY 10011. **Website:** www.spencerhillpress.com. Spencer Hill Press is an independent publishing house specializing in sci-fi, urban fantasy, and paranormal romance for young adult readers. "Our books have that 'I couldn't put it down!' quality." Guidelines online.

NEEDS "We are interested in young adult, new adult, and middle grade sci-fi, psych-fi, paranormal, or urban fantasy, particularly those with a strong and interesting voice."

HOW TO CONTACT Check website for open submission periods.

STAR BRIGHT BOOKS

13 Landsdowne St., Cambridge MA 02139. (617)354-1300. **Fax:** (617)354-1399. **E-mail:** lolabush@starbrightbooks.com. **Website:** www.starbrightbooks. com. **Contact:** Lola Bush. Estab. 1994. Star Bright Books accepts unsolicited mss and art submissions. "We welcome submissions for picture books and longer works, both fiction and particularly nonfiction." Also beginner readers and chapter books. Currently seeking bios, math infused books. Catalog online.

TERMS Pays advance. as well as flat fee Responds in several months.

STERLING PUBLISHING CO., INC.

1166 Avenue of the Americas, 17th Floor, New York NY 10036. (212)532-7160. **Website:** www.sterlingpublishing.com. "Sterling publishes highly illustrated, accessible, hands-on, practical books for adults and children. Our mission is to publish high-quality books that educate, entertain, and enrich the lives of our readers." Publishes hardcover and paperback originals and reprints. Catalog online. Guidelines online.

NEEDS Publishes fiction for children.

HOW TO CONTACT Submit to attention of "Children's Book Editor."

TERMS Pays royalty or work purchased outright. Offers advances (average amount: $2,000).

TIPS "We are primarily a nonfiction activities-based publisher. We have a picture book list, but we do not publish chapter books or novels. Our list is not trend-driven. We focus on titles that will backlist well. "

STONE ARCH BOOKS

1710 Roe Crest Rd., North Mankato MN 56003. **Website:** www.stonearchbooks.com. Catalog online.

NEEDS Imprint of Capstone Publishers.Young readers, middle readers, young adults: adventure, contemporary, fantasy, humor, light humor, mystery, science fiction, sports, suspense. Average word length: young readers—1,000-3,000; middle readers and early young adults—5,000-10,000.

HOW TO CONTACT Submit outline/synopsis and 3 sample chapters. Electronic submissions preferred. Full guidelines available on website.

TERMS Work purchased outright from authors.

TIPS "A high-interest topic or activity is one that a young person would spend their free time on without adult direction or suggestion."

STONE BRIDGE PRESS

P.O. Box 8208, Berkeley CA 94707. **E-mail:** sbp@stonebridge.com. **Website:** www.stonebridge.com. **Contact:** Peter Goodman, publisher. Estab. 1989. "Independent press focusing on books about Asia, primarily Japan and China, in English (business, language, culture, literature, animation)." Publishes hardcover and trade paperback originals. Books: 60-70 lb. offset paper; web and sheet paper; perfect bound; some illustrations. Distributes titles through Consortium. Promotes titles through social media and Internet announcements, blogs, special-interest magazines and niche tie-ins to associations. Catalog online. Do not send children's books. Do not send proposals that are outside our key Asia-related subject areas. No poetry.

NEEDS Experimental, gay/lesbian, literary, Asia-themed. "Primarily looking at material relating to Asia, especially Japan and China. "

HOW TO CONTACT Does not accept unsolicited mss. Accepts queries by e-mail.

TERMS Pays royalty on wholesale price. Responds to queries in 4 months; mss in 8 months.

TIPS "Query first before submitting. Research us first and avoid sending mss not in our subject area. Generic and bulk submissions will be ignored. No poetry. Looking also for graphic novels, not manga or serializations."

STONESLIDE BOOKS

Stoneslide Media LLC, P.O. Box 8331, New Haven CT 06530. **Website:** www.stoneslidecorrective.com. Estab. 2012. "We like novels with strong character development and narrative thrust, brought out with writing that's clear and expressive." Publishes trade paperback and electronic originals. Book catalog and guidelines online.

NEEDS "We will look at any genre. The important factor for us is that the story use plot, characters, emotions, and other elements of storytelling to think and move the mind forward."

HOW TO CONTACT Submit proposal package via online submission form including: synopsis and 3 sample chapters.

TERMS Pays 20-80% royalty. Responds in 1-2 months.

TIPS "Read the Stoneslide Corrective to see if your work fits with our approach."

SUBITO PRESS

University of Colorado at Boulder, Dept. of English, 226 UCB, Boulder CO 80309-0226. **E-mail:** subitopressucb@gmail.com. **Website:** www.subitopress.org. Subito Press is a non-profit publisher of literary works. Each year Subito publishes one work of fiction and one work of poetry through its contest. Publishes trade paperback originals. Guidelines online.

HOW TO CONTACT Submit complete ms to contest.

TIPS "We publish 2 books of innovative writing a year through our poetry and fiction contests. All entries are also considered for publication with the press."

SUNBURY PRESS, INC.

PO Box 548, Boiling Springs PA 17007. **E-mail:** info@sunburypress.com. **E-mail:** proposals@sunburypress.com. **Website:** www.sunburypress.com. Estab. 2004. Sunbury Press, Inc., headquartered in Mechanicsburg, PA is a publisher of trade paperback, hard cover and digital books featuring established and emerging authors in many fiction and non-fiction categories. Sunbury's books are printed in the USA and sold through leading booksellers worldwide. "Please use our online submission form." Publishes trade paperback and hardcover originals and reprints; electronic originals and reprints. Catalog and guidelines online. Online submission form.

IMPRINTS Sunbury Press (history and nonfiction); Milford House Press (murder mysteries, historical fiction, young adult fiction); Hellbender Books (horror, thrillers); Brown Posey Press (literary fiction, art); Ars Metaphysica (religion, spiritual, metaphysical, visionary fiction); Speckled Egg Press (juvenile fiction/nonfiction).

NEEDS "We are seeking manuscripts for our three fiction imprints: Milford House Press, Brown Posey

Press, and Hellbender Books." Does not want vampires, zombies, erotica.

HOW TO CONTACT Please use our online submission service.

TERMS Pays 10% royalty on wholesale price. Responds in 3 months.

TIPS "We are a rapidly growing small press with six diverse imprints. We currently have over 250 authors and 500 works under management."

SUNSTONE PRESS

Box 2321, Santa Fe NM 87504. (800)243-5644. **Website:** www.sunstonepress.com. **Contact:** Submissions Editor. Sunstone's original focus was on nonfiction subjects that preserved and highlighted the richness of the American Southwest but it has expanded its view over the years to include mainstream themes and categories—both nonfiction and fiction—that have a more general appeal. Guidelines online.

HOW TO CONTACT Query with 1 sample chapter.

SWEET CHERRY PUBLISHING

Unit 36, Vulcan Business Complex, Vulcan Rd., Leicester Leicestershire LE5 3EF, United Kingdom. **E-mail:** info@sweetcherrypublishing.com. **E-mail:** submissions@sweetcherrypublishing.com. **Website:** www.sweetcherrypublishing.com. Estab. 2011. Sweet Cherry Publishing is an independent publishing company based in Leicester. "We specialize in middle-grade series. Our aim is to provide children with compelling worlds and engaging characters that they will want to revisit again and again." Send the first 3 chapters or 3,000 words along with a synopsis, author biography, and cover letter detailing your target audience and your plans for further books in the series.

TERMS Offers one-time fee for work that is accepted.

TIPS "Submit a cover letter and a synopsis with 3 sample chapters via email. Please note that we do not accept submissions by post."

TAFELBERG PUBLISHERS

Imprint of NB Publishers, P.O. Box 879, Cape Town 8000, South Africa. (27)(21)406-3033. **Fax:** (27)(21)406-3812. **E-mail:** engela.reinke@nb.co.za. **Website:** www.tafelberg.com. **Contact:** Engela Reinke. General publisher best known for Afrikaans fiction, authoritative political works, children's/youth literature, and a variety of illustrated and nonillustrated nonfiction.

NEEDS Picture books, young readers: animal, anthology, contemporary, fantasy, folktales, hi-lo, humor, multicultural, nature/environment, scient fiction, special needs. Middle readers, young adults: animal (middle reader only), contemporary, fantasy, hi-lo, humor, multicultural, nature/environment, problem novels, science fiction, special needs, sports, suspense/mystery. Average word length: picture books—1,500-7,500; young readers—25,000; middle readers—15,000; young adults—40,000.

HOW TO CONTACT Submit complete ms.

TERMS Pays authors royalty of 15-18% based on wholesale price. Responds to queries in 2 weeks; mss in 6 months.

TIPS "Writers: Story needs to have a South African or African style. Illustrators: I'd like to look, but the chances of getting commissioned are slim. The market is small and difficult. Do not expect huge advances. Editorial staff attended or plans to attend the following conferences: IBBY, Frankfurt, SCBWI Bologna."

NAN A. TALESE

Imprint of Penguin Random House LLC, 1745 Broadway, New York NY 10019. (212)782-8918. **Fax:** (212)782-9000. **Website:** www.nanatalese.com. Nan A. Talese publishes nonfiction with a powerful guiding narrative and relevance to larger cultural interests, and literary fiction of the highest quality. Publishes hardcover originals.

NEEDS Well-written narratives with a compelling story line, good characterization and use of language. We like stories with an edge.

HOW TO CONTACT *Agented submissions only.*

TERMS Pays variable royalty on retail price. Pays varying advance.

TIPS "Audience is highly literate people interested in story, information and insight. We want well-written material submitted by agents only. See our website."

TANTOR MEDIA

Recorded Books, 6 Business Park Rd., Old Saybrook CT 06475. (860)395-1155. **Fax:** (860)395-1154. **E-mail:** rightsemail@tantor.com. **Website:** www.tantor.com. **Contact:** Ron Formica, director of acquisitions. Estab. 2001. Tantor Media, a division of Recorded Books, is a leading audiobook publisher, producing more than 100 new titles every month. We do not publish print or e-books. Publishes audiobooks only. Catalog online. Not accepting print or e-book queries. We only publish audiobooks.

We are not publishing print/e-book titles.

TERMS Responds in 2 months.

TEXAS TECH UNIVERSITY PRESS

1120 Main St., Second Floor, Box 41037, Lubbock TX 79415. (806)742-2982. **Fax:** (806)742-2979. **E-mail:** ttup@ttu.edu. **Website:** www.ttupress.org. Estab. 1971. Texas Tech University Press, the book publishing office of the university since 1971 and an AAUP member since 1986, publishes nonfiction titles in the areas of natural history and the natural sciences; 18th century and Joseph Conrad studies; studies of modern Southeast Asia, particularly the Vietnam War; costume and textile history; Latin American literature and culture; and all aspects of the Great Plains and the American West, especially history, biography, memoir, sports history, and travel. In addition, the Press publishes several scholarly journals, acclaimed series for young readers, an annual invited poetry collection, and literary fiction of Texas and the West. Guidelines online.

NEEDS Fiction rooted in the American West and Southwest, Jewish literature, Latin American and Latino fiction (in translation or English).

☾ THISTLEDOWN PRESS LTD.

410 2nd Ave., Saskatoon SK S7K 2C3, Canada. (306)244-1722. **Fax:** (306)244-1762. **E-mail:** editorial@thistledownpress.com. **Website:** www.thistledownpress.com. **Contact:** Allan Forrie, publisher. Estab. 1975. "Thistledown originates books by Canadian authors only, although we have co-published titles by authors outside Canada. We do not publish children's picture books." Book catalog on website. Guidelines online.

NEEDS Young adults: adventure, anthology, contemporary, fantasy, humor, poetry, romance, science fiction, suspense/mystery, short stories. Average word length: young adults—40,000.

HOW TO CONTACT Submit outline/synopsis and sample chapters. *Does not accept mss.* Do not query by e-mail. "Please note: we are not accepting middle years (ages 8-12) nor children's manuscripts at this time." See Submission Guidelines on Website.

TERMS Pays authors royalty of 10-12% based on net dollar sales. Pays illustrators and photographers by the project (range: $250-750). Rarely pays advance. Responds to queries in 6 months.

TIPS "Send cover letter including publishing history and SASE."

THUNDERSTONE BOOKS

6575 Horse Dr., Las Vegas NV 89131. **E-mail:** info@thunderstonebooks.com. **Website:** www.thunderstonebooks.com. **Contact:** Rachel Noorda, editorial director. Estab. 2014. "At ThunderStone Books, we aim to publish children's books that have an educational aspect. We are not looking for curriculum for learning certain subjects, but rather stories that encourage learning for children, whether that be learning about a new language/culture or learning more about science and math in a fun, fictional format. We want to help children to gain a love for other languages and subjects so that they are curious about the world around them. We are currently accepting fiction and nonfiction submissions. Picture books without accompanying illustration will not be accepted." Publishes hardcover, trade paperback, mass market paperback, and electronic originals. Catalog available for SASE. Guidelines available.

NEEDS Interested in multicultural stories with an emphasis on authentic culture and language (these may include mythology).

HOW TO CONTACT "If you think your book is right for us, send a query letter with a word attachment of the first 50 pages to info@thunderstonebooks.com. If it is a picture book or chapter book for young readers that is shorter than 50 pages send the entire manuscript."

TERMS Pays 5-15% royalties on retail price. Pays $300-1,000 advance. Responds in 3 months.

☾⊘ TIGHTROPE BOOKS

Toronto ON , Canada. **E-mail:** tightropeasst@gmail.com. **Website:** www.tightropebooks.com. Estab. 2005. Publishes trade paperback originals.

☾ Press is going out of business and not accepting new manuscripts.

❹ TIN HOUSE BOOKS

2617 NW Thurman St., Portland OR 97210. (503)473-8663. **Fax:** (503)473-8957. **E-mail:** masie@tinhouse.com. **Website:** www.tinhouse.com. **Contact:** Masie Cochran, editor; Tony Perez, editor. "We are a small independent publisher dedicated to nurturing new, promising talent as well as showcasing the work of established writers." Distributes/promotes titles through W. W. Norton. Publishes hardcover originals, paperback originals, paperback reprints. Guidelines online.

HOW TO CONTACT *Agented mss only.* "We no longer read unsolicited submissions by authors with no representation. We will continue to accept submissions from agents."

TERMS Responds to queries in 2-3 weeks; mss in 2-3 months.

TITAN PRESS

2150 Pickwick Dr. #455, Camarillo CA 93011. **E-mail:** titan91416@yahoo.com. **Website:** https://www.facebook.com/RVClef. **Contact:** Romana Von Clef, editor. Estab. 1981. Little literary publisher. Publishes hardcover and paperback originals.

HOW TO CONTACT Does not accept unsolicited mss. Query with SASE. Include brief bio, list of publishing credits.

TERMS Pays 20-40% royalty. Responds to queries in 3 months.

TIPS "Look, act, sound, and *be* professional."

⊘ TOP COW PRODUCTIONS, INC.

3812 Dunn Dr., Culver City CA 90232. **Website:** www.topcow.com. Guidelines online.

HOW TO CONTACT *No unsolicited submissions.* Prefers submissions from artists. See website for details and advice on how to break into the market.

TOR BOOKS

Tom Doherty Associates, 175 Fifth Ave., New York NY 10010. **Website:** www.tor-forge.com. Tor Books is the "world's largest publisher of science fiction and fantasy, with strong category publishing in historical fiction, mystery, western/Americana, thriller, YA." Book catalog available. Guidelines online.

HOW TO CONTACT Submit first 3 chapters, 3-10 page synopsis, dated cover letter, SASE.

TERMS Pays author royalty. Pays illustrators by the project.

TORREY HOUSE PRESS

150 S. State St., Ste. 100 Ofc. 36, Salt Lake City UT 84111. **E-mail:** kirsten@torreyhouse.com. **Website:** www.torreyhouse.org. **Contact:** Kirsten Allen. Estab. 2010. Torrey House Press is an independent nonprofit publisher promoting environmental conservation through literature. Publishes hardcover, trade paperback, and electronic originals. Catalog online. Guidelines online.

NEEDS Torrey House Press publishes literary fiction and creative nonfiction about the world environment and the American West.

HOW TO CONTACT Submit proposal package including: synopsis, complete ms, bio.

TERMS Pays 5-15% royalty on retail price. Responds in 4-6 months.

TIPS Include writing experience (none okay).

✪ TOUCHWOOD EDITIONS

The Heritage Group, 103-1075 Pendergast St., Victoria BC V8V 0A1, Canada. (250)360-0829. **Fax:** (250)386-0829. **E-mail:** edit@touchwoodeditions.com. **Website:** www.touchwoodeditions.com. **Contact:** Renée Layberry, Editor. Publishes trade paperback, originals and reprints. Book catalog and guidelines online.

HOW TO CONTACT Submit bio/CV, marketing plan, TOC, outline, word count.

TERMS Pays 15% royalty on net price. Responds in 6 months to queries.

TIPS "Our area of interest is western Canada. We would like more creative nonfiction and fiction from First Nations authors, and welcome authors who write about notable individuals in Canada's history. Please note we do not publish poetry."

✪ TRADEWIND BOOKS

202-1807 Maritime Mews, Granville Island, Vancouver BC V6H 3W7, Canada. (604)662-4405. **Website:** www.tradewindbooks.com. "Tradewind Books publishes juvenile picture books and young adult novels. Requires that submissions include evidence that author has read at least 3 titles published by Tradewind Books." Publishes hardcover and trade paperback originals. Book catalog and ms guidelines online.

NEEDS Average word length: 900 words.

HOW TO CONTACT Send complete ms for picture books. *YA novels by Canadian authors only. Chapter books by US authors considered.* For chapter books/Middle Grade Fiction, submit the first three chapters, a chapter outline and plot summary.

TERMS Pays 7% royalty on retail price. Pays variable advance. Responds to mss in 2 months.

TRIANGLE SQUARE

Seven Stories Press, 140 Watts St., New York NY 10013. (212)226-8760. **Fax:** (212)226-1411. **E-mail:** info@sevenstories.com. **Website:** https://www.sevenstories.com/imprints/triangle-square. Triangle Square is a children's and young adult imprint of Seven Story Press.

HOW TO CONTACT Send a cover letter with 2 sample chapters and SASE. Send c/o Acquisitions.

TU BOOKS

Lee & Low Books, 95 Madison Ave., Suite #1205, New York NY 10016. **Website:** www.leeandlow.com/imprints/3. **Contact:** Stacy Whitman, publisher. Estab. 2010. The Tu Books imprint spans many genres: science fiction, fantasy, mystery, contemporary, and more. We don't believe in labels or limits, just great stories. Join us at the crossroads where fantasy and real life collide. You'll be glad you did. Publishes young adult and middle grade novels and graphic novels: science fiction, fantasy, contemporary realism, mystery, historical fiction, and more, with particular interest in books with strong literary hooks. Also seeking middle grade and young adult nonfiction. Catalog available online. Please see our full submissions guidelines online.

○ For new writers of color, please be aware of the New Visions Award writing contest, which runs every year from May-August. Previously unpublished writers of color and Native American writers may submit their middle grade and young adult novels and graphic novels. See submission guidelines for the contest online.

NEEDS "Our focus is on fiction and narrative nonfiction centering people of color or Native people. We are interested in both middle grade stories for ages 8 to 12 and young adult stories for ages 12 to 18. Occasionally a manuscript might fall between these two categories; if your manuscript does, let us know. We look for fantasy set in worlds inspired by non-Western folklore or culture, contemporary mystery and fantasy set all over the world, and science fiction that centers the possibilities for people of color or Native people in the future. We also selectively publish realism and narrative nonfiction that explores the contemporary and historical experiences of people of color or Native people. We welcome intersectional narratives that feature LGBTQIA and disabled people as heroes in their own stories. Stacy Whitman and Cheryl Klein both acquire titles for Tu Books, and we ask that you identify which of them you wish to consider your submission. As loose rules of thumb, Cheryl has a more literary bent and does not acquire graphic novels, while Stacy has a more commercial focus and does not acquire narrative nonfiction." Not seeking picture books or chapter books.

HOW TO CONTACT Please include a synopsis and first three chapters of the novel. Do not send the complete ms. Mss should be typed doubled-spaced. Mss should be accompanied by a cover letter that includes a brief biography of the author, including publishing history. The letter should be addressed to either Stacy Whitman or Cheryl Klein, and should also state if the ms is a simultaneous or an exclusive submission. "We're looking for middle grade (ages 8-12) and young adult (ages 12 and up) books. We are not looking for chapter books (ages 6 to 9) at this time. Be sure to include full contact information on the cover letter and first page of the manuscript. Page numbers and your last name/title of the book should appear on subsequent pages."

TERMS Advance against royalties. Pays advance. Responds only if interested.

TUMBLEHOME LEARNING

P.O. Box 71386, Boston MA 02117. **E-mail:** info@tumblehomelearning.com. **E-mail:** submissions@tumblehomelearning.com. **Website:** www.tumblehomelearning.com. **Contact:** Pendred Noyce, editor. Estab. 2011. Tumblehome Learning helps kids imagine themselves as young scientists or engineeers and encourages them to experience science through adventure and discovery. "We do this with exciting mystery and adventure tales as well as experiments carefully designed to engage students from ages 8 and up." Publishes hardcover, trade paperback, and electronic originals. Catalog available online. Guideliens available on request for SASE.

NEEDS "All our fiction has science at its heart. This can include using science to solve a mystery (see *The Walking Fish* by Rachelle Burk or *Something Stinks!* by Gail Hedrick), realistic science fiction, books in our Galactic Academy of Science series, science-based adventure tales, and the occasional picture book with a science theme, such as appreciation of the stars and constellations in *Elizabeth's Constellation Quilt* by Olivia Fu. A graphic novel about science would also be welcome."

HOW TO CONTACT Submit completed ms electronically.

TERMS Pays authors 8-12% royalties on retail price. Pays $500 advance. Responds in 1 month to queries and proposals, and 2 months to mss.

TIPS "Please don't submit to us if your book is not about science. We don't accept generic books about animals or books with glaring scientific errors in the first chapter. That said, the book should be fun to read and the science content can be subtle. We work closely with authors, including first-time authors, to edit and improve their books. As a small publisher, the greatest benefit we can offer is this friendly and respectful partnership with authors."

TUPELO PRESS

P.O. Box 1767, North Adams MA 01247. (413)664-9611. **Website:** www.tupelopress.org. **Contact:** Sarah Russell, administrative director. Estab. 2001. "We're an independent nonprofit literary press. We publish book-length poetry, poetry collections, translations, short story collections, novellas, literary nonfiction/ memoirs and novels." Guidelines online.

NEEDS "For Novels—submit no more than 100 pages along with a summary of the entire book. If we're interested we'll ask you to send the rest. We accept very few works of prose (3 or 4 per year)."

HOW TO CONTACT Submit complete ms. **Charges a $45 reading fee.**

TERMS Standard royalty contract. Pays advance in rare instances.

☮ TURNSTONE PRESS

Artspace Building, 206-100 Arthur St., Winnipeg MB R3B 1H3, Canada. (204)947-1555. **Fax:** (204)942-1555. **Website:** www.turnstonepress.com. **Contact:** Submissions Assistant. Estab. 1976. "Turnstone Press is a literary publisher, not a general publisher, and therefore we are only interested in literary fiction, literary nonfiction—including literary criticism—and poetry. We do publish literary mysteries, thrillers, and noir under our Ravenstone imprint. We publish only Canadian authors or landed immigrants, we strive to publish a significant number of new writers, to publish in a variety of genres, and to have 50% of each year's list be Manitoba writers and/or books with Manitoba content." Guidelines online.

HOW TO CONTACT "Samples must be 40 to 60 pages, typed/printed in a minimum 12 point serif typeface such as Times, Book Antiqua, or Garamond."

TERMS Responds in 4-7 months.

TIPS "As a Canadian literary press, we have a mandate to publish Canadian writers only. Do some homework before submitting works to make sure your subject matter/genre/writing style falls within the publishers area of interest."

TWILIGHT TIMES BOOKS

P.O. Box 3340, Kingsport TN 37664. **E-mail:** publisher@twilighttimesbooks.com. **Website:** www.twilight-timesbooks.com. **Contact:** Andy M. Scott, managing editor. Estab. 1999. "We publish compelling literary fiction by authors with a distinctive voice." Published 5 debut authors within the last year. Averages 120 total titles; 15 fiction titles/year. Member: AAP, IBPA, PAS, SPAN, SLF. Guidelines online.

HOW TO CONTACT Accepts unsolicited mss. Do not send complete mss. Queries via e-mail only. Include estimated word count, brief bio, list of publishing credits, marketing plan.

TERMS Pays 8-15% royalty. Responds in 4 weeks to queries; 2 months to mss.

TIPS "The only requirement for consideration at Twilight Times Books is that your novel must be entertaining and professionally written."

TWO DOLLAR RADIO

Website: www.twodollarradio.com. **Contact:** Eric Obenauf, editorial director. Estab. 2005. Two Dollar Radio is a boutique family-run press, publishing bold works of literary merit, each book, individually and collectively, providing a sonic progression that "we believe to be too loud to ignore." Targets readers who admire ambition and creativity. Range of print runs: 2,000-7,500 copies.

HOW TO CONTACT Submit entire, completed ms with a brief cover letter, via Submittable. No previously published work. No proposals. No excerpts. There is a $2 reading fee per submission. Accepts submissions every other month (January, March, May, July, September, November).

TERMS Advance: $500-1,000.

TIPS "We want writers who show an authority over language and the world that is being created, from the very first sentence on."

❶❷ TYNDALE HOUSE PUBLISHERS, INC.

351 Executive Dr., Carol Stream IL 60188. (800)323-9400. **Fax:** (800)684-0247. **Website:** www.tyndale.com. Estab. 1962. "Tyndale House publishes practical, user-friendly Christian books for the home and family." Publishes hardcover and trade paperback originals and mass paperback reprints. Guidelines online.

NEEDS "Christian truths must be woven into the story organically. No short story collections. Youth books: character building stories with Christian perspective. Especially interested in ages 10-14. We primarily publish Christian historical romances, with occasional contemporary, suspense, or standalones."

HOW TO CONTACT *Agented submissions only. No unsolicited mss.*

TERMS Pays negotiable royalty. Pays negotiable advance.

TIPS "All accepted manuscripts will appeal to Evangelical Christian children and parents."

UNBRIDLED BOOKS

8201 E. Highway WW, Columbia MO 65201. **E-mail:** michalsong@unbridledbooks.com. **Website:** unbridledbooks.com. **Contact:** Greg Michalson. Estab. 2004.

"Unbridled Books is a premier publisher of works of rich literary quality that appeal to a broad audience."

HOW TO CONTACT Please query first by e-mail. "Due to the heavy volume of submissions, we regret that at this time we are not able to consider uninvited mss."

TIPS "We try to read each ms that arrives, so please be patient."

UNIVERSITY OF ALASKA PRESS

P.O. Box 756240, Fairbanks AK 99775-6240. (907)474-5831 or (888)252-6657. **Fax:** (907)474-5502. **Website:** www.uaf.edu/uapress. Estab. 1967. "The mission of the University of Alaska Press is to encourage, publish, and disseminate works of scholarship that will enhance the store of knowledge about Alaska and the North Pacific Rim, with a special emphasis on the circumpolar regions." Publishes hardcover originals, trade paperback originals and reprints. Book catalog available free. Guidelines online.

NEEDS Alaska literary series with Peggy Shumaker as series editor. Publishes 1-3 works of fiction/year.

HOW TO CONTACT Submit proposal.

TERMS Responds in 2 months to queries.

TIPS "Writers have the best chance with scholarly nonfiction relating to Alaska, the circumpolar regions and North Pacific Rim. Our audience is made up of scholars, historians, students, libraries, universities, individuals, and the general Alaskan public."

UNIVERSITY OF GEORGIA PRESS

Main Library, Third Floor, 320 S. Jackson St., Athens GA 30602. (706)369-6130. **Fax:** (706)369-6131. **Website:** www.ugapress.org. **Contact:** Mick Gusinde-Duffy, executive editor; Walter Biggins, executive editor; Pat Allen, acquisitions editor; Beth Snead, assistant acquisitions editor. Estab. 1938. University of Georgia Press is a mid-sized press that publishes fiction only through the Flannery O'Connor Award for Short Fiction competition. Publishes hardcover originals, trade paperback originals, and reprints. Book catalog and guidelines online.

NEEDS Short story collections published in Flannery O'Connor Award Competition.

TERMS Pays 7-10% royalty on net receipts. Pays rare, varying advance. Responds in 2 months to queries.

TIPS "Please visit our website to view our book catalogs and for all manuscript submission guidelines."

UNIVERSITY OF IOWA PRESS

100 Kuhl House, 119 W. Park Rd., Iowa City IA 52242. (319)335-2000. **Fax:** (319)335-2055. **E-mail:** james-mccoy@uiowa.edu. **Website:** www.uiowapress.org. **Contact:** James McCoy, director. Estab. 1969. The University of Iowa Press publishes both trade and academic work in a variety of fields. Publishes hardcover and paperback originals. Book catalog available free. Guidelines online.

NEEDS Currently publishes the Iowa Short Fiction Award selections. "We do not accept any fiction submissions outside of the Iowa Short Fiction Award. See www.uiowapress.org for contest details."

UNIVERSITY OF MICHIGAN PRESS

839 Greene St., Ann Arbor MI 48106. (734)764-4388. **Fax:** (734)615-1540. **Website:** www.press.umich.edu. **Contact:** Mary Francis, editorial director. "In partnership with our authors and series editors, we publish in a wide range of humanities and social sciences disciplines." Guidelines online.

NEEDS In addition to the annual Michigan Literary Fiction Awards, this publishes literary fiction linked to the Great Lakes region.

HOW TO CONTACT Submit cover letter and first 30 pages.

UNIVERSITY OF NORTH TEXAS PRESS

1155 Union Circle, #311336, Denton TX 76203. (940)565-2142. **Fax:** (940)565-4590. **E-mail:** karen.devinney@unt.edu. **Website:** untpress.unt.edu. **Contact:** Ronald Chrisman, director; Karen De Vinney, assistant director. Estab. 1987. "We are dedicated to producing the highest quality scholarly, academic, and general interest books. We are committed to serving all peoples by publishing stories of their cultures and experiences that have been overlooked. Currently emphasizing military history, Texas history, music, Mexican-American studies." Publishes hardcover and trade paperback originals and reprints. Book catalog for 8 ½×11 SASE. Guidelines online.

NEEDS "The only fiction we publish is the winner of the Katherine Anne Porter Prize in Short Fiction, an annual, national competition with a $1,000 prize, and publication of the winning ms each Fall."

TERMS Responds in 1 month to queries.

TIPS "We publish series called War and the Southwest; Texas Folklore Society Publications; the Western Life Series; Practical Guide Series; Al-Filo: Mexican-American studies; North Texas Crime and Criminal Justice; Katherine Anne Porter Prize in Short Fiction; and the North Texas Lives of Musicians Series."

UNIVERSITY OF TAMPA PRESS

The University of Tampa, 401 W. Kennedy Blvd., Tampa FL 33606. (813)253-6266. **E-mail:** utpress@ut.edu.

Website: www.ut.edu/tampapress. **Contact:** Richard Mathews, editor. Estab. 1952. "We are a small university press publishing a limited number of titles each year, primarily in the areas of local and regional history, poetry, and printing history. We do not accept e-mail submissions." Publishes hardcover originals and reprints; trade paperback originals and reprints. Book catalog online.

TERMS Does not pay advance. Responds in 3-4 months to queries.

UNIVERSITY OF WISCONSIN PRESS

1930 Monroe St., 3rd Floor, Madison WI 53711. **E-mail:** kadushin@wisc.edu; gcwalker@wisc.edu. **Website:** uwpress.wisc.edu. **Contact:** Gwen Walker, executive editor (gcwalker@wisc.edu); Dennis Lloyd, director (dlloyd2@wisc.edu). Estab. 1937. See submission guidelines on our website.

HOW TO CONTACT Query with SASE or submit outline, 1-2 sample chapter(s), synopsis.

TERMS Pays royalty. Responds in 1-3 weeks to queries; 3-6 weeks to proposals. Rarely comments on rejected work.

TIPS "Make sure the query letter and sample text are well-written, and read guidelines carefully to make sure we accept the genre you are submitting."

USBORNE PUBLISHING

83-85 Saffron Hill, London EC1N 8RT, United Kingdom. (44)207430-2800. **Fax:** (44)207430-1562. **E-mail:** mail@usborne.co.uk. **Website:** www.usborne.com. "Usborne Publishing is a multiple-award-winning, worldwide children's publishing company publishing almost every type of children's book for every age from baby to young adult."

NEEDS Young readers, middle readers: adventure, contemporary, fantasy, history, humor, multicultural, nature/environment, science fiction, suspense/mystery, strong concept-based or character-led series. Average word length: young readers—5,000-10,000; middle readers—25,000-50,000; young adult—50,000-100,000.

HOW TO CONTACT *Agented submissions only.*

TERMS Pays authors royalty.

TIPS "Do not send any original work and, sorry, but we cannot guarantee a reply."

VÉHICULE PRESS

P.O.B. 42094 BP Roy, Montreal QC H2W 2T3, Canada. (514)844-6073. **E-mail:** sd@vehiculepress.com. **E-mail:** admin@vehiculepress.com. **Website:** www.vehiculepress.com. **Contact:** Simon Dardick, nonfic-tion; Carmine Starnino, poetry; Dimitri Nasrallah, fiction. Estab. 1973. "Montreal's Véhicule Press has published the best of Canadian and Quebec literature-fiction, poetry, essays, translations, and social history." Publishes trade paperback originals by Canadian authors mostly. Book catalog for 9 x 12 SAE with IRCs.

IMPRINTS Signal Editions (poetry); Esplanade Editions (fiction).

NEEDS No romance or formula writing.

HOW TO CONTACT Query with SASE.

TERMS Pays 10-15% royalty on retail price. Pays $200-500 advance. Responds in 4 months to queries.

TIPS "Quality in almost any style is acceptable. We believe in the editing process."

VERTIGO

DC Universe, Vertigo-DC Comics, 1700 Broadway, New York NY 10019. **Website:** www.vertigocomics.com. At this time, DC Entertainment does not accept unsolicited artwork or writing submissions.

VIKING

Imprint of Penguin Random House LLC. 1745 Broadway, New York NY 10019. (212)782-9000. **Website:** www.penguinrandomhouse.com. Estab. 1925. Viking publishes a mix of academic and popular fiction and nonfiction. Publishes hardcover and originals.

HOW TO CONTACT *Agented submissions only.*

TERMS Pays 10-15% royalty on retail price.

VIKING CHILDREN'S BOOKS

Imprint of Penguin Random House LLC. 1745 Broadway, New York NY 10019. (212)782-9000 **Website:** www.penguinrandomhouse.com. "Viking Children's Books is known for humorous, quirky picture books, in addition to more traditional fiction. We publish the highest quality fiction, nonfiction, and picture books for pre-schoolers through young adults." *Does not accept unsolicited submissions.* Publishes hardcover originals.

NEEDS All levels: adventure, animal, contemporary, fantasy, history, humor, multicultural, nature/environment, poetry, problem novels, romance, science fiction, sports, suspense/mystery.

HOW TO CONTACT *Accepts agented mss only.*

TERMS Pays 2-10% royalty on retail price or flat fee. Pays negotiable advance. Responds in 6 months.

TIPS "No 'cartoony' or mass-market submissions for picture books."

A⊘ VILLARD BOOKS

Penguin Random House, 1745 Broadway, New York NY 10019. (212)572-2600. **Website:** www.penguinrandomhouse.com. Estab. 1983. "Villard Books is the publisher of savvy and sometimes quirky, best-selling hardcovers and trade paperbacks."

NEEDS Commercial fiction.

HOW TO CONTACT *Agented submissions only.*

TERMS Pays negotiable royalty. Pays negotiable advance.

A⊘ VINTAGE ANCHOR PUBLISHING

Penguin Random House, 1745 Broadway, New York NY 10019. **Website:** www.penguinrandomhouse.com.

HOW TO CONTACT *Agented submissions only.*

TERMS Pays 4-8% royalty on retail price. Average advance: $2,500 and up.

VIVISPHERE PUBLISHING

675 Dutchess Turnpike, Poughkeepsie NY 12603. (845)463-1100, ext. 314. **Fax:** (845)463-0018. **E-mail:** cs@vivisphere.com. **Website:** www.vivisphere.com. **Contact:** Submissions. Estab. 1995. Vivisphere Publishing is now considering new submissions from any genre as follows: game of bridge (cards), nonfiction, history, military, new age, fiction, feminist/gay/lesbian, horror, contemporary, self-help, science fiction and cookbooks. Publishes trade paperback originals and reprints and e-books. Book catalog and ms guidelines online.

○ "Cookbooks should have a particular slant or appeal to a certain niche. Also publish out-of-print books."

HOW TO CONTACT Query with SASE.

TERMS Pays royalty. Responds in 6-24 months.

⊘ VIZ MEDIA LLC

P.O. Box 77010, San Francisco CA 94107. (415)546-7073. **Website:** www.viz.com. "VIZ Media, LLC is one of the most comprehensive and innovative companies in the field of manga (graphic novel) publishing, animation and entertainment licensing of Japanese content. Owned by three of Japan's largest creators and licensors of manga and animation, Shueisha Inc., Shogakukan Inc., and Shogakukan-Shueisha Productions, Co., Ltd., VIZ Media is a leader in the publishing and distribution of Japanese manga for English speaking audiences in North America, the United Kingdom, Ireland, and South Africa and is a global ex-Asia licensor of Japanese manga and animation. The company offers an integrated product line including magazines such as *Shonen*

Jump and *Shojo Beat*, graphic novels, and DVDs, and develops, markets, licenses, and distributes animated entertainment for audiences and consumers of all ages."

HOW TO CONTACT "At the present, all of the manga that appears in our magazines come directly from manga that has been serialized and published in Japan."

WASHINGTON WRITERS' PUBLISHING HOUSE

P.O. Box 15271, Washington DC 20003. **Website:** www.washingtonwriters.org. Estab. 1975. Guidelines online.

NEEDS Washington Writers' Publishing House considers book-length mss for publication by fiction writers living within 75 driving miles of the U.S. Capitol, Baltimore area included, through competition only. Mss may include previously published stories and excerpts. "Author should indicate where they heard about WWPH."

HOW TO CONTACT Submit an electronic copy by e-mail (use PDF, .doc, or rich text format) or 2 hard copies by snail mail of a short story collection or novel (no more than 350 pages, double or 1-1/2 spaced; author's name should not appear on any ms pages). Include separate page of publication acknowledgments plus 2 cover sheets: one with ms title, poet's name, address, telephone number, and e-mail address, the other with ms title only. Include SASE for results only; mss will not be returned (will be recycled).

TERMS Offers $1,000 and 50 copies of published book plus additional copies for publicity use.

A⊘ WATERBROOK MULTNOMAH PUBLISHING GROUP

10807 New Allegiance Dr., Suite 500, Colorado Springs CO 80921. (719)590-4999. **Fax:** (719)590-8977. **Website:** www.waterbrookmultnomah.com. Estab. 1996. Publishes hardcover and trade paperback originals. Book catalog online.

HOW TO CONTACT *Agented submissions only.*

TERMS Pays royalty. Responds in 2-3 months.

WHITAKER HOUSE

1030 Hunt Valley Circle, New Kensington PA 15068. **E-mail:** publisher@whitakerhouse.com. **Website:** www.whitakerhouse.com. **Contact:** Editorial Department. Estab. 1970. Publishes hardcover, trade paperback, and mass market originals. Book catalog online. Guidelines online.

IMPRINTS Whitaker Espanol, SmartKidz.

NEEDS All fiction must have a Christian perspective.

HOW TO CONTACT Query with SASE.

TERMS Pays 5-15% royalty on wholesale price. Responds in 3 months.

TIPS "Audience includes those seeking uplifting and inspirational fiction and nonfiction."

✪ WHITECAP BOOKS, LTD.

210 - 314 W. Cordova St., Vancouver BC V6B 1 E8, Canada. (604)681-6181. **Fax:** (905)477-9179. **Website:** www.whitecap.ca. "Whitecap Books is a general trade publisher with a focus on food and wine titles. Although we are interested in reviewing unsolicited ms submissions, please note that we only accept submissions that meet the needs of our current publishing program. Please see some of most recent releases to get an idea of the kinds of titles we are interested in." Publishes hardcover and trade paperback originals. Catalog and guidelines online.

NEEDS No children's picture books or adult fiction.

HOW TO CONTACT See guidelines.

TERMS Pays royalty. Pays negotiated advance. Responds in 2-3 months to proposals.

TIPS "We want well-written, well-researched material that presents a fresh approach to a particular topic."

WHITE MANE KIDS

73 W. Burd St., Shippensburg PA 17257. (717)532-2237. **Fax:** (717)532-6110. **E-mail:** marketing@whitemane. com. **Website:** www.whitemane.com. **Contact:** Harold Collier, acquisitions editor. Estab. 1987. Book catalog and writer's guidelines available for SASE.

IMPRINTS White Mane Books, Burd Street Press, White Mane Kids, Ragged Edge Press.

NEEDS Middle readers, young adults: history (primarily American Civil War). Average word length: middle readers—30,000. Does not publish picture books.

HOW TO CONTACT Query.

TERMS Pays authors royalty of 7-10%. Pays illustrators and photographers by the project. Responds to queries in 1 month, mss in 6-9 months.

TIPS "Make your work historically accurate. We are interested in historically accurate fiction for middle and young adult readers. We do *not* publish picture books. Our primary focus is the American Civil War and some America Revolution topics."

⑤ THE WILD ROSE PRESS

P.O. Box 708, Adams Basin NY 14410-0708. (585)752-8770. **E-mail:** queryus@thewildrosepress.com. **Website:** www.thewildrosepress.com. **Contact:** Rhonda Penders, editor-in-chief. Estab. 2006. Publishes paperback originals, reprints, and e-books in a POD format. Guidelines online.

HOW TO CONTACT *Does not accept unsolicited mss.* Send query letter with outline and synopsis of up to 5 pages. Accepts all queries by e-mail. Include estimated word count, brief bio, and list of publishing credits. Agented fiction less than 1%. Always comments on rejected mss.

TERMS Pays royalty of 7% minimum; 40% maximum. Sends prepublication galleys to author. Responds to queries in 4 weeks; mss in 12 weeks.

TIPS "Polish your manuscript, make it as error free as possible, and follow our submission guidelines."

⊘⊘ WILLIAM MORROW

HarperCollins, 195 Broadway, New York NY 10007. (212)207-7000. **Fax:** (212)207-7145. **Website:** www.harpercollins.com. Estab. 1926. "William Morrow publishes a wide range of titles that receive much recognition and prestige—a most selective house." Book catalog available free.

NEEDS Publishes adult fiction. Morrow accepts only the highest quality submissions in adult fiction. *No unsolicited mss or proposals.*

HOW TO CONTACT *Agented submissions only.*

TERMS Pays standard royalty on retail price. Pays varying advance.

WOODBINE HOUSE

6510 Bells Mill Rd., Bethesda MD 20817. (301)897-3570. **Fax:** (301)897-5838. **E-mail:** info@woodbinehouse.com. **Website:** www.woodbinehouse.com. **Contact:** Acquisitions Editor. Estab. 1985. Woodbine House publishes books for or about individuals with disabilities to help those individuals and their families live fulfilling and satisfying lives in their homes, schools, and communities. Publishes trade paperback originals. Guidelines online.

NEEDS Receptive to stories re: developmental and intellectual disabilities, e.g., autism and cerebral palsy.

HOW TO CONTACT Submit complete ms with SASE.

TERMS Pays 10-12% royalty. Responds in 3 months to queries.

TIPS "Do not send us a proposal on the basis of this description. Examine our catalog or website and a couple of our books to make sure you are on the right track. Put some thought into how your book could be marketed (aside from in bookstores). Keep cover letters concise and to the point; if it's a subject that interests us, we'll ask to see more."

WORLD WEAVER PRESS

Albuquerque NM 87154. **Website:** www.worldweaverpress.com. **Contact:** WWP Editors. Estab. 2012. World Weaver Press publishes digital and print editions of speculative fiction at various lengths for adult, young adult, and new adult audiences. "We believe in great storytelling." Catalog online. Guidelines on website.

NEEDS "We believe that publishing speculative fiction isn't just printing words on the page — it's the act of weaving brand new worlds. Seeking speculative fiction in many varieties: protagonists who have strength, not fainting spells; intriguing worlds with well-developed settings; characters that are to die for (we'd rather find ourselves in love than just in lust)." Full list of interests on website. Not currently open to full-length fiction. Check anthology submission guidelines for short fiction calls.

HOW TO CONTACT Not currently open for queries. Full guidelines will be updated approximately one month before queries re-open. Frequently open for submissions for themed short story anthologies. Check website for details.

TERMS Average royalty rate of 39% net on all editions. No advance. Responds to query letters within 3 weeks. Responses to mss requests take longer.

WORTHYKIDS

Hachette Book Group, 6100 Tower Circle, Suite 210, Franklin TN 37067. (615)932-7600. **E-mail:** idealsinfo@worthypublishing.com. **Website:** www.worthypublishing.com. Estab. 1944. "WorthyKids is an imprint of Hachette Book Group and publishes 20-30 new children's titles a year, primarily for 2-8 year-olds. Our backlist includes more than 400 titles, including The Berenstain Bears, VeggieTales, and Frosty the Snowman. We publish picture books, activity books, board books, and novelty/sound books covering a wide array of topics, such as Bible stories, holidays, early learning, history, family relationships, and values. Our bestselling titles include *The Story of Christmas, The Story of Easter, The Sparkle Box, Seaman's Journal, How Do I Love You?, God Made You Special, The Berenstain Bears' Please and Thank You Book,* and *My Daddy and I.* Through our dedication to publishing high-quality and engaging books, we never forget our obligation to our littlest readers to help create those special moments with books."

NEEDS WorthyKids/Ideals publishes fiction and nonfiction picture books for children ages 2 to 8. Subjects include holiday, faith/inspirational, family values, and patriotic themes; relationships and values; and general fiction. Picture book mss should be no longer than 800 words. Board book mss should be no longer than 250 words.

HOW TO CONTACT Editors will review complete mss only; please do not send query letters or proposals. Previous publications, relevant qualifications or background, and a brief synopsis of your manuscript may be included in a cover letter. Please send copies only—we cannot be responsible for an original ms. Include your name, address, and phone number or e-mail address on every page. Do not include original art or photographs. We do not accept digital submissions via e-mail or other electronic means. Send complete mss to: WorthyKids, Attn: SUBMISSIONS, 6100 Tower Circle, Suite 210, Franklin TN 37067.

TERMS Due to the high volume of submissions, we are only able to respond to unsolicited manuscripts of interest to our publishing program. We cannot discuss submissions by telephone or in person and we cannot provide detailed editorial feedback.

WORTHY KIDS/IDEALS BOOKS

6100 Tower Circle, Suite 210, Franklin TN 37067. **Website:** www.idealsbooks.com. Estab. 1944.

NEEDS Picture books: animal, concept, history, religion. Board books: animal, history, nature/environment, religion. Worthy Kids/Ideals publishes for ages birth to 8, no longer than 800 words.

HOW TO CONTACT Submit complete ms.

YELLOW SHOE FICTION SERIES

LSU Press, P.O. Box 25053, Baton Rouge LA 70894. **Website:** www.lsu.edu/lsupress. **Contact:** Michael Griffith, editor. Estab. 2004.

"Looking first and foremost for literary excellence, especially good manuscripts that have fallen through the cracks at the big commercial presses. I'll cast a wide net."

HOW TO CONTACT Does not accept unsolicited mss. Accepts queries by mail, Attn: James W. Long.

TERMS Pays royalty. Offers advance.

ZEBRA BOOKS

Kensington, 119 W. 40th St., New York NY 10018. (212)407-1500. **E-mail:** esogah@kensingtonbooks.com. **Website:** www.kensingtonbooks.com. **Contact:** Esi Sogah, senior editor. Zebra Books is dedicated to women's fiction, which includes, but is not limited to romance. Publishes hardcover originals, trade paperback and mass market paperback originals and reprints. Book catalog online.

HOW TO CONTACT Query.

ZUMAYA PUBLICATIONS, LLC

3209 S. Interstate 35, Austin TX 78741. (512)333-4055. **Fax:** (512)276-6745. **E-mail:** business@zumayapublishing.com. **E-mail:** acquisitions@zumayapublications.com. **Website:** www.zumayapublications.com. **Contact:** Elizabeth K. Burton. Estab. 1999. Zumaya Publications is a digitally-based micro-press publishing mainly in on-demand trade paperback and e-book formats in an effort to reduce environmental impact. "We currently offer approximately 190 fiction titles in the mystery, SF/F, historical, romance, LGBTQ, horror, and occult genres in adult, young adult, and middle reader categories. In 2016, we plan to officially launch our graphic and illustrated novel imprint, Zumaya Fabled Ink. We publish approximately 10-15 new titles annually, at least five of which are from new authors. We do *not* publish erotica or graphic erotic romance at this time. We accept only electronic queries; all others will be discarded unread. A working knowledge of computers and relevant software is a necessity, as our production process is completely digital." Publishes trade paperback and electronic originals. Catalog online. Guidelines online. "We do not accept hard-copy queries or submissions."

○ Zumaya was publishing diversity before it became a thing, and is always looking for fiction that presents the wonderful multiplicity of cultures in the world in ways that can lower the divisions that are too often keeping us from understanding one another. We also love books about people who are often either overlooked altogether or presented in clichéd ways. A romance between two 80-year-olds? Bring it on. A police procedural where the officers have happy home lives? Yes, please. We like the idea of having fiction that reflects the manifold realities of people everywhere, even if the world they inhabit resides only in the author's imagination.

IMPRINTS Zumaya Arcane (New Age, inspirational fiction & nonfiction), Zumaya Boundless (GLBTQ); Zumaya Embraces (romance/women's fiction); Zumaya Enigma (mystery/suspense/thriller); Zumaya Thresholds (YA/middle grade); Zumaya Otherworlds (SF/F/H), Zumaya Yesterdays (memoirs, historical fiction, fiction, western fiction); Zumaya Fabled Ink (graphic and illustrated novels).

NEEDS "We are open to all genres, particularly GLBT and YA/middle grade, historical and western, New Age/inspirational (no overtly Christian materials, please), non-category romance, thrillers. We encourage people to review what we've already published so as to avoid sending us more of the same, at least, insofar as the plot is concerned. While we're always looking for good mysteries, especially cozies, mysteries with historical settings, and police procedurals, we want original concepts rather than slightly altered versions of what we've already published. We do not publish erotica or graphically erotic romance at this time." Does not want erotica, graphically erotic romance, experimental, literary (unless it fits into one of our established imprints).

HOW TO CONTACT A copy of our rules of submission is posted on our website and can be downloaded. They are rules rather than guidelines and should be read carefully before submitting. It will save everyone time and frustration.

TERMS Pay 20% of net on paperbacks, net defined as cover price less printing and other associated costs; 50% of net on all e-books. Does not pay advance. Responds in 3 months to queries and proposals; 6 months to mss.

TIPS "We're catering to readers who may have loved last year's best seller but not enough to want to read 10 more just like it. Have something different. If it does not fit standard pigeonholes, that's a plus. On the other hand, it has to have an audience. And if you're not prepared to work with us on promotion and marketing, particularly via social media, it would be better to look elsewhere."

CONTESTS & AWARDS

///

In addition to honors and, quite often, cash prizes, contests and awards programs offer writers the opportunity to be judged on the basis of quality alone, without the outside factors that sometimes influence publishing decisions. New writers who win contests may be published for the first time, while more experienced writers may gain public recognition for an entire body of work.

Listed here are contests for almost every type of fiction writing. Some focus on form, such as short stories, novels, or novellas, while others feature writing on particular themes or topics. Still others are prestigious prizes or awards for work that must be nominated.

SELECTING AND SUBMITTING TO A CONTEST

Use the same care in submitting to contests as you would sending your manuscript to a publication or book publisher. Deadlines are very important, and, where possible, we've included this information. For some contests, deadlines were only approximate at our press deadline, so be sure to write, call, or look online for complete information.

Follow the rules to the letter. If, for instance, contest rules require your name on a cover sheet only, you will be disqualified if you ignore this and put your name on every page. Find out how many copies to send. If you don't send the correct amount, by the time you are contacted to send more, it may be past the submission deadline. An increasing number of contests invite writers to query by e-mail, and many post contest information on their websites. Check listings for e-mail and website addresses.

One note of caution: Beware of contests that charge entry fees that are disproportionate to the amount of the prize. Contests offering a $10 prize and charging $7 in entry fees are a waste of your time and money.

AEON AWARD

Albedo One/Aeon Press, Aeon Award, Albedo One & Yellow Brick Road, 8 Bachelor's Walk, Dublin D1, Ireland. (353)1-8730177. **E-mail:** fraslaw@yahoo.co.uk. **Website:** www.albedo1.com. **Contact:** Frank Ludlow, Event Coordinator.. Estab. 2004.. Prestigious fiction-writing competition for short stories in any speculative fiction genre such as fantasy, science fiction, horror, or anything in-between or unclassifiable. Annual Deadline: November 30. Contest begins January 1. Grand Prize: €1,000; 2nd Prize: €200; 3rd Prize: €100. The top 3 stories are guaranteed publication in *Albedo One*. Costs: €8.50 entry fee. Judged by Ian Watson, Priya Sharma, Juliet E. McKenna, and Michael Carroll.

AESTHETICA ART PRIZE

Aesthetica Magazine, P.O. Box 371, York YO23 1WL, United Kingdom. (+44)1904 629 137. **E-mail:** info@ aestheticamagazine.com; artprize@aestheticamagazine.com. **Website:** www.aestheticamagazine.com. The Aesthetica Art Prize is a celebration of excellence in art from across the world and offers artists the opportunity to showcase their work to wider audiences and further their involvement in the international art world. There are 4 categories: Photograpic & Digital Art, Three Dimensional Design & Sculpture, Painting & Drawing, Video Installation & Performance. See guidelines at Artwork & Photography, Fiction, and Poetry. See guidelines at www.aestheticamagazine. com. The Aesthetica Art Prize is a celebration of excellence in art from across the world, and offers artists the opportunity to showcase their work to wider audiences and further their involvement in the international art world. Deadline: August 31. Prizes include: £5,000 main prize courtesy of Hiscox; £1,000 Student Prize courtesy of Hiscox; group exhibition and publication in the Aesthetica Art Prize Anthology. Entry fee is £24 and permits submission of 2 works in one category. Costs: £24. The panel comprises influential art figures; including curators, academics and artists whose expertise spans all media.

AHWA FLASH & SHORT STORY COMPETITION

AHWA (Australian Horror Writers Association), **E-mail:** ahwacomps@australianhorror.com; ahwa@australianhorror.com. **Website:** www.australianhorror. com. **Contact:** Competitions Officer. Competition/ award for short stories and flash fiction. Looking for horror stories, tales that frighten, yarns that unsettle readers in their comfortable homes. All themes in this genre will be accepted, from the well-used (zombies, vampires, ghosts etc) to the highly original, so long as the story is professional and well written. Deadline: May 31. Prize: The authors of the winning Flash Fiction and Short Story entries will each receive paid publication in *Midnight Echo*, the Magazine of the AHWA, and an engraved plaque. Costs: $5 for flash fiction, $10 for short story; free for AHWA members. Judged by previous winners.

ALABAMA STATE COUNCIL ON THE ARTS INDIVIDUAL ARTIST FELLOWSHIP

201 Monroe St., Suite 110, Montgomery AL 36130. (334)242-4076, ext. 236. **Fax:** (334)240-3269. **E-mail:** anne.kimzey@arts.alabama.gov. **Website:** www.arts. state.al.us. **Contact:** Anne Kimzey, Literary Arts Program Manager. Recognizes the achievements and potential of Alabama writers. Deadline: March 1. Applications must be submitted online by eGRANT. Costs: No entry fee. Judged by independent peer panel. Fellowship recipients notified by mail and announced on website in June.

MARIE ALEXANDER POETRY SERIES

English Department, 2801 S. University Ave., Little Rock AR 72204. **E-mail:** mariealexandereditor@ gmail.com. **Website:** mariealexanderseries.com. **Contact:** Nickole Brown.. Annual contest for a collection of previously unpublished prose poems or flash fiction by a U.S. writer. Deadline: July 31. Open to submissions on July 1. Prize: $1,000, plus publication.

ALLIGATOR JUNIPER AWARD

Alligator Juniper/Prescott College, 220 Grove Ave., Prescott AZ 86301. (928)350-2012. **Fax:** (928)776-5102. **E-mail:** alligatorjuniper@prescott.edu. **Website:** www.prescott.edu/alligatorjuniper/national-contest/index.html. **Contact:** Skye Anicca, Managing Editor.. Annual contest for unpublished fiction, creative nonfiction, and poetry. Open to all age levels. Each entrant receives a personal letter from staff regarding the status of their submission, as well as minor feedback on the piece. Deadline: October 1. Prize: $1,000 plus publication in all three categories. Finalists in each genre are recognized as such, published, and paid in copies. Costs: $15. Judged by distinguished writers in each genre and Prescott College writing students enrolled in the Literary Journal Practicum course.

AMERICAN ASSOCIATION OF UNIVERSITY WOMEN YOUNG PEOPLE'S LITERATURE AWARD

4610 Mail Service Center, Raleigh NC 27699-4610. (919)807-7290. **E-mail:** michael.hill@ncdcr.gov. **Website:** www.ncdcr.gov. **Contact:** Michael Hill, Awards Coordinator.. Annual award. Book must be published during the year ending June 30. Submissions made by author, author's agent. or publisher. SASE for contest rules. Recognizes the year's best work of juvenile literature by a North Carolina resident. Deadline: July 15. Prize: Awards a cup to the winner and winner's name inscribed on a plaque displayed within the North Carolina Office of Archives and History. Judged by 3-judge panel.

○ Competition receives 10-15 submissions per category.

AMERICAN LITERARY REVIEW CONTESTS

American Literary Review, P.O. Box 311307, University of North Texas, Denton TX 76203-1307. (940)565-2755. **E-mail:** americanliteraryreview@gmail.com. **Website:** www.americanliteraryreview.com. Contest to award excellence in short fiction, creative nonfiction, and poetry. Multiple entries are acceptable, but each entry must be accompanied with a reading fee. Do not put any identifying information in the file itself; include the author's name, title(s), address, e-mail address, and phone number in the boxes provided in the online submissions manager. Short fiction: Limit 8,000 words per work. Creative Nonfiction: Limit 6,500 words per work. Deadline: October 1. Submission period begins June 1. Prize: $1,000 prize for each category, along with publication in the Spring online issue of the *American Literary Review*. Costs: $15 reading fee for one short story, one creative nonfiction entry, or up to 3 poems.

AMERICAN-SCANDINAVIAN FOUNDATION TRANSLATION PRIZE

The American-Scandinavian Foundation, 58 Park Ave., New York NY 10016. (212)779-3587. **E-mail:** grants@amscan.org; info@amscan.org. **Website:** www.amscan.org. **Contact:** Carl Fritscher, Fellowships & Grants Officer.. The annual ASF translation competition is awarded for the most outstanding translations of poetry, fiction, drama, or literary prose written by a Scandinavian author born after 1900. Deadline: June 15. Prize: The Nadia Christensen Prize includes a $2,500 award, publication of an excerpt in *Scandinavian Review*, and a commemorative bronze medallion. The Leif and Inger Sjöberg Award, given to an individual whose literature translations have not previously been published, includes a $2,000 award, publication of an excerpt in *Scandinavian Review*, and a commemorative bronze medallion.

SHERWOOD ANDERSON FICTION AWARD

Mid-American Review, Mid-American Review, Dept. of English, Box WM, BGSU, Bowling Green OH 43403. (419)372-2725. **Fax:** (419)372-4642. **E-mail:** mar@bgsu.edu. **Website:** www.bgsu.edu/midamericanreview. **Contact:** Abigail Cloud, Editor-in-Chief.. Offered annually for unpublished mss (6,000 word limit). Contest is open to all writers not associated with a judge or *Mid-American Review*. Deadline: December 15, 2019. Prize: $1,000, plus publication in the Spring issue of *Mid-American Review*. Four finalists: Notation, possible publication. Costs: $10. Judged by editors and a well-known writer (Aimee Bender or Anthony Doerr). Judged by Charles Yu in 2017. 2017-2018 judges: Alexander Weinstein and Dara Wier.

ANNUAL WRITING CONTEST

Lumina, the literary journal of Sarah Lawrence College., Sarah Lawrence College Slonim House, One Mead Way, Bronxville NY 10708. **E-mail:** lumina@gm.slc.edu. **Website:** www.luminajournal.com/contest. Annual writing contest in poetry, fiction, or creative nonfiction (varies by year). Please visit website in August/September for complete and updated contest rules. Deadline varies by year. Usually in the early fall. Prize: Cash. Costs: $12.

ARTIST TRUST FELLOWSHIP AWARD

1835 12th Ave., Seattle WA 98122. (209)467-8734, ext. 11. **Fax:** (866)218-7878. **E-mail:** info@artisttrust.org. **Website:** www.artisttrust.org. **Contact:** Miguel Guillen, Program Manager.. Fellowships award $7,500 to practicing professional artists of exceptional talent and demonstrated ability. The Fellowship is a merit-based, not a project-based, award. Recipients present a Meet the Artist Event to a community in Washington state that has little or no access to the artist and their work. Awards 14 fellowships of $7,500 and 2 residencies with $1,000 stipends at the Millay Colony. Deadline: January 17. Applications available December 3. Prize: $7,500.

ARTS & LETTERS PRIZES

Arts & Letters Journal of Contemporary Culture, Campus Box 89, GC&SU, Milledgeville GA 31061. (478)445-1289. **E-mail:** al.journal@gcsu.edu. **Website:** al.gcsu.edu. **Contact:** The Editors.. Offered annually for unpublished work. Deadline: March 31. Prize: $1,000 prize for each of the four major genres. Fiction, poetry, and creative nonfiction winners are published in Fall or Spring issue. The prize-winning, one-act play is produced at the Georgia College campus (usually in March). Costs: $20/entry (payable to GC&SU). Judged by the editors (initial screening); see website for final judges and further details about submitting work.

$ AUTUMN HOUSE POETRY, FICTION, AND NONFICTION PRIZES

5530 Penn Ave., Pittsburgh PA 15206. (412)362-2665. **E-mail:** info@autumnhouse.org. **Website:** autumnhouse.org. **Contact:** Christine Stroud, Editor-in-Chief. Estab. 1998. Offers annual prize and publication of book-length ms with national promotion. Submission must be unpublished as a collection, but individual poems, stories, and essays may have been previously published elsewhere. Considers simultaneous submissions. "Autumn House is a nonprofit corporation with the mission of publishing and promoting poetry and other fine literature. We have published books by Sherrie Flick, Ed Ochester, Gerald Stern, Sharma Shields, Clifford Thompson, Danusha Lameris, Cameron Barnett, Dickson Lamb, Harrison Candelaria Fletcher, Ada Limon, and many others." Deadline: June 30. Prize: The winner (in each of 3 categories) will receive book publication, $1,000 advance against royalties, and a $1,500 travel/publicity grant to promote his or her book. Costs: $30/ms. Judged by Cornelius Eady (poetry), Aimee Bender (fiction), and Paul Lisicky (nonfiction).

AUTUMN HOUSE PRESS FULL-LENGTH FICTION PRIZE

Autumn House Press, 5530 Penn Ave., Pittsburgh PA 15206. **E-mail:** info@autumnhouse.org. **Website:** autumnhouse.org. Fiction submissions should be approximately 200-300 pages. All fiction sub-genres (short stories, short-shorts, novellas, or novels), or any combination of sub-genres, are eligible. All finalists will be considered for publication. Deadline: June 30. Prize: Winners will receive book publication, $1,000 advance against royalties, and a $1,500 travel grant. Costs: $30. Judged by Aimee Bender (final judge).

AWP AWARD SERIES

Association of Writers & Writing Programs 5700 Rivertech Ct, Suite 225 , 20737-1250, 5700 Rivertech Ct, Suite 225, Riverdale Park MD 22030. **E-mail:** supriya@awpwriter.org. **Website:** www.awpwriter.org. **Contact:** Supriya Bhatnagar, Director of Publications.. AWP sponsors the Award Series, an annual competition for the publication of excellent new book-length works. The competition is open to all authors writing in English, regardless of nationality or residence, and is available to published and unpublished authors alike. Offered annually to foster new literary talent. Deadline: Postmarked between January 1 and February 28. Prize: AWP Prize for the Novel: $2,500 and publication by New Issues Press; Donald Hall Prize for Poetry: $5,500 and publication by the University of Pittsburgh Press; Grace Paley Prize in Short Fiction: $5,500 and publication by the University of Massachusetts Press; and AWP Prize for Creative Nonfiction: $2,500 and publication by the University of Georgia Press. Costs: $30 for nonmembers; $20 for members. Creative Nonficton: Debra Monroe; Novel:Bonnie Jo Campbell; Poetry: Natasha D. Trethewey; Short Fiction: Dan Chaon.

BALCONES FICTION PRIZE

Austin Commmunity College, Department of Creative Writing c/o Joe O'Connell, 4400 College Park Dr,, Round Rock TX 78665. (512)584-5045. **E-mail:** joconne@austincc.edu. **Website:** www.austincc.edu/crw/html/balconescenter.html. **Contact:** Joe O'Connell. Awarded to the best book of literary fiction published the previous year. Books of prose may be submitted by publisher or author. Send three copies. Deadline: January 31. Prize: $1,500, winner is flown to Austin for a campus reading. Costs: $30 reading fee.

BARD FICTION PRIZE

Bard College, P.O. Box 5000, Annandale-on-Hudson NY 12504-5000. (845)758-7087. **Fax:** (845)758-7917. **E-mail:** bfp@bard.edu. **Website:** www.bard.edu/bfp. **Contact:** Irene Zedlacher.. Estab. 2001. The Bard Fiction Prize is awarded to a promising, emerging writer who is an American citizen aged 39 years or younger at the time of application. The Bard Fiction Prize is intended to encourage and support young writers of fiction to pursue their creative goals and to provide an opportunity to work in a fertile and intellectual environment. Deadline: June 15. Prize: $30,000 and appointment as writer-in-residence at Bard College for 1 semester. Judged by a committee of 5 judges (authors associated with Bard College).

MILDRED L. BATCHELDER AWARD

Association for Library Service to Children, Division of the American Library Association, 50 E. Huron St., Chicago IL 60611-2795. (800)545-2433. **Fax:** (312)280-5271. **Website:** www.ala.org/alsc/awardsgrants/book-media/batchelderaward. Estab. 1966. The Batchelder Award is given to the most outstanding children's book originally published in a language other than English in a country other than the United States, and subsequently translated into English for publication in the US. The purpose of the award, a citation to an American publisher, is to encourage international exchange of quality children's books by recognizing US publishers of such books in translation. Deadline: December 31.

BELLEVUE LITERARY REVIEW GOLDENBERG PRIZE FOR FICTION

Bellevue Literary Review, NYU Dept of Medicine, 550 First Ave., OBV-A612, New York NY 10016. (212)263-3973. **E-mail:** info@blreview.org; stacy@blreview.org. **Website:** www.blreview.org. **Contact:** Stacy Bodziak, managing editor. The BLR prizes award outstanding writing related to themes of health, healing, illness, the mind and the body. Annual competition/award for short stories. Receives about 200-300 entries per category. Submit online. Guidelines available in February. Accepts inquiries by e-mail, phone, mail. Submissions open March 1st. Results announced in December and made available to entrants with SASE, by e-mail, on website. Winners notified by mail, by e-mail. Deadline: July 1. Prize: $1,000 and publication in *The Bellevue Literary Review*. Honorable mention winners receive $250 and publication. Costs: $20, or $30 to include 1-year subscription. BLR editors select semi-finalists to be read by an independent judge who chooses the winner. Previous judges include Nathan Englander, Jane Smiley, Francine Prose, Andre Dubus III, Ha Jin, and Geraldine Brooks.

⭕ GEORGE BENNETT FELLOWSHIP

Phillips Exeter Academy, 20 Main Street, Exeter NH 03833-2460. **E-mail:** teaching_opportunities@exeter.edu. **Website:** www.exeter.edu/bennettfellowship. Annual award for fellow and family to provide time and freedom from material considerations to a person seriously contemplating or pursuing a career as a writer. Applicants should have a ms in progress that they intend to complete during the fellowship period. Ms should be fiction, nonfiction, novel, short stories, or poetry. Duties: To be in residency at the Academy for the academic year; to make oneself available informally to students interested in writing. Committee favors writers who have not yet published a book with a major publisher. Deadline: November 30. A choice will be made, and all entrants notified in mid-April. Cash stipend (currently $15,260), room and board. Costs: $15 application fee. Application form and guidelines on website. Judged by committee of the English Department.

BINGHAMTON UNIVERSITY JOHN GARDNER FICTION BOOK AWARD

Creative Writing Program, Binghamton University, Binghamton University, Department of English, General Literature, and Rhetoric, Library North Room 1149, P.O. Box 6000, Binghamton NY 13902-6000. (607)777-2713. **E-mail:** cwpro@binghamton.edu. **Website:** http://binghamton.edu/english/creative-writing/. **Contact:** Maria Mazziotti Gillan, Director. Estab. 2001. Contest offered annually for a novel or collection of fiction published in previous year in a press run of 500 copies or more. Each book submitted must be accompanied by an application form. Publisher may submit more than 1 book for prize consideration. Send 2 copies of each book. Guidelines available on website. Deadline: February 1 $1,000. Judged by a professional writer not on Binghamton University faculty.

🌀 JAMES TAIT BLACK MEMORIAL PRIZES

English Literature, University of Edinburgh, School of Literatures, Languages, and Cultures, 50 George Square, Edinburgh EH8 9LH, Scotland. (44-13)1650-3619. **E-mail:** s.strathdee@ed.ac.uk. **Website:** https://www.ed.ac.uk/events/james-tait-black. Estab. 1919. Open to any writer. Entries must be previously published. Winners notified by phone, via publisher. Contact department of English Literature for list of winners or check website. Accepts inquiries by e-mail or phone. Deadline: December 1 Two prizes each of £10,000 are awarded: one for the best work of fiction, one for the best biography or work of nature, published during the calendar year January 1 to December 31. Judged by professors of English Literature, with the assistance of teams of postgraduate readers.

THE BLACK RIVER CHAPBOOK COMPETITION

Black Lawrence Press, 279 Claremont Ave, Mount Vernon NY 10552. **E-mail:** editors@blacklawrencepress.com. **Website:** www.blacklawrence.com. **Contact:** Kit Frick, senior editor. Twice each year Black Lawrence Press will run the Black River Chapbook Competition for an unpublished chapbook of poems or short fiction between 16-36 pages in length. Spring deadline: May 31. Fall deadline: October 31. Prize: $500, publication, and 10 copies. Costs: $15. Judged by a revolving panel of judges, in addition to the Chapbook Editor and other members of the BLP editorial staff.

🐚 THE BOARDMAN TASKER PRIZE FOR MOUNTAIN LITERATURE

The Boardman Tasker Charitable Trust, 8 Bank View Rd., Darley Abbey Derby DE22 1EJ, UK. 01332 342246. **E-mail:** steve@people-matter.co.uk. **Website:** www.boardmantasker.com. **Contact:** Steve Dean. Offered annually to reward a work with a mountain theme, whether fiction, nonfiction, drama, or poetry, written in the English language (initially or in translation). Subject must be concerned with a mountain environment. Previous winners have been books on expeditions, climbing experiences, a biography of a mountaineer, and novels. Guidelines available in January by e-mail or on website. Entries must be previously published. Open to any writer. The award is to honor Peter Boardman and Joe Tasker, who disappeared on Everest in 1982. Deadline: August 1 £3,000 Judged by a panel of 3 judges elected by trustees.

BOSTON GLOBE-HORN BOOK AWARDS

The Boston Globe, Horn Book, Inc., 300 The Fenway, Palace Road Building, Suite P-311, Boston MA 02115. (617)278-0225. **Fax:** (617)278-6062. **E-mail:** bghb@hbook.com; info@hbook.com. **Website:** www.hbook.com/bghb/. Estab. 1967. Offered annually for excellence in literature for children and young adults (published June 1-May 31). Categories: picture book, fiction and poetry, nonfiction. Judges may also name up to 2 honor books in each category. Books must be published in the US, but may be written or illustrated by citizens of any country. The Horn Book Magazine publishes speeches given at awards ceremonies. Guidelines for submitting books online. Deadline: May 15 Prize: $500 and an engraved silver bowl; honor-book recipients receive an engraved silver plate. Judged by a panel of 3 judges selected each year.

BOULEVARD SHORT FICTION CONTEST FOR EMERGING WRITERS

Boulevard Magazine, Boulevard Emerging Writers Contest, PMB #325, 6614 Clayton Rd., Richmond Heights MO 63117. (314)862-2643. **Website:** www.boulevardmagazine.org. **Contact:** Jessica Rogen, Editor. Estab. 1985. Offered annually for unpublished short fiction to a writer who has not yet published a book of fiction, poetry, or creative nonfiction with a nationally distributed press. Holds first North American rights on anything not previously published. Open to any writer with no previous publication by a nationally known press. Guidelines for SASE on website. Deadline: December 31. Prize: $1,500, and publication in one of the next year's issues. Costs: $16 fee/story, includes 1-year subscription to Boulevard.

🐚 THE BRIDPORT PRIZE

P.O. Box 6910, Bridport, Dorset DT6 9QB, United Kingdom. **E-mail:** info@bridportprize.org.uk; kate@bridportprize.org.uk. **Website:** www.bridportprize.org.uk. **Contact:** Kate Wilson, Bridport Prize Programme Manager. Estab. 1973. Award to promote literary excellence, discover new talent. Categories: Short stories, poetry, flash fiction, first novel. Deadline: May 31 each year. Prize: £5,000; £1,000; £500; various runners-up prizes and publication of approximately 13 best stories and 13 best poems in anthology; plus 6 best flash fiction stories. 1st Prize of £1,000 for the best short, short story of under 250 words. £1,000 plus up to a year's mentoring for winner of Peggy Chapman-Andrews Award for a first novel. A second anthology containing extracts of the twenty long-listed novels will be published for the first time in 2019. Costs: £9 for poems, £10 for short stories, £8 for flash fiction, and £20 for novels until December 31; from January 1: £10 for poems, £12 for short stories, £9 for flash fiction and £20 for novels. Judged by 1 judge for short stories (in 2019, Kirtsty Logan), 1 judge for poetry (in 2019, Holly McNish) and 1 judge for flash fiction (in 2019 Kirsty Logan). The Novel award is judged by a group comprising representatives from The Literary Consultancy, A.M. Heath Literary Agents, and (in 2019) judge Naomi Wood.

🐚 BRITISH CZECH AND SLOVAK ASSOCIATION WRITING COMPETITION

24 Ferndale, Tunbridge Wells Kent TN2 3NS, England. **E-mail:** prize@bcsa.co.uk. **Website:** www.bcsa.co.uk/competitions. Estab. 2002. Annual contest

for original writing (entries should be 1,500-2,000 words) in English on the links between Britain and the Czech/Slovak Republics, or describing society in transition in the Republics since 1989. Entries can be fact or fiction. Topics can include history, politics, the sciences, economics, the arts, or literature. Deadline: End of July. Winners announced in November. Prize: 1st Place: £400; 2nd Place: £150.

CALIFORNIA BOOK AWARDS

Commonwealth Club of California, 110 The Embarcadero, San Francisco CA 94105. (415)597-6700. **Fax:** (415)597-6729. **E-mail:** bookawards@commonwealthclub.org. **Website:** https://www.commonwealthclub.org/events/california-book-awards. **Contact:** Priscilla Vivio, bookawards@commonwealthclub.org, pvivio@commonwealthclub.org. Estab. 1931. Offered annually to recognize California's best writers and illuminate the wealth and diversity of California-based literature. Award is for published submissions appearing in print during the previous calendar year. Can be nominated by publisher or author. Open to California residents (or residents at time of publication). Deadline: December 22. Prize: Medals and cash prizes to be awarded at publicized event, annually in June for previous year submissions. Judged by 12-15 California professionals with a diverse range of views, backgrounds, and literary experience.

JOHN W. CAMPBELL MEMORIAL AWARD FOR BEST SCIENCE FICTION NOVEL OF THE YEAR

1445 Jayhawk Blvd, Suite 3001, University of Kansas, Lawrence KS 66045. (785)864-2518. **E-mail:** Gunn.SF.Center@gmail.com. **Website:** www.sfcenter.ku.edu/campbell.htm. **Contact:** Chris McKitterick. Estab. 1973. Honors the best science fiction novel of the year. Deadline: Check website. Prize: Campbell Award trophy. Winners receive an expense-paid trip to the Campbell Conference to receive their award. Their names are also engraved on a permanent trophy. Judged by a jury.

✪ CANADIAN AUTHORS ASSOCIATION AWARD FOR FICTION

192 Spadina Avenue, Suite 107, Toronto ON M5T 2C2, Canada. **Website:** www.canadianauthors.org. **Contact:** Anita Purcell, executive director. Estab. 1975. Award for full-length, English language literature for adults by a Canadian author. Deadline: January 15. Prize: $1,000. Judging: Each year a trustee for each

award appointed by the Canadian Authors Association selects up to 3 judges. Identities of the trustee and judges are confidential.

✪ CANADIAN AUTHORS ASSOCIATION EMERGING WRITER AWARD

192 Spadina Avenue, Suite 107, Toronto ON M5T 2C2, Canada. **Website:** www.canadianauthors.org. **Contact:** Anita Purcell, Executive Director. Estab. 2006. Annual award for a writer under 30 years of age deemed to show exceptional promise in the field of literary creation. Deadline: January 15. Prize: $500. Judging: Each year a trustee for each award appointed by the Canadian Authors Association selects up to 3 judges. Identities of the trustee and judges are confidential.

KAY CATTARULLA AWARD FOR BEST SHORT STORY

Texas Institute of Letters, P.O. Box 609, Round Rock TX 78680. **E-mail:** tilsecretary@yahoo.com. **Website:** www.texasinstituteofletters.org. Offered annually for work published January 1-December 31 of previous year to recognize the best short story. The story submitted must have appeared in print for the first time to be eligible. Writers must have been born in Texas, must have lived in Texas for at least 2 consecutive years, or the subject matter of the work must be associated with Texas. See website for guidelines. Deadline: January 10. Prize: $1,000.

✪ PEGGY CHAPMAN-ANDREWS FIRST NOVEL AWARD

The Bridport Prize, The Bridport Prize, P.O. Box 6910, Dorset DT6 9QB, United Kingdom. **E-mail:** info@bridportprize.org.uk. **Website:** www.bridportprize.org.uk. **Contact:** Kate Wilson, Programme Manager. Estab. 1973. Award to promote literary excellence and new writers. Enter first chapters of novel, up to 8,000 words (minimum 5,000 words) plus 300 word synopsis. Deadline: May 31. Prize: 1st Place: £1,000 plus mentoring & possible publication; Runner-Up: £500. Costs: £20. Judged in 2019 by Naomi Wood with The Literary Consultancy & A.M. Heath Literary Agents.

✪ THE CITY OF VANCOUVER BOOK AWARD

Cultural Services Dept., Woodward's Heritage Building, 111 W. Hastings St., Suite 501, Vancouver BC V6B 1H4, Canada. (604)871-6634. **Fax:** (604)871-6005. **E-mail:** marnie.rice@vancouver.ca; culture@vancouver.ca. **Website:** https://vancouver.ca/people-programs/

city-of-vancouver-book-award.aspx. Estab. 1989. The annual City of Vancouver Book Award recognizes authors of excellence of any genre that reflect Vancouver's unique character, rich diversity and culture, history and residents. The book must exhibit excellence in one or more of the following areas: content, illustration, design, format. Deadline: May 22. Prize: $3,000. Costs: $20/entry. Judged by an independent jury.

CLOUDBANK BOOKS

Vern Rutsala Book Contest, Cloudbank Books, P.O. Box 610, Corvallis OR 97339. (541) 752-0075. **E-mail:** michael@cloudbankbooks.com. **Website:** www. cloudbankbooks.com. **Contact:** Michael Malan. Estab. 2009. *Cloudbank* is a 96-to-112 page print journal published annually. Included are poems, flash fiction, and book reviews. Regular submissions and contest submissions are accepted. The annual Vern Rutsala Book Contest results in a published book of poetry and/or flash fiction, plus monetary prize. Deadlines: Submissions for the journal's annual Cloudbank Contest are accepted from Nov. 1 through the last day in February. Non-contest submissions for the journal are accepted through April 30. Submissions for the Vern Rutsala Book Contest are accepted from July 1 through Oct. 31. The Cloudbank Contest prize is $200 and publication. Two contributors' copies are sent to all writers whose work appears in the magazine. The Vern Rutsala Book Contest winner receives $1,000 and publication of the manuscript. Costs: To fee for the Cloudbank Contest is $15. All writers entering the Contest receive a two-issue subscription to *Cloudbank*. The fee for the Vern Rutsala Book Contest is $25. Submissions can be sent by mail or via Submittable. The Cloudbank Contest is judged by Editor Michael Malan and editorial staff. The Vern Rutsala Book Contest has an outside judge.

○ Submissions for the journal—poetry and flash fiction—are accepted via Submittable and by mail. Complete guidelines are available at the website. There are two contests—one for *Cloudbank* (the journal) and one entitled the Vern Rutsala Book Contest.

THE DANAHY FICTION PRIZE

Tampa Review, University of Tampa, Tampa Review, 401 W. Kennedy Blvd., Tampa FL 33606-1490. (813)253-6266. **E-mail:** utpress@ut.edu. **Website:** www.ut.edu/TampaReview. Estab. 2006. Annual award for the best previously unpublished short fic-

tion. Deadline: December 31. Prize: $1,000, plus publication in *Tampa Review* and 1-year subscription to *Tampa Review*. Costs: $20. Judging is by the editors of Tampa Review.

☙ DEBUT DAGGER

Crime Writers' Association, Debut Dagger, Dea Parkin, CWA Secretary, The Writing House, 3 Dale View, Chorley Lancashire PR7 3QJ, United Kingdom. **E-mail:** secretary@thecwa.co.uk. **Website:** https:// thecwa.co.uk/the-debuts/. **Contact:** Dea Parkin. Estab. 1998. Annual competition for unpublished crime writers. Submit the opening 3,000 words of a crime novel, plus a 1,000-1,500 word synopsis. Open to any writer without agent representation who has not had a full-length novel traditionally published. (Self-published only is acceptable, including the novel entry itself.) To bring new writers to the attention of publishers and create opportunities for crime novelists of the future. Deadline: February 28. Submission period begins November 1. Prize: £500. All shortlisted entrants will, with their permission, have their entry sent to interested UK literary agents and publishers, and receive brief feedback on their entries. Any changes to the above will be posted to the website. Costs: £36. Judged by a panel of top crime editors and agents as well as the CWA's head of Criminal Critiques. The shortlisted entries are sent to agents. Any changes to the above will be posted to the website.

WILLIAM F. DEECK MALICE DOMESTIC GRANTS FOR UNPUBLISHED WRITERS

Malice Domestic, P.O. Box 8007, Gaithersburg MD 20898-8007. **E-mail:** malicegrants@comcast.net. **Website:** www.malicedomestic.org. **Contact:** Harriette Sackler, Malice Domestic Grants Chair. Estab. 1989. Offered annually for unpublished work in the mystery field. Malice awards 1 grant to unpublished writers in the Malice Domestic genre at its annual convention in May. The competition is designed to help the next generation of Malice authors get their first work published and to foster quality Malice literature. Malice Domestic literature is loosely described as mystery stories of the Agatha Christie type; i.e., traditional mysteries. These works usually feature no excessive gore, gratuitous violence, or explicit sex. Deadline: November 1. Prize: $2,500, plus a comprehensive registration to the following year's convention and 2 nights' lodging at the convention hotel.

DIAGRAM/NEW MICHIGAN PRESS CHAPBOOK CONTEST

New Michigan Press, P.O. Box 210067, English, ML 445, University of Arizona, Tucson AZ 85721. **E-mail:** nmp@thediagram.com. **Website:** www.thediagram. com. **Contact:** Ander Monson, editor. Estab. 1999. The annual *DIAGRAM*/New Michigan Press Chapbook Contest offers $1,000, plus publication and author's copies, with discount on additional copies. Deadline: April 26. Prize: $1,000, plus publication. Finalist chapbooks also considered for publication. Costs: $20. Judged by editor Ander Monson.

DIAGRAM/NEW MICHIGAN PRESS CHAPBOOK CONTEST

Department of English, University of Arizona, New Michigan Press, P.O. Box 210067, Tucson AZ 85721-0067. **E-mail:** nmp@thediagram.com; editor@thediagram.com. **Website:** www.thediagram.com/contest. html. **Contact:** Ander Monson, editor. Estab. 2000. Contest for prose, poetry, or hybrid manuscript (images ok) between 18-44 pages. Deadline: April 28. Check website for more details. Prize: $1,000 and publication. Typically we also published 3-5 finalist chapbooks. Costs: $20. Judged by editor Ander Monson.

DOBIE PAISANO WRITER'S FELLOWSHIP

The Graduate School, The University of Texas at Austin, Attn: Dobie Paisano Program, 110 Inner Campus Drive Stop G0400, Austin TX 78712-0531. (512)232-3612. **Fax:** (512)471-7620. **E-mail:** gbarton@austin. utexas.edu. **Website:** www.utexas.edu/ogs/Paisano. **Contact:** Gwen Barton. Sponsored by the Graduate School at The University of Texas at Austin and the Texas Institute of Letters, the Dobie Paisano Fellowship Program provides solitude, time, and a comfortable place for Texas writers or writers who have written significantly about Texas through fiction, nonfiction, poetry, plays, or other mediums. The Dobie Paisano Ranch is a very rural and rustic setting, and applicants should read the guidelines closely to ensure their ability to reside in this secluded environment. Deadline: January 15. Applications are accepted beginning December 1 and must be post-marked no later than January 15. The Ralph A. Johnston memorial Fellowship is for a period of 4 months with a stipend of $6,250 per month. It is aimed at writers who have already demonstrated some publishing and critical success. The Jesse H. Jones Writing Fellowship is for a period of approximately 6 months with a stipend of $3,000 per

month. It is aimed at, but not limited to, writers who are early in their careers. Costs: Application fee: $20 for one fellowship; $30 for both fellowships.

THE EMILY CONTEST

West Houston RWA, Houston TX **E-mail:** emily.contest@whrwa.com. **Website:** www.whrwa.com. Annual award to promote publication of previously unpublished writers of romance. Open to any writer who has not published in a given category within the past 3 years. The mission of The Emily is to professionally support writers and guide them toward a path to publication. Deadline: October 2. Submission period begins September 1. Prize: $100. Costs: $25 for members of WHRWA, $35 for all others. Final judging done by an editor and an agent.

☉ THE FAR HORIZONS AWARD FOR SHORT FICTION

The Malahat Review, University of Victoria, P.O. Box 1800, Stn CSC, Victoria BC V8W 3H5, Canada. (250)721-8524. **E-mail:** malahat@uvic.ca. **E-mail:** horizons@uvic.ca. **Website:** www.malahatreview.ca. **Contact:** L'Amour Lisik, Marketing and Circulation Manager. Open to "emerging short fiction writers from Canada, the US, and elsewhere" who have not yet published their fiction in a full-length book (48 pages or more). Deadline: May 1 of odd-numbered years. Prize: $1,000 CAD, publication in fall issue of *The Malahat Review*. Announced in fall on website, Facebook page, and in quarterly e-newsletter *Malahat Lite*. Costs: $25 CAD for Canadian entries; $30 USD for US entries; $35 USD from Mexico and outside North America; includes a 1-year subscription to *The Malahat Review*. $15 for additional entries, no limit.

THE VIRGINIA FAULKNER AWARD FOR EXCELLENCE IN WRITING

Prairie Schooner, 110 Andrews Hall, University of Nebraska-Lincoln, Lincoln NE 68588-0334. (402)472-0911. **Fax:** (402)472-1817. **E-mail:** PrairieSchooner@ unl.edu. **Website:** www.prairieschooner.unl.edu. **Contact:** Kwame Dawes. Offered annually for work published in *Prairie Schooner* in the previous year. Categories: short stories, essays, novel excerpts, and translations. Prize: $1,000. Judged by editorial board.

THE WILLIAM FAULKNER-WILLIAM WISDOM CREATIVE WRITING COMPETITION

Faulkner - Wisdom Competition, Pirate's Alley Faulkner Society, Inc., Faulkner – Wisdom Competition, 624 Pirate's Alley, New Orleans LA 70116. (504)586-1609. **E-mail:** faulkhouse@aol.com. **Website:** https://faulknersociety.org. **Contact:** Rosemary James, Award Director. Estab. 1992. See guidelines posted at www.wordsandmusic.org. Deadline: May 31. Prizes: $750-7,500 depending on category. Costs: Charges $10-45, depending on category for entry fees. Writers who wish to submit books exceeding 125,000 words will pay an additional amount (see website). Judged by established authors, literary agents, and acquiring editors.

FINELINE COMPETITION FOR PROSE POEMS, SHORT SHORTS, AND ANYTHING IN BETWEEN

Mid-American Review, Dept. of English, Bowling Green State University, Bowling Green OH 43403. (419)372-2725. **E-mail:** mar@bgsu.edu. **Website:** www.bgsu.edu/midamericanreview. **Contact:** Abigail Cloud, Editor-in-Chief. Offered annually for previously unpublished submissions. Contest open to all writers not associated with current judge or *Mid-American Review.* Deadline: June 1. Prize: $1,000, plus publication in fall issue of *Mid-American Review;* 10 finalists receive notation plus possible publication. Costs: $10 for up to 3 prose poems or short shorts; all participants receive prize issue. Judge will be a contemporary writer of note.

FOREWORD'S INDIES BOOK OF THE YEAR AWARDS

Foreword Magazine, Attn Foreword INDIES, Foreword Reviews, 413 E 8th St, Traverse City MI 49686. (231)933-3699. **Website:** www.forewordreviews.com. **Contact:** Michele Lonoconus. Estab. 1998. Awards offered annually. In order to be eligible, books must have a current-year copyright and be independently published, which includes university presses, privately held presses, and self-published authors. International submissions are welcome. New editions of previously published books are eligible if significant content has been changed and the book has a new ISBN. Reissued editions in new formats are not eligible. *Foreword's* INDIES Book of the Year Awards were established to bring increased attention from librarians, booksellers, and avid readers to the literary achievements of independent publishers and their authors. Deadline: January 15th. Prize: $1,500 cash will be awarded to a Best Fiction and Best Nonfiction choice. Costs: We offer a $79 Early Bird entry fee for books registered through June 30th. Choose a second (or third,

or fourth) category for the same book and the fee drops to $59 for each additional submission. Through September 30th, the fee is $89 per entry and $69 for additional categories. After September 30th, the fee is $99 per entry and $79 for additional categories. Our awards process is unique and well-respected because we assemble a jury of volunteer booksellers and librarians to make the final judgment on the books and who select winners based on their experience with readers. Their decisions also take into consideration editorial excellence, professional production, originality of the narrative, author credentials relative to the subject matter, and the value the title adds to its genre.

SOEURETTE DIEHL FRASER AWARD FOR BEST TRANSLATION OF A BOOK

P.O. Box 609, Round Rock TX 78680. **E-mail:** tilsecretary@yahoo.com. **Website:** http://texasinstituteofletters.org. Offered every 2 years to recognize the best translation of a literary book into English. Translator must have been born in Texas or have lived in the state for at least 2 consecutive years at some time. Deadline: January 10. Prize: $1,000.

☺ FREEFALL SHORT PROSE AND POETRY CONTEST

Freefall Literary Society of Calgary, 922 9th Ave. SE, Calgary AB T2G 0S4, Canada. **E-mail:** editors@freefallmagazine.ca. **Website:** www.freefallmagazine.ca. **Contact:** Ryan Stromquist, Managing Editor. Offered annually for unpublished work in the categories of poetry (5 poems/entry) and prose (3,000 words or less). Recognizes writers and offers publication credits in a literary magazine format. Contest rules and entry form online. Acquires first Canadian serial rights; ownership reverts to author after one-time publication. Deadline: December 31. Prize: 1st Place: $500 (CAD); 2nd Place: $250 (CAD); 3rd Place: $75; Honorable Mention: $25. All prizes include publication in the spring edition of *FreeFall Magazine.* Winners will also be invited to read at the launch of that issue, if such a launch takes place. Honorable mentions in each category will be published and may be asked to read. Travel expenses not included. Costs: $25. Judged by current guest editor for issue (who are also published authors in Canada).

THE GHOST STORY SUPERNATURAL FICTION AWARD

The Ghost Story, P.O. Box 601, Union ME 04862. **E-mail:** editor@theghoststory.com. **Website:** www.theghoststory.com. **Contact:** Paul Guernsey. Estab. 2015. Biannual contest for unpublished fiction. "Ghost stories are welcome, of course—but submissions may involve *any* paranormal or supernatural theme, as well as magic realism. What we're looking for is fine writing, fresh perspectives, and maybe a few surprises in the field of supernatural fiction." Deadline: April 30 and September 30. Winner receives $1,000 and publication. Two Honorable Mentions each win $250 plus publication. Costs: $20. Judged by the editors of *The Ghost Story*.

GIVAL PRESS NOVEL AWARD

Gival Press, LLC, P.O. Box 3812, Arlington VA 22203. (703)351-0079. **E-mail:** givalpress@yahoo.com. **Website:** www.givalpress.submittable.com. **Contact:** Robert L. Giron. Estab. 2005. Offered every other year, with the next deadline being May 30, 2020 and book publication in 2021, for a previously original unpublished novel (not a translation). Guidelines by phone, on website, via e-mail, or by mail with SASE. Results announced late fall of same year. Winners notified by phone. Results made available to entrants with SASE, by e-mail, on website. Enter via portal: www.givalpress.submittable.com. Purpose is to award the best literary novel. Deadline: May 30, 2020. Prize: $3,000, plus publication of book with a standard contract and author's copies. Costs: $50. Final judge is announced after winner is chosen. Entries read anonymously.

GIVAL PRESS SHORT STORY AWARD

Gival Press, Gival Press Short Story Award; Gival Press, LLC; Att'n: Robert L. Giron, Editor, P.O. Box 3812, Arlington VA 22203. (703)351-0079. **E-mail:** givalpress@yahoo.com. **Website:** www.givalpress.submittable.com. **Contact:** Robert L. Giron, Editor-in-Chief. Estab. 2004. Annual literary, short-story contest. Entries must be unpublished. Open to anyone who writes original short stories, which are not a chapter of a novel, in English. Receives about 100-150 entries per category. Guidelines available online, via e-mail, or by mail. Results announced in the fall of the same year. Winners notified by phone. Results available with SASE, by e-mail, and on website. Enter via portal: www.givalpress.submittable.com. Recognizes the best literary short story. Deadline: August 8. Prize: $1,000 and publication on website. Costs: $25 entry fee; make checks payable to Gival Press, LLC. Judged anonymously.

☼ JOHN GLASSCO TRANSLATION PRIZE

Literary Translators' Association of Canada, ATTLC | LTAC; Concordia University, LB-601, 1455 de Maisonneuve Boulevard West, Montréal QC H3G 1M8, Canada. (514)848-2424, ext. 8702. **E-mail:** info@attlc-ltac.org. **Website:** attlc-ltac.org/john-glassco-translation-prize. **Contact:** Glassco Prize Committee. Estab. 1981. Offered annually for a translator's first book-length literary translation into French or English, published in Canada during the previous calendar year. The translator must be a Canadian citizen or permanent resident. Eligible genres include fiction, creative nonfiction, poetry, and children's books. Deadline: July 9. Prize: $1,000 and a 1-year membership to LTAC.

☼ GOVERNOR GENERAL'S LITERARY AWARDS

Canada Council for the Arts, 150 Elgin St., P.O. Box 1047, Ottawa ON K1P 5V8, Canada. (800)263-5588, ext. 5573 or (613)566-4414, ext. 5573. **Website:** ggbooks.ca. Estab. 1937. The Canada Council for the Arts provides a wide range of grants and services to professional Canadian artists and art organizations in dance, media arts, music, theatre, writing, publishing, and the visual arts. The Governor General's Literary Awards are given annually for the best English-language and French-language work in each of 7 categories, including fiction, non-fiction, poetry, drama, young people's literature (text), young people's literature (illustrated books), and translation. Deadline: Depends on the book's publication date. See website for details. Prize: Each GG winner receives $25,000. Non-winning finalists receive $1,000. Publishers of the winning titles receive a $3,000 grant for promotional purposes. Evaluated by fellow authors, translators, and illustrators. For each category, a jury makes the final selection.

☼ MARJORIE GRABER-MCINNIS SHORT STORY AWARD

ACT Writers Centre, ACT Writers Centre, Gorman Arts Centre, Ainslie Ave., Braddon ACT 2612, Australia. (02)6262 9191. **Fax:** (02)6262 9191. **E-mail:** admin@actwriters.org.au. **Website:** www.actwriters.org.au. Open theme for a short story with 1,500-3,000 words. Guidelines available on website. Open only to unpublished emerging writers residing within the ACT or region. Deadline: October 26. Submissions period begins in early September. Prize: $600 and publication. 5 runners-up receive book prizes. All winners may be published in the ACT Writers Centre newsletter and on the ACT Writers Centre website.

Costs: $10 for ACT Writers Centre members and $15 for non-members.

SUE GRANZELLA HUMOR PRIZE

Category in the Soul-Making Keats Literary Competition, The Webhallow House, 1544 Sweetwood Dr., Broadmoor Vlg. CA 94015-2029. **E-mail:** soulkeats@mail.com. **Website:** www.soulmakingcontest.us. **Contact:** Eileen Malone. Deadline: November 30. Prize: First Place: $100; Second Place: $50; Third Place: $25. Costs: $5. Judged by Sue Granzella.

GREAT LAKES COLLEGES ASSOCIATION NEW WRITERS AWARD

The Great Lakes Colleges Association, 535 W. William St., Suite 301, Ann Arbor MI 48103. (734)661-2350. **Fax:** (734)661-2349. **E-mail:** wegner@glca.org. **Website:** https://glca.org/glcaprograms/new-writers-award. **Contact:** Gregory R. Wegner, Director of Program Development: wegner@glca.org.. Estab. 1970. The Great Lakes Colleges Association (GLCA) is a consortium of 13 independent liberal arts colleges in Ohio, Michigan, Indiana, and Pennsylvania. The Award's purpose is to celebrate literary achievement in a writer's first-published volume of fiction, poetry, or nonfiction. Deadline: June 25, 2019. Any work received with a postmark after this date will not be accepted. Prize: Honorarium of at least $500 from each member college that invites a winning to give a reading on its campus. Each award winner receives invitations from several of the 13 colleges of the GLCA to visit campus. At these campus events an author will give readings, meet students and faculty, and occasionally visit college classes. In addition to the $500 honorarium for each campus visit, travel costs to colleges are paid by the GLCA's member colleges. Costs: No entry fee. Publisher must submit four copies of the submitted volume to be considered by judges and an author's signed statement agreeing to visit GLCA colleges if invited as the winning writer of the award. Judged by professors of literature and writers in residence at GLCA colleges.

○ Annual award for a first published volume of poetry, fiction, and creative nonfiction.

GREEN PIECES PRESS ARIZONA LITERARY CONTEST BOOK AWARDS

Green Pieces Press, 6939 East Chaparral Rd., Paradise Valley AZ 85253-7000. (480)219-4559. **E-mail:** Director@AzLiteraryContest.com. **Website:** www.AzLiteraryContest.com. **Contact:** Lisa Aquilina, publisher.

Estab. 1980. Green Pieces Press is honored to receive the baton from its contest predecessor and sponsor a refreshed, retooled 2019 annual literary competition for published books, unpublished novels, and Arizona Book of the Year. Cash prizes awarded ($1,000 Book of the Year) from Green Pieces Press. First Place in each of the nine categories ($200), Second Place $100, Third Place $50. All category finalists in 2019 have their literary works published in the *Arizona Literary Magazine 2020*. NEW PRIZE in 2019 for Unpublished Novel category. All Finalists have their completed manuscript submitted to Ingram Elliot Book Publishers for consideration and potential award of a standard, traditional publishing contract. All published work must have 2018 or 2019 copyright date at time of submission. Deadline: September 1, 2019. Begins accepting submissions January 1, 2019. Finalists notified by Labor Day weekend. Prizes: Grand Prize, Arizona Book of the Year Award: $1,000. All categories: 1st Prize: $200; 2nd Prize: $100; 3rd Prize: $50. Unpublished Novel finallists also have their manuscripts submitted to IngramElliott Book Publishers for consideration to be awarded traditional publishing contract. Features in *Arizona Literary Magazine 2020*. Costs: Each submission: Unpublished novel/novella-$50; Memoir-$50; Inspirational, Spiritual, Religion-$50; History-$50; Children's Picture Book-$50; Mystery & Suspense/Crime Fiction-$50; Romance Fiction-$50; Sci Fi & Fantasy-$50; Graphic Novel-$50; Multiple entries by same author accepted in all categories. Judged by nationwide published authors, editors, literary agents, and reviewers. Winners announced prior to Thanksgiving 2019. International entries encouraged; only caveat, all entries must be written in English.

○ Competition receives approximately 1,000+ entries per year. Submissions welcome from authors worldwide. All entries must be published or written in English. The Contest Directors reserve the right not to award a prize in any or all categories if the entries received are insufficient for viable competition and/or entries received do not meet international literary standards.

GUGGENHEIM FELLOWSHIPS

John Simon Guggenheim Memorial Foundation, John Simon Guggenheim Memorial Foundation, 90 Park Ave., New York NY 10016. (212)687-4470. **E-mail:** fellowships@gf.org. **Website:** www.gf.org. Estab. 1925. Often characterized as "midcareer" awards, Guggenheim Fellowships are intended for men and women who have already demonstrated exceptional capacity for productive scholarship or exceptional creative ability in the arts. Fellowships are awarded through two annual competitions: one open to citizens and permanent residents of the United States and Canada, and the other open to citizens and permanent residents of Latin America and the Caribbean. Candidates must apply to the Guggenheim Foundation in order to be considered in either of these competitions. The Foundation receives between 3,500 and 4,000 applications each year. Although no one who applies is guaranteed success in the competition, there is no prescreening: all applications are reviewed. Approximately 200 Fellowships are awarded each year. Deadline: September 17.

🌑 HADOW STUART SHORT STORY COMPETITION

Fellowship of Australian Writers (WA), FAWWA, PO Box 6180, Swanbourne WA 6910, P.O. Box 6180, Swanbourne WA 6910, Australia. (61)(08)9384-4771. **Fax:** (61)(08)9384-4854. **E-mail:** fellowshipaustralianwriterswa@gmail.com. **Website:** www.fawwa.org. Annual contest for unpublished short stories (maximum 3,000 words). Reserves the right to publish entries in a FAWWA publication or on website. Guidelines online or for SASE. Deadline: June 1. Submissions period begins April 1. Prize: 1st Place: $1,000; 2nd Place: $300; 3rd Place: $100. Costs: $15/story (maximum of 3).

HAMMETT PRIZE

International Association of Crime Writers, North American Branch, 243 Fifth Avenue, #537, New York NY 10016. **E-mail:** crimewritersna@gmail.com. **Website:** www.crimewritersna.org.. **Contact:** J. Madison Davis. Award for crime novels, story collections, or nonfiction by 1 author. "Our reading committee seeks suggestions from publishers, and they also ask the membership for recommendations." Nominations announced in January; winners announced in fall. Winners notified by e-mail or mail and recognized at awards ceremony. For contest results, send SASE or e-mail. Award established to honor a work of literary excellence in the field of crime writing by a US or Canadian author. Deadline: December 15. Prize: Trophy. Judged by a committee of members of the organization. The committee chooses 5 nominated books, which are then sent to 3 outside judges for a final selection. Judges are outside the crime-writing field.

WILDA HEARNE FLASH FICTION CONTEST

Big Muddy: A Journal of the Mississippi River Valley, WHFF Contest, Southeast Missouri State University Press, One University Plaza, MS 2650, Cape Girardeau MO 63701. (573)651-2044. **E-mail:** upress@semo.edu. **Website:** www.semopress.com. **Contact:** James Brubaker, publisher. Annual competition for flash fiction, held by Southeast Missouri State University Press. Deadline: October 1. Prize: $500 and publication in *Big Muddy: A Journal of the Mississippi River Valley*. Costs: $15. The Editors

DRUE HEINZ LITERATURE PRIZE

University of Pittsburgh Press, Drue Heinz Literature Prize, University of Pittsburgh Press, 7500 Thomas Blvd., 4th Floor, Pittsburgh PA 15260. **Fax:** (412)383-2466. **E-mail:** info@upress.pitt.edu. **Website:** www.upress.pitt.edu. Estab. 1981. Offered annually to writers who have published a book-length collection of fiction or a minimum of 3 short stories or novellas in commercial magazines or literary journals of national distribution. Does not return mss. Manuscripts must be received during May and June 2019. That is, they must be postmarked on or after May 1 and on or before June 30th. Prize: $15,000. Judged by anonymous nationally known writers such as Robert Penn Warren, Joyce Carol Oates, and Margaret Atwood.

LORIAN HEMINGWAY SHORT STORY COMPETITION

P.O. Box 2011 c/o Cynthia. D. Higgs: Key West Editorial, Key West FL 33045. **E-mail:** shortstorykeywest@hushmail.com. **Website:** www.shortstorycompetition.com. **Contact:** Eva Eliot, editorial assistant. Estab. 1981. Offered annually for unpublished short stories up to 3,500 words. Guidelines available via e-mail, or online. Award to encourage literary excellence and the efforts of writers whose voices have yet to be heard. Deadline: May 15. Prizes: 1st Place: $1,500, plus publication of his or her winning story in *Cutthroat: A Journal of the Arts*; 2nd-3rd Place: $500; honorable mentions will also be awarded. Costs: $15/story postmarked by May 1; $20/story postmarked by May 15. Judged by a panel of writers, editors, and literary scholars selected by author Lorian Hemingway. Lorian Hemingway is the competition's final judge.

TONY HILLERMAN PRIZE

Wordharvest, St. Martin's Press, 175 Fifth Avenue, New York NY 10010. (505)471-1565. **E-mail:** tonyhillermanprize@stmartins.com. **Website:** www.wordharvest.com. **Contact:** Anne Hillerman and Jean Schaumberg, Co-organizers. Estab. 2006. Awarded annually, and sponsored by St. Martin's Press, for the best first mystery set in the Southwest. Murder or another serious crime or crimes must be at the heart of the story, with the emphasis on the solution rather than the details of the crime. Honors the contributions made by Tony Hillerman to the art and craft of the mystery. Deadline: January 2. Prize: $10,000 advance and publication by St. Martin's Press. Nominees will be selected by judges chosen by the editorial staff of St. Martin's Press, with the assistance of independent judges selected by organizers of the Tony Hillerman Writers Conference (Wordharvest), and the winner will be chosen by St. Martin's editors.

ERIC HOFFER AWARD

Hopewell Publications, LLC, P.O. Box 11, Titusville NJ 08560-0011. **Fax:** (609)964-1718. **E-mail:** info@hopepubs.com. **Website:** www.hofferaward.com. **Contact:** Dawn Shows, EHA Coordinator. Annual contest for previously published books. Recognizes excellence in independent publishing in many unique categories: Art (titles capture the experience, execution, or demonstration of the arts); Poetry (all styles); Chapbook (40 pages or less, artistic assembly); General Fiction (nongenre-specific fiction); Commercial Fiction (genre-specific fiction); Science Fiction/Fantasy; Historical Fiction; Short Story/Anthology; Mystery/Crime; Children (titles for young children); Middle Reader; Young Adult (titles aimed at the juvenile and teen markets); Culture (titles demonstrating the human or world experience); Memoir (titles relating to personal experience); Business (titles with application to today's business environment and emerging trends); Reference (titles from traditional and emerging reference areas); Home (titles with practical applications to home or home-related issues, including family); Health (titles promoting physical, mental, and emotional well-being); Self-help (titles involving new and emerging topics in self-help); Spiritual (titles involving the mind and spirit, including relgion); Legacy Fiction and Nonfiction (titles over 2 years of age that hold particular relevance to any subject matter or form); E-book Fiction; E-book Nonfiction. Open to any writer of published work within the last 2 years, including categories for older books. This contest recognizes excellence in independent publishing in many unique categories. Also awards the Montaigne Medal

for most though-provoking book, the Da Vinci Eye for best cover, and the First Horizon Award for best new authors. Results published in the US Review of Books. Deadline: January 21. Grand Prize: $2,500; honors (winner, runner-up, honorable mentions) in each category, including the Montaigne Medal (most thought-provoking), da Vinci Art (cover art), First Horizon (first book), and Best in Press (small, academic, micro, self-published). Costs: Charges $60; $40 for chapbook.

TOM HOWARD/JOHN H. REID FICTION & ESSAY CONTEST

Winning Writers, 351 Pleasant St., PMB 222, Northampton MA 01060-3961. (866)946-9748. **Fax:** (413)280-0539. **E-mail:** adam@winningwriters.com. **Website:** www.winningwriters.com. **Contact:** Adam Cohen, president. Estab. 1993. Since 2001, Winning Writers has provided expert literary contest information to the public. Sponsors four contests. One of the "101 Best Websites for Writers" (*Writer's Digest*). Open to all writers. Submit any type of short story or essay. Both published and unpublished works are welcome. If you win a prize, requests nonexclusive rights to publish your submission online, in e-mail newsletters, in e-books, and in press releases. Deadline: April 30. Prizes: Two 1st prizes of $2,000 will be awarded, plus 10 honorable mentions of $100 each. Top 12 entries published online. The top two winners will also receive one-year gift certificates from the contest co-sponsor, Duotrope (a $50 value). Costs: $20. Judged by Dennis Norris II, assisted by Lauren Singer Ledoux.

THE JULIA WARD HOWE/BOSTON AUTHORS AWARD

The Boston Authors Club, The Boston Authors Club, Boston Authors Club, Attn. Mary Cronin, 2400 Beacon Street, Unit 208, Chestnut Hill MA 02467. **E-mail:** bostonauthors@aol.com. **Website:** www.bostonauthorsclub.org. **Contact:** Alan Lawson. Estab. 1900. This annual award honors Julia Ward Howe and her literary friends who founded the Boston Authors Club in 1900. It also honors the membership over 110 years; consisting of novelists, biographers, historians, governors, senators, philosophers, poets, playwrights, and other luminaries. Boston Authors Club has been awarding the Julia Ward Howe Prizes (named after the Club's first President) to outstanding adult and young-reader books for over 20 years. These awards recognize exceptional books by Boston-area authors in four separate categories: Fiction, Nonfiction, Poetry, and the

Young Reader category. Deadline: January 31. Prize: $1,000. Costs: $35 per title. Judged by the members.

HENRY HOYNS & POE-FAULKNER FELLOWSHIPS

Creative Writing Program, 219 Bryan Hall, P.O. Box 400121, University of Virginia, Charlottesville VA 22904-4121. (434)924-6074. **Fax:** (434)924-1478. **E-mail:** creativewriting@virginia.edu. **Website:** creativewriting.virginia.edu. **Contact:** Barbara Moriarty, Administrative Assistant.. Two-year MFA program in poetry and fiction; all students receive fellowships and teaching stipends that total $20,000 in both years of study. Sample poems/prose required with application. Optional third year with partial funding. Deadline: December 15. Costs: Students must apply to the UVA Graduate School of Arts and Sciences, which has a current application fee of $85.

L. RON HUBBARD'S WRITERS OF THE FUTURE CONTEST

Author Services, Inc., L. Ron Hubbard's Writers of the Future Contest, 7051 Hollywood Blvd., Los Angeles CA 90028. (323)466-3310. **Fax:** (323)466-6474. **E-mail:** contests@authorservicesinc.com. **Website:** www.writersofthefuture.com. **Contact:** Joni Labaqui, Contest Director. Estab. 1983. Foremost competition for new and amateur writers of unpublished science fiction or fantasy short stories or novelettes. Offered to find, reward and publicize new speculative fiction writers so they may more easily attain professional writing careers. Open to writers who have not professionally published a novel or short novel, more than 2 novelettes, or more than 3 short stories. Entry stories must be unpublished. Limit 1 entry per quarter. This is an international contest. Results announced quarterly in e-newsletter. Winners notified by phone. Contest has 4 quarters. There shall be 3 cash prizes in each quarter. In addition, at the end of the year, the 4 first-place, quarterly winners will have their entries rejudged, and a grand prize winner shall be determined. Deadline: December 31, March 31, June 30, September 30. Prize (awards quarterly): 1st Place: $1,000; 2nd Place: $750; and 3rd Place: $500. Annual grand prize: $5,000. Costs: No entry fee. Judged by David Farland (initial judge), then by a panel of 4 professional authors.

CAROL OTIS HURST CHILDREN'S BOOK PRIZE

Westfield Athenaeum, 6 Elm St., Westfield MA 01085. (413)562-6158, Ext. 5. **Website:** www.westath.org. **Con-**tact: Sarah Scott, Youth Services Librarian. Estab. 2007. The Carol Otis Hurst Children's Book Prize honors outstanding works of fiction and nonfiction, including biography and memoir, written for children and young adults through the age of 18, which exemplify the highest standards of research, analysis, and authorship in their portrayal of the New England Experience. The prize will be presented annually to an author whose book treats the region's history as broadly conceived to encompass one or more of the following elements: political experience, social development, fine and performing artistic expression, domestic life and arts, transportation and communication, changing technology, military experience at home and abroad, schooling, business and manufacturing, workers and the labor movement, agriculture and its transformation, racial and ethnic diversity, religious life and institutions, immigration and adjustment, sports at all levels, and the evolution of popular entertainment. The public presentation of the prize will be accompanied by a reading and/or talk by the recipient at a mutually agreed upon time during the spring immediately following the publication year. Deadline: December 31. Prize: $500.

INK & INSIGHTS WRITING CONTEST

Critique My Novel, 1802 S Lincoln, Amarillo TX 79102. **E-mail:** contest@inkandinsights.com. **Website:** https://inkandinsights.com. **Contact:** Catherine York, contest administrator. Estab. 2012. Ink & Insights is a writing contest geared toward strengthening the skills of independent writers by focusing on feedback. Each entry is assigned four judges who specialize in the genre of the manuscript. They read, score, and comment on specific aspects of the segment. The top three mss in the Master and Nonfiction categories move on to the Agent Round and receive a guaranteed read and feedback from a panel of agents. Deadline: May 30 (regular entry), June 30 (late entry). Prize: Prizes vary depending on category. Every novel receives personal feedback from four judges. Costs: Early bird entry: $35; Regular entry: $40; Late entry: $45. Judges listed on website, including the agents who will be helping choose the top winners of the Master category.

INTERNATIONAL LITERACY ASSOCIATION CHILDREN'S AND YOUNG ADULT'S BOOK AWARDS

P.O. Box 8139, 800 Barksdale Rd., Newark DE 19714-8139. (302)731-1600, ext. 221. **E-mail:** kbaughman@

reading.org. **E-mail:** committees@reading.org. **Website:** www.literacyworldwide.org. **Contact:** Kathy Baughman. The ILA Children's and Young Adults Book Awards are intended for newly published authors who show unusual promise in the children's and young adult's book field. Awards are given for fiction and nonfiction in each of 3categories: primary, intermediate, and young adult. Books from all countries and published in English for the first time during the previous calendar year will be considered. Deadline: March 15. Prize: $1,000.

THE IOWA REVIEW AWARD IN POETRY, FICTION, AND NONFICTION

The Iowa Review, University of Iowa, 308 English-Philosophy Building, Iowa City IA 52242. **E-mail:** iowa-review@uiowa.edu. **Website:** www.iowareview.org. *The Iowa Review* Award in Poetry, Fiction, and Nonfiction presents $1,500 to each winner in each genre and $750 to runners-up. Winners and runners-up published in *The Iowa Review*. Deadline: January 31. Submission period begins January 1. Costs: $20. Make checks payable to *The Iowa Review*. Enclose additional $10 (optional) for year-long subscription. Judges for the 2019 Awards are Kiki Petrosino (poetry), Rebecca Makkai (fiction), and Roxane Gay (nonfiction).

THE IOWA SHORT FICTION AWARD & JOHN SIMMONS SHORT FICTION AWARD

Iowa Writers' Workshop, Iowa Writers' Workshop, 507 N. Clinton St., 102 Dey House, Iowa City IA 52242-1000. **Website:** www.uiowapress.org. **Contact:** James McCoy, Director. Annual award to give exposure to promising writers who have not yet published a book of prose. Open to any writer. Current University of Iowa students are not eligible. No application forms are necessary. Announcement of winners made early in year following competition. Winners notified by phone. No application forms are necessary. Do not send original ms. Include SASE for return of ms. Deadline: September 30. Submission period begins August 1. Prize: Publication by University of Iowa Press. Judged by senior Iowa Writers' Workshop members who screen mss; published fiction author of note makes final selections.

Ⓢ JAPAN-U.S. FRIENDSHIP COMMISSION PRIZE FIR THE TRANSLATION OF JAPANESE LITERATURE

Japanese Literary Translation Prize, Columbia University, Donald Keene Center, c/o Department of East Asian Languages and Cultures, 407 Kent Hall MC 3907, 1140 Amsterdam Ave., New York NY 10027, USA. **Website:** http://www.keenecenter.org/. **Contact:** Yoshiko Niiya, Program Coordinator. Estab. 1979. The Donald Keene Center of Japanese Culture at Columbia University annually awards Japan-U.S. Friendship Commission Prizes for the Translation of Japanese Literature. A prize is given for the best translation of a modern work or a classical work, or the prize is divided between equally distinguished translations. Deadline: June 3. Prize: $6,000.

Ⓞ Translations must be book-length Japanese literary works: novels, collections of short stories, manga, literary essays, memoirs, drama, or poetry. Works may be unpublished manuscripts, works in press, or books published during the 2 years prior to the prize year.

JESSE H. JONES AWARD FOR BEST WORK OF FICTION

P.O. Box 609, Round Rock TX 78680. **E-mail:** tilsecretary@yahoo.com. **Website:** http://texasinstituteofletters.org. Offered annually by Texas Institute of Letters for work published January 1-December 31 of year before award is given to recognize the writer of the best book of fiction entered in the competition. Writers must have been born in Texas, have lived in the state for at least 2 consecutive years at some time, or the subject matter of the work should be associated with the state. Deadline: January 10. Prize: $6,000.

JAMES JONES FIRST NOVEL FELLOWSHIP

Wilkes University, James Jones First Novel Fellowship, c/o M.A./M.F.A. in CreativeWriting, Wilkes University, 84 West South Street, Wilkes-Barre PA 18766. (570)408-4547. **Fax:** (570)408-3333. **E-mail:** jamesjonesfirstnovel@wilkes.edu. **Website:** www.wilkes.edu/. Offered annually for unpublished novels (must be works-in-progress). This competition is open to all U.S. citizens who have not previously published novels. The award is intended to honor the spirit of unblinking honesty, determination, and insight into modern culture exemplified by the late James Jones. Deadline: March 15. Submission period begins October 1. Prize: $10,000; 2 runners-up awards of $1000 each may be given. Costs: A $30 check/money order, payable to Wilkes University, not to James Jones First Novel Fellowship, must accompany each entry. For online submissions, add a $3.00 processing fee.

JUNIPER PRIZE FOR FICTION

University of Massachusetts Press, 180 Infirmary Way, 4th Fl., Amherst MA 01003. (413)545-2217. **Fax:** (413)545-1226. **E-mail:** info@umpress.umass.edu; cjandree@umpress.umass.edu. **E-mail:** juniperprize@ umpress.umass.edu. **Website:** www.umass.edu/umpress. **Contact:** Courtney Andree. Estab. 2004. The Juniper Prize for Fiction is awarded annually to two original manuscripts of fiction: one short story collection and one novel. The University of Massachusetts Press publishes the winning manuscripts and the authors receive a $1,000 award upon publication. Deadline: September 30. Submissions period begins August 1. Winners announced online in April on the press website. Prize: $1,000 cash and publication. Costs: $30.

THE LAWRENCE FOUNDATION AWARD

Prairie Schooner, 110 Andrews Hall, University of Nebraska-Lincoln, Lincoln NE 68588-0334. (402)472-0911. **Fax:** (402)472-9771. **E-mail:** prairieschooner@ unl.edu. **Website:** www.prairieschooner.unl.edu. Offered annually for the best short story published in Prairie Schooner in the previous year. Only work published in *Prairie Schooner* in the previous year is considered. Work is nominated by editorial staff. Results announced in the Spring issue. Winners notified by mail in February or March. Prize: $1,000. Judged by editorial staff of *Praire Schooner*.

LAWRENCE FOUNDATION PRIZE

Michigan Quarterly Review, 0576 Rackham Bldg., 915 E. Washington St., Ann Arbor MI 48109-1070. (734)764-9265. **E-mail:** mqr@umich.edu. **Website:** www.michiganquarterlyreview.com. **Contact:** H.R. Webster, managing editor. Estab. 1978. This annual prize is awarded by the *Michigan Quarterly Review* editorial board to the author of the best short story published in *MQR* that year. The prize is sponsored by University of Michigan alumnus and fiction writer Leonard S. Bernstein, a trustee of the Lawrence Foundation of New York. Approximately 20 short stories are published in *MQR* each year. Prize: $1,000. Judged by editorial board.

✪ THE STEPHEN LEACOCK MEMORIAL MEDAL FOR HUMOUR

Bette Walker, 149 Peter St. N., Orillia ON L3V 4Z4, Canada. (705)326-9286. **E-mail:** awardschair@leacock.ca. **Website:** www.leacock.ca. **Contact:** Bette Walker, Award Committee, Stephen Leacock Associates. The Leacock Associates awards the prestigious Leacock Medal for the best book of literary humor written by a Canadian and published in the current year. The winning author also receives a cash prize of $15,000, thanks to the generous support of the TD Financial Group. 2 runners-up are each awarded a cash prize of $3,000. Deadline: Postmarked before December 31. Prize: $15,000. Costs: $200.

LEAGUE OF UTAH WRITERS WRITING CONTEST

The League of Utah Writers, The League of Utah Writers, P.O. Box 64, Lewiston UT 84320. (435)755-7609. **E-mail:** luwcontest@gmail.com; luwriters@gmail.com. **Website:** www.luwriters.org. Estab. 1935. Open to any writer, the LUW Contest provides authors an opportunity to get their work read and critiqued. Multiple categories are offered; see website for details. Entries must be the original and unpublished work of the author. Winners are announced at the Annual Writers Round-Up in September. Those not present will be notified by e-mail. Deadline: May 31. Submissions period begins March 1. Prize: Cash prizes are awarded. Costs: Vary depending on category. Judged by professional authors and editors from outside the League.

LES FIGUES PRESS NOS BOOK CONTEST

Les Figues Press, c/o Los Angeles Review of Books, 6671 Sunset Blvd., Suite 1521, Los Angeles CA 90028. (323)734-4732. **E-mail:** info@lesfigues.com. **Website:** www.lesfigues.com. **Contact:** Teresa Carmody, Founding Editor. Les Figues Press creates aesthetic conversations between writers/artists and readers, especially those interested in innovative/experimental/avant-garde work. The Press intends in the most premeditated fashion to champion the trinity of Beauty, Belief, and Bawdry. Deadline: March 20 (submissions open until midnight PST) Prize: $1,000, plus publication by Les Figues Press. Costs: $25 ($40 for international entrants who choose to receive a book).

💲 FENIA AND YAAKOV LEVIANT MEMORIAL PRIZE IN YIDDISH STUDIES

Modern Language Association of America, Leviant Memorial Prize, Modern Language Association, 85 Broad Street, Suite 500, New York NY 10004-2434. (646)576-5141. **Fax:** (646)458-0030. **E-mail:** awards@ mla.org. **Website:** www.mla.org. **Contact:** Coordinator of book prizes. Offered in even-numbered years for an outstanding English translation of a Yiddish literary work or the publication of a scholarly work. Cultural studies, critical biographies, or edited works in the field of Yiddish folklore or linguistic studies are eligible to compete. See website for details on which they are accepting. Deadline: May 1. Prize: A cash prize and a certificate, to be presented at the Modern Language Association's annual convention in January.

LITERAL LATTÉ FICTION AWARD

Literal Latté, 200 E. 10th St., Suite 240, New York NY 10003. **E-mail:** litlatte@aol.com. **Website:** www.literal-latte.com. **Contact:** Edward Estlin, contributing editor. Estab. 1994. Award to provide talented writers with 3 essential tools for continued success: money, publication, and recognition. Offered annually for unpublished fiction (maximum 20,000 words). Guidelines online. Open to any writer. Deadline: January 30. Prize: 1st Place: $1,000 and publication in *Literal Latté*; 2nd Place: $300; 3rd Place: $200; also up to 7 honorable mentions. All winners published in *Literal Latté*. Costs: $10 per story; $15 for two. The Editors

LITERAL LATTE SHORT SHORTS CONTEST

Literal Latté, Literal Latté Awards, 200 E. 10th St., Suite 240, New York NY 10003. **E-mail:** litlatte@aol.com. **Website:** www.literal-latte.com. **Contact:** Jenine Gordon Bockman, Editor. Estab. 1994. Keeping free thought free since 1994. Deadline: June 30. Prize: $500. Costs: $10 for up to 3 shorts; $15 reading fee for up to 6 shorts. Judged by the editors.

⟳ Annual contest. Send unpublished shorts, 2,000 words max. All styles welcome. Name, address, phone number, e-mail address (optional) on cover page only. Include SASE or e-mail address for reply. All entries considered for publication.

THE HUGH J. LUKE AWARD

Prairie Schooner, 110 Andrews Hall, University of Nebraska-Lincoln, Lincoln NE 68588-0334. (402)472-0911. **Fax:** (402)472-1817. **E-mail:** prairieschooner@unl.edu. **Website:** www.prairieschooner.unl.edu. **Contact:** Kwame Dawes. Prize: $250. Judged by editorial staff of *Prairie Schooner*.

THE MARY MACKEY SHORT STORY PRIZE CATEGORY

Soul-Making Keats Literary Competition, The Webhallow House, 1544 Sweetwood Dr., Broadmoor Village CA 94015-2029. **E-mail:** soulkeats@mail.com. **Website:** www.soulmakingcontest.us. **Contact:** Eileen Malone. Open annually to any writer. Deadline: November 30. Prize: Cash prizes. Costs: $5/entry (make checks payable to NLAPW).

⟳ THE MALAHAT REVIEW NOVELLA PRIZE

The Malahat Review, University of Victoria, P.O. Box 1800 STN CSC, Victoria BC V8W 3H5, Canada. (250)721-8524. **E-mail:** malahat@uvic.ca. **E-mail:** novella@uvic.ca. **Website:** malahatreview.ca. **Contact:** L'Amour Lisik, Marketing and Circulation Manager.. Held in alternate (even-numbered) years with the Long Poem Prize. Offered to promote unpublished novellas. Obtains first world rights. After publication, rights revert to the author. Open to any writer. Deadline: February 1 (even years). Prize: $1,500 CAD and one year's subscription. Winner published in summer issue of *The Malahat Review* and announced on website, Facebook page, and in quarterly e-newsletter *Malahat Lite*. Costs: $35 CAD for Canadian entrants; $40 US for American entrants; $45 US for entrants from elsewhere (includes a 1-year subscription to *Malahat*). $15 for additional entries, no limit. Three recognized literary figures are assigned to judge the contest each year.

⬤ THE MAN BOOKER PRIZE

Four Colman Getty PR, Marion Fraser, Four Culture, 20 St Thomas Street, London SE1 9BF, United Kingdom. (44)020 3697 4256. **Website:** www.themanbookerprize.com. **Contact:** Marion Fraser. Estab. 1968. Books are only accepted through UK publishers. However, publication outside the UK does not disqualify a book once it is published in the UK. Open to any full-length novel (published October 1-September 30). No novellas, collections of short stories, translations, or self-published books. Open to citizens of the Commonwealth or Republic of Ireland. Deadline: June 14. Prize: £50,000; Each shortlisted author receives £2,500. Judges appointed by the Booker Prize Management Committee.

⟳ MANITOBA BOOK AWARDS

Manitoba Writers' Guild, c/o Manitoba Writers' Guild, 218-100 Arthur St., Winnipeg MB R3B 1H3, Canada. (204)944-8013. **E-mail:** info@manitobabookawards.com. **Website:** www.manitobabookawards.com. **Contact:** Ellen MacDonald. Estab. 1983. The awards honor books written by Manitobans, published in Manitoba or about Manitoba. More than $30,000 in prizes is awarded each year to Manitoba writers. The Manitoba Book Awards celebrates literary excellence, originality and diverse talent. Some of Canada's best writers have springboarded to national and international acclaim after winning the Manitoba Book Awards. Previous winners include: Carol Shields (1993), David Bergen (1993,1996, 2009), Miriam Toews (1998, 2000), Margaret Sweatman (1991, 2001), Sandra Birdsell (1992), Jake MacDonald (2002), Allan Levine (2010), Barbara Huck (2014) and Wab Kinew (2016). The 18 awards to be presented at the 29th annual Manitoba Book Awards include Alexander Kennedy Isbister Award for Non-Fiction/Prix Alexander-Kennedy-Isbister pour les études et les essais, Beatrice Mosionier Aboriginal Writer of the Year Award /Prix Beatrice-Mosionier pour l'écrivain.e autochtone de l'année (English/Français/Indigenous Languages), Carol Shields Winnipeg Book Award/Prix littéraire Carol-Shields de la ville de Winnipeg, The Chris Johnson Award for Best Play by a Manitoba Playwright /Prix Chris-Johnson pour la meilleure pièce par un dramaturge manitobain, Eileen McTavish Sykes Award for Best First Book, John Hirsch Award for Most Promising Manitoba Writer/Prix John-Hirsch pour l'écrivain manitobain le plus prometteur, Lansdowne Prize for Poetry / Prix Lansdowne de poésie, Le Prix Littéraire Rue-Deschambault, Manuela Dias Book Design and Illustration Awards/Prix Manuela—Dias de conception graphique et d'illustration en édition—4 categories, Margaret Laurence Award for Fiction, Mary Scorer Award for Best Book by a Manitoba Publisher/Prix Mary-Scorer pour le meilleur livre par un éditeur du Manitoba, McNally Robinson Books for Young People Awards—2 categories, McNally Robinson Book of the Year Award, and Lifetime Achievement Award—English/Français. Deadline: December 1 and January 15. Prize: Several prizes up to $5,000 (CAD). Costs: $25 per category. Jurors selected by the Manitoba Writers' Guild.

◯ Melanie Matheson, Executive Director of the Manitoba Writers' Guild, said, "Manitoba is blessed with an abundance of world class writers and these awards are a tremendous boon to both writers and to the industry. We celebrate that."

MASS CULTURAL COUNCIL ARTIST FELLOWSHIP PROGRAM

Mass Cultural Council, Mass Cultural Council, 10 St. James Ave., #302, Boston MA 02116-3803. (617)727-3668. **Fax:** (617)727-0044. **E-mail:** mcc@art.state.ma.us. **Website:** www.massculturalcouncil.org; http://artsake.massculturalcouncil.org. **Contact:** Dan Blask, Program Officer. Awards in poetry, fiction/creative nonfiction, and dramatic writing (among oth-

er discipline categories) are given in recognition of exceptional original work (check website for award amount). Looking to award artistic excellence and creative ability, based on work submitted for review. Judged by independent peer panels composed of artists and arts professionals.

MARY MCCARTHY PRIZE IN SHORT FICTION

Sarabande Books, 822 E. Market St., Louisville KY 40206. (502)458-4028. **Fax:** (502)458-4065. **E-mail:** info@sarabandebooks.org. **Website:** www.sarabandebooks.org. **Contact:** Sarah Gorham, editor-in-chief. Annual competition to honor a collection of short stories, novellas, or a short novel. Prize: $2,000 and publication (standard royalty contract).

THE MCGINNIS-RITCHIE MEMORIAL AWARD

Southwest Review, Southern Methodist University, P.O. Box 750374, Dallas TX 75275-0374. (214)768-1037. **Fax:** (214)768-1408. **E-mail:** swr@mail.smu.edu. **Website:** www.smu.edu/southwestreview. **Contact:** Greg Brownderville, editor-in-chief. The McGinnis-Ritchie Memorial Award is given annually to the best works of fiction and nonfiction that appeared in the magazine in the previous year. Mss are submitted for publication, not for the prizes themselves. Guidelines for SASE or online. Prize: $500. Judged by Greg Brownderville.

❺ MCKNIGHT ARTIST FELLOWSHIPS FOR WRITERS, LOFT AWARD(S) IN CHILDREN'S LITERATURE/CREATIVE PROSE/POETRY

The Loft Literary Center, 1011 Washington Ave. S., Suite 200, Open Book, Minneapolis MN 55415. (612)215-2575. **Fax:** (612)215-2576. **E-mail:** loft@loft.org. **Website:** www.loft.org. **Contact:** Bao Phi. The Loft administers the McKnight Artists Fellowships for Writers. Five $25,000 awards are presented annually to accomplished Minnesota writers and spoken word artists. Four awards alternate annually between creative prose (fiction and creative nonfiction) and poetry/spoken word. The fifth award is presented in children's literature and alternates annually for writing for ages 8 and under and writing for children older than 8. The awards provide the writers the opportunity to focus on their craft for the course of the fellowship year. Prize: $25,000, plus up to $3,000 in reimbursement for a writer's retreat or conference. The judge is announced after selections are made.

MEMPHIS MAGAZINE FICTION CONTEST

Memphis Magazine, Fiction Contest, c/o *Memphis* magazine, P.O. Box 1738, Memphis TN 38101. (901)521-9000, ext. 451. **Fax:** (901)521-0129. **E-mail:** fiction@memphismagazine.com. **Website:** www.memphismagazine.com. The Very Short Story Contest will recognize ten winning entries annually, every month except February and August. Authors are strongly encouraged to bring Memphis or the Mid-South into their stories. Entries accepted throughout the year. $200 gift certificate at Novel, a Memphis independent bookstore.

DAVID NATHAN MEYERSON PRIZE FOR FICTION

Southwest Review, Southern Methodist University, P.O. Box 750374, Dallas TX 75275-0374. (214)768-1037. **Fax:** (214)768-1408. **E-mail:** swr@smu.edu. **Website:** www.smu.edu/southwestreview. **Contact:** Greg Brownderville, editor-in-chief. Annual award given to a writer who has not published a first book of fiction, either a novel or collection of stories. Deadline: May 1 (postmarked). Prize: $1,000 and publication in the *Southwest Review*. Costs: $25/story.

A MIDSUMMER TALE

E-mail: editors@toasted-cheese.com. **E-mail:** amtcontest19@toasted-cheese.com. **Website:** www.toasted-cheese.com. **Contact:** Theryn Fleming, Editor. Estab. 2002. A Midsummer Tale is open to non-genre fiction and creative nonfiction. There is a different theme each year. Entries must be unpublished. Accepts inquiries by e-mail. Deadline: June 21. Results announced on July 31. Winners notified by e-mail. List of winners on website. Prize: Amazon gift certificates and publication in Toasted Cheese. Costs: No entry fee. Entries are blind-judged by at least one Toasted Cheese editor

☐ "Non-genre fiction" means literary or mainstream fiction. No science fiction, fantasy, mystery, horror, thriller, romance, western, or other genre fiction, please. Follow all contest guidelines.

MILKWEED NATIONAL FICTION PRIZE

1011 Washington Ave. South, Open Book, Suite 300, Minneapolis MN 55415. (612)332-3192. **Fax:** (612)215-2550. **E-mail:** editor@milkweed.org. **Website:** www.milkweed.org. **Contact:** Patrick Thomas, Editor and Program Manager. Annual award for unpublished works. Mss should be one of the following: a novel, a collection of short stories, one or more novellas, or a combination of short stories and one or more novel-

las. Deadline: Rolling submissions. Check website for details. Prize: Publication by Milkweed Editions and a cash advance of $5,000 against royalties, agreed upon in the contractual arrangement negotiated at the time of acceptance. Judged by the editors.

MILKWEED PRIZE FOR CHILDREN'S LITERATURE

Milkweed Editions, 1011 Washington Ave. S., Suite 300, Minneapolis MN 55415. (612)332-3192. **Fax:** (612)215-2550. **E-mail:** editor@milkweed.org. **Website:** www.milkweed.org. Milkweed Editions will award the Milkweed Prize for Children's Literature to the best mss for young readers that Milkweed accepts for publication during the calendar year by a writer not previously published by Milkweed. All mss for young readers submitted for publication by Milkweed are automatically entered into the competition. Recognizes an outstanding literary novel for readers ages 8-13, and encourage writers to turn their attention to readers in this age group. Prize: $10,000 cash, in addition to a publishing contract negotiated at the time of acceptance. Judged by the editors of Milkweed Editions.

MINNESOTA BOOK AWARDS

The Friends of the Saint Paul Public Library, 1080 Montreal Ave., Suite 2, St. Paul MN 55116. (651)222-3242. **Fax:** (651)222-1988. **E-mail:** mnbookawards@thefriends.org. **Website:** www.mnbookawards.org. **Contact:** Bailey Veesenmeyer: bailey@thefriends.org. Estab. 1988. A year-round program celebrating and honoring Minnesota's best books, culminating in an annual awards ceremony. Recognizes and honors achievement by members of Minnesota's book and book arts community. Deadline: Books should be entered by 5 p.m. on the third Friday in November.

MISSISSIPPI REVIEW PRIZE

Mississippi Review, Mississippi Review Prize, 118 College Dr., #5144, Hattiesburg MS 39406-0001. (601)266-4321. **Fax:** (601)266-5757. **E-mail:** msreview@usm.edu. **Website:** www.mississippireview.com. Annual contest starting August 1 and running until January 1. Winners and finalists will make up next spring's print issue of the national literary magazine *Mississippi Review*. Each entrant will receive a copy of the prize issue. Deadline: January 1. Prize: $1,000 in fiction and poetry. Costs: $15 mail submission; $16 online submission. Judged by Andrew Malan Milward in fiction, and Angela Ball in poetry.

MONTANA PRIZE IN FICTION

Cutbank Literary Magazine, *CutBank*, University of Montana, English Dept., LA 133, Missoula MT 59812. **E-mail:** editor.cutbank@gmail.com. **Website:** www.cutbankonline.org. **Contact:** Allison Linville, Editor-in-Chief. The Montana Prize in Fiction seeks to highlight work that showcases an authentic voice, a boldness of form, and a rejection of functional fixedness. Deadline: January 15. Submissions period begins November 9. Prize: $500 and featured in the magazine. Costs: $20. Judged by a guest judge each year.

JENNY MCKEAN MOORE VISITING WRITER

Department of English, George Washington University, Phillips Hall, 801 22nd St. NW, Suite 643, Washington DC 20052. (202)994-6180. **Fax:** (202)994-7915. **E-mail:** engldept@gwu.edu; lpageinc@gwu.edu. **Website:** https://english.columbian.gwu.edu/activities-events. **Contact:** Lisa Page, Director of Creative Writing. The position is filled annually, bringing a visiting writer to The George Washington University. During each semester the Writer teaches 1 creative-writing course at the university as well as a community workshop. Seeks someone specializing in a different genre each year—fiction, poetry, creative nonfiction. Annual stipend between $50,000 and $60,000, plus reduced-rent townhouse on campus (not guaranteed). Application deadline: December 12. Annual stipend varies, depending on endowment performance; most recently, stipend was $60,000, plus reduced-rent townhouse (not guaranteed).

THE HOWARD FRANK MOSHER SHORT FICTION PRIZE

Vermont College of Fine Arts, 36 College St., Montpelier VT 05602. (802)828-8517. **E-mail:** hungermtn@vcfa.edu. **Website:** www.hungermtn.org. **Contact:** Cameron Finch, managing editor. Estab. 2002. The Howard Frank Mosher Short Fiction Prize is an annual contest for short fiction. Deadline: March 1. Prize: One first place winner receives $1,000 and online publication. One runner-up receives $100 and online publication. Other finalists are considered for print publication. Costs: $20.

NATIONAL BOOK AWARDS

The National Book Foundation, 90 Broad St., Suite 604, New York NY 10004. (212)685-0261. **E-mail:** nationalbook@nationalbook.org. **Website:** www.nationalbook.org. The National Book Foundation and the National Book Awards celebrate the best of American literature, expand its audience, and enhance the cultural value of great writing in America. The contest offers prizes in 4 categories: fiction, nonfiction, poetry, and young people's literature. Books should be published between December 1 and November 30 of the previous year. Deadline: Submit entry form, payment, and a copy of the book by May 15. Prize: $10,000 in each category. Finalists will each receive a prize of $1,000. Costs: $135/title. Judged by a category specific panel of 5 judges for each category.

NATIONAL OUTDOOR BOOK AWARDS

921 S. 8th Ave., Stop 8128, Pocatello ID 83209. (208)282-3912. **E-mail:** wattron@isu.edu. **Website:** www.noba-web.org. **Contact:** Ron Watters. Nine categories: History/biography, outdoor literature, instructional texts, outdoor adventure guides, nature guides, children's books, design/artistic merit, natural history literature, and nature and the environment. Additionally, a special award, the Outdoor Classic Award, is given annually to books which, over a period of time, have proven to be exceptionally valuable works in the outdoor field. Application forms and eligibility requirements are available online. Applications for the Awards program become available in early June. Deadline: August 22. Prize: Winning books are promoted nationally and are entitled to display the National Outdoor Book Award (NOBA) medallion. Costs: $85.

NATIONAL READERS' CHOICE AWARDS

Oklahoma Romance Writers of America (OKRWA), **E-mail:** nrca@okrwa.com. **Website:** www.okrwa.com. **Contact:** Kathy L Wheeler, NRCA Chair. Estab. 1990. To provide writers of romance fiction with a competition where their published novels are judged by readers. See the website for categories and descriptions. Additional award for best first book. All entries must have an original copyright date during the current contest year. Entries will be accepted from authors, editors, publishers, agents, readers, or whoever wants to fill out the entry form, pay the fee, and supply the books. No limit to the number of entries, but each title may be entered only in one category. Open to any writer published by an RWA approved non-vanity/non-subsidy press. For guidelines, send e-mail or visit website. Deadline: October 1st. Prize: Plaques and finalist certificates awarded at the awards banquet hosted at the Annual National Romance Writers

Convention. Costs: $35 per entry, plus $5 for Best First Book Category. Judged by readers.

NATIONAL WRITERS ASSOCIATION NOVEL CONTEST

The National Writers Association, NWA Novel Contest, 10940 S. Parker Rd. #508, Parker CO 80134. E-mail: natlwritersassn@hotmail.com. Website: www.nationalwriters.com. Contact: Sandy Whelchel, Director. Open to any genre or category. Open to any writer. Contest begins December 1. Annual contest to help develop creative skills, recognize and reward outstanding ability, and increase the opportunity for the marketing and subsequent publication of novel mss. Deadline: April 1. Prize: 1st Place: $500; 2nd Place: $250; 3rd Place: $150. Costs: $35. Judged by editors and agents.

NATIONAL WRITERS ASSOCIATION SHORT STORY CONTEST

NWA Short Story Contest, 10940 S. Parker Rd., #508, Parker CO 80134. E-mail: natlwritersassn@hotmail.com. Website: www.nationalwriters.com. Estab. 1971. The purpose of the National Writers Assn. Short Story Contest is to encourage the development of creative skills, recognize and reward outstanding ability in the area of short story writing. July 1 (postmarked) Prize: 1st Prize: $250; 2nd Prize: $100; 3rd Prize: $50; 4th-10th places will receive a book. 1st-3rd place winners may be asked to grant one-time rights for publication in *Authorship* magazine. Honorable Mentions receive a certificate. Costs: $15 per submission. Judging will be based on originality, marketability, research, and reader interest. Copies of the judges' evaluation sheets will be sent to entrants furnishing an SASE with their entry.

THE NELLIGAN PRIZE FOR SHORT FICTION

Colorado Review/Center for Literary Publishing, Colorado State University, 9105 Campus Delivery, Dept. of English, Colorado State University, Ft. Collins CO 80523-9105. (970)491-5449. E-mail: creview@colostate.edu. Website: https://nelliganprize.colostate.edu. Contact: Stephanie G'Schwind, editor. Estab. 2004. Annual competition/award for short stories. Receives approximately 1,000 stories. All entries are read blind by Colorado Review's editorial staff. Ten to fifteen entries are selected to be sent on to a final, outside judge. Stories must be unpublished and between 10 and 50 pages. "The Nelligan Prize for Short Fiction was established in memory of Liza Nelligan, a writer, editor, and friend of many in Colorado State University's English Department, where she received her master's degree in literature in 1992. By giving an award to the author of an outstanding short story each year, we hope to honor Liza Nelligan's life, her passion for writing, and her love of fiction." Deadline: March 14. Prize: $2,000 and publication of story in *Colorado Review*. Costs: $15, send checks payable to Colorado Review; payment also accepted via our online submission manager link from website (add $2 to submit online). Judged by a different writer each year. 2019 judge is Joan Silber.

THE NEUTRINO SHORT-SHORT CONTEST

Passages North, Passages North, Northern Michigan University, 1401 Presque Isle Ave., Marquette MI 49855. (906)227-1203. Fax: (906)227-1096. E-mail: passages@nmu.edu. Website: www.passagesnorth.com. Contact: Jennifer Howard. Offered every 2 years to publish new voices in literary fiction, non-fiction, hybrid-essays, and prose poems (maximum 1,000 words). Guidelines available for SASE or online. Deadline: April 15. Submission period begins February 15. Prize: $1,000, and publication for the winner; 2 honorable mentions also published; all entrants receive a copy of *Passages North*. Costs: $15 for up to 3 poems. 2019: Tarfia Faizullah

NEW ENGLAND BOOK AWARDS

NEIBA, 1955 Massachusetts Ave., #2, Cambridge MA 02140. (617)547-3642. Fax: (617)547-3759. E-mail: ali@neba.org. Website: www.newenglandbooks.org. Contact: Nan Sorensen, Administrative Coordinator. Estab. 1990. All books must be either written by a New-England-based author or be set in New England. Eligible books must be published between September 1, 2017 and August 31, 2018 in either hardcover or paperback. Submissions made by New England booksellers and publishers. Submit written nominations only; actual books should not be sent. Award is given to a specific title: fiction, non-fiction, children's, or young adult. The titles must be either about New England, set in New England. or by an author residing in the New England. The titles must be hardcover, paperback original, or reissue that was published between September 1 and August 31. Entries must be still in print and available. Deadline: June 14. Prize: Winners will receive $250 for literacy to a charity of their choice. Costs: $25 fee per title for non-member submissions; NEIBA members free. Judged by NEIBA membership.

NEW LETTERS LITERARY AWARDS

New Letters, University of Missouri-Kansas City, 5101 Rockhill Rd., Kansas City MO 64110-2499. (816)235-1168. E-mail: newletters@umkc.edu. **Website:** www.newletters.org/writers-wanted/writing-contests. **Contact:** Ashley Wann. Estab. 1986. Award has 3 categories (fiction, poetry, and creative nonfiction) with 1 winner in each. Offered annually for previously unpublished work. For guidelines, send an SASE to *New Letters*, or visit http://www.newletters.org/writers-wanted/writing-contests. Deadline: May 18. 1st place: $1,500, plus publication in poetry and fiction category; 1st place: $2,500, plus publication in essay category. Costs: $24 entry fee. Judged by regional writers of prominence and experience. Final judging by someone of national repute. Previous judges include Maxine Kumin, Albert Goldbarth, Charles Simic, and Janet Burroway.

NEW LETTERS PRIZE FOR FICTION

New Letters, University of Missouri-Kansas City, *New Letters* Awards for Writers, UMKC, University House, 5101 Rockhill Rd., Kansas City MO 64110-2499. (816)235-1168. E-mail: newletters@umkc.edu. **Website:** www.newletters.org/writers-wanted/writing-contests. **Contact:** Ashley Wann. Estab. 1986. Offered annually for the best short story to discover and reward new and upcoming writers. Buys first North American serial rights. Open to any writer. Deadline: May 18. 1st Place: $1,500 and publication in a volume of *New Letters*. Costs: $24 entry fee.

NEW MILLENNIUM AWARDS FOR FICTION, POETRY, AND NONFICTION

New Millennium Writings, New Millennium Writings, 340 S Lemon Ave #6906, Walnut CA 91789. (865)254-4880. **Website:** www.newmillenniumwritings.org. **Contact:** Alexis Williams, Editor and Publisher. Estab. 1996. No restrictions as to style, content, or number of submissions. Previously published pieces acceptable if online or under 5,000 print circulation. Simultaneous and multiple submissions welcome. Deadline: Postmarked on or before January 31 for the Winter Awards and June 23 for the Summer Awards. Prize: $1,000 for Best Poem; $1,000 for Best Fiction; $1,000 for Best Nonfiction; $1,000 for Best Flash Fiction (Short-Short Fiction). Costs: $20; see website regarding fee information for multiple entries.

NEW SOUTH WRITING CONTEST

English Department, Georgia State University, P.O. Box 3970, Atlanta GA 30302-3970. **E-mail:** newsoutheditors@gmail.com. **Website:** newsouthjournal.com/contest. **Contact:** Anna Sandy, editor-in-chief. Offered annually to publish the most promising work of up-and-coming writers of poetry (up to 3 poems) and fiction (9,000-word limit). Rights revert to writer upon publication. Guidelines online. Deadline: April 15. Prize: 1st Place: $1,000 in each category; 2nd Place: $250 Costs: $15. Judged by Natalie Eilbert in poetry and SJ Sindu in prose.

NORTH CAROLINA ARTS COUNCIL REGIONAL ARTIST PROJECT GRANTS

North Carolina Arts Council, Dept. of Natural and Cultural Resources, MSC #4632, Raleigh NC 27699-4634. (919)807-6512. **Fax:** (919)807-6532. **E-mail:** david.potorti@ncdcr.gov. **Website:** www.ncarts.org. **Contact:** David Potorti, literature and theater director. See website for contact information for the consortia of local arts councils that distribute these grants. Deadline: Dates vary in fall/spring. Prize: $500-3,000 awarded to writers to pursue projects that further their artistic development. These grants are awarded through consortia of local arts councils. See our website for details.

NORTH CAROLINA WRITERS' FELLOWSHIPS

North Carolina Arts Council, NC Department of Natural and Cultural Resources, North Carolina Arts Council, Mail Service Center #4632, Raleigh NC 27699-4632. (919)814-6512. **E-mail:** david.potorti@ncdcr.gov. **Website:** www.ncarts.org. **Contact:** David Potorti, literature and theater director. The North Carolina Arts Council offers fellowship grants to support writers of fiction, creative non-fiction, poetry, spoken word, playwrighting, screenwriting and literary translation. Offered every even-numbered year to support writers of fiction, creative non-fiction, poetry, spoken word, playwriting, screenwriting and literary translation. See website for guidelines and other eligibility requirements. Deadline: November 1 of even-numbered years. Next deadline is Nov. 1, 2020. Prize: $10,000 grant. Reviewed by a panel of literature professionals (writers and editors).

NORTHERN CALIFORNIA BOOK AWARDS

Northern California Book Reviewers Association, Northern California Book Awards, c/o Poetry Flash, 1450 Fourth St. #4, Att'n: NCBR, Berkeley CA 94710. (510)525-5476. **E-mail:** ncbr@poetryflash.org; editor@poetryflash.org. **Website:** www.poetryflash.org.

Contact: Joyce Jenkins, Executive Director. Estab. 1981. Annual Northern California Book Award for outstanding book in literature; open to books published in the current calendar year by Northern California authors. NCBR presents annual awards to Bay Area (northern California) authors annually in fiction, nonfiction, poetry, and children's literature. Encourages writers and stimulates interest in books and reading. Deadline: January 18. Prize: $100 honorarium and award certificate. Judging by voting members of the Northern California Book Reviewers.

❂ NOVA WRITES COMPETITION FOR UNPUBLISHED MANUSCRIPTS

Writers' Federation of Nova Scotia, 1113 Marginal Rd., Halifax NS B3H 4P7. (902)423-8116. **Fax:** (902)422-0881. **E-mail:** programs@writers.ns.ca. **Website:** www.writers.ns.ca. **Contact:** Robin Spittal, Communications and Development Officer. Estab. 1975. Annual program designed to honor work by unpublished writers in all 4 Atlantic Provinces. Entry is open to writers unpublished in the category of writing they wish to enter. Prizes are presented in the fall of each year. Categories include: short form creative nonfiction, long form creative nonfiction, novel, poetry, short story, and writing for children/young adult novel. Judges return written comments when competition is concluded. Deadline: January 3. Prizes vary based on categories. See website for details. Costs: $25 per entry.

❧ SEAN O'FAOLAIN SHORT STORY COMPETITION

The Munster Literature Centre, Frank O'Connor House, 84 Douglas Street, Cork , Ireland. +353-0214319255. **E-mail:** munsterlit@eircom.net. **Website:** www.munsterlit.ie. **Contact:** Patrick Cotter, artistic director. Purpose is to reward writers of outstanding short stories. Deadline: July 31. Prize: 1st prize €2,000; 2nd prize €500. Four runners-up prizes of €100 (approx $146). All six stories to be published in *Southword Literary Journal*. First-Prize Winner offered week's residency in Anam Cara Artist's Retreat in Ireland. Costs: $20.

FRANK O'CONNOR AWARD FOR SHORT FICTION

descant, Texas Christian University's literary journal, descant, c/o TCU Department of English, Box 298300, Fort Worth TX 76129. **E-mail:** descant@tcu.edu. **Website:** www.descant.tcu.edu. **Contact:** Matthew Pitt, Editor. Offered annually for an outstanding story accepted for publication in the current edition of the journal. Publication retains copyright but will transfer it to the author upon request. Deadline: April 1. Open to submissions September 1. Prize: $500. Costs: No entry fees.

OHIOANA BOOK AWARDS

Ohioana Library Association, 274 E. First Ave., Suite 300, Columbus OH 43201-3673. (614)466-3831. **Fax:** (614)728-6974. **E-mail:** ohioana@ohioana.org. **Website:** www.ohioana.org. **Contact:** David Weaver, executive director. Estab. 1942. Offered annually to bring national attention to Ohio authors and their books, published in the last year. (Books can only be considered once.) Categories: Fiction, nonfiction, juvenile, poetry, and books about Ohio or an Ohioan. Deadline: December 31. Prize: $1,000 cash prize, certificate, and glass sculpture. Judged by a jury selected by librarians, book reviewers, writers and other knowledgeable people.

OHIOANA WALTER RUMSEY MARVIN GRANT

Ohioana Library Association, 274 E. First Ave., Suite 300, Columbus OH 43201. (614)466-3831. **Fax:** (614)728-6974. **E-mail:** ohioana@ohioana.org. **Website:** www.ohioana.org. **Contact:** David Weaver, executive director. Award to encourage young, unpublished writers 30 years of age or younger. Competition for short stories or novels in progress. Deadline: January 31 Prize: $1,000.

OKLAHOMA BOOK AWARDS

200 NE 18th St., Oklahoma City OK 73105. (405)521-2502. **Fax:** (405)525-7804. **E-mail:** connie.armstrong@libraries.ok.gov. **Website:** www.odl.state.ok.us/ocb. **Contact:** Connie Armstrong, executive director. Estab. 1989. This award honors Oklahoma writers and books about Oklahoma. Awards are presented to best books in fiction, nonfiction, children's, design and illustration, and poetry books about Oklahoma or books written by an author who was born, is living or has lived in Oklahoma. SASE for award rules and entry forms. Winner will be announced at banquet in Oklahoma City. The Arrell Gibson Lifetime Achievement Award is also presented each year for a body of work. Deadline: January 10. Prize: Awards a medal. Costs: $25. Judging by a panel of 5 people for each category, generally a librarian, a working writer in the genre, booksellers, editors, etc.

⑤ ON THE PREMISES CONTEST

On The Premises, LLC, 4323 Gingham Court, Alexandria VA 22310. **E-mail:** questions@onthepremises. com. **Website:** www.onthepremises.com. **Contact:** Tarl Kudrick or Bethany Granger, co-publishers. *On the Premises* aims to promote newer and/or relatively unknown writers who can write creative, compelling stories told in effective, uncluttered, and evocative prose. Each contest challenges writers to produce a great story based on a broad premise that the editors supply as part of the contest. Deadline: Short story contests held twice a year; smaller mini-contests held four times a year; check website for exact dates. Prize: 1st Prize: $220; 2nd Prize: $160; 3rd Prize: $120; Honorable Mentions receive $60. All prize winners are published in *On the Premises* magazine in HTML and PDF format. Costs: There are no fees for entering our contests. Judged by a panel of judges with professional editing and writing experience.

○ OPEN SEASON AWARDS

The Malahat Review, University of Victoria, P.O. Box 1700, Stn CSC, Victoria BC V8V 2Y2, Canada. (250)721-8524. **Fax:** (250)472-5051. **E-mail:** malahat@ uvic.ca. **Website:** www.malahatreview.ca. **Contact:** L'Amour Lisik, publicity manager. The Open Season Awards accepts entries of poetry, fiction, and creative nonfiction. Winners published in the spring issue of *The Malahat Review*, announced in the winter on our website, social media pages, and in our monthly e-newsletter, *Malahat lite*. Deadline: November 1. Prize: $6,000 over three categories (poetry, fiction, creative nonfiction) and publication in *The Malahat Review*. Costs: $35 CAD for Canadian entries; $40 USD for US entries ($45 USD for entries from Mexico and outside North America). $10 for each additional entry, any genre, no limit to how many times you can send in additional entries. Includes a 1-year print subscription to *The Malahat Review*.

OREGON BOOK AWARDS

925 SW Washington St., Portland OR 97205. (503)227-2583. **Fax:** (503)241-4256. **E-mail:** la@literary-arts.org. **Website:** www.literary-arts.org. **Contact:** Susan Denning, director of programs and events. The annual Oregon Book Awards celebrate Oregon authors in the areas of poetry, fiction, nonfiction, drama and young readers' literature published between August 1 and July 31 of the previous calendar year. Awards are available for every category. See website for details. Deadline: August 26. Prize: Grant of $2,500. (Grant money could vary.) Judged by writers who are selected from outside Oregon for their expertise in a genre. Past judges include Mark Doty, Colson Whitehead and Kim Barnes.

OREGON LITERARY FELLOWSHIPS

925 S.W. Washington, Portland OR 97205. (503)227-2583. **E-mail:** susan@literary-arts.org. **Website:** www. literary-arts.org. **Contact:** Susan Moore, Director of programs and events. Oregon Literary Fellowships are intended to help Oregon writers initiate, develop, or complete literary projects in poetry, fiction, literary nonfiction, drama, and young readers literature. Writers in the early stages of their career are encouraged to apply. The awards are merit-based. Deadline: Last Friday in June. Prize: $3,000 minimum award, for approximately 8 writers and 2 publishers. Judged by out-of-state writers

⑤ KENNETH PATCHEN AWARD FOR THE INNOVATIVE NOVEL

Eckhard Gerdes Publishing, 1110 Varsity Blvd., Apt. 221, DeKalb IL 60115. **E-mail:** egerdes@experimentalfiction.com. **Website:** www.experimentalfiction. com. **Contact:** Eckhard Gerdes. This award will honor the most innovative novel submitted during the previous calendar year. Kenneth Patchen is celebrated for being among the greatest innovators of American fiction, incorporating strategies of concretism, asemic writing, digression, and verbal juxtaposition into his writing long before such strategies were popularized during the height of American postmodernist experimentation in the 1970s. Deadline: All submissions must be postmarked between January 1 and July 31. Prize: $1,000 and 20 complimentary copies. Costs: $25 entry fee. Judged by novelist Dominic Ward.

THE PATERSON FICTION PRIZE

The Poetry Center at Passaic Community College, One College Blvd., Paterson NJ 07505. (973)684-6555. **Fax:** (973)523-6085. **E-mail:** mgillan@pccc.edu. **Website:** www.pccc.edu/poetry. **Contact:** Maria Mazziotti Gillan, executive director. Offered annually for a novel or collection of short fiction published the previous calendar year. For more information, visit the website or send SASE. Deadline: February 1. Prize: $1,000.

THE KATHERINE PATERSON PRIZE FOR YOUNG ADULT AND CHILDREN'S WRITING

Hunger Mountain, Vermont College of Fine Arts, 36 College St., Montpelier VT 05602. (802)828-8517. **E-mail:** hungermtn@vcfa.edu. **Website:** www.hungermtn.org. **Contact:** Cameron Finch, managing editor. Estab. 2002. The annual Katherine Paterson Prize for Young Adult and Children's Writing honors the best in young adult and children's literature. Submit young adult or middle grade mss, and writing for younger children, short stories, picture books, poetry, or novel excerpts, under 10,000 words. Guidelines available on website. Deadline: March 1. Prize: $1,000 and publication for the first place winner; $100 each and publication for the three category winners. Costs: $20. Judged by a guest judge every year.

JUDITH SIEGEL PEARSON AWARD

Judith Siegel Pearson Award, c/o Department of English, Wayne State University, Attn: Royanne Smith, 5057 Woodward Ave., Ste. 9408, Detroit MI 48202. **E-mail:** fm8146@wayne.edu. **Website:** https://wsuwritingawards.submittable.com/submit. **Contact:** Donovan Hohn. Offers an annual award for the best creative or scholarly work on a subject concerning women. The type of work accepted rotates each year: nonfiction in 2018; fiction in 2019; drama in 2020, poetry in 2021. Open to all interested writers and scholars. Only submit the appropriate genre in each year. Deadline: February 22. Prize: $500. Judged by members of the writing faculty of the Wayne State University English Department.

WILLIAM PEDEN PRIZE IN FICTION

The Missouri Review, 357 McReynolds Hall, Columbia MO 65211. (573)882-4474. **Fax:** (573)884-4671. **E-mail:** mutmrcontestquestion@moreview.com. **Website:** www.missourireview.com. **Contact:** Michael Nye, managing editor. Offered annually for the best story published in the past volume year of the magazine. All stories published in *The Missouri Review* are automatically considered. Guidelines online or for SASE. Prize: $1,000 and a reading/reception.

PEN CENTER USA LITERARY AWARDS

PEN Center USA, P.O. Box 6037, Beverly Hills CA 90212. (323)424-4939. **E-mail:** awards@penusa.org. **E-mail:** awards@penusa.org. **Website:** www.penusa.org. Offered for work published or produced in the previous calendar year. Open to writers living west of the Mississippi River. Award categories: fiction, poetry, research nonfiction, creative nonfiction, translation, young adult, graphic literature, drama, screenplay, teleplay, journalism. Deadline: See website for details. Prize: $1,000. Costs: $35 entry fee per submission.

PEN/FAULKNER AWARD FOR FICTION

PEN/Faulkner Foundation, 641 S Street NW, Third Floor, Washington DC 20001. (202)898-9063. **E-mail:** shahenda@penfaulkner.org. **Website:** www.penfaulkner.org. **Contact:** Shahenda Helmy, Programs & Logistics Director. Offered annually for best book-length work of fiction by an American citizen published in a calendar year. Deadline: October 31. Prize: $15,000 (one Winner); $5,000 (4 Finalists).

PENGUIN RANDOM HOUSE CREATIVE WRITING AWARDS

One Scholarship Way, P.O. Box 297, St. Peter MN 56082. (212)782-9348. **Fax:** (212) 782-5157. **E-mail:** creativewriting@penguinrandomhouse.com. **Website:** www.penguinrandomhouse.com/creativewriting. **Contact:** Melanie Fallon Hauska, director. Offered annually for unpublished work to NYC public high school seniors. 72 awards given in literary and nonliterary categories. Four categories: poetry, fiction/drama, personal essay, and graphic novel. Applicants must be seniors (under age 21) at a New York high school. No college essays or class assignments will be accepted. Deadline: February 3 for all categories. Graphic Novel extended deadline: March 1st. Prize: Awards range from $500-10,000. The program usually awards just under $100,000 in scholarships.

THE PINCH LITERARY AWARDS

Literary Awards, The Pinch, Department of English, The University of Memphis, Memphis TN 38152-6176. (901)678-4591. **Website:** www.pinchjournal.com. Offered annually for unpublished short stories of 5,000 words maximum or up to three poems. Guidelines on website. Cost: $20, which is put toward one issue of *The Pinch*. Deadline: March 15. Prize: 1st place Fiction: $1,500 and publication; 1st place Poetry: $1,000 and publication. Offered annually for unpublished short stories and prose of up to 5,000 words and 1-3 poems. Deadline: March 15. Open to submissions on December 15. Prizes: $1,000 for 1st place in each category. Costs: $20 for initial entry, $10 each for subsequent entries.

PNWA LITERARY CONTEST

Pacifc Northwest Writers Association, PMB 2717, 1420 NW Gilman Blvd., Suite 2, Issaquah WA 98027. (452)673-2665. **Fax:** (452)961-0768. **E-mail:** pnwa@pnwa.org. **Website:** www.pnwa.org. Annual literary contest with 12 different categories. See website for details and specific guidelines. Each entry receives 2 critiques. Winners announced at the PNWA Summer Conference, held annually in mid-July. Deadline: February 20. Prize: 1st Place: $600; 2nd Place: $300; 3rd Place: $100. Costs: $35 for PNWA members; $50 for non-members. Judged by an agent or editor attending the conference.

○ POCKETS FICTION-WRITING CONTEST

P.O. Box 340004, Nashville TN 37203-0004. (615)340-7333. **Fax:** (615)340-7267. **E-mail:** pockets@upperroom.org. **Website:** www.pockets.upperroom.org. **Contact:** Lynn W. Gilliam, senior editor. Designed for 6- to 12-year-olds, *Pockets* magazine offers wholesome devotional readings that teach about God's love and presence in life. The content includes fiction, scripture stories, puzzles and games, poems, recipes, colorful pictures, activities, and scripture readings. Freelance submissions of stories, poems, recipes, puzzles and games, and activities are welcome. The primary purpose of *Pockets* is to help children grow in their relationship with God and to claim the good news of the gospel of Jesus Christ by applying it to their daily lives. *Pockets* espouses respect for all human beings and for God's creation. It regards a child's faith journey as an integral part of all of life and sees prayer as undergirding that journey. Deadline: August 15. Submission period begins March 15. Prize: $500 and publication in magazine.

EDGAR ALLAN POE AWARD

1140 Broadway, Suite 1507, New York NY 10001. (212)888-8171. **E-mail:** mwa@mysterywriters.org. **Website:** www.mysterywriters.org. Estab. 1945. Mystery Writers of America is the leading association for professional crime writers in the United States. Members of MWA include most major writers of crime fiction and nonfiction, as well as screenwriters, dramatists, editors, publishers, and other professionals in the field. Purpose of the award: Honor authors of distinguished works in the mystery field. Previously published submissions only. Submissions should be made by the publisher. Work must be published/produced the year of the contest. Deadline: November 30. Prize: Awards ceramic bust of "Edgar" for winner; certificates for all nominees. Judged by active status members of Mystery Writers of America (writers).

THE KATHERINE ANNE PORTER PRIZE FOR FICTION

Nimrod International Journal, The University of Tulsa, 800 S. Tucker Dr., Tulsa OK 74104. (918)631-3080. **Fax:** (918)631-3033. **E-mail:** nimrod@utulsa.edu.

Website: www.utulsa.edu/nimrod. **Contact:** Eilis O'Neal. Estab. 1978. Postmark Deadline: April 30. 1st Place: $2,000 and publication; 2nd Place: $1,000 and publication. Costs: $20, includes a 1-year subscription (2 issues) to *Nimrod*; make checks payable to *Nimrod*. Judged by the *Nimrod* editors, who select the finalists, and a recognized author, who selects the winners.

PRAIRIE SCHOONER BOOK PRIZE

Prairie Schooner and the University of Nebraska Press, Prairie Schooner Prize Series, 123 Andrews Hall, Lincoln NE 68588-0334. (402)472-0911. **E-mail:** PSBookPrize@unl.edu. **Website:** prairieschooner.unl.edu. **Contact:** Kwame Dawes, editor. Annual competition/award for poetry and short story collections. Deadline: March 15. Prize: $3,000 and publication through the University of Nebraska Press. Costs: $25.

PRESS 53 AWARD FOR SHORT FICTION

Press 53, 560 N. Trade St., Suite 103, Winston-Salem NC 27101. (336)770-5353. **E-mail:** kevin@press53.com. **Website:** www.press53.com. **Contact:** Kevin Morgan Watson, Publisher. Estab. 2014. Awarded to an outstanding, unpublished collection of short stories. Deadline: December 31. Submission period begins September 1. Finalists and winner announced no later than May 1. Publication in October. Prize: Publication of winning short story collection, $1,000 cash advance and 50 copies of the book. Costs: $30 via Submittable or by mail. Judged by Press 53 publisher Kevin Morgan Watson.

PRIME NUMBER MAGAZINE AWARDS

Press 53, 560 N. Trade St., Suite 103, Winston-Salem NC 27101. (336)770-5353. **E-mail:** kevin@press53.com. **Website:** www.press53.com. **Contact:** Kevin Morgan Watson, publisher. Awards $1,000 each for poetry and short fiction. Deadline: April 15. Submission period begins January 1. Finalists and winners announced by August 1. Winners published in Prime Number Magazine in October. Prize: $1,000 cash. All winners receive publication in Prime Number Magazine online. Costs: $15 via Submittable. Judged by industry professionals to be named when the contest begins.

☼ PRISM INTERNATIONAL ANNUAL SHORT FICTION, POETRY, AND CREATIVE NONFICTION CONTESTS

PRISM International, Creative Writing Program, UBC, Buch. E462, 1866 Main Mall, Vancouver BC V6T 1Z1, Canada. **E-mail:** promotions@prismmagazine.ca. **Website:** www.prismmagazine.ca. **Contact:**

Claire Matthews. Estab. 1959. Offered annually for unpublished work to award the best in contemporary fiction, poetry, drama, translation, and nonfiction. Works of translation are eligible. Guidelines are available on website. Acquires first North American serial rights upon publication, and limited web rights for pieces selected for website. Open to any writer except students and faculty in the Creative Writing Department at UBC, or people who have taken a creative writing course at UBC within 2 years of the contest deadline. Entry includes subscription. Deadlines: Creative Nonfiction: July 15; Fiction: January 15; Poetry: October 15. Prize: All grand prizes are $1,500, $600 for first runner up, and $400 for second runner up. Winners are published. Costs: $35 Canadian entries, $40 US entries, and $45 International entries; $5 each additional entry. Entries accepted via Submittable at http://prisminternational.submittable.com/submit or by mail.

✪ PRISM INTERNATIONAL ANNUAL SHORT FICTION CONTEST

Creative Writing Program, UBC, Buch. E462 - 1866 Main Mall, Vancouver BC V6T 1Z1, Canada. (604)822-2514. **Fax:** (604)822-3616. **Website:** prismmagazine.ca/contests. **Contact:** Jessica Johns, executive editor, promotions. Offered annually for unpublished work to award the best in contemporary fiction. Works of translation are eligible. Guidelines by SASE, by e-mail, or on website. Acquires first North American serial rights upon publication, and rights to publish online for promotional or archival purposes. Open to any writer except students and faculty in the Creative Writing Department at UBC, or people who have taken a creative writing course at UBC with the 2 years prior to the contest deadline. Deadline: January 31. Prize: 1st Place: $1,500; 1st Runner-up: $600; 2nd Runner-up: $400; winner is published. Costs: $35 CAD entries; $40 US entries; $45 international entries; $5 each additional entry (outside Canada, pay US currency); includes subscription.

PURPLE DRAGONFLY BOOK AWARDS

Story Monsters LLC, 4696 W Tyson St, Chandler AZ 85226-2903. (480)940-8182. **Fax:** (480)940-8787. **E-mail:** linda@storymonsters.com. **Website:** www.dragonflybookawards.com. **Contact:** Cristy Bertini, contest coordinator. Estab. 2009. The Purple Dragonfly Book Awards were conceived with children in mind. Not only do we want to recognize and honor accomplished authors in the field of children's literature, but we also want to highlight up-and-coming, newly published authors, and younger published writers. Divided into 55 distinct subject categories ranging from books on the environment and cooking to sports and family issues, and even marketing collateral that complements a book, the Purple Dragonfly Book Awards are geared toward stories that appeal to children of all ages. We are looking for books that are original, innovative and creative in both content and design. A Purple Dragonfly Book Awards seal on your book's cover, marketing materials, or website tells parents, grandparents, educators, and caregivers that they are giving children the very best in reading excellence. Our judges are industry experts with specific knowledge about the categories over which they preside. Being honored with a Purple Dragonfly Book Award confers credibility upon the winner and gives published authors the recognition they deserve and provide a helping hand to further their careers. Deadline: May 1. The grand prize winner will receive a $500 cash prize, a certificate commemorating their accomplishment, 100 Grand Prize seals, a one-hour marketing consulting session with Linda F. Radke, a news release announcing the winners sent to a comprehensive list of media outlets, and a listing on the Dragonfly Book Awards website. All first-place winners of categories will be put into a drawing for a $100 prize. In addition, each first-place winner in each category receives a certificate commemorating their accomplishment, 25 foil award seals, and mention on Dragonfly Book Awards website. All winners receive certificates and are listed in Story Monsters Ink magazine. Costs: Early bird pricing: $60/category before March 1. Fee is $65/category after March 1. Judged by industry experts with specific knowledge about the categories over which they preside.

PUSHCART PRIZE

Pushcart Press, P.O. Box 380, Wainscott NY 11975. (631)324-9300. **Website:** www.pushcartprize.com. **Contact:** Bill Henderson. Estab. 1976. Published every year since 1976, The Pushcart Prize - Best of the Small Presses series "is the most honored literary project in America. Hundreds of presses and thousands of writers of short stories, poetry and essays have been represented in the pages of our annual collections." Little magazine and small book press editors (print or online) may make up to six nominations from their year's publicatoins by the deadline. The nominations may be any combination of poetry, short fiction, essays or literary whatnot. Editors may nominate self-contained portions of books — for instance, a chapter from a novel. Deadline: December 1.

☯ THOMAS H. RADDALL ATLANTIC FICTION AWARD

Writers' Federation of Nova Scotia, 1113 Marginal Rd., Halifax NS B3H 4P7, Canada. (902)423-8116. **Fax:** (902)422-0881. **E-mail:** director@writers.ns.ca. **Website:** www.writers.ns.ca. **Contact:** Marilyn Smulders, executive director. Estab. 1990. The Thomas Head Raddall Atlantic Fiction Award is awarded for a novel or a book of short fiction by a full-time resident of Atlantic Canada. Deadline: First Friday in December. Prize: Valued at $25,000 for winning title.

DAVID RAFFELOCK AWARD FOR PUBLISHING EXCELLENCE

National Writers Association, 10940 S. Parker Rd., #508, Parker CO 80134. **E-mail:** natlwritersassn@hotmail.com. **Website:** www.nationalwriters.com. **Contact:** Sandy Whelchel. Contest is offered annually for books published the previous year. Published works only. Open to any writer. Guidelines for SASE, by e-mail, or on website. Winners will be notified by mail or phone. List of winners available for SASE or visit website. Purpose is to assist published authors in marketing their works and to reward outstanding published works. Deadline: May 15. Prize: Publicity tour, including airfare, valued at $5,000. Costs: $100.

☯ THE RBC BRONWEN WALLACE AWARD FOR EMERGING WRITERS

The Writers' Trust of Canada, 460 Richmond St. W., Suite 600, Toronto ON M5C 1P1, Canada. (416)504-8222. **Fax:** (416)504-9090. **E-mail:** djackson@writerstrust.com. **Website:** www.writerstrust.com. **Contact:** Devon Jackson. Presented annually to a Canadian writer under the age of 35 who is not yet published in book form. The award, which alternates each year between poetry and short fiction, was established in memory of Bronwen Wallace and honours her wish to help more writers achieve success at a young age. Prize: $10,000. Two finalists receive $2,500 each.

☯ THE RED HOUSE CHILDREN'S BOOK AWARD

Red House Children's Book Award, 123 Frederick Road, Cheam, Sutton, Surrey SM1 2HT, United Kingdom. E-mail: info@rhcba.co.uk. **Website:** www.redhousechildrensbookaward.co.uk. **Contact:** Sinead Kromer, national coordinator. Estab. 1980. The Red House Children's Book Award is the only national book award that is entirely voted for by children. A shortlist is drawn up from children's nominations and any child can then vote for the winner of the three categories: Books for Younger Children, Books for Younger Readers and Books for Older Readers. The book with the most votes is then crowned the winner of the Red House Children's Book Award. Deadline: December 31.

RHODE ISLAND ARTIST FELLOWSHIPS AND INDIVIDUAL PROJECT GRANTS

Rhode Island State Council on the Arts, State of Rhode Island, One Capitol Hill, 3rd Floor, Providence RI 02908. (401)222-3880. **Fax:** (401)222-3018. **E-mail:** Cristina.DiChiera@arts.ri.gov. **Website:** www.arts.ri.gov. **Contact:** Cristina DiChiera, director of individual artist programs. Annual fellowship competition is based upon panel review of poetry, fiction, and playwriting/screenwriting manuscripts. Project grants provide funds for community-based arts projects. Rhode Island artists who have lived in the state for at least 12 consecutive months may apply without a nonprofit sponsor. Applicants for all RSCA grant and award programs must be at least 18 years old and not currently enrolled in an arts-related degree program. Online application and guidelines can be found at www.arts.ri.gov/grants/guidelines/. Deadline: April 1 and October 1. Fellowship awards: $5,000 and $1,000. Grants range from $500-5,000, with an average of around $1,500. Judged by a rotating panel of artists.

HAROLD U. RIBALOW PRIZE

Hadassah Magazine, Hadassah WZOA, 40 Wall St., 8th Floor, New York NY 10005. (212)451-6286. **Fax:** (212)451-6257. **E-mail:** magtemp3@hadassah.org. **Website:** www.hadassahmagazine.org. **Contact:** Deb Meisels, coordinator. Offered annually for English-language (no translation) books of fiction (novel or short stories) on a Jewish theme published the previous year. Books should be submitted by the publisher. Administered annually by *Hadassah Magazine*. Deadline: April 15. The official announcement of the winner will be made in the fall.

☯ THE ROGERS WRITERS' TRUST FICTION PRIZE

The Writers' Trust of Canada, 460 Richmond St. W., Suite 600, Toronto ON M5V 1Y1, Canada. (416)504-

8222. **Fax:** (416)504-9090. **E-mail:** djackson@writerstrust.com. **Website:** www.writerstrust.com. **Contact:** Devon Jackson. Awarded annually to the best novel or short story collection published within the previous year. Presented at the Writers' Trust Awards event held in Toronto each fall. Open to Canadian citizens and permanent residents only. Deadline: July 18. Prize: $50,000 and $5,000 to 4 finalists.

ETHEL ROHAN NOVEL EXCERPT PRIZE CATEGORY

Soul-Making Keats Literary Competition Category, The Webhallow House, 1544 Sweetwood Dr., Broadmoor Vlg. CA 94015-2029. **E-mail:** soulkeats@mail.com. **Website:** www.soulmakingcontest.us. **Contact:** Eileen Malone. Open annually to any writer. Ongoing Deadline: November 30. Prize: 1st Place: $100; 2nd Place: $50; 3rd Place: $25. Costs: $5/entry (make checks payable to NLAPW).

LOIS ROTH AWARD

Modern Language Association, 85 Broad Street, suite 500, New York NY 10004-2434. (646)576-5141. **Fax:** (646)458-0030. **E-mail:** awards@mla.org. **Website:** www.mla.org. Offered in odd-numbered years for an outstanding translation into English of a book-length literary work. Translators need not be members of the MLA. Deadline: April 1. Prize: A cash award and a certificate to be presented at the Modern Language Association's annual convention in January.

ERNEST SANDEEN PRIZE IN POETRY AND THE RICHARD SULLIVAN PRIZE IN SHORT FICTION

University of Notre Dame, Dept. of English, 356 O'Shaughnessy Hall, Notre Dame IN 46556-5639. (574)631-7526. **Fax:** (574)631-4795. **E-mail:** creativewriting@nd.edu. **Website:** http://english.nd.edu/creative-writing/publications/sandeen-sullivan-prizes. **Contact:** Director of Creative Writing. Estab. 1994. The Sandeen & Sullivan Prizes in Poetry and Short Fiction is awarded to the author who has published at least one volume of short fiction or one volume of poetry. Awarded biannually, but judged quadrennially. Submissions Period: May 1 - September 1. Prize: $1,000, a $500 award and a $500 advance against royalties from the Notre Dame Press. Costs: $15.

SANTA FE WRITERS PROJECT LITERARY AWARDS PROGRAM

Santa Fe Writers Project, 369 Montezuma Ave., #350, Santa Fe NM 87501. **E-mail:** info@sfwp.com. **Web-site:** www.sfwp.com. **Contact:** Andrew Gifford. Estab. 1998. Annual contest seeking fiction and nonfiction of any genre. The Literary Awards Program was founded by a group of authors to offer recognition for excellence in writing in a time of declining support for writers and the craft of literature. Past judges have included Benjamin Percy, Jayne Anne Phillips, Robert Olen Butler, Emily St. John Mandel, and David Morrell. Deadline: July 15th. Prize: $2500 and publication. Costs: $30. Judged by Carmen Maria Machado in 2019.

SASKATCHEWAN BOOK AWARDS

315-1102 8th Ave., Regina SK S4R 1C9, Canada. (306)569-1585. **E-mail:** director@bookawards.sk.ca. **Website:** www.bookawards.sk.ca. **Contact:** Courtney Bates-Hardy, executive director. Estab. 1993. Saskatchewan Book Awards celebrates, promotes, and rewards Saskatchewan authors and publishers worthy of recognition through 14 awards, granted on an annual or semiannual basis. Awards: Fiction, Nonfiction, Poetry, Scholarly, First Book, Prix du Livre Français, Regina, Saskatoon, Indigenous Peoples' Writing, Indigenous Peoples' Publishing, Publishing in Education, Publishing, Children's Literature/Young Adult Literature, Book of the Year. November 1. Prize: $2,000 (CAD) for all awards except Book of the Year, which is $3,000 (CAD). Costs: $50 per award entered. Juries are made up of writing and publishing professionals from outside of Saskatchewan.

> Saskatchewan Book Awards is the only provincially focused book award program in Saskatchewan and a principal ambassador for Saskatchewan's literary community. Its solid reputation for celebrating artistic excellence in style is recognized nationally.

THE SATURDAY EVENING POST GREAT AMERICAN FICTION CONTEST

The Saturday Evening Post Society, 1100 Waterway Blvd., Indianapolis IN 46202. **E-mail:** fictioncontest@saturdayeveningpost.com. **Website:** www.saturdayeveningpost.com/fiction-contest. "In its nearly 3 centuries of publication, *The Saturday Evening Post* has included fiction by a who's who of American authors, including F. Scott Fitzgerald, William Faulkner, Kurt Vonnegut, Ray Bradbury, Louis L'Amour, Sinclair Lewis, Jack London, and Edgar Allan Poe. The *Post*'s fiction has not just entertained us; it has played a vital role in defining who we are as Americans. In launching this contest, we are seeking America's next great, unpublished voices." Deadline: July 1. The winning story will receive $500 and publication in the magazine and online. Five runners-up will be published online and receive $100 each. Costs: $10.

ALDO AND JEANNE SCAGLIONE PRIZE FOR A TRANSLATION OF A LITERARY WORK

Modern Language Association, 85 Broad Street, suite 500, New York NY 10004-2434. (646)576-5141. **Fax:** (646)458-0030. **E-mail:** awards@mla.org. **Website:** www.mla.org. **Contact:** Coordinator of Book Prizes. Offered in even-numbered years for an outstanding translation into English of a book-length literary work. Deadline: April 1. Prize: A cash award and a certificate to be presented at the Modern Language Association's annual convention in January.

○ THE SCARS EDITOR'S CHOICE AWARDS

Scars Publications, **E-mail:** editor@scars.tv. **Website:** http://scars.tv (contest direct link http://scars.tv/contests.htm). **Contact:** Janet Kuypers, editor/publisher (whom all reading fee checks need to be made out to). Estab. annually. Award to showcase good writing in an annual book. Prize: Publication of story/essay and 1 copy of the book. Costs: $19/short story and $15/poem.

◐   If you have difficulties sending emails through to a scars.tv address, send it to janetkuypers@gmal.com and explain the email problem and specifically what you were writing about.

THE MONA SCHREIBER PRIZE FOR HUMOROUS FICTION AND NONFICTION

3940 Laurel Canyon Blvd., #566, Studio City CA 91604, USA. **E-mail:** brad.schreiber@att.net. **Website:** www.bradschreiber.com. **Contact:** Brad Schreiber.. Estab. 2000. Established in 2000 to honor Mona Schreiber, a writer and teacher. Entry fees are the same as in 2000 and money from entries helps pay for prizes. The purpose of the contest is to award the most creative humor writing, in any form, under than 750 words, in either fiction or nonfiction, including but not limited to stories, articles, essays, speeches, shopping lists, diary entries, or anything else writers dream up. Complete rules and previous winning entries on website. Deadline: December 1. Prize: 1st Place: $500; 2nd Place: $250; 3rd Place: $100. Costs: $5 fee per entry (checks payable to Mona Schreiber Prize). PayPal fee is $7 using email address of brad. schreiber@att.net. Foreign entries may include US

currency or checks drawn on US banks. Judged by Brad Schreiber, journalist, consultant, instructor, author of, among other books, the humor-writing, how-to *What Are You Laughing At?*

SCREAMINMAMAS MAGICAL FICTION CONTEST

1911 Cleveland St., Hollywood FL 33020. **E-mail:** screaminmamas@gmail.com. **Website:** www.screaminmamas.com/contests. **Contact:** Darlene Pistocchi, editor/managing director. This contest celebrates moms and the magical spirit of the holidays. If you had an opportunity to be anything you wanted to be, what would you be? Transport yourself! Become that character and write a short story around that character. Can be any genre. Length: 800-3,000 words. Open only to moms. Deadline: June 30. Prize: Publication.

SCREAMINMAMAS VALENTINE'S DAY CONTEST

1911 Cleveland St., Hollywood FL 33020. **E-mail:** screaminmamas@gmail.com. **Website:** www.screaminmamas.com/contests. **Contact:** Darlene Pistocchi, editor/managing director. "Looking for light romantic comedy. Can be historical or contemporary—something to lift the spirits and celebrate the gift of innocent romance that might be found in the everyday life of a busy mom." Length: 600-1,200 words. Open only to moms. Deadline: June 30. Prize: Publication. Costs: $5.

MARY WOLLSTONECRAFT SHELLEY PRIZE FOR IMAGINATIVE FICTION

Rosebud, ROSEBUD MAGAZINE; ROSEBUD, INC., C/O Rosebud Magazine, N3310 Asje Rd., Cambridge WI 53523, USA. (608)423-9780. **E-mail:** jrodclark@rsbd.net. **Website:** www.rsbd.net. **Contact:** J. Roderick Clark, editor. Estab. 1993. Publishes eclectic mix of poetry, fiction and nonfiction. Genres with a literary feel okay. The Shelley Award is presented for any kind of unpublished imaginative fiction/short stories, 4,000 words or less. Entries are welcome any time. Acquires first rights. Open to any writer. Deadline: June 15 in even years. Prize: Grand Prize: $1,000. 4 runner-ups receive $100. All winners published in *Rosebud*. Costs: $30/story. Judged by editor Rod Clark in 2016.

◑⑤ SHORT GRAIN CONTEST

P.O. Box 3986, Regina SK S4P 3R9, Canada. (306)791-7749. **E-mail:** grainmag@skwriter.com. **Website:** www.grainmagazine.ca/short-grain-contest. **Contact:** Jordan Morris, business administrator (inquiries only). The annual Short Grain Contest includes a category for poetry of any style up to 100 lines and fiction of any style up to 2,500 words, offering 3 prizes. Deadline: April 1. Prize: $1,000, plus publication in *Grain Magazine*; 2nd Place: $750; 3rd Place: $500. Costs: $40 CAD; $50 for US and $60 for international entrants, in US or CAD funds; includes 1-year subscription to *Grain Magazine*.

AWARD WINNING PUB SKIPPING STONES HONOR (BOOK) AWARDS

P.O. Box 3939, Eugene OR 97403, USA. (541)342-4956. **Fax:** (541)342-4956. **E-mail:** editor@skippingstones. org. **Website:** www.skippingstones.org. **Contact:** Arun N. Toké. Estab. 1994. *Skipping Stones* is a well respected, multicultural literary magazine now in its 29th year. Annual award to promote multicultural and/or nature awareness through creative writings for children and teens and their educators. Seeks authentic, exceptional, child/youth friendly books that promote intercultural, international, intergenerational harmony, or understanding through creative ways. Deadline: February 29. Prize: Honor certificates; gold seals; reviews; press release/publicity. Costs: $50. Judged by a multicultural committee of teachers, librarians, parents, students and editors.

AWARD WINNING PUB SKIPPING STONES YOUTH AWARDS

P.O. Box 3939, Eugene OR 97403-0939. (541)342-4956. **Fax:** (541)342-4956. **E-mail:** editor@skippingstones. org. **Website:** www.skippingstones.org. **Contact:** Arun N. Toké. Annual awards to promote creativity as well as multicultural and nature awareness in youth. Deadline: June 25. Prize: Publication in the autumn issue of *Skipping Stones*, honor certificate, subscription to magazine, plus 5 multicultural and/or nature books. Costs: $5/entry. Make checks payable to Skipping Stones. Judged by editors and reviewers at *Skipping Stones* magazine.

THE BERNICE SLOTE AWARD

Prairie Schooner, 110 Andrews Hall, PO Box 880334, Lincoln NE 68588-0334. (402)472-0911. **Fax:** (402)472-1817. **E-mail:** PrairieSchooner@unl.edu. **Website:** www.prairieschooner.unl.edu. **Contact:** Kwame Dawes. Offered annually for the best work by a beginning writer published in *Prairie Schooner* in the previous year. Celebrates the best and finest writing that they have published for the year. Prize: $500. Judged by editorial staff of *Prairie Schooner*.

BYRON CALDWELL SMITH BOOK AWARD

The University of Kansas, Hall Center for the Humanities, 900 Sunnyside Ave., Lawrence KS 66045. (785)864-4798. **E-mail:** vbailey@ku.edu. **Website:** www.hallcenter.ku.edu. **Contact:** Victor Bailey, director. Offered in odd years. To qualify, applicants must live or be employed in Kansas and have written an outstanding book published within the previous 2 calendar years. Translations are eligible. Guidelines for SASE or online. Deadline: March 1. Prize: $1,500.

JEFFREY E. SMITH EDITORS' PRIZE IN FICTION, NONFICTION AND POETRY

The Missouri Review, 357 McReynolds Hall, UMC, Columbia MO 65201. (573)882-4474. **Fax:** (573)884-4671. **E-mail:** contest_question@moreview.com. **Website:** www.missourireview.com. **Contact:** Editor. Offered annually for unpublished work in 3 categories: fiction, essay, and poetry. Guidelines online or for SASE. Deadline: October 16. Prize: $5,000 and publication for each category winner. Costs: $24, includes a 1-year digital subscription; $30, includes a 1-year print subscription.

KAY SNOW WRITING CONTEST

Willamette Writers, Willamette Writers, 2108 Buck St., West Linn OR 97068. (503)305-6729. **Fax:** (503)344-6174. **E-mail:** reg@willamettewriters.com. **Website:** www.willamettewriters.org. Willamette Writers is the largest writers' organization in Oregon and one of the largest writers' organizations in the United States. It is a non-profit, tax-exempt Oregon corporation led by volunteers. Elected officials and directors administer an active program of monthly meetings, special seminars, workshops, and an annual writing conference. Continuing with established programs and starting new ones is only made possible by strong volunteer support. The purpose of this annual writing contest, named in honor of Willamette Writer's founder, Kay Snow, is to help writers reach professional goals in writing in a broad array of categories and to encourage student writers. Deadline: April 23. Submission deadline begins January 15. Prize: One first prize of $300, one second place prize of $150, and a third place prize of $50 per winning entry in each of the six categories. Student first prize is $50, $20 for second place, $10 for third. Costs: $10-$15, no fee for student entries (grades 1-12).

SOCIETY OF MIDLAND AUTHORS AWARD

Society of Midland Authors, P.O. Box 10419, Chicago IL 60610-0419. **E-mail:** marlenetbrill@comcast.net. **Website:** www.midlandauthors.com. **Contact:** Marlene Targ Brill, awards chair. Since 1957, the Society has presented annual awards for the best books written by Midwestern authors. The Society began in 1915. The Society of Midland Authors (SMA) Award is presented to one title in each of 6 categories: adult nonfiction, adult fiction, adult biography and memoir, children's nonfiction, children's fiction, and poetry. There may be honor book winners as well. Books and entry forms must be mailed to the 3 judges in each category; for a list of judges and the entry and payment forms, visit the SMA website. Do not mail books to the society's P.O. box. The fee can be sent to the SMA P.O. box or paid via Paypal. Deadline: The first Saturday in January for books from the previous year. Prize: $500 and a plaque that is awarded at the SMA banquet in May in Chicago. Honorary winners receive a plaque. Costs: $25 entry fee. Check the SMA website for each year's judges at the end of October.

STONY BROOK SHORT FICTION PRIZE

Stony Brook Southampton, 239 Montauk Highway, Southampton NY 11968. **Website:** www.stonybrook. edu/fictionprize. Deadline: March 15. Prize: $1,000.

STORY MONSTER APPROVED BOOK AWARDS

Story Monsters LLC, 4696 W. Tyson St., Chandler AZ 85226. (480)940-8182. **Fax:** (480)940-8787. **E-mail:** linda@storymonsters.com. **E-mail:** cristy@story-monsters.com. **Website:** www.dragonflybookawards. com. **Contact:** Cristy Bertini. The Story Monsters Approved! book designation program was developed to recognize and honor accomplished authors in the field of children's literature that inspire, inform, teach, or entertain. A Story Monsters seal of approval on your book tells teachers, librarians, and parents they are giving children the very best. Kids know when they see the Story Monsters Approved! seal, it means children their own age enjoyed the book and are recommending they read it, too. How do they know that? Because after books pass a first round of rigorous judging by industry experts, the books are then judged by a panel of youth judges who must also endorse the books before they can receive the official seal of approval. There is no deadline to enter. Books are sent for judging as they are received. The Book of the Year winner will receive a feature interview and a full-page ad in Story Monsters Ink® magazine, a certificate commemorating their accomplishment, and 50 Story Monsters Approved! seals. All authors earning a Story Monsters Approved! designation receive a certificate commemorating their accomplishment; 50 award seals, a news release sent to a comprehensive list of media outlets, and listings on our website and in Story Monsters Ink® magazine. Costs: $65 per entry, per category. Our judging panel includes industry experts in the fields of education and publishing, and student judges.

STORYSOUTH MILLION WRITERS AWARD

E-mail: terry@storysouth.com. **Website:** www.storysouth.com. **Contact:** Terry Kennedy, editor. Estab. 2003. Annual award to honor and promote the best fiction published in online literary journals and magazines during the previous year. Most literary prizes for short fiction have traditionally ignored web-published fiction. This award aims to show that world-class fiction is being published online and to promote to the larger reading and literary community. Deadline: August 15. Nominations of stories begins on March 15. Prize: Prize amounts subject to donation. Check website for details.

THEODORE STURGEON MEMORIAL AWARD FOR BEST SHORT SF OF THE YEAR

Center for the Study of SF, 1445 Jayhawk Blvd, Room 3001, University of Kansas, Lawrence KS 66045. (785)864-2518. **Fax:** (785)864-1159. **E-mail:** cssf@ku.edu. **Website:** sfcenter.ku.edu/sturgeon.htm. **Contact:** Kij Johnson, professor and associate director. Estab. 1987. Award to "honor the best science fiction short story of the year." Prize: Trophy. Winners receive expense-paid trip to the University and have their names engraved on the pernmanent trophy.

☉ SUBTERRAIN MAGAZINE'S LUSH TRIUMPHANT LITERARY AWARDS COMPETITION

P.O. Box 3008 MPO, Vancouver BC V6B 3X5, Canada. (604)876-8710. **Fax:** (604)879-2667. **E-mail:** subter@portal.ca. **Website:** www.subterrain.ca. Estab. Magazine est. 1988; Lush Triumphant est. 2002. Entrants may submit as many entries in as many categories as they like. Fiction: Max of 3,000 words. Poetry: A suite of 5 related poems (max of 15 pages). Creative Nonfiction (based on fact, adorned with fiction): Max of 4,000 words. Deadline: May 15. Prize: Winners in each category will receive $1,000 cash (plus payment for publication) and publication in the Winter issue. First runner-up in each category will be published in the Spring issue of *subTerrain*. Costs: $30.00/entry includes a 1-year subscription to *subTerrain*.

SYDNEY TAYLOR MANUSCRIPT COMPETITION

Association of Jewish Libraries, Sydney Taylor Manuscript Award Competition, 204 Park St., Montclair NJ 07042-2903. **E-mail:** stmacajl@aol.com. **Website:** www.jewishlibraries.org/main/Awards/SydneyTaylorManuscriptAward.aspx. **Contact:** Aileen Grossberg. Estab. 1985. This competition is for unpublished writers of juvenile fiction. Material should be for readers ages 8-13. The manuscript should have universal appeal and reveal positive aspects of Jewish life that will serve to deepen the understanding of Judaism for all children. To encourage new fiction of Jewish interest for readers ages 8-13. Deadline: September 30. Prize: $1,000. Judging by qualified judges from within the Association of Jewish Libraries.

THE TEXAS INSTITUTE OF LETTERS LITERARY AWARDS

E-mail: Betwx@aol.com. **Website:** www.texasinstituteofletters.org. Estab. 1936. The Texas Institute of Letters gives annual awards for books by Texas authors and writers who have produced books about Texas, including Best Books of Poetry, Fiction, and Nonfiction. Awards are also given for best Short Story, Magazine or Newspaper Article, Essay, and best Books for Children and Young Adults. Work submitted must have been published in the year stipulated, and entries may be made by authors or by their publishers. Complete guidelines and award information is available on the Texas Institute of Letters website.

THREE CHEERS AND A TIGER

E-mail: editors@toasted-cheese.com. **Website:** tclj.toasted-cheese.com. **Contact:** Stephanie Lenz, editor. Contestants are to write a short story (following a specific theme) within 48 hours. Contests are held first weekend in Spring (mystery) and first weekend in Fall (science fiction/fantasy). Word limit announced at the start of the contest, 5 pm ET. Contest-specific information is announced 48 hours before the contest submission deadline. Results announced in April and October. Winners notified by e-mail. List of winners on website. Prize: Amazon gift certificates and publication. Costs: Contest is free to enter. Blind-judged by *Toasted Cheese* editors. Each judge uses his or her own criteria to choose entries.

THE THURBER PRIZE FOR AMERICAN HUMOR

77 Jefferson Ave., Columbus OH 43215. **Website:** www.thurberhouse.org. This award recognizes the art of humor writing. Deadline: March 31. Prize: $5,000 for the finalist, non-cash prizes awarded to two runners-up. Judged by well-known members of the national arts community.

TORONTO BOOK AWARDS

City of Toronto c/o Toronto Arts & Culture, Cultural Partnerships, City Hall, 9E, 100 Queen St. W., Toronto ON M5H 2N2, Canada. **E-mail:** shan@toronto.ca. **Website:** www.toronto.ca/book_awards. Estab. 1974. The Toronto Book Awards honor authors of books of literary or artistic merit that are evocative of Toronto. Deadline: April 30. Prize: Each finalist receives $1,000 and the winning author receives $10,000 ($15,000 total in prize money available).

STEVEN TURNER AWARD FOR BEST FIRST WORK OF FICTION

6335 W. Northwest Hwy., #618, Dallas TX 75225. **Website:** www.texasinstituteofletters.org. Offered annually for work published January 1-December 31 for the best first book of fiction. Deadline: normally first week in January; see website for specific date. Prize: $1,000.

ANNUAL VENTURA COUNTY WRITERS CLUB SHORT STORY CONTEST

Ventura County Writers Club Short Story Contest, P.O. Box 3373, Thousand Oaks CA 91362. **E-mail:** vcwc.contestchair@gmail.com. **Website:** www.venturacountywriters.com. **Contact:** Contest Chair. Estab. 1999. Annual short story contest for youth and adult writers. High school division for writers still in school. Adult division for those 18 and older. Club membership not required to enter and entries accepted worldwide as long as fees are paid, story is unpublished and in English. Enter through website. Winners get cash prizes and are published in club anthology. Deadline: November 15. Adult Prizes: 1st Place: $500; 2nd Place: $250; 3rd Place: $125. High School Prizes: 1st Place: $100; 2nd Place: $75; 3rd Place: $50. Costs: Submission fee for each story submitted: $15 U.S. for adult VCWC members; $25 U.S. for adult non-members; and $10 for high school students. PayPal, credit or debit cards are accepted.

Usually receives less than 500 entries.

WAASNODE SHORT FICTION PRIZE

Passages North, Department of English, Northern Michigan University, 1401 Presque Isle Ave., Marquette MI 49855. (906)227-1203. **Fax:** (906)227-1096. **E-mail:** passages@nmu.edu. **Website:** www.passagesnorth.com. **Contact:** Jennifer Howard. Offered every 2 years to publish new voices in literary fiction (maximum 10,000 words). Guidelines for SASE or online. Submissions accepted online. Deadline: April 15. Submission period begins February 15. Prize: $1,000 and publication for winner; 2 honorable mentions are also published; all entrants receive a copy of *Passages North*. Costs: $15 reading fee/story, make checks payable to Northern Michigan University. Judged by Anne Valente in 2018.

WABASH PRIZE FOR FICTION

Sycamore Review, Department of English, 500 Oval Dr., Purdue University, West Lafayette IN 47907. **E-mail:** sycamore@purdue.edu; sycamorefiction@purdue.edu. **Website:** www.sycamorereview.com/contest/. **Contact:** Kara Krewer, editor-in-chief. Annual contest for unpublished fiction. Deadline: November 15. Prize: $1,000 and publication. Costs: $20 reading fee; $5 for each additional story.

THE JULIA WARD HOWE AWARD

The Boston Authors Club, 33 Brayton Road, Brighton MA 02135. (617)783-1357. **E-mail:** alan.lawson@bc.edu. **Website:** www.bostonauthorsclub.org. **Contact:** Alan Lawson, president. Julia Ward Howe Prize offered annually in the spring for books published the previous year. Two awards are given: one for adult books of fiction, nonfiction, or poetry, and one for children's books, middle grade and young adult novels, nonfiction, or poetry. No picture books or subsidized publishers. There must be two copies of each book submitted. Deadline: January 15. Prize: $1,000 in each category. Several books will also be cited with no cash awards as Finalists or Highly Recommended. Costs: $25/title.

THE WASHINGTON WRITERS' PUBLISHING HOUSE FICTION PRIZE

Washington Writers' Publishing House, P.O. Box 15271, Washington DC 20003. **E-mail:** wwphpress@gmail.com. **Website:** www.washingtonwriters.org. Fiction writers living within 75 miles of the Capitol are invited to submit a ms of either a novel or a collection of short stories (no more than 350 pages, double-spaced). Deadline: November 15. Submission period begins July 1. Prize: $1,000 and 50 copies of the book. Costs: $25 reading fee.

THE ROBERT WATSON LITERARY PRIZE IN FICTION AND POETRY

The Robert Watson Literary Prizes, *The Greensboro Review*, MFA Writing Program, 3302 MHRA Building, Greensboro NC 27402-6170. (336)334-5459. **E-mail:** tgr@uncg.edu. **Website:** www.greensbororeview.org. **Contact:** Terry Kennedy, editor. Offered annually for fiction (up to 25 double-spaced pages) and poetry (up to 10 pages). Entries must be unpublished. Open to any writer. Deadline: September 15. Prize: $1,000 each for best short story and poem. Costs: $14. Judged by editors of *The Greensboro Review*.

🌏 WESTERN AUSTRALIAN PREMIER'S BOOK AWARDS

State Library of Western Australia, Perth Cultural Centre, 25 Francis St., Perth WA 6000, Australia. (61)(8)9427-3151. **E-mail:** premiersbookawards@slwa.wa.gov.au. **Website:** pba.slwa.wa.gov.au. **Contact:** Karen de San Miguel. Estab. 1982. Annual competition for Australian citizens or permanent residents of Australia, or writers whose work has Australia as its primary focus. Categories: children's books, digital narrative, fiction, nonfiction, poetry, scripts, writing for young adults, West Australian history, and Western Australian emerging writers. Deadline: January 31. Prize: Awards $25,000 for Premier's Prize; awards $15,000 each for the Children's Books, Digital Narrative, Fiction, and Nonfiction categories; awards $10,000 each for the Poetry, Scripts, Western Australian History, Western Australian Emerging Writers, and Writing for Young Adults; awards $5,000 for People's Choice Award.

WESTERN HERITAGE AWARDS

National Cowboy & Western Heritage Museum, 1700 NE 63rd St., Oklahoma City OK 73111-7997. (405)478-2250. **Fax:** (405)478-4714. **Website:** www.nationalcowboymuseum.org. **Contact:** Jessica Limestall. Estab. 1961. The National Cowboy & Western Heritage Museum Western Heritage Awards were established to honor and encourage the legacy of those whose works in literature, music, film, and television reflect the significant stories of the American West. Accepted categories for literary entries: western novel, nonfiction book, art book, photography book, juvenile book, magazine article, or poetry book. The WHA are presented annually to encourage the accurate and artistic telling of great stories of the West through 16 categories of western literature, television, film and music; including fiction, nonfiction, children's books and poetry. See website for details and category definitions. Deadline: November 30. Prize: Awards a Wrangler bronze sculpture designed by famed western artist, John Free. Costs: $50. Judged by a panel of judges selected each year with distinction in various fields of western art and heritage.

WESTERN WRITERS OF AMERICA

271 CR 219, Encampment WY 82325. (307)329-8942. **E-mail:** wwa.moulton@gmail.com. **Website:** www.westernwriters.org. **Contact:** Candy Moulton, executive director. Estab. 1953. Eighteen Spur Award categories in various aspects of the American West. The nonprofit Western Writers of America has promoted and honored the best in Western literature with the annual Spur Awards, selected by panels of judges. Awards, for material published last year, are given for works whose inspirations, image and literary excellence best represent the reality and spirit of the American West. Deadline: January 4. Costs: No fee. Judged by independent Judges.

WESTMORELAND POETRY & SHORT STORY CONTEST

Westmoreland Arts & Heritage Festival, 252 Twin Lakes Road, Latrobe PA 15650-9415. (724)834-7474. **Fax:** (724)850-7474. **E-mail:** info@artsandheritage.com. **Website:** www.artsandheritage.com. **Contact:** Diane Shrader. Offered annually for unpublished work. Two categories: Poem and Short Story. Short story entries no longer than 4,000 words. Family-oriented festival and contest. Deadline: February 17. Prizes: Award: $200; 1st Place: $125; 2nd Place: $100; 3rd Place: $75. Costs: $10/story or for 2 poems; both categories may be entered for $20.

WILLA LITERARY AWARD

Women Writing the West, 8547 East Arapaho Rd., #J-541, Greenwood Village CO 80112-1436. **E-mail:** 2019willachair@gmail.com. **Website:** www.womenwritingthewest.org. **Contact:** Carmen Peone. The WILLA Literary Award honors the year's best in published literature featuring women's or girls' stories set in the West. Women Writing the West (WWW), a nonprofit association of writers and other professionals writing and promoting the Women's West, underwrites and presents the nationally recognized award annually (for work published between January 1 and December 31). The award is named in honor of Pulitzer Prize winner Willa Cather, one of the country's foremost novelists. The award is given in 8 categories: historical fiction, contemporary fiction, original softcover fiction, creative nonfiction, scholarly nonfiction, poetry, children's fiction and nonfiction and young adult fiction/nonfiction. Entry forms available on the website. Deadline: November 1–February 1. Prize: $150 and a trophy. Finalist receives a plaque. Both receive digital and sticker award emblems for book covers. Notice of Winning and Finalist titles mailed to more than 4,000 booksellers, libraries, and others. Award announcement is in early August, and awards are presented to the winners and finalists at the annual WWW Fall Conference. Also, the eight winners will participate in a drawing for 2 two week all expenses paid residencies donated by Playa at Summer Lake in Oregon. Costs: $65. Judged by professional librarians not affiliated with WWW.

TENNESSEE WILLIAMS/NEW ORLEANS LITERARY FESTIVAL CONTESTS

Tennessee Williams/New Orleans Literary Festival, 938 Lafayette St., Suite 514, New Orleans LA 70113. (504)581-1144. **E-mail:** info@tennesseewilliams.net. **Website:** www.tennesseewilliams.net/contests. **Contact:** Paul J. Willis. Annual contests for: Unpublished One Act, Unpublished Short Fiction, Unpublished Flash Fiction, and Unpublished Poem. "Our competitions provide writers a large audience during one of the largest literary festivals in the nation." Deadline: October 1 (One Act, Fiction); October 15 (Poetry, Very Short Fiction) Prize: One Act: $1,500, staged read at the next festival, VIP All-Access Festival pass, and publication in Bayou. Poetry: $1,000, public reading at next festival, VIP all-access pass, publication in Louisiana Cultural Vistas Magazine. Fiction: $1,500, public reading at next festival, publication in Louisiana Literature, VIP all-access pass. Very Short Fiction: $500, publication in the New Orleans Review, VIP all-access past. Costs: $25 entry fee for One Act and Fiction submissions; $20 entry fee for Poetry submissions; $10 entry fee for Very Short Fiction. Judged by special guest judges, who change every year. See website for full details.

WISCONSIN INSTITUTE FOR CREATIVE WRITING FELLOWSHIP

6195B H.C. White Hall, 600 N. Park St., Madison WI 53706. **E-mail:** sbbishop@wisc.edu. **Website:**

creativewriting.wisc.edu/fellowships.html. **Contact:** Sean Bishop, graduate coordinator. Estab. 1986. Fellowship provides time, space and an intellectual community for writers working on first books.Since 2012, we have also considered applicants who have published only one full-length collection of creative writing prior to the application deadline, although unpublished authors remain eligible, and quality of writing remains the near-exclusive criterion for selection. Receives approximately 300 applicants a year for each genre. Judged by English Department faculty and current fellows. Candidates can have up to one published book in the genre for which they are applying. Open to any writer with either an M.F.A. or Ph.D. in creative writing. Results announced on website by May 1. Deadline: Last day of February. Open to submissions on February 1. Prize: $38,000 for a 9-month appointment. Costs: $50, payable to the Dept. of English; see website for payment instructions.

THOMAS WOLFE PRIZE AND LECTURE

North Carolina Writers' Network, Thomas Wolfe Fiction Prize, Great Smokies Writing Program, Attn: Nancy Williams, CPO #1860, UNC, Asheville NC 28805. **Website:** englishcomplit.unc.edu/wolfe. Estab. 1999. The Thomas Wolfe Fiction Prize honors internationally celebrated North Carolina novelist Thomas Wolfe. The prize is administered by Tommy Hays and the Great Smokies Writing Program at the University of North Carolina at Asheville. Deadline: January 30. Submissions period begins December 1. Prize: $1,000 and potential publication in *The Thomas Wolfe Review*. Costs: $15 fee for members of the NC Writers' Network, $25 for non-members.

TOBIAS WOLFF AWARD FOR FICTION

Bellingham Review, Mail Stop 9053, Western Washington University, Bellingham WA 98225. (360)650-4863. **E-mail:** bellingham.review@wwu.edu. **Website:** www.bhreview.org. **Contact:** Susanne Paola Antonetta, editor-in-chief; Bailey Cunningham, managing editor. Offered annually for unpublished work. Guidelines available on website; online submissions only. Categories: novel exceprts and short stories. Deadline: March 15. Submissions period begins December 1. Prize: $1,000, plus publication and subscription. Costs: $20 entry fee for 1st entry; $10 for each additional entry.

THE WORD AWARDS

The Word Guild, The Word Guild, Suite # 226, 245 King George Rd, Brantford ON N3R 7N7, Canada. 800-969-9010 x 1. **E-mail:** info@thewordguild.com. **E-mail:** info@thewordguild.com. **Website:** www.thewordguild.com. **Contact:** Karen deBlieck. The Word Guild is an organization of Canadian writers and editors who are Christian, and who are committed to encouraging one another and to fostering standards of excellence in the art, craft, practice and ministry of writing. Memberships available for various experience levels. Yearly conference Write Canada (please see website for information) and features keynote speakers, continuing classes and workshops. Editors and agents on site. The Word Awards is for work published in the past year, in almost 30 categories including books, articles, essays, fiction, nonfiction, novels, short stories, songs, and poetry. Please see website for more information. Deadline: January 15. Prize $50 CAD for article and short pieces; $100 CAD for book entries. Finalists book entries are eligible for the $5,000 Grace Irwin prize. Costs: Short Piece Entries: Members: $30 CAD + HST (per short piece entered); Non Members: $60 CAD + HST (per short piece entered). Book Entries: Members: $55 CAD + HST (per title entered); Non Members: $110 + HST (per title entered). Judged by industry leaders and professionals.

WORLD FANTASY AWARDS

P.O. Box 43, Mukilteo WA 98275. **E-mail:** sfexecsec@gmail.com. **Website:** www.worldfantasy.org. **Contact:** Peter Dennis Pautz, president. Offered annually for previously published work in several categories, including life achievement, novel, novella, short story, anthology, collection, artist, special award-pro and special award-nonpro. Works are recommended by attendees of current and previous 2 years' conventions and a panel of judges. Awards to recognize excellence in fantasy literature worldwide. Deadline: June 1. Prize: Trophy. Judged by panel.

WORLD'S BEST SHORT-SHORT STORY CONTEST, NARRATIVE NONFICTION CONTEST & SOUTHEAST REVIEW POETRY CONTEST

The Southeast Review, Florida State University, English Department, Tallahassee FL 32306. **E-mail:** southeastreview@gmail.com. **Website:** www.southeastreview.org. **Contact:** Erin Hoover, editor. Estab.

1979. Annual award for unpublished short-short stories (500 words or less), poetry, and narrative nonfiction (6,000 words or less). Visit website for details. Deadline: March 15. Prize: $500 per category. Winners and finalists will be published in *The Southeast Review*. Costs: $16 reading fee for up to 3 stories or poems, or 1 narrative essay.

WOW! WOMEN ON WRITING QUARTERLY FLASH FICTION CONTEST

WOW! Women on Writing, P.O. Box 2832, Winnetka CA 91396. **E-mail:** contestinfo@wow-womenonwriting.com. **Website:** www.wow-womenonwriting.com/contest.php. **Contact:** Angela Mackintosh, editor. Contest offered quarterly. "We are open to all themes and genres, although we do encourage writers to take a close look at our literary agent guest judge for the season if you are serious about winning." Deadline: August 31, November 30, February 28, May 31. Prize: 1st place: $400 cash prize, $25 Amazon gift certificate, story published on WOW! Women On Writing, interview on blog; 2nd place: $300 cash prize, $25 Amazon gift certificate, story published on WOW! Women On Writing, interview on blog; 3rd place: $200 cash prize, $25 Amazon gift certificate, story published on WOW! Women On Writing, interview on blog; 7 runners up: $25 Amazon gift certificate, story published on WOW! Women on Writing, interview on blog; 10 honorable mentions: $20 gift certificate from Amazon, story title and name published on WOW!Women On Writing. Costs: $10. Judged by a different guest every season, who is either a literary agent, acquiring editor or publisher.

WRITER'S DIGEST ANNUAL WRITING COMPETITION

Writer's Digest, a publication of Active Interest Media, Inc., 5720 Flatiron Pkwy., Boulder CO 80301. **E-mail:** writersdigestwritingcompetition@aimmedia.com. **Website:** www.writersdigest.com. Writing contest with 9 categories: Inspirational Writing (spiritual/religious, maximum 2,500 words); Memoir/Personal Essay (maximum 2,000 words); Magazine Feature Article (maximum 2,000 words);Children's/Young Adult Fiction (maximum 2,000 words) Short Story (genre, maximum 4,000 words); Short Story (mainstream/literary, maximum 4,000 words); Rhyming Poetry (maximum 32 lines); Nonrhyming Poetry (maximum 32 lines); Stage Play/TV/Movie Script (first 15 pages and 1-page synopsis). Entries must be original, in English, unpublished/unproduced (except for Magazine Feature Articles), and not accepted by another publisher/producer at the time of submission. Writer's Digest retains one-time publication rights to the winning entries in each category. Deadline: May (early bird); June. Grand Prize: $5,000 and a trip to the Writer's Digest Conference to meet with editors and agents; 1st Place: $1,000; 2nd Place: $500; 3rd Place: $250; 4th Place: $100; 5th Place: $50; Sixth through Tenth place winners in each category:$25; and more. Costs: Poetry entry—$20 for the first entry; $15 for each additional poetry entry. Manuscript entry—$30 for the first entry; $25 for each additional manuscript entry. Poetry entry—$25 for the first entry; $20 for each additional poetry entry. Manuscript entry—$35 for the first entry; $30 for each additional manuscript entry.

WRITER'S DIGEST SELF-PUBLISHED BOOK AWARDS

Writer's Digest, 5720 Flatiron Pkwy., Boulder CO 80301. **E-mail:** writersdigestselfpublishingcompetition@aimmedia.com. **Website:** www.writersdigest.com. **Contact:** Nicole Howard. Estab. 1992. Contest open to all English-language, self-published books for which the authors have paid the full cost of publication, or the cost of printing has been paid for by a grant or as part of a prize. Categories include: Mainstream/Literary Fiction, Genre Fiction, Nonfiction, Inspirational (spiritual/new age), Life Stories (biographies/autobiographies/family histories/memoirs), Children's Books, Reference Books (directories/encyclopedias/guide books), Poetry, and Middle-Grade/Young Adult Books. Judges reserve the right to re-categorize entries. Judges reserve the right to withhold prizes in any category. All winners will be notified in October. Early bird deadline: April 2. Prizes: Grand Prize: $8,000, a trip to the Writer's Digest Conference, promotion in *Writer's Digest*, 10 copies of the book will be sent to major review houses, and a guaranteed review in *Midwest Book Review*; 1st Place (9 winners): $1,000 and promotion in *Writer's Digest*; Honorable Mentions: promotion on writersdigest.com. All entrants will receive a brief commentary from one of the judges. Costs: $99; $85/additional entry.

WRITER'S DIGEST SELF-PUBLISHED E-BOOK AWARDS

Writer's Digest, 5720 Flatiron Pkwy., Boulder CO 80301. **E-mail:** writersdigestselfpublishingcompetition@aimmedia.com. **Website:** www.writersdigest.com. **Con-**

tact: Nicole Howard. Estab. 2013. Contest open to all English-language, self-published e-books for which the authors have paid the full cost of publication, or the cost of publication has been paid for by a grant or as part of a prize. Categories include: Mainstream/Literary Fiction, Genre Fiction, Nonfiction (includes reference books), Inspirational (spiritual/new age), Life Stories (biographies/autobiographies/family histories/memoirs), Children's Books, Poetry, and Middle-Grade/Young Adult Books. Judges reserve the right to re-categorize entries. Judges reserve the right to withhold prizes in any category. All winners will be notified by December 31. Early bird deadline: August 1; Deadline: September 4. Prizes: Grand Prize: $5,000, promotion in *Writer's Digest* and more; 1st Place (9 winners): $1,000 and promotion in *Writer's Digest*; Honorable Mentions: Promotion on writersdigest.com. All entrants will receive a brief commentary from one of the judges. Costs: $99; $85/additional entry.

WRITER'S DIGEST SHORT SHORT STORY COMPETITION

Writer's Digest, 5720 Flatiron Pwky., Boulder CO 80301. **E-mail:** WritersDigestWritingCompetition@aimmedia.com. **Website:** www.writersdigest.com. **Contact:** Nicole Howard. Looking for fiction that's bold, brilliant, and brief. Send your best in 1,500 words or fewer. All entries must be original, unpublished, and not submitted elsewhere at the time of submission. *Writer's Digest* reserves one-time publication rights to the 1st-25th winning entries. Winners will be notified by Feb. 28. Early bird deadline: November 15. Final deadline: December 15. Prize: 1st Place: $3,000 and a trip to the Writer's Digest Conference; 2nd Place: $1,500; 3rd Place: $500; 4th-10th Place: $100; 11th-25th Place: $50 gift certificate for writersdigestshop.com. Costs: $25.

WRITERS-EDITORS NETWORK INTERNATIONAL WRITING COMPETITION

CNW Publishing, P.O. Box A, North Stratford NH 03590-0167. **E-mail:** contestentry@writers-editors.com. **E-mail:** info@writers-editors.com. **Website:** www.writers-editors.com. **Contact:** Dana K. Cassell, executive director. Annual award to recognize publishable talent. New categories and awards for 2018: Nonfiction (unpublished or self-published; may be an article, blog post, essay/opinion piece, column, nonfiction book chapter, children's article or book chapter); fiction (unpublished or self-published; may be a short story, novel chapter, Young Adult [YA] or children's story or book chapter); poetry (unpublished or self-published; may be traditional or free verse poetry or children's verse). Guidelines available online. Deadline: March 15. Prize: 1st Place: $150 plus one year Writers-Editors membership; 2nd Place: $100; 3rd Place: $75. All winners and Honorable Mentions will receive certificates as warranted. Most Promising entry in each category will receive a free critique by a contest judge. Costs: $10 (active or new WEN/FFWA members) or $20 (nonmembers) for each fiction or nonfiction entry; $3 (members) or $5 (nonmembers) for each poem; or $10 for 3 poems (members), $15 for 3 poems (nonmembers). Judged by editors, librarians, and writers.

◑ WRITERS' GUILD OF ALBERTA AWARDS

Writers' Guild of Alberta, Percy Page Centre, 11759 Groat Rd., Edmonton AB T5M 3K6, Canada. (780)422-8174. **Fax:** (780)422-2663. **E-mail:** mail@writersguild.ca. **Website:** writersguild.ca. **Contact:** Executive Director. Offers the following awards: Wilfrid Eggleston Award for Nonfiction; Georges Bugnet Award for Fiction; Howard O'Hagan Award for Short Story; Stephan G. Stephansson Award for Poetry; R. Ross Annett Award for Children's Literature; Gwen Pharis Ringwood Award for Drama; Jon Whyte Memorial Essay Award; James H. Gray Award for Short Nonfiction. Deadline: December 31. Prize: Winning authors receive $1,500; short piece prize winners receive $700.

WRITERS' LEAGUE OF TEXAS BOOK AWARDS

Writers' League of Texas, 611 S. Congress Ave., Suite 200A-3, Austin TX 78704. (512)499-8914. **Fax:** (512)499-0441. **E-mail:** sara@writersleague.org. **Website:** www.writersleague.org. **Contact:** Sara Kocek. Open to Texas authors of books published the previous year. To enter this contest, you must be a Texas author. "Texas author" is defined as anyone who (whether currently a resident or not) has lived in Texas for a period of 3 or more years. This contest is open to indie or self-published authors as well as traditionally-published authors. Deadline: February 28. Open to submissions October 7. Prize: $1,000 and a commemorative award. Costs: $60/title; $40 for WLT members.

☼ THE WRITERS' TRUST ENGEL/FINDLEY AWARD

The Writers' Trust of Canada, 460 Richmond St. W., Suite 600, Toronto ON M5V 1Y1, Canada. (416)504-8222. **Fax:** (416)504-9090. **E-mail:** djackson@writerstrust.com. **Website:** www.writerstrust.com. **Contact:** Devon Jackson. The Writers' Trust Engel/Findley Award is presented annually at The Writers' Trust Awards Event, held in Toronto each fall, to a Canadian writer for a body of work in hope of continued contribution to the richness of Canadian literature. Open to Canadian citizens and permanent residents only. Prize: $25,000.

WRITERSWEEKLY.COM'S QUARTERLY 24-HOUR SHORT STORY CONTEST

WritersWeekly.com, BookLocker.com, Inc., 200 2nd Ave. S., #526, St. Petersburg FL 33701. **E-mail:** writersweekly@writersweekly.com. **Website:** https://www.24HourShortStoryContest.com/. **Contact:** Angela Hoy, Publisher. Estab. 1997. A popular and fun quarterly contest in which registered entrants receive an assigned topic at start time (usually noon Central Time on a Saturday), and have 24 hours to write and submit a story on that topic. All submissions must be returned via e-mail. Each contest is limited to 500 people. Upon registration, entrant will receive guidelines and details on competition, including submission process. All past topics and winners are listed on the website, as well as the contest rules and hints for winning. Deadline: Quarterly—see website for dates. Prize: 1st Place: $300 + a publishing contract; 2nd Place: $250; 3rd Place: $200. There are also 20 honorable mentions and 60 door prizes (randomly drawn from all participants). The top 3 winners' entries are posted on WritersWeekly.com (non-exclusive electronic rights only). Writers retain all rights to their work. See website for full details on prizes. Costs: $5. Judged by Angela Hoy (publisher of WritersWeekly.com and Booklocker.com).

☼ "We love surprise endings!"

LAMAR YORK PRIZE FOR FICTION AND NONFICTION CONTEST

The Chattahoochee Review, Georgia Perimeter College, 2101 Womack Rd., Dunwoody GA 30338-4497. (770)274-5479. **E-mail:** gpccr@gpc.edu. **Website:** thechattahoocheereview.gpc.edu. **Contact:** Anna Schachner, Editor. Offered annually for unpublished creative nonfiction and nonscholarly essays and fic-tion up to 5,000 words. *The Chattahoochee Review* buys first rights only for winning essay/ms for the purpose of publication in the summer issue. Deadline: January 31. Submission period begins October 1. Prize: 2 prizes of $1,000 each, plus publication. Costs: $15 fee/entry; subscription included in fee. Judged by the editorial staff of *The Chattahoochee Review*.

ZOETROPE: ALL-STORY SHORT FICTION COMPETITION

Zoetrope: All-Story, Zoetrope: All-Story, Attn: Fiction Editor, 916 Kearny St., San Francisco CA 94133. (415)788-7500. **E-mail:** contests@all-story.com. **Website:** www.all-story.com/contests.cgi. Acclaimed annual short fiction competition. Considers submissions of short stories no longer than 5,000 words. Deadline: October 1. Submission period begins July 1. Prizes: 1st place: $1,000 and publication on website; 2nd place: $500; 3rd place: $250. Costs: $25.

ZONE 3 FICTION AWARD

Zone 3, Austin Peay State University, P.O. Box 4565, Clarksville TN 37044. (931)221-7031. **Fax:** (931)221-7149. **E-mail:** wallacess@apsu.edu. **Website:** www.apsu.edu/zone3/contests. **Contact:** Susan Wallace, Managing Editor. Annual contest for unpublished fiction. Open to any fiction writer. Deadline: April 1. Prize: $250 and publication.

CONFERENCES & WORKSHOPS

///

Why are conferences so popular? Writers and conference directors alike tell us it's because writing can be such a lonely business—at conferences writers have the opportunity to meet (and commiserate) with fellow writers, as well as meet and network with publishers, editors, and agents. Conferences and workshops provide some of the best opportunities for writers to make publishing contacts and pick up valuable information on the business, as well as the craft, of writing.

The bulk of the listings in this section are for conferences. Most conferences last from one day to one week and offer a combination of workshop-type writing sessions, panel discussions, and a variety of guest speakers. Topics may include all aspects of writing from fiction to poetry to scriptwriting, or they may focus on a specific type of writing, such as those conferences sponsored by the Romance Writers of America (RWA) for writers of romance or by the Society of Children's Book Writers and Illustrators (SCBWI) for writers of children's books.

Workshops, however, tend to run longer—usually one to two weeks. Designed to operate like writing classes, most require writers to be prepared to work on and discuss their fiction while attending. An important benefit of workshops is the opportunity they provide writers for an intensive critique of their work, often by professional writing teachers and established writers.

Each of the listings here includes information on the specific focus of an event as well as planned panels, guest speakers, and workshop topics. It is important to note, however, some conference directors were still in the planning stages for 2020 when we contacted them. If it was not possible to include 2020 dates, fees, or topics, we provided the most up-to-date information available so you can get an idea of what to expect. For the most current information, it's best to check the conference website about three months before the date(s) listed.

WRITING AND CREATIVITY: A SEVEN-DAY RETREAT FOR WOMEN

Bar Harbor, Maine Sept. 7-14, 2019, Yorktown Heights NY 10598. (914)962-4432. **E-mail:** emily@emilyhanlon.com. **Website:** https://www.thefictionwritersjourney.com/writing-retreats.html. **Contact:** Emily Hanlon, Novelist and Writing Coach. Estab. 1998.

Each day, we weave our writing and our creativity together, while we explore the journey of fiction writers as women. Or I should say, "journeys," because though there's a surprising degree of similarity among our journeys, we also discover and share differences that we've experienced. Whether you're a writer who's just beginning to write or one who's been creating fiction for decades, this sharing of experiences is truly illuminating…it makes the twists and turns of one's own path as a writer more comprehensible, less daunting, more rewarding, more fun. Whatever your writing experience, you'll become a part of this Circle of Women Writers who are open to the daring, passion, and fun of creativity!

COSTS See website for current costs. https://www.thefictionwritersjourney.com/accommodations-and-dining.html

ACCOMMODATIONS Private and semi-private rooms with ocean view.

ADDITIONAL INFORMATION For brochure, visit website. https://www.thefictionwritersjourney.com/writing-retreats.html

AGENTS & EDITORS CONFERENCE

Writers' League of Texas, 611 S. Congress Ave., Suite 200 A-3, Austin TX 78704. (512)499-8914. **E-mail:** michael@writersleague.org. **Website:** www.writersleague.org/38/conference. **Contact:** Michael Noll, program director. Estab. 1982.

COSTS Registration for the 2019 conference opens in November for WLT members and n December for everyone.

ACCOMMODATIONS Discounted rates are available at the conference hotel.

ALABAMA WRITERS' CONCLAVE

AL **Website:** www.alabamawritersconclave.org. **Contact:** T.K. Thorne, president. Estab. 1923.

COSTS Membership is only $25 a year and provides with with a informative newsletter and reduced fees for the conference and other events. Previous fees for the conference: $175 for members and $225 for non-members. Discount $30 for seniors/students. Includes 2 meals. Critique fee: $25 for members and $30 for non-members.

ADDITIONAL INFORMATION "We have major speakers and faculty members who conduct intensive, energetic workshops. Our annual writing contest guidelines and all other information are available online."

ALASKA CONFERENCE FOR WRITERS & ILLUSTRATORS

Alaska Writers Guild, SCBWI Alaska, & RWA Alaska, P.O. Box 670014, Chugiak AK 99567. **E-mail:** alaskawritersguild.awg@gmail.com. **Website:** alaskawritersguild.com.

ALGONKIAN WRITER RETREAT AND NOVEL WORKSHOP

2020 Pennsylvania Ave. NW, Suite 443, Washington DC 20006. **E-mail:** info@algonkianconferences.com. **Website:** algonkianconferences.com.

COSTS 5 Days for $1095.00 - Tuition, Consults, Lodging, and Meals

AMERICAN CHRISTIAN WRITERS CONFERENCES

P.O. Box 110390, Nashville TN 37222. (800)219-7483 or (615)331-8668. **E-mail:** acwriters@aol.com. **Website:** www.acwriters.com. **Contact:** Reg Forder, director. Estab. 1981.

COSTS Costs vary and may depend on type of event (conference or mentoring retreat).

ACCOMMODATIONS Special rates are available at the host hotel (usually a major chain like Holiday Inn).

ADDITIONAL INFORMATION E-mail or call for conference brochures.

ARKANSAS WRITERS' CONFERENCE

1815 Columbia Dr., Conway AR 72034. (501)833-2756. **E-mail:** breannacone1@yahoo.com. **Website:** www.arkansaswritersconference.org. **Contact:** Brenda Iannacone.

COSTS $30 registration fee if received by May 20, 2019. $35 on-site registration fee.

ACCOMMODATIONS Special discount room rate of $99. Call 501-945-8792 to reserve a room by Friday, May 10, 2019, to take advantage of this discount.

ARTIST-IN-RESIDENCE NATIONAL PARKS

E-mail: acadia_information@nps.gov. **Website:** www.nps.gov/subjects/arts/air.htm. **Contact:** Artist-In-Residence Coordinator.

ADDITIONAL INFORMATION See website for contact information for individual parks.

ART WORKSHOPS IN GUATEMALA

4758 Lyndale Ave. S., Minneapolis MN 55419. (612)825-0747. **E-mail:** info@artguat.org. **Website:** www.artguat.org. **Contact:** Liza Fourre, director. Estab. 1995.

COSTS See website. Includes tuition, lodging, breakfast, and ground transportation.

ADDITIONAL INFORMATION For brochure/guidelines, visit website, e-mail, or call.

ASPEN SUMMER WORDS WRITERS CONFERENCE & LITERARY FESTIVAL

Aspen Words, 110 E. Hallam St., Suite 116, Aspen CO 81611. (970)925-3122. **Fax:** (970)925-5700. **E-mail:** aspenwords@aspeninstitute.org. **Website:** www.aspenwords.org. **Contact:** Caroline Tory. Estab. 1976.

COSTS Non-Juried 5-Day Writing Workshop: $1525.00. 3-Day Readers Retreat: $425. Financial aid is available on a limited basis.

ADDITIONAL INFORMATION To apply for a juried workshop, see website for an application and complete guidelines.

ASSOCIATION OF WRITERS & WRITING PROGRAMS CONFERENCE & BOOKFAIR

Association of Writers & Writing Programs, University of Maryland, 5700 Rivertech Court, Suite 225, Riverdale Park MD 20737-1250. (301)226-9711. **Fax:** (301)226.9797. **E-mail:** conference@awpwriter.org; events@awpwriter.org. **Website:** www.awpwriter.org/awp_conference. Estab. 1973.

ADDITIONAL INFORMATION Upcoming conference locations include San Antonio (March 4-7, 2020), Kansas City (March 3-6, 2021) and Philadelphia (March 23-26, 2022).

ATLANTA WRITERS CONFERENCE

Atlanta Writers Club, Westin Atlanta Airport Hotel, 4736 Best Rd., Atlanta GA 30337. **E-mail:** awconference@gmail.com. **Website:** www.atlantawritersconference.com. **Contact:** George Weinstein. Estab. 2008.

COSTS Manuscript critiques are $170 each (2 spots/waitlists maximum). Pitches are $70 each (2 spots/waitlists maximum). There's no charge for waitlists unless a spot opens. Query letter critiques are $70 (1 spot maximum). Other workshops and panels may also cost extra; see website. The "all activities" option is $620 and includes 2 manuscript critiques, 2 pitches, and 1 of each remaining activity.

ACCOMMODATIONS A block of rooms is reserved at the conference hotel. Booking instructions will be sent in the registration confirmation e-mail.

ADDITIONAL INFORMATION A free shuttle runs between the airport and the hotel.

AUSTIN FILM FESTIVAL & CONFERENCE

1801 Salina St., Suite 210, Austin TX 78702. (512)478-4795 or (800)310-3378. **Fax:** (512)478-6205. **Website:** www.austinfilmfestival.com. **Contact:** Conference Director. Estab. 1994.

COSTS Austin Film Festival offers 4 badge levels for entry, and access to the conference depends on the badge level. Go online for offers and to view the different options available with each badge.

AWP ANNUAL CONFERENCE AND BOOKFAIR

MS 1E3, George Mason Univ., Fairfax VA 22030. (703)993-4317. **E-mail:** conference@awpwriter.org. **Website:** https://www.awpwriter.org/awp_conference/overview. Estab. 1967.

COSTS Early registration fees: $40 student; $140 AWP member; $160 non-member.

ACCOMMODATIONS Provides airline discounts and rental-car discounts.

ADDITIONAL INFORMATION AWP Annual Conference & Bookfair, Los Angeles, CA 2016. Annual. Conference duration: 4 days. AWP holds its Annual Conference in a different region of North America in order to celebrate the outstanding authors, teachers, writing programs, literary centers, and small press publishers of that region. The Annual Conference typically features 350 presentations: readings, lectures, panel discussions, and forums plus hundreds of book signings, receptions, dances, and informal gatherings. The conference attracts more than 8,000 attendees and more than 500 publishers. All genres are represented. "We will offer 175 panels on everything from writing to teaching to critical analysis." In 2009, Art Spiegelman was the keynote speaker. Others readers were Charles Baxter, Isaiah Sheffer, Z.Z. Packer, Nareem Murr, Marilynne Robinson; 2008: John Irving, Joyce Carol Oates, among others.

BALTIMORE COMIC-CON

Baltimore Convention Center, 1 West Pratt St., Baltimore MD 21201. (410)526-7410. **E-mail:** general@baltimorecomiccon.com. **Website:** www.baltimorecomiccon.com. **Contact:** Marc Nathan. Estab. 1999.

COSTS General admission, VIP, celebrity, and Ringo Awards tickets are available at baltimorecomiccon.com/tickets.

ACCOMMODATIONS Does not offer overnight accommodation. Provides list of area hotels and lodging options offering associated discounts.

ADDITIONAL INFORMATION For brochure, visit website.

BALTIMORE WRITERS' CONFERENCE

English Department, Liberal Arts Bldg., Towson University, 8000 York Rd., Towson MD 21252. (410)704-5196. **E-mail:** prwr@towson.edu. **Website:** baltimorewritersconference.org. Estab. 1994.

○ This conference has sold out in the past.

ACCOMMODATIONS Hotels are close by, if required.

ADDITIONAL INFORMATION Writers may register through the website. Send inquiries via e-mail.

BAY TO OCEAN WRITERS CONFERENCE

P.O. Box 1773, Easton MD 21601. (410)482-6337. **E-mail:** eswapresident@gmail.com. **Website:** https://easternshorewriters.org/Bay-To-Ocean-Conference. Estab. 1998.

COSTS Adults: $100-120. Students: $55. A paid ms review is also available; details on website. Includes continental breakfast and networking lunch.

ADDITIONAL INFORMATION Registration is on website. Pre-registration is required; no registration at door. Conference usually sells out 1 month in advance. Conference is for all levels of writers.

BLOCKBUSTER PLOT INTENSIVE WRITING WORKSHOPS (SANTA CRUZ)

Santa Cruz CA **E-mail:** contact@blockbusterplots.com. **Website:** www.blockbusterplots.com. **Contact:** Martha Alderson (also known as the Plot Whisperer), instructor. Estab. 2000.

COSTS Costs vary based on the time frame of the retreat/workshop.

ACCOMMODATIONS Updated website provides list of area hotels and lodging options.

ADDITIONAL INFORMATION Accepts inquiries by e-mail.

JAMES BONNET'S STORYMAKING: THE MASTER CLASS

Santa Monica CA (310)451-5418. **E-mail:** bonnet@storymaking.com. **Website:** www.storymaking.com. **Contact:** James Bonnet. Estab. 1990.

ACCOMMODATIONS Provides a list of area hotels or lodging options.

ADDITIONAL INFORMATION For brochure, e-mail, visit website, or call. Accepts inquiries by e-mail, phone, and fax. James Bonnet is the author of *Stealing Fire From the Gods: The Complete Guide to Story for Writers and Filmmakers.*

BOOKS-IN-PROGRESS CONFERENCE

Carnegie Center for Literacy and Learning, 251 W. Second St., Lexington KY 40507. (859)254-4175. **E-mail:** ccll1@carnegiecenterlex.org. **Website:** carnegiecenterlex.org. **Contact:** Laura Whitaker, program director. Estab. 2010.

○ "Personal meetings with faculty (agents and editors) are only available to full conference participants. Limited slots available. Please choose only one agent; only one pitching session per participant."

ACCOMMODATIONS See website for list of area hotels.

BREAD LOAF IN SICILY WRITERS' CONFERENCE

Middlebury College, Middlebury College, Middlebury VT 05753. (802)443-5286. **Fax:** (802)443-2087. **E-mail:** blsicily@middlebury.edu. **Website:** www.middlebury.edu/bread-loaf-conferences/blsicily. Estab. 2011.

COSTS $3,265/$3,010 (as a contributor with manuscript/as an auditor without manuscript). Includes the conference program, transfer to and from Palermo Airport, 6 nights of lodging, 3 meals daily (except for Wednesday), wine reception at the readings, and an excursion to the ancient ruins of Segesta. The charge for an additional person is $1,900. There is a $20 application fee and a deposit.

ACCOMMODATIONS Accommodations are single rooms with private bath. Breakfast and lunch are served at the hotel, and dinner is available at select Erice restaurants. A double room is possible for those who would like to be accompanied by a spouse or significant other.

ADDITIONAL INFORMATION Application deadline for 2019 conference: October 15, 2018-April 15, 2019 or until spaces fill. Rolling admissions. Space is limited.

BREAD LOAF WRITERS' CONFERENCE

Middlebury College, Middlebury College, Middlebury VT 05753. (802)443-5286. **Fax:** (802)443-2087.

E-mail: blwc@middlebury.edu. **Website:** www.middlebury.edu/bread-loaf-conferences/bl_writers. Estab. 1926.

COSTS $3,525 for general contributors and $3,380 for auditors. Both options include room and board.

ACCOMMODATIONS Bread Loaf campus of Middlebury College in Ripton, Vermont.

ADDITIONAL INFORMATION The application deadline for the 2019 conference: October 15, 2018-February 15, 2019; there is a $20 application fee.

BYRON WRITERS FESTIVAL

Northern Rivers Writers' Centre, P.O. Box 1846, Byron Bay New South Wales 2481, Australia. (61) (02)6685-5115. **Website:** www.byronwritersfestival.com. **Contact:** Edwina Johnson, director. Estab. 1997.

COSTS See website for details. Costs vary for early bird registration, NRWC members, students, and children.

CALIFORNIA CRIME WRITERS CONFERENCE

Sisters in Crime Los Angeles and Southern California Mystery Writers of America, DoubleTree by Hilton Los Angeles—Westside, 6161 W. Centinela Avenue, Culver City CA 90230, USA. **E-mail:** ccwconference@gmail.com. **E-mail:** ccwconference@gmail.com. **Website:** www.ccwconference.org. **Contact:** Sisters in Crime/Los Angeles and SoCal Mystery Writers of America. Estab. 1995.

"Sisters in Crime Los Angeles and the Southern California Mystery Writers of America invite emerging and established mystery writers for a weekend of invaluable guidance, insight, and community. Whether your novel is brewing in your imagination, ready to publish, or you already have several published books under your belt, our workshops, presented by agents, editors, award-winning authors, and crime investigation professionals, are geared to elevate your mystery writing skills and foster relationships on your path to publication and beyond."

COSTS $355 visit website for further details. Online and mail-in registration close May 31, 2019.

CAMPBELL CONFERENCE

University of Kansas Gunn Center for the Study of Science Fiction, Wesoce Hall, 1445 Jayhawk Blvd., Lawrence KS 66045. (785)864-2518. **E-mail:** campbellconference@gmail.com, gunn.sf.center@gmail.com. **Website:** www.sfcenter.ku.edu/courses.htm. Estab. 1978.

ACCOMMODATIONS Housing is available for workshop attendees. Several airport shuttle services offer reasonable transportation from the Kansas City International Airport to Lawrence.

ADDITIONAL INFORMATION All are welcome to attend the Campbell Conference. Admission to the workshops (we now offer five) requires application and is very selective. See website for guidelines and full information. The original workshop is intended for writers who have just started to sell their work or need that extra bit of understanding or skill to become a published writer, and the advanced workshops are for those who have previously attended.

CAPE COD WRITERS CENTER ANNUAL CONFERENCE

P.O. Box 408, Osterville MA 02655. (508)420-0200. **E-mail:** writers@capecodwriterscenter.org. **Website:** www.capecodwriterscenter.org. **Contact:** Nancy Rubin Stuart, executive director.

COSTS Costs vary, depending on the number of courses selected, beginning at $125. Several scholarships are available.

ACCOMMODATIONS Resort and Conference Center of Hyannis, Massachusetts.

CELEBRATION OF SOUTHERN LITERATURE

Southern Lit Alliance, 301 E. 11th St., Suite 301, Chattanooga TN 37403. (423)267-1218. **Fax:** (866)483-6831. **Website:** www.southernlitalliance.org.

CENTRAL OHIO FICTION WRITERS ANNUAL CONFERENCE

Romance Writers of America, P.O. Box 24254, Dayton OH 45424. **E-mail:** susan_gee_heino@yahoo.com; cofwpresident@gmail.com. **Website:** www.cofwevents.org. **Contact:** Jeanne Estridge, 2019 President. Estab. 1990.

COSTS Please see our website for current membership information.

CENTRUM'S PORT TOWNSEND WRITERS' CONFERENCE

P.O. Box 1158, Port Townsend WA 98368. (360)385-3102. **E-mail:** info@centrum.org. **Website:** centrum.org/the-port-townsend-writers-conference. **Contact:** Jordan Hartt, director of programs. Estab. 1974. P.O. Box 1158, Port Townsend, WA 98368. (360)385-3102. **Fax:** (360)385-2470. **E-mail:** info@centrum.org; jhartt@centrum.org. **Website:** www.centrum.org. Estab. 1974. Annual. Conference held mid-July. Average attendance: 180. Conference to promote poetry, fiction, and creative nonfiction "featuring many of the nation's leading writers." Two different workshop options: "New Works" and "Works-in-Progress." Site: The conference is held at Fort Worden State Park on the Strait of Juan de Fuca. "The site is a Victorian-era military fort with miles of beaches, wooded trails, and recreation facilities. The park is within the limits of Port Townsend, a historic seaport and arts community, approximately 80 miles northwest of Seattle, on the Olympic Peninsula." Guest speakers participate in addition to full-time faculty.

COSTS Tuition for the conference is $200-700. Admission to afternoon workshops is $200-300. Register online.

ACCOMMODATIONS "Modest room and board facilities on site." Provides list of area lodging options.

ADDITIONAL INFORMATION Brochures/guidelines available for SASE or on website. "The conference focus is on the craft of writing and the writing life, not on marketing."

CHRISTOPHER NEWPORT UNIVERSITY WRITERS' CONFERENCE & WRITING CONTEST

(757)269-4368. **E-mail:** eleanor.taylor@cnu.edu. **Website:** writers.cnu.edu. Estab. 1981.

ACCOMMODATIONS Provides list of area hotels.

CLARION SCIENCE FICTION AND FANTASY WRITERS' WORKSHOP

Arthur C. Clarke Center for Human Imagination, University of California, San Diego, 9500 Gilman Dr., #0445, La Jolla CA 92093. (858)534-2115. **E-mail:** clarion@ucsd.edu. **Website:** clarion.ucsd.edu. **Contact:** Program Coordinator. Estab. 1968.

COSTS See website for current costs. Application fee is $55 before February 15 and $70 after. "Financial aid is awarded based on a combination of merit, need, and the criteria established by donors for particular funds. They range in size from $100 to over $3000, though most are between $500 and $1500."

ACCOMMODATIONS Participants make their own travel arrangements to and from the campus. Campus residency is required. Participants are housed in semi-private accommodations (private bedroom, shared bathroom) in student apartments. The workshop fee includes room and board and 3 meals a day at a campus dining facility.

ADDITIONAL INFORMATION "Workshop participants are selected on the basis of their potential for highly successful writing careers. Applications are judged by a review panel composed of the workshop instructors. Applicants submit an application and 2 complete short stories, each between 2,500 words and 6,000 words. The application deadline (typically, March 1) is posted on the Clarion website." Information available in September. For additional information, visit website.

CLARION WEST WRITERS WORKSHOP

P.O. Box 31264, Seattle WA 98103. (206)322-9083. **E-mail:** info@clarionwest.org. **Website:** www.clarionwest.org. **Contact:** Neile Graham, workshop director. Estab. 1984.

"Students write their own stories every week while preparing critiques of all the other students' work for classroom sessions. This gives participants a more focused, professional approach to their writing. The core of the workshop remains speculative fiction, and short stories (not novels) are the focus."

COSTS $4,200 (for tuition, housing, most meals). Numerous scholarships are available. Students apply through our website and must submit 20-30 pages of ms with four-page biography and $60 fee ($35 if received by February 10).

ACCOMMODATIONS Students stay on-site in workshop housing near the University of Washington.

ADDITIONAL INFORMATION Information available in fall. For brochure/guidelines, send SASE, visit website, e-mail, or call.

CONFLUENCE

P.O. Box 3681, Pittsburgh PA 15230. **Website:** parsecsff.org/confluence. Estab. 1996.

DETROIT WORKING WRITERS ANNUAL WRITERS CONFERENCE

Detroit Working Writers, P.O. Box 1105, Royal Oak MI 48068. **E-mail:** conference@detworkingwriters.org. **Website:** dww-writers-conference.org. Estab. 1961.

"Detroit Working Writers was founded on June 5, 1900, as the Detroit Press Club, the city of Detroit's first press club. Today, more than a century later, it is a 501(c)(6) organization and the state of Michigan's oldest writers organization."

COSTS Costs vary, depending on early bird registration and membership status within the organization.

❶ DRAGON CON

P.O. Box 16459, Atlanta GA 30321. **Website:** www.dragoncon.org.

❶ EMERALD CITY COMICON

3333 184th St. SW. Suite G, Lynnwood WA 98037. (425)744-2767. **Fax:** (425)675-0737. **E-mail:** info@emeraldcitycomicon.com; ksalierno@reedexpo.com. **Website:** www.emeraldcitycomicon.com. **Contact:** Kristen Salierno, operations manager. Estab. 2002.

COSTS Prices vary based on day.

ACCOMMODATIONS Offers discounted rate at Roosevelt Hotel, Crowne Plaza, and Red Lion in Seattle.

FESTIVAL OF FAITH AND WRITING

Department of English, Calvin College, 1795 Knollcrest Circle SE, Grand Rapids MI 49546. (616)526-6770. **E-mail:** ffw@calvin.edu. **Website:** festival.calvin.edu. Estab. 1990.

ACCOMMODATIONS Shuttles are available to and from local hotels. Shuttles are also available for overflow parking lots. A list of hotels with special rates for attendees is available on the conference website. High school and college students can arrange on-campus lodging by e-mail.

FLORIDA CHRISTIAN WRITERS CONFERENCE

Word Weavers International, Inc., P O Box 520224, Longwood FL 32752. (407)615-4112. **E-mail:** floridacwc@aol.com. **Website:** floridacwc.net. **Contact:** Eva Marie Everson and Mark T. Hancock. Estab. 1988.

COSTS Ranges: $275 (daily rate—in advance, includes lunch and dinner; specify days) to $1,495 (attendee and participating spouse/family member in same room). Scholarships offered. For more information or to register, go to the conference website.

ACCOMMODATIONS Offers private rooms and double occupancy as well as accommodations for participating and non-participating family members. Meals provided, including awards dessert banquet Saturday evening. For those flying into Orlando or Sanford airports, FCWC provides a shuttle to and from the conference center.

FLORIDA ROMANCE WRIITERS FUN IN THE SUN CONFERENCE

Florida Romance Writers, P.O. Box 550562, Fort Lauderdale FL 33355. **E-mail:** frwfuninthesun@yahoo.com. **Website:** frwfuninthesunmain.blogspot.com. Estab. 1986.

THE GLEN WORKSHOP

Image Journal, St. John's College, 1160 Camino Cruz Blanca, Santa Fe NM 87505. (206)281-2988. **Fax:** (206)281-2335. **E-mail:** glenworkshop@imagejournal.org. **Website:** glenworkshop.com. Estab. 1995.

COSTS See costs online. "Lodging and meals are included with registration at affordable rates. A low-cost 'commuter' rate is also available for those who wish to camp, stay with friends, or otherwise find their own food and lodging." A limited number of partial scholarships are available.

ACCOMMODATIONS Offers dorm rooms, dorm suites, and apartments.

ADDITIONAL INFORMATION "Like *Image*, the Glen is grounded in a Christian perspective, but its tone is informal and hospitable to all spiritual wayfarers. Depending on the teacher, participants may need to submit workshop material prior to arrival (usually 10-25 pages)."

GOTHAM WRITERS WORKSHOP

writingclasses.com, 555 Eighth Ave., Suite 1402, New York NY 10018. (212)974-8377. **E-mail:** contact@gothamwriters.com. **Website:** www.writingclasses.com. Estab. 1993.

ADDITIONAL INFORMATION See the website for courses, pricing, and instructors.

GREEN LAKE CHRISTIAN WRITERS' CONFERENCE

W2511 State Rd. 23, Green Lake Conference Center, Green Lake WI 54941. (920)294-3323. **E-mail:** program@glcc.org. **E-mail:** kriswood@glcc.org. **Website:** glcc.org. **Contact:** Cindy Manske, Conference Planning Coordinator, Kris Wood, conference director. Estab. 1948.

COSTS Check website for updated pricing.

ACCOMMODATIONS Hotels, lodges, and all meeting rooms are air conditioned. Affordable rates, excellent meals.

ADDITIONAL INFORMATION Brochure and scholarship info available online, or contact Kris Wood.

GREEN MOUNTAIN WRITERS CONFERENCE

47 Hazel St., Rutland VT 05701. (802)236-6133. **E-mail:** ydaley@sbcglobal.net. **E-mail:** yvonnedaley@me.com. **Website:** vermontwriters.com. **Contact:** Yvonne Daley, director. Estab. 1998.

○ "We offer the opportunity to learn from some of the nation's best writers at a small, supportive conference in a lakeside setting that allows one-on-one feedback. Participants often continue to correspond and share work after conferences."

COSTS $525 before April 15; $575 before May 15; $600 before June 1. Partial scholarships are available.

ACCOMMODATIONS Dramatically reduced rates at the Mountain Top Inn and Resort for attendees. Close to other area hotels and bed-and-breakfasts in Rutland County, Vermont.

ADDITIONAL INFORMATION Participants' mss can be read and commented on at a cost. Sponsors contests and publishes a literary magazine featuring work of participants. Brochures available on website or e-mail.

HAMPTON ROADS WRITERS CONFERENCE

Hampton Roads Writers, P.O. Box 56228, Virginia Beach VA 23456. (757)639-6146. **E-mail:** hrwriters@cox.net. **Website:** hamptonroadswriters.org. Estab. 2008.

COSTS Costs vary. There are discounts for members, for early bird registration, for students, and more.

HEDGEBROOK

P.O. Box 1231, Freeland WA 98249. (360)321-4786. **Fax:** (360)321-2171. **Website:** www.hedgebrook.org. **Contact:** Vito Zingarelli, residency director. Estab. 1988.

ADDITIONAL INFORMATION Takes applications 6 months in advance.

HIGHLAND SUMMER CONFERENCE

P.O. Box 7014, Radford University, Radford VA 24142. **E-mail:** tburriss@radford.edu. **Website:** tinyurl.com/q8z8ej9. **Contact:** Dr. Theresa Burriss. Estab. 1978.

HIGHLIGHTS FOUNDATION FOUNDERS WORKSHOPS

814 Court St., Honesdale PA 18431. (877)288-3410. **Fax:** (570)253-0179. **E-mail:** klbrown@highlights-foundation.org. **E-mail:** jo.lloyd@highlightsfounda-tion.org. **Website:** highlightsfoundation.org. **Contact:** Kent L. Brown, Jr.. Estab. 2000.

○ "Applications will be reviewed and accepted on a first-come, first-served basis. Applicants must demonstrate specific experience in the writing area of the workshop they are applying for—writing samples are required for many of the workshops."

COSTS Prices vary based on workshop. Check website for details.

ACCOMMODATIONS Coordinates pickup at local airport. Offers overnight accommodations. Participants stay in guest cabins on the wooded grounds surrounding Highlights Founders' home adjacent to the house/conference center.

ADDITIONAL INFORMATION Some workshops require pre-workshop assignment. Brochure available for SASE, by e-mail, on website, by phone, by fax. Accepts inquiries by phone, fax, e-mail, SASE. Editors attend conference.

HIGHLIGHTS FOUNDATION WRITERS WORKSHOPS

814 Court St., Honesdale PA 18431. (570)253-1192. **Fax:** (570)253-0179. **E-mail:** jo.lloyd@highlights-foundation.org. **Website:** highlightsfoundation.org. Estab. 1985.

ACCOMMODATIONS Private lodging on-site, included in workshop tuition.

ADDITIONAL INFORMATION Most workshops offer attendees the option of submitting a ms for review at the conference. Workshop brochures/guidelines are available upon request.

INDIANA UNIVERSITY WRITERS' CONFERENCE

Lindley Hall 215, 150 South Woodlawn Avenue, Bloomington IN 47405. (812)855-1877. **E-mail:** writecon@indiana.edu. **Website:** https://www.pw.org/content/indiana_university_writers_conference. **Contact:** Bob Bledsoe, Director. Estab. 1940.

COSTS The cost for the Poetry, Fiction Workshops is $385-670, depending on workshop. Lodging and meals are not included; lodging is available in campus dormitories for $50 per night or in the campus hotel for $134 per night. The registration fee is $30; general registration is first come, first served. To apply for a workshop, submit 8-10 pages of poetry or 15-20 pages of prose; admissions are made on a rolling basis. Visit the website for more information.

ACCOMMODATIONS Information on accommodations available on website.

ADDITIONAL INFORMATION Follow the conference on Twitter at @iuwritecon.

⊕ **INTERNATIONAL COMIC-CON**

Comic-Con International, P.O. Box 128458, San Diego CA 92112. (619)491-2475. **Fax:** (619)414-1022. **E-**

mail: cci-info@comic-con.org. **Website:** www.comic-con.org/cci. **Contact:** Gary Sassaman, director of print/publications. Comic-Con International, P.O. Box 128458, San Diego, CA 92112-8458. (619)491-2475. **Fax:** (619)414-1022. **E-mail:** cci-info@comic-con.org. **Website:** www.comic-con.org/cci/. Annual. Conference duration: 4 days. Average attendance: 104,000. "The comics industry's largest expo, hosting writers, artists, editors, agents, publishers, buyers and sellers of comics and graphic novels." Site: San Diego Convention Center. "Nearly 300 programming events, including panels, seminars and previews on the world of comics, movies, television, animation, art, and much more. We're also, of course, featuring Golden and Silver Age creators, sf/fantasy writers and artists, and longtime Comic-Con friends." Previous special guests included Ray Bradbury, Forrest J. Ackerman, Sergio Aragones, John Romita Sr., J. Michael Straczynski, Daniel Clowes, George Perez.

COSTS Prices vary. Check website for full costs.

ACCOMMODATIONS Does not offer overnight accommodations. Provides list of area hotels or lodging options. Special conference hotel and airfare discounts available. See website for details.

ADDITIONAL INFORMATION For brochure, visit website. Agents and editors participate in conference.

INTERNATIONAL MUSIC CAMP CREATIVE WRITING WORKSHOP

111 11th Ave. SW, Minot ND 58701. (701)838-8472. **Fax:** (701)838-1351. **E-mail:** info@internationalmusiccamp.com. **Website:** www.internationalmusiccamp.com. **Contact:** Christine Baumann and Tim Baumann, camp directors. Estab. 1956.

COSTS Fees vary based on activities. Check website for full details.

ACCOMMODATIONS Airline and depot shuttles are available upon request. Housing is included in the fee.

ADDITIONAL INFORMATION Program information is available on the website. Welcomes questions via e-mail.

◕◎ INTERNATIONAL WOMEN'S FICTION FESTIVAL

Via Cappuccini 8E, Matera , Italy. (39)0835-312044. **Fax:** (39)333-5857933. **E-mail:** contact@womensfictionfestival.com. **Website:** www.womensfictionfestival.com. **Contact:** Elizabeth Jennings. Estab. 2004.

COSTS Registration costs vary. Check website for full details.

ACCOMMODATIONS The conference is held at Le Monacelle, a restored 17th century convent. Conference travel agency will find reasonably priced accommodation. A paid shuttle is available from the Bari Airport to the hotel in Matera.

IOWA SUMMER WRITING FESTIVAL

The University of Iowa, 250 Continuing Education Facility, University of Iowa, Iowa City IA 52242. (319)335-4160. **Fax:** (319)335-4039. **E-mail:** iswfestival@uiowa.edu. **Website:** https://iowasummerwritingfestival.org/. Estab. 1987.

COSTS See website for registration and conference fees.

ACCOMMODATIONS Accommodations available at area hotels. Information on overnight accommodations available by phone or on website.

ADDITIONAL INFORMATION Brochures are available in February. Inquire via e-mail or on website. "Register early. Classes fill quickly."

IWWG SPRING BIG APPLE CONFERENCE

International Women's Writing Guild, (917)720-6959. **E-mail:** iwwgquestions@iwwg.org. **Website:** www.iwwg.org.

IWWG ANNUAL SUMMER CONFERENCE

(917)720-6959. **E-mail:** iwwgquestions@gmail.com. **Website:** https://iwwg.wildapricot.org/events. **Contact:** Dixie King, executive director. Estab. 1976. 2017 dates: July 7-14. Location: Pennsylvania. More information to come. Average attendance: 500 maximum. Open to all women. Around 65 workshops offered each day.

COSTS Varies. See website for details.

ACCOMMODATIONS Check website for updated pricing.

ADDITIONAL INFORMATION Choose from 30 workshops in poetry, fiction, memoir and personal narrative, social action/advocacy, and mind-body-spirit. Critique sessions; book fair; salons; open readings. No portfolio required.

JACKSON HOLE WRITERS CONFERENCE

P.O. Box 1974, Jackson WY 83001. (307)413-3332. **E-mail:** jhwritersconf@gmail.com. **Website:** jacksonholewritersconference.com. Estab. 1991.

COSTS $375 thru May 12, 2019; critiques additional.

ACCOMMODATIONS Accommodations not included.

ADDITIONAL INFORMATION Held at the Center for the Arts in Jackson, Wyoming, and online.

JAMES RIVER WRITERS CONFERENCE

2319 E. Broad St., Richmond VA 23223. (804)433-3790. **E-mail:** info@jamesriverwriters.org. **Website:** www.jamesriverwriters.org. **Contact:** Katharine Herndon. Estab. 2003.

○ The James River Writers conference is frequently recognized for its friendly atmosphere and southern hospitality.

COSTS Check website for updated pricing.

KACHEMAK BAY WRITERS' CONFERENCE

Kachemak Bay Campus—Kenai Peninsula College/University of Alaska Anchorage, Kenai Peninsula College—Kachemak Bay Campus, 533 E. Pioneer Ave., Homer AK 99603. (907)235-7743. **E-mail:** KachemakBayWritersConf@alaska.edu. **Website:** http://writersconf.kpc.alaska.edu/.

○ Previous keynote speakers have included Natasha Trethewey, Dave Barry, Amy Tan, Jeffrey Eugenides, and Anne Lamott.

COSTS See the website. Some scholarships available.

ACCOMMODATIONS Homer is 225 miles south of Anchorage, Alaska, on the southern tip of the Kenai Peninsula and the shores of Kachemak Bay. There are multiple hotels in the area.

KENTUCKY WOMEN WRITERS CONFERENCE

University of Kentucky College of Arts & Sciences, 232 E. Maxwell St., Lexington KY 40506. (859)257-2874. **E-mail:** kentuckywomenwriters@gmail.com. **Website:** kentuckywomenwriters.org. **Contact:** Julie Wrinn, director. Estab. 1979.

COSTS $200 for general admission and a workshop and $125 for admission with no workshop.

ADDITIONAL INFORMATION Sponsors prizes in poetry ($300), fiction ($300), nonfiction ($300), playwriting ($500), and spoken word ($500). Winners are also invited to read during the conference. Pre-registration opens May 1.

KENTUCKY WRITERS CONFERENCE

Southern Kentucky Book Fest, WKU South Campus, 2355 Nashville Rd., Bowling Green KY 42101. (270)745-4502. **E-mail:** sara.volpi@wku.edu. **Website:** www.sokybookfest.org. **Contact:** Sara Volpi.

○ Since the event is free, interested attendees are asked to register in advance. Information on how to do so is on the website.

KENYON REVIEW WRITERS WORKSHOP

Kenyon Review, Kenyon College, Gambier OH 43022. (740)427-5208. **Fax:** (740)427-5417. **E-mail:** kenyonreview@kenyon.edu; writers@kenyonreview.org. **Website:** www.kenyonreview.org/workshops. **Contact:** Anna Duke Reach, director. Estab. 1990.

COSTS Fiction, literary nonfiction, poetry, nature writing, translation: $2,295. Teachers: $1,795. All rates include tuition and room and board.

ACCOMMODATIONS The workshop operates a shuttle to and from Gambier and the airport in Columbus, Ohio. Offers overnight accommodations. Participants are housed in Kenyon College student housing.

ADDITIONAL INFORMATION Application includes a writing sample. Admission decisions are made on a rolling basis. Starting in November, workshop information is available online. For a brochure, send e-mail, visit website, call, or fax. Accepts inquiries by SASE, e-mail, phone, and fax.

◎ KILLER NASHVILLE

P.O. Box 680759, Franklin TN 37068. (615)599-4032. **E-mail:** contact@killernashville.com. **Website:** www.killernashville.com. Estab. 2006.

COSTS $399 for general registration. Includes network lunches on Friday and Saturday and special sessions with best-selling authors and industry professionals.

ADDITIONAL INFORMATION Additional information about registration is provided online.

KINDLING WORDS EAST

Burlington VT **Website:** www.kindlingwords.org.

KINDLING WORDS WEST

Breckenridge CO **Website:** www.kindlingwords.org.

LAS VEGAS WRITER'S CONFERENCE

Henderson Writers' Group, P.O. Box 92032, Henderson NV 89009. (702)953-5675. **E-mail:** confcoord@hendersonwritersgroup.com. **Website:** www.lasvegaswritersconference.com. Estab. 2001.

COSTS Costs vary depending on the package. See the website. There are early bird rates through January 31.

ADDITIONAL INFORMATION Agents and editors participate in conference.

LEAGUE OF UTAH WRITERS' ANNUAL

WRITER'S CONFERENCES

Spring Conference and Quills Conference, 1042 East Fort Union Blvd. #443, Midvale UT 84047. (385)434-0355. **E-mail:** president@leagueofutahwriters.org. **Website:** https://www.leagueofutahwriters.com. **Contact:** Johnny Worthen. Estab. 1935.

○ The Spring Conference is held at Utah State University in the Eccles Conference Center. The Quills Conference is held at Salt Lake City Marriott University Park.

COSTS Spring Conference is $25 early bird pricing. Quills Conference starts at $230. See website for details.

THE MACDOWELL COLONY

100 High St., Peterborough NH 03458. (603)924-3886. **Fax:** (603)924-9142. **E-mail:** admissions@macdowellcolony.org. **Website:** www.macdowellcolony.org. Estab. 1907.

COSTS Artists are responsible for travel to and from the Colony. Travel reimbursement and stipends are available for participants of the residency, based on need. There are no residency fees.

ACCOMMODATIONS Exclusive use of a private studio and bedroom are provided for each artist in residence.

◉ MAGNA CUM MURDER

Magna Cum Murder Crime Writing Festival, E.B. and Bertha C. Ball Center, Ball State University, 400 Minnetrista Pkwy., Muncie IN 47306. (765)285-8975. **Fax:** (765)747-9566. **E-mail:** ebball@bsu.edu. **Website:** www.magnacummurder.com. Estab. 1994.

COSTS Check website for updates.

MENDOCINO COAST WRITERS' CONFERENCE

P.O. Box 2087, Fort Bragg CA 95437. **E-mail:** info@mcwc.org. **Website:** www.mcwc.org. **Contact:** Lisa Locascio, Executive Director. Estab. 1989.

COSTS $575 registration includes morning intensives, afternoon panels and seminars, social events, and most meals. Scholarships available. Opt-in for consultations and Publishing Boot Camp. Early application advised.

ACCOMMODATIONS Many lodging options in the scenic coastal area.

ADDITIONAL INFORMATION "Take your writing to the next level with encouragement, expertise, and inspiration in a literary community where authors are also fantastic teachers." General registration opens March 1.

MIDWEST WRITERS WORKSHOP

Muncie IN 47306. (765)282-1055. **E-mail:** midwestwriters@yahoo.com. **Website:** www.midwestwriters.org. **Contact:** Jama Kehoe Bigger, director.

COSTS $155-425. Some meals included.

ADDITIONAL INFORMATION See website for more information. Keep in touch with the MWW at facebook.com/midwestwriters and twitter.com/midwestwriters.

MONTEVALLO LITERARY FESTIVAL

Comer Hall, Station 6420, University of Montevallo, Montevallo AL 35115. (205)665-6420. **Fax:** (205)665-6420. **E-mail:** murphyj@montevallo.edu. **Website:** www.montevallo.edu/arts-sciences/college-of-arts-sciences/departments/english-foreign-languages/student-organizations/montevallo-literary-festival. **Contact:** Dr. Jim Murphy, director. Estab. 2003.

MONTROSE CHRISTIAN WRITERS' CONFERENCE

Montrose Bible Conference, 218 Locust St., Montrose PA 18801. (570)278-1001 or (800)598-5030. **Fax:** (570)278-3061. **E-mail:** mbc@montrosebible.org. **Website:** www.montrosebible.org. Estab. 1990.

COSTS Tuition is around $200.

ACCOMMODATIONS Will meet planes in Binghamton, New York, and Scranton, Pennsylvania. On-site accommodations: room and board $360-490/conference, including food (2018 rates). RV court available.

ADDITIONAL INFORMATION "Writers can send work ahead of time and have it critiqued for a small fee." The attendees are usually church related. The writing has a Christian emphasis. Conference information available in April. For brochure, visit website, e-mail, or call. Accepts inquiries by phone or e-mail.

MOONLIGHT AND MAGNOLIAS WRITER'S CONFERENCE

Georgia Romance Writers, P.O. Box 1484, Buford GA 30515. **Website:** www.georgiaromancewriters.org/mm-conference. Estab. 1982.

COSTS Registration Closes September 8, 2019. $270-320 visit website for exact amount; early bird ends August 1, 2019.

JENNY MCKEAN MOORE COMMUNITY WORKSHOPS

English Department, George Washington University, Phillips Hall, 801 22nd St. NW, Suite 643, Washington DC 20052. (202)994-6180. **Fax:** (202)994-6637. **E-mail:** engldept@gwu.edu; lpageinc@aol.com. **Website:** www.gwu.edu/~english/creative_jennymckean-moore.html. **Contact:** Lisa Page, director of creative writing. Estab. 1976.

ADDITIONAL INFORMATION Admission is competitive and by decided by the quality of a submitted ms.

⊙ MOUNT HERMON CHRISTIAN WRITERS CONFERENCE

P.O. Box 413, Mount Hermon CA 95041. **E-mail:** info@mounthermon.org. **Website:** writers.moun-thermon.org. **Contact:** Kathy Ide, director. Estab. 1969.

ACCOMMODATIONS Options include modern cabins (with full kitchens) or lodges (similar to hotel rooms), available in economy, standard, and deluxe. See website for pricing.

MUSE AND THE MARKETPLACE

Grub Street, 162 Boylston St., 5th Floor, Boston MA 02116. (617)695-0075. **E-mail:** info@grubstreet.org. **Website:** museandthemarketplace.com.

The Muse and the Marketplace is designed to give aspiring writers a better understanding of the craft of writing fiction and nonfiction, to prepare them for the changing world of publishing and promotion, and to create opportunities for meaningful networking. On all 3 days, prominent and nationally recognized, established and emerging authors lead sessions on the craft of writing—the "muse" side of things—while editors, literary agents, publicists, and other industry professionals lead sessions on the business side—the "marketplace."

ACCOMMODATIONS Boston Park Plaza Hotel.

NAPA VALLEY WRITERS' CONFERENCE

Napa Valley College, 1088 College Ave., St. Helena CA 94574. (707)967-2900 ext. 4. **E-mail:** info@napawritersconference.og. **Website:** www.napawritersconference.org. **Contact:** Catherine Thorpe, managing director. Estab. 1981.

On Twitter as @napawriters and on Facebook as facebook.com/napawriters.

COSTS Applications for admission to the 2019 conference are now closed as of April 30, 2019.

The total participation fee for the 2019 program is $1,025, and includes daily breakfast and lunch, two dinners, wine tastings, and attendance at all conference events.

$25 reading fee–Pay with your application.

$1,025 participation fee–due on acceptance, non-refundable after June 5.

Financial Assistance: A limited number of grants are available to cover all or part of the conference participation fee, with awards made on the basis of merit and need.

NATIONAL WRITERS ASSOCIATION FOUNDATION CONFERENCE

10940 S. Parker Rd., #508, Parker CO 80138. **E-mail:** natlwritersassn@hotmail.com. **Website:** www.nationalwriters.com. **Contact:** Sandy Whelchel, executive director. Estab. 1926.

ADDITIONAL INFORMATION Awards for previous contests will be presented at the conference. Brochures/guidelines are available online or by SASE.

NETWO WRITERS CONFERENCE

Northeast Texas Writers Organization, P.O. Box 962, Mt. Pleasant TX 75456. (469)867-2624 or (903)573-6084. **E-mail:** jimcallan@winnsboro.com. **Website:** www.netwo.org. Estab. 1987.

COSTS $55 for members, $75 for non-members, $80 to join NETWO and attend conference.

ACCOMMODATIONS See website for information on area motels and hotels.The conference is held at the Titus County Civic Center in Mt. Pleasant, Texas.

ADDITIONAL INFORMATION Conference is co-sponsored by the Texas Commission on the Arts. See website for current updates.

NEW JERSEY ROMANCE WRITERS PUT YOUR HEART IN A BOOK CONFERENCE

P.O. Box 513, Plainsboro NJ 08536. **Website:** www.njromancewriters.org/conference.html. Estab. 1984.

NIMROD JOURNAL'S CONFERENCE FOR READERS AND WRITERS

800 S. Tucker Dr., Tulsa OK 74104. (918)631-3080. **E-mail:** nimrod@utulsa.edu. **Website:** www.utulsa.edu/nimrod. **Contact:** Eilis O'Neal, editor-in-chief. Estab. 1978.

COSTS $60. Lunch provided. Scholarships are available for students.

ADDITIONAL INFORMATION *Nimrod International Journal* sponsors the Katherine Anne Porter Prize for fiction and the Pablo Neruda Prize for poetry. Poetry and fiction prizes: $2,000 each and publication (top prize); $1,000 each and publication (other winners). Deadline: must be postmarked no later than April 30.

NORTH CAROLINA WRITERS' NETWORK FALL CONFERENCE

P.O. Box 21591, Winston-Salem NC 27120. (336)293-8844. **E-mail:** mail@ncwriters.org. **Website:** www.ncwriters.org. Estab. 1985.

COSTS Approximately $260 (all days, with meals).

NORTHERN COLORADO WRITERS CONFERENCE

407 Cormorant Ct., Fort Collins CO 80525. (970)227-5746. **E-mail:** april@northerncoloradowriters.com. **Website:** www.northerncoloradowriters.com. Estab. 2006.

COSTS Prices vary depending on a number of factors. See website for details.

ACCOMMODATIONS Conference hotel offers rooms at a discounted rate.

NORWESCON

100 Andover Park W. Suite 150-165, Tukwila WA 98188. (425)243-4692. **E-mail:** info@norwescon.org. **Website:** www.norwescon.org. Estab. 1978.

ACCOMMODATIONS Conference is held at the Doubletree Hotel Seattle Airport.

ODYSSEY FANTASY WRITING WORKSHOP

P.O. Box 75, Mont Vernon NH 03057. (603)673-6234. **E-mail:** jcavelos@odysseyworkshop.org. **Website:** www.odysseyworkshop.org. **Contact:** Jeanne Cavelos. Estab. 1996.

Since its founding in 1996, the Odyssey Writing Workshop has become one of the most highly respected workshops for writers of fantasy, science fiction, and horror in the world. Top authors, editors and agents have served as guests at Odyssey. Fifty-nine percent of graduates have gone on to be professionally published. Among Odyssey's graduates are *New York Times* bestsellers, Amazon bestsellers, and award winners.

COSTS $2,060 tuition, $195 textbook, $892 housing (double room), $1,784 housing (single room), $40 application fee, $600 food (approximate), $1,000 optional processing fee to receive college credit.

ACCOMMODATIONS Most students stay in Saint Anselm College apartments to get the full Odyssey experience. Each apartment has 2 bedrooms and can house a total of 2 to 3 people (with each bedroom holding 1 or 2 students). The apartments are equipped with kitchens, so you may buy and prepare your own food, which is a money-saving option, or you may eat at the college's Coffee Shop or Dining Hall. Wireless internet access and use of laundry facilities are provided at no cost. Students with cars will receive a campus parking permit.

ADDITIONAL INFORMATION Students must apply and include a writing sample. Application deadline: April 1. Students' works are critiqued throughout the 6 weeks. Workshop information available in October. For brochure/guidelines, send SASE, e-mail, visit website, or call.

OHIO KENTUCKY INDIANA CHILDREN'S LITERATURE CONFERENCE

Northern Kentucky University, 405 Steely Library, Highland Heights KY 41099. (859)572-6620. **Fax:** (859)572-5390. **E-mail:** smithjen@nku.edu. **Website:** https://swonlibraries.org/mpage/oki. **Contact:** Jennifer Smith.

COSTS $85; includes registration/attendance at all workshop sessions, continental breakfast, lunch, and author/illustrator signings. Manuscript critiques are available for an additional cost. E-mail or call for more information.

OREGON CHRISTIAN WRITERS SUMMER CONFERENCE

1075 Willow Lake Rd. N., Keizer OR 97303. **E-mail:** summerconference@oregonchristianwriters.org. **Website:** www.oregonchristianwriters.org. **Contact:** Lindy Jacobs, summer conference director. Estab. 1989.

COSTS $550 for OCW members, $595 for nonmembers. Registration fee includes all classes, workshops, and 2 lunches and 3 dinners. Lodging additional. Full-time registered attendees may also pre-submit 3 proposals for review by an editor (or agent) through the conference, plus sign up for a half-hour mentoring appointment with an author.

ACCOMMODATIONS Conference is held at the Red Lion on the River Hotel. Attendees wishing to stay at the hotel must make a reservation through the hotel. A block of rooms is reserved at a special rate and held until mid-July. The hotel reservation link is posted on the website in late spring. Shuttle bus transportation is provided from Portland Airport (PDX) to the hotel, which is 20 minutes away.

ADDITIONAL INFORMATION Conference details posted online beginning in January. All conferees are welcome to attend the Cascade Awards ceremony, which takes place Wednesday evening during the conference. For more information about the Cascade Writing Contest for published and unpublished writers—opens February 14. Please check the website for details.

OUTDOOR WRITERS ASSOCIATION OF AMERICA ANNUAL CONFERENCE

2814 Brooks St., Box 442, Missoula MT 59801. (406)728-7434. **E-mail:** info@owaa.org. **Website:** owaa.org. **Contact:** Jessica Seitz, conference and membership coordinator. Estab. 1927.

COSTS Full 3 Days - $249; 2 Days - $200; One Day - $100.

OZARK CREATIVE WRITERS, INC. CONFERENCE

P.O. Box 9076, Fayetteville AR 72703. **E-mail:** ozarkcreativewriters@ozarkcreativewriters.com. **Website:** www.ozarkcreativewriters.com.

○ A full list of sessions and speakers is online. The conference usually has agents and/or editors in attendance to meet with writers.

COSTS Full Conference Early Bird Registration: $185.00; after August 25:$ 248.00. Conference Only Registration: $140.00; after August 25: $150.00.

PACIFIC COAST CHILDREN'S WRITERS WHOLE-NOVEL WORKSHOP: FOR ADULTS AND TEENS

P.O. Box 244, Aptos CA 95001. **Website:** www.childrenswritersworkshop.com. Estab. 2003.

COSTS Visit website for tiered fees (includes lodging, meals), schedule, and more; e-mail Director Nancy Sondel via the contact form.

WILLIAM PATERSON UNIVERSITY SPRING WRITER'S CONFERENCE

English Department, Preakness Hall 349, 300 Pompton Rd., Wayne NJ 07470. (973)720-3067. **Fax:** (973)720-2189. **E-mail:** parrasj@wpunj.edu. **Website:** wpunj.edu/mfa. **Contact:** John Parras. Estab. 1998.

COSTS $50-75, depending on registration type.

PENNWRITERS CONFERENCE

P.O. Box 685, Dalton PA 18414. **E-mail:** conference-co@pennwriters.org; info@pennwriters.org. **Website:** pennwriters.org/conference. Estab. 1987.

○ As the official writing organization of Pennsylvania, Pennwriters has 8 different areas with smaller writing groups that meet. Each of these areas sometimes has their own, smaller event during the year in addition to the annual writing conference.

ACCOMMODATIONS Costs vary. Pennwriters members in good standing get a slightly reduced rate.

ADDITIONAL INFORMATION Sponsors contest. Published authors judge fiction in various categories. Agent/editor appointments are available on a first-come, first-served basis.

PHILADELPHIA WRITERS' CONFERENCE

P.O. Box 7171, Elkins Park PA 19027. (215)619-7422. **E-mail:** info@pwcwriters.org. **Website:** pwcwriters.org. Estab. 1949.

○ Offers 14 workshops, usually 4 seminars, several "manuscript rap" sessions, a Friday Roundtable Forum Buffet with speaker, and the Saturday Annual Awards Banquet with speaker. Attendees may submit mss in advance for criticism by the workshop leaders and are eligible to submit entries in more than 10 contest categories. Cash prizes and certificates are given to first and second place winners, plus full tuition for the following year's conference to first place winners.

ACCOMMODATIONS See website for details. Hotel may offer discount for early registration.

ADDITIONAL INFORMATION Accepts inquiries by e-mail. Agents and editors attend the conference. Many questions are answered online.

PIKES PEAK WRITERS CONFERENCE

Pikes Peak Writers, P.O. Box 64273, Colorado Springs CO 80962. (719)244-6220. **E-mail:** registrar@pikespeakwriters.com. **Website:** www.pikespeakwriters.com/ppwc. Estab. 1993.

COSTS $405-465 (includes all 7 meals).

ACCOMMODATIONS Marriott Colorado Springs holds a block of rooms at a special rate for attendees until late March.

ADDITIONAL INFORMATION Readings with critiques are available on Friday afternoon. Registration forms are online; brochures are available in January. Send inquiries via e-mail.

PNWA SUMMER WRITERS CONFERENCE
Writers' Cottage, 317 NW Gilman Blvd. Suite 8, Issaquah WA 98027. (425)673-2665. **E-mail:** pnwa@pnwa.org. **Website:** www.pnwa.org. Estab. 1955.

COSTS See website for costs and early bird registration.

RETREAT TO THE SPRINGS!
Beckman Communications, 2836 Westbrook Dr., Cincinnati OH 45211. **E-mail:** whbeckman@gmail.com. **Website:** https://wendyonwriting.com/2017/03/31/write-in-yellow-springs/. **Contact:** Wendy Hart Beckman. Estab. 2000.

COSTS $195 for instruction. Participants procure their own lodging and meals.

ACCOMMODATIONS John Bryan Community Center (http://www.yellowspringsohio.org/venue/john-bryan-community-center/) for classes. Many hotels available in the area with numerous restaurants within walking distance.

ADDITIONAL INFORMATION The 2018 retreat features Ann Hagedorn (creative nonfiction), Donna MacMeans (romance), Jason Sanford (sci-fi/fantasy), and Valerie Coleman (self-publishing).

ROCKY MOUNTAIN FICTION WRITERS COLORADO GOLD CONFERENCE
Rocky Mountain Fiction Writers, Denver Renaissance Hotel, Denver CO **E-mail:** conference@rmfw.org. **Website:** www.rmfw.org. **Contact:** Pamela Nowak and Susan Brooks. Estab. 1982.

COSTS Available on website.

ACCOMMODATIONS Special rates will be available at conference hotel.

ADDITIONAL INFORMATION Pitch appointments available at no charge. Add-on options include agent and editor critiques, master classes, pitch coaching, query letter coaching, special critiques, and more.

ROMANCE WRITERS OF AMERICA NATIONAL CONFERENCE
14615 Benfer Rd., Houston TX 77069. (832)717-5200. **Fax:** (832)717-5201. **E-mail:** info@rwa.org. **Website:** www.rwa.org/conference. **Contact:** Donna Mathoslah, Membership Services Administrator. Estab. 1981.

COSTS $499-724 depending on your membership status as well as when you register.

ADDITIONAL INFORMATION Annual RTA awards are presented for romance authors. Annual Golden Heart awards are presented for unpublished writers.

⬤ SAGE HILL WRITING EXPERIENCE
324-1831 College Avenue, Regina Saskatchewan S4P 4V5, Canada. (306)537-7243. **E-mail:** sage.hill@sasktel.net. **Website:** sagehillwriting.ca.

ACCOMMODATIONS Located at Lumsden, 45 kilometers outside Regina.

ADDITIONAL INFORMATION See the website for pricing and current course offerings.

SAN DIEGO STATE UNIVERSITY WRITERS' CONFERENCE
SDSU College of Extended Studies, 5250 Campanile Dr., San Diego State University, San Diego CA 92182. (619)594-2099. **Fax:** (619)594-8566. **E-mail:** sdsuwritersconference@mail.sdsu.edu. **Website:** ces.sdsu.edu/writers. Estab. 1984.

SAN FRANCISCO WRITERS CONFERENCE
Hyatt Regency Embarcadero, San Francisco (925) 420-6223. **E-mail:** barbara@sfwriters.org. **E-mail:** See website at www.SFWriters.org for event details, SFWC Writing Contest, Poetry Summit and scholarship submissions.. **Website:** sfwriters.org. **Contact:** Barbara Santos, marketing director. Estab. 2003.

⬤ Keynoters for 2019 include Catherine Coulther, Jose Antonio Vargas, and Jane Friedman. Attendees can take educational sessions and network with the 100+ presenters from the publishing world. Free editorial and PR consults, exhibitor hall, pitching and networking opportunities available throughout the four-day event. Also several free sessions offered to the public. See website for details or sign up for the SFWC Newsletter for updates.

COSTS Full registration is $895 with a $795 early bird registration rate until December 31, 2018

ACCOMMODATIONS The Hyatt Regency Embarcadero offers a discounted SFWC rate (based on availability. Use Code WR19). Call directly: (415) 788-1234. Across from the Ferry Building in San Francisco, the hotel is located so that everyone arriving at the Oakland or San Francisco airport can take the BART to the Embarcadero exit, directly in front of the hotel.

ADDITIONAL INFORMATION "Present yourself in a professional manner, and the contacts you will make will be invaluable to your writing career. Fliers, details, and registration information are online."

SANTA BARBARA WRITERS CONFERENCE

27 W. Anapamu St., Suite 305, Santa Barbara CA 93101. (805)568-1516. **E-mail:** info@sbwriters.com. **Website:** www.sbwriters.com. Estab. 1972.

COSTS $150 for single-day; $699 for full conference.

ACCOMMODATIONS Hyatt Santa Barbara.

ADDITIONAL INFORMATION Register online or contact for brochure and registration forms.

☼ SASKATCHEWAN FESTIVAL OF WORDS

217 Main St. N., Moose Jaw Saskatchewan S6H 0W1, Canada. (306)691-0557. **E-mail:** amanda@festivalofwords.com. **Website:** www.festivalofwords.com. Estab. 1997.

COSTS Passes are available for $175 ($200 after June 1) for a full pass, $100 for a flex pass, and $55 for a student pass. Learn more about passes on our website. We also have tickets available for events from $10-30 and free events too!

SCBWI—CENTRAL-COASTAL CALIFORNIA; FALL CONFERENCE

E-mail: cencal@scbwi.org. **Website:** cencal.scbwi.org. **Contact:** Rebecca Langston-George, Regional Advisor. Estab. 1971.

○ SCBWI—NEW JERSEY; ANNUAL SUMMER CONFERENCE

New Jersey NJ **Website:** newjersey.scbwi.org. **Contact:** Regional Advisor Tisha Hamiliton,; Co-Assistant Regional Advisor Rosanne Kurstedt; Co-Assistant Regional Advisor Kelly Calabrese.

COSTS Registration for 2019 is now closed.

SCBWI WINTER CONFERENCE ON WRITING AND ILLUSTRATING FOR CHILDREN

4727 Wilshire Blvd #301, Los Angeles CA 90010. (323)782-1010. **Fax:** (323)782-1892. **E-mail:** scbwi@scbwi.org. **Website:** www.scbwi.org. **Contact:** Stephen Mooser. Estab. 2000.

COSTS See website for current cost and conference information; $525-675.

ADDITIONAL INFORMATION SCBWI also holds an annual summer conference in August in Los Angeles.

SEWANEE WRITERS' CONFERENCE

735 University Ave., 119 Gailor Hall, Stamler Center, Sewanee TN 37383. (931)598-1654. **E-mail:** swc@sewanee.edu. **Website:** www.sewaneewriters.org. **Contact:** Adam Latham. Estab. 1990.

COSTS $1,100 for tuition, and $700 for room, board, and activity costs.

ACCOMMODATIONS Participants are housed in single rooms in university dormitories. Bathrooms are shared by small groups.

SITKA CENTER FOR ART AND ECOLOGY

56605 Sitka Dr., Otis OR 97368. (541)994-5485. **Fax:** (541)994-8024. **E-mail:** info@sitkacenter.org. **Website:** www.sitkacenter.org. **Contact:** Mindy Chaffin, program manager. Estab. 1970.

COSTS Workshops are generally $25-505; they do not include meals or lodging.

ACCOMMODATIONS Does not offer overnight accommodations. Provides a list of area hotels or lodging options.

ADDITIONAL INFORMATION Brochure available in February of each year; request a copy by e-mail or phone, or visit website for listing. Accepts inquiries in person or by e-mail, phone, or fax.

SLEUTHFEST

Mystery Writers of America Florida, **E-mail:** sleuthfestinfo@gmail.com. **Website:** sleuthfest.com.

SOUTHAMPTON CHILDREN'S LITERATURE CONFERENCE

Stony Brook Southampton MFA in Creative Writing, 239 Montauk Hwy., Southampton NY 11968. (631)632-5030. **Fax:** (631)632-2578. **Website:** www.stonybrook.edu/mfa/clc/. **Contact:** Carla Caglioti, Executive Director, Southampton Graduate Arts Campus, Interim Co-Director, Creative Writing and Literature. Estab. 2007. 239 Montauk Hwy., Southampton NY 11968-6700. (631)632-5030. **Fax:** (631)632-2578. **E-mail:** southamptonwriters@notes.cc.sunysb.edu. **Website:** www.stonybrook.edu/writers. Annual conference held in July. "The seaside campus of Stony Brook Southampton is located in the heart of the Hamptons, a renowned resort area only 70 miles from New York City. During free time, participants can draw on inspiration from the Atlantic beaches or explore the charming seaside towns."

COSTS Fees vary. 2019 fees available online.

ACCOMMODATIONS On-campus housing, doubles and small singles with shared baths, is modest but comfortable. Supplies list of lodging alternatives.

ADDITIONAL INFORMATION Applicants must complete an application and submit a writing sample of original, unpublished work. Details available online. Accepts inquiries by e-mail, phone.

THE SOUTHAMPTON WRITERS CONFERENCE

Stony Brook Southampton MFA in Creative Writing Program, 239 Montauk Hwy., Southampton NY 11968. (631)632-5007. **E-mail:** christian.mclean@stonybrook.edu. **Website:** www.stonybrook.edu/writers. **Contact:** Christian McLean. Estab. 1976.

COSTS 5-day workshop only: $1,495. 5-day workshop plus residency: $1,995 (12 days total). 12-day workshop: $1,995. 12-day residency: $500. 12-day lecture series: $500 (does not include afternoon faculty-led workshop).

ACCOMMODATIONS Participants can stay on campus in air-conditioned dorms.

SOUTH CAROLINA WRITERS WORKSHOP

4711 Forest Dr., Suite 3, P.M.B. 189, Columbia SC 29206. **E-mail:** scwwliaison@gmail.com. **Website:** www.myscwa.org. Estab. 1991.

SOUTHEASTERN WRITERS ASSOCIATION—ANNUAL WRITERS WORKSHOP

E-mail: southeasternwriters@gmail.com. **Website:** www.southeasternwriters.org. Estab. 1975.

Instruction offered for novel writing, short fiction, young adult, humor, columns, poetry, memoir, and self-publishing. Includes agent in residence, publisher in residence, and photographer for author head shots.

COSTS Cost of workshop: $445 for 4 days or lower prices for daily tuition or early bird special. (See website for tuition pricing.)

ACCOMMODATIONS Lodging at Epworth and throughout St. Simons Island. Visit website for more information.

SPACE (SMALL PRESS AND ALTERNATIVE COMICS EXPO)

Back Porch Comics, P.O. Box 20550, Columbus OH 43220. **E-mail:** bpc013@gmail.com. **Website:** www.backporchcomics.com/space.htm. **Contact:** Bob Corby, founder.

COSTS Admission is free.

ADDITIONAL INFORMATION For brochure, visit website. Editors participate in conference.

COMMUNITY OF WRITERS AT SQUAW VALLEY

Community of Writers at Squaw Valley, P.O. Box 1416, Nevada City CA 95959. (530)470-8440 or (530)583-5200 (summer). **E-mail:** info@communityofwriters.org. **Website:** www.communityofwriters.org. **Contact:** Brett Hall Jones, Executive Director. Estab. 1969.

Annual conference held in July. 2019 dates: July 8-15. Conference duration: 7 days. Average attendance: 124. "Workshops in fiction, nonfiction, and memoir assist talented writers by exploring the art and craft as well as the business of writing." Offerings include daily morning workshops led by writer-teachers, editors, or agents of the staff, limited to 12-13 participants; seminars; panel discussions of editing and publishing; craft colloquies; lectures; and staff readings. Past themes and panels included "The Nation of Narrative Prose: Telling the Truth in Memoir and Personal Essay" and "Anatomy of a Short Story." The workshops are held in a ski lodge at the foot of a ski area. Literary agent speakers have recently included Michael Carlisle, Susan Golomb, Joy Harris, Mary Evans, B.J. Robbins, Janet Silver, and Peter Steinberg. Agents and editors attend/participate.

COSTS Tuition is $1,350, which includes 6 dinners. Limited financial aid is available.

ACCOMMODATIONS The Community of Writers rents houses and condominiums in the Squaw Valley for participants to live in during the week of the conference. Single room (1 participant): $790/week. Double room (twin beds, room shared by conference participant of the same gender): $490/week. Multiple room (bunk beds, room shared with 2 or more participants of the same gender): $325/week. All rooms subject to availability; early requests are recommended. Can arrange airport shuttle pickups for a fee.

SUMMER WRITING PROGRAM

Naropa University, 2130 Arapahoe Ave., Boulder CO 80302. (303)245-4862. **Fax:** (303)546-5287. **E-mail:** swp@naropa.edu. **Website:** www.naropa.edu/swp. **Contact:** Kyle Pivarnik, special projects manager. Estab. 1974.

COSTS See website for pricing information.

ADDITIONAL INFORMATION Writers can elect to take the Summer Writing Program for noncredit, graduate credit, or undergraduate credit. The registration procedure varies, so participants should consider which option they are choosing. All participants can elect to take any combination of the first, second, third, and fourth weeks. To request a catalog of upcoming programs or to find additional information, visit the website. Naropa University welcomes participants with disabilities.

TAOS SUMMER WRITERS' CONFERENCE

Department of English Language and Literature, MSC 03 2170, 1 University of New Mexico, Albuquerque NM 87131. (505)277-5572. **E-mail:** nmwriter@unm.edu. **Website:** taosconf.unm.edu. **Contact:** Sharon Oard Warner, founding director. Estab. 1999.

COSTS Week-long workshop registration: $700. Weekend workshop registration: $400. Master classes: $1,350-1,625. Publishing consultations: $175.

♋ THE UNIVERSITY OF WINCHESTER WRITERS' FESTIVAL

University of Winchester, Winchester Hampshire S022 4NR, United Kingdom. (44)(0)1962-827238. E-mail: sara.gangai@winchester.ac.uk. **Website:** www.writersfestival.co.uk. **Contact:** Sara Okaya Gangai, festival director. Estab. 1980.

COSTS See festival program.

ACCOMMODATIONS On-site student single en-suite accommodation available. Also, a range of hotels and bed and breakfasts nearby in the city.

ADDITIONAL INFORMATION Lunch, and tea/coffee/cake included in the booking cost. Dinner can be booked separately. All dietary needs catered for.

THRILLERFEST

P.O. Box 311, Eureka CA 95502. **E-mail:** kimberlyhowe@thrillerwriters.org; infocentral@thrillerwriters.org. **Website:** www.thrillerfest.com. **Contact:** Kimberley Howe, executive director. Estab. 2006.

COSTS $160-1,260, depending on which events are selected. Various package deals are available, and early bird pricing is offered beginning September of each year.

TIN HOUSE WORKSHOPS

Tin House Winter Workshops, *Tin House*, 2601 NW Thurman St., Portland OR 97210. (503)219-0622. **E-mail:** lance@tinhouse.com. **Website:** www.tinhouse.com/workshop. **Contact:** Lance Cleland. Estab. 2003.

Applications are read by a board composed of Tin House Workshop staff and previous Tin House Scholars. All applications will be read by at least three readers and acceptance is based on the strength and promise of the writing sample, as well as how much the board feels an applicant might benefit from the Workshop and contribute to the community. Scholarships are offered for both our Winter and Summer Workshops.

COSTS Winter: $25 application fee; $1,500 for program/transportation/room & board;. Payment plans are available. Summer: $25 application fee; $1,600 for tuition; $300 for room/board, $400 to audit.

ACCOMMODATIONS The Summer Workshop takes place at Reed College, located on 100 acres of rolling lawns, winding lanes, and magnificent old trees in the southeast area of Portland, Oregon, just minutes from downtown and twelve miles from the airport.

Summer Workshop participants are housed in the dormitories of Reed College near the center of campus. Unless requested, all rooms are singles, with shared bathrooms (private stalls) on each floor. ADA accessible rooms are available.

The Winter Workshops are held at the Sylvia Beach Hotel. Located in the Nye Beach district of Newport, OR, the property sits on a 45-foot bluff overlooking the Pacific, with coastal panoramas that include the famed Yaquina Head Lighthouse. A true hotel for book lovers, the Sylvia Beach Hotel offers 21 literary-themed rooms. Once registered for the workshop, your room will be assigned through a lottery.

ADDITIONAL INFORMATION Attendees must apply; all information available online.

TMCC WRITERS' CONFERENCE

Truckee Meadows Community College, 7000 Dandini Blvd., Reno NV 89512. (775)673-7111. **E-mail:** wdce@tmcc.edu. **Website:** wdce.tmcc.edu. Estab. 1991.

ACCOMMODATIONS Contact the conference manager to learn about accommodation discounts.

ADDITIONAL INFORMATION "The conference is open to all writers, regardless of their level of experience. Brochures are available online and mailed in January. Send inquiries via e-mail."

UCLA EXTENSION WRITERS' PROGRAM

11020 Kinross Ave, Kinross Building South, Los Angeles CA 90024. (310)825-9415. **Fax:** (310)206-7382. **E-mail:** writers@uclaextension.edu. **Website:** www.uclaextension.edu/writers. Estab. 1891. 10995 Le Conte Avenue, #440, Los Angeles CA 90024. (310)825-9415. **Fax:** (310)206-7382. **E-mail:** writers@uclaextension.edu. **Website:** www.uclaextension.edu/writers. **Contact:** Nutschell Windsor, program manager. Courses held year-round with 1-day or intensive weekend workshops to 12-week courses. Writers Studio held in February. 9-month master classes are also offered every fall. "The diverse offerings span introductory seminars to professional novel and script completion workshops. The annual Writers Studio and a number of 1-, 2- and 4-day intensive workshops are popular with out-of-town students due to their specific focus and the chance to work with industry professionals. The most comprehensive and diverse continuing education writing program in the country, offering over 550 courses a year, including screenwriting, fiction, writing for the youth market, poetry, nonfiction, playwriting and publishing. Adult learners in the UCLA Extension Writers' Program study with professional screenwriters, fiction writers, playwrights, poets, and nonfiction writers, who bring practical experience, theoretical knowledge, and a wide variety of teaching styles and philosophies to their classes." Site: Courses are offered in Los Angeles on the UCLA campus, in the 1010 Westwood Center in Westwood Village, at the Figueroa Courtyard in downtown Los Angeles as well as online.

COSTS Depends on length of the course.

ACCOMMODATIONS Students make their own arrangements. Out-of-town students are encouraged to take online courses.

ADDITIONAL INFORMATION Some advanced-level classes have ms submittal requirements; see the UCLA Extension catalog or visit website.

UNICORN WRITERS CONFERENCE

17 Church Hill Rd., Redding CT 06896, USA. (203)938-7405. **E-mail:** unicornwritersconference@gmail.com. **Website:** www.unicornwritersconference.com. **Contact:** Jan L. Kardys, chair. Estab. 2010.

○ "The forty pages for manuscript reviews are read in advance by your selected agents/editors, but follow the submission guidelines on the website. Check the genre chart for each agent and editor before you make your selection."

ACCOMMODATIONS Held at Reid Castle, Purchase, New York. Directions available on event website.

ADDITIONAL INFORMATION The first self-published authors will be featured on the website, and the bookstore will sell their books at the event.

UNIVERSITY OF WISCONSIN AT MADISON WRITERS INSTITUTE

21 N. Park St., Madison WI 53715. (608)265-3972. **E-mail:** laurie.scheer@wisc.edu. **Website:** uwwritersinstitute.wisc.edu. Estab. 1990.

COSTS $265-345, depending on discounts and if you attend one day or multiple days.

VERMONT STUDIO CENTER

P.O. Box 613, 80 Pearl Street, Johnson VT 05656. (802)635-2727. **Fax:** (802)635-2730. **E-mail:** info@vermontstudiocenter.org. **Website:** www.vermontstudiocenter.org. **Contact:** Gary Clark, President. Estab. 1984. P.O. Box 613, Johnson VT 05656. (802)635-2727. **Fax:** (802)635-2730. **E-mail:** info@vermontstudiocenter.org. **Website:** www.vermontstudiocenter.org. **Contact:** Gary Clark, writing program director. Estab. 1984. Ongoing residencies. Conference duration: From 2-12 weeks. Average attendance: 55 writers and visual artists/month. "The Vermont Studio Center is an international creative community located in Johnson, Vermont, and serving more than 600 American and international artists and writers each year (50 per month). A Studio Center Residency features secluded, uninterrupted writing time, the companionship of dedicated and talented peers, and access to a roster of two distinguished Visiting Writers each month. All VSC Residents receive three meals a day, private, comfortable housing and the company of an international community of painters, sculptors, poets, printmakers and writers. Writers attending residencies at the Studio Center may work on whatever they choose—no matter what month of the year they attend." Visiting writers have included Ron Carlson, Donald Revell, Jane Hirshfield, Rosanna Warren, Chris Abani, Bob Shacochis, Tony Hoagland, and Alice Notley.

COSTS The total cost of supporting an artist or writer for 4 weeks at VSC is $4,950, which includes a private bedroom, 24-hour access to a private studio space, access to our Visiting Artists and Writers program, 20 hot meals per week, and round-the-clock fresh fruit, hot and cold beverages, and breakfast cereal. No VSC resident is required to pay this cost in full. All successful applicants' residency fees are subsidized thanks to the generous support of our donors and foundation partners. The current full (subsidized) fee is $4,250* for a 4-week residency and ranges down to $0 for those who are awarded a fellowship. Financial support is available to 100% of admitted residents who request it. *We are very grateful to any residents who opt to pay this fee in full, as it allows us to offer more financial assistance to talented artists and writers who would otherwise be unable to attend our program. Generous fellowship and grant assistance is available.

ACCOMMODATIONS Accommodations available on site. "Residents live in single rooms in 10 modest, comfortable houses adjacent to the Red Mill Building. Rooms are simply furnished and have shared baths. Complete linen service is provided. The Studio Center is unable to accommodate guests at meals, overnight guests, spouses, children, or pets."

ADDITIONAL INFORMATION Fellowships application deadlines are February 15, June 15, and October 1. Writers are encouraged to visit website for more information. May also e-mail, call, fax.

WESLEYAN WRITERS CONFERENCE
Wesleyan University, 294 High St., Room 207, Middletown CT 06459. (860)685-3604. **Fax:** (860)685-2441. **E-mail:** agreene@wesleyan.edu. **Website:** www.wesleyan.edu/writing/conference. **Contact:** Anne Greene, director. Estab. 1956.

ACCOMMODATIONS Meals are provided on campus. Lodging is available on campus or in town.

ADDITIONAL INFORMATION Ms critiques are available but not required.

WHIDBEY ISLAND WRITERS' CONFERENCE
P.O. Box 1289, Langley WA 98260. (360)331-0307. **E-mail:** http://writeonwhidbey.org. **Website:** http://writeonwhidbey.org.

WILDACRES WRITERS WORKSHOP
233 S. Elm St., Greensboro NC 27401. (336)255-8210. **E-mail:** judihill@aol.com. **Website:** www.wildacreswriters.com. **Contact:** Judi Hill, director. Estab. 1985.

COSTS $850 for Workshop only; $1,300 for Workshop & Retreat. Prices include room (double)/no private rooms, meals, workshop, and all evening programs. Balance is due June 1. No exceptions. Check the website for more info.

ADDITIONAL INFORMATION Include a one-page writing sample with registration.

WILLAMETTE WRITERS CONFERENCE
5331 SW Macadam Ave.
Suite 258, PMB 215, Portland OR 97239. (971) 200-5382. **E-mail:** conf.chair@willamettewriters.org. **Website:** willamettewriters.com/wwcon/; willamettewriters.org; wilwrite@Willamettewriters.org. Estab. 1981.

COSTS Pricing schedule available online. Conference price includes breakfast, lunch, and an appetizer reception on Friday and Saturday. Workshops on Friday, Saturday, and Sunday are included — first come, first serve. No additional registration is required for workshops. You must sign up at an additional cost to participate in Master Classes and Sunday Intensives.

WINTER POETRY & PROSE GETAWAY
Murphy Writing of Stockton University, 30 Front Street, Hammonton NJ 08037, USA. (609)626-3594. **E-mail:** info@wintergetaway.com. **Website:** www.stockton.edu/wintergetaway; stockton.edu/murphy-writing. **Contact:** Amanda Murphy, Director. Estab. 1994.

COSTS See website or call for past fee information. Scholarships available.

ACCOMMODATIONS Room packages at the historic Stockton Seaview Hotel are available.

ADDITIONAL INFORMATION Previous faculty has included Julianna Baggott, Christian Bauman, Laure-Anne Bosselaar, Kurt Brown, Mark Doty (National Book Award winner), Stephen Dunn (Pulitzer Prize winner), Dorianne Laux, Carol Plum-Ucci, James Richardson, Mimi Schwartz, Terese Svoboda, and more.

WISCONSIN BOOK FESTIVAL
Madison Public Library, 201 W. Mifflin St., Madison WI 53703. (608)229-2081. **E-mail:** bookfest@mplfoundation.org. **Website:** www.wisconsinbookfestival.org. **Contact:** Conor Moran. Estab. 2002.

COSTS All festival events are free.

WISCONSIN WRITERS ASSOCIATION
Wisconsin Writers Association, Inc., WI **E-mail:** barrymwightman@gmail.com. **Website:** www.wiwrite.org. **Contact:** Barry Wightman, President. Estab. 1948. 9708 Idell Ave., Sparta WI 54656. (608)269-8541. **E-mail:** registration@wrwa.net. **Website:** www.wrwa.net. **Contact:** Nate Scholze, Fall Conference Coordinator; Roxanne Aehl, Spring Conference Coordinator. Estab. 1948. Annual. Conferences held in May and September "are dedicated to self-improvement through speakers, workshops and presentations. Topics and speakers vary with each event." Average attendance: 100-150. "We honor all genres of writing. Fall conference is a two-day event featuring the Jade Ring Banquet and awards for six genre categories. Spring conference is a one-day event."

COSTS $80-100.

ACCOMMODATIONS Rooms available at the host conference center.

WOMEN WRITERS WINTER RETREAT

Steele Mansion B&B, 348 Mentor Avenue, Painesville OH 44077. (440)463-4633. **E-mail:** deencr@aol.com. **Website:** www.deannaadams.com. Estab. 2007.

COSTS Visit website for details.

WORDHARVEST WEBINARS FOR WRITERS

1063 Willow Way, Santa Fe NM 87507. (505)795-1590. **E-mail:** wordharvest@wordharvest.com. **Website:** www.wordharvest.com. **Contact:** Anne Hillerman and Jean Schaumberg, cofounders. Estab. 2004.

COSTS Check website for current pricing.

WRITEAWAYS

Durham NC **E-mail:** writeawaysinfo@gmail.com. **Website:** https://www.writeaways.com. **Contact:** Mimi Herman. Estab. 2013.

COSTS North Carolina workshop: Price TBA (check web site for the latest information). France and Italy: $2,350 single room, $2,100 shared rooms. The Grand Tour (France and Italy): $4,200 each single room, $4,000 each shared room.

ACCOMMODATIONS North Carolina: The Whitehall, Camden, North Carolina. France: Chateau du Pin, near Champtocé-sur Loire (18 miles west of Angers). Italy: Villas Cini and Casanova, near Bucine, between Siena and Arezzo.

🐚 WRITE IT OUT

P.O. Box 704, Sarasota FL 34230. (941)359-3824. **E-mail:** rmillerwio@gmaill.com. **Website:** www.writeitout.com. **Contact:** Ronni Miller, director. Estab. 1997.

COSTS Costs vary by workshop.

ADDITIONAL INFORMATION Conference information available year round. For brochures/guidelines e-mail, call, or visit website. Accepts inquiries by phone, e-mail.

WRITE ON THE RIVER

8941 Kelsey Lane, Knoxville TN 37922. **E-mail:** bob@bobmayer.org. **Website:** www.bobmayer.org. **Contact:** Bob Mayer. Estab. 2002.

COSTS Varies; depends on venue. Please see website for any updates.

ADDITIONAL INFORMATION Limited to 4 participants, and focused on their novel and marketability.

WRITE ON THE SOUND

WOTS, City of Edmonds Arts Commission, Frances Anderson Center, 700 Main St., Edmonds WA 98020. (425)771-0228. **E-mail:** wots@edmondswa.gov. **Website:** www.writeonthesound.com. **Contact:** Laurie Rose, Conference Organizer or Frances Chapin, Edmonds Arts Commission Mgr. Estab. 1985.

🗨 Past attendee says, "I came away from every session with ideas to incorporate into my own writer's toolbox. The energy was wonderful because everyone was there for a single purpose: to make the most of a weekend for writers, whatever the level of expertise. I can't thank all the organizers, presenters, and volunteers enough for a wonderful experience."

COSTS $90-300 (not including optional fees).

ACCOMMODATIONS Best Western Plus/Edmonds Harbor Inn is a conference partner.

ADDITIONAL INFORMATION Schedule posted on website late spring/early summer. Registration opens mid-July. Attendees are required to select the sessions when they register. Wait lists for conference and manuscript appointments are available.

WRITER'S DIGEST ANNUAL CONFERENCE

Active Interest Media, Inc., 5720 Flatiron Pkwy., Boulder CO 80301. **E-mail:** writersdigestconference@aimmedia.com. **Website:** www.writersdigestconference.com. **Contact:** Taylor Sferra. Estab. 1995.

COSTS Cost varies by location and year. There are typically different pricing options for those who wish attend the pitch slam and those who just want to attend the conference education.

ACCOMMODATIONS A block of rooms at the event hotel is reserved for guests. See the travel page on the website for more information.

WRITERS IN PARADISE

Eckerd College, 4200 54th Ave. S., St. Petersburg FL 33711. (727)386-2264. **E-mail:** wip@eckerd.edu. **Website:** writersinparadise.com. Estab. 2005.

COSTS See website for cost information.

ADDITIONAL INFORMATION Application materials are due in November and required of all attendees.

WRITERS OMI AT LEDIG HOUSE

55 Fifth Ave., 15th Floor, New York NY 10003. (212)206-6114. **E-mail:** writers@artomi.org. **Website:** www.artomi.org.

ACCOMMODATIONS Residents provide their own transportation. Offers overnight accommodations.

ADDITIONAL INFORMATION "Agents and editors from the New York publishing community are invited for dinner and discussion. Bicycles, a swimming pool, and nearby tennis court are available for use."

WRITERS STUDIO AT UCLA EXTENSION

1010 Westwood Blvd., Los Angeles CA 90024. (310)825-9415. **E-mail:** writers@uclaextension.edu. **Website:** writers.uclaextension.edu/programs-services/writers-studio. **Contact:** Katy Flaherty. Estab. 1997.

ADDITIONAL INFORMATION For more information, call or e-mail.

THE WRITERS' WORKSHOP

THE RENBOURNE EDITORIAL AGENCY, 387 Beaucatcher Rd., Asheville NC 28805. (828)254-8111. **E-mail:** writersw@gmail.com. **Website:** www.twwoa.org. Estab. 1985.

○ "We have exceptional editors on hand to finetune your work for publication. We do it all—content, line, and copy editing—with a fine-tooth comb. We accept most genres, and we specialize in novels, memoirs, and creative nonfiction."

COSTS For editorial services: usually $4 per page (double spaced) for a thorough editing, or $3 per page for a read-through and revision suggestions.

ADDITIONAL INFORMATION Also sponsors annual contests in poetry, literary fiction, memoirs, and essay. For guidelines, see website.

WRITE-TO-PUBLISH CONFERENCE

WordPro Communication Services, 9118 W. Elmwood Dr., Suite 1G, Niles IL 60714. (847)296-3964. **E-mail:** lin@writetopublish.com. **Website:** www.writetopublish.com. **Contact:** Lin Johnson, director. Estab. 1971.

COSTS See the website for current costs.

ACCOMMODATIONS Campus residence hall rooms available. See the website for current information and costs.

ADDITIONAL INFORMATION Conference information available in late January or early February. For details, visit website, or email brochure@writetopublish.com. Accepts inquiries by e-mail, phone.

WRITING AND ILLUSTRATING FOR YOUNG READERS CONFERENCE

1480 E. 9400 S., Sandy UT 84093. **E-mail:** staff@wifyr.com. **Website:** www.wifyr.com. Estab. 2000. BYU, conferences and workshops, 348 HCEB, BYU, Provo UT 84602-1532. (801)422-2568. **Fax:** (801)422-0745. **E-mail:** cw348@byu.edu. **Website:** http://wifyr.byu.edu. **Contact:** Conferences & Workshops. Estab. 2000. Annual. 5-day workshop held in June of each year. The workshop is designed for people who want to write or illustrate for children or teenagers. Participants focus on a single market during daily 4-hour morning writing workshops led by published authors or illustrators. Afternoon workshop sessions include a mingle with the authors, editors, and agents. Workshop focuses on fiction for young readers: picture books, book-length fiction, fantasy/science fiction, nonfiction, mystery, illustration, and general writing. Site: Conference Center at Brigham Young University in the foothills of the Wasatch Mountain range.

○ Guidelines and registration are on the website.

ACCOMMODATIONS A block of rooms is available at the Best Western Cotton Tree Inn in Sandy, UT, at a discounted rate. This rate is good as long as there are available rooms.

ADDITIONAL INFORMATION There is an online form to contact this event.

WRITING FOR THE SOUL

Jerry B. Jenkins Christian Writers Guild, P.O. Box 88288, Black Forest CO 80908. (866)495-7551. **Fax:** (719)494-1299. **E-mail:** jerry@jerryjenkins.com. **Website:** www.jerryjenkins.com.

THE HELENE WURLITZER FOUNDATION

P.O. Box 1891, Taos NM 87571. (575)758-2413. **Fax:** (575)758-2559. **E-mail:** hwf@taosnet.com. **Website:** www.wurlitzerfoundation.org. **Contact:** Nic Knight, executive director. Estab. 1954.

ACCOMMODATIONS Provides individual housing in fully furnished studios/houses (casitas), rent- and utility-free. Artists are responsible for transportation to and from Taos, their meals, and materials for their work. Bicycles are provided upon request.

GLOSSARY

ADVANCE. Payment by a publisher to an author prior to the publication of a book, to be deducted from the author's future royalties.

ADVENTURE STORY. A genre of fiction in which action is the key element, overshadowing characters, theme, and setting. The conflict in an adventure story is often man against nature. A secondary plot that reinforces this kind of conflict is sometimes included.

ALL RIGHTS. The rights contracted to a publisher permitting a manuscript's use anywhere and in any form without additional payment to the writer.

AMATEUR SLEUTH. The character in a mystery, usually the protagonist, who does the detection but is not a professional private investigator or police detective.

ANTHOLOGY. A collection of selected writings by various authors.

ASSOCIATION OF AUTHORS' REPRESENTATIVES (AAR). An organization for literary agents committed to maintaining excellence in literary representation.

AUCTION. Publishers sometimes bid against each other for the acquisition of a manuscript that has excellent sales prospects.

BACKLIST. A publisher's books not published during the current season but still in print.

BIOGRAPHICAL NOVEL. A life story documented in history and transformed into fiction through the insight and imagination of the writer. This type of novel melds the elements of biographical research and historical truth into the framework of a novel, complete with dialogue, drama, and mood. A biographical novel resembles historical fiction, save for one aspect: Characters in a historical novel may be fabricated and then placed into an authentic setting; characters in a biographical novel have actually lived.

BOOK PRODUCER/PACKAGER. An organization that may develop a book for a publisher based upon the publisher's idea or may plan all elements of a book, from its initial concept to writing and marketing strategies, and then sell the package to a book publisher and/or movie producer.

CLIFFHANGER. Fictional event in which the reader is left in suspense at the end of a chapter or episode, so that interest in the story's outcome will be sustained.

CLIP. Sample, usually from a newspaper or magazine, of a writer's published work.

CLOAK-AND-DAGGER. A melodramatic, romantic type of fiction dealing with espionage and intrigue.

COMMERCIAL. Publishers whose concern is salability, profit, and success with a large readership.

CONTEMPORARY. Material dealing with popular current trends, themes, or topics.

CONTRIBUTOR'S COPY. Copy of an issue of a magazine or published book sent to an author whose work is included.

CO-PUBLISHING. An arrangement in which the author and publisher share costs and profits.

COPYEDITING. Editing a manuscript for writing style, grammar, punctuation and factual accuracy.

COPYRIGHT. The legal right to exclusive publication, sale, or distribution of a literary work.

COVER LETTER. A brief letter sent with a complete manuscript submitted to an editor.

"COZY" (OR "TEACUP") MYSTERY. Mystery usually set in a small British town, in a bygone era, featuring a somewhat genteel, intellectual protagonist.

ELECTRONIC RIGHTS. The right to publish material electronically, either in book or short story form.

ELECTRONIC SUBMISSION. A submission of material by e-mail or on computer disk.

ETHNIC FICTION. Stories whose central characters are black, Native American, Italian-American, Jewish, Appalachian, or members of some other specific cultural group.

EXPERIMENTAL FICTION. Fiction that is innovative in subject matter and style; avant-garde, non-formulaic, usually literary material.

EXPOSITION. The portion of the story line, usually the beginning, where background information about character and setting is related.

E-ZINE. A magazine that is published electronically.

FAIR USE. A provision in the copyright law that says short passages from copyrighted material may be used without infringing on the owner's rights.

FANTASY (TRADITIONAL). Fantasy with an emphasis on magic, using characters with the ability to practice magic, such as wizards, witches, dragons, elves, and unicorns.

FANZINE. A noncommercial, small-circulation magazine usually dealing with fantasy, horror or science-fiction literature and art.

FIRST NORTH AMERICAN SERIAL RIGHTS. The right to publish material in a periodical before it appears in book form, for the first time, in the United States or Canada.

FLASH FICTION. *See* short short story.

GALLEY PROOF. The first typeset version of a manuscript that has not yet been divided into pages.

GENRE. A formulaic type of fiction such as romance, western, or horror.

GOTHIC. This type of category fiction dates back to the late eighteenth and early nineteenth centuries. Contemporary gothic novels are characterized by atmospheric, historical settings and feature young, beautiful women who win the favor of handsome, brooding heroes—simultaneously dealing successfully with some life-threatening menace, either natural or supernatural. Gothics rely on mystery, peril, romantic relationships, and a sense of foreboding for their strong, emotional effect on the reader. A classic early gothic novel is Emily Brontë's *Wuthering Heights*.

GRAPHIC NOVEL. A book (original or adapted) that takes the form of a long comic strip or heavily illustrated story of forty pages or more, produced in paperback. Though called a novel, these can also be works of nonfiction.

HARD-BOILED DETECTIVE NOVEL. Mystery novel featuring a private eye or police detective as the protagonist; usually involves a murder. The emphasis is on the details of the crime, and the tough, unsentimental protagonist usually takes a matter-of-fact attitude toward violence.

HARD SCIENCE FICTION. Science fiction with an emphasis on science and technology.

HIGH FANTASY. Fantasy with a medieval setting and a heavy emphasis on chivalry and the quest.

HISTORICAL FICTION. A fictional story set in a recognizable period of history. As well as telling the stories of ordinary people's lives, historical fiction may involve political or social events of the time.

HORROR. Howard Phillips (H.P.) Lovecraft, generally acknowledged to be the master of the horror tale in the twentieth century and the most important American writer of this genre since Edgar Allan Poe, distinguishes horror literature from fiction based entirely on physical fear and the merely gruesome. It is that atmosphere—the creation of a particular sensation or emotional level—that, according to Lovecraft, is the most important element in the creation of horror literature. Contemporary writers enjoying considerable success in horror fiction include Stephen King, Robert Bloch, Peter Straub, and Dean Koontz.

HYPERTEXT FICTION. A fictional form, read electronically, that incorporates traditional elements of storytelling with a nonlinear plot line, in which the reader determines the direction of the story by opting for one of many author-supplied links.

IMPRINT. Name applied to a publisher's specific line (e.g., Owl, an imprint of Henry Holt).

INTERACTIVE FICTION. Fiction in book or computer-software format where the reader determines the path the story will take by choosing from several alternatives at the end of each chapter or episode.

INTERNATIONAL REPLY COUPON (IRC). A form purchased at a post office and enclosed with a letter or manuscript to an international publisher, to cover return postage costs.

JUVENILES, WRITING FOR. This includes works intended for an audience usually between the ages of two and eighteen. Categories of children's books are usually divided in this way: (1) picture books and storybooks (ages two to eight); (2) young readers or easy-to-read books (ages five to eight); (3) middle readers or middle grade (ages nine to eleven); (4) young adult books (ages twelve and up).

LIBEL. Written or printed words that defame, malign, or damagingly misrepresent a living person.

LITERARY AGENT. A person who acts for an author in finding a publisher or arranging contract terms on a literary project.

LITERARY FICTION. The general category of fiction that employs more sophisticated technique, driven as much or more by character evolution than action in the plot.

MAINSTREAM FICTION. Fiction that appeals to a more general reading audience, versus literary or genre fiction. Mainstream is more plot-driven than literary fiction and less formulaic than genre fiction.

MALICE DOMESTIC NOVEL. A mystery featuring a murder among family members, such as the murder of a spouse or a parent.

MANUSCRIPT. The author's unpublished copy of a work, usually typewritten, used as the basis for typesetting.

MASS MARKET PAPERBACK. Softcover book on a popular subject directed to a general audience and sold in drugstores and groceries as well as in bookstores.

MIDDLE READER. Also called *middle grade*. Juvenile fiction for readers aged nine to eleven.

MS(S). Abbreviation for *manuscript(s)*.

MULTIPLE SUBMISSION. Submission of more than one short story at a time to the same editor. *Do not make a multiple submission unless requested.*

MYSTERY. A form of narration in which one or more elements remain unknown or unexplained until the end of the story. The modern mystery story contains elements of the mainstream novel: a convincing account of a character's struggle with various physical and psychological obstacles in an effort to achieve his goal, good characterization, and sound motivation.

NARRATION. The account of events in a story's plot as related by the speaker or the voice of the author.

NARRATOR. The person who tells the story, either someone involved in the action or the voice of the writer.

NEW AGE. A term including categories such as astrology, psychic phenomena, spiritual healing, UFOs, mysticism, and other aspects of the occult.

NOIR. A style of mystery involving hard-boiled detectives and bleak settings.

NOM DE PLUME. French for "pen name"; a pseudonym.

NONFICTION NOVEL. A work in which real events and people are written [about] in novel form, but are not camouflaged, as they are in the roman à clef.

NOVELLA (ALSO NOVELETTE). A short novel or long story, approximately 20,000–50,000 words.

#10 ENVELOPE. 4" × 9½" envelope, used for queries and other business letters.

OFFPRINT. Copy of a story taken from a magazine before it is bound.

ONETIME RIGHTS. Permission to publish a story in periodical or book form one time only.

OUTLINE. A summary of a book's contents, often in the form of chapter headings with a few sentences outlining the action of the story under each one; sometimes part of a book proposal.

OVER THE TRANSOM. A phrase referring to unsolicited manuscripts, or those that come in "over the transom."

PAYMENT ON ACCEPTANCE. Payment from the magazine or publishing house as soon as the decision to print a manuscript is made.

PAYMENT ON PUBLICATION. Payment from the publisher after a manuscript is printed.

PEN NAME. A pseudonym used to conceal a writer's real name.

PERIODICAL. A magazine or journal published at regular intervals.

PLOT. The carefully devised series of events through which the characters progress in a work of fiction.

POPULAR FICTION. Generally, a synonym for category or genre fiction; i.e., fiction intended to appeal to audiences for certain kinds of novels. Popular, or category, fiction is defined as such primarily for the convenience of publishers, editors, reviewers, and booksellers who must identify novels of different areas of interest for potential readers.

PRINT ON DEMAND (POD). Novels produced digitally one at a time, as ordered.

PROOFREADING. Close reading and correction of a manuscript's typographical errors.

PROOFS. A typeset version of a manuscript used for correcting errors and making changes, often a photocopy of the galleys.

PROPOSAL. An offer to write a specific work, usually consisting of an outline of the work and one or two completed chapters.

PROTAGONIST. The principal or leading character in a literary work.

PSYCHOLOGICAL NOVEL. A narrative that emphasizes the mental and emotional aspects of its characters, focusing on motivations and mental activities rather than on exterior events. The psychological novelist is less concerned about relating what happened than about exploring why it happened. The term is most often used to describe twentieth-century works that employ techniques such as interior monologue and stream of consciousness. Two examples of contemporary psychological novels are Judith Guest's *Ordinary People* and Mary Gordon's *The Company of Women*.

PUBLIC DOMAIN. Material that either was never copyrighted or whose copyright term has expired.

PULP MAGAZINE. A periodical printed on inexpensive paper, usually containing lurid, sensational stories or articles.

QUERY. A letter written to an editor to elicit interest in a story the writer wants to submit.

READER. A person hired by a publisher to read unsolicited manuscripts.

READING FEE. An arbitrary amount of money charged by some agents and publishers to read a submitted manuscript.

REGENCY ROMANCE. A subgenre of romance, usually set in England between 1811 and 1820.

REMAINDERS. Leftover copies of an out-of-print book, sold by the publisher at a reduced price.

REPORTING TIME. The number of weeks or months it takes an editor to report back on an author's query or manuscript.

REPRINT RIGHTS. Permission to print an already published work whose rights have been sold to another magazine or book publisher.

ROMAN À CLEF. French "novel with a key." A novel that represents actual living or historical characters and events in fictionalized form.

ROMANCE NOVEL. A type of category fiction in which the love relationship between a man and a woman pervades the plot. The story is often told from the viewpoint of the heroine, who meets a man (the hero), falls in love with him, encounters a conflict that hinders their relationship, then resolves the conflict. Romance is the overriding element in this kind of story: The couple's relationship determines the plot and tone of the book.

ROYALTIES. A percentage of the retail price paid to an author for each copy of the book that is sold.

SASE. Self-addressed stamped envelope.

SCIENCE FICTION (VS. FANTASY). It is generally accepted that, to be science fiction, a story must have elements of science in either the conflict or setting (usually both). Fantasy, on the other hand, rarely utilizes science, relying instead on magic, mythological and neo-mythological beings, and devices and outright invention for conflict and setting.

SECOND SERIAL (REPRINT) RIGHTS. Permission for the reprinting of a work in another periodical after its first publication in book or magazine form.

SELF-PUBLISHING. In this arrangement, the author keeps all income derived from the book, but he pays for its manufacturing, production, and marketing.

SERIAL RIGHTS. The rights given by an author to a publisher to print a piece in one or more periodicals.

SERIALIZED NOVEL. A book-length work of fiction published in sequential issues of a periodical.

SETTING. The environment and time period during which the action of a story takes place.

SHORT SHORT STORY. A condensed piece of fiction, usually under 1,000 words.

SIMULTANEOUS SUBMISSION. The practice of sending copies of the same manuscript to several editors or publishers at the same time. Some editors refuse to consider such submissions.

SLANT. A story's particular approach or style, designed to appeal to the readers of a specific magazine.

SLICE OF LIFE. A presentation of characters in a seemingly mundane situation that offers the reader a flash of illumination about the characters or their situation.

SLUSH PILE. A stack of unsolicited manuscripts in the editorial offices of a publisher.

SOCIAL FICTION. Fiction written with the purpose of bringing positive changes in society.

SOFT/SOCIOLOGICAL SCIENCE FICTION. Science fiction with an emphasis on society and culture versus scientific accuracy.

SPACE OPERA. Epic science fiction with an emphasis on good guys versus bad guys.

SPECULATION (OR SPEC). An editor's agreement to look at an author's manuscript with no promise to purchase.

SPECULATIVE FICTION (SPECFIC). The all-inclusive term for science fiction, fantasy, and horror.

SUBSIDIARY. An incorporated branch of a company or conglomerate (e.g., Alfred Knopf, Inc., a subsidiary of Random House, Inc.).

SUBSIDIARY RIGHTS. All rights other than book publishing rights included in a book contract, such as paperback, book club, and movie rights.

SUBSIDY PUBLISHER. A book publisher who charges the author for the cost of typesetting, printing, and promoting a book. Also called a *vanity publisher*.

SUBTERFICIAL FICTION. Innovative, challenging, nonconventional fiction in which what seems to be happening is the result of things not so easily perceived.

SUSPENSE. A genre of fiction where the plot's primary function is to build a feeling of anticipation and fear in the reader over its possible outcome.

SYNOPSIS. A brief summary of a story, novel or play. As part of a book proposal, it is a comprehensive summary condensed in a page or page and a half.

TABLOID. Publication printed on paper about half the size of a regular newspaper page (e.g., the *National Enquirer*).

TEARSHEET. Page from a magazine containing a published story.

THEME. The dominant or central idea in a literary work; its message, moral, or main thread.

THRILLER. A novel intended to arouse feelings of excitement or suspense. Works in this genre are highly sensational, usually focusing on illegal activities, international espionage, sex, and violence. A thriller is often a detective story in which the forces of good are pitted against the forces of evil in a kill-or-be-killed situation.

TRADE PAPERBACK. A softbound volume, usually around 5" × 8", published and designed for the general public, available mainly in bookstores.

UNSOLICITED MANUSCRIPT. A story or novel manuscript that an editor did not specifically ask to see.

URBAN FANTASY. Fantasy that takes magical characters, such as elves, fairies, vampires, or wizards, and places them in modern-day settings, often in the inner city.

VANITY PUBLISHER. See subsidy publisher.

VIEWPOINT. The position or attitude of the first- or third-person narrator or multiple narrators, which determines how a story's action is seen and evaluated.

WESTERN. Genre with a setting in the West, usually between 1860 and 1890, with a formula plot about cowboys or other aspects of frontier life.

WHODUNIT. Genre dealing with murder, suspense, and the detection of criminals.

WORK-FOR-HIRE. Work that another party commissions you to do, generally for a flat fee. The creator does not own the copyright and therefore cannot sell any rights.

YOUNG ADULT (YA). The general classification of books written for readers twelve and up.

ZINE. A small, noncommercial magazine, often one- or two-person operations run from the home of the publisher/editor. Themes tend to be specialized, personal, experimental, and often controversial.

GENRE GLOSSARY

Definitions of Fiction Subcategories

///

The following were provided courtesy of The Extended Novel Writing Workshop, created by the staff of Writers Online Workshops (www.writersonlineworkshops.com).

MYSTERY SUBCATEGORIES

The major mystery subcategories are listed below, each followed by a brief description and the names of representative authors, so you can sample each type of work. Note that we have loosely classified "suspense/thriller" as a mystery category. While these stories do not necessarily follow a traditional "whodunit" plot pattern, they share many elements with other mystery categories.

AMATEUR DETECTIVE. As the name implies, the detective is not a professional detective (private or otherwise), but is almost always a professional something. This professional association routinely involves the protagonist in criminal cases (in a support capacity), gives him or her a special advantage in a specific case, or provides the contacts and skills necessary to solve a particular crime. (Jonathan Kellerman, Patricia Cornwell, Jan Burke)

CLASSIC MYSTERY (WHODUNIT). A crime (almost always a murder) is solved. The detective is the viewpoint character; the reader never knows any more or less about the crime than the detective, and all the clues to solving the crime are available to the reader.

COURTROOM DRAMA. The action takes place primarily in the courtroom; protagonist is generally a defense attorney out to prove the innocence of his or her client by finding the real culprit.

COZY. A special class of the amateur detective category that frequently features a female protagonist. (Agatha Christie's Miss Marple stories are the classic example.) There is less onstage violence than in other categories, and the plot is often wrapped up in a final scene where the detective identifies the murderer and explains how the crime was solved. In contemporary stories, the protagonist can be anyone from a chronically curious housewife to a mystery-buff clergyman to a college professor, but he or she is usually quirky, even eccentric. (Susan Isaacs, Andrew Greeley, Lillian Jackson Braun)

ESPIONAGE. The international spy novel is less popular since the end of the Cold War, but stories can still revolve around political intrigue in unstable regions. (John le Carré, Ken Follett)

HEISTS AND CAPERS. The crime itself is the focus. Its planning and execution are seen in detail, and the participants are fully drawn characters that may even be portrayed sympathetically. One character is the obvious leader of the group (the "brains"); the other members are often brought together by the leader specifically for this job and may or may not have a previous association. In a heist, no matter how clever or daring the characters are, they are still portrayed as criminals, and the expectation is that they will be caught and punished (but not always). A caper is more lighthearted, even comedic. The participants may have a noble goal (something other than personal gain) and often get away with the crime. (Eric Ambler, Tony Kenrick, Leslie Hollander)

HISTORICAL. May be any category or subcategory of mystery, but with an emphasis on setting, the details of which must be diligently researched. But beyond the historical details (which must never overshadow the story), the plot develops along the lines of its contemporary counterpart. (Candace Robb, Caleb Carr, Anne Perry)

JUVENILE/YOUNG ADULT. Written for the 8–12 age group (middle grade) or the 12 and up age group (young adult), the crime in these stories may or may not be murder, but it is serious. The protagonist is a kid (or group of kids) in the same age range as the targeted reader. There is no graphic violence depicted, but the stories are scary and the villains are realistic. (Mary Downing Hahn, Wendy Corsi Staub, Cameron Dokey, Norma Fox Mazer)

MEDICAL THRILLER. The plot can involve a legitimate medical threat (such as the outbreak of a virulent plague) or the illegal or immoral use of medical technology. In the former scenario, the protagonist is likely to be the doctor (or team) who identifies the virus and procures the antidote; in the latter he or she could be a patient (or the relative of a victim) who uncovers the plot and brings down the villain. (Robin Cook, Michael Palmer, Michael Crichton, Stanley Pottinger)

POLICE PROCEDURALS. The most realistic category, these stories require the most meticulous research. A police procedural may have more than one protagonist since cops rarely work alone. Conflict between partners, or between the detective and his or her superiors, is a common theme. But cops are portrayed positively as a group, even though there may be a couple of bad or ineffective law enforcement characters for contrast and conflict. Jurisdictional disputes are still popular sources of conflict as well. (Lawrence Treat, Joseph Wambaugh, Ridley Pearson, Julie Smith)

PRIVATE DETECTIVE. When described as "hard-boiled," this category takes a tough stance. Violence is more prominent, characters are darker, the detective—while almost always licensed by the state—operates on the fringes of the law, and there is often open resentment between the detective and law enforcement. More "enlightened" male detectives and a crop of contemporary females have brought about new trends in this category. (For female P.I.s: Sue Grafton, Sara Paretsky; for male P.I.s: John D. MacDonald, Lawrence Sanders)

SUSPENSE/THRILLER. Where a classic mystery is always a whodunit, a suspense/thriller novel may deal more with the intricacies of the crime, what motivated it, and how the villain (whose identity may be revealed to the reader early on) is caught and brought to justice. Novels in this category frequently employ multiple points of view and have broader scopes than more traditional murder mysteries. The crime may not even involve murder—it may be a threat to global economy or regional ecology; it may be technology run amok or abused at the hands of an unscrupulous scientist; it may involve innocent citizens victimized for personal or corporate gain. Its perpetrators are kidnappers, stalkers, serial killers, rapists, pedophiles, computer hackers, or just about anyone with an evil intention and the means to carry it out. The protagonist may be a private detective or law enforcement official, but is just as likely to be a doctor, lawyer, military officer, or other individual in a unique position to identify the villain and bring him or her to justice. (James Patterson, John J. Nance)

TECHNO-THRILLER. These are replacing the traditional espionage novel and feature technology as an integral part of not just the setting but the plot as well.

WOMAN IN JEOPARDY. A murder or other crime may be committed, but the focus is on the woman (and/or her children) currently at risk, her struggle to understand the nature of the danger, and her eventual victory over her tormentor. The protagonist makes up for her lack of physical prowess with intellect or special skills and solves the problem on her own or with the help of her family (but she runs the show). Closely related to this category is romantic suspense. But, while the heroine in a romantic suspense is certainly a "woman in jeopardy,"' the mystery or suspense element is subordinate to the romance. (Mary Higgins Clark, Mary Stewart, Jessica Mann)

ROMANCE SUBCATEGORIES

These categories and subcategories of romance fiction have been culled from the *Romance Writer's Sourcebook* (Writer's Digest Books) and Phyllis Taylor Pianka's *How to Write Romances* (Writer's Digest Books). We've arranged the "major" categories below, with the subcategories beneath them, each followed by a brief description and the names of authors who write in each category, so you can sample representative works.

CATEGORY OR SERIES. These are published in "lines" by individual publishing houses (such as Harlequin); each line has its own requirements as to word length, story content, and amount of sex. (Debbie Macomber, Nora Roberts, Glenda Sanders)

CHRISTIAN. With an inspirational Christian message centering on the spiritual dynamic of the romantic relationship and faith in God as the foundation for that relationship; sensuality is played down. (Janelle Burnham, Ann Bell, Linda Chaikin, Catherine Palmer, Dee Henderson, Lisa Tawn Bergen)

GLITZ. So called because they feature generally wealthy characters with high-powered positions in careers that are considered glamorous—high finance, modeling/acting, publishing, fashion—and are set in exciting or exotic (often metropolitan) locales, such as Monte Carlo, Hollywood, London, or New York. (Jackie Collins, Judith Krantz)

HISTORICAL. Can cover just about any historical (or even prehistorical) period. Setting in the historical is especially significant, and details must be thoroughly researched and accurately presented. For a sampling of a variety of historical styles, try Laura Kinsell (*Flowers from the Storm*), Mary Jo Putney (*The Rake and the Reformer*), and Judy Cuevas (*Bliss*). Some currently popular periods/themes in historicals are:

- **GOTHIC:** Historical with a strong element of suspense and a feeling of supernatural events, although these events frequently have a natural explanation. Setting plays an important role in establishing a dark, moody, suspenseful atmosphere. (Phyllis Whitney, Victoria Holt)
- **HISTORICAL FANTASY:** With traditional fantasy elements of magic and magical beings, frequently set in a medieval society. (Amanda Glass, Jayne Ann Krentz, Kathleen Morgan, Jessica Bryan, Taylor Quinn Evans, Carla Simpson, Karyn Monk)
- **EARLY AMERICAN:** Usually Revolution to Civil War, set in New England or the South, but "frontier" stories set in the American West are quite popular as well. (Robin Lee Hatcher, Ann Maxwell, Heather Graham)
- **NATIVE AMERICAN:** Where one or both of the characters are Native Americans; the conflict between cultures is a popular theme. (Carol Finch, Elizabeth Grayson, Karen Kay, Kathleen Harrington, Genell Dellim, Candace McCarthy)
- **REGENCY:** Set in England during the Regency period from 1811 to 1820. (Carol Finch, Elizabeth Elliott, Georgette Heyer, Joan Johnston, Lynn Collum)

MULTICULTURAL. Most currently feature African-American or Hispanic couples, but editors are looking for other ethnic stories as well. Multiculturals can be contemporary or historical and fall into any subcategory. (Rochelle Alers, Monica Jackson, Bette Ford, Sandra Kitt, Brenda Jackson)

PARANORMAL. Containing elements of the supernatural or science fiction/fantasy. There are numerous subcategories (many stories combine elements of more than one) including:

- **TIME TRAVEL:** One or more of the characters travels to another time—usually the past—to find love. (Jude Deveraux, Linda Lael Miller, Diana Gabaldon, Constance O'Day-Flannery)
- **SCIENCE FICTION/FUTURISTIC:** S/F elements are used for the story's setting: imaginary worlds, parallel universes, Earth in the near or distant future. (Marilyn Campbell, Jayne Ann Krentz, J.D. Robb [Nora Roberts], Anne Avery)
- **CONTEMPORARY FANTASY:** From modern ghost and vampire stories to "New Age" themes such as extraterrestrials and reincarnation. (Linda Lael Miller, Anne Stuart, Antoinette Stockenberg, Christine Feehan)

ROMANTIC COMEDY. Has a fairly strong comic premise and/or a comic perspective in the author's voice or the voices of the characters (especially the heroine). (Jennifer Crusie, Susan Elizabeth Phillips)

ROMANTIC SUSPENSE. With a mystery or psychological thriller subplot in addition to the romance plot. (Mary Stewart, Barbara Michaels, Tami Hoag, Nora Roberts, Linda Howard, Catherine Coulter)

SINGLE TITLE. Longer contemporaries that do not necessarily conform to the requirements of a specific romance line and therefore feature more complex plots and nontraditional characters. (Mary Ruth Myers, Nora Roberts, Kathleen Gilles Seidel, Kathleen Korbel)

YOUNG ADULT (YA). Focus is on first love with very little, if any, sex. These can have bittersweet endings, as opposed to the traditional romance happy ending, since first loves are often lost loves. (YA historical: Nancy Covert Smith, Louise Vernon; YA contemporary: Kathryn Makris)

SCIENCE FICTION SUBCATEGORIES

Peter Heck, in his article "Doors to Other Worlds: Trends in Science Fiction and Fantasy," which appears in the 1996 edition of *Science Fiction and Fantasy Writer's Sourcebook* (Writer's Digest Books), identifies some science fiction trends that have distinct enough characteristics to be defined as categories. These distinctions are frequently the result of marketing decisions as much as literary ones, so understanding them is important in deciding where your novel idea belongs. We've supplied a brief description and the names of authors who write in each category. In those instances where the author writes in more than one category, we've included titles of appropriate representative works.

ALTERNATE HISTORY. Fantasy, sometimes with science fiction elements, that changes the accepted account of actual historical events or people to suggest an alternate view of history. (Ted Mooney, *Traffic and Laughter*; Ward Moore, *Bring the Jubilee*; Philip K. Dick, *The Man in the High Castle*)

CYBERPUNK. Characters in these stories are tough outsiders in a high-tech, generally near-future society where computers have produced major changes in the way society functions. (William Gibson, Bruce Sterling, Pat Cadigan, Wilhelmina Baird)

HARD SCIENCE FICTION. Based on the logical extrapolation of real science to the future. In these stories the scientific background (setting) may be as, or more, important than the characters. (Larry Niven)

MILITARY SCIENCE FICTION. Stories about war that feature traditional military organization and tactics extrapolated into the future. (Jerry Pournelle, David Drake, Elizabeth Moon)

NEW AGE. A category of speculative fiction that deals with subjects such as astrology, psychic phenomena, spiritual healing, UFOs, mysticism, and other aspects of the occult. (Walter Mosley, *Blue Light*; Neil Gaiman)

SCIENCE FANTASY. Blend of traditional fantasy elements with scientific or pseudoscientific support (genetic engineering, for example, to "explain" a traditional fantasy creature like the dragon). These stories are traditionally more character driven than hard science fiction. (Anne McCaffrey, Mercedes Lackey, Marion Zimmer Bradley)

SCIENCE FICTION MYSTERY. A cross-genre blending that can either be a more-or-less traditional science fiction story with a mystery as a key plot element, or a more-or-less traditional whodunit with science fiction elements. (Philip K. Dick, Lynn S. Hightower)

SCIENCE FICTION ROMANCE. Another genre blend that may be a romance with science fiction elements (in which case it is more accurately placed as a subcategory within the romance genre) or a science fiction story with a strong romantic subplot. (Anne McCaffrey, Melanie Rawn, Kate Elliott)

SOCIAL SCIENCE FICTION. The focus is on how the characters react to their environments. This category includes social satire. (George Orwell's *1984* is a classic example.) (Margaret Atwood, *The Handmaid's Tale*; Ursula K. Le Guin, *The Left Hand of Darkness*; Marge Piercy, *Woman on the Edge of Time*)

SPACE OPERA. From the term "horse opera," describing a traditional good-guys-versus-bad-guys western, these stories put the emphasis on sweeping action and larger-than-life characters. The focus on action makes these stories especially appealing for film treatment. (The Star Wars series is one of the best examples; also Samuel R. Delany.)

STEAMPUNK. A specific type of alternate-history science fiction set in Victorian England in which characters have access to 20th-century technology. (William Gibson; Bruce Sterling, *The Difference Engine*)

YOUNG ADULT. Any subcategory of science fiction geared to a YA audience (12–18), but these are usually shorter novels with characters in the central roles who are the same age as (or slightly older than) the targeted reader. (Jane Yolen, Andre Norton)

FANTASY SUBCATEGORIES

Before we take a look at the individual fantasy categories, it should be noted that, for purposes of these supplements, we've treated fantasy as a genre distinct from science fiction. While these two are closely related, there are significant enough differences to warrant their separation for study purposes. We have included here those science fiction categories that have strong fantasy elements, or that have a significant amount of crossover (these categories appear in both the science fiction and the fantasy supplements), but "pure" science fiction categories are not included below. If you're not sure whether your novel is fantasy or science fiction, consider this definition by Orson Scott Card in *How to Write Science Fiction and Fantasy* (Writer's Digest Books): "Here's a good, simple, semi-accurate rule of thumb: If the story is set in a universe that follows the same rules as ours, it's science fiction. If it's set in a universe that doesn't follow our rules, it's fantasy. Or in other words, science fiction is about what could be but isn't; fantasy is about what couldn't be."

But even Card admits this rule is only "semi-accurate." He goes on to say that the real boundary between science fiction and fantasy is defined by how the impossible is achieved: "If you have people do some magic, impossible thing [like time travel] by stroking a talisman or praying to a tree, it's fantasy; if they do the same thing by pressing a button or climbing inside a machine, it's science fiction."

Peter Heck, in his article "Doors to Other Worlds: Trends in Science Fiction and Fantasy," which appears in the 1996 edition of the *Science Fiction and Fantasy Writer's Sourcebook* (Writer's Digest Books), does note some trends that have distinct enough characteristics to be defined as separate categories. These categories are frequently the result of marketing decisions as much as literary ones, so understanding them is important in deciding where your novel idea belongs. We've supplied a brief description and the names of authors who write in each category, so you can sample representative works.

ARTHURIAN. Reworking of the legend of King Arthur and the Knights of the Round Table. (T.H. White, *The Once and Future King*; Marion Zimmer Bradley, *The Mists of Avalon*)

CONTEMPORARY (ALSO CALLED "URBAN") FANTASY. Traditional fantasy elements (such as elves and magic) are incorporated into an otherwise recognizable modern setting. (Emma Bull, *War for the Oaks*; Mercedes Lackey, *The SERRAted Edge*; Terry Brooks, the Word & Void series)

DARK FANTASY. Closely related to horror but generally not as graphic. Characters in these stories are the "darker" fantasy types: vampires, witches, werewolves, demons, etc. (Anne Rice; Clive Barker, *Weaveworld*, *Imajica*; Fred Chappell)

FANTASTIC ALTERNATE HISTORY. Set in an alternate historical period (in which magic would not have been a common belief) where magic works, these stories frequently feature actual historical figures. (Orson Scott Card, *Alvin Maker*)

GAME-RELATED FANTASY. Plots and characters are similar to high fantasy, but are based on a particular role-playing game. (Dungeons and Dragons; Magic: The Gathering; World of Warcraft)

HEROIC FANTASY. The fantasy equivalent to military science fiction, these are stories of war and its heroes and heroines. (Robert E. Howard, the Conan the Barbarian series; Elizabeth Moon, *Deed of Paksenarrion*; Michael Moorcock, the Elric series)

HIGH FANTASY. Emphasis is on the fate of an entire race or nation, threatened by an ultimate evil. J.R.R. Tolkien's Lord of the Rings trilogy is a classic example. (Terry Brooks, David Eddings, Margaret Weis, Tracy Hickman)

HISTORICAL FANTASY. The setting can be almost any era in which the belief in magic was strong; these are essentially historical novels where magic is a key element of the plot and/or setting. (Susan Schwartz, *Silk Roads and Shadows*; Margaret Ball, *No Earthly Sunne*; Tim Powers, *The Anubis Gates*)

JUVENILE/YOUNG ADULT. Can be any type of fantasy, but geared to a juvenile (8–12) or YA audience (12–18); these are shorter novels with younger characters in central roles. (J.K. Rowling, Christopher Paolini, C.S. Lewis)

SCIENCE FANTASY. A blend of traditional fantasy elements with scientific or pseudoscientific support (genetic engineering, for example, to "explain" a traditional fantasy creature like the dragon). These stories are traditionally more character driven than hard science fiction. (Anne McCaffrey, Mercedes Lackey, Marion Zimmer Bradley)

HORROR SUBCATEGORIES

Subcategories in horror are less well defined than in other genres and are frequently the result of marketing decisions as much as literary ones. But being familiar with the terms used to describe different horror styles can be important in understanding how your own novel might be best presented to an agent or editor. What follows is a brief description of the most commonly used terms, along with names of authors and, where necessary, representative works.

DARK FANTASY. Sometimes used as a euphemistic term for horror in general, but also refers to a specific type of fantasy, usually less graphic than other horror subcategories, that features more "traditional" supernatural or mythical beings (vampires, werewolves, zombies, etc.) in either contemporary or historical settings. (Contemporary: Stephen King, *Salem's Lot*; Thomas Tessier, *The Nightwalker*. Historical: Brian Stableford, *The Empire of Fear* and *Werewolves of London*)

HAUNTINGS. "Classic" stories of ghosts, poltergeists, and spiritual possessions. The level of violence portrayed varies, but many writers in this category exploit the reader's natural fear of the unknown by hinting at the horror and letting the reader's imagination supply the details. (Peter Straub, *Ghost Story*; Richard Matheson, *Hell House*)

JUVENILE/YOUNG ADULT. Can be any horror style, but with a protagonist who is the same age as, or slightly older than, the targeted reader. Stories for middle grades (8–12 years old) are scary, with monsters and violent acts that might best be described as "gross," but stories for young adults (12–18) may be more graphic. (R.L. Stine, Christopher Pike, Carol Gorman)

PSYCHOLOGICAL HORROR. Features a human monster with horrific, but not necessarily supernatural, aspects. (Thomas Harris, *The Silence of the Lambs*, *Hannibal*; Dean Koontz, *Whispers*)

SPLATTERPUNK. Very graphic depiction of violence—often gratuitous—popularized in the 1980s, especially in film. (*Friday the 13th*, *Halloween*, *Nightmare on Elm Street*, etc.)

SUPERNATURAL/OCCULT. Similar to the dark fantasy, but may be more graphic in its depiction of violence. Stories feature satanic worship, demonic possession, or ultimate evil incarnate in an entity or supernatural being that may or may not have its roots in traditional mythology or folklore. (Ramsey Campbell; Robert McCammon; Ira Levin, *Rosemary's Baby*; William Peter Blatty, *The Exorcist*; Stephen King, *Pet Sematary*)

TECHNOLOGICAL HORROR. "Monsters" in these stories are the result of science run amok or technology turned to purposes of evil. (Dean Koontz, *Watchers*; Michael Crichton, *Jurassic Park*)

PROFESSIONAL ORGANIZATIONS

AGENTS' ORGANIZATIONS

ASSOCIATION OF AUTHORS' AGENTS (AAA) Curtis Brown, Haymarket House, 28-29 Haymarket, London SW1Y 4SP. (020)7393-4420. E-mail: wiseoffice@curtisbrown.co.uk. Website: www.agentsassoc.co.uk.

ASSOCIATION OF AUTHORS' REPRESENTATIVES (AAR) 302A West 12th Street, #122, New York, NY 10014. E-mail: administrator@aaronline.org. Website: aaronline.org.

ASSOCIATION OF TALENT AGENTS (ATA) 9255 Sunset Blvd., Suite 930, Los Angeles, CA 90069. (310)274-0628. Fax: (310)274-5063. E-mail: info@agentassociation.com. Website: www.agentassociation.com.

WRITERS' ORGANIZATIONS

ACADEMY OF AMERICAN POETS 75 Maiden Lane, Suite 901, New York, NY 10038. (212)274-0343. Fax: (212)274-9427. E-mail: academy@poets.org. Website: www.poets.org.

AMERICAN CRIME WRITERS LEAGUE (ACWL) E-mail: info@acwl.org. Website: www.acwl.org.

AMERICAN MEDICAL WRITERS ASSOCIATION (AMWA) 30 West Gude Drive, Suite 525, Rockville, MD 20850-4347. (240)238-0940. Fax: (301)294-9006. E-mail: amwa@amwa.org. Website: www.amwa.org.

AMERICAN SCREENWRITERS ASSOCIATION (ASA) E-mail: info@americanscreenwriters.com. Website: www.americanscreenwriters.com.

AMERICAN TRANSLATORS ASSOCIATION (ATA) 225 Reinekers Lane, Suite 590, Alexandria, VA 22314. (703)683-6100. Fax: (703)683-6122. E-mail: ata@atanet.org. Website: www.atanet.org.

EDUCATION WRITERS ASSOCIATION (EWA) 3516 Connecticut Avenue NW, Washington, DC 20008. (202)452-9830. Website: www.ewa.org.

THE ASSOCIATION OF GARDEN COMMUNICATORS (GWA) 355 Lexington Avenue, 15th Floor, New York, NY 10017. (212)297-2198. Fax: (212)297-2149. E-mail: info@garden writers.org. Website: www.gardenwriters.org.

HORROR WRITERS ASSOCIATION (HWA) P.O. Box 56687, Sherman Oaks, CA 91413. (818)220-3965. E-mail: hwa.contact@gmail.com. Website: www.horror.org.

THE INTERNATIONAL WOMEN'S WRITING GUILD (IWWG) 5 Penn Plaza, PMB #19059, New York, NY 10001. (917)720-6959. E-mail: iwwgquestions@gmail.com Website: iwwg. wildapricot.org.

MYSTERY WRITERS OF AMERICA (MWA) 1140 Broadway, Suite 1507, New York, NY 10001. (212)888-8171. Fax: (212)888-8107. Website: www.mysterywriters.org.

NATIONAL ASSOCIATION OF SCIENCE WRITERS (NASW) P.O. Box 7905, Berkeley, CA 94707. (510)647-9500. E-mail: editor@nasw.org. Website: www.nasw.org.

ORGANIZATION OF BLACK SCREENWRITERS (OBS) 3010 Wilshire Boulevard, #269, Los Angeles, CA 90010. E-mail: contactus@obswriter.com. Website: www.obswriter.com.

OUTDOOR WRITERS ASSOCIATION OF AMERICA (OWAA) 615 Oak Street, Suite 201, Missoula, MT 59801. (406)728-7434. E-mail: info@owaa.org. Website: www.owaa.org.

POETRY SOCIETY OF AMERICA (PSA) 15 Gramercy Park, New York, NY 10003. (212)254-9628. Website: www.poetrysociety.org.

POETS & WRITERS 90 Broad St., Suite 2100, New York, NY 10004. (212)226-3586. Fax: (212)226-3963. Website: www.pw.org.

ROMANCE WRITERS OF AMERICA (RWA) 14615 Benfer Road, Houston, TX 77069. (832)717-5200. E-mail: info@rwa.org. Website: www.rwa.org.

SCIENCE FICTION AND FANTASY WRITERS OF AMERICA (SFWA) P.O. Box 3238, Enfield, CT 06083-3238. Website: www.sfwa.org.

SOCIETY OF AMERICAN BUSINESS EDITORS AND WRITERS (SABEW) Walter Cronkite School of Journalism and Mass Communication, Arizona State University, 555 North Central Avenue, Suite 406E, Phoenix, AZ 85004-1248 (602)496-7862. E-mail: sabew@sabew.org. Website: www.sabew.org.

SOCIETY OF AMERICAN TRAVEL WRITERS (SATW) 1 Parkview Plaza, Suite 800, Oakbrook Terrace, IL 60181. E-mail: info@satw.org. Website: www.satw.org.

SOCIETY OF CHILDREN'S BOOK WRITERS & ILLUSTRATORS (SCBWI) 4727 Wilshire Boulevard, Suite 301, Los Angeles, CA 90010. (323)782-1010. E-mail: scbwi@scbwi.org. Website: www.scbwi.org.

WESTERN WRITERS OF AMERICA (WWA) E-mail: wwa.moulton@gmail.com. Website: www.westernwriters.org.

INDUSTRY ORGANIZATIONS

AMERICAN BOOKSELLERS ASSOCIATION (ABA) 333 Westchester Avenue, Suite S202, White Plains, NY 10604. (914)406-7500. Fax: (914)417-4013. E-mail: info@bookweb.org. Website: www.bookweb.org.

AMERICAN SOCIETY OF JOURNALISTS & AUTHORS (ASJA) 355 Lexington Avenue, 15th Floor, New York, NY 10017-6603. (212)997-0947. Website: www.asja.org.

THE ASSOCIATION FOR CHRISTIAN RETAIL (CBA) 1365 Garden of the Gods Road, Suite 105, Colorado Springs, CO 80907. (800)252-1950. Fax: (719)272-3510. E-mail: info@cbaonline. org. Website: cbaonline.org.

THE ASSOCIATION FOR WOMEN IN COMMUNICATIONS (AWC) 1717 East Republic Road, Suite A, Springfield, MO 65804. (417)886-8606. Fax: (417)886-3685. E-mail: becky@club-managementservices.com. Website: www.womcom.org.

ASSOCIATION OF AMERICAN PUBLISHERS (AAP) 71 Fifth Avenue, Second Floor, New York NY 10003. (212)255-0200. Fax: (212)255-7007. Or: 455 Massachusetts Avenue NW, Suite 700, Washington, DC 20001. (202)347-3375. Fax: (202)347-3690. Website: publishers.org.

ASSOCIATION OF WRITERS & WRITING PROGRAMS (AWP) George Mason University, 4400 University Drive, MSN 1E3, Fairfax, VA 22030. (703)993-4301. Fax: (703)993-4302. E-mail: awp@awpwriter.org. Website: www.awpwriter.org.

THE AUTHORS GUILD 31 East 32nd Street, Seventh Floor, New York, NY 10016. (212)563-5904. Fax: (212)564-5363. E-mail: staff@authorsguild.org. Website: www. authorsguild.org.

CANADIAN AUTHORS ASSOCIATION (CAA) 6 West Street North, Suite 203, Orilla, ON L3V 5B8 Canada. (705)325-3926. E-mail: admin@canadianauthors.org. Website: www.canadi-anauthors.org.

DRAMATISTS GUILD OF AMERICA 1501 Broadway, Suite 701, New York, NY 10036. (212)398-9366. Fax: (212)944-0420. Website: www.dramatistsguild.com.

NATIONAL LEAGUE OF AMERICAN PEN WOMEN (NLAPW) Pen Arts Building and Art Museum, 1300 17th St. NW, Washington DC 20036-1973. (202)785-1997. Fax: (202)452-8868. E-mail: contact@nlapw.org. Website: www.nlapw.org.

NATIONAL WRITERS ASSOCIATION (NWA) 10940 South Parker Road, #508, Parker, CO 80134. E-mail: natlwritersassn@hotmail.com. Website: www.nationalwriters.com

NATIONAL WRITERS UNION (NWU) 256 West 38th Street, Suite 703, New York, NY 10018. (212)254-0279. Fax: (212)254-0673. E-mail: nwu@nwu.org. Website: www.nwu.org.

PEN AMERICA 588 Broadway, Suite 303, New York, NY 10012. (212)334-1660. E-mail: info@pen.org. Website: www.pen.org.

PLAYWRIGHTS GUILD OF CANADA (PGC) 401 Richmond Street West, Suite 350, Toronto, ON M5V 3A8 Canada. (416)703-0201. Fax: (416)703-0059. E-mail: info@playwrightsguild.ca. Website: www.playwrightsguild.ca.

VOLUNTEER LAWYERS FOR THE ARTS (VLA) 1 East 53rd Street, New York, NY 10022. (212)319-2787, ext.1. E-mail: vlany@vlany.org. Website: www.vlany.org.

WOMEN IN FILM (WIF) 6100 Wilshire Boulevard, Suite 710, Los Angeles, CA 90048. (323)935-2211. Fax: (323)935-2212. E-mail: info@wif.org. Website: www.wif.org.

WOMEN'S NATIONAL BOOK ASSOCIATION (WNBA) P.O. Box 237, FDR Station, New York NY 10150. (866)610-9622. Fax: (212)208-4629. E-mail: info@wnba-books.org. Website: www.wnba-books.org.

WRITERS' GUILD OF ALBERTA (WGA) Main Floor, Percy Page Centre, 11759 Groat Road NW, Edmonton AB T5M 3K6 Canada. (780)422-8174. Fax: (780)422-2663 (Attn: Writers' Guild of Alberta). E-mail: mail@writersguild.ca. Website: writersguild.ab.ca.

WRITERS GUILD OF AMERICA, EAST (WGA) 250 Hudson Street, Suite 700, New York, NY 10013. (212)767-7800. Fax: (212)582-1909. E-mail: gbynoe@wgaeast.org. Website: www.wgaeast.org.

WRITERS GUILD OF AMERICA, WEST (WGA) 7000 West Third Street, Los Angeles, CA 90048. (323)951-4000, (800)548-4532. Website: www.wga.org.

THE WRITERS' UNION OF CANADA (TWUC) 600-460 Richmond Street West, Toronto, ON M5V 1Y1 Canada. (416)703-8982. Fax: (416)504-9090. E-mail: info@writersunion.ca. Website: www.writersunion.ca.

LITERARY AGENTS
SPECIALITIES INDEX

CATEGORY INDEX

GENERAL INDEX